The Handbook of
Fixed Income Securities

The Handbook of Fixed Income Securities

SECOND EDITION

Frank J. Fabozzi

and

Irving M. Pollack

Editors

1987

DOW JONES-IRWIN
Homewood, Illinois 60430

ISBN 0-87094-745-1
Library of Congress Catalog Card No. 86–50815

Printed in the United States of America

5 6 7 8 9 0 K 4 3 2 1 0 9 8 7

FJF's corner
    To the memory of my grandparents,
    Lucia and Francesco Fabozzi
    Maria and Biagio Falzone

IMP's corner
    To my family,
    Shirley, Janet,
    and Joan

Foreword

Although buy-and-hold is a realistic option for investors who buy equities, it is an act of wanton imprudence for investors in debt securities. Ultimately, of course, a debt security reverts to cash, and thereafter earns nothing for its owner. Well before the maturity date, however, its entire pattern of market behavior changes with the passage of time. This means that active management of fixed income securities is an inescapable responsibility.

Lenders of money have two other factors to worry about. First, will the borrower meet all payments of interest and principal when due? Second, how much will those payments buy in terms of goods, services, and financial assets as the repayments come in?

From these three painfully obvious considerations—the impact of time, the credit-worthiness of the borrower, and the relation of predetermined dollar payments to a changing price level—stems an extraordinarily complex collection of tools, techniques, risk and return calculations, and forecasting models for the active manager to worry about. In a world in which the variety of issuers and issues seems to proliferate continuously, this is no job for people who are seeking soft berths.

It is, indeed, an area where constant study is essential. What happens in any given market, in any given moment, or in any given economic environment is relevant for all the other markets, moments, and environments. Our learning requirements give us no surcease.

This volume is essential for those who recognize the importance of meeting those requirements. It leaves no stone unturned, and has about the most skilled stone-turners one would want to put to this particular task. Whether we turn to it for a guide to action, for a grasp of the facts, or for an understanding of fundamental theory, the answers we seek are here.

Peter L. Bernstein
President of Peter L. Bernstein Inc.,
and Editor of
The Journal of Portfolio Management

Preface

Dynamic changes in the financial markets in recent years have intensified the interest of investors in fixed income securities. In the late 1960s interest rates began to rise, making fixed income securities more competitive with other investment vehicles such as common stock. As rates continued to rise throughout the 1970s and early 1980s and as erratic monetary policy caused interest rates to fluctuate substantially, borrowers began issuing fixed income contracts that offered more attractive investment characteristics to an investing public that had become concerned with committing funds in a volatile interest rate environment. Moreover, improved techniques for managing fixed income portfolios in such an investment climate were developed.

This book is designed to provide extensive coverage of not only the wide range of fixed income securities but also investment strategies and the interest rate environment. It is intended for both the novice investor and the professional money manager. Each chapter is written by an authority on the subject. Many of these authorities have written books, monographs, and/or articles in leading journals on their topic.

The *Handbook* is divided into eight parts. Part 1 provides investment information with which an investor must be familiar in order to understand the risks and rewards associated with fixed income securities and portfolios. The securities—money market instruments, U.S. Treasury and agency obligations, corporate bonds, preferred stock, municipal securities, zero-coupon securities, domestic floating rate securities, mortgages, pass-through securities, collateralized mortgage obligations, and convertible securities—are explained in Part 2. Credit analysis of corporate bonds and municipal securities is the subject of Part 3. Fixed income portfolio management strategies are explained in Part 4, followed by comprehensive coverage of options and futures and their roles in portfolio management in Part 5. The chapters in Part 6 cover international fixed income instruments and global fixed income investing, with special attention given to the Deutschemark and ECU bond markets. The determinants of the level of interest rates, corporate/Treasury spreads, and the term structure of interest rates are the subjects of Part 7. Also included in Part 7 is an explanation of interest-rate forecasting techniques. Part 8 explains how interest-rate swaps can be used by a portfolio manager and gives the mathematics necessary to understand the interest-rate swap market. The appendix to the book summarizes the various fixed income indexes.

Money managers must justify their management fees to clients. Consequently, eventually all money managers must explain to their clients how much *value* they've added to portfolio performance above and beyond what could have been realized from a passive management strategy. Similarly, as editors of this book, we must justify to our current clients (those who have purchased the first edition of the *Handbook*) why they should *not* follow a passive book buying strategy of simply continuing to use the first edition and saving on the advisory fee (the cost of the second edition). That is, what value have we added to the book? First, we expanded the number of chapters from 47 to 58, 23 of which are new chapters. Although all of the chapters carried over from the first edition have been updated, five of the chapters have been substantially revised. The exhibit on pages x and xi summarizes the differences between the first and second editions.

We extend our deep personal appreciation to the contributing authors, the editorial advisory board, and the following individuals who provided us with assistance in this project:

David Askin (*Drexel Burnham Lambert*); Jackson Breaks (*Merrill Lynch*); John Ezell (*Charter Atlantic Corp.*); David Fisher (*Salomon Brothers Inc*); Jack Clark Francis (*Bernard Baruch College, CUNY*); William H. K. Fung (*Shearson Lehman Brothers*); Joseph Gaziano (*Merrill Lynch*); Laurie Goodman (*Citibank Investment Bank*); Michael Granito (*J.P. Morgan Investment Management*); Jim Hight (*Bear Stearns*); Richard Howe (*Constitutional Capital*); Andrew Kalotay (*Salomon Brothers*); Tony Kao (*Chrysler*); James Kennedy (*Merrill Lynch Capital Markets*); David Kidwell (*Tulane University*); Graham Lord (*MathTech*); David McLaughlin (*Chase Investment Counsel*); Roger McMahon (*RMJ Securities*); Eileen Moran (*PSG&E*); Sharmin Mossavar-Rahmani (*Shearson Lehman Investment Management*); David Muntner (*First Boston*); Benjamin J. Neuhausen (*Arthur Andersen & Co.*); Fred Price (*Bear Stearns*); Thomas Radwanski (*Lafayette College*); Frank Reilly (*University of Notre Dame*); Ronald J. Ryan (*Ryan Financial Strategy Group*); Michael Smirlock (*University of Pennsylvania*); Rob Smith (*Bear Stearns*); Andrea Tractenberg (*Merrill Lynch Capital Markets*);

Oldrich Vasichek (*Gifford Fong Associates*); Charles Webster (*Fordham University*); Leslie Webster (*Chase Manhattan Bank*); M. Didi Weinblatt (*Merrill Lynch Capital Markets*).

   An editorial footnote is needed to explain the use of the pronoun *he* in some parts of the *Handbook*. In most instances, when referring to a person the contributors used the term *investor*. It became necessary, however, to use a pronoun at certain times. The pronoun *he* was selected by contributors for convention. They felt that alternatives such as *he/she* or *he or she* or *s(he)* are awkward. The use of the generic *he* throughout this *Handbook*, then, is meant to include both sexes.

Frank J. Fabozzi
Irving M. Pollack

SUMMARY OF DIFFERENCES BETWEEN FIRST AND SECOND EDITIONS

The first edition has 47 chapters and two appendixes, divided into the following 4 parts:

PART 1: General Investment Information
PART 2: Securities and Instruments
PART 3: Bond Investment Management
PART 4: Interest Rate and Interest-Rate Forecasting

The second edition has 58 chapters and an appendix, divided into the following 8 parts:

PART 1: General Investment Information
PART 2: Securities and Instruments
PART 3: Credit Analysis
PART 4: Fixed Income Portfolio Management
PART 5: Options and Futures and Their Role in Fixed Income Portfolio Management
PART 6: International Bond Investing
PART 7: Interest-Rate Determinants and Interest-Rate Forecasting
PART 8: Interest-Rate Swaps

Contributing Authors

Carl R. Beidleman, Ph.D. Allen C. DuBois Professor of Finance, Lehigh University

Richard Bookstaber, Ph.D. Vice President, Morgan Stanley & Co.

Peter E. Christensen Managing Director, PaineWebber Incorporated

Bruce M. Collins Vice President, Shearson Lehman Brothers, Inc.

Noreen M. Conwell Assistant Vice President, Merrill Lynch, Pierce, Fenner & Smith, Inc.

Frank J. Fabozzi, Ph.D., C.F.A., C.P.A. Visiting Professor, Sloan School of Management, Massachusetts Institute of Technology

Sylvan G. Feldstein, Ph.D. Vice President, Merrill Lynch Capital Markets

Michael G. Ferri, Ph.D. Edward J. and Louise E. Mellen Chair in Finance, John Carroll University

H. Gifford Fong President, Gifford Fong Associates

Philip H. Galdi, C.P.A. Vice President, Merrill Lynch Capital Markets

Lawrence A. Garber, LL.B., LL.M., C.P.A. President, Woodcliff Consultants, Inc.

T. Dessa Garlicki, Ph.D. Assistant Professor of Finance, Bentley College

Gary L. Gastineau Manager of the Options Portfolio Service, Kidder, Peabody, & Co., Inc.

Steven Guterman Vice President Mortgage Research, Salomon Brothers Inc

Margaret Darasz Hadzima, C.F.A. Vice President, Bonds, Scudder, Stevens & Clark

Victor J. Haghani Interest Rate Arbitrage Group, Salomon Brothers Inc

Jane Tripp Howe, C.F.A. Consultant

Tran Q. Hung Vice President, Merrill Lynch Capital Markets

David P. Jacob Research Manager, Morgan Stanley & Co.

Michael D. Joehnk, Ph.D., C.F.A. Professor of Finance, Arizona State University

Frank J. Jones, Ph.D.   Vice President, Kidder, Peabody & Co., Inc.

James L. Kochan   Vice President and Manager, Merrill Lynch, Pierce, Fenner & Smith, Inc.

Robert W. Kopprasch, Ph.D., C.F.A.   Vice President, Salomon Brothers Inc

Mark N. Landau   Vice President, Wood Gundy Inc.

Martin L. Leibowitz, Ph.D.   Managing Director, Bond Portfolio Analysis Group, Salomon Brothers Inc

A. Michael Lipper, C.F.A.   President, Lipper Analytical Services, Inc.

John G. Macfarlane   Director, Salomon Brothers Inc

Howard S. Marks, C.F.A.   Managing Director, Trust Company of the West

William J. Marshall, Ph.D.   Associate Director, Financial Strategies Group, Goldman Sachs & Co.

Richard W. McEnally, Ph.D., C.F.A.   Professor of Finance, University of North Carolina

William C. Melton, Ph.D.   Vice President and Senior Economist, IDS Financial Services, Inc.

Gregory J. Parseghian   Vice President, The First Boston Corporation

Mark Pitts, Ph.D.   Senior Vice President, Shearson Lehman Brothers, Inc.

John C. Ritchie, Jr., Ph.D.   Professor of Finance, Temple University

Daniel R. Ross   Vice President, Salomon Brothers Inc

Harry C. Sauvain, D.S.C.   University Professor Emeritus of Finance, Indiana University

Christina Seix, C.F.A.   Director of Bond Management, MacKay-Shields Financial Corporation

Dexter Senft   Managing Director, Fixed Income Research, The First Boston Corporation

Janet Showers, Ph.D.   Vice President, Salomon Brothers Inc

Corneila M. Small   Managing Director, Scudder, Stevens & Clark

David A. Smilow

Marcia Stigum, Ph.D.   Stigum & Associates, New York

Kenneth H. Sullivan   Managing Director, Drexel Burnham Lambert, Inc.

Eric M.P. Tang   Vice President, Gifford Fong Associates

Alden L. Toevs, Ph.D. Vice President, Director of Mortgage Research, Morgan Stanley & Co.

Michael Waldman Director & Manager of Mortgage Research, Salomon Brothers Inc

Arthur Williams III, C.F.A. Managing Director, Simms Capital Management, Ltd.

Richard S. Wilson Vice President, Merrill Lynch Capital Markets

Benjamin Wolkowitz, Ph.D. Vice President, Morgan Stanley & Co.

Alling Woodruff, C.F.A. Vice President, Lipper Analytical Services, Inc.

W. David Woolford, C.F.A. Vice President, Prudential Insurance Company of America

Jess B. Yawitz, Ph.D. Director, Financial Strategies Group, Vice President, Fixed Income Division, Goldman Sachs & Co.

Contents

Part 3
Credit Analysis 501

Accumulation Return. The "Market" Portion of a Bond's
Capital Gain. Measures of Volatility. The Horizon Volatility Factor.

Misuse of Financial Futures and Options Markets. Conclusion.

The Target for Hedges with Short Holding Periods. How the Basis Affects the Target Rate for a Hedge. A More General Approach to the Target. Basis Risk. A Digression: Hedges that Do Not Minimize Risk. Cross Hedging: *The Hedge Ratio. Changing Yield Spreads: The Regression. Deriving the Target for a Cross Hedge. Cross Hedging Summarized.* Monitoring and Evaluating the Hedge. Summary.

Generic Equivalent Cash Flow Approach (GECA). Varia-
tions on the Generic Theme: *Floating-Rate Variations. Fixed-
Rate Variations. Effective Date.* Nonpar Swaps. Conclusion.
Appendix.

PART 1

General Investment Information

1

An Introduction to Fixed Income Securities

Michael D. Joehnk, Ph.D., C.F.A.
Professor of Finance
Arizona State University

Ever since interest rates began to climb in the late 1960s, the appeal of various types of fixed income securities has increased in a similar fashion. Today such securities as bonds, preferred stock, and convertible issues are found in an increasing number of investment portfolios and are being actively used to fulfill a variety of investor objectives. Basically two things have occurred to alter the investment appeal of fixed income securities: (1) interest rates moved to levels that were highly competitive with other securities, and (2) at the same time, these market rates began to fluctuate widely and provided investors with attractive capital gains opportunities. Such behavior was, of course, predictable since the yields and price performance of good- to high-grade fixed income securities are sensitive to changes in market interest rates. This book is devoted exclusively to fixed income securities—to the substantial return opportunities inherent in this investment vehicle, to the various investment strategies that can be employed, and to the different kinds of fixed income securities that are available to portfolio managers. The present chapter provides an introduction to and an overview of fixed income securities; in it, we'll look at reasons for investing in fixed income securities, the market for these securities, sources of risk exposure, and the type of risk-return relationship to expect with such investment vehicles.

WHY INVEST IN FIXED INCOME SECURITIES?

Like any other type of investment vehicle, bonds and other forms of fixed income securities provide investors with two kinds of income: (1) They provide current income, and (2) they can often be used to generate

3

varying amounts of capital gains. The current income, of course, is derived from the periodic receipt of interest and/or dividend payments. Capital gains, in contrast, are earned whenever market interest rates fall. A basic trading rule in the market for fixed income securities is that interest rates and security prices move in opposite directions.[1] When interest rates rise, prices fall; and when rates drop, prices move up. So it is possible to buy fixed income securities at one price and, if market interest-rate conditions are right, to sell them some time later at a higher price. Of course, it is also possible to incur a capital loss should market rates move against the investor. Taken together, the current income and capital gains earned from bonds and other types of fixed income securities can lead to *attractive and highly competitive investor yields.*

In addition to their yields, fixed income securities are a versatile investment outlet. They can be used conservatively by those who primarily (or exclusively) seek high current income as a way to supplement their income sources. Or they can be used aggressively for trading purposes by those who actively go after capital gains. Fixed income securities have long been regarded as excellent vehicles for those seeking current income, but it has only been since the advent of high and volatile interest rates that they have also become recognized as excellent trading vehicles. This is so because investors have found that the number of profitable trading opportunities has increased substantially as wider and more frequent swings in interest rates began to occur. Finally, because of the generally high quality of many fixed income securities, they can also be *used for the preservation and long-term accumulation of capital.* Many investors regularly and over the long haul commit all or a major portion of their investment funds to fixed income securities because of this investment attribute. Some investors, in fact, may never use any other type of investment vehicle.

Advantages and Disadvantages of Ownership

One of the advantages of investing in fixed income securities is the highly competitive rates of return that are available, even with nominal amounts of trading and minimal risk exposure. Another advantage is the occasional opportunity to realize substantial capital gains. Also attractive to some investors are the tax advantages that can be obtained with certain types of issues; municipal obligations are perhaps the best known in this regard, but there are also some unusual tax advantages to Treasury and agency issues.[2]

On the other side, there are disadvantages to investing in fixed income securities. For the individual investor, one of the biggest disad-

---

[1] The reason for this relationship is explained in Chapter 4.

[2] See Chapters 8, 9 and 12.

vantages is the relatively large denomination of many of these issues. Another is that the coupons or dividend rates are fixed for the life of the issue[3] and therefore cannot move up over time in response to the ravages of inflation. In fact, inflation is probably the biggest worry for fixed income investors. Not only does inflation erode the purchasing power of the principal portion of the investment, but it also has a strong influence upon the behavior of interest rates. That is, inflation can lead to violent swings in interest rates and, in so doing, produce violent swings in the market behavior of fixed income securities, all of which can cause substantial capital losses. A final disadvantage is the often inactive secondary markets for some of these securities, which tends to limit the amount of aggressive trading and speculation that can take place.

What Are the Choices?

Fixed income securities derive their name from the fact that their level of current income, as defined by the issue's coupon or dividend rate, is fixed for a stipulated period of time, usually the life of the issue. In essence, the security's claim on the income of the issuer is set at a fixed amount. A 12 percent coupon on a $1,000 bond means that the issuer has to pay the bondholder $120 per year for the use of the money— nothing more, nothing less. Likewise, a $5 dividend rate on a preferred stock means the same thing: that the issuer is required to pay "rent" of precisely $5 per year for each share of preferred stock outstanding.

Investors and portfolio managers can select from a number of different types of fixed income securities; these include:

- Money market instruments
    Short-term debt securities, such as Treasury bills, commercial paper, CDs, money market certificates
- Bonds
    Treasury issues
    Agency issues
    Municipal bonds
    Corporate bonds
    Mortgage-backed securities
    Institutional obligations
    International bonds
- Preferred stock
- Convertible issues
    Convertible bonds
    Convertible preferreds

---

[3] There are exceptions, such as floating- and variable-rate instruments. See Chapter 14.

- Investment company shares (mutual funds)
  - Open- and closed-end funds
  - Investment trusts
- Interest-rate futures
- Put and call options on fixed income securities

Although each of the listed types will be reviewed in detail in later chapters, a perusal of the above list reveals that investors/portfolio managers can find fixed income securities with short-term maturities (money market instruments), or they can choose to go long term (with bonds, preferreds, and convertibles). In addition, they can acquire a position in a managed portfolio of fixed income securities via a mutual fund, or they can deal in financial assets that are linked to the price behavior of certain kinds of fixed income securities by trading financial futures or put and call options.

Briefly, money market instruments are low-risk, highly liquid, short-term, unsecured IOUs that are issued by banks, nonfinancial corporations, the U.S. Treasury, various agencies of the U.S. government, and state and local governments. The minimum denominations of these securities are relatively large (seldom are they less than $10,000), and trading lots can be substantial (usually $100,000–$250,000 or more). Major money market instruments include U.S. Treasury bills, federal funds, Eurodollars, negotiable certificates of deposit, commercial paper, bankers acceptances, repurchase agreements, and notes and bills issued by federal agencies and municipal governments.

Like the money market, the bond market is immense. The largest sector is the market for issues of the U.S. Treasury. The fastest growing sector of the U.S. bond market is that for mortgage-backed securities.

The municipal sector is another part of the bond market; this is the "tax-exempt" segment wherein state and local government bonds are traded.[4] The major nongovernmental sector of the market is the corporate segment. The market for corporates is customarily subdivided into several segments, which include industrials (the most diverse of the groups); public utilities (the dominant group in terms of volume of new issues); rail and transportation bonds; and financial issues (bonds issued by banks and other financial institutions). Not only is there a full range of bond quality available in the corporate market, but it also has the widest range of different types of issues—from first mortgage bonds and convertible issues to serial bonds and variable-rate notes. By far the smallest segment of the market, institutional bonds are marketed by a

---

[4] Municipal issuers include states, counties, cities, and other political subdivisions, such as school districts and industrial development authorities. These issues are considered tax exempt, since the interest they pay is free from federal income taxation and normally from taxation by the state and local authorities in the state in which they were issued.

variety of private, nonprofit institutions, such as schools, hospitals, and churches. Many of the issuers are affiliated with religious orders, and hospitals make up the primary source of issues.[5]

Although preferred stocks are actually a form of equity, they are considered fixed income securities because their level of current income is fixed (i.e., they carry a fixed dividend, which is paid quarterly). Most outstanding issues are utility issues, although there is a growing number of industrial preferreds. One attraction of preferreds as a form of fixed income security is the fact that 85 percent of preferred dividends received by corporations are tax exempt (leading to yields on preferred stocks that are normally slightly *less* than comparable corporate bonds). Convertible securities, initially issued as bonds or preferreds, are subsequently convertible into shares of the issuing firm's common stock. So long as the convertible is outstanding, it has the same underlying attributes of any other fixed income security (bond or preferred), except that under certain conditions its price behavior is linked to movements in the underlying common stock.

In addition to investing directly into various types of fixed income securities, investors can also invest indirectly into these securities via investment company shares (such as mutual funds) and interest-rate futures and debt options. A money fund is a mutual fund that invests in a portfolio of money market instruments. There are also fully managed bond funds available, or if that's not to their liking, investors can buy units in an investment trust, which represents little more than an interest in an *unmanaged* (limited life) portfolio of corporate or municipal bonds. Interest-rate futures and debt options provide a vehicle for speculating on the behavior of interest rates and hedging risk.

Equity versus Fixed Income Investments

As the above review suggests, fixed income investors and portfolio managers have a vast array of investment vehicles to choose from. This is in sharp contrast to equity investors, who basically have five alternatives: common stocks; options, such as warrants and puts and calls; mutual funds; stock-index futures; and when the conditions are right, convertible securities.

Although the investment objectives may be the same in either case, investing in equity securities is not at all like investing in fixed income securities. To begin with, the analytical and selection process for equity

---

[5] Institutional bonds are not discussed in this book, primarily because the market is so small and there is a definite paucity of interest in the market on the part of institutional investors. Such obligations are issued, in serial form, by a variety of private nonprofit (often religious-affiliated) institutions. Even though these obligations have a virtually spotless default record, they regularly provide returns that are 1 to 1½ percentage points above comparable corporates.

securities is far more complex and less certain. That is, the dividend and price performance of common stock is subject to not only economic and market forces, but also corporate and financial variables; the net result is considerable uncertainty in formulating future expectations. High-grade fixed income securities, in contrast, are heavily influenced by a single variable—the behavior of interest rates—which simplifies the credit analysis and selection process. (This is not to suggest, however, that the task is an easy one! Rather, because there is less variability between returns of individual securities, the actual selection process with fixed income securities is a bit less uncertain.) Unfortunately, forecasting interest rates is not an easy task in itself, and the task is made even more difficult by the presence of a *complex structure of yield spreads* (which is constantly changing with movements in interest rates).

Equity investors seek high levels of return from capital gains and current income, and the same can certainly be said of investors/ portfolio managers who deal in fixed income securities. Clearly, on a risk-return continuum, fixed income investors have just as many options to choose from as equity investors—they can select the bluest of blue chips or, if they are so inclined, decide to go with very high risk, speculative vehicles.[6] Moreover, the introduction of aggressive management strategies to fixed income securities (such as the use of margin, bond swaps, interest-rate speculation, interest-rate futures, and debt options), as well as techniques for controlling risk, has enhanced the investment appeal of fixed income securities and improved the return potential of such portfolios. Although equities have historically been viewed as superior investment vehicles relative to fixed income securities, the comparative advantage seems to have shifted dramatically in the past decade or so. For example, the widely quoted study by Lawrence Fisher and James Lorie reveals that, over the 40-year period from 1926 to 1965, the average rate of return from common stocks was a hefty 9.3 percent.[7] When these rates of return are contrasted with those available from bonds, the latter appear meager indeed. The Hickman[8] study of bond returns over the 44-year period ending in 1943 shows an annual rate of return of 5.6 percent,

---

[6] A special type of speculative bond vehicle is the high yield or so-called "junk bond." In some circles of Wall Street, the junk bond is simply a low-rated, speculative-grade obligation that lacks the bond merits and characteristics of investment-grade issues. They offer high yields but also possess high exposure to risk, reflecting doubt by bond analysts about an issuer's ability to keep up interest payments and eventually pay back the face value of the bond. Unlike investment-grade fixed income securities, the fortunes of junk bonds are closely tied to the future outlook of the issuing firm or municipality (the movements of interest rates often have little, if any, effects on the price behavior of junk bonds). High yield bonds are covered in Chapters 23 and 35.

[7] Lawrence Fisher and James H. Lorie, "Rates of Return on Investments in Common Stock: The Year-by-Year Record, 1926–65," *Journal of Business*, July, 1968, pp. 291–316.

[8] W. Braddock Hickman, *Corporate Bond Quality and Investor Experience*, a study by the National Bureau of Economic Research (Princeton, N.J.: Princeton University Press, 1958).

whereas Lawrence Fisher and Roman Weil[9] suggest that only about 3.5 percent was earned on bonds over the period 1926 to 1968.

The situation began to change, however, as the decade of the 1960s came to a close. To wit, in a more recent study, Roger Ibbotson and Rex Sinquefield showed that although stocks have dominated the investment universe over the long run, the comparative annual returns from 1969 through 1980 favored fixed income securities about half of the time.[10] The lofty and violent yields that prevailed during this period have created a whole new investment environment in which fixed income obligations have become more competitive with equities for the investor's dollar. Further, aggressive bond management tactics are becoming more widely adopted, and as a result the returns on fully managed portfolios are improving accordingly. In fact, this more aggressive approach to bond portfolio management was reviewed in an article by Daniel Ahearn, who showed that in the first half of the 1970s fully managed bond portfolios far outperformed the Standard & Poor's 500 Stock Average.[11] Thus, bonds and other forms of fixed income securities have come into their own and are today viewed as competitive with the equity side of the market.

AN OVERVIEW OF THE MONEY AND CAPITAL MARKETS

Fixed income securities are found in both the money and capital markets. Essentially, short-term debt instruments with maturities of one year or less are traded in the money market, whereas the capital markets deal in financial claims with maturities greater than one year. Such instruments not only include long-term debt obligations but equity securities as well. Looking only at the fixed income securities component the capital market dominates the money market in terms of size (the former is perhaps two to three times the size of the latter), though the money market holds the upper hand with respect to overall quality of the obligations traded and the liquidity/marketability of the instruments.

The money market is the economic arena in which short-term credit instruments are bought and sold; it is a vital part of our nation's financial system. It is the market in which commercial banks and other businesses adjust their liquidity positions, the Federal Reserve conducts its mone-

---

[9] Lawrence Fisher and Roman L. Weil, "Coping with the Risk of Interest-Risk Fluctuations: Returns to Bondholders from Naive and Optimal Strategies," *Journal of Business,* October 1971, pp. 408–31.

[10] Roger G. Ibbotson and Rex A. Sinquefield, *Stocks, Bonds, Bills and Inflation: The Past and The Future (1981 Edition),* (Charlottesville, Va.: Financial Analysts Research Foundation, 1981).

[11] Daniel S. Ahearn, "The Strategic Role of Fixed Income Securities," *Journal of Portfolio Management,* Spring 1975, pp. 12–16.

tary policy, and the federal government sells its debt to finance day-to-day operations. In the money market, businesses, governments, and sometimes individuals borrow or lend funds for short periods—usually 1 day to 120 days. Actually, the money market consists of a collection of markets, each trading distinctly different financial instruments. There is no formal organization, such as the New York Stock Exchange. Central to the activity of the money market are the dealers and brokers who specialize in one or more money market instruments; such dealers buy securities for their own position and sell from their security inventories when a trade takes place. Generally speaking, money market instruments are financial claims that have low default risk, short maturities, and high marketability.

The most important function of the money market is to provide a vehicle that enables economic units to adjust their liquidity positions. Almost every economic unit—financial institution, business corporation, or governmental body—has a recurring problem of liquidity management. Money market instruments allow these units to bridge the gap between cash receipts and cash expenditures, thereby solving their liquidity needs. More than anything else, an efficiently functioning money market provides liquidity to the economy, which ultimately fosters the flow of funds to the most important use throughout the nation.

In contrast to the money markets, capital markets involve financial claims with relatively high degrees of price risk. They include common and preferred stocks, debt securities with maturities greater than one year and mutual funds. Capital markets facilitate the transfer of funds from savers to borrowers, and in so doing, they enhance the economic development and vitality of the country. Because of the lengthy maturities that exist with the securities, the existence of a secondary market is especially important because it allows investors and financial institutions to alter the liquidity, composition, and risk of their portfolios in response to new information and/or to changes in general market conditions. Such secondary markets provide the needed liquidity to the capital markets. After all, conditions change, and individual and institutional investors need ways to alter their investment positions.

RISK EXPOSURE IN FIXED INCOME SECURITIES

Investors in fixed income securities are exposed to a variety of potential risks. Depending upon the investment particulars and market climate, some types of risks are going to be more important than others, and some may be of insignificant importance. The major sources of risk include the following:

Interest-rate risk
Purchasing-power risk
Market risk

Liquidity (or marketability) risk
Business risk (or risk of default)
Issue-specific risks
    Reinvestment risk
    Call risk
    Price risk

The most important of these is interest-rate risk, which measures the variability of bond returns/prices as caused by changes in the level of interest rates. Because of the relationship between bond prices and interest rates, no segment of the market (except perhaps for the highly speculative issues) is free of this important and powerful force. The price stability of investment-grade securities is mainly a function of interest-rate stability and, therefore, interest-rate risk. Purchasing-power and market risk are closely related to interest-rate risk. Purchasing-power risk is linked to inflation and the loss of purchasing power over time; market risk, in contrast, is the effect of the market (in general) upon the price behavior of securities. In the latter case, since virtually all segments of the market for fixed income securities are responsive to interest rates, it follows that market risk is directly related to interest-rate risk. Also, though purchasing power may decline over time with a given level of inflation, what is more important to bond investors is the impact of inflation on yields and prices. For although the level of inflation affects the promised yield, *changes* in the rate of inflation (or inflation expectations) lead to changes in the level of interest rates and therefore changes in the prices of seasoned issues.

Marketability risk has to do with the liquidity of an obligation and the ease with which the issue can be sold at or near prevailing market prices. Smaller issues and those with thin secondary markets will often experience marketability difficulties and are therefore subject to such risk. Marketability is important in defining the yield performance of an obligation—the greater the assumed marketability risk, the greater the required yield. Finally, business risk is the risk of default as reflected by the financial and operating risks of the issuer. Business risk is relevant to corporate fixed income securities (bonds, preferred stocks, and convertibles) as well as municipal and institutional obligations. Fortunately, ratings by commercial rating companies are available to help in measuring the amount of business risk exposure. They are not perfect, but they do provide an excellent starting point for the assessment of such risk exposure. The quality of an obligation as reflected in ratings by commercial rating companies has an influence on the promised yield of a security—the lower the default risk, the higher the assigned rating and the lower the prevailing yield to maturity. Business risk, along with marketability risk, has an *insignificant* impact on price behavior because it only affects prevailing levels of yields. In contrast, interest-rate risk and purchasing-power risk can have *dramatic* effects on the price behavior of an obligation over time and therefore are extremely important to investors in fixed income securities.

The final source of risk is, like default risk, issue specific and has more of an impact on the prevailing level of yields than changes in yield (and therefore price behavior). One of these is reinvestment risk, which has to do with the ability of an investor to reinvest principal and/or coupon/dividend receipts at an attractive rate. It is a particularly important risk for those investors holding short-term securities as well as obligations that derive a major portion of their return from coupon, for example, high-coupon, high-yielding premium bonds. For such investors, the rate of return that can be obtained on reinvested proceeds over the life or investment horizon of a security can have a substantial effect on the level of yield actually realized from an investment. In fact, depending upon the coupon and maturity of an obligation, reinvestment results can represent as much as half (or more) of the total return on an investment and therefore have a dramatic effect on determining whether or not realized yield will live up to promised yield.[12]

Call risk is another form of risk to which some fixed income investors are exposed. Whenever a security, such as a bond, carries a call feature that gives the issuer the right to retire the obligation prior to the maturity date, investors face the risk that the issue will be called out from under them, in which case, they will be left with no alternative but to reinvest the funds in less attractive (lower yielding) investment vehicles. This is an especially important feature for investors holding current coupon or premium bonds during periods when interest rates are falling, and the likelihood of a call (for refunding purposes) is increasing. Finally, there is price risk—a type of exposure that is obviously linked to movements in interest rates, but that can have a greater or lesser impact on price behavior depending upon the maturity of the obligation held. Other things being equal, price risk increases as the term to maturity of an obligation increases. Thus, short-term money market instruments have much less exposure to price risk than long issues and therefore are considered attractive when interest rates are rising. In contrast, the prices of long maturities will fluctuate over wide ranges with movements in interest rates and, as a result, are used by investors who are going after capital gains during periods of declining interest rates.

As we noted above, some risks have a primary impact on price behavior, and others effect differential yields at a given time. Certainly, both categories of risk will effect holding-period returns. Interest rate, purchasing power, and market risk are reflected in comparative price behavior over time. Other things being equal, the greater the change in interest rates, the greater the impact on the market value/price of an

---

[12] See Chapter 4.

obligation. Liquidity, business risk, and issue-specific risk, in contrast, are reflected in differential promised yields. For example, the higher the default risk, the greater the comparative promised yield of an obligation at any time. The same can be said of an issue that lacks marketability, or one that has substantial call or reinvestment risk.

AN OVERVIEW OF THE BOOK

This book is organized into four parts. Part 1 provides a review of the basic features of fixed income securities, including yield measures and price volatility, as well as their tax treatment. An overview of the determinants of interest rates is also presented.

Part 2 gives in-depth coverage of the various fixed income instruments currently traded. Starting with money market instruments, the debt obligations examined include Treasury obligations, agency issues, corporate bonds, preferred stock, tax-exempt securities, domestic floating-rate securities, zero-coupon bonds, mortgage pass-through securities, collateralized mortgage obligations, convertible bonds, and fixed income funds. Part 3 provides an analytical framework for evaluating the creditworthiness of corporate bonds, including high-yield bonds (commonly referred to as "junk bonds"), municipal bonds, and tax-exempt, short-term instruments.

Fixed income portfolio management is the subject of Part 4. The basic tools of fixed income portfolio management discussed in this part are horizon analysis, yield-curve analysis and performance measurement. Some of the strategies included are immunization, dedication, indexing, and high-yield portfolio management. Part 5 covers the role of options and futures in fixed income management. The chapters cover not only exchange-traded options and futures, but also options embedded in fixed income securities. International bond investing—the instruments, markets, and strategies—is the subject of Part 6.

A detailed treatment of interest-rate determinants-level of interest rates and yield spreads—is presented in Part 7. Also included in Part 7 are chapters dealing with "Fed watching" and interest-rate forecasting. The two chapters in Part 8 are on interest-rate swaps. The first discusses interest-rate swaps and the second presents the mathematics underlying these swaps. The appendix to the book documents the various bond indexes.

2

Features of Fixed Income Securities

Michael G. Ferri, Ph.D.
Edward J. and Louise E. Mellen Chair
in Finance
John Carroll University

The purpose of this chapter is to explore some of the most important features of bonds and preferred stock and to provide the reader with a taxonomy of terms and concepts that will be of assistance in the reading of the specialized chapters to follow. We will first offer a discussion of the attributes of bonds and proceed later to an account of analogous aspects of preferred stock.

BONDS

Type of Issuer

One of the most important characteristics of a bond is the nature of its issuer. Though foreign governments and firms do raise capital in the American financial markets, the three largest issuers of debt are domestic corporations, municipal governments, and the federal government and its agencies. Within each of these classes of issuer, however, one can find additional and significant differences. Domestic corporations, for example, include regulated utilities as well as unregulated manufacturers. Further, each firm may sell differing kinds of bonds: Some debt may be publicly placed, other bonds may be sold directly to one or only a few buyers; some debt is collateralized by specific assets of the company, and other debt may be unsecured. Municipal debt is also varied: "general obligation" bonds (or GOs in the jargon of the bond market) are backed by the full faith, credit, and taxing power of the governmental unit issuing them; "revenue bonds," on the other hand, have a safety or creditworthiness that depends upon the vitality and success of the particular entity (such as hospitals or water systems) within the municipal government issuing the bond. Within the federal government, many departments and agencies have the authority to sell bonds. The U.S. Treasury has the most voracious appetite for debt, but the bond market often receives calls from such units as the Export-Import Bank, the Federal Home Loan Bank, and other agencies of the federal government.

It is important for the investor to realize that, by law or practice or both, these different borrowers have developed different ways of raising debt capital over the years. As a result, the distinctions among the various types of issuers correspond closely to differences among bonds in yield, denomination, safety, maturity, tax status, and such important provisions as the call privilege and sinking fund. As we discuss the key features of fixed income securities, we will point out how the characteristics of the bonds vary with the obligor or issuing authority. A more extensive discussion is provided in the chapters in Section II that explain the various instruments.

Maturity

A key feature of any bond is its *term to maturity*, the number of years during which the borrower has promised to meet the conditions of the debt (which are contained in the bond's *indenture*). A bond's maturity is the date on which the debt will cease to exist and the firm will redeem the issue by paying the face value or principal. One indication of the importance of the maturity is that the code word or name for every bond contains its maturity (and coupon). Thus, the title of the Exxon bond due or maturing in 1998 is given as "Exxon 6.5 percent '98." In practice, the words *maturity, term,* and *term to maturity* are used interchangeably to refer to the number of years remaining in the life of a bond. Technically, however, maturity denotes the date the bond will be redeemed, and term or term-to-maturity denotes the number of years until that date.

A bond's maturity is crucial for several reasons. First, maturity indicates the expected life of the instrument or the number of periods during which the holder of the bond can expect to receive the coupon payments and the number of years before the principal will be paid. Second, the yield on a bond depends substantially on its maturity.[1] Third, the volatility of a bond's price is closely associated with maturity: Changes in the market level of rates will wrest much larger changes in price from bonds of long maturity than from otherwise similar debt of shorter life.[2] Finally, bonds with long terms may be safer than debt with shorter matu-

---

[1] See Chapters 6 and 53 for a fuller account of the relationship between maturity and yield.

[2] Chapter 4 discusses this point in detail.

rities: The issuers of longer-term bonds have a higher likelihood of finding favorable conditions for retirement, which usually occurs through a refinancing, than the obligors whose bonds have a short life.

When considering a bond's maturity, the investor should be aware of any provisions that modify, or permit the issuer to modify, the maturity of a bond. Though corporate bonds are typically *term bonds* (issues that have a single maturity), they contain arrangements by which the firm either can or must retire the debt early, in full or in part. Many corporates, for example, give the issuer a *call privilege*, which permits the firm to redeem the bond before the scheduled maturity under certain conditions (these conditions are discussed below). Some U.S. government bonds have the same provision. Many industrials and some utilities have *sinking-fund provisions*, which mandate that the firm must retire a goodly portion of the debt, in a prearranged schedule, during its life and before the stated maturity. Typically, municipal bonds are *serial bonds* or, in essence, bundles of bonds with differing maturities. (Some corporates are of this type, too.)

Usually, the maturity of a corporate bond is between 10 and 30 years; the shorter maturities are more characteristic of banking or financial issues, and utilities are more likely to employ the longer maturities. Government bonds range in life from 1 to 20 or more years (though, technically, Treasury issues of 1 to 10 years are called notes), but the number of bonds with maturities exceeding 10 years is relatively small. The "term component" of municipal debt—the longest lived part of the serial issue—tends to have a maturity between 15 and 20 years.

Coupon and Principal

A bond's *coupon* is the periodic interest payment made to owners during the life of the bond. The coupon is always cited, along with maturity, in any quotation of a bond's price. Thus, one might hear about the "Alabama Power 7.875 due in 2002" or the "Sears 8 due in 2006" in discussions of current bond trading. In these examples, the coupon cited is in fact the *coupon rate* or rate of interest that, when multiplied by the *principal* or face value of the bond, provides the value of the coupon payment. Typically, but not universally, half of the coupon payment is made in semiannual installments. Most bonds are "bearer bonds" whose investors clip coupons and send them to the obligor for payment. Some bonds are "registered issues," and their owners receive the payment automatically at the appropriate time. A small class of industrial bonds, called income bonds, contain a provision that permits the firm to omit or delay the payment of interest if the firm's earnings are too low. Because it combines the riskiness of equity with the limited return of debt, this kind of bond is not popular with many investors. Since 1980, some corporations and municipalities have issued "zero-coupon" debts.[3]

One reason that debt financing is popular with corporations is that the interest payments are tax-deductible expenses. As a result, the true aftertax cost of debt to a profitable firm is usually much less than the stated coupon interest rate. The level of the coupon on any bond is typically close to the level of yields for issues of its class at the time the bond is first sold to the public. Although some original-issue, deep-discount bonds have been offered to the market, firms usually try to set the coupon at a level that will make the market price close to par value. This goal can be accomplished by placing the coupon rate near the prevailing market rate.

To many investors, the coupon is simply the amount of interest they will receive each year. However, the coupon has another major impact on an investor's experience with a bond. The coupon's size influences the volatility of the bond's price: The larger the coupon, the less the price will change in response to a shift in market interest rates. Thus, the coupon and the maturity have opposite effects on the variability of a bond's price.[4]

The *principal* or *face value* of a bond is the amount to be repaid to the investor either at maturity or at those times when the bond is called or retired according to sinking-fund provisions. But the principal plays another role, too. It is the basis on which the coupon or periodic interest rests; the coupon is the product of the principal and the coupon rate. For most corporate issues, the face value is $1,000; many government bonds have larger principals, up to $10,000 or $25,000; and most municipal bonds come in denominations of $5,000.

Yields

Participants in the bond market use two calculations to describe the expected or present return on a bond. The first, and simpler, calculation is the *current yield,* which is the ratio of the coupon to the current price. For example, a bond with a price of 91 (which is 91 percent of par, or $910 for a corporate bond with a face value of $1,000) and a coupon of 9.5 (or 9.5 percent of par) has a current yield of 10.44 percent. *The Wall Street Journal*'s tables for trading in the bond market report this yield.

Despite its wide use and simplicity, the current yield is deficient because it neglects the principal to be paid at maturity. To account for this rather large cash flow, investors utilize the conceptually and compu-

---

[3] See Chapter 13.
[4] See Chapter 4 for more analysis of this point.

tationally more complex measure of *yield-to-maturity*. The yield-to-maturity, often referred to as yield, is the rate of interest an investor would have to earn if an investment equal to the price of the bond were capable of generating the semiannual coupon payments and the principal of the bond in exactly the yearly pattern promised by the issuer. For example, suppose a bond is selling at $961.60 and has a coupon of $80 per year for the next 20 years. The holder of such a bond would expect to receive $40 every six months for 20 years and $1,000 at the end of the 20th year. What rate of interest on an investment of $961.60 would be able to produce those cash flows and leave nothing after the payment of the $1,000? The answer is a yearly compounding rate of 8.4 percent, which is the yield-to-maturity of this bond.

The yield-to-maturity is an application of the discounting technique known as internal rate of return (or IRR). The IRR of any series of payments is that discount rate that makes the present value of the payments just equal to the price or cost of the asset that generates the flows. The yield and the price of any bond are inversely related: As the price of the bond rises, the yield falls, and vice versa. For example, had the price of the bond in the preceding example been $1,010.00, the yield would have been 7.90 percent; and if the price had been $847.80, the yield would have been 9.40 percent. Yield must rise if price falls because any given future cash flows can be generated with a lower investment *if* the yearly, compounded rate of interest increases. Similarly, yield would fall as price rose because it would take a smaller rate of interest to generate set future cash flows if the initial investment were to increase.[5]

Price Quotes

As we mentioned above, the prices of most bonds are quoted as percentages of par value or face value.[6] To convert the price quote into a dollar figure, one simply multiplies the price by the par value. The following table will illustrate the matter. Thus a bond with a par of $1,000 and a price of "91¾" has a market value or price of $917.50.

Par Value	Price Quote	Price as a Percentage of Par	Price in Dollars
$ 1,000	91¾	91.75%	$ 917.50
5,000	102½	102.5	5,125.00
10,000	87¼	87.25	8,725.00
25,000	100⅞	100.875	25,218.75

---

[5] Further discussion of this principle may be found in Chapter 4.

[6] The exception to this rule is certain municipal issues, which are quoted on a yield basis. This point will receive some more attention in Chapter 12.

Call and Refunding Provisions

If a bond's indenture contains a *call feature* or *call provision,* the issuing firm or governmental entity retains the right to retire the debt, fully or partially, before the scheduled maturity. The chief benefit of such a feature is that it permits the borrower, should market rates fall, to replace an old bond with a lower interest cost issue. The call feature has added value for corporations and municipalities, which may in the future wish to escape the restrictions that frequently characterize their bonds (about the disposition of assets or collateral). The call feature provides an additional benefit to corporations, which might want to use unexpectedly high levels of cash to retire outstanding bonds or might wish to restructure their balance sheets.

The call provision is detrimental to investors, who run the risk of losing a high-coupon bond when rates begin to decline. When the borrower calls the issue, the investor must find other outlets, which presumably would have lower yields than the bond just withdrawn through the call privilege. Another problem for the investor is that the prospect of call limits the appreciation in a bond's price that could be expected when interest rates start to slip.

Because the call feature benefits the issuer and potentially disadvantages the lender, callable bonds carry higher yields than bonds that cannot be retired before maturity. This difference in yields is likely to grow when investors believe that market rates are about to fall and that the borrower may be tempted to replace a high-coupon debt with a new, low-coupon bond. (Such a transaction is called refunding.) However, the higher yield alone, is not sufficient compensation to the investor for the call privilege. Thus the price at which the bond may be called, termed the *call price,* is normally higher than the principal or face value of the issue. The difference between call price and principal is the *call premium,* whose value may be as much as one year's interest in the first few years of a bond's life and may decline systematically thereafter.

An important limitation on the borrower's right to call is the *period of call protection* or *deferment period,* which is a specified number of years in the early life of the bond during which the issuer may not call the debt. Such protection is another concession to the investor and comes in two forms. Some bonds are *noncallable* (often abbreviated NC) for any reason during the deferment period; other bonds are nonrefundable (NR) for that time. The distinction lies in the fact that nonrefundable debt may be called for reasons of merger or reorganization if the firm uses unborrowed or internally generated funds for the transaction. The market attaches a higher value to the protection from refunding, even though it is less extensive than the provision of noncallability.

Variations in call protection mirror the type of issuer of the bond. Industrial debt is usually nonrefundable for 10 years but immediately callable for other reasons. Public utility bonds tend to be noncallable for five years. Treasury bonds with 20 years to maturity are noncallable for at least the first 15 years, and debt of federal agencies has protection against call for 10 years. Municipal bonds tend to offer 10 years of protection against call. It is important to note that debt from federal sources is seldom called or refunded for purposes of saving interest payments; rather, government debt managers attempt to refund debt in a way that is consistent with stability in the capital markets.

Some years ago, *Barron's* carried an article on refunding entitled "The Unwelcome Call." A firm's exercise of its call privilege is unwelcome because of its impact on an investor's return. The following example will illustrate the point. Suppose an investor is holding a bond with an 11 percent coupon and 13 years of remaining maturity. The expected return seven years ago when the bond was purchased at par ($1,000) was 11 percent. The deferment period, now passed, was set at five years. Suppose further that the company can now float a new 20-year bond for a rate of 9 percent and that the call premium on the old debt is $85 (and initially was $110, or one year's interest).

In the investor's view, the existence of the call has two unpleasant consequences. First, the market value of the bond cannot exceed par plus call premium, or $1,085. If the firm did not have the option to buy at that price, the value of the bond would have risen to more than $1,150, which is the present value of the remaining interest payments and principal, discounted at the current market rate of 9 percent. But no investor will pay more than $1,085, the price at which the firm can force a bondholder to sell. The second consequence is that the realized return is lower than the originally expected 11 percent. The yearly return from initial purchase to call, seven years later, is approximately 11.8 percent, which is the discount rate equating the purchase price of $1,000 to the present value of seven years of $110 in coupons and a call price of $1,085. However, if the investor reinvests the proceeds in a bond of like risk and relatively similar maturity, he can expect only a return of 9 percent per year over the remaining 13 years of the original planning period. Hence, in the absence of any shift in rates, the investor's likely return from the original investment and the forced second one is rather substantially below the 11 percent originally expected when the investor bought the bond with limited protection from call.

The example has raised the question of when the firm might find it profitable to refund an issue. It is important for investors to understand the process by which a firm decides whether it ought to retire an old bond and issue a new one. A simple and brief example will illustrate that process and introduce the reader to the kinds of calculations to make when trying to predict whether a bond will be refunded.

Suppose a firm's outstanding debt consists of $30 million in a bond with a coupon of 10 percent, a maturity of 15 years, and a lapsed deferment period. The firm can now issue a bond, with a similar maturity, for an interest rate of 7.8 percent. Assume that the issuing expenses and legal fees amount to $200,000. The call price on the old bond is $1,050.

The firm must pay, adjusted for taxes, the sum of call premium and expenses. This sum is $850,000, given that the tax rate is 50 percent and the call premium is $1.5 million.[7] Such a transaction would save the firm a yearly sum of $330,000 in interest (which equals the interest of $3 million on the old bond less the $2.34 million on the new, adjusted for taxes) for the next 15 years.[8] The rate of return on a payment of $850,000 now in exchange for a yearly savings of $330,000 per year for 15 years is about 38 percent. This rate exceeds the firm's aftertax cost of debt (now at 7.8 percent times .5 or 3.9 percent) and makes the refunding a profitable transaction.[9]

Sinking-Fund Provision

The *sinking-fund provision*, which is typical for publicly and privately issued industrial bonds and not uncommon among certain classes of utility debt, requires the obligor to retire a certain amount of the outstanding debt each year. Generally, the retirement occurs in one of two ways. The firm may purchase the amount of bonds to be retired in the open market if their price is below par, or the company may make payments to the trustee empowered to monitor the indenture and the trustee will call a certain number of bonds chosen by lottery. In the latter case, the investor would receive the prearranged call price, which is usually very close to par value. The schedule of retirements varies considerably from bond to bond. Some issuers, particularly in the private-placement market, retire most if not all of their debt before maturity. In the public market, some companies may retire as little as 20 percent or 30 percent of the outstanding par value before maturity. Further, many companies write a deferment period into the indenture, permitting them to wait five years or more before beginning the process of sinking-fund retirements. Government debt is generally free of this provision.

It is generally conceded that sinking-fund provisions redound, on balance, to the benefit of the investor. The sinking-fund requirement assures an orderly retirement of the debt so that the final payment, at

---

[7] Both expenses are tax-deductible expenses for the firm. The total expense is the call premium of $1.5 million plus the issuing expenses and legal fees of $200,000. The aftertax cost is equal to the before-tax cost times (1 − tax rate). Hence the aftertax cost is $1.7 million times (1 − .5), or $850,000.

[8] The new interest expense would be $30 million times .078. The aftertax cost of the interest expense is $660,000 times (1 − .5).

[9] Most analysts believe that the "hurdle rate" for refunding must be the aftertax cost of debt, which equals the product of the yield-to-maturity and (1 − marginal tax rate of the firm).

maturity, will not be too large. Second, the provision enhances the liquidity of some debt, especially the smaller issues and Eurobonds, which have thin secondary markets. Third, the prices of bonds with this requirement are presumably more stable because the issuer may become an active participant on the buy side when prices fall. For these reasons, the yields on bonds with sinking-fund provisions tend to be less than those on bonds without them, all else being the same.

Sometimes, however, the sinking fund can work to the disadvantage of an investor. Suppose that an investor is holding one of the early bonds to be called for a sinking fund. All of the time and effort put into analyzing the bond would now have become wasted, and the investor would have to choose new instruments for purchase. Also, an investor holding a bond with a high coupon at the time rates begin to fall is still forced to relinquish the issue. For this reason, in times of high interest rates one might find investors demanding higher yields from bonds with sinking funds than from other debt.

The sinking-fund provision may also harm the investor's position through the *doubling option,* which is part of many corporate bond indentures. With this option, the corporation is free to retire twice the amount of debt the sinking fund requires and to do it at the call price set for sinking-fund matters. Of course, the firm will exercise this doubling option only if the price of the bond exceeds the sinking-fund price (usually near par), and this happens when rates are relatively low. If, as is typically the case, the sinking-fund provision becomes operative before the lapse of the call-deferment period, the firm can retire much of its debt with the doubling option and can do so at a price far below that of the call price it would have to pay in the event of refunding. The impact of such activity on the investor's position is obvious: The firm can redeem at or near par many of the bonds that appear to be protected from call and that have a market value above the face value of the debt.

Convertible Debt

A *convertible bond* is one that can, after a lapse of a deferment period, be exchanged for specified amounts of common stock in the issuing firm: The conversion cannot be reversed, and the terms of the conversion are set by the company in the bond's indenture. The most important term is *conversion price* or *conversion ratio,* which dictates the number of shares of common to which the holder of the convertible has a claim. For example, one convertible issue of Burlington Industries matures in 2008 and has a coupon rate of 8.75 percent; this bond has a conversion ratio of 20.619 shares for one bond, or a conversion price of $48.50 per share. Typically, the conversion ratio falls through time, in a schedule contained in the indenture.

The *conversion value* is the market value of the shares into which the bond can be converted. At issuance, the value is less than the face value of the bond, and the difference between them is the *conversion premium*. If the value of the stock grows over time, then the difference begins to favor conversion from fixed income to common stock.

Should investors delay conversion despite a rising price of common, the firm can exert a certain amount of pressure on the bondholders by exercising the call privilege, which is a part of almost all convertible debt. The specified call price is usually equal to or less than par plus one year's interest and can accordingly be much less than the market value of the common stock, which may have appreciated since the convertible was first issued. Another form of pressure on the investor to convert has already been mentioned—the conversion ratio falls through time as the conversion price rises. Investors thus have an incentive not to keep the fixed income security too long in the face of a rising common stock price.

Companies issue convertible bonds for several reasons. The conversion feature produces a yield on the bond that is below that of otherwise similar "straight" or nonconvertible issues. Also, the interest on a convertible may appeal to many investors who want the cash flow and safety of a bond while still enjoying the prospects of capital gains should the company's stock begin to perform well. In addition, convertibles offer a firm a chance to avoid dilution in earnings per share, which a new equity issue might bring about. Such a consideration would be important to a firm about to embark on a project whose earnings will not materialize for some time. By using convertible debt instead of new common, the firm can expect that its number of shares will not increase until investors see improved earnings and higher prices for common stock. Convertible bonds are also tempting to management that believes the market is underestimating its firm's potential. Though small and aggressive firms have been ready to use this financing tool, some large concerns have also employed convertible debt as a funding mechanism.

Convertibles offer investors the relatively safe income of a bond as well as the opportunity for capital gains should the price of the stock do well. Thus a convertible bond is like a straight bond with a very long call option. As a result, convertibles often have higher prices than nonconvertible debt of similar characteristics. Convertibles are especially attractive to those institutions forbidden by regulatory agencies from holding common stock. By buying convertibles these institutions can participate in the stock market even though they are holding bonds.

Anyone interested in convertibles should take notice of two potential problems. First, the yields on convertibles, as mentioned above, are substantially below that of straight debt. Second, convertibles tend to be *subordinated debentures,* a form of debt that has a somewhat residual claim on the firm's income and assets in the case of liquidation. In fact subordinated debt usually has a lower credit rating than otherwise similar bonds. Thus, even though the convertible bond promises the relatively safe income of a fixed income security, the investor should realize that it is often a junior debt and inferior to other forms of debt in important respects. Techniques for analyzing convertible bonds are discussed in Chapter 19.

Warrants

A *warrant* is an option a firm issues that permits the owner to buy, from the firm, a certain number of shares of common stock at a specified price. It is not uncommon for publicly held corporations to issue warrants with new bonds. Firms issue bonds sweetened by warrants in order to decrease the cost of debt and, eventually, to increase the amount of equity in the firm when investors exercise their warrants. Though many small and marginal firms issue bonds with warrants, it is not uncommon for large firms to employ this technique in raising new debt capital.

One of the most valuable aspects of a warrant is that it has a rather long life: Most warrants are in effect for at least two years from issuance, and some are perpetual.[10] Another key feature of the warrant is the *exercise price*, the value for which the warrant holder can buy stock from the corporation. This price is normally set at 15 percent or so above market price of common at the time the bond is issued. Frequently, the exercise price will rise through time, according to the schedule in the bond's indenture. Another important characteristic of the warrant is its *detachability*. Detachable warrants can be sold to third parties who can exercise them with the firm. These warrants are often actively traded on the American Stock Exchange. Other warrants can be exercised only by the bondholder, and these are called nondetachable warrants.

The chief benefit to the investor is the financial leverage the warrant provides. The following example illustrates the point. Suppose that a company's warrant that allows the holder to buy one share of common has an exercise price of $55, that its market value is $3, and that it is detachable. Suppose further that the price of the stock is now $50. If the price of the underlying common were to rise to $60, or an increase of 20 percent, the price of the warrant would rise to at least $5 (the difference between the market value of the stock and the price at which the warrant holder can get shares from the company). The warrant's value would then have risen by more than 66 percent. The prospect of such large gains explains why bonds with warrants are more attractive to investors than is similar debt without warrants. Hence the price of a

---

[10] This long life contrasts sharply with the three to nine months during which call options on common stock, similar to warrants, are exercisable.

bond with a warrant is higher (and its yield is lower) than that of an otherwise similar bond without a warrant. A further discussion of warrants appears in Chapter 19.

PREFERRED STOCK

Preferred stock is a form of equity or ownership in a publicly held corporation. As the term implies, the claims of the holders of preferred stock are superior in some important ways to those of the owners of the other form of equity, common shares. The firm must pay dividends on preferreds before it is free to distribute earnings to holders of common stock. Also, in the event of liquidation, the owners of preferreds have a prior claim on any assets that may remain after the creditors have been satisfied. One difference between preferred and common is that holders of preferred are not normally permitted a voting power in the management of the firm.

The dividend on a preferred stock is, like the coupon on a bond, a fixed payment. A preferred with a dividend of 8 percent and a par value of $100 (which is a typical value) would receive $8 per year. However, the dividend is unlike the coupon on a bond in that the firm is not legally bound to pay the dividend. The company may decide to omit or delay the dividend without suffering the legal consequences it would meet if it omitted a coupon payment. Some dividends are cumulative, which means that the firm must eventually pay arrearages on any previously omitted dividend payments. Other dividends are noncumulative, and the firm may skip them without the liability of having to pay them later. A very small number of preferreds, called participating, entitle the investor to receive extra dividends in the case when common dividends exceed the level of dividends on preferred issues.

Public utilities are the prime issuers of preferred stock. Their aim in using this hybrid security is to increase the equity portion of their balance sheet or to prepare the way for a later flotation of new debt. Industrial concerns use preferred primarily in the special cases of merger or acquisition. The type of preferred used then is *convertible preferred*, which will be discussed later. Industrial firms find preferred an unsuitable form of financing because the dividend payments are not tax deductible, as are interest payments on bonds. If the tax rate of a firm is near 50 percent, then the true aftertax cost of debt capital is nearly half as large as the rate on preferred equity. Utilities, by contrast, have an easier time passing costs along to customers and consequently are not reluctant to employ preferred stock in their capital structure.

The expected rate of return on preferred stock is easy to calculate. Because it is a form of equity and a perpetuity, preferred stock has no maturity or principal to be redeemed (with the exceptions of some cases to be analyzed later). Thus the price of preferred is simply the discounted value of an unlimited series of fixed dividend payments. It can be shown that the return on preferred is approximately equal to the ratio of the dividend to the price. (This calculation resembles the current yield on bonds discussed above.) For example, if the Duke Power preferred with a dividend of $8.70 has a price of $61, then its yield is 14.26 percent. This figure is the one reported in *The Wall Street Journal* table of trades from the preceding day on the market. As is the case with bonds, the price and yield of preferred stock vary inversely: A rise in yield brings about a fall in price, and vice versa. Further, the yields on preferreds tend to correspond closely to and move in concert with the yields on other long-term fixed income securities. Any utility may have more than one preferred stock outstanding at any time, and the different instruments are designated by their dividend level. For example, Duke Power currently has at least four preferreds outstanding—one with a dividend of 8.7 percent, another with a dividend of 8.2 percent, a third with a dividend of 2.69 percent, and so on.

Preferreds have a number of characteristics that are analogous to those discussed above in connection with corporate bonds. The first is the call provision. By such a provision the issuer has the right to redeem, under certain circumstances and at a price near par plus one year's dividend, the outstanding preferred stock. Normally the issuer will be motivated to call the stock when rates fall below the level in effect when the preferred stock was first issued. Again, as in the case of bonds, saved payments are the goal of early retirement. Also the issuer has usually granted the investor a deferment period during which the stock cannot be called. As in the case of bonds, the actual call provisions can vary considerably from stock to stock, company to company, and time to time.

Preferred stock also often contains a sinking-fund provision, which mandates that the issuer retire a given percentage of the issue at scheduled periods after issuance. Investors holding a stock with this provision tend to calculate its yield in a manner similar to the yield-to-maturity on bonds. Obviously, a preferred stock with a sinking fund bears a strong resemblance to a typical corporate bond: Both have fixed, periodic payments, both have maturities, and both have large par value payments at the time of maturity.

Finally, as mentioned above, some preferred stock is convertible into shares of common of the issuing company. This instrument has been popular in the arrangement of mergers and acquisitions. If an acquiring company offers convertible preferreds in exchange for common stock in the acquired firm, the owners of that stock have no immediate tax liability. By accepting the convertible preferred, the owners of the acquired firm can receive a steady stream of high dividends and decide when, and to what extent, they might want to convert into common shares of the acquiring firm.

One more interesting facet of preferred stock requires mention here. The dividends from preferred stock are not fully taxable if the owner of the stock is a corporation. As a result of this rule, corporations tend to be active buyers of the preferreds of other companies, particularly the utilities. This point will be treated in greater detail in Chapter 11.

SUMMARY

This chapter has provided an introduction to some of the fundamental attributes of bonds and preferred stock. The chapter has explored, in a preliminary way, such matters as the yields and pricing of these instruments, the motivation behind the issuance of the securities, and the key features of the assets. We have examined to some extent the impact on the investor's experience of such characteristics as call features, sinking-fund provisions, and convertibility. It is our hope that this chapter will supply the reader with a general knowledge of the instruments and provide a conceptual and terminological background for the later chapters that will investigate, in some detail, each of the features discussed above.

The bond market has become a very exciting investment arena. A decade of high and volatile interest rates has had two important effects: (1) It has created a variability in bond prices and returns that have offered both large gains and large risks to its investors; and (2) the recent past has encouraged issuers and investors alike to experiment with unusual types of debt and fixed income securities.

3

Federal Income Tax Treatment of Fixed Income Securities*

Frank J. Fabozzi, Ph.D., C.F.A., C.P.A.
Visiting Professor
Sloan School of Management
Massachusetts Institute of Technology

A knowledge of federal income tax rules governing security transactions is essential to understand how fixed income securities are priced and why certain institutions and individuals participate in particular segments of the market. Several examples will make this clear.

First, as explained in this chapter, bonds selling below their redemption value that were issued after July 18, 1984 are treated differently than bonds issued prior to that date. This difference in the tax treatment makes the bonds issued prior to July 18, 1984 more attractive than those issued after that date, resulting in a lower pretax yield compared to post-July 18, 1984 issues also selling below their redemption value.

As another example, consider bonds that are exempt from Federal income taxes. These bonds will sell at a lower yield relative to taxable bonds because of the tax-exempt feature. Some institutions, such as pension funds, do not pay taxes and are not interested in tax-exempt bonds. However, institutions that are subject to federal income taxes, such as commercial banks and insurance companies, will alter how they participate in the market for taxable and tax-exempt bonds depending on their expected marginal tax rate.

Not only does the prevailing tax law have an impact on fixed income security prices, but so also will anticipated changes in the tax law. For example, when there is a likelihood that tax rates may be reduced for

---

* At the time of this writing, legislation has been proposed to eliminate the preferential treatment of capital gains. Should this legislation be passed, the discussion of the capital gains treatment may no longer be appropriate.

individuals, the price of tax-exempt bonds may fall (yield rise) because the tax-exempt feature has less value to individuals. As another example, the threat that the Internal Revenue Service may disallow the tax-exempt status of a particular municipal (tax-exempt) bond because of some perceived violation by the issuer will drive down the price of that bond so as to increase its yield.

This chapter explains the federal income tax treatment of fixed income security transactions. The tax rules applicable to interest-rate options and futures are described in Chapter 47. It is impossible to cover all of the nuances in the tax code that affect fixed income security prices and the tax provisions specifically applicable to certain institutions. Some of these are covered in other chapters of this book. Since the tax law changes, it is important for investors to investigate how those changes will impact their current portfolio and investment philosophy.

SOME DEFINITIONS

Gross Income, Adjusted Gross Income, and Taxable Income

Investors often use the term *income* in a very casual way. The Internal Revenue Code (IRC), however, provides a more precise definition of income. The IRC distinguishes between gross income, adjusted gross income and taxable income. *Gross income* is all income that is subject to income tax. For example, interest income and dividends are subject to taxation. However, there is a statutory exemption for interest from certain types of debt obligations, as explained later in this chapter. For such obligations, interest income is not included in gross income. Gross income for an individual and a corporation is determined in the same manner.

Adjusted gross income is gross income minus certain business and other deductions. For example, for investors an important deduction from gross income to arrive at adjusted gross income is the long-term capital gain deduction. This deduction will be discussed later in this chapter.

Taxable income is the amount on which the tax liability is determined. It is found by subtracting the personal exemption allowance and other permissible deductions (other than those deductible in arriving at adjusted gross income) from adjusted gross income. For a corporation, all permissible deductions are treated as business deductions. Therefore, adjusted gross income is meaningless for a corporation.

Tax Basis of a Capital Asset, Capital Gain, and Capital Loss

The IRC provides for a special tax treatment on the sale or exchange of a capital asset. The instruments described in this book—debt obligations, preferred stock, and shares of investment companies specializing in fixed income securities—would qualify as capital assets in the hands of a qualified owner. In order to understand the tax treatment of a capital asset, the tax *basis* of a capital asset must first be defined. In most instances the *original basis* of a capital asset is the taxpayer's total cost on the date it is acquired.[1] The *adjusted basis* of a capital asset is its original basis increased by capital additions and decreased by capital recoveries.

The proceeds received from the sale or exchange of a capital asset are compared to the adjusted basis to determine if the transaction produced a capital gain or capital loss. If the proceeds exceed the adjusted basis, the taxpayer realized a *capital gain;* on the other hand, a *capital loss* is realized when the adjusted basis exceeds the proceeds received by the taxpayer.

Classification of Taxpayers: Dealers, Traders, Investors

For tax purposes, taxpayers are classified as either dealers, traders, or investors. The classification is important because it determines whether capital gain or loss provisions are applicable and the treatment of transaction costs.[2]

Traders and investors are entitled to realize capital gains and losses. Dealers, on the other hand, are not. In the case of dealers the securities held are considered inventory, and any gains or losses are treated as ordinary gains or losses rather than capital gains or losses.[3] A dealer in securities is a merchant of securities who is regularly engaged in the acquisition of securities and subsequent resale to customers with a view to the gains and profits that may be derived as a result of such transactions. A dealer may be an individual, partnership, or corporation.

A trader is a person who buys and sells for his or her own account rather than the account of a customer, and the frequency of such transacting is such that the person may be said to be engaged in such activi-

---

[1] When securities are purchased in a package, it is necessary to unbundle the package in order to determine the basis for each security. The general rule for determining the basis of each security is to allocate the cost of the package based upon the total fair market value of the unit immediately after the acquisition. For example, suppose that a unit package containing one bond and one share of preferred stock is purchased for $950. Immediately after the acquisition, the bond sells for $900 and the preferred stock for $85. The total value of the unit is therefore $985. The original basis of the bond is then 91.4 percent ($900 divided by $985) of the acquisition cost, or $868.30 (.914 times $950). The original basis of the preferred stock is $81.70 (.086 times $950).

[2] The classification is also important because it determines whether "wash sale" provisions are applicable. (A wash sale is defined in footnote 19.)

[3] There is an exception. If a dealer (1) clearly designates that certain securities are being held for investment purposes when the securities are acquired, and (2) does not hold the securities primarily for sale to customers in the ordinary course of business after the designation, then gains or losses on the designated securities qualify for capital gain and loss treatment.

ties as a trade or business. Investors, like traders, transact for their own accounts. However, transactions are occasional and much less than required in a trade or business.

Regardless of the classification of the taxpayer, expenses incurred to acquire a security are treated as part of the acquisition cost. Selling expenses, however, are handled differently for traders and investors compared with dealers. Traders and investors must deduct the selling expenses from the sale price when determining whether a capital gain or loss is realized. For dealers, selling expenses are deducted as a business expense.

INTEREST INCOME

Interest received by a taxpayer is included in gross income, unless there is a specific statutory exemption indicating otherwise. Therefore, if a taxpayer purchases $10,000 in par value of a corporate bond that has a coupon rate of 12 percent, the taxpayer expects to receive $1,200 per year. If that amount is actually paid by the issuer in the tax year, it is included in gross income.

Interest received on debt issued by any state or political subdivision thereof,[4] the District of Columbia, any possession of the United States, and certain local and urban agencies operating under the auspices of the Department of Housing and Urban Development is not included in gross income.

The statutory exemption of the interest received from debtors who are state and local governments (both referred to as municipalities in this chapter) is supposedly based upon the reciprocal immunity doctrine of the United States Constitution. This doctrine holds that states cannot interfere in the operations of the federal government, and the latter cannot interfere in the operations of the former. By taxing interest income on municipal obligations, it is argued that the ability of the state to finance its operations would be impaired. Although the exemption is still part of the Internal Revenue Code, many political analysts believe that since the passage of the 16th Amendment to the Constitution, the exemption has been based upon political reasons rather than on constitutional grounds.

Likewise, interest paid on debt issued by the U.S. government is exempt from income taxation by state and local governments but not from federal income taxes. Interest income by U.S. territories, the District of Columbia, and certain local urban agencies operating under HUD

---

[4] Because of financing practices by some state and local governments that Congress viewed as abusive, Congress imposed limitations on the issuance of tax-exempt obligations in various amendments to the Internal Revenue Code of 1954. The limitations involved industrial development bonds and arbitrage bonds. See Chapter 12.

is also exempt from all state and local income taxes. Most states exempt the interest income from their own debt obligations, agencies, and political subdivisions from state and local income taxes. States may exempt the interest income from obligations of other states and political subdivisions.

As explained in Chapter 4, a portion of the income realized from holding a fixed income security may be in the form of capital appreciation, rather than interest income. The tax treatment of the income component that represents capital appreciation differs depending on when the bond was issued. Prior to the The Deficit Reduction Act of 1984, any capital appreciation that did not represent original-issue discount (to be discussed later) was generally treated as a capital gain.[5] As explained later in this chapter, the IRC provides for favorable tax treatment for certain capital gains. The 1984 act still allows this tax treatment for bonds issued on or prior to July 18, 1984; however, for bonds issued after that date, part of the capital appreciation will be treated as ordinary income. This tax treatment of income from holding a debt instrument will have a major impact on the aftertax return realized by an investor. Because of the importance of distinguishing between income in the form of a capital gain (or loss) and interest income, the investor must be familiar with certain rules set forth in the IRC. These rules are summarized later in this chapter.

Unlike debt instruments whose interest payments are taxable, the capital gain portion of a tax-exempt bond is unattractive for an investor who seeks tax-free income. This is because although the coupon interest received is exempt from federal income taxation, the capital gain portion is subject to taxation, albeit at a lower rate than coupon interest received from a taxable obligation. This point should be kept in mind when considering the acquisition of a tax-exempt obligation.[6]

Accrued Interest

Usually, bond interest is paid semiannually. The interest earned by the seller from holding the bond until the disposal date is called *accrued interest*. For example, if a corporate bond whose issuer promises to pay $60 on June 1 and December 1 for a specified number of years is sold on October 1, the seller is usually entitled to accrued interest of $40 ($60 times ⅔) for the four months that the seller held the bond.

---

[5] This is not true for original-issue discount obligations issued by individuals.

[6] As explained in Chapter 12, there is a formula suggested for determining the equivalent taxable yield for a tax-exempt obligation. This formula is only an approximation because it assumes that all of the income is tax free.

Let us look at the tax position of the seller and the buyer, assuming that our hypothetical bond is selling for $900 in the market and that the seller's adjusted basis for this bond is $870. The buyer must pay the seller $940, $900 for the market price plus $40 of accrued interest. The seller must treat the accrued interest of $40 as interest income. The $900 is compared to the seller's adjusted basis of $870 to determine whether the seller has realized a capital gain or capital loss. Obviously, the seller has realized capital appreciation of $30. When the buyer receives the December 1 interest payment of $60, only $20 is included in gross income as interest income. The basis of the bond for the buyer is $900, not $940.

Not all transactions involving bonds require the payment of accrued interest by the buyer. This occurs when the issuer of the bond is in default of principal or interest, or if the interest on the bonds is contingent on sufficient earnings of the issuer.[7] Such bonds are said to be quoted *flat*. The acquisition price entitles the buyer to receive the principal and unpaid interest for both past scheduled payments due and accrued interest. Generally, for bonds quoted flat, all payments made by the issuer to the buyer are first considered as payments to satisfy defaulted payments or unpaid contingent interest payments and accrued interest before acquisition. Such payments are treated as a return of capital. As such, the proceeds reduce the cost basis of the bond. On the other hand, accrued interest after the acquisition date is considered interest income when received.

For example, suppose the issuer of a corporate bond is in default of two scheduled interest payments of $60 each. The interest payments are scheduled on April 1 and October 1. The bond is sold for $500 on August 1. Assume that on October 1 of the year of acquisition the issuer pays the bondholder $120. The buyer would treat the payment as a return of capital of $120, since it represents the two defaulted interest payments. Hence the adjusted basis of the bond is $380 ($500 minus $120) and is not considered interest income. Suppose that two weeks later the issuer pays an additional $60 to the bondholder. This payment must then be apportioned between accrued interest before the acquisition date of August 1 and accrued interest after the acquisition date. The latter is $20, since the bond was held by the buyer for two months. Thus $40 of the $60 payment reduces the adjusted basis of $380 prior to the second payment to $340 and is not treated as interest income. The $20 of accrued interest since the acquisition date is treated as interest income.

---

[7] A bond whose interest is contingent upon sufficient earnings by the issuer is called an *income bond* and is discussed in Chapter 10.

Bond Purchased at a Premium

When a bond is purchased at a price greater than its redemption value at maturity, the bond is said to be purchased at a premium.[8] For a taxable bond purchased by a nondealer taxpayer, the taxpayer may elect to amortize the premium ratably over the remaining life of the security. In the case of a convertible bond selling at a premium, however, the amount attributable to the conversion feature may not be amortized. The amount amortized reduces the amount of the interest income that will be taxed. In turn, the basis is reduced by the amount of the amortization.

For a tax-exempt bond, the premium *must* be amortized. Although the amount amortized is not a tax-deductible expense since the interest is exempt from taxation, the amortization reduces the original basis.

For example, suppose on January 1, 1981, a calendar-year taxpayer purchased *taxable* bonds for $10,500. The bonds have a remaining life of 10 years and a $10,000 redemption value at maturity. The coupon rate is 7 percent. The premium is $500. The taxpayer can amortize this premium over the 10-year remaining life. If so, the amount amortized would be $50 per year ($500 divided by 10).[9] The coupon interest received of $700 ($10,000 times .07) would then be effectively reduced by $50 so that $650 would be reported as interest income. At the end of 1981, the first year, the original basis of $10,500 is reduced by $50 to $10,450. By the end of 1985 the bond would be held for five years. The adjusted basis would be $10,250 ($10,500 minus $250). If the bond is held until retired by the issuer at maturity, the adjusted basis would be $10,000, and consequently there would be no capital gain or loss realized. If the taxpayer does not elect to amortize the premium, the original basis is not changed. Consequently, at maturity the taxpayer would realize a capital loss of $500.

Had our hypothetical bond been a tax-exempt bond, the premium would have had to be amortized. The coupon interest of $700 would be tax exempt, and the amortization of $50 would not be a tax-deductible expense.[10] Instead, the basis would be adjusted each year.

---

[8] A bond will sell at a premium so that the effective interest rate of the bond is adjusted to reflect the prevailing interest rate on securities of comparable risk and remaining maturity. For a further discussion, see Chapter 4.

[9] There is a method that provides the precise value of the amount that should be amortized each year. This is known as the constant-yield (or scientific) method and is explained later in this chapter. However, this method provides lower amortization in the earlier years than the straight-line method of amortization used in the example. Consequently, the straight-line method is preferred for taxable bonds if the taxpayer elects to amortize the premium.

[10] In the case of tax-exempt bonds, the scientific method of amortization would be preferred, since the adjusted basis would be higher than if the straight-line method were used. Consequently there would be a greater capital loss or smaller capital gain if the bonds were sold before maturity.

As an illustration of the amortization for a bond purchased some time during the tax year rather than at the beginning of the tax year, let's take an actual case. In April 1981 Albany County South Mall 10s maturing 4/1/85 sold for approximately $270,285. The redemption value at maturity per bond was $250,000. Suppose that a calendar-year taxpayer purchased the bond on April 1, 1981. The premium was $20,285 ($270,285 minus $250,000).

The number of months remaining to maturity was 48 (four years times 12 months). Consequently, the monthly amortization was $422.60. At the end of 1981 the original basis of $270,285 was reduced by the amortization corresponding to the number of months the bond was held for in 1981. Since the bond was held for nine months (April 1 to December 31), the original basis was reduced by $3,803.40 ($422.60 times nine months). Hence, the adjusted basis was $266,481.60 ($270,285 minus $3,803.40) at the end of 1981.

Suppose the bond was sold on October 31, 1982, and the taxpayer received $260,000. To determine whether there was a capital gain or loss, the adjusted basis must be ascertained. Since the bond was held for 19 months, amortization was $8,029.40 ($422.60 times 19 months) and the adjusted basis was $262,255.60 ($270,285 minus $8,029.40). Hence the taxpayer would realize a capital loss of $2,255.60, the difference between the adjusted basis of $262,255.60 and the proceeds received of $260,000.

So far in our illustration we have used the original basis and the remaining number of years to maturity to determine the amount to be amortized. In the case of a callable taxable bond acquired after January 1, 1957, the taxpayer must elect to compute the amortization based upon the earlier call date *if a smaller deduction results compared to using the number of years remaining to maturity.* For example, suppose an investor purchased a bond that has 10 years remaining to maturity for $1,300. The redemption value at maturity is $1,000; however, the bond may be called in six years for $1,150. If the bond is a taxable bond, then the first election the investor must make is whether or not to amortize the premium. If the investor elects to amortize the premium, then the investor must elect to base the amount of the amortization on the call price and date rather than on the redemption value at maturity if the deduction is less. If the amount amortized is based on the redemption value at maturity, then the annual amount deducted would be $30, since the premium is $300 and there are 10 years remaining to maturity. If the earlier call date is used, the amount of the premium is $150. The annual deduction is $25 per year, since there are six years to the call date.

Should a bond be called before its maturity date, any unamortized portion of the premium is treated as an ordinary loss in the year the bond is called. For example, consider our hypothetical 10-year bond that is callable in 6 years. If the bond were actually called in the sixth year, an investor who did not elect to amortize the premium would realize an ordinary loss of $150 (original basis of $1,300 minus call price of $1,150). Notice what happens if the premium is amortized. Amortization based upon the maturity date would result in a capital gain of $30.[11] Of course, amortization based upon the call date would have generated neither a capital gain nor loss.

As noted earlier, no portion of the premium attributable to the conversion feature of a convertible bond may be amortized. For example, suppose a 15-year convertible bond with a 9.5 percent coupon rate is selling for $1,400. The investor must determine what portion of the premium is due to the conversion value. Suppose the investor determines that nonconvertible bonds with the same quality rating and years remaining to maturity are selling to yield 8.1 percent, A 15-year bond priced to yield 8.1 percent would sell for $1,120.30 per $1,000 of redemption value at maturity.[12] Consequently, the premium that the investor may elect to amortize is based upon $1,120.30, *not* $1,400.

Bond Purchased at a Discount

A bond purchased at a price less than its redemption value at maturity is said to be bought at a *discount*. The tax treatment of the discount depends upon whether the discount represents *original-issue discount* or a bond that was not sold at an original-issue discount but is purchased in the secondary market at a market discount.

Original-issue discount bonds. When bonds are issued, they may be sold at a price that is less than their redemption value at maturity. Such bonds are called original-issue discount bonds. The difference between the redemption value and the purchase price is the original-issue discount. Each year a portion of the original-issue discount must be amortized (accrued) and included in gross income. There is a corresponding increase in the adjusted basis of the bond.

The tax treatment of an original-issue discount bond depends on its issuance date. For obligations issued prior to July 2, 1982, the original-issue discount must be amortized on a straight-line basis each month and included in gross income based on the number of months the bond is held in that tax year. For obligations issued on or after July 2, 1982, the amount of the original-issue discount amortized is based on the constant-yield method (also called the effective or scientific method) and included in gross income based on the number of days in the tax year that the bond is held. With this method for determining the amount of the original-issue discount to be included in gross income, the interest

---

[11] The adjusted basis would be the original basis of $1,300 minus the amount amortized over the six years of $180 ($30 times six). The capital gain is therefore the call price of $1,150 minus the adjusted basis of $1,120.

[12] See Chapter 4 for the pricing of bonds.

for the year is first determined by multiplying the adjusted basis by the yield at issuance. From this interest, the coupon interest is subtracted. The difference is the amount of the original-issue discount amortized for the year. The same amount is then added to the adjusted basis.

To illustrate the tax rules for original-issue discount bonds, consider a bond with a 4-percent coupon rate (interest paid semiannually), maturing in five years, that was issued for $7,683, and has a redemption value of $10,000. The yield-to-maturity for this hypothetical bond is 10 percent. The original-issue discount is $2,317 ($10,000 − $7,683). Suppose that the bond was purchased by an investor on the day it was issued, January 1, 198X. First, assume that this hypothetical bond was issued prior to July 2, 1982. The investor is required to amortize the original-issue discount of $2,317 on a straight-line monthly basis. Since there are 60 months to maturity, the prorated monthly interest on a straight-line basis is $38.62 ($2,317 ÷ 60). Since the hypothetical bond is assumed to be purchased on January 1, the annual interest that must be reported from the amortization of the original-issue discount *each year* is $464 ($38.62 × 12). The total interest reported each year from holding this bond is $464 plus the coupon interest of $400 ($10,000 × .04). Exhibit 1 shows the amortization of the original-issue discount for each six-month period. Notice that, if the bond is held to maturity, there is no capital gain or loss since the adjusted basis will equal the redemption value of $10,000. If the bond is held for two years and six months, in the third year the investor reports $232 ($38.62 × 6) of interest income from amortization of the original-issue discount. The adjusted basis is $8,844. If the proceeds from the sale of the bond exceed $8,844, the investor realizes a capital gain. A capital loss is realized if the proceeds from the sale are less than $8,844.

Suppose instead that the bond was issued after July 2, 1982. The constant-yield method is used to determine the amortization and the adjusted basis. The procedure is as follows. Each six months, the investor of this hypothetical bond is assumed to realize for tax purposes interest equal to 5 percent of the adjusted basis. The 5 percent represents one half of the 10 percent yield to maturity. The original investment is the purchase price of $7,683. In the first six months the bond is held, the investor realizes for tax purposes interest equal to 5 percent of $7,683, or $384. The coupon payment for the first six-month period that the bond is held is $200. Therefore, $184 ($384 − $200) is assumed to be realized (although not received) by the investor. This is the amount of the original-issue discount amortized. The amount that will be reported as gross income from holding this bond for six months is $200 in coupon interest plus the $184 of the original-issue discount amortized. The adjusted basis for the bond at the end of the first six months will equal the original-issue price of $7,683 plus the amount of the original-issue discount amortized, $184. Thus, the adjusted basis is $7,867.

EXHIBIT 1 Amortization Schedule for an Original-Discount Bond Issued
Prior to July 2, 1982

Characteristics of hypothetical bond:

Coupon	= 4 percent
Interest payments	= semiannual
Issue price	= $7,683
Redemption value	= $10,000
Years to maturity	= 5
Yield to maturity	=10 percent
Original-issue discount	= $2,317
Monthly amortized market discount (straight-line method)	= $38.62
Six-month amortized market discount	= $232
Basis at time of purchase	= $7,683

		For the Period		
Period Held (Years)	Adjusted Basis*	Gross Income Reported	Coupon Interest	Original-Issue Discount Amortized
0.5	$ 7,916	$432	$200	$232
1.0	8,148	432	200	232
1.5	8,380	432	200	232
2.0	8,612	432	200	232
2.5	8,844	432	200	232
3.0	9,076	432	200	232
3.5	9,308	432	200	232
4.0	9,540	432	200	232
4.5	9,772	432	200	232
5.0	10,000	432	200	232

* Adjusted basis at the end of the period. The adjusted basis is found by adding $232 to the previous period's adjusted basis.

Let's carry this out for one more six-month period. If the bond is held for another six months, the amount of interest that the investor is expected to realize for tax purposes is 5 percent of the adjusted basis. Since the adjusted basis at the beginning of the second six-month period is $7,867, the interest is $393. The coupon interest for the second six months is $200. Therefore, the amount of the original-issue discount amortized for the second six-month period is $193 ($393 − $200). The $393 reported for holding the bond for the second six months is $200 in coupon interest and $193 in amortization of the original-issue discount. The adjusted basis at the end of the second six-month period is $8,060— the previous adjusted basis of $7,867 plus $193. If this bond, which was assumed to be purchased on January 1, 198X, is sold on December 31, 198X, interest income would be $777, consisting of $400 of coupon interest and $377 of the original-issue discount amortized. If this bond is sold on December 31, 198X, for $8,200, there would be a capital gain of $140, the difference between the sale proceeds of $8,200 and the adjusted basis of $8,060.

Exhibit 2 shows the amount of the original-issue discount that must be reported as gross income for each six-month period that the bond is held and the adjusted basis at the end of the period. Notice that amortization is lower in the earlier years, gradually increasing over the life of the bond on a compounding basis. For the pre-July 2, 1982 rules, the dollar amortization is constant each year. Note also that, if a bond is sold after 2.5 years, the adjusted basis is $8,700 using the constant-yield method, but $8,844 (see Exhibit 1) using the straight-line method. The constant-yield method results in a greater capital gain.

The 1984 act requires the holders of original-issue discount tax-exempt bonds to amortize the original-issue discount using the constant-

---

EXHIBIT 2 Amortization Schedule for an Original-Discount Bond Issued After July 2, 1982

Characteristics of hypothetical bond:
Coupon	= 4 percent
Interest payments	= semiannual
Issue price	= $7,683
Redemption value	= $10,000
Years to maturity	= 5
Yield to maturity	=10 percent
Original-issue discount	= $2,317
Basis at time of purchase	= $7,683

Amortization based on constant-yield method

		For the Period		
Period Held (Years)	Adjusted Basis*	Gross Income Reported†	Coupon Interest	Original-Issue Discount Amortized‡
0.5	$ 7,867	$384	$200	$184
1.0	8,060	393	200	193
1.5	8,263	403	200	203
2.0	8,476	413	200	213
2.5	8,700	424	200	224
3.0	8,935	435	200	235
3.5	9,182	447	200	247
4.0	9,441	459	200	259
4.5	9,713	472	200	272
5.0	10,000	486	200	286

* Adjusted basis at the end of the period. The adjusted basis is found by adding the original-issue discount amortized for the period to the previous period's adjusted basis.

† The gross income reported is equal to the coupon interest for the period plus the original-issue discount amortized for the period.

‡ By the constant yield method, it is found as follows:

(Adjusted basis in previous period × .05) − $200

yield method. However, the amount of the original-issued discount amortized is not included as part of gross income because all interest is
exempt from federal income taxes. The amount of the original-issue
discount is added to the adjusted basis.

The original-issue discount rules do not apply in two cases. The first
is the case of Series EE and E U.S. government savings bonds. The
holders of these bonds may elect to have the original-issue discount on
these bonds taxed when the bonds are redeemed rather than having the
accrued interest taxed annually. The second exception is for noninterest-
bearing obligations such as Treasury bills and many other taxable short-
term obligations with no more than one year to maturity. When these
obligations are held by investors who report for tax purposes on a *cash*
rather than an accrual basis, the discount is not recognized until redeemed or sold. However, there are restrictions on the deductibility of
interest to carry such obligations, as explained later in this chapter.

There are three more points the investor should be familiar with
when dealing with original-issue discount bonds. First, original-issue
discount is treated as zero if the discount is less than one fourth of 1
percent of the redemption value at maturity multiplied by the number of
complete years to maturity. For example, suppose a bond maturing in 20
years is initially sold for $990 for each $1,000 of redemption value at
maturity. The discount is $10. The redemption value multiplied by the
number of years to maturity is $20,000. The original-issue discount is
.0005 of $20,000. Since it is less than one fourth of 1 percent (.0025), the
original-issue discount is treated as zero; that is, the investor does not
have to amortize the discount and report it as gross income. Instead, the
rule discussed in the next section is applicable. Second, if an original-
issue discount bond is sold before maturity, subsequent holders must
continue to amortize the original-issue discount. The third point to keep
in mind is that an investor may have to pay taxes on interest included in
gross income but not received in cash. *Consequently, original-issue discount obligations are unattractive for portfolios of investors subject to taxation.*

**Bond purchased at a market discount with no original-issue dis-
count.** When a bond is purchased at a market discount and there is no
original-issue discount, the tax treatment depends on whether the bond
was issued on or prior to July 18, 1984, or after. For bonds issued before
that date, any capital appreciation is treated as a capital gain. If there is a
loss, it is a capital loss. For example, suppose that the hypothetical bond
used to illustrate the original-issue discount rules is not an original-issue
discount bond. Instead, suppose that the bond was issued 25 years ago
at par ($10,000) and 20 years later the price of the bond declined to
$7,683 because of a rise in interest rates. If this bond is purchased by an
investor for $7,683 and sold 2.5 years later for $9,000, the investor will
realize a capital gain of $1,317. As discussed later, this capital gain
would be treated as a long-term capital gain and afforded preferential

tax treatment. No amortization of the discount is required even though a portion of the capital appreciation really represents a form of interest.

The 1984 act changed the tax treatment for *taxable* bonds issued after July 18, 1984. Any capital appreciation must be separated into a portion that is attributable to interest income (as represented by bond amortization) and a portion that is attributable to capital gain. The portion representing interest income is taxed as ordinary income when the bond is sold. This is called accrued market discount. Unlike original-issue discount, the amount of the market discount that represents interest income (that is, bond amortization) is not taxed until the bond is sold. Accrued market discount can be determined using either the straight-line method or the constant-yield method.

Exhibit 3 shows the tax consequences for five assumed selling prices for the hypothetical bond that has been used in the examples above. The results are shown for bonds issued before and after July 18, 1984. The results are also shown for the constant-yield and straight-line methods.

Two implications are evident from Exhibit 3. First, from a tax perspective, taxable bonds issued before July 18, 1984, and selling at a discount will be more attractive than bonds issued after that date and selling at a discount. This will be reflected in the market price of those bonds. Consequently, investors that are in low marginal tax rates will find that they may be overpaying for bonds issued before July 18, 1984. The second implication is that it is not in the best interest of the investor to select the straight-line method to compute the accrued market discount because the capital gain will be lower than if the constant-yield method is elected.

Because of the difference in the tax treatment of original-issue discount bonds and market-discount bonds, prior to purchase the investor should check the type of bond and when it was issued.

DIVIDENDS

Preferred stock and investment companies specializing in fixed income securities are discussed later in this book. Both investment vehicles pay dividends rather than interest. The general rule applicable to these investment vehicles are discussed in this section.

Corporations make cash distributions to shareholders. Not all cash distributions, however, are taxed. For individual taxpayers, only that portion of the distribution representing dividends is included in gross income, subject to a $100 dividend exclusion for a single return and $200 for a joint return.

A *dividend* is defined as a payment made by a corporation out of earnings and profits in the year of distribution or earnings and profits accumulated in all years prior to the date of distribution. Dividend in-

---

EXHIBIT 3 Tax Treatment of Market Discount Bond for Five Assumed
Selling Prices

Characteristics of hypothetical bond:
     Coupon   = 4 percent
     Interest payments   = semiannual
     Bond price   = $7,683
     Redemption value   = $10,000
     Years to maturity   = 5
     Yield to maturity   = 10 percent
Market discount   = $2,317
Basis at time of purchase = $7,683
Bond sold after 2.5 years

Bond issued before July 18, 1984

Sale Price	Accrued Market Discount	Capital Gain (Loss)
$9,500	$ 0	$1,817
9,000	0	1,317
8,700	0	1,017
7,683	0	0
7,000	0	(693)

Bond issued after July 18, 1984, with amortization based on constant-yield method

Sale Price	Accrued Market Discount	Capital Gain (Loss)
$9,500	$1,017	$ 800
9,000	1,017	300
8,700	1,017	0
7,683	1,017	(1,017)
7,000	1,017	(1,700)

Bond issued after July 18, 1984, with amortization based on straight-line method

Sale Price	Accrued Market Discount	Capital Gain (Loss)
$9,500	$1,161	$ 656
9,000	1,161	156
8,700	1,161	(144)
7,683	1,161	(1,161)
7,000	1,161	(1,844)

come is taxed as ordinary income. Any portion of a distribution that does not represent a dividend or a redemption of stock is treated as a return of capital. No tax is paid on that portion; instead, the basis of the stock is reduced by that amount.[13]

Corporate recipients of dividend payments must include the entire amount in gross income. However, there is a special deduction that a corporation can take against dividend payments.[14] A corporate taxpayer is entitled to a deduction equal to (1) 85 percent of a dividend received from a domestic corporation[15] and (2) 100 percent of the dividend received from a corporation that is a member of a controlled group with the recipient corporation. For this reason, the treasurer of a corporation contemplating a fixed income investment would prefer a high-quality preferred stock issue to a high-quality, long-term debt instrument.

Dividends are also paid by regulated investment companies, such as a mutual fund.[16] Investment companies sell their own securities to the public and reinvest the proceeds in a large number of securities. The shareholder of an investment company participates in the return generated from holding and transactions involving these securities. The return earned by the investment company can therefore be in the form of interest, dividends, or capital gains. However, the dividend from an investment company to its shareholders is designated by the investment company in a written notice to its shareholders not later than 45 days after the close of the taxable year as either ordinary dividends or capital gains. Ordinary dividends are treated in the same way as preferred stock dividends. However, any portion of the dividend that represents tax-exempt income realized by the investment company is under certain conditions tax-exempt to the shareholder.[17] The amount classified as a capital gain is considered a long-term capital gain and treated accordingly as explained later in this chapter.

Not all of the long-term capital gain realized by the investment company is actually paid in cash to the shareholders. In that case, the investment company will pay the income tax on that portion retained. The shareholder, however, is deemed to have paid the tax on the undistributed capital gain, which can be refunded or credited to the shareholder. Moreover, the shareholder increases the basis of the share of the investment company by an amount equal to the excess of the long-term

---

[13] If the distribution that is not a dividend exceeds the adjusted basis, it is treated as a capital gain.

[14] Section 243(a) of the IRC.

[15] There is a limitation based upon the taxable income of the corporation.

[16] Section 852(a) of the IRC sets forth specific requirements for a regulated investment company to be granted special tax treatment.

[17] Section 852(b)(5) of the IRC specifies the conditions for the tax-exempt portion of interest income to be tax free to the shareholder.

capital gains over the capital gains tax included in the shareholder's total long-term capital gains.[18]

CAPITAL GAIN AND LOSS TREATMENT

Once a capital gain or capital loss is determined for a capital asset, there are special rules for determining the impact on adjusted gross income. The tax treatment for individuals and nondealer corporations is explained in this section.

Capital Gain and Loss Treatment for Individuals

To determine the impact of transactions involving capital assets on adjusted gross income, it is first necessary to ascertain whether the sale or exchange has resulted in a capital gain or loss that is long term or short term. The classification depends on the length of time the capital asset is held by the taxpayer. For capital assets acquired after June 22, 1984, the general rule is that if a capital asset is held for six months or less, the gain or loss is a short-term capital gain or loss.[19] A long-term capital gain or loss results when the capital asset is held for one day more than six months, or longer. For capital assets acquired before June 22, 1984, the holding period for a long-term capital gain is one day more than one year.

Second, all short-term capital gains and losses are combined to produce either a *net short-term capital gain* or a *net short-term capital loss*. The same procedure is followed for long-term capital gains and losses. Either a *net long-term capital gain* or a *net long-term capital loss* will result.

Third, an overall *net capital gain* or *net capital loss* is determined by combining the amounts in the previous step. If the result is a net capital gain, the entire amount is added to gross income. However, net long-term capital gains are given preferential tax treatment. A deduction is allowed from gross income in determining adjusted gross income. The permissible deduction is 60 percent of the excess of net long-term capital gains over net short-term capital losses.[20] Exhibit 4 provides six illustrations of the treatment of a net capital gain.

---

[18] Section 852(b)(3)(D) of the IRC.

[19] An exception to this general rule applies to wash sales. A wash sale occurs when "substantially identical securities" are acquired within 30 days before or after a sale or the securities *at a loss*. In such cases, the loss is not recognized as a capital loss. Instead, the loss is added to the basis of the securities that caused the loss. The holding period for the new securities in connection with a wash sale then includes the period for which the original securities were held. The rule is not applicable to an individual who is a trader, nor to an individual or corporate dealer.

[20] A capital gain deduction taken by an individual could result in a minimum tax liability.

EXHIBIT 4 Tax Treatment of a Net Capital Gain for an Individual

	Illustration Number					
	(1)	(2)	(3)	(4)	(5)	(6)
1. Net long-term capital gain (loss)	$35,000	$35,000	$35,000	$ 0	($3,000)	($8,000)
2. Net short-term capital gain (loss)	(15,000)	15,000	0	15,000	15,000	15,000
3. Net capital gain: increase in gross income	$20,000	$50,000	$35,000	$15,000	$12,000	$7,000
4. Excess of net long-term capital gain over net short-term capital loss	$20,000	$35,000	$35,000	$ 0	$ 0	0
5. Capital gains deduction (60 percent of line 4)	(12,000)	(21,000)	(21,000)	0	0	0
6. Increase in adjusted gross income (line 3 minus line 5)	8,000	29,000	14,000	15,000	12,000	7,000

If there is a net capital loss, it is deductible from gross income. The amount that may be deducted, however, is limited to the lesser of (1) $3,000 (but $1,500 for married taxpayers filing separate returns), (2) taxable income without the personal exemption and without capital gains and losses minus the zero bracket amount, and (3) the total of net short-term capital loss plus half the net long-term capital loss. The third limitation is the so-called $1 for $2 rule and is the basic difference between the tax treatment of net short-term capital losses and net long-term capital losses. The former is deductible dollar for dollar, but the latter requires $2 of long-term capital loss to obtain a $1 deduction.

Because of the difference in the tax treatment of net long-term capital losses and net short-term capital losses, the order in which these losses are deductible in a tax year is specified by the Treasury. First, net short-term capital losses are used to satisfy the limitation. Any balance to satisfy the limitation is then applied from net long-term capital losses using the $1 for $2 rule. Any unused net short-term or net long-term capital losses are carried over on a dollar-for-dollar basis.[21] When they are carried over, they do not lose their identity but remain either short term or long term. These losses can be carried over indefinitely until they are all utilized in subsequent tax years.

Exhibit 5 provides 10 illustrations of the net capital loss deduction rule. In the illustrations it is assumed that taxable income as defined in (2) above is greater than $3,000, and the taxpayer, if married, is not filing a separate return.

Capital Gain and Loss Treatment for Corporations

The procedure for determining a net capital gain or loss for corporations is the same as that for individuals. The tax treatment of any net capital gain or loss differs from that of individuals in the following two ways.

First, a corporation is not entitled to a net capital gain deduction for the excess of net long-term capital gains over net short-term capital losses. Instead the excess is subject to an alternative tax computation that limits the tax to 28 percent of the gain.[22] The tax attributable to the excess of net long-term capital gains over net short-term capital losses is the lesser of (1) the tax liability on the taxable income when the excess is included in taxable income (i.e., regular tax computation), and (2) the tax liability on taxable income that is reduced by the excess, plus a 28 percent tax on the excess. The latter tax computation is the alternative tax computation.

---

[21] However, in determining the amount of the net capital loss deduction in a future tax year, the $1 for $2 rule applies.

[22] The minimum tax can raise the effective tax rate on net capital gains to 29.7 percent.

EXHIBIT 5   Tax Treatment of a Net Capital Loss for an Individual

	(1)	(2)	(3)	(4)	(5)	(6)	(7)	(8)	(9)	(10)
					Illustration Number					
1. Net long-term capital gain (loss)	$ 0	($7,000)	($7,000)	($7,000)	($3,000)	($4,000)	$6,000	($4,000)	($12,000)	$ 4,000
2. Net short-term capital gain (loss)	(5,000)	0	(5,000)	(2,000)	(1,000)	0	(7,000)	1,000	2,000	(14,000)
3. Net capital loss	$5,000	$7,000	$12,000	$9,000	$4,000	$4,000	$1,000	$3,000	$10,000	$10,000
4. Capital loss deduction*	3,000	3,000	3,000	3,000	2,500	2,000	1,000	1,500	3,000	3,000
5. Long-term capital loss carryover	0	1,000	7,000	5,000	0	0	0	0	4,000	0
6. Short-term capital loss carryover	2,000	0	2,000	0	0	0	0	0	0	7,000

* Assumes that the taxpayer (1) is not married or if married is not filing a separate return, and (2) has taxable income without the personal exemption and without capital gains and losses minus the zero bracket amount greater than $3,000.

Second, no deduction is allowed for a net capital loss. However, net capital losses can be carried back to three preceding taxable years and carried forward five taxable years to offset any net capital gains in those years.[23] Although there are exceptions, the general rule is that any unused net capital loss after the fifth subsequent year can never be used by a corporate taxpayer. Net capital losses are not carried over in character. Instead, they are carried over as a short-term capital loss.

DEDUCTIBILITY OF INTEREST EXPENSE INCURRED TO ACQUIRE OR CARRY SECURITIES

Some investment strategies involve the borrowing of funds to purchase or carry securities. Although interest expense on borrowed funds is a tax-deductible expense, the investor should be aware of the following three rules relating to the deductibility of interest expense to acquire or carry securities.

First, there are limits on the amount of current interest paid or accrued on debt to purchase or carry a market discount bond. It is limited by the amount of any income from the bond. Any interest expenses that remain can be deducted in the current year only to the extent that they exceed the amortized portion of the market discount. The amount of the interest expense that is disallowed can be deducted either (1) in future years if there is net interest income and an election is made, or (2) when the bond is sold.

To illustrate this limitation, suppose that interest expense incurred to carry a market discount bond is $500 for the current year, the coupon interest from that bond is $200, and the amortized portion of the market discount is $140. The investor is entitled to deduct $200 (the amount of the coupon interest.) In addition, since the remaining interest expense of $300 ($500 − $200) exceeds the amortized portion of the market discount of $140 by $160, an additional $160 may be deducted. Thus, the total interest expense that may be deducted in the current year is $360. The $140 can be deducted in future years, if it does not exceed the limit, or when the bond is sold.

There is an exception to the above rule. An investor can elect to have the amortized portion of the market discount taxed each year. In that case, the entire interest expense to purchase or carry the bond is tax deductible in the current year. For example, if an investor elects to include the $140 of amortized market discount as gross income in the current year, he or she may deduct the $140 as current interest expense.

---

[23] There is a limitation on the amount that can be carried back. The amount cannot cause or increase a net operating loss in the taxable year it is carried back to. Net capital losses are applied to the earliest year as a carry-back or carry-over.

Second, the IRC specifies that interest paid or accrued on "indebtedness incurred or continued to purchase or carry obligations, the interest on which is wholly exempt from taxes," is not tax deductible. It does not make any difference if any tax-exempt interest is actually received by the taxpayer in the taxable year. In other words, interest expense is not deductible on funds borrowed to purchase or carry tax-exempt securities. The nondeductibility of interest expenses also applies to debt incurred or continued in order to purchase or carry shares of a regulated investment company (e.g., mutual fund) that distributes exempt interest dividends.

To understand why interest related to debt incurred to purchase or carry tax-exempt obligations is disallowed as a deduction, consider the following example. Suppose a taxpayer in the 50 percent marginal tax bracket borrows $100,000 at an annual interest cost of 12 percent, or $12,000. The proceeds are then used to acquire $100,000 of municipal bonds at par with a coupon rate of 8 percent, or $8,000 interest per year. If the $12,000 interest expense were allowed as a tax-deductible expense, the aftertax cost of the interest expense would be $6,000. Since the interest received from holding the municipal bonds is $8,000, the taxpayer would benefit by $2,000 after taxes.

Finally, there is a limitation on investment interest deductions equal to $10,000 plus investment income.

4

Bond Yield Measures and Price Volatility Properties

Frank J. Fabozzi, Ph.D., C.F.A., C.P.A.
Visiting Professor
Sloan School of Management
Massachusetts Institute of Technology

To make investment decisions, the investor must be capable of determining the yield on an investment. A bond may provide three sources of income to an investor over the time it is held: (1) the contracted periodic interest payments, (2) interest from the reinvestment of the periodic interest payments, and (3) capital gain (or loss) resulting from the disposal of the security. Several measures of the yield on a bond are discussed in this chapter. Since a measure may not take into account all three sources of income offered by a bond, the investor should understand the drawback of each measure. In Chapter 27, a more thorough treatment of bond yield measures is presented. Special yield measures are computed for money market instruments, and they are discussed in Chapter 7.

A fundamental relationship illustrated in this chapter is that the price of a fixed income security moves in the opposite direction of the change in the yield that investors require. Consequently, as market participants require a higher (lower) yield, the price of a bond falls (rises). However, not all bonds change by the same magnitude for a given change in yield. The response of bond prices to a change in yield depends upon certain characteristics of the bond. The characteristics that influence bond price volatility are discussed in this chapter.

To appreciate the bond yield measures and price volatility properties, the investor should understand the concepts of compound interest and present value. The following two sections discuss these concepts.

COMPOUND INTEREST

One of history's wealthiest bankers, Baron Rothschild, was once asked if he could name the Seven Wonders of the World. Although he responded he could not, he did tell his questioner what he thought was the Eighth Wonder of the World. "The Eighth Wonder should be utilized by all of us to accomplish what we want," he stated. "It is compound interest."[1]

The concept of compound interest is very simple. When a principal is invested, interest is earned on the principal in the first period. In subsequent periods interest is earned on not only the original principal invested but also on the interest earned in previous periods. Thus interest is being earned on an amount that is increasing over time.

For example, suppose that $1,000 is invested today earning 8 percent interest compounded annually. The amount at the end of one year will be $1,080 ($1,000 times 1.08). The $80 represents the interest earned for one year. If the principal and interest are reinvested for another year, the amount at the end of the second year will be $1,166.40 ($1,080 times 1.08). The amount at the end of two years can be broken down as follows:

Original principal	$1,000.00
First year's interest	80.00
Second year's interest on original principal	80.00
Second year's interest on interest ($80 times .08)	6.40
	$1,166.40

Reinvestment of $1,166.40 for a third year would produce $1,259.71 ($1,166.40 times 1.08). The third-year interest of $93.31 ($1,166.40 times .08) is comprised of $80 interest on the original principal of $1,000 plus $13.31 interest on the $166.40 interest earned in the first two years.

It is the interest on interest that explains the snowballing effect of money to multiply itself under compound interest. To highlight this point, suppose the $1,000 is invested for 50 years earning 8 percent interest compounded annually. The amount at the end of 49 years would be $43,427. Just how this amount is determined will be explained later. At the end of 50 years, the amount will be $46,901 ($43,427 times 1.08). The interest in the 50th year is $80 interest on the original principal plus $3,394 interest on the $42,427 interest earned in the first 49 years.

Had interest been based on simple interest, the investment would not have grown as much compared to compound interest. With simple interest, only interest on the original principal is realized. Interest is not

---

[1] Loraine L. Blaire, *Your Financial Guide for Living* (Englewood Cliffs, N.J.: Prentice-Hall, 1963), p. 62.

earned on the interest earned in previous years. For example, if $1,000 is invested earning 8 percent simple interest for two years, the amount at the end of the second year will be $1,160. The amount is composed of the original principal of $1,000 plus two years of simple interest of $80 per year. Recall that if interest is compounded, the amount at the end of the second year is $1,166.40. The difference between simple interest and compound interest is only $6.40 in this example. However, as the time increases over which the principal is invested, the difference between the amount resulting from simple and compound interest is no longer trivial. For example, at the end of 50 years, simple interest would produce an amount equal to $5,000 ($1,000 plus 50 times $80), but the amount assuming compound interest would be $46,901!

Computing Future Value

To determine the future value of a principal invested today, the following formula is used:

$$FV = P(1 + r)^n$$

where

FV = future value
P = original principal invested
r = the nominal or simple interest rate (as a decimal)
n = number of periods

The expression $(1 + r)^n$ means multiply $(1 + r)$ by itself n times. For example, if n is 4, then the expression $(1 + r)^4$ is

$$(1 + r) \text{ times } (1 + r) \text{ times } (1 + r) \text{ times } (1 + r)$$

ILLUSTRATION 1. What is the future value of $80 invested today earning 10 percent compounded annually for six years?

In terms of the formula for future value, P is $80, n is 6, and r is 10 percent. The expression $(1 + .10)^6$ is then:

$$(1.10) \times (1.10) \times (1.10) \times (1.10) \times (1.10) \times (1.10) = 1.7716$$

Hence

$$FV = \$80 \ (1.7716) = \$141.73$$

(End of Illustration 1.)

It can become quite tedious to compute the value for the expression $(1 + r)^n$. Most calculators have an option that computes this value. Alternatively, there are tables available that provide the value of $(1 + r)^n$. Exhibit 1 is an abridged future value table that provides the value of $(1 + r)^n$. Notice that at the intersection of the 10 percent column and 6 period row, the value is 1.7716. This is the same value computed for $(1.10)^6$ in Illustration 1.

Thus far it has been assumed that interest is compounded annually. When interest is compounded more than one time per year, the formula provided above can still be used. It is only necessary to adjust the interest rate and the number of compounding periods. The interest rate per compounding period is calculated by dividing the annual interest rate by the number of times interest is compounded per year. Multiplying the number of times interest is compounded per period by the number of years gives the number of periods that should be used. Thus the formula given above becomes:

$$FV = P \left(1 + \frac{r}{m}\right)^{Nm}$$

where

    m = number of times interest is compounded each year
    N = number of years

For example, suppose interest is assumed to be compounded quarterly for five years. The adjusted interest rate to be used in the formula and the table is the annual interest rate (r) divided by four (m). The number of compounding periods is five years (N) times four (m) or 20.

ILLUSTRATION 2. Instead of assuming annual compounding in Illustration 1, suppose interest is compounded semiannually (i.e., twice per year). The adjusted interest rate is 5 percent (10 percent divided by 2). The number of compounding periods is 12 (2 times 6). From Exhibit 1, the future value of $1 assuming 5 percent interest compounded per period for 12 periods is 1.7959. Hence, the future value of $80 is

$$FV = \$80 \ (1.7959)$$
$$= \$143.67$$

When interest was assumed to be compounded annually, the future value was $141.73. Compounding more times within a year results in more interest on interest and therefore a greater future value. (End of Illustration 2.)

Computing Future Value of an Ordinary Annuity

An annuity is a series of equal dollar payments for a specified number of periods. An annuity for which payment occurs at the end of the period is referred to as an *ordinary annuity*.[2] In this chapter, when we refer to an annuity we mean an ordinary annuity.

---

    [2] An annuity in which the payment occurs at the beginning of the period is called an *annuity due*.

EXHIBIT 1 Future Value of $1 at the End of n Periods

								Interest rate							
Period	1%	2%	3%	4%	5%	6%	7%	8%	9%	10%	11%	12%	13%	14%	15%
1	1.0100	1.0200	1.0300	1.0400	1.0500	1.0600	1.0700	1.0800	1.0900	1.1000	1.1100	1.1200	1.1300	1.1400	1.1500
2	1.0201	1.0404	1.0609	1.0816	1.1025	1.1236	1.1449	1.1664	1.1881	1.2100	1.2321	1.2544	1.2769	1.2996	1.3225
3	1.0303	1.0612	1.0927	1.1249	1.1576	1.1910	1.2250	1.2597	1.2950	1.3310	1.3676	1.4049	1.4429	1.4815	1.5209
4	1.0406	1.0824	1.1255	1.1699	1.2155	1.2625	1.3108	1.3605	1.4116	1.4641	1.5181	1.5735	1.6305	1.6890	1.7490
5	1.0510	1.1041	1.1593	1.2167	1.2763	1.3382	1.4026	1.4693	1.5386	1.6105	1.6851	1.7623	1.8424	1.9254	2.0114
6	1.0615	1.1262	1.1941	1.2653	1.3401	1.4185	1.5007	1.5869	1.6771	1.7716	1.8704	1.9738	2.0820	2.1950	2.3131
7	1.0721	1.1487	1.2299	1.3159	1.4071	1.5036	1.6058	1.7138	1.8280	1.9487	2.0762	2.2107	2.3526	2.5023	2.6600
8	1.0829	1.1717	1.2668	1.3686	1.4775	1.5938	1.7182	1.8509	1.9926	2.1436	2.3045	2.4760	2.6584	2.8526	3.0590
9	1.0937	1.1951	1.3048	1.4233	1.5513	1.6895	1.8385	1.9990	2.1719	2.3579	2.5580	2.7731	3.0040	3.2519	3.5179
10	1.1046	1.2190	1.3439	1.4802	1.6289	1.7908	1.9672	2.1589	2.3674	2.5937	2.8394	3.1058	3.3946	3.7072	4.0456
11	1.1157	1.2434	1.3842	1.5395	1.7103	1.8983	2.1049	2.3316	2.5804	2.8531	3.1518	3.4785	3.8359	4.2262	4.6524
12	1.1268	1.2682	1.4258	1.6010	1.7959	2.0122	2.2522	2.5182	2.8127	3.1384	3.4984	3.8960	4.3345	4.8179	5.3502
13	1.1381	1.2936	1.4685	1.6651	1.8856	2.1329	2.4098	2.7196	3.0658	3.4523	3.8833	4.3635	4.8980	5.4924	6.1528
14	1.1495	1.3195	1.5126	1.7317	1.9799	2.2609	2.5785	2.9372	3.3417	3.7975	4.3104	4.8871	5.5347	6.2613	7.0757
15	1.1610	1.3459	1.5580	1.8009	2.0789	2.3966	2.7590	3.1722	3.6425	4.1772	4.7846	5.4736	6.2543	7.1379	8.1371
16	1.1726	1.3728	1.6047	1.8730	2.1829	2.5404	2.9522	3.4259	3.9703	4.5950	5.3109	6.1304	7.0673	8.1372	9.3576
17	1.1843	1.4002	1.6528	1.9479	2.2920	2.6928	3.1588	3.7000	4.3276	5.0545	5.8951	6.8660	7.9861	9.2765	10.761
18	1.1961	1.4282	1.7024	2.0258	2.4066	2.8543	3.3799	3.9960	4.7171	5.5599	6.5435	7.6900	9.0243	10.575	12.375
19	1.2081	1.4568	1.7535	2.1068	2.5270	3.0256	3.6165	4.3157	5.1417	6.1159	7.2633	8.6128	10.197	12.055	14.231
20	1.2202	1.4859	1.8061	2.1911	2.6533	3.2071	3.8697	4.6610	5.6044	6.7275	8.0623	9.6463	11.523	13.743	16.366
21	1.2324	1.5157	1.8603	2.2788	2.7860	3.3996	4.1406	5.0338	6.1088	7.4002	8.9491	10.803	13.021	15.667	18.821
22	1.2447	1.5460	1.9161	2.3699	2.9253	3.6035	4.4304	5.4365	6.6586	8.1403	9.9335	12.100	14.714	17.861	21.644
23	1.2572	1.5769	1.9736	2.4647	3.0715	3.8197	4.7405	5.8715	7.2579	8.9543	11.026	13.552	16.627	20.361	24.891
24	1.2697	1.6084	2.0328	2.5633	3.2251	4.0489	5.0724	6.3412	7.9111	9.8497	12.239	15.178	18.788	23.212	28.625
25	1.2824	1.6406	2.0938	2.6658	3.3864	4.2919	5.4274	6.8485	8.6231	10.834	13.585	17.000	21.230	26.461	32.918
26	1.2953	1.6734	2.1566	2.7725	3.5557	4.5494	5.8074	7.3964	9.3992	11.918	15.080	19.040	23.990	30.166	37.856
27	1.3082	1.7069	2.2213	2.8834	3.7335	4.8223	6.2139	7.9881	10.245	13.110	16.739	21.324	27.109	34.389	43.535
28	1.3213	1.7410	2.2879	2.9987	3.9201	5.1117	6.6488	8.6271	11.167	14.421	18.580	23.883	30.633	39.204	50.065
29	1.3345	1.7758	2.3566	3.1187	4.1161	5.4184	7.1143	9.3173	12.172	15.863	20.624	26.749	34.616	44.693	57.575
30	1.3478	1.8114	2.4273	3.2434	4.3219	5.7435	7.6123	10.062	13.267	17.449	22.892	29.959	39.116	50.950	66.211

When realized compound yield is discussed later in this chapter, it will be helpful to have a means of quickly computing the future value of an ordinary annuity. Therefore the computation of the future value of an ordinary annuity will be illustrated.

ILLUSTRATION 3. Suppose that today (time period 0) you expect to receive $40 every six months for the next seven years. Each payment will be made at the end of the period. That is, you will receive the first payment at the end of period one, the second payment at the end of period two, and so on. Exhibit 2 illustrates the timing of the 14 payments of $40. Suppose that each time a $40 payment is received it can be invested for the remainder of the 14 periods and that the interest rate earned each six months is 5 percent. What is the future value of this ordinary annuity?

For each payment of $40 the number of periods that it can be invested must be determined. Then the future value of each $40 investment must be computed. The total future value is the sum of the future value of the 14 investments of $40. As shown in Exhibit 2, the future value of this ordinary annuity is $783.93. (End of Illustration 3.)

Rather than go through the lengthy computations shown in Exhibit 2, a shortcut procedure is available. Tables are available that provide the future value of an ordinary annuity of $1 per period. Exhibit 3 is an abridged version. The value from the table should then be multiplied by the annuity payment, $40 in Illustration 3, to obtain the future value of the annuity. For example, from Exhibit 3 the future value of an ordinary annuity of $1 per period for 14 periods assuming a 5 percent interest rate per period is 19.598. Hence the future value of an ordinary annuity of $40 is $40 times 19.598, or $783.92.

If a table is not available or if a table does not include the interest rate needed, the following formula can be used to obtain the future value of an ordinary annuity of $1 per period:

$$\text{FV of an ordinary annuity of \$1} = \frac{(1 + r)^n - 1}{r}$$

where

n = number of payments
r = simple interest rate per period

For example, if r is 5 percent and n is 14, the future value of an ordinary annuity of $1 per period is

$$\frac{(1 + .05)^{14} - 1}{.05} = 19.5986$$

EXHIBIT 2 Future Value of an Ordinary Annuity of $40 Per Period for 14 Periods

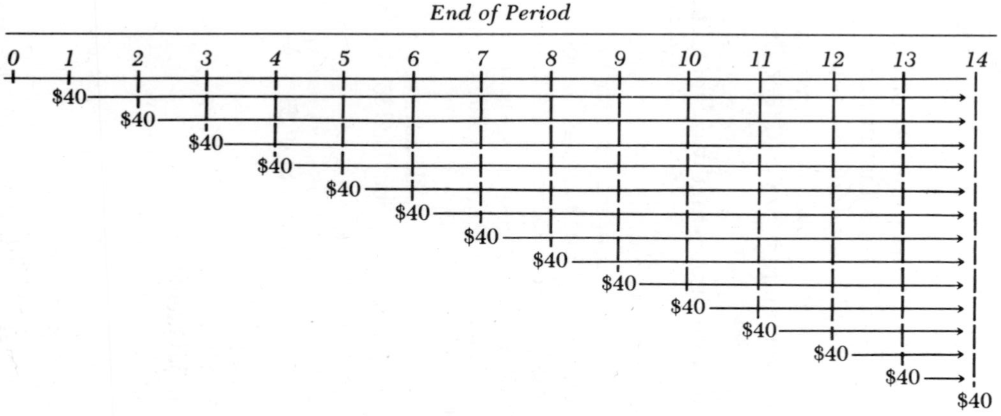

End of Period

Future Value at the End of Period 14

Number of Periods Invested	FV of $1 at 5 Percent from Exhibit 1	FV of $40
13	1.8856	$ 75.42
12	1.7959	71.84
11	1.7103	68.41
10	1.6289	65.16
9	1.5513	62.05
8	1.4775	59.10
7	1.4071	56.28
6	1.3401	53.60
5	1.2763	51.05
4	1.2155	48.62
3	1.1576	46.30
2	1.1025	44.10
1	1.0500	42.00
0	1.0000	40.00
Total future value		$783.93

EXHIBIT 3 Future Value of an Ordinary Annuity of $1 per Period for n Periods

Number of Periods						Interest Rate									
	1%	2%	3%	4%	5%	6%	7%	8%	9%	10%	11%	12%	13%	14%	15%
1	1.0000	1.0000	1.0000	1.0000	1.0000	1.0000	1.0000	1.0000	1.0000	1.0000	1.0000	1.0000	1.0000	1.0000	1.0000
2	2.0100	2.0200	2.0300	2.0400	2.0500	2.0600	2.0700	2.0800	2.0900	2.1000	2.1100	2.1200	2.1300	2.1400	2.1500
3	3.0301	3.0604	3.0909	3.1216	3.1525	3.1836	3.2149	3.2464	3.2781	3.3100	3.3421	3.3744	3.4069	3.4396	3.4725
4	4.0604	4.1216	4.1836	4.2465	4.3101	4.3746	4.4399	4.5061	4.5731	4.6410	4.7097	4.7793	4.8498	4.9211	4.9934
5	5.1010	5.2040	5.3091	5.4163	5.5256	5.6371	5.7507	5.8666	5.9847	6.1051	6.2278	6.3528	6.4803	6.6101	6.7424
6	6.1520	6.3081	6.4684	6.6330	6.8019	6.9753	7.1533	7.3359	7.5233	7.7156	7.9129	8.1152	8.3227	8.5355	8.7537
7	7.2135	7.4343	7.6625	7.8983	8.1420	8.3938	8.6540	8.9228	9.2004	9.4872	9.7833	10.089	10.405	10.730	11.066
8	8.2857	8.5830	8.8923	9.2142	9.5491	9.8975	10.259	10.636	11.028	11.435	11.859	12.299	12.757	13.232	13.726
9	9.3685	9.7546	10.159	10.582	11.026	11.491	11.978	12.487	13.021	13.579	14.164	14.775	15.416	16.085	16.785
10	10.462	10.949	11.463	12.006	12.577	13.180	13.816	14.486	15.192	15.937	16.722	17.548	18.420	19.337	20.303
11	11.566	12.168	12.807	13.486	14.206	14.971	15.783	16.645	17.560	18.531	19.561	20.654	21.814	23.044	24.349
12	12.682	13.412	14.192	15.025	15.917	16.869	17.888	18.977	20.140	21.384	22.713	24.133	25.650	27.270	29.001
13	13.809	14.680	15.617	16.626	17.713	18.882	20.140	21.495	22.953	24.522	26.212	28.029	29.985	32.088	34.351
14	14.947	15.973	17.086	18.291	19.598	21.015	22.550	24.214	26.019	27.975	30.095	32.392	34.883	37.581	40.504
15	16.096	17.293	18.598	20.023	21.578	23.276	25.129	27.152	29.360	31.772	34.405	37.279	40.418	43.842	47.580
16	17.257	18.639	20.156	21.824	23.657	25.672	27.888	30.324	33.003	35.949	39.190	42.753	46.672	50.980	55.717
17	18.430	20.012	21.761	23.697	25.840	28.212	30.840	33.750	36.973	40.544	44.501	48.883	53.739	59.117	65.075
18	19.614	21.412	23.414	25.645	28.132	30.905	33.999	37.450	41.301	45.599	50.396	55.749	61.725	68.394	75.836
19	20.810	22.840	25.116	27.671	30.539	33.760	37.379	41.446	46.018	51.159	56.940	63.439	70.749	78.969	88.211
20	22.019	24.297	26.870	29.778	33.066	36.785	40.995	45.762	51.160	57.275	64.203	72.052	80.947	91.024	102.44
21	23.239	25.783	28.676	31.969	35.719	39.992	44.865	50.422	56.764	64.002	72.265	81.698	92.470	104.76	118.81
22	24.471	27.299	30.536	34.248	38.505	43.392	49.005	55.456	62.873	71.402	81.214	92.502	105.49	120.43	137.63
23	25.716	28.845	32.452	36.617	41.430	46.995	53.436	60.893	69.531	79.543	91.148	104.60	120.20	138.29	159.27
24	26.973	30.421	34.426	39.082	44.502	50.815	58.176	66.764	76.789	88.497	102.17	118.15	136.83	158.65	184.16
25	28.243	32.030	36.459	41.645	47.727	54.864	63.249	73.105	84.700	98.347	114.41	133.33	155.62	181.87	212.79
26	29.525	33.670	38.553	44.311	51.113	59.156	68.676	79.954	93.323	109.18	128.00	150.33	176.85	208.33	245.71
27	30.820	35.344	40.709	47.084	54.669	63.705	74.483	87.350	102.72	121.09	143.08	169.37	200.84	238.49	283.56
28	32.129	37.051	42.930	49.967	58.402	68.528	80.697	95.338	112.96	134.20	159.82	190.69	227.95	272.88	327.10
29	33.450	38.792	45.218	52.966	62.322	73.639	87.346	103.96	124.13	148.63	178.40	214.58	258.58	312.09	377.16
30	34.784	40.568	47.575	56.084	66.438	79.058	94.460	113.28	136.30	164.49	199.02	241.33	293.20	356.78	434.74

PRESENT VALUE

The notion that money has time value is one of the basic concepts in investment management. Money has time value because of the opportunity to invest money received at some earlier date at some interest rate. As a result, money to be received in the future is less valuable than money that could be received at an earlier date.

Computing Present Value

The process of determining the amount that must be set aside today in order to have a specified future value is called *discounting*. The amount that must be set aside today in order to have a specified future value is called the present or discounted value. The formula for the present value of $1 in the future is:

$$PV = \frac{FV}{(1 + r)^n}$$

where

PV = present value
FV = future value
  r = interest rate or discount rate
  n = number of periods

Note that the formula for the present value is derived by solving the formula for the future value of $1 for the original principal, P, and demonstrates that the present value procedure is the reverse of the future value calculations demonstrated above.

ILLUSTRATION 4. Suppose an investor expects to receive $1,000 seven years from now. Assuming the investor can earn 12 percent compounded annually on any sum invested today, what is the present value of this future sum?

Using the formula for present value, we have FV = $1,000, r = 12 percent, and n = 7. The expression $(1 + .12)^7$, found in Exhibit 1, is 2.2107. Hence the present value is

$$PV = \frac{\$1,000}{2.2107}$$

$$= \$452.35$$

By placing $452.35 today into an investment that earns 12 percent compounded annually, the investor will have $1,000 at the end of seven years. (End of Illustration 4.)

Present value tables are also available. Exhibit 4 shows the present value of $1, which is found by dividing one by $(1 + r)^n$, as mentioned

EXHIBIT 4 Present Value of $1

Discount rate

Period	1%	2%	3%	4%	5%	6%	7%	8%	9%	10%	11%	12%	13%	14%	15%	16%	18%	20%
1	.9901	.9804	.9709	.9615	.9524	.9434	.9346	.9259	.9174	.9091	.9009	.8929	.8850	.8772	.8696	.8621	.8475	.8333
2	.9803	.9612	.9426	.9246	.9070	.8900	.8734	.8573	.8417	.8264	.8116	.7972	.7831	.7695	.7561	.7432	.7182	.6944
3	.9706	.9423	.9151	.8890	.8638	.8396	.8163	.7938	.7722	.7513	.7312	.7118	.6931	.6750	.6575	.6407	.6086	.5787
4	.9610	.9238	.8885	.8548	.8227	.7921	.7629	.7350	.7084	.6830	.6587	.6355	.6133	.5921	.5718	.5523	.5158	.4823
5	.9515	.9057	.8626	.8219	.7835	.7473	.7130	.6806	.6499	.6209	.5935	.5674	.5428	.5194	.4972	.4761	.4371	.4019
6	.9420	.8880	.8375	.7903	.7462	.7050	.6663	.6302	.5963	.5645	.5346	.5066	.4803	.4556	.4323	.4104	.3704	.3349
7	.9327	.8706	.8131	.7599	.7107	.6651	.6227	.5835	.5470	.5132	.4817	.4523	.4251	.3996	.3759	.3538	.3139	.2791
8	.9235	.8535	.7894	.7307	.6768	.6274	.5820	.5403	.5019	.4665	.4339	.4039	.3762	.3506	.3269	.3050	.2660	.2326
9	.9143	.8368	.7664	.7026	.6446	.5919	.5439	.5002	.4604	.4241	.3909	.3606	.3329	.3075	.2843	.2630	.2255	.1938
10	.9053	.8203	.7441	.6756	.6139	.5584	.5083	.4632	.4224	.3855	.3522	.3220	.2946	.2697	.2472	.2267	.1911	.1615
11	.8963	.8043	.7224	.6496	.5847	.5268	.4751	.4289	.3875	.3505	.3173	.2875	.2607	.2366	.2149	.1954	.1619	.1346
12	.8874	.7885	.7014	.6246	.5568	.4970	.4440	.3971	.3555	.3186	.2858	.2567	.2307	.2076	.1869	.1685	.1372	.1122
13	.8787	.7730	.6810	.6006	.5303	.4688	.4150	.3677	.3262	.2897	.2575	.2292	.2042	.1821	.1625	.1452	.1163	.0935
14	.8700	.7579	.6611	.5775	.5051	.4423	.3878	.3405	.2992	.2633	.2320	.2046	.1807	.1597	.1413	.1252	.0985	.0779
15	.8613	.7430	.6419	.5553	.4810	.4173	.3624	.3152	.2745	.2394	.2090	.1827	.1599	.1401	.1229	.1079	.0835	.0649
16	.8528	.7284	.6232	.5339	.4581	.3936	.3387	.2919	.2519	.2176	.1883	.1631	.1415	.1229	.1069	.0930	.0708	.0541
17	.8444	.7142	.6050	.5134	.4363	.3714	.3166	.2703	.2311	.1978	.1696	.1456	.1252	.1078	.0929	.0802	.0600	.0451
18	.8360	.7002	.5874	.4936	.4155	.3503	.2959	.2502	.2120	.1799	.1528	.1300	.1108	.0946	.0808	.0691	.0508	.0376
19	.8277	.6864	.5703	.4746	.3957	.3305	.2765	.2317	.1945	.1635	.1377	.1161	.0981	.0829	.0703	.0596	.0431	.0313
20	.8195	.6730	.5537	.4564	.3769	.3118	.2584	.2145	.1784	.1486	.1240	.1037	.0868	.0728	.0611	.0514	.0365	.0261
21	.8114	.6598	.5375	.4388	.3589	.2942	.2415	.1987	.1637	.1351	.1117	.0926	.0768	.0638	.0531	.0443	.0309	.0217
22	.8034	.6468	.5219	.4220	.3418	.2775	.2257	.1839	.1502	.1228	.1007	.0826	.0680	.0560	.0462	.0382	.0262	.0181
23	.7954	.6342	.5067	.4057	.3256	.2618	.2109	.1703	.1378	.1117	.0907	.0738	.0601	.0491	.0402	.0329	.0222	.0151
24	.7876	.6217	.4919	.3901	.3101	.2470	.1971	.1577	.1264	.1015	.0817	.0659	.0532	.0431	.0349	.0284	.0188	.0126
25	.7798	.6095	.4776	.3751	.2953	.2330	.1842	.1460	.1160	.0923	.0736	.0588	.0471	.0378	.0304	.0245	.0160	.0105
26	.7720	.5976	.4637	.3607	.2812	.2198	.1722	.1352	.1064	.0839	.0663	.0525	.0417	.0331	.0264	.0211	.0135	.0087
27	.7644	.5859	.4502	.3468	.2678	.2074	.1609	.1252	.0976	.0763	.0597	.0469	.0369	.0291	.0230	.0182	.0115	.0073
28	.7568	.5744	.4371	.3335	.2551	.1956	.1504	.1159	.0895	.0693	.0538	.0419	.0326	.0255	.0200	.0157	.0097	.0061
29	.7493	.5631	.4243	.3207	.2429	.1846	.1406	.1073	.0822	.0630	.0485	.0374	.0289	.0224	.0174	.0135	.0082	.0051
30	.7419	.5521	.4120	.3083	.2314	.1741	.1314	.0994	.0754	.0573	.0437	.0334	.0256	.0196	.0151	.0116	.0070	.0042

above. The columns show the interest or discount rate. The rows show the number of periods. The present value of $1 obtained from Exhibit 4 is then *multiplied* by the future value to determine the present value. For example, the present value of $1,000 seven years from now assuming 12 percent interest compounded annually is

$$PV = \$1,000 \ (PV \ of \ \$1 \ from \ Exhibit \ 4)$$
$$= \$1,000 \ (.4523)$$
$$= \$452.30$$

There are two facts you should note about present value. Look again at Exhibit 4. Select any interest rate and look down the column. Notice that the present value decreases. That is, the greater the number of periods over which interest could be earned, the less must be set aside today for a given dollar amount to be received in the future. Next select any period and look across the row. As you look across, the interest rate increases and the present value decreases. The reason is the higher the interest rate that can be earned on any amount invested today, the less must be set aside to obtain a specified future value.

So far, the present value of a single future sum has been illustrated. The principle is the same if there is a series of future sums at different times. Each future sum must be discounted individually to obtain its present value. Then the present values are added to obtain the present value for the series of future sums.

Computing Present Value of an Ordinary Annuity

In the case of an annuity, it is a simple task to compute the present value of the series. Exhibit 5 provides the present value of an ordinary annuity of $1 for n periods for selected interest rates. As noted earlier in this chapter, the payments occur at the end of each period in the case of an ordinary annuity.[3] The present value of an ordinary annuity is computed by multiplying the value from Exhibit 5 by the annuity payment.

ILLUSTRATION 5. Suppose an investor makes a bond investment that is expected to pay interest of $80 at the end of each year for the next seven years and $1,000 at the end of the seventh year. What is the present value of this investment if the investor seeks a 12 percent return?

The present value of this investment can be computed in two steps. First, the present value of $80 per year is computed using the present

---

[3] The present value of an annuity due of $1 per period can be obtained from Exhibit 5 as follows: (1) find the present value for n minus one payment in Exhibit 5 and (2) add $1 to the value found in (1). For example, the present value of an annuity due of $1 for five years at 5 percent interest is the present value of an ordinary annuity of $1 for four years from Exhibit 5 ($3.5460) plus $1, or $4.5460.

EXHIBIT 5 Present Value of an Ordinary Annuity of $1 per Period for n Periods

Number of Periods	1%	2%	3%	4%	5%	6%	7%	8%	9%	10%	11%	12%	13%	14%	15%
1	0.9901	0.9804	0.9709	0.9615	0.9524	0.9434	0.9346	0.9259	0.9174	0.9091	0.9009	0.8929	0.8850	0.8772	0.8696
2	1.9704	1.9416	1.9135	1.8861	1.8594	1.8334	1.8080	1.7833	1.7591	1.7355	1.7125	1.6901	1.6681	1.6467	1.6257
3	2.9410	2.8839	2.8286	2.7751	2.7232	2.6730	2.6243	2.5771	2.5313	2.4869	2.4437	2.4018	2.3612	2.3216	2.2832
4	3.9020	3.8077	3.7171	3.6299	3.5460	3.4651	3.3872	3.3121	3.2397	3.1699	3.1024	3.0373	2.9745	2.9137	2.8550
5	4.8534	4.7135	4.5797	4.4518	4.3295	4.2124	4.1002	3.9927	3.8897	3.7908	3.6959	3.6048	3.5172	3.4331	3.3522
6	5.7955	5.6014	5.4172	5.2421	5.0757	4.9173	4.7665	4.6229	4.4859	4.3553	4.2305	4.1114	3.9976	3.8887	3.7845
7	6.7282	6.4720	6.2303	6.0021	5.7864	5.5824	5.3893	5.2064	5.0330	4.8684	4.7122	4.5638	4.4226	4.2883	4.1604
8	7.6517	7.3255	7.0197	6.7327	6.4632	6.2098	5.9713	5.7466	5.5348	5.3349	5.1461	4.9676	4.7988	4.6389	4.4873
9	8.5660	8.1622	7.7861	7.4353	7.1078	6.8017	6.5152	6.2469	5.9952	5.7590	5.5371	5.3282	5.1317	4.9464	4.7716
10	9.4713	8.9826	8.5302	8.1109	7.7217	7.3601	7.0236	6.7101	6.4177	6.1446	5.8892	5.6502	5.4263	5.2161	5.0188
11	10.3676	9.7868	9.2526	8.7605	8.3064	7.8869	7.4987	7.1390	6.8052	6.4951	6.2065	5.9377	5.6870	5.4527	5.2337
12	11.2551	10.5753	9.9540	9.3851	8.8633	8.3838	7.9427	7.5361	7.1607	6.8137	6.4924	6.1944	5.9177	5.6603	5.4206
13	12.1337	11.3484	10.6350	9.9856	9.3936	8.8527	8.3577	7.9038	7.4869	7.1034	6.7499	6.4235	6.1218	5.8424	5.5831
14	13.0037	12.1062	11.2961	10.5631	9.8986	9.2950	8.7455	8.2442	7.7862	7.3667	6.9819	6.6282	6.3025	6.0021	5.7245
15	13.8651	12.8493	11.9379	11.1184	10.3797	9.7122	9.1079	8.5595	8.0607	7.6061	7.1909	6.8109	6.4624	6.1422	5.8474
16	14.7179	13.5777	12.5611	11.6523	10.8378	10.1059	9.4466	8.8514	8.3126	7.8237	7.3792	6.9740	6.6039	6.2651	5.9542
17	15.5623	14.2919	13.1661	12.1657	11.2741	10.4773	9.7632	9.1216	8.5436	8.0216	7.5488	7.1196	6.7291	6.3729	6.0472
18	16.3983	14.9920	13.7535	12.6593	11.6896	10.8276	10.0591	9.3719	8.7556	8.2014	7.7016	7.2497	6.8399	6.4674	6.1280
19	17.2260	15.6785	14.3238	13.1339	12.0853	11.1581	10.3356	9.6036	8.9501	8.3649	7.8393	7.3658	6.9380	6.5504	6.1982
20	18.0456	16.3514	14.8775	13.5903	12.4622	11.4699	10.5940	9.8181	9.1285	8.5136	7.9633	7.4694	7.0248	6.6231	6.2593
21	18.8570	17.0112	15.4150	14.0292	12.8212	11.7641	10.8355	10.0168	9.2922	8.6487	8.0751	7.5620	7.1016	6.6870	6.3125
22	19.6604	17.6580	15.9369	14.4511	13.1630	12.0416	11.0612	10.2007	9.4424	8.7715	8.1757	7.6446	7.1695	6.7429	6.3587
23	20.4558	18.2922	16.4436	14.8568	13.4886	12.3034	11.2722	10.3711	9.5802	8.8832	8.2664	7.7184	7.2297	6.7921	6.3988
24	21.2434	18.9139	16.9355	15.2470	13.7986	12.5504	11.4693	10.5288	9.7066	8.9847	8.3481	7.7843	7.2829	6.8351	6.4338
25	22.0232	19.5235	17.4131	15.6221	14.0939	12.7834	11.6536	10.6748	9.8226	9.0770	8.4218	7.8431	7.3300	6.8729	6.4642
26	22.7952	20.1210	17.8768	15.9828	14.3752	13.0032	11.8258	10.8100	9.9290	9.1609	8.4881	7.8957	7.3717	6.9061	6.4906
27	23.5596	20.7069	18.3270	16.3296	14.6430	13.2105	11.9867	10.9352	10.0266	9.2372	8.5478	7.9426	7.4086	6.9352	6.5135
28	24.3164	21.2813	18.7641	16.6631	14.8981	13.4062	12.1371	11.0511	10.1161	9.3066	8.6016	7.9844	7.4412	6.9607	6.5335
29	25.0658	21.8444	19.1885	16.9837	15.1411	13.5907	12.2777	11.1584	10.1983	9.3696	8.6501	8.0218	7.4701	6.9830	6.5509
30	25.8077	22.3965	19.6004	17.2920	15.3725	13.7648	12.4090	11.2578	10.2737	9.4269	8.6938	8.0552	7.4957	7.0027	6.5660

Discount rate

value of an ordinary annuity table, Exhibit 5. The present value is $365.10, as shown below:

PV of $80 per year for seven years
  = $80 (PV of $1 per year at 12 percent from Exhibit 5)
  = $80 (4.5638)
  = $365.10

Next, the present value of $1,000 seven years from now is determined using a 12 percent discount rate. The present value is $452.30 as shown earlier. Therefore the present value of the investment is $817.40 ($365.10 plus $452.30). The investor who pays more than $817.40 will realize a return that is less than 12 percent; however, a rate of return greater than 12 percent will be realized if the investor can acquire the investment at a cost of less than $817.40. (End of Illustration 5.)

ILLUSTRATION 6. Suppose that the bond investment in the previous illustration will still pay $80 each year; however, the interest will be received in two equal installments every six months. The investor seeks a 6 percent semiannual rate of return from this investment. The present value is then $814.10, as shown below:

PV of $40 for 14 six-month periods
  = $40 (PV of $1 each six months at 6 percent from Exhibit 5)
  = $40 (9.2950)
  = $371.80

PV of $1,000 at the end of 14 six-month periods
  = $1,000 (PV of $1 at 6 percent from Exhibit 4)
  = $1,000 (.4423)
  = $442.30

Present value of investment = $371.80 + $442.30
  = $814.10

(End of Illustration 6.)

There is also a general formula that can be used to compute the present value of an ordinary annuity of $1. The formula is[4]

---

[4] For an annuity due, the corresponding formula is

$$\left[\frac{1 - \dfrac{1}{(1 + r)^{n-1}}}{r} \right] + 1$$

Present value of an ordinary annuity of $1 $= \dfrac{1 - \dfrac{1}{(1 + r)^n}}{r}$

To illustrate the use of this formula, let us compute the present value of an ordinary annuity of $1 for seven years assuming 12 percent interest compounded annually ($r = .12$ and $n = 7$).

$$\frac{1 - \dfrac{1}{(1.12)^7}}{.12} = \frac{1 - .4523492}{.12} = 4.5638$$

YIELD MEASURES

As stated at the outset of this chapter, there are three potential sources of income to an investor who holds a bond: (1) the contracted interest payments (i.e., coupon payments), (2) income from the reinvestment of the periodic interest payments, and (3) capital gain (or loss) from disposal of the security. The four yield measures discussed below—current yield, yield-to-maturity, yield-to-call, and realized compound yield—take one or more of these sources into consideration when determining the investor's return on investment.

The following hypothetical bond will be used to illustrate the yield measures:

Years to maturity = 7
Coupon rate = 8 percent
Market price = $814.10
Redemption value at maturity = $1,000
Frequency of interest payments = semiannual

Since this bond is selling below its redemption value at maturity (or par value), the bond is said to be selling at a *discount.*

Current Yield

The current yield relates the annual dollar coupon interest to the market price. It can be expressed mathematically as follows:

$$\text{Current yield} = \frac{\text{Annual dollar coupon interest}}{\text{Market price}}$$

For our hypothetical bond, the current yield is

$$\frac{\$80}{\$814.10} = 0.098 = 9.8 \text{ percent}$$

The current yield exceeds the coupon rate when a bond is selling at a discount. The opposite is true when a bond is selling at a premium. For example, if the market price of our hypothetical bond is $1,089 rather than $814.10, the current yield is 7.3 percent ($80 divided by $1,089).

The drawback of the current yield is that it does not take into consideration the two other sources of income—reinvestment of interest and capital gain (or loss). To illustrate the latter source, suppose the bond is held to maturity. At that time, the issuer will redeem the bond for $1,000. The investor who purchased the bond for $814.10 will realize a capital gain of $185.9 ($1,000 minus $814.10). Had the bond been purchased for $1,089, there would be a capital loss of $89.

Yield-to-Maturity

Unlike the current yield, the yield-to-maturity does take into account any capital gain or loss. The yield-to-maturity does consider the reinvestment of the contracted interest payments; *however, it implicitly assumes that these payments are reinvested at the yield-to-maturity.*

The yield-to-maturity is the discount rate that equates the present value of the promised cash flow (coupon payments plus redemption value at maturity) to the market price.[5] Thus the yield-to-maturity takes the time value of money into consideration. When a yield-to-maturity is quoted, the market price used to make the computation is the offer price.

Let us go through the computation of the yield-to-maturity once. Later it will be explained how this yield can be determined without the necessary trial-and-error computations given below. The worksheet for determining the yield-to-maturity for our hypothetical bond is shown as Exhibit 6. Now remember what our objective is—to determine the discount rate that equates the present value of the 14 payments of $40 every six months (beginning six months from now) plus the present value of the redemption value of $1,000 at maturity to the market price of the bond ($814.10).

---

[5] The general formula for the yield-to-maturity for a bond paying interest semiannually is:

$$P = \sum_{t=1}^{2n} \frac{C/2}{\left(1 + \frac{r}{2}\right)^t} + \frac{R}{\left(1 + \frac{r}{2}\right)^{2n}}$$

where

    P = price of bond
    n = number of years to maturity
    C = annual dollar coupon interest
    r = yield-to-maturity
    R = redemption value of bond at maturity

EXHIBIT 6 Worksheet for the Computation of the Yield-to-Maturity of an 8 Percent Coupon Bond—Maturing in Exactly Seven Years, and Priced at $814.10

Discount Rate (percent)	PV of an Annuity of $1 for 14 Periods*	PV of an Annuity of $40 for 14 Periods†	PV of $1 14 Periods Hence‡	PV of $1,000 14 Periods Hence§	Total PV of Cash Flow
4%	$10.5631	$422.52	$.5775	$577.50	$1,000.02
5	9.8986	395.94	.5051	505.10	901.04
6	9.2950	371.80	.4423	442.30	814.10
7	8.7455	349.82	.3878	387.80	737.62
8	8.2442	329.77	.3405	340.50	669.82

* From Exhibit 5.
† $40 times PV of an annuity of $1 for 14 periods.
‡ From Exhibit 4.
§ $1,000 times PV of $1 14 periods hence.

An arbitrary starting point of 5 percent was selected. The present value of the promised cash flow is $901.04. This discount rate produces a present value that is greater than the bond's market price of $814.10. Since a higher discount rate lowers the present value, a higher discount rate must be tried. Skipping 6 percent for the moment, we see that a 7 percent discount rate produces a present value for the promised cash flow that is less than the market price. Consequently, the discount rate we are searching for must be less than 7 percent, but greater than 5 percent. When a 6 percent rate is used, the present value of the promised cash flow is equal to the market price. But 6 percent is *not* the yield-to-maturity because the time period in the discounting process is six months. To annualize the yield, the *convention* is to double the discount rate. The yield-to-maturity of our hypothetical bond is therefore 12 percent.[6]

---

[6] Technically, the yield should be annualized using the following formula:

$$(1 + \text{Discount rate})^2 - 1$$

In our example, we would find the annualized yield to be

$$(1.06)^2 - 1 = 1.1236 - 1 = .1236, \text{ or } 12.36 \text{ percent}$$

The discrepancy between the yield-to-maturity as conventionally computed (i.e., doubling of the semiannual discount rate) and the correct procedure for annualizing explains why bonds carrying a coupon rate equal to the prevailing market interest rate may be selling slightly below par.

This convention also presents problems when comparing bonds that do not have the same number of coupon payments per year. This can be corrected by adjusting the conventional yield-to-maturity as follows:

$$\text{Adjusted yield-to-maturity} = \left(1 + \frac{\text{Conventional yield-to-maturity}}{m}\right)^m - 1$$

where

m is the number coupon interest payments per annum

For example, if the conventional yield-to-maturity for three hypothetical bonds that pay interest annually, semiannually, and monthly is 12 percent, the adjusted yield-to-maturity would be as follows:

If annual, m = 1

$$\text{Adjusted yield-to-maturity} = \left(1 + \frac{.12}{1}\right)^1 - 1 = .12$$

If semiannual, m = 2

$$\text{Adjusted yield-to-maturity} = \left(1 + \frac{.12}{2}\right)^2 - 1 = .1236$$

If monthly, m = 12

$$\text{Adjusted yield-to-maturity} = \left(1 + \frac{.12}{12}\right)^{12} - 1 = .1268$$

The calculation becomes more complicated when the next coupon payment is not six months from the time the bond is purchased. For example, consider a bond that pays interest on January 1 and July 1. Suppose that the bond is purchased on March 14. Then the buyer must pay the seller accrued interest from January 1 to March 14.[7] Once the accrued interest is computed, the yield-to-maturity is then found by determining the discount rate that makes the present value of the promised cash flow from the bond equal to the market price *plus* the accrued interest.

Fortunately, the tedious calculations necessary to compute the yield-to-maturity can be avoided by using a financial calculator that is preprogrammed to make the calculation. If one is not available, tables are available. The tables are part of a book usually referred to as a yield book, basis book, or bond value tables. Sample pages from a yield book are shown in Exhibit 7.

The yield book is organized as follows. Each page corresponds to a coupon rate. A yield book may increment the coupon rate by one eighth or one fourth of 1 percent. Exhibits 7(a), 7(b), and 7(c) are three sample pages from a yield book for an 8 percent coupon rate. The top row of each page indicates the time remaining to maturity. The time increments can be given in terms of months, quarters, six months, or years. In the yield book from which the pages were abstracted, monthly periods are used up to 5 years, quarterly to 10 years, and semiannually to 40 years. (The bold number on the pages refers to the number of years, and the number after the hyphen refers to the number of months.) In the first column, the yield-to-maturity ("yield") is given.

The values appearing within the table are the bond values expressed as a percentage of par value. For example, at the intersection of 7–0 and 10.00 is 90.10. This value is interpreted as follows: A bond with a coupon rate of 8 percent, seven years remaining to maturity, and priced to yield 10 percent will sell for 90.10 percent of its par value. For a bond with a par value of $1,000, this means that the bond will sell for $901.00. Notice the agreement of this value with the present value found in Exhibit 6. When the 8 percent coupon bond with seven years remaining to maturity is discounted at 5 percent, which corresponds to a 10 percent yield-to-maturity, the present value of the bond is found to be $901.02.

Let us return to our original task of using the yield book to find the yield-to-maturity given the coupon rate, remaining time to maturity,

---

[7] Just how much the accrued interest will be depends on the type of bond. For corporate and Treasury securities, accrued interest is computed on an actual calendar day basis. For agency securities, it is computed as if each year had 360 days and each month 30 days. Chapters 8 and 9 show how accrued interest is computed for Treasury and agency securities, respectively.

EXHIBIT 7 Sample Pages from a Yield Book

YEARS and MONTHS — 8%

Yield	3-5	3-6	3-7	3-8	3-9	3-10	3-11	4-0
4.00	112.65	112.94	113.23	113.51	113.79	114.08	114.36	114.65
4.20	111.97	112.25	112.51	112.78	113.05	113.32	113.59	113.86
4.40	111.30	111.56	111.81	112.06	112.31	112.56	112.82	113.07
4.60	110.63	110.88	111.11	111.34	111.58	111.81	112.05	112.29
4.80	109.97	110.20	110.41	110.63	110.85	111.07	111.30	111.52
5.00	109.31	109.52	109.72	109.93	110.13	110.34	110.55	110.76
5.20	108.66	108.86	109.04	109.23	109.42	109.61	109.80	110.00
5.40	108.01	108.19	108.36	108.53	108.71	108.88	109.06	109.24
5.60	107.36	107.53	107.69	107.84	108.00	108.17	108.33	108.50
5.80	106.72	106.88	107.02	107.16	107.31	107.45	107.60	107.75
6.00	106.09	106.23	106.36	106.48	106.61	106.75	106.88	107.02
6.10	105.77	105.91	106.03	106.15	106.27	106.39	106.52	106.65
6.20	105.46	105.59	105.70	105.81	105.93	106.05	106.17	106.29
6.30	105.14	105.27	105.37	105.48	105.58	105.70	105.81	105.93
6.40	104.83	104.95	105.04	105.14	105.24	105.35	105.46	105.57
6.50	104.52	104.63	104.72	104.81	104.91	105.00	105.11	105.21
6.60	104.21	104.31	104.39	104.48	104.57	104.66	104.75	104.85
6.70	103.90	104.00	104.07	104.15	104.23	104.32	104.40	104.50
6.80	103.60	103.68	103.75	103.82	103.90	103.98	104.06	104.14
6.90	103.29	103.37	103.43	103.50	103.56	103.64	103.71	103.79
7.00	102,98	103.06	103.11	103.17	103.23	103.30	103.37	103.44
7.10	102.68	102.75	102.79	102.85	102.90	102.96	103.02	103.09
7.20	102.38	102.44	102.48	102.52	102.57	102.62	102.68	102.74
7.30	102.07	102.13	102.16	102.20	102.24	102.29	102.34	102.39
7.40	101.77	101.82	101.85	101.88	101.92	101.96	102.00	102.05
7.50	101.47	101.51	101.54	101.56	101.59	101.62	101.66	101.70
7.60	101.17	101.21	101.22	101.24	101.27	101.29	101.32	101.36
7.70	100.88	100.91	100.91	100.93	100.94	100.96	100.99	101.02
7.80	100.58	100.60	100.60	100.61	100.62	100.63	100.65	100.68
7.90	100.28	100.30	100.30	100.30	100.30	100.31	100.32	100.34
8.00	99.99	100.00	99.99	99.98	99.98	99.98	99.99	100.00
8.10	99.70	99.70	99.68	99.67	99.66	99.66	99.66	99.66
8.20	99.40	99.40	99.38	99.36	99.35	99.34	99.33	99.33
8.30	99.11	99.10	99.07	99.05	99.03	99.01	99.00	99.00
8.40	98.82	98.81	98.77	98.74	98.72	98.69	98.68	98.66
8.50	98.53	98.51	98.47	98.43	98.40	98.37	98.35	98.33
8.60	98.24	98.22	98.17	98.13	98.09	98.06	98.03	98.00
8.70	97.96	97.93	97.87	97.82	97.78	97.74	97.71	97.68
8.80	97.67	97.63	97.57	97.52	97.47	97.42	97.39	97.35
8.90	97.39	97.34	97.28	97.22	97.16	97.11	97.07	97.03
9.00	97.10	97.05	96.98	96.92	96.85	96.80	96.75	96.70
9.10	96.82	96.76	96.69	96.61	96.55	96.49	96.43	96.38
9.20	96.54	96.48	96.39	96.32	96.24	96.18	96.11	96.06
9.30	96.26	96.19	96.10	96.02	95.94	95.87	95.80	95.74
9.40	95.98	95.91	95.81	95.72	95.64	95.56	95.49	95.42
9.50	95.70	95.62	95.52	95.42	95.34	95.25	95.17	95.10
9.60	95.42	95.34	95.23	95.13	95.04	94.95	94.86	94.79
9.70	95.14	95.05	94.94	94.84	94.74	94.64	94.55	94.47
9.80	94.87	94.77	94.66	94.54	94.44	94.34	94.25	94.16
9.90	94.59	94.49	94.37	94.25	94.14	94.04	93.94	93.85
10.00	94.32	94.21	94.08	93.96	93.85	93.74	93.63	93.54
10.20	93.77	93.66	93.52	93.39	93.26	93.14	93.03	92.92
10.40	93.23	93.11	92.96	92.81	92.68	92.55	92.42	92.31
10.60	92.69	92.56	92.40	92.24	92.10	91.96	91.82	91.70
10.80	92.16	92.02	91.84	91.68	91.52	91.37	91.23	91.10
11.00	91.63	91.48	91.29	91.12	90.95	90.79	90.64	90.50
11.20	91.10	90.94	90.75	90.56	90.39	90.22	90.06	89.91
11.40	90.58	90.41	90.21	90.01	89.83	89.65	89.48	89.32
11.60	90.06	89.88	89.67	89.47	89.27	89.08	88.90	88.73
11.80	89.55	89.36	89.13	88.92	88.72	88.52	88.33	88.15
12.00	89.04	88.84	88.60	88.38	88.17	87.96	87.77	87.58

(a)

8% — **YEARS** and MONTHS

Yield	6-3	6-6	6-9	7-0	7-3	7-6	7-9	8-0
4.00	121.92	122.70	123.45	124.21	124.95	125.70	126.42	127.16
4.20	120.69	121.42	122.12	122.84	123.53	124.23	124.91	125.59
4.40	119.47	120.16	120.82	121.49	122.13	122.79	123.41	124.06
4.60	118.28	118.92	119.53	120.15	120.75	121.36	121.94	122.54
4.80	117.09	117.69	118.25	118.84	119.39	119.96	120.50	121.05
5.00	115.92	116.47	117.00	117.54	118.05	118.57	119.07	119.58
5.20	114.77	115.28	115.76	116.25	116.72	117.21	117.66	118.14
5.40	113.62	114.09	114.53	114.99	115.42	115.86	116.28	116.71
5.60	112.50	112.93	113.32	113.74	114.13	114.53	114.91	115.31
5.80	111.38	111.77	112.13	112.51	112.86	113.23	113.56	113.92
6.00	110.28	110.63	110.95	111.30	111.60	111.94	112.24	112.56
6.10	109.74	110.07	110.37	110.69	110.98	111.30	111.58	111.89
6.20	109.19	109.51	109.79	110.10	110.37	110.67	110.93	111.22
6.30	108.66	108.95	109.22	109.50	109.76	110.04	110.28	110.56
6.40	108.12	108.40	108.64	108.91	109.15	109.41	109.64	109.90
6.50	107.59	107.85	108.08	108.33	108.55	108.79	109.00	109.24
6.60	107.06	107.30	107.51	107.75	107.95	108.18	108.37	108.59
6.70	106.53	106.76	106.95	107.17	107.35	107.57	107.74	107.95
6.80	106.01	106.22	106.39	106.60	106.76	106.96	107.12	107.31
6.90	105.49	105.68	105.84	106.03	106.18	106.36	106.50	106.68
7.00	104.98	105.15	105.29	105.46	105.59	105.76	105.89	106.05
7.10	104.46	104.62	104.74	104.90	105.01	105.16	105.28	105.42
7.20	103.95	104.10	104.20	104.34	104.44	104.57	104.67	104.80
7.30	103.45	103.57	103.66	103.78	103.87	103.99	104.07	104.19
7.40	102.94	103.05	103.13	103.23	103.30	103.41	103.47	103.57
7.50	102.44	102.54	102.59	102.68	102.74	102.83	102.88	102.97
7.60	101.94	102.02	102.06	102.14	102.18	102.26	102.29	102.37
7.70	101.45	101.51	101.54	101.60	101.62	101.69	101.71	101.77
7.80	100.96	101.00	101.02	101.06	101.07	101.12	101.13	101.17
7.90	100.47	100.50	100.50	100.53	100.52	100.56	100.55	100.58
8.00	99.98	100.00	99.98	100.00	99.98	100.00	99.98	100.00
8.10	99.50	99.50	99.47	99.47	99.44	99.45	99.41	99.42
8.20	99.02	99.01	98.96	98.95	98.90	98.90	98.85	98.84
8.30	98.54	98.52	98.45	98.43	98.37	98.35	98.29	98.27
8.40	98.06	98.03	97.95	97.91	97.84	97.81	97.73	97.70
8.50	97.59	97.54	97.45	97.40	97.31	97.27	97.18	97.14
8.60	97.12	97.06	96.95	96.89	96.79	96.73	96.64	96.58
8.70	96.66	96.58	96.46	96.39	96.27	96.20	96.09	96.03
8.80	96.19	96.10	95.97	95.88	95.76	95.67	95.55	95.47
8.90	95.73	95.63	95.48	95.38	95.24	95.15	95.02	94.93
9.00	95.28	95.16	95.00	94.89	94.74	94.63	94.48	94.38
9.10	94.82	94.69	94.52	94.40	94.23	94.11	93.95	93.84
9.20	94.37	94.23	94.04	93.91	93.73	93.60	93.43	93.31
9.30	93.92	93.76	93.57	93.42	93.23	93.09	92.91	92.78
9.40	93.47	93.30	93.10	92.94	92.74	92.58	92.39	92.25
9.50	93.03	92.85	92.63	92.46	92.24	92.08	91.88	91.73
9.60	92.59	92.39	92.16	91.98	91.76	91.58	91.37	91.21
9.70	92.15	91.94	91.70	91.50	91.27	91.09	90.86	90.69
9.80	91.71	91.49	91.24	91.03	90.79	90.59	90.36	90.18
9.90	91.28	91.05	90.78	90.57	90.31	90.11	89.86	89.67
10.00	90.84	90.61	90.33	90.10	89.83	89.62	89.36	89.16
10.20	89.99	89.73	89.43	89.18	88.89	88.66	88.38	88.16
10.40	89.14	88.86	88.54	88.27	87.96	87.71	87.42	87.18
10.60	88.31	88.01	87.66	87.38	87.05	86.78	86.46	86.21
10.80	87.48	87.16	86.79	86.49	86.14	85.85	85.52	85.25
11.00	86.67	86.32	85.94	85.62	85.25	84.94	84.59	84.31
11.20	85.86	85.50	85.09	84.75	84.37	84.05	83.68	83.38
11.40	85.06	84.68	84.26	83.90	83.50	83.16	82.78	82.46
11.60	84.28	83.88	83.43	83.06	82.64	82.29	81.89	81.56
11.80	83.50	83.08	82.62	82.23	81.79	81.43	81.01	80.67
12.00	82.73	82.29	81.82	81.41	80.96	80.58	80.15	79.79

(b)

YEARS and MONTHS — 8%

Yield	30-6	31-0	31-6	32-0	32-6	33-0	33-6	34-0
4.00	170.12	170.71	171.28	171.84	172.39	172.94	173.47	173.99
4.20	165.01	165.53	166.05	166.55	167.04	167.52	168.00	168.46
4.40	160.12	160.59	161.05	161.49	161.93	162.36	162.78	163.19
4.60	155.45	155.86	156.27	156.67	157.06	157.43	157.80	158.17
4.80	150.98	151.34	151.70	152.05	152.40	152.73	153.06	153.38
5.00	146.70	147.02	147.34	147.65	147.95	148.24	148.53	148.81
5.20	142.60	142.88	143.16	143.43	143.69	143.95	144.20	144.45
5.40	138.67	138.92	139.16	139.40	139.63	139.85	140.07	140.28
5.60	134.91	135.12	135.33	135.54	135.74	135.93	136.12	136.30
5.80	131.30	131.49	131.67	131.84	132.02	132.18	132.34	132.50
6.00	127.84	128.00	128.16	128.31	128.45	128.60	128.73	128.87
6.10	126.16	126.31	126.46	126.59	126.73	126.86	126.99	127.11
6.20	124.52	124.66	124.79	124.92	125.04	125.16	125.28	125.39
6.30	122.92	123.04	123.16	123.28	123.39	123.50	123.61	123.71
6.40	121.34	121.45	121.56	121.67	121.77	121.87	121.97	122.06
6.50	119.80	119.90	120.00	120.10	120.19	120.28	120.37	120.45
6.60	118.28	118.38	118.47	118.56	118.64	118.72	118.80	118.88
6.70	116.80	116.89	116.97	117.05	117.12	117.20	117.27	117.34
6.80	115.35	115.43	115.50	115.57	115.64	115.70	115.77	115.83
6.90	113.93	114.00	114.06	114.12	114.18	114.24	114.30	114.35
7.00	112.53	112.59	112.65	112.71	112.76	112.81	112.86	112.91
7.10	111.17	111.22	111.27	111.32	111.36	111.41	111.45	111.49
7.20	109.83	109.87	109.91	109.96	110.00	110.03	110.07	110.11
7.30	108.51	108.55	108.59	108.62	108.66	108.69	108.72	108.75
7.40	107.22	107.26	107.29	107.32	107.34	107.37	107.40	107.42
7.50	105.96	105.99	106.01	106.03	106.06	106.08	106.10	106.12
7.60	104.72	104.74	104.76	104.78	104.80	104.81	104.83	104.85
7.70	103.51	103.52	103.54	103.55	103.56	103.57	103.59	103.60
7.80	102.32	102.32	102.33	102.34	102.35	102.36	102.37	102.37
7.90	101.15	101.15	101.16	101.16	101.16	101.17	101.17	101.17
8.00	100.00	100.00	100.00	100.00	100.00	100.00	100.00	100.00
8.10	98.88	98.87	98.87	98.86	98.86	98.86	98.85	98.85
8.20	97.77	97.76	97.75	97.75	97.74	97.73	97.73	97.72
8.30	96.69	96.68	96.66	96.65	96.64	96.63	96.62	96.61
8.40	95.63	95.61	95.59	95.58	95.57	95.55	95.54	95.53
8.50	94.58	94.56	94.54	94.53	94.51	94.49	94.48	94.46
8.60	93.56	93.54	93.52	93.49	93.48	93.46	93.44	93.42
8.70	92.55	92.53	92.50	92.48	92.46	92.44	92.42	92.40
8.80	91.57	91.54	91.51	91.49	91.46	91.44	91.42	91.40
8.90	90.60	90.57	90.54	90.51	90.48	90.46	90.43	90.41
9.00	89.65	89.61	89.58	89.55	89.52	89.50	89.47	89.45
9.10	88.71	88.68	88.64	88.61	88.58	88.55	88.53	88.50
9.20	87.80	87.76	87.72	87.69	87.66	87.63	87.60	87.57
9.30	86.90	86.86	86.82	86.78	86.75	86.72	86.69	86.66
9.40	86.01	85.97	85.93	85.89	85.86	85.83	85.79	85.76
9.50	85.14	85.10	85.06	85.02	84.98	84.95	84.92	84.88
9.60	84.29	84.24	84.20	84.16	84.12	84.09	84.05	84.02
9.70	83.45	83.40	83.36	83.32	83.28	83.24	83.21	83.17
9.80	82.63	82.58	82.53	82.49	82.45	82.41	82.38	82.34
9.90	81.82	81.77	81.72	81.68	81.64	81.60	81.56	81.53
10.00	81.02	80.97	80.92	80.88	80.84	80.80	80.76	80.72
10.20	79.47	79.42	79.37	79.33	79.28	79.24	79.20	79.16
10.40	77.97	77.92	77.87	77.82	77.78	77.74	77.70	77.66
10.60	76.52	76.47	76.42	76.37	76.33	76.28	76.24	76.20
10.80	75.12	75.07	75.02	74.97	74.92	74.88	74.84	74.80
11.00	73.77	73.71	73.66	73.61	73.57	73.52	73.48	73.44
11.20	72.46	72.40	72.35	72.30	72.26	72.21	72.17	72.13
11.40	71.19	71.13	71.08	71.03	70.99	70.94	70.90	70.86
11.60	69.96	69.91	69.86	69.81	69.76	69.72	69.68	69.64
11.80	68.77	68.72	68.67	68.62	68.57	68.53	68.49	68.45
12.00	67.62	67.57	67.52	67.47	67.42	67.38	67.34	67.30

(c)

SOURCE: Reproduced from Publication #63, *Expanded Bond Values Table,* copyright 1970, pages 873, 876, and 883, Financial Publishing Company, Boston, Mass.

and market price of the bond. First, locate the page in the yield book that corresponds to the coupon rate and time remaining to maturity for the bond whose yield is sought. Second, look down the column corresponding to the time remaining to maturity until the market price of the bond (expressed as a percentage of par value) is found. Finally, look across the row to obtain the yield.

The procedure can be illustrated using our hypothetical bond. Exhibit 7(b) represents the appropriate page of the yield book, since it contains bond values for a bond with a coupon rate of 8 percent and seven years remaining to maturity. The market price of our hypothetical bond is $814.10, or 81.41 percent of par. Looking down column 7–0 we find the value of 81.41 in the row corresponding to a yield of 12 percent. This, of course, agrees with our previous computation that indicated the yield-to-maturity for our hypothetical bond to be 12 percent.

Everything went smoothly in our illustration. The exact time remaining to maturity was on the table, and so was the exact market price. Suppose instead that our hypothetical bond had seven years and one month remaining to maturity and a market price of $904. Neither input needed to determine the yield-to-maturity is included on the sample page. What can be done in such cases? The yield-to-maturity can be approximated by interpolating the values presented in the yield book. Such an approach may be satisfactory for a investor with a small sum to invest. However, for a portfolio manager with substantial funds to invest, such an approach would be inadequate. In such instances, bond traders and portfolio managers usually use financial calculators.

Yield-to-maturity for zero-coupon bonds. Although a zero-coupon bond does not pay interest, the computation of its yield-to-maturity is based on semiannual cash flows, so that the computed yield can be compared to the yield for coupon securities. For example, suppose that a 5-year zero-coupon bond with a maturity value of $1,000 is selling for $675.56. The yield-to-maturity is found by finding the interest rate that will make the present value of $1,000 *ten periods* from now equal to $675.56. The interest rate that will accomplish this is 4 percent. The yield-to-maturity is then double this interest rate, or 8 percent.

Yield relationships. The investor should be cognizant of the following relationships for the coupon rate, current yield, and yield-to-maturity:

Price of the Bond	Relationship
Selling at par	Coupon rate = Current yield = Yield-to-maturity
Selling at a discount	Coupon rate < Current yield < Yield-to-maturity
Selling at a premium	Coupon rate > Current yield > Yield-to-maturity

Yield-to-maturity for nontraditional bonds. In this book bonds with cash-flow characteristics that differ from that of traditional bonds will be discussed. Two examples are mortgage-related securities and floating-rate securities. The calculation of the yield-to-maturity or its equivalent for such securities is beyond the scope of this introductory chapter.[8] Nevertheless, the principles set forth in this chapter underlie the various "yield" approaches for evaluating these securities.

Yield-to-maturity for a bond portfolio. So far we have focused on the yield-to-maturity for an individual bond. The yield-to-maturity for a bond portfolio is computed in two steps. In the first step, the cash flow from all the bonds in the portfolio is computed. In the second step, the discount rate that makes the present value of the portfolio's cash flow equal to the market value of the portfolio is found. Adjusting the discount rate to an annual basis gives the portfolio's yield-to-maturity, commonly referred to as the portfolio's *internal rate of return.*

Yield-to-Call

As explained in Chapter 2, a bond may be called by the issuer before maturity. Consequently, a conservative investor will compute the yield on a bond in two ways: (1) assuming the bond is held to maturity, and (2) assuming the bond is called by the issuer. The latter yield is referred to as the yield-to-call. A conservative investor uses the lower of the two yields in determining the promised "yield" on the bond because it represents a minimum yield that may be realized.

At the outset, it must be noted that the yield-to-call, like the yield-to-maturity, is a traditional measure that is *not* a good measure to employ in order to evaluate the investment merits of alternative bonds available to the investor. This is so for two reasons. First, it assumes the coupon interest payments before the issue is called will be reinvested at a rate equal to the yield-to-call. Hence it suffers from the same problem as the yield-to-maturity. Second, it does not recognize what will happen to the proceeds after the bond is called. Consequently, since the yield-to-maturity assumes a time commitment of funds greater than the yield-to-call, a direct comparison of these two yields is inappropriate. These drawbacks of the yield-to-call are discussed in the next section. In this section, the yield-to-call is explained.

The yield-to-call is defined as the discount rate that equates the present value of the promised cash flow if the bond is called (coupon

---

[8] For a discussion of yield approaches for mortgage pass-through securities, see Chapter 16. Also see Michael Waldman and Mark Gordon, "Determining the Yield of a Mortgage Security," Chapter 10 in Frank J. Fabozzi, *The Handbook of Mortgage-Backed Securities* (Chicago, IL: Probus Publishing, 1985). For floating-rate securities, see David Muntner, "Evaluation Floating Rate Notes: II." Chapter 10 in Frank J. Fabozzi (ed.) *Floating Rate Securities: Instruments, Investment Characteristics and Portfolio Strategies* (Chicago, IL: Probus Publishing, 1986).

payments plus call price) to the market price. To illustrate the computation of the yield-to-call, suppose our hypothetical bond is selling for $1,089.37 instead of $814.10. Further, assume the bond is callable three years from now at 104.2 (i.e., $1,042). A trial-and-error approach can be used to determine the yield-to-call for this bond. If a 3 percent discount rate is used, the present value is the market price of $1,089.37, as shown below:

$$\begin{bmatrix} \text{PV of an annuity of \$1} \\ \text{for six periods at 3 percent} \end{bmatrix} \times \begin{bmatrix} \text{Semiannual} \\ \text{coupon rate} \end{bmatrix}$$

$$5.4172 \qquad\qquad \times \quad \$40 \qquad\qquad = \$ \ 216.69$$

plus

$$\begin{bmatrix} \text{PV of \$1 six periods} \\ \text{hence at 3 percent} \end{bmatrix} \times \begin{bmatrix} \text{Call price} \end{bmatrix}$$

$$.8375 \qquad\qquad \times \quad \$1,042 \qquad\qquad = \quad \underline{\ \ 872.68}$$

Present value of bond if called $\qquad\qquad\qquad\qquad = \$1,089.37$

Doubling the discount rate gives the yield-to-call. Hence the yield-to-call is 6 percent.

The yield-to-maturity for the bond can be found using the yield book. From Exhibit 7, we find that an 8 percent coupon bond with seven years remaining to maturity and a price of 108.91 offers a yield-to-maturity of 6.4 percent. Since our hypothetical bond has a market price of 108.94, its yield-to-maturity is approximately 6.4 percent. A conservative investor would use the yield-to-call as the "yield," since it is less than the yield-to-maturity.

When the call price is greater than the maturity value, which it usually is when a bond may be called, there are methods for approximating the yield-to-call.[9] Since there are specialized yield-to-call books published and pocket calculators with preprogrammed features to compute the yield on an investment, the approximation methods are not discussed in this chapter. It may not be necessary, however, to compute the yield-to-call. Remember that if the yield-to-call is greater than the yield-to-maturity, then the latter is the minimum "yield."

Realized Compound Yield

When using the yield-to-maturity as a measure of investment return, it is assumed that the coupon interest can be reinvested at a rate equal to

---

[9] See Sidney Homer and Martin L. Leibowitz, *Inside the Yield Book* (Published jointly: Englewood Cliffs, N.J.: Prentice-Hall, and New York: New York Institute of Finance, 1972), pp. 164–67.

the yield-to-maturity. That is, if the yield-to-maturity is 12 percent, it is assumed that the coupon interest payments can be reinvested to yield 12 percent.

Importance of interest-in-interest. To see the importance of the interest-on-interest component on total return, consider a bond selling at par with seven years remaining to maturity and carrying a 12 percent coupon rate. The total return for this bond consists of two sources: (1) coupon interest of $60 every six months for seven years and (2) interest from the reinvestment of the coupon interest. Since the bond is assumed to be selling at par, there is no capital gain or loss.

The future value generated from the reinvestment of coupon interest at 12 percent annually can be found by multiplying the future value of an annuity of $1 by the semiannual coupon interest. Thus for the bond under examination we have:

$$
\left[\begin{array}{l} \text{FV of \$60 for 14} \\ \text{six-month periods} \end{array} \right] = \$60 \times \left[\begin{array}{l} \text{FV of \$1 each six months at} \\ \text{6 percent interest from Exhibit 5} \end{array} \right]
$$
$$
= \$60 \times 21.015
$$
$$
= \$1,261
$$

The coupon interest is $840 ($60 times 14). Hence the balance, $421 ($1,261 minus $840), represents the interest-on-interest component of the total return. For this bond, interest-on-interest accounts for 33 percent ($421 divided by $1,261) of the total return.

The importance of the interest-on-interest component becomes greater the longer the maturity. For example, if the 12 percent coupon bonds selling at par had a remaining life of 30 years instead of 7 years, the total return would be $31,987. Since coupon interest payments are $3,600 ($60 times 60 semiannual coupon payments), interest-on-interest is $28,387 ($31,987 minus $3,600) or 89 percent of the total return.

For a bond selling at a discount from par, interest-on-interest makes up less of the total return for bonds of equal time remaining to maturity and the same yield-to-maturity. This can be illustrated with the hypothetical bond used to illustrate the computation of the yield-to-maturity. Recall that the bond carries an 8 percent coupon rate, has seven years remaining to maturity, and has a market price of $814 (rounded to the nearest dollar). The yield-to-maturity for this bond is 12 percent. The total return consists of (1) coupon interest payments of $560, (2) interest-on-interest of $281, and (3) a capital gain of $186 ($1,000 minus $814). The interest-on-interest component accounts for 27 percent of the total return ($281 divided by $1,027). For the 12 percent, seven-year par bonds, the interest-on-interest component makes up 33 percent of the total return.

The interest-on-interest component of a long-term bond selling at a discount would be a substantial portion of the bond's total return, just as in the case of a bond selling at par. In fact the longer the term of the bond, the less important is the capital gain component compared with the other two components. For example, a bond with 30 years remaining to maturity, carrying a coupon rate of 8 percent, and selling at $677 will have a yield-to-maturity of 12 percent. The total return for this bond is $21,648, consisting of: (1) coupon interest payments of $2,400, (2) interest-on-interest of $18,925, and (3) a capital gain of $323. The capital gain component is only 1.5 percent of the total return. For the seven-year bond selling at a discount, the capital gain component represented 18 percent of the total return. The interest-on-interest component for the 30-year bond selling at a discount is about 87 percent, which is approximately the same as in the case of the 30-year bond selling at par.

As would be expected, bonds selling at a premium are more dependent upon the interest-on-interest component of the total return.

Because of the importance of the rate that the coupon interest is assumed to be reinvested, a measure of return that can be used for investment decisions must take into account interest-on-interest. Homer and Leibowitz suggest a comprehensive measure that takes into consideration all three sources of a bond's return.[10] The measure they suggest reveals the fully compounded growth rate of an investment under varying reinvestment rates. They call this measure the *realized compound yield.*

Computing the realized compound yield. The steps to compute the realized compound yield are as follows:

1. Compute the total future dollars that will be received from the investment. This is equal to the sum of the coupon payments, the interest-on-interest from reinvesting the coupon payments at an assumed reinvestment rate, and the redemption value.
2. Divide the amount found in the previous step by the investment. The resulting amount is the future value per dollar invested.
3. Find the interest rate that produces the future value per dollar invested. This can be done by using a future value of $1 table such as Exhibit 1 or by solving the following equation:

$$\text{(Future value per dollar invested)}^{\frac{1}{\text{no. of periods}}} - 1$$

4. Since interest is assumed to be paid semiannually, double the interest rate found in the previous step. The resulting interest rate is the realized compound yield.

The 12 percent, seven-year bond selling at par will be used to demonstrate the computation of the realized compound yield. The reinvestment rate assumed is 10 percent. The steps are as follows:

---

[10] Homer and Leibowitz, *Inside the Yield Book.*

1. The total future dollars to be received consists of the coupon interest and interest-on-interest of $1,176[11] and the redemption value of $1,000. Hence the total future dollars to be received is $2,176.
2. Since the investment is $1,000, the future value per $1 invested is $2.176 ($2,176 divided by $1,000).
3. From Exhibit 1 it can be seen that the interest rate that will produce a future value of $2.176 for a $1 investment made for 14 periods is between 5 and 6 percent. Using the formula, or consulting a more detailed table, the interest rate of 5.7 percent would produce a future value of $2.17.
4. Doubling 5.7 percent we get a realized compound yield of 11.4 percent.

Properties of the realized compound yield. One property of the realized compound yield is that it will be between the yield-to-maturity and the reinvestment rate. Therefore when the reinvestment rate is the same as the yield-to-maturity, the realized compound yield is the same as the yield-to-maturity. When the reinvestment rate is greater than the yield-to-maturity, the realized compound yield will be greater than the yield-to-maturity. The realized compound yield will be less than the yield-to-maturity when the reinvestment rate is less than the latter.

The difference in basis points[12] between the realized compound yield and the yield-to-maturity depends not only on the reinvestment rate but also on the remaining life of the bond and the coupon rate. The longer the term-to-maturity, the more important will be the interest-on-interest component for a given coupon rate and yield-to-maturity. Consequently, the longer the term of a bond, the closer its realized compound yield will be to the reinvestment rate. On the other hand, the shorter the maturity, the closer the realized compound yield will be to the yield-to-maturity.

For a given term-to-maturity and yield-to-maturity, the lower the coupon rate, the less of a bond's total return depends on the interest-on-interest component. Therefore, holding all other factors constant, the realized compound yield will deviate from the yield-to-maturity by less basis points for a given reinvestment rate the lower the coupon rate. For

---

[11]
$$\begin{bmatrix} \text{FV of \$60 for 14} \\ \text{six-month periods} \end{bmatrix} = \$60 \times \begin{bmatrix} \text{FV of \$1 each six months} \\ \text{at 5 percent interest from Exhibit 3} \end{bmatrix}$$
$$= \$60 \times 19.598$$
$$= \$1,176$$

Note that since the annual reinvestment rate is assumed to be 10 percent, a 5 percent semiannual interest rate is used in the future value computation.

[12] Bond market participants express interest rate changes or spreads in terms of basis points. A basis point is equal to .01 percent. Therefore, 100 basis points are equal to 1 percent.

a zero coupon bond, the realized compound yield is equal to the yield-to-maturity.

Exhibit 8 shows the realized compound yield under different assumptions for the reinvestment rate for the four bonds discussed in this section. The reader can verify the properties of the realized compound yield stated in the preceding discussion.

EXHIBIT 8 Realized Compound Yields for 7-Year and 30-Year Bonds with a 12 Percent Yield-to-Maturity: Coupon Rates 12 Percent and 8 Percent

Reinvestment Rate	Realized Compound Yield* 7-Year Bonds		30-Year Bonds	
	12 Percent Coupon, Price = 100	8 Percent Coupon, Price = 81.41	12 Percent Coupon, Price = 100	8 Percent Coupon, Price = 677
8%	10.8%	11.1%	9.3%	9.4%
10	11.4	11.6	10.6	10.8
12	12.0	12.0	12.0	12.0
14	12.6	12.5	13.3	13.3
16	13.2	13.0	15.0	14.9

* The yield-to-maturity for each bond is 12 percent.

Application to callable bonds selling at a premium.   Realized compound yield should also be used to measure the minimum yield for a callable bond selling at a premium. As discussed in the previous section, the selection of a minimum yield based upon the lesser of the yield-to-maturity and yield-to-call is deficient because it does not consider the reinvestment opportunities available to the investor. A proper analysis would consider the realized compound yield assuming the bond is not called and assuming the bond is called. Using the callable bond discussed in the previous section, the realized compound yield approach will be illustrated. Information about the callable bond is summarized below:

> Coupon rate = 8 percent
> Time remaining to maturity = seven years
> Market price = $1089.40
> Time to first call = three years
> Call price = $1,042
> Yield-to-maturity = 6.4 percent
> Yield-to-call = 6 percent
> Crossover yield = 6.8 percent

To compute the realized compound yield, the reinvestment rate must be specified. It is assumed in this illustration that the coupon interest and principal, if the bond is called, can be reinvested earning 5 percent per annum (2.5 percent semiannually).

The realized compound yield if the bond is *not* called and held to maturity is 6 percent as shown below:

1. The total future dollars to be received consists of the coupon interest and interest-on-interest of $661 and the redemption value at maturity of $1,000. The total future dollars to be received is therefore $1,661.
2. The future value per $1 invested is $1.52 ($1,661 divided by $1,089.4).
3. From Exhibit 1 it can be seen that the interest rate that will produce a future value of $1.52 if $1 is invested for 14 periods is 3 percent.
4. Doubling 3 percent we obtain the realized compound yield of 6 percent.

The realized compound yield if the bond is called is 5.4 percent as shown below:

1. Determination of the total future dollars to be received if the bond is called requires several computations, each of which is explained below.

    a. *Coupon interest and interest-on-interest up to the call date:* There are six coupon payments of $40 per period between the contemplated acquisition date and the call date. The future value of the coupon interest and interest-on-interest assuming the $40 coupon interest payments are reinvested at 2.5 percent per period is $256.
    b. *Future value at maturity of coupon interest and interest-on-interest expected up to the call date:* The $256 computed in the previous step can be reinvested for the remaining number of periods until maturity earning 2.5 percent per period. Since there are eight periods (four years) between the call date and maturity, $256 will grow to $312.[13]
    c. *Coupon interest and interest-on-interest to maturity for the funds reinvested after the bond is called:* The call price is $1,042. This amount can be reinvested earning 5 percent per annum. The annual coupon interest from the reinvestment of the funds would be $52.10 ($1,042 times .05) or $26.05 semiannually. Reinvesting $26.05 for eight periods earning 2.5 percent per period would give $228 at the end of eight periods.

---

[13] The future value of $1 invested for eight periods at 2.5 percent is 1.2184.

The total future dollars to be received is b plus c plus the redemption value of $1,042. Hence the total future dollars to be received is $1,582 ($312 + $228 + $1,042).

2. The future value per dollar invested is $1.45 ($1,582 divided by $1,089.40).
3. From Exhibit 1 it can be seen that the interest rate that will produce a future value of $1.45 for a $1 investment made for 14 periods is between 2 and 3 percent. The approximate rate is 2.7 percent.[14]
4. Doubling 2.7 percent we get a realized compound yield if the bond is called of 5.4 percent.

The minimum yield is therefore 5.4 percent, the realized compound yield if the bond is called.

BOND PRICE VOLATILITY

From our discussion of the time value of money, it should be clear that the price of a bond changes in the opposite direction from the change in the yield required by investors. For example, if a 9 percent coupon bond with 20 years remaining to maturity is selling at 100 (par) to yield 9 percent, the price of the bond will decrease to 91.42 if market yields increase by 100 basis points to 10 percent. The increase in market yields decreases the price of the bond by 8.58 percent. If, on the other hand, market yields decline by 100 basis points to 8 percent, the price of the bond will increase by 9.9 percent to 109.90. In addition the change in the price of the bond will be greater the greater the change in the yield required by investors. For example, for the 9 percent coupon, 20-year bond, an increase in market yields from 9 percent to 11 percent (a 200 basis point increase) will result in a decrease in the price of the bond from 100 to 83.95. Hence, for a 200 basis point increase in yield, the price of the bond will fall by 16.05 percent compared with 8.58 percent for a 100 basis point increase in yield.

For a given initial market yield and a given change in basis points, the percentage change in the price of the bond will depend upon certain characteristics of the bond. The relationship between bond price volatility and these characteristics of a bond are illustrated in the remainder of this chapter.

Before proceeding, it is important to understand that the volatility we will be discussing is the change that will result from an *instantaneous* change in market yields. Even if market yields do not change, the price of a bond selling at a premium or discount will change due to the passage of time. For example, consider a bond with a 7 percent coupon

---

[14] $1.027^8 = 1.4521$

rate, 20 years remaining to maturity, and selling at 81.60 to yield 9 percent. If the bond is held for one year and market yields remained at 9 percent, the price of the bond would increase to 81.95, since it would have 19 years remaining to maturity. The increase in price from 81.60 to 81.95 results from an accretion process that will eventually increase the price of the bond to its par value at maturity. For a bond selling at a premium, the price of a bond decreases as it approaches maturity if market yields remain constant. Consider, for example, a bond with a coupon rate of 12 percent, 20 years remaining to maturity, and selling for 127.60 to yield 9 percent. The price of the bond after one year has passed will be 127.07 if market yields do not change. This results from the amortization of the premium. The relationship between the price of a bond and the remaining time to maturity assuming that market yields are unchanged is shown in Exhibits 9 and 10.

EXHIBIT 9 Time Path of the Value of a 7 Percent Coupon, 20-Year Bond If the Required Yield Begins and Remains at 9 Percent

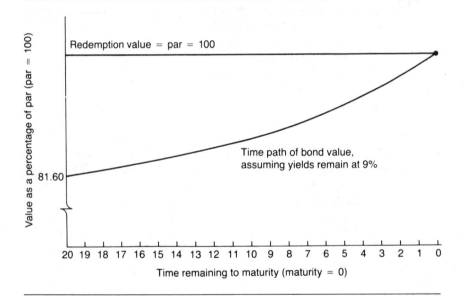

Bond Price Volatility and Coupon Rate

For a given maturity and initial market yield, the volatility of a bond's price increases as the coupon rate decreases. This is illustrated in Exhibit 11. The term to maturity is 20 years, and the initial yield is 9 percent. The price of the bond for coupon rates between 5 percent and 12 percent at 1 percent increments for eight hypothetical changes in the market yield

EXHIBIT 10   Time Path of the Value of a 12 Percent Coupon, 20-Year
Bond if the Required Yield Begins and Remains at 9 Percent

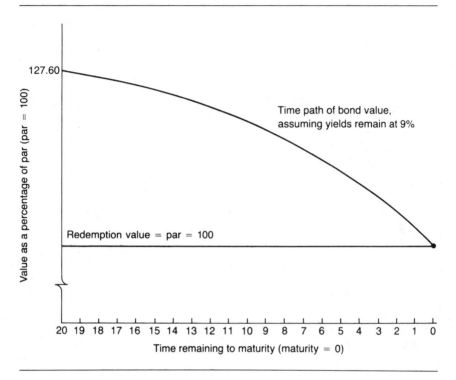

are shown in the top panel of Exhibit 11. In the second panel, the percentage change in the price of the bond is shown.

An implication of this property of price volatility is that bonds selling at a discount are more responsive to changes in market yield, all other factors equal, compared with bonds selling at or above par. Moreover, the deeper the discount resulting from the divergence between the coupon rate and market yield, the greater the responsiveness of the bond's price to changes in market yield. The greatest price response is offered by zero-coupon bonds. From a purely capital gain or loss perspective, therefore, investors would avoid bonds selling at a discount if interest rates are expected to rise; however, bonds selling at a discount are attractive if interest rates are anticipated to decline.

Notice in Exhibit 11 that the percentage change in the price of a bond is not the same for both an increase and decrease of the same number of basis points. The percentage increase in price when rates decline is greater than the percentage decrease in price when rates increase. The difference between the percentage change in price increases as the

EXHIBIT 11 Bond Price Volatility for Bonds Yielding 9 Percent and 20 Years to Maturity

				Coupon Rate				
	5 Percent	6 Percent	7 Percent	8 Percent	9 Percent	10 Percent	11 Percent	12 Percent
Initial Price	$63.20	$72.40	$81.60	$90.80	$100.00	$109.20	$118.40	$127.60
Price If Yield Changes by:								
−200 bp	$78.64	$89.32	$100.00	$110.68	$121.36	$132.03	$142.71	$153.39
−100	70.31	80.21	90.10	100.00	109.90	119.79	129.69	139.59
−50	66.61	76.15	85.69	95.23	104.77	114.31	123.85	133.39
−10	63.86	73.13	82.39	91.66	100.93	110.19	119.46	128.73
+10	62.54	71.68	80.82	89.95	99.09	108.22	117.36	126.49
+50	60.03	68.91	77.80	86.68	95.56	104.44	113.32	122.20
+100	57.10	65.68	74.26	82.84	91.42	100.00	108.58	117.16
+200	51.86	59.88	67.91	75.93	83.95	91.98	100.00	108.02
Percentage Change in Price If Yield Changes by:								
−200 bp	+24.43%	+23.37%	+22.55%	+21.89%	+21.36%	+20.91%	+20.53%	+20.21%
−100	+11.25	+10.79	+10.42	+10.13	+9.90	+9.70	+9.54	+9.40
−50	+5.40	+5.18	+5.01	+4.88	+4.77	+4.68	+4.60	+4.54
−10	+1.04	+1.01	+0.97	+0.95	+0.93	+0.91	+0.90	+0.89
+10	−1.04	−0.99	−0.96	−0.94	−0.91	−0.90	−0.88	−0.87
+50	−5.02	−4.82	−4.66	−4.54	−4.44	−4.36	−4.29	−4.23
+100	−9.65	−9.28	−9.00	−8.77	−8.58	−8.42	−8.29	−8.18
+200	−17.94	−17.29	−16.78	−16.38	−16.05	−15.77	−15.54	−15.34
Ratio of Percentage Price Change to Yield Movement in Basis Points If Yield Changes by:								
−200 bp	−.1222%	−.1169%	−.1128%	−.1095%	−.1068%	−.1046%	−.1027%	−.1011%
−100	−.1125	−.1079	−.1042	−.1013	−.0990	−.0970	−.0954	−.0940
−50	−.1080	−.1036	−.1002	−.0976	−.0954	−.0936	−.0920	−.0908
−10	−.1040	−.1010	−.0970	−.0950	−.0930	−.0910	−.0900	−.0890
+10	−.1040	−.0990	−.0960	−.0940	−.0910	−.0900	−.0880	−.0870
+50	−.1004	−.0964	−.0932	−.0908	−.0888	−.0872	−.0858	−.0846
+100	−.0965	−.0928	−.0900	−.0877	−.0858	−.0842	−.0829	−.0818
+200	−.0897	−.0865	−.0839	−.0819	−.0803	−.0789	−.0777	−.0767

amount of the change in basis points increases. This is due to the convexity property of the price/yield profile. Convexity will be discussed in the next chapter.

The change in the price of the bond, however, is only one consideration in evaluating the investment merits of a particular bond issue. Recall that even though interest rates may decline so that the price of the bond increases, the interest-on-interest component of the bond's total return will decrease due to the lower reinvestment rate. It seems that we are missing an important element in assessing the relative attractiveness of a bond issue. That element is the period of time the investor plans to hold the bond. This period is commonly referred to as the investor's investment horizon. In Chapter 28 a framework for evaluating the attractiveness of a bond for a given investment horizon is explained.

Bond Price Volatility and Maturity

The volatility of the price of a bond increases the longer the remaining term to maturity, all other factors constant. For a bond yielding 9 percent and with a coupon rate of 9 percent, this property is illustrated in Exhibit 12.[15]

An implication of this property of price volatility is that if interest rates are expected to increase, bond prices will decrease by a greater percentage for long-term bonds compared to short-term bonds, all other factors constant. Therefore, from a purely capital loss perspective, an investor will avoid long-term bonds (holding everything else constant) if interest rates are expected to rise. Conversely, since the percentage change in prices of long-term bonds will increase by a greater percentage than short-term bonds, investors will prefer long-term bonds from a purely capital gain perspective when interest rates are projected to fall.

Once again, remember that the capital gain or loss resulting from a change in market yield is only one component of the total return from holding a bond. The technique discussed in Chapter 28 can be employed to evaluate the relative investment merit of holding a bond over the investor's investment horizon given the investor's projection about the future movement of interest rates.

Bond Price Volatility and Duration

A pitfall with using the maturity of a bond as a measure of the timing of its cash flow is that it only takes into consideration the final payment. To overcome this shortcoming, Professor Frederick R. Macaulay in 1938

---

[15] Once again it can be seen that the percentage change in price is not symmetrical for a given change in basis points and a given maturity, except for very small changes. The difference in the percentage change in price decreases as the maturity increases.

EXHIBIT 12 Bond Price Volatility for 9 Percent Coupon Bonds Selling at Par

	Years to Maturity						
	1	5	10	15	20	25	30
Initial Price	$100.00	$100.00	$100.00	$100.00	$100.00	$100.00	$100.00
Price If Yield Changes by:							
−200 bp	$101.90	$108.32	$114.21	$118.39	$121.36	$123.46	$124.94
−100	100.94	104.06	106.80	108.65	109.90	110.74	111.31
−50	100.47	102.00	103.32	104.19	104.77	105.15	105.40
−10	100.09	100.40	100.65	100.82	100.93	101.00	101.04
+10	99.91	99.61	99.35	99.19	99.09	99.02	98.98
+50	99.53	98.05	96.82	96.04	95.56	95.25	95.06
+100	99.07	96.14	93.77	92.31	91.42	90.87	90.54
+200	98.15	92.46	88.05	85.47	83.95	83.07	82.55
Percentage Change If Yield Changes by:							
−200 bp	+1.90%	+8.32%	+14.21%	+18.39%	+21.36%	+23.46%	+24.94%
−100	+0.94	+4.06	+6.80	+8.65	+9.90	+10.74	+11.31
−50	+0.47	+2.00	+3.32	+4.19	+4.77	+5.15	+5.40
−10	+0.09	+0.40	+0.65	+0.82	+0.93	+1.00	+1.04
+10	−0.09	−0.39	−0.65	−0.81	−0.91	−0.98	−1.02
+50	−0.47	−1.95	−3.18	−3.96	−4.44	−4.75	−4.94
+100	−0.93	−3.86	−6.23	−7.69	−8.58	−9.13	−9.46
+200	−1.85	−7.54	−11.95	−14.53	−16.05	−16.93	−17.45
Ratio of Percentage Price Change to Yield Movement in Basis Points If Yield Changes by:							
−200 bp	−.0095%	−.0416%	−.0711%	−.0920%	−.1068%	−.1173%	−.1247%
−100	−.0094	−.0406	−.0680	−.0865	−.0990	−.1074	−.1131
−50	−.0094	−.0400	−.0664	−.0838	−.0954	−.1030	−.1080
−10	−.0090	−.0400	−.0650	−.0820	−.0930	−.1000	−.1040
+10	−.0090	−.0390	−.0650	−.0810	−.0910	−.0980	−.1020
+50	−.0094	−.0390	−.0636	−.0792	−.0888	−.0950	−.0988
+100	−.0093	−.0386	−.0623	−.0769	−.0858	−.0913	−.0946
+200	−.0093	−.0377	−.0598	−.0727	−.0803	−.0847	−.0873

suggested using a measure that would account for all cash flows expected.[16] The measure he suggested, known as *duration*, is a weighted average term-to-maturity where the cash flows are in terms of their present value. Mathematically, duration is measured as follows:

$$\text{Duration} = \frac{\text{PVCF}_1\,(1)}{\text{PVTCF}} + \frac{\text{PVCF}_2\,(2)}{\text{PVTCF}} + \frac{\text{PVCF}_3\,(3)}{\text{PVTCF}} + \cdots + \frac{\text{PVCF}_n\,(n)}{\text{PVTCF}}$$

where

PVCF_t = the present value of the cash flow in period t discounted at the prevailing yield-to-maturity

t = the period when the cash flow is expected to be received

n = remaining number of periods until maturity

PVTCF = total present value of the cash flow from the bond where the present value is determined using the prevailing yield-to-maturity

For a bond in which there are no sinking-fund or call effects and in which interest is paid semiannually, the cash flow for periods 1 to n − 1 is just one half of the annual coupon interest. The cash flow in period n is the semiannual coupon interest plus the redemption value. The discount rate is one half the prevailing yield-to-maturity. The resulting value is in half years when semiannual interest payments are used in the computation. To obtain duration in terms of years, duration in half years is divided by two.[17] Since the price of a bond is equal to its cash flow discounted at the prevailing yield-to-maturity, PVTCF is nothing more than the current market price *including accrued interest*.

Exhibit 13 shows how the duration of a 7 percent coupon bond with eight years to maturity and selling for $887.70 to yield 9 percent is computed assuming coupon interest is paid semiannually. The duration for this bond is 6.1335 years.

Properties of duration. Four properties of a bond's duration should be noted. First, for coupon bonds, the duration of a bond is less than its maturity. Second, for zero-coupon bonds the duration is the number of years to maturity. Third, the duration of a bond decreases the greater the coupon rate. Finally, as market yields increase, the duration of a bond decreases. These properties are demonstrated in the next chapter.

Relationship between duration and bond price. The specific link between a bond's duration and its bond price volatility for small changes

---

[16] Frederick R. Macaulay, *Some Theoretical Problems Suggested by the Movement of Interest Rates, Bond Yields, and Stock Prices in the United States Since 1865* (New York: National Bureau of Economic Research, 1938).

[17] In general, if there are m coupon payments per year, then duration in years is computed by dividing the duration based on m payments per year by m.

EXHIBIT 13   Worksheet for Computation of the Duration of a 7 Percent Coupon Bond with Eight Years to Maturity Selling at $887.70 to Yield 9 Percent (semiannual interest payments assumed)

Period	Cash Flow	PV at 4.5 Percent	PVCF	PVCF× Period
1	$ 35	.9569	$ 33.4915	$ 33.4915
2	35	.9157	32.0495	64.0990
3	35	.8763	30.6705	92.0115
4	35	.8386	29.3510	117.4040
5	35	.8025	28.0875	140.4375
6	35	.7679	26.8765	161.2590
7	35	.7348	25.7180	180.0260
8	35	.7032	24.6120	196.8960
9	35	.6729	23.5515	211.9635
10	35	.6439	22.5365	225.3650
11	35	.6162	21.5670	237.2370
12	35	.5897	20.6395	247.6740
13	35	.5643	19.7505	256.7565
14	35	.5400	18.9000	264.6000
15	35	.5167	18.0845	271.2675
16	1035	.4945	511.8075	8,188.9200
			$887.6935	$10,889.4080

$$\text{Duration in half years} = \frac{10,889.4080}{887.6935}$$

$$= 12.2671$$

$$\text{Duration in years} = \frac{12.2671}{2}$$

$$= 6.1335$$

in interest rates was demonstrated by Professors Michael Hopewell and George Kaufman.[18] They show that

Percentage change in bond's price

$$= -(\text{Modified duration}) \times \left(\frac{\text{Change in market yield in basis points}}{100} \right)$$

where modified duration is

$$\frac{\text{duration}}{1 + \left(\dfrac{\text{market yield}}{\text{no. of coupon payments per year}} \right)}$$

[18] Michael H. Hopewell and George C. Kaufman, "Bond Price Volatility and Term to Maturity: A Generalized Respecification," *American Economic Review*, September 1973, pp. 749–53.

For example, the duration of the 7 percent coupon bond with eight years to maturity and selling to yield 9 percent is 6.1335. Hence modified duration is

$$\frac{6.1335}{1 + \left(\frac{.09}{2}\right)} = 5.8694$$

The percentage decline in the bond's price if market yields *rise* by 50 basis points is 2.93 percent as shown below:

$$= -(5.8694) \times \left(\frac{+50}{100}\right)$$
$$= -2.93 \text{ percent}$$

Other applications of duration. The use of duration as a measure of the responsiveness of a bond's price to a change in market yields is only one application of how this concept can be used in bond portfolio management. Another important application deals with the trade-off that arises as interest rates change over the investor's investment horizon. As noted several times earlier, as interest rates increase, the price of the bond declines, but the portion of the total return from interest-on-interest increases. When interest rates decrease over the investor's investment horizon, the opposite is true. The portion of the total return resulting from interest-on-interest decreases, but the price of the bond increases. To immunize a bond portfolio from this interest-rate risk so as to achieve a targeted return over an investment horizon, it has been demonstrated that the duration of the portfolio should be set equal to the investment horizon. This application of duration is discussed in Chapter 31.

SUMMARY

This chapter explained the basic elements of bond yield mathematics. In addition to illustrating how each yield measure is computed, the drawback of the conventional yield-to-maturity measure is explained and a better measure, the realized compound yield, is introduced. The investor should now understand why the yield-to-maturity only provides a *promised yield* and that yield will not necessarily be equal to the return realized by the investor at the end of the investor's investment horizon. A further discussion of a bond's total return is provided in Chapter 27, and a framework for evaluating the investment merit of a bond over the investor's investment horizon is discussed in Chapter 28.

The factors that influence the volatility of a bond's price are also explained in this chapter. The duration of a bond is a concept with important implications for bond portfolio management. Although this concept is introduced in this chapter, a more detailed treatment is provided in the next chapter.

5

Understanding Duration
and Volatility

Robert W. Kopprasch, Ph.D., C.F.A.
Vice President
Salomon Brothers Inc

Duration is not a new concept: It was first described by Frederick Macaulay in 1938.[1] After being rediscovered in the 1970s, duration has become one of the most commonly used tools of fixed income managers. One use is immunization, when a portfolio of assets is selected such that its duration equals the duration of the liability portfolio. With a slight modification, duration provides a good estimate of the volatility or sensitivity of the market value of a bond portfolio to changes in interest rates.[2] Many managers measure the risk of their portfolios by reference to the duration. And, as a volatility measure, duration is often used in constructing hedges and in weighting arbitrage trades.[3]

Despite its wide use, duration is not always fully understood. As a result, trades are sometimes incorrectly weighted, and portfolio volatilities are not estimated correctly. This chapter will provide a basic review and reference document on duration and trade weighting. Wherever

---

[1] Frederick Macaulay, *Some Theoretical Problems Suggested by the Movements of Interest Rates, Bond Yields and Stock Prices in the United States Since 1856.* (National Bureau of Economic Research, 1938).

[2] J. R. Hicks, *Value and Capital* (Oxford: Clarendon Press, 1939).

[3] For an interesting review of the path taken by duration from 1938 to its current use in the financial community, see Martin L. Leibowitz, "How Financial Theory Evolves in the Real World—Or Not: The Case of Duration and Immunization," *The Financial Review,* 18 (November 1983).

possible, a nonmathematical approach is used. The next section describes *Macaulay duration*, which is used in immunization, both by reference to a formula and a graphic presentation. This section also discusses how duration varies with maturity, yield, and coupon level, and how it changes over time. The second section presents *modified duration*, which is more appropriate for volatility measures and trade weighting. The third section shows the mechanics of *volatility weighting*. The relationship of duration to both the "price value of a basis point" and the "yield value of $\frac{1}{32}$ (or $\frac{1}{8}$)" is described in this section. The fourth section discusses *convexity*, which is related to the change in duration introduced by yield changes. The final section discusses duration with respect to nonbond and complex bond securities.

MACAULAY DURATION

In the bond market, securities are commonly referred to by their maturities. While this is a useful benchmark, it is deficient, because it measures only when the final cash flow is paid and ignores all of the interim flows. Frederick Macaulay attempted to create a better measure than maturity of the interest rate risk of a portfolio. He described a measure he called duration, which measures the weighted average time until cash flow payment. The weights are the present values of the cash flows themselves. The formula for duration follows:[4]

$$
D = \frac{\displaystyle\sum_{t=1}^{m} \frac{tC_t}{(1 + r)^t}}{\displaystyle\sum_{t=1}^{m} \frac{C_t}{(1 + r)^t}}
\tag{1}
$$

The formula is simply a weighted-average calculation. The time until the receipt (t) of each cash flow is multiplied by the present value[5] of the cash flow ($C_t/(1 + r)^t$). The sum of these components is divided by the sum of the weights, which is also the full price (including accrued interest) of the bond.[6]

Some useful insights can be drawn by examining the formula. For example, consider a zero-coupon bond. For a zero-coupon bond, all of

---

[4] The formula shown here is technically for use only on coupon dates. The more general form of this equation and an alternative closed-form solution are shown in the Appendix.

[5] This version of duration uses the (periodic) yield of the security as the discount rate for all of the present-value calculations, rather than spot rates for the particular maturities. As a result, it is frequently referred to as the "flat yield curve" duration.

[6] Because r is a periodic rate (for example, a semiannual discount rate) and t = number of periods, the formula provides a duration in periods, not years. The result must be converted to years. See the Appendix.

the C_ts are zero, except for the final payment, and the formula reduces to:

$$D = \frac{\dfrac{mC_m}{(1 + r)^m}}{\dfrac{C_m}{(1 + r)^m}} \qquad (2)$$

$$= m$$

that is, the duration equals the maturity.[7]

The Analog Presentation of Duration

Despite the potential insights that can be drawn from the formula, it is probably more helpful to pictorially look at duration. Exhibit 1 shows the

---

EXHIBIT 1 Cash Flows and Present Values of a Seven-Year 12 Percent Bond

---

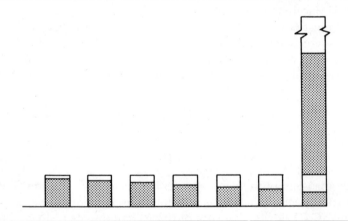

---

cash flows of a seven-year 12 percent annual pay bond: The shaded area of each cash flow represents the present value of that cash flow. (These values are used in the calculation of duration.) We can extend this diagram into an imaginary physical device that will reveal many of the properties of duration without involving mathematics.

We can view Exhibit 1 as a series of containers resting on a board or seesaw. The size (capacity) of each container is the nominal amount of the cash flow to be received at that time, and each is filled to the present value of its cash flow. The distance between the centers of each cash

---

[7] See footnote 6.

flow container represents the amount of time between the cash flows. Thus, horizontal *distance* is actually a measure of *time*. If an investor was evaluating the bond on a coupon date, the first container would be placed one full period from the investor, the second two periods, etc. The duration would be the distance from the investor to the point at which we could place a fulcrum and balance the whole system (see Exhibit 2). The duration of this seven-year 12 percent annual pay bond is approximately 5.1 years.

EXHIBIT 2   Cash Flows and the Duration Fulcrum

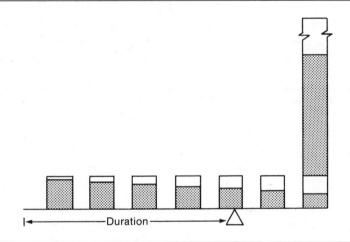

These present-value diagrams can also demonstrate that the duration of a zero-coupon bond is equal to its maturity. Because there is only one cash flow, the balance point must lie at that cash flow. Changes in yields and the elapsing of time will not change this "duration equals maturity" relationship for zero-coupon bonds.

This approach to understanding duration offers some insights that are not available without resorting to mathematics, and we will return to this type of diagram throughout the chapter.

Duration and Maturity for Nonzero-Coupon Bonds

Consider what happens as the maturity of the bond in Exhibits 1 and 2 is lengthened to eight years, nine years and so on. Each lengthening adds another coupon payment at the new maturity and moves the redemption payment out one period. The present value of the redemption payment also declines, because the time to maturity increases. The balance point starts moving to the right: The duration increases as the redemption payment is moved, but by less and less for each additional year because of the diminishing weight of the redemption payment. (The duration of a 100-year annual-pay 12 percent bond at par is only 9.33.) As the maturity is lengthened further, the bond begins to look more like a perpetual annuity, the duration of which is given by:[8]

$$D = \frac{1 + r}{r} \qquad (3)$$

This duration versus maturity pattern is shown in Exhibit 3; however, **this applies only to par and premium bonds.**

The duration pattern for discount bonds is more complex. Very low-coupon bonds have a duration pattern that lies close to the zero-coupon pattern (D = m) up to a reasonably long maturity. For very long maturities, however, even a low-coupon bond begins to resemble a perpetual annuity. For an extreme example, consider a ½ percent coupon bond. If

EXHIBIT 3 Duration of Par and Premium Bonds

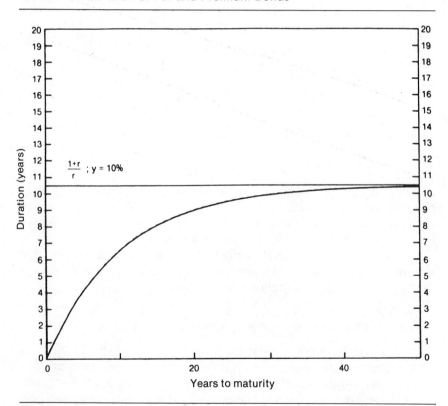

[8] See footnote 6.

the maturity was 20 years, the duration would be approximately 17 years at 10 percent yield, because the coupons are relatively insignificant, compared with the redemption payment. If the maturity was 100 years, however, the bond would act like an annuity, because the redemption payment would be so distant. The duration would be 10.6 years, very close to the perpetual annuity duration of 10.5 years. Thus, the duration can actually decrease with increasing maturity, approaching the duration of a perpetual annuity from above. This pattern is shown in Exhibit 4. Note, however, that the maturity range that can

EXHIBIT 4 Duration of Discount Bonds

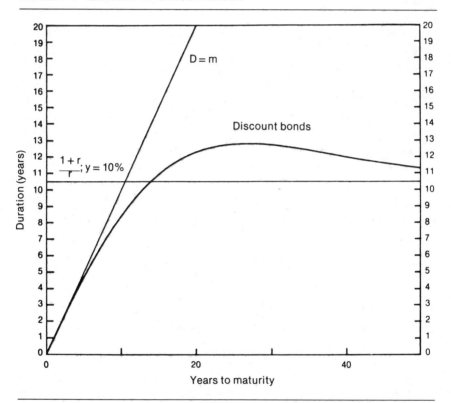

exhibit a decreasing duration is fairly long, although not quite as long as the longest utility bonds. Within the more usual range of bond maturities, the basic pattern (though not the level) shown in Exhibit 3 applies even to discount bonds. Therefore, we will refer to Exhibit 3 as the basic duration versus maturity pattern, even though long-maturity discount bonds can behave differently. For comparison, the patterns of premium, par, and discount bonds are shown in Exhibit 5.

EXHIBIT 5 Duration versus Maturity—Premium, Par, and Discount Bonds

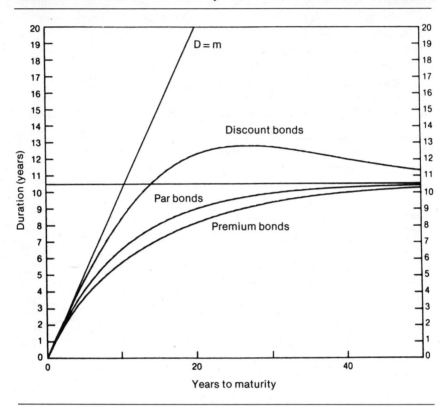

The Effect of the Yield Level

The equation for Macaulay duration shown in Equation 1 includes a yield term; thus, it is natural to expect that the yield level will affect duration. Using Exhibit 2 as a guide, consider how the exhibit would change as the yield increased. All of the present values would decline, but the cash flows that are the farthest away would show the largest proportional decrease.[9] As a result, the early cash flows would have a

---

[9] In general, a cash flow n periods away has a present value of $C/(1 + r)^n$, where C = cash flow and r = periodic discount rate. If r is changed to r', the present value changes to $C/(1 + r')^n$. This yield change causes the original present value $C/(1 + r)^n$ to be multiplied by $(1 + r)^n/(1 + r')^n$. If rates have increased ($r' > r$), this factor is less than one, thereby decreasing the present value. This adjustment factor becomes smaller as a function of n, so that distant cash flows (high n) are proportionately decreased the most. If yields have decreased ($r' < r$), then the adjustment factor is greater than one and increases the present value of the cash flows, again having the greatest effect when n is high.

greater weight relative to the later cash flows, and the fulcrum would have to be moved to the left (shorter duration) to keep the system in balance.

As rates decline, the opposite effect occurs. All of the cash flows increase in value, but the longest ones increase at the greatest rate. At the extreme of 0 percent yield, the present values equal the cash flows, and the redemption payment has a much greater effect, moving the balance point further to the right (longer duration). It may help to remember that duration changes in the same direction as price when yield changes.

Another indication of the effect of the yield level is Equation 3, which was given earlier for the duration of a perpetual annuity. This is the limiting value for duration for bonds, and it depends solely on the yield level ($D = (1 + r)/r$). When r is smaller, $(1 + r)/r$ is larger, and the maximum duration is longer than at higher yield levels, as shown in Exhibit 6 for par bonds.

EXHIBIT 6 Effect of Yield Level

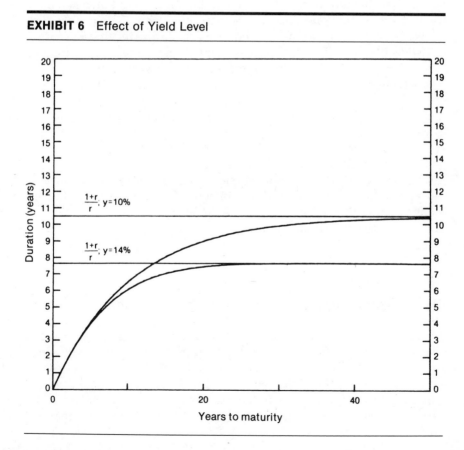

The Effect of the Coupon Frequency

While most domestic corporate bonds have coupons that are paid semi-annually, other securities may pay annually (Eurobonds, for example), quarterly, or monthly. How does the coupon payment frequency affect the duration? Referring to the seesaw diagrams, imagine that every coupon was divided into two parts and that one of the parts was paid one-half period earlier than the other. On the diagram, this represents a shift of weight to the left, as part of each coupon is paid earlier. This shift to the left moves the balance point to the left; thus, increasing the coupon frequency shortens the duration. Decreasing the frequency lengthens the duration.

Duration as Time Elapses (and Maturity Approaches)

Consider the duration of a par bond as time elapses and the bond's maturity decreases (holding yield constant). Using Exhibit 3 as a guide, we can see that duration will initially decline slowly, and then at a more rapid pace as the bond approaches maturity. Using the example from above of a 12 percent annual-pay bond at par, during the first 93 years of a 100-year bond's life, the duration drops from 9.33 to 5.11, or by only about 4.2 years. Yet the duration must decline to zero in the next seven years (when the bond matures), so the duration drop in the last seven years (5.11) exceeds the decline in the first 93 years. This is shown in Exhibit 7, which is similar to Exhibit 3 with the lower scale (X-axis) reversed.

Charts similar to those in Exhibits 3 and 7 are often used as standard illustrations of the duration versus maturity and duration through time relationships, but they are not complete. The curves are actually drawn through a series of duration values for coupon dates, so we must determine whether the curve is an accurate reflection of duration values for the time between coupon payments.

Duration between Coupon Dates

We will return to the analog device to determine what happens to duration as time elapses between coupon payments (with no change in yield). Using Exhibit 2 as a guide, consider what happens as one day elapses. Each cash flow and the original duration fulcrum are now one "day" closer to the investor. If the position of the fulcrum does not change relative to the cash flows, then the duration (the time from the "investor" to the fulcrum) will have decreased by one day. As we will show, this is the case: The fulcrum's position will *not* have changed relative to the cash flows.

EXHIBIT 7   Duration versus Passage of Time—100-Year 12 Percent
Annual-Pay Bond at Par

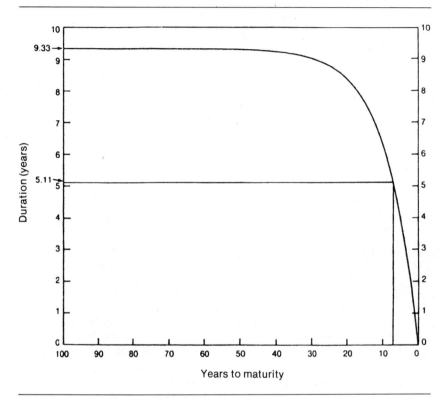

As one day elapses (with no change in yield level), all of the cash flows will increase in present value, because the discounting period is being shortened. An equivalent way to view this is to say that the original present value of each cash flow increases at the yield rate for one day. Thus, each present value is multiplied by $(1 + r)^t$, where r is the periodic rate and t is the fraction of the coupon period that has elapsed. While the values will not expand by the same dollar amounts, they will all increase in proportion to their original values. In other words, the original diagram of present values is still accurate, except that the scale has changed slightly. As the original diagram remains an accurate picture of the present values, the duration fulcrum will lie in the same position (relative to the cash flows) as the original fulcrum, except that now the investor is one day closer to the fulcrum. Thus, as time elapses between coupon dates (or any cash flow dates), duration shortens by the same amount of time that elapsed. After each day, the duration will be one day shorter.

EXHIBIT 8 Cash Flows and Present Values Immediately before
Coupon Payment

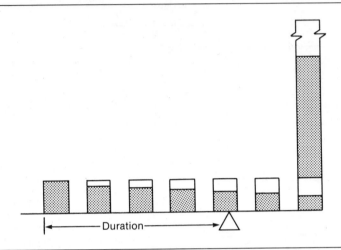

We now have to consider what happens as the coupon date approaches. As before, each day that elapses brings the fulcrum one day closer (that is, duration shortens by one day). Exhibit 8 shows the situation immediately before the coupon date, when the duration has shortened by almost the whole coupon period, which is typically six months. Exhibit 9 shows the effect of the payment of the coupon. The coupon is no longer part of the bond's cash flows and, thus, is not a factor in its duration.[10] To bring the system into balance after the coupon is paid, the fulcrum must be moved to the right (as shown in Exhibit 10) and the duration increases. Except for the extreme maturity range of Exhibit 4, this increase is less than the time between coupon payments; thus, the duration shows a slight decline from one coupon date to the next (as in Exhibit 7).

With this new information, the duration versus time pattern can now be redrawn more accurately (see Exhibit 11 for an example of a semiannual bond). The downward-sloping straight line segments represent the duration decreasing between coupon dates, with the upward jumps occurring on the coupon dates. This sawtooth duration pattern normally evokes a question about the volatility of the bond, namely

---

[10] The payment of the coupon does not alter the duration of the investor's portfolio if the cash remains in the portfolio. We can think of the investor as piling all of his cash on the seesaw at his viewing point. When the coupon suddenly turns to cash, no change occurs in the balance point (fulcrum) of the portfolio. In effect, the investor now has two holdings: cash, with a duration of zero, and a bond, the duration of which has just increased. The combined duration will equal that of the bond at the instant before the payment.

EXHIBIT 9   The Effect of the Coupon Payment

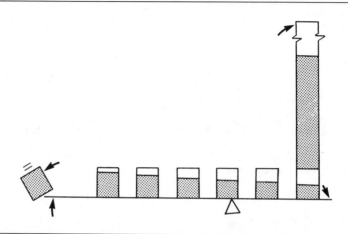

EXHIBIT 10   Coupon Payment Increases Duration

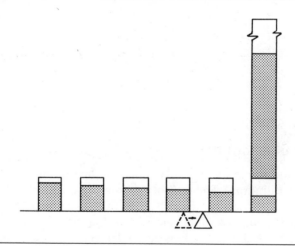

whether the volatility follows a similar pattern.[11] As described more fully in the third section, the answer is no: Volatility follows a smooth path as time elapses (at constant yield).

---

[11] Volatility, as used here, refers to the absolute sensitivity (for example, in price points) of a bond's price to changes in interest rates. In contrast, the term volatility in *Inside the Yield Book* usually referred to percentage sensitivity. Sidney Homer and Martin L. Leibowitz, Ph.D., *Inside the Yield Book* (Prentice-Hall, Inc. and New York Institute of Finance, 1972.)

EXHIBIT 11   Duration through Time—Last Eight Coupon Periods of a
Semiannual Bond

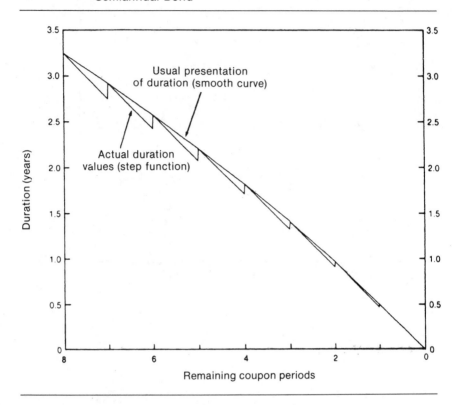

Remaining coupon periods

Duration of a Portfolio

Portfolio duration is a weighted average of the durations of the individual security durations. The weights are the present values (full prices) of the securities divided by the full price of the entire portfolio, and the duration that results is often referred to as a "market-weighted" duration. This approach is actually very similar to the determination of duration of a single bond, in which the bond is considered a portfolio of zero-coupon instruments. The duration of each payment (time to maturity) is multiplied by its present value divided by the value of the whole bond.

The duration of a portfolio has the same application as duration for an individual security: It can be used in structuring immunized portfolios and (when modified) to estimate percentage volatility. It is quite likely, however, that a portfolio may exhibit more convexity than individual securities. This will be covered in the fifth section.

MODIFIED DURATION

While Macaulay duration is appropriate for use in immunization, another measure—modified duration—is better as a volatility measure. Modified duration *appears* to be a slightly modified form of Macaulay duration, but it was actually developed by Hicks in 1939 without any reference to duration. The formula for modified duration is:

$$D_{mod} = \frac{D}{1 + y/_f} \tag{4}$$

where D = Macaulay duration
y = yield to maturity (in decimal form)
f = discounting periods per year
y/f = periodic yield (in decimal form)

For semiannual pay bonds, this formula becomes:

$$D_{mod} = \frac{D}{1 + y/_2} \tag{5}$$

Modified duration can be used to estimate the percentage price volatility of a fixed income security. The relationship follows:

$$\frac{\Delta P}{P} \times 100 = -D_{mod} \times \Delta Y \tag{6}$$

percentage price change = − modified duration × yield change
(in absolute percentage points)

The following section illustrates its use in trade weighting. At this point, however, it is useful to point out several important features about duration and volatility. As mentioned above, modified duration, not Macaulay duration, is appropriate for volatility measurements. Second, modified duration provides a measure of *percentage* price volatility, not absolute-dollar volatility. Third, the percentage volatility applies to the *full price* of the security (including accrued interest), not the quoted (flat) price. These points will be explained more fully in the following section.

VOLATILITY WEIGHTING FOR HEDGING, BOND SWAPS, AND ARBITRAGE

The motivations for entering hedging, bond swaps, and arbitrage transactions are usually quite different. The hedger is usually attempting to minimize a risk that cannot otherwise be conveniently eliminated. The bond swapper is attempting to increase return by swapping into a security that is expected to outperform (even in the absence of a general market move) the original position over some specified time horizon.

The arbitrageur is creating an entirely new position to capitalize on an expected realignment of yield spreads. Despite these differing motivations, however, volatility weighting is similarly used in all three cases.[12]

In its simplest form, hedging attempts to offset price changes in one security (resulting from a change in the level of rates) with equal changes in another. Because most securities in the debt market are positively correlated with one another in terms of price movement, a short position normally offsets a long position. However, as the securities may not have identical price changes even if they experience identical yield changes, some ratio of the short to the long other than 1:1 is usually necessary.

Many bond swaps and arbitrage transactions attempt to capitalize on an expected realignment of yield-spread relationships. Unless these trades are properly weighted, however, it is possible to suffer a loss even when the spread moves in the predicted manner within the time horizon specified. These losses usually result from the realization of the target spread at a different level of the market, causing the differential bond price movements from one market level to another to far outweigh the spread movement. As a result, the trade must be insulated from changes in market level by volatility weighting.

Volatility weighting is occasionally and unfortunately referred to as "duration weighting," leading some to assume—incorrectly—that the ratio of the durations is the proper hedge ratio. Duration *can* be used to weight trades, but it is more complex than the simple ratio of the durations. In the sections that follow, we determine the correct weighting for one bond versus another. This ratio is appropriate for hedging one bond with the other, swapping from one to another (except for rate-anticipation swaps) or establishing an arbitrage position.

We will discuss three different methods of weighting a transaction. The methods to be analyzed include: Weighting by price value of a basis point, yield value of $1/32$ (or $1/8$), and the correct use of duration. An example will confirm that the three methods are equivalent.

The Hedge Ratio

The objective of weighting the position is to equalize the total changes in value of the two offsetting positions. We can state this symbolically as follows:

$$\Delta P_t = HR \times \Delta P_h \tag{7}$$

where ΔP_t = the price change of the target security (to be hedged)
ΔP_h = the price change of the hedge vehicle
HR = the hedge ratio

---

[12] Obviously, the weighting is different for a rate-anticipation swap, in which the investor hopes to capitalize on a market move rather than be insulated from it.

$HR \times \Delta P_h$ is, therefore, the total change in value of the position in the hedge vehicle. This value must equal the change in the target security.

Equation 7 can be rewritten as:

$$HR = \frac{\Delta P_t}{\Delta P_h}$$

We can expand this to:

$$HR = \frac{\Delta P_t}{\Delta Y_t} \times \frac{\Delta Y_t}{\Delta Y_h} \times \frac{\Delta Y_h}{\Delta P_h} \qquad (8)$$

where $\dfrac{\Delta P_t}{\Delta Y_t}$ = change in price of security t for a given change in yield

$\dfrac{\Delta Y_t}{\Delta Y_h}$ = expected change in yield on security t relative to a change in security h

$\dfrac{\Delta Y_h}{\Delta P_h}$ = reciprocal of $\dfrac{\Delta P_h}{\Delta Y_h}$, which has a meaning analogous to $\dfrac{\Delta P_t}{\Delta Y_t}$ above

How is this formula related to hedge ratios determined using the price value of a basis point, yield value of $\frac{1}{32}$ (or $\frac{1}{8}$) of duration? As shown below, this formula can be utilized regardless of which approach is deemed easier or more convenient by the hedger.

Price Value of a Basis Point

The measure known as the price value of a basis point (PVBP) or, alternatively, as the dollar value of a 0.01 (DV.01), is simply the change in price for a bond that corresponds to a change in yield to maturity of one basis point (0.01%). Exhibit 12 shows the price-yield curve pattern that is common to noncallable bonds and expands this to present the graphic interpretation of PVBP, which is a direct measure of price volatility relative to yield change. Exhibit 12 also demonstrates that a given bond has a greater price sensitivity to a given yield change when rates are low.

We can use the PVBP to determine the appropriate volatility weighting for trades. For example, assume that the price of one bond would change by 0.08 (from 98.60 to 98.68, for example) if its yield moved by one basis point, and we wished to hedge that change by taking a position in a security that would change by 0.06 per basis point. If we assume that both securities will change by the same number of basis points, then it is obvious that we need 1.3333 units of the hedge vehicle per unit of target security. Thus, if yields changed by 10 basis points, we would expect that the target security would change by approximately 0.80, and 1.3333 hedge vehicle units, changing by 0.60 each for 10 basis

EXHIBIT 12 Price-Yield Curve and Price Value of Basis Point (PVBP)

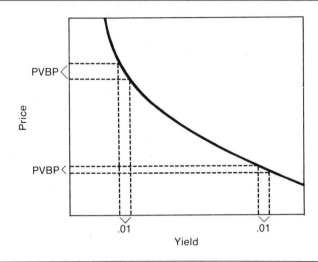

points, would also change by 0.80 (that is, 1.3333×0.60). How does this intuitive approach compare with Equation 8 above?

$$HR = \frac{\Delta P_t}{\Delta Y_t} \times \frac{\Delta Y_t}{\Delta Y_h} \times \frac{\Delta Y_h}{\Delta P_h}$$

$$= PVBP_t \times \frac{\Delta Y_t}{\Delta Y_h} \times 1/PVBP_h$$

$$= \frac{PVBP_t}{PVBP_h} \times \frac{\Delta Y_t}{\Delta Y_h}$$

$\Delta Y_t/\Delta Y_h$ is simply the change in yield of security t relative to the change in yield of security h. We will use the term *yield beta* to express this value and will write it as B_t. In this example, the two securities are assumed to have the same yield changes, so B_t equals one. Therefore,

$$HR = \frac{PVBP_t}{PVBP_h} \times B_t$$

$$= \frac{.08}{.06} \times 1.0 \tag{9}$$

$$= 1.3333$$

Equation 9 is the general form of the hedging equation when the weighting is done by price values of one basis point.

Yield Value of 1/32

Many Treasury bond traders use yield value of 1/32 for weighting trades. (Weighting by yield value of ⅛ seems to be most common in the corporate bond area and probably dates back to the use of yield books. In a yield book, prices were listed by ⅛s, and then the yields for those prices were shown. It was quite easy to determine the yield change for a ⅛ change in price, but there was no direct way to determine the price value of a basis point.) Exhibit 13 presents the yield value of 1/32 and shows

EXHIBIT 13   Yield Value of 1/32

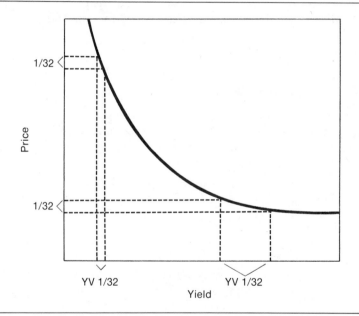

that this is an inverse measure of volatility. A high value indicates low price volatility (and vice versa), because it means that a large yield change is necessary to produce a 1/32 price change.

The hedge ratio is determined by dividing the yield value of 1/32 (YV 1/32) of the hedge security by the yield value of the target security. Note that the positions of the hedge vehicle and the target security are reversed (from denominator to numerator, and vice versa) when compared with the PVBP method (because YV 1/32 is an inverse measure of volatility). We can also return to Equation 8 to see why this occurs.

$$HR = \frac{\Delta P_t}{\Delta Y_t} \times \frac{\Delta Y_t}{\Delta Y_h} \times \frac{\Delta Y_h}{\Delta P_h}$$

$$= \frac{1}{\dfrac{\Delta Y_t}{\Delta P_t}} \times \frac{\Delta Y_t}{\Delta Y_h} \times \frac{\Delta Y_h}{\Delta P_h}$$

$$= \frac{\dfrac{\Delta Y_h}{\Delta P_h}}{\dfrac{\Delta Y_t}{\Delta P_t}} \times \frac{\Delta Y_t}{\Delta Y_h}$$

$\Delta Y_h / \Delta P_h$ is the change in the yield of security h for a given change in the price of h (see Exhibit 13). If we choose to make the price change by 1/32 (or ⅛), then Y_h will be the yield value of 1/32 (or ⅛). Thus,

$$HR = \frac{(YV\frac{1}{32})_{hedge}}{(YV\frac{1}{32})_{target}} \times B_t \tag{10}$$

Using Duration in Volatility Weighting

As mentioned earlier, duration can be used to determine hedge ratios, but the procedure is somewhat more cumbersome than using PVBP or YV 1/32. Several aspects of duration must be considered when using duration to determine a hedge ratio:

1. Neither Macaulay duration nor modified duration are measures of absolute price volatility. However, modified duration is a measure of percentage price volatility.
2. Modified duration is a measure of the percentage price volatility of the *full* price (including accrued interest).

Because the goal of a hedge ratio is to equate the dollar price changes in two positions, several steps must be taken to determine the hedge ratio with duration. First, the modified duration must be determined. Second, the full price of the bond must be determined. Third, the percentage price volatility must be turned into a dollar price volatility. As an example, consider a bond trading at par, with three points of accrued interest, which has a Macaulay duration of 8.23 years and a yield of 12 percent. In order to determine the dollar price volatility for one basis point, we will use Equation 6. (Because we are concerned only with the magnitude of the price change, and not the sign, we have dropped the minus sign shown in Equation 6.)

$$\frac{\Delta P}{P} \times 100 = D_{mod} \times \Delta Y$$

Remember that ΔY is expressed in absolute percentage points and that P represents the full price.

Rearranging, we obtain:

$$\Delta P = D_{mod} \times \Delta Y \times P/100$$

$$= \frac{8.23}{1.06} \times .01 \times 103/100 \qquad (11)$$

$$= .08$$

Note that this could be the same bond as was used earlier, which had a PVBP of 0.08. Since most investors use computer software to determine the duration, it would be far simpler to have the software provide the PVBP, which can be used directly in a hedge ratio calculation.

The same process is required to determine the price volatility of the hedge vehicle. The ratio of the two values (see Equation 9) is the hedge ratio. The process takes several extra steps to determine the same ratio given directly by use of PVBP.

We can modify the hedge ratio equation on page 104 by substituting Equation 11 for each ΔP:

$$HR = \frac{\Delta P_t}{\Delta P_h} = \frac{D_{t\,mod} \times P_t}{D_{h\,mod} \times P_h}$$

Duration Can Mislead—A Treasury Bond Example

In this section, hedge ratios for several different pairings of Treasury bonds are calculated. In most hedging or arbitrage examples, at least one of the bonds used is an "on the run" issue—a recently issued, current-coupon bond. The examples that are presented below were not selected to be realistic; rather, they make a point about duration. The four Treasury bonds are shown in Exhibit 14.

EXHIBIT 14 Treasury Hedge Example—August 1, 1985

Bond	Coupon	Maturity	Price	Yield	Duration
A	12.625	15 May 95	111 13/32	10.709	5.955
B	8.000	15 Aug 01	78 22/32	10.828	8.060
C	8.250	15 May 05	78 26/32	10.874	8.741
D	10.750	15 Aug 05	98 06/32	10.968	8.448

Assume that an investor holding bond B wishes to hedge it by shorting bond D. Of the securities shown, this does not appear to be a bad choice, because the two bonds have similar maturities (and, therefore, low yield curve reshaping risk) and similar durations. The closeness of their durations might lead the investor to believe that the bonds have similar price volatility and that a hedge ratio near 1.0 (that is, 1.0 : 1) would be appropriate. However, use of the methods discussed in the previous sections results in a hedge ratio of 0.79, rather than 1.0.

Suppose that the investor wanted to hedge bond B with bond A, a bond having a duration two years shorter. Must he use a hedge ratio greater than 1.0 to counter the low volatility of bond A as indicated by its duration? The answer is no, because the hedger is interested in dollar volatility, not percentage volatility. The hedge ratio is 0.977 (see Exhibit 16).

Exhibit 15 repeats Exhibit 14 but adds some important information for hedging. The PVBP column provides a direct indication of the dollar

EXHIBIT 15 Treasury Hedge Example—August 1, 1985

Bond	Coupon	Maturity	Price	Yield	Duration	YV 1/32	PVBP
A	12.625	15 May 95	111 13/32	10.709	5.955	0.4846	0.064482
B	8.000	15 Aug 01	78 22/32	10.828	8.060	0.4961	0.062988
C	8.250	15 May 05	78 26/32	10.874	8.741	0.4679	0.066784
D	10.750	15 Aug 05	98 06/32	10.968	8.448	0.3938	0.079345

volatility of each bond, which is exactly the figure that the hedger needs. As shown earlier, the same figure can be obtained in several steps by using duration. As long as duration is used correctly, the results will be the same. (Because duration is often available to only two decimal places, there may be some rounding error.)

Using the information in the PVBP column, we can verify that the hedge ratio for hedging B with D is 0.79 (0.062988/0.079345). Similarly, the ratio for hedging B with A is 0.977 (0.062988/0.064482).

A matrix of hedge ratios is shown in Exhibit 16. The target securities are shown across the top, and the hedge vehicles are down the side. The hedge ratio for hedging bond D with bond A is the top right value, or 1.23. Note that all of the values on the diagonal (top left to bottom right) are 1.0, indicating simply that to hedge a bond with a short position in

EXHIBIT 16 Hedge Ratios

		Target Security			
		A	B	C	D
	A	1.000	0.977	1.036	1.230
Hedge	B	1.024	1.000	1.060	1.260
Vehicle	C	0.966	0.943	1.000	1.188
	D	0.813	0.794	0.842	1.000

the same bond, the long and short positions would involve equal par amounts.

A helpful check for hedge-ratio calculations is to determine which bond has more absolute price volatility (higher PVBP, not necessarily duration). If it is the target security, then the hedge ratio should be greater than one, and if it is the hedge security, it should be less than one.

More on the Price Value of a Basis Point

As shown in the first section, Macaulay duration (and thus modified duration) declines linearly through time until a cash flow, if yield is held constant. On cash flow dates, the duration jumps up to a higher value. The question is, if duration and modified duration are measures of risk and volatility, does volatility decline through time and then increase on the cash flow dates?

As time passes and duration decreases, at constant yield, the bond is accruing interest and possibly changing in price (for example, accreting toward par) to reflect the passage of time. The full price (including accrued) is following a pattern opposite that of duration, because it

---

EXHIBIT 17   PVBP versus Duration as Time Elapses

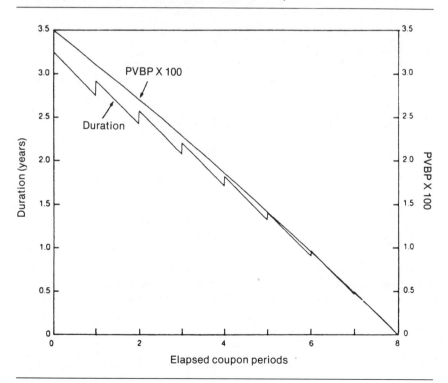

increases through time and then declines on the cash flow date when the accrued drops to zero. Equation 11 shows that the major determinant of the PVBP is the product of the duration and the full price. The PVBP is actually a smooth curve through time, reflecting the decrease in duration coupled with the increase in full price. This is shown in Exhibit 17 for a premium bond.

Another aspect of PVBP that should be mentioned is its relation to coupon level. A higher coupon results in a lower duration—all other factors held constant—but also in a higher price. The higher price is the overpowering factor here, and the volatility, as measured by PVBP, is higher for higher-coupon bonds. Exhibit 18 shows the PVBPs of 20-year bonds with different coupon rates across a variety of yield levels.

EXHIBIT 18 PVBP: Effect of Yield and Coupon

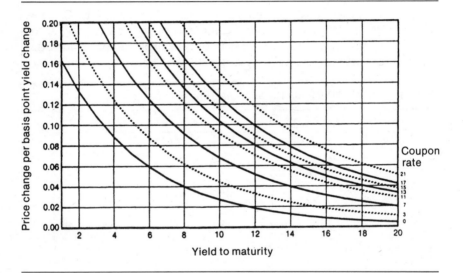

CONVEXITY

The basic price-yield pattern of a straight bond (for example, no options, noncallable, no sinking fund) was shown in Exhibit 13. Because of its shape, it is referred to as convex: The degree of curvature is loosely referred to as the convexity. Convexity is the reason that estimates of price changes using duration or price value of a basis point increase in error as the yield change increases. This section explains why convexity exists.[13]

---

[13] A number of aspects of convexity—magnitude, cost, impact on hedging, and arbitrage—are described in Richard Klotz, *Convexity of Fixed-Income Securities*, Salomon Brothers Inc, New York, October 1985.

Let us compare the price (and duration) changes that occur to three different investments for equal yield moves. The three securities are structured as follows: The first pays a single payment of 162.89 in five years, the second pays 67.00 in three years and 98.99 in seven years, and the third pays 55.13 in one year and 120.33 in nine years. While these securities seem to be quite different, they have at least two characteristics in common—a present value at 10 percent (discounted semiannually) of 100 and a Macaulay duration of 5.0. The cash flows of the securities, along with the duration fulcrums, are shown in Exhibit 19.

EXHIBIT 19   Nominal Flow and Present Value

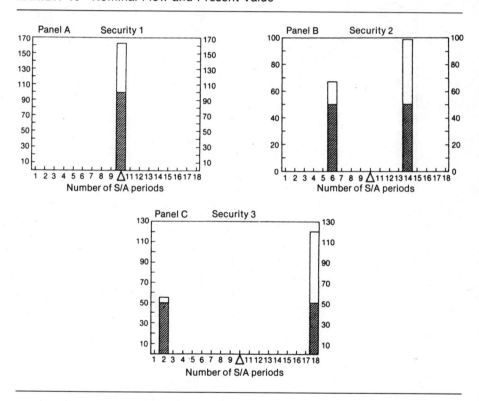

The duration of Security 1 is obviously five years, because it is a zero-coupon bond with a maturity of five years. The duration of Security 2 is also five years, because the present values of each cash flow are the same (50) and are equal distances from the five-year point, so the balance point is five years. A similar argument shows that the duration of Security 3 is also five years.

For small changes in yield, the prices of the three securities change almost identically. For example, if the yield (discount rate) changes to 11 percent, the prices of Securities 1, 2 and 3 become 95.36, 95.38 and 95.43, respectively. If the rate drops to 9 percent, the prices become 104.89, 104.91 and 104.97, respectively. Note that Security 3 shows the smallest price decline (4.57) and the largest price increase (4.97). When viewed over a greater range of yield levels, as shown in Exhibit 20, Security 3

EXHIBIT 20 Prices at Different Yields

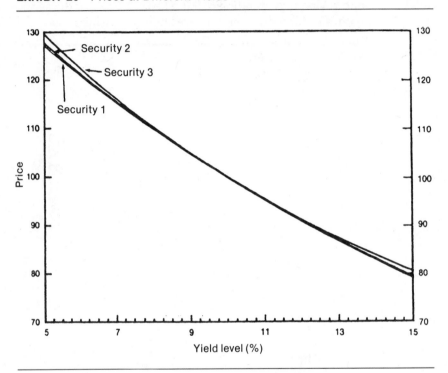

shows that its superiority over the other two securities is not a local phenomenon, but is actually more pronounced for greater yield moves. A summary of values for different yields is shown in Exhibit 21.

Exhibits 20 and 21 demonstrate the convexity patterns of the three securities, but they do not explain why convexity occurs. For this, we will return to the seesaw diagrams. We begin by examining what happens to Security 1 (the least convex), compared with Security 3 (the most convex). As soon as the discount rate changes from 10 percent, both securities start to change in value. For Security 1, with all of the cash flow at only one point, the duration (Macaulay) does not change and remains at 5.0 years. Security 3, with two cash flows, reacts somewhat differently. As the rate changes, the two cash flows change in present

EXHIBIT 21 Prices at Different Yields

Yield (Pct.)	Security 1	Security 2	Security 3
5%	127.25	127.84	129.62
6	121.21	121.56	122.64
7	115.48	115.67	116.24
8	110.04	110.12	110.36
9	104.89	104.91	104.97
10	100.00	100.00	100.00
11	95.36	95.38	95.43
12	90.96	91.02	91.22
13	86.78	86.92	87.33
14	82.80	83.04	83.75
15	79.03	79.38	80.44

value, but the longer flow changes by a greater amount. (Security 3 can be thought of as a portfolio of two zero-coupon bonds. When rates change, the longer zero-coupon bond has a greater proportional price change).

When rates decline, the longer cash flow of Security 3 increases in value more than the shorter one, causing the duration fulcrum to move further to the right to keep the system in balance. As a result, each downward notch in rates has two effects: The price moves more than a comparable (same duration, same present value) zero-coupon bond, and the duration gets longer. This causes the next downward change in rates to have an even greater effect, due to the slightly longer duration and the slightly higher starting price.[14] For example, at 9 percent, the duration of Security 3 is 5.12, versus 5.0 for Security 1. The higher duration results in a greater percentage price move and, because the starting price is now higher, a greater dollar price move. The opposite occurs when rates rise. The longer cash flow declines by more than the shorter one, causing the duration fulcrum to move to the left (shorter). This shorter duration dampens the effect of the next slight upward move in rates. The changes in duration of Security 3 are represented in Exhibit 22, which is exaggerated for illustration purposes.

The duration values for different yield levels are shown in Exhibit 23. Security 3 has the highest duration if rates decline and the lowest if rates rise, giving it the best performance in either market.

---

[14] The durations from the seesaw diagrams are Macaulay durations, not modified durations, so they do not give a direct measure of percentage volatility. However, all of the securities in this example have identical yields; thus, the security with the higher Macaulay duration will also have a higher modified duration.

EXHIBIT 22 Duration as Rates Change

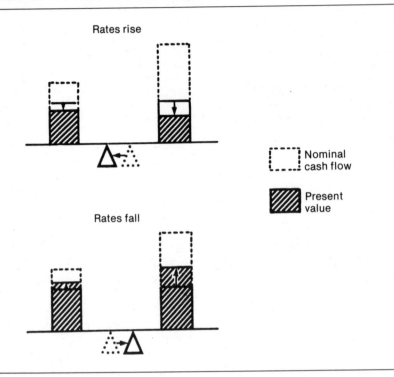

Rates rise

Rates fall

Nominal cash flow

Present value

A More Pronounced Example

The differences in convexity among Securities 1, 2 and 3 are fairly small. A much more extreme example demonstrates the potential of convexity. Let us define a new security, Security 4, which has two cash flows: 95.04 at the end of year one and 257.68 at the end of year 30. The present values of these cash flows are 86.20 and 13.80, respectively. The duration of Security 4 is 5.0 years. Its cash flow pattern and duration are shown in Exhibit 24.

The prices of Security 4 for a variety of yield levels are shown in Exhibit 25, along with the values for Securities 1, 2 and 3. Security 4 is shown to be much more convex than the other securities. The reason is that the two cash flows are spread out much further from the duration point and have (relative to each other) very different reactions to changes in yield level. The result of this dispersion of the present values about the duration point is greater convexity, which is caused by a more rapid change in the duration for a change in yield. The duration of Security 4 for different yield levels is shown versus the other securities

EXHIBIT 23 Duration versus Yield Level

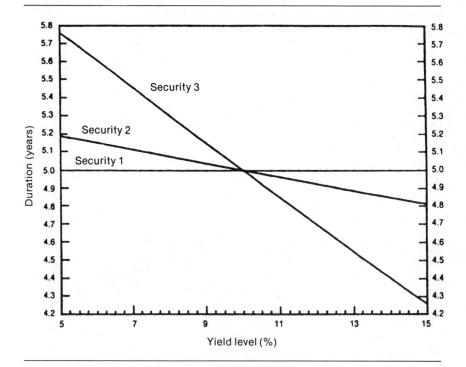

EXHIBIT 24 Security 4—Cash Flow and Duration

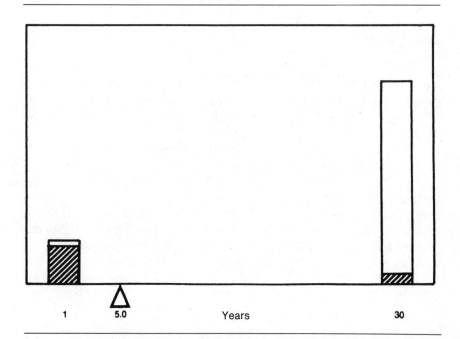

EXHIBIT 25   Prices at Different Yields—Effect of Convexity

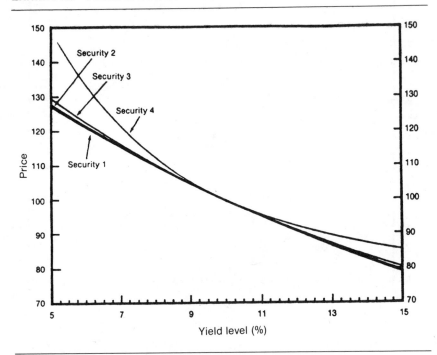

in Exhibits 26 and 27. Exhibit 27 is shown with the same scale as Exhibit 23 for comparison.

Convexity, Real Securities, and the Market

Security 4 demonstrates the extreme of convexity: It is an extreme type of security. It is an exaggerated "barbell," with the cash flows at the limits of the maturity spectrum for most securities. While it is possible to create such a portfolio, several other factors become involved. The yields of 30-year zero-coupon bonds and one-year zero-coupon bonds are often not the same, and the yield on that portfolio may be lower than the yield on a five-year zero-coupon bond, so the extra convexity over a single five-year zero-coupon bond may not be without "cost." It is also difficult to find securities with as much convexity as Security 4. Normal bonds have cash flows that are spread out but not nearly to the extent of Security 4, so they do not exhibit as much convexity. Finally, in all of the examples in this section, the yield on all maturities moved by the same amount. While parallel shifts in the curve occur often enough, they cannot be counted on to deliver the apparent convexity.

EXHIBIT 26 Duration at Different Yields

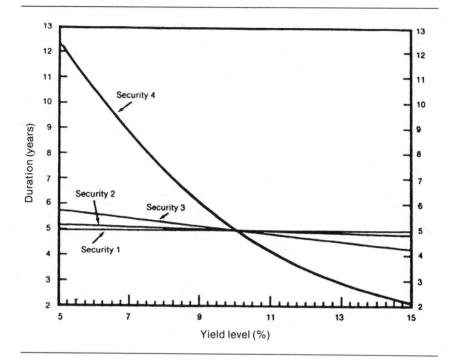

DURATION FOR OTHER SECURITIES

Except for the convexity section, the securities that have been discussed have been straight bonds, with regular, known coupon payments, without call or put provisions, without sinking funds, etc. Duration can be determined for other securities—easily for some and with more difficulty for others.

Money market instruments. Most money market securities, like commercial paper, bankers acceptances, and Treasury bills can be treated as short-term, zero-coupon bonds. As such, their durations are equal to their maturities.

Securities with embedded options. Many securities contain various types of options that affect their price behavior. Callable bond prices tend to cap out as they go much above par, particularly if the call date is near. Putable bonds tend to trade near par (or above) as put dates approach, because the bonds are redeemable. Duration calculations are made difficult by the uncertainty of the cash flows associated with the bonds, in addition to the problem of determining the appropriate yield (to call, maturity, or first-put date) to use.

EXHIBIT 27   Duration at Different Yields

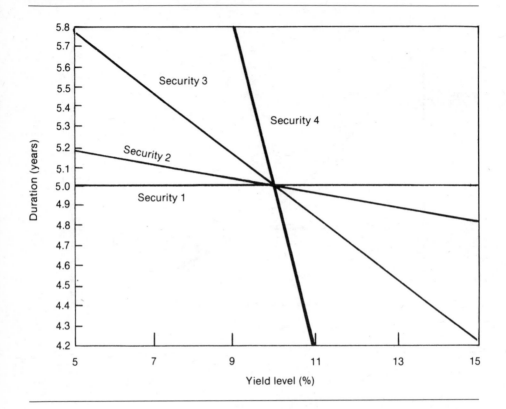

Securities with embedded options must be analyzed with a model of price behavior to properly determine duration. For putable and callable bonds, the model may simply combine the value of the underlying bond with the positive (put) or negative (call) value of the options position. The duration of the combined security is usually determined implicitly by estimating its price response to a change in yield level and then determining the duration that would lead to the same price change. The appropriate yield may still be difficult to determine, however. One suggestion for dealing with this problem is mentioned below.

Mortgages.   The duration of mortgage securities is even more difficult to determine than that of callable bonds. While mortgages could be treated like callable bonds,[15] several complicating factors affect the valuation of the call. First, the cash flows of the mortgage are even more uncertain than those of a callable bond, reflecting the unknown pattern

---

[15] The prepayment option held by the homeowner-borrower is nothing more than an option to call any portion of the outstanding debt at par.

of prepayments that may prevail. Second, the call feature of mortgages is not as totally yield driven as it is for callable bonds, and many prepayments occur even when the option is out of the money.

Because of the difficulties in determining the cash flows, it is difficult to calculate the duration in the traditional sense—the "present-value-weighted time to receipt of cash flow."[16] However, it is more likely that the search for duration is driven by the need to estimate the sensitivity of the mortgage to changes in the market level of rates. One method is to attempt to model the price or yield behavior of the mortgage versus a benchmark for the market, for example, 10-year Treasury notes. This relationship would allow the investor to predict price movements of the mortgage for changes in the market. This type of approach provides a volatility measure that can be substantially lower than the result of the standard calculation for current- and high-coupon mortgages.

Futures contracts. The duration of a futures contract cannot be determined using the standard calculation. There are no definable cash flows associated with a futures contract. We can view a contract as pure volatility, and because there is no cash outflow (price) paid to enter the contract, its percentage volatility (and, thus, its modified duration) is infinite. A long position adds volatility, and a short position reduces volatility in a portfolio.[17] Using the market-weighted approach to duration of a portfolio containing futures, the required calculation would attempt to incorporate a security with an infinite duration and a zero market weight.

A more useful approach is to determine the dollar volatility of the futures contract relative to yield changes in the underlying security or portfolio. This volatility can be added to portfolio volatility for a long position or subtracted for a short position, and the result will be net portfolio volatility. From this value, an implied duration may be computed. Thus, it is not necessary to have an actual duration value of the futures contract, yet the effect on portfolio duration can be determined.

Floaters. Floating-rate securities defy attempts at the standard duration calculation because of the unknown level of the future cash flows. If a sensitivity to rate changes is the objective, however, then a duration can be inferred. If a particular floater is reset every quarter to the then-prevailing three-month rate based on some index, the primary volatility of the floater will be the same as that of a three-month instrument. As time elapses and the coupon payment approaches, the implied primary

---

[16] This definition is merely an interpretation of the formula. Another "definition" often heard is that duration is "the time it takes to receive one half of the present value." This is simply incorrect—and can be shown to be incorrect by reference to Security 4, shown in Exhibit 24.

[17] This is true if the portfolio has "long" price sensitivity. Naturally, if the portfolio is net short, a long position in futures will reduce volatility.

duration will approach zero and will reset to three months on the coupon date. This measure is independent of the maturity of the floater.

Another aspect of the price sensitivity of a floater *is* a function of the maturity. If market spreads change for floaters, then the price change will vary according to the maturity. For example, consider a floater resetting at LIBOR flat, and assume that the market for new floaters from issuers of similar quality is also LIBOR flat. The floater would be priced near par. If the market began demanding new issues (and repriced old ones) at LIBOR + 20 basis points, then the price of this old floater would reflect the number of remaining quarters in which the investor would receive the lower "historic" rate rather than the new rate of LIBOR + 20. In essence, the investor gives up an annuity of 20 basis points, and the price should decline by the present value of this annuity.

In a sense, two volatility measures are needed for floaters: The simple duration, which is the time until next coupon payment and reset, and a "spread duration," which is a function of the maturity and the starting yield level.

Interest-rate swaps. An interest-rate swap can be analyzed as essentially an exchange of two securities, usually involving a fixed-rate and a floating-rate component. In a manner similar to futures contracts, an interest-rate swap contract adds (or subtracts) volatility without involving a purchase "price." As a result, it is impossible to determine duration as a percentage volatility measure, but it is possible to estimate the volatility characteristics of the swap and how entering into the swap affects the duration of an existing portfolio. As a combination of long and short positions in a fixed-rate instrument and a floater, the volatility of the interest-rate swap can be determined by netting the volatilities of each component. This volatility can then be aggregated with the volatility of the portfolio to back into the duration of the portfolio including the swap.

In practice, many "risk-controlled" arbitrages[18] involving swaps are "duration weighted," using only the fixed-payment side of the swap. This is because the floating side is already offset by floating-rate liabilities in the arbitrage portfolio. Thus, the primary volatility at issue is the value of the fixed-rate side of the swap versus the value fixed-rate mortgages, for instance. If the market values of these components are equal and have the same duration, then the position is considered to be properly weighted.

SUMMARY

We had several objectives in writing this report. The first was to explain duration and convexity in a nonmathematical, almost intuitive, frame-

---

[18] See Michael Waldman and Thomas B. Lupo, "Risk-Controlled Arbitrage for Thrift Institutions," *Mortgage-Backed Securities: New Strategies, Applications and Research,* ed. Frank J. Fabozzi (Chicago: Probus Publishing, 1987).

work. The second was to illustrate the correct use of duration for hedging, swapping and arbitrage, and to demonstrate alternative, more convenient, weighting tools (price value of a basis point and yield value of 1/32).

We did not attempt to discuss the nuances of hedging, swapping, or arbitrage[19]—or the effect of taxes.[20] We did not discuss the statistical procedures for estimating a "yield beta." Improper estimation can cause significant profit or loss variation. Indeed, so can bad luck—the estimate based on past history can be statistically correct, but market action may not continue to exhibit the relationship. As a result, a judgment factor can be more important than statistics. Despite these potential problems, the various volatility measures are important tools for all fixed income managers. Correctly used, they can minimize the risk in achieving specific return objectives.

APPENDIX A

Equation 1 given in the text for duration can be used only for evaluation on a coupon date. A more general form that works for any date is:

$$D = \frac{\sum_{t=1}^{m} \frac{(t - 1 + \alpha)C_t}{(1 + r)^{t-1+\alpha}}}{\sum_{t=1}^{m} \frac{C_t}{(1 + r)^{t-1+\alpha}}}$$

where C_t = the tth cash flow
r = periodic discount rate (in decimal form)
α = fraction of a period remaining until the next cash flow anniversary date
($\alpha = 1$ on a cash flow anniversary date)
m = number of cash flow anniversary dates

The formula above gives duration in *periods*, not years. To convert to years, multiply the duration by $1/f$, where f = frequency of coupon payment.

---

[19] See Robert W. Kopprasch, Cal Johnson, and Armand H. Tatevossian, "Strategies for the Asset Manager: Hedging and the Creation of Synthetic Assets," in *Advances in Bond Portfolio Management*, ed. Frank J. Fabozzi and Dessa A. Garlicki (Chicago: Probus Publishing, 1987).

[20] Andrew J. Kalotay, *The After Tax Duration of Original Issue Discount Bonds* (Salomon Brothers Inc, August 8, 1983).

APPENDIX B

A closed form solution for duration, which can be used for any date, is given by:[21]

$$D = \frac{C\left(\alpha + \frac{1}{r}\right)[(1 + r)^m - 1] - Cm + 100r(m - 1 + \alpha)}{C[(1 + r)^m - 1] + 100r}$$

where C = periodic coupon payment in percentage of face value
r = periodic discount rate (in decimal form)
α = fraction of a period remaining until next cash flow anniversary date
(α = 1 if on a cash flow anniversary date)
m = number of cash flow anniversary dates

The formula above gives duration in *periods*, not years. To convert to years, multiply the duration by 1/f, where f = frequency of coupon payment.

---

[21] The author would like to thank Cal Johnson for providing this solution.

6

The Determinants of Interest Rates on Fixed Income Securities

Frank J. Jones, Ph.D.
Vice President
Kidder, Peabody & Company, Inc.

Benjamin Wolkowitz, Ph.D.
Vice President
Morgan Stanley & Co.

This chapter discusses the determination of interest rates on fixed income securities. In discussing the determination of interest rates, first the determination of the general level of interest rates at a specific time, and then the factors that cause differences in interest rates at a specific time are considered. The interest rates on securities issued by the U.S. Department of the Treasury (hereafter Treasury) are commonly accepted as the benchmark interest rates in the U.S. economy and, typically, in the world. Thus a topic related to interest-rate determination, the market for Treasury securities, is also discussed in this chapter.

The interest rates on Treasury securities are commonly accepted as being reflective of the general level of interest rates because there are more of Treasury securities outstanding than of any other securities in the world, the Treasury issues securities of every maturity spectrum on a regular basis, and Treasury securities have virtually no credit risk. The next section in this chapter discusses the primary and secondary markets for Treasury securities.

Following the Treasury security markets section is the discussion of interest-rate determination. This discussion is structured so that the conceptual analysis is followed by applications of the conceptual conclusions. Most of these applications use Treasury securities as the basis for comparison. The first part of this discussion considers the determination of the general level of interest rates, which can be considered "the" interest rate. The three major rationales or theories for interest-rate determination—liquidity preference, loanable funds, and inflation and the real rate of interest—are discussed. A synthesis of these approaches is also provided. A fourth rationale, the "tone of the market," is also reviewed and shown to have an impact on interest rates in the short term.

The second part of the discussion on interest-rate determination discusses the factors that cause differences among interest rates at a specific time, that is, why all interest rates are not equal to the general level of interest rates. There are three such factors or reasons for differences among interest rates.

The first factor is maturity. The impact of maturity on a security's interest rate is considered in the context of three hypotheses, the liquidity hypothesis, the expectations hypothesis, and the segmentation hypothesis.

Second, differences among interest rates on securities at a time also occur due to differences in credit risk. Investors respond to a risk-return trade-off in that the greater the risk associated with a particular security, that is, the less creditworthy the issuer, the greater the required return. This concept of credit risk is explained and illustrated with a number of actual market examples.

A third important reason for differences among interest rates on securities is taxability, with regard to the tax exemption on coupons for municipal securities, the difference in tax treatment between coupon return and capital appreciation, and flower bonds. The subject of taxability and its impact on interest rates is also discussed.

The chapter concludes with an overview of interest-rate determination, which combines all the concepts introduced and demonstrates how they interact to determine market interest rates. This synthesis of theory and actual experience, relying on Treasury issues as a basis for comparison, provides a comprehensive overview of interest-rate determination.

THE CASH MARKET FOR GOVERNMENT SECURITIES

The liabilities of the U.S. Treasury outstanding are greater in magnitude than the liabilities of any other institution in the world. The Treasury has, over time, issued liabilities to raise funds to finance its budget deficits. During recent years there has been a substantial increase in the amount of Treasury liabilities outstanding, as indicated in Exhibit 1.

The Treasury issues marketable and nonmarketable securities, the former representing 75 percent of Treasury liabilities in 1985. This section focuses on marketable Treasury securities.

EXHIBIT 1 Outstanding Treasury Securities (in millions of dollars)

| End of Fiscal Year or Month | Amount Outstanding | | | Securities Held By: | | | | | |
| | | | | Government Accounts | | | The Public | | |
	Total	Public Debt Securities	Agency Securities	Total	Public Debt Securities	Agency Securities	Total	Public Debt Securities	Agency Securities
1980	$ 914,317	$ 907,701	$6,616	$199,212	$197,743	$1,469	$ 715,105	$ 709,958	$5,147
1981	1,003,941	997,855	6,086	209,507	208,056	1,450	794,434	789,799	4,636
1982	1,146,987	1,142,035	4,952	217,640	216,404	1,236	929,346	925,631	3,716
1983	1,381,886	1,377,211	4,675	240,116	239,023	1,092	1,141,770	1,138,188	3,582
1984	1,576,748	1,572,267	4,481	264,159	263,084	1,075	1,312,589	1,309,183	3,406
1984 June	1,517,221	1,512,697	4,525	258,679	257,597	1,083	1,258,542	1,255,100	3,442
July	1,543,117	1,538,602	4,515	260,036	258,953	1,083	1,283,081	1,279,649	3,432
Aug	1,565,140	1,560,649	4,492	256,719	255,640	1,079	1,308,421	1,305,009	3,413
Sept	1,576,748	1,572,267	4,481	264,159	263,084	1,075	1,312,589	1,309,183	3,406
Oct	1,616,010	1,611,537	4,473	282,668	281,594	1,074	1,333,343	1,329,943	3,399
Nov	1,635,510	1,631,041	4,469	282,814	281,738	1,077	1,352,696	1,349,303	3,392
Dec	1,667,425	1,662,966	4,459	290,674	289,600	1,074	1,376,750	1,373,366	3,385
1985 Jan	1,684,364	1,679,916	4,449	294,939	293,863	1,075	1,389,426	1,386,053	3,374
Feb	1,702,793	1,698,358	4,434	297,373	296,300	1,073	1,405,420	1,402,058	3,361
Mar	1,715,148	1,710,731	4,417	296,570	295,499	1,070	1,418,578	1,415,232	3,347
Apr	1,737,119	1,732,717	4,402	301,504	300,434	1,070	1,435,615	1,432,283	3,332
May	1,758,330	1,753,936	4,395	306,383	305,313	1,070	1,451,947	1,448,623	3,325
June	1,779,026	1,774,640	4,386	315,222	314,156	1,067	1,463,804	1,460,484	3,319

SOURCE: Monthly Treasury Statement of Receipts and Outlays of the United States Government.

Because Treasury securities are liabilities of the U.S. Department of the Treasury, and in effect of the U.S. government, they are perceived to have virtually no credit risk. On the basis of credit risk, the yields on Treasury securities are thus lower than those of any private security.

Due to their large volume outstanding, the broad range of maturities available, the low credit risk, and the liquidity of their secondary market, Treasury securities are widely held. Holders of substantial amounts include foreign governments and government agencies, commercial banks, nonbank financial institutions, nonfinancial institutions, and individuals. Because of their unique characteristics and because they are widely held, Treasury debt securities make up a fundamental component of the securities markets and the basis for analyses of these markets.

It is important to distinguish between the two different types of marketable Treasury securities—discount and coupon securities. The fundamental difference between these two types of securities is the form in which the holder receives interest and, as a result, the prices at which they are issued.

On coupon securities explicit interest payments are periodically (typically every six months) made by the Treasury while the securities are outstanding. On the other hand, on discount securities there is no payment of interest by the Treasury to the holders from the time of issue until the maturity day when the principal is repaid. This difference in the way in which interest is paid causes a difference in issue prices between these two types of securities, as discussed below.

According to current Treasury practices, all Treasury securities with maturities of one year or less are issued as discount securities, and all securities with maturities of more than two years are issued as coupon securities. Treasury discount securities are called *bills*. Treasury coupon securities with original maturities between 2 and 10 years are called *notes*, and with maturities of greater than 10 years are called *bonds*.

On coupon securities, the annual coupon is specified before the issue, and an amount equal to half the annual coupon is paid to the holder every six months, beginning six months after the issue date through the maturity date. For example, if a Treasury security is issued with an 8 percent coupon, a $40 payment is made every six months for a maturity value of $1,000.

Consider the issue prices of discount and coupon securities. Both issue prices are related to the maturity value or par value of the security, which is the amount paid by the Treasury to the holder of the security on the maturity day of the security. Since the coupon payment of coupon securities represents the payment of interest during the time the security is outstanding, the initial issue price of a Treasury coupon security is approximately the same as its maturity value. Thus Treasury coupon securities are issued at about par, the maturity value. If interest rates subsequently increase, the coupons of newly issued bonds will be higher, and thus the price of the bonds previously issued at lower coupons will sell at a price below its maturity value, that is "at a discount" to par. Contrarily, if interest rates subsequently decrease, the coupons of newly issued bonds will be lower than the coupon of the previously issued bonds, and thus the price of the bonds previously issued at higher coupons will sell at a price above its maturity value, that is "at a premium" to par. Note that interest rates and prices move in opposite directions.

On the other hand, because no explicit interest is paid on a discount security, the security must be issued at a price that is at a discount to its maturity value such that the difference between the initial discount price and the final maturity price represents the return to the holder of the security.

Exhibit 2 shows the relationship between issue prices and maturity values for Treasury discount and coupon securities.

There are two major components of the Treasury security market: (1) the primary market, that is, the market on which the securities are originally issued, and (2) the secondary market, that is, the market for the postissue trading of these securities.

Primary Market

Marketable securities are typically issued on an auction basis by the Treasury with the assistance of the Federal Reserve System.

The Treasury has found that it can reduce the rate at which it issues its debt, and thus its interest cost, particularly when issuing substantial amounts to fund large budget deficits, by issuing Treasury securities on a regular basis (i.e., having a stable schedule for auctioning securities with specific maturities). Such regularity provides the purchasers of Treasury debt with firm expectations regarding the timing of issuances of the various types of Treasury securities. The regularization of the Treasury funding process has developed such that there are now several regular cycles on which the Treasury auctions and issues specific maturities of debt. A description of these cycles is provided in Exhibit 3. Exhibits 4 and 5 provide examples of Treasury announcements for the auctions and issues of Treasury discount and coupon securities, respectively.

As indicated in Exhibit 3, there are three discount security (Treasury bill) cycles. Every Monday the Treasury auctions 91-day Treasury bills. These bills are issued on the following Thursday and mature on the Thursday 13-weeks (91 days) later. On the same cycle, every Monday the Treasury also auctions 182-day bills, which are issued on the following Thursday and mature on the Thursday 26 weeks, or 182 days, after their issue date. The third Treasury bill cycle is the "year bill" cycle. On

---

EXHIBIT 2   Price Behavior of Treasury Discount and Coupon Securities

A. Treasury discount securities

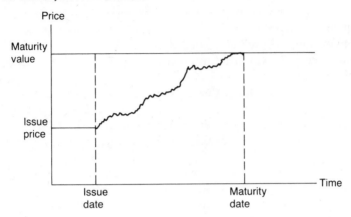

B. Treasury coupon securities

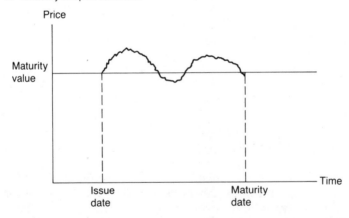

---

this cycle, every fourth Thursday the Treasury auctions a 52-week Treasury bill, which is issued on the following Thursday and matures on the Thursday 52 weeks, or 364 days, later.

Note that initial 91-day and 182-day Treasury bills mature every Thursday, and initial 364-day Treasury bills mature every fourth Thursday. Note also that during the last 91 days of its maturity, an initial 182-day Treasury bill is indistinguishable from an initial 91-day Treasury bill issued 91 days after it. Likewise during the last 182 days of its maturity a 364-day Treasury bill is indistinguishable from an initial 182-day Treasury bill issued 182 days after it.

EXHIBIT 3   Treasury Auction Cycles

Security	Auctioned	Issued
Bills:		
3 month	Every Monday	Following Thursday
6 month	Every Monday	Following Thursday
12 month	Every fourth Thursday	Following Thursday
Notes:		
2 year	End of each month	Following Week
3 year	15th of Feb., May, Aug., and Nov.	Following Week
4 year	Mar., June, Sept., Dec.	Following Week
5 year	Mar., June, Sept., Dec.	Following Week
7 year	Jan., April, July, Oct.	Following Week
10 year	Feb., May, Aug., Nov.	Following Week
Bonds:		
30 year	Feb., May, Aug., Nov.	Following Week

As indicated in Exhibit 3, there are several auction cycles for Treasury coupon issues. Although none of these cycles is immutable, the auction cycles for the 2-year and 4-year Treasury notes and the refunding cycle have been fairly stable during recent years. In addition, there have been 5-year and, until early 1986, 20-year auction cycles.

Since it contains the Treasury long bond, typically 30 years in maturity, the refunding cycle is most important. The Treasury refunding cycle involves the issue of three coupon securities, typically a short note, a long note, and a long bond, during the February, May, August, and November quarterly cycle months. The securities to be auctioned and issued on the Treasury refunding cycle during the February, May, August and November quarterly cycle months are usually announced late in the month prior to auction, as illustrated in Exhibit 5. The three securities are auctioned on different days early in the refunding month and issued on the 15th day of the month. Typically the three issues include, with slight deviations, a 3½-year Treasury note (the short note), a 10-year Treasury note (the long note), and a long bond, which has usually had 30 years to maturity and 25 years to call.[1]

Both Treasury bills and Treasury coupon issues are sold on an auction basis. Treasury bills are auctioned on a yield basis wherein the bids are expressed on a bank discount basis with not more than two decimal

---

[1] By statute, the Treasury cannot issue bonds with coupons greater than 4.25 percent, which limits its ability to issue long-term debt. Originally, with respect to this statute, a bond was defined as any security over 5 years in maturity; as of 1976 a bond is now defined as any security over 10 years. Congress has granted exemptions to the ceiling on an annual basis.

EXHIBIT 4 Treasury Bill Offering Announcement

FEDERAL RESERVE BANK OF NEW YORK
Fiscal Agent of the United States

Circular No. **9919**
September 11, 1985

OFFERING OF TWO SERIES OF TREASURY BILLS

$7,200,000,000 of 91-Day Bills, To Be Issued September 19, 1985, Due December 19, 1985
$7,200,000,000 of 182-Day Bills, To Be Issued September 19, 1985, Due March 20, 1986

To All Banking Institutions, and Others Concerned,
in the Second Federal Reserve District:

Following is the text of a notice issued by the Treasury Department:

The Department of the Treasury, by this public notice, invites tenders for two series of Treasury bills totaling approximately $14,400 million, to be issued September 19, 1985. This offering will result in a paydown for the Treasury of about $2,675 million, as the maturing bills total $17,080 million (including the 16-day cash management bills issued September 3, 1985, in the amount of $3,004 million). Tenders will be received at Federal Reserve Banks and Branches and at the Bureau of the Public Debt, Washington, D.C. 20239, prior to 1:00 p.m., Eastern Daylight Saving time, Monday, September 16, 1985. The two series offered are as follows:

91-day bills (to maturity date) for approximately $7,200 million, representing an additional amount of bills dated June 20, 1985, and to mature December 19, 1985 (CUSIP No. 912794 JK1), currently outstanding in the amount of $7,033 million, the additional and original bills to be freely interchangeable.

182-day bills (to maturity date) for approximately $7,200 million, representing an additional amount of bills dated March 21, 1985, and to mature March 20, 1986 (CUSIP No. 912794 JX3), currently outstanding in the amount of $8,529 million, the additional and original bills to be freely interchangeable.

The bills will be issued on a discount basis under competitive and noncompetitive bidding, and at maturity their par amount will be payable without interest. Both series of bills will be issued entirely in book-entry form in a minimum amount of $10,000 and in any higher $5,000 multiple, on the records either of the Federal Reserve Banks and Branches, or of the Department of the Treasury.

The bills will be issued for cash and in exchange for Treasury bills maturing September 19, 1985. Tenders from Federal Reserve Banks for their own account and as agents for foreign and international monetary authorities will be accepted at the weighted average bank discount rate of accepted competitive tenders. Additional amounts of the bills may be issued to Federal Reserve Banks, as agents for foreign and international monetary authorities, to the extent that the aggregate amount of tenders for such accounts exceeds the aggregate amount of maturing bills held by them. Federal Reserve Banks currently hold $1,701 million as agents for foreign and international monetary authorities, and $3,799 million for their own account. Tenders for bills to be maintained on the book-entry records of the Department of the Treasury should be submitted on Form PD 4632-2 (for 26-week series) or Form PD 4632-3 (for 13-week series).

Each tender must state the par amount of bills bid for, which must be a minimum of $10,000. Tenders over $10,000 must be in multiples of $5,000. Competitive tenders must also show the yield desired, expressed on a bank discount rate basis with two decimals, e.g., 7.15%. Fractions may not be used. A single bidder, as defined in Treasury's single bidder guidelines, shall not submit noncompetitive tenders totaling more than $1,000,000.

Banking institutions and dealers who make primary markets in Government securities and report daily to the Federal Reserve Bank of New York their positions and in borrowings on such securities may submit tenders for account of customers, if the names of the customers and the amount for each customer are furnished. Others are only permitted to submit tenders for their own account. Each tender must state the amount of any net long position in the bills being offered if such position is in excess of $200 million. This information should reflect positions held as of 12:30 p.m., Eastern time, on the day of the auction. Such positions would include bills acquired through "when issued" trading, and futures and forward transactions as well as holdings of outstanding bills with the same maturity date as the new offering, e.g., bills with three months to maturity previously offered as six-month bills. Dealers, who make primary markets in Govern-

ment securities and report daily to the Federal Reserve Bank of New York their positions in and borrowings on such securities, when submitting tenders for customers, must submit a separate tender for each customer whose net long position in the bill being offered exceeds $200 million.

A noncompetitive bidder may not have entered into an agreement, nor make an agreement to purchase or sell or otherwise dispose of any noncompetitive awards of this issue being auctioned prior to the designated closing time for receipt of tenders.

Payment for the full par amount of the bills applied for must accompany all tenders submitted for bills to be maintained on the book-entry records of the Department of the Treasury. A cash adjustment will be made on all accepted tenders for the difference between the par payment submitted and the actual issue price as determined in the auction.

No deposit need accompany tenders from incorporated banks and trust companies and from responsible and recognized dealers in investment securities for bills to be maintained on the book-entry records of Federal Reserve Banks and Branches. A deposit of 2 percent of the par amount of the bills applied for must accompany tenders for such bills from others, unless an express guaranty of payment by an incorporated bank or trust company accompanies the tenders.

Public announcement will be made by the Department of the Treasury of the amount and yield range of accepted bids. Competitive bidders will be advised of the acceptance or rejection of their tenders. The Secretary of the Treasury expressly reserves the right to accept or reject any or all tenders, in whole or in part, and the Secretary's action shall be final. Subject to these reservations, noncompetitive tenders for each issue for $1,000,000 or less without stated yield from any one bidder will be accepted in full at the weighted average bank discount rate (in two decimals) of accepted competitive bids for the respective issues. The calculation of purchase prices for accepted bids will be carried to three decimal places on the basis of price per hundred, e.g., 99.923, and the determinations of the Secretary of the Treasury shall be final.

Settlement for accepted tenders for bills to be maintained on the book-entry records of Federal Reserve Banks and Branches must be made or completed at the Federal Reserve Bank or Branch on the issue date, in cash or other immediately-available funds or in Treasury bills maturing on that date. Cash adjustments will be made for differences between the par value of the maturing bills accepted in exchange and the issue price of the new bills. In addition, Treasury Tax and Loan Note Option Depositaries may make payment for allotments of bills for their own accounts and for account of customers by credit to their Treasury Tax and Loan Note Accounts on the settlement date.

In general, if a bill is purchased at issue after July 18, 1984, and held to maturity, the amount of discount is reportable as ordinary income in the Federal income tax return of the owner at the time of redemption. Accrual-basis taxpayers, banks, and other persons designated in section 1281 of the Internal Revenue Code must include in income the portion of the discount for the period during the taxable year such holder held the bill. If the bill is sold or otherwise disposed of before maturity, the portion of the gain equal to the accrued discount will be treated as ordinary income. Any excess may be treated as capital gain.

Department of the Treasury Circulars, Public Debt Series—Nos. 26-76 and 27-76, Treasury's single bidder guidelines, and this notice prescribe the terms of these Treasury bills and govern the conditions of their issue. Copies of the circulars, guidelines, and tender forms may be obtained from any Federal Reserve Bank or Branch, or from the Bureau of the Public Debt.

This Bank will receive tenders for both series prior to 1:00 p.m., Eastern Daylight Saving time, Monday, September 16, 1985, at the Securities Department of its Head Office and at its Buffalo Branch. Tender forms for both series are enclosed. Please be sure to use them to submit tenders and return them in the enclosed envelope. Forms for submitting tenders directly to the Treasury are available from the Government Bond Division of this Bank. Tenders not requiring a deposit may be submitted by telegraph, subject to written confirmation; no tenders may be submitted by telephone. Settlement must be made in cash or other immediately available funds or in Treasury securities maturing on or before the issue date. Treasury Tax and Loan Note Option Depositaries may make payment for Treasury bills by credit to their Treasury Tax and Loan Note Accounts.

Results of the last weekly offering are shown on the reverse side of this circular.

E. GERALD CORRIGAN,
President.

EXHIBIT 4 *(concluded)*

RESULTS OF LAST WEEKLY OFFERING OF TREASURY BILLS
(TWO SERIES TO BE ISSUED SEPTEMBER 12, 1985)

RANGE OF ACCEPTED COMPETITIVE BIDS:	13-week bills maturing December 12, 1985			:	26-week bills maturing March 13, 1986		
	Discount Rate	Investment Rate 1/	Price	:	Discount Rate	Investment Rate 1/	Price
Low	7.18%	7.41%	98.185	:	7.38% a/	7.77%	96.269
High	7.23%	7.47%	98.172	:	7.40%	7.79%	96.259
Average	7.22%	7.46%	98.175	:	7.39%	7.78%	96.264

a/ Excepting 1 tender of $125,000.

Tenders at the high discount rate for the 13-week bills were allotted 21%.
Tenders at the high discount rate for the 26-week bills were allotted 41%.

TENDERS RECEIVED AND ACCEPTED
(In Thousands)

Location	Received	Accepted	:	Received	Accepted
Boston	$ 46,745	$ 46,745	: $	85,175	$ 45,175
New York	17,953,775	5,930,810	:	20,385,590	6,045,515
Philadelphia	30,870	30,870	:	21,520	21,520
Cleveland	49,995	49,130	:	299,050	105,550
Richmond	62,575	53,455	:	83,560	52,085
Atlanta	57,605	51,605	:	89,855	47,705
Chicago	1,372,105	332,515	:	1,209,980	229,055
St. Louis	67,800	27,800	:	99,310	59,310
Minneapolis	49,745	49,745	:	46,650	31,900
Kansas City	167,430	98,680	:	61,375	61,375
Dallas	42,415	33,465	:	30,770	20,770
San Francisco	1,094,170	190,170	:	1,106,100	84;235
Treasury	306,100	306,100	:	400,400	400,400
TOTALS	$21,301,330	$7,201,090	:	$23,919,335	$7,204,595
Type					
Competitive	$17,910,350	$3,810,110	:	$20,594,970	$3,880,230
Noncompetitive	1,156,250	1,156,250	:	1,159,365	1,159,365
Subtotal, Public	$19,066,600	$4,966,360	:	$21,754,335	$5,039,595
Federal Reserve	1,824,730	1,824,730	:	1,800,000	1,800,000
Foreign Official Institutions	410,000	410,000	:	365,000	365,000
TOTALS	$21,301,330	$7,201,090	:	$23,919,335	$7,204,595

1/ Equivalent coupon-issue yield.

EXHIBIT 5 Treasury Coupon Security Offering Announcement

FEDERAL RESERVE BANK
OF NEW YORK
Fiscal Agent of the United States

Circular No. **9903**
August 1, 1985

TREASURY ANNOUNCES AUGUST QUARTERLY FINANCING

To All Banking Institutions, and Others Concerned,
in the Second Federal Reserve District:

The following is quoted from a statement issued yesterday by the Treasury Department:

The Treasury will raise about $9,400 million of new cash and refund $12,341 million of securities maturing August 15, 1985, by issuing $8,500 million of 3-year notes, $6,750 million of 10-year notes, and $6,500 million of 30-year bonds. The $12,341 million of maturing securities are those held by the public, including $1,409 million held, as of today, by Federal Reserve Banks as agents for foreign and international monetary authorities.

The 10-year note and 30-year bond being offered today will be eligible for exchange in the STRIPS program and, accordingly, may be divided into their separate Interest and Principal Components and maintained on the book-entry records of the Federal Reserve Banks and Branches. Once a security is in the STRIPS form, the components may be maintained and transferred in multiples of $1,000. Financial institutions should consult their local Federal Reserve Bank or Branch for procedures for requesting securities in STRIPS form.

The three issues totaling $21,750 million are being offered to the public, and any amounts tendered by Federal Reserve Banks as agents for foreign and international monetary authorities will be added to that amount. Tenders for such accounts will be accepted at the average prices of accepted competitive tenders.

In addition to the public holdings, Government accounts and Federal Reserve Banks, for their own accounts, hold $3,275 million of the maturing securities that may be refunded by issuing additional amounts of the new securities at the average prices of accepted competitive tenders.

Printed on the reverse side is a table summarizing the highlights of the offerings.

The 10-year note and the 30-year bond will be eligible for conversion to STRIPS (Separate Trading of Registered Interest and Principal of Securities). Information about this feature is set forth in the Treasury Department's official offering circulars, copies of which will be furnished upon request directed to the Government Bond Department (Tel. No. 212-791-6619). Questions regarding procedures for requesting securities in STRIPS form should be directed to H. John Costalos, Manager, Securities Transfer Department (Tel. No. 212-791-5986) or Daniel Bolwell, Chief, Securities Transfer Division (Tel. No. 212-791-5379).

In addition, enclosed are copies of the forms to be used in submitting tenders.

This Bank will receive tenders at the Securities Department of its Head Office and at its Buffalo Branch on the dates and times specified on the reverse side of this circular as the deadlines for receipt of tenders. *All competitive tenders,* whether transmitted by mail or by other means, must reach this Bank or its Branch by that time on the specified dates. However, for investors who wish to submit noncompetitive tenders and who find it more convenient to mail their tenders than to present them in person, the official offering circular for each offering provides that *noncompetitive* tenders will be considered timely received if they are mailed to this Bank or its Branch under a postmark no later than the date preceding the date specified for receipt of tenders.

Bidders submitting noncompetitive tenders should realize that it is possible that the average price may be above par, in which case they would have to pay more than the face value for the securities.

Payment with a tender may be made in cash, by check, in Treasury securities maturing on or before the issue date of the securities being purchased, by a charge to an institution's reserve account at this Bank, or, in the case of Treasury Tax and Loan Note Option Depositaries, by credit to a Treasury Tax and Loan Note Account. Payment by check must be in the form of an official bank check, a Federal funds check (a check drawn by a depository institution on its Federal Reserve account), or a personal check, which need not be certified. All checks must be drawn payable to the Federal Reserve Bank of New York; *checks endorsed to this Bank will not be accepted.*

Recorded messages provide information about Treasury offerings and about auction results: at the Head Office — Tel. No. 212-791-7773 (offerings) and Tel. No. 212-791-5823 (results); at the Buffalo Branch — Tel. No. 716-849-5158 (offerings) and Tel. No. 716-849-5046 (results). Additional inquiries regarding this offering may be made by calling, at the Head Office, Tel. No. 212-791-6619, or, at the Buffalo Branch, Tel. No. 716-849-5016.

E. GERALD CORRIGAN, *President.*

EXHIBIT 5 *(concluded)*

**HIGHLIGHTS OF TREASURY
OFFERINGS TO THE PUBLIC
AUGUST 1985 FINANCING
TO BE ISSUED AUGUST 15, 1985**

	3-Year Notes	10-Year Notes	30-Year Bonds
Amount Offered:			
To the public	$8,500 million	$6,750 million	$6,500 million
Description of Security:			
Term and type of security	3-year notes	10-year notes	30-year bonds
Series and CUSIP designation	Series T-1988 (CUSIP No. 912827 SN3)	Series C-1995 (CUSIP No. 912827 SP8)	Bonds of 2015 (CUSIP No. 912810 DS4)
CUSIP Nos. for STRIPS Components	Not applicable	Listed in Attachment A of offering circular	Listed in Attachment A of offering circular
Maturity date	August 15, 1988	August 15, 1995	August 15, 2015
Interest rate	To be determined, based on the average of accepted bids	To be determined, based on the average of accepted bids	To be determined, based on the average of accepted bids
Investment yield	To be determined at auction	To be determined at auction	To be determined at auction
Premium or discount	To be determined after auction	To be determined after auction	To be determined after auction
Interest payment dates	February 15 and Ausust 15	February 15 and August 15	February 15 and August 15
Minimum denomination available	$5,000	$1,000	$1,000
Amount Required for STRIPS	Not applicable	To be determined after auction	To be determined after auction
Terms of Sale:			
Method of sale	Yield auction	Yield auction	Yield auction
Competitive tenders	Must be expressed as an annual yield, with two decimals, e.g., 7.10%	Must be expressed as an annual yield, with two decimals, e.g., 7.10%	Must be expressed as an annual yield with two decimals, e.g., 7.10%
Noncompetitive tenders	Accepted in full at the average price up to $1,000,000	Accepted in full at the average price up to $1,000,000	Accepted in full at the average price up to $1,000,000
Accrued interest payable by investor	None	None	None
Payment through Treasury Tax and Loan (TT&L) Note Accounts	Acceptable for TT&L Note Option Depositaries	Acceptable for TT&L Note Option Depositaries	Acceptable for TT&L Note Option Depositaries
Payment by non-institutional investors	Full payment to be submitted with tender	Full payment to be submitted with tender	Full payment to be submitted with tender
Deposit guarantee by designated institutions	Acceptable	Acceptable	Acceptable
Key Dates:			
Receipt of tenders	**Tuesday, August 6, 1985, prior to 1:00 p.m., EDST**	**Wednesday, August 7, 1985, prior to 1:00 p.m., EDST**	**Thursday, August 8, 1985, prior to 1:00 p.m., EDST**
Settlement			
a) cash or Federal funds	Thursday, August 15, 1985	Thursday, August 15, 1985	Thursday, August 15, 1985
b) readily collectible check	Tuesday, August 13, 1985	Tuesday, August 13, 1985	Tuesday, August 13, 1985

places (e.g., 8.45 percent). Bids are taken by the Treasury and securities allocated from the lowest yield to higher yields until the Treasury has allocated the total amount of the announced issue. The successful bids are awarded at their actual yield. Those who submit a higher bid yield than the highest accepted by the Treasury are not allocated bills. Bids may also be made on a noncompetitive basis. Such bids include no bid yield, only a quantity. These bids are completely allocated at the average yield of the successful bids. Noncompetitive bids are usually made by small, noninstitutional investors.

Different auction methods have been used by the Treasury for auctioning coupon issues. The most common auction method is to require the bids to be made on a *yield* basis, to two decimal points, for example 11.27 percent. The Treasury then allocates the securities, beginning with the lowest bid to the highest yield until the announced amount is fully subscribed. The average yield of those receiving an allocation is used to determine the coupon of the newly issued bonds. The coupon is usually set slightly less than the average yield so that the new bonds are issued at a slight discount to par. The price paid by each successful bidder is determined from the coupon on the issue established by the Treasury and the yield bid by the particular bidder.

If the current yield on an outstanding bond of approximately the same maturity as that which the Treasury plans to auction is approximately the same as the coupon on the outstanding issue (that is, the issue is trading at about par), the Treasury may announce the reissue of this outstanding security (i.e., an additional amount of this outstanding security is auctioned).

Secondary Market

The secondary market for Treasury securities is the most liquid financial market in the world. This market is "made" by a group of U.S. government securities dealers who continually provide bids and offers on outstanding Treasuries. A current list of primary reporting dealers as specified by the Federal Reserve Bank of New York (FRBNY) is provided in Exhibit 6.

Dealers continuously provide bids and offers on specific outstanding government securities, buying for and selling from their inventories. Dealers' earnings are derived from three sources. First, dealers profit from their market making through the difference in their bid/ask quotes, the spread. The bid/ask spread is a measure of the liquidity of the market for the issue, as discussed below. Second, to the extent that dealers hold inventories, they also profit from price appreciation of their inventories (or price depreciation of securities they have shorted) but experience a loss from their inventory positions if prices decline. Finally, dealers may profit on the basis of "carry," the difference between the interest return

EXHIBIT 6 List of the Government Securities Dealers Reporting to the Market Reports Division of the Federal Reserve Bank of New York (as of May 1986)

Bank of America NT & SA
Bankers Trust Company
Bear, Stearns & Co.
Carroll McEntee & McGinley Incorporated
Chase Manhattan Government Securities, Inc.
Chemical Bank
Citibank, N. A.
Continental Illinois National Bank & Trust Company of Chicago
Crocker National Bank
Dean Witter Reynolds Inc.
Discount Corporation of New York
Donaldson, Lufkin & Jenrette Securities Corporation
Drexel Burnham Lambert Government Securities Inc.
The First Boston Corporation
First Interstate Bank of California
First National Bank of Chicago
Goldman, Sachs & Co.
Greenwich Capital Markets, Inc.
Harris Trust and Savings Bank
E. F. Hutton & Company, Inc.
Irving Securities Inc.
J. P. Morgan Securities Holdings Inc.
Kidder, Peabody & Co., Incorporated
Kleinwort Benson Government Securities, Inc.
Aubrey G. Lanston & Co., Inc.
Lehman Government Securities, Inc.
Manufacturers Hanover Trust Company
Merrill Lynch Government Securities Inc.
Morgan Stanley & Co., Incorporated
Northern Trust Company
Paine Webber Incorporated
Wm. E. Pollock Government Securities, Inc.
Prudential-Bache Securities, Inc.
Refco Partners
Salomon Brothers Inc
Smith Barney Government Securities, Inc.

Note: This list has been compiled and made available for statistical purposes only and has no significance with respect to other relationships between dealers and the Federal Reserve Bank of New York. Qualification for the reporting list is based on the achievement and maintenance of reasonable standards of activity.

on the securities they hold and the financing costs of these securities. Dealers, typically, do not have sufficient capital to own outright the securities they hold in their inventory, so their inventories are financed. When the interest return on the securities they hold is greater than the financing cost, a "positive carry" exists, and thus a profit results from this differential. In the opposite case of "negative carry," dealers experience a loss from carrying their inventory.

Since dealer financing is of a very short maturity and the securities held in inventory are almost always of a longer maturity, the carry is positive when long-term interest rates are higher than short-term interest rates and negative when short-term interest rates are higher than long-term interest rates.[2] Obviously, when carry is negative, the dealers generate a loss on carrying their inventories and attempt to minimize the size of their inventory for this reason.

The typical mechanism for financing Treasury securities is the repurchase agreement, or "repo," which is basically a collaterized loan wherein the Treasury securities owned by the dealer are used as collateral to the lender on the loan to the dealer. Repurchase agreements are typically of very short maturity, commonly one day. Longer repurchase agreements are called term repos. The market for term repos becomes quite thin as the maturity lengthens.

The secondary market for Treasury securities also includes brokers who intermediate between dealers. However, brokers, unlike dealers, do not buy and sell for their own inventories but simply arrange trades between dealers for a commission. The dealers pay the brokers a commission for arranging trades between themselves and others.

Bids and offers in the dealer market for Treasury bills are made on a discount basis, not a price basis, in basis points. (A basis point is 1/100th of 1 percent in discount return; for example, the difference between 10.00 percent and 10.01 percent is one basis point.) Thus a bid/offer quote may be 11.63 percent/11.61 percent. This discount is converted into a price for delivery, as discussed below.

On the other hand, bids and offers for coupon instruments are made on the basis of price to 1/32 of 1 percent of par, which is taken to be $100. For example a quote of 97–19 refers to a price of 97 and 19/32. Thus, on the basis of $100,000 par value, a change in a price of 1 percent is consistent with $1,000 and 1/32 with $31.25.

The government securities dealers work closely with the Federal Reserve System and the Treasury in several ways. First and most importantly, the FRBNY, on behalf of the Board of Governors of the Federal Reserve System (hereafter Fed), conducts its open-market operations and its repo and reverse repo transactions through auctions with the

---

[2] This relationship between short-term and long-term interest rates is the basis for the yield curve, as discussed in the next section.

primary dealers. Such activities are conducted by the FRBNY among the dealers on an auction basis in a matter of minutes. Second, as a basis of its conduct of monetary policy, the FRBNY gets information on a frequent basis form the primary dealers about the condition of the financial markets. Finally, although primary dealers do not underwrite Treasury issues in the same way corporate bonds are underwritten by investment banks, the dealers to a large extent provide the same function. To provide this function dealers frequently bid actively at the auctions and subsequently redistribute the bonds they are allocated to their customers. Of course, if the prices decline before they are redistributed, the dealers experience underwriting losses.

There are two other components of secondary markets, in addition to the market for the spot buying and selling of Treasury securities and the repo market, that are closely associated with the Treasury spot market. The first of these is the market for shorting specific government securities. In this market a dealer or other institution sells a security it does not own, that is, "shorts" the security with an agreement that the security will be returned at some future date. The short accomplishes this by borrowing a security from another dealer or institution. Of course the interest forgone by the lender must be paid by the borrower. There is a fairly active short market for actively traded government securities, but it is confined mainly to government security dealers.[3]

The second component is the "when-issued market," or "W/I market," wherein Treasury securities are traded prior to the time they are issued by the Treasury. The when-issued trading for both Treasury bills and Treasury coupon issues extends from the day the auction is announced until the issue day. All deliveries on when-issued trades occur on the issue day of the Treasury security traded.

The institutional arrangements of the Treasury securities markets are described in this section. Interest rates on Treasury securities are the benchmark interest rates in the U.S. financial system. The next section contains a discussion of the factors affecting interest-rate determination.

INTEREST–RATE DETERMINATION

In this section we shall discuss how interest rates are determined. The first of this section focuses on the determination of "the" interest rate or, alternatively, the general level of interest rates, for which a Treasury security interest rate (either a 91-day Treasury bill rate or a long-term Treasury bond rate) is the benchmark. The second part then considers

---

[3] In many ways the repo transaction is similar to the shorting transaction. However, in the repo transaction the borrower of funds who puts up a Treasury security as collateral is subject to market risk, whereas in the short transaction the borrower of the security is subject to market risk.

why, at any time, a variety of levels of interest rates coexist. This discussion relates to the rationales for structures of interest rates. The concluding part of this section provides an overview of interest-rate determination.[4]

Rationale for Interest-Rate Determination

In a broad sense the economy can be conceived of as being composed of two sectors—the real sector and the financial sector. The real sector is involved with the production of goods and services with physical resources—labor and capital. Important examples of components of the real sector include automobile production, steel production, and housing construction. The financial sector is concerned with the transfer of funds from lenders to borrowers. Important examples of components of the financial sector include commercial banks, insurance companies, and securities dealers.

In the financial sector equilibrium is attained when the demand for borrowed funds equals the supply of loanable funds, as discussed below. The interest rate is the variable that causes this equality or equilibrium.

To an individual deciding whether to currently consume an amount of funds or abstain from consumption and supply the funds to the financial sector (that is, save) the interest rate can be viewed as compensation for abstaining from current consumption. For example, an individual with $100 of disposable income when the interest rate is 10 percent must decide between consuming the $100 today or saving it for one year, after which the individual would have $110 to consume. The $10 of added consumption is in effect a reward for abstaining from current consumption. The greater the reward, that is, the higher the interest rate, the more a saver should be willing to supply loanable funds. In the

---

[4] This chapter discusses interest rates as though the interest rates on securities were directly comparable. Interest rates on all securities, however, are not, without adjustment, directly comparable. Typically, market makers refer to the value of securities in terms of their prices, not their interest rates. The interest rates on the securities are then calculated from their prices. Interest rates are important because they provide a common basis for comparing the returns on securities of different maturities and of different principal values. For these reasons, interest rates are always calculated on an annual basis, typically for $100 of maturity value. However, in calculating interest rates from prices, different assumptions are used for different securities. Thus within the general term *interest rate* are included the returns on several types of securities that are calculated according to different assumptions and are called, alternatively, discount return, yield, bond equivalent yield, repo equivalent yield, and other measures of return. Thus in comparing interest rates on different securities, adjustments must often be made so that the interest rates compared are calculated on the basis of the same assumptions. However, the magnitudes of the differences among interest rates calculated on the basis of different assumptions are in most cases small. This chapter ignores the effect of different assumptions used in calculating interest rates and uses the term *interest rate* as though the returns on all securities were comparable.

aggregate, the supply of loanable funds is directly related to the interest rates, which are reflected in the upward sloping supply curve of Exhibit 7.

EXHIBIT 7   The Supply and Demand of Loanable Funds

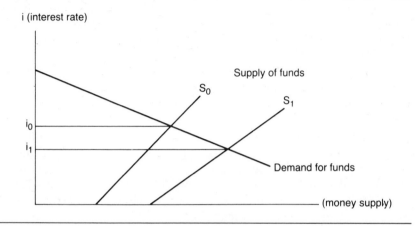

The steepness of this curve depends on the saver's preference for future consumption relative to present consumption. The greater this preference for savings, the flatter the supply curve—the more willing a saver is to save. In this case there is a greater increase in savings for a given increase in interest rates.

To a borrower of funds, the interest rate represents a cost. In the context of the preceding example, at an interest rate of 10 percent, borrowing $100 for one year will cost the borrower $10 in interest. To a business borrower, this $10 interest expense is the cost of borrowing to improve capital plant and equipment. If a business borrower can make operations sufficiently more efficient and consequently more profitable as a result of becoming more capital intensive, then borrowing should occur. The higher the interest rate, however, the greater must be the profitability associated with an investment for it to pay off. Since more investments will pay off at low interest rates than at high interest rates, the demand for funds by borrowers will decline as interest rates rise. For this reason, the demand for funds curve in Exhibit 7 is downward sloping.

The catalyst for achieving equality between the aggregate supply of funds and the aggregate demand for funds in the financial system is the interest rate. The financial sector is not, however, one uniform, homogenous market. Rather the financial sector is composed of a number of financial institutions and markets that, although distinct, are interrelated. Each of these specific components of the financial sector is specialized, attracting funds from specific types of savers and making funds available to specific types of borrowers. There is, however, some substitution in which savers and/or borrowers who usually borrow or lend in one part of the financial sector may switch to a different part because of a change in relative interest rates.

Interest rates bring the supply and demand for funds into equality in each part of the financial system and operate in the same way to bring the total or aggregate supply and demand for funds in the financial system into equality.

Interest rates are not constant, rather they vary over time. Understanding what affects interest rates and why they are variable is key to understanding the operations of the financial sector. The determination of the general level and variability of interest rates is explainable by several different theories or frameworks. The three major theories, liquidity preference, loanable funds, and inflation and the real rate of interest, are described below. In addition to a general conceptual discussion of the theories, a discussion of how these theories can be used in practice is provided. The focus in this section is on the general level of interest rates, not on any particular interest rate.

Liquidity preference. "Liquidity preference" is synonymous with the "demand for money." And, as is the case with the demand for other financial assets and liabilities, the demand for money is dependent on the level of interest rates.

The relationship between the demand for money and interest rates can be explained in two ways. The first relies on a Keynesian construction called the speculative demand for money. In this approach, it is assumed that the investor has as investment alternatives either holding cash, which has a zero return and no risk, or holding a bond that has two forms of return, a coupon return and a potential capital gain or loss. If the capital loss on bonds is large enough to exceed the coupon return, the total return on bonds will be negative, and holding money, even at a zero return, would be preferable.

Since the prices of and interest rates on fixed income securities move inversely, bonds incur a capital loss when interest rates rise and a capital gain when interest rates fall. Thus, when interest rates are low, there will typically be an expectation that they will rise, thus resulting in a capital loss on bonds. In anticipation of such a capital loss, holding cash is preferable. Conversely, if interest rates are presently high, they will typically be expected to decline, so that a capital gain on bonds is anticipated and holding bonds is preferable.

Interest rates affect the relative demand for money and bonds as illustrated by a downward sloping demand curve shown in Exhibit 8. The demand for money increases as the current interest rate decreases because the lower the present interest rate is, the more it is expected to

EXHIBIT 8   The Supply and Demand of Money

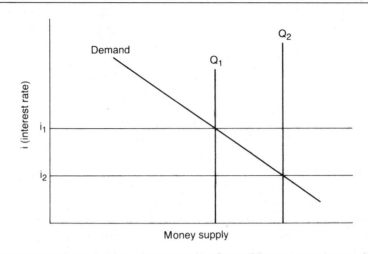

rise, and thus the greater the expected capital loss is and the more investors are inclined to hold money. With respect to Exhibit 8, as the interest rate rises from i_2 to i_1, the quantity of money demanded decreases from Q_2 to Q_1.

A second way to explain the relationship between interest rates and the demand for money is to conceive of the interest rate as the foregone return for holding money instead of an interest-bearing asset. Consequently, the higher the rate of interest, the greater is the return foregone by holding money, and the less money is held. In other words, according to Exhibit 8 as interest rates rise, the cost of holding money rather than an interest-earning asset rises. Consequently, as interest rates rise a smaller amount of money is held.

According to either explanation, the liquidity preference theory of interest rates explains the level of the interest rate in terms of the supply and demand for money. Thus if the Fed increases(decreases) the supply of money and there is no change in the demand relationship, the interest rate will decrease(increase). Again referring to Exhibit 8, increasing the supply of money from Q_1 to Q_2 while leaving the demand relationship unchanged results in a lower equilibrium interest rate. In general, an increase in the supply or a decrease in the demand for money will cause interest rates to decline, whereas a decrease in supply or an increase in demand will cause interest rates to rise.

The liquidity preference theory of interest-rate determination can be used for determining both short-term and long-term changes in interest rates.

A partial, short-term analysis of interest-rate determination is based solely on tracking and analyzing short-term movements in the money supply. Since the Fed has the primary responsibility for determining the money supply, there has developed a school of interest-rate analysts commonly known as Fed watchers who continually monitor and interpret the Fed's activities to infer from these activities the Fed's intentions regarding future activities that will affect the money supply and, consequently, interest rates.[5] The weekly money supply statistics announced by the Fed on Thursday afternoons and widely disseminated by the financial press are carefully examined for indications of changes in Fed policy that could affect interest rates. Exhibit 9 provides a weekly table of Federal Reserve money supply statistics. An additional discussion of how the Fed's money supply data are interpreted is provided below.

In addition to watching and interpreting the market money supply data, the Fed's open-market operations and their effect on the federal funds rate are continuously monitored. As an example, the following discussion appeared in *The Wall Street Journal* (January 20, 1982):

> Some specialists said the recent rise in the funds rate reflected an apparently tougher stance adopted by the Fed late last month in supplying reserves to the banking system. And many contend the recent surge in the money supply will force the Fed to get even tougher.

A longer-term application of the liquidity preference theory is based on the relationship between the money supply and the level of Gross National Product (GNP). This relationship is formally expressed by the equation: $M \times V = P \times Y$ (called the quantity theory of money), where V is the velocity of money, P is the price level, and Y is real gross national product. The product of P and Y, $P \times Y$, is nominal GNP, referred to simply as GNP.

According to this theory, if the level of the money supply over some future time period is less(greater) than the actual amount needed to support the expected level of GNP, then the level of interest rates is likely to rise(fall). It is due to this relationship that economic forecasters go through the complex exercise of predicting GNP and the money supply and their interrelationship in order to provide forecasts of interest rates.[6]

Predicting GNP and money supply relationships is usually conducted in the context of large econometric models of the U.S. economy. These multiequation models attempt to capture the complex interactions in the economy that result in the determination of interest rates, GNP, and money supply. The results of such models are frequently the basis for long-range financial planning by corporations and others.

---

[5] Fed watching is the subject of Chapter 55.

[6] See Chapter 56 for a thorough discussion of interest-rate forecasting.

EXHIBIT 9   Weekly Federal Reserve Money Supply Statistics (May 16, 1986)

Federal Reserve
All data in millions of dollars

	Latest Week	Previous Week	Year Ago
Monetary Aggregates			
M-1 *as of May 5	$654,700	$648,600	577,700
Adj. Mon.Base (St.Louis Fed) *(5/7)	241,900	239,600	222,700
Reserve Position, Eight New York Banks Daily averages for two weeks ended May 7			
Excess (Deficit) Reserves (Incl. carryover)	3	28	33
Borrowings at Federal Reserve	0	0	0
Net Federal Funds Purchases	R 8,016	9,720	6,029
Basic Reserve Surplus (Deficit)	R (8,013)	(9,686)	(5,996)
Federal Reserve Credit Daily averages, week ended May 14			
Gov'ts. and Agencies Held Outright	186,829	187,376	173,233
Gov'ts. and Agencies Under Repurchase	0	3,596	0
Float	788	R 644	589
Other Assets	16,678	R 16,535	12,793
Other Factors Affecting Reserves Daily averages, week ended May 14			
Gold Stock	11,085	11,088	11,091
Special Drawing Rights	4,732	4,718	4,618
Currency in Circulation	196,392	R 195,185	182,900
Treasury Deposits	4,591	7,246	6,890
Other Items			
Gov't. Securities Held by Fed for Foreign accounts as of May 14	145,598	145,787	118,116
Business Loans, National**, Apr. 28	258,737	R 256,611	252,167
Commercial Paper, National, May 7	303,972	R 300,309	257,501
Ten New York Banks, Balance Sheet Items Wednesday, May 7			
Loans and Leases, Adjusted	158,348	R 161,546	147,720
Business Loans**	57,977	57,988	62,552
Treasury and Agency Securities	10,675	10,673	12,295
Tax-Exempt Securities	13,254	13,262	8,643
Demand Deposits	53,548	R 58,584	44,634
Nontransaction Balances	91,377	R 91,395	85,688
Time Deposits Larger than $100,000	34,684	R 34,880	33,842

R Revised.   * Seasonally adjusted.   ** Excluding acceptances.   n.a. Not available.

SOURCE: *The New York Times,* May 16, 1986.

Loanable funds.   The loanable funds theory of interest-rate determination is based on the reasoning related to the supply and demand for loanable funds provided at the beginning of this section. This theory of interest-rate determination depends on the supply of funds available for lending by savers and the demand for such loanable funds by borrowers. As indicated above, as the return to lending rises (as interest rates rise), the supply of loanable funds increases. Conversely, when interest rates decline, the return to lenders declines; thus so does the supply of such funds.

Since interest rates represent a cost to borrowers, the opposite relationship applies to borrowers: As interest rates rise, borrowers' demand for funds decreases, and as interest rates decline, borrowers' demand for funds increases. These relationships are illustrated by Exhibit 10.

EXHIBIT 10   The Supply and Demand of Loanable Funds

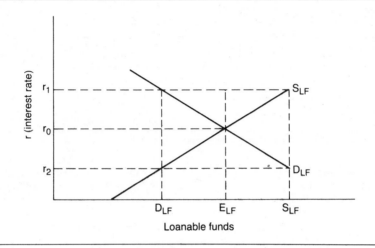

Loanable funds

In Exhibit 10 the equilibrium level of interest rates is r_0, and the quantity of funds lent and borrowed at that rate is E_{LF}. If the interest rate were initially higher than r_0, for example r_1, then the supply of funds, S_{LF}, would exceed the demand, D_{LF}, at that rate. This excess supply of funds would exert downward pressure on interest rates, causing them to decrease to r_0, the point at which supply and demand would be in equilibrium. Alternately, if rates were below the equilibrium level, for example at r_2, then the demand would exceed the supply. The effect of market pressures in this case would be to cause interest rates to increase again to the equilibrium level, r_0.

The loanable funds theory of interest-rate determination applies to aggregate borrowing and lending in the economy. If, at a given interest rate, intended aggregate borrowing is greater than intended aggregate lending, then interest rates will rise. Then the actual measured levels of borrowing and lending at the higher level of interest rates will be equal. If intended aggregate borrowing is less than intended aggregate lending, interest rates will decline until the actual measured levels of borrowing and lending will be equal at the lower level of interest rates.

To apply the loanable funds theory, aggregate borrowing and lending is typically divided into its components or sectors, as illustrated in Exhibit 11. Even though some borrowers and lenders can shift among types and maturities of sources and uses of funds and some cannot, a structure or taxonomy such as shown in Exhibit 11 can be used in either case for determining aggregate borrowing and lending. This structure is useful for summarizing actual, measured aggregate borrowing and lending for past years, as done for 1979–1984 in Exhibit 11; as indicated above, borrowing and lending must be equal.

The structure is also useful for forecasting interest rates.[7] For this purpose, an estimate is developed of the expected or intended levels of borrowing and lending of each type shown in Exhibit 11 over a period of time. Then the sum of all types of borrowing (aggregate borrowing) is compared with the sum of all types of lending (aggregate lending). If the former is greater than the latter, interest rates are forecast to increase. And due to the increase in interest rates, actual borrowing would be less than expected borrowing and actual lending would be greater than expected lending. Then, ex post, actual measured borrowing and lending would be equal. For example, the data in Exhibit 11 provide estimates of the actual measured sources and uses of funds in 1985 after interest rates changed to their equilibrium levels.

Often, instead of developing as complete a taxonomy of borrowing and lending as described above, analysts focus on only the major types of borrowing and lending, such as federal government borrowing, business borrowing, and mortgage borrowing. Then by forecasting increases or decreases in these types of borrowing, analysts assess whether there will be upward or downward pressures on the interest rate.

A popularization of the application of the loanable funds theory on a sectoral basis is referred to as "crowding out." Large federal deficits require the U.S. Department of the Treasury to increase the amount of debt it has outstanding; and the issue of Treasury debt is alleged to compete with privator-sector borrowing, assuming a fixed supply of available credit. Thus an increase in the demand for funds by the Treasury causes interest rates to increase and forces out the private-sector issues. An example of the crowding out application of the loanable funds theory appeared in *The Wall Street Journal* (1981):

> Many dealers said they continue to be concerned about the size of the Treasury's financing needs. Traders also expressed nervousness over recent increases in short-term interest rates. But many said they remain confident

---

[7] See Chapter 56.

EXHIBIT 11 Summary of Supply and Demand for Credit ($ billions)

	1979	1980	1981	1982	1983	1984E	1985P	Amt. Out. 31 Dec 84E
Net Demand								
Privately held mortgages	$113.1	$84.2	$73.7	$15.9	$83.7	$148.5	$136.4	$1,485.5
Corporate and foreign bonds	35.7	40.2	34.9	39.1	37.9	50.5	45.3	656.9
Total long-term private	148.8	124.3	108.6	54.9	121.7	199.0	181.7	2,142.4
Short-term business borrowing	98.0	67.1	117.3	47.5	60.1	141.6	153.2	1,006.7
Short-term other borrowing	49.3	11.2	37.7	27.7	60.5	97.9	120.7	695.5
Total short-term private	147.2	78.3	155.0	75.2	120.6	239.5	273.9	1,702.2
Privately held federal debt	76.2	118.7	123.0	214.1	241.0	257.3	277.9	1,728.1
Tax-exempt notes and bonds	27.8	31.9	29.5	63.9	54.3	66.5	63.2	542.8
Total government debt	104.0	150.6	152.4	278.0	295.3	323.8	341.1	2,270.9
Total Net Demand for Credit	$400.0	$353.3	$416.0	$408.1	$537.6	$762.4	$796.7	$6,115.6
Net Supply*								
Thrift institutions	$56.5	$54.5	$27.8	$31.3	$136.8	$155.8	$171.7	$1,117.1
Insurance, pensions, endowments	77.9	88.2	89.2	107.1	96.1	105.3	105.4	1,190.2
Investment companies	29.3	15.9	72.4	52.4	6.0	49.9	58.0	261.3
Other nonbank finance	27.8	13.1	28.8	4.9	12.0	50.6	41.3	307.8
Total nonbank finance	191.4	171.7	218.1	195.6	250.9	361.5	376.5	2,876.3
Commercial banks	122.2	101.4	107.6	107.2	140.2	169.0	164.8	1,761.6
Nonfinancial corporations	7.0	1.8	18.4	13.6	22.8	12.6	23.1	160.6
State and local governments	7.1	0.6	2.0	10.3	17.2	11.0	9.7	93.6
Foreign investors	−4.6	23.2	16.3	18.1	28.5	30.7	30.8	283.2
Subtotal	323.1	298.7	362.4	344.8	459.5	584.8	604.8	5,175.3
Residual: households direct	76.9	54.6	53.7	63.3	78.1	177.6	191.9	940.4
Total Net Supply of Credit	$400.0	$353.3	$416.0	$408.1	$537.6	$762.4	$796.7	$6,115.6
Memo								
Net issuance corporate stock	$−1.9	$18.2	$11.9	$19.5	$27.8	$−89.1	$−26.8	$2,030.0
Total credit and stock	398.1	371.5	427.9	427.6	565.3	673.3	769.9	8,145.6
Percentage of Total Absorbed by								
Households	56.2%	42.9%	40.1%	28.8%	40.6%	45.8%	44.3%	
Nonfinancial business	24.3	25.3	25.1	18.5	15.0	9.6	15.2	
Financial institutions	7.3	10.1	11.8	4.4	8.4	−2.7	5.1	
Government	7.9	15.6	17.6	45.7	33.5	46.4	34.2	
Foreigners	4.3	6.1	5.4	2.6	2.5	0.9	1.2	

* Excludes funds for equities and other demands not tabulated above.
SOURCE: "1985 Prospects for Financial Markets," (Salomon Brothers Inc, Dec. 11, 1984) p. 26.

that bond prices will rebound early next year, mainly because they anticipate further evidence of erosion in the economy.

And another example appeared in a *New York Times* story (1981):

Unusually heavy year-end Government borrowings continued to weigh on
the money market last week, raising short-term rates a point on average
and reducing prices of longer-term coupon securities as much as two
points, or $20 for each $1,000 of face value.

Thus the crowding-out concept derives from the loanable funds
theory but focuses only on Treasury borrowing. Most applications of
loanable funds use an intermediate approach between a complete taxonomy of sources and uses of funds and only a single use of funds; they
consider a few major uses of funds and perhaps changes in the aggregate supply of funds.

Inflation and the real rate of interest. Interest rates represent a
rate of return for lenders and a cost to borrowers. To be a meaningful
representation of cost or return, however, interest rates should be related to the rate of change of prices. The significance of this relationship
can be considered by the following example. Consider a saver who has
placed $5,000 in a money market fund earning a return of 12 percent per
year. At the end of a year the saver has $5,600, a 12 percent increase in
purchasing power. If, however, the price level had increased by 10
percent per year, then the net increase in purchasing power of the
savings would be only 2 percent.

The 12 percent return on the savings is referred to as the nominal
rate of interest, since it measures the percent increase in the nominal
number of dollars earned or paid over a period of time. The measure of
change in purchasing power of 2 percent is referred to as the real rate of
interest since it measures the real change in purchasing power. The
difference between these two rates is the rate of inflation. Thus the real
rate of interest (IR) equals the nominal rate of interest (IN) minus the
rate of inflation (DP): $IR = IN - DP$.

From the lender's perspective, the real rate of interest represents the
increase in real purchasing power resulting from foregone consumption—savings. From the borrower's perspective, the real rate of interest
represents the real cost of borrowing. The inflation component of the
nominal rate of interest the borrower pays on the borrowed funds represents a deterioration of the principal of the loan (often described as
paying back in cheap dollars), not a real cost of borrowed funds. A
business should as a rule continue to borrow and invest until the real
rate of return on investments equals the real rate of interest paid on
borrowing.

Thus there are two major determinants of the real rate of interest.
The first is the return on investment—the return to capital. If a business
can improve its efficiency of operations and earn a higher rate of return

from investment, it will be inclined to pay a higher real rate of return on borrowed funds. The other influence is the preference of consumers. The more consumers want to consume currently rather than forego consumption, the higher the real rate of return will have to be to induce them to alter their plans and save.

Then the real rate of interest and the rate of inflation jointly determine the nominal rate of interest. The effect of the rate of inflation on the nominal rate of interest is to cause the nominal rate to change so that the real rate is unaffected by the rate of inflation. Lenders, unless subject to a "dollar illusion," are concerned with the return of the real purchasing power on their savings rather than the nominal return. Such concern causes consumers to negotiate for nominal rates that keep their real rate of return at least constant. Thus, to the extent their savings are sensitive to the real rate of interest, an increase in inflation without a corresponding increase in the real rate of interest will cause a decrease in savings. Consequently, there is upward pressure on the nominal rate of interest during periods of inflation, which prevents the real rate of interest from decreasing below its original level. To prevent savings from decreasing requires an increase in the nominal rate equal to the increase in the rate of inflation.

Inflation has a somewhat similar effect on the willingness of borrowers to pay a higher nominal rate of interest for funds. Inflation affects the return on investment by affecting the prices of goods and services produced. An investment earning a given amount net of the interest on borrowings will earn a higher nominal amount after inflation because the value of the goods and services produced by the investment have been inflated. If the interest payments on the borrowings do not increase as well, then the real rate of return on investment will also increase. Presumably, under such circumstances borrowers will continue to increase their demand for funds until the nominal cost of borrowing has increased such that the real cost is at its preinflation level.

Over time, however, the real rate of interest may change for two reasons. First, the real rate of interest, since it is the real return on capital, may decrease during recessions because of a substantial amount of unused capital and a low return to the used capital. Similarly, it may increase during periods of economic growth because all capital is productively employed.

The second reason for changes in the real rate relates to *unexpected* changes in the rate of inflation. The nominal interest rate on a security at any time should reflect the *expected* average rate of inflation over the maturity of the security. If the financial markets *expect* a higher rate of inflation in the future, nominal interest rates should increase to reflect these expectations. However, if inflation changes unexpectedly, the initial nominal rate of interest will not correctly reflect the change, and the actual real rate of interest over the period will be different from the normal level of the real rate in the opposite direction of the unexpected change in the rate of inflation.

Consider the following example. Between times T_0 and T_1 the nominal rate of interest is 8 percent, the rate of inflation is 5 percent, and the real rate of interest is 3 percent. Assume these are the normal levels.

Assume that at T_1 the rate of inflation *unexpectedly* increases to 6 percent. Since the change is unexpected, the nominal rate does not change, and thus the real rate of interest decreases to 2 percent. Assume that by T_2 the financial markets recognize the change in the rate of inflation and the nominal rate of interest increases to 9 percent, restoring the real rate of interest to 3 percent.

At T_3 the rate of inflation *unexpectedly* decreases to its original level of 5 percent. Because the change is unexpected, the nominal rate remains at 9 percent, so the real rate increases to 4 percent. By T_4 the financial market recognizes the change in the rate of inflation, the nominal rate of interest decreases to 8 percent, and the real rate of interest decreases to its original normal level of 3 percent. Thus, although expected changes in the rate of inflation should have no effect on the real rate of interest, unexpected changes in inflation will cause the real rate of interest to change in the opposite direction.

Typically, interest rates are referred to in nominal terms. Similarly, interest-rate determination models relate to the nominal rate of interest. As discussed above, the nominal rate of interest and the rate of inflation are directly related. Since the nominal rate of interest is, by definition, equal to the real rate of interest plus the rate of inflation, the rate of inflation is a major component of the level of the nominal rates of interest. In fact, given the levels of inflation and interest rates that have been observed during the last decade, changes in the nominal rate of interest have been due in greater measure to changes in inflation than to changes in the real rate of interest.

Exhibit 12 provides a plot of the real rate of interest from 1965 until recently. Calculations of the real rate of interest can be made from different measures of the rate of inflation and different interest rates, although in concept the measure of the inflation rate used should be the expected inflation rate over the maturity of the security whose interest rate is used. The interest rate can be either a short-term or a long-term interest rate. Very often the inflation rate used is based on an average over several previous periods or a projection of the trend of the past inflation rate into the future. The real rate of interest in the plot in Exhibit 12 equals the average prime rate charged by banks minus the contemporaneous change in the Consumer Price Index (CPI). Alternatively, the real rate plotted could have been the long-term Treasury bond rate minus an expected long-term rate of inflation.

Exhibit 12 shows that there has been considerable variation in the real rate of interest, the difference between the interest rate and the

EXHIBIT 12 The Real Rate of Interest

Percent

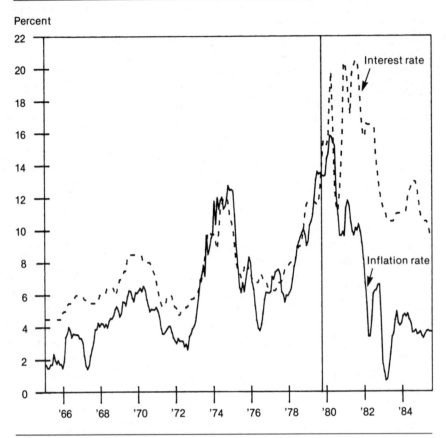

* Interest rate: Average prime rate charged by banks.
† Inflation rate: Consumer price movement, six-month spans (annual rate).
SOURCE: U.S. Commerce Department.

inflation rate. These changes in the real rate have been due both to changes in the strength of the economy and errors in inflationary expectations.[8] Although the correlation is less than perfect, the real rate of interest tends to be low during recessions and high during periods of economic strength.

To summarize, in models of the determination of the nominal rate of interest, the factors that affect the rate of inflation and the real rate of

---

[8] Some observers claim that the real rate of interest has been high in recent years because the real rate contains a risk premium to account for the increased volatility of interest rates since October 1979, when the Fed announced that it would devote more attention to controlling the money supply and less to controlling the interest rate.

interest should be considered separately. Since there has been even greater volatility in the rate of inflation than in the real rate of interest, an accurate determination of the rate of inflation is an important part of an accurate determination of the nominal rate of interest.

Synthesis. The three different theories or rationales of the level of interest rates that were described in this section are not exclusive but, rather, are compatible and complementary ways of considering interest-rate determination. The liquidity preference theory, which considers the supply and demand for money, and the loanable funds theory, which considers the supply of and demand for loanable funds, are equivalent ways of considering interest-rate determination. A model that included both money and loanable funds would show that these two theories would determine the same interest rate. The impact of the inflation and the real rate of interest theory on the level of interest rates is complementary to the other two explanations by introducing the effect of inflation to either. Thus the three theories described in this section should be viewed as a unified approach to interest-rate determination.

Tone of the market. The factors discussed above that affect interest rates—the supply and demand for money, the supply and demand for funds, and the inflation rate—are objective in nature. These fundamental factors undoubtedly determine the level of interest rates after some lag. But there is another type of influence on interest rates that responds very quickly—within hours, or even minutes, and at times includes subjective as well as objective factors—this type of influence is called the tone of the market.

The tone of the market determines the very short-run direction and volatility of interest rates and is due to actions by professionals in the interest-rate markets, mainly dealers in government securities, corporate bonds, and municipal bonds, and also large institutional investors in these securities. The professionals continually monitor the nation's and the world's economic, political, and social condition and quickly assess their likely impacts on interest rates. In particular, they watch for changes in the condition of the nation's economic goals, inflation, unemployment, economic growth, and balance of payments and watch for changes in economic policies, monetary policy, and fiscal policy. Even more specifically, they monitor the volume of new issues of Treasury, corporate, and municipal debt that will be brought to the market in the next few days and weeks, and Fed open-market operations and monetary policy.

By monitoring and quickly assessing the likely impact of these factors on interest rates, the professionals are able to rapidly alter their portfolio strategies in view of new information. If dealers and portfolio managers expect interest rates to increase, they reduce the size of their portfolio to avoid losses, thus lowering the demand for securities and increasing interest rates. In response to the same expectations, they may reduce their holdings of long-term securities but increase their holdings of short-term securities, thus increasing long-term rates relative to short-term rates, a normal phenomenon during times of rising interest rates. Through these portfolio activities, the expectation that interest rates will rise actually causes interest rates to rise, at least for a short period of time. If interest rates are expected to decrease, the opposite will occur.

At times professionals may respond not only to recent information but to expectations or anticipations of future information. Operating on the basis of future information is more subjective than operating after the release of new information. And at times the psychology of the market may be counter to the fundamental factors: Professionals may expect future information that will reverse interest-rate trends based on recently available data.

The tone of the market, whether determined by objective (fundamental) or subjective (psychological) factors, affects interest rates very quickly. And activities by professionals that set the tone of the market by quickly translating new information or expectations of future information into present interest-rate changes add to the efficiency of the financial markets.

The following quote from *The Wall Street Journal* indicates the nature and importance of the tone of the market:

Bond prices swung widely as speculators stepped up their involvement in the credit markets.

The Treasury recently offered 8⅜ percent bonds of 2008, for example opened at 99^{22}/32 bid, 99^{24}/32 asked, traded as high as 100 bid, 100^{4}/32 asked only to finish the session at their opening levels.

The earlier firming came as dealers purchased inventory for possible mark-ups in any subsequent resumption of the strong price rally of the past two weeks.

The Structures of Interest Rates

It is often asked what determines or affects "the" interest rate as if there were a single interest rate. However, from the financial markets it is obvious that there is not one but several interest rates. And although these interest rates may move, in general, in the same direction at the same time, the amounts of their movements and at times even the direction of their movements may differ substantially. Thus the spreads, or differences, between interest rates vary. These observations are illustrated by Exhibit 13.

This section discusses the factors that tend to make interest rates differ among themselves. These factors are often the basis for the "structures" of interest rates. There are three different structures of interest rates, and even if securities are identical in every other respect, their

EXHIBIT 13   Plot of Interest Rates

MONEY MARKET RATES

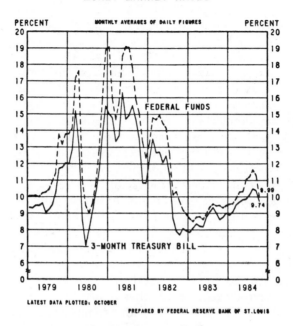

PREPARED BY FEDERAL RESERVE BANK OF ST.LOUIS

LONG-TERM INTEREST RATES

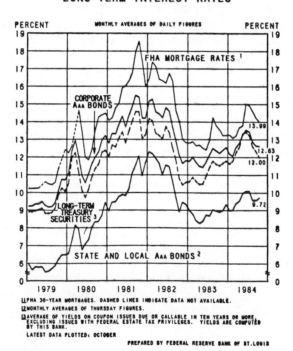

PREPARED BY FEDERAL RESERVE BANK OF ST.LOUIS

SOURCE: *Monetary Trends*, Federal Reserve Bank of St. Louis

interest rates may differ because of maturity, credit risk, and taxability. These three structures of interest rates are discussed below.

Maturity structure (term structure) of interest rates.[9]   This section considers the relationship between a security's interest rate and its term to maturity. This relationship is usually referred to as the maturity structure or term structure of interest rates. A common analytical construct in this context is the yield curve (or term-structure curve), which is a curve illustrating the relationship between the interest rate and the maturity of securities that are identical in every way other than maturity.

There are three distinct explanations of the relationship between the maturities of securities and their interest rates.

Liquidity hypothesis.   Although there are several aspects to a security's liquidity, the major aspect is the security's potential for capital gain or loss, often called market risk. The major determinant of a security's market risk is its maturity, since the longer the security's maturity, the greater the price change for a given change in its interest rate. For example, the prices of Treasury bonds are more volatile than the prices of Treasury bills.

Since there is a trade-off between the risk and the return on a security, investors typically require a higher return to invest in a security with higher risk. Because a security with a longer maturity has greater market risk and, for this reason, less liquidity, interest rates should increase with maturity as a compensation to investors. This relationship between the level of interest rates and the maturity of a security is called the liquidity preference hypothesis and is illustrated in Exhibit 14. This hypothesis does not purport to be a complete explanation of the term structure of interest rates, but only a complement to the other explanations described below.

Expectations hypothesis.   The expectations hypothesis begins with a premise considered in a preceding section, that lenders desire to maximize their return from providing funds and borrowers desire to minimize their cost of borrowing funds. However, unlike the preceding discussion, the expectations hypothesis explicitly considers how lenders and borrowers attain their objectives over a period of time rather than just at any moment in time.

To consider the temporal aspect of maximizing investment return and minimizing borrowing cost and how these decisions affect the relationship between interest rates and maturities, consider a two-period planning horizon. Consider each period to be one year, although it could be any other discrete period of time. A lender considering strategy over this two-period planning horizon has two alternatives—either to purchase a security with a maturity equal to the two periods or purchase

---

[9] For a more detailed discussion of this subject, see Chapter 53.

EXHIBIT 14   Liquidity Preference: The Relationship between the Level of Interest Rates and Maturity

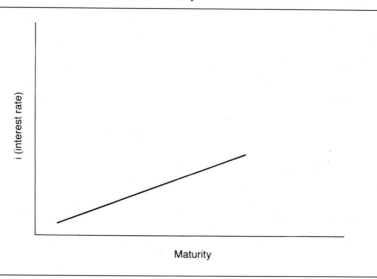

a security with a one-period maturity with the intention of reinvesting for an additional period at the end of the first period. The lender's decision will depend on a comparison of the currently available two-period interest rate with the average of the currently available one-period rate and the expected one-period rate, one period hence. Obviously, the lender will select the strategy with the higher anticipated return.

The borrower who is planning over the same two-period horizon is also faced with two alternatives—either to issue a security with a two-period maturity or to issue a one-period security with the intention of issuing another one-period security, one period hence. The borrower's decision will be based on the total cost of funds over the two periods. If the two-period interest rate is less than the average of the current one-period rate and the one-period rate expected one period hence, then the borrower will issue a two-period security. Otherwise, the borrower will sequentially issue two, one-period securities.

The decisions made separately by lenders and borrowers will affect the relative interest rates over the two-period horizon. For example, if the two-period interest rate exceeds the average of the one-period rate and the expected one-period rate one period hence, then all lenders would choose to invest for two periods and all borrowers would sequentially issue two, one-period securities. As a consequence, there would be an excess supply of funds in the two-period market, causing the two-period interest rate to decrease, and an excess demand for funds in the one-period market, causing the one-period interest rate to increase. According to the expectations hypothesis, the interest rates will continue to change until the current two-period rate equals the effective rate for two sequential one-period securities. Under this circumstance, both borrowers and lenders will be indifferent between a single two-period transaction and two sequential one-period transactions, and thus interest rates will be in equilibrium.

The expectations hypothesis is also applicable to a larger number of periods. However, the basic conclusion that the current long-term rate should equal the average of the current and expected future short-term rates remains the same. As a result, borrowers and lenders will be indifferent between relying on a long-term security or a series of short-term securities.

The expectations hypothesis does not imply that all interest rates will be equal, only that the average of the observed and anticipated short-term rates will equal the long-term rate. If interest rates are expected to remain stable, however, so that future short-term rates are expected to equal the currently observed short-term rate, then current interest rates across all maturities will be equal, as illustrated by the yield curve shown in Exhibit 15. This is a "flat" yield curve.

EXHIBIT 15 Flat Yield Curve

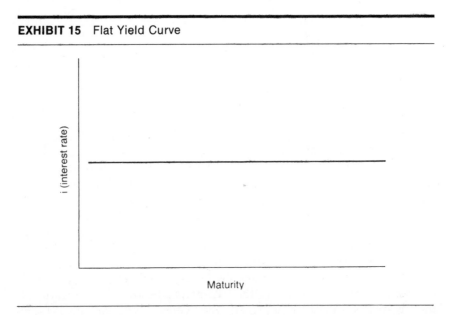

If rates are expected to increase, the shape of the yield curve will be different. With an anticipated increase in interest rates, lenders will purchase short-term securities so that they can earn the higher anticipated rate after their initial short-term-maturity security matures and they subsequently reinvest in another short-term security at a higher rate, and also so that they avoid the capital losses that longer-term securities would incur when interest rates rise. Borrowers, on the other hand, would be induced to issue long-term securities in order to lock in the currently low rates for a long period of time, thereby eliminating the need for issuing new securities at the higher rates. These actions of lenders and borrowers would result in an excess supply of short-term funds, causing short-term rates to decrease, and an excess demand for long-term funds, causing short-term rates to increase. These pressures on short- and long-term interest rates would produce an upward-sloping yield curve as illustrated in Exhibit 16.

EXHIBIT 16   Upward-Sloping Yield Curve

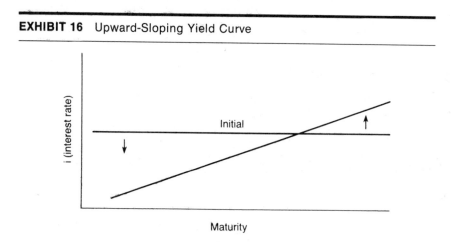

According to the expectations hypothesis, these pressures on interest rates will continue until, again, the current long-term interest rate equals the average of the current and expected short-term rates. For example, if the current one-year rate is 12 percent, the expected one-year rate one year hence is 13 percent, and the expected one-year rate two years hence is 14 percent, then the current two-year rate would be 12.5 percent, and the current three-year rate should be the average of these three one-year rates, 13 percent.[10] Thus the yield curve based on the current one-year, two-year, and three-year rates would be upward sloping.

The explanation is similar if interest rates are expected to decrease in the future. In this case, lenders would purchase only long-term securities in an attempt to lock in currently high interest rates before rates decrease and to reap the capital gain that would result from the decrease

---

[10] This example ignores the effect of compound interest.

in interest rates. Borrowers, on the other hand, would issue only short-term securities, thereby paying currently high rates for a short period of time with the expectation of subsequently issuing longer term securities when rates decrease. Consequently, there would be an excess supply of funds in the long-term market and an excess demand for funds in the short-term market, which would cause long-term interest rates to decrease and short-term interest rates to increase. These pressures on interest rates would result in a downward-sloping, or inverted, yield curve as illustrated in Exhibit 17.

EXHIBIT 17 Downward-Sloping Yield Curve

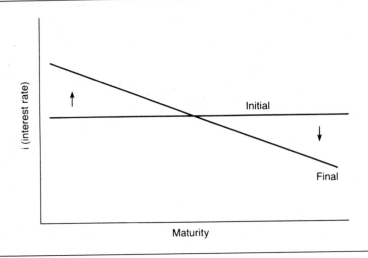

As indicated above, the liquidity hypothesis is not intended to be a complete explanation of the term structure of interest rates. Rather it is intended to supplement the expectations hypothesis. The combined effects of the liquidity hypothesis and the expectations hypothesis are shown in Exhibit 18.

The expectations hypothesis produces a horizontal yield curve when interest rates are normal, an upward-sloping yield curve when interest rates are low, and a downward-sloping yield curve when interest rates are high. Supplementing the expectations hypothesis with the liquidity hypothesis, which always predicts an upward-sloping yield curve, provides an upward bias to a yield curve based only on the expectations hypothesis. Indeed upward-sloping yield curves have historically been the most frequently observed, and for this reason upward-sloping yield curves are frequently referred to as normal yield curves. During recessionary periods, when interest rates are low and are ex-

EXHIBIT 18   Expectations Hypothesis plus Liquidity Hypothesis

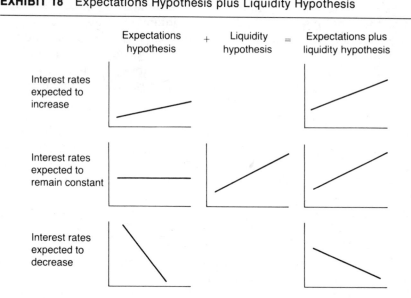

pected to increase, the yield curve has a steep upward slope. When the economy is strong, credit is tight, and interest rates are high, however, downward-sloping yield curves are observed. Both observations are consistent with the expectations hypothesis.

Segmentation hypothesis. The basis for the segmentation hypothesis is the antithesis of the basis for the expectations hypothesis. Whereas the expectations hypothesis assumes that both borrowers and lenders are able to alter the maturity structure of their portfolios, each group shifting among the maturities of their respective borrowings or investments, the segmentation hypothesis assumes that both borrowers and lenders are constrained to particular segments of the maturity spectrum for institutional and legal reasons. For such market participants, shifting among maturities is not feasible, and therefore various maturity securities are not considered to be substitutes for one another, independent of the levels of the various interest rates.

In practice, there are numerous financial market participants whose borrowings or investments are, for a variety of reasons, constrained to only one portion of the maturity spectrum. For example, pension fund managers and insurance companies have a relatively small amount of their investments in short-maturity securities, whereas commercial banks and thrifts have a relatively small amount of their investments in long-term bonds.

If indeed the market is segmented so that borrowers and lenders active in the market for one maturity are unlikely to be active in the market for any other maturity, then the interest rate associated with a particular maturity would have to be the result of the supply and demand pressures for only that maturity. Consequently, a change in supply and demand factors in one maturity will affect the interest rate for only that maturity and have no impact on the interest rate for any other maturity.

The segmentation hypothesis and the expectations hypothesis are competing, incompatible explanations of the relationship between interest rates and maturities on securities. For technical reasons, resolving which is the more correct explanation of the relationship is an intractable problem. In reality there are probably some elements of both theories that are correct while neither one is completely correct in explaining the relationship. In particular, it is unlikely that all borrowers and lenders are locked into one portion of the available maturity structure and unable to switch to another when interest rates dictate. Alternatively, there are undoubtedly some market participants who are restricted to particular segments of the maturity structure.

Either hypothesis could provide correct conclusions without the hypothesis holding in its extreme version. For example, for the expectations hypothesis to apply, not all borrowers and lenders have to be able to shift among maturities on the basis of relative interest rates, only enough to affect the relative interest rates. Similarly, for the segmentation hypothesis to apply, not all borrowers and lenders have to be restricted to particular segments of the maturity range, only enough so that the interest rates associated with each maturity segment are influenced by different supply-and-demand considerations. Observers of debt markets have noted characteristics supportive of both hypotheses in their less-than-extreme versions. However, most observers tend to support the expectations hypothesis complemented by the liquidity hypothesis as the dominant explanation for the observed relationship between interest rates and maturity.

The combined expectations-hypothesis/liquidity-hypothesis description of the maturity structure of interest rates can be applied to the actual behavior of the financial markets. The conclusions that can be drawn from a combination of the expectations hypothesis and the liquidity-preference hypothesis are that when the level of interest rates is normal the yield curve will have a slight upward slope—the long-term rates will be slightly greater than short-term rates. When the general level of interest rates is low, the term structure will have a steeper upward slope. Finally, when the level of interest rates is high, the term structure will have a downward slope. Pragmatically, the segmentation hypothesis adds nothing that either contradicts or supports this observation.

Empirical observations support conclusions derived from the expectations and the liquidity hypotheses. Exhibits 19, 20, and 21 show yield curves on different dates with various slopes. Note that the general level of interest rates is higher for the downward-sloping yield curve.

EXHIBIT 19   Yield Curve—November 29, 1984

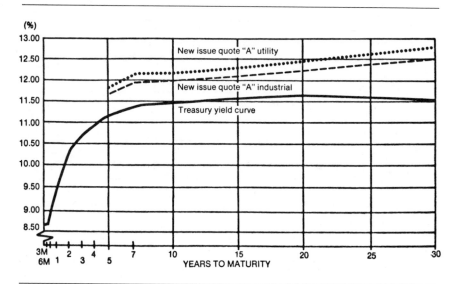

SOURCE: Paine, Webber Fixed Income Research.

Credit risk.   The two major characteristics of a security are return and risk. In turn, there are two major types of risk, market risk and credit risk. Market risk refers to the volatility of the price of a security due to changes in the general level of interest rates. The market risk of a security is thus determined primarily by its maturity, since the longer the maturity, the greater the price change of the security for a given magnitude of interest-rate change in the opposite direction. Thus the term structure of interest rates relates to the market risk of a security. This section considers the other type of risk, credit risk.

The credit risk of a security is a measure of the likelihood that the issuer of the security, the borrower, will be unable to pay the interest or principal on the security when due. Credit risk is thus a measure of the creditworthiness of the issuer of the security. Federal securities, that is, issues of the U.S. Department of the Treasury, have the lowest credit risk. Federal agencies are perceived to have the next lowest credit risk because they are backed by the federal government. Corporate securities are rated lower than federal agencies with respect to credit risk. The

EXHIBIT 20 Yield Curve—September 3, 1981

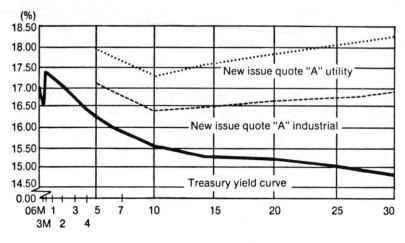

YEARS TO MATURITY

SOURCE: Paine, Webber Fixed Income Research.

EXHIBIT 21 Yield Curve—August 5, 1982

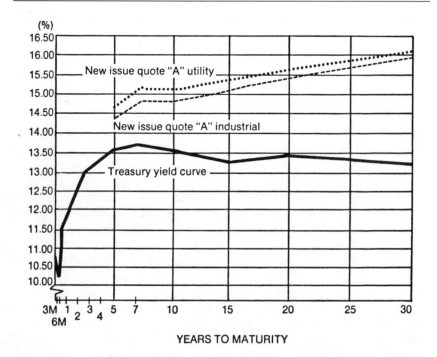

YEARS TO MATURITY

SOURCE: Paine, Webber Fixed Income Research.

relative credit risks of long-term corporate securities are rated by several private financial corporations. Exhibit 22 describes the rating categories of the two major ones—Moody's and Standard & Poor's.

EXHIBIT 22 Corporate Bond Rating Categories*

Standard & Poor's Rating Categories†	Description
AAA (Aaa)	Bonds rated AAA have the highest rating assigned by Standard & Poor's to a debt obligation. Capacity to pay interest and repay principal is extremely strong.
AA (Aa)	Bonds rated AA have a very strong capacity to pay interest and repay principal and differ from the highest rated issues only in small degree.
A (A)	Bonds rated A have a strong capacity to pay interest and repay principal, although they are somewhat more susceptible to the adverse effects of changes in circumstances and economic conditions than bonds in higher rated categories.
BBB (Baa)	Bonds rated BBB are regarded as having an adequate capacity to pay interest and repay principal. Whereas they normally exhibit adequate protection parameters, adverse economic conditions or changing circumstances are more likely to lead to a weakened capacity to pay interest and repay principal for bonds in this category than for bonds in higher rated categories.
BB (Ba) B (B) CCC (CCa) CC (Ca)	Bonds rated BB, B, CCC and CC are regarded, on balance, as predominantly speculative with respect to capacity to pay interest and repay principal in accordance with the terms of the obligation. BB indicates the lowest degree of speculation and CC the highest degree of speculation. While such bonds will likely have some quality and protective characteristics, these are outweighed by large uncertainties or major risk exposures to adverse conditions.
C	The rating C is reserved for income bonds on which no interest is being paid.
D	Bonds rated D are in default, and payment of interest and/or repayment of principal is in arrears.
Plus(+) or minus(−):	The ratings from ''AA'' to ''B'' may be modified by the addition of a plus or minus sign to show relative standing within the major rating categories.

---

  * These Standard & Poor's corporate bond rating categories also apply to municipal bonds.
  † The ratings in parentheses refer to the corresponding ratings of Moody's Investors Service, Inc.
  SOURCE: Standard & Poor's Corporation.

Although the creditworthiness of different issuers of bonds affect the bonds' credit risk, even different bonds of the same issuer can have different credit risk depending on the characteristics of the specific bond. For example, a debenture, an unsecured bond, may have a higher credit risk than a bond that is collateralized by real or financial assets or a sinking-fund bond of the same issuer.

Some money market instruments are also rated by private financial corporations.[11] Both Standard & Poor's and Moody's rate commercial paper issues. For example, the grades usually acceptable to commercial paper investors are Standard & Poor's A–1, A–2, and A–3 and Moody's Prime–1, Prime–2, and Prime–3. Exhibit 23 provides descriptions of the

---

EXHIBIT 23 Standard & Poor's Commercial Paper Rating Definitions

Rating Category	Description
A	Issues assigned this highest rating are regarded as having the greatest capacity for timely payment. Issues in this category are delineated with the numbers 1, 2, and 3 to indicate the relative degree of safety.
A–1	This designation indicates that the degree of safety regarding timely payment is either overwhelming or very strong. Those issues determined to possess overwhelming safety characteristics will be denoted with a plus (+) sign designation.
A–2	Capacity for timely payment on issues with this designation is strong. However, the relative degree of safety is not as high as for issues designated "A–1."
A–3	Issues carrying this designation have a satisfactory capacity for timely payment. They are, however, somewhat more vulnerable to the adverse effects of changes in circumstances than obligations carrying the higher designations.
B	Issues rated "B" are regarded as having only an adequate capacity for timely payment. However, such capacity may be damaged by changing conditions or short-term adversities.
C	This rating is assigned to short-term debt obligations with a doubtful capacity for payment.
D	This rating indicates that the issue is either in default or is expected to be in default upon maturity.

Standard & Poor's commercial paper rating categories. However, other money market instruments, such as domestic bank negotiable certificates of deposit (CDs), are not rated by these agencies.

Interest rates are higher for securities with greater credit risk, since investors have to be compensated for the additional risk. Consequently, the interest rate on a Treasury security is less than that on a AAA corporate security, which is in turn less than that on an A corporate security, all with the same maturity. These spreads tend to widen when interest rates are high and to narrow when interest rates are low. This is consistent with a "flight to quality," an increased preference by investors for low credit-risk instruments when interest rates are high and investors perceive low credit-risk borrowers as vulnerable. Money mar-

---

[11] Money market instruments are described in Chapter 7.

ket spreads similarly show a widening when interest rates are high and a narrowing when interest rates are low, that is, a flight to quality at high interest rates.

The credit-risk structure of interest rates explains variations in the interest rates on various securities of the same maturity due to differences in the credit risk of the issuers and issues. In addition, the size of the spreads between securities with high credit risk and low credit risk varies with the level of interest rates.

Taxability structure. There are three aspects of taxability that cause interest rates on different securities to differ at a specific time.

Tax-exempt municipals. The coupon payments on Treasury and corporate bonds are subject to federal income tax. Consequently, the aftertax yield on Treasury and corporate bonds is less than the coupon yield by an amount determined by the bondholder's tax bracket. The federal government does not tax the coupon payment on state and local securities.[12] Since municipal securities are tax exempt, their aftertax yield is the same as their pretax yield. Because investors are concerned with aftertax rather than pretax yields, municipal securities can be issued with lower coupons than the coupons on similar Treasury or corporate securities. For example, to an investor in the 30 percent tax bracket, a 7 percent municipal security selling at par has the same aftertax yield as a 10 percent Treasury or corporate security.

Thus, municipal bond interest rates differ from the interest rates on Treasury and corporate bonds because of the difference in taxability. The yield spread is always positive, that is, the yield on Treasury bonds is higher than the yield on municipal bonds.

The magnitude of the spread changes over the interest-rate cycle for two reasons. First, municipal bonds have a higher credit risk than Treasury bonds, and the phenomenon related to the flight to quality discussed in the last section is applicable. Here the flight to quality is from municipals to Treasuries when interest rates are high. In this case, however, since the rate on Treasury bonds is higher than the rate on municipal bonds, the flight to Treasury bonds during times of high interest rates tends to narrow the spread.

In addition, the spread between Treasury and municipal bond yields changes over the interest-rate cycle for reasons of taxability. The spread is the absolute difference between the Treasury and the municipal bond interest rates. However, the tax rate as it is applied to the coupon on Treasury securities has a relative or proportional effect. Thus, for example, to an investor in the 50 percent tax bracket a 4 percent

---

[12] State and local governments cannot tax the coupon payments of federal securities, but this exemption is not as important as the federal exemption on state and local government securities because the income tax rates of state and local governments are lower than federal income tax rates.

municipal security has the same aftertax yield as an 8 percent Treasury security, for a spread of 4 percent. However, a 6 percent municipal security has the same aftertax yield as a 12 percent Treasury security, for a spread of 6 percent. Similarly, an 8 percent municipal security has the same aftertax yield as a 16 percent Treasury security, for a spread of 8 percent. Thus, because of the proportional nature of the federal income tax structure, the absolute spread between Treasury and municipal bonds varies over the interest-rate cycle, being larger when interest rates are high and smaller when interest rates are low.

Overall, since due to the flight to quality the spread between Treasury and municipal bonds narrows when interest rates are high, and due to the proportional nature of the income tax, the spread widens when interest rates are high. Thus the two effects are countervailing. Based on the historical Treasury bond/municipal bond interest-rate spreads, the latter effect of interest rates on the spread dominates the former effect.

The spread between municipal and Treasury bonds may also vary structurally due to changes in tax legislation that affect the level of the personal income tax and the attractiveness of other tax shelters that compete with municipal securities as tax-reducing investments.

Level of coupon. A second aspect of taxability also causes interest rates among different securities, even of the same issuer and maturity, to differ *for bonds issued on or before July 18, 1984.* This aspect is the magnitude of the coupon of the security.

As explained in Chapter 3, although coupon payments on Treasury and corporate bonds are taxed at the ordinary income tax rate, capital gains are taxed at a preferential tax rate. If a bond is acquired after July 22, 1984 and held for more than six months, the long-term capital gains tax, which is 40 percent of the personal income tax rate, will apply. The holding period to qualify for a long-term capital gain for a bond purchased on or before July 22, 1984 is more than one year. For a bond issued on or before July 18, 1984 and held to maturity, therefore, the aftertax value of 1 percent of pretax coupon return is less to an investor than the aftertax value of 1 percent of pretax capital gains. This does not apply to bonds issued after July 18, 1984 that are held to maturity.[13]

The yield-to-maturity of a bond, as it is commonly calculated, includes both the coupon return and the return due to capital gain or loss (the difference between the current market price and the par value of the bond) on an annual basis as if the security were held to maturity. If, for example, a 30-year security with an $80 coupon is selling for $1,000, its 8 percent yield-to-maturity is entirely due to the coupon return. If another

---

[13] The rules concerning capital gain treatment briefly discussed here do not apply to original issue discount bonds. These rules are discussed in Chapter 3.

30-year security with a $60 coupon issued on or before July 18, 1984, is initially selling for $773.77 for an 8 percent yield-to-maturity, its yield-to-maturity consists of a 7.75 percent coupon return, and the remainder is due to the capital gain over the 30-year life. Since this low-coupon "discount security" (a security selling for less than its maturity value of $1,000) has a portion of its return due to capital gains, which is taxed at a lower rate, the aftertax return on the low-coupon discount bond is greater than that of the high-coupon bond selling at "par" (its maturity value of $1,000). Therefore, the price of the discount bond will be bid up, and thus the yield-to-maturity at its new actual trading price will be somewhat less than the 8 percent yield on the par bond. The lower yield on the discount bond will compensate for its more favorable tax treatment.[14] Thus, low-coupon discount bonds normally sell at a yield somewhat lower than high-coupon bonds selling at par or at a premium (at a price greater than its maturity value) or even at a smaller discount because of this tax advantage. The yield spread, almost without exception, is positive (the yield on the high-coupon bond is greater than the yield on the low-coupon bond).

Flower bonds. Several Treasury bonds issued during the 1950s and early 1960s exhibit an attractive tax feature. These bonds, known as flower bonds, are acceptable *at par* in payment of federal estate taxes when owned by the decedent at death.[15] These bonds were issued with low coupons. Due to this tax advantage, the (pretax) yields on these bonds are lower than on other Treasury bonds without the estate-tax eligibility provision.

Interest rate structure: A summary. Factors that affect interest rates tend to affect all interest rates in generally the same way. For this reason, discussions of the determinants of interest rates often seem as if there were a single interest rate. This section provides the transition from the consideration of a single interest rate to the actual multiplicity of interest rates observed in the financial world.

There are three major structures of interest rates that contribute to the multiplicity of interest rates observed: the maturity structure, the credit-risk structure, and the taxability structure. There are, in addition, other factors that cause differences in interest rates. One such factor is the liquidity of the security, often measured by the size of the bid/ask spread (the smaller the spread, the more liquid the security). The liquidity of a security may depend on the size of the original issue or the time

---

[14] If the bond had been issued after July 22, 1984, the entire appreciation realized at maturity would be treated as ordinary income. See Chapter 3. Also note that at the time of this writing, Congress is considering the elimination of the favorable capital gains tax treatment.

[15] See Chapter 8 for the conditions imposed by the Treasury to use flower bonds to pay federal estate taxes.

since the original issue. Securities tend to be less liquid if the original-issue size was small and as the time since original issue increases. These aspects of liquidity supplement the market-risk aspect discussed above.

The fundamental factors that affect these three structures, and changes in the relationships among interest rates on the basis of these structures over the interest-rate cycle, are discussed in this section.

Overview of Interest-Rate Determination

Four potentially exclusive rationales for determining the level of "the" interest rate: liquidity preference, loanable funds, inflation and the real rate of interest, and the tone of the market have been discussed. The perspective was on the factors that affect the general level of interest rates at a specific time, not on the differences among various interest rates at a specific time. We then discussed the structures of interest rates, the factors that tend to, given the general level of interest rates, affect the differences among specific interest rates at a specific time. As discussed, the three major factors are the maturity, the credit risk, and the taxability of the specific security. Now we shall integrate these various perspectives on interest-rate determination.

Most models of interest-rate behavior, whether used for explaining past interest-rate behavior or forecasting future interest-rate behavior, and whether they are judgmental or econometric models, incorporate elements of the liquidity preference, loanable funds, and inflation and the real rate of interest rationales. Thus these three rationales are viewed as complimentary rather than competitive as explanations for interest-rate behavior. There are, however, some differences in the applicability of these three rationales and also the tone of the market rationale depending on whether the short-run or long-run responses of interest rates are being considered and whether short-term or long-term interest rates are being considered.

Liquidity preference is an important explanation of very short-run changes in interest rates, particularly changes in short-term interest rates in response to changes in the money supply. Money supply announcements made by the Federal Reserve Bank of New York every week are closely watched, and the financial markets respond quickly to them.

The nature of the response of interest rates, particularly short-term interest rates, to money supply announcements has changed significantly during the last decade. If it was announced a decade ago that money supply had increased significantly, interest rates declined and vice versa, as expected by the liquidity preference rationale. However, today when an announcement is made that money supply has increased significantly, interest rates usually increase rather than decrease, and vice versa. There are two reasons for this change in response.

First, since the mid-1970s the Federal Reserve System has, as an important part of its implementation of monetary policy, set ranges for future money-supply growth. It then conducts monetary policy so that the actual money-supply growth fits within these ranges. Thus an announcement of a large increase in the money supply is now interpreted by the markets as requiring the Federal Reserve System to subsequently tighten money-supply growth to keep the money-supply growth within the announced ranges. The markets, thus anticipating a subsequent decline in money-supply growth, respond by making interest rates increase in response to the expected tightening. Here again the liquidity preference rationale is operable, but now the market responds to expectations of subsequent money-supply growth rather than to the announcement of the past money-supply growth.

The second reason for the change in response is that inflation has become a more important force in determining interest rates. In view of the quantity theory of money, there is an important relationship between money supply and inflation. Thus an announcement of a high growth in the money supply often causes market participants to conclude that inflation will accelerate, at least if this money-supply growth rate continues, thus causing interest rates to increase due to the inflation and real rate of interest rationale. For both of these reasons, interest rates now often increase rather than decrease when there is an announcement of an increase in the money supply.

Essentially, all explanations of the level of interest rates include some measure of the money supply as a determinant, particularly for short-term interest rates, and particularly for short-run changes. The liquidity preference rationale, however, is also used for determining the level of interest rates on a longer term basis. This use is implemented, as discussed above, in the context of the quantity theory of money: $M \times V = P \times Y$. By forecasting a likely growth in the money supply, M, and a likely range of increases in real GNP, Y, an assumption about the likely range of inflation, P, can be made from the quantity theory. From this rate of inflation and an assumption about the real rate of interest, the nominal rate of interest can be determined. This conceptual construction obviously relies jointly on the liquidity preference and the inflation and real rate of interest rationales of interest-rate determination.

The loanable funds rationale is typically used to explain and forecast interest rates on a long-term basis and applies, in general, to both long- and short-term interest rates. By developing a taxonomy of the likely sources and uses of funds over a period of time, as provided above, and including an assumption about changes in the money supply, a forecast of potential imbalances between the supply and demand for funds can be made. Projected imbalances of supply over demand are then used as the basis for forecasting a decrease in interest rates and of demand over supply for forecasting an increase in interest rates.

It is in this context that crowding out (borrowing by the federal government sector, which makes borrowing by the private sector more expensive or impossible) is considered. In addition, increased borrowing by the business or consumer sectors put upward pressures on interest rates, and vice versa. In the loanable funds context, short- and long-term sources and uses of funds are typically aggregated, thus implicitly assuming substitutability among securities of various maturities.

With the higher levels of inflation seen in the late 1970s and early 1980s, the inflation and real rate of interest rationale has become very important in explaining the nominal level of interest rates. As discussed, although they are attributable both to variations in inflation and variations in the real rate of interest, variations in the nominal rate of interest are more attributable to the former than the latter. Thus, the real rate of interest might vary over a range of from −1 percent to 4 percent, and inflation might vary over a range of 5 percent to 15 percent. Therefore, including a measure of inflation in an explanation for the general level of interest rates is essential.

However, it is more difficult to include an accurate measure of the determinants of the real rate of interest. In general, the real rate of interest tends to vary over the business cycle, being high during periods of prosperity and low during periods of recession. Most explanations of the general level of interest rates include inflation explicitly but do not consider the real rate of interest explicitly.

Thus most explanations of the general level of interest rates include elements of the liquidity preference, loanable funds, and the inflation and real rate of interest rationales, although there are some differences in emphasis depending on whether short-term or long-term interest rates and whether short-term changes or long-term changes in the rates are being considered. The "tone of the market" rationale should also be considered in determining interest rates, although typically only for very short run changes and mainly in the short-term interest rates. Therefore models that forecast quarterly interest rates often do not include the tone of the market.

Having determined the general level of interest rates, or "the" interest rate, by the methods summarized above, consideration can be given to determining specific interest rates on specific securities. To make this determination, given the general level of interest rates, the maturity, the identity of the issuer, and the taxability of the specific security must be considered—that is, the interest rate on the specific security must be considered with respect to the three structures of interest rates discussed above. In relating a specific interest rate to the general level of interest rates, two issues must be considered: (1) the normal spread between the specific interest rate and an interest rate reflective of the general level of interest rates, such as the 91-day Treasury bill rate or the long-term Treasury bond rate, and (2) variations in the magnitude in this spread over the interest-rate cycle.

The conclusions of the three maturity structures of interest rates are as follows. When the level of interest rates is low, interest rates increase with maturity (the term structure of interest rate curve has a positive slope). And when the level of interest rates is high, interest rates decrease with maturity (the term structure of interest rate curve has a negative slope). Thus short-term interest rates vary through a much wider range than the long-term interest rates, as illustrated in Exhibit 24.

EXHIBIT 24   Interest-Rate Variability by Maturity

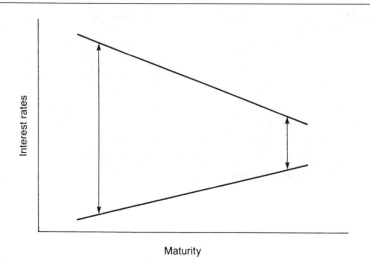

Maturity

And thus the spread between short-term and long-term interest rates (long term minus short term) varies considerably over the interest-rate cycle and becomes less positive (or more negative) as interest rates increase.

With respect to the identity of the issuer, the greater the credit risk of the issuer, the higher the interest rate on the security. It is in this regard that Treasury securities are the benchmark for interest rates. The Treasury has the lowest credit risk of any issuer, and thus Treasury securities have the lowest adjustment for credit risk. Different issues of the same issuer may also have different credit risks due to the nature of the securities. The spread between high credit-risk interest rates and low credit-risk interest rates (high credit risk minus low credit risk) increases with the level of interest rates, due to a "flight to quality" when interest rates are high.

Finally, the taxability of the issue must be considered. The most important aspect of taxability relates to municipal securities whose coupons are exempt from the federal income tax. Due to this tax exemption, actual pretax interest rates on municipals are lower than on Treasury and corporate securities. Because taxes are on a relative or proportionate basis, the spread between Treasury and municipal securities (Treasury rate minus municipal rate) widens (narrows) as the level of interest rates increases (decreases).

Another aspect of taxability at the time of this writing relates to the magnitude of the coupon, which determines the degree of the discount or the premium of a security, since coupon income is taxed as personal income and capital appreciation as capital gains. Thus the higher the coupon on a security, the higher will be its interest rate to compensate for the greater tax liability. Finally, flower bonds have lower yields due to their estate-tax advantages.

Overall, the determination of interest rates occurs in two steps. First, the general level of interest rates is determined by the eclectic combination of the methods described above. Second, the appropriate spread between the interest rate on the specific security being considered and the general level of interest rates is determined by considering the factors that affect the structures of interest rates. The benchmark interest rate used in such spread analysis is typically the interest rate on a U.S. Treasury debt security.

PART 2

Securities and Instruments

7

Money Market Instruments

Marcia Stigum, Ph.D.
Stigum & Associates, New York

In this chapter we examine money market instruments (negotiable short-term debt securities) in which individuals and business firms invest. Treasury bills, issued by the U.S. Treasury, are the most important class of such securities in the United States, but there are others: commercial paper, bankers' acceptances, and negotiable certificates of deposit. Short-term municipal obligations are discussed in Chapter 12.

OVERVIEW OF THE MONEY MARKET

The U.S. money market is a huge and significant part of the nation's financial system in which banks and other participants trade hundreds of billions of dollars every working day. Where those billions go and the prices at which they are traded affect how the U.S. government finances its debt, how business finances its expansion, and how consumers choose to spend or save.

The money market is a wholesale market for low-risk, highly liquid, short-term IOUs. It is a market for various sorts of debt securities rather than equities. The stock in trade of the market includes a large chunk of the U.S. Treasury's debt and billions of dollars worth of federal agency securities, negotiable bank certificates of deposit, bankers' acceptances, municipal notes, and commercial paper. Within the confines of the money market each day, banks, both domestic and foreign, actively trade in multimillion-dollar blocks, billions of dollars of federal funds and Eurodollars; and banks and nonbank dealers are each day the recipients of billions of dollars of secured loans through the *repo market*. State and municipal governments also finance part of their activities in this market.

The money market efficiently accomplishes vital functions every day. One function is shifting vast sums of money between banks. This shifting is required because the major money market banks need a lot more funds than they obtain in deposits, and many smaller banks have more money deposited with them than they can profitably use internally. The money market also provides a means by which the surplus funds of cash-rich corporations and other institutions can be funneled to banks, corporations, and other institutions that need short-term money. In addition, in the money market the U.S. Treasury can fund huge quantities of debt with ease. And the market provides the Federal Reserve System (also known as the Fed) with an arena in which to carry out open-market operations destined to influence interest rates and the growth of the money supply. The varied activities of money market participants also determine the structure of short-term interest rates, for example, what the yields on Treasury bills of different maturities are and how much commercial paper issuers have to pay to borrow. The latter rate is an important cost to many corporations, and it influences in particular the interest rate that a consumer who buys a car on time will have to pay on the loan. Finally, one might mention that the U.S. money market is becoming increasingly an international short-term capital market.

Anyone who observes the money market soon picks out a number of salient features. First and most obviously, it is not one market but a collection of markets for several distinct and different instruments. What makes it possible to talk about *the* money market is the close interrelationships that link all these markets.

A second salient feature is the numerous and varied cast of participants. Borrowers in the market include foreign and domestic banks, the Treasury, corporations of all types, the Federal Home Loan Banks and other federal agencies, dealers in money market instruments, and many states and municipalities. The lenders include almost all of the above plus insurance companies, pension funds—public and private—and various other financial institutions. And often standing between borrower and lender is one or more of a varied collection of brokers and dealers.

Another key characteristic of the money market is that it is a wholesale market. Trades are big and the people who make them are almost always dealing for the account of some substantial institution. Because of the sums involved, skill is of the utmost importance, and money market participants are skilled at what they do. In effect the market is made by extremely talented specialists in very narrow professional areas. A bill trader extraordinaire may have only vague notions as to what the Euromarket is all about, and the Eurospecialist may be equally vague on other sectors of the market.

Another principal characteristic of the money market is honor.

Every day traders, brokers, investors, and borrowers do hundreds of billions of dollars of business over the phone, and however a trade may appear in retrospect, people do not renege. The motto of the money market is: *My word is my bond.* Of course, because of the pace of the market, mistakes do occur, but no one ever assumes that they are intentional, and mistakes are always ironed out in what seems the fairest way for all concerned.

The most appealing characteristic of the money market is innovation. Compared with our other financial markets, the money market is very unregulated. Someone who wants to launch a new instrument or to try brokering or dealing in a new way in existing instruments *does it.* And when the idea is good, which it often is, a new facet of the market is born.

TREASURY BILLS

Treasury bills (known more familiarly as T bills or bills) represent about 40 percent of the total marketable securities issued by the Treasury. These securities are held widely by financial business firms, nonfinancial corporations, and to some extent, by individuals. Nevertheless, despite their huge volume and wide distribution among different investor groups, T bills were relatively unknown to the average investor until the late 1960s, when the growing disparity between bill yields and savings deposit rates began drawing small investors into the bill market.

All T bills are negotiable, noninterest-bearing securities with an original maturity of one year or less. T bills are currently issued in three-month, six-month and one-year maturities.[1] Bills are currently offered by the Treasury in minimum denominations of $10,000, with multiples of $5,000 thereafter. Bills used to be issued by the Treasury in the form of *bearer certificates.* Accordingly, to prove ownership of a bill, the owner had to produce it. The Treasury and the Federal Reserve System then made it possible to hold bills in *book-entry form.* Since 1977 the Treasury has offered bills *only* in book-entry form.

Bills are always issued at a discount from face value, and the amount of the discount is determined in bill auctions held by the Fed each time the Treasury issues new bills. At maturity, bills are redeemed by the Treasury for full face value. Thus investors in bills earn returns because they receive more for the bills at maturity than they paid for them at issue. This return is treated for federal tax purposes as ordinary interest income and, as such, is subject to full federal taxation at ordinary rates; it is, however, specifically *exempt* from state and local taxation.

---

[1] For tactical debt management purposes, the Treasury occasionally meets cash flow gaps by issuing very short-term "cash management bills."

Yield Calculations for T Bills[2]

To illustrate how T bill yields are calculated, we assume that an investor who participates in an auction of new Treasury *year bills* picks up $1 million of them at 10 percent. What this means is that the Treasury sells the investor $1 million of bills maturing in one year at a price approximately 10 percent below their face value. The "approximately" qualifier takes a little explaining. Offhand one would expect the amount of the discount to be the face value of the securities purchased times the rate of discount times the *fraction of the year* the securities will be outstanding. In our example, the discount calculated this way would equal $1 million times 10 percent times one full year, which amounts to $100,000. That figure, however, is incorrect for two reasons. First, the year bill is outstanding not for a year but for 52 weeks, which is 364 days. Second, the Treasury calculates the discount as if a year had only 360 days. So the fraction of the year for which the security is outstanding is 364/360, and the true discount on the security is:

$$\left(\begin{array}{c} \text{Discount on \$1 million of} \\ \text{year bills issued at 10 percent} \end{array} \right) = \$1,000,000 \times 0.10 \times \frac{364}{360}$$
$$= \$101,111.11$$

Because the Treasury calculates the discount as if the year had 360 days, our investor gets his bills at a discount that exceeds $100,000 even though he invests for only 364 days. The price he pays for his bills equals *face value minus the discount,* i.e.,

$$\left(\begin{array}{c} \text{Price paid for \$1 million of} \\ \text{year bills bought at 10 percent} \end{array} \right) = \$1,000,000 - \$101,111.11$$
$$= \$898,888.89$$

Generalizing from this example, we can construct formulas for calculating both the discount from face value and the price at which T bills will sell, depending on their current maturity and the discount at which they are quoted. Let

$$D = \text{discount from face value}$$
$$F = \text{face value}$$
$$d = \text{rate of discount}$$
$$t = \text{days to maturity}$$
$$P = \text{price}$$

Then

$$D = F \left(\frac{d \times t}{360} \right)$$

---

[2] For a complete description, see Marcia Stigum in collaboration with John Mann, *Money Market Calculations: Yields, Break-Evens, and Arbitrage* (Homewood, Ill.: Dow Jones-Irwin, 1981).

and

$$P = F - D = F\left(1 - \frac{d \times t}{360}\right)$$

Equivalent bond yield. If an investor lent $1 million for one 365-day year and received at the end of the year $100,000 of interest plus the $1 million of principal invested, we would—calculating yield on a *simple interest basis*—say that he had earned 10 percent.[3] Using the same approach—return earned divided by principal invested—to calculate the return earned by our investor who bought a 10 percent year bill, we find that, on a simple interest basis, he earned significantly *more than* 10 percent. Specifically,

$$\left(\begin{array}{c}\text{Return on a simple interest basis on} \\ \text{\$1 million 10 percent year bills held to maturity}\end{array}\right) = \frac{\$101,000.11}{\$898,888.89} \div \frac{364}{365}$$

$$= 11.28 \text{ percent}$$

In this calculation, because the bill matures in 364 days, it is necessary to divide by the fraction of the year for which the bill is outstanding to annualize the rate earned.

Treasury notes and bonds, which—unlike bills—are *interest bearing*, pay the holder interest equal to the face value times the interest (i.e., *coupon*) rate at which they are issued. Thus, an investor who bought $1 million of Treasury notes carrying a 10 percent coupon would receive $100,000 of interest during each year the securities were outstanding.

The way yields on notes and bonds are quoted, 10 percent notes selling at *par* (i.e., face value) would be quoted as offering a 10 percent yield. An investor who bought these notes would, however, have the opportunity to earn more than 10 percent simple interest. The reason is that interest on notes and bonds is paid in semiannual installments, which means that the investor can invest, during the second six months of each year, the first semiannual interest installment.

To illustrate the effect of this on return, consider an investor who buys at issue $1 million of 10 percent Treasury notes. Six months later, he receives $50,000 of interest, which we assume he reinvests at 10 percent. Then at the end of the year, he receives another $50,000 of interest plus interest on the interest he has invested; the latter amounts to $50,000 times 10 percent times the one-half year he earns that interest. Thus, his total dollar return over the year is:

$$\$50,000 + (0.10)(\$50,000)(0.5) + \$50,000 = \$102,500$$

---

[3] By *simple interest* we mean interest paid once a year at the end of the year. There is no compounding as, for example, on a savings account.

and the percentage return that he earns, expressed in terms of simple interest, is

$$\frac{\$102,500}{\$1,000,000} = 10.25 \text{ percent}$$

Note that what is at work here is *compound interest*; any quoted rate of interest yields more dollars of return, and is thus equivalent to a higher simple interest rate, the more frequently interest is paid and the more compounding that can thus occur.

Because return can mean different things depending on the way it is quoted and paid, an investor can meaningfully compare the returns offered by different securities only if these returns are stated on a comparable basis. With respect to *discount* and *coupon* securities, the way yields are made comparable in the money market is by restating yields quoted on a *discount basis*—the basis on which T bills are quoted—in terms of *equivalent bond yield*—the basis on which yields on notes and bonds are quoted.

We calculated above that an investor in a year bill would, on a simple interest basis, earn 11.28 percent. This is slightly higher than the rate he would earn measured on an equivalent bond yield basis. The reason is that equivalent bond yield understates, as noted, the true return on a simple interest basis that the investor in a coupon security would earn if he reinvested interest. When adjustment is made for this understatement, the equivalent bond yield offered by a 10 percent year bill turns out to be something less than 11.28 percent. Specifically, it is 10.98 percent.

The formula for converting yield on a bank discount basis to equivalent bond yield is complicated for discount securities that have a current maturity of longer than six months, but that is no problem for investors and other money market participants because bill yields are always restated on dealers' quote sheets in terms of equivalent bond yield at the *asked* rate (see Exhibit 1).

On bills with a current maturity of six months or less, equivalent bond yield is the simple interest rate yielded by a bill. Let

$$d_b = \text{equivalent bond yield}$$

Then, on a security quoted at the discount rate d, equivalent bond yield is given by

$$d_b = \frac{365 \times d}{360 - (d \times t)}$$

For example, on a three-month bill purchased at 8 percent, equivalent bond yield is

$$d_b = \frac{365 \times 0.08}{360 - (0.08 \times 91)} = 8.28 \text{ percent}$$

EXHIBIT 1 Selected Quotes on U.S. Treasury Bills, October 21, 1982

Billions Outstanding	Days to Maturity	Maturity	Discount (percent) Bid	Discount (percent) Asked	Dollar Price	Equivalent Bond Yield
10.2	3	10/28/82	7.20	7.00	99.942	7.10
10.4	32	11/26/82	7.24	7.14	99.365	7.29
15.9	66	12/30/82	7.52	7.42	98.640	7.63
11.1	87	1/20/83	7.62	7.52	98.183	7.73
10.8	122	2/24/83	7.85	7.75	97.374	8.07
10.9	150	3/24/83	7.95	7.85	96.729	8.23
10.9	178	4/21/83	8.00	7.90	96.094	8.34
5.3	206	5/19/83	8.20	8.10	95.365	8.57
6.3	290	8/11/83	8.45	8.35	93.274	8.93
7.0	346	10/6/83	8.32	8.28	92.042	8.93

From the examples we have considered, it is clear that the yield on a discount security is *significantly less* when measured on a discount basis than when measured in terms of equivalent bond yield. The absolute divergence between these two measures of yield is, moreover, not constant. As Exhibit 2 shows, the greater the yield and the longer the maturity of the security, the greater the divergence.

EXHIBIT 2 Comparisons, at Different Rates and Maturities, of Rates of Discount and Equivalent Bond Yields

Yields on a Discount Basis (percent)	Equivalent Bond Yields (percent) 30-Day Maturity	Equivalent Bond Yields (percent) 182-Day Maturity	Equivalent Bond Yields (percent) 364-Day Maturity
6	6.114	6.274	6.375
8	8.166	8.453	8.639
10	10.227	10.679	10.979
12	12.290	12.952	13.399
14	14.362	15.256	15.904

Money market yield. Equivalent bond yield on a bill is calculated on the basis of a 365-day year. Bill rates are—to make them directly comparable to rates on CDs and other interest-bearing, money market instruments—often converted to a simple interest rate on a 360-day-year basis. That number, dubbed *money market yield*, is obtained by substituting 360 for 365 in the above equation for equivalent bond yield; specifically,

$$\left(\begin{array}{c} \text{money market yield} \\ \text{on a bill} \end{array} \right) = \frac{360 \times d}{360 - (d \times t)}$$

Fluctuations in a Bill's Price

Normally, the price at which a bill sells will rise as the bill approaches maturity. For example, to yield 9 percent on a discount basis, a six-month bill must be priced at $95.45 per $100 of face value. For the same bill three months later (three months closer to maturity) to yield 9 percent, it must have risen in price to $97.72. The moral is clear: If a bill always sold at the same yield throughout its life, its price would rise steadily toward face value as it approached maturity.

A bill's yield, however, is unlikely to be constant over time; instead, it will fluctuate for two reasons: (1) changes may occur in the general level of short-term interest rates, and (2) the bill will move along *the yield curve*.[4] Let's look at each of these factors.

Short-term interest rates. T bills are issued through auctions in which yields (discounted prices) are bid. The rate of discount determined at auction on a new bill issue depends on the level of short-term interest rates prevailing at the moment of the auction. The reason is straightforward. Investors who want to buy bills at the time of a Treasury auction have two alternatives—to buy new bills or to buy existing bills from dealers. This being the case, investors will not bid for new bills a rate of discount lower than that available on existing bills. If they did, they would be offering to buy new bills at a price higher than that at which they could buy existing bills. Also, investors will not bid substantially higher rates of discount (lower prices) than those prevailing on existing bills. If they did, they would not obtain bills, since they would surely be underbid by others trying to get just a slightly better return than that available on existing securities. Thus, the prevailing level of short-term rates determines, within a narrow range, the discount established on new bills at issue. However, the going level of short-term rates is not constant over time. It rises and falls in response to changes in economic activity, the demand for credit, investors' expectations, and monetary policy as set by the Federal Reserve System.

If the going level of short-term rates (which establishes the rate at which a bill is initially sold) falls after a bill is issued, then this bill—as

---

[4] Investors and dealers in bills would like to know how much the price of a given bill would fluctuate if its yield changed by one basis point. It is common that dealer quote sheets show the change in the price of the bill for a one-basis-point change per $1 million of face value of bills. The formula to find the "value of an 01 per million" face value on a discount security denoted "V_{01}", is

$$= .0001 \, (1,000,000) \left(\frac{t}{360} \right).$$

long as its price doesn't change—will yield more than new bills. Therefore, buyers will compete for this bill, and in doing so, they will drive up its price and thereby force down its yield until the bill sells at a rate of discount equal to the new, lower going interest rate. Conversely, if short-term rates rise after a bill is issued, the unwillingness of buyers to purchase any bill at a discount less than that available on new issues will drive down its price and thereby force up its yield.

The yield curve. Even if the going level of short-term interest rates does not change while investors hold bills, it would be normal for the rate at which they could sell their bills to change. The reason lies in the *yield curve*. How this works is a function of several factors, described below.

In choosing among alternative securities, an investor considers three things: risk, liquidity, and return. Purchase of a money market instrument exposes an investor to two sorts of risk: (1) *credit risk:* Will the issuer pay off at maturity? and (2) *price risk:* If the investor later sold the security, might he have to do so at a loss because interest rates had subsequently risen? Most money market investors are risk averse, which means that they will accept lower yields to obtain lower risk.

The price risk to which bills and other money market instruments expose the investor is *larger* the *longer* their current maturity. To see why, suppose that short-term interest rates rise a full percentage point across the board; then the prices of all bill issues will drop, *but the price drop will be greater, the longer an issue's current maturity.* For example, a 1 percentage point rise in market rates would cause a three-month bill to fall only $2,500 in price per $1 million of face value, whereas the corresponding price drop on a nine-month bill would be $7,600 per $1 million of face value.

Yield Realized on Sales before Maturity

If an investor buys one-year bills at 10 percent and holds them to maturity, he will earn, on a discount basis, precisely 10 percent over the holding period. If, alternatively, he sells the bills before maturity, he will earn 10 percent over the holding period only if he sells at 10 percent, a relatively unlikely outcome. If he sells at a lower rate, he will get a higher price for his bills than he would have if he had sold them at 10 percent, and he will therefore earn more than 10 percent. If, on the other hand, he sells at a rate higher than 10 percent, he will earn something less than 10 percent.

The holding period yield as a simple interest rate that an investor earns on bills purchased at one rate and subsequently sold at another can be calculated using the formula

$$i = \frac{\text{Sales price} - \text{Purchase price}}{\text{Purchase price}} \div \frac{t}{365}$$

where t equals the number of days held. To illustrate, assume that an investor buys $1 million of one-year bills at 10 percent and sells them three months later at 10.25 percent. His holding-period yield would be

$$i = \frac{\$924,166.67 - \$898,888.89}{\$898,888.89} \div \frac{91}{365} = 11.23\%$$

COMMERCIAL PAPER

Commercial paper, whoever the issuer and whatever the precise form it takes, is an unsecured promissory note with a fixed maturity. In plain English, the issuer of commercial paper (the borrower) promises to pay the buyer (the lender) some fixed amount on some future date. But the issuer pledges no assets—only his liquidity and established earning power—to guarantee that he will make good on his promise to pay. Traditionally, commercial paper resembled in form a Treasury bill; it was a negotiable, noninterest-bearing note issued at a discount from face value and redeemed at maturity for full face value. Today, however, a lot of paper is interest-bearing. For the investor the major difference between bills and paper is that paper carries some small risk of default because the issuer is a private firm, whereas the risk of default on bills is zero for all intents and purposes.

Firms selling commercial paper frequently expect to roll over their paper as it matures; that is, they plan to get money to pay off maturing paper by issuing new paper. Since there is always the danger that an adverse turn in the paper market might make doing so difficult or inordinately expensive, most paper issuers back their outstanding paper with *bank lines of credit;* they get a promise from a bank or banks to lend them at any time an amount equal to their outstanding paper. Issuers normally pay for this service in one of several ways: by holding at their line banks compensating deposit balances equal to some percentage of their total credit lines; by paying an annual fee equal to some small percentage of their outstanding lines; or through some mix of balances and fees.

Issuers of Paper

Financial and nonfinancial firms (e.g., public utilities, manufacturers, retailers) issue paper. Paper issued by nonfinancial firms, referred to as *industrial paper,* accounts for about 32 percent of all paper outstanding. Such paper is issued, as in the past, to meet seasonal needs for funds and also as a means of interim financing (i.e., to obtain funds to start investment projects that are later permanently funded through the sale of long-term bonds). In contrast to industrial borrowers, finance companies have a continuing need for short-term funds throughout the year;

they are now the principal borrowers in the commercial paper market, accounting for roughly 48 percent of all paper.

In the recent years of tight money, bank holding companies have also joined finance companies as borrowers in the commercial paper market. Many banks are owned by a holding company, an arrangement offering the advantage that the holding company can engage in activities in which the bank itself is not permitted. Commercial paper is sold by bank holding companies primarily to finance their nonbank activities in leasing, real estate, and other lines. However, funds raised through the sale of such paper can also be funneled into the holding company's bank, if the latter is pinched for funds, through various devices, such as the sale of bank assets to the holding company.

Issuing Techniques

All industrial paper is issued through paper dealers. Currently there are eight major paper dealers in the country; their main offices are in financial centers—New York, Chicago, and Boston—but they have branches throughout the country. Also there are a number of smaller regional dealers. Typically, dealers buy up new paper issues directly from the borrower, mark them up, and then resell them to investors. The current going rate of markup is very small, an eighth of 1 percent per annum. Generally, paper issues are for very large amounts, and the minimum round lot in which most dealers sell is $250,000. Thus the dealer market for commercial paper is a meeting ground for big corporate borrowers and for large investors (the latter including financial corporations, nonfinancial corporations, and pension funds).

Finance companies and banks occasionally place their paper through dealers, but most such paper (over 80 percent) is placed directly by the issuer with investors. A big finance company, for example, might place $1 million or more of paper with an insurance company or with a big industrial firm that had a temporary surplus of funds. In addition to these large-volume transactions, some finance companies and banks also sell paper in relatively small denominations directly to small business firms and individual investors, as will be discussed later in this section.

Paper Maturities

Maturities on commercial paper are generally very short—one to three months being the most common on dealer-placed paper. Generally, dealers prefer not to handle paper with a maturity of less than 30 to 45 days because, on paper of such short maturity, their markup (which is figured on a percent *per annum* basis) barely covers costs. However, to accommodate established borrowers, they will do so. Paper with a maturity of more than 270 days is rare because issues of such long maturity have to be registered with the SEC.

Finance companies that place their paper directly with large investors generally offer a wide range of maturities—3 to 270 days. Also they are willing to tailor maturities to the needs of investors and will often accept funds for very short periods, for example for a weekend. Finance companies that sell low-denomination paper to individual investors generally offer maturities ranging from 30 to 270 days on such paper. These companies also issue longer-maturity short-term notes that have been registered with the SEC.

Paper Yields

Some paper bears interest, but much does not. The investor who buys noninterest-bearing paper gets a return on his money because he buys his paper at a discount from face value, whereas the issuer redeems the paper at maturity for full face value. Yields on paper are generally quoted in eighths of 1 percent, for example, at 7⅛ percent per annum. Paper rates, whether the paper is interest-bearing or not, are quoted on a *bank discount basis,* as in the case of bills.

Bill rates vary over time, rising if business demand for credit increases or if the Fed tightens credit, falling in the opposite cases. The yields offered by paper issuers follow much the same pattern of bill yields except that paper yields are, if anything, even more volatile than bill yields.

The reason paper rates fluctuate up and down in step with the yields on bills and other money-market securities is simple. Paper competes with these other instruments for investors' dollars. Therefore, as yields on bills and other money market securities rise, paper issuers must offer higher rates in order to sell their paper. In contrast, if bill yields and other short-term rates decline, paper issuers can and do ease the rates they offer.

The volatility of paper rates has important consequences for the investor. First, it means that the attractiveness of paper as an investment medium for short-term funds varies over the interest rate cycle. It also means that the rate you get on paper bought today tells you relatively little about what rate you would get if you were to roll over that paper at maturity. Paper yields offered in the future may be substantially higher or lower than today's rates, depending on whether money is tightening or easing.

Risk and Ratings

Investors thinking of buying paper should consider not only the *return* it yields, but also whether there is any *risk* that they will not get timely payment on their paper when it matures. Basically there are two situations in which an issuing company might fail to pay off its maturing paper: (1) it is solvent, but lacks cash, and (2) it is insolvent. How great are the chances that either situation will occur?

Since the early 1930s, the default record on commercial paper has been excellent. In the case of dealer paper, one reason is that, after the 1920s, the many little borrowers who had populated the paper market were replaced by a much smaller number of large, well-established firms. This gave dealers, who were naturally extremely careful about whose paper they handled, the opportunity to examine much more thoroughly the financial condition of each issuer with whom they dealt.

Since 1965 the number of firms issuing at any time a significant quantity of paper to a wide market has increased from 450 to 1,200; of these about 130 are currently non-U.S. borrowers. Only five issuers of commercial paper have failed over the last decade. Three of these five were small domestic finance companies that got caught by tight money; in each case the losses to paper buyers were small, $2–$4 million. The fourth firm that failed was a Canadian finance company that had sold paper in the U.S. market; losses on its paper totaled $35 million. The fifth failure, one that shook the market, was that of the Penn Central, which at the time it went under had $82 million of paper outstanding.

Although the payments record on paper is good, the losses that have occurred make it clear that an individual putting money into paper has the right—more strongly, the responsibility—to ask: How good is the company whose paper I am buying? Because of the investor's very real need for an answer, and because of the considerable time and money involved in obtaining one, rating services have naturally developed. Today a large proportion of dealer and direct paper is rated by one or more of three companies: Standard & Poor's, Moody's, and Fitch.

Paper issuers willingly pay the rating services to examine them and rate their paper, since a good rating makes it easier and cheaper for them to borrow in the paper market. The rating companies, despite the fact that they receive their income from issuers, basically have the interests of the investor at heart for one simple reason: the value of their ratings to investors and thereby their ability to sell rating services to issuers depend on their accuracy. The worth to an issuer of a top rating is the track record of borrowers who have received that rating.

Each rating company sets its own rating standards, but their approaches are similar. Every rating is based on an evaluation of the borrowing company's management and on a detailed study of its earnings record and balance sheet. Just what a rating company looks for depends in part on the borrower's line of business; the optimal balance sheet for a publishing company would look quite different from that of a finance company. Nonetheless, one can say in general that the criteria for a top rating are strong management, a good position in a well-established industry, an upward trend in earnings, adequate liquidity, and the ability to borrow to meet both anticipated and unexpected cash needs.

Since companies seeking a paper rating are rarely in imminent danger of insolvency, the principal focus in rating paper is on *liquidity*—can the borrower come up with cash to pay off his maturing paper? Here what the rating company looks for is ability to borrow elsewhere than in the paper market and especially the ability to borrow short-term from banks. Today, for a company to get a paper rating, its paper must be backed by bank lines of credit.

Different rating firms grade borrowers according to different classifications. Standard & Poor's, for example, rates companies from A for highest quality to D for lowest. It also subdivides A-rated companies into three groups according to relative strength, A-1 down to A-3. Fitch rates firms F-1 (highest grade) to F-4 (lowest grade). Moody's uses P-1, P-2, and P-3, with P-1 being their highest rating.

Rates and Tiering

In the early 1960s, when the commercial paper market was small, all issuers paid similar rates to borrow there. Then, after the Penn Central's failure and periods of extremely tight money, investors became very credit conscious; they wanted top names, and rate tiering developed in the market. That tiering today is a function not only of issuers' commercial paper ratings but of their long-term bond ratings. The market distinguishes between A-1 issuers with a triple-A bond rating and those with only a double-A bond rating. Many investors want to buy only unimpeachable credits; looking up an issuer's bond rating is a quick way for an investor to check the credit of an issuer with whom he is unfamiliar.

The spread at which A-1, P-1 paper trades to A-2, P-2 paper varies depending on economic conditions. When money is tight and people are more concerned than normal about risk in general and credit risk in particular, they may drive the yield on A-2 paper 200 point basis points above that on A-1 paper; this occurred in the summer of 1982. When—after a period of tight money—rates begin to fall, investors, seeking to maintain past portfolio yields, tend to become yield buyers; they switch out of lower-yielding, top-rated paper into higher-yielding, second-tier paper. As they do, they drive down the spread between A-1 and A-2 paper so that, by the time money eases, it may be only ⅜ or even ¼. Whether money is easy or tight, no institutional investors will buy P-3 paper from dealers.

Commercial paper yields slightly more than Treasury bills of comparable maturity, the spread being widest when money is tight. There are two reasons. First, paper exposes the investor to a small credit risk. Second, commercial paper is much less liquid than bills because there is no active secondary market in it.

Dealer Paper

Close to 40 percent of all commercial paper is issued through dealers. Most of the paper placed through dealers is industrial paper, but some of it is issued by smaller finance companies, bank holding companies, and muni borrowers. Issuers who sell through dealers tell the dealer each day how much they want to sell and in what maturities. The dealer's sales force, in turn, tells the firm's retail customers what names and maturities are available and what rates are.

The standard fee dealers charge issuers of commercial paper who sell through them is ⅛ of 1 percent which works out to $3.47 per 1 million per day. In exchange for this fee, the dealer assumes several responsibilities vis à vis both issuers and investors. First, every dealer carefully checks the credit of each firm that sells paper through him. The dealer has a fiduciary responsibility to do this. He also wants to ensure that he does not tarnish his own good name in the eyes of either issuers or investors by selling paper of an issuer who goes bankrupt. A second responsibility of a dealer is to introduce the name of a new issuer to investors. He does this by having his sales force constantly show the name to investors and explain to them who the issuer is and what its credit is.

Some sophisticated issuers will themselves set the scale of rates to be offered on their paper in different maturity ranges. And if they do not want money badly, they may post rates slightly off the market in an attempt to pick up some cheap money. Most issuers, however, rely on the dealer to determine what rates should be posted on their paper. Dealers all compete with each other for issuers, and for this reason they all try to post the lowest rates at which it is possible to sell whatever quantity of paper an issuer who sells through them wants sold.

If an issuer permits a dealer to decide what rates will be offered on his paper, the dealer in turn assumes an obligation to position at these rates any of that issuer's paper that goes unsold. Normally a dealer finances paper thus acquired through dealer loans. Such financing is expensive, and carry is sometimes negative; dealers prefer to position as little paper as possible. Said one dealer, "Over the last four or five years, when we have had to take into position paper that we could not sell, we have actually made money on doing so despite the inverted yield curve. We are not, however, in business to make money that way. Every day I come to work, I would be thrilled if we just broke even on carry. If you make it, fine. If you don't, it is a cost of doing business."

On longer-term, higher-rate paper, a dealer's carry might be positive, especially if he finances in the RP market. Most dealers, however, are loath to position paper to earn carry profits or to speculate; they believe they should reserve their capacity to borrow for financing the paper—in amounts that cannot be predicted—that they might have to position as an obligation to their issuers. Also, some dealers think that if positioning long paper that an issuer wants to sell seems an attractive speculation because they expect rates to fall, it is their responsibility to advise the issuer that he would be better off issuing short paper.

Dealers don't like to sell very short-dated paper because their transaction costs can easily exceed the fee they earn selling such paper, but to avoid positioning paper, they will occasionally sell even one-day paper. Also, at times they will, if necessary, *break rates* to get paper sold; that is, offer rates above those they have posted.

Secondary Market

Every dealer who sells commercial paper stands ready to buy back paper sold through him at the going market rate for paper of that grade and current maturity plus ⅛ or so. Also, if an investor wants paper of an issuer who is not selling on a particular day, a dealer will attempt to find an investor who holds that issuer's paper and swap him out of it to generate supply.

Thus there is some secondary trading in dealer-issued commercial paper; such paper is, however, nowhere near as liquid as other money market instruments. An investor who holds commercial paper cannot really count on getting a bid on it from more than one dealer, and an ⅛ bid above the market is a wide spread.

The failure for an active secondary market to develop in commercial paper has several causes. Commercial paper outstanding is even more heterogeneous than bank CDs outstanding and thus more difficult to trade actively in the secondary market. Also, many buyers of commercial paper are hold-to-maturity investors, so the demands made on dealers to take back paper are minimal. One major dealer estimated that "buy backs" at his shop run to only 1 to 1½ percent of the paper they place.

LOC Paper

Some smaller or less well-known domestic firms and a number of foreign firms borrow in the commercial paper market by issuing LOC (line of credit) paper. This paper is backed by normal bank lines *plus* a letter of credit from a bank stating that the bank will pay off the paper at maturity if the borrower does not. Such paper is also referred to as *documented discount notes.*

Obtaining a letter of credit to back its paper may permit an issuer to get a P-1 rating on LOC paper, whereas on its own paper it would get only a P-3 rating or no rating. Documented discount notes, which represent only a small fraction of commercial paper outstanding, have been issued by firms that sell nuclear fuel or energy derived from it, leasing companies, REITs, mortgage companies, U.S. subsidiaries of Japanese trading companies, and a number of foreign companies.

Borrowers who get an LOC could not get into the market without it. It is not that they are not creditworthy. Some are foreign companies who do not care to disclose all their financials to the general public, but do not mind disclosing them to their dealers or to the rating agencies. Other LOC borrowers are just not large enough to get a rating. U.S. subsidiaries of Japanese companies make extensive use of LOC paper because they are not sufficiently big and self-sufficient to get a rating: The parent company could guarantee the subsidiary's paper but prefers to have the subsidiary get a LOC to back it. The cost of a letter of credit runs anywhere from ½ to ¾, whereas the cost of normal lines is more like ¼.

Direct Issue Paper

About 50 percent of all commercial paper outstanding is placed directly by the issuer with investors. Firms issuing their paper direct—less than 80 do so—are mostly large finance companies and bank holding companies. Some of these finance companies, such as GMAC, Sears, Roebuck Acceptance Corporation, and Ford Motor Credit, are captive finance companies that borrow primarily to finance the credit sales of the parent industrial company. Others, such as Household Finance, Beneficial Finance, and Associates Corporation of North America, are independent finance companies.

The major incentive for an issuer to go direct is that, by doing so, it escapes the dealer's ⅛ commission. For a firm with $200 million of commercial paper outstanding, this would amount to a savings of $250,000 a year. However, the direct issuer has to set up its own sales organization. A firm with a top credit rating can sell a huge amount of commercial paper through a small sales force—three to six people. Thus, for such a firm, it pays to go direct when the average amount of paper it has outstanding climbs to around $200 to $250 million. A few issuers who are big borrowers in the paper market continue to use a dealer either because they anticipate selling long-term debt to reduce their short-term borrowing or because the amount of paper they have outstanding varies sharply during the year.

Direct issuers determine each day how much they need to borrow, what maturities they want, and what rates they will post. Then they communicate their offerings to investors in three ways. All of the big directs post their rates on Telerate. In addition, their sales representatives call various investors. As one such representative noted, "There are a large number of A-1, P-1 issuers who are posting the same rates. So the sales representative's job is partly to develop personal relationships that will distinguish his firm in investors' eyes from the crowd."

The third way that the top direct issuers sell their paper is by posting their rates on bank money desks. Banks are forbidden by Glass-Steagall from acting as dealers in commercial paper, but they can and do post rates for issuers and arrange sales of their paper to investors.[5] The banks do this partly to service clients who use them to invest surplus funds. By posting paper rates, the banks can offer such clients a full menu of money market instruments. Also, direct issuers typically purchase large backup lines from banks that post their paper rates.

The rates that a direct issuer has to pay are a function of its name, credit rating, and use of the market. A nonprime borrower that uses the market extensively will have to pay up.

Once a direct issuer posts rates, it carefully monitors sales throughout the day by its own sales force and on bank money desks. When money market conditions are volatile, an issuer may change its posted rates several times a day to ensure that it gets whatever amount it set out to borrow. Also, if an issuer achieves that goal early in the day, it will typically lower its rates to make its paper unattractive to investors and thereby stem any further inflow of funds.

Most issuers will break rates for a large investor if they want money. Some, when they are just entering the market, will also consistently offer selected large investors rates slightly above their posted rates. The prevalence of rate breaking tends to increase when money is tight and to decrease when it is easy.

An issuer who fails to borrow as much as it had intended to can always fall back on its bank lines. Also, when money is easy and the demand for bank loans is slack, some banks will position short-term paper at a rate equal to the Fed funds rate plus a small markup; this is a way of giving the issuer a cut-rate loan.

A more recent development is banks offering fixed-rate advances priced off money market rates to commercial paper issuers and other borrowers of short-term money. The availability of such loans is likely to be particularly helpful to big direct issuers who on a given day may find themselves $100 or $200 million short.

Prepayments

The big direct issuers of commercial paper will all prepay on paper they have issued if the investor needs money before the paper he or she has purchased matures. Some issuers do this at no penalty. Others will prepay at the rate that the investor would have gotten on the day paper was purchased if paper had been bought for the period the investor actually held it. The no-penalty system would seem to invite abuse— to encourage investors to buy, whenever the yield curve is upward

---

[5] Glass-Steagall does not preclude banks from dealing in muni commercial paper, but so far at least, it is nonbank dealers who have developed this market and have a lock on it.

sloping, paper of a longer maturity than that for which they intend to invest in order to get a higher rate. Issuers, however, figure that game out quickly and don't let an investor get away with it for long.

One reason issuers are so willing to prepay is that most do not want investors to sell their paper to a dealer for fear that the dealer's later resale of that paper might interfere with their own sales. Still a few of the largest issuers, GMAC in particular, will occasionally sell longer-term paper to dealers who position it for carry profits and as a speculation.

Master Notes

Bank trust departments have many small sums to invest short term. To provide them with a convenient way to do so, the major direct issuers of commercial paper offer bank trust departments what are called *master notes*. A master note is a variable-rate demand note on which the issuer typically pays the rate he is posting for 180-day money, that rate plus ¼, or some similar formula rate.

A bank trust department with whom an issuer has opened a master note invests monies from various trust accounts in it. Then each day the bank advises the issuer what change, if any, has occurred in the total amount invested in the note. From a trust department's point of view, a master note provides such a convenient way for investing small sums to any date that it typically keeps the balance in any note issued to it close to the limit imposed by the issuer on the size of the note; daily variations in the size of a large master note—say, one for $15 million—might be no more than $100,000.

For the issuer, master notes provide a dependable source of funds and reduce bookkeeping costs. Money obtained through a master note, however, is expensive for the issuer because the rate paid is based on the 180-day rate; most issuers limit the amount of master notes they issue to some percentage—typically well below half—of their total outstandings.

A and B notes. Because bank trust departments keep master notes filled up most of the time, some direct issuers said to them, "Look, you have a master note for x million, and most of the time you have it 90 percent full. Let's call the top half of that note an *A note;* you can take money out of it on demand. The bottom half of the note we will call a *B note;* on that part you have to give us a 13-month notice to withdraw funds."

The advantage to the issuer of this arrangement, which is now common among direct issuers, is that the issuer gets cheap money that he can record on his balance sheet as *long-term* debt. From the trust department's point of view, the arrangement provides a high rate on what is really short-term money because different monies are constantly being shifted into and out of the overall note.

Issuers of B notes argue that such debt is not commercial paper but rather a private placement. Still such debt is recorded in money market statistics as commercial paper. A few issuers who do not offer B notes fear that by doing so they would be making an offering that, due to its term and the lack of a prospectus, would not comply with SEC regulations. Because of the attraction of B notes to the issuer, many issuers who offer master notes to bank trust departments will not issue an A note unless they also get a B note.

Before it got into serious financial difficulties, W. T. Grant had a number of master notes outstanding with bank trust departments. While it had closed them out before its bankruptcy, that event did cause a number of bank trust departments to question whether they should not invest cash balances in trust accounts in an institutional money fund rather than in a master note. An institutional money fund offers a bank trust department the same convenient subaccounting that a master note does and a comparable yield. In addition an institutional money fund has the advantage over a master note that it offers, instead of exposure to a single credit risk, *diversity of credit risk.*

Secondary Market

Secondary market trading, uncommon in dealer-issued paper, occurs with increasing frequency in direct-issue paper. Big finance companies such as GMAC, and big bank holding companies, such as Citicorp, have huge amounts of paper outstanding, some of which has been issued in large blocks that mature on a given day.[6] Money market dealers, who trade BAs and CDs, sometimes position such paper as a rate play. This practice has become so common that at least one broker of money markets, Garvin, has started to broker blocks of commercial paper among dealers.

BANKERS' ACCEPTANCES

The *Bankers' acceptance (BA)* is an unknown instrument outside the confines of the money market. Moreover, explaining BAs isn't easy because they arise in a variety of ways out of a variety of transactions. The best approach is to use an example.

Suppose a U.S. importer wants to buy shoes in Brazil and pay for them four months later, after she has had time to sell them in the United States. One approach would be for the importer to simply borrow from her bank; however, short-term rates may be lower in the open market. If

---

[6] Taking its cue from the Treasury, Citi's holding company auctions $150 million of its commercial paper every Wednesday.

they are, and if the importer is too small to go into the open market on her own, then she can go the bankers' acceptance route.

In that case she has her bank write a letter of credit for the amount of the sale and then sends this letter to the Brazilian exporter. Upon export of the shoes, the Brazilian firm, using this letter of credit, draws a time draft on the importer's U.S. bank and discounts this draft at its local bank, thereby obtaining immediate payment for its goods. The Brazilian bank in turn sends the time draft to the importer's U.S. bank, which then stamps "accepted" on the draft; that is, the bank guarantees payment on the draft and thereby creates an *acceptance*. Once this is done, the draft becomes an irrevocable primary obligation of the accepting bank. At this point, if the Brazilian bank did not want cash immediately, the U.S. bank would return the draft to that bank, which would hold it as an investment and then present it to the U.S. bank for payment at maturity. If, on the other hand, the Brazilian bank wanted cash immediately, the U.S. bank would pay it and then either hold the acceptance itself or sell it to an investor. Whoever ended up holding the acceptance, it would be the importer's responsibility to provide her U.S. bank with sufficient funds to pay off the acceptance at maturity. If the importer should fail for any reason, her bank would still be responsible for making payment at maturity.

Our example illustrates how an acceptance can arise out of a U.S. import transaction. Acceptances also arise in connection with U.S. export sales, trade between third countries (e.g., Japanese imports of oil from the Middle East), the domestic shipment of goods, and domestic or foreign storage of readily marketable staples. Currently most BAs arise out of foreign trade; the latter may be in manufactured goods, but more typically is in bulk commodities, such as cocoa, cotton, coffee, or crude oil, to name a few. Because of the complex nature of acceptance operations, only large banks that have well-staffed foreign departments act as accepting banks.

Bankers' acceptances closely resemble commercial paper in form. They are short-term (270 days or less), noninterest-bearing notes sold at a discount and redeemed by the accepting bank at maturity for full face value. The major difference between bankers' acceptances and paper is that payment on paper is guaranteed by only the issuing company, but payment on bankers' acceptances is also guaranteed by the accepting bank. Thus bankers' acceptances carry slightly less risk than commercial paper. The very low risk on acceptances is indicated by the fact that to date no investor in acceptances has ever suffered a loss.

Yields on bankers' acceptances are quoted on a bank discount basis, as in the case of commercial paper. Yields on bankers' acceptances closely parallel yields on paper. Also, both rates are highly volatile, rising sharply when money is tight and falling in an equally dramatic fashion when conditions ease. This means that when money is tight, yields on bankers' acceptances are very attractive.

The big banks through which bankers' acceptances originate generally keep some portion of the acceptances they create as investments. The rest are sold to investors through dealers or directly by the bank itself. Major investors in bankers' acceptances are other banks, foreign central banks, and Federal Reserve banks.

Many bankers' acceptances are written for very large amounts and are obviously out of the range of the small investor; certainly this includes all acceptances that pass through the hands of dealers. However, acceptances in amounts as low as $5,000 or even $500 are not uncommon. Some accepting banks offer these low-denomination acceptances to their customers as investments. An individual investing in a $25,000 acceptance may in fact be buying a single small acceptance arising out of one transaction, or be buying a bundle of even smaller acceptances that have been packaged together to form a round-dollar amount. Frequently, bankers' acceptances are available in still smaller odd-dollar amounts. The investor who puts money into an odd-dollar acceptance should be prepared to experience some difficulty in rolling over the funds. Also the availability of bankers' acceptances varies both seasonally and over the cycle. Generally, availability is greatest when money is tight and banks prefer not to tie up funds in acceptances.

The easiest and cheapest way to buy a bankers' acceptance is from an accepting bank. In that case, service charges will be zero. The rate you get will, of course, be less than the rate that a $1 million investor gets, but when money is tight, it may nevertheless be quite good—as much as twice the rate you would get on a savings account. If you don't live in the vicinity of an accepting bank, you can have your bank purchase acceptances for you through its correspondent bank. Here you are likely to run into a service charge, and its effect on yield should be carefully calculated.

The rates offered on bankers' acceptances, like those on paper, vary from day to day. Also they may vary slightly on a given day from one accepting bank to another. Thus a few calls to shop for rates are in order if you decide to invest in acceptances.

Since payment on acceptances is guaranteed by both the accepting bank and the ultimate borrower, investing in acceptances exposes an individual to minimal risk. For small acceptances, as for paper, there is no secondary market. Thus an investor who needs cash cannot sell a bankers' acceptance to another investor but can use it as collateral for a bank loan. Also, if the investor's need for cash is really pressing, chances are that the accepting bank will be willing to buy back the acceptance early.

NEGOTIABLE CERTIFICATES OF DEPOSIT

A negotiable CD is simply a receipt from a bank for funds deposited at that bank for some specified period of time at some specified rate of return. Today, the major issuers of negotiable CDs are large, nationally known money market banks, principally in New York and Chicago. In addition to these prime borrowers, there are also a number of less well known regional banks that issue CDs. A *Eurodollar CD* resembles a domestic CD except that instead of being the liability of a domestic bank, it is the liability of the London branch of a domestic bank, or of a British bank, or some other foreign bank with a branch in London. Although many of the Eurodollar CDs issued in London are purchased by other banks operating in the Euromarket, a large portion of the remainder are sold to U.S. corporations and other domestic institutional investors. Many Euro CDs are issued through dealers and brokers who maintain secondary markets in these securities. The Euro CD market is younger and smaller than the market for domestic CDs, but it has grown rapidly since its inception. The most recent development in the "Eurodollar" CD market is that some large banks have begun offering such CDs through their Caribbean branches.[7]

Foreign banks issue dollar-denominated CDs not only in the Euro market but also in the domestic market through branches established there. CDs of the latter sort are frequently referred to as Yankee CDs; the name is derived from Yankee bonds, which are bonds issued in the domestic market by foreign borrowers.[8]

CDs can have any maturity longer than 30 days, and some 5- and 7-year CDs have been sold (these pay interest semiannually). Most CDs, however, have an *original maturity* of one to three months. Generally the CD buyer, who may be attempting to fund a predictable cash need—say, provide for a tax or dividend payment—can select his or her own maturity date when making the deposit.

Until May 1973, the Fed, under Regulation Q, imposed lids on the rates that banks could pay on large-denomination CDs of different maturities. Today these lids are past history, and the general level of yields on negotiable CDs is determined by conditions of demand and supply in the money market. Since holding a CD exposes the investor to a small risk of capital loss (the issuing bank might fail), prime-name negotiable CDs, in order to sell, have to be offered at rates approximately one eighth of a point above the rate on T bills of comparable maturity. Of course, in actual practice there is no one CD rate prevailing at any one time. Each issuing bank sets a range of rates for different maturities, normally with an upward-sloping yield curve. On a given day a bank at which loan demand is especially strong, and which therefore needs money, may set rates slightly more attractive than those posted by other banks. Posted rates are not fixed rates; big investors can and do haggle with banks over the rate paid.

---

[7] A CD issued, for example, in Nassau is technically a Euro CD because the deposit is held in a bank branch outside the United States.

[8] Yankee bonds are discussed in Chapter 49.

Generally prime-name banks can attract funds more cheaply than other banks, the rate differential being 1 percentage point or less. Foreign banks pay still higher CD rates. In comparing CD rates with yields on other money market instruments, note that CDs are *not* issued at a discount. It takes $1 million of deposits to get a CD with a $1 million face value. CDs typically pay interest at maturity. Thus rates quoted on CDs correspond to yield in the terms in which the investor normally thinks—what we call equivalent bond yield.

Recently banks have introduced on a small scale a new type of negotiable CD, *variable-rate CDs*. The two most prevalent types are six-month CDs with a 30-day *roll* (on each roll date, accrued interest is paid and a new coupon is set) and one-year paper with a three-month roll. The coupon established on a variable-rate CD at issue and on subsequent roll dates is set at some amount (12.5 to 30 basis points, depending on the name of the issuer and the maturity) above the average rate (as indicated by the composite rate published by the Fed) that banks are paying on new CDs with an original maturity equal to the length of the roll period.

We can sum up our discussion of risk, liquidity, and return on negotiable CDs by saying that CDs are slightly riskier than T bills. They are also slightly less liquid, since the spread between bid and asked prices is narrower in the bill market than in the secondary CD market; the reason for this difference is that in the bill market the commodity traded is homogeneous and buying and selling occur in greater volume.

CDs, however, compensate for these failings by yielding a somewhat higher return than do bills. Euro CDs offer a higher return than do domestic CDs. The offsetting disadvantages are that they are less liquid and expose the investor to some extra risk because they are issued outside the United States. Yankee CDs expose the investor to the extra (if only in perception) risk of a foreign name, and they are also less liquid than domestic CDs. Consequently Yankee CDs trade at yields close to those on Euro CDs. Although variable-rate CDs offer the investor some interest-rate protection, they have the offsetting disadvantage of illiquidity because they trade at a concession to the market. During their last *leg* (roll period) variable-rate CDs trade like regular CDs of similar name and maturity.

How precisely does an investor buy and sell CDs? Since the minimum denomination for readily marketable CDs is $1 million, it is probably safe to ignore that question here. The market for negotiable CDs is one sector of the money market in which the individual investor certainly is not going to participate *directly*. The investor may, however, become an *indirect* participant, which is why we have discussed negotiable CDs here. One of the most attractive liquid, high-yielding investments available to the individual investor is putting money into a money market fund, an institution that is likely to invest heavily, in some cases exclusively, in bank CDs.[9]

Computing the Yield of a CD, Given Its Price

Almost all CDs issued in the domestic market have a maturity at issue of less than one year and pay simple interest on a 360-day basis.[10] The rate of interest paid is the coupon rate, and interest is paid at maturity. In the formulas presented for CDs, the following convention will be adopted. *Price P is always taken to be price per $1 of face value, with accrued interest, if any, included.*[11]

CDs are always quoted, at issue and in the secondary market, in terms of yield on a simple interest basis. The following formula is for the rate of return that a CD offered at a price P will yield an investor.

$$y = \left(\frac{1 + c\dfrac{t_{im}}{360}}{P} - 1 \right) \frac{360}{t_{sm}}$$

where

y = yield on the CD
c = coupon rate
t_{sm} = days from settlement to maturity
t_{im} = days from issue to maturity

For example, suppose that an investor buys a CD that carries a coupon rate of 10 percent and has an original maturity of 90 days and a current maturity of 60 days. If the price P is 1.009024, the yield is 9.5 percent as shown below.

$$y = \left(\frac{1 + .100\dfrac{90}{360}}{1.009024} - 1 \right) \frac{360}{60} = .095$$

There are two points to note about the formula for computing the yield on a CD. First, if a CD is bought on its issue date, then $P = 1$, and the expression for the yield reduces to the coupon rate (c), as would be expected. Second, the fact that CDs pay interest on the basis of a 360-day year should not be forgotten when CD yields are compared with those on other interest-bearing securities, such as government notes and bonds, that pay interest on a 365-day basis. To convert from a 365- to a

---

[9] Money market funds are described in Chapter 20.

[10] As noted above, the exceptions are variable-rate CDs and a few long-term issues that have been floated at various times.

[11] The formulas presented in this section are derived in Stigum, *Money Market Calculations,* pp. 71–80.

360-day basis, the yield on a CD must be multiplied by 1.014.[12] Therefore, getting a year's interest over 360 days is worth 1.4 extra basis points for every 1 percent interest.

Computing Price, Given Yield

Using the formula for the yield on a CD, a formula for the price at which a CD will trade in the secondary market if it is offered at a yield y can be determined. Solving, we have

$$P = \left(\frac{1 + c \dfrac{t_{im}}{360}}{1 + y \dfrac{t_{sm}}{360}} \right)$$

Let's use the CD from the yield formula example, given the price, to show how the foregoing formula is applied. The price P is 1.009024, as shown below:

$$P = \left(\frac{1 + 0.100 \dfrac{90}{360}}{1 + 0.095 \dfrac{60}{360}} \right) = 1.009024$$

Breaking Out Accrued Interest

Separating the price P paid for a CD into principal and interest is easily done. Let

a_i = accrued interest
t_{is} = days from issue to settlement

On a CD accrued interest is given by the expression

$$a_i = c \frac{t_{is}}{360}$$

and

$$\text{Principal per \$1 of face value} = P - c \frac{t_{is}}{360}$$

Applying these formulas to the preceding example, we find that

$$a_i = 0.10 \frac{30}{360} = 0.083333$$

and

Principal = 1.009024 − 0.083333
= 1.000691

---

[12] The conversion factor is found by dividing 365 by 360.

Notice that the CD in our example is selling at a premium. This is to be expected since it was traded at a *yield well below* its coupon.

Holding Period Yield

Intuition, which seems to be invariably wrong in money market calculations, suggests that an investor who bought a CD at 10 percent and sold it before maturity at the same rate would earn 10 percent over the holding period. In fact, the investor would earn *less*. The reason is our old friend, compounding. It crops up because interest is not paid by the issuer on the CD until some period after the investor sells it; the CD is priced at sale, however, so that the buyer will earn the offered yield on an amount equal to the principal paid *plus* accrued interest.

Consider first a CD that is bought by an investor at issue and later sold before maturity. The rate of simple interest (i) earned by the investor over the holding period is

$$i = \left(\frac{1 + c\,\dfrac{t_{im}}{360}}{1 + y\,\dfrac{t_{sm}}{360}} - 1 \right) \frac{360}{t_{is}}$$

where

t_{is} = days from issue to settlement on the sale
y = rate at which the CD is sold

For example, an investor buys a 90-day CD carrying a 10 percent coupon at issue and sells it 30 days later at a 10 percent yield. The return earned is not 10 percent but a lower figure, 9.83 percent. The calculation is:

$$i = \left(\frac{1 + 0.10\,\dfrac{90}{360}}{1 + 0.10\,\dfrac{60}{360}} - 1 \right) \frac{360}{60} = 9.83 \text{ percent}$$

A Secondary CD

The yield on a CD purchased in the secondary market and sold before maturity can be calculated using a similar but slightly more complex formula shown below:

$$i = \left(\frac{1 + y_1\,\dfrac{t_1}{360}}{1 + y_2\,\dfrac{t_2}{360}} - 1 \right) \frac{360}{t_1 - t_2}$$

where

y_1 = purchase rate
y_2 = sale rate
t_1 = days from purchase to maturity
t_2 = days from sale to maturity

Sensitivity of Return to Sale Rate and Length of Holding Period

The figures in Exhibit 3 show what return (i) an investor would earn by selling a six-month CD purchased at 9 percent after various holding

EXHIBIT 3 The Rate of Return (i) Earned by an Investor on a 9 Percent, Six-Month CD when Sold at Various Rates after Various Holding Periods

Holding Period (days)	Sale Rate, y				
	11 Percent	*10 Percent*	*9 Percent*	*8 Percent*	*7 Percent*
30	−0.96%	3.84%	8.67%	13.55%	18.46%
60	4.82	6.77	8.74	10.71	12.70
90	6.81	7.80	8.80	9.80	10.81
120	7.86	8.36	8.87	9.38	9.88
150	8.59	8.73	8.93	9.14	9.35
179	8.99	8.99	9.00	9.00	9.01

periods and at various rates. Notice first the column labeled 9 percent. It shows that if the investor resells the CD at the purchase rate, the return earned will be higher the longer the holding period is (that is, the closer the sale date is to the date on which the CD matures and accrued interest is paid out).

Suppose an investor sells a CD at a rate below the rate at which he bought it. He will receive a capital gain and earn over the holding period a return higher than the yield at which he bought the CD. As the columns labeled 8 percent and 7 percent show, this effect becomes smaller the longer the holding period is. If, conversely, the investor sells the CD at a rate *above* that at which he purchased it, the effect is the opposite and also decreases as the holding period is lengthened.

The reason the impact of the sale rate on the return earned by the investor diminishes as the holding period increases is: The longer the holding period, the shorter is the time in which the buyer of the CD will earn the rate at which he or she buys the CD, and therefore the smaller will be the impact of that rate on the principal amount the investor pays for the CD.

Compounding

We have noted that selling a CD before maturity tends to reduce the yield earned by the investor over the holding period. If the investor *fully* reinvests the proceeds (principal *plus* accrued interest) from the sale of the CD, this effect will be offset by the opportunity for compounding of interest earnings created by the sale and subsequent repurchase.

To illustrate, an investor who purchased at issue a 182-day CD at 9 percent and sold it 91 days later at 9 percent would earn a yield of 8.80 percent over that period. If the investor immediately fully reinvested the sale proceeds ($1.022750 per $1 of face value) in a 9 percent, 91-day CD, total earnings over the 182-day investment period would be identical with what would have been earned by holding to maturity the 182-day, 9 percent CD originally bought.

REPOS AND REVERSES

A variety of bank and nonbank dealers act as market makers in governments, agencies, CDs, and BAs. Because dealers, by definition, buy and sell for their own accounts, active dealers will inevitably end up holding some securities. They will, moreover, buy and hold substantial positions if they believe that interest rates are likely to fall and that the value of these securities is therefore likely to rise. Speculation and risk taking are an inherent and important part of being a dealer.

While dealers have large amounts of capital, the positions they take are often several hundred times that amount. As a result, dealers have to borrow to finance their positions. Using the securities they own as collateral, they can and do borrow from banks at the dealer loan rate. For the bulk of their financing, however, they resort to a cheaper alternative, entering into *repurchase agreements* (*RPs* or *repos*, for short) with investors.

Much RP financing done by dealers is on an overnight basis. It works as follows: The dealer finds a corporation or other investor who has funds to invest overnight. He sells this investor, say, $10 million of securities for roughly $10 million, which is paid in Federal funds to his bank by the investor's bank against delivery of the securities sold. At the same time, the dealer agrees to repurchase these securities the next day at a slightly higher price. Thus, the buyer of the securities is in effect making the dealer a one-day loan secured by the obligations sold to him. The difference between the purchase and sale prices on the RP transaction is the interest the investor earns on his loan. Alternatively, the purchase and sale prices in an RP transaction may be identical; in that case, the dealer pays the investor some explicit rate of interest.

Often a dealer will take a speculative position that he intends to hold for some time. He might then do an RP for 30 days or longer. Such agreements are known as *term* RPs.

From the point of view of investors, overnight loans in the RP market offer several attractive features. First, by rolling overnight RPs, investors can keep surplus funds invested without losing liquidity or incurring a price risk. Second, because RP transactions are secured by top-quality paper, investors expose themselves to little or no credit risk.

The overnight RP rate generally is less t1an the Fed funds rate. The reason is that the many nonbank investors who have funds to invest overnight or very short term and who do not want to incur any price risk, have nowhere to go but the RP market because (with the exception of S&Ls) they cannot participate directly in the Fed funds market. Also, lending money through an RP transaction is safer than selling Fed funds because a sale of Fed funds is an unsecured loan.

On term, as opposed to overnight, RP transactions, investors still have the advantage of their loans being secured, but they do lose some liquidity. To compensate for that, the rate on an RP transaction is generally higher the longer the term for which funds are lent.

Banks that make dealer loans fund them by buying Fed funds, and the lending rate they charge—which is adjusted daily—is the prevailing Fed funds rate plus a one-eighth to one-quarter markup. Because the overnight RP rate is lower than the Fed funds rate, dealers can finance their positions more cheaply by doing RP than by borrowing from banks.

A dealer who is bullish on the market will position large amounts of securities. If he's bearish, he will *short* the market, that is, sell securities he does not own. Since the dealer has to deliver any securities he sells whether he owns them or not, a dealer who shorts has to borrow securities one way or another. The most common technique today for borrowing securities is to do what is called a *reverse RP*, or simply a *reverse*. To obtain securities through a reverse, a dealer finds an investor holding the required securities; he then buys these securities from the investor under an agreement that he will resell the same securities to the investor at a fixed price on some future date. In this transaction, the dealer, besides obtaining securities, is extending a loan to the investor for which he is paid some rate of interest.

An RP and a reverse are identical transactions. What a given transaction is called depends on who initiates it; typically, if a dealer hunting money does, it's an RP; if a dealer hunting securities does, it's a reverse.

A final note: The Fed uses reverses and RPs with dealers in government securities to make adjustments in bank reserves.

CONSIDERATIONS IN MANAGING A SHORT-TERM PORTFOLIO

A short-term portfolio is always managed within certain investment *parameters* that establish limits with respect to: (1) the types of instruments the portfolio may buy; (2) the percentage of the portfolio that may be invested in any one of these instruments (in Treasury bills the limit might be 100 percent, whereas in Certificates of Deposits (CDs), which are less liquid, it might be much lower); (3) the kind of exposure to names and credit risk the portfolio may assume (which banks' CDs and which issuers' commercial paper it may buy and how much of each name it may buy); (4) whether the portfolio may invest in Euros and foreign names; (5) how far out on the maturity spectrum the portfolio may extend; (6) whether the portfolio may short securities or repo securities; and (7) whether the portfolio may use futures and options. The investment parameters within which every short-term portfolio operates are set by the client.

Maturity Choice

A good portfolio manager *cannot* avoid making explicit interest rate predictions and basing his maturity choices upon them. As one portfolio manager pointed out, "The mistake many people make is to think that they do not have to make a forecast. But buying a 90-day bill and holding it to maturity *is* making a forecast. If you think that rates are going to move up sharply and soon, you should be sitting in overnight RP; and then when rates move up, you buy the 90-day bill."

Making rate predictions is important not only because an implicit rate prediction underlies every maturity choice a portfolio manager makes, but because good portfolio managers feel as a group that the way yield on a large portfolio can most effectively be increased is by positioning correctly along the maturity spectrum—by recognizing which maturity sectors of the market are cheap (have relative value), which are expensive, and by buying or selling accordingly.

Riding the yield curve. The best way to illustrate the kind of dividends yielded by maturity choices based on an explicit prediction of how interest rates might move is with a few concrete examples. Let's start by illustrating how a technique commonly used to raise return— namely, *riding the yield curve*—must be based on an explicit prediction of how short-term rates might change.

The yield curve graphically portrays the relationship between yield and current maturity. Normally, the yield curve is positively or upward sloped, indicating that the longer the time to maturity, the higher the yield. The idea of riding the yield curve is to increase return, when the yield curve is positively sloped, by buying a security out on the shoulder of the yield curve and holding that security until it can be sold at a gain because its current maturity has fallen and the yield at which it is currently trading has consequently decreased. Note that the main threats to the success of such a strategy are that short-term rates might rise across the board or that the yield curve might invert at the very short end.

Assume that an investor has funds to invest for three months. The six-month (180-day) bill is trading at 7.90, and the three-month (90-day) bill is trading at 7.50 (Exhibit 4). The alternatives the investor is choosing between are: (1) to buy the 90-day bill and mature it, and (2) to buy the

---

EXHIBIT 4 Yield Curve in an Example of Riding the Yield Curve

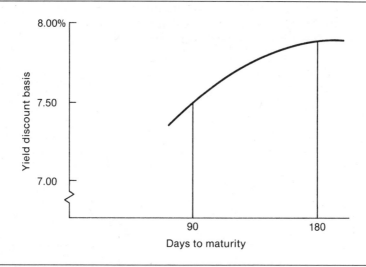

---

six-month bill and sell it three months hence. To assess the relative merits of these two strategies, the investor does a *break-even analysis.*

On $1 million of bills, a 90-day basis point (a basis point earned for 90 days) is worth $25.[13] If the investor bought the six-month bill, he would earn 40 basis points more than if he bought the three-month bill. Thus he could sell out the six-month bill after three months at a rate 40 basis points above the rate at which he bought it, that is, at 8.30, and still earn as many *dollars* on his investment as he would have if he had bought and matured the three-month bill (Exhibit 5). Therefore the rate on the three-month bill three months hence would have to rise above 8.30 before holding the six-month bill for three months would pay out fewer dollars than buying and maturing the three-month bill.

How likely is this to occur? Note that because of the slope of the yield curve (a 40-basis-point drop between the six-month and three-month bill rates), the rate at which the three-month bill trades three months hence would be 7.50 if no change occurred in interest rates, 80

---

[13] The formula using the notation adopted in the previous chapter is:

$$D = (\$1,000,000) \left(\frac{d \times t}{360} \right)$$

The calculation is as follows:

$$(\$1,000,000) \left(\frac{0.001 \times 90}{360} \right) = \$25$$

EXHIBIT 5   Dollar Calculations of Return in Example of Riding the Yield Curve

I.   Buy $1 million of 90-day bills at 7.50% and hold to maturity.

Face value	$1,000,000	Discount at purchase	$18,750
−Purchase price	981,250	−Discount at maturity	0
Return	$ 18,750	Return	$18,750

II.   Buy $1 million of 180-day bills at 7.90% and sell at breakeven yield of 8.30%.

Sale price	$979,250	Discount at purchase	$39,500
−Purchase price	960,500	−Discount at sale	20,750
Return	$ 18,750	Return	$18,750

III.   Buy $1 million of 180-day bills at 7.90% and sell at 7.50%.

Sale price	$981,250	Discount at purchase	$39,500
−Purchase price	960,500	−Discount at sale	18,750
Return	$ 20,750	Return	$20,750

basis points below the break-even rate of 8.30. Thus the investor has 80 basis points of protection, and the question he has to ask in making his choice is: How likely is it that the Fed will tighten in the next three months so sharply that the three-month bill will rise 80 basis points, from 7.50 to 8.30? If his answer is that it is highly unlikely, then he would buy the six-month bill and ride the yield curve.

Note that if the investor buys the three-month bill and matures it, he will earn $18,750 on each $1 million of bills he buys (see Exhibit 5). If, alternatively, he opts to ride the yield curve and does so successfully (i.e., buys the six-month bill and is able, because the Fed does not tighten, to sell out at 7.50), he will earn $20,750, which exceeds $18,750 by $2,000. This $2,000 equals the extra 80 90-day basis points he earns; 40 because the six-month bill is bought at a 40-basis point spread to the three-month bill, and 40 because he is able to sell it three months later at a rate 40 basis points below the rate at which he bought it.

Actually the investor riding the yield curve in our example has more protection than we indicated. The reason is that, when he buys the six-month bill, he invests fewer dollars than when he buys the three-month bill. So on a *simple interest basis,* he would earn an annualized return of 7.75 if he bought and matured the three-month bill, whereas if he bought the six-month bill at 7.90 and sold it at the break-even level of 8.30, he would earn an annualized return, again on a simple interest, 365-day-year basis, of 7.92, which is greater. To earn an annualized return of only 7.75 on the funds invested in the six-month bill, the investor would have to sell it out after three months at a discount of 8.46, which is 96 basis points above 7.50. The first break-even calculation we made on a dollar-return basis is easier to make, but this second more refined calculation is the one the investor who wants to maximize yield should make.

SUMMARY

Money managers must be familiar with the alternative investments in which excess cash may be invested and the return and risk characteristics of each instrument. In this chapter, the investment characteristics of several money market instruments are discussed. In addition to describing the investment characteristics of each instrument, procedures for converting the quoted yields to yields that can be used to compare investment returns among money market instruments are discussed. Finally, an overview of the factors of managing a short-term portfolio and the importance of the maturity choice are discussed.

8

U.S. Treasury Notes and Bonds

Marcia Stigum, Ph.D.
Stigum & Associates

Frank J. Fabozzi, Ph.D., C.F.A., C.P.A.
Visiting Professor
Sloan School of Management
Massachusetts Institute of Technology

The U.S. government securities market, which used to be stuffy and humdrum, has evolved over the last decade and a half into the most active, exciting, and innovative sector of the fixed income market. The reasons are several. The tightening and easing of policies by the Fed began to create wide swings in interest rates. "Back in the old days," noted one dealer, "bonds had no sex appeal. They were not going to change much in price so you bought them, clipped the coupon, and matured them. Then suddenly, because of big fluctuations in interest rates, it became possible for portfolio managers and dealers to make money positioning and trading governments."

The huge and consistent growth of the federal debt has also contributed to the evolution of the government market by creating more supply and attracting more players into the market.[1] So, too, did the freedom in which the government market operates. Ironically, the government market, unlike all other securities markets except the municipal market, is not regulated by the SEC. Thus, it is a market in which the street, which likes to innovate, has had a free hand to do so, and it has done so repeatedly. Over the last decade, the development of the reverse market[2] and the specific issues market has made transactions by dealers and

---

[1] For a discussion of the growth of the federal deficit, see Ronald J. Ryan, "The Treasury Debt Story," in *The Handbook of Treasury Securities*, ed. Frank J. Fabozzi (Chicago: Probus Publishing, 1986), Chapter 2.

[2] Reverses (or reverse purchase agreements) are used by dealers to borrow securities they have shorted.

portfolio managers, unheard of 10 years ago, commonplace. The government market is one of the few markets in which it is possible to run large short positions—to make money on a negative attitude—and growth of the reverse market has made shorting simpler, cheaper, and more attractive. Also, introduction of trading in bill, note, and bond futures and options has opened up a host of new strategies for dealing, investing, and speculating in governments; and it has attracted many new participants to the market.

ATTRACTION TO INVESTORS

Treasury securities, commonly referred to as *governments,* offer investors several advantages. First, because they are constantly traded in the secondary market in large volume and at narrow spreads, they are highly *liquid.* Second, governments are considered to be free from credit risk because it is inconceivable that the government would default on these securities in a situation short of destruction of the country. Third, interest income on governments is exempt from state and local income taxation. Because of these advantages, governments normally offer yields below those of other debt obligations. Municipal obligations are an exception because they offer a still more attractive tax advantage. However, as in the case of other marketable debt instruments, governments are subject to interest-rate risk, reinvestment risk, and purchasing-power risk.

THE SECURITIES

Treasury notes have an *original* maturity of 2 to 10 years. The Treasury currently auctions six different notes, 2-, 3-, 4-, 5-, 7-, and 10-year notes, on a regular cycle. Notes are available in registered and book-entry form. When the Treasury wants to encourage individuals to invest in a new note issue, it sets the minimum denomination at $1,000. At other times it sets it at $5,000. Notes are also available in $10,000, $100,000, and $1 million denominations. In the interdealer market for notes, $1 million is a round lot, trades for $5 million occur routinely, and trades for even larger amounts are common. The note market is a wholesale market, except for sales to individuals and small portfolio managers who typically buy to hold to maturity. Trades in the note market are done for both regular and cash settlement.

Treasury bonds have an original maturity of more than 10 years and are issued in registered and book-entry form. They come in denominations of $1,000, $5,000, $10,000, $100,000, and $1 million. Interdealer trades in bonds are usually for $500,000 or more, and the bond market, like the note market, is largely a wholesale market in which institutions buy and sell. Bond trades are normally done for regular settlement.

Currently, the Treasury auctions 30-year bonds on a regular cycle. A lack of market interest caused the Treasury to stop auctioning a 15-year bond in October 1980. In January 1981 the Treasury began auctioning 20-year bonds but discontinued this practice in May 1986.

Treasury notes are not callable, but many government bond issues outstanding are callable. Generally the call date is five years before maturity. On old low-coupon issues, the call provision is of small importance, but new high-coupon issues might conceivably be called someday.

A number of old *low-coupon* government bonds that currently sell at substantial *discounts* carry a special feature. They are acceptable at par in payment of federal estate taxes when owned by the decedent at the time of death. These bonds are known as "flower bonds."

In October 1984, the first Treasury notes targeted for the foreign market were issued. Foreign targeted investor notes (TINs) pay interest annually and are registered in the name of an international financial organization.

ISSUING PRACTICES

Treasury notes and bonds are issued through *exchanges* of new issues for maturing issues (refundings) and through *auctions* of new issues for cash.

Before the recent years of huge federal deficits and constant Treasury trips to the market for more cash, the Treasury made frequent exchange offerings. In a straight exchange offer, the Treasury sought to refund maturing securities by offering their holders new securities with the same par value. In an *advance refunding* or *pre-refunding*, the Treasury offered to holders of an outstanding issue the opportunity to exchange their securities for new securities of the same par value as long as one year in advance of maturity. The purpose of such straight exchange offerings was to encourage existing bondholders to roll over their bonds, thereby permitting Treasury refundings to be carried out with minimal disruption to the market. In the case of pre-refundings, an additional objective was to reduce Treasury borrowing costs by taking advantage of the interest rate cycle; the Treasury would pre-refund when interest rates were expected to rise, and pre-refunding consequently looked cheap relative to refunding at maturing. Exchange offerings were usually made on generous terms so that issues for which exchange offerings were made tended to rise in value, reflecting the *rights* value they acquired through the exchange offering. The practice of exchange offerings also led to speculative demand for issues that were considered likely candidates for pre-refunding. In recent years, exchange offerings have become uncommon. One reason is that the Treasury, because of its large and constant borrowings, no longer has the flexibility necessary to carry out such operations.

Yield Auctions

To sell new notes and bonds, the Treasury currently relies on auctions carried out by the Federal Reserve System.[3] Prior to September 1974, the Treasury always set coupons on new note and bond issues, and then auctioned them off on the basis of price bids. Naturally the higher the price bid, the lower the yield to maturity for the buyer, and vice versa. The *stop-out* price—below which bids were not accepted—was determined by the bids received and by the amount of securities the Treasury wanted to sell. Typically, each successful bidder paid the price he bid, but the Treasury did hold two *Dutch auctions* in which all successful bidders paid the stop-out pric ·. In all price auctions, noncompetitive bids were accepted; and with the exception of the Dutch auctions, noncompetitive bidders paid a price equal to the average of the competitive bids accepted.

Typically, the Treasury announces a new issue a week or more before the auction date. Under the *price-auction* system, at the time a new issue was announced, the Treasury set the coupon on the issue in line with market rates so that the new issue's price, determined through auction, would be at or near par. If rates moved away from the levels prevailing on the announcement day, the prices bid on the auction day would, reflecting this, move away from par. For example, if rates fell between the announcement of an issue and the auction, bid prices would be above par, whereas if rates rose, bids would be below par. As interest rates became more volatile, deviations of bid prices from par became a problem. In August 1974 one Treasury issue was sold at 101 while another failed to sell out because the Treasury received too few bids at or above the minimum price it would accept. The Treasury feared that above-par prices would discourage some bidders and that below-par prices would place purchasers in an unanticipated tax position (the amount of the discount at issue being taxable at maturity as ordinary income). Another problem with price auctions was that, when the Treasury set coupons, the market tended to move to them, so that price auctions disturbed the market. To solve both problems and to ensure that its issues sold out, the Treasury moved in late 1974 to a new technique in which would-be buyers bid *yields* instead of prices.

In a yield auction for notes and bonds, the Treasury announces the

---

[3] During the one- to two-week period between the time a new Treasury note or bond issue is auctioned and the time the securities sold are actually issued, securities that have been auctioned but not yet issued trade actively on a *when-issued* basis. They also trade *wi* during the announcement to auction period.

new issue a week or more before the auction. At that time it tells the market what amount of securities it will issue, when they will mature, and what denominations will be available. *Competitive* bidders bid yields to two decimal points (e.g., 10.53) for specific quantities of the new issue. After bids are received, the Treasury determines the stop-out bid on the basis of both the bids received and the amount it wishes to borrow. It then sets the coupon on the security to the nearest ⅛ of 1 percent necessary to make the average price charged to successful bidders equal to 100.00 or less. Once the coupon on the issue is established, each successful bidder is charged a price (discount, par, or premium) for his securities; the price is determined so that the yield-to-maturity on the securities a bidder gets equals the yield he bid. *Noncompetitive* bidders pay the average price of the accepted competitive tenders.

SECONDARY MARKET

Little trading in outstanding notes and bonds occurs on organized stock exchanges. The New York Stock Exchange lists a few issues, and the American Exchange (AMEX) offers odd-lot trading in a few others, but neither exchange moves much volume.[4] The real secondary market for bills, notes, and bonds is the dealer-made market, in which huge quantities of bills, notes, and bonds are constantly traded under highly competitive conditions at small margins.

In the note market yields are quoted in 32nds, but quotes can be refined to 64ths through the use of *pluses;* an eight+ bid, for example, means that the bid is eight and one-half 32nds, which is ¹⁷⁄₆₄. (Exhibit 1 gives the decimal equivalent of each 8th, 16th, 32nd and 64th.) On dealers' runs for notes with less than a year to run, the normal spread between the bid and asked is ¹⁄₃₂. On notes in the one- to two-year area, the spread widens to ¹⁄₁₆, and on notes beyond one year, it is typically ⅛, except on new issues that are very actively traded. Quotes on notes are normally good for $1 million, but trades much larger and smaller are also done.

A dealer's daily quote sheet for several Treasury notes and bonds is reproduced in Exhibit 2. Each issue is identified in the first four columns, the "N" and "B" denoting a note and bond, respectively. The bid and asked quotes are shown in the next two columns, the difference representing the spread. The number following the decimal indicates the number of 32nds. For example, for the first issue shown in Exhibit 2, the asked price is 103.05. The "05" following the decimal is ⁵⁄₃₂, or

---

[4] AMEX trading in odd lots of governments is primarily for the convenience of brokers. If the broker uses a dealer to execute a small buy or sell order, the dealer's fee eats up most of the commission that the broker charges the investor. In contrast, on bond trades executed on an exchange by a member firm, transaction costs to the broker are minimal.

EXHIBIT 1 Decimal Equivalents

8ths	16ths	32nds	64ths	Decimal equivalent	8ths	16ths	32nds	64ths	Decimal equivalent
			1	.015625				33	.515625
		1	2	.031250			17	34	.531250
			3	.046875				35	.546875
	1	2	4	.062500		9	18	36	.562500
			5	.078125				37	.578125
		3	6	.093750			19	38	.593750
			7	.109375				39	.609375
1	2	4	8	.125000	5	10	20	40	.625000
			9	.140625				41	.640625
		5	10	.156250			21	42	.656250
			11	.171875				43	.671875
	3	6	12	.187500		11	22	44	.687500
			13	.203125				45	.703125
		7	14	.218750			23	46	.718750
			15	.234375				47	.734375
2	4	8	16	.250000	6	12	24	48	.750000
			17	.265625				49	.765625
		9	18	.281250			25	50	.781250
			19	.296875				51	.796875
	5	10	20	.312500		13	26	52	.812500
			21	.328125				53	.828125
		11	22	.343750			27	54	.843750
			23	.359375				55	.859375
3	6	12	24	.375000	7	14	28	56	.875000
			25	.390625				57	.890625
		13	26	.406250			29	58	.906250
			27	.421875				59	.921875
	7	14	28	.437500		15	30	60	.937500
			29	.453125				61	.953125
		15	30	.468750			31	62	.968750
			31	.484375				63	.984375
4	8	16	32	.500000	8	16	32	64	1.000000

.156250 percent (see Exhibit 1). Therefore the asked price is 103.156250 percent of par. For a $100,000 par value, the price is $103,156.25 ($100,000 times 1.03156250). The change in the asked price (in 32nds) from the previous trading day is then shown. Three yield measures are shown—yield-to-maturity, current yield, and realized compound yield—each based on the asked price. The yield value of $\frac{1}{32}$nd, which as explained in Chapter 5 is a measure of bond price volatility, is also shown. Duration, which is another measure of bond price volatility, is shown on some dealer quote sheets. Other information reported in Exhibit 2 is the accrued interest per $1,000 of par value, the high and low price of the issue over its life, the issue date, the auction yield, and the size of the issue.

EXHIBIT 2 Excerpt from a Dealer's Quote Sheet

			Delivery Date: 6/28/85			Today's Date: 6/27/85					Quotation Date: 6/26/85				
						Yield									
Sec. Nb.	Rate	Maturity	Bid	Asked		To Mat	Curr.	Real.*	Yield 1/32	Accrued Interest†	High	Low	Issue Date	Auction Yield	Pub. Held
125	10¾ N	8/15/90	103.03	103.05	+13	9.94	10.04	9.41	.007759	39.495856	105.15	76.08	8/15/80	10.81	2751
32	11½ N	10/15/90	105.17	105.19	+13	10.10	10.66	9.53	.007488	23.251366	108.08	90.00	10/ 5/83	11.61	5000
130	13.00 N	11/15/90	111.11	111.12	+13	10.19	11.51	9.57	.007165	15.543478	114.02	86.18	11/17/80	13.07	4751
14	11¾ B	2/15/ 1	106.23	106.25	+19	10.84	10.58	9.22	.003982	43.169890	112.04	76.00	1/12/81	11.83	1500
132	13⅛ B	5/15/ 1	117.06	117.10	+29	10.82	11.04	9.21	.003670	15.692935	121.21	84.06	4/ 2/81	13.21	1750

* Realized yield is based on a reinvestment rate equal to the current 6 month bill, bond equivalent yield, for securities with less than 6 months to maturity.

† per $1,000 par value.

In the note market, an issue is current from the time it is auctioned until it is replaced by another issue. Thus, the new two-year note is current for a month, and new four-year note for a quarter. A current issue trades much more actively than other issues until it becomes distributed or is replaced by a new issue. Although notes range in original maturity from 2 to 10 years, there are at any time only five or six current issues that are relatively new and actively traded at narrow spreads. Moreover, before the Treasury undertook its program of regularization of debt issuance, there were even fewer.

Many investors roll notes to stay in the current issue. Sometimes they will even give up coupon just to stay in a note that is active enough so that they can get a bid on size in a market that is quiet or going down. Staying in the current note allows the investor to increase yield by moving out on the yield curve while still maintaining liquidity. Dealers, too, like to position current issues. As one noted, "When I go long or short, I like to stay as current as possible because that is where most people have buying and selling interest."

In longer notes, the market sometimes would go for months without a new issue, something that would be unimaginable in the bill market. When this occurred, trading in this market area tapered off. Where and when the Treasury chooses to issue its new debt also affect the yield curve. For example, before the three-year note was added to the issues sold in the quarterly refunding, a trader of long notes commented, "We are going six months with no auction of a three-year note. That will drive down the yield on the three-year note relative to yields on other issues around it."

Coupons with a current maturity of a year or less are not actively traded. Part of the reason is that brokerage is much less on bills than on coupons. Also, the bill market naturally tends to be active because there are so many bill auctions. Another reason short coupons trade inactively is that it is difficult for government dealers to staff all their major chairs, so they put rookie trainees on short coupons—often in a bank, it's someone who has graduated from the Fed funds desk.

Not all issues trade strictly on the yield curve. One of the reasons is the varying reception that different issues receive in the auction. It also depends on the volume in which it was offered to the market.

Treasury long bonds extend in maturity well past the year 2000. Long bonds are much more volatile in price than short instruments, and the risks in positioning them are commensurately greater. As a result it was always typical for traders of long governments to hedge the bulk of their positions. Especially before the advent of bond futures, many bond traders, if they bought $1 million of long bonds from a customer and could not immediately resell them, would short a similar active issue and then wait and unwind the position when they could. In the view of other traders this sort of trading is wasted activity.

In recent years spreads in the bond market have narrowed because

(1) individual issues are so much bigger these days; (2) the Board provides traders with so much liquidity; and (3) so much volume is transacted in the market. These days it is not unusual for a big shop to trade well in excess of $1 billion of bonds a day.

In 10- to 30-year coupons, virtually every issue is active because customers have positions in virtually all of them. They do a lot of swaps between securities to increase their total rate of return over a year. This is in sharp contrast to the situation in the note market. In the 10 years and under area there are only two active issues within a given area that the Treasury sells: two 10s, two 7s, two 5s, two 4s, two 3s, and two 2s. The premium placed on active note issues is phenomenal compared to that placed on more active long issues. The premium on active note issues is created by speculators who prefer to always trade the most active issues because they can get in and out of them with the greatest ease.

The end users of securities, buyers who intend to hold them to maturity or at least stay with a given security for some period, will buy off the run securities on which they can get some pick up in yield.

Computing Accrued Interest on Treasury Notes and Bonds

Government notes and bonds pay interest semiannually[5] on the basis of a 365-day year. The first coupon date on a government note or bond is determined at issue; the second is the same day of the month six months hence. Thus, if a security's first coupon date is May 15, its second will be November 15. This pattern continues throughout the life of the security. At each coupon date, an amount equal to half the coupon rate (c) times the face value of the security, i.e., c/2 per $1 of face value, is paid to the security holder.[6]

Interest on governments is accrued during each coupon period on an *actual day basis;* that is, a fixed sum of interest is accrued each day during the coupon period until an amount equal to c/2 per $1 of face value is reached on the coupon date.

The number of days in a coupon period is referred to as its *basis,* and the amount of daily interest that accrues during any coupon period is calculated as follows: Let

$$B = \text{basis, i.e., number of days in the coupon period}$$
$$c = \text{coupon rate}$$

---

[5] An exception is foreign targeted issue notes (TINs) in which interest is paid annually.

[6] For calculation of accrued interest when the first coupon period is irregular, see Marcia Stigum, *Money Market Calculations: Yields, Break-Evens, and Arbitrage* (Homewood, IL: Dow Jones-Irwin, 1981), pp. 105–106.

then

$$\left(\begin{array}{c}\text{Interest accrued per day}\\ \text{per \$1 of face value}\end{array}\right) = \frac{c}{2B}$$

The number of days between one day in a month and the same day six months later is never precisely half a year—182.5 days. Therefore, consecutive coupon periods are always unequal in length; one might be 181 days, the next 184 days. Since consecutive coupon periods always have different bases, *the interest that accrues per day on a government always differs by a small amount between consecutive coupon periods.*

When a government note or bond is traded, the buyer pays the dollar price quoted plus accrued interest as of the settlement date. The formula for calculating accrued interest on a government is as follows:

EXHIBIT 3 Year-by-Returns on U.S. Treasury Notes and Bonds: 1960–84

Year End	Notes	Bonds
1960	10.14%	13.78%
1961	2.07	0.97
1962	5.07	6.89
1963	2.14	1.21
1964	4.00	3.51
1965	1.43	0.71
1966	5.02	3.65
1967	1.79	−9.19
1968	4.51	−0.26
1969	−0.97	−5.08
1970	15.13	12.10
1971	8.20	13.23
1972	4.23	5.68
1973	2.47	−1.11
1974	6.50	4.35
1975	8.38	9.19
1976	11.92	16.75
1977	2.29	−0.67
1978	3.22	−1.16
1979	4.64	−1.22
1980	4.55	−3.95
1981	9.70	1.85
1982	23.79	40.35
1983	7.52	0.68
1984	13.29	15.43

SOURCE: Roger G. Ibbotson, Laurence B. Siegel, and Kathryn S. Love, "World Wealth: Market Values and Returns," *The Journal of Portfolio Management* (Fall 1985), p. 11.

Let

a_i = accrued interest *per dollar* of face value

t_{is} = days from issue or last coupon to settlement

then

$$a_i = c \frac{t_{is}}{2B}$$

For example, suppose that a government note paying interest on May 30th and November 30th has a 7⅛ percent coupon and is traded for settlement on August 10th. The number of days from the last coupon payment (May 30th) to settlement is 71 days (t_{is}). The basis in the coupon period is 183 days. Then, accrued interest on this security would be:

$$a_i = 0.07125 \frac{71}{2(183)}$$
$$= 0.013822 \text{ per } \$1 \text{ of face value.}$$

The only difficulty in making this calculation is determining t_{is} and B. One way to do that is to use a financial calculator programmed to calculate the number of days between two dates. An alternative is to use a financial calendar.

REALIZED YIELDS ON TREASURY NOTES AND BONDS

As explained in Chapter 4, the quoted yield-to-maturity is a promised yield. It reflects the yield if the security is held to maturity and if coupon interest payments are reinvested at the yield-to-maturity. We conclude this chapter with a review of realized yields on Treasury coupon securities.

Exhibit 3 presents the *realized* annual total return on notes and bonds from 1960 to 1984. The annual compound return for Treasury notes and bonds was 6.32 and 4.70 percent, respectively, with a standard deviation of 5.27 and 9.70 percent.[7] Due to periods of rising interest rates in the 1970s and in 1980, the shorter term of Treasury notes resulted in their better performance relative to Treasury bonds. Over the same period, the compound return of intermediate-term corporate bonds was 6.37 percent with a standard deviation of 7.15 percent; for long-term corporate bonds the compound return was 5.03 percent with a standard deviation of 11.26 percent.[8]

---

[7] Roger G. Ibbotson, Laurence B. Siegel, and Kathryn S. Love, "World Wealth: Market Values and Returns," *The Journal of Portfolio Management* (Fall 1985), pp. 4–23.

[8] Ibbotson, Siegel and Love, p. 17.

EXHIBIT 4   Total Returns of Treasury Notes and Bonds: 1/1/80 to 12/31/85

Issue	Price Return	Income Return	Reinvestment Return	Total Return	Annualized Total
2 year	6.04%	69.93%	37.39%	113.36%	13.46%
3 year	5.02	69.83	36.24	111.09	13.26
4 year	5.03	70.99	37.55	113.56	13.48
5 year	7.04	71.10	39.76	117.90	13.8€
7 year	8.18	71.59	41.54	121.32	14.16
10 year	8.51	71.20	41.41	121.12	14.14
20 year*	21.65	59.89	39.84	121.38	14.16
30 year	11.10	70.16	42.80	124.06	14.39
Ryan Index†	8.09	70.61	40.27	118.97	13.95

* 20-year was first auctioned on 1/06/81. Totals may not add up due to rounding.
† The Ryan Index is an equally weighted index of current coupon Treasuries published by Ryan Financial Strategy Group.
SOURCE: Sharmin Mossavar-Rahmani, "Performance of the Treasury Market in the 1980s," in *The Handbook of Treasury Securities*, ed. Frank J. Fabozzi (Chicago: Probus Publishing, 1986), Chapter 3.

EXHIBIT 5   Monthly Total Return Volatility of Treasury Notes and Bonds (by year)

Issue	1980	1981	1982	1983	1984	1985
2 year	2.89%	2.02%	1.17%	0.79%	0.98%	0.73%
3 year	3.55	2.54	1.53	1.09	1.29	1.02
4 year	3.85	2.78	1.75	1.36	1.66	1.35
5 year	4.45	3.13	2.09	1.60	1.98	1.66
7 year	4.42	3.62	2.44	2.04	2.42	2.16
10 year	4.84	4.31	2.53	2.60	2.83	2.68
15 year*	5.14	4.90	3.27	—	—	—
20 year†	—	5.35	3.27	3.34	3.45	3.35
30 year	5.74	5.49	3.17	3.44	3.53	3.59
Ryan Index‡	4.25	3.65	2.26	2.07	2.19	2.02

* 15-year returns end 4/14/83. Last 15-year was auctioned on 10/07/80.
† 20-year was first auctioned on 1/06/81.
‡ The Ryan Index is an equally weighted index of current coupon Treasuries published by Ryan Financial Strategy Group.
SOURCE: Sharmin Mossavar-Rahmani, "Performance of the Treasury Market in the 1980s," in *The Handbook of Treasury Securities*, ed. Frank J. Fabozzi (Chicago: Probus Publishing, 1986), Chapter 3.

Total returns of Treasury coupon issues from January 1980 to December 1985 by maturity are shown in Exhibit 4. The three sources of return (price, coupon income, and reinvestment) are also shown. Note the importance of the reinvestment return (or in terms of the discussion in Chapter 4, interest-on-interest return). Finally, Exhibit 5 shows the monthly total return volatility of Treasury coupon securities by year from 1980 to 1985.

9

Securities of Federal Government Agencies and Sponsored Corporations

Marcia Stigum, Ph.D.
Stigum & Associates, New York

The market for securities of federal government agencies and sponsored corporations, commonly referred to in Wall Street lingo as *agencies*[1], while smaller than that for governments, has become in recent years an active and important sector of the fixed income market. In this chapter federal agency securities are discussed.

ATTRACTION TO INVESTORS

Federal agency securities are attractive to a wide range of investors for a number of reasons. First, most agency issues are backed either *de jure* or *de facto* by the federal government, so the credit risk attached to them is zero or negligible. Second, many agency issues offer the tax advantage that interest income on them, like interest income on governments, is exempt from state and local income taxation.

Normally, agencies trade at some spread to Treasury issues of the same maturity. This spread varies considerably depending on supply conditions and the tightness of money. In recent years agencies with a two-year maturity have offered investors a yield advantage over governments that ranged from 3 to 87 basis points. For agencies with a 10-year maturity, the highs and lows of the yield advantage over governments were 134 and 7 basis points, respectively. The spread at which agencies trade in relation to governments also appears to reflect differences in the liquidity of the two sorts of instruments.

---

[1] In this chapter the securities of federal government agencies and sponsored corporations are simply referred to as federal agency, or just agency, securities.

THE FEDERAL FINANCING BANK

As federal agencies proliferated, their borrowings from the public caused several problems. One had to do with calendar scheduling. Each year federal agencies issue substantial quantities of new debt. Agency issues compete with each other and with Treasury issues for investors' funds, and an uneven flow of agency and Treasury issues to the market could result in rates being driven up one week and down the next. To avoid this, the Treasury schedules the timing and size of both its own and agency issues to ensure a reasonably smooth flow of federal issues to the market. In 1973 minor federal agencies made 75 separate offerings, so many that it made Treasury calendar scheduling of new issues difficult. Another problem resulting from the proliferation of federal agencies was that the new small agencies constantly being created by Congress were not well known to investors; and because of their small size, their issues were less liquid than Treasury issues. Consequently, small agencies had to pay relatively high borrowing rates.

To deal with these problems, in 1973 Congress set up the *Federal Financing Bank* (FFB), a government institution supervised by the Secretary of the Treasury. The FFB buys up the debt issues of the smaller agencies, and its clientele currently includes about 20 separate agencies, essentially all federal agencies except for the seven major ones.

The FFB was supposed to obtain funds by issuing securities fully backed by the government in a fashion similar to the way the Treasury issues its securities. It tried this approach once with an offering of short-term bills. This offering was bid for by dealers and others at yields close to those prevailing on T bills, but the issue fell in price in the secondary market, which was discouraging to both dealers and the Treasury. Some dealers felt that, if the FFB had continued to issue its securities, they would—after five or six issues—have been accepted by investors as equal to Treasury issues and would have sold at yields no higher than those on Treasury issues. The Treasury, however, seems to have doubted this; one reason was that FFB offerings would have been smaller than Treasury offerings and consequently less liquid. In any case, the FFB discontinued its public offerings and now borrows from the Treasury. Today only seven major federal agencies still issue new securities to the market. Some of the smaller agencies, which now borrow from the FFB, do, however, still have a few long-term issues outstanding.

PRACTICES AND TYPES OF AGENCY SECURITIES ISSUED

Among the agencies still issuing securities to the public, practices and types of securities issued vary considerably. One can, however, make a few generalizations. Each federal agency establishes a fiscal agent through which it offers its securities, all of which are negotiable. Agency issues are not sold directly to investors by these fiscal agents. Instead they are sold through a syndicate of dealers, who distribute the agency's securities to investors and participate in making a secondary market for these securities.

Agency securities come in varying forms: short-term notes sold at a discount and interest-bearing notes and bonds. Agency bonds are frequently issued with the title *debenture*. Any bond is an interest-bearing certificate of debt. A mortgage bond is a bond secured by a lien on some specific piece of property. A debenture is a bond secured only by the general credit of the issuer.

Interest on agency securities and principal at maturity are usually payable at any branch of the issuing agency, at any Federal Reserve bank or branch, and at the Treasury. Agency bonds are typically not callable.

Like Treasury securities, agency securities are issued under the authority of an act of Congress. Therefore, unlike private offerings, they are exempt from registration with the Securities and Exchange Commission (SEC). Typically agency issues are backed by collateral in the form of cash, U.S. government securities, and the debt obligations that the issuing agency has acquired through its lending activities. A few agency issues are backed by the full faith and credit of the U.S. A number of others are guaranteed by the Treasury or supported by the issuing agency's right to borrow funds from the Treasury up to some specified amount. Finally, there are agency securities with no direct or indirect federal backing.

The major federal agencies still offering securities differ considerably in mission and method of operation, so we have organized our survey of them by function: first the mortgage-related agencies and then the farm credit agencies.

The four major mortgage-related agencies are the Federal Home Loan Banks, the Federal National Mortgage Association, the Government National Mortgage Association, and the Federal Home Loan Mortgage Corporation. Only the first is discussed here. The others are discussed in Chapter 16.

Housing Credit Agencies

Federal Home Loan Banks. Behind the nation's commercial banks stands the Federal Reserve System, which regulates member banks, acts as a lender of last resort, and otherwise facilitates a smooth operation of the banking system. Behind the nation's S&Ls stands a somewhat similar institution, the *Federal Home Loan Bank* system. The FHLB, created in 1932, is composed of 12 regional banks and a central board in Washington.

S&Ls, savings banks, and insurance companies may all become

members of the FHLB system; federally chartered S&Ls are required to do so. Currently about 3,400 S&Ls belong to the FHLB system; these S&Ls hold over 98 percent of the total assets in all S&Ls in the country.

The Federal Home Loan Banks are owned by the private S&Ls that are members of the system, just as the 12 Federal Reserve Banks are owned by their member banks. The private ownership, however, is only nominal since the FHLB, like the Fed, operates under federal charter and is charged by Congress with regulating member S&Ls and with formulating and carrying out certain aspects of government policy with respect to the savings and loan industry. Thus the Federal Home Loan Banks are in fact an arm of the federal government.

In addition to overseeing member S&Ls, the FHLB also lends to member S&Ls just as the Fed lends to commercial banks. Here, however, the similarity ends. The Fed obtains money to lend to banks at the discount window by monetizing debt. The Federal Home Loan Banks have to borrow the money they lend to member S&Ls. Most of the money S&Ls provide to home buyers comes from their depositors. The FHLB lends to member S&Ls primarily to augment this source of funds. In a nutshell, the FHLB borrows money in the open market, then re-lends it to S&Ls, which in turn either relend it again to home buyers or, in recent years, use it to offset deposit outflows.

The main security issued by the FHLB is consolidated *bonds*, "consolidated" referring to the fact that the bonds are the joint obligation of all 12 Federal Home Loan Banks. FHLB bonds have a maturity at issue of one year or more, pay interest semiannually, and are not callable. They are issued in book-entry form and are now sold in denominations of $10,000, $25,000, $100,000, and $1 million. FHLB bonds often appear on dealers' quote sheets as *FHLB notes*. The FHLB used to issue short-term, interest-bearing notes, but it switched some time ago to the sale of discount notes to raise short-term money. These discount notes have a minimum denomination of $50,000 and maturities under one year.

FHLB securities are backed by qualified collateral in the form of secured advances to member S&Ls, government securities, insured mortgages, etc. FHLB securities are *not* guaranteed by the U.S. government. However, they are the obligation of the FHLB system, which plays a key federal role in regulating and assisting the S&L industry. Given this role and the importance of the S&L industry to the economy, it is inconceivable that the U.S. government would ever permit the FHLB to default on outstanding securities.

Interest income from FHLB securities is subject to full federal taxes, but is specifically exempt from state and local taxation.

Farm Credit Agencies

The production and sale of agricultural commodities require large amounts of credit. So, too, does the acquisition by farmers of additional land and buildings. To assure an adequate supply of credit to meet these needs, the government has put together over time the Farm Credit Administration. This administration, which operates as an independent agency of the U.S. government, oversees the Farm Credit System, which operates in all states plus Puerto Rico. Under this system, the country is divided into 12 farm credit districts. In each of these, there is a Federal Land Bank, a Federal Intermediate Credit Bank, and a Bank for Cooperatives, each supplying specific types of credit to qualified borrowers in its district. To obtain funds, these 37 banks plus a Central Bank for Cooperatives all issue securities through a common fiscal agency in New York City.

Before discussing the obligations of the Bank for Cooperatives, Federal Land Banks, and Federal Intermediate Credit Banks, let's first discuss the Consolidated Systemwide obligations of the Federal Credit Banks.

Consolidated Systemwide discount notes and bonds of the Farm Credit Banks were first introduced in January 1975 and August 1977, respectively. These obligations are the secured joint and several obligations of the 37 Farm Credit Banks. The smallest denomination for the discount notes is $50,000 and is issued in bearer form. The maturities on these obligations range from 5 to 270 days. Consolidated Systemwide bonds are issued each month with maturities of six and nine *months*. About six times a year, longer term bonds are issued. For maturities of less than 13 months, they are issued in multiples of $5,000. For longer maturities, bonds are issued in multiples of $1,000. Bonds are issued in book-entry form. Interest income from Consolidated Systemwide discount notes and bonds is subject to full federal income taxation but is specifically exempt from state and local income taxes.

Banks for Cooperatives. The 12 district Banks for Cooperatives, organized under the Farm Credit Act of 1933, make seasonal and term loans to cooperatives owned by farmers, engage in purchasing farm supplies, provide business services to farmers, and market farm output. These loans may provide working capital or finance investments in buildings and equipment. The Central Bank for Cooperatives participates in large loans made by individual district banks. Initially the Banks for Cooperatives were owned by the U.S. government. Since 1955, however, government capital has been replaced by private capital, and ownership is now private.

The major means by which the Banks for Cooperatives finance new loans is through the sale of consolidated collateral trust debentures (*co-ops*). These debentures, which are not callable, are typically offered to investors once a month. They are available in bearer and book-entry form, and the smallest denominations available are $5,000 and $10,000; however, new issues are available in book-entry form in multiples of $1,000. Many recent issues have had an original maturity of six months and pay interest at maturity, but longer term (two to five years) co-ops have also been issued.

All debentures issued by the Banks for Cooperatives must be secured by acceptable collateral in the form of cash, Treasury securities, and notes or other obligations of borrowers from the banks. Also, each bank is examined at least annually by the Farm Credit Administration. Obligations of these banks are not, however, guaranteed either directly or indirectly by the U.S. government. Nevertheless, given the semiofficial status of the Banks for Cooperatives and the government's high degree of concern for agriculture, it seems unlikely, to say the least, that the government would permit these banks to default on their securities.

Interest income from debentures issued by the Banks for Cooperatives is subject to full federal income taxation but is specifically exempt from state and local income taxes.

Federal Land Banks. The 12 Federal Land Banks were organized under the Federal Farm Loan Act of 1916. These banks extend first mortgage loans on farm properties and make other loans through local Federal Land Bank (FLB) associations. Mortgage loans must be made on the basis of appraisal reports and may not exceed 65 percent of the appraised value of the mortgaged property. Maturities on FLB loans may run from 5 to 40 years, but most have original maturities of around 20 years. Although the Federal Land Banks were set up under government auspices, all government capital in these banks has been replaced by private capital, and they are now owned by the FLB associations, which in turn are owned by the farmers who have obtained FLB loans through these associations.

The Federal Land Banks obtain funds to lend out primarily by issuing Consolidated Federal Farm Loan bonds and by occasional short-term borrowings between bond issues. Since 1963, all FLB bond issues have been noncallable. These securities range in maturity from a few years to 15 years. Most have an original maturity of longer than one year. Securities with a maturity of less than five years are available in bearer and book-entry form. Those with a maturity of more than five years are also available in registered form. Interest on FLB bonds is payable semiannually. The smallest denominations available are $1,000, $5,000, and $10,000. All new issues, however, are available in book-entry form only, in multiples of $1,000.

S&Ls are placed in an uncomfortable position whenever interest rates rise because the nature of their business is to borrow short and lend long. Federal Land Banks are in a somewhat similar situation since maturities on the loans they extend tend to be longer than the original maturities of the bonds they issue. To avoid the danger inherent in this position, Federal Land Banks now write only *variable-rate* mortgages. This approach enables them to keep loan income in line with borrowing costs whether interest rates rise or fall.

FLB bonds must be backed with collateral in the form of cash, Treasury securities, or notes secured by first mortgages on farm properties. Federal Land Banks are examined at least annually by the Farm Credit Administration. Their securities are not guaranteed either directly or indirectly by the U.S. government. However, their semiofficial status makes it extremely unlikely that the government would ever permit default on their securities.

Income from FLB bonds is subject to full federal income taxation but is exempt from state and local income taxation.

Federal Intermediate Credit Banks. The 12 Federal Intermediate Credit Banks (FICB) were organized under the Agricultural Credit Act of 1923. Their job is to help provide short-term financing for the seasonal production and marketing of crops and livestock and for other farm-related credit purposes. These banks do not lend directly to farmers. Instead they make loans to and discount agricultural and livestock paper for various financial institutions that lend to farmers.[2] These institutions include commercial banks, production credit associations organized under the Farm Credit Act of 1933, agricultural credit corporations, and incorporated livestock loan companies. Originally, Federal Intermediate Credit Banks were government owned, but like the other farm credit banks discussed above, today their ownership is wholly private.

Although FICBs are authorized to borrow from commercial banks and to rediscount agricultural paper with the Fed, the principal source of their funds is monthly sales of consolidated collateral trust debentures. These debentures are available in bearer and book-entry form and come in denominations of $5,000, $10,000, $50,000, $100,000 and $500,000. New issues are available in book-entry form only, in multiples of $1,000. The Federal Intermediate Credit Banks are authorized to issue securities with a maturity of up to five years, but many of their obligations are issued with nine-month maturities with interest payable at maturity. Farmers may order and purchase FICB securities directly from the production credit associations of which they are members. Otherwise FICB securities are sold through dealers, as in the case of other agency securities.

FICB debentures are backed by collateral in the form of Treasury securities, other farm credit agency securities, cash, and the notes, discounted obligations, and loans that these banks acquire through their lending activities. Federal Intermediate Credit Banks are regularly examined by the Farm Credit Administration. *Their securities are not guaranteed by the government, but as in the case of the institutions discussed above, their semiofficial status offers considerable assurance to the investor that the government would not permit default on FICB debentures.*

---

[2] *Discounting agricultural paper* means buying up farmers' loan notes at a discount.

Interest income on FICB debentures is subject to full federal income taxation but exempt from state and local income taxation.

COMPUTING ACCRUED INTEREST FOR AGENCIES

Federal agency securities are quoted in the same way as governments. However, on agencies, *interest accrues as if the year has 360 days and every month has 30 days*. This method of accruing interest, which is also used on municipal securities, is referred to as a 30/360 basis.

A general formula for computing accrued interest on all securities that pay interest on a 30/360-day basis is[3]:

$$a_i = c\,\frac{t_{is}}{360}$$

where

a_i = accrued interest *per dollar* of face value

c = coupon rate

t_{is} = days *assumed* to have elapsed from issue or last coupon date to settlement date

To illustrate how this method of accruing interest works, suppose an agency with a 9½ percent coupon rate that pays semiannual interest on August 27 and February 27 is purchased for settlement on April 9. Recalling that agencies accrue interest as if every month has 30 days and the familiar rhyme, "Thirty days hath September, April, June, . . . ," it is easy to come up with the following numbers:

	Days from Last Coupon to Settlement	Days from Settlement to Maturity
Assumed in calculating accrued interest	42	138
Actual	41	140

As can be seen, because February has 28 days and seven other months have 31 days, significant discrepancies can arise between the number of days that is *assumed* to exist in a certain period for purposes of accruing interest on an agency security and the number of days that *actually* exists in that period.

To determine how much interest per dollar of face value had accrued as of April 9, we divide the coupon rate by 360 (the assumed

---

[3] In contrasting this formula with the one we gave in the previous chapter for calculating a_i on a short government, note that on an agency the basis in the current coupon period is always assumed to be 180 days.

number of days in the year) and then multiply by 42 (the assumed number of days from the last coupon date to the settlement date). This gives us

$$a_i = 0.095 \; \frac{42}{360} = 0.011083 \text{ per \$1 of face value.}$$

THE SECONDARY MARKET

The secondary market in agency securities, like the secondary market in governments, is made by dealers trading with retail and with each other. There are, however, significant differences between the two markets. These result in large part from the fact that agency issues are smaller than Treasury issues and are traded less actively.

Several primary dealers in governments are in the market every day trading agencies, but many others are sometimes players who will position when they like a spot in the agency market and otherwise ignore it.

Dealer's positions in agencies are much smaller than those in governments. Also in agencies, as in government notes and bonds, dealers sometimes assume net short positions, so the technical condition of the agency market, like that of the government note market, can become bone dry in particular sectors.

Interdealer quotes in agencies are good for only $500,000, and a lot of trades of that size are done. A $5 million trade is a big trade in the agency market except on a new or short-term issue. A $10 million trade is a rarity.

Spreads are wider in agencies than in governments, and agencies are consequently less liquid. An agency run includes the two newest FHLB issues, the two newest Federal Land Bank issues, the most recent Federal Intermediate Credit Bank issue, and the most recent Bank for Cooperatives issue. For on-the-run agency issues, the typical spread is 1/32 for a one-year maturity, 1/32 to 2/32nds for a two- to three-year maturity, and as much as 4/32nds for a 10-year bond. As issues get seasoned, these spreads widen. One reason is that currently many investors in agencies are trust accounts, state and local governments, and commercial banks that mature the securities they buy and rarely do swaps.

In recent years agencies have become, if anything, less liquid than they used to be. A problem with agency securities is that the agencies issuing them have not increased the size of their issues as the Treasury has done. On $400 and $500 million agency issues, once an issue gets distributed, it gets illiquid. Noted one trader,

> "I would like to see the agencies reopen issues and build up an issue to two or three billion in size. People have offered this concept to the agency fiscal agents who seem to have rejected it. There are so many agency issues that it is hard to keep track of them, and many are so small. What develops a really

liquid market is the ability to short an issue because then you always have someone—an arbitrageur—there willing to buy it back at a price. But an arbitrageur has to be crazy to short agency issues. You can't borrow enough of them to do it. Whereas I can short almost any Treasury issue on the list and know I can borrow it at a price, I can't do that in agencies.

The illiquidity of agency paper is reflected in the fact that in inactive issues spreads can be virtually anything.

10

Corporate Bonds

Frank J. Fabozzi, Ph.D, C.F.A., C.P.A.
Visiting Professor
Sloan School of Management
Massachusetts Institute of Technology

Harry C. Sauvain, D.S.C.
University Professor Emeritus of Finance
Indiana University

Richard S. Wilson
Vice President
Merrill Lynch Capital Markets

John C. Ritchie, Jr., Ph.D.
Professor of Finance
Temple University

A corporate bond is a long-term promissory note given under seal, usually as part of a mass borrowing arrangement. The essential features are relatively simple. The issuer promises to pay a specified percentage of par value on designated dates (known as coupon payments)[1] and to repay par or face value (principal) of the bond at maturity.[2] Failure to pay either the principal or interest when due constitutes legal default and court proceedings can be instituted to enforce the contract. Bondholders, as creditors, have a prior legal claim over common and preferred stockholders as to both income and assets of the corporation for the principal and interest due them, and may have a prior claim over

---

[1] Income bonds, zero-coupon bonds, and floating-rate debt are exceptions to this general statement.

[2] While no such issues have been offered in the United States, the British Consuls have no maturity date. They contract to pay a stipulated interest rate forever.

other creditors if liens or mortgages are involved. It is important to recognize, however, that a superior legal status will not prevent bondholders from suffering financial loss when the ability of a corporation to generate cash flow adequate to pay its obligations is seriously eroded.

Bond prices can and do undergo sizeable changes, as the general level of interest rates changes, reflecting changing supply and demand conditions for loanable funds. Bonds can be acquired for income, emphasizing the relative sureness and attractiveness of periodic interest receipts and tending to ignore price fluctuations. On the other hand, fixed income securities can be among the most speculative investment vehicles available when bought on margin or when a low-quality issue is purchased.

Corporate bonds are usually issued in denominations of $1,000 and multiples thereof. In common usage, a corporate bond is assumed to have a par value of $1,000 unless otherwise explicitly specified. A security dealer who says he or she has five bonds to sell means five bonds each of $1,000 principal amount. If the promised rate of interest (coupon rate) is 6 percent, the annual amount of interest on each bond is $60 and the semiannual interest is $30.

THE CORPORATE TRUSTEE

The promises of corporate bond issuers and the rights of investors who buy them are set forth in great detail in contracts generally called *bond indentures*. If bondholders were handed the complete indenture, they would have trouble understanding the legalese, and even greater difficulty in determining from time to time whether the corporate issuer is keeping all the promises made. These problems are solved for the most part by bringing in a corporate trustee as a third party to the contract. The indenture is made out to the corporate trustee as a representative of the interests of bondholders; that is, it acts in a fiduciary capacity for investors who own the bond issue.

A corporate trustee is a bank or trust company with a corporate trust department and officers who are experts in performing the functions of a trustee. This is no small task. The corporate trustee must, at the time of issue, authenticate the bonds issued—that is, keep track of all the bonds sold and make sure that they do not exceed the principal amount authorized by the indenture. It must then be a watchdog for the bondholders by seeing to it that the issuer complies with all the covenants of the indenture. These covenants are many and technical, and they must be watched during the entire period that a bond issue is outstanding. We will describe some of these covenants in subsequent pages.

It is very important that corporate trustees be competent and financially responsible. To this end we have a federal statute known as the Trust Indenture Act, which requires that for all corporate bond offerings in the amount of more than $5 million sold in interstate commerce there must be a corporate trustee. The indenture must include adequate requirements for performance of the trustee's duties on behalf of bondholders; there must be no conflict between the trustee's interest as a trustee and any other interest it may have; and there must be provision for reports by the trustee to bondholders. If a corporate issuer fails to pay interest or principal, the trustee must declare a default and take such action as may be necessary to protect the rights of bondholders. If the corporate issuer has promised in the indenture always to maintain an amount of current assets equal to two times the amount of current liabilities, the trustee must watch the corporation's balance sheet and see that the promise is kept. If the issuer fails to maintain the prescribed amounts, the trustee must take action on behalf of the bondholders.

The terms of bond issues set forth in bond indentures are always a compromise between the interests of the bond issuer and those of investors who buy bonds. The issuer always wants to pay the lowest possible rate of interest and to be tied up as little as possible with legal convenants. Bondholders want the highest possible interest rate, the best security, and a variety of covenants to restrict the issuer in one way or another. As we discuss the provisions of bond indentures, keep this opposition of interests in mind and see how compromises are worked out in practice.

BOND CLASSIFICATIONS

Five main classification categories of bonds will serve to organize this section of the chapter: (1) by issuing agency; (2) by purpose of issue; (3) by method of interest payment; (4) in terms of security for the bonds; and (5) by method of repayment. These classifications have proved useful for purposes of organizing an analysis of bonds, by grouping issues in terms of similar investment characteristics and/or pointing attention to important considerations.

Bonds Classified by Issuing Agency

The four general classifications of corporate bonds used by bond information services (such as Moody's) are public utilities, transportations, industrials, and banks and finance companies. Finer breakdowns are often made by analysts to create more homogeneous groupings. For example, public utilities are subdivided into electric power companies, gas distribution companies, water companies, and telephone companies. Transportations can be further subdivided into airlines, railroads, and trucking companies. Like public utilities, transportations are typically regulated by state and/or federal government agencies. Industrials are the catchall class, and the most heterogeneous of the groupings with respect to investment characteristics. Industrials include all kinds of manufacturing, merchandising, and service companies.

Exhibit 1 indicates the amounts raised by various of these classifications through bond issues during the period 1979 through 1985.

Bonds Classified by Purpose of Issue

Bond titles are typically self-explanatory. For example, a prior-lien bond gives a lien ahead of already outstanding mortgage bonds, and is issued with the consent of the first mortgage bondholders in time of financial difficulty. The mortgage bondholders sublimate their interests in the hope that an injection of new funds will enable the corporation to again operate successfully. A refunding bond is issued to replace an already outstanding issue. While bond titles may be misleading at times, investors should be interested in the purpose of the issue when evaluating its desirability.

Bonds Classified by Method of Interest Payment

The three most common classifications of this type are *coupon* or *bearer bonds*, *registered bonds*, and *income bonds*.

A *coupon* or *bearer bond* is a bond to which is attached, at the time of issue, one coupon for each interest payment.

The bondholder clips the respective coupon on each interest date and deposits it with a bank for collection. The owner's name does not appear on the bond and the issuer does not keep a record of owners. Since such bonds are transferred simply by delivery, they are called bearer bonds; whoever lawfully has possession is the owner. Since endorsement is not necessary for transfer of ownership of such bonds, unusual care must be taken to prevent them from being lost or stolen. Bondholders should keep a record of the number appearing on each bond they hold. Many bonds outstanding today are bearer bonds, and some may be exchanged at the option of the holder for registered bonds. However, in recent years corporations have been issuing bonds only in registered form.

A *registered bond* differs from a coupon or bearer bond in that the owner's name appears on the bond. The issuing corporation records the number and current owner of each bond, and such bonds are transferable only by endorsement by an owner. Registered bonds may be fully registered, or registered as to principal only. In the case of fully registered bonds interest is paid by check by the issuing corporation on promised interest dates to the registered owners. Bonds that are registered as to principal only, however, have coupons attached for each interest payment that must be clipped and deposited for collection as with bearer bonds.

Income Bonds

Bonds contain a promise to pay a stipulated amount of interest periodically to bondholders. Ordinarily, failure to make an interest payment in full is a default, or breach of contract. *Income bonds*, on the other hand, contain a promise to pay a stipulated interest, but payment is contingent on earnings being sufficient for the purpose. The bond indenture sets forth the items to be deducted from revenue in determining earnings for purposes of interest payments to the holders of income bonds. Repayment of the principal, however, is not subject to sufficient earnings.

The interest payments are declared by the board of directors, just as dividends are declared on preferred stock and common stock. The discretion allowed the board of directors in declaring interest varies. Some bond indentures require that the board must declare and pay interest if earned. Other indentures permit the board to allocate a portion of the earnings that the board considers appropriate for capital expenditures or other purposes before determining the amount of interest to declare.[3]

Interest may be cumulative or noncumulative. In the former case, the issuer contracts that interest not paid on schedule, or any unpaid part of the interest, must be paid in the future. Usually, there is a limitation to the amount that may be accumulated of three times the annual coupon rate.[4] If interest payments are noncumulative, interest not paid on scheduled dates is just forgotten. Income bonds may be convertible. They may be callable and require sinking-fund payments. They may or may not be subordinated to other debt incurred by the issuer.[5] Because interest is contingent on earnings, income bonds are traded flat (i.e., without accrued interest).

Initially, income bonds were the product of the reorganization of bankrupt railroads. Income bonds issued in this way, known as adjustment bonds, were considered highly speculative because of the uncertainty surrounding the issuer's ability to repay the principal and make the scheduled interest payments. However, in the 1950s, some firms began issuing income bonds because of the tax advantage of this form of financing to the issuer. The tax advantage is that interest, unlike dividends, is a tax-deductible expense thereby reducing the aftertax cost of funds to the issuer. Although there were a few cases in which new money was raised by issuing income bonds, most of these bonds were issued in exchange for preferred stock.

Surprisingly, corporations have shunned the use of income bonds in spite of recommendations by some members of the investment commu-

---

[3] Benjamin Graham, David L. Dodd, and Sidney Cottle, *Security Analysis*, 4th ed. (New York: McGraw-Hill, 1962) pp. 393–94.

[4] Ibid., p. 331.

[5] John J. McConnell and Gary G. Schlarbaum, "Another Foray Into the Backwaters of the Market," *The Journal of Portfolio Management*, Fall 1980, p. 62.

EXHIBIT 1 Corporate Bonds By Type of Issue, 1978–1984 (billion of dollars)

	1979	1980	1981	1982	1983	1984E	1985P	Amt. Out. 31 Dec 84E
Straight Publicly Issued Corporate Debt								
Public utility	$5.3	$6.9	$7.8	$8.9	$6.3	$4.8	$4.9	
Communications	3.7	5.9	3.9	1.1	3.1	0.5	0.9	
Transportation	0.8	1.4	0.7	0.7	0.7	1.2	1.4	
Industrial	5.9	10.3	9.2	9.2	5.3	8.9	17.4	
Sales finance	1.6	3.7	2.5	4.8	4.1	9.1	9.9	
Other finance and real estate	3.0	2.0	2.1	2.9	4.2	2.8	2.7	
Commercial banks	2.2	2.2	1.8	3.9	6.6	8.3	8.3	
Commercial and miscellaneous	0.7	2.1	1.2	2.3	3.8	5.8	5.1	
Total public straight issues	23.2	34.6	29.3	33.7	34.0	41.4	50.6	
Merger exch. bonds for stock	1.6	0.9	1.1	3.6	4.9	16.9	10.4	
Maturing public straights	5.5	4.4	6.1	7.6	6.8	6.4	13.9	
Calls	0.0	0.2	0.4	2.7	2.0	1.5	3.4	
Sinking fund retirements	2.5	4.8	5.8	4.5	6.8	8.4	5.6	
Debt/equity swaps	0.0	0.0	0.7	5.9	2.0	0.9	0.2	
Net increase in public straights	$16.8	$26.1	$17.4	$16.7	$21.3	$41.2	$38.0	$391.7
Straight Privately Issued Debt*								
Public utility	$3.8	$1.7	$3.6	$1.8	$1.5	$1.7	$2.0	
Communications	0.5	0.5	0.3	0.4	0.0	0.0	0.0	
Transportation	4.3	3.0	2.4	1.9	1.0	0.7	0.1	
Industrial	6.0	4.9	5.9	7.8	6.5	4.5	3.4	
Sales finance	1.4	1.2	1.3	2.0	7.6	2.5	0.4	
Other finance and real estate	0.0	0.0	0.0	0.0	0.1	0.9	0.1	
Commercial banks	0.8	0.7	0.8	2.5	1.4	0.9	0.4	
Commercial and miscellaneous	1.5	1.8	0.8	0.7	2.4	3.1	3.1	
Total private straight issues	18.4	13.9	15.1	17.1	20.5	14.2	9.5	
Maturing private straights	4.7	4.8	5.2	5.6	6.9	5.8	5.7	
Net increase in private straights	$13.7	$9.1	$9.9	$11.5	$13.6	$8.4	$3.8	$180.9

Convertible Bonds

Public utility	$0.0	$0.0	$0.1	$0.0	$0.3	$0.1	$0.2	
Communications	0.0	0.2	0.4	0.5	0.5	0.0	0.0	
Transportation	0.2	0.2	0.0	0.3	0.6	0.1	0.1	
Industrial	0.3	2.8	2.4	0.7	2.2	1.9	3.4	
Sales finance	0.0	0.0	0.0	0.0	0.1	0.1	0.3	
Other finance and real estate	0.0	0.5	0.1	0.4	0.4	0.0	0.0	
Commercial banks	0.1	0.1	0.3	0.0	0.1	0.1	0.3	
Commercial and miscellaneous	0.0	0.3	1.2	0.9	2.2	1.8	3.0	
Total convertible issues	$0.6	$4.0	$4.4	$3.0	$6.5	$4.2	$7.3	
Merger exch. bonds for stocks	1.4	0.8	1.0	3.1	0.0	0.0	0.0	
Calls	0.4	0.4	2.2	0.6	6.1	2.0	2.4	
Conversions	0.2	0.2	1.1	1.3	1.2	3.0	3.7	
Net increase in convertibles	1.4	4.2	2.2	4.2	−0.8	−0.8	1.2	21.6
Net Increase in Corporate Bonds	**$31.8**	**$39.3**	**$29.4**	**$32.4**	**$34.2**	**$48.7**	**$43.0**	**$594.1**
Memo: Sector Analysis								
Nonfinancial corporations	$22.6	$28.9	$23.0	$22.0	$16.5	$24.5	$23.6	$445.8
Finance companies	5.1	4.0	1.4	2.1	7.1	11.3	9.8	81.6
Commercial banks	1.7	2.0	1.9	4.8	6.7	9.3	7.5	39.7
Savings and loan associations	1.4	0.4	−0.5	0.2	0.0	−0.1	0.1	3.5
REITS	0.0	−0.2	−0.7	0.0	0.0	0.0	0.0	0.7
Other finance and real estate	1.0	4.3	4.3	3.3	3.9	3.7	2.0	22.8
Net Increase in Corporate Bonds	**$31.8**	**$39.3**	**$29.4**	**$32.4**	**$34.2**	**$48.7**	**$43.0**	**$594.1**

* Many private placements have equity features.

SOURCE: Henry Kaufman, James McKeon, and Nancy Kimelman, *1985 Prospects for Financial Markets* (New York: Salomon Brothers Inc, December 11, 1984), p. 29.

nity calling for greater use.[6] The late Benjamin Graham suggested that the reluctance of corporations to issue income bonds occurs because management may believe such offerings are associated with financially weak companies, since historically these bonds often arise out of reorganization. In a 1974 study Sidney Robbins found that the professional money managers he surveyed were reluctant to acquire income bonds for their portfolios.[7] In fact, he found a number of professional money managers who had never heard of income bonds!

Income bonds have more of the characteristics of preferred stock than of a bond.[8] Therefore, they should be evaluated in the same way preferred stock is evaluated. Before leaving our discussion of income bonds, however, it is worth noting the conclusions of an empirical study by John McConnell and Gary Schlarbaum of the performance of income bonds:

> One moral that may be derived from this study is that those institutional portfolio managers that have shunned income bonds as an inferior investment may wish to rethink their position. Although investments in income bonds are unlikely to provide superior performance, they may add a dimension of diversification not currently present in institutional portfolios. In an age of "market funds" and optimal diversification strategies, this added element of diversification may merit consideration. Our results would certainly support such a conclusion.[9]

SECURITY FOR BONDS

Shylock demanded a pound of flesh as his security. Investors who buy corporate bonds don't go quite that far, but they do like some kind of security. Either real property (using a mortgage) or personal property may be pledged to offer security beyond that of the general credit standing of the issue. In fact the kind of security, or the absence of a specific pledge of security, is usually indicated by the title of a bond issue.

Mortgage Bond

If you are a reader of *The Wall Street Journal*, you may have seen an advertisement for "$50,000,000 issue of Metropolitan Edison, First Mort-

---

[6] See for example: Leo Barnes, "A Do-It-Yourself Way to Cut Taxes," *Business Week*, May 5, 1975, pp. 21–22; and Harold Bierman and B. Brown, "Why Corporations Should Consider Income Bonds," *Financial Executive*, October 1967, pp. 74–78.

[7] Sidney Robbins, *An Objective Look at Income Bonds* (Boston: Envision Press, 1974).

[8] Preferred stock is discussed in Chapter 11.

[9] McConnell and Schlarbaum, "Another Foray Into the Backwaters of the Market," pp. 64–65.

gage Bonds, 9 percent Series, due December 1, 2008." That title tells you several things about this bond issue.

It tells you that the issuer has granted the bondholders a first-mortgage lien on substantially all of its properties. That is good from the viewpoint of bondholders. But in return, the issuer got a lower rate of interest on the bonds than if the issue were unsecured. A debenture issue (i.e., unsecured debt) of the same company might have carried an interest rate of 9.25 percent to 9.375 percent. A *lien* is a legal right to sell mortgaged property to satisfy unpaid obligations to bondholders. In practice, foreclosure of a mortgage and sale of mortgaged property is unusual. If a default occurs, there is usually a financial reorganization of the issuer in which provision is made for settlement of the debt to bondholders. The mortgage lien is important, though, because it gives the mortgage bondholders a very strong bargaining position relative to other creditors in determining the terms of a reorganization.

Often first-mortgage bonds are issued in series with bonds of each series secured equally by the same first mortgage. The title of the bond issue mentioned above includes "9 percent Series," which tells you that the issue is one of a series. Many companies, particularly public utilities, have a policy of financing part of their capital requirements continuously by long-term debt. They want some part of their total capitalization in the form of bonds because the cost of such capital is ordinarily less than that of capital raised by sale of stock. So, as a principal amount of debt is paid off, they issue another series of bonds under the same mortgage. As they expand and need a greater amount of debt capital, they can add new series of bonds. It is a lot easier and more advantageous to issue a series of bonds under one mortgage and one indenture than it is to create entirely new bond issues with different arrangements for security. This arrangement is called a *blanket mortgage.* When property is sold or released from the lien of the mortgage, additional property or cash may be substituted or bonds may be retired in order to provide adequate security for the debtholders.

When a bond indenture authorizes the issue of additional series of bonds with the same mortgage lien as those already issued, the indenture imposes certain conditions that must be met before an additional series may be issued. Bondholders do not want their security impaired; these conditions are for their benefit. It is common for a first-mortgage bond indenture to provide that property acquired by the issuer subsequent to granting of the first mortgage lien shall be subject to the first-mortgage lien. This is termed the *after-acquired clause.* Then the indenture usually permits the issue of additional bonds up to some specified percentage of the value of the after-acquired property, such as 60 percent. The other 40 percent, or whatever the percentage may be, must be financed in some other way. This is intended to assure that there will be additional assets with a value significantly greater than the amount of additional bonds secured by the mortgage. Another customary kind of restriction on issue of additional series is a requirement that earnings in an immediately preceding period must be equal to some number of times the amount of annual interest on the new series plus interest on all outstanding series. For this purpose, *earnings* are usually defined as earnings before income tax. The number of times interest must be earned may be one and a half, two, or some other number. Still another common provision is that additional bonds may be issued to the extent that earlier series of bonds have been paid off.

You seldom see a bond issue with the term *second mortgage* in its title. The reason is that this term has a connotation of weakness. Sometimes companies get around that difficulty by using such words as *first and consolidated mortgage bonds, first and refunding,* or *general and refunding.* Usually this language means that a bond issue is secured by a first mortgage on some part of the issuer's property, but by a second or even third lien on other parts of its assets. A general and refunding mortgage bond generally is secured by a lien on all of the company's property *subject* to the prior lien of first mortgage bonds.

Collateral Trust Bonds

Some companies do not own fixed assets or other real property and so have nothing on which they can give a mortgage lien to secure bondholders. Instead, they own securities of other companies; they are *holding companies* and the other companies are *subsidiaries*. To satisfy the desire of bondholders for security, they pledge stocks, notes, bonds, or whatever other kind of obligations they own. These assets are termed *collateral*, (or personal property), and bonds secured by such assets are *collateral trust bonds*. Some companies own both real property and securities. They may use real property to secure mortgage bonds and use securities for collateral trust bonds.

The legal arrangement for collateral trust bonds is much the same as that for mortgage bonds. The issuer delivers to a corporate trustee under a bond indenture the securities pledged, and the trustee holds them for the benefit of the bondholders. When voting common stocks are included in the collateral, the indenture permits the issuer to vote the stocks so long as there is no default on its bonds. This is important to issuers of such bonds because usually the stocks are those of subsidiaries, and the issuer depends on the exercise of voting rights to control the subsidiaries.

Indentures usually provide that, in event of default, the rights to vote stocks included in the collateral are transferred to the trustee. Loss of the voting right would be a serious disadvantage to the issuer because it would mean loss of control of subsidiaries. The trustee may also sell the securities pledged for whatever prices they will bring in the market and apply the proceeds to payment of the claims of collateral trust bond-holders. These rather drastic actions, however, are not usually taken immediately upon an event of default. The corporate trustee's primary responsibility is to act in the best interests of bondholders, and their interests may be served for a time at least by giving the defaulting issuer a proxy to vote stocks held as collateral and thus preserve the holding company structure. It may also defer sale of collateral when it seems likely that bondholders would fare better in a financial reorganization than they would by sale of collateral.

Collateral trust indentures contain a number of provisions designed to protect bondholders. Generally, the market or appraised value of the collateral must be maintained at some percentage of the amount of bonds outstanding. The percentage is greater than 100 so that there will be a margin of safety. If collateral value declines below the minimum percentage, additional collateral must be provided by the issuer. There is almost always provision for withdrawal of some collateral provided other acceptable collateral is substituted.

Collateral trust bonds may be issued in series in much the same way that mortgage bonds are issued in series. The rules governing additional series of bonds require that adequate collateral must be pledged, and there may be restrictions on the use to which the proceeds of an additional series may be put. All series of bonds are issued under the same indenture and have the same claim on collateral.

Equipment Trust Certificates

The desire of borrowers to pay the lowest possible rate of interest on their obligations generally leads them to offer their best security and to grant lenders the strongest claim on it. Many years ago the railway companies developed a way of financing purchase of cars and locomotives called *rolling stock* in a way that enabled them to borrow at just about the lowest rates in the corporate bond market.

Railway rolling stock has for a long time been regarded by investors as excellent security for debt. This equipment is sufficiently standard-ized that it can be used by one railway as well as another. And it can be readily moved from the tracks of one railroad to those of another. There is generally a good market for lease or sale of cars and locomotives. The railroads have capitalized on these characteristics of rolling stock by developing a legal arrangement for giving investors a legal claim on it that is different from, and generally better than, a mortgage lien.

The legal arrangement is one that vests legal title to railway equip-ment in a trustee, which is better from the standpoint of investors than a first-mortgage lien on property. A railway company orders some cars and locomotives from a manufacturer. When the job is finished, the manufacturer transfers the legal title to the equipment to a trustee. The trustee leases it to the railroad that ordered it and at the same time sells *equipment trust certificates* in an amount equal to a large percentage of the purchase price. Money from sale of certificates is paid to the manufacturer. The railway company makes an initial payment of rent equal to the balance of the purchase price, and the trustee gives that money to the manufacturer. Thus the manufacturer is paid off. The trustee collects lease rental money periodically from the railroad and uses it to pay interest and principal on the certificates. These interest payments are known as dividends. The amounts of lease rental payments are worked out carefully so that they are enough to pay the equipment trust certificates. At the end of some period of time, such as 15 years, the certificates are paid off, the trustee sells the equipment to the railroad for some nominal price, and the lease is terminated.

The beauty of this arrangement from the viewpoint of investors is that the railroad does not legally own the rolling stock until all the certificates are paid. In the event the railroad does not make the lease rental payments, there is no big legal hassle about foreclosing a lien. The trustee owns the property and can take it back because failure to pay the rent breaks the lease. The trustee can lease the equipment to another railroad and continue to make payments on the certificates from new lease rentals.

This description emphasizes the legal nature of the arrangement for securing the certificates. In practice, these certificates are regarded as obligations of the railway company that leased the equipment and are shown as liabilities in its balance sheet. In fact, the name of the railway appears in the title of the certificates. In the ordinary course of events, the trustee is just an intermediary who performs the function of holding title, acting as lessor, and collecting the money to pay the certificates. It is significant that even in the worst years of depression, railways have paid their equipment trust certificates, though they did not pay bonds secured by mortgages.

Although the railway companies developed the equipment trust device, it has also been used by companies engaged in providing other kinds of transportation. The trucking companies, for example, finance purchase of huge fleets of trucks in the same manner; air transportation companies use this kind of financing to purchase transport planes; and international oil companies use it to buy the huge tankers that bring oil across the oceans.

Debenture Bonds

After all the emphasis upon security, you might think that Shylock-minded investors would not buy bonds without something to secure them. But not so! Investors often buy large issues of unsecured bonds just as they buy first-mortgage bonds. These unsecured bonds are termed *debentures*. However, investors generally get higher rates of interest on debentures than on well-secured bonds, or they get the privilege of converting them into common stock of the issuer.

Debenture bonds are not secured by a specific pledge of designated property, but that does not mean that they have no claim on property of issuers or on their earnings. Debenture bondholders have the claim of general creditors on all assets of the issuer not pledged specifically to secure other debt. And they even have a claim on pledged assets to the extent that these assets have value greater than necessary to satisfy secured creditors. In fact, if there are no pledged assets and no secured creditors, debenture bondholders have first claim on all assets along with other general creditors.

These unsecured bonds are sometimes issued by companies that are so strong financially and have such a high credit rating that to offer security would be gilding the lily. Such companies can simply turn a deaf ear to investors who want security and still sell their debentures at relatively low interest rates. But debentures are sometimes also issued by companies that have already sold mortgage bonds and given liens on most of their property. These debentures rank below the mortgage bonds or collateral trust bonds in their claim on assets, and investors may regard them as relatively weak. This is the kind that bears the higher rates of interest.

Even though there is no pledge of security, the indentures for debenture bonds contain a variety of provisions designed to afford some protection to investors. Frequently the amount of a debenture bond issue is limited to the amount of the initial issue. This limit is to keep issuers from weakening the position of debenture holders by running up additional unsecured debt. Sometimes additional debentures may be issued, provided that the issuer has earned its bond interest on all existing debt plus the additional issue, a specified number of times in a recent accounting period. If a company has no secured debt, it is customary to provide that debentures will be secured equally with any secured bonds that may be issued in the future. This is known as the *negative pledge clause.* Some provisions of debenture bond issues are intended to give the corporate trustee early warning of deterioration in the issuer's financial condition. The issuer may be required always to maintain a specified minimum amount of net working capital—the excess of current assets over current liabilities—equal to not less than the amount of debentures outstanding. The corporate trustee must watch the issuer's balance sheets and, upon failure to maintain the required amount of net working capital, take whatever action is appropriate in the interest of debenture holders. Another common restriction is one limiting the payment of cash dividends by the issuer. Another limits the proportion of current earnings that may be used to pay dividends.

Subordinated and Convertible Debentures

You might think that debenture bonds have about the weakest possible claim on assets and earnings of a corporate issuer, but that is not so. Some companies have issued *subordinated debenture bonds*. The term *subordinated* means that such an issue ranks after secured debt, after debenture bonds, and often after some general creditors in its claim on assets and earnings. Owners of this kind of bond stand last in line among creditors when an issuer fails financially.

Because subordinated debentures are weaker in their claim on assets, issuers would have to offer a higher rate of interest unless they also offer some special inducement to buy the bonds. The inducement is an option to convert bonds into stock of the issuer at the discretion of bondholders. If the issuer prospers and the market price of its stock rises substantially in the market, the bondholders can convert bonds to stock worth a great deal more than they paid for the bonds. This conversion privilege may also be included in the provisions of debentures that are not subordinated. Convertible securities are discussed in Chapter 19.

The bonds may be convertible into something other than the common stock of the issuer. For example, the convertible subordinated debentures of Hi-G, Inc. 13½s due 4/15/2001 are convertible into shares of its subsidiary, Computer Magnetics. The Sun Company, Inc., subordinated exchangeable debentures 10¾s due 4/1/2006 are exchangeable into common stock of Becton, Dickinson and Company. Sun had acquired 32 percent of Becton in 1978. There are also issues indexed to silver or its cash equivalent at the time of maturity or redemption. Sunshine Mining Company has sold four such offerings, and HMW Industries floated an issue in 1981. Such commodity-backed bonds are discussed in more detail later.

Guaranteed Bonds

Sometimes a corporation may guarantee the bonds of another corporation.[10] Such bonds are referred to as guaranteed bonds. The guarantee, however, does not mean that these obligations are free of default risk. The safety of a guaranteed bond depends upon the financial capability of the guarantor to satisfy the terms of the guarantee, as well as the financial capability of the issuer. The terms of the guarantee may call for the guarantor to guarantee the payment of interest and/or repayment of the principal. A guaranteed bond may have more than one corporate guarantor. Each guarantor may be responsible for not only its pro rata share, but also the entire amount guaranteed by the other guarantors.

---

[10] There are debt obligations in which the guarantor is a federal agency. For example, certain mortgage-backed issues, discussed in Chapter 16, are guaranteed by a federal agency.

The debentures of Exxon Pipeline Company due 2004 are unconditionally guaranteed by Exxon Corporation and as such carry the triple-A rating of its guarantor. The joint venture of Gulf Oil and Texaco, called Pembroke Capital Company, is guaranteed by the two partners. The offering of $200 million, which represented the first public offering of a project-financed venture, received a triple-A rating because of its guarantors. (This issue has since been downgraded to Ba1/B by Moody's and Standard & Poor's.) Guaranteed bonds in which the guarantor is another corporation are prevalent in the railroad field. In order to lease the road of another company, a railroad company may have to agree to guarantee the debt of the company from whom it is leasing the road.

PROVISIONS FOR PAYING OFF BONDS

What would you pay for a bond that promises to pay interest in the amount of $50 or $60 a year from now to eternity but does not promise ever to repay principal? The right to receive interest in perpetuity may very well be worth $1,000, depending upon the current level of interest rates in the market, but investors generally dislike the absence of a promise to pay a fixed amount of principal on some specified date in the future; therefore, there is no such thing as a "perpetual bond" in the U.S. financial markets.

Most corporate bonds are *term bonds;* that is, they run for a term of years and then become due and payable. The term may be long or short. Generally, obligations due in less than 10 years from date of issue are called *notes.* Most corporate borrowing takes the form of bonds due in 20 to 30 years. Term bonds may be retired by payment at final maturity, or retired prior to maturity if provided for in the indenture. Serial bonds mature periodically.

Call and Refund Provisions

One important question in negotiation of terms of a new bond issue is whether the issuer shall have the right to redeem the *entire amount* of bonds outstanding on a date before maturity. Issuers generally want to have this right, and investors do not want them to have it. Both sides think that at some time in the future the general level of interest rates in the market may decline to a level well below that prevailing at the time bonds are issued. If so, issuers want to redeem all of the bonds outstanding and replace them with new bond issues at lower interest rates. But this is exactly what investors do not want. If bonds are redeemed when interest rates are low, investors have to take their money back and reinvest it at a low rate.

The usual practice is a provision that denies the issuer a right to redeem bonds during the first 5 or 10 years following the date of issue if the proceeds from the redemption are from lower-cost funds obtained with issues ranking equally with or superior to the debt to be redeemed. This type of redemption is called refunding. However, while most long-term issues have these refunding bars or prohibitions, they are usually immediately callable, in whole or in part, if the source of funds is from other than lower interest cost money. Such sources may include retained earnings, the proceeds from a common stock sale, or funds from the disposition of property. While the redemption price is often at a premium, there are many cases where the call price is 100 percent of par.

Many short- to intermediate-term bonds and notes are not callable for the first three to seven years (in some cases, not callable for the life of the issue). Thereafter, they may be called for any reason. Bond market participants often confuse refunding protection and call protection. Call protection is much more absolute in that bonds cannot be redeemed for any reason. Refunding restrictions only provide protection against one type of redemption as mentioned above. Failure to recognize this difference has resulted in unnecessary losses for some investors.

Long-term industrial issues generally have 10 years of refunding protection but are immediately callable. Electric utilities most often have 5 years of refunding protection although, during times of high interest rates, issues with 10 years of refunding protection have been sold. Long-term debt of the former members of the Bell Telephone System have 5 years of call protection.

As a rule, corporate bonds are callable at a premium above par. Generally, the amount of the premium declines as the bond approaches maturity. The initial amount of the premium may be as much as one year's interest or as little as interest for half a year. When less than the entire issue is called, the specific bonds to be called are selected randomly or on a pro rata basis. If the bonds selected on a random basis are bearer bonds, the serial number of the certificates is published in *The Wall Street Journal* and major metropolitan dailies.

Outright Redemptions

For want of a better term we will use *outright redemptions* to describe the call of debt at general redemption prices. In the spring of 1973 Bristol-Myers Company called for redemption at 107.538 one-third, or $25 million, of its 8⅝ percent Debentures due 1995. Trading as high as 111 in 1972 and about 108–109 when the call was announced, there were obviously some capital losses involved. Some market participants were confused by the call as they did not know the difference between nonrefundable and currently callable.

In 1977, NCR Corporation redeemed $75 million of its 9¾ percent Debentures due 2000 at 107.88. The bonds were trading at 111–111½. The company was in a strong cash position and projected cash flow was substantially in excess of expected capital spending plans. Thus NCR took action to improve its balance sheet and to reduce leverage through the call of this debt.

And, of course, in 1983 a good example of an industrial redemption was Archer Daniels Midland Company 16 Percent Sinking Fund Debentures due May 15, 2011. The bonds were sold May 12, 1981 at 99½ and had the standard redemption/refunding provisions, i.e., currently callable but nonrefundable prior to May 15, 1991. On June 1, 1983, the company announced the call of the bonds for August 1 at 113.95 plus accrued interest. On May 31 the bonds traded at 120. The source of the funds, according to the company, was from the two common stock offerings in January and June. While bondholders brought legal action, the court allowed the redemption to proceed. On August 6, 1984, Archer Daniels Midland sold $100 million of 13 percent sinking-fund debentures due 8/1/2014 at 97.241 for a yield of 13.375 percent. The financial press reported that the investor reception was lukewarm. Would you like to guess one of the reasons for this?

Sinking-Fund Provision

Term bonds may be paid off by operation of a *sinking fund*. Those last two words are often misunderstood to mean that the issuer accumulates a fund in cash, or in assets readily sold for cash, that is used to pay bonds at maturity. It had that meaning many years ago, but too often it happened that the money supposed to be in a sinking fund was not all there when it was needed.[11] In modern practice there is no fund, and *sinking* means that money is applied periodically to redemption of bonds before maturity. Corporate bond indentures require the issuer to retire a specified portion of an issue each year. This kind of provision for repayment of corporate debt may be designed to liquidate all of a bond issue by maturity date, or it may be arranged to pay only a part of the total by the end of the term. If only a part is paid, the remainder is called a *balloon maturity*.

The issuer may satisfy the sinking-fund requirement in one of two ways. A cash payment of the face amount of the bonds to be retired may be made by the corporate debtor to the trustee. The latter then calls the bonds by lot for redemption. Bonds have serial numbers, and numbers may be randomly selected for redemption. Owners of bonds called in this manner turn them in for redemption; *interest payments stop at the redemption date*. Alternatively, the issuer can deliver to the trustee bonds with a total face value equal to the amount that must be retired. The

---

[11] For a brief history of sinking funds, see F. Corine Thompson and Richard L. Norgaard, *Sinking Funds: Their Use and Value* (New York: Research Foundation of Financial Executives Institute, 1967).

bonds are purchased by the *issuer* in the open market. This option is elected by the issuer when the bonds are selling below par. Some corporate bond indentures, however, prohibit the open market purchase of the bonds by the issuer.

Many electric utility bond issues can satisfy the sinking-fund requirement by a third method. Instead of actually retiring bonds, the company may certify to the trustee that it has utilized unfunded property credits in lieu of the sinking fund. That is, it has made property and plant investments that have not been utilized for issuing bonded debt. For example, if the sinking-fund requirement is $1 million, it may give the trustee $1 million in cash to call bonds; it may deliver to the trustee $1 million of bonds it purchased in the open market; or it may certify that it made additions to its property and plant in the required amount, normally $1,667 of plant for each $1,000 sinking-fund requirement. In this case, it could satisfy the sinking fund with certified property additions of $1,667,000.

The issuer is granted a special call price to satisfy any sinking-fund requirement. Usually, the sinking-fund call price is the par value if the bonds were originally sold at par. When issued at a price in excess of par, the sinking-fund call price generally starts at the issuance price and scales down to par as the issue approaches maturity.

There are two advantages of a sinking-fund requirement from the bondholder's perspective. First, default risk is reduced due to the orderly retirement of the issue before maturity. Second, if bond prices decline as a result of an increase in interest rates, price support will be provided by the issuer or its fiscal agent, since it must enter the market on the buy side in order to satisfy the sinking-fund requirement. However, the disadvantage is that the bonds may be called at the special sinking-fund call price at a time when interest rates are lower than rates prevailing at the time of issuance. In that case, the bonds will be selling in the market above par but may be retired by the issuer at the special call price that may be equal to par value.

Usually, the periodic payments required for sinking-fund purposes will be the same for each period. Gas company issues often have increasing sinking-fund requirements. However, a few indentures might permit variable periodic payments, where the periodic payments vary based upon prescribed conditions set forth in the indenture. The most common condition is the level of earnings of the issuer. In such cases, the periodic payments vary directly with earnings. An issuer prefers such flexibility; however, an investor may prefer fixed periodic payments because of the greater default risk protection provided under this arrangement.

Many corporate bond indentures include a provision that grants the issuer the option to retire double the amount stipulated for sinking-fund retirement.[12] This *doubling option* effectively reduces the bondholder's call protection since when interest rates decline, the issuer may find it economically advantageous to exercise this option at the special sinking fund call price to retire a substantial portion of an outstanding issue.

With the exception of finance companies, industrial issues almost always include sinking-fund provisions. Finance companies, on the other hand, almost always do not. The inclusion or absence of a sinking-fund provision in public utility debt obligations depends upon the type of public utility. Pipeline issues almost always include sinking-fund provisions, whereas telephone issues do not. Electric utility companies have varying sinking-fund provisions. There can be a mandatory sinking fund where bonds have to be retired or, as mentioned above, a nonmandatory sinking fund in which it may utilize certain property credits for the sinking-fund requirement. If the sinking fund applies to a particular issue it is called a specific sinking fund. There are also nonspecific sinking funds (also known as funnel, tunnel, blanket, or aggregate sinking funds) where the requirement is based upon the total bonded debt outstanding of an issuer. Generally, it might require a sinking-fund payment of 1 percent of all bonds outstanding as of year end. The issuer can apply the requirement to one particular issue or to any other issue or issues. Again, the blanket sinking fund may be mandatory (bonds have to be retired) or nonmandatory (whereby it can utilize unfunded property additions). Companies with blanket sinking funds include Alabama Power Company, Georgia Power Company, Consumers Power Company, and Pacific Gas and Electric Company, among others. In some years they might actually retire bonds while in other years they may certify unfunded property additions. The blanket sinking fund of Baltimore Gas and Electric Company is mandatory.

Maintenance and Replacement Funds

Calls under maintenance and replacement fund (M&R) provisions first occurred in 1977/78. They shocked bondholders as calls were thought to be unlikely under these provisions, which were little known and used. However, due to the steep decline in interest rates in 1985 and early 1986, some electric utility companies decided to make use of the M&R calls again. Now investors recognize this type of redemption, but since the calls were around the par level and the bonds with above market level coupons were trading at higher prices, the results still hurt.

---

[12] Martin L. Leibowitz, "An Analytic Approach to the Bond Market," in *Financial Analysts Handbook I: Methods, Theory and Portfolio Management,* ed. Sumner N. Levine (Homewood, Ill.: Dow Jones-Irwin, 1975), p. 233.

Florida Power & Light Company retired $63.7 million out of $125 million of its 10⅛ percent bonds due March 1, 2005 at 100.65 on September 2, 1977 through the M&R provisions. The regular redemption price at the time was 110.98 and the issue was well within the refunding period which expired on February 28, 1980 (call price starting March 1, 1980 was 109.76).

In 1977 and 1978 Carolina Power & Light deposited nearly $79 million with its trustee under the M&R fund provisions. The company, on June 2, 1978, called $46 million of its privately-held 11⅛ percent bonds due 1994 and $32.7 million of the public 11 percent bonds of 1984 at the special redemption price of par. The company's announcement stated:

> The funds deposited were derived at the time from cash flow, however, if it is assumed that the eventual result is the replacement of the interest cost of the bonds to be redeemed with bonds at a probable interest cost of about 9 percent for 30 years, it is apparent that there will be a significant reduction of interest costs with an attendant improvement in fixed-charge coverages. The security of the total body of bondholders is improved and the maturities lengthened. These debt management actions are a positive demonstration to customers, stockholders and regulators that the management of the company continues to exercise appropriate cost control measures.

Of course, some bondholders objected to the retirements claiming that as the calls were within the refunding protected periods the companies were barred from these special debt redemptions. They also claimed that the prospectuses and offering statements were unclear. However, a *careful* reading of the prospectuses would reveal that the debt could be redeemed at the special redemption prices for the replacement fund or from certain other deposited cash. The general redemption prices applied to other redemptions provided that none of the bonds could be redeemed *at the general redemption price* prior to the end of the refunding protected period if such redemption was for the purpose or in anticipation of refunding the bonds through the use of borrowed funds at a lower interest cost. The M&R provisions were allowed exceptions and the courts have upheld the companies' rights to redeem bonds in accordance with their terms.

Not all electric utility companies provide maintenance and replacement fund requirements for all of their mortgage debt. Some of the more recent, high coupon issues lack the M&R provisions, although, as long as some of the older issues are still outstanding with these clauses, the M&R provisions apply. A number of issues that are subject to M&R clauses may be retired at the higher general redemption price and not the lower special call price. Others are protected from M&R redemption through the end of the refunding protected period and in some cases certain property credits *must* be used before cash could be deposited with the trustee.

Redemption Through the Sale of Assets and Other Means

As mortgage bonds are secured by property, we want the integrity of the collateral to be maintained. We would not want a company to sell a plant (which has been pledged as collateral) and then to use the proceeds for a distribution to shareholders. Therefore, release and substitution of property clauses are found in most bond indentures.

Wisconsin Michigan Power retired $9.9 million of its 9¼ percent Bonds due 2000 on February 28, 1977, through the release of property clause at a redemption price of 100.97. On June 30, 1976, the company sold its gas business for $16,920,000 to an affiliate, Wisconsin Natural Gas. Of the proceeds, $16,520,000 was deposited with the trustee under the mortgage per the release and substitution of property clause and a portion of these funds was released to the company against certified property additions. The balance was used to redeem the 9¼s as interest rates dropped to a level where the company thought it was to its advantage to retire high-coupon debt.

On December 7, 1983, Virginia Electric and Power Company said it would redeem its $100 million 15¾ percent bonds due April 1, 1989, (the highest public coupon) with the proceeds (so-called "release moneys") from the sale of ownership interests in some nuclear facilities. Property sales are not unusual for electric utility companies and a number have been negotiated in recent years.

Many mortgage indentures and secured loan agreements provide for the retirement of debt at special redemption prices if all or substantially all of the property subject to the lien of the mortgage is taken by the power of eminent domain or disposed of by the order of or to any governmental authority or is destroyed. We are not aware of any calls because of eminent domain but in 1984 Pacific Power & Light announced the sale of an electric distribution system to the Emerald People's Utility District for $25 million. The company stated that it intended to apply these proceeds to the redemption of half of the $50 million outstanding of the 14¾ percent bonds of 2010 at the special call price of 100. It is interesting to note that the 14¾ percent bonds was NOT the highest coupon issue in the capitalization; it had some 18 percent bonds of 1991. However, under the special provisions for the retirement of bonds concerning property sold to a governmental authority, bonds were required to be retired, either through purchase or redemption at the special call price, *but* the 18 percent issue was excepted from these provisions. Further, the issue was also protected from call at the general redemption price prior to October 15, 1986, under these special provisions.

On December 13, 1983, InterNorth, Inc. announced the call on February 1, 1984, of $90.5 million out of $200 million of its 17½ percent Debentures due August 1, 1991, at the regular redemption price of

112.32. The refunding protected period expires September 30, 1988. However, the proceeds were obtained from the sale of its Northern Propane Gas Co. unit. As these are unsecured debentures and not mortgage bonds, there is no release and substitution of property clause and no special call price. On October 1, 1984, it redeemed another $23,875,000 of these 17½ percent Debentures at 109.86 with funds obtained from the December, 1983 sale of two tanker ships.

Serial Bonds

Some corporate obligations are so arranged that specified principal amounts become due on specified dates. Such issues are called serial bonds. Equipment trust certificates, discussed earlier, are structured as serial bonds. The advantage of a serial bond issue from the investor's point of view is that the repayment schedule will match the decline in the value of the equipment used as collateral. Hence, default risk is reduced. In addition, the potential investor can select from a spectrum of maturity dates.

As an example of a serial bond, consider the Equipment Trust certificates of the Union Pacific Railroad Company carrying a coupon rate of 13⅛ percent and maturing annually beginning September 1, 1981, and ending September 1, 1995. The total amount of the issue is $25.5 million. The amount maturing annually is $1.7 million. The yields at the time of issuance, May 20, 1981, varied by maturity as shown below:

September 1	Yield (Percent)
1981	13.45
1982	13.45
1983	13.55
1984	13.45
1985	13.40
1986	13.35
1987	13.20
1988–1995	13.15

HIGH INTEREST RATES, INFLATION, AND RELATED FEATURES

The high interest rates that prevailed in the U.S. capital market in the late 70s and early 80s made the cost of borrowing for issuers of even the highest quality rating expensive. To reduce the cost of debt funds for their corporate clients, investment bankers designed packages to make long-term debt instruments more attractive to investors. Original-issue deep-discount bonds, such as zero-coupon bonds, were first offered. These issues were attractive to certain institutional investors who antici- pated that interest rates would decline and sought to lock in the then existing rate of interest. Variable- or floating-rate notes, which were pioneered in 1974, were revived for investors who sought protection against further advances in interest rates. Original-issue deep-discount bonds and variable-rate bonds are discussed in Chapters 13 and 14, respectively. Other features, such as warrants to purchase additional bonds from the issuer and "put" bonds made their debut which permit the bondholder to sell the issue back to the issuer at par at designated times.

As a sweetener to attract investors so that their bonds may be floated at a reduced cost, *equity kickers* have been included in offerings. The various forms of equity kicker are: options to convert the issue to common stock of the issuer or another entity related to the issuer, war- rants to acquire common stock from the issuer, and unit packages of debt issues and common stock. Convertible and exchangeable bonds were briefly described earlier in this chapter, and the analysis of these securities is explained in Chapter 19. Convertible securities have been around a long time and do not represent a new investment vehicle. Neither do common stock warrants, which grant the holder the option to acquire from the issuer a specified number of shares at a specified price within a designated period of time. Common stock warrants are also discussed in Chapter 19. As an example of the last form of equity kicker, consider the Pettibone Corporation 20-year subordinated deben- tures carrying a coupon of 12.375 percent. When this issue, rated dou- ble-A by Moody's, was sold in August 1980, it included six shares of its issuer's common stock for each $1,000 par value bond.

Commodity-backed bonds, indexed to the price of silver, were first issued during Spring, 1980 by Sunshine Mining Company. By the end of 1985 it had four issues outstanding. Three are indexed to the value of 50 ounces of silver and the other is indexed to 58 ounces of silver. Similar issues by other companies could be linked to gold, other precious metals, or natural resources. In fact, such issues could be linked to anything that has the potential for rising in value at a faster rate than the cost of living. Commodity bonds would offer potential protection from a run-up in interest rates (especially during periods of high inflation) that would erode traditional bond values, depending on the price perfor- mance of the underlying collateral. Such bonds could also have a tax advantage over traditional bonds, since appreciation of the collateral above purchase price of the bond would be taxed at the lower capital gain tax rate at maturity. Moreover, the cost of storing and insuring the underlying asset is absorbed by the issuing company. If substantial price appreciation of the underlying asset is not realized, the investor would be better off to buy traditional bonds and get the higher interest rates offered. Therefore, interest in issuing and purchasing such issues will wane unless inflation and interest rates are relatively high.

SOURCES OF INFORMATION ABOUT CORPORATE BOND OFFERINGS

For a new corporate bond offering, an investor can obtain a prospectus. The prospectus is a statement filed by the issuer with the Securities and Exchange Commission containing all of the pertinent information about the security being offered and the company offering the security.

Summary information about a new offering is provided in *Moody's Bond Survey*. This service is published weekly and provides information on the business of the issuer, how the issuer will use the proceeds, the quality rating of the issue as assigned by Moody's, denominations available, the form of the security (registered or bearer), exchange options, security for the bonds, guarantees, call provisions, sinking-fund requirements, restrictions on management, and statistical highlights about the issuer. This service not only provides information on new offerings, but also on proposed offerings. *Creditweek*, published weekly by Standard & Poor's, provides similar information. These weekly publications are usually carried by local libraries.

For seasoned issues, major contractual provisions are provided in *Moody's Manuals* or Standard & Poor's *Corporation Records*. To obtain basic information about a seasoned corporate issue, the investor can check the monthly publication by either Moody's (*Moody's Bond Record*) or Standard & Poor's (*Standard & Poor's Bond Guide*).

YIELDS ON CORPORATE BONDS

Differences in Yields by Bond Ratings

At any one time, the yields that investors obtain by purchasing bonds in the market vary according to how investors' estimate the uncertainty of future payment of dollar amounts of interest and principal exactly as set forth in bond indentures. This uncertainty is often called *financial risk* because it depends upon the financial ability of issuers to make those payments. If an issuer can pay, it will. Failure by a company to pay usually means intervention of a court of law on behalf of bondholders and court supervision of conduct of the business. In any event, a default is a disaster for an issuer.

Professional bond investors have ways of analyzing information about companies and bond issues to estimate the uncertainty of future ability to pay. These techniques are explained in Chapter 22. However, most individual bond investors and some institutional bond investors make no such elaborate studies. In fact, they rely largely upon bond ratings published by several organizations that do the job of bond analysis and express their conclusions by a system of ratings. Two widely used systems of bond ratings are those of Moody's Investors Service and Standard & Poor's Corporation. In both systems the term *high-grade* means low in financial risk, or, conversely, high in probability of future payments. The highest grade bonds are designated by Moody's by the letters *Aaa*, and by Standard & Poor's by *AAA*. The next highest grade is *Aa* or *AA;* then for the third grade both agencies use *A*. The next three grades are designated *Baa* or *BBB, Ba* or *BB,* and *B*. There are also *C* grades. Bonds rated AAA are said to be *prime* or "gilt edge," AA bonds are of *high quality,* single A issues as *upper medium grade* and BBB debt *medium grade*. These four categories are referred to as *investment grade bonds*. Lower rated bonds are said to have speculative elements or to be *distinctly speculative*. Chapter 6 provides more information about these bond ratings.

Both Moody's and Standard & Poor's publish periodically average yields at market prices on a number of long-term corporate bond issues grouped by ratings. These average yields by category always show the lowest yields on triple-A bonds, somewhat higher yields on double-A bonds, then still higher yields on single-A bonds. There is a relatively large differential between the average yield on single-A and triple-B bonds. Exhibit 2 presents the average promised yields[13] from 1976 to 1985 as reported by Moody's for its top four quality ratings.

EXHIBIT 2 Average Promised Yields on Corporate Bonds by Quality Rating: 1976–1985*

Year	Aaa	Aa	A	Baa
1976	8.43%	8.75%	9.09%	9.75%
1977	8.02	8.24	8.49	8.97
1978	8.73	8.92	9.20	9.49
1979	9.63	9.94	10.20	10.69
1980	11.94	12.50	12.89	13.67
1981	14.17	14.75	15.29	16.04
1982	13.79	14.41	15.43	16.11
1983	12.04	12.42	13.10	13.55
1984	12.71	13.26	13.74	14.19
1985	11.37	11.82	12.28	12.72

*The annual yields are the average of the monthly averages as reported in *Moody's Bond Record.*

---

[13] Recall from Chapter 4 the difference between promised yields and realized yields.

These data on bond yields by rating categories provide empirical evidence that bond investors demand and obtain higher promised rates of return for high levels of financial risk. The differences in average yields between rating categories are measures of how much more they demand. The principle is that investors are averse to risk; they can be induced to take a little more risk only by the probability of a little more return on investment.

There is also empirical evidence that the yields actually realized by investors in corporate bonds over long periods of time vary in size according to rating categories. The classic study of realized yields to maturity on bonds was made a long time ago for the period 1900 through 1943. The study included issues in initial amounts of $5 million or more publicly offered during that period. It showed that realized yields on bonds rated in the first three rating categories at the time of issue were approximately 5 percent, but yields on triple-B bonds averaged 5.7 percent and on even lower rated bonds it rose to higher levels.[14] The flatness of the curve for the three highest rating categories may be attributed chiefly to defaults on even highly rated bonds during the Great Depression of the 1930s. For the past several decades there have been relatively few defaults on bonds initially rated in the first three rating categories, which means that yields at time of issue have been approximately realized.

Yields and Call Provisions

The right of the issuer to call all or part of the issue is advantageous from the issuer's perspective but potentially harmful to the bondholder's economic interests. To induce an investor to purchase a callable corporate bond, the issuer must offer a yield above that of otherwise comparable noncallable corporate bonds. After the initial offering, market participants in the secondary market will continue to price a callable bond so that its yield is greater than that of noncallable bonds that are otherwise comparable.

The size of the yield premium between callable and noncallable bonds depends upon several factors. Most important is the expectations of market participants as to the course of future interest rates. If market participants expect interest rates to decline sufficiently below the coupon rate on the issue so that it would be economical for the corporate issuer to refund it, there will be a substantial yield premium between callable and noncallable bonds. On the other hand, if interest rates are anticipated to rise or not fall appreciably below the coupon rate on the issue, the amount of the yield premium will be negligible. Empirical

---

[14] W. Braddock Hickman, *Statistical Measures of Corporate Bond Financing Since 1900* (Princeton, N.J.: National Bureau of Economic Research, 1960), pp. 394, 579, and 580.

studies that examined yields on callable and noncallable public utility bonds support this view.

The nature of the call provision of an issue also determines the amount of the yield premium. As noted earlier, the corporate bond indenture may include a deferred-call provision. One would expect that, other things equal, the longer the deferment period, the lower the yield premium to compensate for the issuer's right to call. This belief is supported by empirical studies that examined yields on utility bonds. One study, however, found that the length of deferment per se is not an important determinant of the yield premium; instead, it is the kind of early protection provided[15]—that is, whether there is protection against both noncallability and nonrefundability.

As explained earlier, the inclusion of a sinking-fund requirement has advantages and disadvantages to the bondholder. During a period of relatively high interest rates, one study found that the disadvantage (the loss of income if the issue is called for sinking-fund purposes) dominated the advantages of a sinking-fund requirement.[16] As a result, a yield premium on corporate bond issues in which a sinking-fund requirement is included in the indenture was observed.

The call price can be expected to influence the yield premium between callable and noncallable bonds because it is an important determinant of the cost to the corporate issuer of refunding the issue. The greater the dollar premium over the par value to call the issue, the more expensive it will be for the issuer to refund the issue for a given drop in interest rates. Therefore, the less likely it will be that the issuer will call the issue, the higher the call price.[17]

The yield premium between callable and noncallable bonds is also found to be influenced by the number of years to maturity (the longer the maturity the higher the yield premium) and the quality of the issuer (the yield premium increases as quality decreases).

Realized Total Returns on High-Quality Long-Term Corporate Bonds: 1926–81

Recall that the yields offered in the market only reflect promised yields. A recent study, however, estimated the total return (coupon interest

---

[15] Michael G. Ferri, "How Do Call Provisions Influence Bond Yields?" *The Journal of Portfolio Management*, Winter 1979, pp. 55–57. His study is based upon a sample of newly issued industrial and public utilities in 1976, a period of high interest rates. His finding agrees with a survey that Arleigh P. Hess, Jr., and Willis J. Winn conducted of bond fund managers—*The Value of the Call Privilege* (University of Pennsylvania, 1962.)

[16] Ferri.

[17] Ferri uses the ratio of the coupon rate to the call price as a measure of protection against the issuer calling the issue. He finds this measure, which he calls the refunding rate, to be the most important determinant of the yield premium of the various call-protection measures he examines.

plus the change in market value) for high-quality long-term corporate bonds from 1926 to 1981.[18] The results, along with the total return for long-term U.S. government bonds, are presented in Exhibit 3.[19] The total returns adjusted for inflation are also presented for the two instruments.

EXHIBIT 3 Year by Year Total Returns for High-Quality Long-Term Corporate Bonds and Long-Term U.S. Government Bonds: 1926–1981

| | Unadjusted Total Returns | | Inflation-Adjusted Total Returns | |
Year	Long-Term Government Bonds	Long-Term Corporate Bonds	Long-Term Government Bonds	Long-Term Corporate Bonds
1926	0.0777	0.0737	0.0937	0.0896
1927	0.0893	0.0744	0.1112	0.0963
1928	0.0010	0.0284	0.0103	0.0380
1929	0.0342	0.0327	0.0318	0.0304
1930	0.0466	0.0798	0.1127	0.1480
1931	−0.0531	−0.0185	0.0458	0.0837
1932	0.1684	0.1082	0.2999	0.2330
1933	−0.0008	0.1038	−0.0071	0.0973
1934	0.1002	0.1384	0.0777	0.1154
1935	0.0498	0.0961	0.0193	0.0644
1936	0.0751	0.0674	0.0621	0.0545
1937	0.0023	0.0275	−0.0285	−0.0039
1938	0.0553	0.0613	0.0850	0.0912
1939	0.0594	0.0397	0.0623	0.0442
1940	0.0609	0.0339	0.0507	0.0240
1941	0.0093	0.0273	−0.0807	−0.0644
1942	0.0322	0.0260	−0.0560	−0.0618
1943	0.0208	0.0283	−0.0109	−0.0036
1944	0.0281	0.0473	0.0069	0.0257
1945	0.1073	0.0408	0.0831	0.0177
1946	−0.0010	0.0172	−0.1595	−0.1439
1947	−0.0263	−0.0234	−0.1083	−0.1056
1948	0.0340	0.0414	0.0059	0.0129
1949	0.0645	0.0331	0.0837	0.0517
1950	0.0006	0.0212	−0.0547	−0.0351
1951	−0.0394	−0.0269	−0.0933	−0.0816

[18] Roger G. Ibbotson and Rex A. Sinquefield, *Stocks, Bonds, Bills and Inflation: The Past and the Future* (Charlottesville, Va.: Financial Analysts Federation, 1981).

[19] The total returns for corporate bonds are measured for high-quality bonds with approximately 20 years to maturity. For the U.S. government bond portfolio, the target maturity is also 20 years. Ibbotson and Sinquefield try to control for factors that might produce abnormal returns in U.S. government bonds due to favorable tax benefits, impaired marketability, or special call or redemption features.

EXHIBIT 3 *(concluded)*

	Unadjusted Total Returns		Inflation-Adjusted Total Returns	
Year	Long-Term Government Bonds	Long-Term Corporate Bonds	Long-Term Government Bonds	Long-Term Corporate Bonds
1952	0.0116	0.0352	0.0027	0.0261
1953	0.0363	0.0341	0.0299	0.0277
1954	0.0719	0.0539	0.0771	0.0590
1955	−0.0130	0.0048	−0.0167	0.0010
1956	−0.0559	−0.0681	−0.0824	−0.0944
1957	0.0745	0.0871	0.0429	0.0550
1958	−0.0610	−0.0222	−0.0772	−0.0391
1959	−0.0226	−0.0097	−0.0371	−0.0243
1960	0.1378	0.0907	0.1211	0.0747
1961	0.0097	0.0482	0.0030	0.0412
1962	0.0689	0.0795	0.0560	0.0665
1963	0.0121	0.0219	−0.0043	0.0054
1964	0.0351	0.0477	0.0229	0.0354
1965	0.0071	−0.0046	−0.0120	−0.0235
1966	0.0365	0.0020	0.0027	−0.0308
1967	−0.0919	−0.0495	−0.1190	−0.0779
1968	−0.0026	0.0257	−0.0478	−0.0206
1969	−0.0508	−0.0809	−0.1058	−0.1345
1970	0.1210	0.1837	0.0628	0.1225
1971	0.1323	0.1101	0.0955	0.0742
1972	0.0568	0.0726	0.0221	0.0373
1973	−0.0111	0.0114	−0.0913	−0.0706
1974	0.0435	−0.0306	−0.0708	−0.1373
1975	0.0919	0.1464	0.0205	0.0717
1976	0.1675	0.1865	0.1143	0.1324
1977	−0.0067	0.0171	−0.0701	−0.0477
1978	−0.0116	−0.0007	−0.0942	−0.0841
1979	−0.0122	−0.0418	−0.1295	−0.1558
1980	−0.0395	−0.0262	−0.1470	−0.1349
1981	0.0185	−0.0096	−0.0666	−0.0924

SOURCE: Roger G. Ibbotson and Rex A. Sinquefield, *Stocks, Bonds, Bills and Inflation: The Past and the Future* (Charlottesville, Va.: Financial Analysts Research Foundation, 1982).

The results support the expected risk-return relationship between the two securities. The total return holding long-term corporates exceeded that for long-term U.S. governments. This is expected because the latter are free of default risk. The average default premium between long-term corporate and long-term governments is .17 percent.

Exhibit 4 shows the total rate of return on high-quality, long-term corporate bonds for all yearly holdings from 1926 to 1981.

EXHIBIT 4   Rates of Return from All Yearly Holding Periods from 1926 to 1981

LONG-TERM CORPORATE BONDS : TOTAL RETURNS

RATES OF RETURN FOR ALL YEARLY HOLDING PERIODS FROM 1926 TO 1981
(PERCENT PER ANNUM COMPOUNDED ANNUALLY)

TO THE END OF	FROM THE BEGINNING OF 1926	1927	1928	1929	1930	1931	1932	1933	1934	1935	1936	1937	1938	1939	1940	1941	1942	1943	1944	1945
1926	7.4																			
1927	7.4	7.4																		
1928	5.9	5.1	2.8																	
1929	5.2	4.5	3.1	3.3																
1930	5.8	5.4	4.7	5.6	8.0															
1931	4.4	3.9	3.0	3.1	2.9	-1.9														
1932	5.3	5.0	4.5	4.9	5.5	4.3	10.8													
1933	6.0	5.8	5.5	6.0	6.7	6.3	10.6	10.4												
1934	6.8	6.7	6.6	7.3	8.1	8.1	11.7	12.1	13.8											
1935	7.1	7.0	7.0	7.6	8.3	8.4	11.2	11.3	11.7	9.6										
1936	7.1	7.0	7.0	7.5	8.1	8.1	10.3	10.1	10.0	8.2	6.7									
1937	6.7	6.6	6.5	7.0	7.4	7.4	9.0	8.6	8.2	6.3	4.7	2.7								
1938	6.6	6.6	6.5	6.9	7.3	7.2	8.6	8.2	7.8	6.3	5.2	4.4	6.1							
1939	6.4	6.4	6.3	6.6	6.9	6.8	8.0	7.6	7.1	5.8	4.9	4.3	5.0	4.0						
1940	6.2	6.2	6.1	6.3	6.6	6.5	7.5	7.0	6.6	5.4	4.6	4.1	4.5	3.7	3.4					
1941	6.0	5.9	5.8	6.1	6.3	6.1	7.0	6.6	6.1	5.0	4.3	3.8	4.0	3.4	3.1	2.7				
1942	5.8	5.7	5.6	5.8	6.0	5.8	6.6	6.2	5.7	4.7	4.0	3.6	3.8	3.2	2.9	2.7	2.6			
1943	5.6	5.5	5.4	5.6	5.8	5.6	6.3	5.8	5.4	4.5	3.9	3.5	3.6	3.1	2.9	2.7	2.7	2.8		
1944	5.6	5.5	5.4	5.5	5.7	5.5	6.1	5.8	5.3	4.5	4.0	3.6	3.8	3.4	3.3	3.2	3.4	3.8	4.7	
1945	5.5	5.4	5.3	5.5	5.6	5.4	6.0	5.6	5.2	4.5	4.0	3.7	3.8	3.5	3.4	3.4	3.6	3.9	4.4	4.1
1946	5.3	5.2	5.1	5.3	5.4	5.2	5.7	5.3	5.0	4.3	3.8	3.5	3.6	3.3	3.2	3.1	3.2	3.3	3.5	2.9
1947	5.0	4.9	4.7	4.8	4.9	4.7	5.2	4.8	4.4	3.7	3.3	2.9	3.0	2.6	2.4	2.3	2.2	2.2	2.0	1.1
1948	4.9	4.8	4.7	4.8	4.9	4.7	5.1	4.8	4.4	3.8	3.3	3.0	3.1	2.8	2.6	2.5	2.5	2.5	2.4	1.9
1949	4.9	4.8	4.6	4.7	4.8	4.6	5.0	4.7	4.3	3.7	3.3	3.1	3.1	2.8	2.7	2.6	2.6	2.6	2.6	2.2
1950	4.8	4.7	4.5	4.6	4.7	4.5	4.9	4.5	4.2	3.6	3.2	3.0	3.0	2.8	2.6	2.6	2.6	2.6	2.5	2.1
1951	4.5	4.3	4.2	4.3	4.3	4.2	4.5	4.1	3.8	3.2	2.9	2.6	2.6	2.3	2.2	2.1	2.0	2.0	1.8	1.4
1952	4.4	4.3	4.2	4.2	4.3	4.1	4.4	4.1	3.8	3.3	2.9	2.7	2.7	2.4	2.3	2.3	2.2	2.2	2.1	1.7
1953	4.4	4.3	4.2	4.2	4.3	4.1	4.4	4.1	3.8	3.3	2.9	2.7	2.7	2.5	2.4	2.3	2.3	2.3	2.2	1.9
1954	4.4	4.3	4.2	4.3	4.3	4.2	4.4	4.1	3.8	3.4	3.1	2.9	2.9	2.7	2.6	2.5	2.5	2.5	2.5	2.2
1955	4.3	4.2	4.1	4.1	4.2	4.0	4.3	4.0	3.7	3.2	2.9	2.7	2.7	2.5	2.4	2.4	2.4	2.3	2.3	2.1
1956	3.9	3.8	3.7	3.7	3.7	3.6	3.8	3.5	3.2	2.8	2.4	2.2	2.2	2.0	1.9	1.7	1.7	1.6	1.6	1.3
1957	4.1	4.0	3.8	3.9	3.9	3.7	4.0	3.7	3.4	3.0	2.7	2.5	2.5	2.3	2.2	2.2	2.1	2.1	2.1	1.9
1958	3.9	3.8	3.6	3.7	3.7	3.5	3.7	3.5	3.2	2.8	2.5	2.3	2.3	2.1	2.0	1.9	1.9	1.8	1.8	1.6
1959	3.7	3.6	3.5	3.5	3.5	3.4	3.6	3.3	3.0	2.6	2.3	2.2	2.1	1.9	1.8	1.8	1.7	1.7	1.6	1.4
1960	3.9	3.8	3.7	3.7	3.7	3.6	3.7	3.5	3.3	2.9	2.6	2.4	2.4	2.3	2.2	2.1	2.1	2.1	2.0	1.8
1961	3.9	3.8	3.7	3.7	3.7	3.6	3.8	3.5	3.3	2.9	2.7	2.5	2.5	2.4	2.3	2.2	2.2	2.2	2.2	2.0
1962	4.0	3.9	3.8	3.8	3.9	3.7	3.9	3.7	3.5	3.1	2.9	2.7	2.7	2.6	2.5	2.5	2.5	2.5	2.5	2.3
1963	4.0	3.9	3.8	3.8	3.8	3.7	3.9	3.6	3.4	3.1	2.9	2.7	2.7	2.6	2.5	2.5	2.5	2.5	2.5	2.3
1964	4.0	3.9	3.8	3.8	3.8	3.7	3.9	3.7	3.5	3.1	2.9	2.8	2.8	2.7	2.6	2.6	2.6	2.6	2.6	2.5
1965	3.9	3.8	3.7	3.7	3.7	3.6	3.8	3.6	3.3	3.0	2.8	2.7	2.7	2.5	2.5	2.5	2.4	2.4	2.4	2.3
1966	3.8	3.7	3.6	3.6	3.6	3.5	3.7	3.5	3.2	2.9	2.7	2.6	2.6	2.5	2.4	2.4	2.4	2.4	2.3	2.2
1967	3.6	3.5	3.4	3.4	3.4	3.3	3.4	3.2	3.0	2.7	2.5	2.3	2.3	2.2	2.1	2.1	2.1	2.0	2.0	1.9
1968	3.5	3.4	3.3	3.4	3.4	3.2	3.4	3.2	3.0	2.7	2.5	2.3	2.3	2.2	2.2	2.1	2.1	2.1	2.0	1.9
1969	3.3	3.2	3.1	3.1	3.1	2.9	3.1	2.9	2.7	2.4	2.2	2.0	2.0	1.9	1.8	1.7	1.7	1.7	1.6	1.5
1970	3.6	3.5	3.4	3.4	3.4	3.3	3.4	3.2	3.1	2.8	2.6	2.5	2.5	2.3	2.3	2.3	2.2	2.2	2.2	2.2
1971	3.7	3.6	3.6	3.6	3.6	3.5	3.6	3.4	3.3	3.0	2.8	2.7	2.7	2.6	2.6	2.5	2.5	2.5	2.5	2.4
1972	3.8	3.7	3.6	3.7	3.7	3.6	3.7	3.5	3.4	3.1	2.9	2.8	2.8	2.7	2.7	2.7	2.7	2.7	2.7	2.6
1973	3.7	3.7	3.6	3.6	3.6	3.5	3.6	3.5	3.3	3.0	2.9	2.8	2.8	2.7	2.6	2.6	2.6	2.6	2.6	2.5
1974	3.6	3.5	3.4	3.4	3.5	3.4	3.5	3.3	3.1	2.9	2.7	2.6	2.6	2.5	2.5	2.4	2.4	2.4	2.4	2.3
1975	3.8	3.7	3.7	3.7	3.7	3.6	3.7	3.6	3.4	3.2	3.0	2.9	2.9	2.8	2.8	2.8	2.8	2.8	2.8	2.7
1976	4.1	4.0	3.9	4.0	4.0	3.9	4.0	3.9	3.7	3.5	3.4	3.3	3.3	3.2	3.2	3.2	3.2	3.2	3.2	3.2
1977	4.0	4.0	3.9	3.9	3.9	3.9	4.0	3.8	3.7	3.5	3.3	3.2	3.2	3.2	3.1	3.2	3.2	3.1	3.2	3.1
1978	4.0	3.9	3.8	3.8	3.9	3.8	3.9	3.7	3.6	3.4	3.2	3.2	3.2	3.1	3.1	3.1	3.1	3.1	3.1	3.0
1979	3.8	3.7	3.7	3.7	3.7	3.6	3.7	3.6	3.4	3.2	3.1	3.0	3.0	2.9	2.9	2.9	2.9	2.9	2.9	2.8
1980	3.7	3.6	3.5	3.6	3.6	3.5	3.6	3.4	3.3	3.1	2.9	2.8	2.9	2.8	2.7	2.7	2.7	2.7	2.7	2.7
1981	3.6	3.5	3.5	3.5	3.5	3.4	3.5	3.3	3.2	3.0	2.8	2.8	2.8	2.7	2.7	2.6	2.6	2.6	2.6	2.6

CORPORATE DEBT MATURITY

Investors' perceptions of what constitutes short- and long-term maturity for bonds has undergone considerable change over time. A Merrill Lynch survey[20] of bond market personnel determined that securities with a maturity up to one year were considered as cash equivalents. Short-term bonds meant issues maturing between one and five years;

---

[20] Richard S. Wilson, *Maturity: A Look at the Maturity Structure of the Corporate Bond Market* (New York: Merrill Lynch, Pierce, Fenner & Smith, Inc., Corporate Bond Research Department, August, 1981).

EXHIBIT 4 *(concluded)*

LONG—TERM CORPORATE BONDS : TOTAL RETURNS

RATES OF RETURN FOR ALL YEARLY HOLDING PERIODS FROM 1926 TO 1981
(PERCENT PER ANNUM COMPOUNDED ANNUALLY)

TO THE END OF	1946	1947	1948	1949	1950	1951	1952	1953	1954	1955	1956	1957	1958	1959	1960	1961	1962	1963	1964	1965
1946	1.7																			
1947	-0.3	-2.3																		
1948	1.1	0.8	4.1																	
1949	1.7	1.7	3.7	3.3																
1950	1.8	1.8	3.2	2.7	2.1															
1951	1.0	0.9	1.7	0.9	-0.3	-2.7														
1952	1.4	1.3	2.0	1.5	0.9	0.4	3.5													
1953	1.6	1.6	2.3	1.9	1.6	1.4	3.5	3.4												
1954	2.0	2.1	2.7	2.5	2.3	2.4	4.1	4.4	5.4											
1955	1.9	1.9	2.4	2.2	2.0	2.0	3.2	3.1	2.9	0.5										
1956	1.1	1.0	1.4	1.0	0.7	0.5	1.1	0.5	-0.4	-3.2	-4.8									
1957	1.7	1.7	2.1	1.8	1.7	1.6	2.3	2.1	1.8	0.6	0.7	8.7								
1958	1.4	1.3	1.7	1.4	1.2	1.1	1.7	1.4	1.0	-0.1	-0.3	3.1	-2.2							
1959	1.2	1.2	1.5	1.2	1.0	0.9	1.3	1.0	0.6	-0.3	-0.5	1.7	-1.6	-1.0						
1960	1.7	1.7	2.0	1.8	1.7	1.7	2.2	2.0	1.8	1.2	1.4	3.5	1.8	3.9	9.1					
1961	1.9	1.9	2.2	2.1	2.0	2.0	2.4	2.3	2.2	1.7	1.9	3.8	2.6	4.2	6.9	4.8				
1962	2.2	2.3	2.6	2.5	2.4	2.4	2.9	2.9	2.8	2.5	2.8	4.5	3.6	5.1	7.3	6.4	7.9			
1963	2.2	2.3	2.6	2.5	2.4	2.4	2.9	2.8	2.7	2.4	2.7	4.1	3.4	4.5	6.0	5.0	5.0	2.2		
1964	2.4	2.4	2.7	2.6	2.4	2.4	3.0	3.0	2.9	2.7	2.9	4.2	3.6	4.6	5.7	4.9	4.9	3.5	4.8	
1965	2.2	2.3	2.5	2.4	2.4	2.4	2.8	2.7	2.4	2.4	2.6	3.7	3.1	3.8	4.7	3.8	3.A	2.1	2.1	-0.
1966	2.1	2.1	2.4	2.3	2.2	2.2	2.6	2.5	2.4	2.2	2.4	3.3	2.7	3.4	4.0	3.2	2.9	1.7	1.5	-0.
1967	1.8	1.8	2.0	1.9	1.8	1.8	2.1	2.0	1.9	1.6	1.7	2.5	1.9	2.4	2.9	2.0	1.5	0.3	-0.2	-1.
1968	1.8	1.8	2.0	1.9	1.9	1.8	2.1	2.0	1.9	1.7	1.8	2.5	2.0	2.4	2.8	2.1	1.7	0.7	0.4	-0.
1969	1.4	1.4	1.6	1.4	1.3	1.3	1.5	1.4	1.3	1.0	1.1	1.7	1.1	1.4	1.7	0.9	0.4	-0.6	-1.1	-2.
1970	2.0	2.0	2.2	2.1	2.1	2.1	2.3	2.3	2.2	2.0	2.1	2.8	2.4	2.7	3.1	2.5	2.3	1.4	1.5	0.
1971	2.4	2.4	2.6	2.5	2.5	2.5	2.8	2.7	2.7	2.5	2.7	3.3	3.0	3.4	3.7	3.3	3.1	2.6	2.6	2.
1972	2.5	2.6	2.8	2.7	2.7	2.7	3.0	2.9	2.9	2.8	2.9	3.6	3.2	3.6	4.0	3.6	3.5	3.0	3.1	2.
1973	2.5	2.5	2.7	2.6	2.6	2.6	2.9	2.9	2.8	2.7	2.8	3.4	3.1	3.5	3.8	3.4	3.3	2.9	2.9	2.
1974	2.3	2.3	2.5	2.4	2.4	2.4	2.6	2.5	2.4	2.4	2.5	3.1	2.7	3.0	3.3	2.9	2.8	2.4	2.4	2.
1975	2.7	2.7	2.9	2.9	2.8	2.9	3.1	3.1	3.1	3.0	3.1	3.6	3.4	3.7	4.0	3.7	3.6	3.3	3.3	3.
1976	3.2	3.2	3.4	3.4	3.4	3.4	3.7	3.7	3.6	3.5	3.6	4.3	4.1	4.5	4.8	4.5	4.5	4.3	4.4	3.
1977	3.1	3.2	3.3	3.3	3.3	3.4	3.6	3.7	3.6	3.6	3.7	4.3	4.1	4.5	4.8	4.5	4.5	4.3	4.4	4.
1978	3.0	3.1	3.2	3.2	3.2	3.2	3.5	3.5	3.4	3.4	3.5	4.2	4.0	4.3	4.6	4.4	4.4	4.3	4.1	4.
1979	2.8	2.8	3.0	3.0	2.9	2.9	3.2	3.2	3.2	3.1	3.2	4.0	3.8	4.1	4.4	4.1	4.1	3.8	4.0	3.
1980	2.6	2.7	2.8	2.8	2.8	2.8	3.0	3.0	2.9	2.8	2.9	3.6	3.4	3.7	3.9	3.7	3.6	3.4	3.4	3.
1981	2.5	2.6	2.7	2.7	2.6	2.7	2.8	2.8	2.8	2.7	2.8	3.2	3.0	3.2	3.4	3.1	3.1	2.8	2.8	2.

TO THE END OF	1966	1967	1968	1969	1970	1971	1972	1973	1974	1975	1976	1977	1978	1979	1980	1981
1966	0.2															
1967	-2.4	-5.0														
1968	-0.8	-1.3	2.4													
1969	-2.7	-3.6	-2.9	-8.1												
1970	1.2	1.5	3.7	4.3	18.4											
1971	2.8	3.3	5.5	6.5	14.6	11.0										
1972	3.4	4.0	5.8	6.7	12.1	9.1	7.3									
1973	3.1	3.6	5.0	5.6	9.3	6.4	4.2	1.1								
1974	2.4	2.7	3.9	4.1	6.7	3.9	1.7	-1.0	-3.1							
1975	3.6	4.0	5.1	5.5	8.0	6.0	4.8	4.0	5.4	14.6						
1976	4.9	5.4	6.6	7.1	9.4	8.0	7.4	7.5	9.7	16.6	18.6					
1977	4.6	5.0	6.1	6.5	8.4	7.1	6.4	6.3	7.6	11.4	9.9	1.7				
1978	4.2	4.6	5.5	5.8	7.5	6.2	5.5	5.2	6.0	8.4	6.4	0.8	-0.1			
1979	3.6	3.9	4.7	4.8	6.2	5.0	4.2	3.8	4.3	5.8	3.7	-0.9	-2.1	-4.2		
1980	3.2	3.4	4.1	4.2	5.4	4.2	3.4	3.0	3.2	4.3	2.4	-1.3	-2.3	-3.4	-2.6	
1981	2.9	3.1	3.7	3.8	4.9	3.7	3.0	2.5	2.7	3.6	1.8	-1.2	-2.0	-2.6	-1.8	-1.0

SOURCE: Roger G. Ibbotson and Rex A. Sinquefield, *Stocks, Bonds, Bills and Inflation: The Past and The Future* (Charlottesville, Va.: Financial Analysts Research Foundation, 1982).

intermediate-term issues were generally considered those with maturities ranging from 5 to 12 years; and any bond with a maturity over 12 years was considered long term.

Merrill Lynch found that there has been an increased issuance of shorter-term debt in recent years, as suggested by the shortening of average maturity of corporate bonds in Exhibit 5. Much of the relative decline has been attributed to greater amounts of shorter maturity debt outstanding. Moreover, investor preference for shorter maturity is a major determining factor causing corporations to issue less long-term

---

EXHIBIT 5 Average Maturity of Corporate Bonds, 1974–1984

Year	Merrill Lynch Corporate Master Index	New Issues
1974	20.08	19.93
1975	19.07	17.99
1976	18.80	20.39
1977	18.72	22.83
1978	18.52	23.10
1979	18.23	22.01
1980	18.16	18.42
1981	17.55	15.60
1982	17.42	12.90
1983	15.83	15.37
1984	15.00	9.87

SOURCE: Richard S. Wilson, *Bond Market Comment* 8, no. 3 (New York: Merrill Lynch, Fixed Income Research Department, January 18, 1985), p. 3.

---

debt.[21] Investor preference for shorter maturities, beginning in the 1970s, is attributable mainly to increased interest rate and market risk because of increased volatility of bond prices caused by higher interest rates.

The shorter maturity structure of corporate debt also increases the pressures on corporate financial managers. It becomes increasingly difficult to match long-lived assets with long-term liabilities. Years ago, a matching of assets and liabilities was deemed the proper course for corporations to follow. Now, that isn't necessarily so. The more frequent refinancings necessary to replace a heavier volume of maturing debt also add to the burden of the corporate financial officer and to the pressures on the corporate bond market. More of a company's cash flow might have to be directed to paying off these obligations as they become due.

THE BOND MARKETS

It is easy to buy bonds. All you need to know at a minimum is the telephone number of a broker-dealer firm with whom you have established an account. It is better, though, if you know something about the bond markets and how they operate. Familiarity with markets may affect your choice of bond issues and enable you to minimize the cost of buying and selling.

---

[21] Richard S. Wilson, *Bond Market Comment*, Vol. 8, No. 3 (New York: Merrill Lynch, Fixed Income Research Department, January 18, 1985), p. 3.

Billions of dollars of new corporate bonds are sold each year in the primary market—the market for new issues. As soon as a new bond issue is publicly offered, investors begin to buy and sell in the secondary market—the market for outstanding issues.

The secondary market for bonds is a big one. You may not hear as much about it as about the stock markets, but there are more corporate bond issues listed on the New York Stock Exchange than there are stock issues. The dollar value of daily bond trading on the exchanges and in the over-the-counter market appears to be not much less than the value of trading in stocks on the exchanges. The reason the bond market is inconspicuous to the public is that it is mostly an institutional market wherein life insurance companies, pension funds, and savings institutions quietly buy and sell large amounts of bonds with little or no publicity.

There are really two bond markets. One is the *exchange market*, where certain members make a market in listed issues. The other is the *over-the-counter market*, which is a market made by dealer firms in their offices. The exchange market for bonds is chiefly the New York Stock Exchange. The over-the-counter market is chiefly in New York City, but there are many firms all over the country who buy and sell securities as dealers.

In discussing the bond markets one must differentiate clearly between brokers and dealers. Brokers execute orders for accounts of customers; they are agents and get a commission for their services. Dealers buy and sell for their own accounts. When they buy, they take the risk of reselling at a loss. Dealers "make a market" when they quote a bond continuously. A *quote* is a bid and an offer. The *bid* is the price a dealer will pay for bonds of an issue to whomever may want to sell to the dealer; and the *offer* is the price at which a dealer will sell bonds to whomever may want to buy from the dealer. The offer is always higher than the bid; that is, the dealer buys at a lower price than that at which he or she sells, and so makes a profit. The difference between bid and offer prices is the dealer's *spread*.

The Exchange Market

If you look only at the number of bond issues listed on the New York Stock Exchange—about 3,750 at the end of 1984—and at the market value of listed bonds—approximately $1 trillion—you would conclude that the exchange market is the big market. In fact, it is not. A very large percentage of all bond trading, including listed issues, is over the counter. We cannot be precise about this because there are no published data on the volume of over-the-counter trading.

The difference between the size of the two markets is partly a matter of historical development and partly of adaptation to the requirements of institutional investors. The organized security markets developed chiefly as stock markets because, during a long period of history, there was a broad public interest in stocks. However, it has long been the custom for the larger corporate bond issues to be listed on the New York Stock Exchange (NYSE), and a number of member firms do business as specialists in bonds. Dealers in the over-the-counter market have developed a larger and broader market chiefly because they have the capital required to assume the risk of buying and selling large amounts of bonds for their own accounts. They have benefited by the great growth in bond investment by institutional investors during the past several decades.

The New York Stock Exchange assists its bond specialists by requiring that member firms execute customers' orders for nine bonds or fewer on the floor of the exchange unless a better price can be obtained off the floor. The exchange market has also been aided by installation of the Automated Bond System, which provides quotes by its bond specialists in all listed issues to broker-dealer firms that subscribe to the service. Leading newspapers publish daily a record of prices at which NYSE-listed bond issues were traded on the preceding business day. Examination of this information is a good way to learn more about the bond market. Exhibit 6 shows part of the record of trading in NYSE bond issues on a randomly selected day.

The first task is to identify corporate issuers. Most of us can read "ATT" to mean American Telephone and Telegraph Company, but what is the name of the issuer abbreviated to "CPoM"? You may have to refer to one of the bond-rating booklets published monthly by Moody's or Standard & Poor's to get the full name. The particular bond issue is indicated by the interest rate and year of maturity; thus, "ATT 7s01" means an issue bearing interest at 7 percent and due in the year 2001. In the next column reading from left to right is the current yield on the issue. *Notice that this is not the yield to maturity.* In some instances you find the letters *cv* instead of current yield. The letters mean that the bond is *convertible*. The conversion option affects market price and distorts current yield. Sometimes the letter *f* appears in the column for current yield. This means that the bond is *traded flat*; that is, a purchaser does not have to pay a seller accrued interest from the bond's last interest payment date to date of purchase. All other bonds are traded with accrued interest. Bonds traded flat are in default, or for some other reason the next interest payment is particularly uncertain. Moving to the right, you see a number that indicates the total volume of trading in an issue during the day. Scan that column and you see that trading in some issues has been only 5 or 10 bonds and that many listed issues do not appear in this table of prices because there was no trading during the day. Then you come to the high, low, and closing prices for the day. For some issues these three numbers are all the same, which usually means

EXHIBIT 6 Sample Page from *The Wall Street Journal*

52 THE WALL STREET JOURNAL WEDNESDAY, MAY 14, 1986

NEW YORK EXCHANGE BONDS

Tuesday, May 13, 1986

Total Volume $38,380,000

SALES SINCE JANUARY 1

	1986	1985	1984
	$4,343,804,000	$3,150,276,000	$2,525,532,000

Issues traded	Domestic		All Issues	
	Tue.	Mon.	Tue.	Mon.
Issues traded	911	932	916	941
Advances	306	391	309	339
Declines	384	391	385	393
Unchanged	221	205	222	209
New highs	50	62	51	63
New lows	8	8	9	4

Dow Jones Bond Averages

	—1986—		—1985—		——Tuesday——				
	High	Low	High	Low	1986	1985	1984		Net Chg.
20 Bonds	91.39	9¼99	91.94	83.73	91.39	−0.27	76.21	65.38	+0.19
10 Utilities	91.77	−0.15	73.50	59.80	90.31	59.43	81.85		+0.37
10 Industrial	91.02	−0.38	78.92	70.97	76.22	69.61	84.82		+0.02

New York Exchange Bonds quotation tables (Corporation Bonds, Volume $38,290,000) and continuation columns of bond listings.

that only one transaction took place during the day. In the last column is the net change in closing price on the day of the report relative to the closing price on the most recent previous day the bond issue was traded.

The OTC Market

The over-the-counter (OTC) market is hard to describe in precise language because it does not exist in a particular place, it has no listed issues, and there is no published information about the prices at which bonds are traded or about the volume of trading. Any dealer can make a market for a bond issue without having to be a member of an exchange or even a member of the National Association of Securities Dealers (the organization to which most broker-dealer firms belong).

The heart of the over-the-counter market is a group of perhaps two dozen large dealer firms located in New York City that make *wholesale* markets in large numbers of bond issues. Their market is called wholesale because for the most part they deal only with other wholesalers and with broker-dealer firms that have *retail* orders from their own customers to execute as brokers. Wholesalers also deal directly with large institutional investors, who buy and sell in large lots, such as 100 bonds or more.

Some years ago the National Association of Securities Dealers (NASD)—which is both a trade association and a governing organization—developed a computerized system by which dealers may enter their bids and offers for issues in which they make a market and subscribers can read these quotations on cathode-ray tubes in their offices. The system is called *NASDAQ* (for National Association of Security Dealers Automated Quotation service). A broker-dealer firm with an order to execute for a customer can learn instantly the highest bid and lowest offer for the issue in which he or she is interested and then execute the order by telephone. This is much more efficient than the old system of telephoning around to several dealers for quotes.

DIFFERENCES IN THE QUALITY OF MARKETABILITY

Any bond that is quoted continually by a dealer is a *marketable bond;* there is a market for it. But sophisticated investors want to know much more than that; they want to know how good is the market. It may be inferred that a bond quoted by only one dealer in Kansas City has a poor market and that one quoted by half a dozen large wholesalers in New York City has an excellent market. There are gradations between poor and excellent. It is useful to recognize differences in the quality of markets for different bond issues.

The principal basis for grading securities in marketability is the size of the spread between dealers' bid and asked prices. A narrow spread—

say, three eighths to one half of 1 percent—indicates an excellent market. A wide spread—such as 2 or 3 percent—means a poorly marketable issue. The principal determinant of the size of spread is not so much the number of dealers, as suggested above, but the usual volume of trading in an issue. The number of dealers is more or less proportionate to volume of trading. If there is a lot of business in a bond issue, there are a lot of dealers seeking the business. The size of the spread, too, is related to the volume of trading. A large volume of trading and a large number of dealers make a highly competitive market in which spreads are pressed downward. In the actively traded issues, dealers take less risk when they buy bonds and carry them in inventory. Usually, price changes in any short period are small, and a dealer who wishes to do so can unload bonds. In addition, active trading distributes the dealer's costs over many transactions.

The easiest and most direct way to learn the size of dealers' spreads on bond issues is to ask a broker-dealer who subscribes to NASDAQ to tell you the quotes on some bond issues, and also the number of dealers quoting an issue. Short of access to NASDAQ, you can learn something from the data on daily trading in NYSE-listed bonds. Look at the volume of trading for some of the bonds listed in Exhibit 6. You can see that the volume in most issues was less than 30 bonds, but volume in American Telephone and Telegraph 8¾s, due 2000, was 213 bonds. This suggests a small spread in dealers' quotes. In fact that issue is usually quoted with a spread of only three eighths of 1 percent. Another issue with a volume of 10 bonds is usually quoted with a spread of more than 1 percent.

The reason for differentiating between bond issues in grades of marketability is that high marketability costs money. Other things being equal, investors prefer the highly marketable issues, and accordingly will pay slightly more for them. A slightly higher price means a slightly lower yield. An investor who buys in the bond market and expects to sell in the market after some period of time needs high marketability. Only by trading in highly marketable issues can the investor minimize transaction costs. Consider, for example, the cost of buying and selling a bond that is usually quoted with a spread of one half of 1 percent. The cost of a *round trip*—that is, a purchase and a sale—is only 1 percent for the dealer. In addition, a broker's commission on a round trip is likely to be about one half of 1 percent. The sum is about 1.5 percent. In comparison, the cost of a round trip in a poorly marketable issue might be twice as much.

Many investors do not need high marketability. They buy new corporate bond issues when they are first offered to the public at the public offering price. The cost of public distribution is paid by the issuer. Then they usually hold bonds until they are redeemed at par or a premium over par when bonds are called before maturity. Thus they pay no dealer's spread and no commission. The round trip is free. On exceptional occasions such investors elect to sell bonds in the market and have to pay for a one-way trip back.

There is also another category of corporate bond investors who buy in the secondary market and seek to realize capital gains by sale in the market at a higher price; there is speculation in bonds just as there is in stocks. Clearly this category of investors needs highly marketable issues in order to minimize the transaction costs.

SUMMARY

The category of securities described by the term *corporate bonds* includes a great variety of investment instruments. Under this heading you find bond issues generally regarded as bearing very little risk of payments in dollar amounts and others that are distinctly speculative. You find a wide range of obligations in length of the period to maturity from those due within a few days to issues that may have as much as 30 to 40 years to maturity. There are bonds secured by first mortgages on issuers' plant and equipment and those that have no specific pledge of security. There are obligations designed for particular categories of issuers, such as equipment-trust obligations for transportation companies and collateral-trust bonds for holding companies. Provisions for redemption vary widely. There are bonds that are not callable before maturity and those that are callable at any time after a specified period of notice. Most, but not all, corporate bonds have sinking funds to retire bonds from time to time during the period to maturity.

It is not surprising, then, that corporate bonds of all these varieties appeal to investors of many varieties. Life insurance companies buy more corporate obligations than any other category of investors, but other institutions, such as pension funds, trust funds, mutual funds, and casualty insurance companies, are important on the demand side of the market. Although financial institutions make up the principal market, many individuals find corporate issues of one kind or another suitable for their personal investment portfolios.

11

Nonconvertible Preferred Stock

Richard S. Wilson
Vice President
Merrill Lynch Capital Markets

Harry C. Sauvain, D.C.S.
University Professor Emeritus of Finance
Indiana University

This chapter reviews straight, nonconvertible preferred stock issues, i.e., those issues that have fixed dividends. Preferred stock that is convertible into common shares is discussed in Chapter 19. Adjustable rate preferred stock is discussed in Chapter 14.

THE ESSENTIAL NATURE OF PREFERRED STOCKS

Preferred stock is a class of stock with preferences over the common stock of the issuer. It is an equity-type security and not a debt instrument. These preferred equity instruments can be traced back to the mid-16th century in England and to before 1850 in the United States. However, they first came into prominence in the 1890s during the formation of the giant trusts and industrial combinations. Preferences at first concerned dividend rights, but later other provisions were added giving the shares additional features and preferences over the common equity. Preferred shares have some of the characteristics of debt securities (although ranking below debt in the capital structure of a corporation) including priority over common shares in liquidation of the issuer. For the sake of convenience, the term *preferred* will refer to all classes of senior equity securities unless specifically noted.

EXHIBIT 1 Profile of the Public Preferred Stock Market (as of 12/31/84)

	Total Public Market	Industrial and Transportation	Finance	Electric Utility	Gas and Other Utilities	Telephone
No. of issues	1,298	121	25	1,013	92	47
Percent of total issues	100.00%	9.32%	1.93%	78.04%	7.09%	3.62%
Total par or stated value ($MM)	$36,871.04	$8,138.35	$1,422.61	$24,356.01	$1,276.64	$1,677.33
Percent of total par value	100.00%	22.07%	3.86%	66.06%	3.46%	4.55%
No. listed: NYSE/ASE	544	85	17	400	30	12
No. of issues with sinking funds	370	72	13	205	69	11
Percent sinking-fund issues	28.51%	59.50%	52.00%	20.24%	75.00%	23.40%
Size of issues						
$100MM and larger	35	19	4	9	0	3
$50MM to $99.99MM	183	22	9	143	5	4
$25MM to $49.99MM	314	17	7	274	12	4
$10MM to $24.99MM	382	18	2	299	52	11
Under $10MM	384	45	3	288	23	25
Call Features						
No. noncallable/life	14	2	0	10	2	0
No. currently callable	1,102	98	15	863	81	45

No. with call/refunding protection	177	20	6	140	9	2
Dividend rates (percent)						
12 percent and higher	154	15	3	127	7	2
8.00 percent to 11.99 percent	454	34	15	358	37	10
Under 8.00 percent	690	72	7	528	48	35
of which noncallables are:						
12 percent and higher	0	0	0	0	0	0
8.00 percent to 11.99 percent	2	2	0	0	0	0
Under 8.00 percent	12	0	0	10	2	0
Standard & Poor's rating						
AA	213	12	1	190	3	7
A	376	21	9	276	45	25
BBB	352	17	2	296	37	0
BB	213	16	1	193	3	0
B	38	9	0	28	1	0
CCC	4	4	0	0	0	0
CC	1	1	0	0	0	0
C	29	2	0	23	0	4
D	1	1	0	0	0	0
Not rated	71	38	12	7	3	11

PROFILE OF THE PREFERRED STOCK MARKET

At the end of 1984 there were nearly 1,300 straight preferred stock issues outstanding in the U.S. market with a total par or stated value of approximately $36.9 billion (see Exhibit 1). In comparison, the total market for publicly issued corporate debt is about 5,000 issues with a par value of some $360 billion. The electric utility industry has 78 percent of the preferred issues and about two thirds of the par value followed, at a distant second, by industrial and transportation issues. There are few issues of over $100 million and most are under $50 million in size.

In the last few years the issuance of new straight preferred stock has been on the decline as investors and issuers found adjustable rate dividend preferreds more attractive. In 1984 only 11 straight issues with a par value of $455.5 million came to market. This is down from $1,503 million (31 issues) in 1983 and $2,207 million (50 issues) in 1982 (see Exhibit 2).

EXHIBIT 2 Public Straight Preferred Stock Financing ($ millions)

Year	Amount	Year	Amount
1971	$1,900.8	1972	$2,324.4
1973	2,328.5	1974	1,725.5
1975	2,508.5	1976	1,949.1
1977	1,921.0	1978	1,394.5
1979	1,317.5	1980	1,960.5
1981	1,220.3	1982	2,207.1
1983	1,502.8	1984	455.5

PREFERRED STOCK RATINGS

Differences between the terms of preferred stock issues and the financial ability of corporate issuers to pay preferred dividends are factors that determine the riskiness of preferred stocks. Investment information services such as Moody's Investors Service and Standard & Poor's Corporation provide a shortcut to the *initial* appraisal by investors of preferreds by publishing ratings for them in much the same manner as they do for bonds. We think it is quite important for investors to be aware of the definitions and meanings of preferred stock ratings, and have listed below the definitions of the preferred stock ratings of the two major rating agencies.

Moody's Preferred Stock Ratings

Because of the fundamental differences between preferred stocks and bonds, a variation of our familiar bond rating symbols is being used in the quality ranking of preferred stock. The symbols, presented below, are designed to avoid comparison with bond quality in absolute terms. Remember that preferred stock occupies a junior position to bonds within a particular capital structure, and that these securities are rated within the universe of preferred stocks.

An issue which is rated **aaa** is considered to be a top-quality preferred stock. This rating indicates good asset protection and the least risk of dividend impairment within the universe of preferred stocks.

An issue which is rated **aa** is considered a high-grade preferred stock. This rating indicates that there is a reasonable assurance that earnings and asset protection will remain relatively well maintained in the foreseeable future.

An issue which is rated **a** is considered an upper-medium grade preferred stock. While risks are judged to be somewhat greater than in the **aaa** and **aa** classifications, earnings and asset protection are, nevertheless, expected to be maintained at adequate levels.

An issue which is rated **baa** is considered medium-grade, neither highly protected nor poorly secured. Earnings and asset protection appear adequate at present but may be questionable over any great length of time.

An issue which is rated **ba** has speculative elements and its future cannot be considered well assured. Earnings and asset protection may be very moderate and not well safeguarded during adverse periods. Uncertainty of position characterizes preferred stocks in this class.

An issue which is rated **b** generally lacks the characteristics of a desirable investment. Assurance of dividend payments and maintenance of other terms of the issue over any long period of time may be small.

An issue which is rated **caa** is likely to be in arrears on dividend payments. This rating designation does not purport to indicate the future status of payments.

An issue which is rated **ca** is speculative in a high degree and is likely to be in arrears on dividends with little likelihood of eventual payment.

c is the lowest rated class of preferred or preference stock. Issues so rated can be regarded as having extremely poor prospects of ever attaining any real investment standing.

Moody's applies numerical modifiers **1, 2,** and **3** in each rating classification. The modifier **1** indicates that the security ranks in the higher end of its generic rating category; the modifier **2** indicates a midrange ranking; and the modifier **3** indicates that the issue ranks in the lower end of its generic rating category.

Standard & Poor's Preferred Stock Ratings

A Standard & Poor's preferred stock rating is an assessment of the capacity and willingness of an issuer to pay preferred stock dividends and any applicable sinking-fund obligations. A preferred stock rating differs from a bond rating in as much as it is assigned to an equity issue, which issue is intrinsically different from, and subordinated to, a debt issue. Therefore, to reflect this difference, the preferred stock rating symbol will normally not be higher than the bond rating symbol assigned to, or that would be assigned to, the senior debt of the same issuer.

The preferred stock ratings are based on the following considerations:

1. Likelihood of payment—capacity and willingness of the issuer to meet the timely payment of preferred stock dividends and any applicable sinking-fund requirements in accordance with the terms of the obligation.
2. Nature of, and provisions of, the issue.
3. Relative position of the issue in the event of bankruptcy, reorganization, or other arrangements affecting creditors' rights.

Ratings are expressed in letters. The highest rating that is assigned by Standard & Poor's to a preferred stock issue is AAA. This rating indicates an extremely strong capacity to pay the preferred stock dividend payments.

A preferred stock rated AA also qualifies as a high-quality fixed income security. The capacity to pay preferred stock dividend payments is very strong, although not as overwhelming as for issues rated AAA.

An issue rated A is backed by a sound capacity to pay the preferred stock dividend payments, although it is somewhat more susceptible to the adverse effects of changes in circumstances and economic conditions.

An issue rated BBB is regarded as backed by an adequate capacity to pay the preferred stock dividend payments. Whereas it normally exhibits adequate protection parameters, adverse economic conditions or changing circumstances are more likely to lead to a weakened capacity to make payments for a preferred stock in this category than for issues in the A category.

Preferred stock rated BB, B, and CCC are regarded, on balance, as predominately speculative with respect to the issuer's capacity to pay preferred stock dividend payments. BB indicates the lowest degree of speculation and CCC the highest degree of speculation. While such issues will likely have some quality and protective characteristics, these are outweighed by large uncertainties or major risk exposures to adverse conditions.

The rating CC is reserved for a preferred stock issue in arrears on dividends or sinking-fund payments but that is currently paying.

A preferred stock rated C is a nonpaying issue.

A preferred stock rated D is a nonpaying issue with the issuer in default on debt instruments.

To provide more detailed indications of preferred stock quality, the ratings from AA to B may be modified by the addition of a plus (+) or minus (−) sign to show relative standing within the major rating categories.

THE TERMS OF THE BARGAIN WITH INVESTORS

There are many terms in the agreement between a corporate issuer and those who own its preferred stock. The terms influence the riskiness of the stock. In the bargaining between a corporation that proposes a public offering of a preferred stock issue and the investment bankers who buy the issue for resale to the public, the prospective issuer wants to give away no more in terms favorable to investors than necessary to raise capital at an acceptable cost. In a broad sense the investment bankers do the bargaining for investors. They want the most favorable terms for investors because they have to sell the stock to them.

Preference of Dividends

The chief preference of preferred over common stock is the preference as to dividends. Straight preferred stock is almost always entitled to dividends at a fixed rate on par value, stated value, or fixed dollar amount per share annually before any dividend can be paid on the issuer's common stock. For example, such dividend may be stated as $2.50 per share ($25 par or stated value) or 10 percent based on some predetermined value. In the latter case, if the par value were $25, the annual dividend would amount to $2.50 per share; if the par value were $50 per share, the annual dividend would be $5; and if the par value were $100 per share, then the annual dividend would be $10. Dividends are normally paid quarterly although there are a few issues with semiannual dividend payments. The amount of the dividend on straight preferred stock is ordinarily limited to that fixed amount or rate of dividend stated in the description of the issue. It is as though the preferred stockholders say to the common stockholders, "Let us have dividends up to the stipulated amount per share before you receive dividends, and regardless of whether you receive them, we will agree that our dividends shall be limited to the stipulated amount per share. You common shareholders can have dividends in an amount only limited by the financial ability of the company to pay them."

Nonparticipating Preferred Stock

Almost all preferred stocks that can be bought in the market today are nonparticipating. This means that the owners of preferred stocks are entitled to the rate or amount of dividend stipulated in the legal provisions describing the class of stock and no more. This limitation, as we have suggested above, is the big thing that is bargained away by purchasers of preferred stock. A company may become very profitable and realize earnings many times the amounts necessary to pay the regular preferred dividend. But this does preferred stockholders no good other than to get a higher rating for their stock. The big earnings go to the common stockholders as dividends.

In the history of the use of investment instruments there are instances of issues of participating preferred stocks. The terms have varied, but the general idea may be illustrated by a provision that after the preferred has received its stipulated dividend and the common has received the same amount of dividend per share as the preferred, money remaining available for dividend payments is distributed in equal amounts per share among both the common and preferred stocks. Such an arrangement is too good for preferred stock from the standpoint of corporate management. It lets preferred stockholders have their cake and eat it, too. Their cake is the preference to dividends; the eating of it is participation with common in larger dividends per share.

One of the few examples of a preferred that participates in the earnings of a corporation over and above the base or stipulated rate is Southern California Edison's 5 percent Original Cumulative Participating Preferred. The par value was originally $25 per share but in 1962, through a rarely used preferred stock split of 3-for-1, the par value was reduced to $8⅓. According to the Moody's *Public Utility Manual*, it "has preference to cumulative dividends of 5 percent annually before payments on preferred or common stock and entitled to participate in any distribution to holders of preferred to the extent that such distribution shall as to any series exceed 5 percent, such participation being cumulative and also entitled to participate with common to the extent that such distribution shall be greater than the highest dividend rate paid on any preferred stock outstanding."

With 480,000 shares outstanding, the 5 percent preferred has a gross par value of $4,000,000 and the minimum dividend would be $200,000, or $0.42 per share. Dividends paid on this stock totaled $792,000 or $1.65 a share in 1974. In 1984 the dividend payments were $1,891,200 or $3.94 per share. This represents an annual increase of 9.12 percent per annum. Common dividends during the same period rose at the same rate from $0.84 to $2.01 a share. At the end of 1974 the common share price (adjusted for splits) was $8¾ and the preferred was 18. At the end of 1984 the share prices were 22¾ and 41½, respectively. The internal rate of return for the 10-year period was 19.73 percent for the common and 17.75 percent for the preferred. Thus this particular preferred has some of the return characteristics of the common shares but also the senior position of a preferred. It is interesting to note that this senior stock is also entitled to participate in liquidation with the common in any balance remaining after the regular cumulative preferred and preference shares have been paid in full, and par has been paid on the common. Of course, it has priority to the regular preferred in the event of liquidation.

Eastern Air Lines Inc. has a 20 percent Participating Noncumulative Preferred Stock which was issued to the employees' trusts in 1984 and 1985. It provides that after payment of dividends on the preferred issues ranking senior to these shares, they will be entitled to annual dividends up to 20 percent of net income available for common stock to a maximum of $26 million per year.

There are a few other issues that also participate with the common shares in the event of the companies' liquidation. This will be discussed under Preference to Assets.

Cumulative Preferred Stock

Noncumulative preferred stock is a lopsided deal in favor of corporate management. The legal language would say, in effect, "If the issuer does not pay the preferred dividend in any dividend period, you just forget about it because you are not going to get it." That would be a very weak preference; management could skip a dividend payment, and the only important adverse consequence would be that the dividend could not be paid on the common stock in the same period. In our financial history there have been few noncumulative preferred stocks of this type, and most of these have probably been the result of corporate reorganizations.

One example of a noncumulative stock was Wabash Railway's 5 percent Series A shares. Between 1915 and 1926 no dividends (or less than the stated amount) were paid even though earnings were available at times for payment. The company reinvested earnings in plant and equipment. When the Board of Directors later wanted to pay dividends on the Series B preferred and the common shares, the Series A holders brought legal action to obtain back and unpaid dividends as they were earned even though not paid. In 1930, the Supreme Court decided in favor of the company, holding that as the earnings were reinvested in plant and equipment and as no dividends were declared, the preferred holders had no right to receive a share of the earnings. Some state statutes (New Jersey for one) provide that preferred dividends are cumulative if there are earnings and no dividends are declared.

There have been a few more issues of noncumulative preferreds where the dividends are paid *only* if earned; if the company records a loss for a year, the dividend is not paid and it is not made up or left to accumulate for payment in future years. The right to the dividend is gone forever and the company has no obligation to make future payment. These are known as *cumulative-to-the-extent-earned* preferreds. However, research of publicly traded preferreds leads us to only one of these noncumulative issues—UNIROYAL, Inc. First Preferred Stock with a par value of $100 per share. Dividends are payable out of each year's earnings at a rate up to $8 per share and are not cumulative, except to the extent earned, payable and unpaid. Payment is made in the year subsequent to the year in which the company had earnings. Exhibit 3 shows the earnings and dividend payments of UNIROYAL for the 1975–84 period.

EXHIBIT 3   UNIROYAL, Inc. (in thousands of dollars)

Year	Net Income	Total Preferred Dividends	Dividends Per Share	Total Common Dividends
1984	$ 77,146	$4,889	$8.00	$ 3,055
1983	66,998	4,889	8.00	nil
1982	25,598	4,889	8.00	nil
1981	51,640	nil	nil	nil
1980	(7,842)	nil	nil	nil
1979	(119,725)	3,667	6.00	nil
1978	6,503	3,667	6.00	9,963
1977	34,961	4,889	8.00	13,283
1976	18,973	4,889	8.00	13,282
1975	23,041	4,889	8.00	17,265

The full dividend based on 1984 earnings was declared on February 20, 1985, with quarterly payments on March 25, June 25, September 25, and December 24, 1985. The policy of the company in the postwar period up through 1977 was to pay $8 per share, of which $4 per share was from earnings of the preceding year. The 1978 payment included $4 from 1977 earnings and $2 from 1978 earnings. The 1979 payment of $6 was from 1978 earnings.

In September 1985, UNIROYAL proposed to the preferred shareholders that they vote to change some of the provisions of the issue. The first would make the shares cumulative whether or not the dividend was earned. The second proposal would be to make the shares redeemable in order to retire 16⅔ percent of the shares each year beginning in 1995.

Cumulative means that when a preferred dividend is not paid (whether or not earned), it accumulates and no dividend may be paid on shares ranking on a parity with or junior to the preferred until all dividend arrearages have been paid on the preferred. The prohibition of dividend payments on common stock when dividends on preferred stock are in arrears is a serious restriction. Common stockholders like their dividends and when common dividends are stopped and cannot be resumed until some sizable amount of preferred dividend arrearages are paid, they direct some very sharp questions to management. This dissatisfaction is also expressed in the stock market with lower share prices.

Usually failure to pay preferred dividends results in other financial restrictions on management. It is common to provide that while preferred dividends are in arrears the issuer may not redeem any shares of stock junior to the preferred. Generally, the terms of preferred stocks also provide that when dividends are in arrears, sinking-fund payments on the preferred and on any junior preferred are suspended and no money may be used to redeem preferred or common stock. The company may not purchase any shares of the preferred except through a purchase offer made to all preferred shareholders. Consumers Power Company is an exception as its corporate charter does not contain any restrictions on the repurchase or redemption of its preferred and preference shares while there are arrearages of dividends on such stock.

Eastern Air Lines Inc. suspended preferred dividends in late 1983 with the last payment being made on August 15, 1983. This action affected the $2.69 Cumulative Preferred, the $3.20 Cumulative Preferred and the $3.00 Cumulative Convertible Junior Preferred. By May 1985 the cumulative arrearages totalled $4.7075 per share for the $2.69 series, $5.60 for the $3.20 series, and $5.25 for the $3.00 junior series. On June 15, Eastern declared partial payment of arrearages in the two senior issues of $1.177 and $1.40, respectively. Similar payments were made on August 15, bringing the arrearages down to $3.026 for the $2.69 issue and to $3.60 for the $3.20 shares. Payments were not made on the $3.00 junior shares so that the dividends accumulated to $6.00 by August 15, 1985. Before any distribution can be made on these junior shares, all accumulated and unpaid dividends and all accumulated and unpaid sinking-fund requirements for the senior stock must be satisfied in full.

A thorough study of preferred stock would include examination of the terms of any bond issues and bank loans of the issuer and of any class of preferred senior to the one being studied. Sometimes these senior securities have provisions prohibiting payment of dividends on junior securities when the issuer's financial condition falls below standards set in these agreements, such as a minimum current ratio or a minimum amount of surplus available for the payment of dividends. In the case of the Western Union Telegraph Company, the December 1984 bank agreements provided that none of its retained earnings was available for the payment of common or preferred dividends or for sinking-fund or redemption purposes for the preferred stock. In 1984, Long Island Lighting Company, as part of its revolving credit agreement with 14 banks, agreed to suspend the declaration of preferred stock dividends payable on and after October 1, 1984 and through December 31, 1985.

In early 1985 the LTV Corporation sought approval from the holders of its 5 percent Subordinated Debentures due January 15, 1988 to the declaration and payment of regular quarterly cash dividends to January

15, 1988 on its preferred stock then outstanding or to be outstanding. The indenture under which the debentures were issued prohibited the payment of dividends and certain other distributions to the aggregate of $15,000,000 plus LTV's accumulated net income subsequent to December 31, 1966. Due to asset write-downs and expected losses, there would be a deficiency in retained earnings under this provision which would preclude the payment of dividends. Declaration of dividends due for payment in the first quarter of 1985 was deferred.

In the proxy statement sent to debenture holders the company stated:

> The Board of Directors and management of the Company strongly recommend that Debentureholders give their approval (to pay cash dividends on the preferred stock). The Company believes that such approval is in the best interests of Debentureholders and the Company because it would enhance the Company's ability to refinance existing debt and raise additional capital in the market place. The ability to pay preferred dividends will also enhance the Company's ability to issue additional preferred stock instead of debt, which, under certain circumstances, may be more beneficial to both the Company and its debentureholders.

On February 6, 1985, the debenture holders approved the company's request and received a payment of $2.50 per $100 principal amount of debentures outstanding. Preferred dividends were declared on February 7 for payment on March 1; regular declarations and payments continued thereafter on the normal quarterly schedule until they were again omitted in the fall of the year.

Preference to Assets

At the time a preferred stock is issued, hardly anyone thinks about the possibility that at some time in the future the issuing corporation may be liquidated or reorganized. However, the lawyers who draw up the terms of security issues consider the possibility and they write in provisions about what happens to a preferred stock in the event the issuer is liquidated either voluntarily or involuntarily in financial failure. A simple preference is that preferred stockholders are entitled to receive, after settlement has been made with creditors and holders of any senior issue of preferred, the par value of the preferred before any distribution is made to common stock or to any junior preferred stock. In the case of stock without par value, an amount per share is stipulated. Sometimes preferred holders are entitled to a larger amount in voluntary liquidation than in involuntary liquidation.

For example, Detroit Edison's 15.68 percent Series Cumulative Preferred has an involuntary liquidation value of $100 per share and a voluntary liquidation value of the amount equal to the optional redemption price applicable at the time of liquidation. In the case of Consumers Power Company's $7.76 Preference Stock, the involuntary liquidation value is $100 per share and the voluntary liquidation value $101.43 a share (the initial offering price).

There are some issues that may participate with the common stock in the event of liquidation. Public Service Electric & Gas Company has a $1.40 Cumulative Dividend Preference Common which is entitled to receive upon the Company's liquidation twice the amount per share that is distributed on each share of common. In the case of Southern California Edison's 5 percent Original Cumulative Participating Preferred Stock, par value $8⅓, it is entitled to par value in the event of liquidation before payment on preferred, preference, or common stock. It is also entitled to participate with the common stock in any balance remaining after the preferred and preference shares have been paid in full, including dividends, and par ($4⅙ has been paid on the common). Finally, Southern California Gas Co. has an issue of 6 percent, $25 par value preferred with asset participation rights. In liquidation or dissolution of the company, holders of the outstanding preferred stock would be entitled to receive the par value for their shares, any accrued dividends, and no more. However, the subject preferred will receive the $25 par value and accrued and unpaid dividends and then will participate on a pro rata basis with the common in the remaining assets after the par value has been paid on the common.

Seldom are corporations voluntarily liquidated, but one such event occurred in 1985 to City Investing Company. On June 28, 1985, it called for redemption, at the liquidation values plus accrued dividends, three series of publicly issued convertible preference stock. Two of the issues were converted by their holders into common shares because the conversion values were substantially in excess of the redemption price. However, holders of the third issue—$2.875 Convertible/Exchangeable Preference Series E—turned their shares in for the $25 redemption price because the conversion worth was only about $17.50 a share.

Wickes Companies and its subsidiary, Gamble-Skogmo, Inc., emerged from a bankruptcy reorganization in early 1985. Wickes' $8.75 Series A Preferred, $100 par value, received 7.459 shares of the new company's common stock. The new common shares were worth $3.53125 per share or a total of $26.34 per share of old preferred. Gamble-Skogmo's $1.75 preferred ($40 par value) received 4.321 shares of the new Wickes' common and the $1.60 preferred ($35 par value) received 3.779 shares. The total market values of these two distributions were $15.26 and $13.34 a share, respectively. If the company had liquidated instead of reorganizing, the distribution to all security holders probably would have been smaller.

Another example of a distribution to preferred holders of a company coming out of bankruptcy proceedings is Itel Corporation. Itel had an issue of $1.44 preferred with a liquidation price of $15.00 per share. Each 100 shares of preferred (total liquidation value of $1,500) received 38.7 shares of common stock of the newly reorganized company. With the new common initially valued at $7.25 a share, the holder received $280.58 worth of stock, or about 18.70 percent of the claim.

Voting Rights

Corporate issuers of preferred stocks are inclined to the view that as long as preferred stockholders receive their dividends regularly, there is no need for them to have voting rights. Investment bankers who underwrite new issues, however, think that the right to vote makes preferred stock more attractive to investors. Sometimes one view prevails and sometimes another. More often than not preferred shares do not carry general voting privileges, but in some cases each preferred share has the same voting rights as the common equity. Southern California Edison's preferred issues have different voting power; some issues have three votes per share and other issues one vote per share.

However, it is common practice to give nonvoting stock a right to elect some number of directors when preferred dividends have been in arrears for some number of dividend periods (usually four or six dividend payments). This is *contingent voting stock;* the voting right is contingent upon the preferred stockholders not getting their dividends. The most common contingent voting right is the right of owners of a class of preferred stock voting as a class to elect two directors. Thus they are assured of representation on the board of a company experiencing financial difficulties. This kind of provision has become common because the New York Stock Exchange requires it as a condition for listing nonvoting preferred stocks. Another kind of contingent voting provision is one that gives preferred stockholders one vote per share along with common stock as soon as dividends are in arrears. Whenever arrears of dividends on contingent voting stock have been paid or settled, the conditional voting right ceases. In 1985 preferred holders elected members to the Board of Directors of Eastern Air Lines and to that of Public Service Company of New Hampshire. In Eastern's case they elected two members of the Board. In the case of Public Service Company of New Hampshire the preferred stockholders as a class elected seven members to serve on the Board and the common shareholders elected six members.

Another variation that appears in the terms of some voting preferreds is one that requires approval of specified corporate acts by preferred shareholders voting as a class whenever dividends have been in arrears for some period of time. For example, approval by two thirds of a class of preferred stock voting as a class may be required for such management proposals as (1) increasing the authorized amount of any class or series of stock that ranks ahead of the preferred as to dividends or as to assets upon liquidation, (2) altering the provisions of the issuer's articles of incorporation, or (3) merging or consolidating with another company in such manner as to adversely affect the rights and preferences of the preferred stock. Preferred stock with such a provision is called vetoing stock because it can veto action proposed by management by withholding approval. The power to veto ceases when arrears of dividends are paid.

Redemption Provisions

Companies that issue preferred stocks think that raising capital in this way is a good idea at the time of issue. It provides capital at a lower cost than an issue of common stock and does not create the fixed obligation of debt. But circumstances change, and a time may come when an issuer of preferred stock finds it desirable to eliminate the preferred from its capitalization. Voting rights, for example, might impair control of a preferred stock issuer by owners of its common shares. Or circumstances might change in such a manner that it would become advantageous to refund a preferred stock with bonds to increase earnings for the common stock. Interest on bonds is a deductible expense in calculating corporate income subject to income taxes, but preferred dividends are not. Such a refunding would change a nondeductible expense (preferred dividends) to a tax-deductible expense (bond interest). Another reason might be that the issuer would want to restructure its capitalization. In 1985 Pacificorp and Atlantic Richfield Company redeemed preferreds for these reasons.

The most important reason for a senior security to be redeemed is that financing costs have declined and this makes it possible for the issuing company to save money through the replacement of high cost issues with lower cost issues. Virtually all issuers of preferred stock make provisions for (1) periodic redemption by a sinking fund arrangement, (2) redemption of stock in whole or in part by call, or (3) by conversion into common stock.

In our survey of preferreds we found only 14 issues that have no call or redemption provisions. These are truly perpetual issues—there is no way other than through reorganization that an issuer can retire the stock against the will of the owner. Of course, it could make open market purchases or ask for tenders of the shares but the stock cannot be involuntarily taken from the investor. There are a few other issues that are not callable at first glance, but they contain sinking-fund features that provide for the periodic retirement of the shares.

The remaining issues have redemption features of one type or another. The bulk are currently callable at any time, in whole or in part, at the option of the issuer at preset prices plus accrued and unpaid dividends up to the call date. Generally, the initial call price is par or the offering price plus the annual dividend or rate. The call price is then reduced periodically to par or the initial offering price at some future date. For example, West Texas Utilities Company's 10.16 percent Preferred Stock ($100 par value) is callable at $110.16 for the first five years, then at $106.77 for the next five years, then at $103.39 for the next five years, and finally at $100.00. Other issues have steadily declining redemption prices. Detroit Edison's 15.68 percent Series ($100 par value) has a steadily declining redemption price schedule from $115.68 for the year ended July 14, 1982, then $113.72 for the next year, and reduced by $1.96 annually to $100.00 starting July 15, 1989.

The aforementioned call schedules are found in most issues but there are exceptions. BankAmerica Corporation has a preferred with an interesting wrinkle. Its Special Series "C" Preferred is callable beginning September 1, 1990, at the "adjusted" stated value. The shares, issued when BankAmerica acquired Seafirst Corporation in July 1983, have a stated value of $25. The acquisition was structured so that if certain of Seafirst's loans resulted in net losses beyond $350 million, the stated value would be reduced to as low as $2. The reduction would occur on September 1, 1988 based on evaluation of the actual and estimated future loan losses, recoveries, and certain legal expenses. At May 31, 1985, loan charge-offs were such that the stated value, if it were adjusted at that date, would be reduced to $8.71. The Company stated that "it appears highly probable that the stated value . . . will be reduced to $2.00 per share in 1988." The dividend on the preferred is $2.875 per annum, but it could be adjusted in September 1988 to as low as $2.25. Thus if the stated value is reduced to $2, the shares will almost certainly be called at the first opportunity. In September 1985 the shares were trading at 15⅜ providing a current yield of 18.70 percent. This is an example of an investment (or a speculation) with a high current return but an expected low total return.

Most new issues provide some type of deferred redemption provision. Some might not be callable under any circumstance for the first 5 to 10 years while others might be currently callable but protected against being called from proceeds of a refunding issue for a certain period. This is similar to provisions found in corporate debt issues. Noncallable is far more absolute than noncallable by refunding and yet many investors fail to make the distinction and treat refunding protection the same as call protection. This could prove to be costly.

To make the distinction clear, many issues currently callable cannot be called for a certain period if the company sells debt or equity securities ranking equally with or superior to the preferred at a lower cost of capital than the outstanding preferred. This is refunding protection; it does not allow the issuer to take advantage of lower money costs on senior issues for a number of years after the sale of the preferred stock. However, if the issuer sells junior preferred or common equity prior to the expiration of the refunding protected period, the proceeds may be used to retire or refund the higher cost preferred.

Commonwealth Edison Company issued 1,000,000 shares of 9.44 percent Cumulative Prior Preferred Stock in June 1970. Less than two years later it redeemed the shares at $110; just prior to the redemption announcement the stock was trading at about $119 to $120 a share. The funds for the redemption came from the sale of common stock and common stock purchase warrants, clearly junior securities. The preferred prospectus stated:

> Prior to August 1, 1980, none of the shares . . . may be redeemed through refunding, directly or indirectly, by or in anticipation of the incurring of any debt or the issuance of any shares of the Prior Preferred Stock or of any other stock ranking prior to or on a parity with the Prior Preferred Stock, if such debt has an interest cost . . . or such shares have a dividend cost . . . less than the dividend cost . . . of the 9.44 percent . . . Stock.

The Company was sued by some institutional holders but the judge decided that the redemption provision did not prohibit redemption directly out of an issue of common shares. Since then other companies have done similar redemptions.

In the decision concerning the Florida Power & Light Company's debt refunding, the judge stated:

> The terms 'redemption' and 'refunding' are not synonymous. A 'redemption' is simply a call of bonds. A 'refunding' occurs when the issuer sells bonds in order to use the proceeds to redeem an earlier issue of bonds. . . . The refunding bond issue being sold is closely linked to the one being redeemed by contractual language and proximity in time so that the proceeds will be available to pay for the redemption. Otherwise, the issuer would be taking an inordinate risk that market conditions would change between the redemption of the earlier issue and the sale of the later issue.

This principle can also be applied to preferred stock redemptions.

Sinking-fund provisions for preferred stocks are similar to those of bonds. They provide for the periodic retirement of stock usually on an annual basis. They often commence on or after the call or refunding protected period has expired but there are instances where the sinking fund operates prior to such expiration. A specific number of shares or a certain percentage of the original issue is specified for retirement annually. Often it will amount to about 2 percent to 8 percent of the original number of shares with 5 percent being the more common requirement. Commonwealth Edison has an issue of $10.875 Preference Stock which requires that all of the shares be retired at par through the sinking fund on November 1, 1989, the date the call-protected period terminates. Thus this issue has another feature that most bonds have, that is, a maturity of sorts. Most sinking funds have provisions allowing the issuer the noncumulative option to increase sinking-fund payments (usually to double the amount at any one time). Sinking-fund payments may be made in shares of stock purchased in the open market or by the call of the required number of shares at the sinking-fund call price, normally par value. There are instances in which a company wishing to retire an entire issue of sinking-fund preferred will call the maximum number of shares allowed for the sinking fund at the lower sinking-fund redemption price and redeem the balance at the normal call price. Failure to make sinking-fund payments is not an act of default as it would be in the case of debt; it is not a cause for bankruptcy.

Many preferred stock market participants refer to issues without sinking funds as perpetual preferreds but this is a misuse of that term. Nonsinking-fund issues need not be perpetual and yet they do not have a date at which they must be retired. Sinking-fund operations can provide some measure of market support if the issuer can come into the open market and purchase stock at less than the redemption price. However, in periods of lower interest and dividend rates and higher preferred prices, a call below market prices can result in capital losses to investors. Shares to be redeemed for the sinking fund are usually selected randomly by lot and not pro rata.

An important consideration for property and casualty insurance companies is a rule by the National Association of Insurance Commissioners allowing qualifying sinking-fund preferred stocks to be valued on the books at cost rather than being marked to the current market price. This accounting or valuation treatment, at least for regulatory or reserve purposes, reduces the impact of market fluctuations on the company's portfolio to the extent that it utilizes sinking-fund preferreds.

Some preferred issues have purchase funds. These are, to some extent, generally optional on the part of an issuer as it will have to use its best efforts to retire a portion of the shares periodically if such shares can be purchased in the open market, or through tender at less than the redemption or liquidation price. If the stock is selling above the applicable price, the purchase fund cannot be put into operation. Again, the purchase fund may provide some market support to the issue in a higher dividend rate environment but when rates are lower the fund is inoperative. In the case of Occidental Petroleum's $15.50 Cumulative Preferred Stock issued in connection with the acquisition of Cities Service Company in 1982, Occidental was required to use its best efforts to purchase shares in the open market at or below the liquidation value with the proceeds derived from certain asset sales in excess of $100 million. Any shares so purchased would then be credited against any sinking-fund payments when the sinking fund became operational.

It is important to read prospectuses carefully. While preferreds are not secured by assets, as is mortgage debt with its release and substitution of property clauses, there have been instances of preferred stock retirement prior to the end of the refunding protected period because of asset sales. A case in point is Crown Zellerbach Corporation's $3.05 Cumulative Preferred Stock, Series B, issued May 19, 1982 at $20 per share. It was protected against refunding prior to April 15, 1987 and had the normal call schedule starting immediately at $23.05, declining to $20 a share in 1997. However, it also had a special provision for its retirement prior to April 15, 1997 if the company sold certain assets aggregating at least $100 million in any 12-month period. The redemption premium under this circumstance was one half the regular redemption premium. It started at $21.52 per share and declined to $20 in 1997. On May 20, 1983, it redeemed this stock at the special redemption price of $21.42 a share; the regular call price at that time was $22.85. The proceeds came from the sale of its interests in Crown Zellerbach Canada Ltd. and a small steamship company. In late October 1982, it announced that it had a preliminary agreement for the sale of these assets and the use of the proceeds should not have come as any surprise to preferred holders. The shares sold at 21⅞ at the end of December and rose as high as 23⅞ in 1983 prior to the retirement of the stock.

MULTIPLE ISSUES OF ONE CLASS OF PREFERRED

Some companies have more than one class of preferred stock. They sold one class at one time and another class at another time. The terms of the two or more classes are determined separately at the time of issuance. When there is more than one class, the question important to investors is: Which stock is senior to another in claim to dividends and assets upon liquidation? A senior preferred may receive dividends when a junior preferred does not. Other rights and limitations of the two or more classes of preferred may differ. This system of multiple classes of preferred makes things complicated for issuers, investors, and the salesmen and stock traders of brokerage firms. Generally speaking, preferred shares are senior to preference shares. Some companies have only one class of senior equity outstanding, while others might have two classes with different priorities. Consolidated Edison has only preferred shares while Consumers Power and a number of other utilities have preferred and preference shares.

Companies that use preferred stocks continually in their capitalizations as a matter of financial policy find that it is easier both for them and for investors to authorize one class of preferred stock with a defined preference as to dividends. This one class of preferred stock may be issued in series from time to time; there may be Series A, Series B, and so on. It is not uncommon for public utility companies to have six or eight or more series of one class of preferred outstanding. What makes this arrangement attractive to investors is that all of the terms of preferred stock that we have been discussing may be different for the various series although they all have the same preference as to dividends. Thus they can choose the series that best suits them. One series may have one stipulated rate of dividends and another series a different rate. For example, Texas Electric Utilities Company has 32 series of straight preferred stock with dividends ranging from $4 (three series of $4 preferred) to $11.32 per share of $100 stated value. This is the result of the January 1, 1984 merger of three operating subsidiaries into one corporate entity.

All of the other terms of a class of preferred stock may differ among the series. One series may be voting and another nonvoting. The terms for sinking-fund redemption and for redemption in whole or in part may vary. One series may be convertible, another not convertible, and a third might have an adjustable-rate, dividend-setting mechanism. Each series is tailored to conditions in the securities markets at the time of issue.

In the early 1970s, electric utility companies made increased use of preference stock. Some utilities were unable to issue preferred shares due to restrictions contained in bond indentures; they simply could not meet the required earnings tests for issuance of additional preferred stock. As there usually are no similar restrictions on the issuance of shares junior to the preferred, classes of preference shares were used. Also, many corporate charters restricted preferred shares to $100 par or stated value. To broaden the market for their stock, some utilities offered preference stock with lower par values such as $10, $20, and $25. The lower prices appealed to many less-sophisticated individual investors as they could buy round lots of 100 shares each instead of odd lots of 1 to 99 shares. While the low prices were primarily of psychological value to the small investor, (100 shares at $25 is the same as 25 shares at $100 each), this allowed companies to take advantage of a pool of capital that was previously not much interested in preferred stocks.

Another device that is used by some issuers to bring the price of their shares down to a level at which individual investors would buy them is the depositary preferred share. The depositary share represents a fractional interest in a whole preferred share that has been deposited with a bank under legal depositary agreements. It entitles the holder proportionately to all of the rights and preferences of the underlying preferred stock. For example, in 1977 Alabama Power Company issued 4,900,000 Depositary Preferred Shares at $10 each which represented an interest in one-tenth of one share of 8.72 percent $100 par preferred stock. In 1985 Harnischfeger Corporation issued 3,000,000 shares of Series B $3.402 Depositary Preferred Shares at $25.00 a share. Each represented a one-fiftieth ownership in the Series B Sinking-Fund Exchangeable Preferred Stock (60,000 shares deposited with the depositary bank). The Company used this financing method as it did not have enough authorized shares of preferred stock to permit a broad distribution. Only 132,500 shares were available of authorized but unissued stock.

TAXABILITY OF PREFERRED STOCK DIVIDENDS

For individual investors the story about taxability of dividends on preferred stocks is short with very little sweetness. Individuals may exclude from taxable income no more than $100 of dividends received during a tax year on all common and preferred stocks. A married couple filing a joint tax return may exclude $200; it does not matter which spouse receives the dividend income.

For corporate investors it is a different story. A corporation may exclude from gross income 85 percent of dividends received from other *domestic* corporations. This exclusion is justified on the ground that it mitigates double taxation of dividends paid by one company to another and then paid to the stockholders of the second company. Dividends by one company are paid after its earnings have been taxed under the federal corporate income tax. Then when received by a second company they would be taxed again as income to that company. This 85 percent exclusion leaves only 15 percent to be taxed in the hands of a corporate owner of preferred stock. This rule only applies to preferreds of banks, utility holding companies, railroads, and industrial and financial concerns. For utility operating companies the deduction is applicable to so-called "new money" issues, i.e., those preferreds sold after October 1, 1942 for purposes other than refunding purposes. Preferreds sold prior to that date and those issued afterwards for debt and preferred refunding purposes are "old money" issues with the dividends-received deduction only 60.208 percent. At the end of 1984 there were 116 electric utility "old money" issues and 21 "partly new money" issues. Gas and water companies had six "old money" and two "partly new money" preferreds while there were seven "old money" telephone issues and three "partly new money" stocks. "Partly new money" issues are those where only a portion of the proceeds was used for refunding purposes.

In order to qualify for the dividends-received deduction a corporation must hold the preferred shares at least 46 days. Also, the deduction may be reduced in the case of "debt-financed portfolio stock." This is stock acquired or carried with indebtedness which is directly attributable to the investment in such shares.

Exhibit 4 is an example of this deduction.

Because "old money" issues are less advantageous to a corporate investor, they will tend to trade at higher yields (lower prices) in order to make the aftertax return comparable to "new money" stock. As higher grade preferreds are primarily owned and traded by corporations because of their tax advantages, it is no wonder that they sell in the market at current yields less than those on good-quality corporate bonds.

Exhibit 5 compares "new money" preferred yields with other yields assuming a corporate marginal tax rate of 46 percent. If we have a preferred with a yield of 11.00 percent, the yield after taxes is 10.24

EXHIBIT 4 Summary of Intercorporate Dividends-Received Deduction

	"New Money"	*"Old Money"*
Dividends received	$1,000.00	$1,000.00
Dividend exclusion:		
Percent	85.00%	60.208%
Amount	$ 850.00	$ 602.08
Amount subject to taxes	$ 150.00	$ 397.92
Marginal tax rate	46%	46%
Taxes paid	$ 69.00	$ 183.04
Effective tax rate	6.90%	18.30%
Dividends retained:		
Percent	93.10%	81.70%
Amount	$ 931.00	$ 816.96

EXHIBIT 5 Comparison of "New Money" Preferred Stock and Other Yields (46 percent marginal tax rate)

Pretax Preferred Return	*Aftertax Preferred Return*	*Pretax Yield Needed to Equal Aftertax Preferred Return*	*Fully Taxable Alternative Investment Yield*
5.00	4.66	8.63	2.70
6.00	5.59	10.35	3.24
7.00	6.52	12.07	3.78
8.00	7.45	13.80	4.32
9.00	8.38	15.52	4.86
10.00	9.31	17.24	5.40
11.00	10.24	18.96	5.94
12.00	11.17	20.69	6.48
13.00	12.10	22.41	7.02
14.00	13.03	24.13	7.56
15.00	13.97	25.87	8.10

percent. In order to obtain this aftertax return from a taxable investment, the yield would have to be 18.96 percent. If you invested in a security with a 11.00 percent current return which is subject to the full tax rate, the net after taxes would be only 5.94 percent.

THE MARKETABILITY OF PREFERRED STOCKS

Preferred stocks that have been publicly distributed are marketable in the sense that they are traded on the stock exchanges and in the over-the-counter market. There is always a dealer or a stock exchange specialist who is willing to quote a bid price (what he will pay if you want to sell) and an offered price (what he will sell it for if you want to buy). But there are marked differences in marketability among preferred stocks, and these differences are important to investors who buy and sell these stocks.

Of the 1,298 issues profiled in Exhibit 1, less than half are listed on the New York or the American Stock Exchanges; the rest trade in the over-the-counter market. While the normal unit of trading is 100 shares on the major stock exchanges, some issues trade in round lots of 10 shares. Investors who wish to buy or sell odd lots (i.e., less than the standard unit of trading) will pay a fraction more or receive a fraction less per share than a round lot transaction. These 10-share issues are indicated in the stock exchange transaction tables with the letter "z" next to the trading volume. The Alabama Power Depositary Preferred Shares (4,900,000 shares outstanding) mentioned earlier trade in 100-share units on the New York Stock Exchange; the 11 percent shares (less than 400,000 shares outstanding) trade in 10-share units. In the first week of September 1985, 9,700 shares of the Depositary shares traded while only 200 shares of the 11 percent stock changed hands.

Exchange listings generally improve an issue's marketability but other factors include the size and the quality ratings. Larger unlisted issues might be more marketable and trade in greater volume than smaller listed issues. The better marketability of larger and higher rated issues is attributed to the fact that many preferred investors are restricted to what they can hold in their portfolios. There are generally more buyers for shares with these characteristics, and trades can take place far easier than for small and non-investment grade issues. The spread between the bid and the asked price is often smaller for highly marketable securities as the volume of trading is greater and the trader or specialist will usually have little trouble in selling the shares to a willing buyer at market prices close to the price at which the shares just previously traded. If it looks as though he would experience difficulty in quickly moving the shares, the bid price would likely be lower and the asked price would likely be higher. We would classify more than half of the issues in Exhibit 1 as small because they have total par values of less than $25 million, indicating issues of 250,000 shares or less ($100 par). In our opinion, while these may be satisfactory holdings for some large institutional investors, they are unsuitable for most individual investment portfolios.

SOURCES OF INFORMATION ABOUT PREFERRED STOCKS

The best source of information about specific preferred stocks is the prospectus that is published when the preferred stock is first issued. Prospectuses contain fairly complete information about the terms of the new preferred issues; however, in many cases (but not all), the information about the operations of the issuers leaves much to be desired. This is due to the shortened prospectus form used by many corporations under the streamlined shelf registration procedures introduced by the Securities and Exchange Commission in 1982.

You can get information about preferred stocks from many of the same sources as for common stocks and bonds. There are manuals published by the two principal rating agencies that rate senior securities. These manuals provide detailed information about corporate issuers and their securities. They are particularly useful for information about the provisions of preferred stocks such as we have been discussing.

The *Standard & Poor's Stock Guide* and *Moody's Bond Record* are monthly publications providing condensed information about many preferred stock issues. You can compare a number of preferreds quickly by using them. They provide in abbreviated form the ratings of the issues, information about the principal terms, current and historical price data, and shares outstanding. In addition, a number of investment brokers also provide research about individual issues and issuers as well as statistical publications.

SUMMARY

A preferred stock is a peculiar kind of security. Generally, it provides a fixed income—the stipulated annual amount—no more or no less. But it is not a bond; it is a right of ownership in a company. There are many possible variations in the terms of the different preferred issues. They are distinctly unlike common stock in that dividends not paid usually accumulate and must be paid before dividends may be paid on the common. But unlike bonds, failure to pay dividends on preferred is not a default as failure to pay bond interest would be. Although not a default, failure to pay preferred dividends may result in imposition of serious financial restrictions upon the issuer. Like bonds, many preferred issues have no voting power as long as dividends are being paid, but they usually gain some limited voting power when dividends are in arrears. A company may have one class of preferred stock and issue it in series with different terms for different series of stock. So it is peculiar because it has some of the characteristics of bonds and some of the characteristics of common equity. It is also peculiar because the exclusion from taxable income of most of the amount of preferred dividends received by corporations causes it to be owned very largely by corporate investors rather than individuals.

12

Municipal Bonds

Sylvan G. Feldstein, Ph.D.
*Vice President and Manager—Municipal Bond
Research Department
Merrill Lynch Capital Markets*

Frank J. Fabozzi, Ph.D., C.F.A., C.P.A.
*Visiting Professor
Sloan School of Management
Massachusetts Institute of Technology*

Municipal bonds are securities issued by state and local governments and their creations such as "authorities" and special districts. Most recent available information indicates that approximately 37,000 different states, counties, school districts, special districts, towns, and other public issuing bodies have issued municipal bonds. Although some investors buy municipal bonds as a way of supporting public improvements such as schools, playgrounds, and parks, the vast majority buy them because interest income from such bonds generally is exempt from federal income taxes. Consequently, municipal bonds are purchased by those who are in high marginal tax brackets, because on an aftertax basis they offer a yield that is greater than comparable bonds that are fully taxable.

Municipal bonds come in a variety of types, with different redemption features, credit risks, and marketability. Consequently, the holder of municipal bonds is exposed to the same risks as the holder of corporate and Treasury bonds: interest-rate risk, reinvestment risk, and call risk. Moreover, the holder of a municipal bond, like the holder of a corporate bond, faces credit risk.

In this chapter we describe the basic characteristics of municipal bonds as well as the municipal bond industry. In Chapters 24 and 25, a framework for evaluating the creditworthiness of municipal securities is presented.

TYPES OF MUNICIPAL OBLIGATIONS

Bonds

In terms of municipal bond security structures, there are basically two different types. The first type is the general obligation bond, and the second is the revenue bond.

General obligation bonds are debt instruments issued by states, counties, special districts, cities, towns, and school districts. They are secured by the issuer's general taxing powers. Usually, a general obligation bond is secured by the issuer's unlimited taxing power. For smaller governmental jurisdictions such as school districts and towns, the only available unlimited taxing power is on property. For larger general obligation bond issuers such as states and big cities, the tax revenues are more diverse and may include corporate and individual income taxes, sales taxes, and property taxes. The security pledges for these larger issuers such as states are sometimes referred to as being *full faith and credit obligations.*

Additionally, certain general obligation bonds are secured not only by the issuer's general taxing powers to create monies accumulated in the general fund but also from certain identified fees, grants, and special charges, which provide additional revenues from outside the general fund. Such bonds are known as being *double barreled* in security because of the dual nature of the revenue sources.

Also, not all general obligation bonds are secured by unlimited taxing powers. Some have pledged taxes that are limited as to revenue sources and maximum property-tax millage amounts. Such bonds are known as *limited-tax general obligation bonds.*

The second basic type of security structure is found in a revenue bond. Such bonds are issued for either project or enterprise financings in which the bond issuers pledge to the bondholders the revenues generated by the operating projects financed. Below are examples of the specific types of revenue bonds that have been issued over the years.

Airport revenue bonds. The revenues securing airport revenue bonds usually come from either traffic-generated sources—such as landing fees, concession fees, and airline apron-use and fueling fees—or lease revenues from one or more airlines for the use of a specific facility such as a terminal or hangar.

College and university revenue bonds. The revenues securing college and university revenue bonds usually include dormitory room rental fees, tuition payments, and sometimes the general assets of the college or university as well.

Hospital revenue bonds. The security for hospital revenue bonds is usually dependent on federal and state reimbursement programs (such as Medicaid and Medicare), third-party commercial payers (such as Blue Cross and private insurance), and individual patient payments.

Single-family mortgage revenue bonds. Single-family mortgage revenue bonds are usually secured by the mortgages and mortgage loan repayments on single-family homes. Security features vary but can include Federal Housing Administration (FHA), Federal Veterans Administration (VA), or private mortgage insurance.

Multifamily revenue bonds. These revenue bonds are usually issued for multifamily housing projects for senior citizens and low-income families. Some housing revenue bonds are usually secured by mortgages that are federally insured; others receive federal government operating subsidies, such as under section 8, or interest-cost subsidies, such as under section 236; and still others receive only local property tax reductions as subsidies.

Industrial development and pollution control revenue bonds. Bonds have been issued for a variety of industrial and commercial activities that range from manufacturing plants to shopping centers. They are usually secured by payments to be made by the corporations or businesses that use the facilities.

Public power revenue bonds. Public power revenue bonds are secured by revenues to be produced from electrical operating plants. Some bonds are for a single issuer, who constructs and operates power plants and then sells the electricity. Other public power revenue bonds are issued by groups of public and private investor-owned utilities for the joint financing of the construction of one or more power plants. This last arrangement is known as a *joint power* financing structure.

Resource recovery revenue bonds. A resource recovery facility converts refuse (solid waste) into commercially saleable energy, recoverable products, and a residue to be landfilled. The major revenues for a resource recovery revenue bond usually are (1) the "tipping fees" per ton paid by those who deliver the garbage to the facility for disposal; (2) revenues from steam, electricity, or refuse-derived fuel sold to either an electric power company or another energy user; and (3) revenues from the sale of recoverable materials such as aluminum and steel scrap.

Seaport revenue bonds. The security for seaport revenue bonds can include specific lease agreements with the benefiting companies or pledged marine terminal and cargo tonnage fees.

Sewer revenue bonds. Revenues for sewer revenue bonds come from hookup fees and user charges. For many older sewer bond issuers, substantial portions of their construction budgets have been financed with federal grants.

Sports complex and convention center revenue bonds. Sports complex and convention center revenue bonds usually receive revenues from sporting or convention events held at the facilities and, in some instances, from earmarked outside revenues such as local motel and hotel room taxes.

Student loan revenue bonds. Student loan repayments under student loan revenue bond programs are sometimes 100 percent guaranteed either directly by the federal government—under the Federal Insured Student Loan program (FISL) for 100 percent of bond principal and interest—or by a state guaranty agency under a more recent federal insurance program, the Federal Guaranteed Student Loan program (GSL). In addition to these two federally backed programs, student loan bonds are also sometimes secured by the general revenues of the specific colleges involved.

Toll road and gas tax revenue bonds. There are generally two types of highway revenue bonds. The bond proceeds of the first type are used to build such specific revenue-producing facilities as toll roads, bridges, and tunnels. For these pure enterprise-type revenue bonds, the pledged revenues usually are the monies collected through the tolls. The second type of highway bond is one in which the bondholders are paid by earmarked revenues outside of toll collections, such as gasoline taxes, automobile registration payments, and driver's license fees.

Water revenue bonds. Water revenue bonds are issued to finance the construction of water treatment plants, pumping stations, collection facilities, and distribution systems. Revenues usually come from connection fees and charges paid by the users of the water systems.

Hybrid and Special Bond Securities

Though having certain characteristics of general obligation and revenue bonds, there are some municipal bonds that have more unique security structures as well. They include the following:

Federal Savings and Loan Insurance Corporation-backed bonds. In this security structure, the proceeds of a bond sale were deposited in a savings and loan association that, in turn, issued a certificate of deposit (CD). The CD was insured by the Federal Savings and Loan Insurance Corporation (FSLIC) up to a limit of $100,000 of combined principal and interest for each bondholder. The savings and loan association used the money to finance low- and moderate-income rental housing developments. While these bonds are no longer issued, there are billions of dollars of these bonds in the secondary market.

Insured bonds. These are bonds that, in addition to being secured by the issuer's revenues, also are backed by insurance policies written by commercial insurance companies. The insurance, usually structured as a surety type insurance policy, is supposed to provide prompt payment to the bondholders if a default should occur.

Lease-backed bonds. Lease-backed bonds are usually structured as revenue-type bonds with annual rent payments. In some instances the rental payments may only come from earmarked tax revenues, student tuition payments, or patient fees. In other instances the underlying lessee governmental unit is required to make annual appropriations from its general fund.

Letter of credit-backed bonds. Some municipal bonds, in addition to being secured by the issuer's cash flow revenues, also are backed by commercial bank letters of credit. In some instances the letters of credit are irrevocable and, if necessary, can be used to pay the bondholders. In other instances the issuers are required to maintain investment quality worthiness before the letters of credit can be drawn upon.

Life care revenue bonds. Life care bonds are issued to construct long-term residential facilities for older citizens. Revenues are usually derived from initial lump-sum payments made by the residents.

Moral obligation bonds. A moral obligation bond is a security structure for state-issued bonds that indicates that if revenues are needed for paying bondholders, the state legislature involved is legally authorized, though not required, to make an appropriation out of general state-tax revenues.

Municipal utility district revenue bonds. These are bonds that are usually issued to finance the construction of water and sewer systems as well as roadways in undeveloped areas. The security is usually dependent on the commercial success of the specific development project involved, which can range from the sale of new homes to the renting of space in shopping centers and office buildings.

New housing authority bonds. These bonds are secured by a contractual pledge of annual contributions from HUD. Monies from Washington are paid directly to the paying agent for the bonds, and the bondholders are given specific legal rights to enforce the pledge. These bonds can no longer be issued.

Tax allocation bonds. These bonds are usually issued to finance the construction of office buildings and other new buildings in formerly blighted areas. They are secured by property taxes collected on the improved real estate.

"Territorial" bonds. These are bonds issued by United States territorial possessions such as Puerto Rico, the Virgin Islands, and Guam. The bonds are tax-exempt throughout most of the country. Also, the economies of these issuers are influenced by positive special features of the United States corporate tax codes that are not available to the states.

"Troubled City" bailout bonds. There are certain bonds that are structured to appear as pure revenue bonds but in essence are not. Revenues come from general purpose taxes and revenues that otherwise would have gone to a state's or city's general fund. Their bond structures were created to bail out underlying general obligation bond issuers from severe budget deficits. Examples are the New York State *Municipal Assistance Corporation for the City of New York Bonds* (*MAC*) and the State of Illinois *Chicago School Finance Authority Bonds.*

Refunded bonds. These are bonds that originally may have been issued as general obligation or revenue bonds but are now secured by an "escrow fund" consisting entirely of direct U.S. government obligations that are sufficient for paying the bondholders. *They are among the safest of all municipal bonds if the escrow is properly structured.*

Notes

Tax-exempt debt issued for periods ranging not beyond three years is usually considered to be short term in nature. Below are descriptions of some of these debt instruments.

Tax, revenue, grant, and bond anticipation notes: TANs, RANs, GANs, and BANs. These are temporary borrowings by states, local governments, and special jurisdictions. Usually, notes are issued for a period of 12 months, though it is not uncommon for notes to be issued for periods as short as 3 months and for as long as three years. TANs and RANs (also known as TRANs) are issued in anticipation of the collection of taxes or other expected revenues. These are borrowings to even out the cash flows caused by the irregular flows of income into the treasuries of the states and local units of government. BANs are issued in anticipation of the sale of long-term bonds.

Construction loan notes: CLNs. CLNs are usually issued for periods up to three years to provide short-term construction financing for multifamily housing projects. The CLNs generally are repaid by the proceeds of long-term bonds, which are provided after the housing projects are completed.

Tax-exempt commercial paper. This short-term borrowing instrument is issued for periods ranging from 30 to 270 days. Generally the tax-exempt commercial paper has backstop commercial bank agreements, which can include an irrevocable letter of credit, a revolving credit agreement, or a line of credit.

In this chapter we shall refer to both municipal bonds and municipal notes as simply municipal bonds.

Newer Market-Sensitive Debt Instruments

Municipal bonds are usually issued with one of two debt retirement structures or a combination of both. Either a bond has a "serial" maturity structure (wherein a portion of the loan is retired each year), or a bond has a "term" maturity (wherein the loan is repaid on a final date). Usually term bonds have maturities ranging from 20 to 40 years and retirement schedules (which are known as sinking funds) that begin 5 to 10 years before the final term maturity.

Because of the sharply upward-sloping yield curve that has existed in the municipal bond market between 1979 and 1986, many investment bankers have introduced innovative financing instruments priced at short or intermediate yield levels. These debt instruments are intended to raise money for long-term capital projects at reduced interest rates. Below are descriptions of some of these more innovative debt structures.

Put or option tender bonds. A "put" or "option tender" bond is one in which the bondholder has the right to return the bond at a price of par to the bond trustee prior to its stated long-term maturity. The put period can be as short as one day and as long as 10 years. Usually, put bonds are backed by either commercial bank letters of credit in addition to the issuer's cash flow revenues or entirely by the cash flow revenues of the issuer.

Super sinkers. A "super sinker" is a specifically identified maturity for a single-family housing revenue bond issue to which all funds from early mortgage prepayments are used to retire bonds. A super sinker has a long stated maturity but a shorter, albeit unknown, actual life. Because of this unique characteristic, investors have the opportunity to realize an attractive return when the municipal yield curve is upward sloping on a bond that is priced as if it had a maturity considerably longer than its anticipated life.

Variable-rate notes. Variable-rate notes have coupon rates that change. When a variable-rate note has a put feature it is called a *variable rate demand obligation* which may be exercised after one day, seven days, quarterly, semiannually, annually or longer. The coupon rate is tied to one of various indexes. Specific examples include percents of the prime rate, the J. J. Kenney Municipal Index, the Merrill Lynch Index, or a percent of the 90-day Treasury bill rate. A bank letter of credit is usually required as liquidity backup for variable rate demand obligations.

A variation of variable-rate obligations is one in which the investor in advance selects the interest rate and interest payment date from 1 up to 90 or 180 days. The security may have a nominal 30-year maturity. Such a bond has a put feature of a variable rate demand obligation and the maturity flexibility of tax-exempt commercial paper. One version of this new investment vehicle is called UPDATES (Unit Priced Demand Adjustable Tax-Exempt Securities).

Zero-coupon bonds. A zero-coupon bond is one in which no coupon interest payments are paid to the bondholder. Instead, the bond is purchased at a very deep discount and matures at par. The difference between the original-issue discount price and par represents a specified compounded annual yield. In the municipal bond market there is also a variant of the zero-coupon bond called a "municipal multiplier" or "compound interest bond." It is a bond that is issued at par and *does* actually have interest payments. However, the interest payments are not distributed to the holder of the bond until maturity. Rather, the issuer agrees to reinvest the undistributed interest payments at the bond's yield to maturity when it was issued. For example, suppose that a 10 percent, 10-year bond with a par value of $5,000 is sold at par to yield 10 percent. Every six months, the maturity value of the bond is increased by 5 percent of the maturity value of the previous six months. So at the end of 10 years, the maturity value of the bond will be equal to $13,267 [= $5,000 $\times$ (1.05)[20]]. In the case of a 10-year zero bond priced to yield 10 percent, the bond would have a maturity value of $5,000 but sell for $1,884 when it is issued.[1]

THE BUYERS OF MUNICIPAL BONDS

The three categories of investors that have dominated the municipal securities market are commercial banks, property and casualty insurance companies, and households. Although these three investor categories have dominated the market since the mid-1950s, the relative participation in each category has shifted.

Households and Mutual Funds (Individual Investors)

Retail investor participation in the municipal securities market has fluctuated widely since 1972. With some interruptions, retail investors' market share has been trending downward; however, in 1981 the trend was reversed and individual investors are now the largest holders of municipal bonds.

Individual investors may purchase municipal bonds and notes directly or through bond funds and tax-exempt unit investment trusts. The $5,000 piece denominations for municipal securities have made unit investment trusts and bond funds very popular investments among those individuals who are unable to purchase securities in large increments.

Commercial Banks

Several studies of the investment behavior of banks indicate that their demand for municipal securities can best be described as a "residual demand."[2] After commercial banks have met their reserve obligations, remaining funds are placed either in loans or income-producing taxable and tax-exempt securities. If loan demand is sufficiently strong, banks may sell portions of their municipal holdings to avert potential liquidity problems. Conversely, when loan demand is weak, banks will tend to increase their purchases of municipals. In this instance, commercial banks attempt to balance reduced borrowing needs with a less cost-

---

[1] Variations on the zero-coupon bond were introduced to allow municipal issuers to circumvent restrictions on the amount of par value that they were legally permitted to issue.

[2] Donald R. Hodgman, *Commercial Bank Loan and Investment Policy* (Urbana, Ill.: University of Illinois Bureau of Economic and Business Research, 1963), pp. 38–40; and Stephen M. Goldfeld, *Commercial Bank Behavior and Economic Activity* (New York: Elsevier-North Holland Publishing, 1966).

intensive investment portfolio consisting of taxable and tax-exempt securities.[3]

Insurance Companies

Purchases of municipal securities by property and casualty insurance companies are primarily a function of their underwriting profits and investment income. Claims on property and casualty companies are difficult to anticipate. Varying court awards for liability suits, the effects of inflation upon repair costs, and the unpredictability of weather are the chief factors that affect the level of claims experienced by property and casualty insurance companies. The profitability of property and casualty insurance companies, in turn, is primarily dependent upon the revenues generated from insurance premiums and investment income and the cost of claims filed. It is important to note that the premiums for various types of insurance are subject to competitive pressures and to approval from state insurance commissioners.

As can be expected then, the profitability of property and casualty companies is very cyclical. Normally, intense price competition follows highly profitable years. During these high-income periods, property and casualty companies typically step up their purchases of municipals in order to shield taxable income. Furthermore, lower rate increases are usually granted by state commissioners during this time. Underwriting losses traditionally begin to exact a toll as premium and investment income fails to keep pace with claims settlement costs. As underwriting losses mount, property and casualty insurance companies begin to curtail their investment in tax-exempt securities. The profitability cycle is completed when property and casualty companies win rate increases from state commissioners after sustaining continued underwriting losses.

THE LEGAL OPINION

Municipal bonds have legal opinions. The relationship of the legal opinion to the safety of municipal bonds for both general obligation and revenue bonds is threefold. First, bond counsel should check to determine if the issuer is indeed legally able to issue the bonds. Second, bond

---

[3] Besides shielding income from federal taxation, commercial banks hold the obligations of state and local governments for a variety of other reasons. Most state and local governments mandate that public deposits at a bank be collateralized. Although Treasury or federal agency securities may be utilized as collateral, the use of municipal bonds and notes is favored. Obligations of state and local governments also may be used as collateral when commercial banks borrow at the discount window of the Federal Reserve. Furthermore, banks frequently serve as underwriters or market makers of municipal securities, and these functions require maintaining inventories of tax-exempt bonds and notes.

counsel is to see that the issuer has properly prepared for the bond sale by having enacted the various required ordinances, resolutions, and trust indentures and without violating any other laws and regulations. This preparation is particularly important in the highly technical areas of determining whether the bond issue is qualified for tax exemption under federal law and whether the issue has not been structured in such a way as to violate federal arbitrage regulations. Third, bond counsel is to certify that the security safeguards and remedies provided for the bond-holders and pledged either by the bond issuer or by third parties, such as banks with letter-of-credit agreements, are actually supported by federal, state, and local government laws and regulations.

The popular notion is that much of the legal work done in a bond issue is boilerplate in nature, but from the bondholder's point of view the legal opinions and document reviews should be the ultimate security provisions. This is because if all else fails, the bondholder may have to go to court to enforce his or her security rights. Therefore, the integrity and competency of the lawyers who review the documents and write the legal opinions that usually are summarized and stated in the official statements are very important.[4]

THE COMMERCIAL CREDIT-RATING OF MUNICIPAL BONDS

Of the municipal bonds that were rated by a commercial rating company in 1929 and plunged into default in 1932, 78 percent had been rated double-A or better, and 48 percent had been rated triple-A. Since then the ability of rating agencies to assess the creditworthiness of municipal obligations has evolved to a level of general industry acceptance and respectability. In most instances, they adequately describe the financial conditions of the issuers and identify the credit-risk factors. However, a small but significant number of recent instances have caused market participants to reexamine their reliance on the opinions of the rating agencies.

As an example, the troubled bonds of the Washington Public Power Supply System (WPPSS) should be mentioned. Two major commercial rating companies—Moody's and Standard & Poor's—gave their highest ratings to these bonds in the early 1980s. Moody's gave the WPPSS Projects 1, 2, and 3 bonds its very highest credit rating of Aaa and the Projects 4 and 5 bonds its rating of A1. This latter investment-grade rating is defined as having the strongest investment attributes within

---

[4] For specific studies on recent problems with legal opinions, see Chapter 11 on contemporary defaults and related problems. Sylvan G. Feldstein and Frank J. Fabozzi, *Dow Jones-Irwin Guide to Municipal Bonds* (Homewood, IL: Dow Jones-Irwin, forthcoming).

the upper medium grade of creditworthiness. Standard & Poor's also had given the WPPSS Projects 1, 2, and 3 bonds its highest rating of AAA and Projects 4 and 5 bonds its rating of A+. While these high-quality ratings were in effect, WPPSS sold over $8 billion in long-term bonds. By 1986 over $2 billion of these bonds were in default.

In fact, since 1975 all of the major municipal defaults in the industry initially had been given investment-grade ratings by these two commercial rating companies. Of course, it should be noted that in the majority of instances ratings of the commercial rating companies adequately reflect the condition of the credit. However, unlike 20 years ago when the commercial rating companies would not rate many kinds of revenue bond issues, today they seem to view themselves as assisting in the capital formation process.[5] The commercial rating companies now receive fairly substantial fees from issuers for their ratings, and they are part of large, growth-oriented conglomerates. Moody's is an operating unit of the Dun & Bradstreet Corporation and Standard & Poor's is part of the McGraw-Hill Corporation.

Today, many institutional investors, underwriters, and traders rely on their own in-house municipal credit analysts for determining the creditworthiness of municipal bonds. However, other investors do not perform their own credit-risk analysis, but, instead, rely upon credit-risk ratings by Moody's and Standard & Poor's. In this section, we discuss the rating categories of these two commercial rating companies.

Moody's Investors Service

The municipal bond rating system used by Moody's grades the investment quality of municipal bonds in a nine-symbol system that ranges from the highest investment quality, which is Aaa, to the lowest credit rating, which is C. The respective nine alphabetical ratings and their definitions are found in the table on page 302.

Municipal bonds in the top four categories (Aaa, Aa, and A, and Baa) are considered to be of investment-grade quality. Additionally, bonds in the Aa through B categories that Moody's concludes have the strongest investment features within the respective categories are designated by the symbols Aa1, A1, Baa1, Ba1, and B1, respectively. Moody's also may use the prefix *Con.* before a credit rating to indicate that the bond security is dependent on (1) the completion of a construction project, (2) earnings of a project with little operating experience, (3)

---

[5] See Victor F. Zonana and Daniel Hertzberg, "Moody's Dominance in Municipals Market is Slowly Being Eroded," *The Wall Street Journal*, November 1, 1981, pp. 1 and 23; and Peter Brimelow, "Shock Waves from Whoops Roll East," *Fortune*, July 25, 1983, pp. 46–48.

Moody's Municipal Bond Ratings

Rating	Definition
Aaa	Best quality; carry the smallest degree of investment risk.
Aa	High quality; margins of protection not quite as large as the Aaa bonds.
A	Upper medium grade; security adequate but could be susceptible to impairment.
Baa	Medium grade; neither highly protected nor poorly secured— lack outstanding investment characteristics and sensitive to changes in economic circumstances.
Ba	Speculative; protection is very moderate.
B	Not desirable investment; sensitive to day-to-day economic circumstances.
Caa	Poor standing; may be in default but with a workout plan.
Ca	Highly speculative; may be in default with nominal workout plan.
C	Hopelessly in default.

rentals being paid once the facility is constructed, or (4) some other limiting condition.[6]

The municipal note rating system used by Moody's is designated by four investment-grade categories of Moody's Investment Grade (MIG):

Moody's Municipal Note Ratings

Rating	Definition
MIG 1	Best quality
MIG 2	High quality
MIG 3	Favorable quality
MIG 4	Adequate quality

A short-term issue having a "demand" feature (i.e., payment relying on external liquidity and usually payable upon demand rather than fixed maturity dates) is differentiated by Moody's with the use of the symbols VMIG1 through VMIG4.

Moody's also provides credit ratings for tax-exempt commercial paper. These are promissory obligations (1) not having an original maturity in excess of nine months, and (2) backed by commercial banks. Moody's

---

[6] It should also be noted that, as of 1984, Moody's applies numerical modifiers 1, 2, and 3 in each generic rating classification from Aa through B to municipal bonds that are issued for industrial development and pollution control. The modifier 1 indicates that the security ranks in the higher end of its generic rating category; the modifier 2 indicates a midrange ranking, and the modifier 3 indicates that the bond ranks in the lower end of its generic rating category.

uses three designations, all considered to be of investment grade, for indicating the relative repayment capacity of the rated issues:

Moody's Tax-Exempt Commercial Paper Ratings

Rating	Definition
Prime 1 (P–1)	Superior capacity for repayment
Prime 2 (P–2)	Strong capacity for repayment
Prime 3 (P–3)	Acceptable capacity for repayment

Standard & Poor's

The municipal bond rating system used by Standard & Poor's grades the investment quality of municipal bonds in a 10-symbol system that ranges from the highest investment quality, which is AAA, to the lowest credit rating, which is D. Bonds within the top four categories (AAA, AA, A, and BBB) are considered by Standard & Poor's as being of investment-grade quality. The respective 10 alphabetical ratings and definitions are the following:

Standard & Poor's Municipal Bond Ratings

Rating	Definition
AAA	Highest rating; extremely strong security.
AA	Very strong security; differs from AAA in only a small degree.
A	Strong capacity but more susceptible to adverse economic effects than two above categories.
BBB	Adequate capacity but adverse economic conditions more likely to weaken capacity.
BB	Lowest degree of speculation; risk exposure.
B	Speculative; risk exposure.
CCC	Speculative; major risk exposure.
CC	Highest degree of speculation; major risk exposure.
C	No interest is being paid.
D	Bonds in default with interest and/or repayment of principal in arrears.

Standard & Poor's also uses a plus (+) or minus (−) sign to show relative standing within the rating categories ranging from AA to BB. Additionally, Standard & Poor's uses the letter *p* to indicate a provisional rating that is intended to be removed upon the successful and timely completion of the construction project. A double dagger (‡) on a mortgage-backed revenue bond rating indicates that the rating is contingent upon receipt by Standard & Poor's of closing documentation confirming investments and cash flows. An asterisk (*) following a credit rating indicates that the continuation of the rating is contingent upon receipt of an executed copy of the escrow agreement.

The municipal note-rating system used by Standard & Poor's grades the investment quality of municipal notes in a four-symbol system that ranges from highest investment quality, SP–1+, to the lowest credit rating, SP–3. Notes within the top three categories (i.e., SP–1+, SP–1, and SP–2) are considered by Standard & Poor's as being of investment-grade quality. The respective ratings and summarized definitions are:

Standard & Poor's Municipal Note Ratings

Rating	Definition
SP–1	Very strong or strong capacity to pay principal and interest. Those issues determined to possess overwhelming safety characteristics will be given a plus (+) designation.
SP–2	Satisfactory capacity to pay principal and interest.
SP–3	Speculative capacity to pay principal and interest.

Standard & Poor's also rates tax-exempt commercial paper in the same four categories as taxable commercial paper. The four tax-exempt commercial paper rating categories are:

Standard & Poor's Tax-Exempt Commercial Paper Ratings

Rating	Definition
A–1+	Highest degree of safety.
A–1	Very strong degree of safety.
A–2	Strong degree of safety.
A–3	Satisfactory degree of safety.

How the Rating Agencies Differ

Although there are many similarities in how Moody's and Standard & Poor's approach credit ratings, there are certain differences in their respective approaches as well. As examples we shall present below some of the differences in approach between Moody's and Standard & Poor's when they assign credit ratings to general obligation bonds.

The credit analysis of general obligation bonds issued by states, counties, school districts, and municipalities initially requires the collection and assessment of information in four basic categories. The first category includes obtaining information on the issuer's debt structure so that the overall debt burden can be determined. The debt burden usually is composed of (1) the respective direct and overlapping debts per capita as well as (2) the respective direct and overlapping debts as percentages of real estate valuations and personal incomes. The second category of needed information relates to the issuer's ability and political discipline for maintaining sound budgetary operations. The focus of attention here is usually on the issuer's general operating funds and whether or not it has maintained at least balanced budgets over the previous three to five years. The third category involves determining the specific local taxes and intergovernmental revenues available to the issuer, as well as obtaining historical information on both tax-collection rates, which are important when looking at property tax levies, and on the dependency of local budgets on specific revenue sources, which is important when looking at the impact of federal revenue sharing monies. The fourth and last general category of information necessary to the credit analysis is an assessment of the issuer's overall socioeconomic environment. Questions that have to be answered here include determining the local employment distribution and composition, population growth, and real estate property valuation and personal income trends, among other economic indexes.

Although Moody's and Standard & Poor's rely on these same four informational categories in arriving at their respective credit ratings of general obligation bonds, what they emphasize among the categories can result at times in dramatically different credit ratings for the same issuer's bonds.

There are major differences between Moody's and Standard & Poor's in their respective approaches toward these four categories, and there are other differences in conceptual factors the two rating agencies bring to bear before assigning their respective general obligation credit ratings. There are very important differences between the rating agencies, and although while there are some zigs and zags in their respective rating policies, there are also clear patterns of analysis that exist and that have resulted in split credit ratings for a given issuer. The objective here is to outline what these differences between Moody's and Standard & Poor's actually are. Furthermore, although the rating agencies have stated in their publications what criteria guide their respective credit-rating approaches, the conclusions here about how they go about rating general obligation bonds are not only derived from these sources, but also from reviewing their credit reports and rating decisions on individual bond issues.

How do Moody's and Standard & Poor's differ in evaluating the four basic informational categories? Simply stated, Moody's tends to focus on the debt burden and budgetary operations of the issuer, and Standard & Poor's considers the issuer's economic environment as the most important element in its analysis. Although in most instances these differences of emphasis do not result in dramatically split credit ratings for a given issuer, there are at least two recent instances in which major differences in ratings on general obligation bonds have occurred.

The general obligation bonds of the Chicago School Finance Authority are rated only Baa1 by Moody's, but Standard & Poor's rates the same bonds AA−. In assigning the credit rating of Baa1, Moody's bases its rating on the following debt- and budget-related factors: (1) The deficit funding bonds are to be retired over a 30-year period, an unusually long time for such an obligation; (2) the overall debt burden is high; and (3) the school board faces long-term difficulties in balancing its operating budget because of reduced operating taxes, desegregation program requirements, and uncertain public employee union relations.

Standard & Poor's credit rating of AA− appears to be based primarily upon the following two factors: (1) Although Chicago's economy has been sluggish, it is still well diversified and fundamentally sound; and (2) the unique security provisions for the bonds in the opinion of the bond counsel insulate the pledged property taxes from the school board's creditors in the event of a school-system bankruptcy.

Another general obligation bond wherein split ratings have occurred is the bond issue of Allegheny County, Pennsylvania. Moody's rates the bonds A, whereas the Standard & Poor's rating is AA.

Moody's A credit rating is based primarily upon four budget-related factors: (1) above-average debt load with more bonds expected to be issued for transportation related projects and for the building of a new hospital, (2) continued unfunded pension liabilities, (3) past unorthodox budgetary practices of shifting tax revenues from the county tax levy to the county institution district levy, and (4) an archaic real estate property assessment system, which is in the process of being corrected.

Standard & Poor's higher credit rating of AA also appears to be based upon four factors: (1) an affluent, diverse, and stable economy with wealth variables above the national medians, (2) a good industrial mix with decreasing dependence on steel production, (3) improved budget operations having accounting procedures developed to conform to generally accepted accounting principles, and (4) a rapid debt retirement schedule that essentially matches anticipated future bond sales.

Are state general obligation bonds fundamentally different from local government general obligation bonds? There is also another difference between the credit rating agencies in how they apply their analytical tools to the rating of state general obligation bonds and local government general obligation bonds. Moody's basically believes that the state and local bonds are not fundamentally different. Moody's applies the same debt- and budget-related concerns to state general obligation bonds as they do to general obligation bonds issued by counties, school districts, towns, and cities. Moody's has even assigned ratings below A to state general obligation bonds. When the state of Delaware was having serious budgetary problems in the period beginning in 1975 and extending through 1978, Moody's gradually downgraded its general obligation bonds from Aa to Baa1. It should be noted that when Moody's downgraded Delaware general obligation bonds to Baa1 and highlighted its budgetary problems, the state government promptly began to address its budgetary problems. By 1982 the bond rating was up to Aa. In May of 1982 Moody's downgraded the state of Michigan's general obligation bonds from A to Baa1 on the basis of weak local economy and the state's budgetary problems. Another example of Moody's maintaining a state credit rating below A was in Alaska, where until 1974 the state general obligation bonds were rated Baa1. Here, Moody's cited the heavy debt load as a major reason for the rating.

Unlike Moody's, Standard & Poor's seems to make a distinction between state and local government general obligation bonds. Because states have broader legal powers in the areas of taxation and policy making that do not require home-rule approvals, broader revenue bases, and more diversified economies, Standard & Poor's seems to view state general obligation bonds as being significantly stronger than those of their respective underlying jurisdictions. Standard & Poor's has never given ratings below A to a state. Additionally, of the 38 state general obligation bonds that both Moody's and Standard & Poor's rated in mid-1986, the latter agency had given ratings of AA or better to 34 states and ratings of A to only four states. On the other hand, Moody's had given ratings of Aa or better to only 30 states, and ratings in the A range to eight states. On the whole for reasons just outlined, it seems that Standard & Poor's tends to have a higher credit assessment of state general obligation bonds than does Moody's. Furthermore, it should be noted that Moody's views these broader revenue resources as making states more vulnerable in difficult economic times to demands by local governments for increased financial aid.

How do the credit-rating agencies differ in assessing the moral obligation bonds?   In more than 20 states, state agencies have issued housing revenue bonds that carry a potential state liability for making up deficiencies in their one-year debt service reserve funds (backup funds), should any occur. In most cases if a drawdown of the debt reserve occurs, the state agency must report the amount used to its governor and the state budget director. The state legislature, in turn, may appropriate the requested amount, though there is no legally enforceable obligation to do so. Bonds with this makeup provision are the so-called moral obligation bonds.

Below is an example of the legal language in the bond indenture that explains this procedure.

In order to further assure the maintenance of each such debt service reserve fund, there shall be annually apportioned and paid to the agency for deposit in each debt service reserve fund such sum, if any, as shall be certified by the chairman of the agency to the governor and director of the budget as necessary to restore such fund to an amount equal to the fund requirement. The chairman of the agency shall annually, on or before December first, make and deliver to the governor and director of the budget his certificate stating the sum or sums, if any, required to restore each such debt service reserve fund to the amount aforesaid, and the sum so certified, if any, shall be apportioned and paid to the agency during the then current state fiscal year.

Moody's views the moral obligation feature as being more literary than legal when applied to legislatively permissive debt service reserve makeup provisions. Therefore, it does not consider this procedure a credit strength. Standard & Poor's, to the contrary, does. It views moral obligation bonds as being no lower than one rating category below a state's own general obligation bonds. Its rationale is based upon the implied state support for the bonds and the market implications for that state's own general obligation bonds should it ever fail to honor its moral obligation.

As for the result of these two different opinions of the moral obligation, there are several municipal bonds that have split ratings. As examples, in mid-1986 the Nonprofit Housing Project Bonds of the New York State Housing Finance Agency, the General Purpose Bonds of the New York State Urban Development Corporation, and the Series A Bonds of the Battery Park City Authority have the Moody's credit rating of Ba, which is a speculative investment category. Standard & Poor's, because of the moral obligation pledge of the state of New York, gives the same bonds a credit rating of BBB+, which is an investment-grade category.

How do the credit-rating agencies differ in assessing the importance of withholding state aid to pay debt service? Still another difference between Moody's and Standard & Poor's involves their respective attitudes toward state-aid security-related mechanisms. Since 1974 it has been the policy of Standard & Poor's to view as a very positive credit feature the automatic withholding and use of state aid to pay defaulted debt service on local government general obligation bonds. Usually the mechanism requires the respective state treasurer to pay debt service directly to the bondholder from monies due the local issuer from the state. Seven states have enacted security mechanisms that in one way or another allow certain local government general obligation bondholders to be paid debt service from the state-aid appropriations, if necessary. In most instances the state-aid withholding provisions apply to general obligation bonds issued by school districts.[7]

---

[7] The states involved are Indiana, Kentucky, New Jersey, New York, Pennsylvania, South Carolina, and West Virginia.

Although Standard & Poor's does review the budgetary operations of the local government issuer to be sure there are no serious budgetary problems, the assigned rating reflects the general obligation credit rating of the state involved, the legal base of the withholding mechanism, the historical background and long-term state legislative support for the pledged state aid program, and the specified coverage of the state aid monies available to maximum debt-service requirements on the local general obligation bonds. Normally, Standard & Poor's applies a blanket rating to all local general obligation bonds covered by the specific state-aid withholding mechanism. The rating is one or two notches below the rating of that particular state's general obligation bonds. Whether the rating is either one notch below or two notches below depends on the coverage figures, the legal security, and the legislative history and political durability of the pledged state-aid monies involved. It should also be noted that, although Standard & Poor's stated policy is to give blanket ratings, a specified rating is only granted when an issuer or bondholder applies for it.

Although Moody's recognizes the state-aid withholding mechanisms in its credit reviews, it believes that its assigned rating must in the first instance reflect the underlying ability of the issuer to make timely debt-service payments. Standard & Poor's, to the contrary, considers a state-aid withholding mechanism that provides for the payment of debt service equally as important a credit factor as the underlying budget, economic, and debt-related characteristics of the bond issuer.

What is the difference in attitudes toward accounting records? Another area of difference between Moody's and Standard & Poor's concerns their respective attitudes toward the accounting records kept by general obligation bond issuers. In May 1980 Standard & Poor's stated that if the bond issuer's financial reports are not prepared in accordance with generally accepted accounting principles (GAAP) it will consider this a "negative factor" in its rating process. Standard & Poor's has not indicated how negative a factor it is in terms of credit rating changes but has indicated that issuers will not be rated at all if either the financial report is not timely (i.e., available no later than six months after the fiscal year-end) or is substantially deficient in terms of reporting. Moody's policy here is quite different. Because Moody's reviews the historical performance of an issuer over a three- to five-year period, requiring GAAP reporting is not necessary from Moody's point of view, although the timeliness of financial reports is of importance.

MUNICIPAL BOND INSURANCE

Municipal bond insurance is a contractual commitment by an insurance company to pay the bondholder any bond principal and/or coupon interest that is due on a stated maturity date, but has not been paid by the bond issuer. Once issued, this municipal bond default insurance usually extends for the term of the bond issue, and it cannot be canceled by the insurance company. A one-time insurance premium (generally paid at the time of original bond issuance) is paid for the insurance policy and is nonrefundable.

The bondholder or trustee who has not received payments for bond principal and/or coupon interest on the stated due dates for the insured bonds must notify the insurance company and surrender to it the unpaid bonds and coupons. Under the terms of the policy, the insurance company is usually obligated to pay the paying agent sufficient monies for the bondholders. These monies must be enough to cover the face value of the insured principal and coupon interest that was due but not paid. Once the insurance company pays the monies, the company becomes the owner of the surrendered bonds and coupons and can begin legal proceedings to recover the monies that are now due it from the bond issuer.

The Insurers

Municipal bond insurance has been available since 1971. Some of the largest and financially strongest insurance companies in the United States are participants in this industry, as well as smaller monoline insurance companies. By mid-1986, approximately 25 percent of all new municipals were insured. The following companies are some of the major municipal bond insurers as of 1986:

American Municipal Bond Assurance Corporation (AMBAC)
Bond Investors Guaranty Insurance Company (BIG)
Financial Guaranty Insurance Corporation (FGIC)
Municipal Bond Insurance Association (MBIA)

Market Pricing of Insured Municipal Bonds

In general, although insured municipal bonds sell at yields lower than they would without the insurance, they tend to have yields substantially higher than Aaa/AAA-rated noninsured municipal bonds.

EQUIVALENT TAXABLE YIELD

An investor interested in purchasing a municipal bond must be able to compare the promised yield on a municipal bond with that of a comparable taxable bond. The following general formula is used to determine the equivalent taxable yield for a tax-exempt bond:

$$\text{Equivalent taxable yield} = \frac{\text{Tax-exempt yield}}{(1 - \text{marginal tax rate})}$$

For example, suppose an investor in the 30 percent marginal tax bracket is considering the acquisition of a tax-exempt bond that offers a tax-exempt yield of 8 percent. The equivalent taxable yield is 11.43 percent, as shown below.

$$\text{Equivalent taxable yield} = \frac{.08}{(1 - .3)} = .1143$$

When computing the equivalent taxable yield, the traditionally computed yield-to-maturity is not the tax-exempt yield if the issue is selling below par (i.e., selling at a discount) because only the coupon interest is exempt from federal income taxes.[8] Instead, the yield-to-maturity after an assumed capital gains tax is computed and used in the numerator of the formula.

The yield-to-maturity after an assumed capital gains tax is calculated in the same manner as the traditional yield-to-maturity. However, instead of using the redemption value in the calculation, the net proceeds after an assumed capital gains tax is used. For example, suppose that on November 1, 1981, an investor purchased $5,000 New York State Housing Finance Agency (NYSHFA) State University 8 percent bonds maturing November 1, 1999, at 66.50, or $3,325 per bond (.6650 times $5,000). The issue has a $5,000 redemption value at maturity, 18 years from November 1, 1981. The yield-to-maturity for this issue is approximately 12.80 percent. Recall from Chapter 3 that the yield-to-maturity is the interest rate that makes the present value of the 36 semiannual interest payments of $200 plus the redemption value of $5,000 equal to the purchase price of $3,325. Assuming a capital gains tax of 20 percent, the net proceeds after the capital gains tax is $4,665.[9] The interest rate that equates the present value of the 36 semiannual interest payments of $200 each and the net proceeds of $4,665 to the purchase price of $3,325 is 12.66 percent.[10] Therefore, 12.66 percent is the yield-to-maturity after a capital gains tax of 20 percent.

There is a major drawback in employing the equivalent taxable yield formula to compare the relative investment merits of a taxable and tax-exempt bond. Recall from the discussion in Chapter 4 that the yield-to-maturity measure assumes that the entire coupon interest can be rein-

---

[8] An investor who purchases a tax-exempt bond at a premium will not be entitled to a capital loss if the bond is held to maturity because the premium must be amortized. See Chapter 3.

[9] The long-term capital gain is $1,675 ($5,000 minus the purchase price of $3,325). The assumed applicable capital gains tax is $355 (20 percent of $1,675). Therefore, the net proceeds after the assumed capital gains tax is $4,665 ($5,000 minus $335).

[10] More accurately, the interest rate is 6.33 percent. Since the interest payments are semiannual, it is traditional to double the rate to obtain the yield. See Chapter 4.

vested at the computed yield. Consequently, taxable bonds with the same yield-to-maturity cannot be compared because the total dollar returns may differ from the computed yield. The same problem arises when attempting to compare taxable and tax-exempt bonds, especially since only a portion of the coupon interest on taxable bonds can be reinvested, although the entire coupon payment is available for reinvestment in the case of municipal bonds. A framework that should be employed to compare taxable and tax-exempt bonds is provided in Chapter 27. The framework is based upon the concept of realized compound yield, which was discussed in Chapter 4.[11]

STATE AND LOCAL TAX TREATMENT[12]

The tax treatment of municipal bonds varies by state. There are three types of tax that can be imposed: (1) an income tax on coupon income, (2) a tax on realized capital gains, and (3) a personal property tax.

There are 43 states that levy an individual income tax, as does the District of Columbia. Six of these states exempt coupon interest on *all* municipal bonds, whether the issue is in state or out of state. Coupon interest from obligations by in-state issuers is exempt from state individual income taxes in 32 states. Five states levy individual income taxes on coupon interest whether the issuer is in state or out of state.

State taxation of realized capital gains is often ignored by investors when making investment decisions. In 42 states, a tax is levied on a base that includes income from capital transactions (i.e., capital gains or losses). Only one state at the time of this writing, Connecticut, technically levies a capital gains tax. In many states where coupon interest is exempt if the issuer is in state, the same exemption will not apply to capital gains involving municipal bonds.

There are 20 states that levy a personal property tax. Of these 20 states, only 11 apply this tax to municipal bonds. The tax resembles more of an income tax than a personal property tax. For example, in Kansas, Michigan and Ohio, personal property taxes are measured on the annual income generated by a bond.

In determining the effective tax rate imposed by a particular state, an investor must consider the impact of the deductibility of state taxes

---

[11] See also Martin L. Leibowitz, "Total Aftertax Bond Performance and Yield Measures for Tax-Exempt Bonds Held in Taxable Portfolios," in *The Municipal Bond Handbook*, Vol. I, eds. Frank J. Fabozzi, Sylvan G. Feldstein, Irving M. Pollack, and Frank G. Zarb (Homewood, Ill.: Dow Jones-Irwin, 1983).

[12] The source of information for this section is from Steven J. Hueglin, "State and Local Tax Treatment of Municipal Bonds," Chapter 4 in *The Municipal Bond Handbook*, Vol. I, eds. Frank J. Fabozzi, et al.

EXHIBIT 1 Yield Levels and Ratios (early February 1984, January 10, 1985 and November 21, 1985)

Issue	February 1984			January 10, 1985			November 21, 1985		
	Municipal Yield	Treasury Yield	Yield Ratio	Municipal Yield	Treasury Yield	Yield Ratio	Municipal Yield	Treasury Yield	Yield Ratio
3 year AAA G.O.	6.25%	10.75%	.58	6.75%	10.30%	.65	5.60%	8.75%	.64
5 year AAA G.O.	6.90	11.40	.60	7.25	11.00	.66	6.25	9.17	.68
10 year AAA G.O.	8.00	11.60	.69	8.25	11.45	.72	7.10	9.60	.74
30 year AAA G.O.	9.00	11.75	.77	9.25	11.50	.80	8.25	9.94	.83

SOURCE: Merrill Lynch, *Bond Market Comment* 8, no. 2 (January 11, 1985) and *Bond Market Comment* 8, no. 47 (November 22, 1985).

EXHIBIT 2 Ratio of Yields on 1-Year Municipal Notes to Yields on 1-Year Treasury Bills

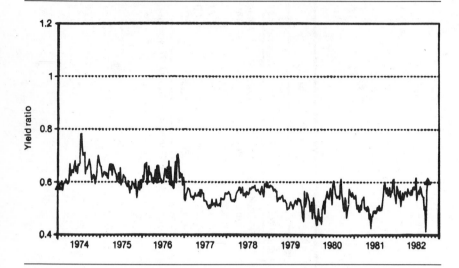

Ratio of Yields on 5-Year AAA G.O. Bonds to Yields on 5-Year Treasury Notes

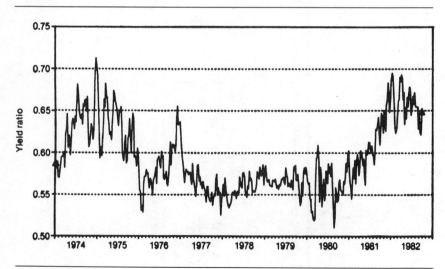

EXHIBIT 2 *(concluded)*

Ratio of Yields on 10-Year AAA G.O. Bonds to Yields on 10-Year Treasury Notes

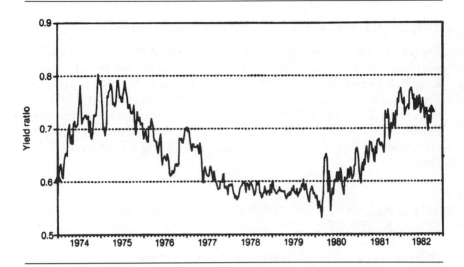

Ratio of Yields on 20-Year AAA G.O. Bonds to Yields on 20-Year Treasury Bonds

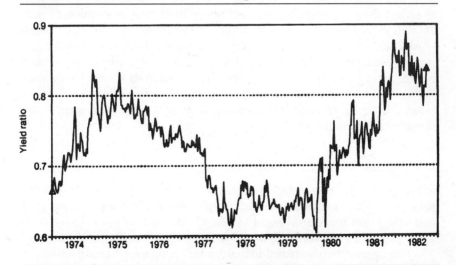

SOURCE: James L. Kochan, "Analyzing Cycles in Municipal Yields: An Institutional Approach," Chapter 22 in *The Municipal Bond Handbook,* Vol. I, eds. Frank J. Fabozzi, et al.

on federal income taxes. Moreover, in 13 states, *federal* taxes are deductible in determining state income taxes.

TREASURY YIELDS VERSUS MUNICIPAL YIELDS

Because of the tax-exempt feature of municipal bonds, the yield on municipal bonds is less than that on Treasuries with the same maturity. Exhibit 1 shows the yield levels and the ratio of municipal yields to Treasury yields for four maturities on February 1984, January 1985 and November 21, 1985. As can be seen, the yield ratio changes over time. Exhibit 2 shows the yield ratio of municipal yields to Treasury yields for maturities of 1 year, 5 years, 10 years and 20 years from mid-1974 to 1982.

YIELD RELATIONSHIPS WITHIN THE MUNICIPAL BOND MARKET

Differences within an Assigned Credit Rating

Bond buyers primarily use the credit ratings assigned by the commercial rating companies, Standard & Poor's and Moody's as a starting point for pricing an issue. The final market-derived bond price is composed of the assigned credit rating by these companies and adjustments by investors to reflect their own analysis of creditworthiness and perception of marketability. For example, as we noted earlier, insured municipal bonds tend to have yields that are substantially higher than noninsured superior-investment-quality municipal bonds even though most insured bonds are given triple-A ratings by the commercial rating companies. Additionally, many investors have geographical preferences among bonds, in spite of identical credit quality and otherwise comparable investment characteristics.

Differences between Credit Ratings

All other factors constant, the greater the credit risk perceived by investors, the higher the return expected by investors. Exhibit 3 shows general obligation municipal bond yields for the two weeks in November 1985, as well as 52-week highs and lows by credit quality and maturity.

The spread between municipal bonds of different credit quality is not constant over time. Reasons for the change in spreads are: (1) the outlook for the economy and its anticipated impact on issuers, (2) federal budget financing needs, and (3) municipal market supply-and-demand factors. During periods of relatively low interest rates, investors

EXHIBIT 3 Yields by Credit Quality and Maturity

	Superior Investment Quality				High Investment Quality				Medium Investment Quality				Low Investment Quality			
	November, 1985		52 Week		November, 1985		52 Week		November, 1985		52 Week		November, 1985		52 Week	
	11/21	11/14	High	Low	11/21	11/14	High	Low	11/21	11/14	High	Low	11/21	11/14	High	Low
New General Obligations																
1 Year	5.00	5.00	6.00	4.50	5.10	5.20	6.10	4.55	5.20	5.40	6.20	4.60	5.40	5.40	6.75	5.40
3 Years	5.60	5.25	7.00	5.25	5.75	5.45	7.25	5.45	5.90	5.65	7.50	5.65	6.65	6.65	7.75	6.65
5 Years	6.25	6.50	7.50	6.25	6.45	6.70	7.60	6.45	6.65	6.90	7.75	6.65	7.65	7.65	8.50	7.25
7 Years	6.75	7.00	8.10	6.75	6.00	7.10	8.75	6.90	7.10	7.35	8.40	7.10	8.15	8.15	9.25	8.15
10 Years	7.10	7.50	8.60	7.10	7.25	7.60	8.80	7.25	7.40	7.80	9.55	7.40	8.75	8.90	9.75	8.50
15 Years	7.80	8.05	9.45	7.80	8.00	8.15	9.60	8.00	8.25	8.40	9.75	8.25	9.12	9.27	10.25	8.55
20 Years	8.15	8.35	9.80	8.15	8.25	8.40	9.95	8.25	8.40	8.60	10.10	8.40	9.25	9.40	10.50	8.63
25 Years	8.20	8.40	9.85	8.20	8.35	8.50	10.00	8.35	8.50	8.75	10.15	8.50	9.37	9.52	10.75	9.37
30 Years	8.25	8.40	9.90	8.25	8.40	8.50	10.05	8.40	8.50	8.75	10.25	8.50	9.50	9.65	10.89	9.50

SOURCE: Merrill Lynch, *Bond Market Comment* 8, no. 47 (November 22, 1985).

sometimes increase their holdings of issues of lower credit quality in order to obtain additional yield. This narrows the spread between high-grade and lower-grade credit issues. During periods in which investors anticipate a poor economic climate, there is often a "flight to quality" as investors pursue a more conservative credit-risk exposure. This widens the spread between high-grade and lower-grade credit issues.

Another factor that causes shifts in the spread between issues of different quality is the temporary oversupply of issues within a market sector. For example, a substantial new-issue volume of high-grade state general obligation bonds may tend to decrease the spread between high-grade and lower-grade revenue bonds. In a weak market environment it is easier for high-grade municipal bonds to come to market than for weaker credits. Therefore, it is not uncommon for high grades to flood weak markets while at the same time there is a relative scarcity of medium- and lower-grade municipal bond issues.

Differences between In-State and General Market

Bonds of municipal issuers located in certain states (for example, New York, California, Arizona, Maryland, and Pennsylvania) usually yield considerably less than issues of identical credit quality that come from other states that trade in the "general market." There are three reasons for the existence of such spreads. First, states often exempt interest from in-state issues from state and local personal income taxes, and interest from out-of-state issues is generally not exempt. Consequently, in states with high income taxes (for example, New York and California), strong investor demand for in-state issues will reduce their yields relative to bonds of issues located in states where state and local income taxes are not important considerations (for example, Illinois, Florida, and New Jersey). Second, in some states, public funds deposited in banks must be collateralized by the bank accepting the deposit. This requirement is referred to as pledging. Acceptable collateral for pledging will typically include issues of certain in-state issuers. For those issues qualifying, pledging tends to increase demand (particularly for the shorter maturities) and reduce yields relative to nonqualifying comparable issues. The third reason is that investors in some states (South Carolina, for example) exhibit extreme reluctance to purchase issues from issuers outside of their state or region. In-state parochialism tends to decrease relative yields of issues from states in which investors exhibit this behavior.

Differences between Maturities

One determinant of the yield on a bond is the number of years remaining to maturity. The yield curve depicts the relationship at a given point in time between yields and maturity for bonds that are identical in every way except maturity. When yields increase with maturity, the yield curve is said to be *normal* or have a *positive slope*. Therefore, as investors lengthen their maturity, they require a greater yield. It is also possible for the yield curve to be "inverted," meaning that long-term yields are less than short-term yields. If short-, intermediate-, and long-term yields are roughly the same, the yield curve is said to be *flat*.

In the taxable bond market, it is not unusual to find all three shapes for the yield curve at different points in the business cycle. However, in the municipal bond market the yield curve is typically normal or upward sloping. Consequently, in the municipal bond market, long-term bonds offer higher yields than short- and intermediate-term bonds.

Another characteristic of the municipal bond yield curve is that yield spreads between maturities are usually wider in the municipal bond market compared with maturity spreads in the taxable market. This is illustrated in Exhibit 4 that contrasts historical maturity spreads between bonds with 30 years and 1 year remaining to maturity for Treasuries and high-grade municipals. These historical maturity spreads were even more dramatic when viewed in terms of percentages, as can be seen in Exhibit 5. This means that potential rewards are greater by lengthening maturity in the municipal bond market compared to the taxable bond market.

EXHIBIT 4 Yield Curve Spreads (30-year/1-year spreads within municipal and Treasury markets)

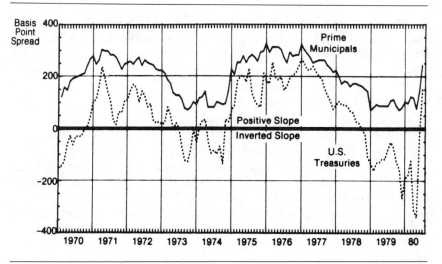

SOURCE: Martin L. Leibowitz, "The Municipal Rolling Yield: A New Approach to the Analysis of Tax-Exempt Yield Curves," Chapter 33 in *The Municipal Bond Handbook*, Vol. I, eds. Frank J. Fabozzi, et al.

EXHIBIT 5 Yield Curve Spreads as Percentage (30-year/1-year spreads as percentage of 1-year rate)

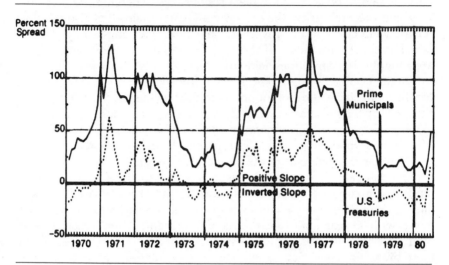

SOURCE: Martin L. Leibowitz, "The Municipal Rolling Yield: A New Approach to the Analysis of Tax-Exempt Yield Curves," Chapter 33 in *The Municipal Bond Handbook*, Vol. I, eds. Frank J. Fabozzi, et al.

THE PRIMARY AND SECONDARY MARKETS

The Primary Market

A substantial number of municipal obligations are brought to market each week. A state or local government can market its new issue by offering them publicly to the investing community or by placing them privately with a small group of investors. When a public offering is selected, the issue is usually underwritten by investment bankers and municipal bond departments of commercial banks. Public offerings may be marketed by either competitive bidding or direct negotiations with underwriters. When an issue is marketed via competitive bidding, the issue is awarded to the bidder submitting the lowest best bid.

Most states mandate that general obligation issues be marketed via competitive bidding; however, this is generally not required for revenue bonds. Usually state and local governments require that a competitive sale be announced in a recognized financial publication, such as *The Bond Buyer*, which is the trade publication of the municipal bond industry. *The Bond Buyer* also provides information on upcoming competitive sales and most negotiated sales as well as the results of the sales of previous weeks.

When an underwriter purchases a new bond issue, it relieves the issuer of two obligations. First, the underwriter is responsible for the distribution of the issue. Second, the underwriter accepts the risk that investors might fail to purchase the issue at the expected prices within the planned time period. The second risk exists because the underwriter may have incorrectly priced the issue and/or because interest rates rise, resulting in a decline in the value of unsold issues held in inventory. The underwriter spread (that is, the difference between the price it paid the issuer for the issue and the price it reoffered the issue to the public) is the underwriter's compensation for undertaking these risks as well as for other services it may have provided the issuer.[13]

An official statement describing the issue and issuer is prepared for new offerings. Exhibits 6 and 7 are cover pages of an official statement for a general obligation and revenue bond, respectively.

The Secondary Market

Although municipal bonds are not listed and traded in formal institutions, as are certain common stocks and corporate bonds on the New York and American stock exchanges, there are very strong and active billion-dollar secondary markets for municipals that are supported by hundreds of municipal bond dealers across the country. Markets are maintained on local credits by regional brokerage firms, local banks, and by some of the larger Wall Street firms. General market names are supported by the larger brokerage firms and banks, many of whom have investment banking relationships with the issuers. Buying and selling decisions are often made over the phone and through municipal bond brokers. For a small fee these brokers serve as intermediaries in the sale of large blocks of municipal bonds among dealers and large institutional investors. These brokers are primarily located in New York City and include Chapdelaine & Company, Drake & Company, the J. J. Kenny Company, and Titus & Donnelly, Inc., among others.

In addition to these brokers and the daily offerings sent out over *The Bond Buyer*'s "munifacts" teletype system, many dealers advertise their municipal bond offerings for the retail market in what is known as *The Blue List*. This is a 100+ -page booklet which is published every weekday by the Standard & Poor's Corporation. In it are listed state municipal bond and note offerings and prices.

In the municipal bond market, an odd lot of bonds is $25,000 (five bonds) or less in par value for retail investors. For institutions, anything below $100,000 in par value is considered an odd lot. Dealer spreads— the difference between the dealer's bid and ask prices—depend on sev-

---

[13] For example, in the case of negotiated offerings there is the value of the origination services provided by the underwriter. Origination services represent the structuring of the issue and planning activities surrounding the offering.

EXHIBIT 6 Official Statement Describing New General Obligation Issue

NEW ISSUE

In the opinion of Bond Counsel, interest on the Bonds will be exempt under existing law from Federal income taxes and from New York State and New York City personal income taxes

$400,000,000

The City of New York

General Obligation Bonds

Fiscal 1985 Series B

Dated: November 15, 1984   Due: November 15, as shown below

Interest will be payable semi-annually, beginning May 15, 1985, and on each November 15 and May 15 thereafter. The Bonds will be issued as registered bonds in the denomination of $5,000 or an integral multiple thereof. Principal of the Bonds and redemption premium, if any, will be payable at the office of the City's Fiscal Agent, Manufacturers Hanover Trust Company, New York, New York, or a successor Fiscal Agent. Interest on the Bonds will be payable by check mailed to the addresses of the registered owners of the Bonds. The Bonds will be subject to redemption prior to maturity as described herein.

Maturity	Amount	Interest Rate	Price	Maturity	Amount	Interest Rate	Price
1985	$14,820,000	6 ½	100%	1998	$ 8,800,000	10⅝	100%
1986	14,820,000	7	100	1999	8,800,000	10⅝	100
1987	14,820,000	7⅜	100	2000	8,800,000	10⅝	100
1988	22,220,000	8⅜	100	2001	8,800,000	10⅝	100
1989	22,220,000	8⅝	100	2002	13,100,000	10⅝	99⅝
1990	8,800,000	9⅜	100	2003	13,200,000	10⅝	99⅝
1991	8,800,000	9⅝	100	2004	13,200,000	10⅝	99⅝
1992	8,800,000	9⅝	100	2005	13,200,000	11	100
1993	8,800,000	9⅞	100	2006	13,200,000	11	100
1994	8,800,000	10	100	2007	13,200,000	11	100
1995	8,800,000	10¼	100	2008	13,200,000	11	100
1996	8,800,000	10½	100	2009	13,200,000	11	100
1997	8,800,000	10⅝	100				

$100,000,000 10⅞% Term Bonds due November 15, 2014 Priced to Yield 11%

(Accrued interest to be added)

The Bonds are offered subject to prior sale, when, as and if issued by the City and accepted by the Underwriters, subject to the approval of the legality of the Bonds by Rogers & Wells, New York, New York, Bond Counsel to the City, and subject to certain other conditions. Certain legal matters in connection with the preparation of this Official Statement will be passed upon for the City by Lord, Day & Lord, New York, New York. Certain legal matters will be passed upon for the Underwriters by Brown, Wood, Ivey, Mitchell & Petty, New York, New York. It is expected that the Bonds will be available for delivery in New York, New York, on or about November 20, 1984.

Merrill Lynch Capital Markets   **Goldman, Sachs & Co.**

Morgan Guaranty Trust Company   **Chase Manhattan Capital Markets**   **Citicorp Capital Markets Group**
of New York   **Corporation**   **Citibank, N.A.**

Bear, Stearns & Co.   **Chemical Bank**   **Dillon, Read & Co. Inc.**

Ehrlich-Bober & Co., Inc.   **E. F. Hutton & Company Inc.**   **PaineWebber**
                                                                                              Incorporated

Prudential-Bache   **L. F. Rothschild, Unterberg, Towbin**   **Salomon Brothers Inc**
Securities

Shearson Lehman/American Express Inc.   **Smith Barney, Harris Upham & Co.**
                                                                              Incorporated

November 9, 1984

EXHIBIT 7   Official Statement Describing New Revenue Issue

NEW ISSUE

In the opinion of Bond Counsel, interest on the Series 1984 Bonds is exempt from all present federal income taxes under existing law except with respect to any Series 1984 Bond for any period during which such Bond is held by a person who is a substantial user of the facilities financed from the proceeds of the bonds being refunded by the Series 1984 Bonds or by a related person as provided in Section 103 b of the Internal Revenue Code of 1954, as amended.

$198,785,000

CITY OF HOUSTON, TEXAS
AIRPORT SYSTEM SUBORDINATE LIEN REFUNDING REVENUE BONDS
SERIES 1984

Dated: November 1, 1984   **Due:** July 1, as shown below

The Series 1984 Bonds are issuable only as fully registered bonds in denominations of $5,000 or any integral multiple thereof. Interest on the Series 1984 Bonds will be payable January 1 and July 1 of each year, commencing July 1, 1985. Principal of and premium, if any, on the Series 1984 Bonds will be payable to the registered holder or owner (the "Holder" or "Owner") at maturity or redemption upon presentation at the principal corporate trust office of The Chase Manhattan Bank, National Association, New York, New York (the "Registrar Paying Agent"). Interest on the Series 1984 Bonds will be payable by check, dated as of the interest payment date, and mailed by the Registrar Paying Agent to Holders as shown on the records of the Registrar Paying Agent as of the fifteenth day of the month next preceding the applicable interest payment date. The Series 1984 Bonds are subject to redemption prior to maturity as described herein.

The Series 1984 Bonds are special obligations of the City of Houston, Texas (the "City") that, subject to the prior and superior lien of any Senior Lien Bonds which may be issued in the future, are payable from and equally and ratably secured by a lien on the Net Revenues of the City's Airport System, as defined and provided in the ordinance authorizing the issuance of the Series 1984 Bonds, and certain funds established pursuant to such ordinance. The Series 1984 Bonds do not constitute an indebtedness or general obligation of the City and are not payable from funds raised or to be raised by taxation.

$57,690,000 Serial Bonds

Year	Amount	Interest Rate	Price	Year	Amount	Interest Rate	Price
1985	$1,170,000	6.25%	100%	1993	$3,860,000	9.75%	100%
1986	2,140,000	7.00	100	1994	4,315,000	9.90	100
1987	2,520,000	7.50	100	1995	4,695,000	10.00	100
1988	2,560,000	8.00	100	1996	5,205,000	10.20	100
1989	2,755,000	8.50	100	1997	5,710,000	10.40	100
1990	2,850,000	9.00	100	1998	6,325,000	10.60	100
1991	3,200,000	9.25	100	1999	6,870,000	10.625	100
1992	3,515,000	9.50	100				

$12,750,000 10.75% Term Bonds due July 1, 2004, Price 100%

$128,345,000 10.875% Term Bonds due July 1, 2013, Price 99.75%

The Series 1984 Bonds are offered when, as and if issued, subject to the approving opinions of the Attorney General of the State of Texas and Vinson & Elkins, Bond Counsel, as to the validity of the issuance of the Series 1984 Bonds under the Constitution and the laws of the State of Texas. Certain legal matters will be passed upon for the Underwriters by their counsel, Mayor, Day & Caldwell, and by Chapman and Cutler, their special counsel. The Series 1984 Bonds are expected to be available for delivery in New York, New York, on or about December 20, 1984.

Merrill Lynch Capital Markets
Shearson Lehman/American Express Inc.

Goldman, Sachs & Co.   **Rauscher Pierce Refsnes, Inc.**

Rotan Mosle Inc.   **Underwood, Neuhaus & Co.**
                                               Incorporated

November 21, 1984

eral factors. For the retail investor, the dealer spread can range from as low as one quarter of one point ($12.50 per $5,000 of par value) on large blocks of actively traded bonds to four points ($200 per $5,000 of par value) for odd lot sales of an inactive issue. The average spread for retail investors seems to be around two points ($100 per $5,000 of par value). For institutional investors, the dealer spread rarely exceeds one half of one point ($25 per $5,000 of par value).

REGULATION OF THE MUNICIPAL SECURITIES MARKET[14]

As an outgrowth of abusive stock market practices, Congress passed the Securities Act of 1933 and the Securities Exchange Act of 1934. The 1934 act created the Securities and Exchange Commission (SEC), granting it regulatory authority over the issuance and trading of *corporate* securities. Congress specifically exempted municipal securities from both the registration requirements of the 1933 act and the periodic reporting requirements of the 1934 act. However, antifraud provisions did apply to offerings of or dealings in municipal securities.

The reasons for the exemption afforded municipal securities appear to have been due to (1) the desire for governmental comity, (2) the absence of recurrent abuses in transactions involving municipal securities, (3) the greater level of sophistication of investors in this segment of the securities markets (that is, institutional investors dominated the market), and (4) the fact that there were few defaults by municipal issuers. Consequently, from the enactment of the two federal securities acts in the early 1930s to the early 1970s, the municipal securities market can be characterized as relatively free from federal regulation.

In the early 1970s, however, circumstances changed. As incomes rose, individuals participated in the municipal securities market to a much greater extent. As a result, public concern over selling practices occurred with greater frequency. For example, in the early 1970s, the SEC obtained seven injunctions against 72 defendants for fraudulent municipal trading practices. According to the SEC, the abusive practices involved both disregard by the defendants as to whether the particular municipal bond offered to individuals were in fact appropriate investment vehicles for the individuals to whom they were offered and misrepresentation or failure to disclose information necessary for individuals to assess the credit risk of the municipal user, especially in the case of revenue bonds. Moreover, the financial problems of some municipal

---

[14] This discussion is drawn from Thomas F. Mitchell, "Disclosure and the Municipal Bond Industry," Chapter 40 and Nancy H. Wojtas, "The SEC and Investor Safeguards," Chapter 42 in *The Municipal Bond Handbook*, Vol. I, eds. Fabozzi, et al.

users, notably New York City, made market participants aware that municipal users have the potential to experience severe and bankruptcy-type financial difficulties.

Congress passed the Securities Act Amendment of 1975 to broaden federal regulation in the municipals market. The legislation brought brokers and dealers in the municipal securities market, including banks that underwrite and trade municipal securities, within the regulatory scheme of the Securities Exchange Act of 1934. In addition, the legislation mandated that the SEC establish a 15-member Municipal Securities Rule Making Board (MSRB) as an independent, self-regulatory agency, whose primary responsibility is to develop rules governing the activities of banks, brokers, and dealers in municipal securities.[15] Rules adopted by the MSRB must be approved by the SEC. The MSRB has no enforcement or inspection authority. This authority is vested with the SEC, the National Association of Securities Dealers, and certain regulatory banking agencies such as the Federal Reserve Bank.

The Securities Act Amendment of 1975 does *not* require that municipal issuers comply with the registration requirement of the 1933 act or the periodic-reporting requirement of the 1934 act. There have been, however, several legislative proposals to mandate financial disclosure. Although none has been passed, there is clearly pressure to improve disclosure. Even in the absence of federal legislation dealing with the regulation of financial disclosure, underwriters began insisting upon greater disclosure as it became apparent that the SEC was exercising stricter application of the antifraud provisions. Moreover, underwriters recognized the need for improved disclosure to sell municipal securities to an investing public that has become much more concerned about credit risk by municipal issuers. Thus it is in the best interest of all parties—the issuer, the underwriter and the investor—that meaningful disclosure requirements be established.

THE CHANGING NATURE OF THE MUNICIPAL BOND INDUSTRY

By the mid-1980s there were three characteristics of the municipal bond industry that distinguished it from what it was in 1960, 1970, and even as recently as 1980. First, municipal bond and note volume increased along with the volatility of interest rates—regardless of the maturity, credit quality, or type of financing structure involved. Second, new financing techniques emerged resulting in more diverse, complex, and

---

[15] For a detailed discussion of the MSRB, see Frieda K. Wallison, "Self-Regulation of the Municipal Securities Industry," Chapter 41 in *The Municipal Bond Handbook*, Vol. I, eds. Fabozzi, et al.

changing bond and note security structures. Third, there was growing reliance on retail investors and on those institutional buyers such as bond funds which catered primarily to individuals.

Increased Volume and Interest-Rate Volatility

A characteristic of the municipal bond industry by the mid-1980s was that it had become a major capital market. As an example, according to *The Bond Buyer*, tax-exempt state and local government long-term debt outstanding by year-end 1960 was only $66 billion, whereas by year-end 1985 it was over $700 billion.[16] This represented a 1,060 percent increase over 25 years. During this same period outstanding U.S. government direct and guaranteed debt increased from $237 billion in 1960 to $1,858 billion by year-end 1985, an increase of 784 percent.[17] With this increased volume has also come a further expansion of the municipal bond industry. Numerous brokerage firms and commercial banks—both national and regional in scope—have entered the municipal bond business. By the 1980s many had extensive municipal securities trading and syndicate departments, public finance, and new business specialists, as well as institutional and retail salesmen and credit analysts. Even the traditional institutional buyers of municipal bonds, such as property and casualty insurance companies, had begun to maintain quasi-trading positions in municipals. An increasing number of investors also began to "buy and trade" municipals, discarding the traditional "buy and hold" investment strategy.

One corollary of this broadening base of market participation was that there were more transitory and speculative forces in the marketplace than in the past. These forces may help explain the volatility of interest rates that characterize the municipal bond and note markets almost on a daily basis as well as the relative lack of sustained trading patterns in many sectors of the market. It should also be noted that the dramatic moves in the business cycle and changing Federal Reserve Board monetary strategies have also been overall contributing factors.

New Financing Techniques

Along with the increased municipal bond volume, issuers and investment bankers have been using new financing techniques and security structures. Additionally, as inflation and U.S. government borrowing increased in the early 1980s, many traditional private sector borrowers began to look to tax-exempt securities—and particularly revenue

---

[16] These data are derived from *The Bond Buyer*.

[17] From data prepared by the Merrill Lynch Securities Research Division.

bonds—as more economical financing vehicles. For instance, in 1970 only 33.5 percent, or $5.959 billion, of the total amount of municipal bonds issued in that year were revenue bonds; in the first 11 months of 1984, 70.3 percent, or $56.859 billion, of all municipals issued were revenue bonds.[18] By 1984, revenue bonds were being used to raise capital for hospitals, major corporations with pollution control projects, airports, seaports, single-family home mortgage lenders, electric utilities, and builders of multifamily housing, among others. Revenue bonds have also been used to provide capital for loans to students and small businesses.

Because of the availability of various federal aid and taxation benefits, many municipal revenue bonds have elaborate bond security structures which could be subject to future adverse congressional actions and IRS interpretations.[19] Housing bonds backed by future federal "Section 8" appropriations and leveraged lease resource recovery revenue bonds incorporating certain tax benefits for the plant vendors are but two examples. Additionally, because of the dramatic changes that occurred in the early 1980s in the U.S. tax code and in specific federal aid programs as the result of Reaganomics, the "state of the art" in structuring revenue bonds has been undergoing constant change. Even state and local government general obligation bond issuers, because of their dependency on numerous intergovernmental aid and revenue sharing programs, developed more complex financial structures.

In addition to the greater reliance on revenue bonds, it should also be noted that investor fears of inflation have eroded confidence in long 20- to 30-year municipals regardless of the particular security structure used. Unlike the U.S. Treasury market where an inverted yield curve existed for much of the late 1970s and early 1980s, the municipal bond market was characterized by having a very steep yield curve—where the yield differentials between 1-year notes and 30-year bonds of equal creditworthiness were at times as wide as 500 basis points.

Because of the widespread investor resistance to buying long municipals, investment bankers introduced several new financing techniques. These included "put" bonds, variable coupon rate bonds, "super sinkers," and "zero" coupon bonds, all described earlier in this chapter. Commercial banks used tax-exempt commercial paper, lines of credit, and letters of credit in structuring new municipal bond and note

---

[18] Data derived from *The Bond Buyer*, December 6, 1984, p. 17.

[19] As an example of the potential role of the IRS, in June of 1980 the Battery Park City Authority sold $97.315 million in construction loan notes which at the time received legal comfort from bond counsel that interest on the notes was exempt from federal income taxation. In November of 1980, however, the IRS held that interest on such notes was not exempt. The issue was not resolved until September 1981 when the Authority and the IRS signed a formal agreement by which the Authority agreed to pay annually to the IRS the arbitrage gains and the IRS, in turn, agreed that the interest paid on the notes was not taxable.

financings. Government bond dealers and investment bankers incorporated "collateralized" repurchase agreements (repos) into several bond and note security structures. The goal of these various innovative structures was either to attract investors to long-term municipal debt instruments and/or to reduce the financing costs for the borrowers.

Increased Importance of the Retail Investor

With the growth of confiscatory federal, state, and local government taxes on personal incomes in the 1960s and 1970s, individuals—particularly upper-income as well as middle-income wage earners—looked to municipal securities as a convenient way to shelter nonearned incomes. The increased bond volume and reduced commercial bank and casualty insurance company earnings which decreased their traditional robust appetites for tax-exempt bonds made municipal yields very attractive for retail investors. As an example, in September of 1982 short-term ready-access municipal note funds offered investors federal tax-free yields of over 6.5 percent compared to 5.5 percent in taxable passbook savings accounts.

Because of the strong demand by retail investors for tax-exemption, certain anomalies in yield relationships began to occur by the early 1980s. During one week in the spring of 1982, Dade County, Florida, sold general obligation bonds due in 25 years at a yield of 14 percent. The bonds were rated A-1 by Moody's and A by Standard & Poor's. During the same week New York City sold 25-year general obligations as well. Its bonds—at the time rated Ba-1 by Moody's and BBB by Standard—sold at a yield of only 14½ percent. This narrow yield spread of 50 basis points resulted from the higher tax burden on individuals in New York. High personal income taxes created strong demands for local municipal bonds which are tax-exempt from state of New York, New York City, and federal income taxes.

Municipal bond funds—which sell primarily to individuals—also became major institutional forces in the marketplace. These institutional buyers, unlike many insurance companies and banks, were "yield" buyers who bought long-term A-rated revenue bonds for their relatively high yields. This preference by the bond funds for A-rated paper along with the weaker market for the high grades, i.e., AA- and AAA-rated bonds, brought about some other very unusual yield relationships. As an example, in 1982 the state of Florida sold 20-year high investment grade, AA-rated general obligations at a yield of 13.90 percent. At the same time the North Carolina Eastern Municipal Power Agency sold 20-year A-rated revenue bonds at a yield of 13¼ percent. As the result of the increased role of retail buyers and the weaker demand by banks and insurance companies for high grades, by the 1980s the market at times priced retail-type weaker credit quality bonds at comparable or lower yields than it did higher quality bonds.

13

Zero-Coupon Securities

Frank J. Fabozzi, Ph.D., C.F.A.
Visiting Professor
Sloan School of Management
Massachusetts Institute of Technology

T. Dessa Garlicki, Ph.D.
Assistant Professor of Finance
Bentley College

The high and volatile interest rates that prevailed in the U.S. capital market in the late 1970s and early 1980s made the cost of borrowing expensive for issuers of even the highest-quality rating. To reduce the cost of debt funds for their corporate and municipal clients, investment bankers designed debt instruments that were more attractive to investors than traditional offerings. One type of security was the zero-coupon fixed income security. This type of security has no coupon payments. Instead, the issuer sells the security at a substantial discount from its maturity value. The interest received by the investor from holding this security to maturity is the difference between the maturity value and the purchase price. The advantage from the investor's point of view is that it eliminates reinvestment risk, allowing the investor to lock in the yield-to-maturity at purchase if the issue is held to maturity. As explained in Chapter 4, reinvestment risk may have a substantial impact on a fixed income security's total return.

ZERO-COUPON SECURITIES AVAILABLE[1]

Zero-coupon securities have been issued by corporations and municipalities. The first public issue of zero-coupon bonds by a corporation was

---

[1] In Chapter 7 several zero-coupon money market instruments are discussed. The focus of the present chapter is on zero-coupon instruments with maturities greater than one year.

on April 22, 1981, by J. C. Penney Company, Inc.[2] The issue was priced at 33.427 percent of par (i.e., $334.27 per $1,000 par value) to yield 14.25 percent. Shortly thereafter, General Motors Acceptance Corporation and IBM Credit Corporation issued zero-coupon notes.

In the municipal market, zero-coupon securities were first issued in the mid-1960s.[3] Legal questions raised by bond attorneys discouraged municipalities from the further issuance of zero-coupon securities. However, the high-interest-rate environment of the early 1980s and the reduced cost potential available with zero-coupon securities saw many such issues brought to market. The first use was in a negotiated sale in 1982 of $68.7 million Massachusetts Bay Transportation Authority bonds, of which $9.95 million of par value were zero-coupon bonds.

To overcome legal restrictions on the amount of par value debt that municipalities were permitted to issue, a variation of the zero-coupon bond was developed in the municipal bond market. This bond is issued at par and *does* actually have interest payments. However, the interest payments are not distributed to the holder of the bond until maturity. Rather, the issuer agrees to reinvest the undistributed interest payments at the bond's yield-to-maturity when it was issued. For example, suppose that a 10 percent, 10-year bond with a par value of $5,000 is sold at par to yield 10 percent. Every six months, the maturity value of the bond is increased by 5 percent of the maturity value of the previous six months. So at the end of 10 years, the maturity value of the bond will be equal to $13,267 (= $5,000 \times [1.05]^{20}$). This type of zero-coupon bond is called a "compound interest bond" or "municipal multiplier." If this bond had been a standard zero-coupon bond priced to yield 10 percent, it would have a maturity value of $5,000 but sell for $1,884 when it was issued.

In August 1982, Merrill Lynch created the first zero-coupon Treasury-derivative security which it marketed as "Treasury Investment Growth Receipts" (TIGRs). Merrill Lynch did this by buying Treasury bonds, stripping off the future coupon payments and principal values, and creating irrevocable trusts with a custodian bank.[4] The custodian bank then issued zero-coupon securities that represented a share in the trust. Each security had a particular maturity value equal to either the coupon or principal payment due on the maturity date of the underlying Treasury security, but no intervening coupon payments. Although the investment vehicles created are not issued by the U.S. Treasury, the

---

[2] A private offering of zero-coupon bonds was made by PepsiCo prior to this offering.

[3] "High Municipal Bond Interest Rates Fuel Rebirth of Zero-Coupon Issues," *The Bond Buyer*, April 5, 1982.

[4] For an explanation of the mathematics of coupon stripping, see Thomas J. Kluber and Thomas Stauffacher, "Zero Coupon Treasury Securities," Chapter 11, in *The Handbook of Treasury Securities*, ed. Frank J. Fabozzi (Chicago: Probus Publishing, 1986).

obligations of the trust—future coupon payments and principal values—are collateralized by U.S. Treasury securities. The investor is exposed to minimal credit (default) risk which is the risk that the custodian bank may go bankrupt.

Other investment banking firms followed suit by creating their own zero-coupon Treasury-derivative securities using the same procedure. For example, in August 1982, Salomon Brothers marketed its "Certificates of Accrual on Treasury Securities" (CATS). Lehman Brothers offered "Lehman Investment Opportunities Notes" (LIONs). Other zero-coupon Treasury-derivative products marketed by various investment banking firms were COUGARs, DOGs, GATORs, EAGLEs, and STARs. Because most of these Treasury receipts, called *trademarks*, were rarely traded by investment banking firms other than the individual firm that issued them, the secondary market was poor. To broaden the market and improve the liquidity of Treasury receipts, a group of primary dealers in the government market agreed to issue a generic Treasury receipt that would not be directly associated with any of the participating dealers. By March 1985, the par value of all zero-coupon Treasury receipts (trademarks and generics) outstanding was $119.8 billion, consisting of $45.1 billion of CATS, $21.1 billion of TIGRs, $9.1 billion of other trademarks and $44.5 billion of generic Treasury receipts.

Prior to June 1982, the Treasury was not a supporter of coupon stripping. In fact, a strongly worded letter from the Federal Reserve Bank of New York to primary government security dealers stated, "in our view trading in Treasury securities stripped of coupons, or trading in the detached coupons themselves, is not a desirable market practice and should be discouraged."[5] The Treasury's objection was that taxpayers were able to undertake transactions involving stripped Treasuries that resulted in a lower tax liability. In June 1982, the Treasury withdrew its objections to coupon stripping when provisions were incorporated into the Tax Equity and Fiscal Responsibility Act of 1982 to eliminate such tax abuses.

Although the U.S. Treasury indirectly benefited from zero programs through heightened demand for its securities for stripping purposes, in August 1984 the Treasury announced its Separate Trading of Registered Interest and Principal of Securities (STRIPS) program. This program allows the stripping of designated Treasury issues for purposes of creating zero-coupon Treasury securities. Initially, the Treasury designated two issues sold on February 15, 1985—the 11¼s of 2/15/95 and 11¼s of 2/15/15—as eligible for stripping under the program. Since then, other issues have been designated including all new Treasury issues of 10 years and longer.

---

[5] See Kluber and Stauffacher.

The zero-coupon Treasury securities created under the STRIPS program are direct obligations of the U.S. government. Thus, there is no default risk. The securities are book-entry securities. This means that the securities are not represented by an engraved piece of paper that is sent to the buyer. Instead, evidence of ownership is maintained in computerized records at the Fed. By the end of August 1985, the par value of securities issued under the STRIPS program was $45 billion.

INVESTMENT CHARACTERISTICS OF ZERO-COUPON SECURITIES

Elimination of Reinvestment Risk

There are three potential sources of a bond's return: (1) the coupon interest payments, (2) income from reinvestment of the coupon interest payments (known as the interest-on-interest component), and (3) changes in capital value realized when the bond is sold or redeemed. Most investors are cognizant of the first and third sources of return. However, as explained in Chapter 4, the second is an important source of a bond's return that is not widely recognized by investors.

The most often cited measure of a bond's total return is its yield-to-maturity.[6] The yield-to-maturity measures a bond's total return if it is purchased today and held until maturity. It assumes that the entire coupon interest will be reinvested when it is received at the same rate as the bond's yield-to-maturity. For example, the yield-to-maturity of an 8 percent coupon bond with 30 years to maturity selling for 67.7 percent of par value today is 12 percent. This assumes that every six months when the coupon interest is received, the investor will reinvest the entire coupon payment for the remaining time to maturity in an investment that will produce a 12 percent return. Therein lies the weakness of the yield-to-maturity. Even if a bond is held to maturity, the actual return will be less than the yield-to-maturity promised when the bond was purchased if (1) the full coupon is not reinvested because part is spent on current consumption or used to pay taxes, and/or (2) the coupon interest is reinvested at a rate that is less than the yield-to-maturity.

The degree of importance of the interest-on-interest component of a bond's total return depends on two factors: (1) the number of years to maturity, and (2) the coupon rate. Holding the coupon rate and yield-to-maturity constant, the longer the number of years to maturity of the bond (that is, the term of the bond), the more important is the interest-on-interest component. For example, for the 8 percent coupon bond

---

[6] See Chapter 4.

with 30 years to maturity which is selling for 67.7 percent of par to yield 12 percent, the interest-on-interest component is 87 percent of the bond's total return. Yet, if an 8 percent coupon bond has only seven years to maturity and is selling for 81.4 percent of par to offer a yield-to-maturity of 12 percent, the interest-on-interest component is 27 percent of the bond's total return. With respect to the coupon rate, the higher the coupon rate for a given number of years to maturity and yield-to-maturity, the greater is the interest-on-interest component. For example, the interest-on-interest component of a 12 percent, seven-year bond selling at par (to yield 12 percent) is 33 percent.

The risk associated with reinvesting the coupon payments of a bond at a rate that is less than its yield-to-maturity is known as reinvestment risk. One way to reduce reinvestment risk and thereby come closer to the promised yield-to-maturity at the time of purchase (assuming, of course, that the issuer does not default) is to buy bonds with a low coupon rate. Although low coupon bonds mitigate reinvestment risk, they do not eliminate it. The elimination of reinvestment risk with a holding period to maturity is only possible with a zero-coupon security as there are no coupons to reinvest.

There is a trade-off however. If interest rates are on average higher between the purchase and redemption dates, an investor would realize a higher realized compound yield[7] with a coupon issue than with a zero-coupon issue.

Price Volatility

Bond prices move in the opposite direction of changes in interest rates. If interest rates rise (fall), bond prices fall (rise). The risk that an investor faces if he must sell a bond prior to maturity is that interest rates may rise and, therefore, the bond price will decline when he goes to sell the bond. This risk is called interest-rate risk. For an investor who expects to hold a bond to maturity, there is no interest-rate risk, but there is reinvestment risk if the bond is a coupon bond.

As explained in Chapter 4, not all bonds have the same interest-rate risk. All other factors constant, the lower the coupon rate, the greater the interest-rate risk. A bond's price volatility (interest-rate risk) is directly related to its duration. The longer the duration of a security, the greater its price volatility. The duration of a zero-coupon security is equal to its term-to-maturity. For a coupon security with the same term-to-maturity, its duration is less than its term-to-maturity. This means that zero-coupon securities have the greatest interest-rate risk for a given maturity.

---

[7] Realized compound yield is discussed in Chapter 4.

While zero-coupon securities expose the investor to greater interest-rate risk than coupon securities with the same maturity, they do offer greater price appreciation potential if interest rates are expected to decline and the instrument is sold prior to its maturity date.

Exhibit 1 shows the monthly total return volatility of Treasury coupon issues and zero-coupon (stripped) Treasury securities in 1985. The

EXHIBIT 1 Comparison of Monthly Total Return Volatility of Coupon and Zero-Coupon Treasury Securities in 1985

Issue	Coupon (Percent)	Zero-Coupon (Percent)
2 Year	0.73	0.71
3 Year	1.02	1.21
4 Year	1.35	1.82
5 Year	1.66	2.07
7 Year	2.16	3.12
10 Year	2.68	4.44
20 Year	3.35	8.31
25 Year	—	8.72
30 Year	3.59	*

* 30-year zero-coupon Treasuries were available only after February 1985 when the 25-year call feature was removed from the 30-year Treasury bond.
SOURCE: Sharmin Mossavar-Rahmani, "Performance of the Treasury Market in the 1980s," Chapter 3, in *The Handbook of Treasury Securities*, ed. Frank J. Fabozzi (Chicago: Probus Publishing, 1986).

volatility of the long-term zero-coupon Treasuries (greater than or equal to 20-years) is more than twice that of the coupon issues. As explained above, the major reason is the greater duration for zero-coupon Treasuries. Another reason is the unpredictable but substantial demand for zero-coupon Treasuries by foreigners, particularly Japanese investors.[8]

Yield Relationships

Because there is no reinvestment risk for investors willing to hold zero-coupon bonds to maturity, it was initially believed that investors would pay more for zero-coupon securities than coupon securities. This would result in a lower yield on zero-coupon securities compared to current coupon bonds with the same maturity.[9] In fact, when stripped Treasur-

---

[8] One reason for the demand by foreigners is the tax advantage that may be available in the country where the foreigner is domiciled. This is discussed later in this chapter.

[9] A current-coupon bond is a bond in which the coupon rate is roughly equal to the prevailing yield-to-maturity of comparable bonds. A current-coupon bond therefore sells for close to par value.

ies were first issued in August 1982, the yield on these investments for maturities of 9 to 10 years was 15 to 20 basis points less than that of Treasury coupon issues with the same maturity. For longer maturities the yield sacrifice was as much as 100 basis points. These yield give-ups did not appear at first glance to be significant concessions by the investor to eliminate reinvestment risk. However, by May 1, 1985, the yield on 9 to 10 year zero-coupon bonds was 25 basis points greater than that on same maturity Treasury issues; for longer maturities the yield gain on zero-coupon Treasuries was as much as 50 basis points. Obviously there was no longer any yield sacrifice for elimination of reinvestment risk. To the contrary, investors were demanding a higher yield on stripped Treasuries relative to coupon Treasuries of identical maturities.

For professional money managers the proper comparison is not against equivalent maturity but against coupon securities of equivalent duration. For a coupon bond, the duration is less than the term-to-maturity whereas for zero-coupon securities, the duration is equal to its term-to-maturity. Investment banking firms and major commercial banks construct a zero-coupon yield curve implied by coupon Treasury securities so that yields on stripped Treasury securities can be compared to their coupon Treasury security duration equivalents.

Exhibit 2 summarizes the yield spread between Treasuries and zero-coupon Treasury derivatives under the Treasury STRIPS program from

---

EXHIBIT 2 Yield Spread Comparisons between Treasuries and STRIPS from 7/85 to 10/85 (in Basis Points)

Treasury Issue	Maturity-Matched Spreads			Duration-Matched Spreads		
	Avg.	High	Low	Avg.	High	Low
2 Year	5	22	−5	5	22	−5
3 Year	17	28	5	0	8	−15
5 Year	30	40	20	10	20	−5
7 Year	30	40	20	−12	−2	−24
10 Year	30	45	10	5	20	−14
20 Year	30	48	−10	−8	2	−19
30 Year	−50	−15	−85	10	20	3

SOURCE: James L. Kochan and Maureen Mooney, "Analysis of and Portfolio Strategies with Zero-Coupon Treasuries", Chapter 12, in *The Handbook of Treasury Securities*, ed. Frank J. Fabozzi (Chicago: Probus Publishing, 1986).

July 1985 to October 1985. Maturity-based and duration-based yield spreads are shown. As can be seen from the narrower spreads between zero-coupon Treasury derivatives and Treasuries based on duration compared to maturity, the market appears to evaluate zero-coupon securities relative to coupon securities of the same duration.

Default Risk

For corporate and municipal zero-coupon securities, there is greater default risk than for coupon securities.[10] The issuer must have funds available to pay off the entire issue at maturity. Many coupon bonds reduce default risk by requiring sinking-fund payments so that a substantial portion of the obligation is redeemed prior to maturity. Zero-coupon bonds do not have this provision.

The issuer of a long-term zero-coupon bond will be exposed to many economic cycles that can adversely affect its ability to pay off the bonds at maturity. If an investor holds a coupon bond in which the issuer subsequently defaults, at least part of the investment will have been recouped from the periodic coupon payments. The holder of a zero, however, will not recover one penny of his or her investment until the bankruptcy litigation is complete.

Moreover, if an investor purchases a bond and the perceived default risk of the issuer increases after the time of purchase, a higher yield will be demanded. With both a coupon and a zero-coupon bond, the price of the bond will decline. However, the decline will be greater for the zero-coupon bond because, as we explained earlier, the lower the coupon, the greater is the price decline for a given rise in interest rates.

Call Risk

Call risk is the risk that the issuer will call the bonds, forcing the investor to reinvest the proceeds at the lower rate prevailing in the market at the time of the call. This risk is therefore tied to reinvestment risk. Another risk associated with call risk is that any capital appreciation potential will be truncated. For example, suppose that a 12 percent coupon bond with seven years to maturity is selling for $1,000 and is callable at $1,080. The yield-to-maturity for this bond is 12 percent. Suppose, also, that interest rates decline to 7 percent. The bond's price would ordinarily rise to $1,273. However, because the bond is callable at $1,080, it may be beneficial for the issuer to call the bond because rates have declined dramatically, thus, the bond's price will not rise to $1,273. No investor will pay this amount because, if the bond is called, the investor would receive only $1,080. *One way an investor can reduce call risk is to purchase low-coupon bonds.*

When a zero-coupon bond is callable, the call price cannot be stated as a percent of the par value. Instead, it is based on the "compound

---

[10] For a discussion of the credit concerns associated with zero-coupon municipal bonds, see Sylvan G. Feldstein and Frank J. Fabozzi, "Zero-Coupon Bonds," Chapter 24, in *The Municipal Bond Handbook*, Volume II, eds. Sylvan G. Feldstein, Frank J. Fabozzi, and Irving M. Pollack, (Homewood, Ill.: Dow Jones-Irwin, 1983).

accreted value" (CAV) of the issue at each possible call date. The CAV is the value of the bond at the call date if the bond grew by its yield-to-maturity when issued.[11] To the CAV is added a premium determined by the issuer when the bond is first issued for each possible call date.

The general formula for the call premium is:

$$CAV \times [1 + (M - Y) \times R]$$

where M is the maturity date, Y is the year the bond may be called, and R is the redemption factor. For example, suppose that a bond that matures on July 1, 2000, can be called on July 1, 1990, and that the redemption factor is .01. Then the call price will be:

$$CAV \times [1 + (2000 - 1990) \times .01] = CAV \times 1.10$$

Therefore, the call price is 110 percent of the CAV.

Tax Treatment

As explained in Chapter 3, the gain from holding a zero-coupon security to maturity is not treated as a capital gain under the U.S. tax code. Even if the bond is sold prior to maturity, only a portion of the capital appreciation above and beyond the interest accrual may be treated as a capital gain and granted preferential tax treatment. In fact, as explained below, the U.S. tax code treatment of zero-coupon securities creates a definite disadvantage of owning a taxable zero-coupon security from a tax perspective. However, in some foreign countries, capital appreciation from holding a zero-coupon bond is granted preferential tax treatment. For example, in Japan the appreciation of a principal repayment zero-coupon bond is considered to be pure capital gains and is not taxed as interest income but rather at a preferential capital gains rate. Consequently, foreign investors in such countries seeking to lock in the high returns prevailing in the U.S. bond market without being exposed to default risk have found long-term stripped Treasury bonds very attractive.

As explained in Chapter 3, for original-issue discount bonds, income taxes must be paid each year on the interest accrued. A zero-coupon security is an original-issue discount security. Consequently, an investor will have to pay taxes on accrued interest each year even though no cash is actually received, resulting in a negative cash flow for the holder. Because of this, taxable zero-coupon securities should be

---

[11]

$$CAV = \text{issue price} \left(1 + \frac{YTM}{2}\right)^n,$$

where YTM = yield to maturity at the time of issuance, and
n = the number of six-month periods from the issuance date to the call date.

purchased only for IRAs, Keogh plans, and portfolios that are exempt from income taxes. The tax disadvantage does not apply to zero-coupon municipal bonds since interest on these bonds is exempt from Federal income taxes.

CONCLUSION

Since early 1980, the market for zero-coupon securities has grown substantially. The investment characteristics that we have discussed in this chapter make them ideal investment vehicles in both active and passive strategies for managing tax-exempt portfolios (and taxable portfolios in the case of municipal zero-coupon securities). Throughout this book examples of the role of these securities in such strategies will be discussed.[12]

---

[12] For an interesting portfolio strategy with GNMA pass-through securities, see Laurie Goodman and Arthur Rones, "GNMA-Zero Combination Strategy to Enhance Portfolio Returns," in *Mortgage-Backed Securities: New Strategies, Applications, and Research,* ed. Frank J. Fabozzi (Chicago: Probus Publishing, forthcoming 1986).

14

Domestic Floating-Rate and Adjustable-Rate Debt Securities

Richard S. Wilson
Vice President
Fixed Income Research Department
Merrill Lynch Capital Markets

This chapter discusses the many varieties of a security called *floating-rate* or *adjustable-rate* debt. It reviews the market for domestic senior securities, which have coupons or interest rates that adjust periodically over their stated life span, with adjustments occurring as often as once a week to as infrequently as every 11 years.

CLASSIFICATION OF FLOATING-RATE DEBT INSTRUMENTS AND SUMMARY OF TERMS

Floating-rate notes (FRNs) is a phrase that embraces a number of types of securities with a similar feature—a coupon or interest rate that is adjusted periodically due to changes in a base or benchmark rate.[1] While the jargon of the investment world will continue to utilize the term to cover all manner of variable-rate debt issues (although there are 37 phrases describing the different types of debt, ranging from annual adjustable-rate notes to variable spread floating-rate notes), they could

---

[1] The United States government issues a form of floating-rate debt, namely the Series EE Savings Bonds. The semiannual interest rate is determined each May and November, and it is based on 85 percent of the average market return for the preceding six months for five-year Treasury bonds with a constant maturity. If held at least five years, the minimum rate will be 7.5 percent. If held for less than five years, interest is earned on a fixed, graduated scale, rising from 5.5 percent after one year to the guaranteed minimum at five years.

very well be classified in two very broad, and at times, overlapping categories.

Thus, floating-rate notes are those instruments whose coupons are based on a short-term rate index (such as the prime rate or the three-month Treasury bill) and reset more than once a year.

Adjustable-rate notes or variable-rate notes (or debentures, bonds, and the like) are debt securities with coupons based on a longer-term index. Coupons are usually redetermined no more than once a year but often a longer time elapses between changes in the interest rates. For example, the base rate might be the two-year Treasury yield, and the coupon would then change every two years to reflect the new level of the Treasury security.

HISTORICAL OVERVIEW

Floating-rate notes originated in Europe and made their appearance in this country in the early 1970s. To the best of our knowledge, the first publicly offered issue was $15 million Mortgage Investors of Washington Floating Rate (8 percent to 12 percent) Senior Subordinated Notes due November 1, 1980, offered on November 1, 1973. This was quickly followed by $20 million First Virginia Mortgage and Real Estate Investment Trust with similar terms.

The big impetus to the market was the Citicorp (a bank holding company) $650 million Floating Rate Notes issued July 30, 1974. The offering was originally structured with the individual investor in mind (Citicorp would be obligated to repurchase any notes offered to it every six months after issuance), and the initial demand was such that it probably could have sold close to $1 billion of the notes. However, opposition from the thrift industry, Congress, and others caused Citicorp to modify the proposed terms so that the date of the first put[2] was June 1, 1976, and semiannually thereafter. It also reduced the size of the final offering. The interest rate on the notes was to be redetermined or readjusted each June and December at 1 percent higher than the Treasury bill rate, except that the minimum rate for the first year was 9.70 percent. The Treasury bill rate at the date of the offering was 7.7 percent.

Citicorp's offering was followed quickly by an issue of Chase Manhattan Corporation. Other corporate borrowers flocked to the trough over the next few months—by year-end 13 issues were outstanding, amounting to $1.36 billion. Issuance of floaters disappeared as rapidly as it made its mark on the investment community, and not one issue was offered for the next three years. Again, in mid-1978, Citicorp tapped the

---

[2] A put is a provision of the debt instrument that gives the holder the right to require the issuer to repurchase the security at certain prices (generally 100 percent of face value) at specific dates prior to the stated maturity.

market with a $200 million, 20-year note issue. This time it did not give the holder the right to put the notes back to the company, and the interest rate was set at a spread above the six-month Treasury bill rate.

In 1979, 18 issues similar to Citicorp's (except that some could be converted into long-term fixed-rate debt) were sold. This was followed by only six offerings for $912 million over the next two years. However, increased market volatility and high interest rates whetted investors' appetites for variable-rate securities, and the market started to mushroom in 1982. The issues range in quality from triple-A down to single-D (the issuer is in default). While most are tied in one way or another with various interest-rate bases, several have been linked to nonfinancial benchmarks, such as the price of West Texas crude oil or the share volume on the New York Stock Exchange. There have also been a few issues convertible into common shares.

SIZE OF THE MARKET

Banks and financial service companies have been the largest issuers of those securities accounting for 71.3 percent of the number of issues and 59.8 percent of the total amount. This is understandable, due to the floating-rate nature and turnover of their financial assets. In effect, they are trying to provide a matching of floating-rate assets with floating-rate liabilities. Exhibit 1 shows the distribution by type of issues.

The most active issuer and largest in terms of amount sold is the highly innovative Citicorp followed by Unocal Corp. and Phillips Petroleum. Lagging far behind in fourth place is Citicorp's archrival, Chase Manhattan Corporation, and in fifth position is Merrill Lynch & Co., Inc.

Exhibit 2 shows volume details for the 265 issues that have been sold to September 30, 1985, by the basis for coupon adjustment. The largest amount—$13,851 billion, or 32.5 percent of the total is based on the one-year and longer Treasury constant maturity.[3] The second largest category, those based on the three-month London interbank offered rate,[4] amounts to $9,178 billion, or 21.5 percent of the total. The smallest segment of the market, $100 billion, is the most recent innovation,

---

[3] The Treasury constant-maturity series is described in the Federal Reserve Statistical Release, H.15(519). Yields on Treasury securities at "constant maturity" are estimated from the Treasury's daily yield curve. This curve, which relates the yield on a security to its time to maturity, is based on the closing market bid yields on actively traded Treasury securities. The constant yield values are read from the yield curve at fixed maturities, currently 1, 2, 3, 4, 5, 7, 10, 20, and 30 years. This method permits estimation of the yield for a 10-year maturity, for example, even if no outstanding security has exactly 10 years remaining to maturity.

[4] LIBOR is the rate at which the major banks in London lend Eurodollar deposits of specific maturities.

EXHIBIT 1 Offerings of Variable-Rate Securities by Issuer Classification as of 9/30/85 (par value dollars in millions-number of issues)

	Banks	Number of Issues	Finance and Related	Number of Issues	International	Number of Issues	Industrial Transportation and Others	Number of Issues	Utilities	Number of Issues	Total $ Million	Total Number of Issues	Percent of Total Amount Issued	Percent of Total Number of Issues
1985 (to 9/30)	$2,700.0	26	$2,785.0	18	$403.5	3	$6,868.6	13	$475.0	4	$13,232.1	64	31.00%	24.15%
1984	$5,295.0	42	$3,315.0	26	$2,500.0	5	$4,652.0	29	$275.0	3	$16,037.0	105	37.57%	39.62%
1983	$3,710.0	20	$1,025.0	9	$100.0	1	$300.0	4	$100.0	1	$5,235.0	35	12.26%	13.21%
1982	$350.0	3	$1,890.0	13	—	—	$775.0	7	—	—	$3,015.0	23	7.06%	8.68%
1981	$250.0	1	$25.0	1	—	—	$85.0	1	—	—	$360.0	3	0.84%	1.13%
1980	$250.0	1	$250.0	1	—	—	$52.0	1	—	—	$552.0	3	1.29%	1.13%
1979	$2,041.5	14	$250.0	2	—	—	$400.0	2	—	—	$2,691.5	18	6.31%	6.79%
1978	$200.0	1	—	—	—	—	—	—	—	—	$200.0	1	0.47%	0.38%
1974	$1,160.0	8	$10.0	1	—	—	$157.5	2	—	—	$1,327.5	11	3.11%	4.15%
1973	—	—	$35.0	2	—	—	—	—	—	—	$35.0	2	0.08%	0.75%
Total	$15,956.5	116	$9,585.0	73	$3,003.5	9	$13,290.1	59	$850.0	8	$42,685.1	265		
Percent of Total	37.38%		22.46%		7.04%		31.14%		1.99%					

Note: Excludes those issues convertible into common stock, certificates of deposit, and those offered on a best-efforts or continuous-offering basis.

money market notes, where the rate is determined by a Dutch auction procedure.

Some of the issues provide the holder with the option of putting the debt back to the borrower at par at certain dates prior to maturity. Generally, to exercise a put option, the holder must notify the issuer or its trustee some time prior to the put date (usually notice of 30 to 60 days is required). Often the put, once exercised, is irrevocable; but a few of the note indentures make it possible for one to withdraw the notification of redemption. This is usually found in issues for which a company might wish to forestall early redemptions by increasing the interest rate above what is determined by the interest-rate-setting mechanism. For example, an issuer might wish to delay or prevent the early redemption of the debt if it has determined that it needs the funds for business activities. By doing so, it will not have to borrow the funds from other sources, thus possibly eliminating expenses associated with another borrowing.

Also, call provisions[5] are not constant among the issues. Some are not optionally redeemable by the issuer for the life of the notes, while other issues can be called two or three years after sale. In some cases, the call provision applies to only part of the time that the issue is outstanding.

Denominations vary among the issues, ranging from a minimum of $1,000 to as large as $100,000, with increments of $1,000 to $100,000. In cases of large minimum denominations where a put is provided, it may be exercised in whole or in part, and, if the latter, the remaining outstanding holding must be at least equal to the required minimum denomination.

There are also some issues that are exchangeable either automatically at a certain date (often five years after issuance) or at the option of the issuer into fixed-rate securities. Most of these issues carry bond ratings below investment grade and must be considered to have speculative elements according to the rating definitions. Generally, the fixed-rate note that is issued on exchange will mature not later than five years after the exchange, or, in some cases, at the maturity date of the variable-rate note. The fixed-rate notes will bear interest based on a premium to the comparable Treasury constant maturity. For example, Chrysler Financial Corporation's Subordinated Exchangeable Variable Rate Notes due 1994 will be exchanged on August 1, 1989 (unless exchanged earlier), for Subordinated Fixed-Rate Notes maturing August 1, 1994. These new notes will bear interest at a rate equal to 124 percent of the base rate, depending on the exchange date. If the exchange takes

---

[5] Call provisions are included in bond contracts to allow the issuer to retire the debt at its convenience. This usually occurs when the general level of interest rates is below the coupon of the subject debt security.

EXHIBIT 2 Offerings of Variable-Rate Securities by Basis of Coupon Adjustment as of 9/30/85 (par value dollars in millions-number of issues)

Date	Prime Rate Commercial Paper and Other S.T.	Num- ber	Money Market Notes	Num- ber	1-Month LIBOR	Num- ber	3-Month LIBOR	Num- ber
1985 (to 9/30)	$150.0	2	$100.0	1	$100.0	1	$5,952.6	21
1984	$2,000.0	3	—		—		$2,825.0	25
1983	$100.0	1	—		—		$400.0	2
1982	—		—		—		—	
1981	—		—		—		—	
1980	—		—		—		—	
1979	—		—		—		—	
1978	—		—		—		—	
1974	$7.5	1	—		—		—	
1973	$35.0	2	—		—		—	
Total	$2,292.5	9	$100.0	1	$100.0	1	$9,177.6	48
Percent of Total	5.37%		0.23%		0.23%		21.50%	

Date	One Year and Longer T.C.M. Rate	Num- ber	Rate Deter- mined by Issuer	Num- ber	Non- Financial and Other Benchmarks	Num- ber	Total	Num- ber
1985 (to 9/30)	$3,801.0	18	$525.0	3	$50.0	1	$13,232.1	64
1984	$6,050.0	41	—		$25.0	1	$16,037.0	105
1983	$1,150.0	9	—		—		$5,235.0	35
1982	$2,015.0	16	—		—		$3,015.0	23
1981	$335.0	2	—		$25.0	1	$360.0	3
1980	$250.0	1	—		$52.0	1	$552.0	3
1979	$250.0	1	—		—		$2,691.5	18
1978	—		—		—		$200.0	1
1974	—		—		—		$1,327.5	11
1973	—		—		—		$35.0	2
Total	$13,851.0	88	$525.0	3	$152.0	4	$42,685.1	265
Percent of Total	32.45%		1.23%		0.36%		65.96%	

Note: Excludes those issues convertible into common stock, certificates of deposit, and those offered on a best-efforts or continuous-offering basis.

place prior to August 1, 1987, the new coupon will be based on the 10-year Treasury constant maturity; if between August 1, 1987, and August 1, 1989, the benchmark rate will be the seven-year Treasury; and if issued on August 1, 1989, the new interest rate will be reflective of the five-year Treasury.

Because the terms of these floating- and variable-rate issues differ, it is suggested that the reader refer to the individual prospectuses for further details.

12-Month LIBOR	Num- ber	91-Day T-Bill Auction Rate	Num- ber	3-Month T-Bill Secondary Mkt. Rate	Num- ber	6-Month T-Bill Auction Rate	Num- ber	6-Month T-Bill Secondary Mkt. Rate	Num- ber
$150.0	2	$2,303.5	14	$100.0	1	—		—	
$125.0	1	$1,450.0	8	$3,562.0	26	—		—	
—		$3,010.0	19	$100.0	1	$475.0	3	—	
—		$1,000.0	7	—		—		—	
—		—		—		—		—	
—		—		$250.0	1	—		—	
—		—		—		—		$2,441.5	17
—		—		—		—		$200.0	1
—		—		$1,320.0	10	—		—	
—		—		—		—		—	
$275.0	3	$7,763.5	48	$5,332.0	39	$475.0	3	$2,641.5	18
0.64%		18.19%		12.49%		1.11%		6.19%	

Percent of Total Dollar Amount Issued	Percent of Total Number of Issues
31.00%	24.15%
37.57%	39.62%
12.26%	13.21%
7.06%	8.68%
0.84%	1.13%
1.29%	1.13%
6.31%	6.79%
0.47%	0.38%
3.11%	4.15%
0.08%	0.75%

DETERMINATION OF THE COUPON

As we have seen, the coupons are based on various benchmarks—ranging from short-term rates, such as the prime rate and one-month commercial paper, to one-year and longer Treasury rates, as well as nonfinancial determinants. There are also several issues where the rate is determined arbitrarily by the issuer. While we cannot go into the details of how every issue's interest rate is determined, we will look at the more important sectors in the market. In many cases, the basic data can be obtained quite easily, with few calculations required. For other issues, the coupon-setting data are more difficult to obtain, and the investor must rely on the trustee or agent bank to announce the rates. The rates are usually published in a newspaper of general circulation in New York City. However, some note agreements do not require the publication of the new rates but require only that such notice be mailed to the registered holder of the security.

91-Day Treasury bill auction rate. FRNs based on this rate first appeared in 1982 and now account for about 19 percent of the market. Interest is usually determined weekly and payable quarterly (the amount of interest payable is usually published retrospectively). Most of the issues have puts at the holders' option. The interest rate obtained may be equal to 100 basis points above the weighted per annum discount rate for the weekly auction of the 91-day Treasury bill, expressed on a bond equivalent basis (this is also known as the *investment basis* or the *coupon equivalent*) based on a 365-day year. The bond equivalent basis converts a yield quoted on a discount basis to one quoted on a coupon basis. The Treasury bill auctions are normally held each Monday, with the interest rate on the notes adjusted on the following day. This rate may be found in the financial sections of many daily newspapers as well as in the weekly report H.15(519)–*Selected Interest Rates*—published by the Board of Governors of the Federal Reserve System.

Three-month Treasury bill secondary market. When floaters first hit the market in 1974, the basis for the coupon was the interest yield equivalent of the secondary market yields of three-month Treasury bills calculated on a 360-day year. In these early floaters, interest was payable and the rate adjusted semiannually; they also provided the holder with a put.

Standard Oil Company of Indiana (now Amoco Corp.) sold $150 million of floating-rate notes due August 1, 1989, on August 15, 1974. The basis for the coupon is 1 percent above the interest yield equivalent of the weekly per annum discount rate for three-month Treasury bills as reported by the Federal Reserve Bank of New York during the 21 calendar days immediately preceding the twentieth day of January or July, as the case may be, prior to the semiannual period for which the interest rate on the notes is being determined. Thus the interest rate determination periods are December 30 through January 19 and June 29 through July 19 of each year.

For example, in the June/July interest rate determination period for 1985 the weekly averages for three-month Treasury bills were:

Week ended Wednesday, July 3	6.91%
Week ended Wednesday, July 10	6.90%
Week ended Wednesday, July 17	7.03%

The calculation for the rate according to the prospectus is as follows:

1. Average of the above rates = 6.9467 × $10,000 (face value) = $694.67,
2. $694.67 × 91/360 = $175.60 (the amount of the discount),
3. $10,000 − $175.60 = $9824.40 (the original sale price),
4. $175.60/$9824.40 = $7.069% (the interest yield equivalent of the arithmetic average of the reported per annum discount rates).

7.069 percent rounded to the nearest five hundredths of a percentage point is 7.05 percent. To this rate we add the 1 percent differential to arrive at the coupon rate of 8.05 percent for the period from August 1, 1985 through January 31, 1986.

The newer floaters in this category (often rated below investment grade) have a slightly different formula in which 365 days are used. Some of these issues have an alternate rate (such as the three-month LIBOR) which, if higher than the Treasury bill rate, will become the rate for the interest period (in some cases subject to a maximum rate).

Six-month Treasury bill secondary market. What used to be known as second-generation floaters—those issued in 1978 and 1979— are based on the interest yield equivalent of the six-month Treasury bill secondary market rates. Again, the base rates are found in the Federal Reserve Report H.15(519) and the calculations are similar to the three-month Treasury bill secondary market, except that 182 days is used, not 91 days.

Treasury constant maturity. The largest issuer category is based on the Treasury constant maturity yields as reported in report H.15(519). While some issues are based on a specific constant maturity, others are based on a constant maturity that is the issuer's choice when future reset dates come about.

LIBOR. Floating rate notes based on the three-month London interbank offered rates (LIBOR) were first issued in the United States in 1983, although Eurodollar LIBOR-based floating-rate securities have been of increasing importance in the foreign debt markets for a number of years.

LOOKING AT YIELDS—EVALUATION METHODS

Bonds with coupons that remain constant to the next put date should be looked at on a yield-to-put basis, whether the put is five months or five years away. Instead of using the maturity date in the calculations, the optional put date is used. This method takes into account any premium or discount amortized or accreted over the remaining term to the put. About half of the presently outstanding issues have puts, but only 82 have coupons that are unchanged to the first optional maturity date.

More complex are those issues where the coupon varies over the time to put or maturity. There are numerous calculations used by investors in evaluating the relative attractiveness, and we will briefly discuss several of them. It is important when comparing issues to make sure that they have similar coupon redetermination *bases* and to be consistent with the method used to reduce distortions that could occur if issues with dissimilar features are analyzed. Comparing a weekly certificate of deposit-based floater with quarterly interest payments to a six-month Treasury bill secondary market-based floater paying interest semiannually would not be acceptable, nor would using one method of calculation for issue A and another for issue B be valid, in our opinion. The issue used in this discussion is a hypothetical one, and the terms and results are shown in Exhibit 3. It should be noted that there are

---

EXHIBIT 3   Hypothetical Issue A

Coupon/maturity	8.70 September 1, 1998
Coupon reset and payment dates	March 1 & September 1
Reset spread	+100 basis points (1.00%)
Base rate	6-month U.S. Treasury bill, interest yield equivalent of the secondary market rate
Price	96.125
Today's assumed base rate	7.75%
Adjusted reset coupon	8.75%
Time remaining to maturity (assuming today is 11/1/85)	12.833 years
Simple current yield	9.05%
Adjusted reset current yield	9.10%
Adjusted spread to base	135 basis points*
Zero-coupon basis—spread from base	129 basis points
Simple or positive margin	135 basis points
Reset or adjusted yield to maturity	9.27%
Spread or reset yield to maturity over base rate	152 basis points

---

* A basis point is equal to one one-hundredth of a percentage point. Thus one percent is equal to 100 basis points.

---

cases where one bond might appear to be the more attractive value under one method or set of assumptions and less attractive under another method and circumstances. Market participants will have to live with these complications.

The current yield method (current interest rate divided by market price) is not a satisfactory measurement for floaters, in our view, because it only reflects the current point in time, assuming both the coupon and the price remain unchanged. When comparing two similar issues with each other, the current yield would not provide much help in determining relative values, especially when there are different coupon reset dates involved. However, if we were to readjust or reset the coupon as of the present time we would get a better guide to the relative attractiveness (all other things being equal). Thus, the simple current yield for issue A is 9.05 percent, and the adjusted reset current yield is 9.10 percent.

While the contractual reset spread to the base rate is plus 100 basis points, the notes are selling at a discount and we are really getting a greater spread or margin. Subtracting the assumed reset rate (7.75 percent) from the adjusted reset current yield (9.10 percent) gives us the adjusted spread to base of 135 basis points. If the notes were selling at par, the adjusted reset spread would be 100 basis points (8.75 percent–7.75 percent).

However, floating-rate notes are not perpetual securities, as are preferred stocks. For issues selling below par, we pick up the discount at maturity (or put date), and for issues selling above par we lose the premium. Therefore, other calculations are used to analyze floaters. For example, one can view the bond as a zero-coupon issue, obtain the yield to maturity on that basis and add it to the reset spread to arrive at the zero-coupon basis-spread from base measurement. Of course, in relative value analysis, the investor must take into consideration the quality of the debt as well as other factors, such as call, sinking-fund, and subordination provisions, if any.

MARKET COMMENT

The first series of floating-rate debt issued in 1974 was met with good investor reception. The prices generally stayed within a few points of par because, at worst (once the put feature became effective), they could be viewed as a short-term dated instrument. Thus, when the 1979 issues were sold, they were well-received by the market. However, these differed from the earlier notes in that they generally lacked puts and, thus, were only intermediate- to long-term instruments with a coupon that was tied to a short-term rate (not necessarily the highest point on the yield curve) and adjusted only every six months. Many of the initial investors apparently failed to take these differences into consideration when purchasing the notes, for they were sorely disappointed by early 1980.

In the last quarter of 1979, interest rates started to rise rather sharply, and they did not peak until March of 1980. These new floaters declined despite upward adjustment of the coupon rate, with some falling to as low as the high 80s. This was due, in part, to the fact that the reset coupon lagged behind current market rates. Also, these floaters did not have put options that would allow the holder to request the issuer to repurchase the securities every six months as the earlier issues had. Just as rapidly as interest rates rose, they dropped dramatically over the next few months, causing an abrupt reversal in the price movement of the notes. Once again rates reversed direction and another sharp price decline occurred. By the end of 1980, new lows were recorded. Without the put feature, the notes failed to hold their own as the market adjusted their yields to compete with returns available on alternate investments. Adding to the pressure on prices was the fact that investors wanted to "get even" after seeing their issues recover in the rally earlier in the year. Only the issues with the puts maintained their value.

Since then, other features were added to the new offerings to reduce price volatility, such as more frequent resetting of the coupon rate and, in the case of variable rate notes, more putable issues. In the latter case, the variables would tend to trade as short- to intermediate-term securities, depending on the length of time to the put date. Generally, the more volatile security would be of a longer maturity, have less frequent coupon readjustments or fixings, and fewer opportunities for the investor to exercise the put option, if any. Also, the smaller the size of the issue and the lower the assigned rating or perceived quality of the debt, the more likely that the debt will be more volatile than larger and better-quality issues, all other things being equal.

Another important factor affecting the aftermarket for these securities (as well as any debt security) is the perceived quality of the issuer. Many of these securities have been downgraded by the rating agencies since they were originally offered. Thus, while a triple-A bank holding company reset spread might have been satisfactory at 100 basis points in 1979, the current rating of double-A might require 125 or more. Of course, if an issue comes under a dark cloud (as Continental Illinois Corporation did in the spring of 1984), investors will dump their bonds into a weak market at steadily declining prices. Despite a put operable on September 15, 1984, Continental's floating rate notes due September 15, 1989, dropped from 96 to 85 in the week ended May 25. Its convertible floaters due in 1987 declined from 87 to 81 at the same time. A month earlier, the putable bonds were at 99¾ and the convertibles at 97⅜. After the Federal Deposit Insurance Corporation stepped in, the notes recovered with most, if not all, of the 1989 issue redeemed at the holders' request in September. The 1987s rose—but not to the levels that existed earlier in the year.

CONCLUSION

Floating-rate and variable-rate debt securities have a place in investment portfolios. In some cases, they can be regarded as a passive substitute for short-term holdings, especially the part of a short-term portfolio that is consistently maintained. For example, if a short-term portfolio fluctuates between $10 million and $50 million but does not drop below the $10 million level, then floaters can be bought for a portion of that more-or-less core or permanent $10 million minimum holding. The variables based on the one-year to seven-year Treasury constant maturity are alternatives to straight intermediate-term issues because the investor has the option of holding the notes or redeeming them. Despite the poor performance of some of the issues, many have maintained their value and fulfilled the objectives of the investor. They can generally be classed as defensive types of instruments. If one expects that short-term rates will remain relatively high or even increase from current levels, then a package of these notes may be held (depending, of course, on the portfolio's goals and parameters). With the issues that have frequent resets of the coupon, the investor is relieved of rolling over short-term paper, thus saving on transaction costs.

15

Mortgages

Dexter Senft
Managing Director, Fixed Income Research
The First Boston Corporation

In order to understand and analyze mortgage-related securities, it is necessary to understand how mortgages operate. In this chapter we examine the types of mortgage loans in existence today, their cash flow, and certain other aspects relevant to the analysis of pass-through securities and collateralized mortgage obligations that are discussed in the next two chapters.

WHAT IS A MORTGAGE?

By definition, a mortgage is a "pledge of property to secure payment of a debt." Typically, property refers to real estate, which is often in the form of a house; the debt is the loan given to the buyer of the house by a bank or other lender. Thus a mortgage might be a "pledge of a house to secure payment of a bank loan." If a homeowner (the *mortgagor*) fails to pay the lender (the *mortgagee*), the lender has the right to foreclose the loan and seize the property in order to ensure that it is repaid.

The form that a mortgage loan takes could technically be anything the borrower and lender agree upon. Traditionally, however, most mortgage loans were structured similarly. There was a fixed rate of interest on the loan for its entire term, and the loan was repaid in monthly installments of principal and interest. Each loan was structured in such a way that the total payment each month (the sum of the principal and interest) was equal, or *level*. We shall refer to this type of loan arrangement as a *traditional* mortgage loan. (There is a growing trend away from this traditional structure, but this is getting ahead of the story.) In a traditional mortgage loan, the terms to be negotiated are the interest rate and the period to maturity. Interest rates vary with the general economic climate, and maturities range from 12 to 40 years, depending on the type of property involved. Most mortgages on single-family homes carry 30-year maturities.

Exhibit 1 illustrates the breakdown of monthly payments between principal and interest on a 30-year, 10 percent traditional mortgage. At first, the mortgage payment is mostly interest. The principal portion increases over time until, at maturity, the payment is almost entirely principal. At all times, however, the sum of the principal and interest payments is the same. Notice that over the course of the loan the borrower pays more dollars as interest than as principal—in fact, total interest is more than twice total principal in this example.

EXHIBIT 1 Monthly Mortgage Payments—Interest/Principal (30-year, 10 percent conventional loan)

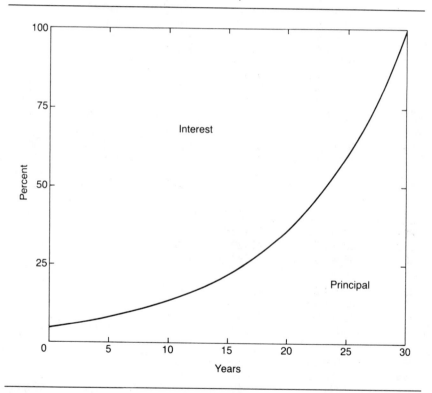

The principal portion of each monthly payment is used to reduce the amount of the loan outstanding. In mortgage terms, the loan is *amortized* over 30 years, and the principal payments each month are known as amortization payments. The amount of the loan that is outstanding at any time is known as the *mortgage balance*. In any month the interest payment equals the interest rate (expressed monthly) times the mortgage balance at the beginning of the month (see Exhibit 2). Often the mortgage balance is expressed as a ratio or percentage of the original loan amount, in which case the mortgage balance runs from 1 (or 100 percent) initially to 0 at maturity. Exhibit 3 shows how the mortgage

---

EXHIBIT 2 Sample Payment Schedule: Traditional Mortgage (10 percent interest rate, 30-year [360-month] term)

| | Mortgage Balance | | Monthly | | |
Month	Dollars	Decimal	Payment	Interest	Principal
0	50000.00	1.00000			
1	49977.88	.99956	438.79	416.67	22.12
2	49955.58	.99911	438.79	416.48	22.30
3	49933.09	.99866	438.79	416.30	22.49
4	49910.41	.99821	438.79	416.11	22.68
5	49887.55	.99775	438.79	415.92	22.87
6	49864.49	.99729	438.79	415.73	23.06
7	49841.24	.99682	438.79	415.54	23.25
8	49817.80	.99636	438.79	415.34	23.44
9	49794.16	.99588	438.79	415.15	23.64
10	49770.33	.99541	438.79	414.95	23.83
. . .	. . .	. . .	. . .	. . .	. . .
100	46567.88	.93136	438.79	388.48	50.30
101	46517.16	.93034	438.79	388.07	50.72
102	46466.02	.92932	438.79	387.64	51.14
103	46414.45	.92829	438.79	387.22	51.57
. . .	. . .	. . .	. . .	. . .	. . .
200	38697.88	.77396	438.79	323.44	115.34
201	38581.57	.77163	438.79	322.48	116.30
202	38464.30	.76929	438.79	321.51	117.27
203	38346.05	.76692	438.79	320.54	118.25
. . .	. . .	. . .	. . .	. . .	. . .
300	20651.61	.41303	438.79	174.30	264.48
301	20384.93	.40770	438.79	172.10	266.69
302	20116.01	.40232	438.79	169.87	268.91
303	19844.86	.39690	438.79	167.63	271.15
. . .	. . .	. . .	. . .	. . .	. . .
355	2140.13	.04280	438.79	21.31	417.47
356	1719.18	.03438	438.79	17.83	420.95
357	1294.72	.02589	438.79	14.33	424.46
358	866.72	.01733	438.79	10.79	428.00
359	435.16	.00870	438.79	7.22	431.56
360	0.00	.00000	438.79	3.63	435.16

Note: Each month, the interest payment is 1/12 of 10 percent of the mortgage balance. The principal payment is the total payment less the interest due. The principal balance is reduced by the amount of the principal payment.

EXHIBIT 3 Examples of Mortgage Balances for Various Loans

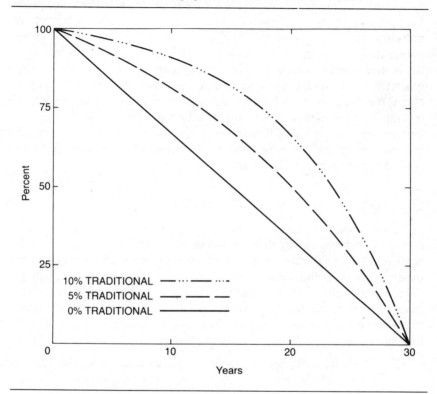

balance for several possible loans would decline over time. Another way to view the mortgage balance is as the amount of the house value the home buyer does not yet own. The amount of a home's value that is owned is referred to as the homeowner's *equity*. Equity can be defined as the difference between the current value of the home and the mortgage balance; as the mortgage balance declines, the equity rises. Equity also increases if the current value of the home increases, due to home improvements, inflation, etc.

Sometimes a mortgagor may want to make a monthly payment that is greater than the amount actually due, with the idea of applying the excess payment to further reducing the loan. Such excess principal payments are called *prepayments* and may be made for several reasons (these reasons will be discussed in detail later). Prepayments result in a direct reduction of the mortgage balance and a direct increase in the amount of equity. Another way to define mortgage balance is that it equals the original loan amount less the total amount of amortization and prepayments to date.

A mortgagor who fails to make a mortgage payment is said to be *delinquent*. Delinquencies can have a variety of causes—the homeowner may have died, become unemployed, bounced a check, or simply forgotten to make the payment. The mortgagee then reminds the homeowner that the payment is overdue and attempts to collect the money. If the matter is not resolved quickly the mortgagee may assess the mortgagor with a late payment charge. Sometimes there is no quick solution, and the mortgagor may become more than one month in arrears. Although most lenders are willing to allow a borrower a few months leeway, in extreme cases it may be necessary for the bank to foreclose the loan, in which case the property is taken from the mortgagor and sold in order to pay off the loan.

QUALIFYING FOR A MORTGAGE

Borrowers who are interested in obtaining mortgage loans must meet certain standards set by the lender in order to be considered creditworthy. The first thing a lender checks is whether the borrower has any other loans or obligations outstanding; if so, these will diminish the borrower's ability to make mortgage payments. Next the lender determines the income and net worth of the borrower. Many mortgage lenders use these classical rules of thumb to determine whether or not a borrower's income is adequate for the mortgage:

1. The total mortgage payment (principal and interest) should not exceed 25 percent of the borrower's total income less any payments owed for other obligations.
2. Total mortgage payments plus other housing expenses should not exceed 33 percent of the borrower's income less payments for other obligations. Other housing expenses include such items as taxes, insurance, utilities, and normal maintenance costs.

Of course, these percentages may vary depending on the lender and the circumstances. In particular, borrowers with relatively high net worth and/or liquid assets will find lenders to be more flexible. Also, in times of high interest rates and tight money, lenders have been known to bend these rules somewhat in order to maintain a certain level of business.

The buyer is usually required to make a down payment on the property in order to qualify for the mortgage. The down payment might range anywhere from 5 to 25 percent of the purchase price. The reason for requiring a down payment is that, in the event the lender is forced to foreclose the loan and sell the property, the mortgage balance will be more easily recovered. In other words, there is room for error if the property is sold—even if it cannot bring the original purchase price on the market, there can still be enough to cover the debt. Lenders use the term *loan to value ratio*, or LTV, to express the amount of protection on the mortgage. LTV is calculated as the ratio of the mortgage balance to the market value of the property and is expressed as a percentage. The lower the LTV, the less the loan amount relative to the property value, and the greater the safety.

The LTV ratio tends to decrease over time. For example, if a buyer makes a 10 percent down payment on a property and mortgages the rest, the LTV is initially 90 percent. Over time, the mortgage balance declines from amortization and prepayments, while the property value tends to increase due to inflation. Both of these changes serve to lower the LTV.

As with income requirements, down payment and LTV requirements depend on certain circumstances. These include not only the net worth of the borrower but the condition and marketability of the property and the availability of credit. Higher LTV ratios are associated with newer, more marketable properties and with easier credit and lower interest rates.

An important (if not obvious) conclusion about qualifying for a mortgage is that it becomes harder when interest rates rise. Because of the income and LTV requirements, smaller mortgage balances are affordable when rates rise, and yet this is also the time when inflation and therefore home purchase prices are rising. As a consequence, all but those buyers with large amounts of cash or equity are squeezed from the market.

MORTGAGE INSURANCE

There are two types of mortgage insurance that may be used when borrowers obtain mortgage financing. One type is originated by borrowers and the other by lenders. Although both have a beneficial effect on the creditworthiness of the borrowers, the latter is of greater importance from the lender's point of view.

The first type of mortgage insurance is taken out by the borrower (borrowers) usually with a life insurance company. The policy provides for the continuing payment of the mortgage after the death of the insured person, thus enabling the survivors to continue living in the house. In the sense that the mortgage might just as well have been paid off with part of the proceeds of ordinary life insurance, this form of mortgage insurance is really only a special form of life insurance. It is cheaper than ordinary life insurance, however, because the death benefit, which is equal to the mortgage balance, declines over time.

The other type of mortgage insurance is taken out by the lender, although borrowers pay the insurance premiums. This policy covers some percentage of the loan amount and guarantees that in the event of a default by the borrower/s the insurance company will pay the amount insured or pay off the loan in full.

An example of how this type of mortgage insurance works is shown in Exhibit 4. Suppose a borrower finances $60,000 of property with a $5,000 down payment and a $55,000 mortgage. The initial LTV ratio is fairly high (91.7 percent), so mortgage insurance is obtained in the amount of $11,000 (20 percent of the loan). Suppose the borrower defaults after five years (the mortgage balance having been paid down to $52,000 by then). Suppose further that the property has deteriorated in condition (or perhaps has been partially destroyed), and its market value falls to $50,000. The bank then turns to the insurance company.

EXHIBIT 4

Situation initially:

$$LTV = \frac{55,000}{60,000} = 91.7\%$$

$11,000 Mortgage insurance obtained

Mortgage:	$55,000	Property
Down payment:	5,000	value:
Total	$60,000	$60,000

Situation after 5 years:

Borrower defaults
Property value falls

Mortgage balance:	Property
$52,000	value:
	$50,000

Option 1: Insurance company pays claim

Lender has	$50,000	Property	Insurance company has
	11,000	Insurance	($11,000) Loss
	(52,000)	Bad debt	
	$ 9,000	Net profit	

Option 2: Insurance company takes title to property

Lender has	$52,000	From insurer	Insurance Company has
	(52,000)	Bad debt	50,000 Property
	0	Net profit	(52,000) Payment to lender
			(2,000) Net loss

Several options are open to the insurance company, perhaps the simplest of which is that it can assist the borrower financially so that the amount in arrears can be paid and no foreclosure is necessary. Assuming this fails, there are two other alternatives. First, the insurance company could pay the claim of $11,000 and let the bank foreclose. The bank, which gets $50,000 for the property and $11,000 insurance, actually makes a profit of $9,000 over the mortgage balance outstanding. A better alternative for the insurance company, however, is to pay off the mortgage balance ($52,000), take title of the property, and sell it (for $50,000). The insurance company thereby loses only $2,000, instead of $11,000. Of course, the insurer could hold the property or even make improvements to it in hope of making a future gain instead of selling it immediately.

The net effect of mortgage insurance from the lender's standpoint is to reduce its risk. The exposure of a lender to loss equals the amount loaned less property value and mortgage insurance. In a sense, the insurance has an effect similar to having a higher down payment because both reduce the lender's exposure to loss. Mortgage insurance is advantageous to borrowers who do not have enough money for a large down payment but who can afford enough down payment and insurance to satisfy the lender.

The cost of the insurance can be passed on to the borrower in several ways. Traditionally, the cost was added to the mortgage rate as an extra one-eighth percent or one-fourth percent, depending on the amount of coverage. As mortgage rates escalated, however, increasing the rate further became less attractive. (In a sense, the insurance company would be increasing the chance of the default it was insuring against.) It has become increasingly common to pay for mortgage insurance in one lump sum at the time of mortgage origination.

It is not necessary to have mortgage insurance in effect for the entire term of a loan. Because the mortgage balance amortizes and the LTV tends to fall over time, the lender may deem mortgage insurance to be unnecessary when the mortgage balance has declined to some predetermined level. At that point, the policy is either cancelled or allowed to expire.

SERVICING

Among the jobs that mortgage lenders must perform in order to ensure that borrowers make timely and accurate payments are sending payment notices, reminding borrowers when payments are overdue, recording prepayments, keeping records of mortgage balances, administering escrow accounts for payment of property taxes or insurance, sending out tax information at year end, and initiating foreclosure proceedings. These functions are collectively known as *servicing* the loans. Many times the original lender, known as the mortgage *originator,* is the one who services the loan, but this is not always the case. Sometimes the mortgage is sold to someone else, and the servicing of the loan may or may not go along with the mortgage.

In the event that one party owns a mortgage and another services it, the servicer receives a fee (the *servicing fee*) for the trouble. Servicing fees usually take the form of a fixed percentage of the mortgage balance outstanding. Although the percentage may vary from one servicer to the next, it is usually in the area of .25 percent to .50 percent. Small servicing fee percentages are usually associated with larger commercial property loans, and larger percentages with smaller residential loans. From the point of view of the owner of the mortgage, the servicing fee comes out of the interest portion of the mortgage payment. For example, if party A owns a 10 percent mortgage being serviced by party B for a three eighths of 1 percent fee, then A is really earning 9⅝ percent (10 percent minus three eighths of 1 percent) on the loan.

In addition to servicing fees, there are occasionally other fees that the servicer may keep. For example, some servicers are entitled to keep late-payment penalties paid by the borrower, foreclosure penalties, and certain other penalty fees. The specific types and amounts of fees that servicers are entitled to receive are set forth in a servicing agreement between the mortgage owner and the servicer.

WHERE DOES MORTGAGE MONEY COME FROM?

The largest single originating group is the savings and loan industry. Savings and loans, together with savings banks and credit unions, constitute the "thrift industry"—so-called because its funds come from the savings accumulated by thrifty depositors. Commercial banks make up the second largest group of originators, and like thrift institutions, the money they put into mortgages comes primarily from deposits. The third major source of mortgage loans is the mortgage company sector, or mortgage banks. Unlike savings banks or commercial banks, mortgage banks do not have depositors. They are in the business of finding other sources of mortgage money, such as thrifts or insurance companies, and making it available for housing construction and ownership. Mortgage bankers' profits come from servicing the loans they originate, plus any profit that can be made from buying and selling the mortgages. The lesser originators of mortgages are insurance companies, pension funds, and various federal, state, and local entities empowered to make mortgage loans.

Knowing who originates mortgages, however, does not really answer the question of where mortgage money comes from. The real lenders of mortgage money are those who *own* mortgages, who are

EXHIBIT 5 U.S. Mortgage Debt Outstanding by Type of Holder, 1975–1984 (billions of dollars)

	1975	1976	1977	1978	1979	1980	1981	1982	1983	1984
Commercial banks	$136.3	$151.3	$179.1	$214.0	$245.2	$263.0	$286.6	$301.3	$328.3	$374.2
Mutual savings banks	76.9	81.8	88.0	94.7	98.9	99.9	100.0	97.8	136.1	160.8
Savings & loans	278.9	322.7	381.1	432.7	475.7	502.8	517.6	483.6	494.8	554.9
Life insurance companies	89.0	91.6	96.8	105.3	118.8	131.1	140.2	142.0	151.0	157.3
Federal agencies	66.5	66.7	70.0	81.9	97.1	114.3	126.2	138.1	147.4	157.8
Mortgage pools and trusts	34.5	49.8	70.3	86.5	119.3	142.3	162.3	216.7	285.1	331.0
Other	119.5	125.4	138.2	157.4	171.9	212.7	210.8	279.0	284.9	294.9
Total	$801.6	$889.3	$1023.5	$1172.5	$1326.9	$1466.1	$1543.7	$1658.5	$1827.6	$2030.9

SOURCE: Federal Reserve Board

somewhat different from those who create them. Mortgage bankers, for example, generally do not want to own mortgages at all—once they create them, they sell the mortgages to someone else. Thrifts and commercial banks prove to be the major holders of mortgages, but there are several other notable ones, such as life insurance companies and households. Exhibit 5 shows the mortgage debt outstanding from 1975 to 1984 by type of holder.

The owner category with by far the largest growth is mortgage pools and trusts. What are these pools and trusts? Essentially, they are collections of mortgages of which shares, or participations, are resold to someone else. (In this sense, mortgage pools and trusts as an ownership category is not very informative.) Mortgage trusts can be created by securities dealers or investment advisors who offer shares in the trust as a form of investment for their clients. Mortgage pools, however, have the lion's share of this category.

WHAT TYPES OF PROPERTIES ARE MORTGAGED?

Virtually all forms of real estate have been mortgaged, but these properties fall into several categories. First, property (and the mortgage on it) can be classified as either residential or nonresidential, depending on whether or not people use the property primarily for living. Residential properties include houses, apartments, condominiums, cooperatives, and mobile homes. These do not necessarily have to be someone's primary residence—for example, summer homes and skiing condominiums are classified as residential properties. Residential properties are subdivided into one- to four-family dwellings and multifamily dwellings for the purposes of Federal Reserve statistics.

Nonresidential properties are subdivided into commercial properties and farm properties. The commercial category encompasses a wide variety of properties, such as office buildings, shopping centers, hospitals, and industrial plants.

Exhibit 6 shows the outstanding amounts of mortgage debt in various years broken out by type of property.

NONTRADITIONAL MORTGAGES

The decade of the 1970s saw the advent of many new and different varieties of mortgages. Unlike traditional mortgages, most of these alternative mortgage instruments (AMIs) do not have level monthly payments, but employ some other (often complicated) scheme. One AMI even provides a way for the homeowner to continually take cash out of equity, as opposed to continually putting cash into it.

What was the impetus for the creation of AMIs, and in what ways are they superior to traditional mortgages? The answers to these questions are related to level and behavior of mortgage interest rates. In the

EXHIBIT 6 U.S. Mortgage Debt Outstanding by Property Type 1950–1984 (billions of dollars)

	Single (1–4) Family	Multi-Family	Commercial	Farm	Total*
1950	$ 45.2	$ 9.3	$ 12.5	$ 6.1	$ 73.1
1955	88.2	13.5	19.3	9.0	130.1
1960	141.9	20.8	33.4	12.8	208.9
1965	220.5	38.2	55.5	21.2	335.4
1970	297.7	60.1	85.5	29.8	473.1
1975	490.8	100.6	159.3	50.9	801.6
1976	556.6	104.5	171.2	57.0	889.3
1977	656.6	111.8	189.3	65.8	1,023.5
1978	761.9	122.0	212.6	76.0	1,172.5
1979	878.9	128.9	236.5	82.7	1,326.9
1980	960.3	137.2	256.5	92.0	1,466.1
1981	1,018.5	144.3	279.1	101.9	1,543.7
1982	1,110.3	140.1	301.4	106.7	1,658.5
1983	1,219.1	150.1	348.9	109.3	1,827.6
1984	1,349.9	164.0	406.1	110.9	2,030.9

SOURCE: Federal Reserve Board
* Totals may not be exact due to rounding.

15 years ending in 1979, mortgage rates doubled from roughly 6 percent levels to 12 percent levels, and by 1981 they had almost tripled to 17 percent. More importantly, the volatility of these rates increased tremendously. Moves of 1 percentage point between the time a loan application was made and the time the loan was closed were not unheard of in 1979. The interest climate resulted in a great deal of risk to both borrower and lender that the rate that seemed plausible one week might be out of line the next week. (Not to mention the next 30 years.) High interest rates combined with the rapid inflation in housing prices to make home financing difficult in general and all but impossible for the first-time buyer. AMIs were created as a way of coping with these problems.

There are literally dozens of different types of AMIs, each with its own peculiar twist. Their names, which are often abbreviated, include GPMs, VRMs, ROMs, RRMs, ARMs, PAMs, FLIPs, WRAPs, and SAMs. The remainder of this chapter will discuss some of the salient features of the more popular AMIs.

Graduated-Payment Mortgages (GPMs)

The only essential difference between the GPM and the traditional mortgage is that the payments on a GPM are not all equal. Graduated payment refers to the fact that GPM payments start at a relatively low level and rise for some number of years. The actual number of years that the payments rise and the percentage increase per year depend on the exact type or plan of the GPM. The five major GPM plans work as follows:

Plan	Term to Maturity (years)	Years That Payments Rise	Percentage Increase per Year
I	30	5	2.5%
II	30	5	5.0
III	30	5	7.5
IV	30	10	2.0
V	30	10	3.0

At the end of the graduation period, the monthly payment is held at its existing level for the remainder of the mortgage term. Exhibit 7 shows the payment schedule on a $50,000, 10 percent, Plan III GPM.

EXHIBIT 7   Mortgage Payment Schedule for a $50,000 Plan III GPM (30-year term, 10 percent mortgage rate)

Year(s)	Monthly Payment
1	$333.52
2	358.53
3	385.42
4	414.33
5	445.40
6–30	478.81

Note: Plan III GPMs call for monthly payments that increase by 7.5 percent at the end of each of the first five years of the mortgage.

The attraction of a GPM is the small payment in its early years. A first-time home buyer who might not be able to afford payments on a traditional mortgage might be able to afford the smaller payments of the GPM, even if both loans were for the same principal amount. Eventually, when the graduation period has ended, homeowners with GPMs make up the difference by paying larger monthly amounts than the traditional mortgages require. The originators of GPMs reason that most home buyers, particularly young, first-time home buyers, have incomes that will increase at least as rapidly as the mortgage payments increase. Thus they should always be able to afford their monthly payments. Exhibit 8 compares the initial and final payments of a traditional mortgage with the five GPM plans, assuming all mortgages have a $50,000 balance and a 10 percent interest rate. Notice that the lowest initial payment is on the Plan III GPM, and in this example it is about $100 less per month than the traditional mortgage in the first year. It is perhaps not surprising that Plan III GPMs are the most popular and accounted for more than 80 percent of all the GPMs originated in late 1978 and early 1979. The Plan III GPM is the only plan to offer a 7.5 percent graduation rate; this is the maximum graduation rate that federally chartered banks can currently offer.

EXHIBIT 8 Comparison of Initial and Final Payments: Traditional Mortgages versus GPMs ($50,000, 10 percent, 30-year mortgages)

Loan Type	Initial Payment	Final Payment
Traditional	$438.79	$438.79
GPM Plan I	400.29	452.88
GPM Plan II	365.29	466.22
GPM Plan III	333.52	478.81
GPM Plan IV	390.02	475.43
GPM Plan V	367.29	493.60

Because GPMs have smaller initial payments than traditional mortgages, they do not pay down their mortgage balances as quickly. The interesting feature of GPMs is that in their early years they do not pay down any principal at all—in fact their mortgage balances actually *increase* for a short period of time. Technically, we would say that they experience "negative amortization" at the outset. To see how this works, consider the first-month payment on the GPM in Exhibit 7.

Interest due for month one is 10 percent per year for one-twelfth year on $50,000 balance or $50,000 $\times$ $\frac{1}{12}$ $\times$ $\frac{10}{100}$ = $416.67
Payment on GPM = $333.52
Principal paid = $333.52 − $416.67 = −83.15
New mortgage balance = $50,000 − (−83.15) = $50,083.15

Another way of viewing this situation is as follows: The amount paid on the mortgage ($333.52) was insufficient to cover even the interest due on the loan ($416.67), so the shortfall ($83.15) is lent to the mortgagor. Thus the new mortgage balance is the sum of the original balance plus the new loan:

$$\$50,000 + \$83.15 = \$50,083.15$$

Of course, the mortgage balance must eventually be reduced to zero. The annual increases in the mortgage payment eventually catch up to and overtake the amount of interest due, and at that time the mort-

EXHIBIT 9 Graduated Payment Mortgage (GPM) Factor Comparison for 10 Percent, 30-Year Loans

Year-End Factors	Ordinary Mortgage	Plan I 5-Year 2.5 Percent	Plan II 5-Year 5.0 Percent	Plan III 5-Year 7.5 Percent	Plan IV 10-Year 2.0 Percent	Plan V 10-Year 3.0 Percent
0	1.00000	1.00000	1.00000	1.00000	1.00000	1.00000
1	.99444	1.00412	1.01291	1.02090	1.00670	1.01241
2	.98830	1.00615	1.02258	1.03769	1.01214	1.02335
3	.98152	1.00582	1.02845	1.04949	1.01614	1.03258
4	.97402	1.00281	1.02987	1.05526	1.01853	1.03985
5	.96574	.99678	1.02612	1.05383	1.01909	1.04484
6	.95660	.98734	1.01640	1.04385	1.01759	1.04725
7	.94649	.97691	1.00567	1.03282	1.01376	1.04669
8	.93533	.96539	.99381	1.02064	1.00732	1.04277
9	.92300	.95266	.98071	1.00719	.99796	1.03504
10	.90938	.93860	.96623	.99233	.98532	1.02299
11	.89433	.92307	.95025	.97591	.96902	1.00606
12	.97771	.90591	.93258	.95777	.95101	.98736
13	.85934	.88696	.91307	.93773	.93111	.96670
14	.83906	.86602	.89151	.91559	.90913	.94388
15	.81665	.84289	.86770	.89113	.88484	.91867
16	.79189	.81733	.84140	.86412	.85802	.89082
17	.76454	.78910	.81233	.83427	.82838	.86005
18	.73432	.75792	.78023	.80130	.79564	.82606
19	.70094	.72347	.74477	.76488	.75948	.78851
20	.66407	.68541	.70559	.72464	.71953	.74703
21	.62333	.64336	.66230	.68019	.67539	.70120
22	.57833	.59692	.61449	.63108	.62663	.65058
23	.52862	.54561	.56167	.57684	.57277	.59466
24	.47370	.48892	.50332	.51691	.51326	.53288
25	.41303	.42631	.43885	.45071	.44752	.46463
26	.34601	.35713	.36764	.37757	.37491	.38924
27	.27197	.28071	.28897	.29678	.29468	.30595
28	.19018	.19629	.20207	.20752	.20606	.21394
29	.09982	.10303	.10606	.10892	.10816	.11229
30	.00000	.00000	.00000	.00000	.00000	.00000

gage balance begins to decrease. In Exhibit 9 the mortgage balances (expressed as ratios to the original loan amount) are shown at the end of each year, for all five GPM plans as well as for a traditional mortgage. Notice that a Plan III GPM has a balance that rises through the end of the fourth year, at which point it declines to zero over the next 26 years. It is interesting to note that the mortgage balance does not go below 1.0 until some time in the 10th year. Exhibit 10 is a graph of the mortgage balances for a traditional mortgage and a Plan III GPM.

GPMs were first introduced by the Federal Housing Administration (FHA) in November 1976, although various legal and technical matters prevented any large-scale issuance until late 1978. In April 1979 GPMs became eligible for pooling into GNMA pass-through securities, and since that time GPMs have accounted for roughly 25–30 percent of all FHA-insured mortgages. In early 1979 the Mortgage Bankers Associa-

EXHIBIT 10 Comparison between Plan III GPM and a
Traditional Mortgage

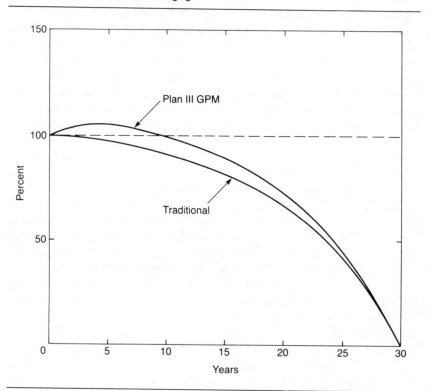

tion of America had predicted that by the end of 1981 GPMs could grow
to half of the FHA-insured mortgages; the disarray of the mortgage
market since 1979 has postponed such an event, but it still appears
feasible.

As interest rates continue to rise, the need for GPMs and similar
vehicles becomes increasingly important to the first-time home buyer or
those with low cash flows. New varieties and plans of GPMs have been
proposed that increase the period that payments rise and/or the graduation rate, thereby making the initial payment progressively smaller. One
GPM proposal called for delaying the time at which payments would
begin to rise—making the payments have a flat-rising-flat pattern. Such
a scheme called for a mortgage balance that would rise for nine years
and not become less than 1.0 until half of the term to maturity had
elapsed.

Pledged-Account Mortgages (PAMs)

Pledged-account mortgages are structured so as to resemble GPMs from the borrower's point of view and traditional mortgages from the lender's point of view. This is engineered by using some or all of the down payment on the property to create a pledged savings account that not only becomes collateral on the loan but also is used to pay off the mortgage. The borrower makes mortgage payments that are initially small; withdrawals from the savings account are then made to supplement the payments. The bank, which receives the sum of the two amounts, gets a level stream of payments, just as it would with a traditional mortgage. PAMs are sometimes referred to as FLIPs (for flexible loan-insurance program), in recognition of the FLIP Mortgage Corporation, which was a pioneer of this type of loan.

Exhibit 11 shows a sample PAM mortgage scheme for a buyer who is interested in a $55,000 house and who has down payment money of $8,767.50. With a traditional mortgage, the buyer would get a mortgage for $46,232.50 (the house price less the down payment); assuming a 10 percent interest rate, this would require a monthly payment of $405.73. In the PAM example, $5,000 of the down payment money is applied to the house directly (leaving $50,000 to be mortgaged), and the remaining $3,767.50 is used to create the pledged savings account, which returns the passbook savings rate (assumed to be 5¼ percent in this example). In the first year of the PAM mortgage, the homeowner pays only $327.89 per month, and an additional $110.90 is taken from the savings account each month. The out-of-pocket expense during the first year is $77.84 less than the traditional mortgage, a saving of 19.2 percent. After each of the first five years of this PAM mortgage, the payment from the borrower rises (6 percent in this case), and the saving relative to the traditional mortgage decreases. As with a GPM, when the graduation period is over, the monthly PAM payment is greater than the payment on the traditional mortgage. (The savings in the early years are paid for in the later years.)

While all of this goes on at the borrower's level, the bank receives a constant monthly sum of $438.79—precisely the amount that the monthly payments on a traditional mortgage for $50,000 would be (also the amount the homeowner pays out of pocket in years 6 through 30, after the savings account is exhausted). From the bank's point of view, the total indebtedness of the borrower equals the mortgage balance less whatever money is in the savings account. Because money is withdrawn from the savings account faster than the mortgage balance is paid down, the total indebtedness of the borrower rises for the first five years. This is analogous to the rise in the mortgage balance of a GPM during the period of negative amortization. If, in this example, we assume that the property value remains at $55,000 (no inflation or improvement), the

EXHIBIT 11 Conventional Mortgage

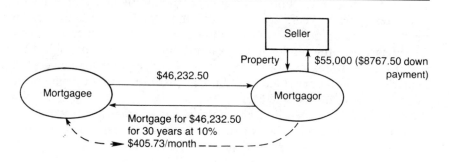

PAM Mortgage

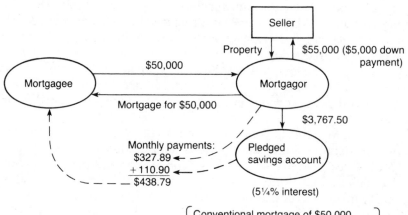

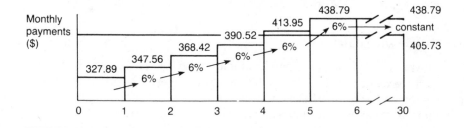

LTV ratio of the mortgage will rise for five years. If the bank had a maximum LTV ratio of 85 percent, then this FLIP mortgage would not be feasible because, even though it is low enough in the first year, the LTV rises above .85 in years two through nine. An LTV maximum of 90 percent would be met, however. In making PAM loans, therefore (and GPMs as well), the lender must examine the maximum possible LTV that the loan can reach in order to determine whether the loan meets the lender's standards or whether additional cash for a down payment or mortgage insurance is called for.

The PAM loan is really an ingenious way of trading net worth (or assets) against income. The borrower who has sufficient cash on hand but faces an income or cash flow shortage for the first few years uses the cash to create the savings account, which subsequently subsidizes the monthly payments and lowers the out-of-pocket cost. The price the borrower pays for this privilege is that the savings account interest rate generally does not yield as much as the mortgage rate costs. The additional cost of a PAM loan over 30 years equals the difference between the mortgage rate and the savings passbook rate on the savings balances for the period of graduation. As with GPMs, however, the PAM could be the best buy in the long run despite these added costs because the costs are repaid in the later years of the mortgage; if inflation is sufficiently high, then the homeowner repays current benefits with inflated future dollars.

Like GPMs, PAMs come in a variety of packages with different terms to maturity, graduation periods, and graduation rates. Because PAMs are designed to meet constraints on income to expense ratios and LTV ratios and take into account such factors as mortgage insurance, property insurance, and taxes, the actual payment schedules vary somewhat from the simple pattern shown in Exhibit 11. Although PAMs do not have the same popularity as GPMs right now (primarily because they are not currently eligible for FHA insurance), the PAM is an interesting form of AMI that deserves closer attention in the future.

Buydown Loans

The buydown loan is extremely similar to the PAM loan described previously, except that it is the seller, not the buyer, who places cash in a segregated account that is subsequently used to augment the buyer's mortgage payments. When newly constructed property is financed in this fashion, the loans may be referred to as builder buydowns, since the seller is the home builder. In general, these loans derive their name from the fact that the seller is using cash to buy down the mortgage rate from a high level to a lower level for some period of time.

The buydown loan is very attractive from the buyer's point of view because it provides the benefit of a PAM loan or a GPM at someone else's expense. It might seem that the seller could pass along the cost of the buydown to the buyer by increasing the price of the house; although this may occur to some small extent, it is not true in general because the mortgage lender places constraints on the maximum LTV ratio. The seller of the home cannot arbitrarily hike the price of the property lest there be a difference of opinion with the lender, who bases the LTV ratio on the appraised value of the property.

What motivation does the seller have, then, to give up part of the profit on the sale in order to create a buydown loan? And would it not be simpler just to reduce the price of the property? The answer to both these questions is that the buydown loan is very often the only financing vehicle that can get the property sold because it is the only type of loan that potential buyers may qualify for. Consider a comparison of two possible ways of financing a $60,000 house (see Exhibit 12), using as alternatives a 30-year traditional loan and a buydown loan. In both cases it is assumed that the prevailing mortgage interest rate is 16 percent, that the home buyer has $10,000 down payment money, and that the home builder is willing to give up $3,000 of its profit. The buydown loan shown in the exhibit is of the "3–2–1" variety, meaning that the buyer pays 3 percent less interest the first year (13 percent in this case), 2 percent less the second year, 1 percent less the third year, and all of the mortgage payment thereafter.

If the builder contributes no money to the sale, the monthly payment (on a $50,000 traditional loan) is $672.38. If the builder simply contributes $3,000 to the purchase (by selling the house for $57,000) the monthly payment on the $47,000 loan is reduced to $632.04. If the $3,000 is used to buy down the interest rate from 16 percent according to the 3–2–1 plan, however, the initial monthly payment is only $547.37 and graduates to $672.38 after three years. The buyer of the house can now apply for the loan based on a monthly payment that is roughly 14 percent less than the payment would have been if the price of the property had simply been lowered, and since the seller is the one who is buying down the rate, no increase in down payment is required. Furthermore, if the escrow account in which the seller's funds are placed pays some rate of interest, then not all of the $3,000 will be necessary to buy down the rate (e.g., if the account pays 8 percent, then only about $2,700 would be needed). Thus the buydown loan can be a cheaper alternative for the seller as well.

Adjustable-Rate Mortgages (ARMs)

The ARM is probably one of the best known alternatives to a traditional, fixed-rate mortgage. While ARMs got off to a relatively slow start in the mid-70s, their use mushroomed in the early 1980s due to changes in ARM structure, thrift regulation, and the shape and level of the Treasury

EXHIBIT 12

Conventional: LTV = .0833

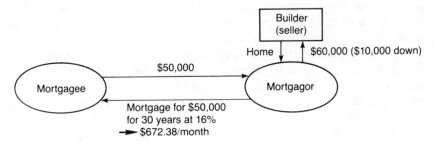

Builder Lowers Sale Price by $3,000: LTV = 0.783

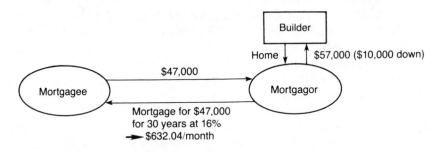

Builder Buys Down Interest Rate:

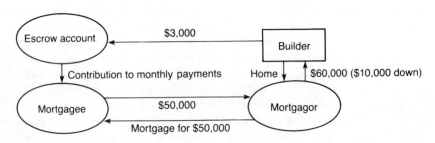

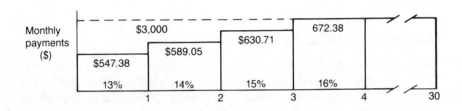

yield curve. In fact, by 1984 it was estimated that roughly two out of every three newly originated mortgages were ARMs of one sort or another.

There are so many different kinds of ARM structures that a comprehensive treatment is impossible. Literally hundreds of different kinds of ARMs have been originated, and more keep arriving on the scene every month. To make matters worse, not all ARMs are even referred to as ARMs. Labels such as VRM (variable-rate mortgage), ROM (rollover mortgage), RRM (renegotiated-rate mortgage) and others are commonly used, with each laying claim to a particular ARM variety or market segment. For our purposes, all of these varieties and labels can be lumped together, and the single term *ARM* will suffice, although the other labels will appear in historical context.

The United States cannot lay claim to the ARM concept. Rollover mortgages (ROMs) have been one of the major financing vehicles in Canada for over 50 years. The exact timing of ARMs' introduction in this country is uncertain, although most analysts would point to California in the early 70s, when the so-called "California VRM" became fairly popular. Before attempting to generalize about the features of ARMs, a detailed look at a typical California VRM will be helpful. The example that follows is a VRM structure that was used by Home Savings and Loan Association, the first lender to issue a pass-through security backed by this type of collateral.

1. The mortgage interest rate is based on the weighted average cost of savings index published by the Federal Home Loan Bank of San Francisco. In general, the spread between the mortgage rate and the index rate is held constant. (When the index changes, the VRM interest rate changes equally.) However, the provisions that follow may prevent this from happening all the time.

2. The mortgage interest rate may change (up or down) only once in any six-month period and may not be changed at all during the first six months.

3. The mortgage interest rate may not change (up or down) more than 0.25 percent (25 basis points) at a time, no matter how much the index changes. Combined with provision 2 above, this means that the mortgage interest rate may not change more than 0.5 percent per year.

4. The mortgage interest rate must change at least 0.1 percent (10 basis points) at a time, except to bring the rate to a level previously impossible because of the 25-basis-point limitation. For example, suppose the index rises 5 basis points from its original level. The VRM rate does not rise because it would not rise the minimum 10 basis points. However, suppose the index rises 30

basis points from its original level. The VRM rate will rise 25 basis points (the maximum) after six months, and the other 5 basis points in another six months.

5. The mortgage interest rate may not rise more than 2.5 percent (250 basis points) higher than its initial level, no matter how much the index rises. In addition, state usury laws may prevent the mortgage rate from exceeding a certain rate.

6. Increases in the mortgage rate are optional on the part of the lender. Decreases, however, are mandatory.

7. Within 90 days of any time the mortgage rate is increased, or at any time the mortgage rate exceeds its initial level, the borrower may prepay the loan in whole or in part without prepayment penalty.

8. Whenever the mortgage rate is increased to a rate higher than its initial level, the borrower may elect to keep his monthly payment constant by extending the maturity of the mortgage. However, the new maturity may not be more than 40 years from the origination date. (In other words, if the loan had an original maturity of 30 years, it cannot be extended more than another 10 years.) Furthermore, if a borrower extends the maturity of the loan and if the mortgage rate is subsequently decreased, the lender may then decrease the maturity by a comparable amount.

As the last provision indicates, ARMs (in this case VRMs) can have maturities that vary as well as interest rates. As an example, suppose a borrower obtains a $50,000 VRM for 30 years with an initial rate of 10 percent. This loan calls for monthly payments of $438.79. If rates rise after six months to 10¼ percent, and the borrower does nothing, monthly payments would rise to $447.99. Provision 8 says that the borrower may have the option to keep monthly payments constant at $438.79, which would extend the maturity of the mortgage an additional five years and one month in order to fully repay the debt. If rates were to rise to 10½ percent, however, the borrower would have to bear some increase in monthly payment, because keeping the payment constant would increase the maturity another 11 years and 9 months, which is more than the maximum allowable extension.

It is impossible to calculate in advance the exact amortization schedule for an ARM, because it will vary with interest rates. In fact, to the extent that the borrower has options to keep payments from rising, two initially identical ARMs based on the same index might follow different schedules depending on borrower preferences. Exhibit 13 displays one example of how a payment schedule for a California VRM might work over its first 30 months.

EXHIBIT 13 VRM: An Example

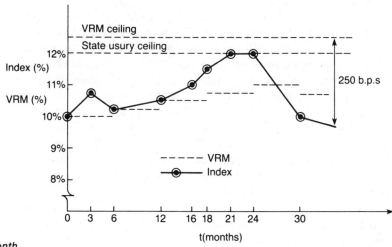

Month

0   Index = 10 percent
         VRM of $50,000 for 30 years at 10 percent = $438.79/month.

3   Index = 10¾ percent
         VRM rate does not change (since less than six months since
         settlement).

6   Index = 10¼ percent
         Borrower may elect to (a) pay $477.99/month (rate increases
         to 10¼ percent—maximum allowed) or (b) pay $438.79/
         month *and* extend maturity by five years, one month (i.e.,
         term increases from 360 to 415 months).
         [Assume (a) is chosen.]

12   Index = 10½ percent
         Borrower may elect to (a) pay $443.14 *and* extend mortgage
         by only 4 years, 11 months (to bring mortgage to 40 years
         past settlement) or (b) pay $448.33/month.
         [Assume (a) is chosen.]

16   Index = 11 percent
         VRM rate cannot increase (since it increased less than six
         months previously).

18   Index = 11½ percent
         Borrower has no option (since maturity is at 40 years).
         Lender elects to increase VRM rate by 25 b.p. maximum to
         10¾ percent. Monthly payment is $452.94.

21   Index = 12 percent
         VRM/usury ceilings apply to VRM rate only.

24   Index = 12 percent
         Notice that VRM rate increased to 11 percent, even though
         the index decreased in the ensuing time period. Monthly
         payments are $462.75.

30   Index = 10 percent
         VRM rate decreases to 10¾ percent. Borrower decides to
         prepay $5,000. However, lender decides to reduce maturity to
         30 years (past settlement). Hence, payments are now $419.87/
         month (instead of $406.96 with a 40-year maturity).

                                      . . . and so on.

Provisions 3 and 5 in the California VRM example are typical of those on a great number of ARMs. The former is referred to as a "periodic cap," because the ARM rate has a maximum increase over any one period. In the above example a period is six months, but other periods, longer and shorter, have been used. The latter provision is known as a "lifetime cap," because the rate is constrained from exceeding a certain rate at any time during the life of the ARM. Most ARMs contain at least one of these types of caps as protection for the borrower against the mortgage rate climbing too far or too fast. However, the caps inherent in the early California VRMs were among the most restrictive ever; it is more common to see periodic caps of 1 or 2 percentage points, and/or lifetime caps of about 5 percent.

Another provision found on many ARMs is negative amortization. The borrower may be able to maintain a constant monthly payment after an interest rate increase by electing to add any interest shortfall to the outstanding mortgage balance. This process is allowed to continue until the mortgage balance reaches a maximum amount (perhaps 120 to 130 percent of the original balance), at which time payments must rise.

Given all of its complexities, it is not obvious why the ARM became so popular as a financing vehicle. From a lender's point of view, the ARM reduces interest-rate risk. To understand why this is so, consider the fact that traditionally, thrift institutions borrow their funds short-term (via deposits, CDs, etc.) and lend the funds long-term (via fixed-rate mortgages). This creates a gap between the maturities of assets and liabilities, and exposes the thrift to the risk that interest rates will rise, thereby raising the cost of funds with no offsetting increase in the rate earned on the mortgage assets. ARMs are one way of dealing with this gap. As interest rates rise, the ARM rate rises, providing the thrift with additional income with which to meet the increased cost of funds. Of course, periodic or lifetime caps may prevent the ARM from being a perfect offset to the gap, but in any event the ARM is far better suited than fixed-rate mortgages to this problem.

Borrowers like ARMs because the lenders express their preference for ARMs in the form of lower initial interest rates. This can be critically important to a potential homeowner for whom a lower rate could mean the difference in qualifying for the loan. Depending on the aggressiveness of the lender, ARMs may carry rates from ½ percent to 2 percentage points or more below the rates posted for fixed-rate financing. Given the protection of interest rate caps, this can be ample enticement for borrowers. Experience has shown that ARMs tend to be most popular when interest rates are highest and home buyers are particularly pinched.

ARMs received a great deal of bad press in the 1983–1984 period due to abuses on the lending side. Overly aggressive lenders were offering so-called teaser rates on their ARMs, in which the initial rate was extremely low for a short period of time (5 percent for the first year was not unheard of), after which the rate reset to the "normal" index. Borrowers flocked to the product, spurred by the fact that at the artificially low initial interest rate, qualifying for the loan became easy. The problems started when the teaser period ended, the rate reset, and the borrower found himself experiencing what became known as payment shock. The teaser-rate ARM has been dubbed the neutron bomb of the mortgage business for its ability to destroy homeowners but leave the property intact. Lenders and their regulators, faced with alarming default and delinquency rates on ARM portfolios, eventually curbed teaser-rate practices.

One problem that remains outstanding for ARMs is standardization. Unlike fixed-rate loans, ARMs are relatively difficult to sell in pooled or security form, especially to buyers outside the thrift industry. The main reason for this is that existing ARMs are so diverse in terms of initial rates, index, interest rate reset frequency, periodic or lifetime caps, and so forth that it is often difficult just finding large quantities of any one kind of ARM. Corporate bond investors are accustomed to floating-rate securities with frequent interest resets, well-known indexes and no rate caps, and therefore are not favorably disposed toward the idiosyncrasies of the ARM market.

Reverse-Annuity Mortgages (RAMs)

The key word to remember when discussing RAMs is *reverse* because, unlike any of the mortgages discussed so far, RAMs do not call for the homeowner to make payments to the bank. Rather, the homeowner (who is still the borrower) receives monthly payments *from* the bank, while the equity in his or her home *decreases*.

Young and first-time borrowers are not the only groups that tend to have cash flow problems from lack of income. Another such group is the elderly, often retired and on a fixed income. In the event that such a person owns (or has substantial equity in) a house, then a RAM provides a way of converting that equity into an income stream. Traditionally this equity could be converted to cash in one of two ways: (1) By selling the house and paying off any outstanding mortgage balance, the homeowner realizes the entire equity in the home in cash; or (2) by taking out a new or second mortgage, the homeowner realizes part of the equity in cash. The RAM goes one step further by allowing homeowners to realize part of their equity in a cash stream, paid to them in monthly installments.

Exhibit 14 illustrates a possible RAM. It involves a homeowner who originally bought her home for $25,000—with a $5,000 down payment and $20,000 mortgage, which has been paid down to a $5,000 balance. The price of the house has risen, due to inflation, to $60,000. The equity

---

EXHIBIT 14 Example of a RAM

Original Mortgage:

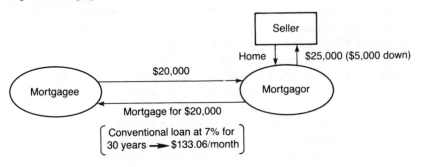

approximately 26½ years

At Origination of RAM:

Current value of home................	$60,000
Mortgage balance........	5,000
Homeowner's equity......	55,000

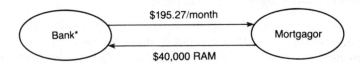

The mortgagor will owe a total of $40,000 to the bank after 10 years.
Cash flows associated with mortgage and RAM:

Before Ram:	−133.06	(outflow = monthly mortgage payment)
For 3½ years after RAM:	+62.21	(net inflow)
For remaining 6½ years of RAM:	+195.77	(RAM monthly payment received)

* The "Bank" may or may not be the original mortgagee.

---

in the home is $60,000 less the $5,000 mortgage balance, or $55,000. The homeowner decides to get a RAM for $40,000 for 10 years at an interest rate of 10 percent. The RAM provides her with a monthly payment of $195.27, which she then uses for food, utilities, home improvements, and/or other expenses. Each year the mortgage balance on the RAM rises to reflect additional payments to the homeowner plus interest on the money lent so far; at the end of 10 years, the mortgage balance is precisely $40,000. Of course, monthly payments on the original mortgage must still be made until it matures. (Often there is no outstanding mortgage when the RAM is originated, so this proviso would not apply.)

From the bank's point of view, the RAM is a continuous series of loans to a homeowner against which the house serves as collateral. Assuming the property keeps the same value, the LTV ratio is continually increasing because the mortgage balance is continually rising. Banks would probably not allow the LTV to get as high as they would for traditional mortgages (i.e., the RAM could not be made for a very high amount relative to the equity) because of the uncertainty of the property value at the end of the RAM's term; as far as the bank is concerned, the property could decline in value and/or deteriorate in condition and marketability.

Shared-Appreciation Mortgages (SAMs)

The SAM loan is another innovation of the early 1980s brought about by high interest rates, and it uses inflation as a way of paying for part of the property. The basic terms are fairly simple. The mortgage lender agrees to provide funds at a greatly reduced rate of interest. In return, the borrower agrees to share part of the increase in the property value with the lender when the loan matures, when the property is sold, or at some other specified time.

At the inception of the SAM program, a one-third participation was popular—the lender would reduce the interest rate by a third (e.g., in a period of 15 percent interest rates the home buyer would obtain a loan at 10 percent) in return for one third of the appreciation in the property value. Over time, the formulas behind SAMs have varied somewhat from the one-third mix. In periods such as 1981 when interest rates were rising in concert with inflation falling, SAM lenders needed to compensate for the imbalance by lowering the percentage reduction in the interest rate, raising the percentage of property appreciation to be shared, or some combination of both.

Exhibit 15 shows the consequences of a SAM loan, assuming the home buyer remains in the home for five years. If the actual percentage increase in the property value (the inflation rate) is close to the prevailing level of interest rates, the cumulative savings over the first five years for the home buyer are roughly the same as the value surrendered at the end of the period. (This example assumes the one-third-type SAM and expresses all costs and benefits in comparable terms.) If inflation turns out to be lower, the homeowner wins in the long run because there is less appreciation in value to surrender; if actual inflation is greater, the

---

EXHIBIT 15 Traditional Loan versus Shared-Appreciation Mortgage (SAM)

- Traditional loan: $50,000 for 30 years @ 15 percent
- One-third SAM: $50,000 for 30 years @ 10 percent one third of appreciation due on sale

Assume: Inflation rate = 12 percent (1 percent per month).
Homeowner sells after five years.
Original down payment = $10,000.

	Traditional Loan	SAM	SAM Benefit
A. Monthly payment	($632.22)	($438.79)	$193.43
B. Total value of payments for five years (assuming 15 percent time value)	(55,998.58)	(38,865.61)	17,132.97
C. Value of house today	60,000.00	60,000.00	—
D. Value of house in five years	109,001.80	109,001.80	—
E. Mortgage balance in five years	(49,360.31)	(48,287.16)	1,073.15
F. One third of appreciation due to bank on SAM	—	(16,333.93)	(16,333.93)
G. Net benefit of SAM in five years (B + E − F)			1,872.19

---

homeowner loses. Of course, the homeowner will never have a problem coming up with the funds to pay the lender if the property is sold because they can be taken from the proceeds of the sale. In the event that the SAM matures or whenever the lender must be repaid without the property being sold, it may be necessary for the homeowner to obtain new financing on the property in order to obtain the required funds.

The attractions of the SAM loan are great to both borrower and lender; the borrower is able to purchase the otherwise unaffordable home, and the lender has the potentially lucrative equity kicker, depending on the rate of inflation. Two factors, though, have prevented SAMs from becoming more popular than they already are. First, although the SAM is simple in concept, the fine print can be onerous. The complications created by property additions or home improvements, for example, can cloud the issue of which portion of the overall increase in property value is really due to inflation and shareable with the lender. Second, SAMs are difficult to package into units and sell as securities because there is such a broad range of formulas and other parameters being used to create them. It is difficult to have mass production of an item for which there is no standardization of parts. Access to the securities markets, which is vital as a liquidity source for mortgage originators, is effectively denied without a fungible product.

The process of creating mortgage securities and the ways of analyzing them are the subjects of the next two chapters.

16

Mortgage Pass-Through Securities

Kenneth H. Sullivan
Managing Director
Drexel Burnham Lambert, Inc.

Bruce M. Collins*

David A. Smilow*

The largest class of mortgage-related securities is the mortgage pass-through certificate. While pass-throughs existed as a legal investment form for decades, they first made sense on a broad scale when several federally supported entities assumed the role of providing credit support and standards of uniformity, which together made the pools of mortgages underlying the pass-throughs more readily marketable. The pooling standards prescribed that all of the mortgages in a pool have similar characteristics, which made the resulting securities easier to analyze, thereby making them more suitable for nontraditional mortgage investors, while the credit support alleviated investor concerns about timely and ultimate collection of amounts due.

Because there are many types of mortgages (e.g., conventional 30-year fixed-rate mortgages, graduated payment mortgages, and 15-year mortgages, among others) a large number of pass-through types have been created. In the following section the principal types traded today are described and compared.

This chapter is designed to serve as a general introduction to mortgage pass-through securities. We present an overview of the structure of these securities by analyzing the factors that affect price, yield, and

---

* This chapter was prepared while the author was an analyst for Mortgage Research at Drexel Burnham Lambert.

average life. We also compare them with other fixed income instruments such as Treasury and corporate securities.

Although mortgage pass-through securities have played a vital role in developing and expanding the secondary mortgage market, the monolithic structure of pass-throughs, that is, the payment stream that features a long life and unpredictable cash flows, has inhibited participation by traditional fixed income investors such as pension funds, bank trust departments, and fund managers. To attract funds at a lower cost than could be obtained by issuing pass-throughs, holders of mortgages began to design "bond-type" alternatives which reduced the term to maturity and provided some certainty regarding the timing of cash flows. Several varieties of *mortgage-backed bonds* have evolved since the mid-1970s, with each succeeding structure designed to focus on the key considerations in issuing mortgage-backed bonds:

- Targeting particular investor groups that have preferences for specific final maturities or average lives that are shorter or longer than those of mortgages.
- Minimizing the amount of collateral required to support the issue while maintaining the integrity of the credit.
- Taking advantage of favorable tax treatment or avoiding the negative tax consequences of certain structures.
- Minimizing accounting leverage as measured by debt ratios to the extent possible while raising funds in the bond market.

In the next chapter, one type of mortgage-backed bond is discussed— the collateralized mortgage obligation.[1]

TERMS AND FEATURES OF THE DIFFERENT TYPES OF MORTGAGE PASS-THROUGHS

Pass-through securities are formed when mortgages are pooled together and undivided[2] interests in the pool are sold. The sale of a pass-through security represents a sale of assets and is not a debt obligation of the originator.[3] The cash flow from the underlying mortgages is "passed through" to the holders of the securities in the form of monthly payments of interest, principal, and prepayments. Prepayments occur

---

[1] For a further discussion of mortgage-backed bonds, see Kenneth H. Sullivan, Llewellyn Miller, and Timothy B. Kiggins, "Mortgage-Backed Bonds," Chapter 7 in Frank J. Fabozzi, ed. *The Handbook of Mortgage-Backed Securities* (Chicago: Probus Publishing, 1985).

[2] Undivided means that each security holder has a proportionate interest in each cash flow generated in the pool.

[3] The reason is that the obligation continues to be that of the borrowers collectively, not the originator through whom the loans were made. Payments on the mortgages never become obligations of an originator unless some kind of explicit "first-loss" arrangement is formalized.

when the holder of an individual mortgage prepays the remaining principal before the final scheduled payment month. Critical to the pricing of pass-throughs are the specific features of that particular pass-through security. In this section, we describe in detail the similarities and differences of various pass-throughs.

Mortgage originators (savings and loans, commercial banks, mortgage companies) are among the most active in pooling mortgages and issuing mortgage-backed securities.[4] The originator can either issue a private pass-through security or file the necessary documents with a guarantor to issue a pass-through security backed by the guarantor. A GNMA (Government National Mortgage Association) security is an example of the latter case. GNMA (commonly called Ginnie Mae) guarantees to the investor the timely payment of interest and principal.

A summary of the terms and features of different types of mortgage pass-throughs is found in Exhibit 1. There are four basic types of mortgage pass-through securities—GNMA pass-throughs, FHLMC participation certificates, FNMA mortgage-backed securities, and private pass-throughs. While all have similar underlying structures, there are several differences among the four types of pass-throughs.

Government National Mortgage Association Pass-Through Securities

The first group of securities is guaranteed by the Government National Mortgage Association. The mortgage pools underlying GNMA pass-through securities are made up of FHA-insured or VA-guaranteed mortgage loans. GNMA pass-throughs are backed by the full faith and credit of the United States government. GNMA is a wholly owned U.S. government corporation within the Department of Housing and Urban Development (HUD) and has the authority to fully guarantee the timely payment of principal and interest on its securities. The pass-through securities guaranteed by GNMA differ according to the nature of the mortgages that comprise the underlying pool.

The GNMA pass-through security is a fully modified pass-through security, which means that, regardless of whether the mortgage payment is received, the holder of the security will receive full and timely payment of principal and interest. The original GNMA pass-through is the most common and liquid pass-through security. It constitutes 80 percent of those outstanding in the market. The GNMA II is the most

---

[4] Pass-throughs are often an attractive alternative to S&Ls in situations where the loans in a pool would trade below par because of their low coupons. By establishing a pass-through security, an S&L can more readily replenish its funds through reverse repurchase agreements. Also, in situations where an S&L wishes to sell assets, the backing of one of the federal agencies and liquidity of the trading markets for pass-throughs can often result in the realization of a higher price for the assets sold.

recent GNMA security. While providing the same guarantees as all GNMA certificates, GNMA II has some differences from GNMA I. First, GNMA IIs are based on multiple-issuer pools,[5] while the original GNMAs are based on single-issuer pools. In addition, the mortgage coupon requirements have been relaxed (a wider range of coupons is permitted in a pool), and there is an additional delay of five days in passing through principal and interest payments because of centralization of the payment facility.

The four additional GNMA securities summarized in Exhibit 1 include the GNMA Midget, GNMA GPM, Mobile Homes, and Projects. The GNMA Midget is an intermediate-term (15 years) security with an assumed average life of 7 years for purposes of quoting yields, and it is similar in structure to the original 30-year GNMA security. The maturity of the underlying mortgages is the primary difference. Because of the maturity difference, which translates into a much shorter average life, the Midget will normally trade at a premium price to a regular GNMA with an equal coupon.

Another security backed by GNMA is the GNMA GPM.[6] The GNMA GPM pass-through security is based on graduated payment mortgages. This market is smaller and less liquid than fixed-rate singlefamily GNMAs. In addition, the cash flows are more complex, and amortization is initially negative. These features have translated into higher yields for the GNMA GPM. It should be noted that the GPM becomes the equivalent of a fixed-rate, fully amortizing, level-payment mortgage after five years. The demographics of the borrowers, however, may be materially different.

The major distinguishing feature for GNMA Mobile Home (MH) pass-through securities from the other GNMA pass-through securities lies in the higher servicing fee. The servicing fee is the difference between the mortgage interest rate and the pass-through coupon rate. The higher servicing fee is the result of several factors. The first is that the "natural" rate for mobile home mortgages is higher than the current production rate for conventional loans. The borrowers are generally less creditworthy and the collateral is not considered as strong as a single family detached home. The second factor is that the payments are more difficult to collect from the borrowers, and policing the borrowers can be

---

[5] Multiple-issuer pools can be arranged by GNMA to accommodate many smaller issuers who may not individually generate the minimum volume of $1 million required to participate in GNMA I.

[6] As explained in the previous chapter, graduated payment mortgages (GPM) differ from conventional mortgages because all payments are not level. Payments start out low and rise for a number of years. GPMs are designed to make housing affordable for first-time home buyers. Because of the low payments in the initial years, GPMs do not pay down as quickly as traditional mortgages. In fact, the smaller payments in the beginning will cause the mortgage balance to increase. This is known as *negative amortization*.

EXHIBIT 1 Features of Selected Mortgage Pass-Through Securities

	GNMA						FHLMC PCs	FNMA MBS
	GNMA I	GNMA II	GNMA Midgets	GNMA GPM	Mobile Homes	FHA Projects		
Type of mortgages	Level payment FHA/VA	Level payment FHA/VA	Level payment FHA/VA	Graduated payment loans (mostly 7.5%)	Level payment FHA/VA	FHA project FHA/VA	95% single family (conventional)	Level payment single family
	New originations	New originations	New originations	New originations	New originations	New originations	New or seasoned conventional loans	New or seasoned conventional loans
Term	90% must be 20 yrs. +	90% must be 20 yrs. +	15 years	30-year original term	4 types ranging from 12–20 yrs.	Most are 40 years	97½% level payment, mostly 30 years (also, a relatively new 15-year term)	30-yr. original term 20-yr. original term (also, a relatively new 15-year term)
Minimum original purchase price	$25,000 ($5,000 increments)	$25,000 ($5,000 increments)	$25,000 ($5,000 increments)	$25,000 ($5,000 increments)	$25,000 ($5,000 increments)	$25,000 ($5,000 increments)	$25,000 ($25,000 increments)	$25,000 ($5,000 increments)

	$1 million, 12 loans	$7 million	$1 million	$1 million	$.5 million	$.5 million, 1 loan	$100 million (except Guarantors Program–$5 million)	$1 million
Minimum pool size								
Geographic characteristics	Highly regional	May be regional or national	Highly regional	Highly regional	Highly regional	Highly regional	National	National
Mortgage coupons allowed (Max. Servicing and Guarantee Fee)	0.5% over P-T rate	0.5% to 1.5% over P-T rate	0.5% over P-T rate	0.5% over P-T rate	3.25% over P-T rate (approx.)	0.25% over P-T rate	0.5% to 2.5% over P-T rate	0.5% to 2.5% over P-T rate
Approximate number of pools outstanding	73,000	3,300	1,925	8,600	5,100	600	12,450	8,150
Approximate dollar amount outstanding (billions)	151.0[a]	8.7[b]	3.4	14.3	3.3[c]	3.0	75.3[d]	33.6[e]
Range of coupons in the market	5.25% to 17.000%	8.00% to 14.50%	7.25% to 13.50%	9.00% to 17.50%	6.00% to 16.75%	8.00% to 14.25%	4.25% to 16.50%	4.00% to 17.00%
Stated delay	45	50	45	50	45	45	75	54
Actual penalty (days)	15	20	15	20	15	15	45	24

[a] Includes $1.7 billion of buydown pools.
[b] Includes $1.1 billion of GPMs, $661 million of 15-year GNMA-IIs, $25 million of Adjustable GNMA-IIs, and $17 million of Mobile Homes.
[c] Includes $17 million of GNMA II Mobil Home pools.
[d] Includes both Regular and Swap/Guarantor PCs, $1.5 billion of 15-year Midgets, $790 million of FHA/VAs, and $385 million of Multi-Family PCs.
[e] Includes $3.0 billion of FHA/VAs, $395 million of Intermediate-Term, and $570 million of Long-Term Assumables.

more costly. Finally, it is important to note that, despite the higher underlying coupons on the mortgages, the GNMA MH pass-through does not show a consistent record of higher prepayment rates than conventional pass-throughs. This, once again, highlights the importance of understanding all of the applicable demographic variables.

The GNMA FHA Projects security is based on longer-term (40 years) multifamily project mortgage loans. Pricing is often based on an average life assumption of 18 years. An additional feature of these securities is that many of the mortgages in the project pools currently outstanding are "putable"[7] back to HUD 20 years from the date of insurance endorsement. Thus, the mortgage loans have what may be interpreted as a minimum return. GNMA projects have historically traded 10 to 40 basis points above the original GNMA yields. Today, however, the put option is no longer available. This should have the effect of increasing the yield differential.

Federal Home Loan Mortgage Corporation Participation Certificate

Another type of pass-through is the Federal Home Loan Mortgage Corporation (FHLMC) participation certificate, or PC. This is commonly known as the "Freddie Mac" PC. FHLMC is the second-largest issuer of pass-through securities. Its PC is based on conventional mortgages (i.e., single-family residential mortgages that are *not* guaranteed by VA or insured by FHA). Some of the features that characterize PCs are (1) prepayments are often more consistent than those of GNMAs because the underlying mortgage pools are often larger; (2) the PC is also a relatively liquid market, although not as liquid as GNMAs; and (3) FHLMC securities have for most of their history traded at higher yields than GNMAs in the secondary markets. PCs can be purchased in the capital markets and can serve as collateral for other activities (e.g., repurchase agreements). Furthermore, FHLMC guarantees the timely payment of interest and ultimate payment of principal on all conventional mortgages that make up the pool.

Whereas GNMA and FNMA (discussed next) guarantee the timely payment of interest and principal, FHLMC guarantees only the timely payment of interest and ultimate payment of principal. This means that FHLMC passes through whatever principal it collects and guarantees payment of the remainder within a year.

The guarantee depends on the ability of FHLMC to satisfy the obligation. Most market participants perceive the credit-worthiness of FHLMC PCs as similar, but not identical, to that of GNMAs despite the

---

[7] A putable security is one in which the holder is granted the option to sell the security back to the issuer at a predetermined price.

fact that GNMAs are backed by the full faith and credit of the U.S. government while FHLMC PCs are not. The higher yield on FHLMC PCs reflects this slight difference in quality.

Federal National Mortgage Association Mortgage-Backed Security

A third type of pass-through security is Federal National Mortgage Association Mortgage-Backed Security (FNMA MBS). FNMA, commonly known as "Fannie Mae," is the newest player in the pass-through security market. It offers a pass-through security similar to the FHLMC PC. FNMA guarantees the timely payment of principal and interest for all securities it issues. This means that there will be no delay in the receipt of either interest or principal. Although FNMA MBSs (mortgage-backed securities) are not backed by the full-faith and credit of the U.S. government, as are GNMAs, it is felt that the U.S. government will not permit FNMA to default. The yields on FNMAs are comparable to those of FHLMC PCs and slightly higher than those of GNMAs. The liquidity of FNMA MBSs is comparable to that of FHLMC PCs.

More recent programs initiated by FNMA include an FHA/VA swap program, an intermediate-term (15-year) pass-through program, and an adjustable rate mortgage pass-through program.

Private Pass-Through Securities

The fourth type of pass-through security is the private pass-through. Because of the low volume of private pass-throughs, they have not been included in Exhibit 1. Approximately $3.3 billion of private pass-throughs have been issued through year-end 1983 by nine different issuers. Private pass-throughs can be issued without guarantees by independent companies, such as commercial banks. This differs from government-related institutions, such as GNMA and FHLMC.

MORTGAGE AND MORTGAGE PASS-THROUGH CASH FLOWS

Before one can compare pass-throughs with other fixed income instruments, one must master the details of how the payments work. The analysis of a pass-through security begins with an examination of the cash flow pattern of the mortgages underlying the pass-through, assuming there are no prepayments. This is the simplest case to analyze. In subsequent examples, the effects of servicing fees (an amount retained by a servicer out of the mortgage cash flow, which reduces the cash flow to pass-through holders) and simulated prepayments are incorporated into the analysis. The mortgage pool used in the following examples is a

$1 million pool of 11 percent mortgages with 30-year maturities. The corresponding pass-through certificate has a 10.5 percent pass-through rate and a .5 percent servicing fee typical of a GNMA pass-through. The servicing fee is retained by the originator of the loans, both to compensate for the cost of collecting the payments and to ensure that the originator has a continuing interest in monitoring the status of the loans.

As explained in the previous chapter, traditional mortgages are fixed-rate loans which are repaid in equal monthly installments of principal and interest. In the early stages of repayment, most of the monthly installment consists of interest. Over time, the interest portion of each payment declines as the principal balance declines until, near maturity, almost all of each payment is principal.

Given the assumption that mortgages are homogeneous, the cash flow patterns from a mortgage pool are consistent with individual mortgages. Exhibit 2(A) shows scheduled cash flow patterns for a $1 million pool of 11 percent, 30-year mortgages under the assumption of no prepayments. Because there is a fixed rate of interest on the loan and no prepayments, the mortgage cash flow is level over all periods.

The cash flow patterns of pass-through certificates are related to, but not identical to, the cash flow from the underlying pool of mortgages. The differences are the deduction of servicing fees and a delay in the receipt of payments. While the minimum monthly cash flow from the mortgage pool is level, the corresponding pass-through cash flow is not. The servicing fee is a percentage of the outstanding principal and, thus, the dollar amount (of servicing fees) is reduced as principal declines. As a consequence, the minimum cash flows for pass-through certificates increase slightly over the term. The cash flow from a pass-through certificate with a 10.5 percent coupon (the difference between the 11 percent and the .5 percent servicing fee) is presented in Exhibit 2(B), which shows that the decline in servicing fees leads to slightly increasing cash flow.

Analysis of the cash flow of both mortgages and pass-through certificates would be straightforward in the absence of prepayments. Since the possibility of prepayments introduces an additional and unpredictable component to cash flow patterns, assumptions must be made concerning the likely prepayment pattern.

Exhibit 3(A) depicts the cash flow patterns for the mortgage pool when prepayments are introduced. Specifically, the cash flow pattern shown in the diagram is based on the assumption of a 12-year prepaid life, which is the "industry standard" for quoting mortgage yields. Under this convention, the first 12 years of the mortgage pool are characterized by cash flows that consist of amortized principal and interest on each of the mortgages in the pool. At the end of the 12th year, the remaining principal balance is assumed to be paid in full. Mortgage yield calculations are made on the assumption of a single prepayment

EXHIBIT 2 Scheduled Cash Flow Patterns for a $1 million Pool of 11 Percent, 30-Year Mortgage and a 10.5 Percent Pass-Through Certificate

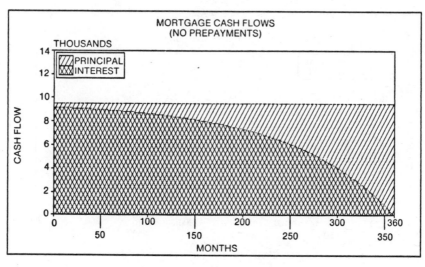

(A)

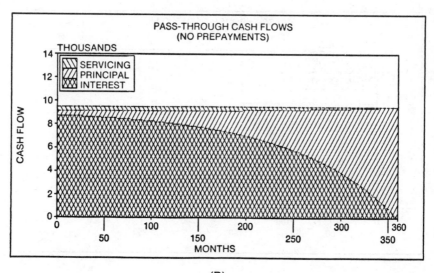

(B)

EXHIBIT 3   Scheduled Cash Flow Patterns for a $1 million Pool of 11 Percent, 30-Year Mortgage and a 10.5 Percent Pass-Through Certificate Assuming a 12-Year Prepaid Life

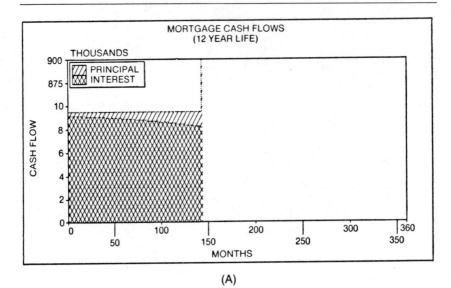

(A)

(B)

"event," much like the maturity of a bond, which takes place at the end of the 12th year.

The 12-year life assumption was derived from and serves as an approximation for the mortgage termination data compiled by the Federal Housing Administration, beginning with 1957 originations. The FHA's analysis of mortgages indicated that mortgages were prepaid on average in the 12th year. Since the mean (or average) life to prepayment was 12 years, mortgage cash flows have traditionally been evaluated on this basis. The 12-year life assumption was adopted by the pass-through certificate market as well. Mortgage yield is, by definition, the calculated yield based on a 12-year life assumption. GNMA quotes, for example, refer to mortgage yield and not cash flow yield, which is dealt with in detail below. Exhibit 3(B) shows the cash flow patterns for a pass-through certificate based on a 12-year life assumption.

The mortgage yield convention was not unrealistic prior to the 1970s. The 1970s, however, brought dramatic increases in the level and volatility of interest rates—as well as demographic changes. Higher and more volatile interest rates altered the prepayment process and led to substantial increases in prepayments in the first 12 years. After a period of high interest rates, such as the most recent experience, any reduction in rates will speed up prepayments of mortgages originated near peaks, because of the benefits of refinancing at a lower rate. Although the application of the 12-year life assumption may have been appropriate for the past periods of stable interest rates with few refinancing opportunities, this is not the case today because the volatility of interest rates is likely to produce highly volatile prepayment rates. For a mortgage pool, prepayment is not a single event, as is the case for an individual mortgage; the prepayments are spread out over time. The shortcoming of the conventional mortgage calculation is that it invariably imposes the same prepayment assumptions, regardless of the age and coupon of the mortgage or the interest rate environment. For example, the conventional mortgage calculation would prescribe the use of a 12-year prepaid life to both of the following GNMAs: a GNMA originated in 1974 with a 7 percent coupon and a GNMA originated in 1981 with a 16 percent coupon. In the first case, the effect of seasoning—the years that have passed since origination—is that the remaining average life is likely to be substantially less than 12 years. In the latter case, the high prepayment rate one could expect, based on current experience, indicates that the "correct" life assumption may be as low as five years. The conventional calculation does not allow the analyst to determine a yield based on a probable economic life of the pass-through.

Changes in prepayment rates are fundamentally important for pass-throughs, as they are for mortgage pools, because of their effect on the yield and pricing of these instruments. Accelerating prepayments have an adverse impact on yields for pass-throughs purchased at a premium.

The opposite is true for discounts. In the GNMA pass-through market, for example, it is known that high-coupon GNMA securities have a faster paydown (prepayment) rate than low-coupon GNMAs; therefore, it is highly misleading to compare high- and low-coupon GNMA yields if both are calculated on a 12-year life.

In summary, the fundamental problem of applying mortgage yields to pass-through certificates is that the cash flow pattern implied by the 12-year life does not conform to the prepayment pattern expected by the marketplace.

There are several alternative methods of addressing the problems associated with the 12-year life assumption. One alternative is to assume the mortgage pool prepays before the 12th year. While this method recognizes that there may be a shorter or longer average life than implied by 12-year prepayments, this alternative has some of the same drawbacks. Although the expected number of years to prepayment is critical for yield determination, it is more appropriate to estimate or assume that a portion of the mortgages is terminated each month over the life of the mortgage pool. The industry first attempted to model prepayments by using the FHA experience rate.[8] This measure of prepayment experience is derived from the FHA probability table for mortgage survivals.

The problems inherent in the FHA experience rate are discussed later in this chapter. An alternative measure of prepayment activity is to assume some constant monthly prepayment rate. This measure assumes a constant fraction of the remaining principal is prepaid each month.

Measures such as a constant prepayment assumption are attempts to deal with the inherent problem of predicting future prepayment rates. Meanwhile analysts are continuing to improve the method of modeling prepayments in order to generate more accurate cash flow projections and more meaningful rate of return calculations. A yield calculation based on modeled prepayments is called a *cash flow yield*.

COMPARISON OF FEATURES OF MORTGAGE PASS-THROUGHS WITH TREASURIES AND CORPORATES

Mortgage-backed securities have certain features that distinguish them from Treasury or corporate fixed income securities. The differences are described in Exhibit 4.

---

[8] The FHA provides mortgage protection insurance. Its derivation of FHA experience is intended to be used for actuarial purposes. The FHA is interested in mortgage termination data in order to determine if it is adequately funded and does not promote its survivorship table as an estimate of future prepayment activity.

EXHIBIT 4 A Comparison of the Features of Pass-Throughs with Those of Treasuries and Corporates

Feature	Mortgage pass-through securities	Treasuries	Corporates	Stripped Treasuries
Range of coupons (premium and discount securities)	Full range.	Full range.	Full range for a few issuers.	Zero coupon; all are discount securities.
Maturities available	Limited to ability to select fast-paying pools or seasoned (short maturity) pools.	Full range.	Full range.	Full range.
Average life	Must be estimated; securities can be prepaid.	Very predictable; most are noncallable.	Minimum average life is predictable and a prepayment penalty helps if called.	Predictable.
Call protection/ prepayments	Complex prepayment pattern; coupon selection can help limit the negative effects of prepayments.	Noncallable (except for certain 30-year bonds).	Usually callable after an initial period of 5 to 10 years.	Noncallable.
Frequency of payments	Monthly payments of interest and a portion of principal.	Semiannual interest payments.	Semiannual (except for Eurobonds which pay annual interest payments).	None until maturity.
Credit risk spectrum	Generally high grade; range from government-guaranteed to A (private pass-throughs).	All are government-guaranteed.	High-grade to speculative.	All are backed by government guarantees.
Liquidity/trading market	Good for many pass-throughs, particularly GNMA, FHLMC, FNMA.	Excellent.	Limited in most cases.	Fair.
Basis for quoting yields	Mortgage yield: monthly payments and a 12-year life (7-year life in certain cases).	Semiannual bond equivalent based on a 365-day year.	Semiannual bond equivalent based on a 360-day year of 12 30-day months.	Semiannual bond equivalent based on either a 360-day or 365-day year depending on the sponsor.

There are two basic differences between Treasuries or corporates and mortgage-backed securities. The most significant difference—and what makes the mortgage-backed security unique—is prepayments. The prepayment patterns inherent in mortgage-backed securities create uncertainties for maturity and yield that are not present in Treasuries and that are limited in corporates. The range of average lives available for pass-throughs, for instance, is limited by the ability to select pools with expectations of higher or lower prepayments.[9] The average life must be estimated for mortgage-backed securities, while it is quite predictable for Treasuries and corporates.

The second principal difference is the frequency of payments. Pass-through securities pay monthly, while Treasuries and corporates pay semiannually. This has present-value implications for mortgage-backed securities. Several other factors must be incorporated into an analysis of pass-throughs as fixed income investments. The most important are discussed in the following sections.

Throughout this section we use average life, as opposed to duration, half life, or other measures of term to compare securities and measure effects of changes in other variables.[10] Duration has gained broad acceptance since it is more easily used to describe the sensitivity of prices to changes in yields; however, it is more difficult to use when comparing mortgage-backed instruments to Treasuries. Treasuries, which are generally bullets (i.e., securities that repay the entire principal at maturity), have maturities and average lives that are equal; thus, no special calculations are required to derive the average life.

Payment Delay

The first issue to examine is the fact that there is an initial payment delay with mortgage pass-through securities. The first mortgage payment is not due from the homeowner until the beginning of the second month after origination (see Exhibit 5). The holder of the corresponding pass-through does not receive his or her first payment, however, until some time into the second month.

---

[9] One motivation for the development of collateralized mortgage obligations (CMOs) was the limited range of maturities available with pass-throughs. CMOs enable investors to select from a broader range of maximum maturities.

[10] Average life is the weighted average time to principal repayment. It is useful as an approximation of a single maturity where the mean or average maturity is used to describe the life of the instrument. Duration is calculated by taking a weighted average of the time periods to receipt of the present value of the cash flows from an investment. (The computation of a bond's duration is illustrated in Chapter 4.) Half life is the period until half of the original principal amount of the pool is repaid.

EXHIBIT 5   Time Line for a GNMA Pass-Through

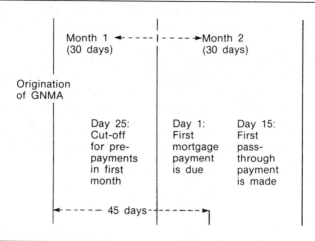

An investor in a GNMA single-family pass-through, for example, does not receive payment until the 15th day of the second month from origination. A GNMA trader will express this 15-day delay as a 45-day delay, indicating the time from origination to first payment. The FNMA security has a stated delay of 54 days. This means the first payment takes place on the 24th day of the second month. A FHLMC security has a 75-day delay.

For a given mortgage yield, as the delay in payments increases, the price of a pass-through declines. At a specific price, a greater delay will decrease the yield.

Monthly Payments

One feature that increases the value of a pass-through of a given coupon, compared to traditional corporate or government debt, is the monthly, rather than semiannual, payment frequency. This feature provides investors with reinvestment opportunities to compound interest monthly, which are not accorded investors in most corporate or government securities. This monthly compounding gives pass-through securities an advantage over other securities. The quoted mortgage yield, however, does not reflect the advantage.

To compare pass-through yields with yields on other securities it is necessary to adjust the mortgage yield upward to its corporate bond equivalent yield (CBE). The CBE allows a standard of comparison for securities with different payment frequencies. In essence, the monthly coupons are treated as if they are collected and reinvested at the mortgage-yield rate until the end of each semiannual or other period. The accumulated amount is larger than the face amount of six monthly coupons.

Exhibit 6 shows the upward adjustment of the mortgage yield. The last column indicates the magnitude of the adjustment. The adjustment is absolutely essential for comparing relative performance of pass-through securities for anyone engaged in intermarket transactions.

EXHIBIT 6 Upward Adjustment of Mortgage Yield Due to Monthly Payments

Mortgage Yield (Percent)	Semiannual Bond Equivalent* (Percent)	Increase in Yield	
		(Basis Points)	(Percent Change)
6.0%	6.08%	+8	+1.33%
8.0	8.13	+13	+1.63
10.0	10.21	+21	+2.10
12.0	12.30	+30	+2.50
13.5	13.89	+39	+2.89
14.0	14.41	+41	+2.93
16.0	16.54	+54	+3.38
18.0	18.69	+69	+3.83

* The higher semiannual bond equivalent reflects monthly compounding of the mortgage yield at the mortgage-yield to an equivalent semiannual payment which includes reinvestment income.

A crucial assumption is made when the yield to maturity is used as a measure of how attractive an investment is. The yield to maturity, including both mortgage yield and corporate bond equivalent, assumes that the contractual periodic payments are reinvested at the yield rate. The reinvestment rate subsequently realized could vary considerably from the yield to maturity. Exhibit 6 shows the effect of various reinvestment rates on the yield realized on a security with monthly payment frequency.

When the reinvestment rate is below the quoted yield to maturity, the realized yield to maturity (also known as the realized compound yield) will be less than the corporate bond equivalent yield. The opposite is true when reinvestment rates exceed the quoted yield to maturity. The last column in Exhibit 7 shows how far the realized yield is likely to vary across a range of reinvestment rate assumptions that do not coincide with the mortgage yield. Careful assessment of mortgage yields requires consideration of the impact reinvestment rate assumptions have on realized return.

EXHIBIT 7 The Effect of Reinvestment Rates on the Realized Increase in Yield from Monthly Payment Frequency (10.5 percent pass-through; 13.5 percent mortgage yield)

Realized Reinvestment Rate (Percent)	Semiannual Bond Equivalent* (Percent)	Semiannual Reinvestment Rate of Return† (Percent)	Yield Relative to Semiannual Bond Equivalent (Basis Points)
0%	13.89%	13.50%	−39
6	13.89	13.67	−22
8	13.89	13.72	−17
10	13.89	13.78	−12
12	13.89	13.84	−5
14	13.89	13.90	+1
16	13.89	13.96	+7

---

* Semiannual bond equivalent is not affected by the reinvestment rate, since its assumed reinvestment rate is the mortgage yield.

† Assumes monthly payments of interest and principal are compounded at the realized reinvestment rate to arrive at a semiannual equivalent payment.

Prepayment Effects

The cash flow pattern of a pass-through security is strongly influenced by prepayments. When the prepayment rate is increased, this shortens average life and skews the cash flow to earlier years. This reduces the investment horizon and affects the realized yield.

If the pass-through security is trading at a premium (i.e., above par), an increase in prepayment rates will reduce the yield because the principal is being returned at par which is less than the initial price. It is beneficial for the investor to retain the high coupon interest for as long as possible. In general, for high-coupon (premium) pass-throughs, as prepayment rates rise, average life falls, which reduces rates of return and yield. When pass-through securities are purchased at a discount, increased prepayment rates serve to enhance the yield. This occurs because average life is shortened, which results in the early return of principal at par, which is more than the initial price.

Seasoning

Seasoning refers to the time since origination or age of a mortgage or the mortgages in a pool. The average age of the mortgage pool is important because of the implications for average life and yield. Seasoning also affects the assumptions made about prepayment rates.

Consider, for example, a typical 12 percent GNMA pass-through security priced at 91 and expected to prepay at .01 percent per month. When the underlying mortgage pool consists of new originations, the security has an average life of 22.45 years and a cash flow yield of 12.23 percent. If, however, the underlying mortgages are seasoned 5 years (i.e., 5 years old) and we expect the prepayment rate to increase to .50 percent per month, then the average life falls to 10.72 years while the cash flow yield increases to 13.79 percent. The prepayment assumption is revised upward for the seasoned case, because we anticipate an increase in prepayment activity over the low levels associated with the first few years of a mortgage pool. Average life is lower and cash flow yield higher, because there are fewer remaining in the term and principal is recovered more quickly.

PREPAYMENTS AND HOW THEY ARE ESTIMATED

The controversy surrounding pass-through securities has focused on the methods of calculating yields for these instruments. Typically, a measure of yield involves calculating the rate of discount that equates some sequence of future cash flows with a market price. In the case of Treasury securities the yield measurement is straightforward because the amount and timing of future cash flows are known. With pass-through securities, prepayments create an element of uncertainty which complicates the projection of cash flows and yield measurement. The purpose of this section is to examine the behavior of pass-through yields under different prepayment assumptions.

Twelve-year prepaid life was the first method used to address this issue. In this section two other widely used benchmarks for prepayments are discussed; FHA experience and constant prepayment assumptions.

Causes of Prepayments

Prepayments occur when a homeowner makes a payment which exceeds the minimum scheduled amount. Most often, though, loans are repaid in full if prepaid at all, and we focus our analysis exclusively on such terminations.

Prepayments can be separated into two general categories—economic and uneconomic. In the first category we include refinancings. Refinancings occur, with some observable lag, when rates fall below the level of previous originations to the extent that homeowners can more than recoup their expenses of refinancing through lower payments on the new loan. When the home is refinanced, the repayment of the old mortgage causes a flow of cash to be passed on to security holders. Since the future level of interest rates is hard to predict with accuracy, the economic component of prepayments will likewise be difficult to predict. Mortgage loans can be prepaid at the homeowner's option at or near the face amount at any time. Therefore, economic prepayments will always be a negative event for pass-through investors since new pass-through coupons will be lower than the coupon previously held.

The second category of prepayments is "uneconomic" prepayments. These occur when a mortgage contract is terminated in an interest rate environment that is not conducive to advantageous refinancings. Uneconomic prepayments include terminations due to default and/or foreclosure, sale of the property (usually a due-on-sale clause is the cause of this kind of prepayment), terminations due to disasters such as floods, fires, and mortgage insurance contracts which pay off balances in the event of a death of a borrower-owner. In general, these are advantageous redemptions for investors since the market value of the mortgage at the time of redemptions will usually be less than the face amount.

Projecting prepayments, i.e., describing prepayments in the form of a model, is a complex problem which depends on both economic variables (such as interest rates, inflation and general affluence), and demographic variables (such as frequency of moves and population trends). An additional layer of complexity is contributed by legislative action. For example, recent legislation has upheld the enforceability of due-on-sale clauses. This will have an important effect in "homogenizing" conventional loans across state lines since individual states had heretofore adopted their own positions on this issue. Also, one class of pass-through remains unaffected by due-on-sale clauses. GNMA pools consist of FHA and VA mortgages which by their terms are "assumable." This fact prevents GNMA investors from obtaining the benefit of the largest category of uneconomic redemptions—those forced by due-on-sale clauses. The careful modeling of prepayments, and the analysis and quantification of the factors affecting prepayments is beyond the scope of this chapter.[11] At the very least, the discussion above should alert participants in the mortgage market to the variety of factors that have an impact on investment values and that many of the factors are correlated.

FHA Experience

FHA experience has become the traditional method for estimating prepayments. It is the best known and most widely used prepayment model. FHA periodically publishes a table of 30 numbers that represent a series of annual survival rates. The table indicates the probability for survival of a mortgage and implicitly tells the percentage of mortgages expected to terminate for any given policy year. The annual rates are interpolated and spread out across each year in monthly intervals. A

---

[11] For a detailed discussion, see David S. Askin, "Forecasting Prepayment Rates for Mortgage Securities," Chapter 11 in Fabozzi, ed., *The Handbook of Mortgage-Backed Securities*.

fundamental problem though is that the FHA experience is based on a single parameter: age of the mortgage. It ignores the coupon and year of origination of the mortgage, among other things. A major consequence of this is that FHA experience more accurately reflects the interest rate environment of the 1960s and 1970s. Furthermore, the usefulness of FHA data is limited in that the statistics are based on assumable FHA and VA mortgages. Thus, for securities other than GNMAs, such as FHLMCs and FNMAs, the data can be misleading.

To accommodate prepayment experience rates that are either faster or slower than those suggested by the FHA table, prepayment rates are expressed as a multiple of the FHA experience rate. "0 percent of FHA" means no prepayments and "100 percent of FHA" refers to the "normal" rate. Any other rate of prepayment can be expressed as a percentage of the normal rate. "200 percent of FHA" means, for example, that a pool is experiencing prepayment at twice the rate of what appears in the table (i.e., 100 percent of FHA). The use of multiples of FHA experience to adjust for mortgage pools that pay faster or slower is problematic because the pools do not follow a consistent pattern. In other words, fast-paying pools do not increase prepayments proportionately across policy years. Nevertheless, FHA experience is widely used throughout the mortgage-backed securities industry. Therefore, it is important to examine the effect of FHA experience assumptions on variables that affect the pricing of mortgage-backed securities.

Constant Prepayment Factors

An alternative measure for prepayments is to assume that the principal is prepaid at some constant rate, which we call the *Conditional Prepayment Rate* (CPR). Several different expressions have been coined to describe this measure, all of which assume a constant fraction of the remaining principal is prepaid each month (or year). This implies that each individual mortgage that makes up the pool is equally likely to prepay. A major difficulty with this type of measure is that it merely quantifies prepayments. This is a subjective decision and is not based on a predictive model. The advantage of a constant measure is its simplicity. It can easily be incorporated into pricing and yield formulas and it can also be easily adjusted to reflect current prepayment conditions.

SUMMARY

Mortgage pass-through securities represent the largest class of a general category of securities that are mortgage-related. The cash flows of underlying mortgages are securitized and "passed through" to the investor in a pass-through security. The market for these securities has grown rapidly, due to the participation of three government agencies: GNMA,

FHLMC, and FNMA. Today's market is characterized by pass-through security types backed by one of these agencies. The cash flow patterns of pass-throughs differentiate them from other securities, such as Treasuries or corporates. Payments are received monthly and there is an option for prepayment of principal. Monthly cash flows provide an opportunity for higher yields through reinvestment. The prepayment option creates uncertain cash flows and, thus, requires careful consideration when estimating performance of the security. These two features explain why, for example, pass-through securities historically have traded at a yield above comparable Treasuries.

17

Collateralized Mortgage Obligations

Gregory J. Parseghian
Vice President
The First Boston Corporation

The collateralized mortgage obligation, or CMO, is a dynamic innovation in mortgage security structure. In the first two years following their introduction in June 1983, CMOs have grown into a $20 billion market. CMOs generally retain many of the yield and credit quality advantages of pass-throughs while eliminating some of the less desirable elements of the traditional mortgage-backed security. Each of the group of bonds issued in a CMO deal is referred to as a *tranche*. The shorter final maturity, enhanced call protection, and semiannual payments found on many CMO tranches make them suitable for some investors who cannot incorporate pass-throughs into their portfolios or strategies. As a result, the profile of participants in the CMO market differs from that of pass-through owners. The wide range of risk and return characteristics found within the universe of CMO securities gives them the potential to meet the needs of a broader investor group than can the more homogeneous pass-through market.

THE CMO PRODUCT

CMOs are bonds that are collateralized by whole loan mortgages or mortgage pass-through securities. In addition to the security afforded by the fully dedicated collateral, some CMO issues also possess minimum reinvestment rate and minimum sinking-fund guarantees. The cash flows generated by the assets in the collateral pool are used to first pay interest and then pay principal to the CMO bondholders.

A key difference between traditional pass-throughs and CMOs is the mechanics of the principal payment process. In a pass-through, each investor receives a pro rata distribution of any principal and interest payments (net of servicing) made by the homeowner. Because mortgages are self-amortizing assets, a pass-through holder receives some return of principal each month. Complete return of principal and the final maturity of the pass-through, however, do not occur until the final mortgage in the pool is retired. This results in a large difference between average life and final maturity as well as a great deal of uncertainty with regard to the timing of principal return.

The CMO structure substitutes sequential retirement of bonds for the pro rata principal return process found in pass-throughs. Subject to the provisions of the individual CMO issues considered, cash flow generated by the underlying collateral (to the extent that it exceeds the amount required to pay interest) is used to retire bonds. Only one class of bonds at a time receives principal. All principal payments go first to the "fastest-pay" tranche of bonds, as stipulated by the prospectus. Following retirement of this class, the next tranche in the sequence then becomes the exclusive recipient of principal. This sequential process continues until the last tranche of bonds is retired.

The effect of the CMO innovation is to utilize cash flows of long maturity, monthly-pay collateral to create securities with short, intermediate and long final maturities and expected average lives. On the offering date of the first FHLMC (A) deal, for example, the final maturities of the tranches ranged from 5 years to 25 years and the expected average lives of the bonds ranged from 3 years to 21 years. The shorter classes clearly hold more appeal than the underlying collateral for investors seeking low exposure to interest-rate risk. Since the shorter tranches must be retired before longer tranches receive principal payments, the longer tranches have a form of call protection. This feature appeals to investors who require less call and reinvestment risk than pass-through securities or whole loans carry.

CMOs are an important innovation because they broaden the range of investment objectives that can be filled by mortgage securities. Prior to the introduction of the FHLMC CMO in June, 1983, the mortgage securities market was dominated by 15- and 30-year final maturity pass-throughs. The inherent problem was that this structure did not meet the needs of the entire universe of fixed income investors. Hence, some market participants were effectively excluded from the major segment of the mortgage securities market. The shorter average life CMO tranches frequently meet the requirements of investors requiring greater predictability of the timing of principal returns. The longer CMO classes offer a greater degree of protection against call and reinvestment risk. The conclusion is that a greater array of investors is able to participate in the mortgage market because of the introduction of CMOs. This is extremely important since investors have limited choices of high quality fixed income securities with higher yields than Treasuries.

THE CMO STRUCTURE

Exhibit 1 illustrates the structure of a typical CMO issue and demonstrates how cash flows get from the collateral to the bondholders. Interest is paid to each of the three tranches of bondholders. Cash flow generated by the collateral, in excess of that required to pay interest to

---

EXHIBIT 1 Cash Flow Diagram for CMO

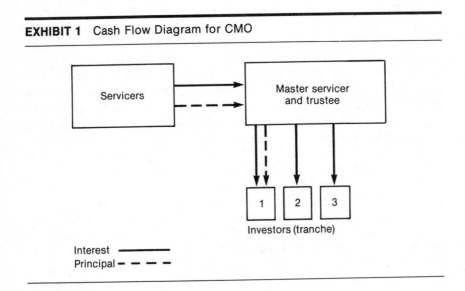

Interest ———
Principal — — — —

---

all bondholders, is paid exclusively to the first tranche bondholders. In this example, it is assumed that monthly cash flows generated by the collateral are reinvested until the semiannual bond payment date. The inclusion of this reinvestment income means that the amount available for the semiannual distribution to bondholders exceeds the sum of the six monthly cash flows from the collateral. Exhibit 2 illustrates the effect on cash flows after the first class is retired. It shows that the second tranche then becomes the exclusive recipient of principal payments.

After the final tranche of the bonds is paid off, any collateral remaining generally reverts back to the issuer in the form of a "residual." Generally, the proceeds initially received by the issuer for the bonds are substantially less than the value of the collateral. Hence, an issuer is dependent upon the residual in order to realize a profit on the transaction. This implies that issuers whose desire is to maximize cash proceeds generally do not issue CMOs, but use pass-throughs or simply sell whole loans.

EXHIBIT 2   After First Tranche Is Retired . . .

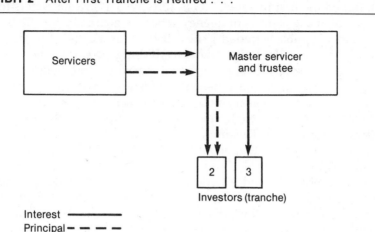

Interest ——————
Principal — — — —

EVOLUTION OF THE CMO

A review of the history of CMO development demonstrates the innovations that have made CMOs an increasingly popular financing alternative and investment vehicle. From the viewpoint of an issuer, one objective is to tailor the cash flows due bondholders to closely resemble those produced by the mortgages. Deviations from this standard generally result in less proceeds at the time of the bond sale relative to the value of the collateral.

CMOs were further enhanced to better suit the requirements of investors. Methods of using whole loan collateral, GPMs and conventional mortgages improved the yields that could be passed through to investors. The introduction of the accrual bond provided a uniquely call-protected mortgage security and enabled larger offerings of three-year and five-year final maturity tranches. The concentration on meeting the liquid asset requirements of thrifts and the needs of insurance companies to fund guaranteed investment contracts (GICs) and other intermediate liabilities had further effects on the CMO structure.

The original FHLMC CMO deal, comanaged by First Boston and Salomon Brothers in June, 1983, was a three-tranche offering with a guaranteed minimum sinking fund. The collateral was level pay whole loans, the credit of which was guaranteed by FHLMC. FHLMC's guaranteed sinking fund was structured to approximate a 100 percent FHA prepayment rate on the underlying collateral.

Pulte Homes, through its subsidiary Guaranteed Mortgage Corporation, issued the first private CMO in July, 1983. ("Private" refers to the absence of any government agency acting as guarantor for the bonds; the security is publicly traded.) The collateral for the Pulte "A" deal, the first offering from the Pulte Guaranteed Mortgage Corporation I shelf, was GNMA level pay (SFs) and graduated payment mortgages (GPMs). In order to overcome the potential problem of insufficient cash flow generation in the early years by the GPMs to service the bonds, Pulte set aside capital with a trustee to cover the greatest possible shortfall due to negative amortization. This fund, referred to as the debt service reserve fund, is an innovation that enabled inclusion of GPM mortgages in the collateral pool.

Subsequent Pulte and American Southwest CMOs began to employ techniques that eliminated the need for the debt service reserve fund. There were two innovations that enabled this to occur. The primary idea was the creation of the accrual bond, a bond that receives neither principal nor interest payments until all previous tranches are fully retired. The accrual bonds are designed to have negative amortization and hence absorb that created by the GPM collateral. Other means of absorbing negative amortization include coupon income from premium mortgages and unscheduled principal return from discount mortgages.

CMOs with semiannual payments to bondholders have a potential problem making coupon payments if large monthly flows of principal from the collateral must be reinvested in a low interest-rate environment. The rating agencies stipulated that a reserve fund be set aside for this risk or that excess mortgages be put up to collateralize the bonds. The "calamity clause," introduced by Pulte Homes, eliminated the need for these measures by stipulating that prepayments beyond a specified rate could be passed through monthly to bondholders.

The next significant step in CMOs involved the collateral included in private deals. Most of the early private CMO deals utilized only GNMA, FNMA, and FHLMC guaranteed pass-throughs. Subsequent deals, however, included conventional mortgages insured by private entities such as MGIC, General Electric and Aetna. CitiMac's CMO offering went several steps further. First, the credit guarantee on the conventional whole loans was provided by Citicorp and CitiMac, the issuer of the CMO. Second, CitiMac guaranteed a minimum sinking fund that approximates an SMM (Single Monthly Mortality), as opposed to an FHA, prepayment rate on the collateral.

Additional innovations in the CMO product have included a wide variety of technical enhancements and new structures. One such concept was that of a monthly pay CMO. Another innovation was to place a REIT (Real Estate Investment Trust) structure on a deal and to sell the interest in residual collateral in the form of stock dividends.

CMOs undoubtedly will undergo additional evolution as the product matures. The next innovation may be that of an expansion of the conduit format, in which an issuer collects collateral from a number of mortgage originators and combines it to collateralize a single, large offering. This concept will appeal to investors who prefer large deal sizes and to issuers who don't wish to issue CMOs solely with their own mortgage production.

SPECIAL FEATURES

The preceding section dealt with CMOs assumed to have the simplest possible structure. There are a large number of special features on various CMOs, however, that must be detailed in order to accurately evaluate the universe of CMO securities.

Guaranteed Minimum Sinking Fund

The speed at which principal is retired on CMO bonds is highly dependent on the cash flow generated by the underlying collateral. Future cash flows from coupon income and amortization of the collateral are known. The rate of prepayments that will be received, however, cannot be predicted with certainty. Hence, the best cash flow that can be guaranteed to be generated by the mortgages is that assuming a zero percent prepayment rate on the collateral.

Some issuers, such as FHLMC and CitiMac, guarantee a minimum repayment schedule on the CMOs which exceeds that guaranteed to be generated by the collateral. If cash flow received from the underlying collateral is insufficient to meet the sinking-fund requirement, then the issuer is obligated to advance an amount sufficient to cover the shortfall. The amount guaranteed to be retired each semiannual period is expressed in the prospectus as a percentage of the remaining principal balance of the CMO. The sinking-fund schedule generally reflects an approximation of a selected FHA or SMM prepayment rate on the underlying collateral. In subsequent periods, issuers generally can recover advances made to the extent that cash flow generated by the collateral exceeds the minimum amount guaranteed to the bondholder.

Exhibit 3 demonstrates the mechanics of the guaranteed minimum sinking-fund feature. In Period 1, the sinking-fund guarantee is assumed to require a principal payment of at least $1,000. The collateral, however, generated cash flow sufficient for only $500 of principal payments, meaning that the issuer had to advance the other $500. In Period 2, the collateral produced enough to cover the guarantee but no excess. In Period 3, another $100 had to be advanced by the issuer, bringing the total advanced to $600. The collateral generated a $200 excess in Period 4. Since advances must be repaid with excess before excess can be applied to retire more bond principal, the entire $200 was retained by the

EXHIBIT 3

Period	[1] Principal Guaranteed to Bondholders	[2] Cash Flow Generated by Collateral in Excess of That Needed for Interest	[3] [2] − [1] Excess(+) or Shortfall(−)	[4] Advance Required by Issuer	[5] Return of Advances	[6] [3] − [5] Excess Paid to Bondholders
1	$1,000	$ 500	$−500	$500	0	N.A.
2	900	900	0	0	0	0
3	800	700	−100	100	0	N.A.
4	700	900	200	0	200	0
5	600	2,000	1,400	0	400	1,000

issuer and used to reduce the $600 in advances outstanding to $400. In Period 5, the first $400 of excess cash flow generated by the collateral is used to return the remaining advance outstanding. The remaining $1,000 of the $1,400 excess may then be used to retire more CMO principal. An additional wrinkle found on some CMOs is that the advance account accrues interest. For purposes of this example, we assumed no such accrual.

The effect of the minimum guaranteed sinking fund is to place a floor on the minimum pace of bond retirement above what can be guaranteed solely by cash flows from the collateral. This feature is particularly valuable in a rising interest rate environment when prepayments tend to decline. A bond with no sinking-fund guarantee may experience a greater lengthening of its expected average life than will a bond with a minimum guaranteed sinking fund. This sinking-fund guarantee limits cash flow and average life uncertainty and adds value to a CMO.

Guaranteed Minimum Reinvestment Rate

In CMOs that make semiannual payments to bondholders, the monthly cash flows generated by the collateral must be reinvested until the payment date to bondholders. The rate earned on the cash flows reinvested can have a material effect on the amount available to pay bondholders and the average life of the CMO tranches. A guaranteed minimum reinvestment rate requires the guarantor (generally a AAA bank or agency) to supplement the reinvestment income if it does not meet the minimum rate. The effect is to quicken the pace of bond retirement relative to what would be retired if there were no guarantee in periods of very low short-term interest rates.

Credit Guarantee on Mortgages

The issuer of a CMO may establish a reserve fund to absorb some or all of the losses upon defaults of the whole loans or pass-throughs in the collateral pool. Generally, this type of guarantee exists only in CMOs such as CitiMac's that are backed by whole loans. In contrast, most bonds issued by home builders need no supplemental credit guarantees since the mortgages are insured by GNMA, FNMA, or FHLMC.

Removal of Excess Cash Flow by Issuer

The issuer of a CMO is always required to pay interest on CMO bonds. In addition, the issuer must pay down enough CMO principal so that the outstanding CMO bonds remain fully collateralized. If cash available on a payment date to bondholders exceeds the sum of required principal and interest payments, then this amount is termed the excess.

There is wide variation among CMO deals on the method by which to calculate and distribute this excess. Some deals allow the issuer to retain the entire excess while others stipulate that the entire amount be distributed to bondholders. Many CMO indentures contain a formula dividing the excess between CMO bondholders and the issuer.

It is clear that distribution of the excess to the bondholder shortens the expected average life of the CMO. Investors should not be alarmed, however, if the indenture provides that the issuer retains part or all of the excess. The yield table for each deal, which generally lists yields, timing of principal payments, final maturity, duration, and average life under a range of collateral prepayment rates, fully reflects the provisions relating to the handling of the excess. Hence, it is critical to scan the yield table in order to gain an understanding of how the various features of a particular CMO work together to influence cash flows.

Special Reserve Fund for Negative Amortization Collateral

Some CMO offerings contain special reserve funds to supplement, if necessary, the cash flows from the portion of collateral that experiences negative amortization, such as would occur with GPMs. This feature is generally termed the "debt service reserve fund." The effect of this feature is to bias upward the speed at which bonds are retired.

Prepayment Reserve Fund

In a CMO that makes semiannual payments to bondholders, the issuer must pay coupon income on the entire principal balance outstanding at the beginning of the six-month period. This can pose difficulty if the reinvestment rate available on monthly principal return from the collateral is less than the coupon rate on the bonds. Some CMOs overcome this hurdle with a calamity clause that allows the issuer to make monthly principal payments to the bondholder.

CMOs without a calamity clause frequently have a prepayment reserve fund. This fund, which represents capital set aside by the issuer at the outset of the deal, is used to supplement the reinvestment income on monthly principal received from the collateral. This supplement may be required to make interest and principal payments to bondholders.

While it is easy at first glance to categorize the preceding special features as good and bad, these labels do not necessarily lead to accurate assessment of the relative value of the particular CMO. For example, excess income removal provisions frequently appear in combination with special reserve funds for negative amortization securities. Under close scrutiny, it becomes apparent that the approximate net effect of the provisions is to cancel out and generate cash flows to bondholders similar to those in more simply structured CMO offerings. The critical yardstick is the yield table, which enables the investor to scrutinize the cash flow characteristics of the bonds under a range of prepayment assumptions on the collateral.

IMPORTANCE OF THE ISSUER

All CMO offerings to date are backed by collateral that is held in trust exclusively for the benefit of bondholders. This means that bondholders retain possession of the collateral in the event of default of the CMO issuer. The credit quality of the CMO issuer is important only to the extent that promises made to bondholders cannot be satisfied by the collateral. Examples of this include guaranteed minimum sinking funds, guaranteed minimum reinvestment rates, and credit guarantees on the underlying collateral. A generalization that can be made is that CMOs issued by home builders tend to be structured to meet obligations to bondholders exclusively with cash flow from the collateral. In contrast, FHLMC, CitiMac and other financial institutions that have issued CMOs more frequently have provisions that may result in bondholder reliance on the issuer to supplement cash flows generated by the collateral.

In a typical builder bond such as the Pulte GMC I and II Series, fully collateralized by GNMA securities, the effective credit quality is that of GNMA. In a CMO offering fully collateralized by FHLMC and/or FNMA pass-throughs, the effective credit of the particular agency is the credit on the bonds. The term *fully collateralized* means that the collateral will generate cash flows sufficient to meet obligations to bondholders under any prepayment and interest rate scenario.

ACCRUAL BONDS

Many CMO issues include one or more tranches that are *accrual bonds*. An accrual bond does not receive any cash payments of principal *or interest* until all tranches preceding it are retired. In effect, an accrual bond is a deferred interest obligation, resembling a zero-coupon bond, prior to the time that the preceding tranches are retired. The accrual bond, also termed the Z-bond, then receives cash payments representing interest and principal on the accrued amount outstanding. This amount is the original principal balance plus the compounded accrued interest. Accrual bonds are purchased most frequently by investors who require the greatest degree of protection against reinvestment and call risk, or who seek the greater price leverage afforded by these classes.

Exhibit 4 demonstrates the effect of an accrual bond in a CMO structure. Interest accrues on but is not paid to the accrual bond (the fourth

EXHIBIT 4   Cash Flow Diagram for CMO with Accrual Bond

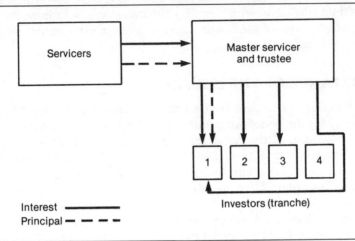

tranche in this example) until the first three tranches are fully retired. The sequential payment of principal concept is not affected by the existence of an accrual bond. Since interest payments on this tranche are deferred, however, the payment of principal on the prior classes is accelerated by the amount of interest deferred on the accrual bond. Exhibit 5 shows that the second tranche in the sequence becomes the sole recipient of principal after the first tranche is retired. One should note that an

EXHIBIT 5   After First Tranche Is Retired . . .

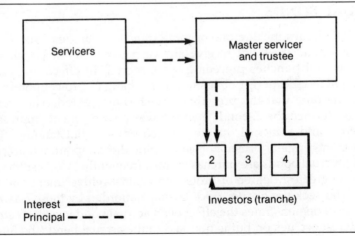

accrual bond need not be the last class, and that some deals had more than one accrual bond tranche.

Settlement of Accrual Bonds

Accrual bonds trade based on price as a percentage of accrued principal amount. A 12 percent accrual bond, for example, has a 6 percent rise in principal amount each semiannual period. The "factor" on this bond begins at 1.0000, rises to 1.0600 in six months and to 1.1236 in one year. The factor continues to rise 6 percent each semiannual period until all previous tranches of bonds are retired and interest on the accrual bond becomes payable.

To determine the market value of an accrual bond on the settlement date of a trade, one must calculate the product of the original face, factor, and dollar price. For example, a one-year old $100,000 original face of a 12 percent accrual bond with a factor of 1.1236 and price of 95 on settlement date has a market value of $106,742 ($100,000 × 1.1236 × .95 = $106,742). Since the factor rises continuously through the accrual period of an accrual bond, there is no need for any additional accrued interest computation.

Most Z-bonds accrue interest over semiannual periods. At the end of the six-month period, on the date of cash payments to other bond-holders, the interest accrued by the Z-bond since the last payment date is transferred to the outstanding principal balance. In the interim between payment dates, the legal principal balance is the amount of principal as of the last payment date. While the legal balance changes only semiannually, the factor associated with the bond for trade settlement purposes changes daily.

The reason for the daily factor system stems from the structure of the Z-bond. In an ordinary fixed income security, accrued interest is valued at par. On a Z-bond, however, accrued interest becomes part of the outstanding principal balance rather than being paid out in cash. Since the outstanding principal amount may trade at a discount or premium to par, the daily factor system was established to take this into account.

Exhibit 6 shows a portion of the factor table for the FHLMC C–4 12.10 percent bond. If a trade was settled on February 15, 1985, for example, the factor was 1.13033041. Hence, the proceeds from $1,000,000 original face at a price of 98 was $1,107,724 ($1,000,000 × 1.13033041 × .98).

When all prior tranches of a CMO offering are retired, the accrual bond begins to receive interest and principal payments. At this point, accrual bonds begin to trade and settle similar to other coupon-paying CMOs. The value at settlement is the product of the price and outstand-

EXHIBIT 6 Accrual Bond CMO Factor Table for FHLMC C–4 12.10 Percent

Date of Settlement	Accrual Factor	Date of Settlement	Accrual Factor	Date of Settlement	Accrual Factor
11/05/84	1.09436235	12/31/84	1.11396687	2/25/85	1.13411052
11/06/84	1.09471880	1/01/85	1.11432332	2/26/85	1.13448853
11/07/84	1.09507525	1/02/85	1.11467977	2/27/85	1.13486654
11/08/84	1.09543169	1/03/85	1.11503621	2/28/85	1.13524455
11/09/84	1.09578814	1/04/85	1.11539266	3/01/85	1.13637858
11/12/84	1.09685747	1/07/85	1.11646200	3/04/85	1.13751262
11/13/84	1.09721392	1/08/85	1.11681844	3/05/85	1.13789063
11/14/84	1.09757037	1/09/85	1.11717489	3/06/85	1.13826864
11/15/84	1.09792681	1/10/85	1.11753133	3/07/85	1.13864665
11/16/84	1.09828326	1/11/85	1.11788778	3/08/85	1.13902466
11/19/84	1.09935260	1/14/85	1.11895712	3/11/85	1.14015869
11/20/84	1.09970904	1/15/85	1.11931356	3/12/85	1.14053670
11/21/84	1.10006549	1/16/85	1.11967001	3/13/85	1.14091471
11/22/84	1.10042193	1/17/85	1.12002645	3/14/85	1.14129273
11/23/84	1.10077838	1/18/85	1.12038290	3/15/85	1.14167074
11/26/84	1.10184772	1/21/85	1.12145224	3/18/85	1.14280477
11/27/84	1.10220416	1/22/85	1.12180868	3/19/85	1.14318278
11/28/84	1.10256061	1/23/85	1.12216513	3/20/85	1.14356079
11/29/84	1.10291705	1/24/85	1.12252157	3/21/85	1.14393880
11/30/84	1.10327350	1/25/85	1.12287802	3/22/85	1.14431681
12/03/84	1.10434284	1/28/85	1.12394736	3/25/85	1.14545084
12/04/84	1.10469928	1/29/85	1.12430380	3/26/85	1.14582886
12/05/84	1.10505573	1/30/85	1.12466025	3/27/85	1.14620687
12/06/84	1.10541217	1/31/85	1.12466025	3/28/85	1.14658488
12/07/84	1.10576862	2/01/85	1.12503826	3/29/85	1.14696289
12/10/84	1.10683796	2/04/85	1.12617229	4/01/85	1.14771891
12/11/84	1.10719440	2/05/85	1.12655030	4/02/85	1.14809692
12/12/84	1.10755085	2/06/85	1.12692831	4/03/85	1.14847493
12/13/84	1.10790730	2/07/85	1.12730633	4/04/85	1.14885294
12/14/84	1.10826374	2/08/85	1.12768434	4/05/85	1.14923095
12/17/84	1.10933308	2/11/85	1.12881837	4/08/85	1.15036498
12/18/84	1.10968952	2/12/85	1.12919638	4/09/85	1.15074300
12/19/84	1.11004597	2/13/85	1.12957439	4/10/85	1.15112101
12/20/84	1.11040242	2/14/85	1.12995240	4/11/85	1.15149902
12/21/84	1.11075886	2/15/85	1.13033041	4/12/85	1.15187703
12/24/84	1.11182820	2/18/85	1.13146444	4/15/85	1.15301106
12/25/84	1.11218465	2/19/85	1.13184246	4/16/85	1.15338907
12/26/84	1.11254109	2/20/85	1.13222047	4/17/85	1.15376708
12/27/84	1.11289754	2/21/85	1.13259848	4/18/85	1.15414509
12/28/84	1.11325398	2/22/85	1.13297649	4/19/85	1.15452310

SOURCE: The First Boston Corporation

ing principal balance. The accrued interest from the latest payment date to the settlement date is added to this product.

EVALUATING CMOs

The objective of most mortgage security analysis is to gain insight and create expectations of the cash flow pattern in various market environments. A three-step process can be employed in applying this type of analysis to CMO securities. The first phase involves examination of the pass-throughs or whole loans that collateralize the offering. The second step is to review the process by which money generated by the collateral flows through to the bondholders in various tranches. The third phase of the analysis involves a determination of the impact of other special features on the expected cash flows to bondholders. Taken together, the three steps in the analysis process seek to make a determination of the likely pace of cash flows to CMO bondholders under various market environments. Generally, greater uncertainty surrounding the timing of cash flows is perceived to represent the risk in a mortgage security. The end result is to evaluate the sufficiency of the yield to compensate the investor for the risks undertaken.

The Underlying Collateral

The following factors should be considered:

1. Average coupon and maturity
2. Range of coupons and maturities
3. Cash flow pattern of mortgages
   a. Level pay
   b. Graduated payment
   c. Other
4. Geographic distribution
5. Due-on-sale provisions
6. Prepayment history if seasoned
7. Amount of collateral relative to amount of bonds

The average and range of coupons and maturities, in combination with the geographic distribution, due-on-sale provisions and prepayment history, are needed to forecast prepayments on the underlying collateral. It is necessary to forecast prepayments under various scenarios because of the impact they have on the amount of cash flow generated by the collateral.

Structure and Seasoning of a CMO

The amount of collateral backing the deal relative to the amount of CMO bonds outstanding is very significant. If a deal becomes over-collateralized, meaning that the amount of collateral exceeds that necessary to make payments to bondholders under any market scenario, the remaining bonds will be paid relatively quickly. If, however, the issuer is empowered to retain excess cash flow generated by the collateral, the bonds would not enjoy as much benefit of expected shortening of average life produced by over-collateralization. A buildup in the amount of collateral relative to the quantity of bonds can be caused by a number of factors. If the reinvestment rate or prepayment rate experience is more favorable than the extremely conservative assumptions employed when constructing the asset pool, then over-collateralization is likely to occur. Another assumption frequently employed is that premium collateral immediately prepays. Hence, if coupon income produced by premium bonds (above that needed to pay interest to CMO bondholders) is used to retire additional bonds, then the remaining principal amount of collateral will be greater than the remaining principal amount of bonds.

The sequential pay feature on CMOs makes the seasoning process even more significant for CMOs than for pass-throughs. As a first tranche is retired, for example, the holders of the second tranche move from no receipt of principal to an environment of rapid principal paydowns. Amortization and prepayments on the underlying collateral and retirements of CMO bond principal have an effect on both the long and short CMO tranches. Faster than anticipated retirement of the first tranche of bonds may shorten the final maturity and expected average life of not only the second tranche but also the longer tranches in the CMO offering. The yield tables, generally revised on the dates of payments to bondholders, reflect the effects of principal retirement and passage of time. Since actual prepayment speeds and expected amortization rates of the underlying collateral change over time, it is critical to use updated yield tables.

Sensitivity to Prepayment Changes

The major risk inherent in a mortgage security is the uncertainty of timing of cash flows. The primary source of uncertainty in a CMO is the prepayment rate on the underlying collateral. In order to determine the likely price sensitivity of a particular CMO to changing prepayments, one must consider several factors.

1. Yield Effect—If the price of a CMO bond differs from par, then the rate of prepayments has an effect on yield. For CMOs trading at a discount, a higher prepayment rate connotes faster retirement of principal and higher yield. A CMO trading at a premium to par suffers a decline in yield if prepayments rise on the underlying collateral.
2. Average Life Effect—Changes in the prepayment rate on the collateral generally impact the average life and final maturity of

a CMO bond. The extent to which this occurs depends upon the structure of the CMO offering.

3. Yield-Spread Effect—Most CMO bonds are quoted in terms of yield spread to the Treasury curve. Changes in the prepayment rate have a dual effect on this relationship. First, the CMO's yield may change if the price differs from par. Second, if the Treasury yield curve has a positive or negative slope, the reference yield on the Treasury curve may change from that originally assumed. A third factor must be considered for in-depth analysis. If prepayment rates rise and a CMO with an original average life assumption of seven years moves to an average life assumption of four years, then the required spread to the Treasury curve may change. Assuming that yield spreads should tighten as the expected average life shortens, this would exert upward pressure on a CMO's price.

4. Special Features—A change in prepayments may trigger a minimum guaranteed sinking fund. To the extent that this fund mitigates the effect of slower prepayments on cash flow to bondholders, it reduces the bond's sensitivity to changing prepayment rates.

The net effect of the factors listed above determines the impact of changing prepayment rates on the price and return of CMOs. An investor must be aware of CMO yield, yield spread to Treasuries, and comparison point on the Treasury yield curve in order to evaluate sensitivity to prepayments. The universe of CMO tranches has vastly differing sensitivities to prepayment rates on underlying collateral. To the extent that this sensitivity causes risk, the investor must be compensated in the form of yield.

The Coupon Rate and Relationship of CMO Price to Par

These factors will determine the current yield and likely impact of increased prepayments on yields and returns. All else equal, a CMO trading at par should have a greater yield spread to Treasuries than a CMO trading at a discount. As in all other fixed income sectors, the incremental call risk in a current coupon relative to a discount coupon requires incremental yield spread to represent fair value. It should be recognized, however, that the speed of retirements will be more dependent on the interest rates of the collateral pool than on the price of the CMO bonds.

Liquidity of CMOs

Exhibit 7 lists the typical bid-ask spreads in terms of points and basis points for a range of CMO securities. Generally, larger size tranches of

EXHIBIT 7 Typical Bid-Ask Spreads

	Bid-Ask Spread	Approximate Basis Points per Spread
Tranche 1 1 to 2-year average life	⅛ of 1 point	10
Tranche 2 3 to 5-year average life	⅛ of 1 point	5
Tranche 3 7 to 10-year average life	¼ of 1 point	5
Tranche 4 10 to 20-year average life	¼ of 1 point	5
Accrual Bond	½ of 1 point	5

frequent CMO issuers have the best liquidity while small tranches of unfamiliar issuers are the least liquid.

EVALUATION OF INVESTOR PROFILE

The most common CMO structure is that of a four-part deal with an accrual bond as the final tranche. Average life expectations of 2-, 5-, 7- and 20-years are commonly associated with the first, second, third, and fourth tranches, respectively. Exhibit 8 presents a breakdown of the investor profile on each tranche.

EXHIBIT 8 Profile of CMO Investors by Tranche*

	Tranche			
	1	2	3	4
Thrifts	37%	17%	6%	3%
Commercial banks	18	12	3	3
Insurance companies	18	37	48	28
Pension funds, bank trust	23	29	40	63
Individuals	2	3	1	2
Other	2	2	2	1
Assumed average life	2 yr	5 yr	7 yr	20 yr

* First Boston estimates

Exhibit 8 shows that thrift institutions, with a large need for short average life products, have purchased 37 percent of first tranche offerings. Commercial banks also purchased a larger share of first tranche bonds than of any other tranche. Insurance companies, pension funds, and bank trust departments own over 40 percent of first tranche bonds. This percentage share, however, is less than their participation in the longer tranches.

Insurance companies dominate ownership of the second and third tranches with 37 percent and 48 percent respective shares of these bonds. Many observers tie insurance companies' interest in the five- and seven-year average life issues with their need to fund intermediate liabilities created by GICs and other products. The participation of thrifts and commercial banks in the intermediate and long tranches is dramatically less than these sectors' ownership of first tranche issues.

Pension fund and bank trust departments are the major buyers of the fourth tranche accrual bonds. These securities provide a higher yield and greater call protection than most other mortgage securities. As such, they are viewed as highly appropriate vehicles by many money managers to fund the retired-lives portion of pension funds.

The fact that the investor profiles among tranches differ greatly underscores the value added of the CMO process. CMOs take long final maturity mortgages and divide the cash flows in a manner that creates short, intermediate and long bonds. Since many of the bonds fit investor objectives that are not suitably filled by pass-throughs, a conclusion is that CMOs have broadened the universe of investors able and willing to buy mortgage securities.

18

The Historical Performance of Mortgage Securities*

Michael Waldman
Director & Manager of Mortgage Research
Salomon Brothers Inc

Steven Guterman
Vice President Mortgage Research
Salomon Brothers Inc

The growth of mortgage pass-through securities in the 1970s, and their acceptance as an investment vehicle by a wide variety of institutional investors led Salomon Brothers Inc to introduce a Total Rate-of-Return Index for these securities in March 1979. This Index allows investors to compare the performance of mortgage pass-throughs with alternative fixed income investments, and the performance of their pass-through portfolios with the "market average" return.

The Index covers periods beginning with January 1, 1972 for GNMA pass-throughs, January 1, 1977 for FHLMC PCs, January 1, 1978 for conventional pass-throughs,[1] July 1, 1979 for FHA-insured project mortgage pools, and January 1, 1982 for FNMA Mortgage-Backed Securities.

---

* The authors would like to express their appreciation to Matthew Kunka for his invaluable assistance in preparing this chapter.

[1] Conventional mortgage pools originated by "private sector" institutions without a government or agency guarantee.

In previous studies,[2] we analyzed the rate-of-return results through June 1980 and June 1981. The period from mid-1981 through 1984 has been one of extraordinary change for the secondary mortgage market:

- The cumulative amount of mortgage pass-through securities issued expanded from $143 billion to $354 billion. Much of this explosive growth resulted from portfolio restructuring at savings and loan associations, following regulatory accounting changes in the industry and the introduction of mortgage "swap" programs by FHLMC and FNMA.
- New types of pass-through securities such as FHLMC Guarantor PCs, FNMA Mortgage-Backed Securities, and intermediate 15-year mortgage pass-throughs were introduced.
- For the first time, massive refinancing of high-coupon mortgages took place and these issues became utilized as short-term investments.
- Deregulation of liabilities created large deposit inflows at thrifts and they returned as buyers of mortgage investments.
- Adjustable-rate mortgages (ARMs) emerged to dominate the primary mortgage market.
- Collateralized mortgage obligations (CMOs) were developed to more efficiently make use of mortgage cash flows.
- The previous three developments combined to lower mortgage origination costs and promoted the strong housing market in 1983–84.
- Rate ceilings on FHA-insured mortgages were removed.
- The yield spreads between mortgage and bond investments underwent wide swings during this period reaching record wide levels in October 1981 as well as record narrow levels in May 1984.

The purpose of this chapter is to extend the rate-of-return results previously discussed through the end of 1984, and to analyze these results for the various market cycles during the 1972–84 period. Comparisons will be made between the Mortgage Index and the Salomon Brothers High-Grade Corporate Bond Index as well as long and 10-year Treasury securities. Finally, some of the relative performance differences within the mortgage pass-through market will be discussed. Some of the key results from this study are as follows:

- Mortgage pass-through investments outperformed high-grade corporate bonds by 43.4 percent from January 1972 to January 1985.

---

[2] Michael Waldman and Steven P. Baum, "The Historical Performance of Mortgage Securities: 1972–1981," Chapter 19 in *The Handbook of Fixed Income Securities,* ed. Frank J. Fabozzi and Irving M. Pollack (Homewood, Ill.: Dow Jones-Irwin, 1983).

- Mortgage pass-throughs outperformed long Treasuries by 70.3 percent from September 1974 to January 1985.
- Mortgage pas-throughs outperformed 10-year Treasuries by 24.1 percent from January 1977 to January 1985.

The return advantage of the mortgage investments resulted from their higher yield and their shorter maturity (versus corporates and long Treasuries) during a period of generally rising rates:

- Within the market, high-coupon mortgage securities trailed lower-coupon issues during market rallies, as the threat of homeowner refinancing limited their price gains, but outperformed them during market declines. This performance contrast became magnified when large-scale refinancing actually occurred in 1983.
- Since 1981, the position of discount FHLMC PCs improved relative to discount GHMAs owing to an increase in the FHLMC investor base and a resumption of faster prepayments.
- FNMA securities improved relative to FHLMC securities as the FNMA MBS program gained acceptance.
- FHA project pools outperformed or matched long Treasuries in seven of eight market cycles owing to a higher yield and a mostly narrowing yield spread.
- GNMA–GPMs trailed single-family GNMAs in total return during the early stages of the GPM market, but have outperformed them since 1981 owing to an improved relative market position.

THE MORTGAGE PASS-THROUGH INDEX

The total return of the Mortgage Index is made up of three components: principal return, interest return, and reinvestment return. Principal return is divided into two parts, a return due to price move and a return resulting from the capture of discount (or premium) from principal paydown, which includes normal amortization and prepayments. Since prepayments on mortgages are statistically uncertain, Salomon Brothers maintains a database of monthly paydowns on all mortgage pass-throughs. Thus, the paydown return over any holding period reflects the actual principal payments on all pools covered by the Index. Reinvestment is "back into the market"; that is, each month's payment of principal and interest is reinvested in the pass-through market in amounts weighed by the overall composition of the market that month.

The composition of the Index is shown in Exhibit 1. The Index currently covers about 93,000 pools, representing approximately $312 billion in issued amount. This encompasses about 86 percent of the total of all outstanding mortgage pass-through pools—the difference arises in large part because the Index does not cover "odd coupon" pass-throughs for which there are no regularly available price quotes, non-single-family pass-throughs other than FHA-insured project mortgage

EXHIBIT 1   Composition of Salomon Brothers Inc Mortgage Pass-Through Index (amount issued, dollars in billions)

January 1	GNMA	FHLMC	Conven-tional	FHA Projects	FNMA	Total
1972	$ 2.4					$ 2.4
1973	3.8					3.8
1974	5.8					5.8
1975	9.1					9.1
1976	16.7					16.7
1977	27.2	$ 0.6				27.8
1978	46.6	5.5	$0.2			52.3
1979	59.6	11.1	0.8			71.5
1980	69.3	15.0	1.2	$0.2		85.7
1981	98.8	17.2	1.4	0.4		117.8
1982	115.3	19.5	1.4	0.9	$ 0.5	137.6
1983	131.5	44.6	1.4	1.5	11.1	190.1
1984	173.6	63.7	1.4	2.1	24.3	265.1
1985	195.0	79.6	1.4	2.1	33.8	311.9

pools, 15-year intermediate mortgages, adjustable-rate mortgages, or "private sector" pass-throughs for which paydown factors and prices are not readily available.

The Index covers GNMAs from the beginning of calendar year 1972. Since paydown figures for GNMAs were not available until March 1972, it was assumed that the paydowns for January and February of that year were at the same rate as in March. With this exception, the Mortgage Index is based entirely on historical paydowns, prices, and market compositions. The yearly total returns for the five major mortgage security categories are summarized in Exhibit 2.

EXHIBIT 2   Annual Total Returns

Year	GNMA	FHLMC	Conven-tional	FHA Projects	FNMA	Mortgage Index
1972	6.1%					6.1%
1973	2.6					2.6
1974	3.9					3.9
1975	10.4					10.4
1976	16.3					16.3
1977	1.5	2.9%				1.6
1978	2.2	4.0	1.9%			2.4
1979	0.2	0.1	0.2			0.1
1980	0.4	0.6	0.0	−1.1%		0.5
1981	1.5	−1.0	0.2	−0.4		1.2
1982	40.1	46.4	41.6	49.0	45.6%	41.4
1983	10.0	12.6	13.9	4.9	13.3	10.9
1984	15.2	17.1	19.9	17.6	16.5	15.8

ANALYSIS OF THE RESULTS

A natural starting point for comparisons with the Mortgage Index is the Salomon Brothers High-Grade Corporate Bond Index, an index similar to the Mortgage Index, covering long-term AAA and AA utility and industrial bonds. For the period from January 1972 to January 1985, the Mortgage Index shows a net advantage in total return of 43.4 percent over the High-Grade Corporate Bond Index (see Exhibits 3 and 4). Al-

EXHIBIT 3 Historical Returns over Calendar Years: High-Grade Corporate Bonds versus Mortgage Securities

	High-Grade Corporate Bond Index	Mortgage Pass-Through Index	Advantage of Mortgage Index
1972	7.3%	6.1%	−1.2%
1973	1.1	2.6	1.5
1974	−3.0	3.9	6.9
1975	14.6	10.4	−4.2
1976	18.6	16.3	−2.3
1977	1.7	1.6	−0.1
1978	−0.1	2.4	2.5
1979	−4.2	0.1	4.3
1980	−2.6	0.5	3.1
1981	−1.0	1.2	2.2
1982	43.7	41.4	−2.3
1983	4.7	10.9	6.2
1984	16.4	15.8	−0.6
13.0-Year Period	135.3%	178.7%	43.4%

most all of this advantage was accrued during market decline periods (1973–74, 1978–81, and 1983). On the other hand, the Bond Index significantly outperformed the Mortgage Index during market rallies (1975–76 and 1982). For 1984, both the Mortgage Index and Bond Index performed similarly, with the Bond Index slightly ahead by 0.6 percent.

An interesting sidelight to these statistics is that in contrast with the Corporate Bond Index, which produced negative rates-of-return for 5 of the 13 years shown, the Mortgage Index provided at least a slim positive return in every calendar year from 1972 to 1984.

That the Mortgage Index should enjoy an overall advantage during this period is not surprising; the Bond Index represents an average maturity of approximately 23 years, while as a general rule, mortgages are intermediate investments—most mortgage pass-throughs are traded to a 12-year prepaid life. Thus, one would expect the shorter Mortgage

EXHIBIT 4 Rate-of-Return by Calendar Year

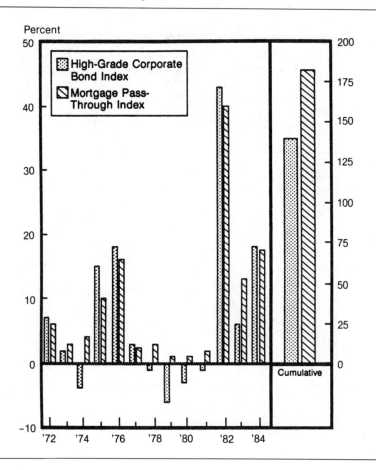

Index to do better during the significant upward trend in interest rates of the past thirteen years. Exhibit 5 shows the cumulative value of the two Indexes (January 1, 1972 = 100). One can clearly see the Mortgage Index gaining its advantage during the market declines that occurred during 1972–74, 1975, 1977–80, 1980–81, and finally 1983–84. The market rallies subsequent to each of these declines were able to partially offset, but not reverse, these advantages.

The performance characteristics of mortgage pass-throughs relative to other fixed-income investments become more apparent when one breaks the period under consideration into market cycles. Exhibit 6 gives the rates-of-return for long Treasury and 10-year Treasury securities, as

EXHIBIT 5   Comparative Rate-of-Return Indexes

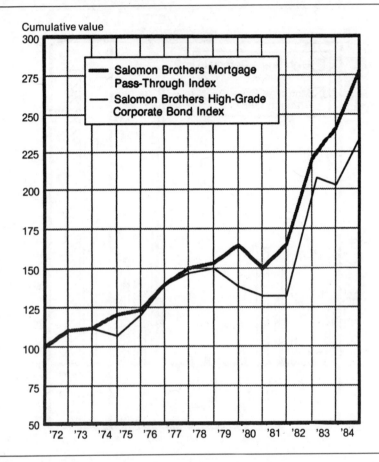

Cumulative value

Legend:
— Salomon Brothers Mortgage Pass-Through Index
— Salomon Brothers High-Grade Corporate Bond Index

well as for the Mortgage and Corporate Bond Indexes, for 12 market cycles.[3] Each phase represents a period from a peak or trough in interest rates to the subsequent extreme point.

Comparison versus Treasury Market

Let us focus now on the comparison between mortgage pass-throughs and long Treasury securities (see Exhibits 7, 8 and 9). Over the 10.3-year

---

[3] Long Treasuries are analyzed beginning with the rally period starting in September 1974, shortly after the issuance of the Treasury 8½s of May 15, 1999. The analysis of 10-year Treasuries starts with the cycle beginning in January 1977, about half a year after the 7⅞ percent notes of May 15, 1986, were issued.

EXHIBIT 6 Historical Returns over Market Cycles

Period Ending First of Month	Market Cycle	Months in Cycle	Total Return			
			Corporate Bond Index	Long Treasuries	10-Year Treasuries	Mortgage Index
Jan 72						
Sep 74	decline	32	−5.4%			−0.1%
Mar 75	rally	6	19.4	14.2%		18.8
Oct 75	decline	7	−2.3	−3.2		−2.6
Jan 77	rally	15	29.6	26.6		25.5
Apr 80	decline	39	−15.8	−18.5	−8.9%	−6.5
Jul 80	rally	3	25.1	24.8	19.0	22.1
Oct 81	decline	15	−21.1	−22.3	−14.8	−19.2
Dec 81	rally	2	19.9	18.3	15.8	21.6
Jul 82	decline	7	−0.0	1.7	2.2	2.7
May 83	rally	10	48.5	41.9	37.2	39.7
Jun 84	decline	13	−10.9	−12.2	−7.8	−2.1
Jan 85	rally	7	24.8	25.6	21.5	21.8
Cumulative Results						
Jan 72–Jan 85			135.3%			178.7%
Sep 74–Jan 85			148.7	108.6%		178.9
			64.4	49.0	68.0%	92.1

period from September 1974 to January 1985, the mortgage pass-throughs provided a substantial net 70.3 percent greater total return. Again, the mortgage securities were ahead in all the market decline cycles, as would be expected given their shorter average maturity. However, the pass-throughs also outperformed the long Treasuries in the 1974–75 rally by a considerable 4.6 percent and during the fall 1981 rally by 3.3 percent. How is this explained?

The answer is that there are two key factors that influence the relative performance of these securities other than their maturity differences. First, mortgage pass-throughs enjoyed a yield advantage over long Treasuries throughout this period on the basis of the monthly-compounded quoted yield, which assumes a 30-year maturity and a 12-year prepaid life. By stating the quoted yield on a semiannually compounded basis, this advantage is even greater.[4] Furthermore, the actual prepayments on mortgage securities were often faster than those needed to produce the quoted yield, thereby widening the yield advantage for pass-throughs trading at a discount.

Second, the changing relationship of the yield spread between these two instruments greatly influenced the return of pass-throughs vis-à-vis long Treasuries. This largely accounted for the surprisingly strong showing of the Mortgage Index during the September 1974–March 1975 rally. For this period, the yield spreads between pass-throughs, as rep-

---

[4] All the yields for mortgage securities shown in the figures, such as those for current coupon GNMAs in Exhibits 7 and 9, will be bond equivalent quoted yields.

EXHIBIT 7 Historical Returns and Spreads over Market Cycles: Long Treasuries versus Mortgage Securities

Period Ending First of Month	Market Cycle	Months in Cycle	Total Return			Yield Spread Relationship			
			Long Treasuries	Mortgage Index	Advantage of Mortgage Index	Long Treasuries Yield	Current Coupon GNMAs	Current Coupon GNMAs Yield*	Basis-Point Spread off Long Treasuries
Sep 74	rally	6	14.2%	18.8%	4.6%	8.70%	9.0%	10.14%	144bp
Mar 75	decline	7	-3.2	-2.6	0.6	7.83	8.0	8.34	51
Oct 75	rally	15	26.6	25.5	-1.1	8.55	8.5	9.41	86
Jan 77	decline	39	-18.5	-6.5	12.0	7.30	7.5	7.53	23
Apr 80	rally	3	24.8	22.1	-2.7	12.27	12.5	14.26	199
Jul 80	decline	15	-22.3	-19.2	3.1	9.94	11.0	11.55	161
Oct 81	rally	2	18.3	21.6	3.3	15.20	17.0	18.53	333
Dec 81	decline	7	1.7	2.7	1.0	13.03	15.0	15.19	216
Jul 82	rally	10	41.9	39.7	-2.2	13.84	15.0	16.38	254
May 83	decline	13	-12.2	-2.1	10.1	10.50	11.5	11.85	135
Jun 84	rally	7	25.6	21.8	-3.8	13.71	13.5	14.80	109
Jan 85						11.58	12.0	12.58	100
10.3-Year Period			108.6%	178.9%	70.3%				

* Bond equivalent yield to 12-year prepaid life.

EXHIBIT 8   Historical Returns over Market Cycles: Long Treasuries versus
Mortgage Securities

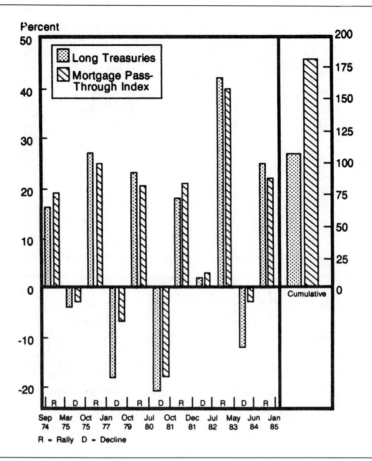

resented by GNMA current coupon securities, and the Treasuries narrowed by 93 basis points (from 144 basis points to 51 basis points). This
narrowing combined with the pass-throughs' yield advantage more
than overcame the greater price volatility of the longer Treasuries in the
rally, and allowed the Mortgage Index to outperform the long Treasuries
by 4.6 percent.

The long bear market from January 1977 through March 1980, with
long Treasury rates rising almost 500 basis points, saw the more defensive mortgage instruments outperform long Treasuries by a cumulative
12.0 percent. For the dramatic market rally in the second quarter of
1980—long Treasury rates fell more than 200 basis points—long Treasuries provided 2.7 percent greater returns.

EXHIBIT 9   Historical Yield Levels: Long Treasuries versus Current
Coupon GNMAs

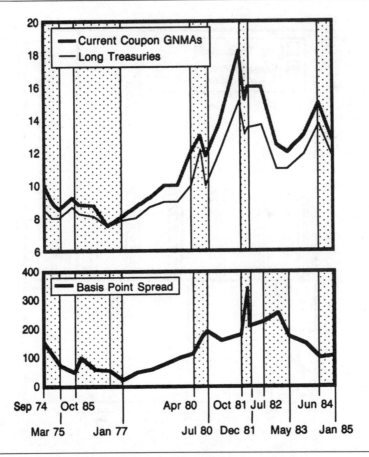

Note: Shaded areas indicate market rally periods.

In July 1980, the market resumed its fall and in October 1981, long
Treasury rates reached their highest levels ever at about 15¼ percent. At
the same time, the yield spreads of GNMAs to long Treasuries widened
to an unprecedented level of more than 300 basis points. Contributing
factors were: an inverted yield curve expanded the spreads of all intermediate investments to long Treasuries; high interest rates and the resulting disintermediation removed thrift institutions as purchasers of
mortgage securities; mortgage prepayment rates declined to an extremely slow 1 percent pace in a severely depressed housing market,
reducing the attractiveness of discount mortgage securities; and a fear

existed that credit problems might lead to large-scale selling of mortgages from the portfolios of failed institutions.

This widening in yield spreads provided the basis for the Mortgage Index to outperform long Treasuries by 3.3 percent in the fall 1981 rally. The yield spread of GNMAs to long Treasuries narrowed by 117 basis points as the Treasury yield curve flattened and lower rates provided a more favorable environment for prepayments. This process repeated in several ways the developments that took place during the September 1974–March 1975 and spring 1980 market rallies.

For the December 1981–June 1982 period, long Treasury rates rose moderately by 81 basis points and mortgages outperformed long Treasuries by 1 percent. Market rates then began to decline in July 1982 and rallied dramatically in August–September. By May 1983, long Treasury rates fell to a cyclical low of near 10¼ percent. For this 10-month period, returns of fixed income investments exploded, reaching levels of 40 percent or more. While the long Treasury return exceeded (by 2.2 percent) that of the Mortgage Index overall, the yield spreads of mortgages to Treasuries narrowed dramatically and many discount mortgage issues outperformed long Treasury bonds.

From May 1983 to June 1984, long Treasury rates rose more than 200 basis points. However, unlike previous market declines, spreads between mortgage securities and long Treasuries tightened considerably. This can be explained by a number of developments that occurred in the housing and mortgage markets. First, the introduction of collateralized mortgage obligations (CMOs) in June 1983 created both a demand for mortgage securities and a direct arbitrage link between mortgage yields and Treasury yields. Second, the deregulation of deposit accounts led to large savings inflows as savings institutions and thrifts reentered the market as purchasers of mortgage securities. Third, adjustable-rate mortgages (ARMs) with low initial rates were aggressively marketed by lenders and became the primary vehicle for housing finance. With ARMs replacing fixed-rate mortgages, the supply of new fixed-rate product was greatly reduced.

Despite the general rise in market interest rates, the average cost of financing a home purchase actually trended downward, because of the tighter spreads between fixed-rate mortgages and Treasuries and the prevalence of low initial rate ARMs. This maintained affordability in the housing market and fostered strong housing activity. As a consequence, mortgage prepayment rates rose, further enhancing the value of discount mortgage securities.

For this period, the Mortgage Index outperformed long Treasuries by a sizable 10.1 percent, because of the shorter maturity of mortgages under rising interest rates and the tightening of spreads.

Some of this advantage was relinquished when the market rallied during the period since June 1984, and—counter to the traditional pat-

EXHIBIT 10 Historical Returns and Spreads over Market Cycles: 10-Year Treasuries versus Mortgage Securities

Period Ending First of Month	Market Cycle	Months in Cycle	Total Return			Yield Spread Relationship			
			10-Year Treasuries	Mortgage Index	Advantage of Mortgage Index	10-Year Treasuries Yield	Current Coupon GNMAs	Current Coupon GNMAs Yield*	Basis-Point Spread off 10-Year Treasuries
Jan 77						6.79%	7.5%	7.53%	74bp
Apr 80	decline	39	−8.9%	−6.5%	2.4%	12.60	12.5	14.26	166
Jul 80	rally	3	19.0	22.1	3.1	9.98	11.0	11.55	157
Oct 81	decline	15	−14.8	−19.2	−4.4	15.76	17.0	18.53	277
Dec 81	rally	2	15.8	21.6	5.8	13.27	15.0	15.19	192
Jul 82	decline	7	2.2	2.7	0.5	14.32	15.0	16.38	206
May 83	rally	10	37.2	39.7	2.5	10.18	11.5	11.85	167
Jun 84	decline	13	−7.8	−2.1	5.7	13.78	13.5	14.80	102
Jan 85	rally	7	21.5	21.8	0.3	11.45	12.0	12.58	113
8-Year Period			68.0%	92.1%	24.1%				

* Bond equivalent yield to 12-year prepaid life.

tern—yield spreads widened. For the latest seven-month period, long Treasuries returned 25.6 percent versus 21.8 percent for the Mortgage Index.

Comparison versus 10-Year Treasuries

Turning our attention to the 10-year Treasuries, we see that for the market decline from January 1977 through April 1980, the Mortgage Index had a net return advantage of 2.4 percent (see Exhibits 10, 11, and 12). The sizable yield advantage of the mortgage securities overcame the widening of spreads between the mortgage investments and 10-year

---

EXHIBIT 11 Historical Returns over Market Cycles: 10-Year Treasuries versus Mortgage Securities

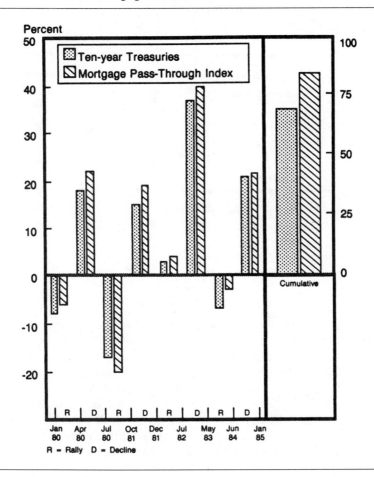

EXHIBIT 12 Historical Yield Levels: 10-Year Treasuries versus Current
Coupon GNMAs

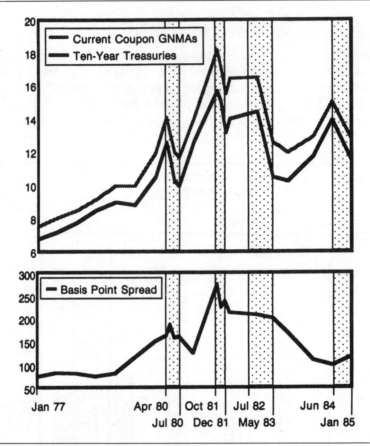

Note: Shaded areas indicate market rally periods.

Treasuries and provided the pass-throughs with a higher total return.
The April–July 1980 rally saw the mortgages maintain their return advantage over the 10-year Treasuries, 22.1 percent to 19 percent.

In the July 1980–October 1981 decline, widening yield spreads resulted in a return for Treasuries (−14.8 percent) that was 4.4 percent higher than that of the Mortgage Index (−19.2 percent). The spread between the GNMA current coupon and the 10-year Treasuries expanded from 157 to 277 basis points during this period. This was the only market cycle in which 10-year Treasuries outperformed the Mortgage Index.

Mortgage security yields improved relative to 10-year Treasuries during the October–December 1981 rally—the GNMA current coupon-to-10-year Treasury yield spread narrowed from 277 basis points to 192 basis points. This improvement and the mortgage pass-throughs' higher yield combined to produce a 5.8 percent greater return for the Mortgage Index.

The pass-throughs maintained a return advantage through the December 1981–July 1982 and July 1982–May 1983 cycles, by 0.5 percent and 2.5 percent, respectively. During the subsequent market decline of May 1983–June 1984, the Mortgage Index outpaced the 10-year Treasuries by a sizable 5.8 percent. Much of this return advantage was a result of spreads between pass-throughs and 10-year Treasuries sharply tightening by 65 basis points.

For the most recent seven-month period since June 1984, mortgage investments returned 21.8 percent versus 21.5 percent for 10-year Treasuries. Overall, the Mortgage Index provided a 24.1 percent cumulative return advantage for the eight-year period from January 1977 to January 1985, with a return of 92.1 percent versus 68.0 percent for the 10-year Treasuries.

PERFORMANCE WITHIN THE MORTGAGE SECURITIES MARKET

The above discussion compared the overall mortgage market returns to those of other investments. However, there have been significant relative performance differences within the market. Exhibit 13 outlines the performance record by market cycle for the five mortgage security categories (GNMAs, FHLMCs, conventional pass-throughs, FHA project pools, and FNMAs) and for selected coupon sectors. Particular comparisons over various periods are highlighted below.

GNMA 7½s versus 9s: January 1976–April 1980

As GNMA 9s traded at premium prices in the 1976 rally, they became less attractive to many investors because of the potential losses on prepayments. As a result, prices on 9s rose less than those on the discount GNMAs and the 9s underperformed the 7½s by 3.4 percent in total return. However, the 9s were a more defensive vehicle during the next January 1977–April 1980 market decline, with a return advantage of 1 percent compared with the 7½s (see Exhibit 14).

GNMA 11½s versus GNMA 15s: October 1981–January 1985

The pattern of high-coupon mortgages outperforming lower-coupon issues during market declines and underperforming them during market

EXHIBIT 13 Historical Returns for Selected Issues

Issue	Jan 72–Sept 74 Decline	Sep 74–Mar 74 Rally	Mar 75–Oct 75 Decline	Oct 75–Jan 77 Rally	Jan 77–Apr 80 Decline	Apr 80–Jul 80 Rally	Jul 80–Oct 81 Decline	Oct 81–Dec 81 Rally	Dec 81–Jul 82 Decline	Jul 82–May 83 Rally	May 83–Jun 84 Decline	Jun 84–Jan 85 Rally
High-grade corporate bonds	-5.4%	19.4%	-2.3%	29.6%	-15.8%	25.1%	-21.1%	19.9%	0.0%	48.5%	-10.9%	24.8%
Long Treasuries		14.2	-3.2	26.6	-18.5	24.8	-22.3	18.3	1.7	41.9	-12.2	25.6
10-year Treasuries					-8.9	19.0	-14.8	15.8	2.2	37.2	-7.8	21.5
Mortgage index	-0.1	18.8	-2.6	25.5	-6.5	22.1	-19.2	21.6	2.7	39.7	-2.1	21.8
GNMA	-0.1	18.8	-2.6	25.5	-6.8	22.3	-19.0	21.5	2.5	38.5	-3.2	22.1
FHLMC					-2.9	20.7	-20.4	22.4	3.9	42.5	0.1	21.7
FNMA										44.2	1.0	20.5
Conventional						23.2	-20.5	21.8	2.6	46.1	0.5	21.4
Discount												
FHA project	0.7	18.3	-2.5	25.3	-6.6	24.1	-21.8	23.4	3.2	48.0	-9.6	25.6
GNMA 8					-3.8	23.7	-20.9	20.5	2.5	41.7	-7.4	24.2
FHLMC 8						22.3	-23.1	24.0	3.2	45.7	-0.8	23.0
FNMA 8½										46.0	-0.5	21.9
GNMA 9			-0.2	21.5	-7.1	21.9	-19.6	21.6	2.9	42.0	-7.4	24.5
GNMA-GPM 9½						24.0	-21.1	21.4	4.2	45.4	-7.0	23.9
Intermediate-Coupon												
GNMA 11½						19.5	-15.5	22.6	1.7	39.7	-2.7	22.1
FHLMC 12						16.3	-15.9	21.3	4.7	41.5	-0.4	21.6
GNMA 13								22.0	1.6	35.8	1.3	19.4
High-Coupon												
GNMA 15								20.0	3.1	26.3	7.9	15.6
FHLMC 15½								17.4	6.8	22.0	12.9	13.4
FHLMC 16¼								16.7	6.1	17.7	14.9	13.2

EXHIBIT 14   GNMA 7½s versus GNMA 9s: January 1976–April 1980

Period Ending First of Month	Market Cycle	Months in Cycle	Total Return			Yield Spread Relationship		
			GNMA 7½s	GNMA 9s	Advantage of 7½s	GNMA 7½s Yield*	GNMA 9s Yield*	Basis Point Spread
Jan 76						8.66%	8.73%	7bp
Jan 77	rally	12	17.9%	14.5%	3.4%	7.52	7.99	47
Apr 80	decline	39	−8.1	−7.1	−1.0	13.40	13.78	38
4.3-Year Period			8.3%	6.4%	1.9%			

* Bond equivalent yield to 12-year prepaid life.

rallies was repeated during later market cycles. This can be illustrated by comparing the performance of GNMA 11½s with GNMA 15s. For the October–December 1981 rally, the 11½s had a return advantage of 2.6 percent, and for the December 1981–July 1982 decline, the 15s had a return advantage of 1.4 percent (see Exhibit 15).

EXHIBIT 15   GNMA 11½s versus GNMA 15s: October 1981–January 1985

Period Ending First of Month	Market Cycle	Months in Cycle	Total Return			Yield Spread Relationship		
			GNMA 11½s	GNMA 15s	Advantage of 11½s	GNMA 11½s Yield*	GNMA 15s Yield*	Basis Point Spread
Oct 81						18.04%	18.33%	29bp
Dec 81	rally	2	22.6%	20.0%	2.6%	14.62	15.19	57
Jul 82	decline	7	1.7	3.1	−1.4	15.92	16.38	46
May 83	rally	10	39.7	26.3	13.4	11.85	14.00	215
Jun 84	decline	13	−2.7	7.9	−10.6	14.68	15.09	41
Jan 85	rally	7	22.1	15.6	6.5	12.51	13.84	133
3.3-Year Period			106.9%	94.9%	12.0%			

* Bond equivalent yield to 12-year prepaid life.

During the next two market cycles, there were enormous swings in the relative total returns of these two issues. From July 1982 to May 1983, market rates fell 400 basis points and GNMA 11½s returned an impressive 39.7 percent. In this environment, many homeowners refinanced their high-rate mortgages—prepayment rates on GNMA 15s rose to a 37 percent annual rate in early 1983—and the price gains of the 15s stalled out in the rally. For the period, GNMA 15s returned only 26.3 percent— 13.4 percent less than for the 11½s.

On the other hand, for the May 1983–June 1984 market decline, the 15s—now used as a short-term investment alternative—maintained their price level to a much greater extent than lower-coupon issues. The 15s provided a positive 7.9 percent return compared with a negative 2.7 percent for the 11½s—an advantage of 10.6 percent.

GNMA 8s versus FHLMC 8s: January 1977–January 1985

A dealer group was established to distribute and trade FHLMC PCs in January 1977. FHLMC PCs are primarily backed by conventional loans which often exhibit faster prepayment rates than the FHA/VA mortgages underlying GNMA pools. In the initial stages of trading the yield spread between FHLMC 8s and GNMA 8s was a positive 15–30 basis points. As investors recognized the value of the faster FHLMC paydowns, prices were bid up and the FHLMC discounts started trading through the GNMAs. Also contributing to the strong performance of FHLMCs during this period was an expansion in the FHLMC investor base as nontraditional investors became familiar with the security. For the January 1977–April 1980 market cycle, FHLMC 8s provided a return advantage of 2.8 percent relative to GNMA 8s (see Exhibits 16, 17, and 18).

EXHIBIT 16   GNMA 8s versus FHLMC 8s: January 1977–January 1985

Period Ending First of Month	Market Cycle	Months in Cycle	Total Return		Advantage of FHLMCs	Yield Spread Relationship		Basis Point Spread
			GNMA 8s	FHLMC 8s		GNMA 8s Yield*	FHLMC 8s Yield*	
Jan 77						7.71%	8.05%	34bp
Apr 80	decline	39	−6.6%	−3.8%	2.8%	13.39	13.39	0
Jul 80	rally	3	23.7	22.3	1.4	10.45	10.67	22
Oct 81	decline	15	−20.9	−23.1	2.2	17.11	18.04	93
Dec 81	rally	2 .	20.5	24.0	3.5	14.21	14.63	42
Jul 82	decline	7	2.5	3.2	0.7	15.16	15.58	42
May 83	rally	10	41.7	45.7	4.0	11.01	11.11	10
Jun 84	decline	13	−7.4	−0.8	6.6	14.40	13.48	−92
Jan 85	rally	7	24.2	23.0	−1.2	12.05	11.44	−61
8 Year Period			84.0%	105.8%	21.8%			

* Bond equivalent yield to 12-year prepaid life.

The yield spread between FHLMCs and GNMAs then turned positive and widened during the July 1980–October 1981 market decline, peaking at close to 100 basis points when the market hit bottom in October 1981. This resulted from FHLMC prepayment rates drastically slowing to the 1 percent level in the severely depressed housing market and from investors' flight to quality as rates rose to historically high levels. From April 1980 to October 1981, GNMA 8s outperformed FHLMC 8s by a cumulative 3.8 percent.

Beginning with the October–December 1981 rally, the yield spread narrowed once again. The strong 1983 housing market brought an increase in mortgage prepayment rates with FHLMC prepayments faster than those of GNMAs. In addition, legislative/judicial and FHLMC policy actions made mortgage due-on-sale clauses generally enforceable for

EXHIBIT 17   Historical Yield Levels: GNMA 8s versus FHLMC 8s

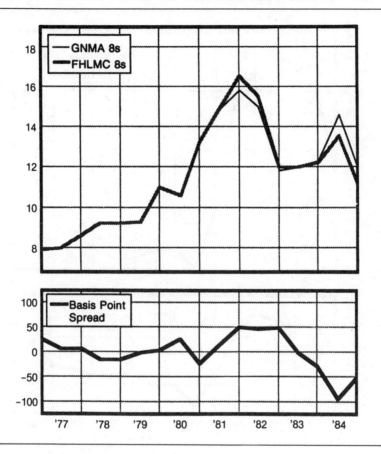

the conventional loans backing FHLMC pools while FHA/VA mortgages remained assumable.

The relative position of discount FHLMCs improved further in 1984, with the yield spread between FHLMC 8s and GNMA 8s turning strongly negative at 60–90 basis points. From October 1981 to January 1985, FHLMC 8s outperformed GNMA 8s by a staggering 26.2 percent, owing to faster prepayments and the realignment of relative market levels.

FNMAs versus FHLMCs: July 1982–January 1985

During the second half of 1981, two new mortgage pass-through programs were introduced—the FHLMC Guarantor PC and the FNMA

EXHIBIT 18 Historical Prepayment Rates: GNMA 8s versus FHLMC 8s

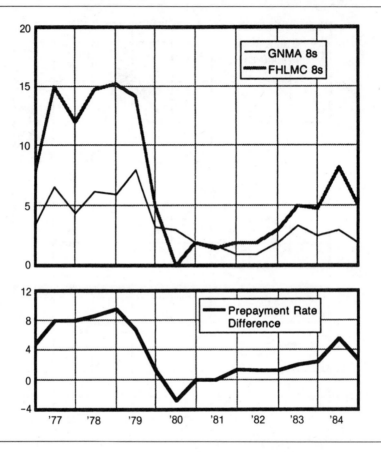

Mortgage-Backed Security. In both programs, pools of mortgages are exchanged for pass-through securities, with FHLMC and FNMA playing the role of guarantor. Most of the pass-throughs are backed by seasoned discount conventional mortgages. The prepayment experience on pools created under these programs has been faster than for GNMA pools and, until the most recent year, than for FHLMC regular pools.

In early 1982, FNMA securities were priced about ⅛-point below comparable coupon FHLMCs (as represented by the 8½ percent coupon securities, see Exhibits 19 and 20). During this period there was some concern about FNMA's credit as FNMA suffered losses in a high interest-rate environment. The credit concerns dissipated when rates fell in the second half of 1982, prompting FNMA MBS prices to rise to the same level as FHLMCs. In 1983, as the market continued to mature, FNMA

EXHIBIT 19   FHLMC 8½s versus FNMA 8½s: July 1982–January 1985

			Total Return			Price Spread Relationship*		
Period Ending First of Month	Market Cycle	Months in Cycle	FHLMC 8½s	FNMA 8½s	Advantage of FNMAs	FHLMC 8½s Price	FNMA 8½s Price	Price Spread
Jul 82						63–08	63–04	−0–04
May 83	rally	10	44.9%	46.0%	1.1%	82–24	82–24	0–00
Jun 84	decline	13	−0.3	0.5	0.8	71–16	71–28	0–12
Jan 85	rally	7	22.2	21.9	−0.3	80–24	80–28	0–04
2.5-Year Period			76.5%	78.9%	2.4%			

* Prices in 32nds.

EXHIBIT 20   Historical Prices: FHLMC 8½s versus FNMA 8½s

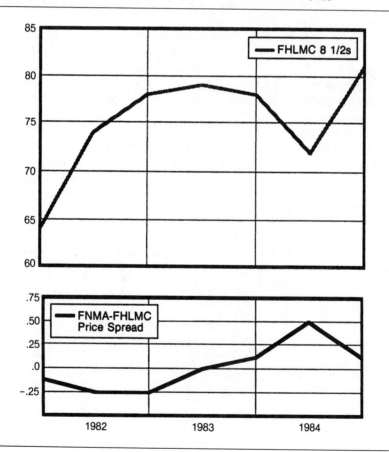

MBSs started trading at a premium in price to FHLMC PCs in recognition of the value of the shorter FNMA delay (54 days to first payment for FNMAs versus 75 days for FHLMCs).

FHA Projects versus Long Treasuries: October 1979–January 1985

GNMA first started auctioning FHA-insured project mortgages originated under the "Tandem program" in 1978. Since then FHA project loans have developed into an actively traded market. The majority of these loans are 7½ percent 40-year mortgages, which trade with an 18-year prepaid life convention. In addition, most of these loans have Section 8 Housing Assistance Payments (HAP) contracts attached. These rent subsidy contracts are either for 5 or 20 years with HUD providing for partial payment of the building tenant's rent.

FHA projects have the distinction among standard mortgage products of having the longest maturity, and unlike other mortgage securities, which trade relative to a 10-year Treasury benchmark, yields are typically compared with long Treasury rates. FHA projects have been used as long-bond substitutes by total return investors and for dedicated and immunized bond portfolios, which have a need for long-term, call-protected investments. Because of a higher yield and a narrowing yield spread, FHA projects have been able to outperform or match long Treasuries in all market cycles since October 1979, with the exception of the April–July 1980 rally. For the overall 5.3-year October 1979–January 1985 period, the projects provided a cumulative return advantage of 26.2 percent (see Exhibits 21 and 22).

EXHIBIT 21 Long Treasuries versus FHA Projects: October 1979–January 1985

			Total Return			Yield Spread Relationship		
Period Ending First of Month	Market Cycle	Months in Cycle	Long Treasuries	FHA Projects	Advantage of FHA Projects	Long Treasuries Yield	FHA Projects*	Basis-Point Spread off Long Treasuries
Oct 79						9.23%	10.75%	152bp
Apr 80	decline	6	−19.3%	−16.4%	2.9%	12.27	14.01	174
Jul 80	rally	3	24.8	24.1	−0.7	9.94	11.38	144
Oct 81	decline	15	−22.3	−21.8	0.5	15.20	17.71	251
Dec 81	rally	2	18.3	23.4	5.1	13.03	14.71	168
Jul 82	decline	7	1.7	3.2	1.5	13.84	15.67	183
May 83	rally	10	41.9	48.0	6.1	10.50	11.33	83
Jun 84	decline	13	−12.2	−9.6	2.6	13.71	14.52	81
Jan 85	rally	7	25.6	25.6	0.0	11.58	12.20	62
5.3-Year Period			47.4%	73.6%	26.2%			

* Bond equivalent yield to 18-year prepaid life.

EXHIBIT 22 Historical Yield Levels: Long Treasuries versus FHA Projects

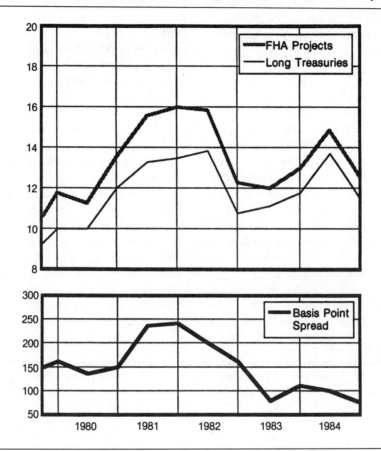

GNMA–GPMs versus Single-Family GNMAs: October 1979–January 1985

HUD first started insuring Graduated Payment Mortgages (GPMs) in 1976. However, it was not until 1979 when they became eligible for GNMA pools, that their volume became significant. To date, $16 billion of GNMA–GPMs have been issued. The majority of these mortgages have 30-year maturities, with annual payment increases of 7½ percent for the first five years and level payments thereafter. The loans have negative amortization for the first few years since the initial GPM payments are not sufficient to cover the interest due. As a result, in the absence of prepayments, a GNMA–GPM will have a slightly longer average life than a single-family GNMA of the same coupon.

GPM prepayments during their early years have been slower than for the corresponding single-family GNMAs. However, the prepayment experience suggests that the prepayment rates of GPMs tend to rise gradually to levels close to those of single-family GNMAs as they approach the end of their five-year graduation period. This trend will bear watching for the next few years as more GPM pools pass over the five-year mark.

In the early stages of the GPM market, GPMs traded 1–2 points below the price of the corresponding GNMA coupon issue. However, the volume and liquidity of GNMA–GPMs were disappointing and during 1980–81, pricing spreads expanded to 3–4 points.

During this period many mortgage market participants focused on the quoted yield based on a 30-year maturity and 12-year prepaid life. This yield calculation assumes a 30-year maturity regardless of the seasoning of the mortgages.[5] The resulting distortion was a minor problem for most GNMA issues in the early 1980s. However, seasoning has a major impact for GNMA–GPMs because of their graduated payment structure. For example, the price of a new 30-year 9½ percent GNMA–GPM would have to be 1¾ points below the price of the comparable single-family GNMA to obtain the same 15 percent bond equivalent

---

EXHIBIT 23 GNMA–SF 9½s versus GNMA–GPM 9½s: October 1979–January 1985

			Total Return			Price Spread Relationship*		
		Months	GNMA–	GNMA–	Advantage	SF	GPM	
Period Ending	Market	in	SF	GPM	of GNMA–	9½s	9½s	Price
First of Month	Cycle	Cycle	9½s	9½s	GPMs	Price	Price	Spread
Oct 79						92–12	91–20	–0–24
Apr 80	decline	6	–11.9%	–15.5%	–3.6%	76–12	72–28	–3–16
Jul 80	rally	3	21.7	24.0	2.3	90–16	88–00	–2–16
Oct 81	decline	15	–18.8	–21.2	–2.3	62–00	59–00	–3–00
Dec 81	rally	2	21.2	21.4	0.2	73–12	70–00	–3–12
Jul 82	decline	7	2.8	4.2	1.4	69–12	67–08	–2–04
May 83	rally	10	42.5	45.4	2.9	89–20	88–24	–0–28
Jun 84	decline	13	–7.1	–7.0	0.1	72–28	72–12	–0–16
Jan 85	rally	7	24.2	23.9	–0.3	84–00	83–12	–0–20
5.3-Year Period			78.3%	75.2%	–3.1%			

* Prices in 32nds.

---

[5] The quoted yield contains inaccuracies with respect to the assumed prepayment pattern of the loans as well as their assumed maturity. Cash flow yields based on constant prepayment rate estimates utilize a more realistic representation of the actual cash flow stream on a mortgage pool than a one-time balloon prepayment and have come into much wider use in recent years.

EXHIBIT 24   Historical Prices: GNMA–SF 9½s versus GNMA–GPM 9½s

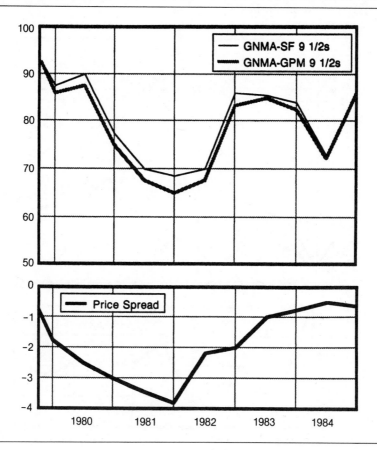

quoted yield. However, if both issues have three years of seasoning, the GPM would have to be priced only ½ point below the single-family GNMA.

During 1982, the market began to adjust the price relationships for the seasoning of the older GPM issues. At the same time, the GPM market developed a broader range of participants and a greater degree of liquidity. As a consequence, the price spread narrowed to approximately one point in this period. Whether the trend will continue so that GNMA–GPMs that are past their graduation periods trade at the same dollar price as single-family GNMAs remains to be seen.

GNMA–GPM 9½s thus trailed GNMA 9½s in total return during the early 1979–81 market period, owing to widening price spreads and slower prepayments. Since October 1981, they have outperformed the

EXHIBIT 25   Historical Prepayment Rates: GNMA–SF 9½s versus
GNMA–GPM 9½s

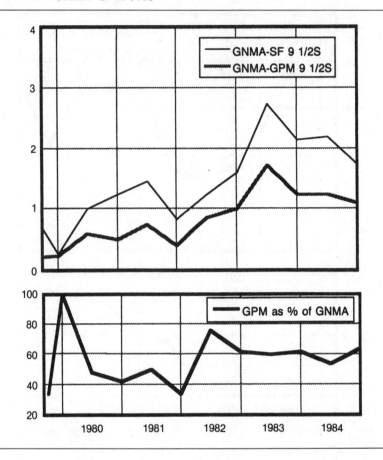

GNMA 9½s as a result of an improving relative market position (Exhibits 23, 24, and 25).

CONCLUSION

Overall, mortgage securities have outperformed each of the other sectors examined (high-grade corporate bond, long Treasuries, and 10-year Treasuries). The main reasons for this are the high relative yield levels of mortgage securities and their shorter average maturity.

The relative performance of mortgages in market cycles has been greatly influenced by changes in yield spreads. Tightening yield spreads enabled mortgages to outperform other fixed-income sectors during the September 1974–March 1975 and October 1981–December 1981 rallies.

Tightening yield spreads also contributed to the sizable performance advantage of mortgages during the May 1983–June 1984 market decline. On the other hand, greater price volatility produced advantages for the longer securities in market rallies when yield spreads failed to narrow. This is evident in the latest June 1984 to January 1985 period.

Much of the improvement in the mortgage market from the low point in the 1981 bear market to date has been the result of structural changes. The deregulation of deposit accounts, the emergence of ARMs as a housing finance force, and the development of CMOs all helped to bring about a housing market recovery and had a direct positive impact on the demand for and supply of mortgage product. The broadened enforceability of mortgage due-on-sale clauses also enhanced the relative value of conventional mortgage-backed securities. These and other developments have created a system of housing finance that should be more resilient in future adverse markets.

There have been wide performance differences within the market. Generally, discount mortgage securities have had the greatest price movements both in market rallies and market declines. Shifts in prepayments have had an important impact on the performance of both high- and low-coupon issues. The posture of thrift institutions has played a major role in the performance of mortgage security investments with the presence or absence of thrift buying being felt most directly in the current coupon sector.

Finally, the pattern of a new security that produces return advantages as it develops market acceptance and liquidity, thereby improving its relative market position, has been repeated several times—first for the GNMA market itself, and then for FHLMC PCs, GNMA–GPMs, FHA project pools, and FNMA MBSs.

19

Convertible Securities and Warrants

John C. Ritchie, Jr., Ph.D.
Professor of Finance
Temple University

A bond or preferred stock may have warrants attached or offer a conversion privilege. In either case, the holder has the right to acquire the common stock of the issuing corporation under specified conditions rather than by direct purchase in the market. One can, however, pay what later proves to be an excessive price for the privilege conferred.

This chapter clarifies the nature of each of these securities, discusses their advantages and disadvantages, and develops an analytical framework aimed at assessing the desirability of acquiring either security by an investor. The investor's point of view, rather than that of the issuer, is emphasized.

CONVERTIBLE SECURITIES

The holder of a convertible bond or preferred stock can exchange the security, at his or her option, for the common stock of the issuer in accordance with terms set forth in the bond indenture. The option to convert is solely at the discretion of the holder and will only be exercised when and if the holder finds such an exchange desirable.[1]

Convertible bonds are typically subordinated debentures; this means that the claims of "senior" creditors must be settled in full before any payment will be made to holders of subordinated debentures in the event of insolvency or bankruptcy. Senior creditors typically include all

---

[1] We will later discuss the possibility of the corporation forcing conversion through exercising a call privilege.

other long-term debt issues and bank loans. Subordinated debentures do, of course, have a priority over common and preferred stockholders. Convertible preferred stocks are equity securities with a priority to dividend payments over common stockholders that offer the opportunity to share in corporate growth.

Although our discussion will consistently refer to convertible bonds, the comments and the approach to analysis of such securities is in general equally applicable to convertible preferred stocks.

Who Issues Convertibles?

The issuers of convertible bonds are classified in Exhibit 1 in terms of broad groupings commonly used by bond analysts and the rating services, such as Standard & Poor's Corporation. It is interesting to note that although utility issues account for the largest portion of total bond issues outstanding in the United States, utilities have chosen not to issue convertible bonds, except for a relatively small amount in 1977, until 1981. Industrial, finance and real estate, and commercial are the largest issuers of convertible bonds.

New cash offerings tend to be greater during periods of rising stock prices, such as in 1972, 1975–76, 1980–81 and 1983. The right to share in future price rises for the common stock is likely to be most highly valued during such a period of bullish expectations, allowing the corporation to offer such securities on favorable terms.

Smaller and more speculative firms, especially when a new venture is being undertaken, often issue convertible bonds in the form of subordinated debentures. The risks inherent in such issues tend to make it difficult to sell straight bonds or common stock at a reasonable cost. Management sweetens the debt issue by giving purchasers a chance to participate in potential profits (which may be large), while having a priority over equity securityholders in the event of financial difficulty.

Advantages and Disadvantages to Issuing Firms

Convertible issues offer two basic potential advantages to the issuer. First, a lower interest cost is incurred and generally less restrictive covenants need be included in the indenture than for a nonconvertible bond issue. In other words, the investor pays for the privilege of speculating on future favorable price changes in the underlying common stock by accepting a lower interest return and a less restrictive debt agreement.

The required yield to sell a convertible relative to that of a nonconvertible issue varies over time and with the issuer. A nonconvertible issue might require a yield-to-maturity that could range from 50 basis points (one half of 1 percent) to 4 percent or more higher than that

EXHIBIT 1 Convertible Bond Issues 1972–1981 (dollars in billions)

Issuing Classification	1972	1973	1974	1975	1976	1977
Public utility	$ 0.0	$ 0.0	$ 0.0	$ 0.0	$ 0.0	$ 0.1
Communications	0.1	0.0	0.0	0.0	0.0	0.0
Transportation	0.1	0.1	0.0	0.0	0.1	0.1
Industrial	0.8	0.1	0.3	0.7	0.8	0.5
Sales finance	N.A.	N.A.	N.A.	0.0	0.0	0.0
Other finance and real estate	0.8	0.4	0.0	0.5	0.0	0.0
Commercial and miscellaneous	0.5	0.0	0.2	0.1	0.1	0.1
Total cash offerings	$ 2.3	$ 0.6	$ 0.5	$ 1.3	$ 1.0	$ 0.8
Plus exchange, net conversion	−1.8	−1.3	0.1	−0.8	−0.5	−0.3
Less calls and other retirements	−0.2	−0.1	−0.2	−0.2	−0.2	−0.1
Net issuance convertible debt	$ 0.3	$−0.8	$ 0.4	$ 0.3	$ 0.3	$ 0.4
Net issuance all corporate bonds	$18.9	$ 13.2	$26.9	$34.0	$33.0	$32.2
Convertible issues as a percent of all corporate issues based on:						
Total cash offerings	12.17%	4.55%	1.86%	3.82%	3.03%	2.48%
Net issuance	1.59	N.M.	1.49	0.88	0.91	1.24

N.A. = Not available.
N.M. = Not marked.
SOURCE: Henry Kaufman, James McKeon, and David Foster, *1985 Prospects for Financial Markets* (New York: Salomon Brothers Inc). Figures for 1972–74 were obtained from the 1978 issue.

offered by a convertible issue.[2] Convertible bonds, moreover, are typically subordinated debt issues. The rating agencies, therefore, have usually rated convertible issues one class below that of a straight debenture issue.[3] This would suggest even higher relative interest-cost savings than suggested by the differentials noted above. The interest-cost saving to a firm will, of course, be highly related to market expectations for the common stock.

Second, a firm may be able to sell common stock at a better price through a convertible bond than by a direct issue. To illustrate, assume a firm is currently earning $5 a common share and that the common stock is selling at $50 per share. The firm believes it can utilize new capital effectively and that it would be preferable to raise equity rather than debt capital. The firm foresees, however, a potential fall in earnings per

---

[2] For example, see Eugene F. Brigham, "An Analysis of Convertible Debentures: Theory and Some Empirical Evidence," *Journal of Finance* (March 1966), pp. 35–54.

[3] George E. Pinches and Kent A. Mingo, "A Multivariate Analysis of Industrial Bond Ratings," *Journal of Finance* (March 1973), pp. 1–18.

1978	1979	1980	1981	1982	1983	1984E	1985P
$ 0.0	$ 0.0	$ 0.0	$ 0.1	$ 0.0	$ 0.3	$ 0.1	$ 0.2
0.0	0.0	0.2	0.4	0.5	0.5	0.0	0.0
0.0	0.2	0.2	0.0	0.3	0.6	0.1	0.1
0.3	0.3	2.8	2.4	0.7	2.2	1.9	3.4
0.0	0.0	0.0	0.0	0.0	0.1	0.1	0.3
0.1	0.0	0.5	0.1	0.4	0.4	0.0	0.0
0.0	0.1	0.4	1.5	0.9	2.3	1.9	3.3
$ 0.4	$ 0.6	$ 4.0	$ 4.5	$ 3.0	$ 6.5	$ 4.2	$ 7.3
−0.5	+1.2	+0.6	−0.1	+1.8	−1.2	−3.0	−3.7
−0.1	−0.4	−0.4	−2.2	−0.6	−6.1	−2.0	−2.4
$−0.2	$ 1.4	$ 4.2	$ 2.2	$ 4.2	$−0.8	$−0.8	$ 1.2
$ 27.6	$31.8	$39.3	$29.4	$32.4	$ 34.2	$ 48.7	$43.0
1.45%	1.89%	10.18%	15.31%	9.26%	19.01%	8.62%	16.98%
N.M.	4.40	10.69	7.48	12.96	N.M.	N.M.	2.79

share if common stock is sold directly because it will take time to bring the new facilities, acquired with the funds raised, on stream. The market might well also fear potential dilution of earnings per share and might not be as optimistic as management about the future of the planned investments. For these reasons, the firm might have to sell new common stock at less than $50 a share. On the other hand, the firm might be able to sell a convertible bond issue at par that can be converted into 20 shares of the firm's common stock. The required interest rate might result in less dilution in earnings per share currently than would a direct stock issue, since the number of shares outstanding would not increase. Further assume that the bonds would be callable at 105 ($1,050 per bond).

If the new capital investments raised earnings per share to $6.50 two years hence, the price of the common stock in the market would increase to $65 a share, assuming a price-earnings ratio of 10 continued to exist. The firm could then call the bonds, forcing conversion. The value of stock received in conversion is $1,300 ($65 per share times 20 shares), which is greater than the cash ($1,050) that would be received by allowing the issuer to call the stock. In effect, the firm sold stock for $50 a share, less issuance costs, through the convertible bonds. The firm, therefore, received a greater price per share than by a direct issue of common stock, at that time, since the market price for a direct issue is expected to be lower and the issuance cost of a common issue is typically higher than for a convertible bond issue. The firm, in other words, would have to issue fewer common shares to raise a given amount by selling convertibles and forcing conversion than by directly selling common stock. Also, interest cost is lowered, sometimes substantially, by offering the convertible privilege.

Convertible securities do have possible disadvantages to the issuer. If the underlying common stock does increase markedly in price, the issuer might have been better off had the financing been postponed and a direct issue made. Moreover, if the price of the common stock drops after the issue of the convertible instrument, conversion cannot be forced and will not occur. The firm, therefore, cannot be sure it is raising equity capital when a convertible issue is made.

Advantages to the Investor

An investor purchasing a convertible security supposedly receives the advantages of a senior security; that is, safety of principal in terms of a prior claim to assets over equity security holders and relative income stability at a known rate. Furthermore, if the common stock of the issuer rises in price, the convertible instrument will usually also rise to reflect the increased value of the underlying common stock. Upside potential can be realized through sale of the convertible bond, without conversion into the stock. On the other hand, if the price of the underlying common stock declines in the market, the bond can be expected to decline only to the point where it yields a satisfactory return on its value as a straight bond. A convertible offers the downside protection that bonds can offer during bad economic times, while allowing one to share in the upside potential for the common stock of a growing firm.

In terms of their dividend yield, convertible bonds also typically offer higher current yield than do common stocks. If the dividend yield on the underlying common stock surpassed the current yield on the convertible bond, conversion would tend to be attractive.

Convertible bonds may have special appeal for financial institutions, notably commercial banks. Commercial banks are not permitted to purchase common stocks for their own account and, therefore, lose the possibility of capital gains through participation in corporate earnings growth. In 1957 approval was given for the purchase of eligible convertible issues by commercial banks if the yield obtained is reasonably similar to nonconvertible issues of similar quality and maturity and they are not selling at a significant conversion premium. Admittedly, commercial banks hold relatively few convertibles, and convertibles typically do sell at a conversion premium.

Convertible bonds have good marketability, as shown by active trading in large issues on the New York Exchange; whereas nonconvertible issues of similar quality are sometimes difficult to follow, since they are traded over the counter.

Disadvantages to the Investor

The investor pays for the convertible privilege by accepting a significantly lower yield-to-maturity than that currently offered by nonconvertible bonds of equivalent quality. Also a call clause can lessen the potential attractiveness of a convertible bond, since the firm may be able to force conversion into the common stock as previously discussed. The possibility of forced conversion limits the speculative appeal.

If anticipated corporate growth is not realized, the purchaser will have sacrificed current yield and may well see the market value of the convertible instrument fall below the price paid to acquire it. A rise in the price of the underlying common stock is necessary to offset the yield sacrifice. For example, prices of convertible bonds rose to very high levels in 1965, but in 1966, when both stock and bond markets declined, many convertible issues declined even more than the stocks into which they were convertible. It appears a speculative premium was built into the price of convertibles in 1965, and the market no longer believed that this premium was justified in 1966.

Investor risk can be markedly heightened by purchasing convertibles on margin. If interest rates rise after purchase, bondholders may receive margin calls, reflecting falling prices of convertible bonds, as happened during the 1966–70 period. Many bonds had to be sold, depressing the market further than purchasers had thought possible based on their estimate of a floor price at which the bonds would sell on a pure yield or straight investment basis.

Analysis of Convertible Bonds

The following factors must be considered when evaluating convertible securities:

1. The appreciation in price of the common stock that is required before conversion could become attractive. This is measured by the *conversion premium ratio.*
2. The prospects for growth in the price of the underlying stock.
3. The downside potential in the event that the conversion privilege proves valueless.
4. The yield sacrifice required to purchase the convertible.

5. The income advantage offered through acquiring the convertible bond, rather than the number of common shares that would be obtained through conversion.
6. The quality of the security being offered.
7. The number of years over which the conversion premium paid to acquire the convertible will be recouped by means of the favorable income differential offered by the convertible relative to the underlying common stock. This is the *break-even time*.

The discussion that follows will concentrate on calculations typically used by analysts to evaluate points 1, 3, 4, 5, and 7 above. The grading of bonds in terms of quality, both by the rating agencies and in terms of financial analysis, is discussed in Chapters 10 and 22. Assessing the prospects for growth in the price of the underlying common stock is the work of fundamental analysis. The techniques of fundamental analysis are reviewed in several well-accepted books.[4]

Convertible Securities: An Illustrative Analysis

Exhibit 2 contrasts the 8⅞s convertible debentures issued by Boeing Corporation that mature in the year 2006 with the $4.50 convertible preferred stock issued by Weyerhaeuser Company. Pertinent calculations contained in the exhibit are explained below.

A few basic definitions are in order before we begin to discuss Exhibit 2. The convertible security contract will either state a conversion ratio or a conversion price. A *conversion ratio* directly specifies the number of shares of the issuing firm's common stock that can be obtained by surrendering the convertible security. Alternatively, the conversion rate may be expressed in terms of a *conversion price*—the price paid per share to acquire the underlying common stock through conversion. The conversion ratio may then be determined by dividing the stated conversion price into the par value of the security:

$$\text{Conversion ratio} = \frac{\text{Par of security}}{\text{Conversion price}}$$

For example, if the conversion price were $20, a holder of such a bond would receive 50 shares of common stock in conversion, assuming a typical par value of $1,000 for the bond.

In some cases, the security contract may provide for changes in the conversion price over time. To illustrate, a conversion price of $20 might

---

[4] For example, see Herbert E. Phillips and John C. Ritchie, *Investment Analysis and Portfolio Selection*, 2d ed. (Cincinnati: South-Western Publishing, 1983), Chapters 7, 17–22, and 24.

EXHIBIT 2 Comparative Data for Two Convertible Securities as of November 30, 1984

	Boeing Corporation 8.87 percent, 2006	Weyerhaeuser $4.50 pref.
Known data:		
Conversion ratio	23.67	1.111
Market price of convertible	$1,340.00	$47.00
Market price of common stock	$ 54.00	$28.00
Dividend per share—common	$ 1.40	$ 1.30
Call price	$1,065.00	$53.00
First call date	6/85	immediately
Yield to maturity, equivalent	12.50%*	11.00%*
Quality nonconvertible	—	—
Calculated data:		
Market conversion price†	$ 56.61	$42.30
Conversion premium per common share	$ 2.61	$14.30
Conversion premium ratio‡	4.83%	51.07%
Current yield—convertible	6.62%	9.57%
Dividend yield—common	2.59%	4.64%
Yield sacrifice on convertible§	6.50%	1.43%
Income differential—total‖	$ 55.56	$ 3.06
Income differential—per share	$ 2.35	$ 2.75
Break-even time	1.11 years	5.2 years
Estimated floor price#	$ 732.68	$40.91

* The average yield to maturity for 25-year corporate bonds rated AA to A by Standard & Poor's and the yield for an outstanding issue of Atlantic Richfield preferred stock in November 1984, coupled with the writer's judgment.

† Market price of the convertible instrument divided by the conversion ratio.

‡ The conversion premium per common share divided by the market price of the common stock.

§ The yield to maturity offered by equivalent nonconvertible securities less the yield offered by the convertible security.

‖ The interest income paid by the convertible instrument less the annual dividend income that would be received by converting into the underlying common shares. This figure expresses the income advantage in holding the convertible bond, rather than the equivalent number of shares of the underlying common stock.

The price at which the convertible would have to sell to offer the yield currently being offered by nonconvertible securities of equivalent risk.

be specified for the first five years, $25 for the next five years, $30 for the next five years, and so on. This, of course, means that a holder of the instrument will be able to obtain fewer shares through conversion each time the conversion price increases. For example, 50 shares can be obtained when the conversion price is $20, but only 40 shares when the conversion price rises to $25. Such a provision forces investors to emphasize early conversion if they intend to convert, and the provision would be reasonable if corporate growth had generally led to a rising value for the common stock over time.

Conversion premium. The *market conversion price* of a convertible instrument represents the cost per share of the common stock if obtained through the convertible instrument, ignoring commissions. For example, the market conversion price of $56.61 calculated for the Boeing Corporation convertible bond is obtained by dividing the market price of the convertible bond ($1,340) by the number of common shares that could be obtained by converting that bond (23.67 shares). Since the market conversion price per common share is higher than the current market price of a common share, the bond is selling at a *conversion premium*, represented by the excess cost per share to obtain the common stock through conversion.

The *conversion premium ratio* shows the percentage increase necessary to reach a *parity price* relationship between the underlying common stock and the convertible instrument. *Conversion parity* is that price relationship between the convertible instrument and the common stock at which neither a profit nor a loss would be realized by purchasing the convertible, converting it, and selling the common shares that were received in conversion, ignoring commissions. At conversion parity the following condition would exist:

$$\frac{\text{Par of security}}{\text{Conversion price}} = \frac{\text{Market price of the convertible}}{\text{Market price of the common}}$$

When the price of the common stock exceeds its conversion parity price, one could feel certain that the convertible security would fluctuate directly with changes in the market price of the underlying common stock. In other words, gains in value of the underlying common stock should then be able to be realized by the sale of the convertible instrument, rather than conversion and sale of the stock itself. The market conversion price, incidentally, is the parity price for a share of common stock obtainable through the convertible instrument.

At the time of this comparative analysis, both instruments sold at a premium, but the premium on the Weyerhaeuser convertible preferred was substantially greater in both relative and absolute terms. If one assumes that the appreciation potentials of the common stocks of both companies were equal (a feeling the market appeared not to hold), the Boeing Corporation bond had a substantial advantage. An increase of only 4.83 percent in the common stock of Boeing was needed to ensure that further increases in the underlying common would be reflected in the price of the convertible bond. Weyerhaeuser common stock, however, would have to rise 51.07 percent before the conversion had an assured value.

There is usually, although not always, some conversion premium present on convertible instruments, which reflects the anticipation of a possible increase in the price of the underlying common stock beyond the parity price. Professional arbitrageurs are constantly looking for situations in which the stock can be obtained more cheaply (allowing for commissions) by buying the convertible instrument than through direct purchase in the market. For example, assume a bond is convertible into 20 shares and can be purchased for $1,000. If the common stock was currently selling at $55 a share, an arbitrageur would buy the convertible and simultaneously short sell the common stock. The arbitrageur would realize a gross profit (before transaction costs) of $100 calculated as follows:

Short sale of 20 shares at $55/share	$1,100
Less purchase cost of bond	1,000
	$ 100

The demand by arbitrageurs for the convertible would continue until the resultant rise in price of the convertible no longer made such actions profitable.

Yield sacrifice.   At the time of this analysis, nonconvertible bonds of equivalent quality to the convertible issued by Boeing Corporation offered a yield of 12.5 percent, or 6.5 percent higher than the yield to maturity offered by the convertible. The yield sacrifice would have to be overcome by a rise in the price of the underlying common stock, or the investor would have been better off to purchase the nonconvertible instrument. The yield sacrifice required by the Weyerhaeuser preferred was significantly lower than that for the Boeing Corporation bonds, thereby requiring less attractive appreciation potential for its common stock during the holding period to make the convertible attractive. Although the Weyerhaeuser instrument offered an advantage in terms of the lower yield sacrifice required, this could have been offset by a more attractive price appreciation potential for the common stock of Boeing Corporation, if that was in fact the case.

Downside risk potential.   The floor price for a convertible is estimated as that value at which the instrument would sell in the market to offer the yield of an equivalent nonconvertible instrument. Boeing Corporation bonds were rated AA by Standard & Poor's Corporation at the time of this analysis, and the average yield paid by AA bonds was used as the required market yield to represent the yield on a nonconvertible bond if issued by Boeing Corporation. An Atlantic Richfield nonconvertible preferred, felt to be of equivalent quality to the Weyerhaeuser issue, yielded 11 percent.

The floor price of the Weyerhaeuser convertible was calculated, therefore, by dividing the annual dividend ($4.50) by 11 percent. Present-value calculations were used to determine the price ($732.68) at which the Boeing Corporation bond would have to sell to yield 12.5 percent to maturity.

The analysis suggests a substantially greater downside risk for Boeing Corporation convertible bonds than for the Weverhaeuser convertible.

One should not place too much emphasis on the estimated floor prices, however. The calculations assume that current yield levels will continue, and this may well not be correct. On the one hand, if yields rise to even higher levels, and the conversion privilege proves worthless, the price of the bonds could fall below the estimated floor price. On the other hand, if yield levels fall, the loss will not be as great as suggested. More importantly, one should not be purchasing convertibles (remember the yield sacrifice) unless one believes the probability is relatively high that the market price of the underlying common will rise and eventually exceed the parity price for that common stock.

Break-even time. Break-even time represents the number of years it will take for the favorable income differential over the common stock offered by the convertible instrument to equal the total dollar conversion premium paid to acquire that convertible instrument. For example, the break-even time for the Boeing Corporation bonds is 1.11 years, calculated as follows:

Interest paid on each $1,000 bond at 8⅞ percent	$88.70
Dividend income offered by 23.67 shares into which each bond is convertible (23.67 shares × 1.40/share)	33.14
Favorable bond income differential	55.56
Favorable income differential per common share (55.56 ÷ 23.67 shares)	$ 2.35
Break-even time equals the conversion premium per share divided by the favorable income differential per share (2.61 ÷ 2.35)	1.11 years

A break-even time exceeding five years is widely regarded by analysts as excessive, other things being equal. The Weyerhaeuser preferred has a significantly longer break-even time, though neither security suggests an excessive break-even time.

Dilution of the Convertible Privilege

A large common stock split or stock dividend could markedly dilute the value of the conversion privilege, unless adjustment of the number of shares received in conversion is made. For example, assume a bond is convertible into 20 shares, and the company undergoes a two-for-one stock split. Recognizing this, the conversion privilege is typically protected by a provision in the bond indenture providing for a pro rata adjustment of the conversion price and/or the conversion ratio, so the exchange ratio would increase to 40 shares after the stock split.

When Should a Convertible Be Converted or Sold?

If the prospects for favorable growth in the underlying common stock or the relative prices and yields of the convertible security and the common stock change significantly, a sale or conversion may be suggested. For example, the dividend obtainable by converting into the common stock of AT&T from the $4 convertible preferred rose to $4.20 a share during

1977. A conversion was then desirable, assuming the investor still wished to retain a claim on the further potential growth of AT&T, since current yield would be increased through conversion by 20 cents per share.

Summary of Convertibles

Some fixed-income securities are convertible into common stock, offering the basic advantages of a senior security (bond or preferred stock) while allowing the holder to participate in potential corporate growth. The investor pays for the conversion privilege by accepting a significantly lower yield than could be obtained by purchasing nonconvertible bonds or preferred stocks. A convertible, moreover, usually sells at a premium over the value of the underlying common stock. If the anticipated growth in the value of the common stock is not realized, the purchaser will have sacrificed yield and may well also see the value of the convertible instrument fall sharply.

There are three distinct areas of analysis that should be undertaken when evaluating a convertible security:

1. The quality of the security should be assessed in the same way as for other nonconvertible senior securities. This requires assessing the ability of the issuing company to meet the fixed charges mandated by the issue under reasonably conceivable adverse economic circumstances.
2. The growth potential for the underlying common stock must be evaluated, since that growth potential offers the basis for generating the added yield necessary to offset the yield sacrifice incurred at the time of purchase and provide a return that makes purchase attractive.
3. Special calculations developed in the illustrative analysis in this chapter should be used to assess the relative attractiveness of the many convertible securities available in the market.

Conversion should be considered when the annual total dividends that would be received from the common shares obtained through conversion exceeds the annual coupon payments offered by the convertible bond. Sale of the convertible security should also be considered when the price of that security exceeds the estimated value of the underlying stock into which it is convertible and/or the prospects for favorable growth in the underlying common stock deteriorate.

COMMON STOCK WARRANTS

A warrant is usually a long-term option, at least when issued, that conveys to the holder the privilege of buying a specified number of shares of the underlying common stock at a specified exercise price at any time on or before an expiration date. The typical warrant originates by attachment to a bond or preferred stock issue, with the intent to lower the cost of capital for the issuing firm and/or make an issue more attractive to investors, thereby improving its marketability. Warrants may also be added to make possible the sale of a marginal-quality issue. In addition, warrants may be issued to corporate employees under a bonus plan or could even be offered as a security in a direct sale.

A warrant that is attached to a bond or preferred stock can only be exercised by the holder of that financial instrument. Such warrants, however, may typically be detached as of a particular date and subsequently traded on their own merits. A number of warrants are now listed by the New York Stock Exchange, and trading in warrants can be expected to increase in volume in the years ahead.[5]

Warrants and Stock Rights Distinguished

Stock purchase rights are created by corporations who issue them to existing common stockholders when making a privileged subscription offering. Stock rights typically allow subscription to new shares on a pro rata basis at a price below the current market price for the common stock, and warrants at the time of issue offer the holder the option to buy the common stock at a price substantially *above* the current market price. Warrants, however, have a long life, often exceeding five years; and stock rights usually have a life of one month or less.

The value of a warrant is usually defined in terms of the probabilities that the future price of the common stock will exceed the option price. The value of stock rights, on the other hand, is measured in terms of the dollar savings per right that can be realized by purchasing the common stock at the preferential price, which is below the current market price.

Warrants and Call Options Distinguished

A call option gives the buyer the right to purchase the underlying common stock from the option seller at a fixed price within a given period. Therefore, it is similar to a warrant. Call options also trade independently from the common stock, as do warrants.

However, call options are written by investors, who will purchase and deliver already outstanding shares of common stock if the option is exercised. Warrants, on the other hand, are issued by business corporations, and the corporation utilizes the instrument as a means of selling a new issue and thereby raising additional capital. Also, warrants may

---

[5] The first warrant to be listed on the NYSE was an AT&T warrant that expired April 1975. Other warrants have since been listed there. Most existing warrants, however, trade over the counter or are listed on the American or Pacific Coast Stock Exchanges.

well have a life of many years, but a call option typically expires within nine months. Finally, warrants are often attached to bonds (or other financial instruments) to make them more attractive when being initially sold.

Leverage and Minimum Values

The price of a warrant is usually quite small in comparison with the current market price of the common stock of the issuer. A given percentage increase in the common stock's price, therefore, may have a magnified percentage effect on the price of the warrant.

For example, assume the common stock of company X is now selling for $50 a share, and an investor expects the price to rise to $100 a share within a few years. Further assume a warrant is outstanding that gives the holder the right to buy a share of common stock of company X for $65 a share at any time during the next 10 years. A warrant currently sells for $10.

An investor who bought the common stock at $50 a share would realize a 100 percent gain (ignoring commissions) plus any dividend income received if the stock rose to $100 in a year. The *minimum value of the warrant* when the stock rises to $100, however, is about $35 ($100 − $65), the saving that can be realized by acquiring the stock through exercise of the warrant rather than by direct purchase. If it were much less than this, arbitrageurs would buy the warrant and short sell the stock to take advantage of the assured gain, thereby forcing the price of the warrant to the minimum value.[6] An investor who had bought a warrant at $10 and sold it at $35 would have realized a gain of 250 percent, substantially exceeding the gain offered by direct purchase of the common stock. Actually, the warrant is likely to be selling for more than $35 when the stock reaches $100 per share because of the speculative enthusiasm such a price rise would tend to generate.

But the value of the warrant may fall sharply, even to zero, if the common stock does not rise in value. Notice that at any price below $65 a share for the common stock, the warrant has no assured minimum value. Suppose the price of the common stock merely stayed at $50 a share, and reduced expectations for future growth in the market reduced the price of a warrant to $5. An investor in the warrants would have lost 50 percent of his or her capital, but an investor in the stock would have no potential current loss and would receive any dividend

---

[6] In the event a warrant entitles the holder to purchase more or less than one share, the formula for calculating the minimum value is $N(MP − EP)$, where N is the number of shares that can be purchased through exercise of the warrant, MP is the market price of a share of the common stock, and EP is the exercise price, or price at which a share of the common stock can be acquired through the warrant.

income paid by the corporation. Furthermore, if the stock does not rise above $65 a share before expiration, the warrant will be worth $0.

Like any leveraged situation, the potential return is increased by purchasing warrants, but risk is also increased.

Warrant Premiums

Warrants tend to sell at a premium over minimum value, reflecting expectations of future increases in the price of the common stock and the leverage potential. The speculative leverage possibilities diminish, however, as the price of the underlying stock rises relative to the exercise price of the warrant and/or as the warrant approaches expiration. This is because the expectation of further substantial gains in the price of the common stock is likely to become less probable in terms of market expectations, leading to lower leverage potential that may not seem worthwhile when one realizes that direct purchase of the common stock would generate dividend income that will not be realized through purchase of the warrant.

The factors affecting the size of the warrant premium have been explored in the financial literature,[7] and are briefly summarized below:

1. The most important factor, of course, is the market's expectations regarding the future price of the underlying common stock. The greater the growth expectations, the larger the premium will be, other things equal.
2. The longer the warrant has to go before reaching the expiration date, the higher the premium is likely to be. Once the life of a warrant exceeds five years, however, it has less chance of further increasing the premium paid.
3. A higher dividend yield offered by the underlying common stock will tend to lower the premium paid, since the sacrificed dividend yield makes purchase of the warrant less attractive.
4. Empirical studies suggest that warrants trading on organized exchanges tend to have higher premiums than those trading over the counter. For similar reasons, the warrants of small companies or those of companies whose stocks are inactively traded tend to have smaller premiums.
5. As the expiration date of the warrant nears, the premium tends to shrink, and the price of the warrant approaches minimum value or zero, whichever is the lower bound.

---

[7] See, for example, J. P. Shelton, "The Relation of the Price of a Warrant to the Price of Its Associated Stock," *Financial Analysts Journal*, May–June and July–August 1967; S. T. Kassonf, "Warrant Price Behavior, 1945–1964, "*Financial Analysts Journal*, January–February 1968; and J. D. Miller, "Longevity of Stock Purchase Warrants," *Financial Analysts Journal*, November–December 1971.

Summary of Warrants

The purchase of a warrant, essentially a means of obtaining a call on a common stock, offers attractive leverage possibilities. A warrant typically sells at a premium over the value represented by the savings that could be made by acquiring the common stock through exercise. If the expected appreciation is not realized on the common stock, an investor in warrants may lose a greater percentage of the capital invested than would have been lost by direct investment in the common stock. On the other hand, investment in warrants may produce a greater percentage gain on the capital committed when the stock does increase in value, than could have been realized by direct investment in the underlying common stock.

20

Fixed Income Funds

A. Michael Lipper, C.F.A.
President
Lipper Analytical Services, Inc.

Alling Woodruff, C.F.A.
Vice President
Lipper Analytical Services, Inc.

INTRODUCTION

By the time you have reached this point in expanding your knowledge of fixed income securities, you probably have learned the following lessons:

1. Fixed income securities are characterized by reasonably predictable income, known credit quality, and maximum maturity.
2. The price one pays for these features does not guarantee any specific investment return prior to maturity, nor does it guarantee the relative attractiveness of returns under conditions of changing interest rates.
3. There are substantial credit and interest-rate risks inherent in the character of fixed income securities.
4. The opportunity to buy any particular bond at a known price and in reasonable quantity is rare after the initial offering.
5. Collecting and reinvesting interest to produce the fabled interest-on-interest return is a time-consuming bore for many investors who are not organized to perform these functions.
6. Basic to the security of all investments in common-law countries is the ability (and willingness) to assert one's right through legal action, which requires expertise and expense.

However, as is often the case, a lesson is nothing more than an identification of problems, the solution of which requires expert and timely action. Many fixed income investors lack the knowledge, resolve, facilities, and most important the buying power, to bring about an orderly solution to their problems. One alternative for individuals and institutions who have this view is the use of fixed income funds. In this chapter we will examine some of the critical elements of funds for the fixed income investor and the types of fixed income funds.

FIXED INCOME FUNDS IN GENERAL

Because of the expertise required for the intelligent selection and management of a fixed income portfolio, it seemed reasonable to set up fixed income funds. Fixed income funds provide diversity by owning a variety of issues. Each fund provides for the safekeeping of cash and securities, the collection of income either for distribution or reinvestment, and income management. These funds have all the characteristics of ownership, including specific legal rights of action.

LEGAL FORMS OF FIXED INCOME INVESTMENT COMPANIES

There are three types of fixed income funds regulated by the Investment Company Act of 1940. All three are subject to regulations prescribed by the Securities and Exchange Commission and to rules of the various states' securities commissions. The distinctions among the three types involve whether the fund has a fixed portfolio of issues and whether it has a fixed number of shares outstanding.

The three types of funds, in terms of their corporate and legal structure, are unit trusts, open-end funds, and closed-end funds. Any one of these types of funds could be the most appropriate for an investor, depending upon the investor's particular requirements. Also, each type of fund has some specific drawbacks in terms of flexibility and exact portfolio focus in respect to maturities, coupons, and quality.

Unit Investment Trusts

Unit investment trusts are fixed portfolios of securities not subject to continuous management. Unit trust portfolios are assembled by an underwriter sponsor, usually a brokerage firm and underwriter of fixed income issues. Upon completion of the sponsors' and fellow underwriters' selling efforts, the sponsor deposits the portfolio with an independent trustee, usually a bank. The trustee holds these issues until they are redeemed, unless their agreement with the fund requires a sale for some very specific reason, for example, a material downgrade in the issue's credit rating.

The trustee collects the income and remits either to shareholders or to the fund sponsor for reinvestment as directed by the shareholder. Unit trusts have a definite termination date, usually between 6 months and 10 years from the offering date. The principal feature of unit trusts is that they are passive investors with a known and preselected portfolio not subject to subsequent management.

The remaining sections of this and the chapter to follow will not deal further with unit investment trusts. Readers who are interested in learning more about these trusts should contact the sponsors of these trusts: John Nuveen & Co. and Merrill Lynch, Pierce, Fenner & Smith, Inc. among others, in addition to their regular securities broker.

Open-End Funds

Open-end fixed income mutual funds, including money market instrument funds, as of June 30, 1985, had total net assets of $329 billion, accounting for 75% of the $440 billion total value of all mutual funds. There are three essential characteristics of an open-end mutual fund, which can be summarized as follows:

1. An open-end fund stands ready on any business day to sell and redeem any of its shares. (In contrast, unit trusts or closed-end funds do not sell additional shares after their initial offering.)
2. Most open-end funds employ an investment adviser who is responsible for making appropriate changes in the portfolio. This produces a changing or dynamic portfolio as compared with the static portfolio of a unit trust.
3. There is a board of directors for each open-end fund. Except in very rare cases these boards have a majority of directors who are not affiliated with the fund or its adviser. These directors, particularly the outside directors, must annually approve the investment advisory contract and other key arrangements for the fund on behalf of its shareholders. (Unit investment trusts have no such safeguards because many of these continuous problems and potential conflicts of interest apparently do not arise.)

Closed-End Funds

The original type of fund, which began in England after the Napoleonic Wars and in the early stages of the Industrial Revolution, was what we in this country call a closed-end fund. In England, however, they are known as investment trusts.

The closed-end investment company, similar to the unit trust, has an initial offering (occasionally followed by subsequent new securities offerings). Following the offering, however, investors who wish to transact in these shares must find through their brokers a willing counterparty (buyer or seller) in order to consumate a trade. Such transactions may take place at prices either above or below the current underlying proportionate asset value of the shareholders' interest in the portfolio. This proportionate interest in the portfolio is calculated by adding up the current market value of all portfolio holdings, deducting any liabilities including accrued expenses, and dividing by the number of shares to determine the net asset value per share. Sales below net asset value are said to be at a discount, and sales above net asset value are said to be at a premium.

The reasons closed-end funds often sell at discounts have been subject to extensive study, but there is no general agreement as to the answer. We take the position that the discount is the bargain rate required to entice a buyer to make a purchase. Because most brokers are not interested in the additional work of finding a new buyer, the discount price mechanism helps to create the inducement. The brokerage commissions charged in such transactions are at the normal rates for equity trades of similar dollar value for the similar type of customer.

SHAREHOLDER SERVICES

The share owner of an investment company share is not only a proportionate owner in the portfolio, but also is recipient of a number of shareholder services imbedded in the ownership rights. Some of these rights are of particular value to a share owner of fixed income funds.

Safekeeping

Most fixed income securities are in bearer form and thus offer opportunities for theft. However, investment companies are required to have independent custodians of securities and cash. Both the custodians, usually major banks, and the registered investment adviser (the investment company's manager) are required to carry fidelity bonds (insurance) at prescribed levels to protect shareholders against losses due to theft, embezzlement, and so on. Fund managements and directors are held responsible for protecting the fund shareholder against frauds or defalcations. Further, the independent auditor is required to physically count the securities belonging to the fund periodically. This in turn, in the case of managed funds, is backed up by a periodic review by the fund's board of directors.

Income Collection

Income collection of interest is an administrative function provided by a fund's custodian included in its charges to the fund. The fund custodian working with an investment adviser is likely to be diligent in efforts to collect at the earliest possible date, permitting immediate reinvestment of these proceeds and producing the highest possible interest-on-interest consistent with the fund's investment policy. In the case of long maturities, interest-on-interest is the largest component of the total return to the bond holder.

Securities and Portfolio Valuations

Information concerning the value of securities and portfolio valuations is another important benefit shareholders in fixed income funds receive. Since fixed income issues are largely traded by dealers in the over-the-counter market, transaction prices are not publicly available, and representative quotations do not reflect true market value, *especially in large size*. Quite often particular issues of fixed income securities become very inactively traded as long-term holders remove the issue from the dealers' trading inventory. Hence the owner of a portfolio of fixed income securities may have some difficulty in determining the value of holdings before an actual sale.

Without periodic valuation of portfolios, investors cannot compare their results with those of other investors or with relevant standards of performance or, perhaps more important, with other alternative opportunities. Investment companies are skilled in developing valuation studies of their portfolios. In the case of open-end-funds, pricing the portfolio valuation is of particular importance because this determines the price that purchasing and redeeming shareholders pay or receive. Errors are to be avoided at all costs, since they may entail significant commercial and legal risks to the investment adviser/portfolio manager. Both the fund's independent auditors and the various regulatory authorities periodically check and verify the calculations. Fund directors also are held responsible for supervision of the valuation process.

Reports to Shareholders

Reports to shareholders are issued periodically. All funds issue them semiannually and annually, and some funds issue them monthly or quarterly. Depending upon the type of fund and type of report, the information provided usually includes the net asset value and income generated by the fund for the period. Other information often provided are a complete portfolio showing current market value (and often historic cost) and a rather complete income statement of the fund. Perhaps the information of greatest value in shareholder reports is the investment adviser's commentary on the performance and characteristics of the portfolio. In some cases the commentary is excellent and can be of material aid to the investor both as an educational device and a guide for investment policy generally.

Information for Tax Reporting

Form 1099 is a report to the Internal Revenue Service issued by each fund in January every year indicating the amount and character of taxable income for each of its shareholders. A copy is supplied to each shareholder. This is very helpful for preparation of the shareholder's income tax return, and supplants a great deal of shareholder record-keeping.

Exchange Privileges

The exchange privilege between one fund and another at zero or nominal cost is an especially valuable service available to shareholders of most funds. Such exchanges are usually, but not always, limited to other funds managed by the same investment adviser but having different investment objectives. Many funds permit such exchanges to be arranged by telephone, subject to prior written authority.

Checkwriting Privilege

Checkwriting is a privilege available on many short-term funds. This permits the shareholder to sign a draft payment order for larger bills (typically in excess of $500). For all practical purposes the draft is a check that is processed through normal banking channels and is presented to the fund's custodian bank for payment through an automatic preauthorized redemption procedure. A particular advantage of the check-redemption feature is that the shareholder continues to earn income until the draft is finally presented (i.e., the shareholder benefits from the "float," rather than the bank).

SOURCES OF INFORMATION ON INVESTMENT COMPANIES

The best sources of information for most purposes are the individual fund report and prospectus (an offering document). Information on no-load funds (funds that do not have a sales charge) should be sought direct from the fund. Most brokerage firms will be happy to provide information on load funds, from which they earn a sales commission.

The No-Load Mutual Fund Association publishes regularly an extensive description, including the addresses and phone numbers of its members, and other sources of information are available.[1]

TYPES OF FIXED INCOME FUNDS

Thus far we have identified funds in terms of their legal and organizational characteristics—unit trusts, open-end funds, and closed-end funds. In this section, we will discuss the various types of long-term funds. In the next section, we will discuss short-term funds that are used for liquidity or short-term reserve purposes.

The shareholder usually chooses a fund based on its investment characteristics. The main characteristics of a fund are determined by the type of securities in its portfolio. Other investment characteristics result from the portfolio manager's use of the individual securities and the expenses to the shareholder of producing the expected returns.

Exhibit 1 sets forth the criteria used by Lipper Analytical Services, Inc. to assign a particular fund to an investment objective category. Notice that the criteria reflect particularly the type of issues that represent the bulk of the securities in the portfolios. The criteria for short-term funds are included for completeness; such funds are discussed more completely in the next section.

Uses, Advantages, and Disadvantages of Different Types of Funds

United States government funds. These funds should be utilized by investors whose primary objective is absolute highest quality, with virtually no risk of default. Securities of the U.S. government are considered to be the highest credit quality available in the marketplace. This is due to the U.S. government history of no defaults, combined with its virtually unlimited ability to print money. Although there may be theoretical risks associated with U.S. government obligations, very few analysts apply credit analysis to the U.S. government financial status.

Subject only to congressional approval of the debt limit, the government always has the ability to pay. One caveat to remember is that the U.S. government cannot be sued without its permission. Due to the very

---

[1] No-Load Mutual Fund Association, 11 Penn Plaza, New York, N.Y. 10001 (212) 563–4540. Twice a year the Investment Dealers Digest (212) 227–1200, 150 Broadway, New York 10038, publishes a mutual fund directory with addresses, phone numbers, and other information on funds. Other sources of information include Investment Company Institute, 1600 M Street, Washington, DC 20036; United Mutual Fund Selector, 210 Newbury Street, Boston, MA 02116; Weisenberger Investment Company Services, 210 South Street, Boston, MA 02111; and Donoghue's Money Fund Report, Holliston, MA 01746.

high perceived quality of U.S. government securities, investors usually accept on U.S. government investments somewhat less yield than available from comparable maturities of the highest quality corporate debt.

Although U.S. government securities pose no credit risk, there is a sizable interest-rate risk on longer term U.S. government securities. Further, the interest is wholly subject to federal income taxes, although exempt from state taxes. These issues are most appropriate for extremely credit-risk-adverse investors, often as a permanent reserve element for the investor's portfolio. The major disadvantage to these funds is their relatively smaller yield compared with portfolios of corporate or tax-exempt bonds.

Funds of Government National Mortgage Association (GNMA) issues. GNMA issues are utilized by investors for many of the same reasons that attract investors to other U.S. government issues. The main difference is that GNMA issues are guaranteed by a specific agency of the U.S. government, rather than directly by the Treasury. Second, because they are mortgage bonds, there is amortization of principal during the holding period. Third, when the owners of homes mortgaged under a GNMA mortgage sell their homes prior to the final maturity date of the mortgage, they must pay the remaining principal value of their debt under the mortgage in full. This money is then transmitted to the owner of the mortgage, who receives cash at an earlier date than expected, and this in turn changes the yield to maturity calculations.

The amortization of principal and liquidation of mortgage prior to termination give GNMA mortgages a more rapid return of borrowed funds than other types of fixed income securities. This is an advantage during periods of rising interest rates but a disadvantage in periods of declining rates. As the decision to sell a home and thus repay a mortgage in full is the homeowner's decision, there is no certainty of early repayment. Sales may accelerate in periods of easy money, and this may be a disadvantage to the investor. Numerous GNMA mutual funds are available, offering the convenience of central collection, accounting, and tax services.

A-rated corporate bond funds. A-rated corporate bond funds are invested primarily in high-quality corporate bonds. For investors willing to take some modest credit risk, these funds usually offer somewhat higher yields than funds invested exclusively in government issues. Experience over many years suggests that these funds provide a better strategic reserve element than do government bond funds.

BBB-rated corporate bond funds. Investors who wish the bulk of their portfolios to be investment-grade issues and can accept some additional credit risk as compared with higher credit-rated bond portfolios may invest in BBB-rated corporate bond funds. In general, these funds have performed better than the A-rated issue funds because of higher

EXHIBIT 1 Criteria for Assignment of Fixed Income Funds to Investment Objectives

Our assignment of funds to a specific investment objective is often a matter of judgment. The prospectus's statement of policy is initially used in assigning the fund to one of the various classifications. As the fund matures and develops, clearly discernible investment policies and practices assume paramount importance in assigning the fund to a specific objective category. Once assigned, funds are not again changed without clear evidence of further change in portfolio management policy. A change in policy may be voted on by the shareholders or by the Board of Directors, or it may become more subtly evident from close observation and analysis of changes in the portfolio. Our *Lipper-Portfolio Analysis Report on Fixed Income Funds* is one of the most useful tools for this purpose. Below are the symbols and definitions we use for each of the fixed income objectives.

Open-end short-term fixed income funds

MM   Money Market Instrument Funds—invest in financial instruments with short maturities. In order to be allowed to use amortized prices and/or dollar rounding, funds must have an average weighted maturity of no more than 120 days. Most funds restrict their longest maturity to one year. However, longer maturity issues with shorter-term optional maturities of under one year have been used.

USS   U.S. Government Short-Term Funds—similar in all respects to money market instrument funds except they restrict their investments to U.S. Treasury and agency issues. Some of these issues may be the underlying security in holdings of repurchase agreements.

SM   Short-Term Municipal Bond Funds—similar to money market instrument funds except tney invest primarily in tax-exempt securities.

BBB/T   Corporate Bond Funds BBB/Trading—similar to the BBB funds except their prospectus permits turnover rates in excess of 100 percent.

GB   General Bond Funds—do not have restrictions other than to keep the bulk of their portfolio in corporate bonds.

HY   High Current Yield Funds—managed with an emphasis on high current (relative) yield. There are no quality or maturity restrictions.

PP   Private Placement Bond Funds—invest in excess of 25 percent of their portfolio in issues that have been placed privately rather than sold to the public via registered offerings.

CV   Convertible Securities Funds—invest the bulk of their portfolios in convertible bonds and convertible preferred shares.

PRF   Preferred Stock Funds—invest 50 percent or more of their assets in preferred shares.

ARP Adjustable Rate Preferred Funds—invest primarily in adjustable rate preferred shares. At least 75 percent of gross income consists of dividends received from domestic corporations.

Open and closed-end long-term fixed income funds
U.S. U.S. Government Funds—invest in U.S. Treasury and Agency issues usually without maturity limits.

GNM GNMA Funds—invest a minimum of 65 percent of their portfolio in Government National Mortgage Association securities.

USM U.S. Mortgage Funds—invest a minimum of 65 percent of their portfolio in mortgages/securities issued or guaranteed as to principal and interest by the U.S. Government.

"A" Corporate Bond Funds A Rated—invest 60 percent of their corporate holdings in "A" rated issues or better.

BBB Corporate Bond Funds BBB Rated—invest 60 percent of their corporate holdings in the top four grades of bonds.

FLX Flexible Income Funds—emphasize income generation by investing in bonds, preferreds, convertibles, and/or common stocks and warrants.

Municipal bond funds
GM General Municipal Bond Funds—invest 60 percent or more of their assets in the top four tax-exempt credit ratings. California (CA), Massachusetts (MA), New York (NY), and Other State (OTH) Municipal Bond Funds—limit at least 80 percent of their investments to those securities which are exempt from taxation of a specified state (double tax-exempt) or city (triple tax-exempt).

IM Intermediate Municipal Bond Funds—generally restrict their holdings of municipal bonds to those with maturities between 2 and 20 years.

HM High Yield Municipal Bond funds—may utilize lower rated municipal bonds for 50 percent of their portfolio.

SOURCE: Lipper Analytical Services, Inc.

interest returns. In portfolios of less than AAA credit, there are opportunities for the credit ratings to be upgraded, which in turn usually leads to higher prices over the ensuing two years, but any downgrading of credit rating often has an immediate impact, lowering the price of the issues. To take advantage of potential or actual credit upgrades and to avoid potential cuts in credit ratings, these funds experience a higher degree of portfolio trading (turnover) than the A-rated issue funds in general.

BBB/trading corporate bond funds.   In the early 1970s, a number of managers believed that by aggressively trading their portfolios, taking advantage of imperfections in the market, they could add significantly to the total returns of their portfolios. Thus when a number of new closed-end bond funds were launched during this period, their policy statements permitted portfolio turnover rates as high as 100 percent annually. In some markets this can create a worthwhile advantage, but in other markets high turnover has not worked. Generally, the most favorable environment for the BBB/trading funds is a market with gradual interest rate trends and with different portions of the market reacting slowly and at different rates of change.

High current yield funds.   When high current income is of primary importance, high current yield funds may be used. Although entailing high principal risk, such funds might be appropriate for a relatively impoverished individual with little or no other source of taxable income. In the past, a number of these funds have been sold without regard to the risk of principal, which is very great on the high current-yield frontier. Usually yields that are high relative to others signify perceived additional risk by investors.

General bond funds.   General bond funds can have strategies and tactics ranging over the whole spectrum of the bond market. This type of fund is appropriate for investors who do not want to restrict their fixed income investment managers.

Convertible securities funds.   These funds invest in hybrid securities that have some characteristics of both fixed income and equity issues. The success of most convertible funds has been attributable to selection of issues convertible into what later proved to be equities that rise in price. In declining equity markets, convertible issues decline at a slower rate than does common stock in the same company. Most of the time they also go up at a somewhat slower rate.

Private placement funds.   Private placement funds offer to the investor a chance to participate in a select portfolio of securities that were not offered to the public. Often these issues can have more attractive terms than those of similar companies available in the public market. These advantages may be higher income, stronger covenants, better conversion privileges, warrants, and so on.

Flexible income funds. Flexible income funds can select any publicly traded securities that pay an income. Thus they have an even broader field of maneuver than the general bond funds. The key to success for such funds is an ability to balance their portfolios between income production and capital preservation.

Municipal bond funds. Municipal bond funds come in many different sizes and shapes, with the same general breakdowns as corporate bond funds in terms of quality and maturity. We believe our description of the three categories of municipal bond funds are self-explanatory. Municipal bond funds may be broken down into subcategories of short-term funds (which will be discussed later in this chapter with money market funds) and intermediate-term funds (maturities 2 to 20 years). High-yield municipal bond funds may utilize lower rated municipal bonds, while general municipal bond funds keep at least 60 percent of their assets in the top four tax-exempt credit ratings.

Investors in municipal bond funds should recognize that these funds may have up to 20 percent of their income from taxable sources and still maintain their designation as tax-exempt funds. Therefore investors should examine carefully the portfolios of these funds if there is a desire for nontaxable income.

Investors in tax-exempt securities should remember that inflation attacks their principal at the same rate as it reduces the purchasing power of money invested in taxable securities. With a lower interest rate on tax-exempt securities than available on taxable securities, there may be a smaller income earned to offset the deterioration of the principal value caused by inflation. At times in the past, one could not earn a "real" tax-exempt income due to the purchasing power decline of the principal value. However, in an environment of lower inflation and higher interest rates, one may be able to earn a real inflation-adjusted rate-of-return on tax exempts.

Preferred stocks funds. Funds specializing in preferred stocks are attractive to corporate buyers due to the 85 percent tax exemption on intercompany dividends on the portfolio of preferred shares they own. Some of these issues are convertible into common stock.

THE STRUCTURE OF THE FIXED INCOME FUND INDUSTRY

Exhibit 2 shows the breakdown of the fixed income fund industry in terms of number of funds and total net assets in each category. As of June 30, 1985 there were 815 fixed income funds with total net assets of $329 billion. This compares with only 451 funds and total net assets of $223 billion just three years earlier.

EXHIBIT 2 Fixed Income Fund Industry as of June 30, 1985 (includes both open- and closed-end funds)

Types of Funds	Number of Funds	Total Net Assets ($ millions)
Short-Term		
Money market instrument funds	206	$165,563.7
Short-term U.S. government funds	92	44,491.3
Short-term municipal bond funds	99	34,953.7
Adjustable-rate preferred funds	14	2,210.5
	411	$247,219.2
Long-Term		
U.S. government funds	32	$ 8,141.7
GNMA funds	22	14,394.5
U.S. mortgage funds	12	3,881.5
Corp. bond funds—A rated	39	4,113.5
—BBB rated	19	2,602.0
—BBB rated/trading	17	1,540.1
General bond funds	19	2,929.6
High current yield funds	39	9,788.5
Private placement bond funds	5	437.2
Convertible securities funds	10	595.1
Preferred stock funds	3	88.2
Flexible income funds	19	1,660.5
	236	$ 50,172.4
Tax-Exempt		
General municipal bond funds	67	$ 14,762.7
California municipal bond funds	17	4,602.7
Massachusetts municipal bond funds	7	308.5
New York State municipal bond funds	16	2,403.1
Other states municipal bond funds	27	541.5
Intermediate municipal bond funds	23	2,974.9
High-yield municipal bond funds	11	5,732.2
	168	31,325.6
Grand Total	815	$328,717.2

SOURCE: Lipper—Fixed Income Fund Performance Analysis

SHORT-TERM MONEY MARKET INSTRUMENT FUNDS

Starting in 1971 a new phenomenon hit both the investment company and fixed income scenes—the short-term money market instrument funds. These funds, generally called money market funds, offer a combination of cash management (liquidity) services and near money market instrument yields. They make available to small investors the economies and high returns of large-scale money market investment and have become major competitors to the more traditional savings institutions.

Nearly all money market funds are available without sales charges (i.e., no-load) and they maintain constant net asset values of $1.00 per share.[2] Their total operating expense ratio average is 0.78 percent annually (May 1985). Altogether their total net asset value of $245 billion (as of June 30, 1985) accounted for 55.7 percent of all open-end mutual fund assets of $440 billion on that date.

Definitions

Three important elements of the money market fund industry should be identified:

1. *General money market instrument funds*—open-end funds that invest in financial instruments with short maturities. In order to be allowed to use amortized prices and dollar rounding, funds must have an average weighted maturity of no more than 120 days. Most funds restrict their longest maturity to one year, with average maturities in the range of 30 to 40 days. However, longer maturity issues with short-term optional maturities of under one year have been used by these funds.

2. *U.S. government short-term funds*—open-end funds that invest in U.S. Treasury and agency issues with maturities averaging about 40 days. Some of these issues may be the underlying security in holdings of repurchase agreements. During periods

---

[2] In order to compete with savings institutions, the marketers of money market instrument funds convinced the Securities and Exchange Commission that their funds should have a fixed net asset value. Income was to be the only variable similar to the experience in bank accounts in which the principal is nominally level. After considerable discussion and rancor, the fund industry and the Securities and Exchange Commission agreed that if funds followed one of two procedures called penny-rounding or amortized cost, it would permit funds to attempt to keep their net asset value at a predetermined level, normally $1 per share.

Valuing a fund's securities by the amortized cost method means that all of the securities in the fund's portfolio will be valued at their amortized cost. Amortized cost is an approximation of market value determined by systematically increasing the carrying value of a security if acquired at a discount, or systematically reducing the carrying value if acquired at a premium, so that the carrying value is equal to maturity value on the maturity date. It does not take into consideration unrealized capital gains or losses.

A penny-rounding fund's net asset value per share will remain constant if all net income that includes interest and similar plus net changes in the value of the portfolio is declared as a dividend each day and net asset value per share is computed to the nearest penny. The latter procedure prevents any net realized gains or losses on portfolio securities from being reflected in net asset value per share unless their accumulation over time would amount to more than a one-half cent per share variance from the fund's central value of $1 per share. The opportunity for such a sizable accumulation to occur is considered minimal due to the fund's portfolio and valuation policies, including the fund's commitment to maintaining a dollar-weighted average portfolio maturity that does not exceed 120 days.

of increasing credit crisis threat, the U.S. government short-term funds tend to attract a major part of the new investment in money funds.

3. *Short-term municipal bond funds*—open-end funds that invest largely, if not exclusively, in fixed income securities paying interest exempt from federal income tax. The maturities in the portfolio are normally limited to one year or less. Most of the short-term municipal bond funds are modeled after the money market funds in that they are priced continuously at a fixed price, normally of $1 per share. The Securities and Exchange Commission will grant the request to use penny rounding and/or amortized cost, which in effect keeps the net asset value even, only to those funds which make an undertaking to keep their average maximum maturity of the portfolio under 120 days.

Usefulness and Growth of Money Market Funds

Development of the money market fund industry has proven of great service not only to the small investor (who never or rarely before had access to the high returns and the many conveniences offered by the industry), but also to large investors, especially institutional, who have become extensive users of money market funds. Accordingly, since its beginning in 1971 the industry has displayed incredible growth, as shown in Exhibit 3.

By the close of 1982 the three categories of short-term funds (money market funds, short-term U.S. government funds, and short-term municipal bond funds) had total net assets of $236 billion as compared with total fixed income fund assets (including closed-end funds) of $258 billion.

This growth was sharply reversed at the beginning of 1983, when the federal ceiling on commercial bank account interest payments was eliminated and banks were permitted to open interest-competitive money market accounts, with the additional advantage of $100,000 FDIC deposit guarantees. Additionally, many banks offered promotional interest rates in excess of prevailing short-term market rates.

This combination initially siphoned a large volume of funds out of the money market mutual funds. After the early promotional period, however, the average yield of bank money market accounts dropped appreciably below average money market mutual fund yields, and has consistently remained lower. Money market funds have since recouped all of their 1983 losses.

In recent years the short-term U.S. government and short-term municipal bond funds have grown at particularly rapid rates, closely following the pattern established by the original money market funds in their

EXHIBIT 3 Total Net Assets and Number of Short-Term Funds Compared with Total Universe of All Fixed Income Funds

	Money Market Funds		Short-Term U.S. Government Funds		Short-Term Municipal Bond Funds		Total Fixed Income Funds*	
	Total Net Assets ($ millions)	Number of Funds	Total Net Assets ($ millions)	Number of Funds	Total Net Assets ($ millions)	Number of Funds	Total Net Assets ($ millions)	Number of Funds
June 30, 1985 (Exhibit 2)	$165,564	206	$44,491	92	$34,954	99	$328,717	815
Year-End								
1984	166,146	203	43,039	93	23,639	95	286,181	759
1983	128,228	186	33,234	97	16,619	69	212,720	609
1982	182,435	174	39,785	93	13,842	43	258,421	529
1981	158,904	121	22,893	39	5,223	26	200,260	380
1980	67,157	84	8,143	25	2,161	13	90,672	305
1979	40,686	67	4,243	13	363	5	58,005	254
1978	9,067	50	1,262	7	31	2	22,081	218
1977	3,028	41	559	7	3	2	14,253	190
1976	2,971	34	335	6	—	—	10,992	148
1975	3,156	23	101	5	—	—	8,692	120
1974	2,178	14	27	2	—	—	6,602	105
1973	79	1	2	2	—	—	4,809	83
1972	0	1	0	1	—	—	3,423	63

* Includes closed-end funds.
SOURCE: Lipper—Fixed Income Fund Performance Analysis.

earlier years. The U.S. government funds have appealed especially to investors seeking optimum short-term safety during periods of increasing strain upon the banking system, while the municipal funds have consistently provided superior yields for top-bracket investors.

In summary, the wide scope of usefulness of the short-term money market funds is indicated by the following examples:

1. To obtain the superior money market instrument rates of return, otherwise available only to large institutional investors.
2. To completely avoid the administrative problem of continuously reinvesting maturing instruments.
3. To obtain broad diversification and competent professional screening of credit risks.
4. To keep funds fully and efficiently invested at all times, via the automatic investment of income and the checkwriting privileges offered by nearly all money market funds.
5. For top tax bracket investors, to obtain yields in excess of the aftertax returns from top quality taxable short-term instruments.

We believe that these many conveniences and economies have become so widely appreciated that the money market fund industry is here to stay in an important way. By mid-year 1985, the $245 billion total value of all money market fund assets accounted for 55.7 percent of the entire $440 billion total assets of all open-end mutual funds. The successful recovery from the initially formidable competition of the new bank money market accounts, and the continued ability to provide superior returns augurs well for continued health and further growth of this important industry.

Selection of a Money Market Fund

As with any investment, the selection criteria for money market funds must satisfy the primary requirements of the investor. Following are some major elements to be considered in the selection process.

The fund management's structure, degree of experience, and capabilities. A breadth of experience in money management and strong research capabilities should be sought. We particularly favor funds equipped to perform their own independent credit research.

Character and scope of the fund's areas of investment. Investment area may spread broadly across the following alternatives or may be closely limited to a few of them:

U.S. Treasury
U.S. government agencies
Issuers guaranteed by U.S. government
Foreign governments
Domestic U.S. banks

Foreign branches of U.S. banks
Foreign banks' U.S. branches
Foreign banks' foreign branches
Bankers' acceptances
Commercial paper issuers
State and municipal governments
Revenue authorities

The investor may wish to avoid certain of these areas due to quality preferences, tax problems, or for other personal reasons.

The investor's own interest-rate expectations. This should influence the choice between funds with relatively short or long average maturities. A money fund will provide the investor with the average market yield available over the length of its average maturity, typically less than 60 days, but possibly longer.

The investor's own income tax status. This is of obvious importance in the selection between taxable and nontaxable types of funds. Some close calculations should be made because it is sometimes most economical to choose taxable funds.

The investor's degree of risk tolerance. There are wide differences in average quality among the funds, with the U.S. government funds generally considered as having the highest quality. The investor who is apprehensive about credit risks should adhere either to U.S. government or to the very highest quality corporate or municipal funds.

Ease of investment and prompt liquidation. Some funds have ascertainable reputations for back-office foul-ups, due to poor organization and/or to excessively large size. A major purpose of money fund investment is instant liquidity, and the investor should be reassured as to that expectation.

Sources of Information on Money Market Funds

There are numerous sources of information on money market funds. Generally, they fall into three categories—funds, newspapers, and specialized publications. The funds themselves will provide a great deal of historic information in terms of yields, performance, periodic portfolios, policies, and so on. This information is found in prospectuses, and annual and interim reports. Current yield information for most funds is usually available on a prerecorded message reached by calling a designated phone number.

Although funds provide primary information about themselves, they do not provide comparative information about competitors. *The Wall Street Journal* and other major newspapers at least once a week publish 7-day and 30-day yields plus the number of days of average maturity for each portfolio. These lists are usually for funds with total net assets in excess of $100 million.

A third source of data, specialized publications, includes the following:

Donoghue's Money Fund Report
  Box 540
  Holliston, MA 01746

Money Market Fund Survey
  51 East 42nd Street
  New York, NY 10017

United Mutual Fund Selector
  210 Newbury Street
  Boston, MA 02116

Wiesenberger Investment Company Services
  210 South Street
  Boston, MA 02111

The first two cover short-term funds exclusively, while the second two publications are more general mutual fund publications. Lipper Analytical Services provides extensive analysis of all types of fixed income funds but its publications are available only to professional financial organizations (e.g., banks, insurance companies, independent counselors, pension plans).

Limited Significance of Past Investment Performance and Yields

Investors should clearly recognize that past investment performance and/or yields do not provide a useful means for selecting funds. Although past results may indicate fund-management expertise under similar future market conditions, they afford no guarantee of future performance, either absolute or relative to other funds or to the market. The volatility of the money market is so great that today's successful strategy, in terms of instruments and maturities, may well prove wrong for tomorrow's markets.

Investors in short-term funds should not be overly concerned with yield differences between the various funds. The yield spread between the highest return fund and the lowest return fund is relatively small as shown in Exhibit 4. The large majority of yields cluster closely around the entire group average. Further, the highest yields quite likely reflect portfolio risk policies which may not be acceptable or appropriate for most investors, while the lowest yields may well reflect prudently desirable policies. Assured liquidity and safety of principal should be the paramount considerations in the selection of money market instrument funds.

EXHIBIT 4   Range in Characteristics of Money Market Instrument Funds
as of June 30, 1985 (153 funds, excluding short-term U.S.
government and municipal bond funds)

	Highest	Lowest	Average
12-month yield (percent)	9.7%	8.0%	8.9%
Average portfolio maturity (days)	82	1	36
Total net assets (millions of dollars)	$17,006	$3.5	$926
Number of holdings (number)	793	12	98
Portfolio structure (percent of total net assets):			
U.S. Treasury bills, notes, repos	100%	0	6%
U.S. government agencies	66	0	1
Bank certificates of deposit			
Total	98	0	20
Foreign banks	98	0	(Note)
Bankers' acceptances	62	0	10
Commercial paper	104	0	57
Letters of credit	67	0	2
Corporation notes	22	0	0
Other assets	58	0	1

Note: 107 of the 153 funds did not hold any foreign bank certificates of deposit, while 10 funds held such paper to the extent of 25 percent or more of total portfolio value. ·
SOURCE: Lipper—Portfolio Analysis Report on Fixed Income Funds

Investors should be fully aware of the very wide range of differences in the structure and characteristics of the many money market funds now available to the investing public. These are dramatically contrasted in Exhibit 4, which shows the highest, lowest, and average characteristics for 153 funds as of June 30, 1985 (excluding short-term U.S. government and municipal bond funds). Note the following remarkable contrasts:

- Yields range only between 8.0 percent and 9.7 percent, averaging 8.9 percent.
- Average portfolio maturity ranges from only one day out to 82 days, averaging 36 days.
- Fund size ranges from a massive $17 billion down to only $3.5 million, averaging $926 million.
- In respect to portfolio structure, in each category of investment at least some (many) funds avoid completely types of investment which account for 100 percent or more of the portfolios of other funds.
- While most of the funds (70 percent) elected not to hold any foreign bank certificates of deposit, 10 funds held such paper to the extent of 25 percent or more of total portfolio value, with a ratio of 98 percent for one fund.

Obviously the funds themselves have access to a wide array of alternatives, and they display widely differing preferences, among which the investor must make his own selection, hopefully well informed and appropriate to his objective.

Some Concluding Remarks about Short-Term Funds

The proliferation of short-term funds and publications that follow them is testimony to their growth and significance. In the past the practice of leaving large balances in checking accounts, brokerage accounts, or low-interest savings accounts was acceptable, since there were no perceived alternatives except for the choices available to the very wealthy and financially sophisticated. With the introduction of money funds in which idle money could earn higher interest rates than in savings accounts and could be accessed through a checkwriting account, all that has changed.

The money fund has probably won a permanent place in the portfolio of most investors. The size of the commitment to money funds will be determined by numerous variables; but especially by the interest rates afforded on the funds compared with other perceived alternatives. We suggest that even if the money funds did not yield a competitive rate, some money would stay in the funds, both for convenience and due to inertia.

For most investors the perceived risk should play a higher role than the maximization of return. As already noted, the spread between the highest and lowest returns is not substantial enough to be the first concern of the investor. Key elements of much greater importance are the interest-rate (maturity) risk and the credit risk.

The interest-rate risk (and opportunity) is a function of being locked into a portfolio when market rates of interest are changing. For example, assume two funds with average maturities of 20 days and 60 days when interest rates begin to rise. The fund with an average maturity of 60 days would not be able to take advantage of the higher yielding paper as quickly as could the shorter-term fund. Further, the portfolio of the longer-term fund would be vulnerable to some market price risk as interest rates rose. If any significant number of its shareholders redeem to go to higher yielding funds, the fund might have to sell some of its assets below their portfolio value, sustaining some capital loss.

The second risk is credit risk. In this case the fear is that the issuer fails to pay principal or interest in a timely fashion as required by its promise or indenture. This is a much smaller risk than the interest-rate risk.

While we do not perceive any substantial risk to short-term fund investors if a risk were to occur, it would be most likely in a period of very low interest rates when some funds for competitive reasons extend maturities and/or accept lower quality credits. These funds would typically be small or have great competitive pressures placed on them.

Despite the cautionary notes expressed, we believe that short-term funds provide an ideal vehicle for idle funds awaiting longer term use, and for emergency reserve funds. During periods of volatile short-term rates, they may well be among the very best of investments.

——————— 21 ———————

Performance and Portfolio Analysis of Fixed Income Funds

A. Michael Lipper, C.F.A.
President
Lipper Analytical Services, Inc.

Alling Woodruff, C.F.A.
Vice President
Lipper Analytical Services, Inc.

INTRODUCTION

The fixed income fund investor who wants to investigate fixed income mutual funds should review a number of different characteristics. Although past performance is no guarantee of future performance, it may prove a useful guide to possible future results, provided that both the portfolio characteristics and the future conditions are similar to the specific past periods measured. There are three significant performance-related items to be measured: income production, capital progress, and some mixture of these into a combined total return. Calculating these three items often reveals a repetitive pattern in the fund's performance. The patterns are most likely to repeat in fixed income funds if the portfolio structure (maturities, quality, and sector) and turnover rates are reasonably constant.

INCOME PRODUCTION

Income production for a fund is normally measured by the amount of net investment income produced per share. Net investment income is the gross income of the fund (interest, dividends, and other income generated) less the expenses of the fund, including management fees.

Most funds choose to qualify as a conduit for tax purposes and, thus pay no income taxes, as the tax liability is transferred entirely to the shareholder. In order to do this they must conform with Subchapter M of the Internal Revenue Code, which requires among other things that they distribute at least 90 percent of their net investment income. As a practical matter, most funds pay out essentially all of their investment income. The method of payment is the declaration of an income dividend.

Most funds have a policy of paying income dividends regularly, and they may choose to pay out dividends daily, monthly, quarterly, semi-annually, or annually. In most cases the shareholder has the option of receiving the dividend in cash or in additional shares of the fund. If the dividend is paid in the form of additional shares, this does not relieve the shareholder of the obligations of reporting the income and paying taxes on the dividends. Most money market funds accrue dividends daily, crediting shareholder accounts at the close of each month.

To determine income production, there are four elements to be measured.

Yield. Yield is the income generated over each 12-month period divided by the ending net asset value. (Variations on this measure may use beginning or an average net asset value.) The current net asset value yield is the common measure of income generation efficiency for comparison purposes among alternative investments.

Growth in income generation. Shifting levels of interest rates, changes in the nature of assets, and changes in fund expenses will cause generated income to fluctuate. Investors should be aware of changing levels of income because a low-yielding fund with growing dividends may fill their needs better than a high-yielding fund with no growth.

Volatility of income. Income volatility is important for the many investors who need a predictable level of income. In a period of widely fluctuating interest rates, different strategies may produce wide changes in income dividends. To determine income production, investors should know whether income will be stable or will vary widely.

Composition of income. Knowing the income composition is also important. Income may come from unreliable sources (bonds of companies close to bankruptcy) or the portfolio composition itself may be changed.

CAPITAL PROGRESS

Capital progress is the performance of the principal of an account—the difference between the beginning cost and the current value. Measuring capital progress works very well for a security or a portfolio of securities, but the measurement is complicated for investment companies because of tax considerations.

As previously mentioned, most funds choose to avoid paying taxes

EXHIBIT 1 A-Rated Corporate Bond Fund Performance for Periods Ending October 31, 1985 (20 top-ranking funds)

Investment Company	Total Reinvestment						Principal Only					
	Percent Chg 9/30/85 to 10/31/85	Rank	Percent Chg 12/31/84 to 10/31/85	Rank	Percent Chg 10/31/84 to 10/31/85	Rank	Percent Chg 9/30/85 to 10/31/85	Rank	Percent Chg 12/31/84 to 10/31/85	Rank	Percent Chg 10/31/84 to 10/31/85	Rank
Sigma Income Shares	2.15	10	18.89	1	23.10	2	−0.37	34	7.62	4	11.43	1
Bond Fund of America	1.82	15	18.85	2	21.95	3	0.90	19	8.43	3	8.08	5
Fort Dearborn Income Sec.	1.57	22	18.72	3	23.37	1	1.57	8	9.72	2	10.88	2
United Bond Fund	2.48	2	17.02	4	19.69	5	1.58	7	6.45	10	6.64	16
GIT A Rated Income	2.21	4	16.47	5	19.97	4	1.36	9	6.67	7	7.88	7
Dreyfus A Bonds Plus	2.17	8	16.35	6	19.59	6	1.30	12	6.53	9	7.52	8
Value Line Bond	2.34	3	16.21	7	19.37	8	−0.32	32	4.48	22	7.33	10
Kemper Income and Cap. Pres.	1.30	27	16.16	8	19.35	9	0.35	29	5.28	17	5.28	23
Merrill Lyn. High Quality	2.17	9	16.15	9	19.56	7	1.28	13	6.03	11	7.06	12
Hutton Inv. SR. Bond	3.01	1	16.10	10	18.83	14	2.10	2	2.76	31	5.17	24
Bond Port. for Endowments	2.20	5	15.98	11	18.97	12	2.20	1	10.10	1	7.05	13
Scudder Target Genl. 1994	1.40	25	15.68	12	18.79	15	0.73	21	7.41	5	8.57	4
J. Hancock Bond	2.20	6	15.39	13	19.23	10	1.33	10	5.78	14	7.35	9
Putnam Income	1.65	21	15.24	14	18.91	13	0.71	23	4.85	20	6.09	18
Lutheran Bro. Income	1.74	17	15.14	15	18.78	16	0.79	20	4.19	25	5.42	21
Excelsior Income Shares	1.73	18	15.12	16	18.98	11	1.73	5	6.02	12	6.67	15
North Star Bond Fund	1.71	19	15.02	17	18.63	17	−0.80	35	3.98	26	7.24	11
Scudder Target Genl. 1990	1.21	28	14.96	18	18.61	18	0.59	24	7.24	6	9.07	3
Bunker Hill Income Sec.	1.07	32	14.85	19	17.86	21	1.07	17	4.41	23	3.71	31
Fidelity Thrift Trust	1.65	20	14.75	20	18.53	19	1.65	6	6.61	8	8.04	6
Averages 36 funds (not all shown)	1.68	36	14.64	34	17.92	34	0.84	36	5.25	34	6.32	34

Note: In the interest of complete comparability, regardless of the Funds' stated objectives, our performance calculations include the reinvestment of all capital gains distributions and income dividends for the indicated period. It is our intention to present total performance results in a manner designed to best serve the portfolio manager without regard to tax consequences or charges to an investor. Yield is calculated monthly using the latest 12 month income dividends and net asset values adjusted for the latest 12 month capital gains distributions. This material has been prepared for the use of professional money managers and is not to be publicly disseminated.

SOURCE: Lipper—Fixed Income Fund Performance Analysis, 10/31/85

by qualifying under Subchapter M of the Internal Revenue Code. These provisions cover not only investment income generated, but also capital gains from securities transactions. Each year, funds have a single opportunity to declare a capital gains dividend. Shareholders have the option of taking the dividend in cash or in additional shares of the fund. In either case the shareholders have a tax liability for the taxes due on the capital gains. After declaring a dividend, the fund calculates the percentage change from the beginning net asset value to the *adjusted* ending net asset value (after the dividend). The preferred measurement technique assumes reinvestment rather than adding back the distributions to net asset value at the end of the period. The reinvestment method gives the investor the benefit of the dividend being reinvested from the "ex-date" to the end of the period. In a period of rising prices, this will improve the performance over the add-back method, and the reverse is true for declining markets.

Although for most comparison purposes fixed income funds should be measured by the use of the total (reinvested) return methodology, certain trust accounts may find a hybrid method useful. Often personal trusts require income generated to go to one class of beneficiaries and the ultimate beneficiaries to eventually receive the remaining principal or capital. To aid the analysis for the remainderman class, in the Lipper—Fixed Income Fund Performance Analysis, performance data are shown for both total return and principal only. In this report, the principal-only calculation reinvests the capital gains only. Exhibit 1 shows both total reinvestment and principal-only performance for a sample of funds keeping the bulk of their assets in A or better credits.

PERIODS TO BE MEASURED

One looks at performance data, in part, to develop an understanding of the past and to aid in looking at the future. As the past is made up of discrete if not overlapping periods, past records should be measured in a similar fashion. In Exhibit 1 three periods with different beginning dates and the same ending dates are measured. Even though this particular table covers a maximum period of 12 months, examine the variability in the ranking columns. Out of 20 funds shown, review the top and bottom two funds for each period and the averages for a total of 36 funds. Below is a further extract from the table comparing the total return calculation data for October and the 10 months ending in October.

Month of October		10 Months	
Rank	Fund	Rank	Fund
1	Merrill Lynch High Quality	1	Sigma Income Shares
2	United Bond Fund	2	Bond Fund of America
19	North Star Bond Fund	19	Bunker Hill Income Sec.
20	Fidelity Thrift Trust	20	Fidelity Thrift Trust

Out of a 20-fund universe, only one of the four funds on the extremities of the performance array was found at the same extreme for the other time period. Thus one must select carefully which periods to measure. If there is a sufficient number of funds operating, one should measure fixed income funds for at least three periods: 1, 5, and 10 years. Also, returns over significant market cycle-periods rather than calendar time periods should be reviewed for significant additional perspective.

PATTERNS

As we indicated earlier, the purpose of performance analysis is to identify historical patterns that may have some significant value in thinking about the future. We have already demonstrated that it is unusual to find in any large universe of funds consistency of outstanding performance. To a large extent those funds who desire to be at the top of any performance league, particularly short-term periods, must also accept the risk of being on the bottom. This follows inevitably from the strategy of taking extreme positions relative to competition. Performance analysis can be extremely valuable in identifying periods when specific funds perform well or poorly versus competition and seeing whether these periods have common characteristics (e.g., rising interest rates, increase in supply of new issues, etc.).

Another pattern one looks for is whether over longer periods of time a fund provides superior returns in periods that contain a number of rising and falling markets. For many long-term investors, funds that go down less than average yet show some gains in rising markets are better investments than ones that have a better performance in rising markets but a substantially greater than average decline in falling markets. Investors very often lose their courage in falling markets and exit at absolutely the wrong time and price. Therefore funds with the greatest decline during that period do the most damage to the investors' capital.

Another use of pattern analysis is to reveal a sharp break in the fund's past performance patterns. This can be caused by a change in portfolio manager, a change in portfolio strategy, or a structural change in the fund's principal investment arena; for example, a decline in the perceived quality of electric utility issues relative to industrial issues.

Perhaps the most important of all patterns which investors should study are the widely differing performance characteristics of different types of fixed income funds. Exhibit 2 shows changes in the annual total return performance of various types of fixed income funds from 1974 through 1985. Note the wide variations in returns over this 11-year period:

1. Over the period as a whole, high current-yield bond funds showed the greatest increase in returns (+390 percent), albeit with considerable quality and maturity risk assumed.

EXHIBIT 2 Relative Performance of Seven Categories of Fixed Income Funds (cumulative performance, December 31, 1974 = 100.00)

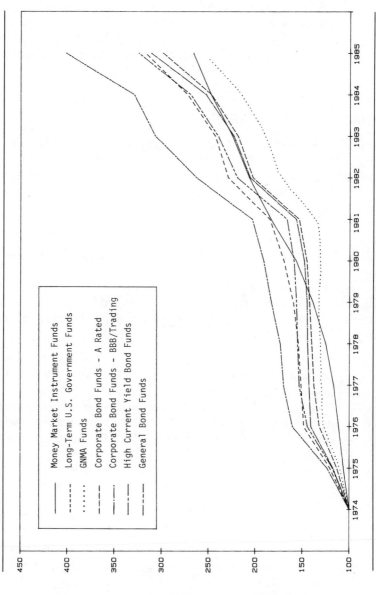

Money Market Instrument Funds
Long-Term U.S. Government Funds
GNMA Funds
Corporate Bond Funds - A Rated
Corporate Bond Funds - BBB/Trading
High Current Yield Bond Funds
General Bond Funds

SOURCE: Lipper—Fixed Income Fund Performance Analysis

2. The increases for all other groups fell within a fairly narrow range, led by general bond funds (+316 percent) and U.S. government funds (+311 percent), with government guaranteed GNMA funds showing the smallest gain (+251 percent).
3. The returns of money market instrument funds increased by 265 percent for the period as a whole. However, during the high inflation years, 1977–1981, their gains were much greater than any of the other six categories.

PORTFOLIO ANALYSIS

Within each fixed income fund category there are funds that display unique performance characteristics, compared with others in the same category. Often the cause for such variations is a significant difference in the structure of the portfolio. Structural analysis of a fixed income fund focuses on type of instrument, maturity, quality, and coupon rate. In general, structural portfolio analysis is even more useful with fixed income funds than with equity funds.

Each quarter Lipper Analytical Services examines the portfolio structure of the fixed income funds. Exhibit 3 shows investment performance, yield, and portfolio structure for 24 A-rated bond funds for the third quarter of 1985. These funds are arranged in descending order of their third quarter total investment returns, with dividends reinvested. Note the following highlights of this exhibit:

1. In total reinvested performance there was a dispersion of 259 basis points for the quarter, from a high of +2.80 percent to a low of +0.21 percent.
2. Twelve-month yields did not array themselves in the same order as overall performance, with the three highest yields well down toward the bottom of the list. This suggests that yields are not a primary determinant of performance.
3. The range of portfolio diversification, as measured by total number of holdings, varies greatly, from a maximum of 162 issues to a mere 6 in one case. The average holding of 52 issues indicates about 2 percent of portfolio per issue. However, the median number of 39 issues, indicating an average holding of about 2.50 percent, appears more representative of the group.
4. The disposition of assets among principal types of holdings also varies widely:
   Cash and money market instrument holdings range from zero to 60 percent of total portfolio value.
   U.S. government bond holdings range from only 2 percent to 91 percent.
   Corporate bond holdings range from zero to 87 percent.

EXHIBIT 3 Corporate Bond Funds—A Rated, Investment Performance, Yield, and Portfolio Structure (3rd quarter 1985)

Total (Reinv. Perf.)	12-Month Yield	No. of Holdings	Total Net Assets $ mil	Investment Company Name	Percent of Total Net Assets							
					Cash and Money Mrkt. Instr.	U.S. Govt. Bonds	Can. Bonds	Other Int. Bonds	Corp. Bonds	Corp. Pfds.	Cv. Bond and Pfd.	Com. Stk. and Other
2.80	10.9	162	410.1	Bond Fund of America	7	37	4	0	51	0	0	1
2.54	10.0	25	15.5	Bond Port for Endowments	10	52	1	2	35	0	0	0
2.43	10.0	22	23.5	North Star Bond Fund	6	79	0	2	13	0	0	0
2.39	10.3	95	164.8	Dreyfus A Bonds Plus	5	22	0	3	70	0	0	0
2.36	9.6	39	21.1	Sigma Income Shares	3	56	0	0	35	2	4	0
2.31	11.3	71	319.0	United Bond Fund	0	39	0	2	59	0	0	0
2.30	11.7	99	225.6	Lutheran Bro. Income	2	57	0	0	41	0	0	0
2.27	10.2	12	70.4	Value Line Bond	3	69	1	0	28	0	0	0
2.11	10.2	108	941.4	J. Hancock Bond	6	13	1	0	80	0	0	0
2.04	11.0	55	135.0	Merrill Lyn. High Quality	10	20	0	5	65	0	0	0
2.03	9.6	23	6.9	Phoenix High Qual. Bond	11	2	0	0	87	0	0	0
1.98	10.0	31	165.2	Vanguard Fi. Inc. Sht. Term	17	29	0	9	45	0	0	0
1.92	12.1	79	118.2	Massmutual Income Inv.	7	31	4	0	58	0	0	0
1.83	12.3	42	134.2	Kemper Income and Cap. Pres.	2	34	0	0	63	0	1	0
1.71	N/A	32	3.7	"New Beginning" Inv. Resv.	60	23	0	0	17	0	0	0
1.70	N/A	6	2.5	The Bond Accumulation	9	91	0	0	0	0	0	0
1.60	9.9	90	218.9	Fidelity Thrift Trust	2	43	0	0	55	0	0	0
1.51	10.9	39	19.0	Pioneer Bond Fund	11	26	14	4	45	0	0	0
1.33	9.4	37	11.6	United Missouri Bk. Bond	25	62	0	0	13	0	0	0
1.28	14.2	32	202.1	Hutton Inv. Sr. Bond R	0	66	0	1	33	0	0	0
1.25	10.2	N/A	231.1	FTP–Fixed Income Port.	5	49	1	0	45	0	0	0
1.08	10.6	20	15.7	Sentinel Bond Fund	20	35	0	0	45	0	0	0
0.81	10.5	65	85.9	Keystone B-1 R	11	25	0	13	43	0	0	0
0.21	10.0	22	19.9	Pro. Income Fund	6	53	0	0	18	0	23	0
1.82	10.6*	52*	148.3	Average	9	42	1	1	43	0	1	0

* Excludes issues for which data are not available (N/A).

R Redemption fee may apply.

SOURCE: Lipper—Portfolio Analysis Report on Fixed Income Funds, Third Quarter, 1985

Only four funds held any convertible securities, but one of these had 23 percent in such issues.

Exhibit 4 shows quality rating and maturity structure for the same 24 A-Rated bond funds shown in Exhibit 3. By definition, these funds maintain at least 60 percent of their assets in A or better quality corporate and/or U.S. government securities. For the group as a whole the average commitments were:

Cash and/or U.S. government bonds	51%
Corporate bonds rated A or better	39
Corporate bonds rated BBB or lower	10
Total	100%

However, there is substantial variation in the extent to which the various managements elect to dip below the A-quality borderline:

- Five funds report no holdings below A-quality.
- Four funds show 25 percent or more of their portfolios below that level, with one reporting 35 percent.

It should be clearly understood that many of these fund managements maintain top-flight credit analysts on their own staffs. Hence their judgments of quality ratings may frequently differ from the Moody's or Standard & Poor's ratings which are generally used.

With higher quality portfolios the management of the maturity schedule is critical to ultimate performance results. In this particular quarter most of the funds that had a significant portion of their portfolios in the longer maturities on average did better than the shorter maturity funds.

In the analysis of bond funds it is important to note substantial changes in the portfolio structure. These often are highlighted and explained in fund management reports to shareholders. For the A-Rated bond funds listed in Exhibits 3 and 4 we show in Exhibit 5 changes of more than 15 percent in various categories of bonds during the third quarter of 1985. In most cases increases in one category were closely matched by decreases in another. These changes were sizable enough to materially alter the overall character of the portfolios.

Still another useful analytical tool is the turnover rate of investments within the portfolio. The particular measure used, prescribed by the Securities and Exchange Commission, is the smaller of sales or purchases of securities divided into the average total net assets. Exhibit 6 shows turnover rates for the 20 top-ranking A-Rated corporate bond funds previously listed in Exhibit 1.

It is evident from the wide range of turnover rates in Exhibit 6 that many different routes may lead to top investment performance. Five funds display extremely high turnover rates, exceeding 100 percent in

EXHIBIT 4 Corporate Bond Funds—A Rated, Portfolio Quality Ratings and Maturity Schedule (3rd quarter 1985)

Rated Percent of Total Net Assts.	Avrge. Coup.	Investment Company Name	Percent of Total Net Assets										
			Ratings					Years to Maturity					
			AAA and AA	A	BBB	BB	B and Under	<1	1–5	6–10	11–20	21–30	30+
52	11.3	Bond Fund of America	13	4	7	11	17	0	8	25	31	28	0
32	11.3	Bond Port. for Endowments	10	9	13	0	0	0	15	29	26	20	0
15	11.5	North Star Bond Fund	11	4	0	0	0	0	56	38	0	1	0
72	12.0	Dreyfus A Bonds Plus	29	25	16	1	1	0	8	42	44	76	0
41	10.1	Sigma Income Shares	17	10	9	3	2	0	0	5	14	76	0
59	11.6	United Bond Fund	30	14	12	2	1	0	1	26	31	29	13
37	14.9	Lutheran Bro. Income	25	0	9	3	0	0	2	5	15	76	3
28	12.7	Value Line Bond	15	10	3	0	0	0	0	3	10	81	3
80	12.6	J. Hancock Bond	15	38	26	1	0	0	9	23	31	26	5
N/A	13.1	Merrill Lyn. High Quality	N/A	N/A	N/A	N/A	N/A	N/A	N/A	N/A	N/A	N/A	N/A
87	N/A	Phoenix High Qual. Bond	13	52	22	0	0	0	0	54	12	23	0
46	10.2	Vanguard Fi. Inc. Sht. Term	30	16	0	0	0	0	73	10	0	0	0
65	11.7	Massmutual Income Inv.	28	8	10	6	13	5	21	29	36	2	0
64	14.3	Kemper Income and Cap. Pres.	32	7	19	3	3	15	20	49	14	0	0
17	9.4	"New Beginning" Inv. Resv.	11	5	1	0	0	N/A	N/A	N/A	N/A	N/A	N/A
91	N/A	The Bond Accumulation	0	0	0	0	0	0	71	20	0	0	0
95	N/A	Fidelity Thrift Trust	62	33	0	0	0	3	19	65	6	5	0
63	11.5	Pioneer Bond Fund	49	8	6	0	0	5	26	21	6	30	0
N/A	N/A	United Missouri Bk. Bond R	N/A	N/A	N/A	N/A	N/A	20	32	22	1	0	0
34	9.8	Hutton Inv. Sr.-Bond R	2	20	10	2	0	0	0	20	22	55	3
28	N/A	FTP-Fixed Income Port.	25	3	0	0	0	2	39	51	3	0	0
53	12.3	Sentinel Bond Fund	34	16	0	0	0	15	19	23	2	21	0
60	11.8	Keystone B-1 R	35	17	8	0	0	0	2	6	9	68	0
41	10.9	Pro Income Fund	14	7	9	5	6	0	13	12	40	29	0
52*	11.7*	Average	26*	13*	8*	1*	1*	2*	19*	26*	16*	25*	1*

* Excludes issues for which data are not available (N/A).
R Redemption fee may apply.
SOURCE: Lipper—Portfolio Analysis Report on Fixed Income Funds, Third Quarter, 1985

EXHIBIT 5 Corporate Bond Funds—A Rated, Portfolio Changes in Excess of 15 Percent (3rd quarter 1985)

Fund Name	Percentage Increase		Percentage Decrease	
FTP-Fixed Income Portfolio	U.S. government bonds	24	Corporate bonds	−22
Keystone B-1	Corporate bonds	43	Canadian bonds	−44
"New Beginning" Inv. Resv.	U.S. government bonds	23	Corporate bonds	−22
Value Line Bond	U.S. government bonds	18		

SOURCE: Lipper—Portfolio Analysis Report on Fixed Income Funds, Third Quarter, 1985.

EXHIBIT 6 Turnover Rates of 20 Top-Ranking A-Rated Corporate Bond Funds

Fund Name	Fiscal Year Ended	Latest Year	Year Before
Bond Fund of America	12/31/84	134%	104%
Bond Portfolio for Endowments	7/31/84	131	190
Bunker Hill Income Securities	9/30/85	92	104
Dreyfus A Bonds Plus	3/31/85	21	5
Excelsior Income Shares	12/31/84	91	64
Fidelity Thrift Trust	12/31/84	80	288
Fort Dearborn Income Securities	9/30/84	10	80
GIT A-Rated Income	3/31/85	94	0
J. Hancock Bond Fund	12/31/84	47	23
Hutton Inv.—SR Bond Fund	12/31/84	477	346
Kemper Income and Capital Pres.	10/31/84	80	68
Lutheran Bro. Income Fund	1/31/85	26	78
Merrill Lynch High Quality	9/30/84	112	145
North Star Bond Fund	3/31/85	22	40
Putnam Income Fund	10/31/84	265	207
Scudder Target Genl.—1990	10/31/84	13	4
Scudder Target Genl.—1994	Commenced operations 4/02/84		
Sigma Income Shares	9/30/84	6	16
United Bond Fund	12/31/84	94	40
Value Line Bond Fund	8/31/85	64	31

SOURCE: Lipper—Directors' Analytical Data, November, 1985.

each of the two years shown, and ranging up to 346 percent and 477 percent in two successive years at the upper extreme.

At the other extreme five funds display rates of less than 50 percent in each of the two years, while others show wide variation from one year to the next. There is no discernible correlation between investment performance and turnover rates but the investor's appraisal of risk and reliability of returns may well be influenced by his judgment in respect to turnover rates.

CONCLUSIONS

Performance analysis of fixed income funds is a useful historical tool, providing an understanding as to what funds and what policies worked well in specific time periods. Portfolio analysis is useful in understanding the performance results.

For most investors a fund that follows consistent basic policies in respect to portfolio structure and turnover rate is likely to produce a more predictable result than one that shifts policy frequently and rapidly, even if the more changeable fund occasionally produces a better result. Another factor favoring the more sedate fund is that chances are greater that the fund that demonstrates more flexibility is likely to change policy after a new trend has already gotten underway, and thus will be playing catch-up ball. On the other hand, a fund that has a consistent policy that has recently had a period of poor relative performance is probably much closer to the point in time when it will have relatively good performance, unless it changes its policy. This unfortunately happens altogether too often at the absolutely wrong time, among funds with highly variable policies.

For investors who have a need to invest in fixed income securities, fixed income funds offer the distinct advantage of buying into an existing portfolio with a known policy, record, and expense structure. Often the fixed income shareholder will, quite inexpensively, have some of the most competent managers in the institutional investment world working for him. The funds are likely to produce substantially superior returns for their shareholders.

PART 3

Credit Analysis

22

Credit Analysis for Corporate Bonds*

Jane Tripp Howe, C.F.A.
Consultant

Traditionally, credit analysis for corporate bonds has focused almost exclusively on the default risk of the bond. That is, what is the chance that the bondholder will not receive the scheduled interest payments and/or principal at maturity. This one-dimensional analysis concerned itself primarily with straight ratio analysis. This approach was deemed appropriate during the time when interest rates were stable and investors purchased bonds with the purpose of holding them to maturity. In this scenario fluctuations in the market value of the bonds due to interest-rate changes were minimal, and fluctuations due to credit changes of the bonds were mitigated by the fact that the investor had no intention of selling the bond before maturity. During the past decade, however, the purpose of buying bonds has changed dramatically. Investors still purchase bonds for security and thereby forego the higher expected return of other assets such as common stock. However, an increasing number of investors buy bonds to actively trade them with the purpose of making a profit on changes in interest rates or in absolute or relative credit quality. The second dimension of corporate bond credit analysis addresses the latter purpose of buying a bond. What is the likelihood of a change in credit quality that will affect the price of the bond? This second dimension of corporate bond analysis deals primarily with the ratios and profitability trends, such as return on equity, operating margins, and asset turnover, generally associated with common stock analysis. In practice, both dimensions of analysis should be applied in corporate bond analysis. In a sense, both dimensions are addressing the same

---
* I wish to thank Richard S. Wilson, vice president, fixed income research, Merrill Lynch, Pierce, Fenner & Smith, for his helpful comments and suggestions.

issue—default or credit risk. However, only by using both dimensions of credit analysis will the analyst address the dual purpose of a bond-holding: security of interest and principal payments and stability or improvement of credit risk during the life of the bond.

Historically, common stock and bond research areas have been viewed as separate. However, with the development of the options theory, the two disciplines are beginning to be viewed as complementary.

The value of the option is a direct function of the company's aggregate equity valuation. As the market value of a company's stock increases, the value of the option increases. Conversely, as the market value of a company's stock declines, so does the value of the option. The practical implication of this theory for corporate bonds analysis is that the perceptions of both markets should be compared before a final credit judgment is rendered. For the analyst who believes that there is a higher level of efficiency in the stock market than in the bond market, particular attention should be paid to the stock price of the company being analyzed. Of interest will be those situations in which the judgment of the two markets differ substantially.

For example, in early 1981 the market to book values of the major chemical companies ranged from .77 to 2.15. The bond ratings of these same companies ranged from Baa/BBB to Aaa/AAA. The interesting point is not the range of either the market to book values or bond ratings, but rather the fact that although there was some correlation between the market/book ratios and bond ratings, there were instances in which there was little or no correlation. The options theory would suggest that there should be more of a relationship between the two. When the relative valuation of the bond as measured by the rating is low compared with the equity valuation as measured by market/book, one or both markets may be incorrectly valuing the company. Given the evidence that bond-rating changes generally lag market moves, it is likely in this case that the bond market is undervaluing the company.

Although there are numerous types of corporate bonds outstanding, three major issuing segments of bonds can be differentiated: industrials, utilities, and finance companies. This chapter will primarily address industrials in its general description of bond analysis and then discuss the utility and finance issues.

INDUSTRY CONSIDERATIONS

The first step in analyzing a bond is to gain some familiarity with the industry. Only within the context of an industry is a company analysis valid. For example, a company growing at 15 percent annually may appear attractive. However, if the industry is growing at 50 percent annually, the company is competitively weak. Industry considerations can be numerous. However, an understanding of the following eight variables should give the general fixed income analyst a sufficient framework to properly interpret a company's prospects.

Economic Cyclicality

The economic cyclicality of an industry is the first variable an analyst should consider in reviewing an industry. Does the industry closely follow GNP growth, as does the retailing industry, or is it recession resistant but slow growing, as is the electric utility industry? The growth in earnings per share (EPS) of a company should be measured against the growth trend of its industry. Major deviations from the industry trend should be the focus of further analysis. Some industries may be somewhat dependent on general economic growth but be more sensitive to demographic changes. The nursing home industry is a prime example of this type of sensitivity. With the significant aging of the U.S. population, the nursing home industry is projected to have above average growth for the foreseeable future. Other industries, such as the banking industry, are sensitive to interest rates. When interest rates are rising, the earnings of banks with a high federal funds exposure underperform the market as their loan rates lag behind increases in the cost of money. Conversely, as interest rates fall, banking earnings outperform the market because the lag in interest change works in the banks' favor.

In general, however, the earnings of few industries perfectly correlate with one economic statistic. Not only are industries sensitive to many economic variables, but often various segments within a company or an industry move countercyclically, or at least with different lags in relation to the general economy. For example, the housing industry can be divided between new construction and remodeling and repair. New construction historically has led GNP growth, but repair and remodeling has exhibited less sensitivity to general trends. Therefore, in analyzing a company in the construction industry, the performance of each of its segments must be compared with the performance of the subindustry.

Growth Prospects

A second industry variable related to that of economic cyclicality is the growth prospects for an industry. Is the growth of the industry projected to increase and be maintained at a high level, such as in the nursing industry, or is growth expected to be stable? Each growth scenario has implications for a company. In the case of a fast-growth industry, how much capacity is needed to meet demand, and how will this capacity be financed? In the case of slow-growth industries, is there a movement toward diversification and/or a consolidation within the industry, such as in the brewing industry? A company operating within a fast-growing industry often has a better potential for credit improvement than does a company whose industry's growth prospects are below average.

Research and Development Expenses

The broad assessment of growth prospects is tempered by the third variable—the research and development expenditures required to maintain or expand market position. The technology field is growing at an above-average rate, and the companies in the industry should do correspondingly well. However, products with a high technological component can become dated and obsolete quickly. Therefore, although a company may be situated well in an industry, if it does not have the financial resources to maintain a technological lead, or at least expend a sufficient amount of money to keep technologically current, its position is likely to deteriorate in the long run. In the short run, however, a company whose R&D expenditures are consistently below industry averages may produce above-average results because of expanded margins.

Competition

Competition within an industry also directly relates to the market structure of an industry and has implications for pricing flexibility. An unregulated monopoly is in an enviable position in that it can price its goods at a level that will maximize profits. Most industries encounter some free market forces and must price their goods in relation to the supply and demand for their goods as well as the price charged for similar goods. In an oligopoly, a pricing leader is not uncommon. General Motors Corporation, for example, performs this function in the automobile industry. A concern arises when a small company is in an industry that is trending toward oligopoly. In this environment, the small company's costs of production may be higher than those of the industry leaders, and yet it may have to conform to the pricing of the industry leaders. In the extreme, a price war could force the smaller companies out of business. This situation is present now in the brewing industry. For the past two decades, as the brewing industry has become increasingly concentrated, the leaders have gained market share at the expense of the small, local brewers. Many small, local brewers have either been acquired or have gone out of business. These local brewers have been at a dual disadvantage: They are in an industry whose structure is moving toward oligopoly, and yet their weak competitive position within the industry largely precludes pricing flexibility.

Sources of Supply

The market structure of an industry and its competitive forces have a direct impact on the fifth industry variable—sources of supply of major production components. A company in the paper industry that has sufficient timber acreage to supply 100 percent of its pulp is preferable to a paper company that must buy all or a large percentage of its pulp. A company that is not self-sufficient in its factors of production but is sufficiently powerful in its industry to pass along increased costs is also in an enviable position. R. J. Reynolds is an example of the latter type of company. Although R. J. Reynolds has major exposure to commodity prices for ingredients, its strong market position has enabled it to pass along increased costs of goods sold.

Degree of Regulation

The sixth industry consideration is the degree of regulation. The electric utility industry is the classic example of regulation. Nearly all phases of a utility's operations are regulated. The analyst should not be as concerned with the existence or absence of regulation per se, but rather with the direction of regulation and the effect it has on the profitability of the company. For the electric utility industry, regulation generally places a cap on earned returns. Other industries, such as the drug industry, also have a high though less pervasive degree of regulation. In the drug industry, however, the threat of increased regulation has been a negative factor in the industry for some time.

Labor

The labor situation of an industry should also be analyzed. Is the industry heavily unionized? If so, what has been the historical occurrence of strikes? When do the current contracts expire, and what is the likelihood of timely settlements? The labor situation is also important in nonunionized companies, particularly those whose labor situation is tight. What has been the turnover of professionals and management in the firm? What is the probability of a firm's employees, such as highly skilled engineers, being hired by competing firms? The more labor intensive an industry, the more significance the labor situation assumes.

Accounting

A final industry factor to be considered is accounting. Does the industry have special accounting practices, such as those in the insurance industry or the electric utility industry? If so, an analyst should become familiar with industry practices before proceeding with a company analysis. Also important is whether a company is liberal or conservative in applying the generally accepted accounting principles. The norm of an industry should be ascertained, and the analyst should be sure to analyze comparable figures.

FINANCIAL ANALYSIS

Having achieved an understanding of an industry, the analyst is ready to proceed with a financial analysis. The financial analysis should be conducted in three phases. The first phase consists of traditional ratio analysis for bonds. The second phase, generally associated with common stock research, consists of analyzing the components of a company's return on equity (ROE). The final phase considers such nonfinancial factors as management and foreign exposure and includes an analysis of the indenture.

Traditional Ratio Analysis

There are numerous ratios that can be calculated in applying traditional ratio analysis to bonds. Of these, eight will be discussed in this section. Those selected are the ratios with the widest degree of applicability. In analyzing a particular industry, however, other ratios assume significance and should be considered. For example, in the electric utility industry, allowance for funds used in construction as a percent of net income is an important ratio that is inapplicable to the analysis of industrial or financial companies.

Pretax interest coverage. Generally, the first ratio calculated in credit analysis is pretax interest coverage. This ratio measures the number of times interest charges are covered on a pretax basis. Fixed-charge coverage is calculated by dividing pretax income plus interest charges by total interest charges. The higher the coverage figure, the safer the credit. If interest coverage is less than 1X, the company must borrow or use cash flow or sale of assets to meet its interest payments. Generally, published coverage figures are pretax as opposed to aftertax because interest payments are a pretax expense. Although pretax interest coverage ratio is useful, its utility is a function of the company's other fixed obligations. For example, if a company has other significant fixed obligations, such as rents or leases, a more appropriate coverage figure would include these other fixed obligations. An example of this is the retail industry, in which companies typically have significant lease obligations. A calculation of simple pretax interest coverage would be misleading in this case because fixed obligations other than interest are significant. The analyst should also be aware of any contingent liabilities, such as a company's guaranteeing another company's debt. For example, there has been a dramatic increase in the insurance industry's guaranteeing of other company's debt. Today, this guaranteed debt exceeds the debt of the industry. Although the company being analyzed may never have to pay interest or principal on the guaranteed debt, the existence of the guarantee diminishes the quality of the pretax coverage. In addition, the quality of the guaranteed debt must be considered.

Once pretax interest coverage and fixed-charge coverage are calculated, it is necessary to analyze the ratios' absolute levels and the numbers relative to those of the industry. For example, pretax interest coverage for an electric utility of 4.5X is consistent with an "AAA" rating, whereas the same coverage for a drug company would indicate a lower rating.

Standard & Poor's 1981–1983 median ratios of pretax interest coverage ranges for the senior debt of industrial companies were as follows:

Rating Classification	Pretax Interest Coverage
AAA	14.84
AA	6.49
A	4.65
BBB	2.87

Leverage. A second important ratio is *leverage*, which can be defined in several ways. The most common definition, however, is long-term debt as a percent of total capitalization. The higher the level of debt, the higher the percentage of operating income that must be used to meet fixed obligations. If a company is highly leveraged, the analyst should also look at its margin of safety. The margin of safety is defined as the percentage that operating income could decline and still be sufficient to allow the company to meet its fixed obligations. Standard & Poor's 1981–1983 median ratios of leverage for the senior debt of industrial companies were as follows:

Rating Classification	Long-Term Debt/Capitalization
AAA	8.81
AA	19.23
A	26.73
BBB	33.54

The most common way to calculate leverage is to use the company's capitalization structure as stated in the most recent balance sheet. In addition to this measure, the analyst should calculate capitalization using a market approximation for the value of the common stock. When a company's common stock is selling significantly below book value, leverage will be understated by the traditional approach.

The degree of leverage and margin of safety varies dramatically among industries. Finance companies have traditionally been among the most highly leveraged companies, with debt to equity ratios of 10/1. Although such leverage is tolerated in the finance industry, an industrial company with similar leverage would have a difficult time issuing debt.

In addition to considering the absolute and relative level of leverage of a company, the analyst should evaluate the debt itself. How much of the debt has a fixed rate, and how much has a floating rate? A company with a high component of debt tied to the prime may find its margins being squeezed as interest rates rise if there is no compensating increase in the price of the firm's goods. Such a debt structure may be beneficial during certain phases of the interest-rate cycle, but it has the disadvantage of precluding a precise estimate of what interest charges for the year will be. In general, a company with a high percentage of floating-rate debt is less preferable than a similarly levered company with a small percentage of floating-rate debt.

The maturity structure of the debt should also be evaluated. What is the percentage of debt that is coming due within the next five years? As this debt is refinanced, how will the company's embedded cost of debt be changed? In this regard, the amount of original-issue discount (OID) debt should also be considered. High quality OIDs were first issued in sizable amounts in 1981, although lower quality OIDs have been issued for some time. This debt is issued with low or zero coupons and at substantial discounts to par. Each year the issuing company expenses the interest payment (coupon times the total principal amount due at maturity) as well as the amortization of the discount. At issuance only the actual bond proceeds are listed as debt on the balance sheet. However, as this debt payable will increase annually, the analyst should consider the full face amount due at maturity when evaluating the maturity structure and refinancing plans of the company.

Cash flow. A third important ratio is cash flow as a percent of total debt. Cash flow is often defined as net income plus depreciation, depletion, and deferred taxes. In calculating cash flow for credit analysis, the analyst should also subtract noncash contributions from subsidiaries. In essence, the analyst should be concerned with cash from operations. Any extraordinary sources or uses of funds should be excluded when determining the overall trend of cash flow coverage. Cash dividends from subsidiaries should also be questioned in terms of their appropriateness (too high or too low relative to the subsidiary's earnings) and also in terms of the parent's control over the upstreaming of dividends. Is there a legal limit to the upstreamed dividends? If so, how close is the current level of dividends to the limit? Standard & Poor's 1981–1983 Median Ratios of Funds From Operations/Long-Term Debt for the senior debt of industrial companies were as follows:

Rating Classification	Funds From Operations/ Long-Term Debt
AAA	262
AA	112
A	63
BBB	41

Net assets.   A fourth significant ratio is net assets to total debt. In analyzing this facet of a bond's quality, consideration should be given to the liquidation value of the assets. Liquidation value will often differ dramatically from the value stated on the balance sheet. At one extreme, consider a nuclear generating plant that has had operating problems and has been closed down and whose chance of receiving an operating license is questionable. This asset is likely overstated on the balance sheet, and the bondholder should take little comfort in reported asset protection. At the other extreme is the forest products company whose vast timber acreage is significantly understated on the balance sheet. In addition to the assets' market value, some consideration should also be given to the liquidity of the assets. A company with a high percentage of its assets in cash and marketable securities is in a much stronger asset position than a company whose primary assets are illiquid real estate.

In addition to the major variables discussed above, the analyst should also consider several other financial variables including intangibles, unfunded pension liabilities, the age and condition of the plant, and working capital adequacy.

Intangibles.   Intangibles often represent a small portion of the asset side of a balance sheet. Occasionally, however, particularly with companies that have or have had an active acquisition program, intangibles can represent a significant portion of assets. In this case, the analyst should estimate the actual value of the intangibles and determine whether this value is in concert with the balance sheet valuation. A carrying value significantly higher than market value indicates a potential for a write-down of assets. The actual write down may not occur until the company actually sells a subsidiary with which the intangibles are identified. However, the analyst should recognize the potential and adjust capitalization ratios accordingly.

Unfunded pension liabilities.   Unfunded pension liabilities can also affect a credit decision. Although a fully funded pension is not necessary for a high credit assessment, a large unfunded pension liability that is 10 percent or more of net worth can be a negative. Of concern is the company whose unfunded pension liabilities are sufficiently high to interfere with corporate planning. For example, a steel company with high unfunded pension liabilities might delay or decide against closing an unprofitable plant because of the pension costs involved. The analyst should also be aware of a company's assumed rate of return on its pension funds and salary increase assumptions. The higher the assumed rate of return, the lower the contribution a company must make to its pension fund, given a set of actuarial assumptions. Occasionally, a company having difficulty with its earnings will raise its actuarial assumption and thereby lower its pension contribution and increase earnings. The impact on earnings can be dramatic. In other cases, companies have attempted to "raid" the excess funds in an overfunded retirement plan to enhance earnings.

Age and condition of plant. The age of a company's plant should also be estimated, if only to the extent that its age differs dramatically from industry standards. A heavy industrial company whose average plant age is well above that of its competitors is probably already paying for its aged plant through operating inefficiencies. In the longer term, however, the age of net plant is an indication of future capital expenditures for a more modern plant. In addition, the underdepreciation of the plant significantly lowers inflation-adjusted earnings.

The Financial Accounting Standards Board Statement Number 33 requires extensive supplementary information from most companies on the effect of changing prices. This information is generally unaudited and there is still no consensus on the best presentation of such data. However, the supplementary information provision does give the analyst an indication of the magnitude of the effects of inflation on a given company. The effects differ dramatically from industry to industry. At one extreme are the high technology and financial firms where the effects are nominal. At the other extreme are the capital intensive industries where the effects are major.

Working capital. A final variable in assessing a company's financial strength concerns the strength and liquidity of its working capital. Working capital is defined as current assets less current liabilities. Working capital is considered a primary measure of a company's financial flexibility. Other such measures include the current ratio (current assets divided by current liabilities) and the acid test (cash, marketable securities, and receivables divided by current liabilities). The stronger the company's liquidity measures, the better able it is to weather a downturn in business and cash flow. In assessing this variable, the analyst should consider the normal working capital requirements of a company and industry. The components of working capital should also be analyzed. Although accounts receivables are considered to be liquid, an increase in the average days a receivable is outstanding may be an indication that a higher level of working capital is needed for the efficient running of the operation.

Analysis of the Components of Return on Equity

Once the above financial analysis is complete, the bond analyst traditionally examines the earnings progression of the company and its historical return on equity (ROE). This section of analysis often receives less emphasis than the traditional ratio analysis. It is equally important, however, and demands equal emphasis. An analysis of earnings growth and ROE is vital in determining credit quality because it gives the analyst necessary insights into the components of ROE and indications of the sources of future growth. Equity analysts devote a major portion of their time examining the components of ROE, and their work should be recognized as valuable resource material.

A basic approach to the examination of the components of return on equity is presented in a popular investment textbook by Jerome B. Cohen, Edward D. Zinbarg, and Arthur Zeikel.[1] Their basic approach breaks down return on equity into four principal components: pretax margins, asset turnover, leverage, and the tax rate. These four variables multiplied together equal net income/stockholders' equity, or return on equity.

$$\left(\frac{\text{Nonoperating pretax income}}{\text{Sales}} + \frac{\text{Operating pretax income}}{\text{Sales}} \right) \times \frac{\text{Sales}}{\text{Assets}} \times \frac{\text{Assets}}{\text{Equity}}$$

$$\times (1 - \text{Tax rate}) = \text{Net Income/Equity}$$

In analyzing these four components of ROE, the analyst should examine their progression for a minimum of five years and at least through a business cycle. The progression of each variable should be compared with the progression of the same variables for the industry, and deviations from industry standards should be further analyzed. For example, perhaps two companies have similar ROE's, but one company is employing a higher level of leverage to achieve its results, whereas the other company has a higher asset-turnover rate. As the degree of leverage is largely a management decision, the analyst should focus on asset turnover. Why have sales for the former company turned down? Is this downturn a result of a general slowdown in the industry, or is it that assets have been expanded rapidly and the company is in the process of absorbing these new assets? Conversely, a relatively high rise in asset-turnover rate may indicate a need for more capital. If this is the case, how will the company finance this growth, and what effect will the financing have on the firm's embedded cost of capital?

The analyst should not expect similar components of ROE for all companies in a particular industry. Deviations from industry norms are often indications of management philosophy. For example, one company may emphasize asset turnover, and another company in the same industry may emphasize profit margin. As in any financial analysis, the trend of the components is as important as the absolute levels.

In order to give the analyst a general idea of the type of ratios expected by the major rating agencies for a particular rating classification, Standard & Poor's medians of key ratios for 1981–1983 by rating category are outlined in Exhibit 1. The analyst should only use this table

---

[1] *Investment Analysis and Portfolio Management* (Homewood, Ill.: Richard D. Irwin, 1977). © Richard D. Irwin, Inc., 1977.

EXHIBIT 1 Three-Year (1981–1983) Medians of Key Ratios by
Rating Category

	AAA	AA	A	BBB	BB	B
Pretax interest coverage	14.84	6.49	4.65	2.87	2.10	1.55
Pretax interest and full rental coverage	8.38	3.97	2.81	2.07	1.73	1.39
Funds from operations/long-term debt	261.61	111.64	62.60	40.61	24.79	16.46
Funds from operations/total debt	162.09	79.43	53.33	36.34	22.65	13.74
Pretax return on average long-term capital employed	26.82	20.68	16.87	12.41	13.73	10.53
Operating income/sales	17.63	13.19	11.24	8.10	10.23	9.65
Long-term debt/capitalization	8.81	19.23	26.73	33.54	46.16	55.37
Total debt/capitalization including short-term debt	14.67	24.40	30.22	36.25	50.07	59.03
Total debt/capitalization including short-term debt (Including 8X rents)	25.62	37.64	43.49	48.13	59.05	68.23
Total liabilities/tangible shareholders' equity and minority interest	65.44	101.57	115.47	127.40	197.54	268.95

Note: These are not meant to be minimum standards.
SOURCE: Standard & Poor's Corporation, 1985.

in the most general applications, however, for two reasons. First, industry standards vary considerably. Second, financial ratios are only one part of an analysis.

Nonfinancial Factors

After the traditional bond analysis is completed, the analyst should consider some nonfinancial factors that might modify the evaluation of the company. Among these factors are the degree of foreign exposure and the quality of management. The amount of foreign exposure should be ascertainable from the annual report. Sometimes, however, specific country exposure is less clear because the annual report often lists foreign exposure by broad geographic divisions. If there is concern that a major portion of revenue and income is derived from potentially unstable areas, the analyst should carefully consider the total revenue and income derived from the area and the assets committed. Further consideration should be given to available corporate alternatives should nationalization of assets occur. Additionally, the degree of currency exposure should be determined. If currency fluctuations are significant, has management hedged its exposure?

The quality and depth of management is more difficult to evaluate. Earnings progress at the firm is a good indication of the quality of management. Negative aspects would include a firm founded and headed by one person who is approaching retirement and has made no plan for succession. Equally negative is the firm that has had numerous changes of management and philosophy. On the other hand, excessive stability is not always desirable. If one family or group of investors owns a controlling interest in a firm, they may be too conservative in terms of reacting to changes in markets. Characteristics of a good management team should include depth, a clear line of succession if the chief officers are nearing retirement, and a diversity of age within the management team.

INDENTURE PROVISIONS

An indenture is a legal document that defines the rights and obligations of the borrower and the lender with respect to a bond issue. An analysis of the indenture should be a part of a credit review in that the indenture provisions establish rules for several important spheres of operation for the borrower. These provisions, which can be viewed as safeguards for the lender, cover such areas as the limitation on the issuance of additional debt, sale and leasebacks, and sinking-fund provisions.

The indentures of bonds of the same industry are often similar in the areas they address. Correlation between the quality rating of the senior debt of a company and the stringency of indenture provisions is not perfect. For example, the debt test is more severe in A securities than in BBB securities. However, subordinated debt of one company will often have less restrictive provisions than will the senior debt of the same company. In addition, more restrictive provisions are also generally found in private placement issues. In analyzing a company's indenture, the analyst should look for the standard industry provisions. Differences in these provisions (either more or less restrictive) should be examined more closely. In this regard, a more restrictive nature is not necessarily preferable if the provisions are so restrictive as to hinder the efficient operation of the company.

Outlined below are the provisions most commonly found in indentures. These provisions are categorized by industry because the basic provisions are fairly uniform within an industry. A general description of the indenture is found in a company's prospectus. However, notification is generally given that the indenture provisions are only summarized. A complete indenture may be obtained from the Trustee who is listed in the prospectus.

Utility Indentures

Security. The security provision is generally the first provision in a utility indenture. This provision specifies the property upon which there is a mortgage lien. In addition, the ranking of the new debt relative to outstanding debt is specified. Generally, the new bonds rank equally with all other bonds outstanding under the mortgage. This ranking is necessary, but it has created difficulty for the issuing companies because some mortgage indentures were written more than 40 years ago. Specifically, because all bondholders must be kept equal, companies must often retain antiquated provisions in their indentures. Often these provisions hinder the efficient running of a company due to structural changes in the industry since the original writing of the indenture. Changes in these provisions can be made, but changes have occurred slowly because of the high percentage of bondholders that must approve a change and the time and expense required to locate the bondholders.

Issuance of additional bonds. The "Issuance of Additional Bonds" provision establishes the conditions under which the company may issue additional first mortgage bonds. Often this provision contains a debt test and/or an earnings test. The debt test generally limits the amount of bonds that may be issued under the mortgage to a certain percentage (often 60 percent) of net property or net property additions, the principal amount of retired bonds, or deposited cash. The earnings test, on the other hand, restricts the issuance of additional bonds under the mortgage unless earnings for a particular period cover interest payments at a specified level.

Although both of these tests may appear straightforward, the analyst must carefully study the definitions contained in the tests. For example, net property additions may be defined as plant that has operating licenses. Over the past decade, although there has been a great deal of nuclear construction, few operating licenses have been granted. Therefore, there is a significant backlog of construction work in progress (CWIP) that has had to be financed and yet may not be operational for some time. This situation can present problems for the company whose indenture requires net plant additions to be licensed and/or used and useful assets. In the extreme case, a company with a heavy nuclear construction program may find itself unable to issue bonds under its mortgage agreement.

In a similar circumstance, a company whose regulatory commission requires a substantial write-down related to nuclear construction may find itself unable to meet a debt test for several years if the write-down is taken in one quarter.

Maintenance and replacement fund. The purpose of a maintenance and replacement fund (M&R) is to assure that the mortgaged property is maintained in good operating condition. To this end, electric utility indentures generally require that a certain percentage of gross operating revenues, a percentage of aggregate bonded indebtedness, or a percentage of the utility's property account be paid to the trustee for the M&R fund. A major portion of the M&R requirement has historically been satisfied with normal maintenance expenditures. To the extent there is a remaining requirement, the company may contribute cash, the pledge of unbonded property additions, or bonds.

The rapid escalation of fuel costs during the 1970s has greatly raised the required levels of many M&R funds which are tied to operating revenues. This situation precipitated a number of bond calls for M&R purposes. Bonds can still be called for this purpose, but investors are more cognizant of this risk and are less likely to pay a significant premium for bonds subject to such a call. Furthermore, M&R requirements are slowly being changed toward formulas that exclude the large portion of operating income attributable to rises in fuel costs. Finally, a number of companies have indicated that they have no intention of using M&R requirements for calling bonds because of the original intent of the provision and also because of the disfavor such an action would generate among bondholders. However, the intent of companies in this regard would certainly be secondary if a call for M&R requirements were ordered by a commission.

Redemption provisions. The redemption, or call, provision specifies during what period and at what prices a company may call its bonds. Redemption provisions vary. Long-term bonds are generally currently callable but nonrefundable for five years. Exceptions to this statement are the longer term issues of the AT&T System, which are noncallable for five years. In the case of intermediate and short-term issues, the noncall provisions generally extend to a year or two prior to maturity. Refunding is an action by a company to replace outstanding bonds with another debt issue sold at a lower interest expense. (Refunding protection does not protect the bondholder from refunding bonds with equity or short-term debt.) The refunding protection is a safeguard for bondholders against their bonds being refunded at a disadvantageous time.

Sinking fund. A sinking fund is an annual obligation of a company to pay the trustee an amount of cash sufficient to retire a given percentage of bonds. This requirement can often be met with actual bonds or with the pledge of property. In general, electric utilities have 1 percent sinking funds that commence at the end of the refunding period. However, there are several variations of the sinking-fund provision with which the analyst (and bondholder) should be familiar in that they could directly affect the probability of bonds being called for sinking-fund purposes. Some companies have nonspecific, or funnel, sinkers. This type of sinker often entails a 1 or 1½ percent sinking fund applicable to all outstanding bonds. The obligation can be met by the stated percentage of each issue outstanding, by cash, or by applying (or funneling) the whole requirement against one issue or several issues.

Other provisions. In addition to the provisions discussed above, the indenture covers the events of default, modification of the mortgage, and the powers and obligations of the trustee. In general, these provisions are fairly standard. However, differences occur that should be evaluated.

Industrial Indentures

Many of the provisions of an industrial indenture are similar to those of a utility's indenture, although specific items may be changed. For example, sinking-fund and redemption provisions are part of an industrial indenture. However, refunding protection for an industrial is generally 10 years (as opposed to 5 years for an electric utility), and sinking funds often have the option to double or more than double their requirements on an annual basis at the option of the company.

In general, there are five indenture provisions that have historically been significant in providing protection for the industrial bondholder.

Negative pledge clause. The negative pledge clause provides that the company cannot create or assume liens to the extent that more than a certain percentage of consolidated net tangible assets (CNTA) is so secured without giving the same security to the bondholders. This provision is important to the bondholders because their security in the specific assets of the company establishes an important protection for their investment. The specific percentage of CNTA that is exempted from this provision is referred to as exempted indebtedness, and the exclusion provides some flexibility to the company.

Limitation on sale and lease-back transactions. The indenture provision limiting sale and lease-back parallels the protection offered by the negative pledge clause, except that it provides protection for the bondholder against the company selling and leasing back assets that provide security for the debtholder. In general, this provision requires that assets or cash equal to the property sold and leased back be applied to the retirement of the debt in question or used to acquire another property for the security of the debtholders.

Sale of assets or merger. The sale of assets or merger provision protects the debtholder in the event that substantially all of the assets of the company are sold or merged into another company. Under these circumstances, the provision generally states that the debt be retired or be assumed by the merged company.

Dividend test. The dividend test provision establishes rules for the payment of dividends. Generally, it permits the company to pay dividends to the extent that they are no greater than net income from the previous year plus the earnings of a year or two prior. Although this provision allows the company to continue to pay dividends when there is a business decline, it assures the debtholders that the corporation will not be drained by dividend payments.

Debt test. The debt test limits the amount of debt that may be issued by establishing a maximum debt/assets ratio. This provision is generally omitted from current public offerings. However, there are numerous indentures outstanding that include this provision. In addition, private placements often include a debt test. When present, the debt test generally sets a limit on the amount of debt that can be issued per dollar of total assets. This limitation is sometimes stated as a percentage. For example, a 50 percent debt/asset limit restricts debt to 50 percent of total assets.

Financial Indentures

Sinking-fund and refunding provisions. Similar to industrial indentures, indentures for finance issues specify sinking-fund and refunding provisions. In general, finance issues with a short maturity are noncallable, whereas longer issues provide 10-year call protection. Occasionally, an issue can be called early in the event of declining receivables. Sinking funds are not as common in finance issues as they are in industrial issues, although they are standard for some companies.

Dividend test. Perhaps the most important indenture provision for a debtholder of a finance subsidiary is the dividend test. This test restricts the amount of dividends that can be upstreamed from a finance subsidiary to the parent and thereby protects the debtholder against a parent draining the subsidiary. This provision is common in finance indentures, but it is not universal. (One notable exception is International Harvester Credit.)

Limitation on liens. The limitation on liens provision restricts the degree to which a company can pledge its assets without giving the same protection to the bondholder. Generally, only a nominal amount may be pledged or otherwise liened without establishing equal protection for the debtholder.

Restriction on debt test. The debt test limits the amount of debt the company can issue. This provision generally is stated in terms of assets and liabilities, although an earnings test has occasionally been used.

UTILITIES

Utilities are regulated monopolies. These companies generally operate with a high degree of financial leverage and low fixed-charge coverage (relative to industrial companies). These financial parameters have been historically accepted by investors due to the regulation of the industry and the belief that there is minimal, if any, bankruptcy risk in those securities because of the essential services they provide. The changing structure of the electric utility industry brought about by increasing investment in nuclear generating units and their inherent risk has changed this belief. Initially, the faltering financial position of General

Public Utilities precipitated by the Three Mile Island nuclear accident and the regulatory delays in making a decision regarding the units highlighted the default risk that does exist in the industry. More recently, the default of several Washington Public Power Supply System issues reemphasized the default risk. In addition, the industry is faced with the acid rain issue and increased uncertainty in construction costs and growth rates. In 1985, Standard & Poor's developed more conservative financial benchmarks for a given rating to reflect the increased risk in the industry.

Segments within the Utility Industry

There are three major segments within the utility industry: electric companies, gas companies, and telephone companies. This chapter will deal primarily with the electric utilities. This segment encompasses most of the variables affecting the industry in general.

Financial Analysis

There are four major financial ratios that should be considered in analyzing an electric utility: leverage, pretax interest coverage, cash flow/spending, and cash flow/capital.

Leverage in the electric utility industry is high relative to industrial concerns. This degree of leverage is accepted by investors because of the historical stability of the industry. The expected ranges for AAA, AA, A, BBB, and BB companies are outlined below:

Rating Classification	Debt Leverage
AAA	Less than 41 percent
AA	39–46 percent
A	44 to 52 percent
BBB	50 to 58 percent
BB	Greater than 56 percent

In calculating the debt leverage of an electric utility, long-term debt/capitalization is standard. However, the amount of short-term debt should also be considered because this is generally variable-rate debt. A high proportion of short-term debt may also indicate the possibility of the near-term issuance of long-term bonds. In addition, several companies guarantee the debt of subsidiaries (regulated or nonregulated). The extent of these guarantees should be considered in calculating leverage.

Fixed-charge coverage for the electric utilities is also low relative to coverage for industrial companies. Standard & Poor's expected ranges for coverage are as follows:

Rating Classification	Expected Pretax Fixed-Charge Coverage
AAA	Greater than 4.5X
AA	3.5–5.0X
A	2.5–4.0X
BBB	1.5–3.0X
BB	Less than 2.0X

These ranges are accepted by investors because of the stability of the industry. However, due to the changing fundamentals of the industry discussed above, perhaps less emphasis should be placed on the exact coverage figures and more on the trend and quality of the coverage.

The utility industry is unique in that its earnings include allowance for funds used during construction (AFUDC). AFUDC is an accounting treatment that allows utilities to recognize income (at a rate determined by individual regulatory commissions) on the amount of funds employed in construction. The percentage that AFUDC represents of total earnings varies significantly from almost zero to well in excess of 70 percent of earnings. Currently, AFUDC generates more than 50 percent of industry earnings. Obviously, the higher the percentage that AFUDC represents of net earnings, the lower the quality of earnings. This becomes evident when the cash flow of a utility is calculated. Often, the cash flow of a utility with substantial AFUDC is less than the dividend requirements of the company. In this instance, the company is returning the capital of the shareholders!

In calculating fixed-charge coverage, the analyst should calculate two sets of coverage figures—fixed-charge coverage including AFUDC and fixed-charge coverage excluding AFUDC, with the latter being more important.

A third important ratio is cash flow/spending. This ratio should be approximated for three years (the general range of an electric company's construction forecast). The absolute level as well as the trend of this ratio gives important insights into the trend of other financial parameters. An improving trend indicates that construction spending is probably moderating, whereas a low cash flow/spending ratio may indicate inadequate rates being approved by the commissions and a heavy construction budget. Estimates for construction spending are published in the company's annual reports. Although these are subject to revision, the time involved in building a generating unit makes these forecasts reasonably reliable. In 1985, Standard & Poor's deemphasized this ratio primarily due to its volatility. Although it will still be considered, Standard & Poor's now emphasizes cash flow/capital as a preferable indicator of cash flow adequacy.

Standard & Poor's ranges for cash flow/spending (suspended in January 1985) and its expected ranges for net cash flow/permanent capital are as follows:

Rating Classification	Expected Cash Flow/Spending	Net Cash Flow/Permanent Capital
AAA	—	Greater than 10 percent
AA	More than 40 percent	7.0–11.0 percent
A	20–50 percent	5.0–8.0 percent
BBB	Less than 30 percent	2.5–6.0 percent
BB	—	Less than 3.0 percent

In calculating cash flow, the standard definition outlined above should be followed. However, AFUDC should also be subtracted, and any cash flow from nonregulated subsidiaries should be segregated and analyzed within the total context of the company. The regulatory commissions take divergent views on nonutility subsidiaries. Some commissions do not regulate these subsidiaries at all, whereas other commissions give inadequate rate relief to an electric utility with a profitable nonutility subsidiary under the premise that the company should be looked at as a whole. In the extreme, the latter view has encouraged companies to sell or spin off some subsidiaries.

Nonfinancial Factors

Although financial factors are important in analyzing any company, nonfinancial factors are particularly important in the electric utility industry and may alter a credit assessment. The five nonfinancial factors outlined below are of particular importance to the utility industry. These are in addition to the nonfinancial factors discussed earlier.

Regulation is perhaps the most important variable in the electric utility industry. All electric companies are regulated. Most are primarily regulated by the state or states within which they operate. If a company operates in more than one state, the analyst should weigh the evaluation of the regulatory atmosphere by revenues generated in each state. In addition, the Federal Energy Regulatory Commission (FERC) regulates interstate operations and the sale of wholesale power. Currently, FERC regulation is considered to be somewhat more favorable than that of the average state regulatory commission.

Regulation is best quantified by recent rate decisions and the trend of these decisions. Although a company being analyzed may not have had a recent rate case, the commission's decisions for other companies operating within the state may be used as a proxy. Regulatory commissions are either appointed or elected. In either case, the political atmosphere can have a dramatic effect on the trend of decisions.

The regulators determine innumerable issues in a rate decision, although analysts often mistakenly focus only on the allowed rate of return on equity or the percentage of request granted. In particular, the commissions determine how much of construction work in progress (CWIP) is allowed into the rate base. A company may appear to have a favorable allowed ROE but be hurt by the fact that only a small portion of the company's capital is permitted to earn that return, while the CWIP earns nothing. Due to the high construction budgets for nuclear generating plants and the length of time these plants are under construction, allowance of CWIP in the rate base is of critical importance. Some companies have more than half of their capital in CWIP that is not permitted to earn a return.

In addition, regulators have a high degree of control over the cash flow of a company through the allowance or disallowance of accounting practices and the speed with which decisions are made on cases.

The source of a company's energy is a second important variable. Currently, a company with a heavy nuclear construction budget is viewed negatively relative to a company with coal units under construction. Not only are the lead times for nuclear construction much longer than for other generating plants, but the risk of licensing delays are significant in nuclear construction. The energy source variable relates to a third variable, the growth and stability of the company's territory. Although above-average growth is viewed positively in an industrial company, it is viewed negatively with respect to an electric utility. An electric utility with above-average growth must necessarily have a high construction budget. To the extent that CWIP is disallowed or only partially allowed in the company's rate base, the company is likely to have declining financial parameters until the unit is operational. A fourth variable, whether a company is a subsidiary of a holding company, should also be considered. Holding company status permits non-utility subsidiaries, but it is not universal that these subsidiaries (if successful) will improve the overall credit quality of the company. This depends on the regulatory atmosphere. Furthermore, when there are several electric utility subsidiaries, the parent is more likely to give relatively large equity infusions to the relatively weak subsidiaries. The stronger subsidiary may have to "support" the other subsidiaries. Finally, holding companies should be analyzed in terms of consolidated debt. Although a particular subsidiary may have relatively strong financial parameters, off-balance sheet financing may lower the overall assessment.

A final nonfinancial factor is the rate structure of a utility. An electric utility with a comparatively low rate structure is generally in a stronger position politically to request rate increases than one with rates higher than national averages, and particularly one with rates higher than regional averages.

FINANCE COMPANIES

Finance companies are essentially financial intermediaries. Their function is to purchase funds from public and private sources and to lend them to consumers and other borrowers of funds. Finance companies earn revenue by maintaining a positive spread between what the funds cost and the interest rate charged to customers. The finance industry is highly fragmented in terms of type of lending and type of ownership. This section will briefly outline the major sectors in the industry and then discuss the principal ratios and other key variables used in the analysis of finance companies.

Segments within the Finance Industry

The finance industry can be segmented by type of business and ownership. Finance companies lend in numerous ways in order to accommodate the diverse financial needs of the economy. Five of the major lending categories are: (1) sales finance, (2) commercial lending, (3) wholesale or dealer finance, (4) consumer lending, and (5) leasing. Most often, companies are engaged in several of these lines rather than one line exclusively. Sales finance is the purchase of third-party contracts that cover goods or services sold on a credit basis. In most cases, the sales finance company receives an interest in the goods or services sold. Commercial finance is also generally on a secured basis. However, in this type of financing, the security is most often the borrower's account receivables. In factoring, another type of commercial lending, the finance company actually purchases the receivables of a company and assumes the credit risk of the receivables.

Dealer or wholesaler finance is the lending of funds to finance inventory. This type of financing is secured by the financed inventory and is short term in nature. Leasing, on the other hand, is intermediate to long-term lending—the lessor owns the equipment, finances the lessee's use of it, and generally retains the tax benefits related to the ownership.

Consumer lending has historically involved short-term, unsecured loans of relatively small amounts to individual borrowers. In part because of the more lenient bankruptcy rules and higher default rates on consumer loans, consumer finance companies have dramatically expanded the percentage of their loans for second mortgages. The lower rate charged individuals for this type of loan is offset by the security and lower default risk of the loan.

There are numerous other types of lending in addition to those described above. Among these are real estate lending and export/import financing.

The ownership of a finance company can significantly impact evaluation of the company. In some instances, ownership is the most important variable in the analysis.

There are three major types of ownership of finance companies: (1) captives, (2) wholly owned, and (3) independents. Captive finance companies, such as General Motors Acceptance Corporation and J. C. Penney Financial, are owned by the parent corporation and are engaged solely or primarily in the financing of the parent's goods or services. Generally, maintenance agreements exist between the parent and the captive finance company under which the parent agrees to maintain one or more of the finance company's financial parameters, such as fixed-charge coverage, at a minimum level. Because of the overriding relationship between a parent and a captive finance subsidiary, the financial strength of the parent is an important variable in the analysis of the finance company. However, captive finance companies can have ratings either above or below those of the parent.

A wholly-owned finance company, such as Associates Corporation of North America, differs from a captive in two ways. First, it primarily finances the goods and services of companies other than the parent. Second, maintenance agreements between the parent and the subsidiary are generally not as formal. Frequently, there are indenture provisions that address the degree to which a parent can upstream dividends from a finance subsidiary. The purpose of these provisions is to prevent a relatively weak parent from draining a healthy finance subsidiary to the detriment of the subsidiary's bondholders.

Independent finance companies are either publicly owned or closely held. Because these entities have no parent, the analysis of this finance sector is strictly a function of the strengths of the company.

Financial Analysis

In analyzing finance companies, several groups of ratios and other variables should be considered. There is more interrelationship between these ratios and variables than for any other type of company. For example, a finance company with a high degree of leverage and low liquidity may be considered to be of high investment quality if it has a strong parent and maintenance agreements. No variable should be viewed in isolation but rather within the context of the whole finance company/ parent company relationship.

Loan loss.　The most important ratio in analyzing a finance company is the relationship of the company's loan loss experience and related variables. Net loan losses are defined as loans deemed uncollectible and therefore written off, less recoveries of loans previously written off. The importance of this ratio is twofold. First, the net loan loss is a major and unpredictable expense variable. Second, a company with an above-average loan loss record has the necessary business expertise to create a loan portfolio of above-average quality. A related variable that should also be evaluated is the company's provision for these losses. A company whose loss provisions are consistently inadequate should be further explored for other indications of liberal accounting.

In evaluating the company's loan loss experience, the analyst must also necessarily consider the quality of the portfolio. Diversification is one measure of portfolio quality. Is the portfolio diversified across different types of loans? If the company is concentrated in or deals exclusively in one lending type, is there geographic diversification? A company that deals exclusively in consumer loans in the economically sensitive Detroit area would not be as favorably viewed as a company with broad geographic diversification. Accounting quality is also an important factor in assessing portfolio quality. The more conservative the accounting for recognition of income, revenue, and loan losses, the better. The security for the loans is also an important variable in portfolio quality. The stronger the underlying security, the higher the loan quality. The analyst should be primarily concerned with the level of loans compared with levels of similar companies and the risk involved in the type of lending. For example, the expected loan loss from direct unsecured consumer loans is higher than for consumer loans secured by second mortgages. However, the higher fees charged for the former type of loan should compensate the company for the higher risk.

Leverage. Leverage is a second important ratio used in finance company analysis. By the nature of the business, finance companies are typically and acceptably more highly leveraged than industrial companies. The leverage is necessary to earn a sufficient return on capital. However, the acceptable range of leverage is dependent on other factors, such as parental support, portfolio quality, and type of business. The principal ratio to determine leverage is total debt to equity, although such variations as total liabilities to equity may additionally be used. In a diversified company with high portfolio quality, a leverage ratio of 5 to 1 is acceptable. On the other hand, a ratio of 10 to 1 is also acceptable for a captive with a strong parent and maintenance agreements. The analyst should always view the leverage of a finance company in comparison with similar companies.

Liquidity. The third important variable in finance company analysis is liquidity. Because of the capital structure of finance companies, the primary cause of bankruptcies in this industry is illiquidity. If for some reason a finance company is unable to raise funds in the public or private market, failure could quickly result. This inability to raise funds could result from internal factors, such as a deterioration in earnings, or from external factors, such as a major disruption in the credit markets. Whatever the cause, a company should have some liquidity cushion. The ultimate liquidity cushion, selling assets, is only a last resort because these sales could have long-term, detrimental effects on earnings. The traditional liquidity ratio is cash, cash equivalents, and receivables due within one year divided by short-term liabilities. The higher this ratio, the higher the margin of safety. Also to be considered are the liquidity of the receivables themselves and the existence of bank lines of credit to provide a company with short-term liquidity during a financial crisis. In general, the smaller and weaker companies should have a higher liquidity cushion than those companies with strong parental backing who can rely on an interest-free loan from the parent in times of market stress.

Asset coverage.   A fourth important variable in the analysis of finance companies that is related to the three variables discussed above is the asset coverage afforded the bondholder. In assessing asset protection, the analyst should consider the liquidation value of the loan portfolio.

Earnings record.   The fifth variable to be considered is the finance company's earnings record. The industry is fairly mature and is somewhat cyclical. The higher the annual EPS growth, the better. However, some cyclicality should be expected. In addition, the analyst should be aware of management's response to major changes in the business environment. The recent more lenient personal bankruptcy rules and the fact that personal bankruptcy is becoming more sociably acceptable have produced significantly higher loan losses in direct, unsecured consumer loans. Many companies have responded to this change by contracting their unsecured personal loans and expanding their portfolios invested in personal loans secured by second mortgages.

Size.   A final factor related to the finance company or subsidiary is size. In general, the larger companies are viewed more positively than the smaller companies. Size has important implications for market recognition in terms of selling securities but also in terms of diversification. A larger company is more easily able to diversify in terms of type and location of loan than is a smaller company, and thereby to lessen the risk of the portfolio.

In addition to an analysis of the financial strength of the company according to the above variables, the analyst must incorporate the net effect of any affiliation the finance company has with a parent. If this affiliation is strong, it may be the primary variable in the credit assessment. The affiliation between a parent company and a finance subsidiary is straightforward; it is captive, wholly owned, or independent. However, the degree to which a parent will support a finance subsidiary is not as straightforward. Traditionally, the integral relationship between a parent and a captive finance subsidiary has indicated the highest level of potential support. However, it is becoming increasingly clear that a wholly-owned finance subsidiary can have just as strong an affiliation. For example, General Electric Credit Corporation (GECC) finances little or no products manufactured by its parent, General Electric Company. However, General Electric receives substantial tax benefits from its consolidation of tax returns with GECC. Additionally, General Electric has a substantial investment in its credit subsidiary. Therefore, although there are no formal maintenance agreements between General

Electric and GECC, it can be assumed that General Electric would protect its investment in GECC if the finance subsidiary were to need assistance. In other instances it may be that the affiliation and maintenance agreements are strong, but the parent itself is weak. In this case, the strong affiliation would be discounted to the extent that parent profitability is below industry standards.

In addition to affiliation, affiliate profitability, and maintenance agreements, the analyst should also examine any miscellaneous factors that could affect the credit standing of the finance company. Legislative initiatives should be considered to determine significant changes in the structure or profitability of the industry.

THE RATING AGENCIES AND BROKERAGE HOUSES

There is no substitute for the fundamental analysis generated by the fixed income analyst. The analyst has many sources of assistance, however. The major sources of assistance are the public rating agencies and brokerage houses that specialize in fixed income research.

Rating Agencies

Three major rating agencies provide public ratings on debt issues: Standard & Poor's Corporation, Moody's Investors Service, and Fitch Investors Service. In particular, Fitch rates a number of banks unrated by the other agencies. In addition, Duff & Phelps, Inc., a Chicago-based research house, has *recently* begun to offer public ratings.

Standard & Poor's (S&P) and Moody's are the most widely recognized and used of the services, although Duff & Phelps and Fitch are frequently cited. S&P and Moody's are approximately the same size, and each rates the debt securities of approximately 2,000 companies. If a company desires a rating on an issue, it must apply to the rating agency. The agency, in turn, charges a one-time fee of generally $5,000 to $20,000. For this fee, the issue is reviewed periodically during the life of the issue and at least one formal review is made annually.

Each of the three rating agencies designate debt quality by assigning a letter rating to an issue. Standard & Poor's ratings go from AAA to D, with AAA obligations having the highest quality investment characteristics and D obligations being in default. In a similar fashion, Moody's ratings extend from Aaa to C, and Fitch's, from AAA to D. Duff & Phelps, on the other hand, assigns numerical ratings from 1 to 14, with 1 analogous to a AAA.

Public ratings are taken seriously by corporate managements, since a downgrade or an upgrade by a major agency can cost or save a corporation thousands of dollars in interest payments over the life of an issue. In the event of downgrade below the BBB or Baa level, the corporation may find its bonds ineligible for investment by many institutions and funds, either by legal or policy constraints. Corporations therefore strive to maintain at least an investment-grade rating (Baa or higher) and are mindful of the broad financial parameters that the agencies consider in deriving a rating.

Many factors promote the use of agency ratings by investors, bankers, and brokers. Among these strengths are the breadth of companies followed, the easy access to the ratings, and the almost universal acceptance of the ratings. On the other hand, the ratings are criticized for not responding quickly enough to changes in credit conditions and for being too broad in their classifications.

The slow response time of the agencies to changes in credit conditions is certainly a valid criticism. There are few instances in which the lag is significant in terms of a dramatic change, but the market generally anticipates rating changes. The rating agencies have become increasingly sensitive to this criticism and have been quicker to change a rating in light of changing financial parameters. On the other hand, the agencies recognize the financial impact of their ratings and their obligation to rate the long-term (as opposed to the short-term) prospects of companies. They therefore have a three- to five-year perspective and purposefully do not change a rating because of short-term fluctuations.

Standard & Poor's has addressed this criticism directly by creating *Creditwatch,* a weekly notice of companies whose credit ratings are under surveillance for rating changes. These potential rating changes can be either positive or negative. The basis for potential change can emanate from a variety of sources, including company and industry fundamentals, changes in the law, and mergers. Duff & Phelps also has a "Watch List" of companies that are potential upgrades or downgrades. Additionally, subscribers to the agencies' services have access to agency analysts to discuss individual companies or industries.

Investors who are concerned that the ratings are too broad in their classifications have several options among the brokerage house services that offer more continuous ratings.

Brokerage-House Services

Numerous brokerage houses specialize in fixed income research. Generally, these services are available only to institutional buyers of bonds. The strength of the research stems from the in-depth coverage provided, the statistical techniques employed, and the fine gradations in rating. On the other hand, the universe of companies that these firms follow is necessarily smaller than that followed by the agencies.

Of particular interest is the methodology employed by Kidder Peabody to quantify risk. Kidder Peabody performs Financial Quality Profiles (FQP) on approximately 200 nonoil industrial companies, a universe of oil companies, and a growing number of finance companies. The FQP analysis concentrates on inflation-adjusted financial parameters. In particular, FQP quantifies the "unit growth fundable" of a company, which is the real growth rate of unit production that a company can sustain without a significant deterioration in its balance sheet. The result of an FQP analysis is a numerical rating ranging from 0 to 125 (93–125 is roughly equivalent to an AAA). The numerical ratings are the quantitative assessment of the firm's financial parameters. Kidder Peabody tempers these ratings with its assessment of other nonfinancial factors, such as management and the outlook for the industry. In 1981 FQP analysis was extended to include forecasted FQP scores. Although several firms will qualitatively discuss the longer term outlook for a company, only FQP quantifies the evaluation.

In spite of the numerous services available, the market continues to demand more fixed income research. To partially satisfy this demand, many independent analysts are evaluating segments of the market previously not covered or inadequately covered. This research is frequently supplied by specialists in independently originated research such as Autranet.

CONCLUSION

This chapter has emphasized a basic methodology in analyzing corporate bonds. A format for analysis is essential. However, analysis of securities cannot be totally quantified, and the experienced analyst will develop a second sense about whether to delve into a particular aspect of a company's financial position or whether to take the financial statements at face value. All aspects of credit analysis, however, have become increasingly important as rapidly changing economic conditions and increasingly severe business cycles change the credit quality of companies and industries.

23

Credit Considerations in Evaluating High Yield Bonds

Jane Tripp Howe, C.F.A.
Consultant

Many analysts shy away from the analysis of high-yield bonds. Perhaps their reticence is a function of the security's lack of a rating or of a rating that is "below investment grade" and therefore publicly documented as having varying degrees of investment risk or elements of speculation. Although the comfort of an investment-grade rating is missing or its assignment is often enough to prohibit the security's inclusion in a portfolio, the potential rewards of this area of credit analysis are well worth the time invested.

The analysis of high-yield, or junk bonds as they are unfortunately nicknamed, is similar to the complete analysis of any other corporate bond, but the emphasis of the analysis must change. Both high-yield and junk bonds are securities that trade primarily on their creditworthiness, as opposed to the level of interest rates. However, an important difference exists between junk and high-yield securities. Both classifications generate high yields. Although the yield of junk bonds reflects the poor quality of the underlying issuer, the yield of many high-yield securities reflects a variety of circumstances, such as small size of a firm or the lack of a credit history. While rating agencies often penalize such a firm by giving it a low rating, the firm may exhibit good credit quality in many areas. It is this difference that presents the challenge to the credit analyst.

The recent expansion of the high-yield market presents an opportunity to the analyst to identify the quality in issues that the majority of analysts have ignored. This process involves in-depth research. Because many high-yield bonds have short histories, the analyst must necessarily make more projections. Overall, the analysis will be heavily weighted to the second dimension of credit analysis discussed in Chapter 22—those aspects which are most commonly associated with the analysis of common stock. In addition, the analyst is often faced with innovative characteristics of the security such as options exercisable only under certain circumstances. These features must be evaluated within the context of the total valuation process.

The artificial differentiation between bonds and the associated technique of credit analysis stem perhaps from some investors' segmentation of the market, whereby the bond portion is the "safe" area in which no risk should be taken. In this framework, potential rewards from bonds are probably not considered. Recent academic papers and numerous studies generated by the securities industry show the fallacy of such reasoning. In a Wharton study, Blume and Keim have shown that from January 1982 to May 1984, a diversified portfolio of high-yield bonds produced higher returns than diversified portfolios of either high-grade bonds or equities.[1] During this period, the lower quality bonds generated an annual return of 20.3 percent. During the same period, A-rated bonds generated 16.6 percent annually, AAA-rated bonds 15.0 percent annually, and equities even less.

If this is the case, why have these credits been so carefully ignored historically by most analysts? There are four major reasons for this inefficient behavior. First, institutional and legal constraints are often imposed on money managers, confining investments to "investment-grade" securities (i.e., those which are rated BBB or higher by the rating agencies). Interestingly, these same money managers often buy the equity of a company whose debt they would not buy. Second, the high-yield market has been well developed for only a few years. Previously, the high-yield market lacked liquidity and stability. Portfolio managers hesitated to invest in this market for portfolios which required liquidity. Third, diversification in the low-grade market has historically been difficult. Until recently the market has been heavily weighted in the railroad industry, as potential issuers relied primarily on bank financing and private placements. Finally, the lack of significant buyers restricted young growth companies from issuing public debt. High-yield securities were therefore associated with junk securities and the behavior was reinforced. A further discussion of these points is given in Chapter 35, along with a history of the high-yield market.

The analysis of high-yield bonds is essentially the same as the complete analysis of investment-grade bonds. However, due to the nature of the company, more time will generally be involved. Extensive market

---

[1] Marshall E. Blume and Donald B. Keim, "Risk and Return Characteristics of Lower-Grade Bonds," Rodney L. White Center for Financial Research (Philadelphia, Pennsylvania, 1984) pp. 3–4.

projections are often required as well as possible explanations for inconsistencies in growth patterns. In addition, the commitment involved in the analysis of high-yield bonds cannot be made to analyze a single credit or even several credits. Because the prices of high-yield bonds change more as a function of changes in creditworthiness (nonmarket risk) than as a function of interest rate changes (market risk), any commitment to high-yield bonds must be made within the context of a portfolio in order to benefit from diversification and lowering of specific risk. The analyst must be familiar with a number of industries to accomplish this.

The importance of diversification and its ability to increase expected return per unit of risk is an accepted tenet of portfolio management. Even portfolio managers who invest solely in high-grade securities will lower their risk by diversifying across industries, coupons, and maturities. The addition of a diversified portfolio of high-yield bonds may add more to a portfolio than the generally perceived higher rate of return. The study by Blume and Keim found that lower-quality bonds experienced less volatility or risk than high-grade bonds or equities over the period studied when risk was defined as the standard deviation of monthly returns.[2] Blume and Keim suggest that this result may be explained by the fact that much of the risk associated with high-yield bonds is nonmarket or firm specific and can therefore be eliminated by diversification.

The implications of this result are far reaching. Many investors, particularly institutional investors, are leery of the high-yield bonds because of the added risk they attribute to these bonds. This avoidance behavior is reinforced by the occasional well-publicized default or bankruptcy. The evidence shows, however, that the investor would be better off in terms of return and possibly lowering of risk with the inclusion of a diversified portfolio of high-yield bonds in a total portfolio. The avoidance behavior may in fact enhance yields. It is unfortunate that well-intentioned bureaucrats occasionally seek to "protect" the public by trying to legislate that certain types of high-yield securities be avoided. They may be increasing the rewards to the investors who do participate in the high-yield market.

Similar to any other bond analysis, the analyst's purpose here is to determine the value of the security. Will the issuing company be able to meet its interest and principal payments? Will the credit quality of the bond change over the life of the issue?

The progression of analysis for a high-yield bond should also be the same as that for any bond as discussed in the previous chapter. The analysis must be rigorous, however, as the margin of safety is generally more narrow. In addition, several areas of analysis should be expanded.

---

[2] Blume and Keim, "Risk and Return Characteristics of Lower-Grade Bonds," p. 4.

Competition

The size of a company has important credit implications. It is well known that many "small" firms file for bankruptcy each year. It should be noted, however, that these firms are not the same "small" firms that are issuing high-yield debt. The firms labeled small by investors are generally small only in relation to the giants of the industry. As the rating agencies favor the very large, well-established firms, the "small" firms suffer by comparison.

In an industry where the leader or leaders can set pricing, a small firm could be at a significant disadvantage. In the scenario where the pricing is set, the small firm must have unit costs approaching, equal, or lower than the pricing leaders. The small firm which is inefficient could not withstand a prolonged pricing war. The leaders in this case could launch a pricing war to gain market share and effectively drive the inefficient producers out of business. In certain circumstances, the small firm may be able to differentiate its product and thereby control a certain segment of the market. However, there is always the threat of competition. The company with a market niche must be monitored to ensure that the niche remains the domain of the company in question.

Cash Flow

One of the most important elements in analyzing a high-yield security is cash flow. In such an analysis, cash flow/long-term debt is not as important as cash flow/total cash requirements. Does the company have enough cash flow to meet its interest payments and to fund necessary research and growth? Does the company have sufficient cash flow to tide it over during a period of weak economic activity? What borrowing capacity is available? The ability to borrow enabled several large firms such as Chrysler and Ford Motor to meet their debt obligation when these companies were producing significant losses. As a result, the companies were granted time to reformulate products and re-position themselves for an upturn in the economy and industry. The smaller firm may not have this advantage. On the other hand, the larger firms which often have the luxury of expanding borrowings during weak markets may be trading on their market name long after their credit quality has deteriorated. The analyst must particularly focus on cash flow in certain leveraged buyout situations. Although the purchaser may have a specific plan for selling assets to reduce debt and related payments, time may be critical. Can the company meet its cash obligations if the sale of assets is delayed? What financial flexibility does the company have in terms of borrowing capacity? Are indenture covenants being met?

Net Assets

In analyzing a bond, the liquidation value of the assets must be ascertained or at least approximated. Are these assets properly valued on the balance sheet? Of particular interest may be real estate holdings. For example, in analyzing the gaming companies, a market assessment of land holdings should be included. On the other hand, one should also consider the likelihood of those assets being available for liquidation, if necessary. To whom do they belong? Are they mortgaged or being used as collateral? Assets are occasionally spun off to the equity owners of the company. In such a circumstance, the bondholders may experience a sudden and dramatic deterioration of credit quality. Other bondholders are secured by specific assets such as railroad cars or a nuclear power station. In these circumstances, the value and marketability of the collateral must be ascertained. Collateral by definition must be specific and so must be the analysis. Ten railroad engines may appear to be secure until it is discovered that the engines are not only obsolete but have not been maintained for a number of years.

Management

Management is a critical element in the assessment of any firm. Given enough time, poor management can bankrupt the most prosperous firm. Conversely, good management is essential to the long-term survival of all firms. Many successful firms were started by employees of the leaders in an industry. The high technology area is an example of this. Often, employees decide to start their own firms for personal profit. Very often the firms are founded by some of the leading engineers or salesmen. While the creative talents and profit motive in these firms may be high, the whole management team must be evaluated. Is there a strong financial manager? Is there a strong marketing manager? Where are the controls? Start-up operations provide high incentives for success. The ownership of a significant portion of the company by management is generally positive. Too often employees of a large firm relate only to their personal paychecks and not to the overall profitability of the firm.

Leverage

Companies which issue high-yield bonds are generally highly leveraged. Leverage per se is not harmful and in many circumstances is beneficial to growth. However, the degree of leverage should be evaluated in terms of its effect on the financial flexibility of the firm. As pointed out in Chapter 22, leverage should be calculated on an absolute and market-adjusted basis. The most common approach to market adjustment is to calculate a market value for the equity of the firm. To the extent that the common stock is selling below book value, leverage will be understated by a traditional approach. Some firms such as Drexel Burnham also adjust the market value of debt in calculating leverage. While this approach is interesting, a consistent approach must be employed when convertibles are considered in the equity equation. The benefit of adjusting the equity side of the leverage equation is clear. As the market values a company's equity upward, the market is indicating a willingness to support more leverage. A similar increase in the market adjustment of a firm's debt may indicate an upward appraisal of creditworthiness or an overall lowering of interest rates. In either case, the company would probably have the opportunity to refinance at a lower cost and thereby increase profitability.

SPECIAL TYPES OF HIGH-YIELD SECURITIES

In addition to the special circumstances involved in analyzing a high-yield security, the analyst is faced with nontraditional forms of financing. This is not surprising. Over the past ten years, the high-yield market has provided the majority of innovative financing. A thorough understanding of the type of security is necessary to complete an evaluation. Some modifications of the security have important implications for the analysis. The modifications and refinements to high-yield securities have been numerous. Several of these modifications are outlined below.

Exchangeable variable rate notes (EVRNs). EVRNs are subordinated, intermediate-term obligations that pay interest quarterly. The interest rate is fixed for a short period. This period is called the "teaser," since the fixed rate is generally set above the rate dictated by the formula. After the fixed-rate period, the rate is adjusted quarterly and is tied to certain benchmarks such as the prime rate or 90-day Treasury bills. Generally, the issuer has the option to exchange the notes for fixed-rate notes, with predetermined features such as maturity, call price, etc. Generally, the issuer must exchange the securities after five years. At the end of 1984, approximately $4.2 billion of high-yield EVRNs were outstanding.

Usable bonds. Usable bonds are securities that are issued with a warrant to purchase the issuing company's common stock. When the warrants are exercised, the bonds can be used at par in lieu of cash. (These bonds are also called synthetic convertibles when they are considered with their respective warrants.) The market value of these securities is sometimes highly correlated to the value of the company's stock and amount of usable bonds outstanding in relation to the amount required for exercise of the warrants. As of December 1984, approximately $5.6 billion of these securities were outstanding.

Springing issues. Springing securities are issues which will change one or more of their characteristics if a certain event occurs. One such issue was a note offering that had springing warrants which would be exercisable only if someone tried to acquire the issuer. Another springing security was originally issued as subordinated debt, but would become senior indebtedness when an old outstanding debenture had been discharged as long as the issuing company was able to create the additional senior indebtedness without violating any covenants of a third outstanding issue. In evaluating springing issues, the analyst must determine the likelihood of the issue's changing form and the value of the change.

Other issues. In recent years, the assortment of high-yield securities has proliferated. Issues have been floated that offer a share of the firm's profits in addition to a stated interest rate as well as issues backed by commodities. Other firms have issued private placements with registration rights.

The variety of financing alternatives is likely to continue to expand. The analyst must evaluate the characteristics of each issue to determine how much, if any, value it adds to the credit. The analysis of low-grade securities often requires additional work. The investor is rewarded for this effort in two ways. The first benefit is enhanced yield. This yield advantage has been significant. Historically, low-grade securities have yielded 300 to 500 basis points more than comparable Treasury issues. The yield advantage versus high-grade corporates has almost been as great. When this advantage is compounded annually, the performance benefit to individuals as well as institutional investors is significant. The advantage is only slightly reduced when default risk is considered. The second benefit of high-yield credit analysis is the likelihood of identifying credits that are improving. These credits will not only provide enhanced yield but also capital appreciation relative to the market. This benefit is familiar to the credit analyst who views his job as identifying improving as well as deteriorating credits.

Performance of High-Yield Securities and Default Risk

Historically, defaults and bankruptcies have been nominal in relation to outstanding U.S. debt. W. Braddock Hickman's study, *Corporate Bond Quality and Investor Experience,* concluded that, on average, during the period 1900–1943, 1.7 percent of all straight public and private debt defaulted. More recent studies have found historic default rates of only approximately .5 percent annually with several years producing no defaults. Recently, defaults have been very low. For the years 1980–1984,

Merrill Lynch estimated annual default rates of straight corporate debt at .10 percent, zero percent, .32 percent, .12 percent, and .12 percent, respectively (see Exhibit 1). When convertibles are included, the default rate increases somewhat.

EXHIBIT 1   Default Rates for Corporate Bonds and Total Corporate Debt Outstanding ($ billions)

	12/84	12/83	12/82	12/81	12/80
Straight Debt	391.7	350.5	329.2	312.5	295.1
Convertible Debt	21.6	22.4	18.2	16.0	11.8
Total	413.3	372.9	347.4	328.5	306.9

Defaults as a Percent of Par Amount of Bonds Outstanding					
	12/84	12/83	12/82	12/81	12/80
Straight Debt	.12	.12	.32	.00	.10
Convertible Debt	.84	.23	1.26	.31	.10
Total	.16	.13	.36	.02	.10

SOURCE: *Presentation on High-Yield Securities*, Merrill Lynch Capital Markets (New York, 1985), pp. 2–6.

It should be noted that in the analysis in Exhibit 1, Merrill Lynch defines default as the "nonpayment of principal and interest under the terms of the original indenture." It also classifies default as "the exchange of outstanding debt for a new issue of debt where interest is payable in common stock or cash and the covenants of the original debenture have been changed."

Regardless of how low default rates are in a given year, the investor who owns the defaulted issue will be greatly impacted if the defaulted issue represents a significant portion of his portfolio. A portfolio must be well diversified to avoid such a negative scenario.

In spite of careful analysis, the investor may be faced with a default or bankruptcy. In such a circumstance, analysis must continue. There have been situations where a defaulting issuer has subsequently resumed payments or issued stock to debt holders that eventually was worth more than the original debt.

BROKERAGE HOUSES AND THE RATING AGENCIES

As with high-grade securities, there is no substitute for sound fundamental analysis. The rating agencies can provide some help. More in-depth research in this area is being generated by the brokerage houses. Drexel Burnham Lambert has traditionally been the leader in this field. As the leading underwriter and market maker, it has significant resources devoted to this market. The research has been very profitable for them. In spite of the profits and the attendant desire of other firms to share in the profits, Drexel has retained a dominant market share. Other firms such as Merrill Lynch have made inroads into this area, with in-depth research and an expanding market making capability.

CONCLUSION

Analysts often classify themselves according to the type of security they analyze. This classification is misleading. An analyst who understands the principles of accounting and credit analysis should feel equally comfortable with high- or low-grade securities. Analysis will never be a rote process. It is only the good analyst who knows when to delve into a specific area exhaustively and when to quickly assess other areas of a company. This intuitive aspect of credit analysis is particularly important in analyzing low-grade credits. It can usually be developed with experience.

24

Guidelines in the Credit Analysis of General Obligation and Revenue Municipal Bonds

Sylvan G. Feldstein, Ph.D.
Vice President and Manager
Municipal Bond Research Department
Merrill Lynch Capital Markets

INTRODUCTION

Although historically the degree of safety of investing in municipal bonds has been considered second only to that of U.S. Treasury bonds, beginning in the 1970s there has developed among many investors and underwriters ongoing concerns about the potential default risks of municipal bonds.

The First Influence: Defaults and Bankruptcies

One concern resulted from the well-publicized, billion-dollar general obligation note defaults in 1975 of New York City. Not only were specific investors threatened with the loss of their principal, but also the defaults sent a loud and clear warning to municipal bond investors in general. That warning was that regardless of the supposedly ironclad legal protections for the bondholder, when issuers, such as large cities, have severe budget-balancing difficulties, the political hues, cries, and financial interests of public employee unions, vendors, and community groups may be dominant forces in the initial decision-making process.

This reality was further reinforced by the new federal bankruptcy law, which took effect on October 1, 1979, and which makes it easier for municipal bond issuers to seek protection from bondholders by filing for bankruptcy. One by-product of the increased investor concern is that since 1975 the official statement, which is the counterpart to a prospectus in an equity or corporate bond offering and which is to contain a summary of the key legal and financial security features, has become more comprehensive. As an example, prior to 1975 it was common for a city of New York official statement to be only 6 pages long, whereas for a bond sale in 1986 it was close to 100 pages long.

The Second Influence: Strong Investor Demand for Tax Exemption

The second reason for the increased interest in credit analysis was derived from the changing nature of the municipal bond market. For most of the decade of the 1970s, the municipal bond market was characterized by strong buying patterns by both private investors and institutions. The patterns were caused in part by high federal, state, and local income tax rates. Additionally, as inflation pushed many investors into higher and higher income tax brackets, tax-exempt bonds increasingly became an important and convenient way for sheltering income. One corollary of the strong buyers' demand for tax exemption has been an erosion of the traditional security provisions and bondholder safeguards that had grown out of the default experiences of the 1930s. General obligation bond issuers with high tax and debt burdens, declining local economies, and chronic budget-balancing problems had little difficulty finding willing buyers. Also, revenue bonds increasingly were rushed to market with legally untested security provisions, modest rate covenants, reduced debt reserves, and weak additional-bond tests. Because of this widespread weakening of security provisions, it has become more important than ever before that the prudent investor carefully evaluate the creditworthiness of a municipal bond before making a purchase.

In analyzing the creditworthiness of either a general obligation or revenue bond, the investor should cover five categories of inquiry. They are questions related to (1) legal documents and opinions (2) politics/management, (3) underwriter/financial advisor, (4) general credit indicators and economics, and (5) red flag, or danger signals.

The purpose of this chapter is to set forth the general guidelines that the investor should rely upon in asking questions about specific bonds.

THE LEGAL OPINION

The popular notion is that much of the legal work done in a bond issue is boilerplate in nature, but from the bondholder's point of view the legal opinions and document reviews should be the ultimate security provisions. This is because, if all else fails, the bondholder may have to go to court to enforce his or her security rights. Therefore, the integrity and competency of the lawyers who review the documents and write the legal opinions that usually are summarized and stated in the official statements are very important.

The relationship of the legal opinion to the analysis of municipal bonds for both general obligation and revenue bonds is threefold. First, the lawyer should check to determine if the issuer is indeed legally able to issue the bonds. Second, the lawyer is to see that the issuer has properly prepared for the bond sale by having enacted the various required ordinances, resolutions, and trust indentures and without violating any other laws and regulations. This preparation is particularly important in the highly technical areas of determining whether the bond issue is qualified for tax exemption under federal law and whether the issue has not been structured in such a way so as to violate federal arbitrage regulations. Third the lawyer is to certify that the security safeguards and remedies provided for the bondholders and pledged either by the bond issuer or by third parties, such as banks with letter-of-credit agreements, are actually supported by federal, state, and local government laws and regulations.

General Obligation Bonds

General obligation bonds are debt instruments issued by states, counties, towns, cities, and school districts. They are secured by the issuers' general taxing powers. The investor should review the legal documents and opinion as summarized in the official statement to determine what specific *unlimited* taxing powers, such as those on real estate and personal property, corporate and individual income taxes, and sales taxes, are legally available to the issuer, if necessary, to pay the bondholders. Usually for smaller governmental jurisdictions, such as school districts and towns, the only available unlimited taxing power is on property. If there are statutory or constitutional taxing power limitations, the legal documents and opinion should clearly describe how they impact the security for the bonds.

For larger general obligation bond issuers, such as states and big cities that have diverse revenue and tax sources, the legal opinion should indicate the claim of the general obligation bondholder on the issuer's general fund. Does the bondholder have a legal claim, if necessary, to the first revenues coming into the general fund? This is the case with bondholders of state of New York general obligation bonds. Does the bondholder stand second in line? This is the case with bondholders of state of California general obligation bonds. Or are the laws silent on the question altogether? This is the case for most other state and local governments.

Additionally, certain general obligation bonds, such as those for water and sewer purposes, are secured in the first instance by user charges and then by the general obligation pledge. (Such bonds are popularly known as being double barreled.) If so, the legal documents and opinion should state how the bonds are secured by revenues and funds outside the issuer's general taxing powers and general fund.

Revenue Bonds

Revenue bonds are issued for either project or enterprise financings that are secured by the revenues generated by the completed projects themselves, or for general public-purpose financings in which the issuers pledge to the bondholders tax and revenue resources that were previously part of the general fund. This latter type of revenue bond is usually created to allow issuers to raise debt outside general obligation debt limits and without voter approvals. The trust indenture and legal opinion for both types of revenue bonds should provide the investor with legal comfort in six bond-security areas:

1. The limits of the basic security.
2. The flow-of-funds structure.
3. The rate, or user-charge, covenant.
4. The priority-of-revenue claims.
5. The additional-bonds test.
6. Other relevant covenants.

Limits of the basic security. The trust indenture and legal opinion should explain what are the revenues for the bonds and how they realistically may be limited by federal, state, and local laws and procedures. The importance of this is that although most revenue bonds are structured and appear to be supported by identifiable revenue streams, those revenues sometimes can be negatively impacted directly by other levels of government. As an example, the Mineral Royalties Revenue Bonds that the state of Wyoming sold in December 1981 had most of the attributes of revenue bonds. The bonds had a first lien on the pledged revenues, and additional bonds could only be issued if a coverage test of 125 percent was met. Yet the basic revenues, themselves, were monies received by the state from the federal government as royalty payments for mineral production on federal lands. The U.S. Congress was under no legal obligation to continue this aid program. Therefore the legal opinion as summarized in the official statement must clearly delineate this shortcoming of the bond security.

Flow-of-funds structure. The trust indenture and legal opinion should explain what the bond issuer has promised to do concerning the revenues received. What is the order of the revenue flows through the various accounting funds of the issuer to pay for the operating expenses of the facility, to provide for payments to the bondholders, to provide for maintenance and special capital improvements, and to provide for debt-service reserves. Additionally, the trust indenture and legal opinion should indicate what happens to excess revenues if they exceed the various annual fund requirements.

The flow of funds of most revenue bonds is structured as *net revenues* (i.e., debt service is paid to the bondholders immediately after revenues are paid to the basic operating and maintenance funds, but before paying all other expenses). A *gross revenues* flow-of-funds structure is one in which the bondholders are to be paid even before the operating expenses of the facility are paid. Examples of gross revenue bonds are those issued by the New York Metropolitan Transportation Authority. However, although it is true that these bonds legally have a claim to the fare-box revenues before all other claimants, it is doubtful that the system could function if the operational expenses, such as wages and electricity bills, were not paid first.

Rate, or user-charge, covenants. The trust indenture and legal opinion should indicate what the issuer has legally committed itself to do to safeguard the bondholders. Do the rates charged only have to be sufficient to meet expenses, including debt service, or do they have to be set and maintained at higher levels so as to provide for reserves? The legal opinion should also indicate whether or not the issuer has the legal power to increase rates or charges upon users without having to obtain prior approvals by other governmental units.

Priority of revenue claims. The legal opinion as summarized in the official statement should clearly indicate whether or not others can legally tap the revenues of the issuer even before they start passing through the issuer's flow-of-funds structure. An example would be the Highway Revenue Bonds issued by the Puerto Rico Highway Authority. These bonds are secured by the revenues from the Commonwealth of Puerto Rico gasoline tax. However, under the commonwealth's constitution, the revenues are first subject to being applied to the commonwealth government's own general obligation bonds if no other funds are available for them.

Additional-bonds test. The trust indenture and legal opinion should indicate under what circumstances the issuer can issue additional bonds that share equal claims to the issuer's revenues. Usually, the legal requirement is that the maximum annual debt service on the new bonds as well as on the old bonds be covered by the projected net revenues by a specified minimum amount. This can be as low as one times coverage. Some revenue bonds have stronger additional-bonds tests to protect the bondholders. As an example, the state of Florida Orlando-Orange County Expressway Bonds have an additional-bonds test that is twofold. First, under the Florida constitution the previous year's *pledged historical revenues* must equal at least 1.33 times maximum annual debt service on the outstanding and to-be-issued bonds. Second, under the original trust indenture *projected revenues* must provide at least 1.50 times estimated maximum annual debt service on the outstanding and to-be-issued bonds.

Other relevant covenants. Lastly, the trust indenture and legal opinion should indicate whether there are other relevant covenants for the bondholder's protection. These usually include pledges by the issuer of the bonds to have insurance on the project (if it is a project-financing revenue bond), to have the accounting records of the issuer annually audited by an outside certified public accountant, to have outside engineers annually review the condition of the capital plant, and to keep the facility operating for the life of the bonds.

In addition to the above aspects of the specific revenue structures of general obligation and revenue bonds, two other developments over the recent past make it more important than ever that the legal documents and opinions summarized in the official statements be carefully reviewed by the investor. The first development involves the mushrooming of new financing techniques that may rest on legally untested security structures. The second development is the increased use of legal opinions provided by local attorneys who may have little prior municipal bond experience. (Legal opinions have traditionally been written by experienced municipal bond attorneys.)

Legally Untested Security Structures and New Financing Techniques

In addition to the more traditional general obligation bonds and toll road, bridge, and tunnel revenue bonds, there are now more nonvoter-approved, innovative, and legally untested security mechanisms. These innovative financing mechanisms include lease-rental bonds, moral obligation housing bonds, take-and-pay power bonds with step-up provisions requiring the participants to increase payments to make up for those that may default, commercial bank-backed letter of credit "put" bonds, and tax-exempt commercial paper. What distinguishes these newer bonds from the more traditional general obligation and revenue bonds is that they have no history of court decisions and other case law to firmly protect the rights of the bondholders. For the newer financing mechanisms, the legal opinion should include an assessment of the probable outcome if the bond security were challenged in court. It should be noted, however, that in most official statements this is not provided to the investor.

The Need for Reliable Legal Opinions

For many years before the 1980s, concern over the reliability of the legal opinion was not as important as it is now. As the result of the numerous bond defaults and related shoddy legal opinions in the 19th century, the investment community demanded that legal documents and opinions be written by recognized municipal bond attorneys. As a consequence, over the years a small group of primarily Wall Street-based law firms and certain recognized firms in other financial centers dominated the industry and developed high standards of professionalism.

In the 1970s, however, more and more issuers began to have their legal work done by local law firms, a few of whom had little experience in municipal bond work. This development, along with the introduction of more innovative and legally untested financing mechanisms has created a greater need for reliable legal opinions. An example of a specific concern involves the documents the issuers' lawyers must complete so as to avoid arbitrage problems with the Internal Revenue Service. On negotiated bond issues, one remedy has been for the underwriters to have their own counsels review the documents and to provide separate legal opinions.

THE NEED TO KNOW WHO *REALLY* IS THE ISSUER

Still another general question to ask before purchasing a municipal bond is just what kind of people are the issuers? Are they conscientious public servants with clearly defined public goals? Do they have histories of successful management of public institutions? Have they demonstrated commitments to professional and fiscally stringent operations? Additionally, issuers in highly charged and partisan environments in which conflicts chronically occur between political parties and/or among factions or personalities within the governing bodies are clearly bond issuers to scrutinize closely, and possibly to avoid. Such issuers should be scrutinized regardless of the strength of the surrounding economic environment.

For General Obligation Bonds

For general obligation bond issuers the focus is on the political relationships that exist on the one hand among chief executives, such as mayors, county executives, and governors, and on the other hand their legislative counterparts. Issuers with unstable political elites are of particular concern. Of course, rivalry among political actors is not necessarily bad. What is undesirable is competition so bitter and personal that real cooperation among the warring public officials in addressing future budgetary problems may be precluded. An example of an issuer that was avoided because of such dissension is the city of Cleveland. The political problems of the city in 1978 and the bitter conflicts between

Mayor Kucinich and the city council resulted in a general obligation note default in December of that year.

For Revenue Bonds

When investigating revenue bond issuers, it is important to determine not only the degree of political conflict, if any, that exists among the members of the bond-issuing body, but also the relationships and conflicts among those who make the appointments to the body. Additionally, the investor should determine whether the issuer of the revenue bond has to seek prior approval from another governmental jurisdiction before the user-fees or other charges can be levied. If this is the case, then the stability of the political relationships between the two units of government must be determined.

An example of the importance of this information can be seen when reviewing the creditworthiness of the water and electric utility revenue bonds and notes issued by Kansas City, Kansas. Although the revenue bonds and notes were issued by city hall, it was the six-member board of public utilities, a separately elected body, that had the power to set the water and electricity utility rates. In the spring of 1981, because of political dissension among the board members caused by a political struggle between a faction on the board of public utilities and the city commissioners (including the city's finance commissioner), the board refused to raise utility rates as required by the covenant. The situation only came under control when a new election changed the makeup of the board in favor of those supported by city hall.

In addition to the above institutional and political concerns, for revenue bond issuers in particular an assessment of the technical and managerial abilities of the staff should be made. The professional competency of the staff is a more critical factor in revenue bond analysis than it is in the analysis of general obligation bonds. This is because unlike general obligation bonds, which are secured in the final instance by the full faith and credit and unlimited taxing powers of the issuers, many revenue bonds are secured by the ability of the revenue projects to be operational and financially self-supporting.

The professional staffs of authorities that issue revenue bonds for the construction of nuclear and other public power-generating facilities, apartment complexes, hospitals, water and sewer systems, and other large public works projects, such as convention centers and sports arenas, should be carefully reviewed. Issuers who have histories of high management turnovers, project cost overruns, or little experience should be avoided by the conservative investor, or at least considered higher risks than their assigned commercial credit ratings may indicate. Additionally, it is helpful, although not mandatory, for revenue bond issuers to have their accounting records annually audited by outside certified public accountants, so as to ensure the investor of a more accurate picture of the issuer's financial health.

ON THE FINANCIAL ADVISOR AND UNDERWRITER

Shorthand indications of the quality of the investment are (1) who the issuer selected as its financial advisor, if any, (2) its principal underwriter if the bond sale was negotiated, and (3) its financial advisor if the bond issue came to market competitively. Additionally, since 1975 many prudent underwriters will not bid on competitive bond issues if there are significant credit-quality concerns. Therefore, it is also useful to learn who was the underwriter for the competitive bond sales as well.

Indentifying the financial advisors and underwriters is important for two reasons.

The Need for Complete, Not Just Adequate, Investment Risk Disclosures

The first reason relates to the quality and thoroughness of information provided to the investor by the issuer. The official statement, or private placement papers if the issue is placed privately, is usually prepared with the assistance of lawyers and a financial advisor or by the principal underwriter. There are industry-wide disclosure guidelines that are generally adhered to, but not all official statements provide the investor with complete discussions of the risk potentials that may result from either the specific economics of the project or the community settings and the operational details of the security provisions. It is usually the author of this document who decides what to either emphasize or downplay in the official statement. The more professional and established the experience of the author to provide the investor with unbiased and complete information about the issuer, the more comfortable the investor can be with information provided by the issuer and in arriving at a credit-quality conclusion.

The Importance of Firm Reputation for Thoroughness and Integrity

By itself, the reputation of the issuer's financial advisor and/or underwriter should not be the determinant credit-quality factor, but it is a fact the investor should consider. This is particularly the case for marginally feasible bond issues that have complex flow-of-funds and security structures. The securities industry is unique as compared with other industries, such as real estate, in that trading and investment commitments are usually made verbally over the phone with a paper trail following days later. Many institutional investors, such as banks, bonds funds, and casualty insurance companies, have learned to judge issuers by the "company" they keep. Institutions tend to be conservative, and they are more comfortable with financial information provided by established financial advisors and underwriters who have recognized reputations for honesty. Individual investors and analysts would do well to adopt this approach as well.

GENERAL CREDIT INDICATORS AND ECONOMIC FACTORS IN THE CREDIT ANALYSIS

The last analytical factor is the health or viability of the economics of the bond issuer or specific project financed by the bond proceeds. The economics cover a variety of concerns. When analyzing general obligation bond issuers, one should look at the specific budgetary and debt characteristics of the issuer as well as the general economic environment. For project-financing, or enterprise, revenue bonds, the economics are primarily limited to the ability of the project to generate sufficient charges upon the users to pay the bondholders. These are known as pure revenue bonds.

For those revenue bonds that rely not upon user charges and fees, but instead upon general purpose taxes and revenues, the analysis should take basically the same approach as for the general obligation bonds. For these bonds the taxes and revenues diverted to the bondholders would otherwise have gone to the state's or city's general fund.

As examples of such bonds, the New York State Municipal Assistance Corporation for the City of New York Bonds (MAC), secured by general New York City sales taxes and annual state-aid appropriations, and the state of Illinois Chicago School Finance Authority Bonds, secured by unlimited property taxes levied within the city of Chicago, are bonds structured to appear as pure revenue bonds; but in essence they are not. They both incorporate bond structures created to bail out the former, New York City, and the latter, Chicago's board of education, from severe budget deficits. The creditworthiness of these bonds is tied to that of their underlying jurisdictions, which have given or have had portions of their taxing powers and general fund revenues diverted to secure the new revenue-type bail-out bonds. Besides looking at the revenue features, the investor therefore must look at the underlying jurisdictions as well.

For General Obligation Bonds

For general obligation bonds, the economics include asking questions and obtaining answers in four specific areas: debt burden, budget soundness, tax burden, and the overall economy.

Debt burden. Concerning the debt burden of the general obligation bond issuer, some of the more important concerns include the determination of the total amount of debt outstanding and to be issued that is supported by the general taxing powers of the issuer as well as by earmarked revenues.

For example, general obligation bonds issued by school districts in New York State and certain general obligation bonds issued by the city of New York are general obligations of the issuer and are also secured by state-aid to education payments due the issuer. If the issuer defaults, the bondholder can go to the state comptroller and be made whole from the next state-aid payment due the local issuer. An example of another earmarked-revenue general obligation bond is the state of Illinois General Obligation Transportation, Series A Bond. Besides being state general obligations, debt service is secured by gasoline taxes in the state's transportation fund as well.

The debt of the general obligation bond issuer includes, in addition to the general obligation bonds outstanding, leases, and "moral obligation" commitments, among others. Additionally, the amount of the unfunded pension liabilities should be determined. Key debt ratios that reveal the burden on local taxpayers include determining the per capita amount of general obligation debt as well as the per capita debt of the overlapping or underlying general obligation bond issuers. Other key measures of debt burden include determining what are the amounts and percentages of the outstanding general obligation bonds as well as the outstanding general obligation bonds of the overlapping or underlying jurisdictions to real estate valuations. These numbers and percentages can be compared to most recent year medians, as well as with the past history of the issuer, to determine whether the debt burden is increasing, declining, or remaining relatively stable.

Budgetary soundness. Concerning the budgetary operations and budgetary soundness of the general obligation bond issuer, some of the more important questions include how well the issuer over at least the previous five years has been able to maintain balanced budgets and fund reserves. How dependent is the issuer on short-term debt to finance annual budgetary operations? How have increased demands by residents for costly social services been handled? That is, how frugal is the issuer? How well have the public-employee unions been handled? They usually lobby for higher salaries, liberal pensions, and other costly fringe benefits. Clearly, it is undesirable for the pattern of dealing with the constituent demands and public-employee unions to result in raising taxes and drawing down nonrecurring budget reserves. Last, another general concern in the budgetary area is the reliability of the budget and accounting records of the issuer. Are interfund borrowings reported? And who audits the books?

Tax burden. Concerning the tax burden, it is important to learn two things initially. First, what are the primary sources of revenue in the issuer's general fund? Second, how dependent is the issuer on any one revenue source? If the general obligation bond issuer relies increasingly upon either a property tax, wage and income taxes, or a sales tax to provide the major share of financing for annually increasing budget appropriations, taxes could quickly become so high as to drive businesses and people away. Many larger northern states and cities with their relatively high income, sales, and property taxes appear to be experiencing this phenomenon. Still another concern is the degree of dependency of the issuer on intergovernmental revenues, such as federal or state revenue sharing and grants-in-aid to finance its annual budget appropriations. Political coalitions on the state and federal levels that support these financial transfer programs are not permanent and could undergo dramatic change very quickly. Therefore, a general obligation bond issuer that currently has a relatively low tax burden but receives substantial amounts of intergovernmental monies should be carefully reviewed by the investor. If it should occur that the aid monies are reduced, as has been occurring under many of President Reagan's legislative programs, certain issuers may primarily increase their taxes, instead of reducing their expenditures to conform to the reduced federal grants-in-aid.

Overall economy. The fourth and last area of general obligation bond analysis concerns the issuer's overall economy. For local governments, such as counties, cities, towns, and school districts, key items include learning the annual rate of growth of the full value of all taxable real estate for the previous 10 years and identifying the 10 largest taxable properties. What kinds of business or activity occur on the respective properties? What percentage of the total property tax base do the 10 largest properties represent? What is the building permit trend for at least the previous five years? What percentage of all real estate is tax exempt, and what is the distribution of the taxable ones by purpose such as residential, commercial, industrial, railroad, and public utility? Last, who are the five largest employers? Concerning the final item, those communities that have one large employer are more susceptible to rapid adverse economic change than communities that have more diversified employment and real estate bases. Additional information that reveals either economic health or decline include determining whether the population of the community over the previous 10 years has been increasing or declining by age, income, and ethnicity and how the monthly and yearly unemployment rates compare with the comparable national averages as well as to the previous history of the community.

For state governments that issue general obligation bonds, the economic analysis should include many of the same questions applied to local governments. In addition, the investor should determine the annual rates of growth on the state level for the previous five years of personal income and retail sales and how much the state has had to borrow from the Federal Unemployment Trust Fund to pay unemployment benefits. This last item is particularly significant for the long-term economic attractiveness of the state, since under current federal law employers in those states with large federal loans in arrears are required to pay increased unemployment taxes to the federal government.

For Revenue Bonds

Airport revenue bonds.   For airport revenue bonds, the economic questions vary according to the type of bond security involved. There are two basic security structures.

The first type of airport revenue bond is one based upon traffic-generated revenues that result from the competitiveness and passenger demand for the airport. The financial data on the operations of the airport should come from audited financial statements going back at least three years. If a new facility is planned, a feasibility study prepared by a recognized consultant should be reviewed. The feasibility study should have two components: (1) a market and demand analysis to define the service area and examine demographic and airport utilization trends and (2) a financial analysis to examine project operating costs and revenues.

Revenues at an airport may come from landing fees paid by the airlines for their flights, concession fees paid by restaurants, shops, newsstands and parking facilities, and from airline apron and fueling fees.

Also, in determining the long-term economic viability of an airport, the investor should determine whether or not the wealth trends of the service area are upward; whether or not the airport is either dependent on tourism or serves as a vital transfer point; whether or not passenger enplanements and air cargo handled over the previous five years have been growing; whether or not increased costs of jet fuel would make such other transportation as trains and automobiles more attractive in that particular region; and whether or not the airport is a major domestic hub for an airline, which could make the airport particularly vulnerable to route changes caused by schedule revisions and changes in airline corporate management.

The second type of airport revenue bond is secured by a lease with one or more airlines for the use of a specific facility, such as a terminal or hangar. The lease usually obligates them to make annual payments sufficient to pay the expenses and debt service for the facility. For many of these bonds, the analysis of the airline lease is based upon the credit quality of the lessee airline. Whether or not the lease should extend as long as the bonds are outstanding depends on the specific airport and facility involved. For major hub airports it may be better not to have long-term leases, since without leases fees and revenues can be increased as the traffic grows regardless of which airline uses the specific facility. Of course, for regional or startup airports, long-term leases with trunk (i.e., major airline) carriers are preferred.

Highway revenue bonds. There are generally two types of highway revenue bonds. The bond proceeds of the first type are used to build specific revenue producing facilities, such as toll roads, bridges, and tunnels. For these pure enterprise revenue bonds, the bondholders have claims to the revenues collected through the tolls. The financial soundness of the bonds depend on the ability of the specific projects to be self-supporting. Proceeds from the second type of highway revenue bond generally are used for public highway improvements, and the bondholders are paid by earmarked revenues, such as gasoline taxes, automobile registration payments, and driver's license fees.

Concerning the economic viability of a toll road, bridge, or tunnel revenue bond, the investor should ask a number of questions.

1. What is the traffic history, and how inelastic is the demand? Toll roads, bridges, and tunnels that provide vital transportation links are clearly preferred to those that face competition from interstate highways, toll-free bridges, or mass transit.
2. How well is the facility maintained? Has the issuer established a maintenance reserve fund at a reasonable level to use for such repair work as road resurfacing and bridge painting?
3. Does the issuer have the ability to raise tolls to meet covenant and debt-reserve requirements without seeking approvals from other governmental actors, such as state legislatures and governors? In those few cases where such approvals are necessary, a question to ask is how sympathetic have these other power centers been in the past in approving toll-increase requests?
4. What is the debt-to-equity ratio? Some toll-road, bridge, and tunnel authorities have received substantial nonreimbursable federal grants that have helped to subsidize their costs of construction. This, of course, reduces the amount of debt that has to be issued.
5. What is the history of labor-management relations, and can public employee strikes substantially reduce toll collections?
6. When was the facility constructed? Generally, toll roads financed and constructed in the 1950s and 1960s tend now to be in good financial condition. This is because the cost of financing was much less than it is today. Many of these older revenue

bond issuers have been retiring their bonds ahead of schedule by buying them at deep discounts to par in the secondary market.
7. If the facility is a bridge that could be damaged by a ship and made inoperable, does the issuer have adequate "use and occupancy" insurance?

Those few toll-road and bridge revenue bonds that have defaulted have done so because of either unexpected competition from toll-free highways and bridges, poor traffic projections, or substantially higher than projected construction costs. An example of one of the few defaulted bonds is the West Virginia Turnpike Commission's Turnpike Revenue Bonds issued in 1952 and 1954 to finance the construction of an 88-mile expressway from Charleston to Princeton, West Virgina. The initial traffic-engineering estimates were overly optimistic, and the construction costs came in approximately $37 million higher than the original budgeted amount of $96 million. Because of insufficient traffic and toll collections, between 1956 and 1979 the bonds were in default. By the late 1970s with the completion of various connecting cross-country highways, the turnpike became a major link for interstate traffic. Since 1979 the bonds have become self-supporting in terms of making interest coupon payments.

Concerning the economics of highway revenue bonds that are not pure enterprise type but instead are secured by earmarked revenues, such as gasoline taxes, automobile registration payments, and driver's license fees, the investor should ask the following questions.

1. Are the earmarked tax revenues based on either state constitutional mandates, such as the state of Ohio's Highway Improvement Bonds, or are they derived from laws enacted by state legislatures, such as the state of Washington's Chapters 56, 121, and 167 Motor Vehicle Fuel Tax Bonds? A constitutional pledge is usually more permanent and reliable.
2. What has been the coverage trend of the available revenues to debt service over the previous 10 years? Has the coverage been increasing, stable, or declining?
3. If the earmarked revenue is gasoline tax, is it based either on a specific amount of cents per gallon of gasoline sold, or as a percentage of the price of each gallon sold? With greater conservation and more efficient cars, the latter tax structure is preferred because it is not as susceptible to declining sales of gasoline and because it benefits directly from any increased gasoline prices at the pumps.

Hospital revenue bonds. Two unique features of hospitals make the analysis of their debt particularly complex and uncertain. The first concerns their sources of revenue, and the second concerns the basic structure of the institutions themselves.

During the past 20 years, the major sources of revenue for most hospitals have been (1) payments from the federal (Medicare) and combined federal-state (Medicaid) hospital reimbursement programs, and (2) appropriations made by local governments through their taxing powers. It is not uncommon for hospitals to receive at least two thirds of their annual revenues from these sources. How well the hospital management markets its service to attract more private-pay patients, how aggressive it is in its third-party collections, such as from Blue Cross, and how conservatively it budgets for the governmental reimbursement payments are key elements for distinguishing weak from strong hospital bonds.

Particularly for community-based hospitals (as opposed to teaching hospitals affiliated with medical schools), a unique feature of their financial structure is that their major financial beneficiaries, physicians, have no legal or financial liabilities if the institutions do not remain financially viable over the long term. An example of the problems that can be caused by this lack of liability is found in the story of the Sarpy County, Nebraska, Midlands Community Hospital Revenue Bonds. These bonds were issued to finance the construction of a hospital three miles south of Omaha, Nebraska, that was to replace an older one located in the downtown area. Physician questionnaires prepared for the feasibility study prior to the construction of the hospital indicated strong support for the replacement facility. Many doctors had used the older hospital in downtown Omaha as a backup facility for a larger nearby hospital. Unfortunately, once the new Sarpy hospital opened in 1976, many physicians found that the new hospital could not serve as a backup because it was 12 miles further away from the major hospital than the old hospital had been. With these physicians not referring their patients to the new Sarpy hospital, it was soon unable to make bond principal payments and was put under the jurisdiction of a court receiver.

The above factors raise long-term uncertainties about many community-based hospitals, but certain key areas of analysis and trends reveal the relative economic health of hospitals that already have revenue bonds outstanding. The first area is the liquidity of the hospital as measured by the ratio of dollars held in current assets to current liabilities. In general, a five-year trend of high values for the ratio is desirable because it implies an ability by the hospital to pay short-term obligations and thereby avoid budgetary problems. The second indicator is the ratio of long-term debt to equity, as measured in the unrestricted end-of-year fund balance. In general, the lower the long-term debt to equity ratio, the stronger the finances of the hospital. The third indicator is the actual debt-service coverage of the previous five years as well as the projected coverage. The fourth indicator is the annual bed-occupancy rates for the previous five years. The fifth is the percentage of physicians at the hospital who are professionally approved (board certified), their respective ages, and how many of them use the hospital as their primary institution.

For new or expanded hospitals, much of the above data is provided to the investor in the feasibility study. One item in particular that should be covered for a new hospital is whether or not the physicians who plan to use the hospital actually live in the area to be served by the hospital. Because of its importance in providing answers to these questions, the national reputation and experience of the people who prepare the feasibility study is of critical concern to the investor.

Housing revenue bonds. For housing revenue bonds the economic and financial questions vary according to the type of bond security involved. There are two basic types of housing revenue bonds— each with a different type of security structure. One is the housing revenue bond secured by *single-family* mortgages, and the other is the housing revenue bond secured by mortgages on *multifamily* housing projects.

Concerning single-family housing revenue bonds, the strongly secured bonds usually have four characteristics.

1. The single-family home loans are insured by the Federal Housing Administration (FHA), Federal Veterans Administration (VA), or an acceptable private mortgage insurer. If the individual home loans are not insured, then they should have a loan-to-value ratio of 80 percent or less.
2. If the conventional home loans have less than 100 percent primary mortgage insurance coverage, an additional 5–10 percent mortgage-pool insurance policy would be required. The private mortgage insurer should be of high quality in terms of company capitalization and in terms of having conservative underwriting standards and limits.
3. In addition to a debt reserve that has an amount of monies equal at least to six months interest on the single-family housing revenue bonds, there is a mortgage reserve fund that has an amount equal at least to 1 percent of the bond issue outstanding.
4. The issuer of the single-family housing revenue bonds is in a region of the country that has either stable or strong economic growth as indicated by increased real estate valuations, personal income, and retail sales, as well as low unemployment rates and relatively low state and local government overall tax burdens.

In the 1970s state agency issuers of single-family housing revenue bonds assumed certain prepayment levels in structuring the bond maturities. In recent years most issuers have abandoned this practice but investors should review the retirement schedule for the single-family mortgage revenue bonds to determine whether or not the issuer has assumed large, lump-sum mortgage prepayments in the early year cash flow projections. And if so, how conservative are the prepayment assumptions, and how dependent is the issuer on the prepayments to meet the annual debt-service requirements?

It should be noted that single-family housing revenue bonds issued by local governments, such as towns, cities, and counties usually have conservative bond-retirement schedules that have not included any home-mortgage prepayment assumptions. Single-family housing revenue bonds issued by states did use prepayment assumptions. This positive feature of local government-issued bonds is balanced somewhat by the facts that the state-issued bonds generally no longer include prepayment assumptions and usually are secured by home mortgages covering wider geographic areas. Additionally, the state issuing agencies usually have professional in-house staffs that closely monitor the home-mortgage portfolios, whereas the local issuers do not. Finally, state issuing agencies have accumulated substantial surplus funds over the years that can be viewed as an additional source of bondholder protection.

For multifamily housing revenue bonds, there are four specific, though overlapping, security structures. The first type of multifamily housing revenue bond is one in which the bonds are secured by mortgages that are federally insured. Usually the federal insurance covers all but the difference between the outstanding bond principal and collectible mortgage amount (usually 1 percent), and all but the *nonasset* bonds (i.e., bonds issued to cover issuance costs and capitalized interest). The attractiveness of the federal insurance is that it protects the investor against bond default within the limitations outlined. The insurance protects the bondholders regardless of whether or not the projects are fully occupied and generating rental payments.

The second type of multifamily housing revenue bond is one in which the federal government subsidizes under the federal Section 8 program all annual costs, including debt service, of the project not covered by tenant rental payments. Under Section 8 the eligible low-income and elderly tenants pay only 15 to 30 percent of their incomes for rent. Since the ultimate security comes from the Section 8 subsidies, which escalate annually with the increased cost of living in that particular geographic region, the bondholder's primary risks concern the developer's ability to complete the project, find tenants eligible under the federal guidelines to live in the project, and then maintain high occupancy rates for the life of the bonds. The investor should carefully review the location and construction standards used in building the project, as well as the competency of the project manager in selecting tenants who will take care of the building and pay their rents. In this regard, state agencies that issue Section 8 bonds usually have stronger in-house management experience and resources for dealing with problems than do the local development corporations that have issued Section 8 bonds. It should be noted that the Federal government has eliminated new appropriations for the Section 8 program and there is little new issuance of tax exempt debt supported by this subsidy program.

The third type of multifamily housing revenue bond is one in which the ultimate security for the bondholder is the ability of the project to generate sufficient monthly rental payments from the tenants themselves to meet the operating and debt-service expenses. Some of these projects may receive governmental subsidies (such as interest cost reductions under the federal Section 236 program and property tax abatements from local governments), but the ultimate security is the economic viability of the project. Key information includes the location of the project, its occupancy rate, whether large families or the elderly will primarily live in the project, whether or not the rents necessary to keep the project financially sound are competitive with others in the surrounding community, and whether or not the project manager has proven records of maintaining good services and of establishing careful tenant selection standards.

A fourth type of multifamily housing revenue bond is one that includes some type of private credit enhancement to the underlying real estate. These credit enhancements can include guarantees by an insurance company, the Federal National Mortgage Association (FNMA), or a bank letter of credit.

Other financial features desirable in all multifamily housing bonds include a debt-service reserve fund, which should contain an amount of money equal to the maximum annual debt service on the bonds, a mortgage reserve fund, and a capital repair and maintenance fund.

Still another feature of many multifamily housing revenue bonds, and particularly of those issued by state housing agencies, is the state moral obligation pledge. Several state agencies have issued housing revenue bonds that carry a potential state liability for making up deficiencies in their one-year debt-service reserve funds, should any occur. In most cases if a drawdown of the debt reserve occurs, the state agency must report the amount used to its governor and state budget director. The state legislature, in turn, may appropriate the requested amount, though there is no legally enforceable obligation to do so. Bonds with this makeup provision are the so-called moral obligation bonds.

The moral obligation only provides a state legislature with permissive authority—*not mandatory authority*—to make an appropriation to the troubled state housing agency. Therefore the analysis should determine (1) whether the state has the budgetary surpluses for subsidizing the housing agency's revenue bonds, and (2) whether or not there is a consensus within the executive and legislative branches of that particular state's government to use state general fund revenues for subsidizing multifamily housing projects.

Industrial revenue bonds. Generally, industrial revenue bonds are issued by state and local governments on behalf of individual corporations and businesses. The security for the bonds usually depends on the economic soundness of the particular corporation or business involved. If the bond issue is for a subsidiary of a larger corporation, one question to ask is whether or not the parent guarantees the bonds. Is it only obligated through a lease, or does it not have any obligation whatsoever for paying the bondholders? If the answer is that the parent corporation has no responsibility for the bonds, then the investor must look very closely at the operations of the subsidiary in addition to those of the parent corporation. Here the investor must determine also whether the bond is guaranteed by the company or is a lease obligation.

For companies that have issued common stock that is publicly traded, economic data is readily available either in the annual reports, or in the 10-K reports that must be filed annually with the Securities and Exchange Commission. For privately held companies, financial data are more difficult to obtain.

In assessing the economic risk of investing in an industrial revenue bond, another question to ask is whether the bondholder or the trustee holds the mortgage on the property. Although holding the mortgage is not an important economic factor in assessing either hospital or low-income, multifamily housing bonds where the properties have very limited commercial value, it can be an important strength for the holder of industrial development revenue bonds. If the bond is secured by a mortgage on a property of either a fast-food retailer, such as MacDonalds, or an industrial facility, such as a warehouse, the property location and resale value of the real estate may provide some protection to the bondholder, regardless of what happens to the company that issued the bonds. Of course, the investor should always avoid possible bankruptcy situations regardless of the economic attractiveness of the particular piece of real estate involved. This is because the bankruptcy process usually involves years of litigation and numerous court hearings, which no investor should want to be concerned about.

Lease-rental bonds. Lease-rental bonds are usually structured as revenue bonds, and annual rent payments, paid by a state or local government, cover all costs including operations, maintenance, and debt service. The public purposes financed by these bond issues include the construction of public office buildings, fire houses, police stations, university buildings, mental health facilities, and highways, as well as the purchase of office equipment and computers. In some instances the rental payments may only come from student tuition, patient fees, and earmarked tax revenues, and the state or local government is not legally obligated to make lease-rental payments beyond the amount of available earmarked revenues. However, for many lease-rental bonds the underlying lessee state, county, or city is required to make annual appropriations from its general fund. For example, the Albany County, New York, Lease Rental South Mall Bonds were issued to finance the construction of state office buildings. Although the bonds are technically general obligations of Albany County, the real security comes from the annual lease payments made by the state of New York. These payments are annually appropriated. For such bonds, the basic economic and financial analysis should follow the same guidelines as for general obligation bonds.

Public power revenue bonds.   Public power revenue bonds are issued to finance the construction of electrical generating plants. An issuer of the bonds may construct and operate one power plant, buy electrical power from a "wholesaler" and sell it "retail," construct and operate several power plants, or join with other public and private utilities in jointly financing the construction of one or more power plants. This last arrangement is known as a joint-power financing structure. Although there are revenue bonds that can claim the revenues of a federal agency (for example, the Washington Public Power Supply System's Nuclear Project No. 2 Revenue Bonds, which if necessary can claim the revenues of the Bonneville Power Administration) and many others that can require the participating underlying municipal electric systems to pay the bondholders whether or not the plants are completed and operating (for example, the Massachusetts Municipal Wholesale Electric Company's Power Supply System Revenue Bonds), the focus here is how the investor determines which power projects will be financially self-supporting without these backup security features.

There are at least five major questions to ask when evaluating the investment soundness of a public power revenue bond.

1. Does the bond issuer have the authority to raise its electric rates in a timely fashion without going to any regulatory agencies? This is particularly important if substantial rate increases are necessary to pay for either new construction or plant improvements.
2. How diversified is the customer base among residential, commercial, and industrial users?
3. Is the service area growing in terms of population, personal income, and commercial/industrial activity so as to warrant the electrical power generated by the existing or new facilities?
4. What are the projected and actual costs of power generated by the system, and how competitive are they with other regions of the country? Power rates are particularly important for determining the long-term economic attractiveness of the region for those industries that are large energy users.
5. How diversified is the fuel mix? Is the issuer dependent on one energy such as hydro dams, oil, natural gas, coal, or nuclear fuel?

Concerning electrical generating plants fueled by nuclear power, the aftermath of the Three Mile Island nuclear accident in 1979 has resulted in greater construction and maintenance reviews and costly safety requirements prompted by the Federal Nuclear Regulatory Commission (NRC). The NRC oversees this industry. In the past, although nuclear power plants were expected to cost far more to build than other types of power plants, it was also believed that, once the generating plants became operational, the relatively low fuel and maintenance costs would more than offset the initial capital outlays. However, with the increased concern about public safety brought about by the Three Mile Island accident, repairs and design modifications are now expected to be made even after plants begin to operate. This of course increases the ongoing costs of generating electricity and reduces the attractiveness of nuclear power as an alternative to the oil, gas, and coal fuels. For ongoing nuclear plant construction projects, the investor should review the feasibility study to see that it was prepared by experienced and recognized consulting engineers and that it has realistic construction, design schedule, and cost estimates.

Resource recovery revenue bonds. A resource recovery facility converts refuse (solid waste) into commercially salable energy, recoverable products, and a residue to be landfilled. The major revenues for a resource recovery bond usually are the "tipping fees" per ton paid monthly by those who deliver the garbage to the facility for disposal; revenues from steam, electricity, or refuse-derived fuel sold to either an electric power company or another energy user; and revenues from the sale of recoverable materials, such as aluminum and steel scrap.

Resource recovery bonds are secured in one of two ways or a combination thereof. The first security structure is one in which the cost of running the resource recovery plant and paying the bondholders comes from the sale of the energy produced (steam, electricity, or refuse-derived fuel) as well as from fees paid by the haulers, both municipal and private, who bring the garbage to the facility. In this financing structure the resource recovery plant usually has to be operational and self-supporting for the bondholders to be paid. The second security structure involves an agreement with a state or local government, such as a county or municipality, which contractually obligates the government to haul or to have hauled a certain amount of garbage to the facility each year for the life of the facility and to pay a tipping fee (service fee) sufficient to operate the facility. The tipping fee must include amounts sufficient to pay bondholders regardless of whether or not the resource recovery plant has become fully operational.

When deciding to invest in a resource recovery revenue bond, one should ask the following questions. First, how proven is the system technology to be used in the plant? *Mass burning* is the simplest method, and it has years of proven experience, primarily in Europe. In mass burning the refuse is burned with very little processing. Prepared fuels and shredding, the next most proven method, requires the refuse to be prepared by separation or shredding so as to produce a higher quality fuel for burning. More innovative and eclectic approaches require the most detailed engineering evaluations by qualified specialists. Second, how experienced and reliable are the construction contractors and facility operators (vendors)? Third, are there adequate safeguards and financial incentives for the contractor/vendor to complete and then maintain the facility? Fourth, what are the estimated tipping fees that will have to be charged, and how do they compare with those at any available nearby landfills? One way for a state resource recovery revenue bond issuer to deal with the latter concern occurred with the Delaware Solid Waste Authority's Resource Recovery Revenue Bonds, Series 1979. The state of Delaware enacted a law requiring that all residential garbage within a specified geographic region be hauled to its plant. Fifth, is the bondholder protected during the construction stage by reserves and by fixed-price construction contracts? Sixth, are the prices charged for the generated energy fixed, or instead are they tied to the changing costs of the fuel sources such as oil and gas in that particular market place?

Because of the uniqueness of the resource recovery technology, there are additional questions that should be asked. First, even if the plant-system technology is a proven one, is the plant either the same size as others already in operation, or is it a larger-scale model that would require careful investor review? Second, if the system technology used is innovative and eclectic, is there sufficient redundancy, or low-utilization assumptions, in the plant design to absorb any unforeseen problems once the plant begins production? Last, in addition to the more routine reserves and covenants—such as debt, maintenance, and special capital improvement reserves along with covenants that commercial insurance be placed on the facility and that the contractor (or vendor) pledge to maintain the plant for the life of the bonds—there should also be required yearly plant reviews by independent consulting engineers. The vendor should be required to make the necessary repairs so that the facility will be operational for the life of the bonds.

For resource recovery revenue bonds that have a security structure involving an agreement with a local government, additional questions for the investor to ask are the following: Is the contractual obligation at a fixed rate, or is the tipping fee elastic enough to cover all the increasing costs of operations, maintenance, and debt service? Would strikes or other *force majeure* events prevent the contract either from being enforceable or preclude the availability of an adequate supply of garbage? Last, the investor should determine the soundness of the budgetary operations and general fund reserves of the local government that is to pay the tipping or service fee. For these bonds, the basic economic analysis should follow the same guidelines as for general obligation bonds.

Student loan revenue bonds. Student loan revenue bonds are usually issued by statewide agencies and are used for purchasing either new guaranteed student loans for higher education, or existing guaranteed student loans from local banks.

The student loans are 100 percent guaranteed. They are either guaranteed directly by the federal government—under the Federal Insured Student Loan (FISL) program for 100 percent of principal and interest— or by a state guaranty agency—under a more recent federal insurance program, the Federal Guaranteed Student Loan (GSL) program. This latter program provides federal reimbursement for a state guaranty agency on an annual basis for 100 percent of the payment on defaulted loans up to approximately 5 percent of the amount of loans being repaid, 90 percent for claims in excess of 5 percent but less than 9 percent, and 80 percent for claims exceeding 9 percent. The federal commitments are not dependent on future congressional approvals. Loans made under the FISL and GSL programs are contractual obligations of the federal government.

Although most student loans have federal government support, the financial soundness of the bond program that issues the student loan revenue bonds and monitors the loan portfolio is of critical importance to the investor. This is because of the unique financial structure of a student loan portfolio. Although loan repayments from the student or, in the event of student default, repayments from the guaranty agency are contractually assured, it is difficult to precisely project the actual loan repayment cash flows. This is because the student does not begin repaying the loan until he or she leaves college or graduate school and all other deferments, such as military service, have ended. Before the student begins the loan repayments, the federal government pays the interest on the loans under prescribed formulas. Therefore the first general concern of the investor should be to determine the strength of the cash flow protection.

The second general concern is the adequacy of the loan guaranty. Under all economic scenarios short of a depression, in which the student loan default rate could be 20 percent or greater, the GSL sliding federal reinsurance scale of 100–90–80 should provide adequate cash flow and bond default protection as long as the student loan revenue bond issuer effectively services the student loan repayments, has established and adequately funded loan-guaranty and debt-reserve funds, employs conservative loan-repayment assumptions in the original bond-maturity schedule, and is required to call the bonds at par if the student loan repayments are accelerated. This latter factor prevents a reinvestment risk for the bondholder.

There are eight specific questions for the investor to ask. (1) What percentage of the student loans are FISL and GSL backed, respectively? (2) Has a loan-guarantee fund been established and funded? Usually a fund that is required to have an amount at least equal to 2 percent of the loan principal outstanding is desirable. (3) Is the issuer required to maintain a debt-reserve fund? Usually, for notes a fund with at least six-months interest, and for bonds a fund with a one-year maximum annual debt-service are desirable. (4) If the bond issuer has purchased portfolios of student loans from local banks, are the local lenders required to repurchase any loans if there are either defaults or improperly originated loans? (5) What in-house capability does the issuer have for monitoring and servicing the loan repayments? (6) What is the historic loan-default rate? (7) How are the operating expenses of the agency met? If federal operating subsidies are received under the "Special Allowance Payment Rate" program, what are the rate assumptions used? In this program the issuer receives a supplemental subsidy, which fluctuates with the 91-day U.S. Treasury bill rate. (8) If a state agency is the issuer, is it dependent on appropriations for covering operating expenses and reserve requirements?

Water and sewer revenue bonds.   Water and sewer revenue bonds are issued to provide for a local community's basic needs and as such are not usually subject to general economic changes. Because of the vital utility services performed, their respective financial structures are usually designed to have the lowest possible user changes and still remain financially viable. Generally, rate covenants requiring that user charges cover operations, maintenance, and approximately 1.2 times annual debt-service and reserve requirements are most desirable. On the one hand, a lower rate covenant provides a smaller margin for either unanticipated slow collections or increased operating and plant maintenance costs caused by inflation. On the other hand, rates that generate revenues in excess of 1.2 times could cause unnecessary financial burdens on the users of the water and sewer systems. A useful indication of the soundness of an issuer's operations is to compare the water or sewer utility's average quarterly customer billings to those of other water or sewer systems. Assuming that good customer service is given, the water or sewer system that has a relatively low customer billing charge generally indicates an efficient operation, and therefore strong bond-payment prospects.

Key questions for the investor to ask include the following. (1) Has the bond issuer through local ordinances required mandatory water or sewer connections? Also, local board of health directives against well water contaminations and septic tank usage can often accomplish the same objective as the mandatory hookups. (2) In regard to sewer revenue bonds in particular, how dependent is the issuer on federal grants either to complete ongoing construction projects or to supplement the cost of future expansions of the sewer system? The level of dependence is particularly important in light of efforts in Congress to reduce the multibillion dollar federal sewage treatment grant program for states and local governments. (3) What is the physical condition of the facilities in terms of plant, lines, and meters, and what capital improvements are necessary for maintaining the utilities as well as for providing for anticipated community growth? (4) For water systems in particular, it is important to determine whether the system has water supplies in excess of current peak and projected demands. An operating system at less than full utilization is able to serve future customers and bring in revenues without having to issue additional bonds to enlarge its facilities. (5) What is the operating record of the water or sewer utility for the previous five years? (6) If the bond issuer does not have its own distribution system, but instead charges other participating local governments that do, are the charges or fees either based upon the actual water flow drawn (for water revenue bonds) and sewage treated (for sewer revenue bonds), or upon gallonage entitlements? (7) For water revenue bonds issued for agricultural regions, what crop is grown? An acre of oranges or cherries in California will provide the grower with more income than will an acre of corn or wheat in Iowa. (8) For expanding water and sewer systems, does the issuer have a record over the previous two years of achieving net income equal to or exceeding the rate covenants, and will the facilities to be constructed add to the issuer's net revenues? (9) Has the issuer established and funded debt and maintenance reserves to deal with either unexpected cash flow problems or system repairs? (10) Does the bond issuer have the power to place tax liens against the real estate of those who have not paid their water or sewer bills? Although the investor would not want to own a bond for which court actions of this nature would be necessary before the investor could be paid, the legal existence of this power usually provides an economic incentive for water and sewer bills to be paid promptly by the users.

Additional bonds should only be issued if the need, cost, and construction schedule of the facility have been certified by an independent consulting engineer and if the past and projected revenues are sufficient to pay operating expenses and debt service. Of course, for a new system that does not have an operating history, the quality of the consulting engineer's report is of the uppermost importance.

RED FLAGS FOR THE INVESTOR

In addition to the areas of analysis described above, certain red flags, or negative trends, suggest increased credit risks.

For General Obligation Bonds

For general obligation bonds, the signals that indicate a decline in the ability of a state, county, town, city, or school district to function within fiscally sound parameters include the following:

1. Declining property values and increasing delinquent tax-payers.
2. An annually increasing tax burden relative to other regions.
3. An increasing property tax rate in conjunction with a declining population.
4. Declines in the number and value of issued permits for new building construction.
5. Actual general fund revenues consistently falling below budgeted amounts.
6. Increasing end-of-year general fund deficits.
7. Budget expenditures increasing annually in excess of the inflation rate.
8. The unfunded pension liabilities are increasing.
9. General obligation debt increasing while property values are stagnant.
10. Declining economy as measured by increased unemployment and declining personal income.

For Revenue Bonds

For revenue bonds, the general signals that indicate a decline in credit quality include the following:

1. Annually decreasing coverage of debt service by net revenues.
2. Regular use of debt reserve and other reserves by the issuer.
3. Growing financial dependence of the issuer on unpredictable federal and state-aid appropriations for meeting operating budget expenses.
4. Chronic lateness in supplying investors with annual audited financials.
5. Unanticipated cost overruns and schedule delays on capital construction projects.
6. Frequent or significant rate increases.
7. Deferring capital plant maintenance and improvements.
8. Excessive management turnovers.
9. Shrinking customer base.
10. New and unanticipated competition.

Analyzing the Creditworthiness of Short-Term Municipal Obligations

Sylvan G. Feldstein, Ph.D.
Vice President and Manager
Municipal Bond Research Department
Merrill Lynch Capital Markets

Frank J. Fabozzi, Ph.D., C.F.A.
Visiting Professor
Sloan School of Management
Massachusetts Institute of Technology

This chapter provides a basic framework for analyzing the various short-term municipal investments available. They include tax, revenue, grant, and bond anticipation notes; construction loan notes; repurchase agreements; and tax-exempt commercial paper.

TAX, REVENUE, GRANT, AND BOND ANTICIPATION NOTES

These notes are temporary borrowings by states, local governments, and special jurisdictions to finance a variety of activities. Notes are issued for a period of 12 months, although it is not uncommon for notes to be issued for periods as short as three months and for as long as three years. There are two general purposes for which notes are issued—to even out cash flows and to temporarily finance capital improvements. Each reason is explained below.

First, many states, cities, towns, counties and school districts, as well as special jurisdictions, borrow temporarily in anticipation of collection of taxes or other expected revenues. Their need to borrow occurs because, while payrolls, bills, and other commitments have to be paid starting at the beginning of the fiscal year, property taxes and other revenues such as intergovernmental grants are due and payable after the beginning of the fiscal year. These notes, identified as "Tax Antici-pation Notes" ("TANs"), "Revenue Anticipation Notes" ("RANs"), or "Grant Anticipation Notes" ("GANs"), are usually used to even out the cash flows which are necessitated by the irregular flows of income into the treasuries of the states and local units of government. In some in-stances, combination Tax and Revenue Anticipation Notes ("TRANs") are issued, which usually are payable from two sources. An example would be the TRANs issued by the state of New York.

The second general purpose for which notes are issued is in antici-pation of the sale of long-term bonds. Such notes are known as "Bond Anticipation Notes" ("BANs"). There are three major reasons why capi-tal improvements are initially financed with BANs.

First, because the initial cost estimates for a large construction pro-ject can vary from the construction bids actually submitted, and since better terms are sometimes obtained on a major construction project if the state or local government pays the various contractors as soon as the work begins, BANs are often used as the initial financing instrument. Once the capital improvement is completed, the bills paid, and the total costs determined, the BANs can be retired with the proceeds of a final bond sale.

Second, issuers such as states and cities that have large, diverse, and ongoing capital construction programs will initially issue BANs, and later retire them with the proceeds of a single long-term bond sale. In this instance, the use of BANs allows the issuer to consolidate various, unrelated financing needs into one bond sale.

The third reason why BANs are sometimes issued is related to mar-ket conditions. By temporarily financing capital improvements with BANs, the issuer has greater flexibility in determining the timing of its long-term bond sale, and possibly avoiding unfavorable market condi-tions.

Evaluating Tax, Revenue, and Grant Anticipation Notes

Tax Anticipation Notes (TANs) are usually secured by the taxes for which they were issued. Counties, cities, towns and school districts, usually issue TANs for expected property taxes. Some governmental units go so far as to establish escrow accounts for receiving the taxes, and use the escrowed monies to pay the noteholders.

Revenue Anticipation Notes (RANs) or Grant Anticipation Notes (GANs) are also usually secured by the revenues for which they were issued—intergovernmental capital construction grants and aid, as well as local taxes other than property taxes. In one extreme case, resulting from the New York City note default in 1975, RANs issued by New York

City for expected educational aid from the state of New York provided for the noteholder to go directly to the state comptroller before monies were sent to the city's treasury, if that was necessary to remedy a default. Most RANs just require the issuer, itself, to use the expected monies to pay the noteholders once they are in hand.

Most TANs, RANs, and GANs issued by states, counties, cities, towns, and school districts are also secured by the "general obligation pledge," which is discussed later in this chapter.

Before recommending purchase of TAN, RAN, or GAN, an analyst should obtain information in five areas. These are in addition to what is required if long-term bonds were being considered for purchase. The five areas are:

1. Determining the reliability of the expected taxes, revenues, or grants.
2. Determining the degree of dependency of the note issuers on the expected monies.
3. Determining the soundness of the issuers' budgetary operations.
4. Determining the problem of "rollovers."
5. Determining the historic and projected cash flows by month.

Each area is discussed below.

Reliability of the expected taxes and revenues. If a TAN is issued in anticipation of property taxes, the analyst should investigate the tax collection rates over the previous five years. Tax collection rates below 90 percent usually indicate serious tax collection problems. Additionally, if the issuer is budgeting 100 percent of the tax levy, but collecting substantially less, serious problems can be expected.

In the case of a RAN or GAN issued in anticipation of state or federal grant monies, the first question to ask is if the grant has been legislatively authorized and committed by the state or federal government. Some RAN issuers (including New York City prior to its RAN defaults in 1975) would issue RANs without having all the anticipated grants committed by the higher levels of government. Other local governments, hard-pressed to balance their budgets, may still follow this practice in order to obtain quick cash through the sale of RANs. As a safeguard, the analyst should make sure the issuer has in its possession a fully signed grant agreement prior to the RAN or GAN sale.

Dependency on expected monies. One measure of the creditworthiness of the TAN or RAN issuer is its degree of dependency on the temporarily borrowed monies. Some jurisdictions for example, limit the amount of TANs that can be issued in anticipation of property taxes to a percentage of the prior year's levy that was actually collected. The state of New Jersey, which has one of the more fiscally conservative local government regulatory codes in the country, limits the annual sale of TANs and RANs by county and municipal governments to no more than 30 percent of the property taxes and various other revenues actually collected in the previous year. School districts may not exceed one half of current expenses. Many other states are more permissive and allow local governments to issue TANs and RANs up to 75 to 100 percent of the monies previously collected, or even expected to be received in the current fiscal year.

Soundness of budgetary operations. Another critical element is the issuer's history of overall prudent and disciplined financial management. The analyst should determine how well the issuer has maintained end-of-year fund balances in its major operating funds over the previous five fiscal years.

The problems of "rollovers." Retiring TANs or RANs with the proceeds of new issues or issuing TANs or RANs to be retired in a fiscal year following the one in which they were originally issued are indications of fiscal problems. Such practices, known as "rollovers," are sometimes used by hard-pressed issuers to disguise chronic operating budget deficits. To leave no doubt as to the soundness of their budgetary operations, many states, local governments, and special jurisdictions have established, either by statute or by administrative policy, that all TANs and RANs issued in one fiscal year must be retired before the end of that fiscal year. Although such a policy reduces the issuer's flexibility in dealing with unexpected emergencies, it helps provide protection to the noteholders against TANs and RANs ever being used for hidden deficit financing. In some circumstances RANs and GANs can be properly issued for periods greater than 12 months, providing the granting agency has established a reimbursement schedule that matches the maturity of the note.

Historical and projected cash flows. The TAN, RAN, or GAN issuer's cash flow history and projections can provide valuable information on creditworthiness. What is initially required is a monthly accounting going back over the previous fiscal year, showing the beginning fund balances, revenues, expenditures, and end-of-month fund balances. The analyst should determine how well the issuer has met its fiscal goals by maintaining at least a balanced budget and meeting all liabilities, including debt service payments.

Cash flow tables on the projected monthly cash flows for the fiscal year in which the TANs or RANs are to be issued should be examined. Of particular importance are whether the issuer has included in the projections sufficient revenues to retire the TANs, RANs, or GANs, including interest payments, and whether the estimated revenues and expenditures amounts are realistic in light of the prior fiscal year's experience.

Evaluating Bond Anticipation Notes

BANs are secured principally by the issuer's access to the municipal bond market—i.e., its ability to issue long-term bonds, the proceeds of which will be used to retire the BANs. Most BANs issued by states, counties, cities, towns and school districts are also secured by the general obligation pledge, which is discussed later in this chapter.

Two factors determine the ability of the issuer to gain market access. Therefore, the analyst should obtain information in these two areas. They are:

1. The creditworthiness of the issuers.
2. Expected future market conditions and the flexibility of the issuers.

Each is discussed below.

Creditworthiness. Because outstanding BANs are retired with the proceeds of long-term bond sales, the creditworthiness of the BANs is directly related to the creditworthiness of the underlying issuer. The analyst must obtain the same credit information he would use for analyzing long-term bonds. In general, the stronger the bond credit quality, the greater is the ability of the BAN issuer to complete long-term bond sales.

Besides determining the credit quality of the underlying bonds, the analyst should also determine the issuer's probable market access and acceptance. That is, in the past how well have the bonds of the issuer been received in the marketplace? Has the issuer had to pay interest costs substantially higher than other bond issuers of similar creditworthiness? How many bids were received for a competitively bid issue? Has the issuer attempted to sell a similar amount of bonds in previous years? Answers to these questions will determine the credit risks involved in the purchase of BANs.

Future market conditions. The BAN investor cannot know in advance what the condition of the market will be when his BANs come due. If the issuer's creditworthiness is at least of investment-grade quality, however, there should be a market for that issuer's bonds. Of course, the weaker the credit quality and the larger the amount of BANs to be retired, the higher the rate of interest would have to be.

If the BANs come due at a time when interest rates in the municipal bond market are rising, the BAN issuer should have the flexibility to retire the maturing BANs with a new BAN issue, rather than long-term bonds. Most state and local government finance regulations recognize this need by allowing BANs to be retired from new BAN issues. The ability of the issuer to do so is directly related to the credit quality of the issuer.

Unlike most TANs, RANs and GANs, BANs can be refunded—i.e.,

rolled over into new BANs. However, prudent issuers are usually limited by local laws to having their BANs outstanding for no longer than five to eight years. If there is no limit as to how long the BANs can be outstanding, the temptation is great for the BAN issuer to avoid funding-out the BANs with a bond issue.

In order to strengthen credit quality and improve marketability, some issuers will use a credit agreement with a nationally reputable banking institution that requires the bank, under certain conditions, to pay the noteholders any outstanding principal and interest due at maturity. The bank would usually issue refunding notes with a specified maturity schedule at that time.

The general obligation pledge. Many TANs, RANs and GANs issued by states, cities, towns, counties, and school districts are secured by the general obligation pledge. What this means is that the issuers are legally obligated to use their full taxing powers and available revenues to pay the noteholders. Therefore, if a city's tax anticipation note is secured by property taxes as well as by the general obligation pledge, and if the city's property tax collection rate that particular year does not generate sufficient taxes to pay the noteholder, the city must use other resources to make the noteholder whole, including available monies in its general fund. Of course, the importance of the general obligation pledge is directly related to the diversification of the issuer's revenue base and lack of dependence on note sales, as well as on the soundness of its budgetary operations.

Many BANs are also secured by the general obligation pledge of the issuer. If the overall credit quality, revenue structure, and market image of the underlying general obligation issuer are stronger than those of the agency or department that has issued the BANs, then the general obligation pledge would be a positive factor, strengthening the issuer's market access for either rolling over the BANs or retiring them with the proceeds of a long-term bond sale.

EVALUATING CONSTRUCTION LOAN NOTES

Construction Loan Notes (CLNs) are usually issued for periods up to three years to provide short-term construction financing for multifamily housing projects. CLNs are generally repaid from the proceeds of long-term bonds, which are provided after the housing projects are completed. There are five major credit risk areas that an analyst should investigate when attempting to determine the degree of insulation from adversity of CLNs.

Status of Federal Insurance

Before CLNs are issued, an analyst should determine if there is Federal Housing Administration (FHA) mortgage insurance already in place.

FHA insurance covers construction loan advances regardless of whether or not the project is completed. This provides comfort to the noteholders should the developer default on his interest or principal payments prior to the maturity of the notes.

State of Permanent Financing

Another key element in the determination of the credit quality of a CLN is whether or not there is an approved permanent financing plan to take out the construction loan notes. Two plans are generally possible.

In one type of financing plan, bonds are originally sold at the same time as the notes. The bond proceeds are placed in escrow pending projection completion, cost certification, and final endorsement for FHA insurance. Once these three events occur, the bond proceed monies can be released and used to pay the noteholders. Bonds that are simultaneously sold with construction loan notes are usually done so under HUD's Section 8-11 (b) program, which is primarily for local issuers.

In the second type of plan, the Government National Mortgage Agency (GNMA) is committed to provide cash—which, along with other required monies such as contributions by the developer—is used to retire the construction loan notes. For the GNMA take-out to occur, the project must be completed, cost certified, and have received final endorsement for FHA insurance.

Cash Flow Protection

For CLNs where bond proceeds are escrowed, and for GNMA issues, temporary investment earnings, interest payments by the developers, and construction payment draw-downs of the CLN proceeds should be based on worst-case assumptions so as to meet all CLN interest payment dates. The cash flow projections should be presented in a format that shows by month the total expected income and expenses. The cash flow projections should also show worst-case scenarios covering periods when mortgage insurance payments and other back-up security features or liquidity enhancements may have to be depended upon. The combination of the investment earnings and interest payments the developer makes on advanced monies should of course be the basis for the financing, but the note trustee should have immediate access to the other security structures as well.

CLNs where a GNMA take-out is planned pose additional concerns. Since the GNMA take-out provides only 97½ percent of the amount needed to retire the construction loan notes, the gap must be accounted for in advance. An analyst should make sure that expected investment earnings, together with cash contributions by the developer, are sufficient. Because the GNMA take-out could occur months before the actual maturity of the construction loan notes, the analyst should also check to see whether investment agreements are in place for the temporary investment of the GNMA monies, or if there is a provision to call the notes following the GNMA takeout.

Construction and Certification Periods

Because of possible construction delays and the time required by FHA/GNMA for the processing of the final mortgage documents, ample time should be allowed between the expected completion date of the project construction and the construction loan note maturity date. A lag of six months or less between targeted construction completion and note maturity is generally not sufficient. Although there may not be a default by the mortgagor on the FHA-insured mortgage loan, a delay in construction or final FHA endorsement could have a negative impact on note security by preventing the timely release of permanent financing funds. The CLN issuer's budget must therefore include a minimum period of approximately eight months between the expected construction completion date and the maturity of the construction loan note.

CLN Investment Agreements

Because many local issuers have limited back-up resources, and the projected investment earnings on the unspent note proceeds play a crucial role in the financing plan, the investment agreement is also a key factor in the credit-risk analysis. If the investment agreement is in the form of a contract with a commercial bank, the bank should be well-capitalized. If the investment agreement takes the form of a repurchase, or "repo," agreement, an analyst must examine certain other factors discussed in the next section.

EVALUATING REPURCHASE AGREEMENTS

A repurchase agreement (or "repo") is a contractual agreement between a municipal issuer (or its bank trustee) and a commercial bank, investment banking firm, or other government bond dealer. In the transaction, the repo issuer (for example, a government bond dealer) receives cash and, in turn, usually provides interest-bearing U.S. government securities to a municipal issuer as collateral for the cash, with the contractual commitment to repurchase the securities at predetermined dates and prices. Construction loan note proceeds, and even cash flow revenues, are often invested through repos until the money is needed to pay either debt service or construction expenses associated with the specific projects. Over the years, investment bankers and municipal issuers have found repos to be attractive short-term investment vehicles, because they can match the maturity of the repo to their specific cash flow needs.

Repos were not generally recognized as pressing credit concerns until the summer of 1982, when a few modestly capitalized government bond dealers that had repos outstanding—Drysdale Securities Corporation, Comark Securities, Inc. and Lombard-Wall, Inc.—experienced severe financial stress. On August 12, 1982, Lombard-Wall filed for court protection under the Federal Bankruptcy Code. Under the automatic-stay provisions of section 362 (a) of the code, as well as a temporary restraining order issued on August 17, no note trustee could sell the collateral securing a Lombard-Wall repo without court approval. In effect, the collateral was frozen.

As an example of the severity of this freeze on individual creditworthiness, one hospital bond issuer had $43.34 million, or 37 percent of its bond proceeds, invested with Lombard-Wall. Another issuer had its total debt reserve fund invested with Lombard under a 30-year repo. Several construction loan note issuers also had whole note issue proceeds invested with Lombard-Wall.

The credit risks for the holders of the notes involved were substantially increased because:

- The bankruptcy court's restraining order on August 17 prevented the sale or disposition of securities received from Lombard-Wall under repurchase or investment agreements without court approval;
- Several of the note issuers were dependent upon these securities to finance construction and related activities; and
- It was not possible to determine future court actions in these areas.[1]

In September 1982, the bankruptcy judge, in an oral opinion concerning an issuer in Pennsylvania, held that the repo collateral belonged to Lombard-Wall.[2] That is, the court considered the collateral used in the repos to be "secured loans" to Lombard-Wall. Before the collateral could be liquidated, the judge would have to agree on the terms of the liquidation and who was to receive the proceeds. It should be noted that on July 10, 1984, the President signed into law the Amendments Bankruptcy Act which exempts repos with a maturity of one year or less or on demand from the automatic stay provisions of the U.S. Bankruptcy Code.

In the Lombard-Wall case, the judge also refused to release the collateral Lombard-Wall borrowed from a third party. At least three

---

[1] This is based on observations at the time of the court proceedings, as well as on interviews with various lawyers involved in the litigations.

[2] "Sale Barred of Lombard-Wall Bonds Used in Repo for Hospital Authority," *American Banker*, September 20, 1982, p. 2 According to the counsel for Dauphin, before the judge's oral decision was typed and signed, the parties involved settled their dispute. Interview with James A. Moyer, Esq., of LeBoeuf, Lamb, Leiby and Macrae, October 4, 1982.

Texas bond issuers—the Lubbock Housing Finance Corporation, the Abilene Housing Finance Corporation, and the Baytown Housing Finance Corporation—received approval to sell only two thirds of their collateral, as the other third had been borrowed by Lombard-Wall from a third party.[3]

Although the great bull bond markets of August and September 1982 helped to bail out Lombard-Wall, at the time over 50 municipal note issuers faced serious financial problems as the result of the bankruptcy. If repos are used in financial transactions, an analyst should consider the following seven factors.

1. Are construction funds, any other proceeds, or project enterprise revenues invested through repos? If so, to what extent is the note issuer dependent on the repo monies? Clearly, construction loan note proceeds, debt reserve funds, mortgage loan repayments, and grant receipts invested in repos are of greater concern than idle funds.

2. Are the repos with well-capitalized, established government bond dealers, investment banking firms, or banking institutions? Repos should not be with under-capitalized government securities arbitrage and trading firms. Inclusion on a trading list approved by the Federal Reserve Bank is not sufficient evidence of creditworthiness.

3. Are the repos fully secured, with collateral which is in negotiable form and in the possession and control of the municipality or trustee? Title to the collateral should at all times be with the trustee.

4. The collateral should only include (a) direct general obligations of the United States or obligations unconditionally guaranteed by the United States; (b) bonds, debentures or notes issued by certain agencies including the Federal Home Loan Banks, Federal Financing Bank, and Federal Home Loan Mortgage Corporation (including participation certificates); and (c) public housing bonds, temporary notes, or preliminary loan notes fully secured by contracts with the United States.

5. Because the vagaries of the bond market impose the risk that the fair market value of the collateral may substantially decline at any time, the collateral should be valued at least monthly; the fair market value of the securities, as stated in the repo agreements, should mean the bid prices as they appear in the "Com-

---

[3] After the court decision, the trustee for the three bond issues used its own resources to remedy the losses resulting from the Lombard-Wall investments. "3 Texas Agencies Will Be Repaid Lombard Funds," *The Bond Buyer*, September 9, 1982, p. 3. It should also be noted that it was reported that the third party involved was the trust department of Bankers Trust (*The Bond Buyer*, September 7, 1982, p. 1).

posite Closing Quotations for Government Securities," published by the Federal Reserve Bank of New York.

6. If the value of the collateral decreases below the level agreed upon under the repurchase agreement and is not replenished immediately after notice, then the note trustees should have the right to sell the respective securities. If the repo issuer defaults in an interest payment, after one business day's notice, the bank trustee should have the option to declare the repo agreement terminated.

7. The repo agreement should state that third parties are not owners of any collateral and that the collateral is free of all liens.

EVALUATING TAX-EXEMPT COMMERCIAL PAPER[4]

This short-term, tax-exempt borrowing instrument is used for periods ranging from 30 to 270 days. Generally, tax-exempt commercial paper has backstop commercial bank agreements, which can include an irrevocable letter of credit, a revolving credit agreement, or a line of credit. If the security does not include a credit "backstop" for the benefit of the investor, the credit risk analysis would follow the guidelines discussed above in regard to tax, revenue, grant, and bond anticipation notes.

The irrevocable letter of credit is the strongest type of investor comfort. It requires the bank to pay necessary amounts to the limits of the letter. Of course, the analyst should review the terms of the agreement carefully, so as to determine whether the letter of credit extends only to defaulted note principal or also includes principal and interest through the date of default on the note.

A revolving credit agreement could have the same creditworthiness as the irrevocable letter of credit. However, the analyst must examine the agreement to see if there are circumstances under which the bank may be released from responsibility. A line of credit agreement is generally the weakest backstop, because it usually has a number of release clauses that allow a bank to avoid providing funds when required. In all the commercial bank supports, the monies are usually provided as a remedy for a default. The investor, or trustees, must present a claim after the default in order to benefit from the backstop.

The Preference Problem

Current bankruptcy law is unclear as to whether a paper holder could be forced to repay the trustee if the tax-exempt commercial paper issuer

---

[4] This discussion is drawn from James J. Goodwin II, "Tax-Exempt Commercial Paper," in Sylvan G. Feldstein, Frank J. Fabozzi, and Irving M. Pollack eds., *The Municipal Bond Handbook*, Volume II (Homewood, Ill.: Dow Jones-Irwin, 1983).

files in bankruptcy and the holder had had a maturity of 90 days or less from such a filing and was "paid" via a rollover of the paper. This could occur even though the investor did not know of the impending bankruptcy of the issuer. Needless to say, the analyst should determine the underlying creditworthiness of the tax-exempt commercial paper issuer, in addition to the commercial bank credit support.

SUMMARY

In this chapter we have discussed the basic security features of different types of municipal short-term investments. These investments range from well-secured instruments with little or no credit risk to those of substantially weaker creditworthiness. While we have indicated the guidelines in evaluating the specific instruments, we have only indicated the basic questions to ask. A review of a specific instrument would require even greater investigation by the analyst.

PART 4

Fixed Income
Portfolio Management

26

Overview of Fixed Income
Portfolio Management

H. Gifford Fong
President
Gifford Fong Associates

Frank J. Fabozzi, Ph.D., C.F.A., C.P.A.
Visiting Professor
Sloan School of Management
Massachusetts Institute of Technology

The investment management process involves a series of integrated activities. These activities are applicable to the management of any investment portfolio—be it that of an institutional or an individual investor. An understanding of the investment management process and fixed income portfolio management will provide a framework for discussing the techniques presented in this section of the book. In the last section of this chapter, we discuss portfolio constraints faced by portfolio managers.

OVERVIEW OF THE INVESTMENT
MANAGEMENT PROCESS

Exhibit 1 provides a diagrammatic representation of the investment management process. The three areas which could be considered the main functional activities of this process are identified—setting investment objectives and policy, portfolio analysis, and asset analysis.

    The first major activity is the setting of investment objectives and policy. For example, for a pension fund this involves the identification of

---

EXHIBIT 1   Investment Management Process

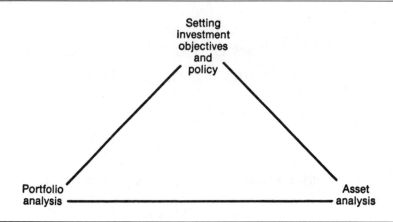

Setting investment objectives and policy

Portfolio analysis

Asset analysis

---

the funding needs of the plan and a policy for pursuing and achieving those needs. The objectives are the goals established by the client. They may take the form of some specific return requirement and the accept-able level of risk. Policy setting takes the form of asset allocation among alternative asset classes so as to achieve the specified objectives. In establishing an investment policy, constraints may be imposed by the client and/or those that regulate the activities of the client.

Under the activity of setting investment objectives and policy we would also include the task of performance measurement and evalua-tion. The performance of the investment manager should be evaluated in light of the investment policy set by the client. Moreover, when an investment manager claims he or she has a specialized skill that will enhance performance given the investment policy set, that claim must be measured and evaluated.

Following the setting of investment objectives and policy, the sec-ond main activity of the investment management process is portfolio analysis. This is essentially the activity of portfolio management. It is, in very formal terms, the method the investment manager uses to con-struct an *optimal* or *efficient* portfolio. An optimal or efficient portfolio is one that provides the greatest *expected* return for a given level of risk, or equivalently, the lowest risk for a given *expected* return.

Asset analysis is the third main activity of the investment manage-ment process. This activity essentially takes the form of individual secu-rity analysis that leads to the construction of an optimal portfolio. There are a number of techniques for accomplishing this such as bond valua-tion.

OVERVIEW OF FIXED INCOME PORTFOLIO MANAGEMENT

Given the background we presented in the previous section, let us now look at the area of concern to us—fixed income portfolio management.

Active Management Strategies

The range of active fixed income portfolio management strategies is wide and subject to much variation. As a basis for discussion, we can identify three broad categories. It should be kept in mind, however, that this categorization serves a pedagogical function and in practice will be subject to significant combination and permutation.

The first category includes those strategies seeking to benefit from temporary price disequilibriums. As bonds trade over time, situations may occur where switching from one bond to another will achieve either a price appreciation or increased yield return as the result of the action. One example is where a bond is swapped or exchanged for another which is identical in all respects except for price. In effect, a lower priced bond is acquired by selling off an identical bond having a higher price. Another approach is similar in nature except that instead of exploiting a price discrepancy, differences in yield are sought. More complicated strategies include evaluating the perceived normal spread relationship between two segments of the bond market. When they become distorted, a trade is made in anticipation of a normal spread reappearing. This would result in a capital appreciation as the price of the acquired security conforms to the "correct" spread.

A basic assumption of the foregoing types of analyses is the belief that the "correction" in the price or yield will occur before overall market conditions change the underlying relationship. This premise is akin to the stock valuation assumption that the price of the undervalued stock will become properly valued before the overall influence of the market changes the relationships between groups of stocks, thus detracting from the superior return of the undervalued stock. The focus is on the unique characteristics of bonds, particularly those relating to creditworthiness, where individual bond valuation is stressed apart from the expectations of the overall market. The period of time over which the undervaluation is corrected is called the workout time. It is over this horizon that the effect of market influences are assumed to be insignificant. We can call this type of activity the valuation approach to bond analysis.

A second category focuses on the effects of overall changes in the market environment. This takes the form of overall changes in interest rates. The key is to anticipate the direction of interest rates. When rates are projected to drop, the longer maturities are sought to maximize capital appreciation. While maximum enhancement of total return can be achieved, forecasting interest rate movements consistently is extremely difficult to achieve.

The third category is actually a method of evaluating the previous two. To assess fully the impact of unique bond characteristics and the effect of the overall market environment, a sensitivity analysis can be pursued. Bond sensitivity analysis combines the influences of the first two categories such that unique characteristics can be evaluated in the context of overall market movements. To overcome the difficulty in interest rate forecasting, multiscenario projections may be used to test the behavior of securities to alternative outlooks.

Passive Management Strategies

Basic to all passive portfolio management strategies is the minimal expectational input in the process. In fact, this is the distinguishing feature of passive versus active strategies. Minimizing expectational requirements limits the total return potential but enhances the ability to be responsive to other needs of the client. This then recognizes the multiobjective situation where seeking the maximum return is tempered by other client-specified requisites. As the facility to generate expectational inputs is the key to active management strategies, the qualities for fulfilling alternative investment objectives is the measure for passive approaches. That there may be a diversity in these other objectives suggests a need for a variety of strategies to accommodate the alternatives. Furthermore, as the needs of the client change so will the requirements of passive approaches. Finally, no single strategy is appropriate across the board and the degree of client responsiveness will vary from situation to situation within the same strategy. This may include meeting the unique risk preference of the investor. For example, a fund sponsor may be satisfied with or even require a portion of his portfolio to be committed to long-term, fixed income securities and be satisfied by the rate of return realized by long-term bonds over a long horizon.

There are two types of passive strategies—*buy-and-hold* and *indexing*. A buy-and-hold strategy is the simplest strategy for passive portfolio management. As the term implies, securities are bought and held to maturity. The main considerations are to be assured that there will be no default and to achieve the highest yield to maturity possible. In the face of fluctuating or rising interest rates, a buy-and-hold approach has a potentially severe disadvantage since there will be a tendency to miss opportunities from anticipated changes in interest rates as well as being subject to a lag in yield to maturity as rates rise. Expectational inputs involve credit analysis to minimize default risk. Advantages include low transaction costs, a better resolution of return over near term horizons, and minimal expectational requirements.

The objective of indexing or index fund strategy is to replicate the performance of the bond market using a proxy which is frequently a designated index. Typically, one of the *Salomon Brothers bond indexes* or *Shearson/Lehman bond indexes* is used. Capital market theory suggests that a portfolio containing every outstanding issue held in proportion to its relative market value will be the efficient portfolio. Efficiency is here defined as the least amount of risk assumed for achieving the overall market return. It follows that if one held a portfolio of securities reflecting the same portfolio characteristics as the market (in the form of an "index"), a favorable risk/return trade-off would be achieved. Presumably, it would be very difficult to outperform the index through expectational inputs, and by combining securities in a portfolio with characteristics similar to the market, the efficiency of the market would be captured. A fundamental issue is the identification of the appropriate index.

Immunization and Cash Flow Matching Strategies

These two strategies can be thought of as a hybrid of active and passive portfolio management strategies. At one extreme, they have a similarity to passive strategies in that there is minimal requirement for expectational inputs and there are unique characteristics which allow addressing a number of investment objectives. At the other extreme, many of the same expectational inputs of active management can be integrated to enhance the expected return. Between these extremes there is a range of alternatives providing varying degrees of blend.

Exhibit 2 provides a schematic representation. At one corner can be

---

EXHIBIT 2   Fixed Income Portfolio Management

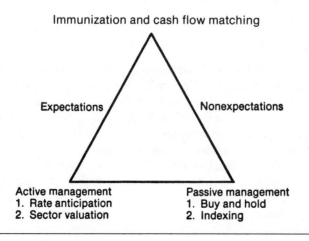

found active management as exemplified by two specific activities, rate anticipation and sector valuation. At another corner is passive management where risk control is the primary emphasis as exemplified by buy-and-hold and indexing strategies. The basic difference between active and passive management is the use of expectational inputs. Active management derives its returns from expectational inputs and as a consequence also experiences higher expected risk. Passive management, in contrast, emphasizes risk control such that the expected return may be lower but the expected associated risk will also be lower due to the reliance on nonexpectational inputs. Immunization and cash flow matching management can be pursued with either emphasis so that if return maximization is the objective then using expectational inputs would be called for. Alternatively, maximum risk control immunization will make use of nonexpectational inputs.

Immunization can be defined as the process of creating a fixed income portfolio having an assured return for a specified time horizon irrespective of interest rate changes. When a portfolio must be constructed to fund a number of liabilities over time, a hybrid management strategy known as a *dedicated portfolio* strategy is appropriate. A dedicated portfolio is a portfolio with a structure designed to fund a schedule of liabilities from portfolio return and asset value, with the portfolio's value diminishing to zero after payment of the last liability. *Multiperiod immunization* and *cash flow matching* are two approaches for dedicating a portfolio.

PORTFOLIO CONSTRAINTS

The return objectives and risk tolerance of investors are modified by investor constraints, some of which are characteristic of a class of investors while others may be unique to a particular institutional or individual investor. In this section we relate the characteristics of fixed income securities and fixed income markets to these investor constraints.

Liquidity Needs

Fixed income securities are looked upon primarily as providing a secure cash flow stream and a fixed maturity. With respect to the allocation of funds among the general investment classes, they are well suited to meeting an investor's needs for continuous and periodic cash flow from income and/or maturing principal. Within the bond portfolio, the degree of liquidity required by investors varies.

For example, despite periods when a life insurance company may encounter liquidity problems due to an aggressive schedule of forward investment commitments, the liquidity needs of this segment of the insurance industry are considerably less than those of property and casualty companies. Even within a given industry, liquidity needs vary.

For example, mature property and casualty insurance companies may be less concerned with liquidity than are newly created companies. In the pension area, the liquidity needs of a pension fund will depend on the current age distribution of future beneficiaries, with relatively young plans of growing firms having less need for liquidity than older plans where considerable benefits must be paid in the near future. Consequently, investors must modify their return objective and risk tolerance because of a basic need for an assured schedule of cash flow from their investment portfolio.

A liquidity reserve may be derived from the cash flow from coupons and maturing fixed income instruments or created and maintained by holding money market instruments, such as Treasury bills and commercial paper. Furthermore, liquidity may be derived from a spaced schedule of maturing obligations over a few months or a few years.

Liquidity can also be achieved by emphasizing or limiting portfolio investments to the most readily marketable and liquid types of bonds; that is, those issues that could be sold quickly with little or no price concession from currently quoted prices. Emphasis on marketability is important, not only for satisfying unanticipated cash flow requirements, but also for pursuing an overall portfolio strategy. For example, to maximize their aftertax return, property and casualty companies constantly shift between taxable and tax-exempts depending on underwriting profits which determine their marginal tax rate. The lack of marketability of portfolio holdings can jeopardize the success of this strategy.

High credit quality and short maturity are the most dominant characteristics of readily marketable bonds. We should also note that round lot holdings—typically $500,000 par value of a corporate issue—are more marketable than odd lots—less than $500,000 par. The marketability of round lots is reflected in the narrower dealer spreads between bid and asked prices than occur for odd lots. Odd lot long bonds typically have wide spreads. On the other hand, Treasury bills and certain other money market instruments can be purchased in odd lots with little or no yield penalty. The yield penalty in the case of corporate bonds places restrictions on the allocation of funds among issues when designing a portfolio under a given strategy. For example, an optimal solution for some strategy may call for the purchase or sale of $200,000 par value of a particular corporate issue. Because of price concessions on odd lot transactions, constraints may have to be imposed to restrict a solution to only portfolio transactions of at least $500,000. Actively managed bond portfolios develop periodic liquidity needs in the form of reserves held in anticipation of a change in yields and bond prices. Minimum market risk is sought with the least sacrifice in interest income.

Liquidity characteristics are determined by:

1. Amount outstanding (dollar amount of the issue of bonds outstanding)—the more the better.

2. Amount closely held (dollar amount of issue)—the less, the better.
3. Coupon level—the closer to the current coupon level the better because there is an investor preference for current coupon securities.
4. Age of issue—recently issued securities tend to be more actively traded.
5. Quality—the higher the better.
6. Terms (such as callability or sinking-fund provisions)—tend to reduce liquidity but if a bond is redeemed by being called, the call feature provides a potential liquidity source.
7. Maturity (duration)—fixed income securities with a maturity or duration of less than one year tend to be more liquid than any longer maturity/duration securities for any given issue.

Tax Considerations

Unlike qualified pension funds, individual investors and financial institutions such as banks and insurance companies are subject to income taxes. Chapter 3 provides an overview of the federal income tax treatment of fixed income securities. Nuances of the tax code with respect to a particular financial institution must be understood by the portfolio manager.

Time Horizon

Each investor has a specified time horizon or period over which the return objectives are intended to be satisfied. The life cycle of the individual investor or the pension fund or the operating cycle of a financial institution or endowment fund largely determines the portfolio time horizon. Fixed income securities have a definite investment life or maturity that can be matched or related to the investor's time horizon. In fact, this certainty of term-to-maturity provides the portfolio manager with a base for fitting expected returns with investor return objectives. Preferred and common stocks, which have a perpetual life, provide no similar certainty or structure.

The essence of fixed income management is to take advantage of this structure. In its most basic form, quality analysis ensures against experiencing default, while more active forms of management seek to exploit cyclical or temporary return opportunities. Time horizon trade-offs, where the relatively certain returns of holding a security to maturity are balanced against a more active trading strategy, must be a continual consideration. For example, if a manager begins to actively manage a portfolio that has employed a buy-and-hold approach, he may jeopardize the high cash flows that had been expected from buying and holding. Similarly, if he decides to actively manage a previously immunized portfolio where coupon reinvestment risk has been balanced against discount accretion, he may jeopardize the original objective sought via immunization. It can be seen from these examples that both the decision to change strategy—and to begin to actively manage—*and* the timing of that decision can be critical to the attainment of fixed income portfolio objectives.

Active strategies are concerned with planning horizons within the portfolio time horizon; hence, the manager is faced with a sequence of decision horizons. Logically, each of these would be concurrently, rather than sequentially, optimized, so that the decision-making process would span multiple horizons instead of one period at a time. However, because of the uncertainty of expectations, considerations beyond the next planning period become very complicated. For example, a three-scenario forecast leads to a nine-scenario projection if two periods are considered at once, since each period-one scenario can lead to three possible period-two scenarios. This would continue to increase by a factor of three with each additional time period. Providing the inputs to and understanding the outputs from such a process would be beyond the capacity of most managers. The solution has been to retain the one-period framework, to continuously monitor the analysis, and to be open to adjustments with the passage of time—especially whenever a change in expectations takes place. A moving window of a desired planning horizon emerges within the overall portfolio time horizon.

Regulatory or Legal Considerations

The environment in which fixed income management must operate includes a number of exogenous constraints.

Regulation of asset allocation. Certain financial institutions are regulated as to the eligible class of assets, the minimum and/or maximum amount that may be placed in a particular asset class, and the maximum amount that may be invested in a given asset. Within an asset class, there may be restrictions on the particular assets eligible for investment.

Regulatory restrictions on the inclusion of certain types of investment vehicles will reduce a portfolio manager's ability to provide a better risk-return trade-off for his client. For example, strategies involving futures and options may allow a portfolio manager to provide a better risk-return trade-off for his clients. Yet, because futures and options are viewed as speculative by some regulators, rather than as tools for controlling portfolio risk, there has often been considerable lag time between the introduction of a new contract and its acceptance by regulators as an eligible investment vehicle. Fortunately, in recent years, as some regulators have become more familiar with the economic role of these instruments, they have broadened their position regarding the use of these relatively new vehicles by the institutions they regulate.

Taking losses.   Because bonds eventually mature at par value, investors, even those who are not legally constrained, are often reluctant to sell a bond at a price below the cost of the bond and realize a capital loss. Many pension funds have bookkeeping practices that inhibit portfolio managers from taking capital losses. This preoccupation with book loss (the difference between cost and market) or even par value loss (the difference between par and market) may appear prudent on the surface. However, for an income-oriented investor in particular, such concerns ignore the opportunity costs involved.

These opportunity costs represent the loss of increase in investment income that could be realized from the sale of a bond and reinvestment of the proceeds in another suitable and higher yielding bond. Such higher yielding opportunities often arise if the investor is willing to lengthen maturity (assuming a positively sloped yield curve) or reduce quality. Less frequently, market inefficiencies provide the observant investor with the opportunity to reinvest at a higher yield without extending or downgrading. For example, sinking-fund bids for industrial bonds frequently provide the opportunity to sell older issues at a premium over current market prices on similar bonds except for sinking-fund purchasing activity.

Most importantly, the opportunity cost must be sufficiently great or, in other words, the yield advantage must be sufficiently large to allow the investor to recover the loss (book or par) out of the additional interest income at or prior to the maturity of the bond sold. Because tax regulation allows the offset of capital gains and losses, as explained in Chapter 3, some taxable investors might adjust the realized loss by the amount of the capital gains tax that could be saved.

The point to be made in this discussion is that fixed income strategies cannot be considered in the abstract. Realistically, depending on the type of investor and the jurisdiction(s) that may be controlling, theoretical optimality may be modified by regulatory constraints.

Unique Considerations of the Investor

Portfolio construction would be sterile without provision for the special requirements of each investor. Some of these have already been covered in the other sections on fixed income portfolio constraints. Beyond these, institutional investors may be concerned with such things as social responsibility issues that may preclude investing in firms that make objectionable products or do business in certain countries; and predefined portfolio structures where the quality and/or maturity range of the portfolio holdings may be restricted. For the individual investor, the status of his or her estate, retirement objectives, and cash flow needs should be taken into account.

SUMMARY

In this chapter we have provided an overview of the investment management process and fixed income portfolio management. The constraints faced by a portfolio manager are also discussed. Various fixed income strategies are illustrated in the following chapters in this section of the book.

27

Total Aftertax Bond Performance and Yield Measures for Taxable Bonds Held in Taxable Portfolios*

Martin L. Leibowitz, Ph.D.

Managing Director
Bond Portfolio Analysis Group
Salomon Brothers Inc

The conventional yield-to-maturity,[1] both in its pretax and aftertax forms, leaves much to be desired as a comprehensive tool for investment analysis and the comparison of relative values. In *Inside the Yield Book*,[2] it was suggested that a total return measure called the realized compound yield could prove useful in evaluating prospective bond purchases and bond swaps.[3] We have since explored the total return to taxable portfo-

---

* Adapted from Martin L. Leibowitz, *Total After-Tax Bond Performance and Yield Measures* (New York: Salomon Brothers Inc, 1974). Although this chapter will explain ways of integrating different tax structures into an analytic investment framework, there will be no attempt to discuss any corporation's specific situations. All tax examples presented here are used strictly for the purpose of illustrating the various analytic techniques and should not be interpreted as necessarily applicable to any given individual or corporate entity. Moreover, the author does not wish to represent himself as being qualified to provide advice relating to tax matters, and neither the author nor Salomon Brothers Inc is in the business of providing such advice.

Although the information in this chapter has been obtained from sources that the author believes to be reliable, Salomon Brothers Inc cannot guarantee its accuracy, and such information may be incomplete or condensed. All opinions and estimates included in this chapter constitute judgment as of this date and are subject to change without notice.

[1] See Chapter 4 for the definition of yield-to-maturity.

[2] Sidney Homer and Martin L. Leibowitz, *Inside the Yield Book* (New York: Prentice-Hall and New York Institute of Finance, 1972).

[3] Bond swaps are discussed in Chapter 29.

lios in some detail. We have found that our realized compound yield approach could be properly extended, in ways that are far from obvious, into the complex world of the taxed portfolio. Once the key concepts of "effective par rate" and "opportunity dollars" were identified, it became clear that this extension was not only possible but could indeed prove to be a most valuable investment tool. In fact, in certain taxed environments this extension proves more informative and provides more counter-intuitive surprises than in the comparable tax-free case.

The purpose of this chapter is to describe how the realized compound yield can be translated into a consistent and useful concept for taxable bonds in taxed bond portfolios and to provide some examples of its application to certain important bond investment situations.[4]

TAX-FREE PORTFOLIOS

Realized Compound Yield for the Tax-Free Portfolio

Before proceeding to the taxed cases, we shall summarize some of the main features of realized compound yield in the tax-free case.

A bond has three basic elements of return: (1) coupon income, (2) principal appreciation, and (3) interest-on-interest. The first two elements are self-explanatory. Interest-on-interest is the indirect return that arises from the compounded reinvestment of the bond's coupon payments at the then available market rates. Since interest-on-interest may well account for more than 70 percent of the overall return for a long-term bond, no evaluation of a bond investment can be complete without giving due consideration to this important factor.

Exhibit 1 shows how a $1 million holding of a 30-year, 7.5 percent par bond generates interest-on-interest from reinvestment of its coupons at an arbitrarily assumed compounding rate of 6 percent. Each semiannual coupon payment will be $37,500. The first such payment is received after six months. It is assumed to be immediately reinvested at 6 percent so that it earns 3 percent over the next six months, or

$$\$37,500 \times .03 = \$1,125$$

Together with the second $37,500 coupon payment, this means that there would be a total accrual of $76,125 available for reinvestment at the end of the first year. At 3 percent over the next six months, these total accrued funds would earn an additional interest-on-interest of

---

[4] For a discussion of tax-exempt bonds in taxable bond portfolios see: Martin L. Leibowitz, "Total Aftertax Bond Performance and Yield Measures for Tax-Exempt Bonds Held in Taxable Portfolios," Chapter 32 in *The Municipal Bond Handbook: Vol. I*, ed. Frank J. Fabozzi, Sylvan G. Feldstein, Irving M. Pollack, and Frank G. Zarb, (Homewood, Ill.: Dow Jones-Irwin, 1983).

$$\$76,125 \times .03 = \$2,284$$

Continuing in this fashion, the interest-on-interest and total amount accrued would grow as shown on Exhibit 1. At the bond's maturity in 25 years, the investor would have received a total of $1,875,000 in direct coupon payments. By reinvesting each of these coupons at the 6 percent rate, compounded semiannually, the investor would have realized an additional $2,354,883 of interest-on-interest. In other words, of the total return of $4,229,883 on the $1 million invested, the factor of interest-on-interest would account for about 56 percent.

The amount of interest-on-interest expected depends on the assumed rate at which coupons are reinvested and compounded over the bond's life. Exhibit 2 shows the dollars of interest-on-interest accumulated from compounding at various fixed rates over the bond's life (e.g., at a 7 percent fixed reinvestment rate, the interest-on-interest would accumulate to $3,037,000 or 62 percent of the bond's total return). At an 8 percent reinvestment rate, the accumulated interest-on-interest becomes $3,850,000, or 67 percent of the total dollar return.

Many investors are surprised by the magnitude of these interest-on-interest figures. Since every bond investment forces a certain cash flow schedule upon the investor, which must either be reinvested or used in some time-valued fashion, this interest-on-interest must be considered in comparing alternative fixed income investments.

Without an assumption on the reinvestment of the coupons, a dollar-and-cents analysis of a bond swap over time will give inconsistent results. In fact, it is literally impossible to determine the compounded dollar-and-cents return from a bond investment without making at least an implicit judgment regarding reinvestment rates.

The concept of realized compound yield as tabulated in Exhibit 2 is one convenient way of characterizing the total return provided by any investment under a given set of reinvestment assumptions. For example, as shown in Exhibit 1, a $1 million investment in a 7.5 percent, 25-year bond, when all coupons are reinvested at 6 percent, will lead to a total dollar return of $4,229,883, above and beyond the repayment of the original $1 million investment. This corresponds to a return of $4.23 for every $1 invested over a period of 25 years, which in turn corresponds to full semiannual compounding at a uniform rate of 6.73 percent. The procedure for computing this rate is explained in Chapter 4. Thus the 7.5 percent, 25-year bond investment can be said to provide a realized compound yield of 6.73 percent at the assumed reinvestment rate of 6 percent. The realized compound yield will always be between the conventional yield-to-maturity and the reinvestment rate.

The realized compound yield is a convenient yardstick for consistently evaluating alternative investments over a range of assumed market conditions. Exhibit 2 shows the realized compound yields associated

EXHIBIT 1 Accrual Schedule for $1 million Par Amount of 25-Year 7.5 Percent Bonds with All Coupons Reinvested at a 6 Percent Rate Compounded Semiannually

Period Start Date	Total Amount Accrued at Start of Period		Reinvestment Rate over Period		Interest-on-Interest	Coupon Payment at End of Period	Total Amount Accrued by End of Period
0 Years 0 Months	$ 0	×	.03	=	$ 0	$ 37,500	$ 37,500
0 Years 6 Months	37,500	×	.03	=	1,125	37,500	76,125
1 Year 0 Months	76,125	×	.03	=	2,284	37,500	115,909
1 Year 6 Months	115,909	×	.03	=	3,477	37,500	156,886
2 Years 0 Months	156,886	×	.03	=	4,707	37,500	199,093
23 Years 6 Months	3,764,869	×	.03	=	112,946	37,500	3,915,315
24 Years 0 Months	3,915,315	×	.03	=	117,459	37,500	4,070,274
24 Years 6 Months	4,070,274	×	.03	=	122,108	37,500	4,229,883
Totals at maturity	$4,229,883				$2,354,883	$1,875,000	
Plus redemption of principal	1,000,000						
Total future value	$5,229,883						

EXHIBIT 2 Effect of the Reinvestment Rate on the Total Dollar Return over the Life of 25-Year, 7.5 Percent Par Bond

Assumed Reinvestment Rate (Semiannual Basis)	Dollars per $1,000 Bond			Interest-on-Interest as Percent of Total Return	Realized Compound Yield
	Coupon Income	Interest-on-Interest	Total Return		
0.0%	$1,875	$ 0	$1,875	0%	4.27%
5.0	1,875	1,781	3,656	49	6.25
6.0	1,875	2,355	4,230	56	6.73
7.0	1,875	3,037	4,912	62	7.24
7.5*	1,875*	3,426*	5,301*	65*	7.50*
8.0	1,875	3,850	5,725	67	7.77
9.0	1,875	4,819	6,694	72	8.33
10.0	1,875	5,976	7,851	76	8.91

* Reinvestment at the conventional yield rate.

with the 7.5 percent, 25-year par bond for one such range of reinvestment conditions. This table demonstrates the sensitivity of bond returns to changes in the reinvestment rate assumption. It is also interesting to note that, when the reinvestment rate is the same as the bond's conventional yield, (i.e., 7.5 percent), the bond's realized compound yield then also coincides with the bond's 7.5 percent *conventional yield-to-maturity*. This equality holds quite generally because the conventional yield computation, when interpreted as the rate of dollars-and-cents accrual of funds, carries the tacit assumption that all cash flows are reinvested (or "time-valued") at the conventional yield rate itself.

Up to this point, we have only discussed "par" bonds. However, all of these concepts hold true for bonds priced at either a premium above par, or at a discount below par.

For example, consider a 25-year, 4 percent bond priced at 60.739 to provide a conventional yield-to-maturity of 7.5 percent. Over its 25-year life, each $1,000 bond would have a return consisting of the locked-in capital gain of $392.61, plus $1,000 in coupon payments (= 25 × $40), plus interest-on-interest arising from the compounded reinvestment of these coupon payments. At a fixed 6 percent reinvestment rate, this interest-on-interest would amount to $1,255.94, so that the total return would become $2,648.55. Since the bond cost $607.39, this would amount to a total return of $4.36 per dollar invested, which corresponds to a fully compounded 6.83 percent rate. Thus this bond investment can be said to provide a prospective realized compound yield of 6.83 percent.

Exhibit 3 shows the discount bond's return per invested dollar and realized compound yield for a range of reinvestment rates. Once again, we see that the realized compound yield coincides with the conventional

EXHIBIT 3 A Comparison of Various Investment Measures (for two bonds with the same 7.5 percent conventional yield-to-maturity—a 25-year, 7.5 percent par bond priced at 100 and a 25-year, 4 percent discount bond priced at 60.739)

Assumed Reinvestment Rate	Conventional Yield-to-Maturity		Total Dollar Return per $1.00 Invested		Realized Compound Yield		Effective Par Rate	
	7.5	4s	7.5s	4s	7.5s	4s	7.5s	4s
0.0%	7.5%	7.5%	$1.88	$2.92	4.27%	4.82%	7.5%	9.17%
5.0	7.5	7.5	3.66	3.86	6.25	6.42	7.5	7.91
6.0	7.5	7.5	4.23	4.36	6.73	6.83	7.5	7.73
7.0	7.5	7.5	4.92	4.96	7.24	7.27	7.5	7.57
7.5*	7.5*	7.5*	5.30*	5.30*	7.50*	7.50*	7.5*	7.50*
8.0	7.5	7.5	5.72	5.66	7.77	7.74	7.5	7.43
9.0	7.5	7.5	6.66	6.53	8.33	8.24	7.5	7.31
10.0	7.5	7.5	7.84	7.55	8.91	8.77	7.5	7.20

* Reinvestment at the conventional yield rate.

yield-to-maturity only when reinvestment takes place at the 7.5 percent yield rate. As reinvestment rates fall below or rise above this 7.5 percent yield rate, the realized compound yields also drop or fall. The same observation holds, of course, for the total return per invested dollar.

In fact, since the realized compound yield is just a mathematical restatement of the total return per invested dollar, every swap improvement in realized compound yield will correspond to an improvement in dollars-and-cents return. This is a critically important characteristic for an investment measure. *As Exhibit 3 illustrates, the conventional yield-to-maturity fails to possess this critical property of accurately reflecting the investment's dollars-and-cents payoff.* In fact, it turns out that for reasonable reinvestment rates, the spread in conventional yields-to-maturity almost always *overstates* the actual difference in this dollars-and-cents return.

By comparing the realized compound yields (or total returns per dollar invested) for the two bonds as shown in Exhibit 3, we see that the discount bond has somewhat less sensitivity than the par bond to variations in reinvestment rate. This reduced variability results from the discount bond's capital gain contribution, which is fixed in advance and hence totally insensitive to reinvestment conditions.

A New Concept: The Effective Par Rate

Conventional judgments of relative long-term investment values are often based upon "yield spreads" between a given security or sector and some benchmark "yield level." This benchmark is often taken to be the new-issue rate for the particular market in question. Since most market movements are communicated in terms of new-issue rates, this capability to "benchmark" yields against new-issue rates has great practical significance. The problem is that such benchmarking comparisons tacitly imply that the conventional yield-to-maturity corresponds to the long-term return provided by a given coupon rate on a par bond. In fact, one might argue further that this benchmarking forms the intuitive basis for the conventional yield-to-maturity (i.e., many investors interpret a conventional yield value as saying that the bonds' dollars-and-cents return is equivalent to that from a par bond having the same yield and maturity. Thus, a 4 percent bond selling on a 7.5 percent conventional yield is taken to be equivalent to a 7.5 percent par bond with regard to long-term return. As Exhibit 3 shows, this will be strictly true only when coupon reinvestment also takes place at 7.5 percent. At reinvestment rates other than the 7.5 percent yield value, the discount 4 percent bond's dollars-and-cents return differs significantly from that of the 7.5 percent par bond.

By its very definition, the realized compound yield values will correctly reflect the differences in dollars-and-cents return. However, the realized compound yield neither fits the intuitively comfortable scale of par bond returns nor can it be conveniently benchmarked against new-issue levels. The "effective par rate" is a new concept that has these two very desirable properties and yet retains the accuracy of the realized compound yield as a consistent measure of dollars-and-cents return.

Put very simply, *the "effective par rate" for a given bond is the coupon rate for that par bond that would produce the same dollars-and-cents return* (and hence the same realized compound yield) *as the given bond under the assumed reinvestment conditions.* Taking an example from Exhibit 3, with reinvestment at 6 percent, the 25-year, 4 percent bond priced at 60.739 (to yield 7.5 percent) provides $4.36 of return for every dollar invested, or a realized compound yield of under 7.5 percent (i.e., 6.83 percent). To obtain this same return from a 25-year par bond, a coupon rate of 7.73 percent would be required. Stated another way, in considering a swap out of the discount 4 percent bond and into the new-issue market, an investor with a 6 percent reinvestment assumption would have to obtain a new-issue rate of at least 7.73 percent in order to break even in terms of the long-term dollars-and-cents return. For this reason, the effective par rate of 7.73 percent can be viewed as the break-even par bond yield for the 4 percent bond under a 6 percent reinvestment assumption.[5]

As we see from this example, the effective par rate provides a measuring tool for the investment manager to immediately benchmark the

---

[5] Martin L. Leibowitz, "New Tools in Bond Portfolio Management," *Trusts and Estates,* January 1973.

bonds in his or her portfolio against new-issue levels. It also provides an intuitively comfortable scale for defining long-term investment value in a manner consistent with dollars-and-cents return. Thus, for a given investor and his or her reinvestment assumptions, all bonds with the same effective par rate over a specified time horizon are completely equivalent in terms of dollars-and-cents return. All such bonds are equivalent not only to each other, but also to the hypothetical par bond having a coupon rate equal to the effective par rate and a maturity spanning the specified time horizon.

The question of yield spread deserves some further discussion. In *Inside the Yield Book,* we observed that the conventional yields-to-maturity tend to overstate the difference in dollars-and-cents return between two bonds. This arises because two bonds at different conventional yields carry the implication of two distinct (and naturally inconsistent) reinvestment-rate assumptions, with the higher rate being ascribed to the higher yielding bond. At a common reinvestment rate, the difference in realized compound yields would usually be less than the conventional yield spread. The magnitude of this contraction depends critically on the investment horizon, but for long-term bonds it would not be surprising to see a 40-basis-point conventional yield spread shrink by a factor of 2 to a 20-basis-point spread in terms of realized compound yields. Although this contraction in the yield spread is indeed an accurate reflection of the basic rate of return, it does require a double shift on the part of the portfolio manager. Not only must the portfolio manager change his or her orientation toward dealing with an explicit reinvestment rate, but must also shift from a conventional scale of values. Thus a 40-basis-point increase in new-issue rates or a 40-basis-point improvement on a swap package now only corresponds to a 20-basis-point improvement in realized compound yield. Hence the meaning of *basis point* in the everyday marketplace would have to differ from the meaning of *basis point* in terms of the personalized realized compound yield measure.

This shift of scale could naturally lead to many problems. For example, a portfolio manager whose market judgment suggests that a 14-basis-point pickup should be attainable might reject a portfolio action resulting in a 7-basis-point pickup in realized compound yield. Yet the 7 basis points of realized compound yield might well correspond to well over 14 basis points in terms of the conventional yield scale ingrained in the manager's past experience and forming the basis for the market judgment.

The effective par rate concept can help resolve this problem of the shifting meaning of a basis point. A given basis point change in conventional yield for a given bond will result in much the same basis-point change in the bond's effective par rate. The level of the effective par rate will, of course, differ from the conventional yield to reflect the impact of the reinvestment assumption on the dollars-and-cents return. These effects are illustrated in Exhibit 4.

EXHIBIT 4 Required Increases in Various Investment Measures to Provide Given Levels of Total Dollar Return (for a 25-year 4 percent bond under a fixed 6 percent reinvestment assumption)

Total Dollar Return per $1 Invested	Required Purchase Price	Required Conventional Yield-to-Maturity		Required Realized Compound Yield		Required Effective Par Rate	
		Level	Increase	Level	Increase	Level	Increase
$4.36	60.739	7.50%		6.83%		7.73%	
4.46	59.591	7.65	+15 B.P.	6.91	+8 B.P.	7.91	+18
4.56	58.585	7.89	+14	6.98	+7	8.08	+17
4.66	57.333	7.93	+14	7.06	+8	8.26	+18
4.76	56.509	8.08	+15	7.13	+7	8.44	+18

The effective par rate thus has many appealing characteristics as a measure of investment value—consistency with dollars-and-cents return, preservation of the interpretation of a yield *level*, maintenance of the intuitive scale for *basis-point spreads* and *changes*, and the convenience of benchmarking against the new-issue market. For all these reasons, it might be argued that it is the effective par rate that should be taken as the natural analogue of the conventional yield value as a consistent and correct measure of dollars-and-cents investment return.

As we shall soon see, this argument in behalf of the effective par rate becomes strongly reinforced when dealing with portfolios subject to taxation.

Realized Compound Yields over the Short Term

Over investment horizons encompassing a bond's maturity, the realized compound yield (or the effective rate) has the great advantage of providing a consistent measure of the dollars-and-cents return. The one uncertainty here is, of course, that of future reinvestment rates. The realized compound yield approach forces the portfolio manager to openly confront this real-life uncertainty and to render explicit judgments as to future level(s) of reinvestment rates consistent with the manager's portfolio structure and purpose. Over investment periods that are shorter than the bond's maturity, a second key element of uncertainty enters the scene: Where will the bond be priced at the end of the review period? Here again, the portfolio manager can use the realized compound yield to confront this uncertainty by exploring the effect of one or more *explicit* assumptions regarding future price (or yield) levels. Once again, the realized compound yield will provide a consistent measure of the dollars-and-cents return that would be obtained under the fulfillment of each of the manager's assumptions.

Exhibit 5 illustrates the computation of realized compound yields for the 25-year, 7.5 percent and 4 percent bonds under the assumption of a

---

EXHIBIT 5   Realized Compound Yields over the Short Term (one year) under the Assumption of a 10-Basis-Point Yield Decline

	25-Year 7.50s	25-Year 4.00s
Original investment per bond (@ 7.50 percent conventional yield)	$1,000.00	$607.39
Two coupons during year	75.00	40.00
Interest-on-interest on one coupon @ 6 percent for ½ year	1.13	.60
Year-end principal appreciation at constant 7.50 percent conventional yield	0.00	5.66
Total dollar gain—without yield move	$ 76.13	$ 46.26
Dollar return per $1.00 invested—without yield move	$ .07613	$ .07616
Realized compound yield—without yield move	7.47%	7.48%
Effective par rate—without yield move	7.50%	7.50%
Year-end principal value at 7.40 percent conventional yield less year-end principal value at 7.50 percent—without yield move	$1,011.15 $1,000.00	$620.86 $613.05
Principal appreciation due to 10 b.p. yield move	$ 11.15	$ 7.81
Dollar return per $1.00 invested due to 10 b.p. yield move	$ .01115	$ .01286
Total dollar return per $1.00 invested—with yield move	$ .08728	$ .08902
Realized compound yield—with yield move	8.55%	8.71%
Effective par rate—with yield move	8.60%	8.77%
Incremental realized compound yield due to 10 b.p. yield move	+108 b.p.	+123 b.p.
Incremental effective par rate due to 10 b.p. yield move	+110 b.p.	+127 b.p.

---

conventional yield move from 7.5 percent to 7.4 percent over the first one-year period. It also shows the corresponding effective par rates. It should be noted that the standard par bond in this computation always has a maturity matched to the review period, no matter what the maturity of the original bond. Thus, under the assumed yield decline over one year, the 4 percent discount bond produces a realized compound yield of 8.71 percent. This in turn corresponds to the realized compound yield of a par bond with a coupon rate of 8.77 percent (the effective par rate) and a maturity of *one year*. Even this simple computation shows a number of more general results. First, over a period as short as one year, the reinvestment effects do not have a chance to develop. Consequently, the realized compound yield and the effective par rate essentially coincide. Moreover, as long as there is no change in yield (i.e., as long as all price changes are due only to amortization at a constant conventional yield), then the conventional yield value will closely approximate the realized compound yield and come even closer to the effective par rate. However, even a relatively small 10-basis-point decline in the conventional yield of a long-term bond will lead to well over 10 times that magnitude of change in both the realized compound yield and the effective par rate. Finally, even with two bonds having the exact same maturity and starting yield value, the bond with the lower coupon will undergo a somewhat greater response to a given yield move.

TAXABLE BONDS IN TAXED PORTFOLIOS

Taxed Portfolios: Sources of Return

The sources of bond return in taxed portfolios include the three basic elements described earlier for the tax-free case—coupons, capital gains or losses, and interest-on-interest. These elements must be adjusted, of course, for the direct effects of taxation. However, most taxed portfolios are subject to a number of other indirect statutory and/or tax factors that can have a significant effect upon the net return derived from a given bond holding or bond purchase. We shall first discuss the three basic elements of return and then later turn to a review of some of the more important indirect factors.

Aftertax Coupon Return

The treatment of coupon return is theoretically straightforward, but can actually present some serious estimation problems in practice. For all bonds purchased at par or at a discount, there is some appropriate marginal income tax rate that can be directly charged against the coupon payments. This marginal tax rate will, of course, depend on both the type of institution, the type of the bond (i.e., fully taxable, state tax exempt, federal tax exempt, federal and state tax exempt, etc.) as well as on the intricacies of the particular institution's operating structure. In fact, determination of the appropriate marginal income tax rate is often a much more complex process than might first appear, and many portfolio managers will confess that they are sometimes hard pressed to obtain usable official estimates for their funds. This problem is, of course, greatly compounded by the fact that most prospective coupon payments will be received—and taxed—in future fiscal years. Ideally, one should develop a sequence of future-estimated income tax rates over the life of the bond. Of course, this is rarely possible except in certain cases where a progressive change in the tax laws is already on the books. In practice, this partial uncertainty is usually dealt with in somewhat the same simplifying manner as the uncertainty regarding future reinvestment rates (i.e., the same fixed tax rate is assumed over the entire life of all of the bonds held in the same tax status). This fixed rate may then be varied over the range of uncertainty in order to explore the effects of various taxation scenarios.

The interaction of the coupon cycle with the tax payment cycle will have some minor impact upon the effective tax rate, but this is one complication that can usually be neglected in practice.

When bonds have been purchased in the secondary market at a premium above par, most institutions have an option regarding their tax treatment. The coupon income can either be taxed fully and directly, and a capital loss taken at maturity, or the purchase premium can be written down year by year, with each year's write-off acting as an offset to the taxable income. When they have such an option, most institutions will elect to obtain the immediate write-off at the more highly taxed income rate. The effect of this write-off option must be correctly treated in analyzing the aftertax coupon flows from premium bonds.[6]

For purposes of our analyses here, we shall assume that an appropriate marginal income tax rate has been chosen for the bond in question. The net coupon rate will then be considered to be the gross coupon flow, with each coupon payment directly reduced by the amount of the tax liability incurred. This is tantamount to treating the bond as possessing an aftertax coupon rate determined by the pretax coupon rates times the income tax "pull-through rate." For example, a 48 percent income tax rate implies a 52 percent pull-through rate. At this tax level, the aftertax coupon rate for the 7.5 percent par bond in Exhibit 5 would be 3.9 percent (= .52 × 7.5 percent), and the discount 4 percent would have an aftertax coupon rate of 2.08 percent (= .52 × 4 percent).

Aftertax Interest-on-Interest

The stream of aftertax coupons will have a time value that can be represented either figuratively or literally by reinvestment at some specified rate. However, the reinvestment rate will itself be subject to taxation. Depending on the nature of the presumed reinvestment process and its relationship to the bond in question, the tax rate for reinvestment might be quite different from the tax rate applied to direct-coupon income. For example, in an insurance company, the bond may be a fully taxable

---

[6] The tax treatment of bonds is discussed in Chapter 3.

corporate issue, but if envisioned future investments involve a heavy mixture of tax-exempts and preferred stocks, then the reinvestment rate selected as well as the applicable tax rate will differ considerably from the values for the bond itself. In fact, wide differences between the average portfolio return and the reinvestment rates may be relatively common in taxed portfolios. Such portfolios frequently exist, at least in part, to meet statutory reserve requirements of some form or another. Consequently, the bond portfolio may not be representative of the highest rates of return available among investment alternatives within the corporate structure. Some portion of the aftertax coupon receipts may, therefore, gravitate toward higher return investment alternatives outside the portfolio. This process would tend to lead toward considerably higher aftertax reinvestment rates.

In any case, a practical point of departure is to once again assume a fixed reinvestment rate, and a fixed tax rate applicable to the reinvestment rate. Although it is usually a good idea to identify these two rates as constituting two distinct assumptions, the net effect is readily seen to be the determination of a single aftertax reinvestment rate.

The same tax rates have a surprisingly disproportionate impact upon the different sources of return. For example, one might at first glance expect that a 48 percent tax rate applied to both coupon and reinvestment income would lead to a comparable reduction in the bond's dollars-and-cents return from these two sources. In fact, although the total coupon return will indeed be reduced by precisely 48 percent, there will be a much more severe reduction in the total interest-on-interest figure. For example, for a pretax reinvestment rate of 6 percent over a 25-year maturity period, the imposition of a 48 percent tax rate will slash the interest-on-interest by 79 percent. At higher pretax reinvestment rates, taxation will have an even more dramatic effect. At a 10 percent reinvestment rate, there will be an 84 percent reduction in the amount of interest-on-interest return.

These results are quite surprising at first, but they are closely related to a well-known property of the compounding process. When the compounding rate is doubled, the total accrual of compound interest over any given period will more than double. Similarly, when the compounding rate is halved, the total interest accrual will undergo a greater than 50 percent reduction. For this reason, reduction of the reinvestment rate through taxation leads to a generally far greater reduction in the total net accrual of interest-on-interest.

This disproportionate impact of taxation dramatically changes the character of the bond's return. Exhibit 6 illustrates these changes for our earlier examples of the 25-year, 7.5 percent par bond and 25-year, 4 percent discount bond, both priced to have a pretax conventional yield of 7.5 percent. A 6 percent pretax reinvestment rate is assumed. Without taxation, the 7.5 percent par bond derives 56 percent of its total return

EXHIBIT 6 The Disproportionate Impact of Taxation on the Components of Return—a 25-Year 7.5 Percent Par Bond and a 25-Year 4 Percent Discount Bond Priced at 60.739 to Yield 7.5 Percent with an Assumed Reinvestment Rate of 6 Percent

	Dollars of Return per $1,000 Bond			As Percent of Total Return	
	Without Taxes	48 Percent Tax Rate	Change	Without Taxes	48 Percent Tax Rate
7.5 percent par bond					
Coupon income	$1,875	$ 975	−48%	44%	67%
Interest-on-interest	2,355	485	−79	56	33
Capital gain	0	0	0	0	0
Total return	$4,230	$1,460	−65%	100%	100%
Total return per $1 invested	$4.23	$1.46	$−2.77		
Realized compound yield	6.73%	3.63%	−310 B.P.		
4 percent discount bond					
Coupon income	$1,000	$ 520	−48%	38%	53%
Interest-on-interest	1,256	259	−79	47	26
Capital gain	393	204	−48	15	21
Total return	$2,649	$ 983	−63%	100%	100%
Total return per $1 invested	$4.36	$1.62	$−2.74		
Realized compound yield	6.83%	3.89%	−294 B.P.		

from interest-on-interest. Taxation of both the coupon and the reinvestment rate at 48 percent leads to 48 percent reduction in coupon income and a 79 percent reduction in interest-on-interest. This results in a cut in the total return of more than 65 percent. Thus the impact of taxation on overall return is greatly magnified through its "leveraged" effect on the reinvestment compounding process.

The structure of the return is, of course, also strongly affected. Without taxation, interest-on-interest accounts for more than half the total return. With the 48 percent tax, the disproportionately reduced interest-on-interest provides only 33 percent of the total aftertax return.

These results suggest that the ultimate "cost of taxation" in dollars and cents may greatly exceed the direct effects of the tax rate.

Aftertax Capital Gain on a Proposed Purchase

We will use the term *capital gain* to refer to any return derived from principal appreciation realized upon a bond's sale or maturity.[7] For

---

[7] We make this point because commercial banks and thrift institutions technically classify all such returns as "*income* derived from security transactions." Since such returns have the same tax rate as fully taxable coupon payments, these institutions sometimes view themselves as not being subject to capital gains tax. This is a matter of terminology, and we wish to make it clear at the outset that our reference to a capital gain and a capital

bonds purchased at par or in the secondary market at a discount, the capital gain is generally measured from the purchase price to the sale price. The bond's maturity has the same effect as a sale at a price of par. For a bond purchased at a premium in the secondary market, the capital gain may be defined in terms of the "adjusted tax cost" or "adjusted tax basis" rather than the purchase cost. This arises when the premium is being amortized year by year as an offset to coupon income. The bond's amortized cost at the time of sale will then be used as an adjusted tax cost in determining the capital gain.[8]

The tax liability associated with principal appreciation becomes due and payable only when the capital gain is realized through the bond's sale or maturity. There may be accounting tax reserves set aside year by year to match a bond's book accretion, but the actual tax liability is triggered by the act of sale.

Apart from maturity, it is the portfolio manager's choice to select the time of sale. Consequently, the manager can theoretically determine, in part, the timing of the flow of capital gains. This capital gains flexibility can prove a primary resource in the management of overall tax liabilities.

For the moment, we shall discuss capital gains in the context of a bond that is being proposed for purchase. Such a bond will be called a P bond, as distinguished from an H bond, which is already held in the portfolio. In terms of our discussion of capital gains, the important point is that the tax cost of a P bond (other than a premium bond) will always be its current market price. Consequently, the capital gain realized over the life of such a P bond will then just coincide with its original price discount from par. The capital gains tax, at the appropriate tax rate, then becomes payable at maturity.

Exhibit 6 illustrates how capital gains taxation at the same 48 percent rate affects the total return from a 4 percent discount bond. The 48 percent taxation reduces the dollars-and-cents value of the capital gain by exactly 48 percent. While this is the same reduction as for coupon income, their effects are quite different. An increased proportion of return from coupon income always means an increased proportion of interest-on-interest. Since interest-on-interest is always reduced by more than the tax rate itself, increased coupon income tends to magnify the impact of taxation because of the associated increase in interest-on-interest. An increased capital gain component, on the other hand, reduces the percentage of return due to coupon income and consequently

---

gains tax relates to the structure of the return as a realized principal appreciation. For purposes of our *terminology*, it does not matter whether or not this realized principal appreciation is taxed at a special capital gains tax rate. Even if it is taxed at the regular income rates, we will still refer to such appreciation as a capital gain and to the relevant tax rate as the capital gains tax rate. As we shall see, it is the structure of the capital gain that counts in the investment analysis.

[8] See Chapter 3.

to interest-on-interest. This acts as a cushion to soften the overall impact of the 79 percent reduction in interest-on-interest. In the extreme limit, for a pure discount bond with a 0 percent coupon, all of the return would be capital gain, and a 48 percent taxation rate would just reduce the overall return by 48 percent. For real-life bonds with only a part of their return due to capital gains, this capital gain component helps to keep the reduction in total return closer to the 48 percent level.

This effect can be seen in Exhibit 6. The 4 percent taxable discount bond has a pretax capital gain component amounting to 15 percent of the total dollar return. Because of this capital gain component, interest-on-interest accounts for only 47 percent of the total return, as opposed to 56 percent of the total return for a 7.5 percent par bond. Consequently, when taxation is imposed, there is a disproportionately greater reduction in the total return of the par bond relative to that of the discount bond.

Thus, even when capital gains are taxed at the same rate as coupons, a discount bond will tend to have a greater aftertax return than a par bond with the same pretax conventional yield. Perhaps a more intuitive view of this effect is that the coupon income is taxed at the point of receipt *prior* to compounding, but the capital gain is taxed only *after* it has already compounded to its full value at maturity.

This added value of the discount bond reveals itself in the conventional yields as well. Under the same tax rate for income and capital gains, a discount bond will have a greater aftertax conventional yield than a par bond with the same pretax conventional yield.[9]

Aftertax Realized Compound Yields

Once there has been a determination of tax rates to be applied to income, reinvestment, and capital gains, one can readily compute the aftertax cash flow and total return over the life of a given P bond. Because we are dealing with a P bond, the original dollar investment clearly corresponds to the bond's current market cost. By dividing the total aftertax return by the market cost, we can determine, as before, the dollars of return per invested dollar. The compound interest tables will then tell us what semiannually compounded interest rate would generate this same level of growth. The result is the aftertax realized compound yield.

Exhibit 6 illustrates the interim steps in this computation for our two sample bonds. As we would expect from the earlier discussion, the

---

[9] Many practitioners may not be fully aware of this fact. This is one of the many excellent points made by William M. Cox in "Aftertax Compounded Yields for Corporate Bonds" (Fort Wayne, Ind.: The Lincoln National Life Insurance Co., 1974).

advantage in realized compound yields of the taxable discount bond over the par bond is increased by the impact of uniform taxation.

Exhibit 7 shows the effect of varying reinvestment-rate and tax-rate assumptions on the realized compound yields of the two sample bonds.[10] Several points of interest emerge from this presentation. The realized compound yields of both bonds are far less sensitive to the reinvestment-rate assumption in the taxed environments than in the portfolios of tax-free owners. This is to be expected in light of the reduced net rate of interest-on-interest. For each tax structure illustrated, except for the tax-free case, the discount bond has a spread advantage over the par bond in terms of realized compound yield. This spread advantage occurs even in the two cases where both income and capital gains are taxed at the same rate. (As would be expected, the discount advantage is largest in those tax structures having the greatest disparity between the income and the capital gains tax rate.) We also observe that the discount bond's spread advantage declines with increasing reinvestment rate. Again, this is to be expected for the same reason as in the tax-free case—higher reinvestment rates place a greater time value on the par bond's relatively larger coupon flow.

The Conventional Aftertax Yield-to-Maturity

To put the aftertax realized compound yield in perspective, we must briefly touch on the conventional aftertax yield. This yield is based upon exactly the same principles as the pretax conventional yield, except that it deals with the bond's aftertax cash flow to maturity. Formally, the aftertax conventional yield will be that discount rate that, when applied to the bond's aftertax cash flow, produces a present value equal to the bond's market cost. In terms of the growth of total dollars-and-cents return, the conventional aftertax yield coincides with the realized compound yield only when the aftertax coupon receipts are assumed to be compounded at an *aftertax* reinvestment rate equal to the aftertax yield value itself. Thus, exactly as in the tax-free situation, the conventional aftertax yield-to-maturity carries its own implicit reinvestment-rate assumption. This will create a discrepancy between the conventional yield and the realized compound yield whenever the appropriate explicit reinvestment-rate assumption differs significantly from the conventional yield level. As noted earlier, such significant differences are not uncom-

---

[10] Some of the tax structures in Exhibit 7 may appear a little odd at this point, but the rationale behind their selection will be presented later. The selection of the specific tax rates used in Exhibit 7 is purely for illustration purposes. The maximum federal tax rate applicable to capital gains is presently 20 percent for individuals and 28 percent for corporations. (See Chapter 3.)

EXHIBIT 7 Comparison of Aftertax Realized Compound and Conventional Yields (for a 25-year 7.5 percent par bond and a 25-year 4 percent discount bond, both priced to provide a conventional pretax yield of 7.5 percent)

| Tax Rates | | Reinvestment Rate | | 7.5 Percent Par Bond | | | 4 Percent Discount Bond | | | Discount Bond's Advantage | |
Coupon and Reinvestment	Capital Gains	Pretax	Aftertax	Realized Compound Yield	Aftertax Conventional Yield	Difference	Realized Compound Yield	Aftertax Conventional Yield	Difference	As Realized Compound Yield	As Conventional Yield
0%	0%	6.0%	6.00%	6.73%	7.50%	+77 B.P.	6.83%	7.50%	+67 B.P.	+10 B.P.	0 B.P.
		7.5	7.50	7.50	7.50	0	7.50	7.50	0	0	0
		9.0	9.00	8.33	7.50	−81	8.24	7.50	−74	−7	0
48	48	6.0	3.12	3.63	3.90	+27	3.89	4.19	+30	+26	+29
		7.5	3.90	3.90	3.90	0	4.11	4.19	+8	+21	+29
		9.0	4.68	4.18	3.90	−28	4.35	4.19	−16	+17	+29
48	30	6.0	3.12	3.63	3.90	+27	4.07	4.43	+36	+44	+53
		7.5	3.90	3.90	3.90	0	4.28	4.43	+15	+38	+53
		9.0	4.68	4.18	3.90	−28	4.51	4.43	−8	+33	+53
48	0	6.0	3.12	3.63	3.90	+27	4.35	4.79	+44	+72	+89
		7.5	3.90	3.90	3.90	0	4.54	4.79	+25	+64	+89
		9.0	4.68	4.18	3.90	−28	4.76	4.79	+3	+58	+89
30	30	6.0	4.20	4.81	5.25	+44	5.02	5.47	+45	+21	+22
		7.5	5.25	5.25	5.25	0	5.39	5.47	+8	+14	+22
		9.0	6.30	5.72	5.25	−47	5.80	5.47	−33	+8	+22
30	0	6.0	4.20	4.81	5.25	+44	5.25	5.79	+54	+44	+54
		7.5	5.25	5.25	5.25	0	5.60	5.79	+19	+35	+54
		9.0	6.30	5.72	5.25	−47	5.98	5.79	−19	+26	+54

mon in taxed portfolios. In such cases, the conventional aftertax yield will be a particularly unreliable guide, with respect to both absolute as well as relative instrument value.

Exhibit 7 shows the relationship between the realized compound yield and the conventional yield for a range of reinvestment rates and tax structures. For example, at a common 48 percent tax rate for both income and capital gains, the conventional aftertax yield turns out to be 3.9 percent for the 7.5 percent par bond and 4.19 percent for the 4 percent bond selling to yield 7.5 percent. By comparison, at an aftertax reinvestment rate of 4.68 percent, the respective realized compound yields are 4.18 percent and 4.35 percent, or 28 and 16 basis points above the conventional yields. This discrepancy would widen further at higher investment rates.

With respect to relative values, the discount bond has a 29-basis-point spread advantage in terms of conventional yields. As in the tax-free case, the conventional aftertax yield tends to exaggerate the rate of return difference between the two bonds. The higher yielding discount bond gets an added advantage through the higher implicit reinvestment rate of 4.19 percent. The magnitude of this effect can be seen in Exhibit 7 when both bonds are subject to a common reinvestment rate of 3.9 percent. The discount bond's spread advantage in terms of realized compound yield then shrinks from 29 to 21 basis points.

Exhibit 7 shows that the conventional yield's overstatement of the discount bond's advantage is highly dependent on the tax structure and reinvestment rate. The most grievous exaggeration of this discount advantage is 31 basis points for the 48 percent income tax rate, 0 percent capital gains tax, and the 4.68 percent reinvestment rate.

The "Coupon" Approximation for the Aftertax Yield

There is occasionally some confusion as to how to compute the conventional aftertax yield. Although the above definition corresponds to the "true yield" in the conventional sense, there is a much simpler computation that is often used to approximate this true yield value. In fact, this approximation technique has become so popular in certain circles that it is sometimes thought to be the standard rather than the approximation. We will illustrate this computation for the case of the discount 4 percent bond with 48 percent income tax and a 30 percent capital gains tax:

1. Subtract pretax coupon rate from pretax yield.

$$7.50 \text{ percent} - 4 \text{ percent} = 3.5 \text{ percent}$$

2. Multiply result by capital gain pull-through rate.

$$3.5 \text{ percent} \times .7 = 2.45 \text{ percent}$$

3. Compute the aftertax coupon rate and add to the above figure.

$$4 \text{ percent} \times .52 = 2.08 \text{ percent}$$
$$2.08 \text{ percent} + 2.45 \text{ percent} = 4.53 \text{ percent}$$

The true yield is 4.43 percent, 10 basis points lower than the approximation.

The approximation works remarkably well for the "48 percent, 30 percent" tax structure, especially for short maturities and relatively modest discounts or premiums. However, the disparities become quite severe for long discount bonds in other tax structures. Exhibit 8 illustrates the problems with pushing this technique too far.

Effective Par Rates in Taxed Portfolios

In the tax-free case, the effective par rate for a given bond was defined to be the coupon (or yield) rate of that par bond that, under the same reinvestment conditions, would match the given bond's total dollars-and-cents return over a specified review period. This same definition extends to the taxed case if we simply add the phrase "under the same reinvestment *and tax conditions.*"

The calculation of the effective par rate is actually quite simple. Taking the example of the 4 percent discount bond illustrated in Exhibit 6, the total aftertax return per dollar invested is $1.62, or a return of $1,618.40 for each $1,000 par bond purchased. The assumed aftertax reinvestment rate is 3.12 percent. The compound interest tables would then tell us that for each $1 of a semiannual aftertax coupon payment, reinvested and compounded semiannually at this 3.12 percent (annual) rate, we would accumulate a total return of $74.896 by the end of the 25-year review period. Dividing $74.896 into the required return of $1,618.40, we see that each coupon payment from the hypothetical par bond must provide $21.61 of aftertax income. Since the tax rate assumed was 48 percent, this would require a pretax coupon payment of

$$\$21.61 \div (.52) = \$41.56$$

or an annual payment of $83.11 per $1,000 par bond. The effective par rate would thus have to be 8.31 percent. In other words, we have a 25-year, 4 percent discount bond selling on the basis of a 7.5 percent conventional pretax yield, a 4.19 percent aftertax conventional yield (from Exhibit 7), and a 3.89 percent aftertax realized compound yield. However, from its effective par rate, we now know that this discount bond will provide the better long-term investment value as long as the comparable new issue market only offers rates below 8.31 percent.

As noted earlier for the tax-free case, the effective par rate provides major advantages in terms of a yardstick with an intuitively comfortable

EXHIBIT 8 The Limitations of a Popular Technique for Approximating the True Conventional Aftertax Yield (all bonds priced for a pretax yield of 7.5 percent)

Maturity	Coupon	Income Tax: 48% / Capital Gains Tax: 30%		48% / 48%		48% / 0%	
		Approximation	True Yield	Approximation	True Yield	Approximation	True Yield
1 Year	4.0%	4.53%	4.52%	3.90%	3.91%	5.58%	5.53%
	6.0	4.17	4.16	3.90	3.90	4.62	4.59
	7.5	3.90	3.90	3.90	3.90	3.90	3.90
5 Years	4.0%	4.53%	4.54%	3.90%	4.02%	5.58%	5.40%
	6.0	4.17	4.16	3.90	3.95	4.62	4.51
	7.5	3.90	3.90	3.90	3.90	3.90	3.90
10 Years	4.0%	4.53%	4.55%	3.90%	4.11%	5.58%	5.24%
	6.0	4.17	4.15	3.90	3.98	4.62	4.42
	7.5	3.90	3.90	3.90	3.90	3.90	3.90
25 Years	4.0%	4.53%	4.43%	3.90%	4.19%	5.58%	4.79%
	6.0	4.17	4.09	3.90	4.00	4.62	4.22
	7.5	3.90	3.90	3.90	3.90	3.90	3.90

scale which can be readily benchmarked against the new issue market. With this extended definition, the added complications of taxation can be consistently integrated with the reinvestment effects and represented through this one simple measure with its direct market significance. Thus the benefits of the "effective par rate" concept are preserved and even enhanced in the case of portfolios subject to taxation.

As set forth in our definition, the effective par rate is a useful new tool that is extremely simple both in conception and computation.

The Taxable Equivalent Yield

There is one closely analogous computation commonly used in hopes of obtaining the same benchmarking objectives. This is the conventional notion of the "taxable equivalent yield" (or as it is sometimes called, the corporate equivalent yield).

The taxable equivalent yield is the coupon rate of a par bond that would provide the same conventional aftertax yield as the given bond. But the conventional aftertax yield of par bonds is always just the aftertax coupon rate (i.e., the coupon rate times the pull-through rate). Hence the taxable equivalent is simply determined by dividing the specified conventional aftertax yield by the pull-through rate. For the above example of the 4 percent discount bond with a conventional aftertax yield of 4.19 percent, the taxable equivalent is simply

$$4.19 \text{ percent} \div (.52) = 8.07 \text{ percent}$$

Exhibit 9 compares the effective par rates and the taxable equivalent yields for the same range of cases as Exhibit 8. For the 7.5 percent par bond, the effective par rate and the taxable equivalent yield coincide at 7.5 percent for all tax structures and all reinvestment rates. This is because both computations, while providing different estimates of aftertax return, relate their respective return estimates to that provided by a par bond. Consequently, both computations will always lead to the original par bond as being its own effective par rate as well as its own taxable equivalent.

On the other hand, the discount bond in Exhibit 9 shows variations as wide as 70 basis points between the effective par rate and the corresponding taxable equivalent. This variation arises from the reinvestment-rate effect. The greatest discrepancy occurs when the explicit reinvestment-rate assumption differs most significantly from the taxable equivalent yield value. This is because the taxable equivalent, like the conventional aftertax yield upon which it is based, carries with it the implicit assumption that reinvestment takes place at a rate equal to its own value.

EXHIBIT 9 Comparison of Effective Par Rates and Conventional Taxable Equivalent Yields for Various Tax Structures and Reinvestment Rates (for a 25-year 7.5 percent par bond and a 25-year 4 percent discount bond both priced to provide a conventional pretax yield of 7.5 percent)

Tax Rates		Reinvestment Rate		7.5 Percent Par Bond			4 Percent Discount Bond			Discount Bond's Advantage	
Coupon and Reinvestment	Capital Gains	Pretax	Aftertax	Effective Par Rate	Conventional Taxable Equivalent	Difference	Effective Par Rate	Conventional Taxable Equivalent	Difference	As Effective Par Rate	As Conventional Taxable Equivalent
0%	0%	6.0%	6.00%	7.5%	7.5%	0 B.P.	7.73%	7.50%	−23 B.P.	+ 23 B.P.	0 B.P.
		7.5	7.50	7.5	7.5	0	7.50	7.50	0	0	0
		9.0	9.00	7.5	7.5	0	7.31	7.50	+19	− 19	0
48	48	6.0	3.12	7.5	7.5	0	8.31	8.07	−24	+ 81	+ 57
		7.5	3.90	7.5	7.5	0	8.14	8.07	− 7	+ 64	+ 57
		9.0	4.68	7.5	7.5	0	7.97	8.07	+10	+ 47	+ 57
48	30	6.0	3.12	7.5	7.5	0	8.91	8.53	−38	+141	+103
		7.5	3.90	7.5	7.5	0	8.67	8.53	−14	+117	+103
		9.0	4.68	7.5	7.5	0	8.45	8.53	+ 8	+ 95	+103
48	0	6.0	3.12	7.5	7.5	0	9.91	9.21	−70	+241	+171
		7.5	3.90	7.5	7.5	0	9.57	9.21	−36	+207	+171
		9.0	4.68	7.5	7.5	0	9.26	9.21	− 5	+176	+171
30	30	6.0	4.20	7.5	7.5	0	8.07	7.81	−26	+ 57	+ 31
		7.5	5.25	7.5	7.5	0	7.87	7.81	− 6	+ 37	+ 31
		9.0	6.30	7.5	7.5	0	7.68	7.81	+13	+ 18	+ 31
30	0	6.0	4.20	7.5	7.5	0	8.71	8.27	−44	+121	+ 77
		7.5	5.25	7.5	7.5	0	8.41	8.27	−14	+ 91	+ 77
		9.0	6.30	7.5	7.5	0	8.15	8.27	+12	+ 65	+ 77

The Tax-Exempt Effective Par Rate

In taxed portfolios, bonds are benchmarked not only against the new issue market of fully taxable issues, but also against markets of bonds having various degrees of tax exemptions. In particular, the fully tax-exempt municipal market almost always serves as an important reference point for taxed portfolios. The common practice is to use the conventional aftertax yield as a yardstick for comparisons with the par market for fully tax-exempt bonds. However, as in all the preceding instances, this comparison can prove highly erroneous when the relevant reinvestment rate differs significantly from the conventional yield value.

The general concept of the effective par rate can overcome this problem by adapting the characteristics of the underlying standard par bond to the new-issue market in question.

A *tax-exempt effective par rate* for a given bond can be defined as the coupon rate of that tax-exempt bond that would produce the same aftertax return as the given bond under the same reinvestment and tax conditions. In the earlier example of the 4 percent discount bond at a 6 percent reinvestment rate and 48 percent taxation, it was found that the aftertax return would be matched by an 8.31 percent fully taxable par bond. The return from such a par bond is identical to that from a tax-exempt par bond with a coupon rate of

$$8.31 \text{ percent} \times .52 = 4.32 \text{ percent}$$

The analogous tax-exempt effective par rate would, therefore, be 4.32 percent. This value can be used to benchmark the taxable discount bond against the level of the tax-exempt market.

In effect, an equivalent definition for *tax-exempt effective par rate* would be the corresponding fully taxable effective par rate multiplied by the pull-through rate on coupon income. This is just the relationship between the taxable equivalent and the conventional aftertax yield. One might, therefore, reverse the definitions and say that the fully taxable effective par rate is just the taxable equivalent of the tax-exempt effective par rate, which in turn is itself based on the aftertax realized compound yield.

As noted earlier, the current practice is to use the conventional aftertax yield for comparison with the tax-exempt market. Therefore, the tax-exempt effective par rate should be compared with this conventional yield. This is done in Exhibit 10 for the same tax structures and reinvestment assumptions as in Exhibits 7 and 9. As would be expected, the two measures coincide in the special case of the 7.5 percent par bond. For the 4 percent discount bond, on the other hand, there are significant discrepancies, ranging up to 36 basis points. Actually Exhibit 10 is just a

EXHIBIT 10 Comparison of Tax-Exempt Effective Par Rates and Conventional Aftertax Yields for Various Tax Structures and Reinvestment Rates (for a 25-year 7.5 percent par bond and a 25-year 4 percent discount bond both priced to provide a conventional pretax yield of 7.5 percent)

Tax Rates		Reinvestment Rate		7.5 Percent Par Bond			4 Percent Discount Bond			Discount Bond's Advantage	
Coupon and Reinvestment	Capital Gains	Pretax	Aftertax	Tax Exempt Effective Par Rate	Conventional Aftertax Yield	Difference	Tax Exempt Effective Par Rate	Conventional Aftertax Yield	Difference	As Effective Par Rate	As Conventional Aftertax Yield
0%	0%	6.0%	6.00%	7.50%	7.50%	0 B.P.	7.73%	7.50%	−23 B.P.	+ 23 B.P.	0 B.P.
		7.5	7.50	7.50	7.50	0	7.50	7.50	0	0	0
		9.0	9.00	7.50	7.50	0	7.31	7.50	+19	− 19	0
48	48	6.0	3.12	3.90	3.90	0	4.32	4.19	−13	+ 42	+29
		7.5	3.90	3.90	3.90	0	4.23	4.19	− 4	+ 33	+29
		9.0	4.68	3.90	3.90	0	4.14	4.19	+ 5	+ 24	+29
48	30	6.0	3.12	3.90	3.90	0	4.63	4.43	−20	+ 73	+53
		7.5	3.90	3.90	3.90	0	4.51	4.43	− 8	+ 61	+53
		9.0	4.68	3.90	3.90	0	4.40	4.43	+ 3	+ 50	+53
48	0	6.0	3.12	3.90	3.90	0	5.15	4.79	−36	+125	+89
		7.5	3.90	3.90	3.90	0	4.98	4.79	−19	+108	+89
		9.0	4.68	3.90	3.90	0	4.82	4.79	− 3	+ 92	+89
30	30	6.0	4.20	5.25	5.25	0	5.65	5.47	−18	+ 40	+22
		7.5	5.25	5.25	5.25	0	5.51	5.47	− 4	+ 26	+22
		9.0	6.30	5.25	5.25	0	5.38	5.47	+ 9	+ 13	+22
30	0	6.0	4.20	5.25	5.25	0	6.10	5.79	−31	+ 85	+54
		7.5	5.25	5.25	5.25	0	5.89	5.79	−10	+ 64	+54
		9.0	6.30	5.25	5.25	0	5.71	5.79	+ 8	+ 46	+54

tax-deflated image of Exhibit 9, since the effective par rate and the conventional taxable equivalent yield can both be viewed as taxable equivalents of Exhibit 10's tax-exempt effective par rate and conventional aftertax yield, respectively.

Aftertax Capital Gain on a Proposed Portfolio Sale

A bond holding in a portfolio subject to taxation has a fundamentally different investment value from the exact same issue not held in that portfolio. This is because the bonds in the portfolio have their unique tax cost. The principal appreciation subject to capital gains taxation will always be measured using this tax cost as a basis. Hence, this tax cost must enter as a critical element in any rational investment decision relating to such a portfolio bond.

For the moment, we shall focus on par and discount bonds and put aside the somewhat more complex case of premium bonds. Then we can say that it is the historical tax cost of the portfolio bond (or H bond, for bond now held) that differentiates it from P bond whose tax cost always coincides with its current market value. Actually, there is a related but even more fundamental difference between the investment analysis of an H bond and that of a P bond. With the P bond, the question of capital gains liability becomes pertinent only at the future review point of possible sale or maturity. For the H bond, on the other hand, there are two times when the capital gains liability becomes relevant: (1) the future point of sale or maturity that would result from continued holding, and (2) the present, in terms of the capital gains liability that would become payable *immediately* if the H bond were to be sold today at its current market value. As we shall soon see, it is the relationship between these two capital gains that determines the total aftertax return over a specified review period.

For given tax and reinvestment assumptions, we can readily compute the H bond's aftertax return from coupon income and from interest-on-interest that would be earned over a review period. The aftertax capital gain at maturity will also be well defined, but it will be based on the bond's tax cost (i.e., its historical purchase price). Consequently, this unadjusted aftertax capital gain figure will reflect the net principal appreciation that took place over the bond's *literal* holding period (i.e., stretching back before the present time to the original date of purchase). However, for comparison with other investment alternatives, our purpose is to identify the capital gains return accruing from holding the bond from *today's* decision point to its future maturity or point of review. Thus we must separate the bond's total capital gains figure into (1) one portion already accrued from its purchase date to today's decision point, and (2) a second portion that will accrue from today forward over the review period. Only this second portion of the capital gains return should enter into our total-return computations for purposes of evaluating investment alternatives.

Actually, this separation is readily performed. The H bond's total pretax capital gain does, after all, consist of the sum of its *past* capital gain from the purchase price to today's market value *plus* its future capital gains from today's market value to its future sale price or maturity value. The capital gains tax liability can be assigned accordingly to each of these components. The net aftertax capital gain can also be divided up in this fashion. Consequently, the H bond's aftertax capital gain over the review period can be taken as the gross principal appreciation from its market value today to its value at the end of the review period, *less* the *increase* in the capital gains tax liability.

For bonds purchased at a discount, this definition will coincide with the net aftertax capital gains from a P bond (as long as there are not anticipated changes in the effective capital gains tax rate). This coincidence arises because the incremental capital gains tax liability for both H bonds and P bonds will always be the same fraction of the incremental capital gain associated with the review period. In particular, when there is no principal appreciation, there will be no increase in the capital gains tax liability, and so the net aftertax capital gain will be zero.

With bonds purchased in the secondary market at a premium, a different situation arises when the tax cost is amortized year by year. In this case, even when the bond's market price remains at the same level, the capital gains tax liability will increase as a result of the dropping tax cost, thus leading to an aftertax capital loss. The rate of amortization of the tax cost will vary with the original time and cost of purchase. Consequently, even for the same change in market value over the review period, the capital gains tax liability accrued for an H bond will generally differ from that accrued for a P bond. In accordance with our definition, this will lead to different aftertax capital gains for premium H bonds and P bonds.

With this general definition of the aftertax capital gain, all sources of aftertax return from an H bond can be computed, and so an H bond's total dollars-and-cents return can be determined for any review period.

In our earlier analysis for P bonds, the next step then consisted in dividing this dollar return by the P bond's market value to determine the return per dollar invested. In the case of the H bond, however, the market value does not constitute directly investable dollars because of the capital gains liability incurred through the act of sale. Therefore, there is some question as to how to proceed with our computation of the return per dollar invested for H bonds, and this leads us to the key concept of "opportunity dollars."

Opportunity Dollars

When an H bond is sold, the portfolio receives its market value in dollars, and it theoretically could use these dollar receipts as a medium of exchange to purchase other bonds in the marketplace. However, when such an H-bond sale also incurs a capital gains tax liability, then some of the immediate dollar receipts must in effect be put aside to pay the added tax liability. This leaves the portfolio with a reduced amount of free dollars available for the pursuit of new investment opportunities. In fact, the funds freely available for new investment would consist of just the market value receipts from the H bond's sale *less* the capital gains tax liability incurred by this act of sale. We will use the term *opportunity dollars* to denote this figure.

This concept of opportunity dollars can be immediately generalized to represent the dollars that *would* be freed for new investment if a given H bond with an "embedded" capital gain *were* to be sold at any given time. Thus, with this more general interpretation, every such H bond in a portfolio has an associated opportunity-dollar value at every point in time.

As an example, suppose a portfolio had purchased our 25-year 4 percent discount bond 5 years ago at a price of 50.739. Today, this H bond would have an embedded capital gain of $100 per bond. If the capital gains tax liability were to be triggered by a sale today, this liability would amount to $48 at a 48 percent capital gains tax rate. Thus the opportunity dollars per bond that would be freed by such a sale today would amount to

$$\$607.39 - \$48.00 = \$559.39$$

Up to this point, we have only discussed the somewhat more cheerful case of bonds with embedded capital gains. What about bonds selling at capital losses relative to their historical tax cost? When such bonds are sold, a capital loss is realized. This loss may in turn be usable as an offset to capital gains in current or future fiscal years. If this offset does in fact lead to a real marginal savings in the portfolio's capital gains tax liability, then this loss will have a concrete positive value. This marginal value of each dollar of loss offset can be represented through an appropriate "capital loss tax rate." The actual value assignable to this capital loss rate will depend critically on several factors relating to the portfolio's overall tax status. This whole subject will be discussed in some detail later. For the moment, however, let us assume that the portfolio has already realized an overwhelming surplus of capital gains in this fiscal year and that any contemplated capital losses may be fully usable as offsets against the existing tax liability. In such a case, the capital loss tax rate will coincide with the assumed capital gain tax rate.

As a concrete example, let us again take the 4 percent discount bond, but now assume that it had been purchased five years earlier at a price of 70.739. Its sale today at a price of 60.739 would then create a capital loss of 10 points, or $100 per bond. At a capital loss tax rate of 48 percent, $48 of this loss would be usable as an offset against existing tax liabilities. Under the presumed conditions, this $48 loss offset would actually free $48 in additional funds that the portfolio could use this fiscal year for new investment purposes. Putting aside the question of the timing of the sale relative to the tax liability cycle, this $48 loss offset then *adds* to the opportunity dollars freed by the H bond's sale. In other words, this H bond's sale would generate an opportunity-dollar value of

$$\$607.39 + \$48.00 = \$655.39$$

This example provides the key to extending the concept of opportunity dollars to include H bonds with embedded tax losses. The opportunity dollar value of such an H bond is its current market value *plus* the product of the embedded capital loss multiplied by the appropriate capital loss tax rate. With this extension, *every* H bond can now be viewed as always having a certain opportunity-dollar value determined by the interplay of market forces with the portfolio's overall tax status.

Up to this point, we have defined the opportunity dollars associated with an H bond as funds that would be freed by its sale. However, every such sale can be considered as a decision between the options of selling the bond, on the one hand, or its continued holding, on the other hand. A decision for continued holding can in turn be viewed as a sort of purchase decision (i.e., the H bond is "purchased" in exchange for the funds that would have been freed by its sale. This means that it is the opportunity dollars that reflect the current "cost" of a decision to continue holding a given H bond. Thus an H bond's opportunity-dollar value can be interpreted in several related ways: (1) as the net usable funds that would be freed by its sale, (2) as the net usable funds that are tied up by its continued holding, and/or (3) as the cost in terms of tax-free exchangeable funds given a decision to purchase its continued holding. Thus, for H bonds, the opportunity-dollar value serves almost precisely the same functions as does the market value for P bonds.

It will be recalled that the preceding section raised the question of how to define the dollars invested in an H bond. It should be clear now that an H bond's opportunity dollars provide a consistent measure for this investment base.

The concept of opportunity dollars also clarifies the determination of an H bond's capital gain over a future review period. Consider the above example of a 4 percent H bond purchased five years earlier at 50.739. At the bond's maturity in 25 years, the total realized capital gain will be

$$\$1,000.00 - \$507.39 = \$492.61$$

or an aftertax gain of

$$\$492.61 \times .52 = \$256.16$$

at a 48 percent capital gains tax rate. However, in accordance with the discussion in the preceding section, the investment return should include only that portion of the capital gain accrued over the *next* 25 years. Since the bond's price today is 60.739, this will amount to

$$\$1,000.00 - \$607.39 = \$392.61$$

for an aftertax capital gains return of

$$\$392.61 \times .52 = \$204.16$$

This calculation can also be expressed in terms of the H bond's opportunity dollars today and at maturity. At its maturity, the H bond will realize a total capital gain amounting to $492.61 and a consequent tax liability of

$$\$492.61 \times .48 = \$236.45$$

The H bond's opportunity value per bond at maturity will therefore be

$$\$1,000.00 - \$236.45 = \$763.55$$

The same H bond's opportunity dollar value today was computed above to be $559.39. Hence, the increase in opportunity dollars over the 25-year period is just

$$\$763.55 - \$559.39 = \$204.16$$

This is the exact same value as the appropriate contribution to the H bond's aftertax return from capital gains over the 25-year review period.

This relationship holds quite generally (for P bonds as well as H bonds): The change in a bond's opportunity-dollar value precisely measures its aftertax capital gain return over any given review period. This relationship holds for premium bonds as well as for discount bonds. It even holds true under the more general case when the effective capital gains (and/or loss) tax rates are expected to undergo changes during the review period.

The Opportunity Yield

With the opportunity dollars as an investment base, we can now proceed to compute an aftertax return per dollar invested for both H bonds and P bonds.

As noted above, the expression "return per dollar invested" is slightly ambiguous for the case of an H bond. However, this ambiguity can be overcome by interpreting an H bond's opportunity dollars as the dollar amount "invested" in its continued holding. Since a P bond's opportunity dollars coincide with its market cost at the time of purchase, we can employ this concept of return per opportunity dollar for *both* H bonds and P bonds. We can then proceed to compute the aftertax return per (opportunity) dollar invested, and move toward the other return measures developed earlier for P bonds.

Staying with the above example of a 4 percent H bond purchased earlier at a price of 50.739, we first determine the total dollars of return over the 25-year review period. The aftertax contributions from coupon income and interest-on-interest will be identical with the $520 and $259 given in Exhibit 6 for the 4 percent P bond. Moreover, the H bond's aftertax capital gain return, when properly allocated to the next 25 years, will also coincide with the $204 associated with the 4 percent P bond. The H bond's total aftertax return will therefore be $983, which in this case of a discount bond is exactly the same value as for the comparable P bond. This equality will not hold for premium bonds or in the face of changes in the structure of capital gains taxation over the review period. The H bond's opportunity dollars was computed earlier to be

$$\$607.39 - \$48.00 = \$559.39$$

Using this amount of opportunity dollars as an investment base, the total aftertax return per invested dollar becomes

$$\$983 \div \$559.39 = \$1.76$$

in comparison with $1.62 for the comparable P bond.

We can now proceed to ask, as before, what fully compounded rate of interest would be needed to provide this same level of return over 25 years of semiannual compounding? For a return per invested dollar of $1.76, the compound interest tables would then supply the rate of 2.05 percent per semiannual period, or 4.1 percent on an annual bond basis. For H bonds, this figure of 4.1 percent is the analogue of the aftertax realized compound yield. However, it does seem useful to distinguish this realized compound yield value as reflecting an investment base measured in opportunity dollars. For this reason, we shall refer to this figure as the opportunity yield.

The opportunity yield as defined here can be applied to both P bonds and H bonds, and hence it can be viewed as a generalization of the aftertax realized compound yield.

Exhibit 11 shows the opportunity yield values for four 25-year 4 percent discount bonds, each identical except for their historical cost basis. The tax and reinvestment structures are the same as used before in Exhibits 7, 9, and 10. As we would expect, Exhibit 11 shows that the historical purchase price is irrelevant when the capital gains and loss are untaxed. It becomes most relevant in those cases where this capital gains taxation is strongest—in the 48 percent case, there is almost a 90 basis point variation in opportunity yields depending only on the historical purchase cost. For this tax case at a 6 percent reinvestment rate, the 10-point capital gain pushes the opportunity yield 21 basis points above the

EXHIBIT 11 Opportunity Yields under Various Tax Structures and Reinvestment Rates (for a 25-year 4 percent bond selling today at 60.739 but purchased earlier)

Tax Rates				Bond's Price at Earlier Purchase Date			
Coupon and Reinvestment	Capital Gain and Loss	Reinvestment Rate		50.739 (H bond with capital gain)	60.739 (P bond)	70.739 (H bond with capital loss)	100.00 (H bond with real capital loss)
		Pretax	Aftertax				
0%	0%	6.00%	6.00%	6.83%	6.83%	6.83%	6.83%
		7.50	7.50	7.50	7.50	7.50	7.50
		9.00	9.00	8.24	8.24	8.24	8.24
48	48	6.00	3.12	4.10	3.89	3.70	3.24
		7.50	3.90	4.33	4.11	3.91	3.44
		9.00	4.68	4.57	4.35	4.15	3.66
48	30	6.00	3.12	4.20	4.07	3.94	3.62
		7.50	3.90	4.41	4.28	4.15	3.82
		9.00	4.68	4.65	4.51	4.38	4.03
48	0	6.00	3.12	4.35	4.35	4.35	4.35
		7.50	3.90	4.54	4.54	4.54	4.54
		9.00	4.68	4.76	4.76	4.76	4.76
30	30	6.00	4.20	5.17	5.02	4.89	4.52
		7.50	5.25	5.55	5.39	5.25	4.87
		9.00	6.30	5.95	5.80	5.65	5.25
30	0	6.00	4.20	5.25	5.25	5.25	5.25
		7.50	5.25	5.60	5.60	5.60	5.60
		9.00	6.30	5.98	5.98	5.98	5.98

P bond case, 40 basis points above the 10-point loss case, and 86 basis points above the opportunity yield for the bond that had been purchased at par.

All four of these bonds actually provide the exact same aftertax return *per bond*. The higher opportunity yield for the bond with the 10-point embedded capital gain is derived from the fact that the same return *per bond* is earned on a smaller investment base of opportunity dollars. This reduction in the opportunity-dollar base occurs because of the tax liability inherent in the embedded capital gain. Hence this bond is a much more valuable "hold" than the other three bonds. The greater opportunity yield reflects this higher holding value. In other words, selling any of the four bonds would entail giving up the same dollars of return, but the opportunity dollars freed would be considerably greater for the bonds with embedded losses.

The H bonds in Exhibit 11 appear to follow the P bond with respect to their opportunity yields' sensitivity to reinvestment-rate effects. In other words, the spreads between the H bond's and the P bond's opportunity yields seem to remain fairly constant as the reinvestment rate varies. In fact, this spread seems to be primarily dependent on the capital gains (and loss) tax rate. Thus for the 48 percent, 30 percent tax structure, the H bond with the 10-point embedded gain and the one with the 10-point embedded loss keep close to a spread of 13–14 basis points above and below the P bond opportunity yield. Very nearly the same spread relationship is maintained for the 30 percent, 30 percent tax structure across all three reinvestment rates.

It should perhaps be reemphasized at this point that the opportunity yield is a completely consistent representation of the aftertax dollars-and-cents return under the assumed tax and reinvestment conditions. Thus, under the same assumptions, an H bond with an opportunity yield of 4.1 percent will always provide a greater aftertax return per invested dollar than a P bond with a smaller opportunity yield, and vice versa. Another way of saying the same thing is to envision the sale of this H bond and the reinvestment of all released opportunity dollars into a new P bond. Unless this new P bond has an opportunity yield exceeding the H bond's 4.1 percent, the swap will turn out to be a loser in terms of dollars-and-cents return under the assumed conditions. Similarly, in comparing any two H bonds, the one with the smaller opportunity yield will prove the better sale, and the one with the higher opportunity yield will always prove the better hold. For a dollars-and-cents comparison of two H bonds, one can always take the model of swapping each of them into a given P bond. The H bond with the lower opportunity yield will always prove the better sale under such a dollars-and-cents evaluation.

Thus the opportunity yield simply, compactly, and consistently integrates the effects of several different elements that affect a bond's investment value: the portfolio's explicit reinvestment rate assumption; its anticipated future tax rates on coupon income, reinvestment, and capital gains and losses; the portfolio's present capital gains tax status; the given bond's position as an H bond or a P bond; and if an H bond, its adjusted tax-cost basis.

The Opportunity Par Rate

The opportunity yield will by its nature have the same problem of intuitive scaling and market benchmarking as the realized compound yield. Once again, to overcome these problems, we can turn to the same device of a hypothetical par bond that would match the bond's level of opportunity yield. This leads us to the effective par rate or, if we wish to stress the fact that the underlying rate of return is based upon an investment base of opportunity dollars, what we might call the opportunity par rate.

Exhibit 12 presents the opportunity par rate values corresponding to the opportunity yield situations of Exhibit 11. Thus, for the 48 percent, 48 percent tax case and a 6 percent reinvestment rate, the H bond with

EXHIBIT 12 Opportunity Par Rates under Various Tax Structures and Reinvestment Rates (for a 25-year 4 percent bond selling today at 60.739 but purchased earlier)

Tax Rates		Reinvestment Rate		Bond's Price at Earlier Purchase Date			
Coupon and Reinvestment	Capital Gain and Loss	Pretax	Aftertax	50.739 (H bond with capital gain)	60.739 (P bond)	70.739 (H bond with capital loss)	100.00 (H bond with real capital loss)
0%	0%	6.0%	6.00%	7.73%	7.73%	7.73%	7.73%
		7.5	7.50	7.50	7.50	7.50	7.50
		9.0	9.00	7.31	7.31	7.31	7.31
48	48	6.0	3.12	9.03	8.31	7.70	6.34
		7.5	3.90	8.83	8.14	7.54	6.21
		9.0	4.68	8.66	7.97	7.39	6.09
48	30	6.0	3.12	9.37	8.91	8.49	7.46
		7.5	3.90	9.12	8.67	8.26	7.26
		9.0	4.68	8.89	8.46	8.06	7.08
48	0	6.0	3.12	9.91	9.91	9.91	9.91
		7.5	3.90	9.57	9.57	9.57	9.57
		9.0	4.68	9.26	9.26	9.26	9.26
30	30	6.0	4.20	8.49	8.07	7.69	6.76
		7.5	5.25	8.27	7.87	7.49	6.59
		9.0	6.30	8.08	7.68	7.32	6.43
30	0	6.0	4.20	8.71	8.71	8.71	8.71
		7.5	5.25	8.41	8.41	8.41	8.41
		9.0	6.30	8.15	8.15	8.15	8.15

the 10-point capital gain is seen to have an opportunity par rate of 9.03 percent. This means that this bond will provide the portfolio with the same aftertax return per invested (opportunity) dollar as a 25-year par bond with a fully taxable 9.03 percent coupon rate. To state it more precisely, any swap out of this H bond and into a new 25-year par bond with any coupon rate below 9.03 percent will turn out to be a loser in terms of dollars-and-cents return.

The opportunity par rate can be a remarkably compact and convenient tool. Suppose that we compute the opportunity par rate for every bond in a given portfolio. Whenever the level of the *comparable* new-issue market exceeds the opportunity par rate of any of the H bonds, then this is an immediate signal that a swap into the new issue would work out profitably in terms of dollars-and-cents return. Moreover, we know that the best swap would, everything else being equal, entail sale of that bond with the lowest opportunity par rate. However, a word of caution is in order. Although it is a convenient point of comparison, the new-issue par market may not represent the best possible P bond sector for a given portfolio.

A tax-exempt opportunity par rate can be computed in the now obvious fashion for benchmarking against the tax-exempt market.

The incorporation of an H bond's capital gains tax liability or loss offset into its investment base dates back to the ideal of the "give-up yield," which has long been used in the management of many commercial bank portfolios. The give-up yield was usually computed as a conventional aftertax yield determined at a price corresponding to what we have called the bond's opportunity dollars. However, this give-up yield failed to include any treatment of explicit reinvestment-rate assumptions.

The opportunity yield concept presented here can be viewed as an integration of the old bank give-up yield with the more recent work on explicit reinvestment rates and realized compound yield.[11]

Tax Losses and Tax Offsets

The estimation of the effective capital gains tax rate for a given portfolio is usually a far more difficult process than it might first appear, even when the tax rate for an isolated capital gain is quite well defined. The actual capital gains tax that can be fairly charged against a contemplated H bond sale depends critically on the overall gain or loss status of the portfolio, not only in the present fiscal year, but over future years as well.

For example, suppose the portfolio carries unrealized losses of such huge proportions as to far outweigh any foreseeable capital gains, and further suppose that the portfolio is blessed with the flexibility to freely realize these losses, as needed, to offset capital gains. In such a situation, the effective capital gains tax rate will be 0 percent! There is no real need for the portfolio to pay a capital gains tax, since by assumption every such gain can be readily offset without depleting the portfolio's resource of losses. By the same token, any particular capital loss realized during this period conveys no special benefit (i.e., it simply adds to an already more-than-abundant resource). Hence the capital loss tax rate would also correspond to 0 percent! It was just this type of situation that motivated the inclusion of the 0 percent capital gains tax cases in Exhibits 7, 9, 10, 11, and 12.

On the other hand, suppose the portfolio has a mountain of unreal-

---

[11] Published references to the give-up yield appear to be rather slim, but there is a mathematically elegant discussion in Robert I. Komar, "Developing a Liquidity Management Model," *Journal of Bank Research* (Spring 1971). On the other hand, there are many references dealing with explicit reinvestment rates and their effects on a bond's total return. (In particular, see: J. Peter Williamson, "Computerized Approaches to Bond Switching," *Financial Analysts Journal* (July–August 1970); and the monograph by Robert H. Cramer and Stephen L. Hawk, *The Consideration of Coupon Levels, Taxes, Reinvestment Rates, and Maturity in the Investment Management of Financial Institutions* (Madison, Wis.: University of Wisconsin-Madison, 1973). These studies explored the area of aftertax cash flows but stopped short of relating these results to the bond's opportunity dollars in terms of an opportunity yield figure.

ized losses, but is unable to take additional tax or book losses in the current fiscal year. Then, any further transactions in the current year should be taxed at the full capital gains rate. However, in future years, if capital losses were to become more freely realizable, then the effective capital gains tax rate might decline to 0 percent.

Another situation would be a portfolio having substantial *realized* losses that have reached the end of their carry-forward period. In other words, the losses will be lost forever unless they are used as offsets in the current fiscal year. If the portfolio does not have an overabundance of *unrealized* losses, then this situation might correspond to a 0 percent effective capital gains tax this year followed by a full capital gains rate next year.

Of course, if a portfolio has already taken an excess of realized capital gains in the current year, and if there is a limited amount of unrealized losses, then any loss taken will be a truly marginal offset and should be valued at the full rate.

In all the above situations, the effective tax rates for capital gains and capital losses were symmetric (i.e., gains and losses both had the same rate in any given year). Moreover, this rate corresponded to either the full capital gains tax rate or to 0 percent. Now one can also envision situations where asymmetric and partial tax rates would be appropriate.

For example, suppose a portfolio has relatively few unrealized losses relative to its unrealized capital gains. However, in terms of *realized* gains and losses, the situation is just the opposite: There is a huge body of capital losses for which the carry forward limit ends in the current fiscal year. The magnitude of these losses far outweighs both the realized and unrealized gains. An incremental capital gain realized this year will therefore be taxed at a marginal rate of 0 percent. An incremental capital loss realized this year would not be marginally useful in the current fiscal year. However, such a loss would be carried forward into subsequent years when the embedded gains would outweigh the available losses. Hence, such a loss might be viewed as having an opportunity-dollar value in excess of 0 percent but below the full capital gains rate that would apply to a needed offset in the present year. In such a case, the marginal-gains rate would be less than the marginal-loss rate. This asymmetry in tax rates creates a corresponding asymmetry in the risk/reward balance. The implications of such an asymmetry for investment policy are fairly evident.

In fact, it could be argued that whenever the unrealized capital gains are out of balance with the losses available as potential offsets, this creates an "asymmetry of resources" with significant implications for portfolio strategy.

In this connection, it is sometimes quite suggestive to look at the portfolio in terms of its overall value in opportunity dollars. This overall value should correspond to the funds remaining following a hypothetical liquidation of the entire portfolio and the payment of any resulting tax liabilities. For example, take the preceding example of a portfolio with carry forward losses that are about to expire. Since the current realized losses outweigh both the realized and unrealized capital gains, the portfolio's current opportunity-dollar value would coincide with its market value. However, in the next fiscal year, if no further action had been taken, the carry-forward losses would have expired and the unrealized capital gains would then exceed the available loss offset. Consequently, liquidation of the portfolio would then result in some net capital gains liability and the opportunity-dollar value would fall below the portfolio's market value. Thus, even if the portfolio's market value remains unchanged over the year, there would be a definite decline in the opportunity-dollar value. This would have the exact same effect as a market decline, and the portfolio would show a reduced opportunity yield over the one-year period. This loss in opportunity yield, of course, reflects the opportunity foregone by not realizing all possible capital gains in the current fiscal year when they could be fully offset against the expiring pool of capital losses.

This whole area of the management of capital gains and losses can obviously become quite intricate and can lead to some thorny estimation problems. However, its difficulty should not lead to its neglect. Theoretically, the subject has many fascinating facets. Practically, it would seem that correct strategic decisions at this level might well have an enormous (and relatively risk-free) impact on the portfolio's total performance.

Indirect Factors Influencing Aftertax Return

The foregoing development of the opportunity yield approach focused on the relatively direct tax factors affecting income, reinvestment, and capital gains or losses. However, there are many indirect factors that can have a powerful and frequently overwhelming influence on the portfolio's return and management strategy. Some of these factors can be readily measured and incorporated into an opportunity yield. Other factors are of a more qualitative nature and probably would defy any effort to introduce them into a formal analytic framework.

One of the more important measurable factors is the "asset tax," which arises in connection with life insurance company portfolios. Many major insurance companies believe that, through the complexities of their taxation structure, they become subject to what amounts to an implicit tax on their portfolio's asset value. Estimates of the magnitude of this asset tax range up to 1 percent. Such an asset tax can readily be incorporated into the opportunity yield measure, and would have a major effect on a bond portfolio strategy. For example, consider a 25-year, 4 percent H bond purchased earlier at a price of par, but selling now at 60.739. At a 30 percent income tax rate, the 4 percent coupon would provide an annual payment of $40 pretax or

$$\$40 \times .70 = \$28$$

aftertax for an aftertax coupon rate of 2.8 percent. The presence of an additional 1 percent asset tax applied to the bond's book value of par would constitute a further tax charge of $10 per bond per year. This would reduce the net aftertax coupon income to

$$\$28 - \$10 = \$18$$

per year, or an after-coupon rate of only 1.80 percent! Moreover, this asset tax is based on the H-bond's inflated book asset value. Suppose the H-bond were sold and then repurchased and put on the books at its present market value of 60.739. The 1 percent asset tax would then amount to $6.07 per year, or a savings of $3.93 per year per bond. In terms of market value, this would constitute a savings of

$$100 \text{ percent} \times (\$3.93 \div \$607.39) = .65 \text{ percent}$$

or 65 basis points of "unnecessary" taxation per year.

Many important but less measurable factors surround the whole issue of realizing book and/or tax losses. As we have seen, it often makes sense to take losses in terms of the direct dollars-and-cents effects. However, the taking of losses can have powerful effects that may reach beyond the confines of the portfolio and have great impact upon the corporation's overall reporting and statutory status. Profits may be adversely affected. The various measures of corporate returns on assets may be reduced. There may be an encroachment upon the level of needed reserves. There are many such circumstances, all of which tend to place limits on the freedom to realize portfolio losses or gains. From the narrower vista of the portfolio, it may seem that such restrictions are purely artificial and have little to do with the true financial realities of the corporation. However, it should be remembered that the financial reporting structure ultimately does have a real economic impact on overall corporate operations regardless of the realities that they may or may not reflect. Obviously, a corporate policy is needed that balances the very real benefits of portfolio loss realization against their possible adverse "reporting" effects. Unfortunately, many taxed portfolios labor under an unexamined and unmeasured dictum that arbitrarily restricts or often prohibits any form of loss realization.

INVESTMENT IMPLICATIONS

The investment implications of the results presented in this chapter are as follows:

1. *Conventional pretax yields and yield spreads can be deceptive for taxed portfolios and can result in apparent yield pickup swaps that actually turn out to be dollars-and-cents losers.*

Consider a swapout of 25-year taxable 4s at 7.5 percent into 25-year taxable 8.5 percent par bonds. Even at a 48 percent, 0 percent tax structure and a 6 percent reinvestment rate, the 100-basis-point yield pickup would appear to be large enough to overwhelm all the fine points and lead to substantial profit. However, Exhibit 9 shows that the 4s have a taxable effective par rate of 9.91 percent. Hence this swap would actually entail a loss of 141 basis points in terms of effective par rate. In terms of dollars-and-cents, this would amount to a loss of $274,000 on a $1,000,000 market value holding over the 25-year period.

2. *The conventional aftertax yields and yield spreads, when computed using the common approximation formulas can prove very unreliable.*

For a 48 percent, 0 percent tax structure, the common "coupon" approximation formula for taxable bonds works out to an aftertax yield estimate of 5.58 percent for a 25-year 4 percent bond priced to yield 7.5 percent. The true *conventional* aftertax yield is 4.79 percent, a discrepancy of 79 basis points. (See Exhibit 8.) For tax-exempts, it can be shown that the popular current yield approximation becomes highly inaccurate for the deeper discount bonds.[12]

3. *The conventional aftertax yields and yield spreads (even when computed exactly) can either overstate or understate or even reverse the actual dollars-and-cents relationship between two bonds.*

In a 48 percent, 48 percent tax structure, suppose a 25-year taxable 4 percent bond is offered at 7.5 percent, and a 25-year taxable new issue is offered at 8.125 percent. The conventional aftertax yields on the 4s is 4.19 percent, leading to a conventional taxable equivalent yield of 8.07 percent. Thus, by the conventional aftertax calculations, the 8.125 percent par bond appears to have a modest yield advantage over the 4s. Actually, at a 9 percent pretax reinvestment rate, using the opportunity yield approach, the 4s would be seen to equate to a 7.97 percent par bond, so that the choice of the par bond would actually lead to a more significant pickup of 16 basis points in effective par rate. On the other hand, at a 6 percent reinvestment rate, the 4s would equate to an 8.31 percent par bond, so that selecting the 8.125 percent par bond would lead to a *loss* of 18 basis points, or about $36,000 on a $1 million investment. (See Exhibit 9.) Even worse, suppose the 4s had been purchased earlier at 10 points below their current market value. Then a swap into the 8.125 percent par bond would actually entail a giveup of 90 basis points in terms of the opportunity par rate, or $175,000 over the next 25 years for each $1 million of net opportunity proceeds (see Exhibit 12).

---

[12] See Leibowitz, "Total Aftertax Bond Performance for Tax-Exempt Bonds Held in Taxable Portfolios," for the investment implications of tax exempts.

The conventional aftertax yields of tax-exempt bonds can also lead to similar important distortions of their investment relationship.

4. *Unlike the conventional yields, the opportunity yield and the opportunity par rate provide investment measures that will be consistent with the dollars-and-cents return to be received under specified portfolio and market conditions.*

The interaction of the effects of taxation, coupon reinvestment, realized and unrealized capital gains and losses, and market actions create quite a complex decision-making environment for the manager of a bond portfolio subject to taxation. The opportunity yield is designed to integrate these factors into a relatively simple and intuitive yardstick that can be readily benchmarked against the marketplace. The validity of the resulting measurements, of course, still depends totally on the validity of the assumptions relating to the portfolio and to market conditions. However, at least the role of these conditions becomes clearer through the need to make these assumptions explicit.

Although the opportunity yields and par rates can be computed manually, they do not represent trivial calculations when performed for large bond portfolios. However, with the assistance of modern computers, opportunity yields can be quickly and accurately determined. Moreover, the use of the computer permits the extension of the opportunity yield approach into the high payoff areas, such as various forms of swap analyses, determination of break-even yields, yield spread studies, loss recovery times, as well as the more complex cash flows resulting from sinking-fund bonds and mortgage-like securities.

5. *Discount bonds have an intrinsic aftertax advantage over par bonds priced at the same conventional pretax yield—even when capital gains are taxed at the same rate as coupon income.*

This is true for conventional aftertax yields and for realized compound yields at virtually any reasonable reinvestment rates. (See Exhibit 10.) Of course, this advantage may well be offset by the yield-spread relationships existing in the market at any given time.

6. *A portfolio with a large reservoir of unrealized losses relative to gains* and *the freedom to realize these losses can, up to a certain point, reduce its effective capital gains tax to 0 percent by offsetting gains with losses.*

No portfolio willingly seeks losses, but once they have occurred, they constitute a valuable resource for tax liability management.

7. *For portfolios with large, usable loss reservoirs, discount bonds with their locked-in capital gain have an even greater structural advantage.*

As always, for any given portfolio, this structural advantage must be evaluated in the context of existing market levels, spreads, and prospects.

8. *Taxation leads to a much greater erosion in dollars-and-cents return than is indicated by the magnitude of the tax rates or any of the aftertax yields.*

A 48 percent, 48 percent tax structure can lead to 65 percent reduction in total aftertax return of taxable bonds, while the conventional yields are reduced by only 48 percent. (See Exhibit 6.) Because of the very nature of the compounding process, the conventional aftertax yields of both taxable and tax-exempt bonds will not fully reflect this dollars-and-cents reduction.

9. *Any tax structure on income greatly reduces the incremental dollars-and-cents return from pure yield pickup swaps (no matter how accurately the yields are figured).*

Without taxes, a swap from a 25-year effective par rate of 7.5 percent to 8 percent would, on a $1 million investment amount to an increased return of $446,000 with reinvestment at a 9 percent rate. Under a 48 percent tax rate on coupon income and reinvestment, this same swap would only provide an additional return of $121,000, a reduction of more than 73 percent of the added return in the tax-free case.

10. *Income taxation renders pure yield pickup swaps far more vulnerable to adverse market moves in yields and/or yield spreads.*

Income taxation reduces the dollars-and-cents accumulation of benefits from pure yield pickup swaps. (See Exhibit 6.) At the same time, it aggravates the aftertax impact of an adverse yield move, particularly in those tax structures where capital gains are taxed at a lower rate than coupon income.

The following, although not demonstrated in this chapter, are other investment implications of the tools discussed in this chapter:[13]

1. *Short and intermediate discounts have a very special advantage, all else being equal, in taxed structures favoring capital gains.*
2. *In selecting potential sale candidates within the discount portion of a portfolio with a tax structure favoring capital gains, there is a strong incentive to focus on the longer maturity bonds.*
3. *The effective volatility of a taxable bond's net return under changes in yields and/or yield spreads is greatly enhanced by any tax structure favorable to capital gains.*

---

[13] See Martin L. Leibowitz, *Total After-Tax Bond Performance and Yield Measures.*

28

Horizon Analysis: An Analytical Framework for Managed Bond Portfolios*

Martin L. Leibowitz, Ph.D.
Managing Director
Bond Portfolio Analysis Group
Salomon Brothers Inc

The fundamental variables of the bond market are interest-rate levels, yield curves, and yield spread relationships. The changing structure of values among these variables forms the sources of investment return. However, as shown in *Inside the Yield Book*[1] and in Chapters 4 and 27 of this book, the conventional yields that the market quotes, observes, and tracks on an everyday basis are very different from the usual portfolio objective of total return. This chapter presents a simple analytic framework for relating the portfolio objective of total return over a given investment horizon to the sources of that return—the basic market variables of interest-rate levels, yield curves, and yield spread relationships. How *horizon analysis* can be applied to yield curve analysis and bond-swap analysis are discussed in Chapters 29 and 30, respectively.[2]

---

* This chapter draws from Martin L. Leibowitz, "Horizon Analysis: A New Analytic Framework for Managed Bond Portfolios," *The Journal of Portfolio Management* (Spring 1975); © Institutional Investor, Inc., 1975.

Although the information in this chapter has been obtained from sources that the author believes to be reliable, Salomon Brothers Inc cannot guarantee its accuracy, and such information may be incomplete or condensed. All opinions and estimates included in this chapter constitute judgment as of this date and are subject to change without notice.

[1] Sidney Homer and Martin L. Leibowitz, *Inside the Yield Book* (New York: published jointly by The New York Institute of Finance and Prentice-Hall, 1972).

[2] Horizon analysis turns out to have an interesting interpretation in terms of the swap classification system described in *Inside the Yield Book* and in Chapter 29 of this book. Using this framework, a given bond swap can be viewed, at each point in time, as a well-defined

THE MIDDLE GROUND OF BOND INVESTMENT

The full impact of the passage of time upon bond investment decisions is often overlooked.

Basically, two vantage points are common among bond market participants: the long view based on some measure of yield-to-maturity and the very short-term view with a primary focus on day-to-day price movements. Surprisingly few investors consistently explore investment horizons extending beyond the current calendar year but earlier than the shortest maturity bond under consideration. At the same time, the most comfortable projections of bond market relationships often imply workout periods extending beyond the immediate months ahead, but rarely further than a few years into the future. This middle ground "between tomorrow and maturity" offers a relatively unscrutinized arena for uncovering new relationships, new values, and consequently, fresh opportunities.

However, there are few convenient analytic tools to aid the investor who wishes to explore this middle ground. The conventional yield book really indicates the levels of return for holders to maturity, and even there, it has its limitations.[3] On the other hand, most studies of price volatility have really dealt with price and yield moves concentrated at a single instant in time. Relatively little has been done to explore the problem of a bond's volatility and return *over time*.

THE THREE BASIC SOURCES OF RETURN

A bond investment provides value from three basic sources—coupon income, interest-on-interest, and capital gains.

Coupon income is taken here to include coupon payments and any accrued interest received should the bond be sold prior to maturity.

Interest-on-interest is the return earned through reinvestment and

---

mixture of components from idealized swap categories. A given swap may thus have different quantifiable components reflecting the effects of pure yield pickup, rate anticipation, changing sector spreads, quality spreads, yield curve effects, and substitution relationships. This enables the bond portfolio manager to associate a proposed portfolio action with the primary sources of its expected return. The manager can then explore the vulnerabilities of this expected return over a range of feasible market conditions. By pursuing this route in a more formal fashion, he or she can begin to define and quantify the various dimensions of risk. Horizon analysis simplifies the computation of certain risk measures, such as break-even points for yield levels and yield spreads. It also suggests a role for "sensitivity ratios" to quantify the risk associated with each market force conflicting with the "target" factor motivating the swap. Horizon analysis also clarifies how the very passage of time leads to dramatic changes in risk structure. See "Horizon Analysis: A New Analytical Framework for Managed Bond Portfolios," *The Journal of Portfolio Management*, Spring 1975, for illustrations.

[3] See Chapter 4.

compounding of this coupon income. Since neither the vehicle nor the rates for this reinvestment process can be specified in advance, the level of accumulation of interest-on-interest is necessarily uncertain. However, interest-on-interest can account for more than 70 percent of the total return for a long-term bond and should therefore be included in every comprehensive evaluation of a bond investment. One convenient, although admittedly simplistic, approach is to assume the availability of a reinvestment rate that is constant over time. The impact of the uncertainty associated with reinvestment can then be explored by varying this rate assumption across some range of feasible values.

The capital gains component of return relates to the increase in the bond's market value. For tax-free portfolios, $1 of capital gains enters into the total return in as direct and as valuable fashion as $1 of coupon income or $1 of interest-on-interest.

These three components of total return apply to any investment medium. As a long-term investment vehicle, bonds are characterized by deriving a significant proportion of their *long-term* return from relatively predictable coupon and redemption flows together with the reinvestment of these flows. On the other hand, over short- and intermediate-term time periods, the more uncertain elements of the capital gain or loss can represent a much more significant proportion of the bond's total return. Consequently, these relatively predictable and relatively uncertain factors must be differentiated in order to develop a good handle on the bond's return over short- to intermediate-term investment horizons. As we shall see, this differentiation leads to an important refinement in the capital gains component.

THE GROWTH OF RETURN OVER TIME

As an example, consider a 10-year 4 percent bond purchased at a price of 67.48 for a conventional yield-to-maturity of 9 percent. One such bond would generate coupon income of $40 over the first year, $80 over a two-year period, and so on. Upon dividing these figures by the original purchase price of $674.80, the cumulative percentage return becomes

$$100 \text{ percent} \times (\$40/\$674.80) = 5.93 \text{ percent}$$

(i.e., just the bond's current yield) over the first year, 11.86 percent over a two-year period, and so forth, as shown in Exhibit 1.

Interest-on-interest results from the reinvestment and compounding of the $20 semiannual coupon payment at the assumed semiannual rate of 3.75 percent (i.e., 7.5 percent annually). For an investment horizon consisting of 10 semiannual compounding periods (i.e., five years), the compound interest tables show that each $1 of periodic payment would grow to a total future value of $11.868. This future value consists

EXHIBIT 1 Growth of Cumulative Percentage Return with Constant Yield Amortization (10-year 4 percent bond purchased at 67.48 for a yield-to-maturity of 9 percent)

	Cumulative Percentage Return			
Investment Horizon	Coupon Income	Interest-on-Interest (at 7.5 percent)	Accumulation Capital Gain	Total "Yield Accumulation" Return
0.0 Years	0.00%	0.00%	0.00%	0.00%
1.0	5.93	0.11	3.14	9.18
2.0	11.86	0.68	6.57	19.11
3.0	17.78	1.75	10.32	29.85
4.0	23.71	3.36	14.41	41.48
5.0	29.64	5.54	18.88	54.06
6.0	35.57	8.34	23.76	67.67
7.0	41.49	11.80	29.08	82.37
8.0	47.42	15.98	34.90	98.30
9.0	53.35	20.94	41.25	115.54
10.0	59.28	26.73	48.19	134.20

Note: Accumulation capital gains based on constant-yield ("scientific") amortization at 9 percent assumed reinvestment rate = 7.5 percent.

of the 10 payments plus the resulting interest-on-interest. Since the bond's semiannual payment is $20, the total future value for this example would be:

$$\$20 \times 11.868 = \$237.36$$

The pure interest-on-interest here is this future value less the 10 coupon payments totaling $200:

$$\$237.36 - \$200 = \$37.36$$

This is the interest-on-interest earned over the five-year investment horizon for each bond. To find the percentage figure shown in Exhibit 1, the above dollar amount must be divided by the cost per bond:

$$100 \text{ percent} \times (\$37.36/\$674.80) = 5.54 \text{ percent}$$

The third component of the bond's return, capital gains, cannot really be viewed solely in terms of some continuous process of growth. The capital gain component has two very different facets, and all bond market participants would be well advised to distinguish between them.

THE ACCUMULATION PORTION OF A BOND'S CAPITAL GAIN

A high-grade discount bond provides a specified capital gain over its life (presuming that there is no danger of default). However, this capital gain does not materialize in a flash at the bond's maturity. Rather it accrues in some fashion on a year-by-year basis throughout the bond's life. Consequently, at each point, prior to a discount bond's maturity, some portion of its capital gain must be attributed to an accretion process, which will ultimately bring the bond's price up to par at maturity. The nature of this *accumulation capital gain* makes it fundamentally different from the *market capital gain* derived through interest-rate movements.

Any formal scheme for distinguishing between these two facets of capital gain must necessarily contain arbitrary features. Nevertheless, as a practical method of analysis, one can make a useful distinction based upon the bond's conventional yield-to-maturity. *Accumulation capital gain* would then be defined as the price appreciation that would take place if the bond's yield-to-maturity remained constant throughout the investment period. Any deviation from this amortized price level can then be ascribed as the market changes affecting the bond's yield value.

Return now to the example of the 10-year 4 percent bond purchased at a 9 percent yield-to-maturity. At the end of a five-year horizon, the bond's remaining life would be five years. From the yield book, a five-year 4 percent bond at the "amortizing" yield of 9 percent would be priced at 80.218 (i.e., an accumulation capital gain of

$$\$802.18 - \$674.80 = \$127.38$$

per bond or a cumulative percentage of

$$100 \text{ percent} \times (\$127.38/\$674.80) = 18.88 \text{ percent}$$

Exhibit 1 shows how this accumulation capital gain grows over time.[4]

THE YIELD ACCUMULATION RETURN

By adding this accumulation capital gain component to the coupon income and interest-on-interest, one obtains an approximate measure of the bond's accumulating return which is *relatively* free from the uncertainties of day-to-day movements in market rates. Consequently, this sum may be called the yield accumulation return.

Exhibit 1 shows how the yield accumulation return and its components grow over longer and longer investment horizons. In the early

---

[4] This constant-yield amortization might, at first, appear to be related to the so-called "scientific amortization" technique used for writing up the book value of a bond purchased at a discount. However, the resemblance is superficial on many counts. Basically, our intent here is to analyze projected market prices at future horizons, and the purpose of scientific amortization is to provide a consistent accounting treatment over portfolio holding periods presumed to cover the bond's remaining life. Thus scientific amortization is always based upon the bond's yield at the time of its original purchase. On the other hand, our accumulation capital gain is based upon the bond's yield at the point of investment decision—which is always *today*.

years, the coupon income provides almost twice as much return as the accumulation capital gain; and the interest-on-interest component is virtually negligible at the outset. As the investment horizon lengthens, the coupon income maintains its constant pace, the interest-on-interest grows in the expected fashion, and the capital gain provides an ever-increasing contribution.

Exhibit 2 provides a clearer view of these growth patterns. Each column here represents the increment to the cumulative percentage re-

EXHIBIT 2 Annual Increments to Cumulative Percentage Return with Constant-Yield Amortization (10-year 4 percent bond purchased at 67.48 for a yield-to-maturity of 9 percent

For Annual Period Ending after	Annual Increment to Cumulative Percentage Return			
	Coupon Income	Interest-on-Interest (at 7.5 percent)	Accumulation Capital Gain	Total "Yield Accumulation" Return
1st Year	5.93%	0.11%	3.14%	9.18%
2nd	5.93	0.57	3.43	9.93
3rd	5.93	1.07	3.75	10.74
4th	5.93	1.61	4.09	11.63
5th	5.93	2.18	4.47	12.58
6th	5.93	2.80	4.88	13.61
7th	5.93	3.46	5.32	14.70
8th	5.93	4.18	5.82	15.93
9th	5.93	4.96	6.35	17.21
10th	5.93	5.79	6.94	18.66
Total	59.28%	26.73%	48.19%	134.20%

Note: Accumulation capital gains based on constant-yield ("scientific") amortization at 9 percent assumed reinvestment rate = 7.5 percent.

turn resulting from extending the investment horizon by one additional year. In particular, it is interesting to note how the accumulation capital gain grows to the point of becoming the largest source of incremental return in the last two years of the bond's life.

It should be noted that the key yardstick is the *cumulative* percentage return (i.e., the net gain in future value represented as a percentage of the current investment base). For various reasons, we have decided to use the cumulative total return figures throughout rather than to translate them into the corresponding annualized *rates* of return.

THE "MARKET" PORTION OF A BOND'S CAPITAL GAIN

The yield accumulation return captures a bond's total return as long as there are no changes in the conventional yield-to-maturity. However, as we know, there are *constant changes* in interest rates, in the relationship between different market sectors, and in the precise relative value attached to individual securities. Apart from all of these factors, a specific bond's character and its role in the general fixed-interest market change with just the simple passage of time. For all these reasons, the investor must carefully study the effects of bond price and yield movements and their contribution to total return.

As it is buffeted by all the dynamics of the marketplace, a bond's actual price may weave many strange patterns over time. However, once a given investment horizon has been selected, there are only two prices that matter for purposes of computing the bond's capital gain over that period—the starting price and the ending price.

Returning to the earlier example of a 10-year, 4 percent bond, Exhibit 3 illustrates a possible price pattern across the page on an abbrevi-

---

EXHIBIT 3   An Abbreviated Yield Book for 4 Percent Bonds Showing How a Bond's Price Movement Can Be Represented as a Constant-Yield Accumulation over Time Plus an Instantaneous Future Yield Move

Yield-to-Maturity	10 Years	9 Years	. . .	5 Years	. . .	1 Years	0 Years
7.00%	78.68	80.22		87.53		97.15	100.00
7.50	75.68	77.39		85.63		96.69	100.00
8.00	72.82	74.68		83.78		96.23	100.00
8.50	70.09	72.09		81.98		95.77	100.00

Actual price pattern over time   Market capital gain

9.00	67.48	69.60		80.22		95.32	100.00

Accumulation capital gain

9.50	64.99	67.22		78.51		94.87	100.00
10.00	62.61	64.92		76.83		94.42	100.00
10.50	60.34	62.74		75.21		93.98	100.00
11.00	58.17	60.64		73.62		93.54	100.00

---

ated yield book. Starting at its purchase price of 67.48 when the bond has a life of 10 years, Exhibit 3 shows the price varying over time and finally winding up five years later at 83.78, resulting in a total capital gain of

$$83.78 - 67.48 = 16.30$$

points, or a cumulative percentage capital gain of

$$100 \text{ percent} \times (16.30/67.48) = 24.16 \text{ percent}$$

Now in determining this bond's yield accumulation return of 54.06 percent over these 5 years, a process of constant-yield amortization was assumed. As shown in Exhibit 3, this amortization process is tantamount to a hypothetical lateral movement across the "9 percent row" in the yield book. Over the five-year investment horizon, this hypothetical amortization process would, by itself, carry the bond's price to 80.22. There, of course, remains the price gap of 3.56 points between this amortized price and the bond's actual price of 83.78. This gap could be theoretically ascribed to a sudden (in fact, a hypothetically instantaneous) jump in yields carrying the bond's price from 80.22 *up* the five-year column to its actual price level of 83.78.

This example can, of course, be generalized. Any price movement over a specified horizon can be theoretically represented as the result of a simple two-step process: (1) a constant-yield amortization over the horizon period (i.e., a lateral movement across one row in the yield book), and (2) an instantaneous yield change taking place at *the end of the investment horizon period* (i.e., a vertical movement up or down one column in the yield book).

Obviously, this two-step representation will *not* provide an accurate description of how the price movement actually took place over time. However, it will provide a mathematically correct result for the total capital gains contribution resulting from any given actual price movement.

The big advantage of this two-step model is that it clearly differentiates the two facets of a bond's capital gain. The first step corresponds to the accumulation capital gain accruing as a result of the passage of time and the bond's consequent march toward its maturity date. The second step corresponds to the effects of any change in the bond's yield. Since most market participants associate such yield changes with market actions, this portion of capital gain component may be referred to as the *market capital gain.*

In terms of cumulative percentage return, the market capital gain is simply added to the yield accumulation return to find the total return. For the example illustrated by price movement in Exhibit 3, the market capital gain of

$$100 \text{ percent } (3.56/67.48) = 5.28 \text{ percent}$$

can be added to the five-year yield accumulation return of 54.06 percent shown in Exhibit 1 to obtain the total cumulative return of 59.34 percent.

With this approach, the total returns can easily be computed over a range of possible yield moves. Exhibit 4 provides such a presentation for yield moves of −100, 0, and +100 basis points by the end of each investment horizon.

EXHIBIT 4 Growth of Cumulative Percentage Return with Market Yield Moves (10-year 4 percent bond purchased at 67.48 for a yield-to-maturity of 9 percent)

Investment Horizon	Total Yield Accumulation Return	Percentage Return from Market Capital Gain Given Yield Move of			Total Cumulative Percentage Return Given Yield Move of		
		−100 B.P.	0 B.P.	+100 B.P.	−100 B.P.	0 B.P.	+100 B.P.
0 years	0%	7.91%	0%	−7.21%	7.91%	0%	−7.21%
1	9.18	7.53	0	−6.92	16.71	9.18	2.26
2	19.11	7.09	0	−6.56	26.20	19.11	12.55
3	29.85	6.57	0	−6.13	36.42	29.85	23.72
4	41.48	5.97	0	−5.62	47.45	11.48	35.86
5	54.06	5.27	0	−5.02	59.33	54.06	49.04
6	67.67	4.48	0	−4.30	72.15	67.67	63.37
7	82.37	3.57	0	−3.46	85.94	82.37	78.91
8	98.30	2.53	0	−2.47	100.83	98.30	95.83
9	115.54	1.34	0	−1.33	116.88	115.54	114.21
10	134.20	0	0	0	134.20	134.20	134.20

Note: Total yield accumulation return based on 7.5 percent reinvestment rate and constant-yield amortization at 9 percent.

MEASURES OF VOLATILITY

Over short-term investment horizons, price changes can often overwhelm all other sources of return. Exhibit 4 illustrates this effect. Every bond market participant needs some sort of handy guide for linking the market yield movements (which he or she follows) to the resulting bond price changes (which he or she feels).

Many practitioners use various simple rules of thumb, for example, "a 10-basis-point move in a 30-year bond corresponds to 1⅜ point change." One of the problems with such rules of thumb is that they tend to become dangerously inaccurate in today's dynamic marketplace. The rule just cited, for example, is really correct only at a 6 percent yield level.

In *Inside the Yield Book* and in Chapter 4 of this book, a series of tabulations were developed to illustrate how the percentage price volatility increased with (1) increasing maturity, (2) higher yield levels, and (3) lower coupon rates. A given bond's volatility was also shown to depend upon the direction and magnitude of the yield move.

Many key aspects of these volatility relationships can be read directly from the pages of the yield book itself. For example, Exhibit 3 shows that a five-year, 4 percent bond with a 9 percent yield carries a price of 80.22. As observed above, a yield decline to 8 percent would result in a price use of

$$83.78 - 80.22 = 3.56$$

points or

$$100 \text{ percent } (3.56/80.22) = 4.44 \text{ percent}$$

relative to the starting price of 80.22. On the other hand, an increase in yield to the 10 percent level results in a price decline of

$$80.22 - 76.83 = 3.39$$

points, or a percentage drop of

$$100 \text{ percent } (3.39/80.22) = 4.23 \text{ percent.}$$

In other words, an upward yield move leads to a somewhat smaller percentage price change than a downward yield move of the same magnitude.

Exhibit 3 illustrates another aspect of price volatility. Suppose the yield of the five-year, 4 percent bond dropped to 8.5 percent. This would lead to a percentage change of

$$100 \text{ percent } \times \left(\frac{81.98 - 80.22}{80.22} \right) = 2.19 \text{ percent.}$$

Dividing this figure by the 50 basis points of yield move, one gets a value of

$$\frac{2.19 \text{ percent}}{50 \text{ B.P.}} = .0439 \text{ percent/B.P.}$$

as the percentage price change per basis-point move. Upon comparing this value with the .0444 percent B.P. obtained with a move of −100 basis points, we further see that it is not possible to *precisely* determine percentage price changes by multiplying the yield move by some constant volatility factor (i.e., each yield move would correspond to a different value for this volatility factor.)

At the same time, this volatility factor approach can provide a fairly close approximation to percentage price changes across a range of different yield moves. For example, averaging the percentage price changes for yield moves of −100 basis points and +100 basis points leads to a figure of

$$\tfrac{1}{2} \times (4.44) \text{ percent } + \tfrac{1}{2} \times (4.23) \text{ percent } = 4.33 \text{ percent}$$

or an average volatility factor of .0433 percent per basis-point move. By applying this average factor to the yield move from 9 percent to 8.5 percent, the approximate percentage price change is found to be

$$-0.433 \text{ percent/B.P. } \times (-50 \text{ B.P.}) = +2.17 \text{ percent}$$

that is, fairly close to the exact value of 2.19 percent found above.

Now there are a number of more sophisticated techniques for finding volatility factors. One such technique is based on the concept of *duration* introduced by Macaulay in 1938.[5] A bond's duration is the weighted average life of all its coupon and principal payments, where the weighting factors consist of present values of each payment. As a measure of average life, duration has many advantages over conventional techniques that only consider principal repayments and even then ignore the time value of different repayment dates. It turns out that, with a simple adjustment, a bond's duration provides a very useful indication of the bond's price volatility. In fact, for small yield moves the (adjusted) duration provides a mathematically *exact* volatility factor.

However, for most investors, Duration is not the easiest thing to compute. For our expository purposes here, the simple average of up and down moves of 100 basis points provides adequate volatility factors. As we shall see, even these approximate volatility factors can fulfill a valuable function in relating projected market movements to the total return expected from different sectors of the bond market. When fine tuning is needed in these computations, there are various computer programs available that can refine the results by incorporating the exact percentage price change associated with each projected yield move.

THE HORIZON VOLATILITY FACTOR

As with most discussions of price volatility, the preceding section focused on *instantaneous* price changes. However, when one wants to determine a bond's total return over an extended investment horizon, then the concept of price volatility must itself be extended beyond the immediate moment. We must proceed from instantaneous volatility to the idea of a *volatility over time*.

This idea of a volatility over time can actually be incorporated quite simply into our two-step representation of capital gains. In this model, all price movements derived from yield changes are relegated to the market capital gain component. Recalling Exhibit 3, all such market price changes are treated *as if* they occurred at the end of the investment horizon. Moreover, they are treated *as if* they began from a future price level obtained through a constant-yield amortization process.

For example, we just found an instantaneous percentage price change of 4.44 percent for a five-year, 4 percent bond moving from 9 percent to 8 percent. However, this percentage price change was measured relative to an investment base of 80.22 (i.e., the price corresponding to a 9 percent yield level for the five-year bond). For the investment problem analyzed in Exhibit 4, the original investment base is the 10-year bond's starting price of 67.48. Over a five-year investment horizon,

---

[5] Duration is discussed in Chapters 4 and 5.

the constant-yield amortization would carry the bond to a price of 80.22. At this point five years hence, a *future* yield move from the 9 percent to the 8 percent level would then produce the price move of

$$83.78 - 80.22 = 3.56$$

points. In terms of points of price, this move is identical to that generated by the same *instantaneous* yield move in a five-year bond. However, as we noted, the investment base is different in these two cases. Suppose we wished to make use of the five-year bond's instantaneous percentage price change of 4.44 percent to help determine the market capital gain return for the 10-year bond over a five-year horizon. Then the investment base must be shifted from the amortized price of 80.22 "backward" to the original price of 67.48. Multiplying the instantaneous percentage price change by the ratio of the two prices will achieve this backward translation, that is,

$$100 \text{ percent} \times (3.56/67.48) = 100 \text{ percent} \times \frac{3.56}{80.22} \times \frac{80.22}{67.48}$$
$$= 4.44 \text{ percent} \times (80.22/67.48)$$
$$= 4.44 \text{ percent} \times (1.1888)$$
$$= 5.28 \text{ percent}$$

This figure coincides with the market capital gain return shown in Exhibit 4 for a −100 basis point yield move over a five-year horizon.

The price ratio used in the above translation, 1.1888, can also be expressed as

$$\frac{100 \text{ percent} + 18.88 \text{ percent}}{100 \text{ percent}}$$

where 18.88 percent is the accumulation capital gain return shown in Exhibit 1 for the five-year horizon. This result can be generalized. The accumulation capital gain return over any horizon period can be used to translate an instantaneous percentage price change at the horizon backward into a figure for the market capital gain return.

Moreover, any measure of instantaneous price *volatility* can be translated backward over an investment horizon in exactly the same manner to obtain a volatility factor for the market capital gain. To differentiate it from the instantaneous volatilities, this figure will be referred to as the *horizon volatility*. As a numerical example, the simple average instantaneous volatility figure of .0433 percent per basis-point move, computed above for the five-year bond, translates into a horizon volatility of

$$\left(\frac{100 \text{ percent} + 18.88 \text{ percent}}{100 \text{ percent}}\right) \times .0433 \text{ percent/B.P.}$$
$$= (1.1888) \times .0433 \text{ percent/B.P.}$$
$$= .0515 \text{ percent/B.P.}$$

Referring to the five-year horizon in Exhibit 4, this horizon volatility of .0515 percent/B.P. would approximate market capital gain resulting from a minus or plus 100 basis-point yield move by plus or minus 5.15 percent, compared with the actual figures of 5.27 percent and −5.02 percent.

The accumulation capital gain is thus seen to act as a magnifier of the instantaneous volatility at the end of the horizon period. Generally speaking, for discount bonds, this effect will boost the horizon volatility above the instantaneous volatility value. Consequently, the longer the horizon period and the larger the accumulation capital gain, the greater will be this magnification effect. On the other hand, for premium bonds, the accumulation capital gain will, of course, be negative, and the horizon volatility will be smaller than the instantaneous volatility, whose own value shrinks with increasing horizon and the consequent shorter maturity.

These volatility factors can also be expressed in terms of the more dramatic scale of "basis points of price move per basis point of yield move." For example, the preceding volatility factor of .0515 percent/B.P. could be restated as 5.15 B.P./B.P., meaning that each basis point of yield move produces approximately 5.15 basis points of incremental return.

The great advantage of the horizon volatility is that it enables a bond's return over a given horizon to be characterized by two readily computed numbers: (1) a yield accumulation return, which depends only upon the selected reinvestment rate, and (2) a horizon volatility factor, from which market capital gain figures can be quickly approximated across any range or combination of projected yield moves.

29

Bond Swaps

Christina Seix, C.F.A.
Director of Bond Management
MacKay-Shields Financial Corporation

Horizon analysis is a sound analytical framework for bond-swap decisions. In volatile markets, it is more important than ever to focus on the sources of expected benefits from a proposed swap and thus identify its potential vulnerabilities. The purpose of this chapter is to present several bond transactions that are common in today's market and to analyze them within the framework of *horizon analysis* (discussed in Chapter 28).

GENERAL COMMENTS

The bond market has undergone a profound change over recent years. Bond prices, which fluctuated in an average daily range of $\pm\frac{1}{16}$ point prior to November 1978, now average $\pm\frac{1}{2}$ to $\pm\frac{3}{4}$ point on a typical trading day. In the past, volatility would heighten as the market was approaching a cyclical turn in interest rates. Currently, whether the market is close to a cyclical turning point or not, managing bond assets is a treacherous exercise. Not only has the market's volatility increased, but many of the key determinants of interest-rate behavior have changed. Interest-rate cycles in the past, for example, were very much related to the disintermediation process in the banking and thrift industries. With recent innovations in the banking system, some of the old barometers are less effective in determining interest-rate pressures.

Monitoring the federal funds rate to gauge the intentions of the Federal Reserve Board has become considerably less important than measuring actual "money" growth. And defining *money* or *transactions balances* in today's economy, which is the commodity whose price we are interested in forecasting, has become a near impossible feat.

The adjustment to this new market has brought with it subtle changes in professional bond management. Among the most apparent are: a general shortening of the performance measurement period (horizon period), larger required-return expectations for executing a given swap, and in some cases, larger percentage moves into and out of the market. That is, a 1- to 2-year measurement period has become more prevalent than the 5- to 10-year horizons of the past. The expected portfolio improvement of holding one bond versus another has to be more significant than in the past to generate a swap action.

Finally, market actions entailing 1 or 2 percent of the portfolio have generally been replaced by 3 and 5 percent commitments. Each of these subtle changes is management's response to the new level of price volatility in today's bond market. A general resetting of priorities in the professional manager's portfolio activities has been an outgrowth of this new environment.

PREPARATION FOR ANALYSIS

One thing that has not changed over this period is the proper measure of portfolio performance. In 1966 The Bank Administration Institute published a comprehensive study on performance measurement that concluded that *total return* was the best measure of overall portfolio growth. Total return is the sum of all investment income plus changes in capital values in a portfolio. It continues to be the critical measure of portfolio improvement.

Moreover, the *realized compound yield* of a specific bond, which is the direct analogy to total return of an entire portfolio, continues to be the best yardstick for a bond-swap decision. This measure was defined in *Inside the Yield Book* by Sidney Homer and Martin L. Leibowitz and is explained in Chapters 4 and 27 of the *Handbook*.

Bond performance has always been determined by three basic factors: (1) position on the *yield curve*, (2) *sector* of the market, and (3) *quality* of the securities held. As of late, position on the yield curve has vastly overridden the other two factors in determining performance. Nevertheless, bond portfolio managers are continually faced with swap decisions involving all three factors. Maintaining a solid analytical framework for day-to-day portfolio decisions is critical during these hectic times. Horizon analysis, as defined in Chapter 28, provides precisely such a framework.

To use horizon analysis, the portfolio manager needs no more information than the standard tools already at hand to manage bond portfolios, namely:

1. Time frame for measuring results (horizon).
2. Today's market levels.

3. Forecast of yield curve (at end of horizon).
4. Forecast of sector spreads (at end of horizon).
5. Forecast of quality spreads (at end of horizon).

It is important to notice that interest-rate projections must be made, implicitly or explicitly, by the bond manager whether or not horizon analysis is to be used. These projections should be internally consistent with an overall economic forecast.

APPLICATION OF HORIZON ANALYSIS TO BOND SWAPS

For ease of classification, we will use the swap types identified in *Inside the Yield Book*.

Applying horizon analysis to the idea of exchanging one bond for another requires that we subdivide our expected return from each bond into three *basic* sources: (1) coupon interest, (2) interest-on-interest, and (3) principal change (from accumulation plus market changes). In the two swap illustrations that follow, a one-year time horizon is assumed. Therefore, the effect of interest-on-interest and the accumulation part of the principal change will be minor.[1]

Intermarket Spread Swap

The motivation on an intermarket spread swap is to take advantage of changing yield spread relationships between various segments of the bond market. Market segments can be differentiated by quality (e.g., Aa versus A public utilities), type of issuer (GNMA versus Treasury), coupon rate, and so on.

The following assumptions are made for the purpose of illustrating an intermarket spread swap:

1. The time horizon is one year.
2. The bond to be sold is a U.S. Treasury bond with a 14⅞ percent coupon rate maturing August 15, 1991, selling at 99.834 to yield 14.9 percent.[2]
3. The bond to be purchased is Texas Eastern Transmission (utility with an A rating) with a 17 percent coupon rate maturing October 1, 1991, selling at 100.929 to yield 16.8 percent.

---

[1] The one-year time horizon is used here for illustrative purposes. This period could be shortened to a calendar quarter (three months) or lengthened to a full interest-rate cycle (approximately four to five years).

[2] The market prices used in the illustrations in this chapter are those that prevailed on September 18, 1981.

4. The projected yield for the two bonds one year hence is 11.75 percent for the Treasury bond and 13.38 percent for the utility.

This swap proposal suggests that we move out of the government sector and into the single A utility sector to take advantage of relatively wide quality and sector spreads that prevail in the current market.

We apply the tools established above in a *horizon analysis* framework as shown in Exhibit 1. This allows us to assess the sources of benefit from holding the Treasuries versus holding the utilities. It further identifies where we may be vulnerable given our projections, if we consummate the transaction.

Horizon analysis clearly reveals the sources of return in this swap. How important is our interest-rate forecast in choosing one bond over the other? In this case, the expected decline in rates only provides a 45-basis-point increment in total return. Spread narrowing between the utility and Treasury sectors helped to a small extent. But the return is improved by 19 basis points, close to 2 percent, by being in one sector of the market versus another. Credit analysis, that is, comfort with A utilities and Texas Eastern in particular, is the focal point for this swap and its main vulnerability. If this issue defaults or if the yield on single A utilities widens significantly versus Treasuries, this swap would hurt portfolio performance. If rates remain the initial level, or even rise further from this point, the difference in total return will still be overwhelmingly governed by the initial differential in coupon income.

Rate Anticipation Swap

In a rate anticipation swap, the portfolio manager designs a swap to protect or benefit from projected changes in market yields. For example, if interest rates are expected to rise (fall), the portfolio manager will shorten (lengthen) maturities.

The following assumptions are made for the purpose of illustrating a rate anticipation swap:

1. The time horizon is one year.
2. The bond to be sold is a U.S. Treasury bond with a 13⅞ percent coupon rate maturing May 15, 2001, selling at 97.358 to yield 14.25 percent.
3. The bond to be purchased is a U.S. Treasury bond with a 16¼ percent coupon maturing August 31, 1983, selling at 100.378 to yield 16 percent.
4. The initial and projected interest rates for U.S. Treasury obligations are given on page 652.

EXHIBIT 1 Intermarket Spread Swap (total return at end of one-year horizon)

Bond	Coupon Income	Interest on Interest at 14 Percent Reinvestment Rate	Accumulation Capital Gain	Total Yield Accumulation Return	Percentage Return from "Market" Capital Gain	Total Return
Sell:						
U.S. Treasury 14⅞ percent 8–15–91 at 14.90 percent/99.834	14.90%	.52%	.01%	15.43%	17.14%	32.57%
Buy:						
Texas Eastern Transmission 17 percent 10–1–91 (A utility) at 16.80 percent/100.929	16.84%	.59%	–.04%	17.39%	17.59%	34.98%
Basis point differential in return	194 b.p.	7 b.p.	–5 b.p.	196 b.p.	45 b.p.	241 b.p.

Computations:	S Bond		P Bond	
	Dollar Return	Percent Return*	Dollar Return	Percent Return*
Initial price	$ 99.834	—	$100.929	—
Projected price	116.952	—	118.645	—
Capital gain (loss)	17.118	17.15%	17.716	17.55%
Portion due to accumulation	.006	.01	–.042	–.04
Portion due to change in market yield	17.112	17.14	17.758	17.59
Coupon interest	14.875	14.90	17.000	16.84
Interest on interest at 14 percent	.521	.52	.595	.59
Total return	$ 32.514	32.57%	$ 35.291	34.98%

* Percent return is derived by dividing each dollar return by the initial price.

EXHIBIT 2 Rate-Anticipation Swap (total return at end of one-year horizon)

Bond	Coupon Income	Interest on Interest at 14 Percent Reinvestment Rate	Accumulation Capital Gain	Total Yield Accumulation Return	Percentage Return from "Market" Capital Gain	Total Return
Sell: U.S. Treasury 13⅞ percent 5-15-11 at 14.25 percent/97.358	14.25%	.50%	.01%	14.76%	18.14%	32.90%
Buy: U.S. Treasury 16¼ percent 8-31-83 at 16 percent/100.378	16.19%	.57%	-.19%	16.57%	5.08%	21.65%
Basis point differential in return	194 b.p.	7 b.p.	-20 b.p.	181 b.p.	-1306 b.p.	-1125 b.p.

Computations:	S Bond		P Bond	
	Dollar Return	Percent Return*	Dollar Return	Percent Return*
Initial price	$ 97.358	—	$100.378	—
Projected price	115.026	—	105.289	—
Capital gain (loss)	17.668	18.15%	4.911	4.89%
Portion due to accumulation	.007	.01	-.193	-.19
Portion due to change in market yield	17.661	18.14	5.104	5.08
Coupon interest	13.875	14.25	16.250	16.19
Interest on interest at 14 percent	.486	.50	.569	.57
Total return	$ 32.029	32.90%	$ 21.730	21.65%

* Percent return is derived by dividing each dollar return by the initial price.

Time to Maturity	Initial	Projected (one year hence)
3 months	15.10%	10.00%
1 year	16.00	10.25
2 years	16.00	10.50
10 years	14.90	11.25
30 years	14.25	12.00

This swap proposal is a move to shorten maturity in order to pick up yield. In a very inverted yield curve environment, it is sometimes argued that when interest rates finally decline, the "snap-down" effect of the yield curve moving to a positive slope may result in better performance from shorter maturities. Exhibit 2 shows the performance of each bond, over a 12-month horizon, given our earlier projections.

The results of this *horizon analysis* clearly show that regardless of the 300-basis-point aggregate shift in the yield curve from a negative to positive slope, the overall decline in interest rates is the critical determinant of the success of the swap. Shortening maturity results in a healthy yield pickup of 181 basis points of income for the year, but this effect is dwarfed by the 1306-basis-point increase in total return that results from the capital gain on the longer maturity instrument.

The vulnerability of this swap is obviously the case where rates decline substantially. On the other hand, if interest rates remain at these levels or trend higher, the give up in total return from not consummating the swap is at least 200 basis points of current yield.

Other Swaps

In the two illustrations cited above, *horizon analysis* has been used to clearly identify the sources of return from different fixed income securities. Homer and Leibowitz have categorized bond swaps into four different types including pure yield pickup swaps, substitution swaps, and the two discussed above (intermarket spread swaps and rate-anticipation swaps). In pure yield pickup swaps, the portfolio manager has no expectations of market changes but is simply interested in increasing yield. In substitution swaps, the portfolio manager swaps from one bond into a similar bond (in terms of quality, coupon, and maturity) when the yield spread inducement exists. The aberration is a result of temporary market imbalances and is expected to reverse itself at some future time.

Although in this chapter we have only analyzed intermarket-spread swaps and rate-anticipation swaps within the context of *horizon analysis*, all swaps can easily be viewed within this framework.

SUMMARY

As the bond market continues to undergo massive shifts in composition, volatility, and overriding fundamentals, it is useful to have a solid analytical framework upon which to base swap decisions. *Horizon analysis* is precisely such a tool.

30

Analysis of Yield Curves*

Martin L. Leibowitz, Ph.D.
Managing Director
Bond Portfolio Analysis Group
Salomon Brothers Inc

THE YIELD CURVE

The traditional "yield curve" plots the yields of fixed income securities against their respective maturities. When the securities plotted are comparable in quality and structure, then the resulting yield curve depicts the available trade-off between yield and maturity. Exhibit 1 illustrates a yield curve for Treasury securities.[1]

The yield curve has many different applications as an investment tool. Some market participants study the yield curve for clues to the market forces acting in the different maturity arenas. Some search for historical analogues by comparing the curve's current shape with similar patterns obtained in the past. Some view the yield curve as reflecting the consensus expectations of the marketplace, and they use mathematical techniques to extract these implicit forecasts. Some gauge the relative value of individual securities by comparing their yield/maturity position relative to current and past yield curves. Many investment managers try to forecast the changing shape of the yield curve so that they can then position their portfolio for maximum performance. Other participants

---

* Reprinted from *Bond Analysis and Selection: The Proceedings of a Seminar on Bond Portfolio Management*, (Charlottesville, Va.: Financial Analysts Research Federation, 1977) pp. 1–21. (Adaptations made by the editors of the *Handbook* with permission of the author.)

[1] The yield curve used in the illustration is that which prevailed on March 29, 1977, for Treasury securities.

EXHIBIT 1 The U.S. Treasury Yield Curve

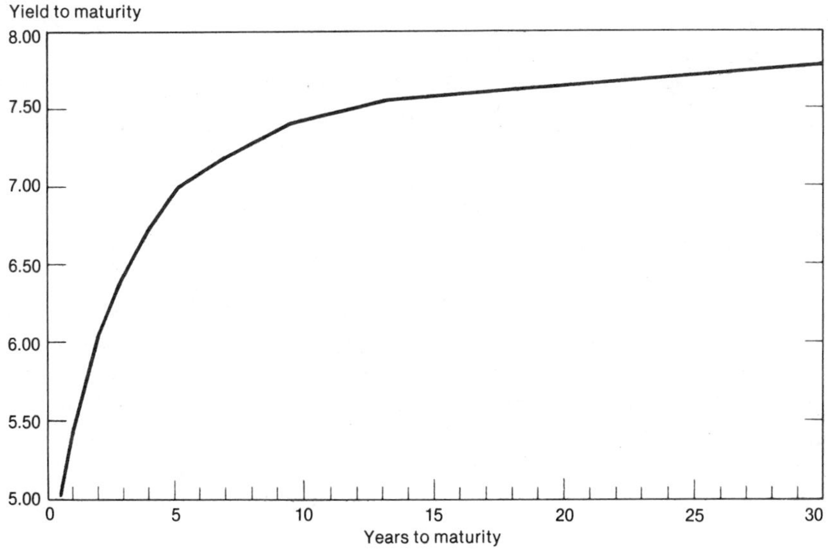

try to find "elbows" in the yield curve, *i.e.*, maturity areas which they consider to represent the most attractive short-term investment.

THE YIELD CURVE AS A RETURN/RISK TRADE-OFF

The most widespread use of the yield curve is probably the one mentioned at the outset—a portrayal of the available trade-off between yield and maturity. In other words, the yield curve indicates how much additional yield can be obtained in exchange for each extension in maturity.

The basic investment problem in any market always comes down to an evaluation of the trade-off between return and risk. Since yield is a measure of total return, and since maturity is closely associated with price volatility, there is a natural temptation to accept the yield curve as depicting this return/risk trade-off. Unfortunately, this interpretation is seriously faulty on several counts.

First of all, there are a number of problems in equating maturity with risk. Maturity is not the only variable determining mathematical price volatility.[2] Price volatility is not the sole determinant of the volatility of return. And volatility of return over short-term periods is not the

---

[2] For a discussion of the factors that affect bond price volatility, see Chapters 4 and 5 on duration.

only (or perhaps even the primary) risk element for many bond portfolios.

With regard to equating yield with return, there is an even more fundamental problem. The concept of total return must refer to a specific investment horizon. Apart from the questions regarding coupon reinvestment,[3] a bond's conventional yield-to-maturity can be used to represent its total return—but only over an investment period coincident with the bond's remaining life.[4] The yield curve, by its very nature, consists of yields over different maturities. Since they do not refer to a common investment horizon, these yield values are not directly comparable as total returns.

As an example, consider a one-year note with a yield of 6 percent and a two-year note with a yield of 7 percent. Over a one-year investment horizon, the one-year, 6 percent note will indeed provide a total return of approximately 6 percent. However, over this same one-year period, the total return provided by the two-year note will depend greatly on its price at year end. At that point, it will be a one-year security, and its price will then be set by the level of one-year yields. As these yields range from 5 percent to 10 percent, the note's total return will range anywhere from 4.29 percent to 8.85 percent. One can see that these total return values can depart widely from the original 7 percent yield level. In fact, the two-year note will provide a 7 percent total return over a one-year period only if one-year rates are 7 percent one year hence. In turn, this would require one-year rates to rise by 100 basis points over the course of the year.

Extrapolating from this example, the total return provided by any security on the yield curve can thus be seen to depend on the yield curve that will prevail at the end of the investment horizon.

HORIZON ANALYSIS APPLIED TO THE YIELD CURVE

Since no one can predict future yield curves with certainty, there is a corresponding uncertainty in the total returns from any security on the yield curve. However, portfolio managers must come to grips with this uncertainty in one way or another. At the very least, they must be able to translate their market judgment(s) into the corresponding total return implications for the various maturity sectors along the yield curve. The technique of "horizon analysis" can prove helpful in this translation process.

Essentially, horizon analysis distinguishes the return achieved un-

---

[3] See Chapter 4 for a discussion of interest-on-interest and its role in computing the total return of a bond.

[4] See Chapter 4 for a discussion of the difference between a promised yield and a realized yield.

der "nominal market conditions" from the return achieved by departures from these nominal conditions. In Chapter 28, the nominal condition was defined to be that of "constant yield over time." Recalling the example of a two-year note with a yield of 7 percent, this "constant-yield" condition would imply a total return of 7 percent over a one-year horizon. If one-year rates actually fell to 6 percent, i.e., 1 percent below the nominal 7 percent level, then the total return would become 7.92 percent. In fact, for every basis point that one-year rates at the horizon fell below the nominal 7 percent level, the total return will be boosted by approximately .92 basis points. This volatility factor of .92 is called the horizon volatility.

There are several advantages in being able to break down prospective return into a "nominal-condition" return plus a return component derived through a "departure-from-the-nominal-condition." First of all, one can distinguish the returns derived through the passage of time from the return achieved through market movements. In fact, by using the horizon volatility factor, changes in market yields can be immediately translated into changes in total return. In the context of a bond or sector swap,[5] horizon analysis allows the swap's incremental return to be decomposed into three basic components:

1. A pure yield pickup component, resulting from the accumulation of the original yields over time, independent of any market changes.
2. A rate anticipation component dependent on the change in overall market levels as magnified by an increase in the horizon volatilities of the two bonds (or sectors).
3. A spread component, determined solely by the changing yield spread relationships between the two bonds or sectors.

In other words, horizon analysis facilitates the manager's ability to relate his judgment regarding conventional market variables—yields, yield spreads, and the changes in yields and yield spreads over time—to total return performance. This structuring also enables the manager to clearly see the effect of departures from his primary expectations, and this can assist in evaluating the nature and magnitude of the risks associated with a contemplated course of action.

It would be most helpful if a simple structuring, along the lines of horizon analysis, could be made applicable to the yield curve.

However, at the outset, the preceding method runs into a problem with its use of the constant yield as a nominal market condition. The very nature of yield curve implies some change in a bond's yield with the passage of time. Consequently, the constant-yield approach must be

---

[5] A sector swap is discussed in Chapter 29.

revised before horizon analysis can even begin to be usefully applied to the yield curve.

The problem is to find a reasonable, convenient, and well-defined yield structure that can serve as a benchmark for nominal market conditions at the end of the investment horizon. There are a number of candidates for this nominal yield structure—the existing yield curve, the implied "forward" yield curve, the individual manager's expected yield curve, etc. However, the simplest approach is to work with the existing yield curve itself.

When the *existing* yield curve is used to define the nominal market conditions at *future* horizons, then each bond's nominal future yield is simply determined by the passage of time along the yield curve. This process is often described as "rolling down the yield curve." For that reason, we refer to this nominal total return as the bond's "rolling yield."

THE ROLLING YIELD

A security's rolling yield can be determined by a relatively simple calculation, at least in theory. Exhibit 2 provides an illustration.

EXHIBIT 2 Calculation of a Rolling Yield (a three-year 6.5 percent par bond rolling down to a 2.5-year yield curve value of 6.3 percent over a six-month horizon)

Coupon income (as percent of par)		3.250%
Reinvestment income (as percent of par)		0.000
Market Appreciation:		
Nominal price six months hence based on yield curve value of 6.3 percent	100.456	
Price today	(100.000)	
Price appreciation	.456	.456
Total return as percent of par		3.706%
Total return as percent of initial market value		3.706%
Annualized total return (rolling yield)		7.410%

Suppose the prevailing yield curve has yield levels of 6.5 percent for three-year maturities and 6.3 percent for 2.5-year maturities. A three-year 6.5 percent bond lying on the yield curve would then be priced at par to yield 6.5 percent. We wish to compute this bond's rolling yield over a six-month investment horizon.

The total return consists of three components—market appreciation, coupon income, and reinvestment income (or more generally, the time value of coupon payments). In this particular example, reinvestment income—usually only a negligible factor over short-term horizons—is completely eliminated.

Coupon income consists of one semiannual coupon payment of 3.25 percent.

The market appreciation is derived from the yield changes associated with rolling down the yield curve for the six-month period. At the end of this period, under the assumed nominal condition of a constant-yield curve, the bond will be priced at the curve's 2.5-year value, i.e., at 6.3 percent. At this yield, the original par bond will be priced at 100.456.[6]

The total points of return (as a percentage of par) thus sum up to 3.706 percent. Since we are dealing with a bond originally priced at par, this 3.706 percent figure also represents the total return as a percentage of initial market value.

Finally, by annualizing this return figure, we obtain the bond's rolling yield of 7.41 percent.

It is interesting to note that this rolling yield of 7.41 percent exceeds the original 6.5 percent conventional yield-to-maturity by 91 basis points!

THE ROLLING YIELD CURVE

The basic yield curve consists of a plot of conventional yield against maturity for a set of comparable securities (e.g., the U.S. Treasury market). When the conventional yield for each security is replaced by the corresponding rolling yield, the resulting plot may be called a rolling yield curve.

Exhibit 3 shows the rolling yield curve, based on a six-month investment horizon, corresponding to the basic yield curve depicted in Exhibit 1. It is instructive to compare Exhibits 1 and 3.

The most striking characteristic of the rolling yield curve is that essentially all the rolling yield values exceed the basic yield curve values for the same maturity. This "boost" in the rolling yield is derived from the process of rolling down to lower yield values over time (see Exhibit 2). This effect will always be seen with positively sloped (i.e., ascending) yield curves. An opposite effect will occur in the case of inverted (i.e., descending) yield curves.

The magnitude of this boost of the rolling yield above the basic yield varies widely across the maturity scale. The basic yield curve of Exhibit 1 has the property that the slope is greatest for the shorter maturities. For

---

[6] To maintain the simplicity of this example, we have purposely neglected a number of practically important problems: determining the exact shape of the yield curve, finding the location over time of individual securities relative to the curve itself, the whole question of transaction costs, etc.

EXHIBIT 3   The Rolling Yield Curve

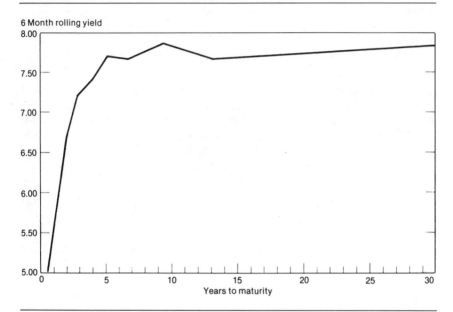

6 Month rolling yield

Years to maturity

---

such yield curves, the roll-down in yield—when measured in basis points—will naturally also be greatest at the shorter maturities. However, the boost in return depends on price volatility as well as the basis-point size of the roll-down. As maturity shortens, the roll-down in basis points may increase, but its effect on return will be partially offset by the decline in price volatility. For example, with a six-month security, there will be no price volatility at all at the six-month horizon. Consequently, there will be no boost in return regardless of the steepness of the underlying yield curve at that point.

This conflict between increasing roll-down and decreasing price volatility will often lead to the boost in return reaching its maximum value at some point among the intermediate maturities. Moreover, when this boost effect is overlaid on a typical positively sloped yield curve, one will often see a peak in the rolling yield curve itself. In Exhibit 3 we see that this peak is reached at the ninth year.

INTERPRETING ROLLING YIELD CURVES

By definition, the rolling yield curve shows the total return that will be realized by each security on the yield curve provided that the yield curve remains exactly constant over the investment horizon.

In contrast to the conventional yields, rolling yields represent total returns over a common investment horizon. Consequently, rolling yields are directly comparable with one another. This comparability of individual rolling yields makes it possible to interpret the rolling yield curve in a number of interesting ways.

The rolling yield curve can be viewed as a plot of nominal returns against maturity. For example, consider the Rolling Yield curve shown in Exhibit 3. Apart from any changes in the underlying yield curve, Exhibit 3 tells us that an investment in a one-year security will provide a total return of 5.62 percent, a two-year security will provide a return of 6.7 percent, etc. Thus, the rolling yield curve depicts the trade-off between comparable *nominal* returns and maturity.

Pursuing this tack one step further, the rolling yield curve also shows the compensation in (nominal) return for a given extension in maturity. Thus, Exhibit 3 shows that a one-year extension from one year to two years increases the rolling yield from 5.62 percent to 6.7 percent, a jump of 108 basis points. However, a one-year extension from four years to five years achieves an improvement in rolling yield from 7.42 percent to 7.71 percent, or 29 basis points.

Similarly, the slope of the rolling yield curve indicates the rate of nominal compensation for every month of extension. (However, as noted earlier, each month of maturity extension incurs different degrees of maturity risk.)

If the rolling yield curve reaches a maximum, then there is no compensation in *nominal* return for further extension of maturity. Any manager extending his maturity beyond this point would presumably have expectations of favorable changes in the yield curve, i.e., lower overall rates and/or a flattening of the curve in the longer maturities.

Peaks in the rolling yield curve are often associated with the so-called elbow points in the underlying yield curve. In fact, one could argue that the common market practice of searching for elbows has value precisely because of this association with maximum or near-maximum rolling yields. By making these relationships explicit, the rolling yield curve can assist in determining the relative risks and rewards of moderate departures from a given elbow point.

The rolling yield curve can also be interpreted as the sequence of short-term returns provided by a security at various points in its life. For example, the 13-year value of 7.67 percent in Exhibit 3 says that a 13-year bond would provide a return of 7.67 percent over the first six-month period—as long as the yield curve remains unchanged. Over the next six months, this same security will generate—again assuming an unchanged yield curve—a return of 7.7 percent, i.e., the rolling yield curve value associated with the 12.5-year maturity. And so on for each succeeding six-month period. This leads to the observation that the security will produce its greatest return over the six-month period that begins when its remaining life has declined to nine years. After this point, the return falls period by period until it reaches the minimum return of 5 percent in the last six-month period. Of course, all of this transpires only under the rather strong assumption that the yield curve remains unchanged over the entire 13 years.

Nevertheless, this interpretation is rather intriguing because it quantifies the concept that there is an optimal time to sell every bond as it rolls down the yield curve.

The rolling yield curve can also be useful in constructing "bridge swaps." By combining two bonds with different maturities, one can create a "bond package" having an average maturity somewhere between the two original bonds. Similarly, this bond package will have an average rolling yield lying somewhere between the rolling yields of the two bonds. In fact, by adjusting the mixture ratio, one can obtain a bond package falling anywhere on a straight line drawn between the rolling yield curve plots of the original two bonds. Suppose this straight line (i.e., the "bridge" across two maturity points) passes significantly below the plot of a third bond on the rolling yield curve. Then, as illustrated in Exhibit 4, a swap out of the appropriately mixed bond package into this third bond can result in an increase in rolling yield while maintaining the same average maturity.

Once again, we must caution that such a swap—like the rolling yield itself—depends upon a constant yield curve. In addition, bond

---

EXHIBIT 4 A Bridge Swap

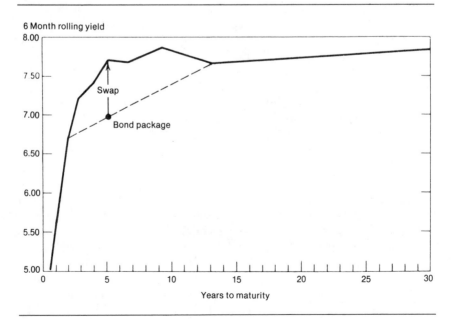

packages with the same average maturity can differ widely in their volatility characteristics.[7]

ROLLING YIELDS AND CHANGING YIELD CURVES

Of course, yield curves do change (sometimes rather violently) and any comprehensive approach to yield curve analysis must deal with the prospect of both expected and unexpected changes.

Any such change will produce realized returns for a given bond that will be higher or lower than its rolling yield. The more adverse the change in the yield curve, the more the realized return will drop below its rolling yield. The more favorable the change in the yield curve, the greater the extent by which the realized return will exceed the rolling yield.

The rolling yield thus serves as benchmark, fully capturing the total return implications of the existing yield curve. One can then focus on potential changes from the existing curve—shifts in overall level as well as sharpenings and/or flattenings at various maturity points. For each maturity, the sum of these changes will result in a given yield move away from the existing curve. Such changes in yield can readily be translated into their approximate value as increments (or decrements) of total return.[8] But the point is that each of these increments (or decrements) of total return must be added to (or subtracted from) the rolling yield.

By serving this role as a total return benchmark for the existing yield curve, rolling yields can help clarify the impact of prospective market changes that may move the yield curve away from its present level and shape.

PARALLEL SHIFTS

The simplest form of yield curve change is the "parallel shift," where all yields undergo exactly the same basis-point move. Exhibit 5 illustrates a parallel shift of +50 basis points in the U.S. Treasury yield curve shown in Exhibit 1.[9]

For any given security, a yield move leads to a corresponding change in price. In turn, this will affect the security's total return over the investment horizon. For the rolling yield, this change is based upon

---

[7] This fundamental problem can be partially overcome by substituting horizon volatility for maturity as a measure of price volatility. (See Chapter 28.)

[8] The horizon volatility for each maturity point provides a handy scaling factor for this translation.

[9] It is interesting to notice that parallel shifts almost never really look "parallel" to the eye.

EXHIBIT 5 Yield Curves under a Parallel Shift of +50 Basis Points

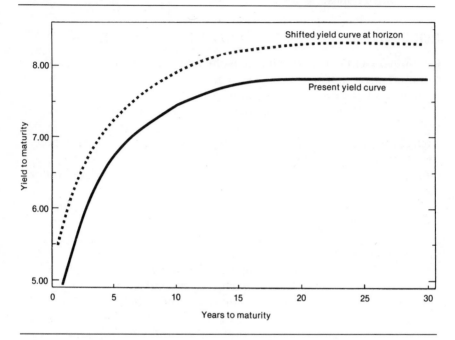

a roll-down of the *existing* yield curve. When the yield curve itself changes, then the additional yield and price move must be incorporated into the total return calculation. This computational process is illustrated in Exhibit 6.

The horizon returns for all securities along the yield curve can be computed in a similar fashion. When these returns are plotted against the original maturity of each security, one obtains a graphic illustration of the effect of changing yield curves.

Exhibit 7 shows the horizon returns for the +50-basis-point parallel shift applied to the yield curve shown in Exhibit 5. Exhibit 7 also shows the rolling yield curve as a benchmark for what the horizon returns would have been without any market changes.

The pattern exhibited in Exhibit 7 can be readily explained in terms of price volatilities. The price impact of a given yield move is determined by the bond's maturity, coupon rate, and its starting yield level.[10] Among these factors, the bond's maturity usually dominates. In particular, for the "current coupon" bonds that comprise the Treasury yield curve, increasing maturity leads to increasing price volatility. In turn,

---

[10] See Chapter 4.

EXHIBIT 6 Calculation of Horizon Return (a three-year 6.5 percent par
bond rolling down to a 2.5-year yield curve value of 6.3
percent over a six-month horizon—followed by a
+50-basis-point parallel shift)

Coupon income (as percent of par)			3.25%
Reinvestment income (as percent of par)			0.00
Market Appreciation:			
Present yield curve value at 2.5 years	6.30%		
Magnitude of parallel shift	+.50		
Yield curve value six months hence at			
2.5 years	6.80%		
Price six months hence based on yield			
curve value of 6.8 percent	99.32	99.32	
Price today @ 6.5 percent		(100.00)	
Price appreciation		−.68	−.68%
Total return as percent of par			2.57%
Total return as percent of initial			
market value			2.57%
Annualized total return (rolling yield)			5.14%

Note: for simplicity, this example is based on rounded values and hence does not
exactly correspond to Exhibit 5.

EXHIBIT 7 Horizon Returns from Parallel Shift

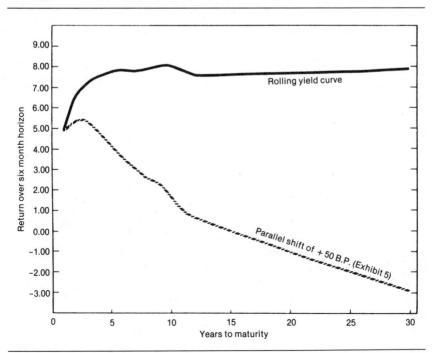

this means that the parallel shift in the yield curve will have increasing price impact at the longer maturities. Consequently, the effect of any parallel shift on returns will always be greatest at the longer end of the curve.

By the same token, at the short end of the yield curve, the effect of a parallel shift will become smaller with decreasing maturity. In fact, for the security whose maturity coincides with the investment horizon, there will be no change whatsoever. In this study, a six-month horizon is used for all examples. The security at this point on the yield curve is the six-month Treasury bill. The rolling yield of the six-month T bill over a six-month horizon is just its original yield (on a bond equivalent basis). Moreover, the six-month T bill will obviously provide this same return over a six-month horizon no matter what changes take place in the yield curve. Consequently, this six-month maturity acts like a fixed point under all yield curve changes.

These volatility responses are clearly evident in Exhibit 7. One has the fixed point at the six-month maturity, where the rolling yield curve and the horizon return curve meet. As the maturity increases, the horizon returns depart farther and farther from the rolling yield, reflecting the increasing volatility of longer bonds. In fact, the *upward* parallel shift in the yield curve has the overall effect of a *downward* angular rotation of the rolling yield curve around the fixed point at the six-month maturity.

For an investor anticipating the parallel shifts shown in Exhibit 7, it is immediately evident that the longer maturities are to be avoided. In general, because of its simple response pattern, the investment implications of any parallel shift are usually quite obvious. There is only one problem. Actual changes in the yield curve rarely take the form of a simple parallel shift across all maturities. When the market moves, the yield curve almost always undergoes some change in shape as well as a shift in level.

CHANGING SHAPES

The reshaping that accompanies a shift movement can often have a surprisingly strong impact on the horizon returns. This is illustrated in Exhibits 8 and 9. Exhibit 8 depicts a market move where the yields in the shorter and intermediate maturities undergo a greater deterioration than yields in the longer maturities. As many investors have learned to their sorrow, such market movements are not uncommon.

Exhibit 9 shows the horizon returns resulting from this reshaping of the yield curve. One can see that in this case, the simple maxim to avoid long maturities could have led the investor astray. In Exhibit 9, the intermediate maturities are hit the hardest in terms of total return. In fact, under this market move, the very worst return is recorded at the thirteenth year, where a relatively high rolling yield value would have been obtained (i.e., if the yield curve had remained unchanged).

EXHIBIT 8   Yield Curves under a Change in Both Shape and Level

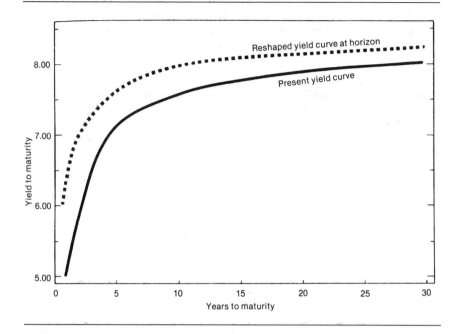

EXHIBIT 9   Horizon Returns from Changing Shape and Level

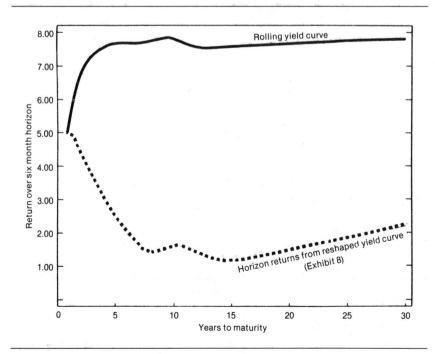

It is useful to contrast the effects of the shape changes shown in Exhibit 8 with the earlier examples of parallel shift. This comparison is facilitated by Exhibit 10, which depicts the respective changes in yields at each maturity. For the parallel shift, the yield change is by definition

EXHIBIT 10   Yield Changes across Maturity

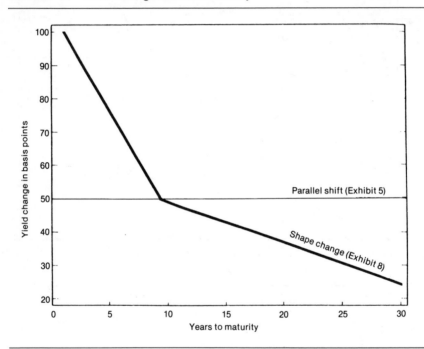

constant at +50 basis points across all maturities. On the other hand, the shape changes of Exhibit 8 result from a strong yield move of +100 basis points at the short end of the curve, with a pattern of decreasing yield changes as maturity increases. By the ninth year, this yield change declines to +50 basis points, and then decreases thereafter at a somewhat slower pace.

Exhibit 11 compares the corresponding horizon returns. One can see that there are two points of coincidence. The first of these is the six-month "fixed point," where the six-month horizon return is unaffected by any change in yields. The second point of coincidence is at the ninth year, where the +50-basis-point yield change occurs in both cases, and naturally results in the same horizon return of +1.7 percent.

Between these two intersection points, the flattening shape change provides a significantly worse horizon return than the parallel shift. This

EXHIBIT 11   Comparison of Horizon Returns

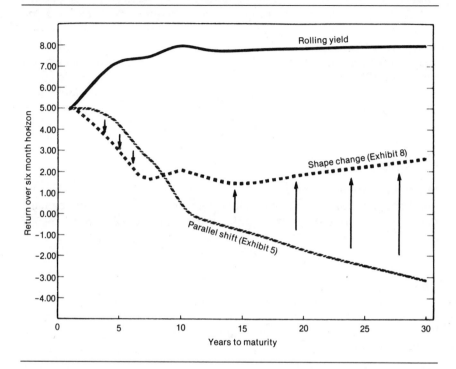

is exactly what we would expect given the respective pattern of yield changes shown in Exhibit 10. At the one-year maturity, the shape change results in a +97-basis-point yield move, over 48 basis points more than the parallel shift. However, because of the limited horizon volatility of the one-year maturity, this leads only to a small difference in horizon returns. On the other hand, at the two-year maturity, the horizon volatility is sufficient to generate a −110-basis-point difference in return for the +40-basis-point difference in the yield changes. The horizon return difference grows to about −150 basis points at the third year. It remains roughly stable around this level until the seventh year. This stability is derived from the compensating effects of increasing volatility against the decreasing difference in the yield change.

At the ninth year, the horizon return curves intersect. After the ninth year, the two factors of less adverse yield changes and increasing horizon volatility work in concert. As a result, the shape change produces an increasingly better return than the parallel shift. By the 30th year, the improvement in horizon return has grown by over 5 percent, from −3 percent for the parallel shift to +2.4 percent for the shape change.

Thus, it is clear that changing yield curve shapes can have powerful impact on horizon returns. Consequently, there is a need for techniques to help the portfolio manager in evaluating the effect of potential shape changes. However, in trying to develop such techniques, one immediately encounters a problem in the bewildering profusion of yield curve shapes that can and do arise in the marketplace. One way to come to grips with this problem is to find a simple way for classifying yield curve movements. The first step in this direction is to break down yield curve changes into a parallel shift followed by a series of sharpenings and flattenings.

Classification of Yield Curve Changes

In Exhibit 8 the intermediate nine-year maturity undergoes a +50-basis-point change. Suppose this nine-year point is selected as a "benchmark maturity" to define the parallel shift component. Then this parallel shift of +50 basis points can be viewed as the first component in the yield curve's total process of change. The remaining changes will then consist of relative "twists" that act to sharpen or flatten the slopes along the curve.

To help visualize this process as it applies to the shape change in Exhibit 8 consider the yield changes plotted in Exhibit 10. In this particular situation, we clearly have the parallel shift of +50 basis points at the ninth year, plus two flattening twists. From the six-month point to the ninth-year benchmark, the yield change declines from +100 basis points to +50 basis points. At the six-month point, this represents a "short-end up-twist" of 50 basis points above and beyond the parallel shift of +50 basis points. Similarly, from the 9th year to the 30th year, the changes decline from +50 basis points to +25 basis points. This 25-basis-point flattening could be viewed as the result of a uniform "long-end down-twist" having a magnitude of 25 basis points when measured in the 30th year.

As Exhibit 10 illustrates, this combination of a parallel shift plus the two twists completely describes the yield curve change. This rather pat fit is, of course, a result of the particular situation chosen for Exhibit 8.

Whenever the yield curve change can be defined in this simple form, the resulting horizon return curve can be visualized as developing from a parallel shift followed by up-twists or down-twists on either side of the benchmark maturity. The parallel shift first leads to a horizon return curve that approximates the angular rotation of the rolling yield. If the shape change consists of a short-end up-twist affecting the maturities preceding the benchmark, then the horizon returns will be depressed below the return levels of parallel shift. The difference in the returns, relative to the parallel shift, will start at zero at the six-month maturity, plummet to some trough value, and then rise to zero again at the benchmark maturity. If a long-end down-twist occurs beyond the benchmark maturity, then the horizon returns will be boosted above the level of the rotated rolling yield curve. The magnitude of this boost will grow with increasing maturity.

On a relative basis, we would see these same effects from up-twists and down-twists regardless of whether the parallel shift was in a positive or negative direction. This has a number of important practical implications. For example, the return from a "bridge swap" tends to be relatively independent from the effects of parallel shifts in either direction. However, up-twists and down-twists can have a severe impact on the profitability of such swaps. Thus, in a short-end up-twist, in the maturities preceding the benchmark, the shorter securities in the bridge will undergo a greater relative upward yield move. In such situations, the horizon return from a bond package can differ significantly from the return provided by the corresponding maturity point on the yield curve.

In the many instances where yield curve changes can be approximated in terms of up-twists or down-twists on either side of an appropriately chosen benchmark security, the horizon returns can be visualized as consisting of three components:

1. The rolling yield curve.
2. An angular rotation of the rolling yield curve to match the shift at the benchmark maturity.
3. The different relative return effects of up-twists or down-twists in the maturities preceding and following the benchmark. These effects can be summarized as follows:
   a. *Short-end up-twist* (i.e., increased rates in maturities preceding the benchmark). This will create a "bulge" depression in relative return, growing in magnitude to a maximum trough level at some maturity between the relative fixed points at six months and the benchmark maturity.
   b. *Short-end down-twist* (i.e., lower relative rates in maturities preceding the benchmark). This will create an upward bulge in relative return, peaking at some interim point between six months and the benchmark.
   c. *Long-end down-twist* (i.e., decreased relative rates in longer maturities beyond the benchmark). The relative return becomes increasingly favorable with the longer maturities.
   d. *Long-end up-twist* (i.e., increased relative rates in the longer maturities beyond the benchmark). The relative return becomes increasingly negative with the longer maturities.

As illustrated in Exhibit 11, these relative return effects from up-twists and/or down-twists can override the shift changes in the overall level of rates. With this classification system for yield curve changes, we

672 / CHAPTER 30

can quickly isolate the key components of return that would affect any contemplated portfolio action.

There are certain patterns of change that cannot be adequately described by a parallel shift followed by only two simple segment twist effects such as in Exhibit 10. However, even complex patterns of change can be approximated (as closely as desired) by a series of up-twists and down-twists over a sufficient number of consecutive maturity segments.

PROPORTIONAL CHANGES IN YIELDS

Up to this point, a yield curve change has been treated as a movement from the present curve to a single, well-defined future curve. In practice, there will always be a certain range of uncertainty surrounding any anticipated future yield curve. It is usually wise to consider how this range of uncertainty can affect the pattern of horizon returns. Once again, this effort can quickly become bogged down in the bewildering range of possible shapes and patterns of change that the market might thrust upon us. However, there is a way to extend the preceding classification system so that it can easily depict the evolution of a wide range of possible future yield curves.

The key assumption is that of "proportional changes" across maturities for each basis point of parallel shift in the benchmark maturity. As an example, consider the pattern of change illustrated in Exhibit 10. When the benchmark nine-year maturity shifts by +50 basis points, the six-month maturity undergoes a change of +100 basis points. Now suppose that the six-month maturity maintained this same change ratio of 2:1 over a range of shifts in the nine-year benchmark. For example, if the nine-year benchmark shifted by only 25 basis points, then the proportional change in the six-month maturity would be 50 basis points. More generally, whatever the benchmark shift, there would be exactly twice that move in the six-month maturity. Similarly, the 30-year maturity would also maintain the same change ratio and would move only 50 basis points for every 100-basis-point shift in the benchmark. In essence, this technique provides a way to define a relative yield response pattern. In this case, the response pattern was based on beliefs that the yield curve will flatten and sharpen in a particular way. This pattern of change could also be made to reflect beliefs regarding the differential volatilities of rates at various maturities. Thus, one could interpret this response pattern as a statement that six-month maturities are twice as volatile in yield as nine-year maturities, etc.

With proportional changes relative to the benchmark defined in this fashion, a whole spectrum of yield curves can be constructed. Exhibit 12 shows the spectrum of yield curves that would be associated with shifts of 0, +10, +20, +30, +40, and +50 basis points in the nine-year

EXHIBIT 12   A Spectrum of Yield Curves

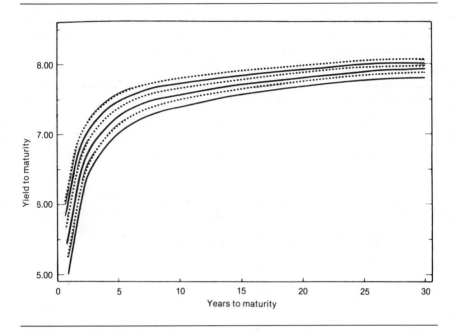

benchmark. Each benchmark shift creates a pattern of change for all maturities in accordance with the proportional changes defined in Exhibit 10.

Different patterns of proportional yield responses might be anticipated if the shift in the yield curve were downward rather than upward. To accommodate this dual pattern, two expected yield curves could be defined—one based on a pessimistic scenario (e.g., Exhibit 8) and the other based on an optimistic scenario. Each curve then determines a pattern of change across maturities (e.g., Exhibit 10). (In fact, the revised yield curve itself can be determined by a small number of estimated changes. For example, the pessimistic yield curve in Exhibit 8 could be defined by three yield changes: +100 basis points at six months, +50 basis points at 9 years and +25 basis points at 30 years.) This pessimistic scenario can then be used to define a pattern of proportional yield change relative to any given benchmark shift in a pessimistic direction. By applying this technique to a sequence of incremental shifts, one can obtain a spectrum of yield curves that move toward and finally coincide with the originally defined pessimistic yield curve (e.g., Exhibit 12).

An identical procedure could then be taken with respect to changes in the optimistic direction.

A SPECTRUM OF HORIZON RETURNS

Each curve in the spectrum shown in Exhibit 12 corresponds to a certain change from the present yield curve. Consequently, each curve will generate a characteristic pattern of horizon returns. This corresponding spectrum of horizon returns is shown in Exhibit 13.

EXHIBIT 13 A Spectrum of Horizon Returns

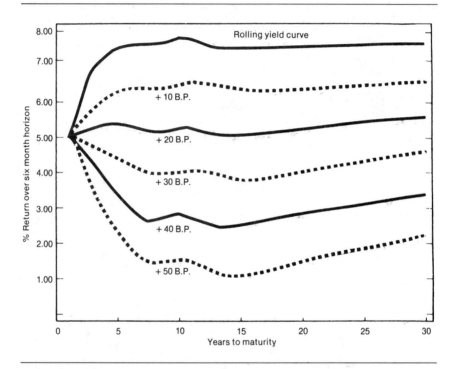

The yield curves of Exhibit 12 are related in an inverse sequence to the horizon returns of Exhibit 13. Thus, the present yield curve (i.e., the one reflecting a scenario of no market movement) lies at the *bottom* of the spectrum in Exhibit 12. The corresponding horizon return graph is the rolling yield curve lying at the *top* of the spectrum in Exhibit 13. By the same token, the most pessimistic yield curve lies at the top in Exhibit 12, while its corresponding horizon return curve is naturally the lowest one in Exhibit 13.

Each of these horizon return curves corresponds to the rotation from a parallel shift followed by the two twist effects. In the two- to nine-year range, the up-twist acts to first straighten out and then to reverse the strong upward slope of the rolling yield curve. In the longer maturities, the different horizon return curves are almost parallel. This is due to the down-twist almost offsetting the volatility increases at the longer maturities. For the 20-basis-point shift, these effects combine to produce a virtually flat return curve.

These spectrums must be recognized as highly simplified approximations of a very complex process. However, they do permit an investor to explore the impact of different kinds of yield curve movements on horizon returns. This exploration can often result in some surprising findings. For example, if Exhibit 13 represented an investor's beliefs, he would see that the longest maturities are not necessarily the most volatile. He would also see that the maturity where the rolling yield reaches its peak, the nine-year maturity, may actually represent quite a high risk sector.

Under the most pessimistic assumption, i.e., the bottom curve, the investor would be reluctant to extend beyond the six-month T bill. However, if his expectations were distributed more equally across all six curves, the investor would clearly extend at least to the one-year T bill and possibly to the third or fourth year. By the same token, unless he had considerable faith in the most optimistic of the six curves, he would probably be reluctant to extend beyond the fifth year. It should be remembered that this example is restricted to the essentially pessimistic spectrum represented in Exhibit 13.

In general, by selecting one or more patterns of proportional yield changes, the investor can explore a wide spectrum of horizon return curves that would result from changing yield curves. The effects of both optimistic and pessimistic changes can then be examined. The impact of various types of shape changes can be studied through alternative patterns of proportional yield changes. By associating different horizons with different degrees of shift in the benchmark maturity, one can visualize the evolution of various return curves over time.

In the final analysis, all investment decisions come down to a trade-off between risk and return. This trade-off is clearly present in decisions relating to the maturity structure of a fixed income portfolio. The current shape of the yield curve and prospective changes in its shape constitute critical factors in this trade-off. With this extension of the rolling yield technique, the investor can examine explicit representations of the risk/return trade-off over a wide range of assumed yield curve conditions.

31

Bond Immunization: An Asset Liability Optimization Strategy

Peter E. Christensen
Managing Director
Fixed Income Research
PaineWebber Incorporated

Frank J. Fabozzi, Ph.D., C.F.A.
Visiting Professor
Sloan School of Management
Massachusetts Institute of Technology

The purpose of this chapter is to review the mechanics and applications of the bond immunization strategy. In the first section, we define immunization as a duration-matching strategy, then compare it to maturity-matching as a less advanced approach to locking in rates. To hedge the reinvestment risk present in maturity-matching, we then explain the single-period immunization strategy and the rebalancing procedures that accompany it. Following single-period immunization, we discuss multiperiod immunization and its applications for the pension, insurance, and thrift markets. Lastly, we review the recent variations on the strategy, including combination matching, contingent immunization, immunization with futures, and immunization with options.

WHAT IS AN IMMUNIZED PORTFOLIO?

Single-period immunization is frequently defined as locking up a fixed rate of return over a prespecified horizon, such as locking up a 10 percent return for a five-year period. It can also be defined as generating a minimum future value at the end of a specified horizon, such as generating $100 million dollars from $50 million five years earlier. With multiperiod immunization, the horizon over which rates are locked in is extended to include multiple periods (such as a schedule of monthly payouts to retirees of a pension plan). Multiperiod immunization is a duration-matching strategy that permits funding of a fixed schedule of a multiple future payouts at a minimum cost (such as funding a $500 million schedule of payouts at a cost of $200 million).

The actuary generally credited with pioneering the immunization strategy, F. M. Reddington, defined immunization in 1952 as "the investment of the assets in such a way that the existing business is immune to a general change in the rate of interest."[1] He also specified a condition for immunization: the average duration of assets must be set equal to the average duration of the liabilities. He thought this matching of durations would immunize a portfolio from the effects of small changes in interest rates. By matching durations on both sides of the balance sheet, he felt that assets and liabilities would be equally price sensitive to changes in the general level of interest rates. For any change in yield, both sides of the ledger should be equally affected; therefore the relative values of assets and liabilities are not changed.

Much later, Lawrence Fisher and Roman Weil defined an immunized portfolio as follows:[2]

> A portfolio of investments is *immunized* for a holding period if its value at the end of the holding period, regardless of the course of rates during the holding period, must be at least as large as it would have been had the interest rate function been constant throughout the holding period.
>
> If the realized return on an investment in bonds is sure to be at least as large as the appropriately computed yield to the horizon, then that investment is immunized.

Fisher and Weil demonstrated that to achieve the immunized result, not only must the average duration of the bond portfolio be set equal to the remaining time in the planning horizon, but the market value of assets must be greater than or equal to the present value of the liabilities discounted at the internal rate of return of the portfolio.

Before reviewing the logic of this portfolio strategy, let's look at maturity-matching as an early approach to locking in a current level of interest rates.

---

[1] F. M. Reddington, "Review of the Principle of Life-Office Valuations," *Journal of the Institute of Actuaries* 78(1952), pp. 286–340.

[2] Lawrence Fisher and Roman Weil, "Coping with the Risk of Interest-Rate Fluctuations: Returns to Bondholders from Naive and Optimal Strategies," *Journal of Business* (October 1971), pp. 408–431.

MATURITY-MATCHING:
THE REINVESTMENT PROBLEM

Suppose an investor wishes to lock in prevailing interest rates for a 10-year period. Should he buy 10-year bonds?

By purchasing 10-year bonds and holding them to maturity, an investor can be certain of receiving all coupon payments over the 10-year period as well as the principal repayment at redemption (assuming no default occurs). These two sources of income are fixed in dollar amounts. The third and final source of income is the interest earned on the semiannual coupon payments. "Interest on coupon" is not fixed in dollar amounts; rather it depends on the many interest-rate environments at the various times of payment.

A reinvestment problem occurs when the reinvestment of coupon income occurs at rates below the yield-to-maturity of the bond at the time of purchase. Note from Exhibit 1 that as interest rates shift instantaneously and remain at the new levels for a 10-year period, the total "holding period" return on a 9 percent par bond due in 10 years will vary considerably. The initial effect will appear in the value of the asset. The immediate result will be a capital gain if rates rise (or loss, if rates fall).

As the holding period increases after a change in rates, the interest-on-coupon component of total return begins to exert a stronger influence. At 10 years, we note that interest on coupon (reinvestment income) exerts a dominance over capital gain (or loss) in determining holding period returns.

Intuitively we know that these relationships make sense. Capital gains appear instantly, whereas changes in reinvestment rates take time to exert their effect on the total holding period return on a bond.

If rates were to jump immediately from 9 percent to 15 percent and a capital loss were to appear today, at what point will that capital loss be made up because the reinvestment of coupon payments is occurring at a higher (15 percent) rate? As illustrated in Exhibit 2, the two "offsetting forces" of market value and reinvestment return equally offset at 6.79 years. This is the duration of the 10-year, 9 percent bond. To earn the original 9 percent target return (the yield-to-maturity at the time of purchase), it is necessary to hold that bond for the period of its duration—6.79 years in our example. If we wish to lock in a market rate of 9 percent for a 10-year period, we would select a bond with a duration of 10 years (not a maturity of 10 years). The maturity for such a par bond in a 9 percent yield environment is roughly 23 years.

From Exhibit 1 we note that regardless of the immediate, one-time interest rate shift, we are still able to earn a 9 percent total return if our holding period is 6.79 years—the duration of the bond. By targeting the duration of a portfolio rather than specific maturities to the prescribed

EXHIBIT 1 Total Return on a 9 Percent, $1,000 Bond Due in 10 Years and Held through Various Holding Periods

Income Source	Interest Rate at Time of Reinvestment	Holding Period in Years					
		1	3	5	6.79*	9	10
Coupon income........	5%	$ 90	$270	$450	$611	$ 810	$ 900
Capital gain or loss ...		287	234	175	100	39	–0–
Interest on interest		1	17	54	105	191	241
Total return........		$ 378	$521	$679	$816	$1,040	$1,141
(and yield).......		(37.0%)	(15.0%)	(11.0%)	(9.0%)	(8.5%)	(8.2%)
Coupon income........	7%	$ 90	$270	$450	$611	$ 810	$ 900
Capital gain or loss ...		132	109	83	56	19	–0–
Interest on interest		2	25	78	149	279	355
Total return........		$224	$404	$611	$816	$1,108	$1,255
(and yield).......		(22.0%)	(12.0%)	(10.0%)	(9.0%)	(8.6%)	(8.5%)
Coupon income........	9%	$ 90	$270	$450	$611	$ 810	$ 900
Capital gain or loss ...		–0–	–0–	–0–	–0–	–0–	–0–
Interest on interest		2	32	103	205	387	495
Total return........		$ 92	$302	$553	$816	$1,197	$1,395
(and yield).......		(9.0%)	(9.0%)	(9.0%)	(9.0%)	(9.0%)	(9.0%)
Coupon income........	11%	$ 90	$270	$450	$611	$ 810	$ 900
Capital gain or loss ...		–112	–95	–75	–56	–18	–0–
Interest on interest		2	40	129	261	502	647
Total return........		$ 20	$215	$504	$816	$1,294	$1,547
(and yield).......		(2.0%)	(6.7%)	(8.5%)	(9.0%)	(9.7%)	(9.8%)

a Duration of a 9 percent bond bought at par and due in 10 years.

EXHIBIT 2 "Offsetting Forces" Principle (9 percent coupon, 30-year maturity bond, rates rise instantly from 9 percent to 15 percent, reinvestment rate is 15 percent)

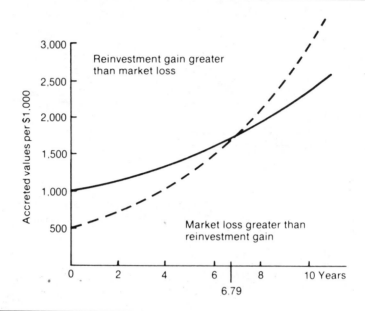

---

investment horizon of 6.79 years, we see the equal offsets of capital gain with lower reinvestment return occurring in the portfolio. This principle of duration-matching together with rebalancing procedures that are used over time allow us to lock in rates and effectively eliminate the reinvestment risk that is associated with the maturity-matching strategy.

SINGLE-PERIOD IMMUNIZATION

The most straightforward approach to funding a single-period liability five years from today is to purchase a five-year, zero coupon bond maturing on the liability payment date. Regardless of future fluctuations in interest rates, the bond, or portfolio of bonds, will be price insensitive (or immune) to changes in rates as the zero coupon securities mature at par on the payment date. Because zero coupons have durations equal to their maturities, the five-year, zero coupon bonds both cash-match and duration-match the single-period liability payment.

If zero coupon bonds have insufficient yield, a portfolio of *coupon-bearing* Treasury, agency, and corporate bonds can be immunized to fund the same single-period payment only if three conditions are met:

(1) the duration of the portfolio of coupon bonds must be set equal to the five-year horizon; (2) the market value of assets must be greater than the present value of liabilities; and (3) the dispersion of the assets must be slightly greater than the dispersion of the liabilities. That is,

(1) $\text{Duration}_{\text{Assets}} \quad = \text{Duration}_{\text{Liabilities}}$
(2) $\text{PV}_{\text{Assets}} \qquad > \text{PV}_{\text{Liabilities}}$
(3) $\text{Dispersion}_{\text{Assets}} \geq \text{Dispersion}_{\text{Liabilities}}$

The Three Conditions for Immunization

Immunization requires that the average durations of assets and liabilities are set equal at all times. Unfortunately, simple matching of durations is not a sufficient condition.

Consider a $200,000 par value zero coupon five-year bond in a 9 percent rate environment as well as a $1 million five-year single-period liability. Obviously the durations of both the assets and liabilities are matched since they are both zero coupon, five-year obligations. However, a $200,000 par value zero coupon, five-year bond cannot realistically compound to $1,000,000 in five years. The required annual rate to compound to $1 million in five years is 38 percent. In a 9 percent rate environment, $643,937 is required in market value of assets to compound to $1 million in five years.

Therefore, a second condition for immunization is necessary; the market value of assets must be greater than or equal to the present value of liabilities, using the internal rate of return (IRR) of the assets as the discount factor in present-valuing the liabilities. The assets, when compounded at the "locked in" immunized rate of 9 percent, will grow to equal or exceed the future value immunized target of $1 million in this example.

To understand the reasons for the third condition for immunization (that the dispersion of assets be greater than or equal to the dispersion of liabilities), it is important to understand the assumptions underlying the Macaulay measure of duration.[3] Since duration is defined as the present value weighted average time to payment on a bond, duration must assume a discount rate (or a series of discount rates) when calculating present value weighted time.

The discount rate assumed in the Macaulay measure of duration is the yield or internal rate of return on the bond or portfolio. By assuming only one discount rate, the Macaulay measure assumes that a flat yield curve prevails at all times, as illustrated in Exhibit 3. If rates shift up, say 100 basis points, the Macaulay duration calculation assumes a parallel shift to another flat yield curve 100 basis points higher.

---

[3] See Chapters 4 and 5 for an explanation of duration and its properties.

EXHIBIT 3   Present Value of Cashflows for Macaulay Duration

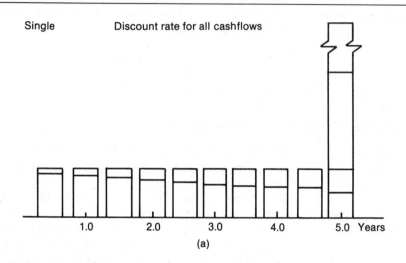

Single   Discount rate for all cashflows

(a)

Yield Curve Assumptions in Macaulay Duration (9 percent, 10-year par bond)

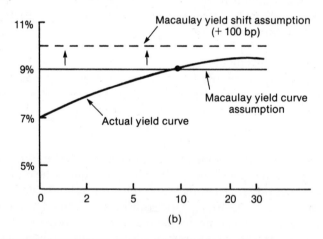

(b)

To meet a target duration of 6.79 years as illustrated in Exhibit 4(a), a portfolio could be constructed as either (1) a barbell of roughly equal amounts of zero-and 13-year duration securities; (2) an even ladder of equal amounts of zero- through 13-year duration securities; or (3) a bullet of only 6.79 year durations. Since the Macaulay duration calculation assumes that a flat yield curve connects every maturity point, the barbell structure incorporates the greatest amount of yield curve risk by concentrating cash flows on both ends of the curve. If the yield curve is

EXHIBIT 4 Maturity Structures for Portfolios—Target Duration of 6.79 Years

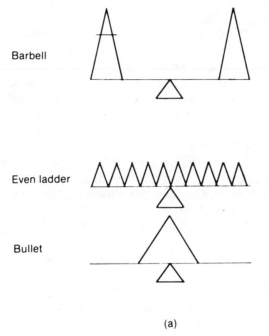

Barbell

Even ladder

Bullet

(a)

U.S. Treasury Zero-Coupon Curve (barbell versus bullet maturity structure)

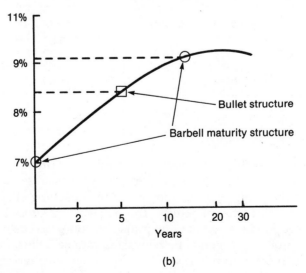

Bullet structure

Barbell maturity structure

(b)

positive or inverted, the barbell structure will violate the assumption of a flat curve more than the even ladder or bullet structure. On the other hand, the bullet structure, by concentrating cash flows at a single maturity point, incorporates a flat slope over the relevant range on the yield curve as shown in Exhibit 4(b).

For single-period immunization, a bullet maturity structure with tight cash flows around the liability date is generally preferred to an even ladder or barbelled portfolio because of the reduced risk exposure to the yield curve becoming steeper or twisting. In fact, to eliminate the risk of pathological shifts in yields, the investor could tighten the cash flows still further and purchase a zero coupon bond to cash-flow-match the single-period liability. Short of that, a bullet structure is the least risky and the barbell the most risky.

Therefore, for immunization the third condition of controlling the degree of barbelling must be incorporated into the process of structuring a portfolio. The measure used to control the barbelling is dispersion—a measure of the variance of cash flows around the duration date (D) of a bond. The mathematical formula for dispersion is as follows:

$$\text{Dispersion} = \frac{\Sigma(t_i - D)^2 PV(CF_i)}{\Sigma PV(CF_i)}$$

The dispersion of a zero coupon bond therefore is zero, while the dispersion of a 30-year current coupon industrial bond can be 80 to 100 years squared as illustrated in Exhibit 5.

EXHIBIT 5 Dispersions of Selected Issues (as of October 22, 1985)

Issuer	Coupon	Maturity	Yield	Maturity	Duration	Dispersion
U.S. Treasury Strip	0	11/15/90	10.00	11/15/90	5.062	.00
U.S. Treasury	9⅝	11/15/90	9.62	11/15/90	4.082	3.31
U.S. Treasury	10⅜	7/15/92	9.97	7/15/92	4.876	5.41
U.S. Treasury	10⅝	8/15/15	10.38	8/15/89	9.435	87.17

Rebalancing Procedures

As time passes, the single-period immunized portfolio must be rebalanced so that the duration of the portfolio is always reset to the remaining life in the planning period to ensure the offsetting effects of capital gains with reinvestment return. This rebalancing procedure requires that the coupon income, matured principal, and proceeds from possible liquidation of longer bonds be reinvested into securities that maintain the duration equal to the *remaining life in the planning period.* Because of the multiple rebalancings required throughout the planning period, the bond portfolio is continually maintained in a duration-matched state and therefore should achieve its target return in spite of periodic shifts in rates.

An immunized bond portfolio, therefore, can be constructed once a time horizon is established. Since duration is inversely related to both the prevailing yields and the coupon rate, it may not be possible to immunize a portfolio beyond a certain number of years using only coupon bearing securities. For example, when bond market yields reached their historic highs in 1981, it was not possible to immunize a bullet liability beyond eight years in the taxable markets with current coupon securities. In early 1986, in a 9 percent rate environment, the maximum lock-up period was closer to 10 years. However, the use of zero coupon securities with long maturities and durations can allow the investor the opportunity to lengthen the planning period over which he can lock in rates.

The actual targeted return on an immunized portfolio will depend on the level of interest rates at the time the program is initiated. Though bond values may for example decline as interest rates rise, the future value of the portfolio (or security) based on the new higher reinvestment rate and lower principal value should still correspond to the original targeted yield. As we demonstrate later in an actual simulation of an immunized portfolio, duration is the key to controlling the equal offset of reinvestment income with asset value as interest rates fluctuate.

The important point to remember is: *The standard deviation of return on an immunized portfolio will be much lower over a given horizon than that on a nonimmunized portfolio—whether measured around a sample mean or promised yield.* With interest-rate risk minimized (when held over an assumed time horizon), the performance of the immunized portfolio is virtually assured, regardless of reinvestment rates.

A SIMULATION OF A SINGLE-PERIOD IMMUNIZED PORTFOLIO[4]

In this section we will illustrate the mechanics of the immunization rebalancing procedures. The parameters for the analysis are as follows:

1. $50 million is available for investment on October 22, 1985.
2. The investment horizon is five years.
3. The only eligible securities are restricted to Treasury notes, bonds and zeroes.
4. The immunized portfolio is rebalanced annually.
5. The yield curve assumptions used in the simulation are presented in Exhibit 6. These yield curves do not represent interest-

---

[4] The following simulation was developed by Richard C. Schwartz.

rate projections. They are used only to subject the immunized portfolio to a wide variety of interest-rate fluctuations over the five-year horizon.

6. A bid/asked spread of a quarter of a point is assumed on all transactions (a quarter point on bond sales, no transaction cost on bond purchases).

EXHIBIT 6 Yield Curve Assumptions for Simulation

	10/15/85	10/15/86	10/15/87	10/15/88	10/15/89	10/15/90
1985	8.13	—	—	—	—	—
1986	8.98	9.27	—	—	—	—
1987	9.52	9.60	10.00	—	—	—
1988	9.79	9.60	10.00	—	—	—
1989	10.01	10.41	10.00	10.00	11.50	—
1990	10.11	10.65	10.00	9.98	11.42	9.00
1991	10.24	10.68	10.00	9.94	11.24	9.10
1992	10.28	10.70	10.00	9.87	10.85	9.00
1993	10.34	10.67	10.00	9.75	10.70	9.20
1994	10.39	10.62	10.00	9.62	10.60	9.35
1995	10.41	10.58	10.00	9.45	10.58	9.50
1996	10.44	10.53	10.00			
1997	10.47	10.46	10.00			
1998	10.50	10.38	10.00			
1999	10.54	10.30	10.00			
2000	10.59	10.24	10.00			
2001	10.62	10.18	10.00			
2002	10.65	10.15	10.00			
2003	10.69	10.12	10.00			

Short-term reinvestment rate

	8.70%	9.50%	10.00%	10.75%	10.25%

The target yield established on October 22, 1985 was 10.41 percent. Exhibit 7 presents the following information for the portfolio at the beginning of each year: (1) the individual issues in the portfolio, including par amount, coupon, maturity, price and yield, (2) the duration of each security and the portfolio, (3) the dispersion of each security and the portfolio, and (4) the market values plus accrued interest. *Notice that the duration of the portfolio is reset each year in order to match the remaining time in the planning horizon.* Exhibits 8 through 12 summarize the actual portfolio transactions each year.

The important conclusion to draw from the above simulation is that the target return for the immunized portfolio was achieved, even in the volatile yield environment envisioned in this scenario. We note from Exhibit 8 that the target yield of 10.41 percent and target future value of

EXHIBIT 7 Portfolio Status at the Beginning of Each Year: Bond Immunization Simulation

October 22, 1985 (Original Portfolio)

Par (000)		Treasury Issue		Market		Duration	Dispersion	Market Value Including Accrued Int.
		Coupon	Maturity	Price	Yield			
$ 5,000	U.S. Treasury	9.625	6/30/89	98.866	9.99	3.098	4.78	$ 5,091,075
5,000	U.S. Treasury	11.500	10/15/90	105.875	9.97	3.952	3.41	5,304,808
2,200	U.S. Treasury	14.625	2/15/92	119.937	10.25	4.420	5.03	2,698,068
5,000	U.S. Treasury	11.750	4/15/92	106.938	10.26	4.766	4.61	5,358,198
5,000	U.S. Treasury	13.750	5/15/92	115.812	10.37	4.452	5.85	6,089,513
5,000	U.S. Treasury	11.875	8/15/93	108.000	10.35	5.300	7.55	5,509,715
2,200	U.S. Treasury	11.750	11/15/93	107.375	10.38	5.273	8.64	2,474,641
5,000	U.S. Treasury	13.125	5/15/94	114.625	10.49	5.340	9.83	6,016,576
5,000	U.S. Treasury	12.625	8/15/94	112.125	10.48	5.637	10.12	5,722,894
4,000	U.S. Treasury	15.750	11/15/ 1	136.187	10.92	7.072	33.11	5,721,393
$43,400	Totals and Averages	12.495%	6/ 2/93	111.890%	10.41	4.997	9.96	$49,986,881
						4.970	9.72	

EXHIBIT 7 *(continued)*

October 22, 1986

Par (000)		Treasury Issue		Market		Duration	Dispersion	Market Value Including Accrued Int.
		Coupon	Maturity	Price	Yield			
$14,000	U.S. Treasury	9.625	6/30/89	97.853	10.55	2.361	3.19	$14,116,852
5,000	U.S. Treasury	11.500	10/15/90	102.792	10.62	3.308	1.76	5,150,658
2,200	U.S. Treasury	14.625	2/15/92	115.603	10.69	3.898	3.18	2,602,720
5,000	U.S. Treasury	11.750	4/15/92	104.349	10.68	4.214	3.07	5,228,748
5,000	U.S. Treasury	13.750	5/15/92	112.615	10.68	3.951	3.87	5,929,663
5,000	U.S. Treasury	11.875	8/15/93	105.795	10.65	4.822	6.16	5,399,465
2,200	U.S. Treasury	11.750	11/15/93	105.450	10.63	4.818	7.12	2,432,291
5,000	U.S. Treasury	13.125	5/15/94	112.897	10.60	4.928	8.38	5,930,176
5,000	U.S. Treasury	12.625	8/15/94	110.600	10.59	5.220	8.99	5,646,644
1,700	U.S. Treasury	15.750	11/15/ 1	142.735	10.15	7.073	35.91	2,542,908
$50,400	Totals and Averages	11.830%	4/29/92	106.670%	10.58	4.002	6.17	$54,980,125
						4.009	6.25	

EXHIBIT 7 *(continued)*

October 22, 1987

Par (000)		Treasury Issue		Market		Duration	Dispersion	Market Value Including Accrued Int.
		Coupon	Maturity	Price	Yield			
$23,000	U.S. Treasury	9.625	6/30/89	99.403	10.00	1.556	2.23	$23,548,471
5,000	U.S. Treasury	11.500	10/15/90	103.781	10.00	2.610	.71	5,200,047
2,200	U.S. Treasury	14.625	2/15/92	115.853	10.00	3.352	2.02	2,608,220
5,000	U.S. Treasury	11.750	4/15/92	106.193	10.00	3.632	2.16	5,320,886
5,000	U.S. Treasury	13.750	5/15/92	113.461	10.00	3.428	2.62	5,971,963
5,000	U.S. Treasury	11.875	8/15/93	108.086	10.00	4.340	5.52	5,514,015
2,200	U.S. Treasury	11.750	11/15/93	107.801	10.00	4.363	6.40	2,484,013
5,000	U.S. Treasury	13.125	5/15/94	114.764	10.00	4.514	7.79	6,023,526
4,600	U.S. Treasury	12.625	8/15/94	112.715	10.00	4.801	8.71	5,292,202
$57,000	Totals and Averages	11.359%	7/31/91	105.758%	10.00	3.004	3.68	$61,963,343
						3.004	3.68	

EXHIBIT 7 *(continued)*

October 22, 1988

Par (000)	Treasury Issue			Market					Market Value Including Accrued Int.
		Coupon	Maturity	Price	Yield	Duration	Dispersion		
$32,000	U.S. Treasury	9.625	6/30/89	99.735	9.99	.664	1.79		$32,869,330
5,000	U.S. Treasury	11.500	10/15/90	102.721	9.95	1.824	.19		5,147,108
2,200	U.S. Treasury	14.625	2/15/92	113.191	9.85	2.721	1.49		2,549,656
5,000	U.S. Treasury	11.750	4/15/92	105.541	9.83	2.964	1.81		5,288,348
5,000	U.S. Treasury	13.750	5/15/92	111.535	9.83	2.820	2.03		5,875,663
5,000	U.S. Treasury	11.875	8/15/93	108.259	9.68	3.773	5.48		5,522,665
2,200	U.S. Treasury	11.750	11/15/93	108.327	9.63	3.827	6.31		2,495,585
5,000	U.S. Treasury	13.125	5/15/94	115.143	9.55	4.025	7.88		6,042,476
2,500	U.S. Treasury	12.625	8/15/94	113.686	9.50	4.309	9.08		2,900,472
$63,900	Totals and Averages	11.073%	3/ 9/91	104.524%	9.75	1.999	2.97		$68,691,302
						2.003	2.99		

EXHIBIT 7 (concluded)

October 22, 1989

Par (000)		Treasury Issue		Market		Duration	Dispersion	Market Value Including Accrued Int.
		Coupon	Maturity	Price	Yield			
$71,400	U.S. Treasury	11.500	10/15/90	100.057	11.43	.953	.02	$71,598,602
2,200	U.S. Treasury	14.625	2/15/92	107.547	10.83	2.011	1.40	2,425,488
800	U.S. Treasury	11.750	4/15/92	102.015	10.80	2.221	1.82	817,928
$74,400	Totals and Averages	11.595%	11/ 4/90	100.300%	11.38	1.000	.08	$74,842,017
						1.001	.08	
			October 22, 1990 (Final Portfolio)					
$2,200	U.S. Treasury	14.625	2/15/92	106.643	9.12	1.221	1.56	$2,405,600
800	U.S. Treasury	11.750	4/15/92	103.535	9.14	1.401	2.02	830,088
$3,000	Totals and Averages	13.858%	3/ 2/92	105.814%	9.13	1.267	.07	$3,235,687
						1.267	1.68	

Notes: (1) CBE = corporate bond equivalent
(2) Two average durations are shown. The first is calculated using the total portfolio's cash flow and discounted by the portfolio IRR. The second is the market value weighted average of the individual securities' duration.

EXHIBIT 8 Bond Immunization Year End Transactions Report, October 22, 1986

1. Income Received During Year:	Coupon Income	+	Interest on Coupon	+	Matured Principal
	$5,421,442		244,345		0

Plus

	Cash Carry Forward	+	Interest on Cash Carry Forward		Total Cash Received
	0		0	=	$ 5,665,788

2. Sell:	Par (000)	Issues	Coupon	Maturity	Yield	Price	Market Value
	2,300	TSY	15.75	11/15/01	10.15	142.735	$3,440,405

		Less Transaction Fees	−5,750
			$3,434,655

3. Available to Reinvest:
$9,100,443

4. Buy:	Par (000)	Issues	Coupon	Maturity	Yield	Price	Market Value
	9,000	TSY	9.625	6/30/89	10.55	97.853	$9,075,119

Cash Carry Forward = (9,100,443 − 9,075,119) $ 25,324

EXHIBIT 9 Bond Immunization Year End Transactions Report, October 22, 1987

1. Income Received During Year:

Coupon Income		Interest on Coupon		Matured Principal
$5,926,750	+	292,739	+	0

Plus

Cash Carry Forward		Interest on Cash Carry Forward		Total Cash Received
25,324	+	2,431	=	$ 6,247,244

2. Sell:

Par (000)	Issues	Coupon	Maturity	Yield	Price	Market Value
400	TSY	12.625	8/15/94	10.00	112.715	$ 460,193
1,700	TSY	15.750	11/15/01	10.00	142.903	2,545,764
				Less Transaction Fees		−5,250
						$3,000,707

3. Available to Reinvest:

$9,247,951

4. Buy:

Par (000)	Issues	Coupon	Maturity	Yield	Price	Market Value
9,000	TSY	9.625	6/30/89	10.00	99.403	$9,214,619

Cash Carry Forward = (9,247,951 − 9,214,619) $ 33,332

EXHIBIT 10 Bond Immunization Year End Transactions Report, October 22, 1988

1. Income Received During Year:

Coupon Income		Interest on Coupon		Matured Principal
$6,474,750	+	333,928	+	0

Plus

Cash Carry Forward		Interest on Cash Carry Forward		Total Cash Received
33,332	+	3,333	=	$ 6,845,343

2. Sell:

Par (000)	Issues	Coupon	Maturity	Yield	Price	Market Value
2,100	TSY	12.625	8/15/94	9.50	113.686	$2,436,396
				Less Transaction Fees		−5,250
						$2,431,146

3. Available to Reinvest: $9,276,489

4. Buy:

Par (000)	Issues	Coupon	Maturity	Yield	Price	Market Value
9,000	TSY	9.625	6/30/89	9.99	99.735	$9,244,499

Cash Carry Forward = (9,276,489 − 9,244,499) $ 31,990

EXHIBIT 11 Bond Immunization Year End Transactions Report, October 22, 1989

1. Income Received During Year:

Coupon Income		Interest on Coupon		Matured Principal
$7,075,875	+	1,462,428	+	32,000,000

Plus

Cash Carry Forward		Interest on Cash Carry Forward		Total Cash Received
31,990	+	3,439	=	$40,573,732

2. Sell:

Par (000)	Issues	Coupon	Maturity	Yield	Price	Market Value
4,200	TSY	11.750	4/15/92	10.80	102.015	$ 4,294,120
5,000	TSY	13.750	5/15/92	10.79	106.462	5,622,013
5,000	TSY	11.875	8/15/93	10.64	103.756	5,297,515
2,200	TSY	11.750	11/15/93	10.61	103.669	2,393,109
5,000	TSY	13.125	5/15/94	10.59	108.974	5,734,026
2,500	TSY	12.625	8/15/94	10.59	107.487	2,745,497
						26,086,280

				Less Transaction Fees		−59,750
						$26,026,530

3. Available to Reinvest: $66,600,262

4. Buy:

Par (000)	Issues	Coupon	Maturity	Yield	Price	Market Value
66,400	TSY	11.500	10/15/90	11.43	100.057	$66,584,694

Cash Carry Forward = (66,600,262 − 66,584,644) $ 15,568

EXHIBIT 12 Bond Immunization Year End Transactions Report, October 22, 1990

1. Income Received During Year:	Coupon Income $8,626,750	+	Interest on Coupon 381,144	+	Matured Principal 71,400,000

Plus

	Cash Carry Forward 15,568	+	Interest on Cash Carry Forward 1,596	=	Total Cash Received $80,425,058

2. Sell:	Par (000)	Issues	Coupon	Maturity	Yield	Price	Market Value
	2,200	TSY	14.625	2/15/92	09.12	106.643	$2,405,600
	800	TSY	11.750	4/15/92	09.14	103.535	830,088
							$3,235,688
					Less Transaction Fees		−7,500
							$3,228,188

3. Available to Reinvest:	$83,653,246

$83,027,095 were exceeded by 16 basis points and $626,151 respectively.[5] We demonstrated in this example that targeted rates may be obtained over a predetermined immunization term, in spite of dramatic fluctuations in market yields.

MULTIPERIOD IMMUNIZATION

In the discussions so far, we have documented how the three conditions are required to create a single-period immunized portfolio. These conditions can be extended to create an immunized portfolio that will satisfy the funding requirements of multiple-period liabilities, such as the monthly payouts to the retired-lives portion of a pension plan.

If a liability schedule were composed of 30 annual payments, it would be possible to create 30 single-period immunized portfolios to fund that schedule. If we then analyzed the overall duration of the 30 asset portfolios, it would equal the duration of the liabilities. As long as the dispersions of assets and liabilities are closely matched and the asset value greater than the present value of liabilities, then the liability schedule should be fully funded and the portfolio immunized.

For example, a retired-lives payout schedule for a pension fund is presented in Exhibit 13. These payouts are summarized in annual amounts, but in practice they are generally converted into monthly numbers (by dividing the annual payouts into 12 equal payments).

Calculating the duration of multiperiod liabilities is not as straightforward as calculating the duration of a single-period liability where the remaining time in the planning horizon is the liability duration. With multiple payout periods, the liability duration is derived by using, as the discount factor, the internal rate of return (IRR) on the assets. Of course, the IRR of the assets is not determinable unless we know the precise portfolio, its duration, and dispersion.

As a result of this simultaneity problem, the construction of an immunized portfolio is an iterative process whereby an IRR guess for the portfolio is advanced; the durations and dispersion of the liabilities are then calculated based on the IRR guess; an optimal immunized portfolio is simulated to match the duration and dispersion estimates; the portfolio IRR is then compared with the estimated IRR, and, if they differ, a new IRR estimate is advanced and the procedure repeated.

A final multiperiod immunized portfolio is presented in Exhibit 14. Note that the 6.91 year duration of the assets is equal to the 6.90 year duration of the liabilities at the portfolio IRR of 9.28 percent. Furthermore the $34,693,591 market value of assets is greater than the

---

[5] Since the initial investment is $49,986,881 and the target yield is 10.41 percent, the target future value is

$$(1.1041)^5 \times \$49,986,881 = \$83,027,095$$

EXHIBIT 13 Retired-Lives Payout Schedule for a Pension Fund:
Multi-period Immunization Illustration

Period Ending	Liability Payments
12/31/86	$ 4,956,660
12/31/87	5,787,470
12/31/88	5,482,992
12/31/89	5,248,992
12/31/90	4,997,004
12/31/91	4,721,004
12/31/92	4,485,000
12/31/93	4,245,996
12/31/94	4,005,996
12/31/95	3,767,004
12/31/96	3,526,000
12/31/97	3,288,004
12/31/98	3,056,373
12/31/99	2,826,996
12/31/00	2,601,996
12/31/01	2,384,004
12/31/02	2,172,996
12/31/03	1,971,000
12/31/04	1,776,996
12/31/05	1,593,996
12/31/06	1,421,004
12/31/07	1,259,004
12/31/08	1,110,000
12/31/09	972,000
12/31/10	845,004
12/31/11	729,000
12/31/12	626,004
12/31/13	533,004
12/31/14	453,000
Totals	$74,269,559

$34,684,891 present value of liabilities; and the 27.46 units of asset dispersion are greater than the 27.10 units of dispersion in the liabilities.

The result of imposing these three conditions is a multiperiod immunized portfolio that is reasonably well protected from the pathological shifting and twisting of future yield curves. If rebalanced properly, the portfolio should be sufficient to fund the entire schedule of liabilities regardless of future rate changes.

Rebalancing Procedures for Multiperiod Portfolios

Just as with a single-period immunized portfolio, a multiperiod portfolio must be rebalanced whenever one of the three conditions is violated. If,

EXHIBIT 14 Multiperiod Immunized Portfolio

| Par (000) | Rating | Issuer | Issue | | Market | | Curr. Yield | Convexity | Duration | Dispersion | IRR | Market Value Including Accrued Int. |
			Coupon	Maturity	Price	Yield						
$ 6,700	AGY	FFCB	13.000	9/ 1/94	121.656	9.26	10.69	37.95	5.406	11.83	9.26	$ 8,576,592
4,300	TSY		11.500	3/31/86	100.280	7.82	11.47	.05	.085	46.45	7.97	4,517,176
5,400	TSY		11.000	11/15/86	102.251	7.64	10.76	.77	.686	38.63	7.62	5,693,847
630	TSY	TSY TR	0.000	5/15/90	70.295	8.55	0.0	18.23	4.208	7.25	8.55	442,858
10,000	TSY	TSY TR	0.000	5/15/97	36.289	9.25	0.0	119.98	11.209	18.57	9.24	3,628,900
10,000	TSY	TSY TR	0.000	11/15/97	34.491	9.30	0.0	130.71	11.713	23.16	9.29	3,449,100
10,000	TSY	TSY TR	0.000	5/15/98	32.767	9.35	0.0	141.69	12.208	28.18	9.34	3,276,700
10,000	TSY	TSY TR	0.000	11/15/98	31.114	9.40	0.0	153.32	12.712	33.78	9.39	3,111,400
6,570	TSY	TSY TR	0.000	2/15/99	30.396	9.40	0.0	159.34	12.964	36.77	9.39	1,997,017
		Totals and										
$63,600	TSY	Averages	3.081%	1/10/96	53.283	9.29	5.78	71.98	6.917	27.46	9.28	$34,693,591

Note the following:
(1) The duration of the assets is 6.917 years. The duration of the liabilities is 6.90 years.
(2) The present value of the assets at the IRR is $34,693,591. The present value of the liabilities at the IRR is $34,684,891.
(3) The dispersion of the assets around the duration date is 27.46. The dispersion of the liabilities around the duration date is 27.10.

for example, the two durations were to wander apart, then the portfolio must be rebalanced to return it to a duration-matched state.

In a multiperiod portfolio, the durations will tend to wander whenever a liability payment comes due. An extreme example might be a $10 million bullet liability due in 1 month (almost zero duration) and a $10 million bullet liability due in 10 years. The average duration of the two liabilities will be about five years.

One month from now, the one month liability will be extinguished and the remaining liability will be 9 years and 11 months. As the asset portfolio has a duration of roughly five years to match what was a 5-year average duration liability, the sudden shift in liability duration from 5 years to approximately 10 years will cause a major duration mismatch and need for a rebalancing.

APPLICATIONS OF THE IMMUNIZATION STRATEGY

The major applications of the immunization strategy have been in the pension, insurance, banking, and thrift industries.

As illustrated in Exhibit 15, the pension market has made widespread use of both single-period and multiperiod immunization. Single-

EXHIBIT 15 Applications for Immunization

	Market		
	PENSION	*INSURANCE*	*BANKING AND THRIFT*
Single Period	Asset strategy (GIC alternative)		
Multiperiod	Funding retired-lives payouts	Funding GICs and structured settlements	Gap management Matched growth
	Single premium buy-outs	Portfolio insurance	Portfolio insurance
	Portfolio insurance		

period immunization is generally employed as an alternative to the purchase of a guaranteed investment contract (GIC) from an insurance company. Both vehicles seek to lock in today's prevailing rates over a finite planning horizon. Immunization has the advantage of liquidity, as the portfolio is composed of marketable securities. GICs are privately written contracts between plan sponsor and insurance company and are not generally traded in the secondary market.

The additional advantage of an immunized portfolio is that the portfolio manager can take advantage of market opportunities in structuring and rebalancing these portfolios by including securities in the portfolio that are attractive on a relative value basis. The investor can actively position the portfolio in sectors and credits he perceives to be cheap or upgrade candidates. By actively positioning the immunized portfolio, he can add incremental value to the portfolio and potentially outperform the illiquid GIC over a fixed planning horizon.

The pension market has also made widespread use of multiperiod immunization. Multiperiod immunization is generally employed to fund a schedule of expected benefit payouts to the retired-lives portion of a defined benefit pension plan. As explained in greater detail in the next chapter on cash flow matching, by matching the durations of an immunized portfolio with corresponding liabilities, the plan sponsor can lock in prevailing rates, raise his actuarial interest-rate assumption, and reduce his cash contributions to the pension fund. Tens of billions of dollars of pension monies went into the immunization and dedication strategies in the early and mid-1980s due to the strong incentive of cash flow savings and the reduced funding risk for the retired segment of the plan.

The insurance market has also made widespread use of the multiperiod immunization strategy for their fixed liability insurance products such as GICs and structured settlements. Since GIC, structured settlement and single premium buy-out assets and liabilities are generally segmented from general account assets and liabilities, the entire line of business can be immunized to minimize interest-rate risk and lock in a spread. Again these portfolios can be actively positioned to take advantage of market opportunities.

Lastly, banks and thrifts have made extensive use of the multiperiod immunization strategy to assist in the management of their asset/liability gap and to assure future duration-matched growth of assets and liabilities.

VARIATIONS TO IMMUNIZATION

There are several variations or enhancements to the immunization strategy including combination-matching; contingent immunization; immunization with futures, options, mortgages, or swaps; and stochastic duration-matching.[6]

The most popular variation of the immunization strategy is combination-matching (horizon-matching). A combination-matched portfolio

---

[6] For a discussion of active strategies with an immunization program, see Chapter 33.

is one that is duration-matched with the added constraint that it be cash-matched in the first few years, usually five years. The advantages of combination-matching over immunization are that liquidity needs are provided for in the initial cash-flow-matched period. Also, most of the positive slope or inversion of a yield curve tends to take place in the first few years. By cash flow matching the initial portion, we have reduced the risk associated with nonparallel shifts of a sloped yield curve.

The disadvantages of combination-matching over immunization are that the cost is slightly greater and the swapping discretion is constrained. The freedom to swap a combination-matched portfolio is partially hampered because the asset durations must be replaced in a swap, and the cash flows in the initial five-year period must be replaced.

A variant strategy to immunization is contingent immunization. The contingent immunization strategy is a blend of active management with immunization, such that a portfolio is actively managed with a lower floor return assured over the horizon.[7]

The floor return, or safety net, is a rate set below the immunized rate, allowing the manager discretion to actively position his portfolio. If the manager incorrectly positions his portfolio and the market moves against him, the portfolio can still be actively managed. If the market continues to move against the portfolio and the floor return is violated, then the manager must commit to an immunized portfolio to assure the floor return over the remainder of the horizon.

Contingent immunization requires an abrupt change in management strategy at the moment the floor return is violated. With dynamic asset allocation (portfolio insurance)[8], the change in strategy is gradual. In this instance, a manager gradually shifts out of his risky asset into a riskless asset to avoid violating his minimum return requirements. An actively managed bond portfolio or equity portfolio is the risky asset. An immunized portfolio, with duration matched to the holding period, can serve as the riskless asset. Overall, the performance of the portfolio of risky and riskless assets replicates the performance that would be obtained were a put option added to the risky portfolio. This synthetic put gives the portfolio maximum upside potential consistent with a prespecified level of protection on the downside.

Immunized portfolios can also be created with the use of futures contracts to replicate the interest sensitivity of an immunized duration.[9] In this form, a desired portfolio can be selected without regard to a target duration, and futures contracts can then be used to replicate the price sensitivity of an immunized portfolio at the desired duration.

---

[7] See Martin L. Leibowitz and Alfred Weinberger, "The Uses of Contingent Immunization," *Journal of Portfolio Management* (Fall 1981), pp. 51–55.

[8] This strategy is discussed in Chapter 44.

[9] See Chapter 45.

Finally, options can be used with immunized portfolios to enhance returns over a specified horizon.[10] Through the use of covered call writing, or long put or call positions, a manager can enhance his return over a specified horizon.

CONCLUSION

Bond immunization is an important risk-control strategy that is used extensively by the pension fund, insurance, banking, and thrift industries. In today's volatile markets, it is imperative that all asset liability gaps be intentional. Immunization provides the tools to measure the interest-rate risk position an institution or a fund is taking with respect to its liabilities; it also provides the tools to minimize that risk when a minimum gap is desired.

---

[10] See Chapter 45.

32

Dedicated Bond Portfolios

Peter E. Christensen
Managing Director
Fixed Income Research
PaineWebber Incorporated

Frank J. Fabozzi, Ph.D., C.F.A.
Visiting Professor
Sloan School of Management
Massachusetts Institute of Technology

INTRODUCTION

Dedication, or cash flow matching as it is also called, is an important portfolio investment strategy in asset/liability management. The applications of dedication include pension benefit funding, defeasement of debt service, structured settlement funding, annuity funding, GIC matching, and funding of other insurance products.

Investors can use dedication to control or even eliminate interest-rate risk by structuring a portfolio of bonds so that the cash flows from the bonds match the projected schedule of payouts on the associated liabilities. In the process, the uncertainty of funding a schedule of liabilities in volatile markets can be substantially minimized.

THE NEED FOR A BROADER ASSET/LIABILITY FOCUS

For financial intermediaries such as banks and insurance companies, there is a well-recognized need for a complete funding perspective. This need is best illustrated by the enormous interest-rate risk assumed by many insurance carriers in the early years of their Guaranteed Investment Contract (GIC) products. A huge volume of compound (zero coupon) and simple interest (annual pay) GICs were issued in three-through seven-year maturities in the positively sloped yield curve environment of the mid-1970s. Proceeds from hundreds of these GIC issuances were reinvested at higher rates in the longer 10- to 30-year private placement, commercial mortgage, and public bond instruments. At the time, industry expectations were that the GIC product would be very profitable because of the large positive spread between the higher "earned" rate on the longer assets and the lower "credited" rate on the GIC contracts.

By pricing GICs on a spread basis and investing the proceeds on a mismatched basis, companies gave little consideration to the rate risk they were assuming in volatile markets. As rates rose dramatically in the late 1970s and early 1980s, carriers were exposed to extreme disintermediation as GIC liabilities matured and the corresponding assets had 20 years remaining to maturity and were valued at only a fraction of their original cost.

As a result of this enormous risk exposure, insurance carriers were induced to adopt a broader asset/liability focus in order to control the interest-rate risk associated with writing a fixed liability product. Dedication has become a very popular matching strategy to control this market risk.

Similarly, in funding pension liabilities, there is also a need for a broad asset/liability focus. Since the future investment performance of a pension fund is unpredictable, actuaries generally incorporate a wide margin of conservatism in the investment return assumptions used in the calculation of annual funding requirements. This conservative approach has sometimes generated current contribution requirements considerably in excess of the amounts ultimately needed. Such excess contributions can cause cash flow or profit squeezes and limit flexibility in tax, expansion, and other planning areas for the sponsoring entity.

Through the use of the dedication strategy to fund the relatively well-defined, retired-lives portion of the pension liability, some of the conservative margin can be eliminated. In the process, current contribution requirements to the pension fund can decline, allowing the plan to sponsor a wider range of policy options.

CASH FLOW MATCHING FOR PENSION FUNDS

The most popular application of the dedicated strategy has been to fund the payout obligations of the retired-lives portion of a pension plan. In the following simulation we illustrate, in detail, the mechanics of the strategy.

Determining the Liabilities

The first step in establishing a dedicated bond portfolio is to determine the schedule of liabilities to be funded. For pension funds, usually it is the expected benefit payouts to a closed block of current retirees that are matched against the cash flows from a dedicated portfolio. Usually the benefit payouts to future retirees can not be projected as accurately. Since future retirees are not included in the closed block, the schedule of payments declines over time as the retirees pass away. Exhibit 1 illustrates the annual schedule of benefit payouts that are expected to be paid to current retirees.

The forecasted payouts are based on the known benefit payouts at retirement for each employee and a number of variables including ex-

EXHIBIT 1 Schedule of Expected Pension Payouts

Year	Dollar Payout
1985 (partial year)	$ 3,750,000
1986	14,916,015
1987	14,427,473
1988	13,445,985
1989	12,435,248
1990	11,754,199
1991	11,384,959
1992	11,028,026
1993	10,654,684
1994	10,408,523
1995	10,355,190
1996	10,236,214
1997	9,953,126
1998	9,670,039
1999	9,302,164
2000	8,748,308
2001	8,621,160
2002	8,209,594
2003	7,893,578
2004	7,435,436
2005	6,993,713
2006	6,579,349
2007	6,145,834
2008	5,732,824
2009	5,322,551
2010	4,983,398
2011	4,615,526
2012	4,257,221
2013	3,892,088
2014	3,537,881
2015	3,216,510
2016	2,934,788
2017	2,659,909
2018	2,385,026
2019	2,123,504
2020	1,447,297
Total	$271,457,335

pected mortality, spouse benefit assumptions, and expected cost-of-living increases. As shown in Exhibit 1, the total payouts in dollars over the 35-year time horizon for the retired employees is $271,457,335.

In addition to funding the retired-lives payouts, the dedicated strategy is frequently applied to a somewhat broader universe of participants that includes retirees plus terminated vested participants. Terminated vested participants are former employees entitled to a benefit commencing sometime in the future. Since these benefit amounts are relatively fixed, they can be easily match funded.

Several pension plans have extended the dedication strategy to include the funding of "anticipated retiree" pension obligations as well. That is, in addition to funding the retired and terminated vested liabilities, the cash-flow-matched design is used to offset liabilities associated with "active" employees aged 50 and greater. Since these benefit payments are not fixed until employees actually retire, the various mortality, termination, and benefit assumptions must be reviewed periodically to insure that actual experience tracks the forecast.

Instead of a downward-sloping liability schedule, the profile of expected benefit payouts for this broad population of plan participants would increase dramatically in the first 10 to 15 years, level off for a brief period, then begin a downward slope. The benefit schedule peaks because the active participants who will be joining the retired population over the next 10 to 15 years are generally greater in number and have higher salaries (due to inflation) than the shrinkage in population of retirees due to mortality. The percentage reduction in actual liability and, hence, in contribution requirements associated with the anticipated retirees, is frequently larger than that for the currently retired population.

Similarly, in the case of insurance companies, a liability schedule will represent monthly projections of fixed payouts for GIC products or structured settlements. Once that schedule is derived, the procedures for match funding a GIC product line are similar to creating a dedicated portfolio for a pension fund.

Setting Portfolio Constraints

With the liability schedule determined, the next step in instituting a dedicated portfolio is to specify portfolio constraints on sector, quality, issue, and lot sizes. As illustrated in Exhibit 2, a portfolio manager may wish to constrain the optimal or least-cost solution to a universe of government, mortgage, and corporate securities rated AAA/A- or better. Similarly, he may wish to constrain mortgages to a maximum of 20 percent of the portfolio. In the simulation that follows, a minimum of 20 percent of the portfolio is constrained to be Treasury and agency securities and a 25 percent maximum is set for each sector of the corporate market.

EXHIBIT 2 Portfolio Constraints

	Minimum	Maximum
Quality*		
Treasury	⎱ 20%	100%
Agency	⎰	100
AAA	0	100
AA	0	100
A	0	50
BBB	0	0
Sector		
Treasury	⎱ 20%	100%
Agency	⎰	100%
Industrial	0	25
Utility	0	25
Telephone	0	25
Bank & finance	0	25
Canadian	0	⎱
Yankee	0	25
World Bank	0	⎰
Euros	0	25
Pass throughs (GNMA only)	0	15
Concentration		
Maximum in one issue		10%
Maximum in one issuer		10
Call		
Spread between coupon and YTM		90 bp
Lot Size		
Conditional minimum		$200,000 (par)
Increment		100,000 (par)
Maximum		Unlimited

* Single A split rated securities allowed.

Note from Exhibit 2 that constraints on lot size are emphasized. Round lot solutions (in lots of 100 bonds or more) are strongly preferred since the actual execution of the portfolio may be accomplished more efficiently without the added costs of odd lot differentials. Also, as the dedicated portfolio is swapped or reoptimized over time, additional odd lot premiums on the sale of such assets are avoided.

The Reinvestment Rate

Since the timing of cash receipts does not always exactly match the timing of cash disbursements, surplus funds generated must be reinvested at an assumed reinvestment rate until the next liability payout date. This reinvestment or rollover rate is of vital importance because it is often preferable to prefund future benefit payments with higher yielding securities than to purchase lower yielding issues that mature closer to the liability payments dates. The more conservative the reinvestment rate, the greater the penalty for prefunding future benefit payouts and therefore, the tighter the cash-flow match. The more aggressive the reinvestment rate, the greater the prefunding in optimal portfolios. Frequently the actuarial investment rate assumption is used. Currently these rates are in the 6 to 9 percent range.

Selecting the Optimal Portfolio

Once the liability schedule, the portfolio constraints, and the reinvestment rate(s) are specified, then an optimal (least cost) portfolio can be structured to fully fund or defease the expected benefit payouts. The optimal portfolio is illustrated in Exhibit 3.

We should note that assembling a dedicated portfolio that has a very high probability of attaining its funding objective over time does require a restricted universe of available issues. The fund manager must avoid questionable credits and, most importantly, avoid those issues that may be called prior to maturity or have large sinking-fund call risk. Defaults and loss of issues prior to maturity would mean that the funding of the liability schedule would not be sufficient. As a result, most current coupon callable bonds are not appropriate for matched portfolios.

The logic used to select the optimal or least-cost portfolio varies among purveyors of the cash-flow-matching service. There are three methods used to identify the optimal portfolio. In order of sophistication, they are stepwise solutions, linear programming, and integer programming. Of the three, integer programming is the most technically advanced and is able to identify the lowest cost round lot solution.

The Cash Flow Match

Exhibit 4 summarizes the cash flow match inherent in the dedicated portfolio in our example. Note that in every year, the cash flow from the maturing principal when added to the coupon income from all securities in the portfolio and the reinvestment income will almost precisely equal the liability requirements specified by the actuary in Exhibit 1. Since almost all cash flow is being paid out to fund the liability payment each month, the portfolio has very little cash to reinvest each period and hence, assumes very little reinvestment risk. The plan can, therefore, lock in a rate of over 11 percent, the rate prevailing at the time of this writing, regardless of the future course of rates.

In this simulation the computer has controlled reinvestment risk by structuring relatively small surplus positions in most years. However, the computer sometimes prefunds distant payouts by reinvesting the proceeds of high yielding shorter maturing issues at the low reinvest-

EXHIBIT 3   The Optimal Portfolio

PAR AMOUNT ($) OR # SHARES	RATING	NAME	COUPON	MATURITY	MARKET PRICE	CURR. YIELD	YIELD	CALL DATA DATE	PRICE	YTC	DURATION	IRR	CBE END YIELD	MARKET VALUE INCLUDING ACCRUED INT.
4,700,000	A3/BBB+	ALCOA	7.000	11/15/96	73.793	A11.15	9.49	11/15/84	100.000	56.55A	7.151	11.14		$3,564,229
5,500,000	A7/BBB+	ALCOA	7.000	4/15/11	62.044	A11.69	11.28	4/15/84	100.000	N/A A	8.795	11.68		$3,233,450
500,000	A1/AA+	ASSOC NA	12.550	5/15/88	107.042	A 9.52	11.72				2.315	9.52		$553,512
3,600,000	A1/A+	BAKER	6.000V	3/15/ 2	60.027	A11.43	10.00	3/15/84	100.000	N/A A	8.492	11.43		$2,259,972
600,000	A3/A	BENE	12.500	12/15/93	110.098	X10.63	11.35				5.413	10.62		$676,213
1,000,000	A3/A	BENE	7.500	5/15/98	76.879	A10.90	9.76	5/15/85	102.600	54.19A	7.538	10.89		$790,665
200,000	A2/A—	CAR P&L	9.750	5/ 1/ 4	87.971	A11.31	11.08	5/ 1/85	105.900	40.29A	8.069	11.30		$182,388
3,000,000	A2/A—	CAR P&L	10.500	5/15/ 9	92.639	A11.40	11.33	5/15/85	108.330	34.24A	8.424	11.39		$2,871,045
6,500,000	A3/A	CAT	6.000V	5/ 1/ 7	56.001	A11.58	10.71	5/ 1/84	100.000	N/A A	9.027	11.57		$3,768,982
500,000	A3/AA	CIT FIN	13.625	8/ 1/88	110.066	A 9.58	12.38				2.506	9.57		$555,818
1,400,000	A2/AA—	CIT FIN	9.850	8/15/04	88.404	A11.35	11.14	8/15/89	102.000	14.17	8.328	11.34		$1,243,402
400,000	AA1/AA	CITI X	10.250	12/15/86	101.563	A 8.92	10.09	12/15/86	100.000	8.92	1.221	8.91		$1,434,794
1,500,000	BAA1/A	CRED FIN	10.750	11/ 1/ 3	100.078	X10.73	10.74				5.380	10.71		$1,539,691
3,900,000	A3/A	CWE	7.625	6/ 1/ 3	72.579	A11.30	10.62	6/ 1/85	104.190	N/A A	8.380	11.29		$2,878,518
300,000	A3/A—	DEERE CR	9.350	10/31/ 3	83.725	A11.50	11.17	10/31/84	104.640	N/A A	8.414	11.34		$220,986
2,000,000	A3/A—	DIASHAM	7.700	12/15/ 1	74.018	A11.20	10.40	12/15/84	104.500	17.34	7.997	11.49		$1,736,833
400,000	A3/A—	FFCB	11.625	7/21/86	103.001	A 8.05	11.29			N/A A	8.264	11.19		$302,489
600,000	AGY	FFCB	7.800	4/ 1/86	99.876	A 8.00	7.81				.863	8.06		$417,041
200,000	AGY	FFCB	8.200	5/ 1/86	100.126	A 7.97	8.19				.567	8.00		$618,626
300,000	AGY	FFCB	10.000	12/ 1/86	101.656	A 8.55	9.84				.649	7.98		$205,673
600,000	AGY	FFCB	10.650	12/ 1/87	102.751	A 9.25	10.36				1.184	8.54		$312,385
500,000	AGY	FFCB	12.875	9/ 1/88	108.500	A 9.55	11.87				2.017	9.25		$632,303
400,000	AGY	FFCB	15.650	10/23/89	118.406	A10.10	13.22				2.460	9.54		$689,410
1,000,000	AGY	FFCB	10.950	1/22/90	103.156	A10.04	10.61				3.144	10.09		$619,635
400,000	AGY	FFCB	14.100	6/ 1/90	114.750	A10.10	12.29				3.582	10.03		$417,247
1,100,000	AGY	FFCB	12.500	4/22/90	108.625	A10.52	11.51				3.599	10.10		$1,182,358
200,000	AGY	FFCB	13.750	7/20/92	114.906	A10.54	11.91				3.915	10.24		$1,606,306
300,000	AGY	FFCB	13.000	9/ 1/94	113.125	A10.69	11.49				4.017	10.52		$359,758
2,300,000	AGY	FFCB	14.250	4/20/94	119.687	A10.69	11.91				4.769	10.53		$233,868
200,000	AGY	FFCB	12.350	3/ 1/94	109.125	A10.69	11.32				5.460	10.68		$2,750,544
800,000	AGY	FHLB	14.250	1/27/86	102.063	A 7.46	12.49				5.307	10.69		$922,126
400,000	AGY	FHLB	12.350	9/25/86	103.938	A 8.31	11.79				5.330	7.43		$412,927
500,000	AGY	FHLB	12.250	8/25/86	106.032	A 8.11	13.77				.411	8.30		$546,062
200,000	AGY	FHLB	14.600	4/25/89	113.062	A 9.89	12.60				.988	8.10		$212,470
900,000	AGY	FHLB	14.550	9/25/89	114.937	A 9.99	12.66				.953	9.88		$1,062,089
800,000	AGY	FHLB	14.125	7/25/89	113.250	A 9.94	12.47				2.893	9.98		$969,613
200,000	AGY	FHLB	12.000	3/11/91	107.719	A10.14	11.14				3.108	9.93		$229,247
500,000	AA1/AA+	FNMA	10.850	4/ 1/87	102.577	A 9.06	10.58				3.147	9.93		$566,762
700,000	AA1/AA+	GMAC	11.000	4/ 1/88	103.174	A 9.58	10.66				4.040	10.14		$749,762
600,000	AA1/AA+	GMAC									1.439	9.06		$646,361

Dedicated Bond Portfolio Analysis

Par	Rating	Issuer	Coupon	Maturity	Price	Yield	Cur Yld	Call Date	Call Price	Call Yld	Dur	Yield	Market Value
15,700,000	AGV	GNMA	10.000	6/ 1/ 9	93.750	11.19	10.67				6.338	11.18	$14,845,222
2,800,000	AA3/AA-	HFC	9.000	7/ 1/ 0	85.826	10.95	10.49	1/ /86	102.000	65.45	7.830	10.94	$698,408
1,000,000	A2/AA+	HSTN L&P	6.250	3/ 1/ 5	85.454	11.40	11.01	3/ 1/85	106.310	N/A A	8.142	11.39	$1,676,094
2,700,000	A1/AA-	HYDRO-Q	14.625	8/15/92	124.431	10.64	13.10				4.137	10.63	$1,260,622
400,000	A1/AA-	HYDRO-Q	16.625	1/15/92	127.636	10.55	13.03				4.367	10.54	$3,246,456
1,200,000	A2/A	ILL PWR	8.625	7/ 1/ 6	78.720	11.30	10.96				4.777	10.54	$518,856
2,000,000	A1/A1+	INTEL	0.000V	5/15/95	34.715	11.20	1.24	7/ 2/84	105.890	N/A A	8.636	11.29	$961,300
5,000,000	A1/A1+	KERR-MCG	7.000V	7/ 1/91	62.297	11.62	11.24	3/15/84	100.000	N/A A	9.706	11.20	$694,300
200,000	A1/AA-	MANITOBA	14.750	7/ 1/91	118.014	10.53	12.50	11/ 1/84	100.000	N/A A	8.893	11.61	$3,230,544
400,000	A2/AA	MARIETTA	7.000V	3/15/11	64.077	11.33	10.92	3/15/84	100.000	N/A A	8.175	10.52	$240,863
700,000	AA3/AA	MERRILLL	13.150	8/ 1/87	106.804	9.19	12.31				1.749	9.18	$269,141
200,000	A2/AA	MERRILLLX	11.250	4/15/88	103.779	9.58	10.84	4/15/88	100.000	9.58	2.259	9.57	$755,043
500,000	A3/A-	NAT MED	12.125	4/ 1/95	109.026	9.26	11.12				5.830	10.59	$216,308
800,000	A1/AA-	NE PWR	9.500	7/ 1/ 8	84.331	11.36	11.19	7/ 1/84	106.640	N/A A	8.629	11.35	$568,706
400,000	A2/A+	NV TEL	8.625	6/15/16	77.440	11.26	11.14	6/15/84	106.170	N/A A	8.088	11.24	$691,904
500,000	AAA/AAA	ONTARIO	16.000	5/ 1/91	124.020	10.59	12.90				4.197	10.58	$1,601,685
300,000	AAA/AAA	ONTARIO	15.750	2/25/92	123.723	10.60	12.73				4.517	10.59	$645,656
900,000	A1/A+	PAC G&E	7.750	6/ 1/ 5	71.837	11.35	10.79	12/ 1/84	104.290	N/A A	8.610	11.34	$1,611,243
1,300,000	A2/BBB+	PAC T&T	9.625	7/15/18	85.551	11.30	11.25	7/15/84	108.440	N/A A	9.087	11.29	$663,777
1,000,000	A1/AA-	PENN P&L	8.250	12/ 1/ 6	75.326	11.34	10.95	12/ 1/84	105.980	N/A A	8.643	11.33	$3,470,165
200,000	A2/A+	QUEBEC	9.875	5/15/ 0	90.188	11.25	10.95	5/15/90	102.500	13.12	7.474	11.24	$1,005,753
600,000	AGV	SEAGRAM	11.375	11/ 1/86	103.087	8.52	11.03				1.094	8.50	$930,682
200,000	AGV	SLMA	11.250	10/ 1/87	103.938	9.12	10.82				1.840	9.12	$213,694
600,000	A3/A	SLMA	10.900	2/28/90	103.125	10.02	10.57				3.503	10.00	$651,565
700,000	A3/A+	TANDY	10.125	2/ 1/87	101.529	8.94	9.97				2.931	9.85	$217,271
300,000	A2/A-	TENNECO	9.625	7/15/18	103.198	9.87	10.66				2.585	9.84	$614,068
5,000,000	A2/A-	TENNECO	8.875	4/15/13	87.275	9.85	10.77	4/15/85	105.610	56.89A	8.026	11.34	$312,252
300,000	A1/A1+	TENNECO	6.000V	12/15/11	54.239	11.55	11.06				2.774	11.58	$784,066
800,000	A1/A1+	TEX CP X	13.250	6/ 1/87	106.433	9.17	12.45	6/ 1/87	100.000	9.17	1.581	11.58	$1,099,984
600,000	A1/A1+	TEX CP X	11.250	1/15/88	102.449	9.56	10.49	1/15/88	100.000	9.56	2.137	9.55	$2,774,350
600,000	A1/A1+	TEX CP X	9.500	4/ 1/89	104.135	9.83	10.80	4/ 1/89	100.000	9.83	2.848	9.82	$877,670
1,000,000	AA3/A+	TEX P&L	9.875	4/ 1/ 5	85.901	11.30	11.06	4/ 1/85		50.37A	8.140	11.29	$622,756
2,000,000	A1/A	TRANS FN	10.500	11/30/85	100.720	7.37	10.42	3/ 1/89	104.220	13.61	7.126	10.94	$1,948,381
640,000	TSV	TSY TR	0.000X	5/15/86	94.589	8.00	0.0				.706	8.03	$605,370
290,000	TSV	TSY TR	0.000X	2/15/86	96.499	7.90	0.0				.463	7.85	$279,847
860,000	TSV	TSY TR	0.000X	11/15/95	34.501	10.70	0.0				10.209	10.69	$296,709
1,000,000	TSV	TSY TR	0.000X	2/15/96	35.085	10.95	0.0				10.461	10.94	$350,853
900,000	TSV	TSY TR	0.000X	2/15/96	31.088	10.95	0.0				10.960	10.94	$279,792
990,000	TSV	TSY TR	0.000X	5/15/96	31.999	10.94	0.0				10.908	10.94	$316,787
810,000	TSV	TSY TR	0.000X	8/15/96	36.018	11.09	0.0				12.463	11.09	$291,756
890,000	TSV	TSY TR	0.000X	2/15/98	26.029	11.10	0.0				13.210	11.09	$231,658
930,000	TSV	TSY TR	0.000X	11/15/98	24.003	11.15	0.0				13.958	11.14	$223,228
750,000	TSV	TSY TR	0.000X	8/15/99	21.989	11.15	0.0				14.209	11.14	$164,917
680,000	TSV	TSY TR	0.000X	11/15/99	21.401	11.15	0.0				14.461	11.14	$145,527
980,000	TSV	TSY TR	0.000X	2/15/ 0	20.828	11.15	0.0				14.461	11.14	$204,114
200,000	TSV	TSY BILL	0.000	9/26/85	99.520	6.40	0.0				.074	6.61	$199,040
120,490,000	Aa2/AA	TOTALS & AVERAGES	8.618%	7/13/ 0	81.137%	11.13	10.62	7/23/86A	102.606%	35.56A	6.437	11.12	$100,358,089

*** THE IMPLEMENTATION OF THIS DEDICATED BOND PORTFOLIO WOULD LOWER THE FUNDING COST FROM ***
*** $133,414,859 TO $100,358,089 FOR A SAVINGS OF $33,056,768 (A REDUCTION OF 25%). ***

*** THE PRESENT VALUE OF THE LIABILITY PAYMENTS, DISCOUNTED AT THE ACTUARIAL (REINVESTMENT) RATE(S) IS $133,414,859. ***

EXHIBIT 4 Cash Flow Report

PROPOSED DEDICATED PORTFOLIO
PORTFOLIO ANALYSIS REPORT

CASHFLOW ANALYSIS

TIME FRAME 8/30/85 — 9/ 1/20

REINVESTMENT RATE 7.00% (CBE)

PERIOD ENDING	OPENING BALANCE (+)	PRINCIPAL	COUPON INCOME (+)	REINVESTMENT INCOME (=)	AVAILABLE CASH (−)	LIABILITY PAYMENTS (=)	ENDING BALANCE
12/31/85		1,176,458	3,611,624	13,990	4,802,072	3,750,000	1,052,072
12/31/86	1,052,072	4,659,093	10,219,717	39,406	15,970,288	14,916,015	1,054,273
12/31/87	1,054,273	4,529,474	9,739,285	35,142	15,358,174	14,427,473	930,701
12/31/88	930,701	4,230,939	9,233,604	53,617	14,448,861	13,454,181	994,680
12/31/89	994,680	3,833,553	8,724,400	62,857	13,615,490	12,444,488	1,171,002
12/31/90	1,171,002	3,537,387	8,230,305	44,746	12,983,440	11,736,087	1,247,353
12/31/91	1,247,353	3,042,519	7,846,892	101,004	12,237,768	11,441,217	796,551
12/31/92	796,551	5,149,035	7,333,578	65,005	13,344,169	10,992,026	2,352,143
12/31/93	2,352,143	2,657,027	6,720,321	70,829	11,800,320	10,660,507	1,139,813
12/31/94	1,139,813	4,566,596	6,314,418	68,809	12,089,636	10,406,503	1,683,133
12/31/95	1,683,133	3,937,852	5,814,420	83,148	11,518,553	10,369,529	1,149,024
12/31/96	1,149,024	8,250,915	5,725,739	180,768	15,306,446	10,333,834	4,972,612
12/31/97	4,972,612	605,915	5,336,976	46,155	10,961,658	9,818,514	1,143,144
12/31/98	1,143,144	4,052,992	5,238,120	57,114	10,491,370	9,480,996	1,010,374
12/31/99	1,010,374	3,072,303	5,038,375	45,720	9,166,772	8,290,441	876,331
12/31/00	876,331	3,444,012	4,825,375	54,968	9,200,686	8,748,308	452,378
12/31/01	452,378	4,988,303	4,490,258	158,834	10,089,773	8,621,160	1,468,613
12/31/02	1,468,613	4,315,372	4,135,161	158,232	10,077,378	8,209,595	1,867,783
12/31/03	1,867,783	4,345,433	3,885,146	86,653	10,185,015	7,893,577	2,291,438
12/31/04	2,291,438	2,378,720	3,543,230	69,755	8,283,143	7,435,437	847,706
12/31/05	847,706	4,715,483	3,146,178	134,598	8,843,965	6,993,713	1,850,252
12/31/06	1,850,252	3,355,999	2,892,930	52,166	8,151,347	6,579,349	1,571,998
12/31/07	1,571,998	7,400,562	2,399,572	293,857	11,665,989	6,145,833	5,520,156
12/31/08	5,520,156	7,749,496	2,112,311	303,019	15,684,982	11,732,824	3,952,158
12/31/09	3,952,158	3,494,559	1,791,980	295,828	9,534,525	5,322,551	4,211,974
12/31/10	4,211,974		1,620,000	159,946	5,991,920	4,983,397	1,008,523
12/31/11	1,008,523	15,400,000	1,431,000	288,758	18,128,281	4,615,526	13,512,755
12/31/12	13,512,755		592,000	823,906	14,928,661	4,257,221	10,671,440
12/31/13	10,671,440		592,000	632,872	11,896,312	3,892,087	8,004,225
12/31/14	8,004,225		592,000	456,590	9,052,815	3,537,881	5,514,934
12/31/15	5,514,934		592,000	291,874	6,398,808	3,216,510	3,182,298
12/31/16	3,182,298	2,400,000	488,500	228,554	6,299,352	2,934,788	3,364,564
12/31/17	3,364,564		385,000	155,707	3,905,271	2,659,909	1,245,362
12/31/18	1,245,362	4,000,000	385,000	144,836	5,775,198	2,385,026	3,390,172
12/31/19	3,390,172			158,764	3,548,936	2,123,504	1,425,432
9/01/20	1,425,432			33,418	1,458,850	1,447,297	11,553
TOTALS:		120,489,997	145,027,746	5,951,145		271,457,335	

*** THE PORTFOLIO CASHFLOW SHOWS NO DEFICITS ON ANY OF THE DATES REPORTED ***

ment rate. This is frequently preferable to purchasing bonds with longer maturities and better matching characteristics, but with lower yields to maturity. Note from Exhibit 4 the large amount of prefunding in the 2014 due to the lack of high-yielding issues in subsequent years.

Pricing the Bonds

It is important to note in Exhibit 4 that neither prices nor yields appear in the analysis. A dedicated portfolio is concerned only with cash flows. As long as all coupon payments are made in a timely fashion and every bond matures on schedule, then all the liabilities specified by the actuary will be fully funded. Though credit ratings on some bonds in a portfolio may deteriorate over time and their market prices drop markedly, the integrity of the dedicated design is still preserved as long as all cash-flow payments are complete and punctual.

Prices and yields enter the analysis only in determining the initial cost of the optimal portfolio as seen in Exhibit 3. In this simulation, all bonds were priced as of August 23, 1985.

It is worth noting that the market value of the bonds in the portfolio as of August 23rd was $100,358,089, and the average yield was 11.12 percent, reflecting the market yields available at the time of this writing.

If none of the bonds in the dedicated portfolio default and if the payout projections are accurate, only $100,358,089 in assets will be required to fully fund the total retired payouts of $271,457,335 that we see illustrated in Exhibit 1.

The Savings to the Pension System

As illustrated in Exhibit 5, using the current actuarial investment rate assumption of 7 percent, the plan must have on hand today $133,424,859 in order to fully fund the $271,457,335 of payouts to retired lives. On the basis of the August 23, 1985 pricing, the portfolio can, with a yield of 11.12 percent, fully fund the same $271,457,335 in liability payouts with an initial investment of only $100,358,089. Purchase of this portfolio would generally give the actuary the comfort level necessary to increase the assumed actuarial investment rate on the retired-lives portion of the fund. In most cases, this increase may go all the way to the funding rate of 11.12 percent.

By raising the assumed rate from 7.00 percent to 11.12 percent on the retired portion of the plan, the plan sponsor has reduced the present value of the accumulated plan benefits by $33,056,768. This actuarial gain or potential savings of $33 million represents a 25 percent reduction from the higher present value required under a 7 percent actuarial assumption.

Increasing the assumed rate on the retired-lives portion of the pen-

---

EXHIBIT 5 Reduced Funding Requirements

	Percent	Dollar Amount
1. Total liabilities	—	$271,457,335
2. Present value of total liabilities at	7.00	133,414,859
3. Portfolio cost (market value) at	11.12	100,358,089
4. Potential savings (2 − 3)	—	33,056,768
5. Percent savings (4/2)	24.78	—
6. Percent savings (4/3)	32.94	—

---

sion fund decreases the present value of the funds promised as future payouts, i.e. the actuarial liability. Reductions in actuarial liability usually translate into reductions in the current funding contribution requirements. The reduction in current contribution due to the dedicated strategy can be substantial.

In our example, the actuarial gain is $33,056,768. Generally, this amount cannot be realized in the form of a reduced contribution all in the first year. Pensions and tax legislation require that the gain be spread over 10 to 30 years. With all other factors remaining constant, the reduction in pension contribution might amount to as much as $5 million per year for each of the next 10 years. However, since every pension plan is different, and different actuarial cost methods treat gains differently, the actual savings to a plan may be of different magnitude than represented by this example.

Reoptimizing a Dedicated Bond Portfolio

It was originally thought that once a dedicated portfolio was structured, it should be passively managed—that is, left untouched as assets roll off in tandem with liabilities. Active management techniques can, however, be applied to dedicated portfolios. In addition to active bond-for-bond swapping and active sector positioning of the portfolio, a cash-matched solution can be entirely reoptimized on a periodic basis.

For example, a portfolio that was "optimized" last year, in last year's rate environment, is not an optimum portfolio in today's rate environment with a new yield curve, yield spreads, and available issues. As seen from Exhibit 6, a new least-cost portfolio can be created one year later to fund the same liability schedule with the same portfolio constraints. Since the new optimum portfolio will be less expensive than the old, a cash take-out can be generated by selling off a portion of the original portfolio and replacing the cash insufficiencies with a new combination of securities. When the take-out is significant such trades are usually executed.

The take-out generated by the computer solution can be guaranteed if the reoptimization is executed through a dealer firm. Frequently

EXHIBIT 6 Take-Out from Reoptimizations

	Market Value (000)	Average Rating	Take-Out (000)
Original dedicated portfolio	$100,000	Aaa/AA+	—
Reoptimized dedicated portfolio	99,100	Aaa/AA+	$900

money managers and third party software vendors work in conjunction with dealer firms to obtain a trader-priced database and guaranteed take-outs. On the other hand, if a reoptimization is simulated on a database of matrix (computer-derived) prices without a dealer firm, the take-out may disappear when market prices are obtained in the actual execution.

Note that the new optimum portfolio will always be cheaper than the original portfolio. If the computer is not able to find a portfolio that is cheaper than the original, it will select the original portfolio again, establishing that it is still the optimum.

Active Management of Dedicated Portfolios[1]

In addition to adding value through comprehensive reoptimizations, bond swaps can be undertaken to pick up yield or to swap out of an undesirable credit.[2] To preserve the integrity of the dedicated portfolio, however, the cash flows associated with the bond being sold must be replaced with those from the bond (or bonds) being purchased. As a result, bonds with identical coupons and maturities can be swapped, or bonds with higher coupons and similar maturities. Bonds with similar coupons and slightly earlier maturities can also be swapped provided an additional cash pay-up is not required.

In addition to swapping, an active manager might add significant value by actively positioning a new dedicated portfolio in cheap sectors of the market. As spreads change, the portfolio can be reoptimized using the computer matching-logic to overweight the newly cheapened sectors of the market and underweight the rich ones.

For example, suppose that an existing $100 million dedicated portfolio could be reoptimized, using the same set of constraints, into a $99.1 million portfolio with a $900,000 take-out. Suppose further that the portfolio manager believes that corporate spreads will widen over the next few months. The manager might desire to temporarily upgrade his port-

---

[1] A further discussion of this topic is presented in the next chapter.
[2] Bond swap strategies are discussed in Chapter 29.

folio from the current average rating of double-A, await the anticipated spread changes, then reverse the trade at a later date.

In this situation, the computer can be instructed, in effect, to spend the $900,000 take-out to buy a higher quality portfolio. Rather than to minimize cost, the computer was instructed to maximize rating, subject to the constraint of spending the full $100 million and cash-flow-matching every liability payment. As shown in Exhibit 7, the result of the restructuring was that the average rating was increased two rating categories from double-A to agency.

EXHIBIT 7   Maximize Quality

	Market Value (000)	Average Rating	Take-Out (000)
Original dedicated portfolio	$100,000	Aaa/AA+	—
Reoptimized dedicated portfolio (minimum cost)	99,100	Aaa/AA+	$900
Reoptimized dedicated portfolio (maximum quality)	100,000	Treasury/Agency	—

Similarly, if rates were expected to rise, the portfolio could be positioned as short as possible by instructing the computer to minimize duration. In Exhibit 8, the duration of the portfolio was shortened almost half a year while still maintaining a cash-flow match. Alternatively, if rates were expected to fall, the $900,000 surplus in the portfolio could be used to maximize duration.

EXHIBIT 8   Minimize Duration

	Market Value (000)	Duration (years)	Percent Decrease
Original dedicated portfolio	$100,000	5.4	—
Reoptimized dedicated portfolio (minimum cost)	99,100	5.4	—
Reoptimized dedicated portfolio (minimize duration)	100,000	4.9	8.3%

Role of Money Manager and Dealer Firm

Both money managers and dealer firms have played important roles in managing and executing cash-flow-matched portfolios. There are relative advantages to selecting a money manager over a dealer firm (and vice versa) in implementing the dedicated strategy. For example, all portfolio optimizations require a database of bonds that is both priced and sized by traders. Most money managers have access only to matrix pricing (computer derived pricing) that is reliable generally within a range of plus or minus 50 basis points. When an optimizer is applied to a matrix priced database of bonds, the optimizer will find the least-cost solution by identifying bonds that are cheap (due to mispricing) and select them in size for the optimal solution. Since the computer-derived solution is not executable at the cheap levels specified in the data base, the "least-cost" solution is not optimal when executed at market rates.

Dealer firms and software vendors with dealer connections are best positioned to simulate, structure, and execute an optimum portfolio due to the accurate pricing and sizing in their databases. However, since dealer firms are not fiduciaries, it is money managers who make the active management decisions about sector positioning, call protection, credit decisions, and spread forecasts.

In short, money managers are in a position to actively swap a portfolio over time to enhance returns. Yet dealers can systematically reoptimize a portfolio and enhance return because of their superior trader priced databases and guaranteed take-outs in a portfolio restructuring. Since both forms of swapping can add substantial value to a portfolio, the combination of money manager and dealer firm working together may be in the client's best interest.

CONCLUSION

Dedication is a very important portfolio investment strategy to control interest-rate risk and lock in prevailing market rates. For insurance companies with fixed liability products such as GICs or structured settlements, cash flow matching has been a popular approach to lock in a spread (or profit) on the entire line of business.

For pension funds, the motivation is to control market risk by fully funding or defeasing the more quantifiable retired liabilities of a plan and locking in a market rate that is well in excess of the actuarial investment return assumption. By raising the actuarial rate to today's market levels on the dedicated portion of the plan, the plan sponsor is able to reduce pension contributions (pension expense), and thereby increase corporate cash flow and reported earnings.

The plan sponsor is also able to eliminate most funding risk (market risk) from a significant part of a plan's liability and eliminate market value fluctuations when reporting surplus asset (or unfunded liability) positions associated with that liability.

33

Actively Managing a Structured Portfolio

Philip H. Galdi, C.P.A.
Vice President
Structured Investments Group
Merrill Lynch Capital Markets

Dedication, immunization, indexing and other portfolio structuring techniques are commonly viewed as passive investment strategies. In a sense, that categorization is appropriate since the decision to follow a "programmed" investment strategy implies less flexibility in actual trading decisions. But by no means do these techniques mandate a buy-and-hold policy or relegate all investment decisions to the computer. Rather, they are most effective when actively monitored to take advantage of return enhancement opportunities.

The decision to establish a structured portfolio is usually made to reduce some element of investment risk. But what is the cost relative to the benefit received? It is the potentially higher returns that *might* be achieved through aggressive active management of investment assets but are foregone in favor of lower risk. Structured portfolios were quite popular in 1984 when it was possible to lock up a 13 to 14 percent internal rate of return on a structure as conservative as a cash-matched dedication. As rates began to decline, however, the opportunity cost associated with a structured portfolio rose. Yet these techniques remain attractive for many purposes. The key is to manage the structured program in such a way as to minimize opportunity cost, and still benefit from lower risk.

This chapter addresses the major ways "active" strategies can improve the performance of "passive" investment techniques, while continuing to meet the objectives of the underlying structured investment program. Also discussed is the process of rebalancing a structured portfolio—a technique necessitated when the original portfolio no longer meets primary objectives. At the conclusion of the chapter, there is a brief discussion of the ways some of these techniques may be applied to active portfolio management strategies as well.

THE OPTIMUM PORTFOLIO

The goal of structuring a portfolio is to select fixed income securities that meet certain investment objectives (e.g., funding future payment obligations, tracking market performance) while taking account of such constraints on security selection as maturity, sector, and quality. There are many possible combinations of available bonds that can meet the primary goal. Therefore, one must apply some additional criteria to the selection process, in order to generate a portfolio that is not only a feasible solution but also the optimal solution.

Structured portfolios are constructed with the aid of linear programming models because there are so many variables to consider. Once the primary objectives and constraints are specified, and the universe of tradable securities identified and priced, the model can quickly select the best solution.

What is the best solution? For some portfolio managers it is the least costly portfolio; for others, it may be the highest yielding portfolio. It may be a portfolio that results in the maximum surplus at the end of the structured program. There are numerous ways to define the optimal solution. Once optimality is defined, however, the computer model can determine which particular securities best meet this definition.

At this point the initial optimal structure has been selected. A passive strategy of buy and hold is possible, provided the original primary goals and constraints continue to be met. But it may also be possible to improve on the optimal solution while continuing to meet the primary goal.

The optimal solution is a moving target. When the portfolio is initially constructed, the securities selected will be determined by (1) availability, and (2) relative pricing of the universe of bonds that meet established criteria. These are both factors that are constantly changing. Of necessity, portfolio selection must focus on bond data at a point in time. Therefore the same program run on two different dates can result in two different optimal portfolios without any change having been made in portfolio constraints or the definition of optimal. Both solutions are adequate in terms of meeting targeted objectives and constraints. Both solutions will be optimal at the time purchased. It is because of the volatility in the fixed income markets that a *more* optimal solution may become available. And it is for this reason that active techniques can be introduced into so-called passive strategies. Even while maintaining the same primary goals and constraints, it may be possible to reconstruct the portfolio to improve on the optimal solution.

RESTRUCTURING A PORTFOLIO AFTER INITIAL STRUCTURING

Once a portfolio has been initially structured, it becomes a candidate for a restructuring. The restructuring process involves a change in the composition of the portfolio such that the aggregate portfolio after all transactions are executed meets original goals and constraints, and performance has been improved. For example, consider a dedication program structured to meet a schedule of future payment obligations at the least possible cost. To qualify, a restructured portfolio would have to continue to generate sufficient cash flow on or before each liability payment date without impairing the overall quality/diversification constraints of the portfolio. In addition, there would have to be either a net cash takeout (i.e., excess cash generated by the transaction over and above the amount required to maintain funding coverage) or an improvement in quality to make the restructuring worth undertaking.

Restructuring opportunities are not a function of time, but rather a result of changing market conditions. Therefore, given no change in liability structure or preferred constraints, there is no set timetable for performing restructuring analyses. Instead the monitoring process focuses more on market conditions with particular emphasis in volatile markets. Conditions that are generally favorable to restructurings are:

1. Availability of more efficient issues.
2. Changes in the shape of the yield curve.
3. Changes in quality or sector spreads.

Availability of more efficient issues. The composition of an optimal portfolio, whatever its primary goal, is largely determined by those issues that are available for purchase at the time the portfolio is established. Thus there is usually some inefficiency in the portfolio since even the "best" portfolio usually can not exactly match, and therefore must overachieve, the constraints set forth. As additional issues become tradable, however, either through a new issuance or because an existing issue in limited supply at the time of the initial structuring has become available for purchase, they can be substituted in the portfolio. Over time then, as illustrated in Exhibit 1, these substitutions can reduce matching inefficiencies.

Changes in the shape of the yield curve. The most efficient match is not always the best solution. For example, one would expect that in a cash-matched structuring, meeting required minimums as opposed to exceeding them should minimize cost. In a normally sloped yield curve environment this is generally true. But when the shape of the yield curve changes, performance can actually be improved by swapping out of a closely matching cash flow structure into a structure where cash is received further in advance of liability payment dates. This will occur

EXHIBIT 1   Potential for More Efficient Dedication as New Issues
Become Available

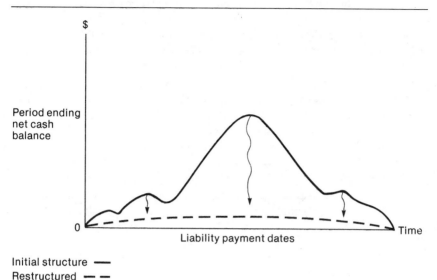

Initial structure ——
Restructured — —

when the benefit of the higher yield on the earlier maturing security outweighs the benefit that is derived from the efficiency of the closer matching security.

The break-even point for determining how much of the yield curve reshaping is necessary to produce a higher return in this manner is largely predicated on the reinvestment assumption that was selected for the initial structuring. For example, if the yield curve is flattening or inverting, a zero percent reinvestment assumption would require a more significant reshaping than a 5 percent or 6 percent assumption, since cash received at the earlier date is assumed to remain idle until used. Of course coupon cash flows must also be considered, further complicating the analysis, and necessitating the use of linear programming models to identify swap opportunities.

Usually the swap involves packaging several issues into a synthetic security that has a cash flow structure similar to the bond being replaced. These types of swaps generally do not require that a complete inversion of the yield curve take place. Depending on the structure of the liabilities being matched, a twist in one segment of the yield curve may be sufficient to produce a swap. Also, as long as there is nonparallel movement somewhere in the yield curve, regardless of direction, swapping can be an ongoing activity. Thus a portfolio might be adjusted after an inversion along one section of the yield curve, with cash flows coming in earlier than required, and then moved back to a more efficient cash match should the yield curve regain its original shape—with cash taken out of the portfolio on each leg of the restructuring and cash flow needs covered at all times.

Changes in quality or sector spreads. The last major factor that can trigger a market-driven restructuring is a change in quality or sector spreads, i.e., movement in the price relationship between quality groups (e.g., agencies versus Treasuries, AAA versus AA, etc.) or sectors of the corporate market (e.g., industrials versus utilities). Certainly restructuring opportunities arise when a shift as dramatic as that shown in Exhibit 2 takes place. Issues in the AAA corporate sector, purchased when the portfolio was initially constructed, could be sold and replaced with the FNMA issue and excess cash withdrawn from the portfolio.

EXHIBIT 2 Swap Potential Due to Changing Price Relationships

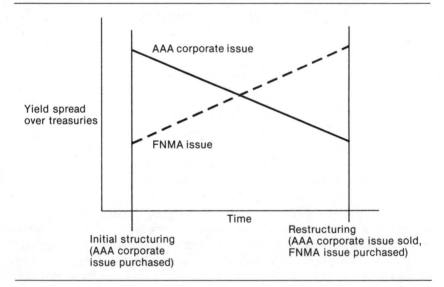

Less dramatic changes in the market are needed to produce swap opportunities when several of the factors discussed so far take place simultaneously. For example, a steepening of the yield curve combined with a narrowing of the spread between AAA and AA corporates may make it possible to upgrade the portfolio by swapping out of the AA issue and into the AAA issue and at the same time generate a cash take-out. Exhibit 3 shows how this compounding element works. Suppose at the time a cash-matched portfolio was established, the two corporate issues shown in Exhibit 3 were both sufficient to meet the required cash

EXHIBIT 3 Compounding Effect of Multiple Market Factors on Dedicated Swap Opportunities

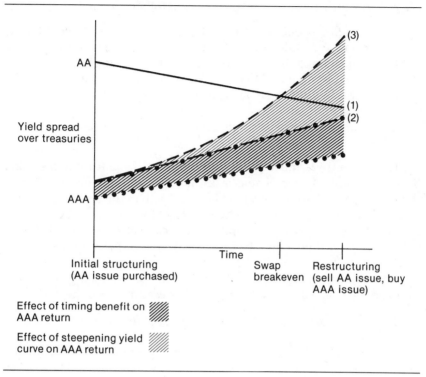

flow structure. The AAA issue more closely matched the liability schedule but that increased efficiency was not enough to offset the higher yield that could be obtained from the AA issue that was purchased for the portfolio.

Subsequent to the initial structuring, market conditions changed and as a result spreads between AAA and AA bonds narrowed. However, by itself, the change in spreads does not provide sufficient benefit to merit a restructuring. Comparing point (1) on the chart to point (2), the AA issue still outperforms the AAA issue. A steepening in the yield curve, however, will further increase the yield of the AAA issue relative to the AA issue since it has a longer term-to-maturity. The combination of factors make the AAA issue more attractive for the portfolio than the AA issue (point (3) versus point (1)) and thus provides an appropriate opportunity for a restructuring. Thus the relative value of two acceptable issues will be a function of their yields relative to each other, the spread over the assumed reinvestment rate, and the timing of cash flows from each respective bond relative to the liability date.

Cash Flow Swaps

A cash flow swap occurs when one or more bonds replace currently held issue(s) in a structured portfolio under the following conditions:

1. Cash flow from the new bond(s) must equal or exceed both the timing and dollar amount of each individual cash flow from the original bond. If cash is received earlier from the new bond(s), it should be assumed to be reinvested until the original bond cash flow dates at the same reinvestment rate used to structure the initial portfolio.
2. Quality of the new bond(s) must equal or exceed the quality of the original bond.

Of course there must be some incremental benefit from executing the swap. Typically the benefit is an immediate cash take-out, that is, the original bond can be sold at a higher price than the cost of the bonds required to replace the lost cash flows (present value swap). Also attractive are those swaps that generate excess cash at future dates (future value swap). Or there might be no cash take-out but an improvement in quality.

A case study will illustrate the effect various restructuring alternatives can have on a dedicated portfolio. The case involved the following:

1. Cash-matching techniques were used to fund the liability schedule as shown in Exhibit 4.
2. Structuring parameters included: 6 percent reinvestment assumption; 25 percent limit on government flow-through zeros (e.g., TIGRS, STRIPS); 50 percent limit on combined agency and corporate issues; 25 percent limit on total corporate issues; 15 percent limit on A-rated issues; no issues rated below A.
3. The portfolio purchased is shown in Exhibit 5 and a summary of aggregate portfolio cash flows appears in Exhibit 6.

Following the initial structuring, a CIT issue maturing in 2005 that had been in limited supply when the portfolio was constructed became available and the swap detailed in Exhibit 7 was executed.

All criteria were met by this swap. Quality was improved, since a AA issue was replaced by a combination of another AA issue and a government flow-through zero. Furthermore, Exhibit 8 shows how the cash generated by the two replacement bonds exceeds the amounts that would have been received on each of the original bond's coupon payment dates and at maturity. Since liabilities were met by the original portfolio, the restructured portfolio will continue to provide more than adequate funding coverage. As shown in Exhibit 8, the earlier receipt of cash flows, caused by the difference in the two bonds' coupon payment and maturity dates, generates additional reinvestment interest. A 6 per-

EXHIBIT 4   Funding Schedule for Sample Dedication

Payment Dates	Liabilities
3/01/86	$ 6,830,000
9/01/86	6,830,000
3/01/87	6,400,000
9/01/87	6,400,000
3/01/88	6,100,000
9/01/88	6,100,000
3/01/89	5,950,000
9/01/89	5,950,000
3/01/90	5,600,000
9/01/90	5,600,000
3/01/91	5,250,000
9/01/91	5,250,000
3/01/92	4,765,000
9/01/92	4,765,000
3/01/93	4,380,000
3/01/94	4,280,000
3/01/95	4,090,000
3/01/96	3,790,000
3/01/97	3,335,000
3/01/98	3,065,000
3/01/99	2,783,000
3/01/00	2,710,000
3/01/01	2,526,000
3/01/02	2,434,000
3/01/03	2,378,000
3/01/04	2,231,000
3/01/05	2,090,000
3/01/06	1,754,000
	$123,636,000

cent reinvestment rate, the same used in the initial structuring, has been applied to cash flows from the new bonds from the time the cash is received until the time cash would have been received from the original bond. Execution of this swap generated net proceeds of $32,969. This is excess funding that can be removed from the structured program and allocated to other investment portfolios with the assurance that the targeted funding schedule will still be met.

Reoptimization

Reoptimization as a restructuring strategy is similar to, but more comprehensive than, cash flow swapping. Rather than examining the structure of individual bonds in the portfolio and using that as a proxy for

EXHIBIT 5 Sample Dedication (scenario A—initial structure)

Issue	Coupon	Maturity	Par Amount (000s)	Yield	Price	Full Price
T Note	9.875	02/15/1986	4,450	7.64480	100.12500	4,638,263.42
T Note	12.375	08/31/1986	4,115	7.72230	102.75000	4,420,882.62
TIGR	0.000	02/15/1987	3,931	8.19170	91.66340	3,603,288.25
TIGR	0.000	08/15/1987	3,928	8.22870	88.00720	3,456,922.82
TIGR	0.000	02/15/1988	3,631	8.47250	84.11800	3,054,324.58
TIGR	0.000	08/15/1988	3,629	8.56840	80.50780	2,921,628.06
T Note	11.375	02/15/1989	3,481	8.42790	107.84375	3,918,667.17
T Note	13.875	08/15/1989	2,680	8.61580	115.90625	3,260,888.18
Tenneco	9.000	09/01/1989	1,000	9.20000	99.37540	1,027,254.00
SLMA	10.900	02/28/1990	3,570	8.97140	106.50000	3,950,135.54
STRIP	0.000	08/15/1990	3,754	8.81070	67.35050	2,528,337.77
Fed. Home L.	11.875	02/25/1991	3,410	9.07010	111.25000	3,951,100.67
Fed. Farm C.	14.700	07/22/1991	24	9.46070	122.12500	31,005.40
T Note	14.875	08/15/1991	3,456	8.94070	125.62500	4,555,334.32
TIGR	0.000	08/15/1991	125	9.10910	60.80910	76,011.38
Fed. Home L.	11.450	02/25/1992	1,620	9.31660	109.75000	1,850,085.00
Priv. Expt.	11.250	02/28/1992	1,770	9.89690	106.07700	1,953,341.03
ITT Fin.	0.000	05/15/1992	1,233	10.14110	53.44500	658,976.85
Fed. Farm C.	13.750	07/20/1992	2,313	9.60090	119.75000	2,924,419.06
Fed. Home L.	10.700	01/25/1993	660	9.38980	106.62500	737,073.33
TIGR	0.000	02/15/1993	2,688	9.35730	52.31670	1,406,272.90
Fed. Farm C.	12.350	03/01/1994	2,280	9.68200	114.75000	2,721,110.31
FNMA Debs	11.500	02/10/1995	2,370	9.60110	111.31250	2,755,454.17
World Bank	0.000	02/15/1996	2,347	10.00550	37.36070	876,855.63
HFC	8.450	01/15/1997	3,706	10.63960	86.00000	3,187,160.00
Honeywell	8.200	12/15/1998	162	10.30700	85.12500	139,009.50
Transam Fin.	9.875	03/01/1999	1,500	9.60500	101.96860	1,584,664.42
Eur. Inv. Bk.	11.875	01/01/2000	1,740	10.64820	108.80300	1,901,207.62
HFC	9.000	07/01/2000	1,795	10.64310	88.00000	1,585,882.50
Niag Mohk.	7.625	02/01/2002	1,850	10.55280	77.57600	1,499,417.81
World Bank	0.000	02/15/2003	1,941	10.50340	17.39660	337,668.01
Eaton Corp.	7.875	12/01/2003	4,219	10.15160	81.37500	3,473,819.13
Std. Oil-Cal.	8.750	07/01/2005	1,000	9.80000	90.94300	912,832.78
			80,378			75,899,294.23

Note: Full price includes accrued interest assuming settlement on 1/15/86

required cash flow minimums, a reoptimization analyzes the entire portfolio relative to the liability schedule, current pricing, and the current universe of tradable issues. As a result, opportunities to make the cash flow structure of the portfolio more efficient can be captured when available.

To illustrate reoptimization, the same hypothetical case study example will be analyzed three months after its initial structuring. All parameters and constraints remained the same as initially; the same universe of tradable bonds were assumed to be available for purchase; and all yields were kept constant except for corporates (AAA, AA, and A)

EXHIBIT 6 Summary Cash-Flow Analysis (scenario A—initial structure)

Period No.	End Date	Portfolio Cash Flows Principal	+ Interest	= Total	− Required Cash Outflows	= Excess	+ Prior Cash Balance	+ Int. on Prior Balance	+ Int. on Current Period Inflows	= Ending Cash Balance
1	3/01/86	4,450,000	2,367,374	6,817,374.00	6,830,000.00	−12,626.00	0.00	0	14,506	1,880.23
2	9/01/86	4,115,000	2,704,836	6,819,836.37	6,830,000.00	−10,163.63	1,880.23	57	11,398	3,171.91
3	3/01/87	3,931,000	2,450,221	6,381,220.75	6,400,000.00	−18,779.25	3,171.91	94	18,670	3,157.08
4	9/01/87	3,928,000	2,450,221	6,378,220.75	6,400,000.00	−21,779.25	3,157.08	95	21,650	3,123.30
5	3/01/88	3,631,000	2,450,221	6,081,220.75	6,100,000.00	−18,779.25	3,123.30	93	18,936	3,373.88
6	9/01/88	3,629,000	2,450,221	6,079,220.75	6,100,000.00	−20,779.25	3,373.88	102	20,815	3,511.66
7	3/01/89	3,481,000	2,450,221	5,931,220.75	5,950,000.00	−18,779.25	3,511.66	104	17,635	2,472.02
8	9/01/89	3,680,000	2,252,239	5,932,238.87	5,950,000.00	−17,761.13	2,472.02	75	17,612	2,397.60
9	3/01/90	3,570,000	2,021,314	5,591,313.87	5,600,000.00	−8,686.13	2,397.60	71	9,333	3,115.92
10	9/01/90	3,754,000	1,826,749	5,580,748.87	5,600,000.00	−19,251.13	3,115.92	94	19,964	3,923.16
11	3/01/91	3,410,000	1,826,749	5,236,748.87	5,250,000.00	−13,251.13	3,923.16	117	10,955	1,744.08
12	9/01/91	3,605,000	1,624,280	5,229,280.12	5,250,000.00	−20,719.88	1,744.08	53	19,410	486.81
13	3/01/92	3,390,000	1,365,476	4,755,476.12	4,765,000.00	−9,523.88	486.81	15	10,081	1,058.18
14	9/01/92	3,546,000	1,173,169	4,719,168.62	4,765,000.00	−45,831.38	1,058.18	32	46,762	2,020.71
15	3/01/93	3,348,000	1,014,150	4,362,149.87	4,380,000.00	−17,850.13	2,020.71	60	16,834	1,064.55
16	9/01/93	2,280,000	1,957,680	4,237,679.75	4,280,000.00	−42,320.25	1,064.55	64	42,761	1,568.88
17	3/01/94	2,370,000	1,676,100	4,046,099.75	4,090,000.00	−43,900.25	1,568.88	94	45,972	3,734.45
18	9/01/94	2,347,000	1,403,550	3,750,549.75	3,790,000.00	−39,450.25	3,734.45	225	39,606	4,115.21
19	3/01/97	3,706,000	1,403,550	5,109,549.75	3,335,000.00	1,774,549.75	4,115.21	247	61,000	1,839,912.12
20	3/01/98	0	1,090,393	1,090,392.75	3,065,000.00	−1,974,607.25	1,839,912.12	110,319	26,557	2,181.33
21	3/01/99	1,662,000	1,090,393	2,752,392.75	2,783,000.00	−30,607.25	2,181.33	131	28,580	284.66
22	3/01/00	1,740,000	928,984	2,668,983.75	2,710,000.00	−41,016.25	284.66	17	41,292	577.70
23	3/01/01	1,795,000	641,584	2,436,583.75	2,526,000.00	−89,416.25	577.70	35	89,734	930.14
24	3/01/02	1,850,000	560,809	2,410,808.75	2,434,000.00	−23,191.25	930.14	56	23,366	1,161.01
25	3/01/03	1,941,000	419,746	2,360,746.25	2,378,000.00	−17,253.75	1,161.01	70	16,540	517.20
26	3/01/04	4,219,000	419,746	4,638,746.25	2,231,000.00	2,407,746.25	517.20	31	75,214	2,483,508.33
27	3/01/05	0	87,500	87,500.00	2,090,000.00	−2,002,500.00	2,483,508.33	148,909	2,170	632,087.27
28	3/01/06	1,000,000	43,750	1,043,750.00	1,754,000.00	−710,250.00	632,087.27	37,899	41,664	1,400.82
		80,378,000	42,151,223	122,529,222.62	123,636,000.00	−1,106,777.38	632,087.27	299,158	809,021	

EXHIBIT 7 Sample Cash Flow Swap (scenario A—two months after initial structuring)

| Issuer | Coupon | Maturity | Par Amount (000s) | | | | Yield | Price | | Full Price |
			Own	Buy	Sell	Net		Bid	Ask	
Buy:										
TIGR	0.000	5/15/05		237		237	9.9000		15.68900	$ 37,183
CIT Fin.	11.500	6/15/05		759		759	10.4000		109.03820	849,421
				996		996				886,604
Sell:										
Std. Oil-Cal.	8.750	7/01/05	1,000		1,000		9.9000	90.15870		919,573
Net Proceeds										$ 32,969

Note: Full price includes accrued interest assuming settlement on 3/15/86.

EXHIBIT 8 Sample Cash Flow Swap (scenario A—two months after initial structuring)

Period No.	End Date	Cash Flow from New Bonds			Original Bond Cash Flows	Excess	Prior Cash Balance	Int. on Prior Balance	Int. on Current Period Inflows	Ending Cash Balance
		Principal +	Interest =	Total	−		+	+	=	
1	7/01/86	0	43,643	43,642.50	43,750.00	−107.50	0.00	0	115	7.21
2	1/01/87	0	43,643	43,642.50	43,750.00	−107.50	7.21	0	122	21.80
3	7/01/87	0	43,643	43,642.50	43,750.00	−107.50	21.80	1	115	29.66
4	1/01/88	0	43,643	43,642.50	43,750.00	−107.50	29.66	1	122	44.93
5	7/01/88	0	43,643	43,642.50	43,750.00	−107.50	44.93	1	115	53.48
6	1/01/89	0	43,643	43,642.50	43,750.00	−107.50	53.48	2	122	69.47
7	7/01/89	0	43,643	43,642.50	43,750.00	−107.50	69.47	2	115	78.75
8	1/01/90	0	43,643	43,642.50	43,750.00	−107.50	78.75	2	122	95.50
9	7/01/90	0	43,643	43,642.50	43,750.00	−107.50	95.50	3	115	105.55
10	1/01/91	0	43,643	43,642.50	43,750.00	−107.50	105.55	3	122	123.12
11	7/01/91	0	43,643	43,642.50	43,750.00	−107.50	123.12	4	115	133.98
12	1/01/92	0	43,643	43,642.50	43,750.00	−107.50	133.98	4	122	152.41
13	7/01/92	0	43,643	43,642.50	43,750.00	−107.50	152.41	5	115	164.17
14	1/01/93	0	43,643	43,642.50	43,750.00	−107.50	164.17	5	122	183.51
15	7/01/93	0	43,643	43,642.50	43,750.00	−107.50	183.51	5	115	196.18
16	1/01/94	0	43,643	43,642.50	43,750.00	−107.50	196.18	6	122	216.48
17	7/01/94	0	43,643	43,642.50	43,750.00	−107.50	216.48	6	115	230.13
18	1/01/95	0	43,643	43,642.50	43,750.00	−107.50	230.13	7	122	251.46
19	7/01/95	0	43,643	43,642.50	43,750.00	−107.50	251.46	7	115	266.14
20	1/01/96	0	43,643	43,642.50	43,750.00	−107.50	266.14	8	122	288.56

EXHIBIT 8 *(concluded)*

Period No.	End Date	Cash Flow from New Bonds			Original Bond Cash Flows	Excess	Prior Cash Balance	Int. on Prior Balance	Int. on Current Period Inflows	Ending Cash Balance
		Principal +	Interest =	Total	−	+	+	=	
21	7/01/96	0	43,643	43,642.50	43,750.00	−107.50	288.56	9	115	304.40
22	1/01/97	0	43,643	43,642.50	43,750.00	−107.50	304.40	9	122	327.97
23	7/01/97	0	43,643	43,642.50	43,750.00	−107.50	327.97	10	115	344.93
24	1/01/98	0	43,643	43,642.50	43,750.00	−107.50	344.93	10	122	369.73
25	7/01/98	0	43,643	43,642.50	43,750.00	−107.50	369.73	11	115	387.94
26	1/01/99	0	43,643	43,642.50	43,750.00	−107.50	387.94	12	122	414.04
27	7/01/99	0	43,643	43,642.50	43,750.00	−107.50	414.04	12	115	433.56
28	1/01/00	0	43,643	43,642.50	43,750.00	−107.50	433.56	13	122	461.04
29	7/01/00	0	43,643	43,642.50	43,750.00	−107.50	461.04	14	115	482.03
30	1/01/01	0	43,643	43,642.50	43,750.00	−107.50	482.03	15	122	510.97
31	7/01/01	0	43,643	43,642.50	43,750.00	−107.50	510.97	15	115	533.37
32	1/01/02	0	43,643	43,642.50	43,750.00	−107.50	533.37	16	122	563.87
33	7/01/02	0	43,643	43,642.50	43,750.00	−107.50	563.87	17	115	587.84
34	1/01/03	0	43,643	43,642.50	43,750.00	−107.50	587.84	18	122	619.99
35	7/01/03	0	43,643	43,642.50	43,750.00	−107.50	619.99	18	115	645.63
36	1/01/04	0	43,643	43,642.50	43,750.00	−107.50	645.63	20	122	679.52
37	7/01/04	0	43,643	43,642.50	43,750.00	−107.50	679.52	20	115	707.04
38	1/01/05	0	43,643	43,642.50	43,750.00	−107.50	707.04	21	122	742.79
39	7/01/05	996,000	43,643	1,039,642.50	1,043,750.00		742.79	22		596.81
—	—	996,000	1,702,058	1,039,642.50	1,043,750.00	4,107.50	742.79	22	3,939	596.81
		996,000	1,702,058	2,698,057.50	2,706,250.00	8,192.50		355	8,435	

which, for purposes of this hypothetical example, were assumed to be trading 15 basis points higher than initially.

The resulting transactions are summarized in Exhibit 9. Assuming an arbitrary five-basis-point spread between bid and ask yields for purposes of pricing issues to be sold out of the original portfolio, net proceeds from the aggregate trades were $22,162 and all constraints continued to be met.

Generally, cash flow swaps will be used as an interim solution. That is, they can be implemented very quickly to take advantage of issues that may become tradable for only a short period of time, or to replace an issue in the portfolio where there is credit or call concern. In this way immediate action can be taken without waiting for a major restructuring to be accomplished.

ACTIVE VERSUS RE-ACTIVE APPLICATION OF RESTRUCTURING TECHNIQUES

Cash flow swaps and reoptimization techniques are only "active" in the sense that there is trading activity in the structured portfolio subsequent to the initial structuring. The portfolio is built to meet certain strict guidelines at the least possible cost, with consideration only given to current market conditions. Then, if the market happens to move favorably after the initial structuring, steps are taken to capitalize on new conditions wherever possible. Accordingly, "active" decisions are only made after the fact.

These types of restructurings are predicated on changes in price relationships between the bonds held in the portfolio and other bonds available for purchase that are also capable of meeting the structuring constraints of the program. If the two groups move in tandem, chances for improvement are limited since cost reductions generated by the higher yields on the new bonds will be offset largely by losses on the sale of the original bonds. Therefore, total performance will be highest when the portfolio has been positioned to take fullest advantage of market movement before it occurs. This calls for truly active decision-making at the onset of the structuring process since one is no longer strictly looking for a mathematical "best" or lowest cost portfolio but rather a portfolio that meets all constraints and is also positioned to take advantage of future market conditions.

An active structuring policy will increase the cost of the portfolio's initial construction because short-term performance may be sacrificed for potentially improved long-term performance. It may appear that doing so defeats the purpose of using a structured approach in the first place, i.e., reducing risk by recognizing the difficulty in trying to accurately predict the market. There is, however, a clear distinction between

EXHIBIT 9 Sample Reoptimization (scenario A—three months after initial structuring, assuming corporate yields increase 25 basis points and all other yields remain constant)

| Issuer | Coupon | Maturity | Par Amount (000s) | | | | | Price | | Full Price |
			Own	Buy	Sell	Net	Yield	Bid	Ask	
Buy:										
T Note	10.000	2/28/87		2,360		2,360	7.8774		101.74337	2,430,644
TIGR	0.000	8/15/87	3,928	11		3,939	8.2287		89.77930	9,876
TIGR	0.000	2/15/88	3,631	11		3,642	8.4725		85.86150	9,445
TIGR	0.000	8/15/88	3,629	12		3,641	8.5684		82.19510	9,863
T Note	11.375	2/15/89	3,481	13		3,494	8.4279		107.27555	14,187
T Note	13.875	8/15/89	2,680	1,007		3,687	8.6158		114.94392	1,180,258
STRIP	0.000	2/15/90		602		602	8.8120		71.82910	432,411
T Note	10.750	8/15/90		5		5	8.7096		107.21591	5,448
Fed. Home L.	11.875	2/25/91	3,410	10		3,420	9.0701		110.80574	11,246
T Note	14.875	8/15/91	3,456	30		3,486	8.9407		124.72186	38,144
Fed. Home L.	11.450	2/25/92	1,620	10		1,630	9.3166		109.44448	11,103
Chase	0.000	5/01/92		274		274	10.2909		54.52270	149,392
Honeywell	8.200	12/15/98	162	460		622	10.5570		83.71580	397,666
STRIP	0.000	2/15/99		1,022		1,022	9.8542		29.08900	297,290
Niag. Mohk.	7.750	8/01/02		1,790		1,790	10.8550		76.48050	1,397,517
McDermott	9.625	3/15/04		190		190	11.0509		88.95720	170,543
			25,997	7,807		33,804				6,565,031

Sell:

Security								
T Note	12.375	8/31/86	4,115	90	4,025	7.7723	101.62806	92,857
TIGR	0.000	2/15/87	3,931	2,460	1,471	8.2418	93.46330	2,299,197
Tenneco	9.000	9/01/89	1,000	1,000		9.5000	98.56440	996,644
SLMA	10.900	2/28/90	3,570	565	3,005	9.0214	106.00017	606,941
Fed. Farm C.	14.700	7/22/91	24	24		9.5107	121.08073	29,873
ITT Fin.	0.000	5/15/92	1,233	101	1,132	10.4411	53.84060	54,379
Fed. Farm C.	13.750	7/20/92	2,313	168	2,145	9.6509	118.89820	205,203
Fed. Home L.	10.700	1/25/93	660	2	658	9.4398	106.17496	2,171
Fed. Farm C.	12.350	3/01/94	2,280	7	2,273	9.7320	114.14900	8,096
FNMA Debs.	11.500	2/10/95	2,370	10	2,360	9.6511	110.78328	11,286
World Bank	0.000	2/15/96	2,347	8	2,339	10.0555	38.09460	3,048
HFC	8.450	1/15/97	3,706	16	3,690	10.9396	84.45640	13,851
Transam Fin.	9.875	3/01/99	1,500	1,500		9.9050	99.76240	1,514,540
Eur. Inv. Bk.	11.875	1/01/00	1,740	121	1,619	10.9482	106.46360	132,972
HFC	9.000	7/01/00	1,795	137	1,658	10.9431	86.12090	121,548
Niag. Mohk.	7.625	2/01/02	1,850	148	1,702	10.8528	75.83700	114,558
World Bank	0.000	2/15/03	1,941	1,941		10.5534	17.70040	343,565
TIGR	0.000	5/15/05	237	237		10.0529	15.38580	36,464
			36,612	8,535	28,077			6,587,194

Net Proceeds $22,162

Note: Full price includes accrued interest assuming settlement on 4/15/86.

aggressively managing a structured portfolio and a purely active management strategy. An actively managed portfolio not only runs the risk of underperforming desired targets, but can also experience negative returns. An aggressively managed structured portfolio, on the other hand, has an established floor—the buy-and-hold alternative—on which to fall back should the market not perform as anticipated. So, as illustrated in Exhibit 10, the maximum potential cost of adopting an

---

EXHIBIT 10 Comparison of Potential Performance Using Minimum Cost versus Sector Weighted Approach for Initial Structuring

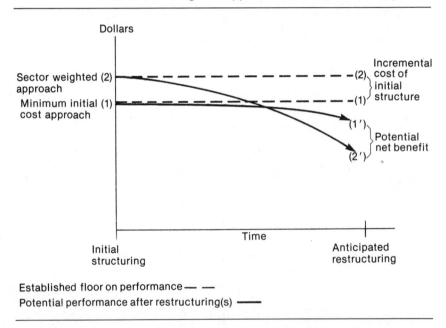

---

aggressive posture with a structured portfolio is known at the outset and limited over the life of the program. An aggressive manager might be willing to bear incremental cost to initially structure the portfolio, shown here as the difference between (1) and (2), in the hopes of generating higher restructuring improvements, or the difference between (1') and (2').

Anticipatory Sector Allocations

Restructuring improvements are maximized by anticipating where price relationships in the market may be changing and then positioning the portfolio to capture those changes when they occur, through reoptimization. This is done by including a minimum weighting of the sector that is perceived to be undervalued and limiting the amount allowed in the overvalued sector. The assessment of relative values is judgmental but will usually be based on a comparison of current versus historical price relationships. Later, when price relationships move to anticipated levels, the previously undervalued sector is sold and replaced with bonds from the sector that was overvalued when the portfolio was first constructed. Of course, these "forced" weightings must also conform to investment policy. For example, an investment policy might permit up to 30 percent of the portfolio to be invested in corporates rated AA or above, provided AA-rated issues alone comprise no more than 15 percent of the portfolio. A minimum cost solution would often call for the purchase of the maximum allowed, in this case 15 percent, in the lower-rated issues since they are higher yielding. If the spread between AA and AAA issues appeared unusually high, there is not much that could be done to position for an anticipated narrowing of spreads since the minimum cost solution would already have recommended purchasing the maximum amount allowed in AAs.

However, if these spreads were unusually narrow and expected to widen significantly, it might be advisable to reduce the cap on AA issues to 10, 5 or even zero percent of the portfolio and to select more AAA issues. Then, assuming spreads do widen, the portfolio is reoptimized using the 15 percent constraint on AA issues, thus remaining within established investment policy and at the same time capitalizing on the price movement between quality sectors.

This approach is illustrated using the case study developed earlier in the chapter. All facts are the same as in the earlier simulations, including the universe of available bonds and pricing data at each respective transaction date. This time however, assume one can anticipate the price movement in the corporate sector (i.e., 15 basis point shift between the initial structuring and a period three months later). To position for the shift in sector spreads, corporates are reduced from 25 percent of the portfolio, the maximum allowed by investment policy, to 10 percent. The resulting portfolio initially purchased under these new parameters is shown in Exhibit 11 with cash flows summarized in Exhibit 12. The cost of the forced sector weighting is $579,219, the difference between the cost of the first portfolio ($75,899,294) and the cost of the repositioned portfolio ($76,478,513). But when the portfolio is reoptimized three months later, as detailed in Exhibit 13, the net cash take-out is $773,036, substantially above the take-out under the first scenario and more than offsetting the higher initial cost. Net funding costs under the two scenarios are summarized in Exhibit 14. It should be noted that some percentage, if not all, of the incremental initial cost of structuring under Scenario B will be recouped even if the market does not move as anticipated since in all probability, the higher quality of this portfolio can still be traded in for corporates at some increased yield.

EXHIBIT 11 Sample Dedicated Portfolio (scenario B—initial structure using anticipatory sector weightings)

Issue	Coupon	Maturity	Par Amount (000s)	Yield	Price	Full Price
T Note	9.875	02/15/1986	4,120	7.64480	100.12500	4,294,302.31
T Note	12.375	08/31/1986	4,095	7.72230	102.75000	4,399,395.94
TIGR	0.000	02/15/1987	3,908	8.19170	91.66340	3,582,205.67
TIGR	0.000	08/15/1987	3,906	8.22870	88.00720	3,437,561.23
TIGR	0.000	02/15/1988	3,608	8.47250	84.11800	3,034,977.44
TIGR	0.000	08/15/1988	3,606	8.56840	80.50780	2,903,111.27
T Note	11.375	02/15/1989	3,459	8.42790	107.84375	3,893,901.10
Tenneco	9.000	09/01/1989	1,000	9.20000	99.37540	1,027,254.00
SLMA	12.850	09/01/1989	2,660	8.84120	112.18750	3,111,416.75
SLMA	10.900	02/28/1990	3,530	8.97140	106.50000	3,905,876.32
T Note	10.750	08/15/1990	1,788	8.70960	107.56250	2,003,130.90
STRIP	0.000	08/15/1990	1,924	8.81070	67.35050	1,295,823.62
Fed. Home L.	11.875	02/25/1991	3,470	9.07010	111.25000	4,020,621.50
T Note	14.875	08/15/1991	3,665	8.94070	125.62500	4,830,816.04
Fed. Home L.	11.450	02/25/1992	3,460	9.31660	109.75000	3,951,416.11
Fed. Farm C.	13.750	07/20/1992	3,585	9.60090	119.75000	4,532,659.90
TIGR	0.000	08/15/1992	53	9.25780	55.10840	29,207.45
Fed. Home L.	10.700	01/25/1993	3,500	9.38980	106.62500	3,908,722.22
Fed. Home L.	12.000	02/25/1994	1,930	9.42140	114.37500	2,297,504.17
Fed. Farm C.	12.350	03/01/1994	997	9.68200	114.75000	1,189,889.03
FNMA Debs.	11.500	02/10/1995	3,090	9.60110	111.31250	3,592,554.17
TIGR	0.000	11/15/1995	3,102	9.55550	39.94380	1,239,056.68
HFC	8.450	01/15/1997	1,076	10.63960	86.00000	925,360.00
STRIP	0.000	02/15/1997	1,615	9.55480	35.53840	573,945.16
STRIP	0.000	02/15/1998	2,521	9.65440	32.00180	806,765.38
STRIP	0.000	02/15/1999	743	9.85420	28.40540	211,052.12
Transam Fin.	9.875	03/01/1999	1,500	9.60500	101.96860	1,584,664.42
STRIP	0.000	02/15/2000	2,316	9.90390	25.62890	593,565.32
TIGR	0.000	11/15/2000	2,102	10.00380	23.50870	494,152.87
STRIP	0.000	02/15/2002	2,041	9.95340	20.96390	427,873.20
World Bank	0.000	02/15/2003	1,986	10.50340	17.39660	345,496.48
Eaton Corp.	7.875	12/01/2003	3,676	10.15160	81.37500	3,026,726.50
Std. Oil—Cal.	8.750	07/01/2005	1,000	9.80000	90.94300	912,832.78
TIGR	0.000	11/15/2005	656	10.00290	14.43220	94,675.23
			85,688			76,478,513.28

Note: Full price includes accrued interest assuming settlement on 1/15/86.

Positioning strategies are not limited to quality or issuer selection. A wide variety of positioning strategies have been employed effectively by users of structured programs. For example, if the portfolio manager's forecast is for interest rates to fall it might be appropriate to place a constraint on coupon levels. Capping coupons and thereby forcing the selection of discount issues implicitly increases the duration of the port-folio (duration moves inversely with coupon). A high duration bond has higher price volatility than a low duration bond. Therefore, if rates do fall as expected, the portfolio will outperform a minimum cost portfolio that had a lower duration. Following the decline in rates, the portfolio can be reoptimized, this time allowing selection of higher coupon issues.

EXHIBIT 12 Summary Cash Flow Analysis (scenario B—initial structure using anticipatory sector weightings)

Period No.	End Date	Portfolio Cash Flows			Cash Outflows	Excess	Prior Cash Balance	Int. on Prior Balance	Int. on Current Period Inflows	Ending Cash Balance
		Principal +	Interest =	Total	−			+	=	
1	3/01/86	4,120,000	2,697,450	6,817,450.37	6,830,000.00	−12,549.63	0.00	0	14,909	2,359.22
2	9/01/86	4,095,000	2,727,979	6,822,978.87	6,830,000.00	−7,021.13	2,359.22	71	9,561	4,970.46
3	3/01/87	3,908,000	2,474,601	6,382,600.75	6,400,000.00	−17,399.25	4,970.46	148	16,812	4,530.83
4	9/01/87	3,906,000	2,474,601	6,380,600.75	6,400,000.00	−19,399.25	4,530.83	137	19,755	5,023.20
5	3/01/88	3,608,000	2,474,601	6,082,600.75	6,100,000.00	−17,399.25	5,023.20	150	17,063	4,837.48
6	9/01/88	3,606,000	2,474,601	6,080,600.75	6,100,000.00	−19,399.25	4,837.48	146	18,917	4,501.33
7	3/01/89	3,459,000	2,474,601	5,933,600.75	5,950,000.00	−16,399.25	4,501.33	134	15,779	4,015.15
8	9/01/89	3,660,000	2,277,870	5,937,870.12	5,950,000.00	−12,129.88	4,015.15	121	8,297	303.99
9	3/01/90	3,530,000	2,061,965	5,591,965.12	5,600,000.00	−8,034.88	303.99	9	7,952	229.83
10	9/01/90	3,712,000	1,869,580	5,581,580.12	5,600,000.00	−18,419.88	229.83	7	18,537	354.00
11	3/01/91	3,470,000	1,773,475	5,243,475.12	5,250,000.00	−6,524.88	354.00	11	9,399	3,238.91
12	9/01/91	3,665,000	1,567,444	5,232,443.87	5,250,000.00	−17,556.13	3,238.91	98	17,901	3,681.23
13	3/01/92	3,460,000	1,294,859	4,754,859.50	4,765,000.00	−10,140.50	3,681.23	110	9,389	3,040.01
14	9/01/92	3,638,000	1,096,774	4,734,774.50	4,765,000.00	−30,225.50	3,040.01	92	32,148	5,054.25
15	3/01/93	3,500,000	850,306	4,350,305.75	4,380,000.00	−29,694.25	5,054.25	150	24,730	240.73
16	3/01/94	2,927,000	1,326,111	4,253,111.50	4,280,000.00	−26,888.50	240.73	14	28,280	1,646.96
17	3/01/95	3,090,000	971,382	4,061,382.00	4,090,000.00	−28,618.00	1,646.96	99	31,174	4,301.35
18	3/01/96	3,102,000	616,032	3,718,032.00	3,790,000.00	−71,968.00	4,301.35	259	69,663	2,254.65
19	3/01/97	2,691,000	616,032	3,307,032.00	3,335,000.00	−27,968.00	2,254.65	135	26,718	1,139.81
20	3/01/98	2,521,000	525,110	3,046,110.00	3,065,000.00	−18,890.00	1,139.81	68	18,801	1,119.52
21	3/01/99	2,243,000	525,110	2,768,110.00	2,783,000.00	−14,890.00	1,119.52	67	14,712	1,008.98
22	3/01/00	2,316,000	376,985	2,692,985.00	2,710,000.00	−17,015.00	1,008.98	61	16,570	624.83
23	3/01/01	2,102,000	376,985	2,478,985.00	2,526,000.00	−47,015.00	624.83	37	47,403	1,050.33
24	3/01/02	2,041,000	376,985	2,417,985.00	2,434,000.00	−16,015.00	1,050.33	63	15,495	593.68
25	3/01/03	1,986,000	376,985	2,362,985.00	2,378,000.00	−15,015.00	593.68	36	15,369	983.15
26	3/01/04	3,676,000	376,985	4,052,985.00	2,231,000.00	1,821,985.00	983.15	59	65,815	1,888,841.96
27	3/01/05	0	87,500	87,500.00	2,090,000.00	−2,002,500.00	1,888,841.96	113,253	2,170	1,765.34
28	3/01/06	1,656,000	43,750	1,699,750.00	1,754,000.00	−54,250.00	1,765.34	106	53,087	708.21
		85,688,000	37,186,660	122,874,659.62	123,636,000.00	−761,340.38		115,641	646,407	

EXHIBIT 13 Sample Reoptimization (scenario B—three months after initial structuring, assuming corporate yields increase 25 basis points and all other yields remain constant)

Issuer	Coupon	Maturity	Par Amount (000s)				Yield	Price		Full Price
			Own	Buy	Sell	Net		Bid	Ask	
Buy:										
T Note	13.875	8/15/89		3,350		3,350	8.6158		114.94392	3,926,378
STRIP	0.000	8/15/89		214		214	8.6634		75.35100	161,251
STRIP	0.000	2/15/90		711		711	8.8120		71.82910	510,705
Priv. Expt.	11.250	2/28/92		487		487	10.1469		104.76350	517,351
Chase	0.000	5/01/92		1,140		1,140	10.2909		54.52270	621,559
TIGR	0.000	2/15/93		3,284		3,284	9.3573		53.51300	1,757,367
Fed. Farm C.	12.350	3/01/94	997	1,074		2,071	9.6820		114.44543	1,245,355
Priv. Expt.	11.250	10/31/95		2,050		2,050	10.3482		105.37590	2,265,909
HFC	8.450	1/15/97	1,076	2,584		3,660	10.8896		84.73480	2,244,134
Pub. S. Elc.	7.000	6/01/98		420		420	10.5036		76.26470	331,255
Honeywell	8.200	12/15/98		463		463	10.5570		83.71580	400,259
Eur. Inv. Bk.	11.875	1/01/00		1,620		1,620	10.8982		106.83250	1,786,261
HFC	9.000	7/01/00		1,658		1,658	10.8931		86.44130	1,476,305
Niag. Mohk.	7.625	2/01/02		1,702		1,702	10.8028		76.14270	1,322,625
Niag. Mohk.	7.750	8/01/02		1,794		1,794	10.8550		76.48050	1,400,640
McDermott	9.625	3/15/04		1,513		1,513	11.0509		88.95720	1,358,058
			2,073	24,064		26,137				21,325,413

Sell:

T Note	12.375	8/31/86	4,095	10	4,085	7.7723	101.62806	10,317
TIGR	0.000	2/15/87	3,908	83	3,825	8.2418	93.46330	77,575
TIGR	0.000	8/15/87	3,906	84	3,822	8.2787	89.72170	75,366
TIGR	0.000	2/15/88	3,608	84	3,524	8.5225	85.78590	72,060
TIGR	0.000	8/15/88	3,606	83	3,523	8.6184	82.10310	68,146
T Note	11.375	2/15/89	3,459	84	3,375	8.4779	107.14598	91,560
Tenneco	9.000	9/01/89	1,000	1,000		9.5000	98.56440	996,644
SLMA	12.850	9/01/89	2,660	2,660		8.8912	111.31055	3,002,637
SLMA	10.900	2/28/90	3,530	785	2,745	9.0214	106.00017	843,272
T Note	10.750	8/15/90	1,788	115	1,673	8.7596	107.03060	125,100
Fed. Home L.	11.875	2/25/91	3,470	120	3,350	9.1201	110.59975	134,699
T Note	14.875	8/15/91	3,665	129	3,536	8.8907	124.48122	163,708
Fed. Home L.	11.450	2/25/92	3,460	625	2,835	9.3666	109.20948	692,499
Fed. Farm C.	13.750	7/20/92	3,585	1,250	2,335	9.6509	118.89820	1,526,809
TIGR	0.000	8/15/92	53	53		9.3078	56.18480	29,778
Fed. Home L.	10.700	1/25/93	3,500	3,500		9.4398	106.17496	3,799,346
Fed. Home L.	12.000	2/25/94	1,930	1,930		9.4714	113.77118	2,227,950
FNMA Debs	11.500	2/10/95	3,090	955	2,135	9.6511	110.78328	1,077,810
TIGR	0.000	11/15/95	3,102	3,102		9.6055	40.69510	1,262,362
STRIP	0.000	2/15/97	1,615	1,615		9.6048	36.18040	584,313
STRIP	0.000	2/15/98	2,521	2,521		9.7044	32.57220	821,145
Transam Fin.	9.875	3/01/99	1,500	1,500		9.9050	99.76240	1,514,540
STRIP	0.000	2/15/00	2,316	2,316		9.9539	26.07630	603,927
TIGR	0.000	11/15/00	2,102	2,102		10.0538	23.91960	502,790
STRIP	0.000	2/15/02	2,041	2,041		10.0034	21.31210	434,980
World Bank	0.000	2/15/03	1,986	1,986		10.5534	17.70040	351,530
Std. Oil-Cal.	8.750	7/01/05	1,000	1,000		10.1000	88.62070	911,485
TIGR	0.000	11/15/05	656	656		10.0529	14.64940	96,100
			73,152	32,389	40,763			22,098,449

Net Proceeds $ 773,036

Note: Full price includes accrued interest assuming settlement on 4/15/86.

EXHIBIT 14

	Scenario A (minimum initial cost)	Scenario B (aggressive positioning)
Initial structuring	$75,899,294	$76,478,513
Less: Restructuring improvements:		
Cash flow swap	32,969	
Reoptimization	22,162	773,036
Net funding cost	$75,844,163	$75,705,477

Another choice to be made in an actively structured investment program is between structuring techniques. As a rule, cost decreases and risk increases as one moves from a cash-matching to a horizon-matching to an immunized approach for funding future liabilities. The decrease in cost should bear some relationship to the additional risk assumed, but as market conditions change the price relationships between these strategies can also fluctuate. Therefore, if immunization is the preferable approach but does not produce a large enough incremental return to compensate for the increased risk, it might make sense to initially structure the investment program using cash-matching or horizon-matching techniques. If and when market conditions make it advantageous, the program can then be restructured using immunization techniques, often resulting in a higher total return than if the higher risk strategy (immunization) had been employed from the outset.

Forecast Weighted Indexing

A fixed income index fund, or a portfolio structured to track the performance of the fixed income market, can also be actively positioned to maximize performance given expectations for future market conditions. The index selected as the proxy for building the portfolio must be one that can easily be segmented into its component parts based on security type (government, agency, corporate, etc.), maturity ranges, coupon ranges, etc. An asset allocation model or some other desired methodology (quantitative, judgmental, or other) is used to make decisions regarding positioning of the portfolio. These decisions are then translated into sector weightings and the indexed portfolio is built to track the average returns of those sub-indexes selected, weighted according to specifications. As market expectations change, sector weightings are adjusted and the portfolio repositioned consistent with the current outlook. This technique enables the portfolio to track returns for the sectors selected while allowing the investment manager to make major strategic decisions regarding positioning of investment assets.

OPTIONAL RESTRUCTURING VERSUS REQUIRED REBALANCING

Active structuring makes it possible to improve investment returns while controlling the risks assumed. The active elements of the investment programs fall within structuring parameters and, in any case, implementation is optional. A different type of restructuring, however, may be mandated as the structured program evolves. Referred to as rebalancings, these adjustments to the portfolio are designed to reestablish a structure that has moved out of line. Common situations that trigger a rebalancing are:

Dedication—changes in estimates of future liabilities; a downgrading or anticipated downgrading in the credit rating of an issue in the dedicated portfolio that causes the portfolio to fall below required minimum levels; inadequate call, reinvestment rate, or mortgage prepayment assumptions.

Immunization—average duration of assets have fluctuated out of step with that of liabilities; all factors listed under dedication.

Indexing—average portfolio characteristics have moved out of line with the targeted index or indexes due to downgrading of issues held in the portfolio, normal changes in the composition of the index, or other factors.

A rebalancing is accomplished in much the same manner as a reoptimization. Current holdings and the universe of available bonds are analyzed using revised constraints to find the currently optimal portfolio. The key difference is that a rebalancing is generally implemented even if it results in a net cost or reduction in performance. This is to ensure that original objectives set out for the program will be met.

ACTIVE OPTIMIZATION

Just as a structured investment program can benefit from active techniques, it is also possible for an active investment program to benefit from structuring techniques. The requirement to match liability cash flows in a dedication, or to match duration of liabilities in an immunization is merely one variable in the linear program that can easily be lifted from the analysis. What is left is a model that can be used to systematically select bonds for an investment portfolio predicated on whatever criteria or objectives the investment manager deems appropriate. Those criteria will, in turn, be driven by his expectations for future market conditions. Examples of criteria that might be targeted include maturity, duration, quality, sector weightings, current yield, and average coupon.

These portfolio characteristics can be used much in the same way as described for anticipatory sector weightings: minimums or maximums are set for key portfolio characteristics. The optimal portfolio is then identified that will meet those targets while maximizing a desired objective such as yield-to-maturity, current yield, etc. Unlike structured programs, however, the solution will not be encumbered with funding requirements.

As an example, an active manager believes that interest rates are about to fall over the short term and then rise. The manager also believes that the industrial sector is undervalued. The current investment portfolio could first be reoptimized to maximize yield to maturity while constraining the solution to (1) lengthen average portfolio duration by a given amount, (2) force a minimum percentage of the portfolio into the industrial sector, and (3) meet investment policy requirements for quality. Then, when the manager believes that interest rates are about to reverse direction, the portfolio is again reoptimized, this time to shorten duration and limit price volatility of the portfolio in preparation for the anticipated drop in prices.

34

A Corporate Bond
Index Fund*

Jane Tripp Howe, C.F.A.
Consultant

The epitome of passive bond management—a buy-and-hold strategy—has been in existence as long as bonds have been. However, with the advent of volatile interest rates in the late 1960s, the theory and practice of active bond management became the dominant force in fixed income management. The trend of fixed income management shifted again in the late 1970s and early 1980s toward passive management. This trend closely paralleled the movement toward passive equity management in the mid-1970s. The development of passive fixed income theory was a major impetus behind this move. However, sponsors' disillusionment with the performance of their fixed income portfolios and a growing belief that interest rates cannot be predicted were perhaps the most important factors in the movement back to passive management. The increasingly unanticipated movement of interest rates and the attendant significant volatility of market values has reinforced this belief and contributed to a significant movement of funds (particularly employee benefit funds) to passive management.

Passive fixed income management today is very different from that practiced historically. A high proportion of "passive" fixed income management has a highly theoretical base and is largely facilitated by specialized computer programs. In addition, the current trend of passive fixed income management is weighted toward portfolio immunization, a technique designed to reduce or eliminate interest-rate risk in a portfolio

* Reprinted in part from "A Corporate Bond Index Fund," *Proceedings*, Center for Research in Security Prices, Graduate School of Business, The University of Chicago, November 1978.

over a given time horizon.[1] However, to the extent that *passive* is defined as diversifying the nonmarket risk in a portfolio and only accepting the market risk of a portfolio, the immunization strategy is not a purely passive strategy, but rather a technique used to structure a portfolio to meet a given fund objective. Contingent or active immunization goes a step further in that this technique permits the active management of a fund as long as the predetermined annual rate of return can be achieved over the entire horizon period. At the point at which interest rates have moved adversely and the predetermined annual rate of return could not be achieved with further adverse interest-rate movements, the portfolio reverts to the immunization mode, and the portfolio is structured so that future interest-rate risk to the horizon will be reduced or eliminated.

The purest passive technique available today is the bond index fund. Its primary objective is to match the performance of the corporate bond universe, rather than to match the liabilities of a given employee benefit fund. This objective is achieved through the continuous matching of the fund with the characteristics of the bond universe. It cannot be achieved with a passive buy-and-hold strategy because this buy-and-hold portfolio will change over time in terms of duration, maturity, and so on. An index fund does not have the immunized fund's guarantee of a close approximation of matching an employee benefit fund's given liabilities. However, it does have the significant advantage of producing the highest level of expected return per unit of risk over a long time horizon. This advantage is similar to the diversification benefit offered by an equity index fund, although the variables used for diversification are different. In practice, because the corporate bond market is more homogeneous than the equity market, the matching of a corporate bond proxy is easier than matching a proxy for the equity market.

In selecting a bond index fund, a sponsor will benefit in at least two additional ways. First, an improvement in performance can be expected due to a reduction in fees and transaction costs. Second, any duplication of managers' efforts will be eliminated. The extent of the savings in terms of fees will depend on the sponsor's current active versus passive fees and also on the extent that fund assets are switched from the higher cost active managers to the lower cost passive managers. Over the life of a fund, the savings in management fees could be substantial.

A more significant savings should be realized in transaction costs. Bonds are typically traded without a commission explicitly stated. However, there is definitely a cost associated with a bond trade, which owners of bonds ultimately pay. Savings to a sponsor in lower transaction costs will be particularly significant to the sponsor of a large pension fund with several active fixed income managers. Each of these managers

---

[1] See Chapter 31.

may report annual turnover in the area of 100 percent. However, it is possible that this estimate of turnover really represents the turning over of the highly liquid issues five or six times per year. Conceivably, the same issues could be bought and sold by the same fund with little or no time interval! It is therefore possible that a manager is doing one of two things: (1) hedging the overall composition of his or her fund by diversifying a portion of it and intensely managing only a portion of it, or (2) actively managing a portion of the fund and essentially ignoring an undiversified core. In either case, the division of active versus passive (if any) fees should be questioned. In effect, the plan sponsor should examine the total composition and activity of his or her portfolio to eliminate duplication of fees and commissions.

THE SELECTION OF A PROXY FOR THE BOND UNIVERSE

Once the decision to invest in a bond index fund has been made, a benchmark or proxy for the bond universe must be selected. This selection process has two parts. First, the appropriate universe must be chosen. This decision is essentially a choice among a corporate bond market, the government market, and a combination of the two. Once this question is resolved, a specific proxy has to be chosen in order that the fund's performance can be evaluated.

The resolution of the first half of the selection process is straightforward. Theoretically, the more comprehensive the proxy, the higher the level of diversification achieved. Therefore, in a theoretical sense, an investor might choose to index the world bond market. Indexing publicly issued corporate bonds is the logical first step for several reasons. First, a major benefit of a bond index fund is that it provides the highest level of expected return for diversification across interest rate as well as default risk. As the government market is generally perceived as presenting no default risk, the inclusion of government securities in an index fund would only increase interest-rate diversification. Therefore, if the choice is between a corporate bond index fund and a government bond index fund, the former would produce the higher level of diversification benefits. Second, if the inclusion of government bonds is desired in order to make the index more comprehensive, it is not clear what weighting they should be allotted. First, a large portion of Treasury debt is nonmarketable and therefore should be excluded from a marketable bond index. In a similar manner, TIGRs should be excluded to avoid double counting of the relevant securities (Merrill Lynch does exclude TIGRs from its Government Master Index). In addition, there is no way of knowing how many TIGRs are outstanding. Finally, to the extent that government issues represent a disproportionately high percentage of the total bond market, a further case can be made for their exclusion from a bond index. As of May 31, 1985, the Treasury and agency component represented 74.7 percent of Merrill Lynch's Corporate and Government Master Index.

Once a corporate bond index has been chosen, the selection of a specific proxy for the corporate bond market must be made. The comprehensiveness of the proxy is a key element in this process, since the purpose of a bond index is to match the risk and return of the entire public corporate bond market to the extent possible. Unfortunately (from a theoretical viewpoint), issues with ratings below BBB should be excluded due to the institutional and legal constraints involved in buying these issues. Therefore, attention should be focused on those indexes covering securities rated BBB and above. Although there are numerous bond indexes published, few are comprehensive.[2] Of these, the Shearson Lehman Brothers (SLB) and Merrill Lynch (ML) Indexes are the most appropriate for use in an index. The most important difference between these and other indexes is the relative comprehensiveness of the SLB and ML indexes. The SLB index tracks all publicly issued industrial, financial, and utility bonds rated Baa or higher that have at least one year until maturity and at least $1 million principal amount outstanding. The issues must be fixed rate and nonconvertible. As of June 1985, this universe contained approximately 4,577 issues with a total market value in excess of $285 billion. The ML index differs from the SLB index in its requirement that an issue have at least $10 million principal amount outstanding. In addition, ML includes transportation as well as Yankee securities. As of May 1985, the universe contained 4,408 issues with a market value of approximately $304 billion. All other well-known public indexes have at least one serious drawback in terms of quality range, coupon, maturity, or industrial classification. Another important difference is the ability of SLB and ML to reflect changes in the market.

Since SLB and ML track all issues in their respective universes, their indexes by definition will reflect all changes in the bond market. Other indexes, on the other hand, use samples of their universes and adjust these samples on an annual or less frequent basis. Therefore, on a month-to-month basis, only the SLB and ML indexes will mirror market changes. This property is important in a dynamic market whose characteristics can change significantly during the course of a year due to such occurrences as sizable calls and refundings or the issuance of a particular type of debt (such as original-issue discount bonds.) For example, if a portion of an issue is retired (such as AT&T 8.75 percent debenture due 5/15/00), such a partial retirement will be reflected in the SLB and ML indexes with a maximum lag of one month. The effect of such a retirement in other indexes is unclear and would depend on such factors as

---

[2] See the appendix to this book for a discussion of bond indexes.

whether the particular bond is in the index and how close the index is to a periodic adjustment. In a similar manner, only the SLB and ML indexes will exactly represent the percentage of upgrades and downgrades occurring in the market.

As of July 28, 1985, the SLB index had an average coupon of 9.61 percent, an average maturity of 14.88 years, and an average duration of 6.46. Additionally, the index had an average rating of A1 by Moody's and AA- by Standard and Poor's. Exhibit 1 further describes the SLB

EXHIBIT 1 The Corporate Bond Market as of June 28, 1985 (components of the Shearson Lehman Bond Index)

Characteristics	Rating				
	Aaa	*Aa*	*A*	*Baa*	*Total*
Percent of total market	5.10	37.30	39.50	18.10	100.00
Average coupon (percent)	7.27	9.30	9.88	10.53	9.61
Average maturity (years)	15.80	15.25	15.12	13.34	14.88
Duration	6.93	6.51	6.50	6.14	6.46
	Industry Classification				
Characteristic	*Industrial*	*Utility*	*Finance*		*Total*
Percent of total market	28.90	45.30	25.80		100.00
Average coupon (percent)	9.88	9.57	9.38		9.61
Average maturity (years)	14.18	18.88	8.65		14.88
Duration	6.51	7.24	5.04		6.46

SOURCE: Shearson Lehman Brothers Inc.

universe by segmenting it according to industrial classifications and Moody's ratings. Although Baa's represent approximately 18 percent of this universe, it should be noted that the additional volatility introduced by Baa securities (as opposed to the indexes that track only Aaa, Aa, and A securities) is largely offset by the lower duration of the Baa group.

PERFORMANCE OF A CORPORATE BOND INDEX

The performance of a corporate bond index fund that matches the SLB or ML indexes should at least match the performance of "active" fixed income managers as a group over the long run. If the corporate market is viewed as a "zero-sum game" (i.e., a game in which the winnings of players are equal to the losses of other players), the long-term aggregate return of all bond managers should approximate the aggregate return of the market. However, to the extent that active managers have higher transaction costs and fees than do passive managers, the bond universe can be expected to perform somewhat better than the median of managed bond funds. To investigate this issue, comparisons will necessarily be imperfect due to the fact that median performance numbers include government securities as well as cash.[3] However, a comparison of the median performance of fixed income managers against the broader based ML and SLB government/corporate indexes suggests that over the long run the logic of indexing is correct. For the year ended December 31, 1984, the median bond manager in the SEI universe returned 14.2 percent compared with 15.2 percent for the SLB government/corporate index and 15.1 percent for the ML government/corporate index. For the five-year period ending September 30, 1979, the indexes also compared favorably with ML (generating 10.0 percent annually) and SLB (generating 10.2 percent annually) versus 9.9 percent for the PIPER median of 200 banks and insurance companies. However, for the ten-year period ended September 30, 1984, SLB matched the PIPER median of 9.4 percent while ML earned 9.0 percent annually.

The nature of these statistics precludes a definitive assessment of whether a fund would increase or decrease its volatility by investing in a bond index fund. This issue has to be answered on an individual account basis.

A comparison of the rates of return and standard deviations of the market indexes versus a long bond proxy does suggest, however, that the diversification advantage is significant. For the eight-year period December 31, 1972, through December 31, 1980, the SLB index produced an annual compound return of +3.8 percent with a monthly mean and standard deviation of +.35 percent and 9.49 percent, respectively. During the same period, the Salomon Brothers index produced an annual compound return of +3.0 percent and had a lower monthly mean of +.29 percent and a higher monthly standard deviation of 10.39 percent. It therefore appears that, at least over this time period, the variability produced by the longer average maturity of the Salomon index is more of a factor than the variability produced by the lower average quality of the SLB index. Comparable variability figures for the median performer of managed funds are unavailable. Medians can be justified as proxies for active fixed income managers. However, the median by its nature will be less volatile than the individual funds that contribute to the median. Furthermore, there will be an unmeasured bias in the median figures to the extent that a certain percent of the assets in the managed funds universe may be reported at book rather than at market value.

This chapter has dealt to this point with the premise that managers collectively cannot outperform the bond market. To address the possibility that one manager or a subgroup of managers could outperform the

---

[3] This comparison difficulty could probably be most easily resolved by including a cash component in the market index.

market is to address the efficiency of the market. There is not available for investigating this subject the voluminous empirical data for bonds that exists for stocks. However, there are two major deductive reasons for concluding that the bond market is probably at least as efficient as the stock market. First, the default risk of a bond is lower than that of a stock in that bondholders' claims in bankruptcy are senior to the claims of stockholders. Second, the fixed parameters of a bond agreement are more precise than those of stocks. Therefore, inefficiencies that arise from events other than credit changes should generally be smaller and more readily identifiable.

THE OPERATIONAL PROCESS OF RUNNING A CORPORATE BOND INDEX

In establishing and running a corporate bond index fund, many of the procedures for running an equity index fund can be used. However, the operational process is more complex for bonds than for stocks, even though the homogeneity of the bond market should make the bond market easier to track. Specifically, relatively greater care should be taken in dealing with the three following areas when establishing a bond index fund.

Characteristics Used for Diversification

In indexing the equity market, only two variables—capitalization and risk decile—need to be used to provide adequate diversification and tracking, although many equity fund managers use many more characteristics. Bonds have many characteristics that affect return, including maturity, duration, quality, capitalization, coupon, industrial classification, sinking fund, and call features, to name a few. There is no precise formula to weight every possible variable. It is clear, however, that a specific assessment must be made in regard to which of these variables should be explicitly taken into consideration and which should be considered implicitly.

Trading

Because bonds are traded over the counter (unlike most stock trading, which is more centralized), there is always going to be a trader's judgment involved in buying for a bond index fund. In this situation, it is important that purchases be made from inventory to the extent possible to avoid creating a demand for a specific bond that will drive up its price. It is also important to try to eliminate prejudices a trader may have about certain credits. One possible way of alleviating this potential problem would be to use a bankruptcy screen as the primary credit guide. In this regard, all companies should be considered purchase candidates with the exception of those companies deemed to be imminent bankruptcy candidates. Because this exception list will generally contain only a few companies, the universe of purchase candidates will approximate the SLB index. Another way of reducing a trader's prejudice is to use the options model as a trading aid.[4] The mathematics of this model have not been sufficiently developed to allow the model to act as the sole credit screen for coupon bonds of complex structures. However, the theory of the model can be used in practice if the trader follows the stock as well as the bond price of a firm.

Reinvestment of Cash Flow

The cash flow from a bond index fund is going to be several times heavier than that generated from an equity index fund. Therefore, relatively frequent and small buying programs will occur in a bond index, and distortions in the overall composition of the fund could occur. Minimization of possible distortions can be achieved through the conscious balancing of purchases among all relevant bond characteristics.

In recent years, computer sampling techniques have been applied to the operational process of running a corporate bond index. Specifically Merrill Lynch's Bond Index Portfolio System attempts to replicate the market or a given sector of the market. A variation of this program attempts to replicate the market in terms of maturity, coupon, and quality, but to modify or "enhance" a fourth variable such as yield.

CONCLUSION

The degree to which indexing should be used by a specific fund depends on account circumstances. The fixed income portion of a fund can be viewed as being composed of several parts. Particularly for a large fund with several managers, a bond index should represent the passive core that is equal to that portion of the fund that is permanently and passively invested in bonds. The sponsor can then add a variety of complementary active and passive strategies that will determine the overall level of risk he or she wants to assume, given account circumstances.

---

[4] The model looks at the relationship of a firm's stock and bond prices and views the firm's bonds as an option to buy the firm from the equity holders. (See Fischer Black and Myron Scholes, "The Pricing of Options and Corporate Liabilities," *The Journal of Political Economy*, May–June 1973, pp. 637–54.

35

High Yield
Bond Portfolios

Howard S. Marks, C.F.A.
Managing Director
Trust Company of the West

In a so-called efficient market, all potential investments are analyzed objectively with equal thoroughness and skill and the *a priori* returns at which they sell are established proportionate to the risks entailed. This is a vast simplification of the relevant theory, but it makes sense and certainly serves adequately as a backdrop against which to search for disequilibria and exceptions from which above-average risk-adjusted gains might be earned. The principal fallout from this formulation of the theory is the suggestion that on viewing any investment that appears to offer returns more than commensurate with the risks, the potential investor should ask, "Why should this be the case? Why am I being offered this chance?"

It appears that such an opportunity may be offered in the high yield sector of the fixed income universe: the yields at which these bonds are available are very high, incorporating large risk premiums, but the actual risks have historically been shown to be modest. It is the purpose of this chapter to describe and define the high yield sector, to attempt to quantify the risks and returns, and to try to explain why this opportunity may exist.

HIGH YIELD BONDS DEFINED

First of all, what are high yield bonds? They are lower rated bonds. "High yield" is a euphemism for bonds that are popularly perceived to entail a substantial probability that the interest payments and principal repayment will not occur as promised. Another, less kind, nickname is "junk bonds." Those in the business regret this nickname, but it does exemplify the attitude that can make unusual profit opportunities available.

Most high yield bonds are corporate bonds. U.S. government bonds and agency obligations have not yet had their creditworthiness impugned (although as of this writing, the expanding yield spread on Federal Farm Credit Bank debt certainly indicates declining confidence). Most municipals have been considered worry-free—at least until New York City's difficulties shook investor confidence and the Washington Public Power Supply System became the first major default in the tax-free area.

Utilities have generally been considered unlikely to default because the essential nature of their product makes it incumbent on the regulators to establish rates which assure their viability. But recently, uncertainties involved in building and operating nuclear generating facilities have been seen to endanger some utility debt. The historic article of faith that no utility can be permitted to default has thus far been tested but not violated.

The greatest number of popularly perceived problem credits, constituting the vast bulk of the high yield bond sector, are found in the industrial and financial areas. By and large, they are bonds that are rated Ba and below by Moody's Investor Services or BB and below by Standard & Poor's, or bonds that are unrated but considered to be equivalent in quality to those rating categories.

What do those ratings mean? In Moody's words, "bonds which are rated Ba are judged to have speculative elements; their future cannot be considered as well assured." It says further that "bonds which are rated B generally lack characteristics of the desirable investment."[1] Standard & Poor's says all bonds rated BB and below are "predominantly speculative with respect to capacity to pay interest and repay principal . . . ."[2] These statements strike fear in the hearts of would-be buyers and tend to discourage investment. Is this appropriate?

One's first reaction might be to question the propriety of assessing the desirability of an investment, as Moody's does, on the basis of the risk alone and without reference to the prospective return. After all, in the efficient market described at the outset, return is logically arrayed opposite risk. Should an investment be condemned solely because it entails high risk or uncertainty? Are venture capital investments which offer success ratios of one-in-twenty or worse necessarily bad investments? The attitude displayed by calling these "junk bonds" implies that an uncertain investment is an undesirable investment. But who among us does not wish that he or she had made an uncertain investment in Apple Computer or in Genentech?

---

[1] *Moody's Bond Record*, Moody's Investors Service, January, 1984. p. 1.

[2] *Standard & Poor's Bond Guide*, Standard & Poor's Corporation, July, 1985. p. 10.

Yet, many bond investors say, "I would never buy a B-rated bond." The implicit statement that a bond of low quality cannot be a good investment, regardless of price or implied return, at once shows why it is reasonable to believe that bargains can be found in low-rated bonds: *prejudice keeps investors from looking at these investment vehicles in the objective, dispassionate way required for a market to be truly efficient.*

TRENDS IN FIXED INCOME INVESTMENTS AND OPPORTUNITIES WITH HIGH YIELD BONDS

Historically, bonds have been a preferred investment of fiduciaries, invested in to provide the secure bedrock for a portfolio. Traditionally, fiduciaries were driven by a doctrine that stressed the avoidance of risk in the absolute and emphasized the preservation of capital. "Prudent man" laws applied penalties if any risky investments were undertaken and were unsuccessful. Further, if a number of risky, but potentially lucrative, investments were made and one failed, the fiduciary could be sued and "surcharged" for the one that failed without being able to offset losses against the profits from the ones that succeeded. Clearly, such a climate provided great incentive to strive to avoid risk. Among the modern concepts that had yet to be invented were risk management, the portfolio approach to investing, real return, opportunity cost, and competitive performance.

In an excellent, related article in the *Financial Analysts Journal,* Dean LeBaron of Batterymarch sought to explain why, despite all of the arguments for market efficiency, departures from efficiency exist and persist. The reason he discussed first and longest is what he calls his "theory of agents." Basically, the problem is that the people who manage money are not the people whose money it is, and they therefore have different incentives. Risk-taking probably will not lead to great rewards for professional money managers if done successfully, but it can certainly produce problems—like termination—if done poorly. "The guiding principle in this environment seems to be that it is better to make a little money conventionally than to run even the smallest risk of losing a lot unconventionally."[3]

Hired money managers—especially in the fixed income world— have traditionally paid dearly for the safety (both financial and personal) they feel accompanies high ratings, and have tried to avoid risk by shunning low-rated bonds despite their high yields and the historic evidence that default is a rare phenomenon.

As time has passed, a number of trends have affected the investment world in ways that have led to alteration of this traditional ap-

---

[3] Dean LeBaron, "Reflections on Market Inefficiency," *Financial Analysts Journal,* May–June 1983, p. 16.

proach toward risk and some increased willingness to consider high yield investing:

- Volatile interest rates have made all fixed income investing more "risky."
- Rate volatility led investors to attempt to anticipate interest rate movements, but success has proved elusive.
- High ratings have not guaranteed an absence of credit losses.
- Professional investors in general have accepted the task of managing risk rather than attempting to avoid it—although traditional fixed income investors have been slow to adopt this approach.
- A public market for low-rated new issues and secondary trades has developed.
- Most important, history has consistently shown that lower rated fixed income portfolio have generated higher returns.

Hopefully, it has been demonstrated above that prejudice is present in a way that can be reasonably believed to have kept high yield bonds underpriced, and that the underpricing that is present makes a review of the sector worthwhile.

HISTORIC DEVELOPMENT

Prior to about 1977, companies that did not qualify for high ratings were unable to issue debt in the public market (due in large part to the prejudices against below-investment grade debt described above). Their choices, for the most part, were limited to taking on bank debt, with its short-term nature, or selling private placement debt to insurance companies, which usually meant accepting severely restrictive covenants.

This is not to say there were no low-rated bonds in the public market. There were many—but they had not been issued as such. They were issued with investment-grade ratings (BBB/Baa or higher) and then were downgraded as their issuers encountered operating difficulties. Above and beyond the previously issued debt of these "fallen angels," exchanges designed to modify the financial structure of troubled companies in a way that would reduce debt service or delay maturities created additional low-rated, publicly-traded bonds.

Beginning in the mid-1970s, pioneering work done primarily at the investment banking firm of Drexel Burnham Lambert led to the conclusion that historic default experience did not justify the traditional aversion to low-rated debt, and that new issues of such securities should be salable. The initial buyers consisted heavily of individuals and high yield mutual funds, who were subsequently joined by pension funds, insurance companies, banks, and savings and loans.

Through this process, a new group of issues has come to share the label "high yield bonds" with the fallen angels. Often called "emerging credits," these are bonds which receive noninvestment grade ratings on issuance rather than as a result of being downgraded. On average, their issuers are smaller and younger than the firms which issued the former high grades. Tables 1 and 2, which document the growth and size of the high yield market, show that compared to the $41.7 billion face value of low-rated bonds outstanding on average during 1984, $31.1 billion came as new issues between 1978 and 1984. While these figures are not directly comparable (because of the departure of some issues from the category due to redemption, bankruptcy, or upgrading), they certainly suggest the importance of the post-1977 new issues in creating the high yield bond market of today.

Clearly there have been major changes during the time period covered by Tables 1 and 2. Low-rated debt has risen from 4.1 percent of the public straight debt outstanding to 11.2 percent, while the rate of growth of outstandings has been three times that of high-rated bonds. In 1984, high yield bonds accounted for 15 percent of new public straight debt issues, up from 6.7 percent in 1978. The size of the average new issue has grown from $29 million in 1978 to $120 million in 1984. And the number of $100 million deals grew from 2 in 1978 to 23 in 1983 and, finally, to 58 in 1984.[4]

TABLE 1   Public Straight Debt Outstanding 1975–1984*
(millions of dollars)

| | | Low Rated Debt | | |
| | | --- | --- | |
Year	Average Par Value-Public Straight Debt	Straight Public Debt	Percent of Public St. Debt	High-Rated Debt
1984	$371,100 (Est.)	$41,700	11.2%	$329,400
1983	339,850	28,223	8.3	311,627
1982	320,850	18,536	5.8	302,314
1981	303,800	17,362	5.7	286,438
1980	282,000	15,125	5.4	266,875
1979	260,600	10,675	4.1	249,925
1978	245,000	9,401	3.8	235,599
1977	228,500	8,479	3.7	220,021
1976	209,900	8,015	3.8	201,885
1975	187,900	7,720	4.1	180,180
Annual Compound Growth Rate	7.9%	20.6%		6.9%

* Not including exchange offers, tax exempts, convertibles, or governments and agencies.
SOURCE: Edward I. Altman and Scott A. Nammacher, *The Anatomy of the High Yield Debt Market* (New York: Morgan Stanley & Co., Inc., 1985), p. 10.

---

[4] Edward I. Altman and Scott A. Nammacher, *The Anatomy of the High Yield Debt Market* (New York: Morgan Stanley & Co., Inc., 1985), p. 11.

TABLE 2 New Straight Domestic Debt Issues: 1978–1984* (millions of dollars)

| | | | High Yield Debt | | | | |
| | Total New Issues—Public Straight Debt | | New Issues of High Yield Debt | | | New Debt Issued in Exchanges | |
Year	Amount	No.	Amount	No.	Percent New Issues $s	Amount	No.
1984	$ 99,416	721	$14,952	124	15.0%	$ 702	10
1983	46,903	511	7,417	86	15.8	486	16
1982	47,798	513	2,798	48	5.9	529	5
1981	41,651	357	1,648	32	4.0	323	2
1980	37,272	398	1,442	43	3.9	646	5
1979	25,678	277	1,307	45	5.0	227	6
1978	22,416	287	1,493	52	6.7	662	12
Total:	$321,134	3,064	$31,057	430		$3,575	56

* Not including exchange offers, tax exempts, convertibles, or governments and agencies.

SOURCE: Edward I. Altman and Scott A. Nammacher, *The Anatomy of the High Yield Debt Market* (New York: Morgan Stanley & Co., Inc., 1985), p. 10.

In recent years, increasing attention has been devoted on the equity side of the investment management industry both to "indexing" portfolios, so that they will mirror the broad universe, and to comparing portfolio diversification against the make-up of popular indexes such as Standard & Poor's 500. In that light, it seems irrational for investors to ignore 11 percent of the public, corporate straight debt market. After all, high yield bonds are as big a part of the bond market as office equipment stocks (IBM, AT&T, Digital Equipment, and Xerox) are of the S&P 500. Rather than dismiss a sector as significant as high yield bonds as "too risky" because the rating agencies say they are, it makes sense to try to ascertain the actual riskiness of these bonds by reviewing the historic experience.

Default Experience

When new high yield issues began to appear in the late 1970s, widespread analysis began. The critical questions, of course, surrounded the magnitude of the risk. Since there was little data on the downgraded bonds and virtually no experience with low-rated new issues, the initial resort was to default data on the overall bond market. Although the relevance of these historic data to the new high yield bonds was uncertain, it was quite easy to demonstrate the simple proposition that default has historically been a very rare occurrence. The results of a number of

TABLE 3 Default Rate—All Straight Corporate Debt

1900–1909	.90%	1940–1949	.40%	1971–1975	.11%
1910–1919	2.00	1950–1959	.04	1976–1980	.06
1920–1929	1.00	1960–1965	.03	1981–1984	.12
1930–1939	3.20	1966–1970	.20		

SOURCE: *The Case for High Yield Bonds* (Beverly Hills, Calif: Drexel Burnham Lambert, March 1985), p. 10.

studies are combined in Table 3, which details the percentage of all outstanding public debt going into default each year by period.

Clearly, default has occurred infrequently, and this is especially true since 1940. In the last 45 years, the default rate for all bonds has averaged .015 percent per year.

For years, until additional data was developed, the typical response was, "But what about defaults on low-rated bonds? Don't those bonds default more often than the overall universe?" In apparent response to such questions, an article in *The Wall Street Journal* on March 6, 1985 was headlined "Study Finds Much Higher Default Rate for 'Junk Bonds' Than for All Issues". It went on to state that the default rate for bonds rated BB or lower has been 20 times higher than on all corporate bonds.[5] The balance of the article and the actual study, however, detailed that the default rate between 1974 and 1984 had been only 1.5 percent of outstanding low-rated straight debt per year. Not only is this default rate modest in absolute terms, but there are reasons why it should be viewed as a conservative (i.e., high) indicator of actual losses. As Altman and Nammacher point out:

> At least 14 of these [54] defaulting firms did not actually file for bankruptcy. In several cases, interest was paid in arrears at a later date either by the firm or by a firm purchasing the defaulted entity. In others, agreements were reached with creditors to restructure the debt.[6]

Additionally, the authors point out that by selling the bonds immediately after bankruptcy, an average of 41 percent of the par value could be recouped and the loss ratio (as opposed to the default ratio) reduced to 1 percent per year. Although the exercise is not performed, joining the two points above should result in a loss ratio which is even lower.

The most specifically focused study of the area has been performed by Drexel Burnham Lambert. The scope of this study was limited to low-

---

[5] Linda Sandler, "Study Finds Much Higher Default Rate for 'Junk Bonds' Than for All Issues," *The Wall Street Journal*, March 6, 1985.

[6] Edward I. Altman and Scott A. Nammacher, "The Default Rate Experience on High Yield Corporate Debt," *Financial Analysts Journal*, July–August 1985, pp. 25–41.

rated bonds issued as such and excluded bonds that were downgraded from investment grade. It also sought to separate the losses on the affected bonds between that part attributable simply to a rise in interest rates and the balance due to credit deterioration, default, or bankruptcy. The conclusions of the study are as follows:

1. Between the start of 1977 and February, 1985, .45 percent of the average amount of high yield debt outstanding was lost in bankruptcies each year on average. There were 19 bankruptcies in the emerging credits, and the average loss was 60 percent from the level at which the bond would have sold based on interest rates alone.

2. The percentage expands to .52 percent if bonds in default but not bankruptcy are added.[7]

My experience is generally in line with the statistics cited above. In a portfolio averaging $450 million which was invested in emerging credits from late 1978 through early 1985, during employment with Citibank and Citicorp Investment Management, a total of $21.4 million is estimated to have been lost in bonds going into bankruptcy. Thus, a total of roughly 5 percent was lost over a period spanning almost seven years, for an average of .7 percent per year. As these losses were calculated from purchase price rather than from investment value based on the level of interest rates, they overstate the loss due to bankruptcy in a period of generally rising interest rates.

I believe these last, personal statistics should be viewed in the following light:

- This experience covers a period which included a double-dip recession which was the most severe contraction since the Depression. Yet the overall loss percentage was absolutely low.
- All of the bankruptcies occurred in the oil industry, which was particularly hard-hit by an exogenous factor: the volatile behavior of OPEC.
- The corresponding observation is that despite the harsh economic climate, there were no bankruptcies among our holdings in the manufacturing, finance, or utility sectors—which numbered in the hundreds of issues.
- Because the oil industry was "defrocked" when prices weakened starting in 1981, portfolios assembled since that time have in many cases been oil-free and, consequently, totally default-free.

There will always be some sector like the oils which is particularly hard-hit for systematic reasons (as were the REITs in the 1970s). But it is

---

[7] *The Case for High Yield Bonds* (Beverly Hills, Calif: Drexel Burnham Lambert, March 1985), p. 11.

cheering that there was no random rash of bankruptcies among the balance of our portfolio holdings due solely to the factors which prompted their low ratings.

When all of the evidence cited above—academic studies, work in the industry, and personal experience—is taken into account, the original conclusion is unchanged; in fact, it is bolstered. On the basis of history, default and bankruptcy occur infrequently, even among the issuers of high yield bonds.

The loss rate is higher than on high-rated bonds, however, so we must examine the adequacy of the yields which are offered as an inducement to bear the risk.

PROMISED YIELDS ON HIGH YIELD BONDS

The argument posed earlier was that high yield bonds, like every other investment, should be considered in terms of the risk and the return which they entail. It was shown above that credit losses in these bonds appear more frequently than they do in higher rated bonds. And it might be argued that as the history is limited to only eight years, the data presented could understate the eventual losses. Thus, it is reasonable to expect that higher *a priori* returns be available if these bonds are to be invested in.

On this topic, there is little disagreement. There has consistently been a substantial, positive spread between the yields-to-maturity at which high yield bonds are available and the yields on higher-rated debt securities.

Table 4 details the average spread between two brokerage firms' high yield bond indexes and U.S. Treasury bonds of comparable maturity.

TABLE 4

	Excess Return over Treasury Bond Offered by	
	DBL 100 Bond Index	*Salomon Bros. "All" High Yield Bonds*
1980	359 b.p.	359 b.p.
1981	394	399
1982	499	526
1983	346	339
1984	319	348
1985	343* (to 9/85)	445 (to 8/85)

* Excludes bonds rated below B
SOURCES: For the DBL 100 Bond Index: *The Case for High Yield Bonds* (Beverly Hills, Calif: Drexel Burnham Lambert, March 1985), p. 6; For Salomon Bros. "All" High-Yield Bonds: Monthly Letters, Salomon Brothers Inc to author, January 1980 to date.

Clearly, the history of the yield spread between high yield bonds and high grade bonds (as exemplified by risk-free Treasuries) shows the persistent presence of what has typically been a 300–400 basis point inducement to take the extra risk. The average spread has been below 300 basis points at the end of only five of the 69 months for which Salomon Brothers has calculated its index, and the lowest of those observations was at 287 basis points.

By all accounts, the promised yield spread on high yield bonds has been far more than enough to compensate for the credit losses which have been experienced to date. It seems reasonable to recognize three specific aspects of the spread.

1. The spread implies higher compound returns over full cycles. This is unaffected by changes in interest rates and interim changes in the spread. If the spread is at the same level at the corresponding point in two cycles, the yield spread will be earned—net of credit losses—for each of the intervening years. Thanks to the power of compound interest, returns grow faster than do rates. $10 million invested at 11 percent for 15 years will grow by $37.8 million. But increase the rate by 28 percent to 14 percent, and the return grows by 62 percent, to $61.4 million.

2. The increased promised yield comes in the form of incremental interest. It is not a hoped-for capital gain which is "on the come." The regular receipt of higher current interest goes a long way to build a solid base for the total return and to render unfavorable relative performance unlikely. As noted investor John Neff has been described as saying:

    . . . of the two components of . . . total return— . . . yield and . . . growth— yield is worth far more because it's "assured today."[8]

3. The increased yield is present as a premium for bearing risk, and it serves that purpose more than admirably. A 350 basis point average spread, for example, means that even if as much as 3½ percent of the portfolio's principal value is lost to credit problems each year, the overall return on a high yield bond portfolio will still match that on a portfolio of Treasury bonds. However, as mentioned earlier, both Drexel and Altman found that roughly 40 percent is recovered when bonds encounter credit difficulty. Thus, if only 60 percent is lost, 5.8 percent of the portfolio's holdings would have to experience default or bankruptcy each year in order to provide 3.5 percent of credit losses. It is when that figure is compared with Drexel's .9 per-

---

[8] Diane Hal Gropper, "How John Neff Does It," *Institutional Investor* (May 1985), p. 88.

cent and Altman's 1.5 percent estimate of the actual default rate that the risk premium can be seen to anticipate much more risk than has historically been present.

What has been described above is a risk premium which appears to more than compensate for the actual risk. The result of that combination should be disproportionately high realized returns. We will next review what the actual return experience has been.

REALIZED RETURNS

With an *a priori* risk premium vastly in excess of the risks which actually materialized, superior realized returns should have come from high yield bonds. And that is exactly what has been witnessed. In fact, the evidence on the subject of returns on low-rated bonds is extensive and appears unanimous.

The classic study in this field was conducted by Braddock Hickman. The Hickman study covered bond experience between 1900 and 1943. Despite the enormous default rates in the Depression, which in 1936 and 1940 reached 15 percent for all bonds[9] and which pushed 42 percent of all BB-, B-, and C-rated bonds outstanding in the 43-year period into default during their life, low-rated bonds had a superior return.

Table 5, which is drawn from Hickman's study, shows the ability of high yields to more than offset high default experience.

In a subsequent study, John Fitzpatrick and Jacobus Severiens reviewed the period 1965–1975.[10] Their findings were similar to Hickman's. Despite the harsh implicit assumption that default results in total loss, systematically higher returns were realized as rating dropped. Table 6 shows the unweighted average yields to maturity for the 11 years reduced by the default rates for B and BB bonds.

A more recent academic study by Marshall Blume and Donald Keim covered the 29 months of January 1982 through May 1984.[11] Their conclusions regarding returns are summarized in Table 7 below:

Finally, a tabulation of actual published results for a number of bond indexes, fund composites, and my investment results at Citicorp is shown in Table 8 and is contrasted against the returns on a single Treasury bond and Salomon Brothers' high-grade bond index.

---

[9] W. B. Hickman, *Corporate Bond Quality and Investor Experience* (Princeton, New Jersey: Princeton University Press, 1958) and, Harold G. Fraine and Robert H. Mills, "Effects of Defaults and Credit Deterioration on Yields of Corporate Bonds," *The Journal of Finance* (September 1961), p. 425.

[10] John D. Fitzpatrick and Jacobus T. Severiens, "Hickman Revisited: The Case for Junk Bonds," *The Journal of Portfolio Management* (Summer 1978), pp. 53–57.

[11] Marshall E. Blume and Donald B. Keim, "Risk and Return Characteristics of Lower Grade Bonds," Rodney L. White Center for Financial Research, University of Pennsylvania, 1985, pp. 3–4.

Table 5 Default Experience and Yields: 1900–1943 Statistics

	Life Span Default Rate	Promised Yield	Realized Yield
AAA	5.9%	4.5%	5.1%
BBB	19.1	4.9	5.0
BB-B-C	42.4	9.5	8.6

SOURCE: John D. Fitzpatrick and Jacobus T. Severiens, "Hickman Revisited: The Case for Junk Bonds," *The Journal of Portfolio Management,* Summer 1978, p. 53.

TABLE 6 Net Realized Annual Yields to Maturity

	B	BB	BBB	A
Average of 11-Year Results	9.4%	8.4%	8.1%	7.1%

SOURCE: Fitzpatrick and Severiens, pp. 53–57.

TABLE 7 Compounded Annual Rates of Return

	Low-Rated*	A	AAA
1/82 through 5/84	20.3%	16.6%	15.0%

* Average of DBL 100 and Salomon Brothers indexes.

TABLE 8 Total Returns

	1984	1983	1982	1981	1980	All Five Years
Salomon Brothers' "All" high yield bonds[a]	8.6%	21.9%	32.4%	3.4%	.4%	12.7%
Drexel Burnham 100[b]	8.5	19.7	32.5	2.7	.9	12.3
Lipper—High current yield mutual funds[c]	7.2	16.8	29.4	6.5	4.7	12.6
Wiesenberger—High yield mutual funds[c]	7.3	16.7	30.3	5.4	4.7	12.5
Citibank high yield fund[d]	5.9	17.7	27.6	7.7	4.9	12.4
Treasury 8⅜% due 2000[b]	13.7	.5	44.2	(2.0)	(4.1)	9.1
Salomon Brothers' High grade index[d]	16.4	4.7	43.8	(1.0)	(2.6)	11.1

[a] Monthly Letters. Salomon Brothers to author.

[b] *The Case for High Yield Bonds* (Beverly Hills, Calif: Drexel Burnham Lambert, March 1985), p. 10.

[c] Edward I. Altman and Scott A. Nammacher, *The Anatomy of the High Yield Debt Market* (New York: Morgan Stanley & Co., Inc., 1985), pp. 20 and 21.

[d] *Annual Reports,* Citibank Investment Management Groups/Citicorp Investment Management, 1980–1985.

The results for the high yield indicators are remarkably consistent and consistently superior. Further, they show an interesting pattern: they were superior when high-grade bonds did poorly and inferior when they did well. Thus, the pattern of returns is worthy of review as well.

VOLATILITY OF RETURNS

The evidence on the volatility of returns runs uniformly in favor of high yield bonds. At the lowest level, this can be seen on inspection. The defensive nature of the returns shown above implies lower volatility.

Viewed statistically, the results are the same. The standard deviation of the annual returns on Citibank's High Yield Fund, for example, was roughly half that on Salomon Brothers' high grade index over the last five years.

	Standard Deviation of Annual Returns 1980–1984
Citibank high yield fund	8.7%
Salomon Brothers high grades	17.1%

Lastly, these conclusions were borne out by Blume and Keim:[12]

	Standard Deviation of Monthly Returns	
	1/82–5/84	1/80–6/84
Lower-Rated Bonds	2.7%	4.1%
A Corporate Bonds	3.5	NA
AAA Corporate Bonds	3.5	4.7

A number of reasons all seem to contribute to this reduced volatility:

- The simple receipt of higher current interest builds a foundation which restricts the downward fluctuation of returns.
- More elegantly put, the higher the coupon and stronger the sinking fund of a bond, *ceteris paribus*, the shorter its duration.
- The cycles in general bond prices, which are forced downward by higher interest rates when the economy strengthens, tend to run counter to the cycles in creditworthiness, which rises in prosperity, and vice versa.
- Bond investors' fluctuating attitudes toward economic events are most often implemented via higher grade bonds.

---

[12] Blume and Keim, "Risk and Return Characteristics of Lower Grade Bonds," Tables 1 and 3.

- The discretionary nature of high yield bond issuance takes some of the pressure off of the outstanding issues when the interest-rate environment is at its worst.

Whatever the reason, high yield bond performance, at least during the 1980s, has been more consistent than has the performance of high grade bonds.

CONCLUSION

All of the evidence concerning high yield bonds is positive. While this conclusion is a strong one, there appear to be no exceptions to the following statements:

- Default, even among high yield bonds, has been rare.
- The yield spread has been and is wide.
- The product of the two, realized return, has been consistently high.
- Return has been earned with above-average consistency.

The above facts argue strongly for investment in high yield bonds.

What could be the catch? What could make investing in high yield bonds a mistake? Put simply, past data would have to be an inaccurate indication of the future.

- There would have to be imperfections in the statistics: survey periods too short or samples too small, for example. But the conclusions are too unanimous for us to suspect previous studies' methodologies.
- The world would have to have changed for the worse. Perhaps one would argue that the business climate will be more treacherous, or that the character of future recessions will be different.
- The universe of bonds may have changed. Could the bonds of today have different risk characteristics than the historic high yield universe in general?
- The sector may have become more efficiently priced. "Junk bond" has become a household word, and the rate of issuance is up sharply. But the yield spread remains high. Unless the default rate rises greatly, therefore, today's returns will continue to more than compensate for the risk.

Perhaps Fitzpatrick and Severiens wrapped it up best:

It is the ability to take advantage of . . . market inefficiency that results in the investment merit of junk bonds. Little reason exists to suppose that this market structure will change. Because of regulation, policy, and custom, most institutional investors shun junk bonds.[13]

---

[13] Fitzpatrick and Severiens, "Hickman Revisited," p. 57.

36

Performance Evaluation in Fixed Income Securities*

Arthur Williams III, C.F.A.
Managing Director
Simms Capital Management, Ltd.

INTRODUCTION

In past and simpler days, investors felt no need to measure fixed income investments to any great extent. It was sufficient to know the quality rating, the interest rate, and term-to-maturity of fixed income investments. As long as these factors suited the objectives of the investor, bonds were held to maturity rather than being actively traded; analysis was unnecessary. For better or worse, those days have long since past. Because of the huge sums invested in fixed income securities, volatility caused by high inflation and high interest rates, and the modern-world need to extract as much as possible from every asset, investors now must take a much more vigorous approach to measuring their fixed income portfolios. In short, performance must be measured. In recent years, significant steps have been made in measuring prices, developing indexes against which performance could be measured, and even constructing approaches that measure not only return, but also risk. The first problem that arises in the measurement of bond portfolios is calculating the value of the fund. That is, before many measurements of return or risk can be performed, the portfolio must be valued. This, in turn, requires an accurate and consistent method of measuring prices. Since there is not a central marketplace for trading bonds, there is no single source of transaction history that can be used for price measure-

---

* For a complete discussion of performance measurement see Arthur Williams III, *Managing Your Investment Manager—The Complete Guide to Selection, Measurement, and Control* (Homewood, Ill.: Dow Jones-Irwin, 1980 and 1986).

ment. Fortunately, as investors have become increasingly interested in measuring portfolios, computerized techniques have been developed for measuring and transmitting bond price information.

MEASURING RETURNS

Once an adequate pricing system is in effect, it is then possible to begin measuring portfolios. One way to do this is to measure a hypothetical portfolio and create an index that can be used for comparison purposes. Chapter 7 deals extensively with how such indexes are created and which indexes are available for use by investors.

The next step in performance measurement is to determine the rate of return earned by the portfolio. Presumably the time-weighted return is desired. For best results, frequent portfolio valuations should be used, and monthly frequency provides excellent results. The time-weighted return (as opposed to the dollar-weighted return, internal rate of return, or yield-to-maturity, all of which are synonymous) is preferred, assuming that the manager has no control over external contributions to or withdrawals from the fund. The time-weighted return is that return that would have been earned on $1 invested in the portfolio at the beginning of the period and maintained throughout. For example, if the market fell significantly and a contribution was received into the portfolio and invested in bonds, the portfolio would grow through the timeliness of the investment. However, assuming the decision to fund the portfolio was made by the owner rather than the manager of the fund, the manager's performance should be calculated independent of this contribution. The time-weighted method correctly calculates return independent of the cash flow.[1]

MEASURING RISK

As investors become more interested in the results of their portfolios, it is no longer adequate to ask how well the portfolio performed without asking how well it performed "relative to the risk taken." Risk measurement provides an entirely new set of problems for investors, since there are many possible definitions of *risk*. As an example, risk can be looked at as potential loss due to default or in terms of loss that would be incurred if interest rates rose above levels at the time of the purchase. For purposes of this chapter, *risk* will be defined as the uncertainty of the portfolio's rate of return or the uncertainty of its future value. For example, even though short-term Treasury bills have no risk of default, they have uncertainty as to rate of return for investors whose time horizon is

---

[1] See a more complete discussion in ibid., pp. 263–284.

greater than the time to maturity of the obligation. Even if the investor's time horizon is equal to the maturity of the instrument owned, the investor will have some uncertainty as to the rate of return, since it will not be known in advance what interest will be earned on the coupon income received on the portfolio. Of course, if the bond carries no coupon (i.e., it is "pure discount" or "zero-coupon") then this factor does not prevail.

One might ask why investors should care about risk in fixed income portfolios, especially if the instruments owned are of high quality and the risk of default is minimal. There are several reasons. First, if a fund has a wrong policy toward risk, its chances of meeting its goal are significantly reduced. Further, since market cycles are so long, it takes many years to find out if a portfolio is successful in meeting its objectives. Consequently, it is difficult to establish a control process whereby results can be monitored and changes instituted when results are unsatisfactory. This makes it especially important to establish the proper risk policy initially in order to avoid what will almost certainly be a disastrous policy if goals are changed as the market fluctuates up and down.

A second reason for measuring risk is to find out if returns are adequate relative to results achieved. Although it is certainly more important to have good results than to have achieved bad results for good reasons, nonetheless, it is important to know whether results are adequate relative to risks, since high risk carries with it the potential for highly unsatisfactory returns.

Finally, in times of high interest rates, returns are especially volatile. It is important to measure risk to be able to provide some protection against this volatility.

Why, instead of measuring risk, should not the investor merely compare returns to hoped-for return, the return of the market, or comparisons with other portfolios? Each of these comparisons is important, but none is sufficient. Absolute objectives are not particularly helpful standards in the short run, since when markets rise all funds tend to exceed these objectives, and in declining markets funds generally fall below these standards. Looking solely at comparisons relative to the market is not satisfactory, either, since in long periods of decline the fund may outperform the market but fail to have sufficient funds to meet its cash requirements. Similarly, when measuring success in relation to the performance of other portfolios, it is possible to do better than everyone else and still have insufficient funds to meet the portfolio's goal.

Sources of Risk in Bond Portfolios

Of course, the primary risk to be concerned about when looking at bond portfolios is that of default. If the issuer is unable to pay interest and principal when due, the portfolio's rate of return will suffer dramatically. Practically speaking, the overwhelming majority of bonds owned by investors are creditworthy. Consequently, the risk of default is usually more obvious in the difference in the yields among bonds of different quality than in the real potential for default. However, it should always be kept in mind that the potential exists for a depression, such as the country has witnessed on several occasions, during which a number of issuers would default.

For bonds that are unlikely to run into these difficulties, two types of uncertainty are apparent. Changes in the general level of interest rates and changes in the "spread" or difference in yield between sectors both provide opportunities for changes in rate of return. A third risk, that arising from changes in reinvestment rate, can also be observed. On one extreme, interest rates might drop sharply thus leading the issue to be called, in which case investors end up owning low-yielding bonds instead of the high-yielding bonds they formerly had. Even in a less dramatic example, the interest-on-interest earned in the portfolio can be substantially less than was originally anticipated.

It should also be noted that there are other risks deriving from special features of bonds. For instance, if a bond is subordinated or has a junior position to that of other creditors, the bond's risk increases. When bonds are convertible into other securities, an additional source of uncertainty of return is introduced. In this case the bond may act more like an equity than like a fixed income security.

Changes in the level of interest rates. When viewing the impact of changes in the general level of interest rates, three laws will be noted. First, as interest rates change, bond prices change also, but in the opposite direction.[2] In other words, as interest rates rise, bond prices decline and vice versa. Second, all other things being equal, bonds with longer-term maturities are more volatile than those with shorter maturities.[3] Finally, bonds with lower coupons are more volatile than those with higher coupons.[4]

Changes in spreads between bond sectors. Bonds can be characterized by their quality, coupon, maturity, and issuer type. Each of these characteristics leads to an assignment by the marketplace of a yield-to-maturity at any point in time. However, just as the overall yield levels in the marketplace can change, the spread or the differential in yields between bonds of different types can also change. This provides an additional uncertainty as to rate of return. The following example demonstrates this phenomenon, which holds true for each of the five characteristics: maturity, quality, coupon, issuer type, and coupon area (discount or premium). Consider bonds A and B, with initial yields of 8

---

[2] See Chapter 4.
[3] See Chapter 4 for illustrations.
[4] See Chapter 4 for illustrations.

percent and 8.1 percent, respectively. The spread is 10 basis points in favor of B. When the spread between the higher yielding bond (B) and the lower yield bond (A) widens, the lower yielding bond is the better performer. If the spread widens by bond B's yield rising, bond B will sustain a capital loss, making bond A, the lower yielding bond, a better performer. If the spread widens by bond A's yield declining, bond A will sustain a capital gain, making it the better performer.

Traditional Risk Measures

Historical or traditional risk measurements of bonds can be divided into two general categories. One looks at the underlying strength of the *issuer*, and the other looks at the characteristics of the *bond issue*. Measurements describing the issuer can be further subdivided into (1) those analyzing the issuer's income or cash flow relative to the amount of debt to be repaid, and (2) others that view liabilities relative to assets. These measures are discussed in Chapter 22.

The analytical techniques discussed above are used primarily in looking at individual securities to determine creditworthiness or value. However, investors are typically more concerned with portfolios than with individual securities, so it is necessary to apply these measurements to portfolios as a whole. This can be done by weighting the individual securities' risk measures by the proportion of the portfolio in each security. For certain nonnumerical measures, such as quality ratings, some sort of numerical translation has to be made. For instance, the highest quality securities can be considered "one," second highest "two," and so on, and then the weighting process can be applied.

New Quantitative Techniques for Measuring Risk

In addition to the traditional measures described previously, new techniques have been developed. Three such risk measures will be considered here. The first uses standard deviation, or total variability, as a measure of risk. The second model uses the beta measurement. Finally, a third model uses "duration" or measures of sensitivity to changes in the level of interest rates.

Standard deviation in the market line analysis. A market line is a method of measuring risk and return using variability of returns as the measure of risk. Exhibit 1 shows a market line analysis for a bond portfolio. The vertical axis of the market line shows return, and the horizontal axis shows variability as measured by the standard deviation of return. (Since standard deviation is an arithmetic, as opposed to geometric, concept, the returns shown are arithmetic rather than geometric. Although this changes the actual measurement of return somewhat, it does not in any way alter the concept of return.) It can be seen from this

EXHIBIT 1 Bond Portfolio Market Line Analysis for Period December 1979 to December 1984

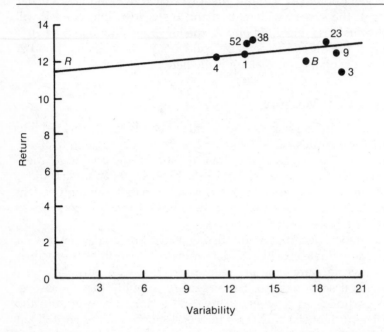

B — BOND PORTFOLIO
R — RISK-FREE 91 DAY U.S. T-BILL
3 — ML 15 YEAR + U.S. T-Bond
4 — ML 3-5 YEAR U.S. T-BOND

1 — ML CORP. AND GOVT. MASTER
9 — ML HIGH-QUAL. LONG-TERM CORP.
23 — ML MED-QUAL. LONG-TERM CORP.
38 — ML HIGH-QUAL. INT.-TERM CORP.
52 — ML MED-QUAL. INT.-TERM CORP.

SOURCE: Merrill Lynch Institutional Sales and Marketing.

framework for measuring risk and return that the most desirable portfolio would be one represented by a point at the upper left part of the graph, signifying a low level of risk and a high level of return.

Utilization of the market line begins with measurement of the risk and return of Treasury bills and the overall bond market (index 1). Treasury bills (represented by R) had a return during the period of a little more than 11 percent and a variability of zero for a one-quarter time horizon. Similarly, a point is shown that represents the risk and return for the overall bond market, as measured by the Merrill Lynch Corporate and Government Master Index. This point shows a return of slightly more than 12 percent, with a variability of about 13 percent. This risk measurement indicates that about two thirds of the time during this period we would have expected the market line to have a return within thirteen percentage points of its average. Put another way, the return would be between −1 percent and +25 percent about two thirds of the time. It should be noted that any return is theoretically possible but that a return above or below two standard deviations (plus or minus 26 percent, or outside the range of −14 percent to +38 percent in this case) would only occur 5 percent of the time.

We have thus described two points on the fixed income spectrum, the risk and return of Treasury bills and the risk and return of the overall bond market. We can now draw a market line showing the risk and return of "market" portfolios with a wide variety of risk levels. This is done by connecting the Treasury bill point with the bond market point and indicating that an investor could achieve a portfolio of any risk level and any return shown on that line merely by combining the appropriate proportions of Treasury bills and the bond market. In other words, a point halfway along the line would have a risk of about 6½ percent and a return halfway between that of bills and that of the market. This portfolio can be constructed by allocating half of fund assets at the beginning of the period to bills and the other half to the bond market as represented by the index. Similarly, any other point on the line can be achieved by combining the appropriate amount of bills and bonds. It must be noted that in order to achieve a point to the right of the bond market, the percentage in Treasury bills must be negative; that is, the investor must borrow money at the risk-free rate and leverage his portfolio. Although this may not be a legal alternative for most funds, it is at least a theoretical alternative and useful from an analytical point of view.

Having drawn a market line for the period December 31, 1979 to December 31, 1984, we note that during this period the line slants upward. This indicates that during the period there was a positive "premium" for bearing risk: The greater the risk that was taken, the better portfolios tended to do. This is the normal long-run expectation.

Beta analysis.　The beta measurement presents the relationship between a portfolio's historic rate of return and the market's historic rate of return, and the slope of the line indicates how volatile the portfolio is relative to the market index.[5] Exhibits 2 and 3 use the beta model to show the relationship between short-term government portfolios and long-term corporate portfolios, both in relation to a broad-based market index. It can easily be seen that the short-term government index has a much flatter slope than that of the long-term corporate index, indicating its lesser volatility, or risk.

Certain difficulties arise in using the beta measurement for bond portfolios and hoping to make judgments about them. First, the choice

---

[5] See Williams, *Managing Your Investment Manager*, pp. 275–279.

EXHIBIT 2

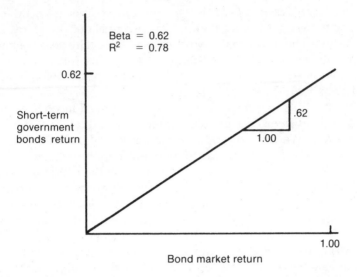

Bond market—Merrill Lynch Master Index of Corporate and Government Bonds (#BOAO) Short-term government—Merrill Lynch Index of Short-Term (1–2.99 years) Treasury Bonds (#G102)

EXHIBIT 3

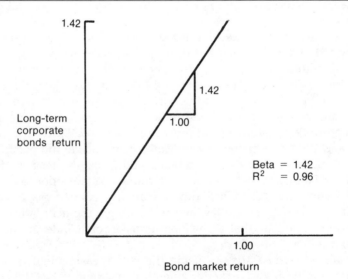

Bond market—Merrill Lynch Master Index of Corporate and Government Bonds (#BOAO) Long-term corporate—Merrill Lynch Index of Long-Term (15 years and over) Corporate Bonds (#C8BO).

of index makes a great deal of difference in the results achieved. Second, the portfolio's characteristics should be stable for the measurement to be highly useful. Since bond portfolios, if no action is taken, are constantly becoming shorter term and hence less risky, this creates difficulties with the measurement. Finally, as will be discussed later, because of these problems it is highly questionable whether the beta analysis can be expanded beyond risk to measure selection and diversification, as can be done with equity portfolios.

The duration model. In recent years, with the increasing emphasis on measuring fixed income portfolios, considerable importance has been attached to an old idea: the concept of duration. Duration measures the average time required for the investor to receive the investment and the interest on it. It is similar to maturity, except that maturity only considers the timing and the amount of the final payment of a bond. Duration, on the other hand, also considers the significant impact on the investor of the timing and magnitude of coupon payments. As explained in Chapters 5 and 6, long-maturity high-coupon bonds have a considerably shorter duration than do long-maturity low-coupon bonds. The significance of duration is that the greater the duration, the more volatile a portfolio's return is with respect to changes in the general level of interest rates. In fact, for small changes in rates the relationship is proportional.

As was noted earlier in the chapter, longer maturity bonds are more volatile than shorter maturity bonds because the time period over which the discounting process takes place is much longer with longer maturity bonds. With low-coupon bonds the percentage of the total return represented by the final payment is much higher, and since the final payment is obviously the longest term payment received, the volatility of the portfolio or bond with respect to changes in interest rates is increased.

The duration measure has several limitations, and these should be noted. First, there are risks to portfolios other than those associated with interest-rate changes. Second, the precise measurement of the portfolio's volatility with respect to interest-rate changes assumes a so-called parallel shift in the yield curve. In other words, if 20-year rates move 1 percent, then a similar change is assumed for 19-year bonds, 10-year bonds, 5-year bonds, and so on. Despite these limitations the duration measure is of considerable use in measuring the risk of fixed income securities.

MEASURING RISK-ADJUSTED RETURN

The rate of return adjusted for the amount of risk taken, also known as the *manager's contribution*, can be calculated by using each of the three measurements shown for calculating portfolio risk. Each of these measurements will be discussed below.

Using Standard Deviation in Market Line Analysis

In the Market Line analysis, a line was drawn representing the risk and return of portfolios consisting of various portions of Treasury bills and the market. This line can be viewed as an unmanaged or "naive" portfolio. In other words, it is possible to suggest that the line represents a market portfolio of a specific risk level and that the market return for a portfolio of that risk level is the one shown on the vertical axis (see Exhibit 1). If the return is above the line, it can be stated that the portfolio achieved a risk-adjusted return above that of the market. If the return is below the line, the portfolio did less well than an unmanaged portfolio of the same risk level. As with all measurements comparing actual performance to a market index, it must be considered that the index has no transaction costs and that real portfolios do. Consequently, all such measurements are somewhat biased against the investment manager operating in the real world.

Using Alpha

Just as with equity portfolios, it is possible to use the alpha, or intercept, to measure risk-adjusted returns.[6] However, this procedure is not recommended because of the following factors: (1) the segmented nature of the bond market, (2) the impact on the portfolio of shifts in the bond yield curve, (3) the varying results that can occur, depending on which index is used to represent the overall bond market, and (4) the changing risk level of the portfolio that occurs as bonds become shorter in maturity and as coupon reinvestment and other funds added to the portfolio change its structure. All of these factors impact the measurement of risk in the portfolio and create the possibility that the alpha is showing a factor representing risk when it is supposedly demonstrating the impact of the manager over and above that indicated by the risk of the portfolio.

Using the Duration Model

With the duration measurement, it is possible to calculate the sensitivity of a portfolio to changes in the general level of interest rates. With this information, it becomes possible to attribute the sources of the portfolio's return to the market effect, the policy effect, the interest-rate anticipation effect, the analysis effect, and the trading effect. In the duration model (Exhibit 4), the rate of return is shown on the vertical axis, and duration is shown on the horizontal axis. This is similar to the market line, except that duration rather than total variability is used as the risk measure. The *market effect* is the base point; it represents the return the

---

[6] See Williams, *Managing Your Investment Manager*, pp. 247–259 and pp. 275–279.

EXHIBIT 4 The Duration Model

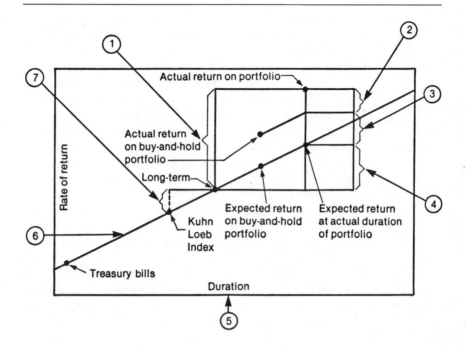

1. The management effect is the improvement in the investment performance of a passive strategy through active bond management. It is the difference between the total bond portfolio return and the expected return at the long-term average average duration.
2. The trading effect is the result of the current quarter's trading, either through effective trade desk operation or short-term selection abilities. It is the difference between the total management effect and the effects attributable to analysis and interest-rate anticipation.
3. The analysis effect, attributable to the selection of issues with better than average long-term prospects, is the difference between the actual return of the buy-and-hold portfolio at the beginning of the quarter and the expected return of that buy-and-hold portfolio.
4. The interest-rate anticipation effect is attributable to changes in portfolio duration resulting from attempts to profit from and ability to predict bond market movements. It is the difference between the expected return at the actual portfolio duration and the expected return at the long-term average duration.
5. Duration, a measure of the average time to the receipt of cash flows from an investment, is a measure of the sensitivity of a bond's price to changes in interest rates. An increase in yields causes a percentage decrease in price equal to the duration times change in yield.
6. The bond market line is a straight line drawn through the return/duration of Treasury bills and the return/duration of the Kuhn Loeb Index.
7. The policy effect is the difference between the long-term duration of a bond portfolio and the duration of a bond market index resulting from long-term investment policy, measured as the return at the long-average less the return on the Kuhn Loeb Index.

Note: The buy-and-hold portfolio is the composition of the portfolio at the beginning of the quarter. It is used to differentiate between trading gains secured within a quarter and long-term analysis gains.

SOURCE: Wilshire Associates, *Pension World*, June 1977.

market achieved during the period being measured. Moving up the line, the long-term average risk level of the portfolio is shown, the difference between the market return and the return of a market portfolio with the fund's policy being the *policy effect*. A manager who expects rates to change will probably shift the duration of the portfolio accordingly. In the example shown (Exhibit 4), higher risk was rewarded as the manager increased the duration of the portfolio above the long-run policy average and achieved a higher rate of return in the process. The difference between the return at the actual duration of the market line and the return at the policy duration, also on the line, is the *interest-rate anticipation effect*. If successful in finding undervalued bonds, the manager's favorable *analysis effect* would be shown as the difference between the rate of return of the initial portfolio—had it been held for the whole period—and a portfolio of the same duration on the market line. Finally, any difference between the actual rate of return earned and the return on the buy-and-hold portfolio is called the *trading effect*. This analysis is extremely interesting, but unfortunately it has limitations. Because measurements are attributed so minutely, it is extremely important that the portfolios be valued precisely and that they be measured whenever any significant cash flow takes place. In other words, the rate of return must be precisely measured for it to be possible to attribute return to the various effects. Also, duration is not a complete measurement of the risk in a portfolio, since it leaves out quality factors. Thus these factors will be attributed to other areas. In addition, the impact on the portfolio from sinking funds, calls, and redemptions will be attributed to trading, whereas they may be due to fortuitous causes. Naturally, since the market line is based on the return and the duration of the market index, precise measurements of the index must also be available. Finally, it should be noted that there is no generally accepted theory that suggests that a straight-line relationship should exist between return and duration. Although the analysis may be extremely ambitious, nonetheless the results being sought are entirely desirable.

Using Traditional Measurements

One recently developed approach to bond measurement uses traditional measurements (see Exhibit 5). This method compares results to the market and to a buy-and-hold portfolio. The difference between the rate of return on the market and the rate of return on the beginning or buy-and-hold portfolio is considered to be the *management differential*. The difference between the rate of return on the beginning portfolio and the actual portfolio is called the *activity factor*. This analysis suggests that the return on a portfolio will equal its beginning yield-to-maturity if nothing else changes. However, interest rates may change, and this impact is measured by looking at the shift in the government bond yield curve from

EXHIBIT 5   Measuring Manager Contribution Using Traditional Analysis

Return Analysis (beginning portfolio):

		Total Return		Adjusted Beginning Yield to Maturity		Interest- Rate Effect		Sector/ Quality Return		Residual
1.	Return of beginning portfolio	0.92%	=	2.14%	+	(3.84%)	+	0.80%	+	1.82%
2.	Market return	(1.25)	=	2.06	+	(4.13)	+	0.87	+	(0.05)
3.	Management differential	2.17%	=	0.08%	+	0.29%	+	(0.07)%	+	1.87%

The manager static portfolio performed considerably better (+2.17 percent) than the market portfolio. This better performance was mainly attributable to 1.87 percent from "other selection effects," which occurred on several bonds. Also, about 0.29 percent additional return was experienced because of the shorter maturity of this portfolio (13.5 years) versus the market average maturity of 19.5 years.

Activity factor:

Total Reported Return	versus	Return on Beginning Portfolio	=	Activity Factor
0.30%		0.92%	=	(0.62%)

Account descriptors:

	Market	Manager
Maturity	19.5 years	13.5 years
Coupon	7.9%	8.2%

SOURCE: Russell Fogler and Peter O. Dietz, Frank Russell & Company, Inc.

the beginning to the end of the period. The impact of this shift is called the *interest-rate effect*. To the extent that the portfolio is weighted differently from the market, any changes in the relationship between quality and issuer type will also have an impact on the portfolio. The difference between the total rate of return of the beginning portfolio and the sum of the beginning yield-to-maturity, the interest rate effect, and the sector/quality effect, is called the *residual effect*, or *other selection effect*. Finally, the difference between the return on the beginning portfolio and the actual return is an *activity* or *swapping factor*.

COMPARISON WITH A BASELINE PORTFOLIO

Some practitioners suggest that it is inappropriate to compare a portfolio's results to a market index or to the results of other funds. Rather, a fund's results should be compared to its objective. The objective is not a simple percentage or dollar amount but a portfolio that meets the needs of the fund sponsor. Assume that a certain fund with assets of $1 million is required to pay $100,000 per year to the sponsor for 10 years. In this case the baseline portfolio might be a U.S. government bond with a 10 percent coupon and a 10-year maturity. It is then possible to compare the results of the portfolio in any period to those that would have been achieved by investing in this bond.

This method has considerable appeal, though it is not easy to put into practice. First, it is not easy for most sponsors to articulate their needs as specifically as the method requires. Second, a portfolio must be found that meets these needs. Third, this portfolio must be measured along with the real portfolio. Nonetheless, at least conceptually, there is considerable merit to this approach. If nothing else, the method forces sponsors to investigate and articulate their needs.

SUMMARY

The measurement of fixed income portfolios has undergone substantial, if not revolutionary, changes in the past 10 years, and there appears to be no letup in sight. As computers and computerized data bases proliferate, this process may even accelerate. In many senses it is long overdue. Although bonds appear to be rather straightforward instruments, the workings of compound interest and changes in relationships within the market provide considerable intricacies in analyzing fixed income instruments. The need for investors to answer the question "For the risk I took, was I amply compensated?" provides the need to measure both risk and risk-adjusted returns. Gains have been made in this area, but more work has to be done, particularly in relation to the specific requirements of individual investors. For if two investors have different time horizons, a very risky portfolio for one may in fact be an extremely conservative portfolio for another. The improvements made in bond indexes and with computerized techniques provide hope that this process can be continued.

37

Measuring Market Timing in Fixed Income Portfolios

Arthur Williams III, C.F.A.
Managing Director
Simms Capital Management, Ltd.

There are two general ways in which investment managers can add return to portfolios. The first is securities selection, and the second is market timing. In equity investment it is debatable whether securities selection is more or less important to long-run success than market timing. This is because individual securities can behave very differently from the market over time. In fixed income securities, the question is not debatable at all. Assuming securities in the portfolio do not default, all bonds tend to behave more or less similarly. Wide swings in portfolio return are, then, a function of variability of the market and the risk posture of the portfolio. This risk posture, whether measured as average maturity, duration, or cash position, is an expression of the investment manager's view of the market outlook relative to the client's ability to bear risk.

Although we all intuitively feel that we know what market timing is, nonetheless, it is a very difficult phenomenon to measure. By market timing is meant changing the allocation between cash and longer term fixed income securities in anticipation of changes in the bond market. For purposes of analysis here, three categories of measuring market timing have been established: *changes in portfolio value, use of market indexes, and measurement of cash flow movements.*

CHANGES IN PORTFOLIO VALUE

Measuring changes in portfolio values involves looking at the portfolio at the beginning of the period and calculating the return that would have been achieved had that same portfolio been held throughout the period. That return can then be compared with the actual return achieved to see whether or not the "unmanaged" buy-and-hold portfolio would have performed better than the managed portfolio. Although this information can certainly be of interest, it is really not a satisfactory measurement of market timing. First, this type of measurement is very sensitive to the beginning point chosen. If the period chosen were one year earlier or one year later, the results might be dramatically different. Also, any aberration in the portfolio's structure at the beginning point impacts the result. More important, this measurement does not distinguish among market timing, the risk level of each asset category, and contributions through selection. Consequently, the measurement has serious deficiencies for investors who are trying to determine the contribution made by timing the market. The impacts of asset category risk level and selection are demonstrated below.

THE USE OF MARKET INDEXES

In order to overcome the biases caused by differences in asset category risk level and selection, it is possible to view the portfolio as being invested not in the actual securities held but in market indexes. In other words, if the portfolio was 70 percent in bonds and 30 percent in cash equivalents, we could assume that the portfolio was invested 70 percent in a bond index and 30 percent in Treasury bills. This appears to be a quite satisfactory solution to the biases introduced by measuring the actual portfolio owned. Someone might suggest that this is not appropriate, since a manager might go from cash into certain long bonds that outperform the market. According to general terminology, however, this manager would be deemed to have had success in selection, as opposed to success in market timing.

Numerous methods can be derived for measuring market timing with the use of indexes.

The Beginning Allocation

It is possible to use the beginning percentage allocation between bonds and cash in order to see whether the portfolio would have performed better over time had the manager maintained the beginning allocation rather than causing or allowing the allocation to change as it did. This method is also very sensitive to the beginning point chosen. It would be possible to repeat this method for each year (or even each quarter or month) of the measurement period. That is to say, we could look at the results from a point starting five years ago, a second point starting four years ago, a third point starting three years ago, and so on. The difficulty with this approach is that the results might be positive for some years and negative for others, and there would be no obvious way of averaging the results for the entire period.

Since this method is sensitive to the beginning point chosen, an improvement can be made by making the beginning point less arbitrary. For instance, if the beginning of a market cycle is used as the beginning point and the end of the market cycle as the end point, the period being measured is both rationally determined and the same for all portfolios. In this case the performance in a market cycle would be measured for the two hypothetical portfolios, one with the average allocation during the cycle and the other with the actual allocation. If the portfolio at the average allocation exceeded the portfolio at the beginning allocation, a positive timing score would result. A drawback of this method is that it cannot be used unless the portfolio was under the manager's control for at least the full market cycle being measured.

The Average Allocation

In order to avoid dependence on the beginning point, it is possible to use the average allocation during the period rather than the allocation at the beginning point. In other words, if the average percentage in bonds and cash equivalents is 70/30, a comparison can be made of the return that would have been achieved by investing in market indexes at the average allocation and comparing it to the return that would have been achieved by investing at the actual quarter-by-quarter allocation that occurred in the portfolio. This method has considerable merit. However, like all of the index methods discussed here, it suffers from two problems: The measurement is "period dependent," and it is sensitive to the level of average allocation. In other words, a manager who behaved exactly the same from 1968 to 1972 as from 1973 to 1977 would show different timing results simply because the bond and cash equivalent markets behaved differently during the two periods. Furthermore, even if we look at only a single period, two funds with significantly different allocations will have different timing measures. This makes it difficult to compare managers over a given period. Such period dependence is the result of a phenomenon that might be called the rebalancing effect. Serious students of performance measurement may wish to study this phenomenon, since it crops up in several different areas of analysis.

The measurement technique is looking at the difference between a portfolio that was rebalanced periodically to a certain allocation level and one that was not rebalanced. This means that if the market rises, the percentage in bonds increases and the rebalancing occurs by selling sufficient bonds to rebalance the desired level. If the market declines, the percentage in bonds also declines, thus making it necessary to rebalance by purchasing additional bonds. As long as the market heads in one direction, rebalancing hurts the portfolio. That is, as long as the market is rising, a policy of selling bonds obviously hurts the portfolio. Similarly, if the market is declining, a policy of purchasing bonds hurts the portfolio. Thus in periods in which the market goes straight up or straight down, the rebalancing strategy works poorly, and the unbalanced portfolio will tend to outperform the rebalanced portfolio. On the other hand, if the market has wide fluctuations but ends up roughly where it started, the rebalancing strategy is effective in increasing returns. This is because the percentage in equities in a rising market is constantly reduced, and at such time as the market declines, the lower level of bonds works to the portfolio's benefit. consequently, in a declining market the policy of rebalancing by purchasing bonds increases the fund's return when the market rebounds to its original position. Thus the rebalancing effect is different in each period measured due to the differences in what the market did during that period. Consequently, a bias is introduced into all measurements that involve rebalancing. Unfortunately, this includes almost all measurements of timing.

A variation of the measurement of looking at the average percentage in bonds versus the actual percentage is to look at the average of a risk measure, such as standard deviation or duration, of the total portfolio in comparison with the period-by-period measures. In other words, the expected returns could be calculated for a portfolio with a duration equal to the average duration over the period, and these returns could be compared to the expected returns from the quarter-by-quarter duration of the portfolio. Again, if the average returns exceed the returns quarter by quarter, a negative timing score results.

The Trend Line Allocation

One of the most difficult problems associated with the measurement of market timing is the need to distinguish between the discretionary activity of the manager and the policies dictated by the sponsor. If the sponsor dictates or suggests a maturity maximum, the measurement of market timing must take this change in policy into account. Otherwise, an impact will be attributed to the manager that should be attributed to the sponsor. Similarly, if the manager changes the long-term policy as to percentage in equities, this change cannot easily be distinguished from attempts at timing.

Regrettably, there is no simple way to measure this phenomenon unless the sponsor precisely and before the fact states an investment policy. It is insufficient for the sponsor to give general guidelines, and of course there is no way to distinguish between the impact of such policy decisions on a manager and the results of subtle comments by the sponsor, such as "I see you've been doing some buying lately; that surprises me, given the market's outlook." One means for eliminating the impact of these policy decisions involves looking not at the average allocation, but at the trend line. That is, if the average, or trend, over time is rising or declining, it is possible to measure the impact of the portfolio's being invested at a higher or lower allocation than that indicated by the trend line. Of course, there is still no way to distinguish between the sponsor's and the manager's impact.

The Perfect Allocation

It is possible to compare the results of a portfolio at actual allocation with the results of a portfolio that had perfect (or always wrong) allocation. Instead of the standard being the beginning point, the average, or the trend line, the standard would be the results obtained from having always been in the highest returning (or the worst returning) asset category. Unfortunately, this measurement is not particularly useful, since it really measures the policy rather than the deviations from the policy that result from the manager's attempts at timing. In a period in which long bonds did well, portfolios with high percentages in long bonds would show up well under this score, even if the manager's activities in deviating from this policy actually hurt the portfolio's results.

All of the measurements using the indexes are affected by the frequency with which the percentage in asset categories is measured and by the stability and magnitude of cash flows. If the portfolio's structure is measured only quarterly and there are longer, infrequent cash flows, the measurement of the asset allocation will be impacted. For instance, if a portfolio is normally 50 percent each in stocks and bonds, and the annual contribution (equal to 10 percent of the portfolio) is received on March 28 and temporarily put in cash equivalents, the portfolio's allocation as of March 31 will be distorted, even though the distortion lasts only a few days.

MOVEMENT OF CASH

In order to eliminate the problems associated with viewing the percentage allocation, some people feel that it is better to look at the movements of cash. This can be done in two ways: looking at purchases and sales and looking at the disposition of new cash in the portfolio.

In applying the first method, if the fund's manager in a given quarter purchased $100 of bonds and sold $30, for a net purchase of $70, this would be regarded as an indication of greater commitment to bonds, and hence the subsequent performance of bonds would be tracked. Although this idea has merit in principle, there are drawbacks. The first drawback is the difficulty of achieving sufficiently detailed information as to when the purchase took place. If the typical system of using mid-month cash flows is utilized, it is possible that the fund manager purchased securities early or late in the month when the situation was more favorable than that suggested by use of the midmonth assumption. Even if the exact timing of bond purchases and sales could be shown, there would still be a need to average purchases on the 5th of the month with sales on the 16th in some intelligent fashion. And if this problem could be solved, there would be the question of how long to track the purchases before deciding that the manager did well or poorly by making them. Should we view the change in the market over the next week, month, year, and so on? Another important limitation of this method is that heavy contributions or withdrawals may dictate making purchases or sales at times when the manager would far prefer to be doing just the opposite.

The second method, tracking new cash added to the portfolio, has two limitations. First, if there is no cash flow activity at all, there is no measurement of market timing, even though there may have been significant attempts at timing the market. Further, a contribution may be used to purchase bonds, whereas shortly before or after this purchase other, more significant sales of bonds may have been made. Obviously, the disposition of contributions does not provide a satisfactory basis for measuring timing. An effort might be made to look at the allocation of contributions as well as the impact of purchases and sales in order to determine the impact of both. However, it is not clear how this would be done, nor would doing it solve the problems of measuring the timing of purchases and sales and the appropriate period for viewing their results.

DOLLAR-WEIGHTED VERSUS TIME-WEIGHTED RETURNS FOR ASSET CATEGORIES

For an asset category (but not for the total portfolio) it is possible to look at the difference between dollar-weighted and time-weighted rates of return. The latter assumes that equal amounts were invested in the asset category during the whole period, whereas the former weights returns by the amount of money invested. Thus if money were moved in and out of the equity portfolio at propitious times, dollar-weighted returns for bonds would exceed time-weighted returns. Conversely, if the timing were poor, dollar-weighted returns would be less than time-weighted returns. It would, however, be difficult to use this method in a portfolio with several asset categories. The measurement could be carried out for each asset sector, though there appears to be no way of combining the results of various sectors unless the portfolio had no external cash flows. If there were no such cash flows, it would be possible to translate the returns into dollars and then combine the dollars in various sectors into a total portfolio measurement. However, if there were external cash flows, there is no obvious way for calculating the average amount of money impacted by the differences between dollar-weighted and time-weighted returns.

DEVIATION FROM "OPTIMUM" AND PRESCRIBED POLICIES

It is possible to establish a "market line" that shows the risk-return relationship available in the marketplace over any period. A longer period could be broken up into shorter periods, over which risk-return ratios for bonds and cash equivalents would each be calculated. The investor's bogey would then become, not the actual return of some hypothetical portfolio, but rather the portfolio with the average risk-return characteristics for the period.

Perhaps the only real method of measuring market timing can be made if the portfolio's owner prescribes a policy and then measures deviations from this policy. If the sponsor says that the policy will be to invest 70 percent in bonds at all times, it is possible to look at the return of a portfolio consisting of market indexes invested at the 70 percent level and to compare its return with that of a portfolio invested at the actual quarter-by-quarter allocations of the fund. Although this method is quite satisfactory in principle, in practice few sponsors prescribe policies sufficiently to permit such a measurement.

SUMMARY

The measurement of the investment manager's contribution to return from market timing is extremely complex, and no bias-free solution appears to exist. Perhaps the only solution, then, is to choose a measurement that is easy to understand and to openly recognize its limitations, so that no one will be misled. With this viewpoint in mind, comparing the return of hypothetical portfolios invested in market indexes at the average allocation with the return of similar portfolios invested at actual allocations appears to be a satisfactory approach.

PART 5

Options and Futures and Their Role in Fixed Income Portfolio Management

38

Overview of Futures and Options

Gary L. Gastineau
Manager of the Options Portfolio Service
Kidder, Peabody & Co., Inc.

OPTIONS AND FUTURES: DERIVATIVE SECURITIES

The concepts of (1) a debt obligation, and (2) a fixed, often periodic, interest payment are the essence of most fixed income securities. These concepts are not difficult for most investors to grasp. The concepts of options and futures contracts on the same fixed income securities are not so simple.

An option on a fixed income security is a right or privilege to buy (a call option) or to sell (a put option) a designated face amount of a particular fixed income security or class of securities during a time period ending on the expiration date of the option. The fixed income security is purchased or sold at the price specified in the option contract, even if the price of the security has changed dramatically by the time the option is exercised. The owner or holder of an option is under no obligation to buy or sell the security and will do so only if exercising the option is preferable to letting the option expire. The seller or writer of the call (or put) option has a contingent obligation to sell (or buy) if the option is exercised. In return for acceptance of this obligation, the seller receives an option premium from the buyer. Options on some fixed income securities are traded on organized exchanges where they can be sold or purchased like any other security. Exchange-listed option positions are usually closed out on the exchange rather than exercised.

A financial (fixed income) futures contract, in contrast to an option contract, imposes a firm obligation on each party to buy or sell a predetermined position in a specific fixed income security or class of securities. Also, in contrast to the options market, no "premium" is paid or received by either party. More detailed descriptions of specific options and futures contracts are available from the exchanges where these contracts are traded and from members of these exchanges.

A rudimentary understanding of the key characteristics of options and futures contracts is helpful in most modern investment analysis and essential to an understanding of the chapters in this section of the book. A brief numerical example illustrating the economics of options and futures contracts should provide the necessary background. This example bears only a passing resemblance to any real option or futures contract. It does, however, serve to highlight some of the significant characteristics of these instruments.

The underlying security that is subject to both options and futures contracts in our example is a 10-year Treasury bond bearing a 10 percent coupon and selling at 95 (or $950 per $1000 face amount). Our hypothetical call option contract would give the owner of the call the right to buy $100,000 face amount of this security, at a price of 96, for a period ending on the expiration date of the option eight months in the future. The buyer of this call option might pay three points ($3,000 per $100,000 face amount of bonds) for the right represented by this call option. If the price of the bond does not rise above 96 by the expiration date, or if it rises above it and falls back before the holder of the call elects to exercise, the call will expire worthless. Prior to exercise or expiration, the price of the call will move up and down with the price of the underlying bond. For example, if the price of the bond rises from 95 to 97, the price of the call might rise from 3 to 4. This price change represents a change from $3,000 to $4,000 on the option covering $100,000 face amount of bonds. Early exercise of such an option would be rare. Most option holders who elect to close their positions prior to the expiration date of the option simply sell the option on the exchange where they bought it.

A futures contract on this same bond will behave quite differently from the option. The purchaser of a call option pays a premium to the seller of the option in return for the right (but not the obligation) to buy the bond at a fixed price on a future date. In contrast, both parties to a futures contract are obligated—the buyer to pay for the bonds and the seller to deliver the bonds at the contract price. These differences between the option contract and the futures contract are important. Whereas the buyer of the option contract is not required to exercise the option, the buyer of the futures contract *is* under an obligation to purchase the securities at the agreed-upon price.

The striking price of an option is standardized by the options exchange to facilitate uniformity in option contract terms. There will rarely be more than five or six different option-striking prices. In the case we have assumed, the exercise price of the option was 96 or $96,000 per $100,000 per face amount of bonds. If the bonds are selling below this price a call option holder will simply let the option expire. The three-point premium ($3,000) will be lost.

Participants in the futures market do not pay a premium. The price at which the buyer agrees to purchase and the seller agrees to deliver is determined in the market place. In this case we assume that the futures price for delivery eight months hence is 95–17. This means that the buyer agrees to purchase and the seller agrees to sell at a price of 95 and 17/32s: ($95,631.25) eight months in the future unless their obligations are cancelled by an offsetting transaction before then.

Neither party to a futures contract pays or receives a premium. In fact, no cash passes between the buyer and seller at the time of the initial transaction. The value of the transaction to each participant is reflected in the futures price they agree upon. This procedure contrasts with the option market wherein the buyer and seller of an option contract exchange a nonrefundable premium. The premium belongs to the option seller whether or not the option is exercised. Parties to a futures contract typically deposit government securities or other collateral with their broker to guarantee that they will fulfill their respective obligations under the contract.

While no cash is required initially, the futures contract must be marked to the market. As the futures price rises (falls) from the 95–17 price, the buyer (seller) will receive a cash credit to his or her account with the broker. This cash may be reinvested at interest. If the futures price falls (rises) the buyer (seller) will have to deposit additional cash with the broker, which will in turn be transferred to the seller (buyer), or interest will be charged on a debit balance. We will have more to say about the differences between options and futures-margin arrangements when we discuss the relative attractiveness of the two markets from the viewpoint of a participant.

Futures contracts are currently available on a variety of fixed income securities ranging from commercial paper, CDs, and Treasury bills on the short end of the yield curve to GNMA certificates, municipal bonds, and Treasury bonds on the long end.[1] Option contracts on several of these futures contracts and options directly on several types of fixed income securities are also available.

Anyone who plans to participate in these markets will need much more extensive and specific information than we have provided here. The example was designed only to help readers unfamiliar with these markets to understand the discussion that follows.

HEDGING—CLASSIC AND MODERN CONCEPTS

Most people understand hedging in options and futures markets to be a mysterious technique to reduce or eliminate risks associated with price

---

[1] See Chapter 39.

fluctuations. Common examples include a farmer who sells futures against a prospective wheat harvest and a manufacturer who purchases copper futures contracts to cover the risks of a fixed-price contract. In contrast to popular wisdom, it is not clear that each of these parties is really eliminating major risks.

The wheat farmer, for example, might lose the crop to adverse weather or pestilence. If crop destruction is widespread and wheat prices rise, the "hedging" attempt would compound the loss of the crop with a loss in the futures market. The manufacturer trying to cover copper requirements and "hedge" the supply price might have problems with currency fluctuations, import restrictions, and political changes in Central Africa. The manufacturer's risks, like the farmer's, might be increased rather than reduced by the futures transaction.

The modern concept of hedging in the options and futures markets focuses on the use of underlying and derivative (futures and options) securities to *control* some element of portfolio or business risk. The notion of control suggests that some participants may increase risks in one way while reducing them in another. Under this very broad but useful definition, the "speculator" who has received so much attention from economists and legislators is probably a very small factor in most markets. By implication, a true speculator is someone who does not adequately understand the magnitude of the risks being taken. Under this definition a market participant would be categorized as a hedger or speculator on the basis of sophistication.

In the following discussion we will examine hedging in the modern sense—the attempted control of portfolio or business risk. Our focus will be on risks associated with interest-rate fluctuations. In thinking about the specific examples of interest-rate risk control we describe, two points should be kept in mind. First, a transaction that reduces interest-rate risk for one party may reduce risk in another way for the other party to the transaction. Second, and seemingly inconsistent with the first point, the total amount of interest-rate risk in the financial system cannot be changed by a transaction in a derivative security, such as a futures or options contract. The key to resolving any inconsistency between these points is that we live in a world where financial markets are derivative to the provision of goods and services and where operating and financial organizations have both asset and liability sides to their balance sheets.

DURATION AND THE CONCEPT OF BOND EQUIVALENCE

As a prelude to understanding the use of options and futures contracts in risk control, the reader needs to have a basic understanding of two important concepts. The first of these concepts, *duration*, is discussed in

Chapters 4 and 5. Although duration has other functions, we use it here as a measure of relative sensitivity to interest-rate fluctuations. A long-term bond with a calculated duration of five years has approximately 10 times the interest-rate risk of a six-month Treasury bill. Although there are credit risk factors that affect the relative riskiness of government and nongovernment securities apart from differences in duration, it is useful to adjust the basic duration number for these additional risk factors and focus on a single measurement of risk. This type of adjustment may seem arbitrary, but more complex techniques for incorporating credit risks do not seem warranted.

Because most other risk factors associated with fixed income securities are correlated with interest-rate fluctuations, a single number for duration modified for differences in credit standing is probably an adequate measurement of risk for most fixed income securities. With appropriate attention to differences in coupons and principal between and among deliverable securities, duration is an adequate interest-rate risk measure in relating futures contracts to a broad range of fixed income securities.

Another concept in addition to duration is necessary to relate the risk characteristics of option contracts to underlying securities. This additional concept is the notion of *bond equivalence.*

The literature on stock options thoroughly describes and documents the concept of the *neutral hedge ratio.*[2] The neutral hedge ratio gets its name from the fact that an option position can be used to neutralize price fluctuations in the underlying security. The neutral hedge ratio is the fractional change in the value of a put or call option in response to a one-point change in the value of the underlying security. Computer services have programs to translate option positions into bond or bill equivalents using the neutral hedge ratio. The fractional change in the option will vary as the distance between the bond price and the striking price changes, but an appropriate risk structure can be maintained by adding to or subtracting from the option position as bond prices move up and down.

The concept of bond equivalence is so important that we will take the time to illustrate it in more detail. In the example we developed earlier to describe the differences between options and futures contracts, we hypothesized a movement in the call option contract from a price of 3 to 4 ($3,000 to $4,000 in terms of the total value of that contract) in response to a move from 95 to 97 ($95,000 to $97,000) in the underlying security. In this very simple example, the value of the option contract changed by half the value of the underlying security. The fraction by which the option changes in response to a move in the underlying

[2] Gary L. Gastineau, *The Stock Options Manual* (New York: McGraw-Hill, 1979), pp. 71–84, 97–111, and 264–267.

security will not always be one half. It could range from a very small fraction if the option is well out-of-the-money to nearly one if the expiration date is near and the option is in-the-money.[3] If the value of the option in the example changes by one half the value of the underlying security, each option is the interest-rate risk equivalent of $50,000 face amount (about $48,000 market value) of the underlying bonds. Two of these call option contracts are equivalent in risk to a $100,000 face amount bond position. They can be used as a substitute for the bond position when an investor buys them or to offset the interest-rate risk of the bond position when the investor sells them.

The calculation of duration and bond equivalence for futures and options is complex. Fortunately, information and software are available through many brokerage firms and some computer services. The quality of this material is uneven, and the wary investor should not accept a computer printout at face value. Once the analytical obstacles are overcome, the incentive to use these instruments in portfolio risk control can be substantial.

USING FINANCIAL INSTRUMENT OPTIONS AND FUTURES CONTRACTS TO CONTROL INTEREST-RATE RISKS

The participants in these markets have widely differing objectives. The following examples illustrate rather than exhaust the possibilities.

Securities Dealers and Underwriters

Securities dealers and underwriters have one of the most difficult interest-rate risk control problems faced by any participant in the fixed income securities markets. Several years ago it was not unusual for a major bond dealer to gain or lose $10 million or more in a relatively short period of time from changes in the value of his or her bond inventory in response to interest-rate fluctuations. Since the introduction and widespread use of financial futures, there have been fewer reported cases of huge losses by bond dealers and underwriters than most observers would have expected given recent dramatic fluctuations in interest rates.

The typical underwriting fee is much larger than the cost of hedging interest risks in the financial futures or options markets. Bond dealers

---

[3] The phrases "in-the-money" and "out-of-the-money" refer to the relationship between the market price of the underlying security and the striking price of the option. An in-the-money option has intrinsic value because the current market price of the bond exceeds the striking price of a call or is below the striking price of a put. For example, a call exercisable at 72 is said to be three points in-the-money when the bond is selling at 75. An out-of-the-money option has no intrinsic value because the current market price is below the striking price of a call or above the striking price of a put.

and underwriters no longer need to take the kind of risks that were almost unavoidable before the introduction of these derivative markets.

Banks

An increasing volume of literature has focused on the potential use of financial futures and options markets by commercial and savings banks.[4] These new markets can be extremely useful in balancing maturities on the asset side of the balance sheet with those on the liability side. The basic risk-management problem for both commercial and savings banks is that their assets are usually of longer duration than their liabilities. Commercial banks have tried to cope with this problem by linking the interest rates on their longer term loans (assets) to the prime rate. The prime rate, in turn, is adjusted to reflect the short-term cost of funds (liabilities). Savings banks and other housing lenders have an even more severe asset/liability mismatch than commercial banks. Variable-rate and renegotiable mortgage loans are helpful, but some lenders have faced adverse reactions when they have tried to raise rates. Increasing rates on a mortgage is often not practical even when it is permitted by the contract. The focus of asset/liability management for deposit institutions has increasingly shifted from changing rates on old loans to offsetting changes in the cost of money through transactions in the financial futures and options markets.

Other Tax-Paying Entities

Nonfinancial corporations. Two important uses of these derivative securities by nonfinancial corporations are corporate cash management and control of the corporation's cost of capital.

To the extent that the relatively long duration of a preferred stock or utility common stock portfolio can be offset with transactions in Treasury bond futures and options, most corporations that expect to have (1) significant cash balances for several years and (2) high marginal tax rates could benefit from a preferred stock or utility common stock hedging program. Corporate taxpayers receive an 85 percent dividend-received deduction. If the corporation's marginal federal tax rate is 46 percent, it pays a 6.9 percent federal tax on a preferred stock or utility common stock dividend. If the interest-rate risk of preferred stocks or utility common stocks is hedged with options or futures, the interest-rate risk

---

[4] For example, John Ezell, "Applications of Debt Options for Banks and Thrifts," in Frank J. Fabozzi, ed., *Winning the Interest Rate Game: A Guide to Debt Options* (Chicago: Probus Publishing, 1985), Chapter 7. Sanford Rose, "Banks Should Look to the Futures," *Fortune,* April 20, 1981, pp. 185–192; and Anthony J. Vignola, "Bank Use of Financial Futures," (New York: Kidder, Peabody & Co, October 1981).

characteristics of the portfolio can approximate those of a portfolio of commercial paper. The aftertax return should be hundreds of basis points higher than the commercial paper return.

Several securities underwriters have begun insulating their corporate clients from interest-rate fluctuations during the period between the decision to sell a debt issue and the actual sale of securities. The underwriter establishes a futures or options position designed to fluctuate in response to interest rates much like the proposed corporate debt issue. When the issue is priced by the underwriter, any gain or loss on the futures or options position is added to or subtracted from the proceeds paid to the issuing company. The underwriter rather than the issuer carries the futures or options position on his or her books to avoid distorting a single year's reported earnings for the issuer. The underwriter offsets the gain or loss on the hedge position against the adjusted underwriting fee. If the corporate client carried the position, it might incur a short-term capital loss, which has limited deductibility for tax purposes.

Individuals. Relatively few individuals face asset/liability mismatches as severe as those that characterize some corporate entities. On the other hand, a growing group of individual participants in the fixed income futures and options markets are high tax bracket individuals who wish to hedge municipal bond portfolios. These individuals want to have the high rates available on long-term municipals without taking the corresponding risk of interest-rate fluctuations. Through careful planning and execution they can achieve extraordinary aftertax returns with interest-rate risk comparable to the risks of municipal project notes.[5]

Individuals who can move quickly might find opportunities to exploit market anomalies through arbitrage-type transactions. The opportunities for this kind of scalping by nonprofessional investors are limited, however. Much individual arbitrage-type participation in fixed income futures and options markets is probably the result of overzealous selling or a misplaced conviction that a few back-of-an-envelope calculations are a match for the computer power and order execution skills of large traders.

Institutional Investors—Exploiting Market Anomalies

So far the groups of investors that seem most likely to benefit from financial futures and options trading are individuals and organizations

---

[5] For a description of this technique, see Gary L. Gastineau, "The Impact of Options and Financial Futures on Municipal Bond Portfolio Management," in *The Municipal Bond Handbook*, Vol. I, ed. Frank J. Fabozzi, Sylvan G. Feldstein, Irving M. Pollack, and Frank G. Zarb (Homewood, Ill.: Dow Jones-Irwin, 1983).

that use these markets much as agribusinesses use agricultural commodity futures markets. Many corporations and high tax bracket individuals can obtain unique tax advantages as well as effective risk control. Most nontaxpaying institutions have done relatively little in these markets to date.

Mutual funds using futures and options contracts may ultimately give their corporate or individual shareholders many of the advantages of direct investment in dividend-paying stocks or municipal debt by passing income to shareholders without changing its character.

For institutional investors unaffected by taxes, such as pension and profit sharing plans and endowment accounts, the advantages of financial futures and options trading are less obvious. The magnitude of market inefficiencies would have to be unusual by any standard for financial futures transactions to appear dramatically more attractive than other means of adjusting the interest-rate risk characteristics of these portfolios. The case for options in a nontaxable account is more tenable if the portfolio is in the hands of a skilled manager. There is little question that the use of options can improve results to the extent that underpriced options are purchased and overpriced options sold as part of a common stock or fixed income portfolio management effort. It should be possible through careful attention to option evaluation to add one or two percentage points to the level of return from a comparable risk, conventional fixed income portfolio.

An additional case for these derivative securities in the management of tax-free portfolios lies in meeting needs for asset-liability matching. This matching can be particularly important for pension plans. Insurance and pension actuaries have begun to work on this concept, and new products and services will undoubtedly appear over the next few years. On balance, it seems probable that the major participants in financial futures and options markets will continue to be securities dealers, banks and other savings institutions, nonfinancial corporations, and individuals. Insurance companies and tax-free institutions will gradually increase their participation.

MISUSE OF FINANCIAL FUTURES AND OPTIONS MARKETS

In our definition of hedging, we suggested that, under the modern concept of hedging, speculators were probably people who really did not understand the risks they were intent on taking. Misuse of financial futures and options markets is essentially a result of failure on the part of market participants to understand the true risk characteristics of the investment strategies and tactics they are using. For example, we suspect that a good deal of the interest in financial futures by pension and profit sharing plans is based on misunderstanding the mathematics of futures markets.

Options frequently become significantly under- or overpriced, but futures contract prices have less tendency to significant misalignment. Anomalies in the futures markets are more likely to arise out of a peculiarity in the delivery process or an unusual and only partly predictable change in government or private financing plans. Anomalies in options markets are more frequent and generally of larger magnitude. Nonetheless, a high degree of skill is required to earn superior returns. Investors seeking to exploit opportunities should expect to pay above-average brokerage commissions or investment management fees. Skill in finding and exploiting these opportunities does not come cheaply.

Apart from misunderstandings and mistaken expectations, the most serious misuse of futures and options markets is to view them as a source of leverage. In our discussion of the concept of bond equivalence, we described how every futures and option position can be translated into an equivalent bond position. Rational investors, whether they view themselves as hedgers or speculators, should translate every fixed income futures and options position into the equivalent of the underlying security. If they would not buy $10 million worth of long-term bonds with cash or by using margin debt, they should not take an equivalent position in the futures or options market.

A less frequent misuse of these markets is in fine-tuning portfolio risk. Although it is *theoretically* possible, through bond equivalence translations, to control risks with an extraordinary degree of precision, the additional transaction costs occasioned by such fine tuning will probably wipe out any advantages. Interest-rate hedging works best when large risks are offset and small risks are accepted.

One final abuse or misuse of fixed income options seems worth noting. A long-held belief that is an article of faith with many stock option market participants is that option sellers enjoy a large and systematic advantage over option buyers. The untruth of this proposition has been amply demonstrated with regard to stock options,[6] but similar demonstrations will probably be necessary with fixed income options. In the meantime, any proposal that an investor "add to income" by selling options should be rejected.

CONCLUSION

The analysis and risk-control techniques used by debt and equity portfolio managers have changed dramatically in recent years. Nowhere has the change been more rapid than in the fixed income markets. Although it is not difficult to find bond portfolio managers whose current ap-

---

[6] Gastineau, *The Stock Options Manual*, pp. 282–312; and Gary L. Gastineau and Albert Madansky, "Why Simulations Are an Unreliable Test of Option Strategies," *Financial Analysts Journal*, September–October 1979, pp. 66–76.

proach would have been considered "time honored" in the 1920s, the parade has passed these managers by. These traditional managers find it nearly impossible to obtain new business because they are unlikely to provide their clients with results that justify a fee.

Today's effective fixed income manager must understand duration, the nuances of bond portfolio immunization, dedicated portfolios, the mathematics of bond yields, and much more. The manager who cannot adapt to new concepts and new techniques will be at a marketing and performance disadvantage. It seems safe to predict that in a few years the manager who does not understand risk-control and risk-adjusted return enhancement with futures and options contracts will be obsolete.

39

Listed Options and Futures Contracts on Fixed Income Securities

Mark Pitts, Ph.D.
Senior Vice President
Shearson Lehman Brothers

Option and futures contracts are financial products created by exchanges. Subject to approval by the regulatory agencies, the exchanges are free to create virtually any contract they please. Not surprisingly then, not all contracts offered by the exchanges are successful. Due to lack of interest by commercial accounts, speculators, or local traders, sufficient volume may never develop in a contract and it will eventually be dropped from trading. In other cases, a contract trades well for several years but then falls from favor due to changes in the economic environment or from increased competition from other contracts. Consequently, futures and options contracts come and go.

This chapter highlights some of the more interesting features of the more important fixed income contracts. (The exchanges will gladly provide more detailed information on these contracts.) Undoubtedly, as economic conditions change, new contracts will be introduced and will flourish, while some of the currently popular contracts will eventually die out.

The primary interest-rate futures and option contracts can be divided into two groups: those based on long- and intermediate-term instruments, and those based on short-term instruments. In the former category, the most heavily traded contracts are the Treasury bond futures contract, the Treasury note futures contract, and the Treasury bond futures option. In the latter category, the most active contracts are the Eurodollar time deposit futures contract, the Treasury bill futures contract, and the Eurodollar futures option contract. There are significant similarities in the contract specifications among the intermediate- and long-term contracts, as well as among the short-term contracts.

Furthermore, the long- and intermediate-term contracts are traded on the Chicago Board of Trade (the Board or CBOT) while the short-term contracts are traded on the International Monetary Market (IMM) of the Chicago Mercantile Exchange (the Merc or CME).

FUTURES CONTRACTS

The Treasury Bond Futures Contract

The T-bond futures contract is by far the most successful of the interest-rate (or commodity) futures contracts. Prices and yields on the T-bond futures contract are always quoted in terms of a (fictitious) 20-year, 8 percent Treasury bond, but the CBOT allows many different bonds to be delivered in satisfaction of a short position in the contract. Specifically, any Treasury bond with at least 15 years to maturity or 15 years to first call, if callable, qualifies for delivery. Consequently, there are usually 20 to 30 outstanding bonds that constitute good delivery.

The T-bond futures contract calls for the short (i.e., the seller) to deliver $100,000 face value of any one of the qualifying Treasury bonds. However, since the coupon and maturity vary widely across the deliverable bonds, the price that the buyer pays the seller depends on which bond the seller chooses to deliver. The rule that the Chicago Board of Trade has adopted adjusts the futures price by a conversion factor that reflects the price the bond would sell for at the beginning of the delivery month if it were yielding 8 percent. Using such a rule, the conversion factor for a given bond and a given delivery month is constant through time and is not affected by changes in the price of the bond. To illustrate, consider the delivery price for the Treasury 12 percent bonds of August 15, 2013 if delivered on the June 1985 contract. At the beginning of June 1985 this bond had 23 years, 2½ months to call. To calculate the conversion factor, the term-to-call is rounded down to the nearest quarter year, in this case giving an even 23 years to call. Since a 23-year, 12 percent bond yielding 8 percent sells for 141.77, the conversion factor for the 12 percent bond for the June 1985 contract is 1.4177 (i.e., 141.77 ÷ 100).

The seller has the right to choose when during the delivery month a delivery will take place and which qualifying bond to deliver. The buyer is then obligated to pay the seller the futures price times the appropriate conversion factor, plus accrued interest on the delivered bond.

Paradoxically, the success of the CBOT T-bond contract can in part be attributed to the fact that the delivery mechanism is not as simple as it may first appear. Implicit in a short position in bond futures, there are several options. First, the seller chooses which bond to deliver. Thus, the seller has a "swap option." If the seller is holding Bond A for delivery, but Bond B becomes cheaper to deliver, he can swap Bond A for Bond B and make a more profitable delivery. Secondly, within some guidelines set by the CBOT, the seller decides when during the delivery month a delivery will take place. He thus has a "timing option" which can be used to his advantage. Finally, the short retains the possibility of making the "wildcard" play. This potentially profitable situation arises due to the fact that the seller can give notice of intent to deliver for several hours after the exchange has closed and the futures settlement price has been fixed. Thus, in a falling market the seller can use the wildcard option to profit from the fact that the delivery price is fixed even if the market is falling. A detailed example of the wildcard play is given in the Appendix.

Each of the seller's options tends to make the contract a bit more difficult to understand, but at the same time they make the contract more attractive to speculators, arbitrageurs, dealers, and anyone else who believes they understand the contract somewhat better than other market participants. Thus, in the case of the T-bond futures contract, complexity has helped provide liquidity.

The Treasury Note Futures Contract

The CBOT Treasury note futures contract was modeled after the CBOT Treasury bond futures contract and resembles it in many respects. The T-note futures contract allows delivery of any note that has a maturity of 6½ to 10 years on the first delivery day of the month. To qualify for delivery the instrument also must have been issued as a Treasury note; thus, old Treasury bonds with a remaining life of 6½ to 10 years do not qualify.

The T-note futures contract offers the seller the same flexibility that the T-bond futures contract offers. By giving proper notice, the seller can deliver at almost any point he chooses during the delivery month. He also chooses which of the qualifying notes to deliver and receives an amount equal to the futures price times the conversion factor for the delivered note (also based on an 8 percent yield), plus accrued interest. There has not, however, been as much of a play in the most deliverable issue for the T-note futures contract as there has been for the T-bond futures contract. It has usually been obvious well in advance which note (or when-issued note) would be delivered by the seller. The note futures contract offers the seller the same wildcard play that is offered by the bond futures contract. Thus, during the delivery month, this idiosyncrasy in the contract specifications can be particularly profitable when prices fall after the exchange has closed.

The Treasury Bill Futures Contract

The Chicago Mercantile Exchange's futures contract on Treasury bills was the first contract on a short-term debt instrument and has been the model for most subsequent contracts on short-term debt. The contract is based on three-month (i.e., 90-day) T bills with a face value of $1,000,000. The contract is quoted and traded in terms of a futures "price," but the futures price is, in fact, just a different way of quoting the futures interest rate. Specifically, the futures price is just the annualized futures rate subtracted from 100. For example, a futures price of 91.00 means that Treasury bills are trading in the futures market at a rate of 9.00 percent. The actual price that the buyer pays the seller is calculated using the usual formula for Treasury bills:

Invoice Price = $1,000,000 × [1 − Rate × (Days to Maturity ÷ 360)]

where the rate is expressed in decimal form. As can be easily verified by this formula, for a 90-day instrument each .01 change in the quoted futures price (i.e., each basis point change in rate) leads to a $25 change in the invoice price.

The T-bill futures contract is considerably simpler than the intermediate- and long-term futures contracts. First, since all T bills of the same maturity are economically equivalent, there is effectively only one deliverable issue, i.e., Treasury bills with three months to maturity. The fact that the three-month bills may be either new three-month bills or older bills that currently have three months of remaining life makes little difference since the new and old issues will trade identically in the cash market. Thus, all the subtleties surrounding conversion factors and most deliverable issues are absent from the T-bill futures market. Furthermore, there is little uncertainty or choice involved in the delivery date because delivery must take place during a very narrow timeframe, usually a three-day period. The rules of the exchange make clear well in advance the exact dates on which delivery will take place. Finally, since there are no conversion factors, there is no wildcard play in the Treasury bill futures market.

Although the T-bill futures contract is simple and thus may not provide as many speculative and arbitrage opportunities as the more complex long- and intermediate-term futures contracts, the T-bill contract does provide a straightforward means of hedging or speculating on the short end of the yield curve. Since the T-bill rate is the benchmark off which other short-term rates are priced, the bill contract fills a well-defined need of many market participants.

The Eurodollar Time Deposit Futures Contract

Eurodollar time deposits are U.S. dollars on deposit outside the United States. As such, they are normally free from reserve requirements and interest-rate ceilings. As the Eurodollar sector of the fixed income market has grown substantially in recent years, so has volume in the Eurodollar time deposit futures contract. Unlike other fixed income futures contracts, the Eurodollar contract does not allow actual delivery. Instead, settlement is made in cash. The final settlement price is determined by the LIBOR rate when trading on the contract is concluded. While this mechanism does not allow one to take or make delivery of an actual LIBOR-based debt instrument, the cash flows from a futures position are such that the contract provides a very good vehicle for hedging or speculating on short-term LIBOR-based debt.

Like the T-bill contract, the quoted futures price for Eurodollar time deposits is equal to 100 minus the annualized yield. Also, each .01 change in the futures price (1 basis point change in yield) carries a value of $25. Settlement on Eurodollar futures takes place on a single day during the delivery month.

The yield on the Eurodollar futures contract is quoted in terms of an add-on, or simple, interest rate. Rates on Eurodollar contracts are thus directly comparable to the rates on domestic CDs. However, to compare the Eurodollar rate to the T-bill rate, one of the rates must be converted so that both rates will be in the same terms.

The Eurodollar futures contract is one of the most widely used contracts. It appeals to many domestic corporations and European commercial banks. Given the high degree of correlation between the Eurodollar rate and many domestic short-term corporate borrowing rates, many hedgers have found the Eurodollar contract to be the best hedging vehicle for a wide range of hedging situations.

OPTIONS ON FUTURES

While futures contracts are relatively straightforward financial instruments, options on futures (or "futures options", as they are commonly called) deserve a little explanation. Options on futures are very similar to other option contracts, but not very similar to futures contracts. Like options on cash (or spot) fixed income securities, both put and call options are available on fixed income futures. The buyer of a call has the right to buy the underlying security at a fixed price. The buyer of a put has the right to sell the underlying security at a fixed price. The option seller (or writer) is obligated to sell the security (in the case of the call) or buy the security (in the case of the put), if the buyer chooses to exercise the option.

An option on a futures contract differs from more traditional options in only one essential way: The underlying instrument is not a spot security, but a futures contract on a security. Thus, for instance, if an option buyer exercises his call, he acquires a long position in futures instead of a long position in a cash security. The seller of the call will be assigned the corresponding short position in the same futures contract. For put options, the situation is reversed. If an option buyer exercises his put, he acquires a short position in futures, and the seller of the put is assigned a long position in futures. The resulting long and short futures positions are like any other futures positions and are subject to daily marking to market.

Whenever one acquires a position in futures, he does so at the current futures price. However, if the strike price on the option does not equal the futures price at the time of exercise, the option seller must compensate the option buyer for the discrepancy. Thus, when a call option is exercised, the seller of the call must pay the buyer the current futures price minus the strike price. On the other hand, the seller of the put must pay the buyer the strike price minus the current futures price. (These transactions are actually accomplished by establishing the futures positions at the strike price, then immediately marking to market.) Note that unlike options on spot securities, the amount of money that changes hands at exercise is only the difference between the strike price and the current futures price. Of course, the option need not be exercised for the owner to reap a profit. In many situations, it will be advisable for the owner of an in-the-money option to close out his position by selling the option instead of exercising it.

The Option on Treasury Bond Futures

The option on the CBOT Treasury bond futures contract is in many respects simpler than the underlying futures contract. Usually, conversion factors, most deliverables, wildcard plays, and other subtleties of the T-bond futures contract need not concern the buyer or seller of options on T-bond futures. Although these factors affect the fair price of the futures contract, their impact is already reflected in the futures price. Consequently, they need not necessarily be reconsidered when buying or selling an option on the futures contract.

The option on the T-bond futures contract is in many respects an option on an index, the "index" being the futures price itself, i.e., the price of the (fictitious) 20-year, 8 percent Treasury bond. Like the futures contract, the nominal size of the contract is $100,000. Thus, for example, with futures prices at 75, a call option struck at 74 has an intrinsic value of $1,000, and a put struck at 80 has an intrinsic value of $5,000.

Unlike Treasury bonds and Treasury bond futures, the premiums on options on Treasury bond futures are quoted in terms of points and 64ths of a point. Thus, an option premium of 1–10 implies a price of $1^{10}/_{64}$ percent of face value, or $1,156.25 (from $100,000 \times 1.15625\%$). Minimum price fluctuations are also $\frac{1}{64}$th of 1 percent.

While an option on a T-bond futures contract is hardly identical to an option on a T bond, it serves much the same purpose. Since spot and futures prices for Treasury bonds are highly correlated, most hedgers and speculators find that options on bond futures provide the essential characteristics needed in a fixed income options contract. Furthermore, given the liquidity of the bond futures market, many users believe that options on bond futures provide distinct advantages over options on cash bonds.

The Option on Eurodollar Futures

Options on Eurodollar futures are based on the quoted Eurodollar futures price (i.e., 100 minus the annualized yield). Like the underlying futures, the nominal size of the contract is $1,000,000 and each .01 change in price carries a value of $25. Likewise, the option premium is quoted in terms of basis points. Thus, for example, an option premium quoted as 25 (or .25) implies an option price of $625; a premium of 125 (or 1.25) implies an option price of $3,125.

Options on Eurodollar futures fill a unique place among hedging products. These options are currently the only liquid option contracts based on a short-term fixed income instrument. Like other debt options, buyers of puts on Eurodollar futures profit as rates move up, while buyers of calls profit as rates move down. Consequently, institutions with liabilities or assets that float off short-term rates can hedge their exposure to fluctuations in short-term rates.

Consider first those institutions that have liabilities that float off short-term rates. These include banks that issue CDs and/or take deposits based on money market rates. Also included are industrial and financial corporations that issue commercial paper, floating-rate notes, or preferred stock that floats off money market rates. Parties to interest-rate swaps who make floating-rate payments fall into the same risk category. Likewise, those who make payments on adjustable-rate mortgages face similar risks.[1] In each instance, as short-term rates increase, the liability becomes more onerous for the issuer. Consequently, the issuers of these liabilities have long sought a means of capping their interest-rate expense. Although options on Eurodollar futures do not extend as far into the future as many issuers would like, they are effective tools for hedging many short-term rates over the near term. Consequently, an institution facing floating-rate liabilities can buy an interest-rate "cap" by buying puts on Eurodollar futures. As rates move up, profits on the put position will tend to offset some or all of the incremental interest expenses.

On the other side of the coin, and facing opposite risks, are the purchasers of floating-rate instruments—that is, the investors who buy money market deposits, floating-rate notes, floating-rate preferred stock, and adjustable-rate mortgages. Investors who roll over CDs or

---

[1] To the extent that the interest-rate payment on an adjustable-rate mortgage has an upper and lower bound, the risk to issuers and investors is limited by the very nature of the instrument.

commercial paper, or receive floating-rate payments in a swap agreement, face the same potential problem. As rates fall, these investors receive less interest income. Consequently, they feel a need to buy interest-rate "floors." The interest-rate floor is nothing other than a call option. As rates fall, calls on debt securities increase in value and tend to offset the lower interest income received by the investor.

In conclusion, options on Eurodollar futures can frequently be used to limit the risk associated with fluctuations in short-term rates. This is accomplished by buying puts (interest-rate caps) if the exposure is to rising rates, or by buying calls (interest-rate floors) if the exposure is to falling rates.

SUMMARY

The foregoing pages address some of the most relevant features of the most actively traded contracts. More detailed information is easily obtained from the exchanges on which the contracts are traded. Less actively traded contracts may also be of interest since they frequently fill unique niches in the fixed income market. For example, the CBOT's municipal bond index futures contract provides a means of hedging and speculating on high quality, long-term municipal bonds. Similarly, a number of other contracts offered by the CBOT have been designed to track the prices of mortgage-backed securities. Also, the Chicago Board Options Exchange and the American Exchange have offered options on spot fixed income securities, as opposed to options on futures on fixed income securities. The list of exchange-traded options and futures contracts changes frequently. By keeping an eye on the financial pages and the exchange literature, potential users can keep abreast of new contracts as they are introduced.

APPENDIX
The Wildcard Delivery

The wildcard delivery play offers potential profits to sellers of T-bond and T-note futures contracts traded on the Chicago Board of Trade. During the delivery period for these contracts, the seller can give notice of intent to deliver up until 8:00 P.M. (Chicago time). The price that the seller receives from the buyer equals the conversion factor for the instrument delivered, times the futures settlement price (determined shortly after the close of the futures market at 2:00 P.M. Chicago time), plus accrued interest. Profit opportunities arise from the fact that up until

8:00 P.M. sellers can choose to make deliveries at prices determined at 2:00 P.M.

To see how the wildcard play can work to the advantage of the seller, suppose an investor buys the 12½ percent Treasury bonds of 8/15/14 and uses the bond futures contract to hedge for an anticipated sale date in September of 1985. Since the conversion factor for the 12½ percent bonds for September 1985 was 1.4749, the hedger would sell 14.75 bond contracts for every $1 million face amount of underlying bonds.

During the delivery period, the hedger may profit from the wildcard delivery play if spot market prices fall after the futures market closes. To illustrate, suppose the hedger holds $100 million face amount of the 12½ percent bonds and is short 1,475 bond contracts. Assume that one day during the delivery period futures close at 78 with the bond simultaneously trading at 115.25. The investor can lift his cash-futures position in either of two ways. He can buy back his futures position and sell the bonds in the cash market. His net position would then be $115,250,000 in cash, plus the gains (or minus the losses) on 1,475 futures contracts. Alternatively, he could deliver bonds in satisfaction of the short futures position. However, in order to make delivery on the futures position, the investor must purchase an additional $47.5 million face value of bonds. If this purchase is made at the close of futures trading, the cost will be $54,743,750 (i.e., 115.25 percent × $47.5 million). From the buyer, he receives $169,687,245 [from $147.5 million (face value) × 1.4749 (the conversion factor) × 78 percent (the futures price)]. This gives a net position of $114,943,495 in cash, plus the gains (or losses) on 1,475 futures contracts.

Obviously, the second alternative is inferior to the first. However, consider what happens if the investor takes no action and bond prices fall after the futures market closes; say, for example, that by 7 P.M. the price of the 12½ bonds fall two points to 113.25. The investor then gives notice of intent to deliver. As before, additional bonds must be purchased, but now the cost is only $53,793,750 (from 113.25 percent × $47.5 million). Receiving $169,687,245 from the buyer, the investor's net position is $115,893,495 in cash, plus the gain (or loss) on 1,475 futures contracts. Of course, if prices do not fall after the close of the futures market (or do not fall sufficiently far), the investor will not give notice of intent to deliver and not buy bonds in the cash market. Consequently, the seller has the option to make delivery if profitable, or carry the position another day if not profitable (unless, of course, the end of the delivery period has been reached).

In essence, the seller has an option. The option gives him the right to sell at a fixed price (the futures settlement price) for a period of six hours, regardless of the price of the underlying asset. In this sense, the wildcard play is much like a daily put option.

Exchange-Traded Options on Fixed Income Securities

Robert W. Kopprasch, Ph.D., C.F.A.
Vice President
Salomon Brothers Inc

Victor J. Haghani
Interest Rate Arbitrage Group
Salomon Brothers Inc

INTRODUCTION

Since the first options contract on Treasury bond futures was traded at the Chicago Board of Trade (CBOT) in October 1982, exchange-traded options on fixed income securities have come into wide use as a means of managing risk and expressing market views. The burgeoning trading volume and broadening variety of securities covered by options has made exchange-traded options on fixed income securities important instruments in their own right. As shown in Exhibit 1, trading volume and month-end open interest has expanded rapidly. This growth in exchange-traded options volume comes in the wake of the success of other exchange-traded fixed income instruments such as Treasury bond futures (CBOT) and Eurodollar time deposit futures (CME).[1]

In addition to the increased liquidity of exchange-traded options, the variety of fixed income securities covered by options contracts has increased. Options on Treasury bonds, notes, and bills, as well as options on Treasury bond futures, Treasury note futures and Eurodollar time deposit rate futures are traded on various exchanges.[2] Many pat-

---

[1] See Robert W. Kopprasch, *An Introduction to Financial Futures on Treasury Securities*, Salomon Brothers Inc, December 1981.

[2] See the appendix, where terms of available exchange-traded options contracts are listed.

EXHIBIT 1   Exchange-Traded Options on Fixed Income Securities

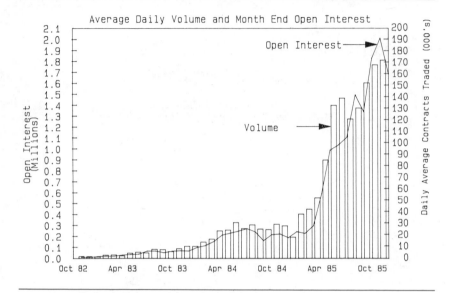

terns of risk and return are made possible by the existence of options at different strike prices and with a range of expiration dates for each underlying security.

The purpose of this chapter is to present a general overview of exchange-traded options, with attention paid to the basics of the option contract and some of the strategies that are possible. Detailed treatment of the valuation of specific contracts is not covered in this chapter.[3]

BASICS OF THE OPTION CONTRACT

There are two basic types or classes of options—puts and calls. A *call* option is the right (but not the obligation) to *buy* a particular security at a specified price (known as the strike price) and usually may be exercised any time until its expiration date. A *put* option is the right (but not the obligation) to *sell* a particular security at a specified price (known as the strike price) and also can normally be exercised until its expiration date. It is important to emphasize the optional nature of these contracts—the holder has the option to exercise the contract if it is in his best interest to

---

[3] See *The Valuation of Options on Fixed Income Securities,* Salomon Brothers Inc, October 1982, or, *Options on Futures on Fixed Income Securities,* Salomon Brothers Inc, December 1983.

do so. If not, the holder will let the option expire and will lose only the premium. On the other hand, the creator or writer of an option contract has an obligation to sell (in the case of a call) or buy (in the case of a put) the securities covered by the contract if the holder exercises the option.

The following are the five basic elements of any options contract:

- *The Underlying Security*—the security that may be purchased (in the case of a call) or sold (in the case of a put) by the option holder until the expiration date. Some option contracts require delivery of actual cash instruments, for instance the 9⅞ percent coupon Treasury bond maturing 11/15/2015. These options are called options on actuals. Where the underlying security is a futures contract (for example, the options on Treasury bond futures), the option is known as an option on futures.
- *The Strike Price*—the price governing the transaction that takes place when an option is exercised.
- *The Expiration Date*—most exchange-traded options are American options, and can be exercised up to and including the expiration date, after which they expire and become worthless. European options can only be exercised on the expiration date of the option, and not before.
- *The Premium*—the price paid for the option.
- *The Size of the Contract*—the amount (usually in par amount) that is covered by one contract.

The Role of the Clearing Corporation

When a trade takes place on an options exchange, the details of the transaction (i.e., number of contracts, price) are agreed to by the actual trading parties, or their agents. However, after the trade clears, the clearing corporation assumes the obligation to perform under the contract. At the same time, however, the investor who is "short" in the contract has an obligation to the clearing corporation. Thus, the clearing corporation stands between the two investors, and its guarantee of performance relieves the option buyer of the necessity of checking the credit of the individual seller of the contract. This is similar to the mechanism used in the futures markets, and was patterned after the futures market system at the time that exchange-traded options on equities were first developed.

The standardized contract, when combined with the clearing corporation system, allows some interesting and useful investment features. First, because all trading must take place through the clearing corporation, trading can be (and is) accomplished without a certificate. The clearing corporation, through its members, maintains records of who is short and who is long, and no certificate is needed to verify this.

Second, when the clearing corporation mechanism is combined with the standardized contracts available on the options exchanges, it also creates the possibility of reversing one's position and negating the responsibility assumed when an options contract was created or sold short. Thus, if an investor wants to offset his position, he merely engages in the opposite transaction for the same option contract. When an investor becomes both short and long in a particular option contract (e.g., an "opening sale" is followed by a "closing purchase"), his position is effectively and contractually eliminated. This mechanism allows sellers to enter into option obligations without the fear of becoming locked into the position if the market moves adversely or if their market projections change. Similarly, option holders need not exercise their options, but can sell them in the secondary market and realize any price and tax benefits that may have accrued to their favor.

Other Fixed Income Options

The over the counter (OTC) market is another forum where options on fixed income securities are bought and sold. The OTC market is a negotiated market where the buyer of the option enters into a direct agreement with the grantor of the option. There are three main areas of activity in OTC debt options. First, there is a large market in options on mortgage-related securities with substantial trading volume. Second, options on specific Treasury issues are bought and sold in large volume over the counter. Third, options on money market instruments have become increasingly important as short-term liability issuance has risen sharply. Although certain institutions are prohibited by specific regulations from buying and/or selling exchange-traded or OTC options, other participants in the debt option market will be faced with a decision as to which type of option to buy or sell. In making such a decision there are several differences between OTC options and exchange-traded options that should be considered. First, some types of asymmetric hedging instruments are only available, for all practical purposes, OTC. These include many of the options on mortgage-related securities, long-term, interest-rate-cap agreements and options on certain specific Treasury issues. Second, in addition to the wider variety of underlying securities on which options are available, OTC option contracts offer greater flexibility than their exchange-traded counterparts since the exercise date(s), strike price(s) and method of payment can be specified exactly as the two parties desire. However, OTC tailor-made option contracts may be difficult to transfer before expiration of the contract, in contrast to exchange-traded options where a publicly quoted two-way market provides a transfer mechanism whereby existing positions may be closed out before expiration. Third, because an OTC option contract is an agreement between principals, the buyer and the seller must each make a credit decision about the other party. The role of the clearing corporation, as described above, and the control procedures enforced by the exchanges allow the participants in the exchange-traded options market to buy and sell contracts without ever having to establish the creditworthiness of the trading counterparty. Fourth, the publicly available quotations on exchange-traded options facilitate the marking to market of existing positions.

In addition to the exchanges and the OTC market, options on debt instruments have been and are available from certain issuers in the corporate and municipal areas. Certain bonds have puts attached to them that allow the holders to redeem them earlier than their stated maturity, usually at par.[4] A number of corporate and municipal issues have come to the market with warrants attached to them. These warrants are actually calls—options that allow the holders to purchase additional fixed income securities at a stated price for some period of time.[5] These options may expire after anywhere from six months to ten years or more, offering coverage far longer than exchange-traded options. However, these types of options can be created only by the issuers of the securities and in the case of puts, are not detachable and cannot be traded separately. These limitations, in conjunction with the advent of exchange-traded and OTC options, have greatly diminished the importance of these types of options, but their volume of issuance remains substantial.

The Intrinsic Value

An option contract's premium can be thought of as having two elements: the intrinsic value (which may be zero) and the time premium. The intrinsic value is merely the immediate exercise value of the option. For example, if a call option has a strike price of 80 and the security is currently selling for 84, the option has an intrinsic value of 4. The time premium is the difference between the option premium and intrinsic value, and its calculation is obvious. If the option described above were selling for 6, the time premium would be 2.

Determining what an option is "worth," as opposed to what its market price is, is more difficult. This estimate of true value will be considered again in the option valuation section in this chapter.[6] First we will concentrate on the intrinsic value of an option as if the option

---

[4] See Robert W. Kopprasch, "Early Redemption (Put) Options on Fixed Income Securities," Chapter 24, in the first edition of *The Handbook of Fixed Income Securities*.

[5] See Robert W. Kopprasch, "Contingent Takedown Options in Fixed Income Securities," Chapter 23 in the first edition of *The Handbook of Fixed Income Securities*.

[6] For more detail, see *The Valuation of Options on Fixed-Income Securities*, Salomon Brothers Inc, October 1982. ·

were held to expiration, because at expiration the time value is zero. At expiration, the actual price will closely approximate intrinsic value because of the arbitrages that would otherwise be possible if these values differed significantly.

PUTS AND CALLS ON FIXED INCOME SECURITIES

The Call Option

In order to illustrate the return patterns associated with a call option, the following example of an option on an actual cash security will be utilized. The analysis of an option on an interest-rate futures contract is largely analogous to the present example and will be discussed later in the paper.

1. *Underlying Security*—8 percent, 30-year bond.
2. *Strike Price*—100.
3. *Expiration Date*—December 19xx.

In option parlance, this option would be known as a December 100. The intrinsic value pattern of this option is shown in Exhibit 2. At all prices below 100, the option's intrinsic value is zero because the security can be purchased in the market for less than it can be purchased via exercising the option. At all prices above 100, the option's intrinsic value

EXHIBIT 2   The Intrinsic Value Pattern of a Call

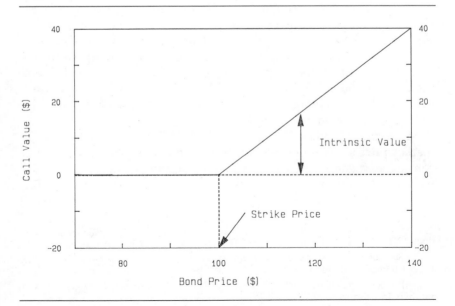

is simply the difference between the market price and the strike price of 100.

Remembering that the intrinsic value is the value that should prevail at or near an option's expiration date, we can also construct a profit chart for an investor if we know the price paid for the option. If an investor paid five points for this option, the resulting profit pattern would be as shown in Exhibit 3.

EXHIBIT 3   The Intrinsic Value and Profit Patterns of a Call

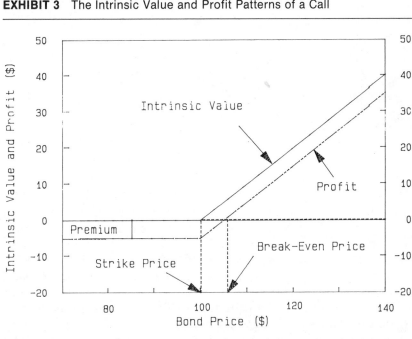

Several elements in Exhibit 3 are important. First, note that the maximum loss to the call option buyer is the premium; no matter how low the ultimate price of the bond, the buyer's loss is limited to five points. Second, the premium paid for the call option also determines the break-even price shown in Exhibit 3. At all prices above the break-even price, the investor shows a profit. This profit is equal to the intrinsic value at expiration less the premium paid for the option. (For ease of presentation, the foregone interest on the capital used to pay the premium is not included in the exhibits. The role of the short-term rate will be discussed later.)

In order to place these charts and concepts into a framework more familiar to the fixed-income investor, they will be restated with yield

EXHIBIT 4 Price-Yield Curve for 8 Percent, 30-Year Bond

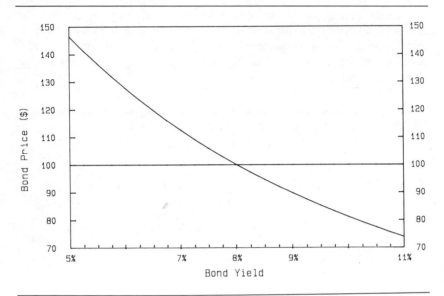

instead of price as the horizontal axis. In Exhibit 4, we see the price yield curve for the deliverable bond which relates the price on the deliverable bond and its yield-to-maturity. (The values for this graph are determined with the option expiration date used as the settlement date.) With Exhibit 4 as a backdrop, it is easy to construct the intrinsic value of a call as a function of yield as is shown in Exhibit 5. The pattern shown illustrates a reversal of the pattern in Exhibit 2 because of the inverse relationship between yield and prices. The slight curvature shown in the intrinsic value line follows that of the price yield curve shown in Exhibit 4. When the option is viewed in this way, we can translate the strike price into a strike yield as shown.

The profit pattern in Exhibit 3 is translated into a yield framework in Exhibit 6, illustrating the profit pattern of a call option versus the yield of the deliverable instrument at expiration. The break-even price in Exhibit 3 translates to a break-even yield in Exhibit 6. It can be seen that the break-even yield is a function of several factors: the premium, which determines how much outflow must be recovered, and the slope of the price yield curve, which determines how much yield movement is necessary to recover that premium. The slope of the price yield curve is a function of the coupon, yield, maturity, and frequency of coupon payment.

The call writer. Let us now consider the other side of the call option transaction, that is, the seller or creator of the call. If the call

EXHIBIT 5   Intrinsic Value of a Call versus Yield at Expiration

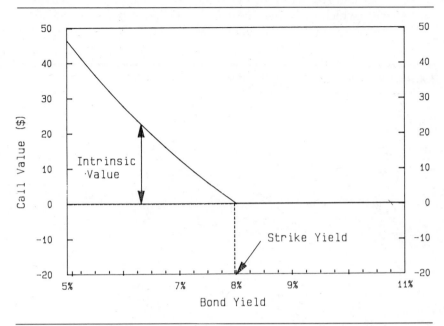

EXHIBIT 6   Profit Pattern of a Call versus Yield at Expiration

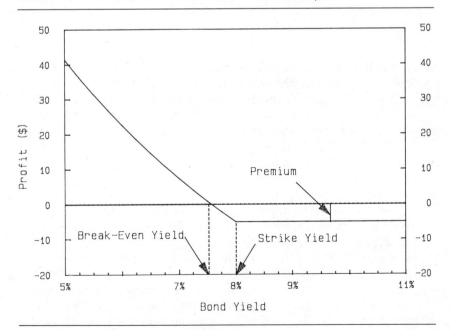

writer has no other position in the market, his profit pattern is like that shown in Exhibit 7. We can see that if the yield at expiration is above the strike yield (which of course means that the price is below the strike price), the option holder will allow the option to expire and the call

---

EXHIBIT 7 The Call Writer's Profit Pattern ("Naked")

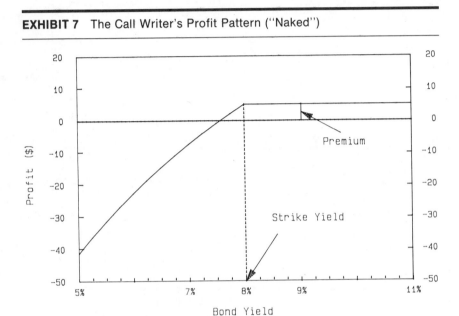

---

writer will have earned the premium. If, on the other hand, the yield at expiration is below the strike yield, the option will be exercised and the call writer will be forced to purchase the security in the marketplace at its now higher price and deliver it at the lower strike price. This will cause a loss of at least some of the premium and perhaps more than the premium. If the yield at expiration is below the break-even yield, the call writer will show an absolute loss.

The reader will note that Exhibit 7 is merely Exhibit 6 rotated around the horizontal zero line. This is not surprising because the call buyer and the call writer are on the opposite sides of the transaction, and whoever "wins" does so at the expense of the other. (Except for transaction costs, option trading is a "zero sum" game.)

It is easy to see that the call writer who has no other position in the market is neutral to bearish, because only if yields remain approximately constant or move upward will the call writer show a profit. If yields decline below the strike yield, some of his premium will be eroded and he may show an absolute loss. The call buyer shown in Exhibit 6, on the other hand, is obviously bullish because his profit comes when yields decline and prices rise.

An alternative approach for the call seller or call writer is to own the security underlying the option when the option is sold. In this case, if yields decline and prices rise, the call seller will not suffer an economic loss in delivering the security to the call holder because he will already own it. (Of course, an opportunity loss occurs.) Only if the security declines in price by an amount sufficient to erode the premium will the call seller (who covers his position with the underlying security) show a real loss. In option terminology, such a call writer is known as a "covered" call writer while the writer who is uncovered is usually referred to as being "naked." Exhibit 8 shows that a security owner who is neutral

EXHIBIT 8   The Covered Call Writer's Profit Pattern

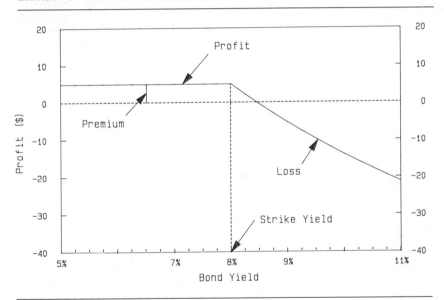

to bearish on the security he holds can sell an option on it and thereby generate some protection for downward price moves. This protection, of course, is equal to the premium income received. Such a strategy may be employed when the holder is restricted from selling the security, due to regulatory or accounting rules, for example.

The Put Option

A put option, as described earlier, is an option to sell a security at a specified price. A put option has value at expiration if the market price of the underlying security is *below* the strike price, allowing the put holder to buy the security in the market and "put" it to the put writer at the higher strike price. The intrinsic value at expiration is thus the difference between the strike price and the market price, if the strike is above the market price, and zero otherwise.

In order to illustrate the intrinsic value and profit patterns of a put, we will utilize a hypothetical put with terms identical to the call example used earlier:

1. *Underlying Security*—8 percent, 30-year bond.
2. *Strike Price*—100.
3. *Expiration Date*—December 19xx.

A chart of the put's intrinsic value, analogous to Exhibit 2 for calls, is shown in Exhibit 9. Exhibit 10 translates this into the yield framework,

---

EXHIBIT 9   The Intrinsic Value of a Put

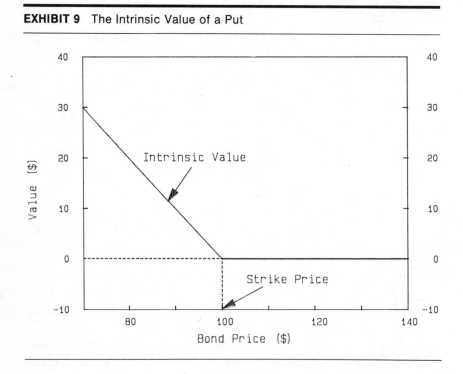

---

and adds a profit line that assumes that the put cost 5 points. The intrinsic value line is adapted directly from the right side of Exhibit 4, in which the price of the security lies below the strike price.

The put writer.   For every put option outstanding, there must be a seller, and that seller guarantees to buy the securities "put" to him if the

EXHIBIT 10   Intrinsic Value and Profit Pattern of a Put versus Yield at Expiration

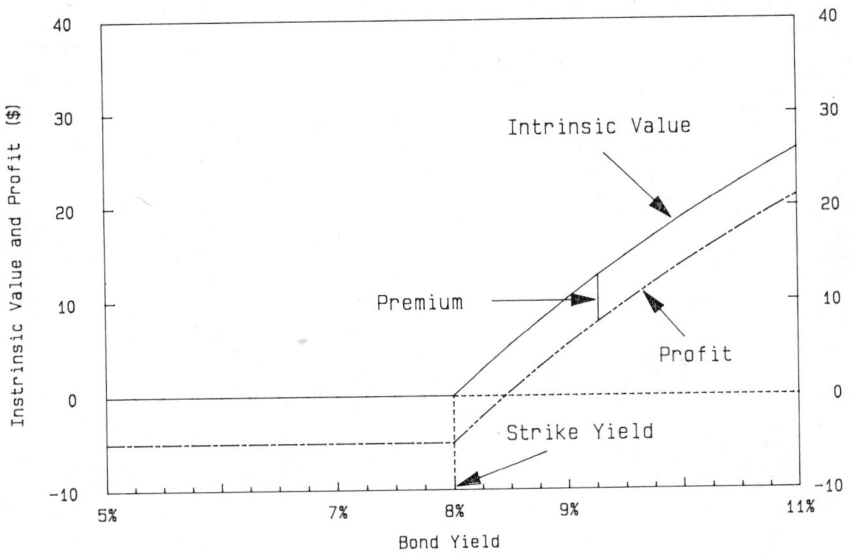

option is exercised. The put seller therefore buys the security at a price higher than the market price whenever a put option is (rationally) exercised. If the strike price is higher than market by more than the premium received for the option, the put seller suffers a loss. This is shown in Exhibit 11.

The put seller's profit pattern, shown in Exhibit 11, exhibits a striking similarity to the covered call writer's profit pattern, shown in Exhibit 8. This illustrates that there exist several paths to equivalent profit patterns when using options. (Several others will be described in later sections.) Furthermore, it suggests that put and call prices may be related to one another to prevent dominance of one return pattern over another. This will also be discussed later in the chapter.

A note on options on money market instruments.   The intrinsic value and profit patterns shown in the preceding sections are based on a *long-term* fixed income security, the price of which is not a linear function of yield. This is the reason for the slight curvature in the patterns. Eurodollar time deposit futures and Treasury bills are quoted on a discount yield basis that relates price and yield in a linear fashion. Thus, the curvature of the figures shown above would disappear if the underlying securities were Eurodollar time deposit futures or Treasury bills (instead of bonds) and if the horizontal axis were shown as quoted discount yield.

EXHIBIT 11 The Put Writer's Profit Pattern ("Naked")

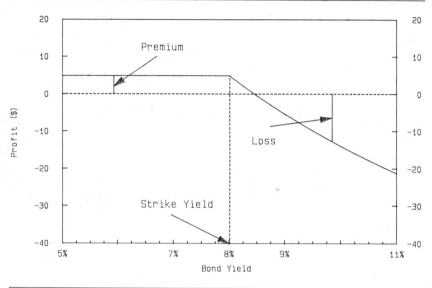

Options Strategies and Tactics

Investors who are familiar with the concepts of the past several sections have undoubtedly considered the "rate anticipation" uses of options. If rates are expected to decline, calls can be purchased and will generate profits if rates fall sufficiently. Similarly, puts will provide profits if purchased prior to a sufficient climb in rates. These approaches to options, as well as hedging (covered later), concentrate on the price movement of the option when profitable, but it is also interesting and useful to consider the times when options expire with no intrinsic value. Several such cases are examined in the following sections.

Prior to studying these options strategies, however, a few notes on terminology may be helpful. When an option has a positive intrinsic value, it is said to be *in-the-money*. Thus, when a call is referred to as in-the-money, the implication is that the market price of the underlying security exceeds the strike price (i.e., the left side of Exhibit 5). An in-the-money put has a strike price that exceeds the market price of the underlying security. Options are referred to as *at-the-money* when the strike price and the market price of the underlying security are equal, or nearly so. An option is *out-of-the-money* when the security must move in a favorable direction (up for calls, down for puts) just to reach the strike price. Thus, the Dec 100 call is out-of-the-money if the underlying bond is trading at 96, but the Dec 100 put on the same bond would be in-the-money.[7]

Viewing Call Options as Alternative Investments[8]

Long-term fixed income investors will discover that call options offer a number of interesting strategies. One of these involves the purchase of calls as an alternative to investment in an equivalent par amount in the long-term sector, with the excess funds being invested in the short-term market. Although we normally think of purchasing calls as being beneficial when prices rise, a somewhat surprising result emerges from an analysis of this strategy.

First, let us consider the cash flows associated with the purchase at par of an 8 percent, 30-year bond (for which one-year put and call options are available). These cash flows are comprised of the 100 outflow, a semiannual inflow of 5, and a redemption of 100 at maturity (see Exhibit 12). To begin our comparative analysis, let us assume that short-term rates approximate 8 percent (i.e., the yield curve is flat) and that a one-year call with a strike price of 100 is available for 5 points.

Let us assume that, instead of buying a bond, the investor buys one call (with a strike of 100) for 5 and invests the remaining 95 in a one-year semiannual coupon instrument. If yields decline and the underlying long-term bond increases in price, the investor would exercise the option and buy the remaining income stream of the bond for 100. The cash flows associated with this approach are shown in Exhibit 13. Note that the first-year income stream is lower because only 95 is invested in the short-term security. The investor would receive 0.20 less semiannually, only 95 at maturity (end of year one), and then would pay 100 (the strike price) for the bond. The net difference between the cash flows in Exhibits 12 and 13 is shown in Exhibit 14. (Note that Exhibit 14 could also describe the situation in which the investor borrowed the money to pay the premium, paid periodic interest on it, and repaid the loan when the option expired.)

The important point of Exhibit 14 is that it shows that the option has a cost that is not offset by any benefits in the future. Now let us consider what happens if rates have increased 200 basis points to 10 percent.

---

[7] This terminology is consistent with that used in the equity option market. In the debt market, where forward trading is more common, these terms are sometimes modified to reflect this "other market." Thus, we use the terms *at-the-money-spot* in the same way equity participants use at-the-money, as well as *in-, at-, and out-of-the-money-forward* to reflect comparisons of the strike price with the forward price of the underlying security, for settlement on the option exercise or exercise settlement date.

[8] This and the following section are based on a talk given by Martin L. Leibowitz at the Financial Analysts Federation Futures Conference, September 1981.

EXHIBIT 12   Cash Flows of an 8 Percent, 30-Year Bond

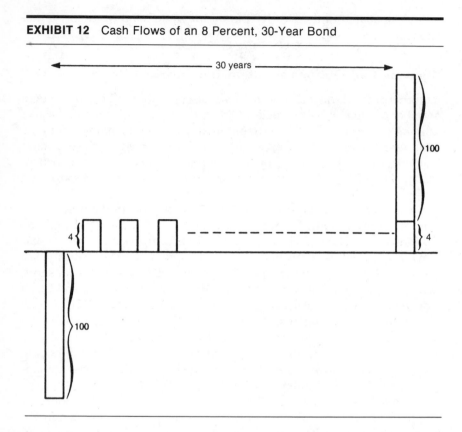

Naturally, the option will be allowed to expire, and if the investor buys a new par bond, the semiannual cash flows will be as shown in Exhibit 15.

When the cash flows of Exhibit 15 are compared to the base case shown in Exhibit 12, the difference takes on the pattern shown in Exhibit 16. The "extra" income results from the increase in yields, and would be even higher if the yield increase had been greater. Thus it appears that the call options, when viewed as an alternative to a long bond purchase, actually provide an option on higher yields, even though calls are usually thought of as profitable when yields decline.[9]

This provides a convenient point at which to mention the effect of short-term rates on option premiums. Consider again the cash-flow diagrams shown in Exhibits 12–14. If short-term rates were higher, the cash flows resulting from the short-term investment shown in Exhibit 13

---

[9] Actually, it is the investment in the short-term security that provides the investor with funds to invest at higher rates (or lower rates) in the future. The role of the call option is to provide a floor on the rate at which the funds will be invested. Thus, it is the combined position (not the call alone) that provides an option on higher yields.

EXHIBIT 13   Cash Flows If Call Option Is Exercised

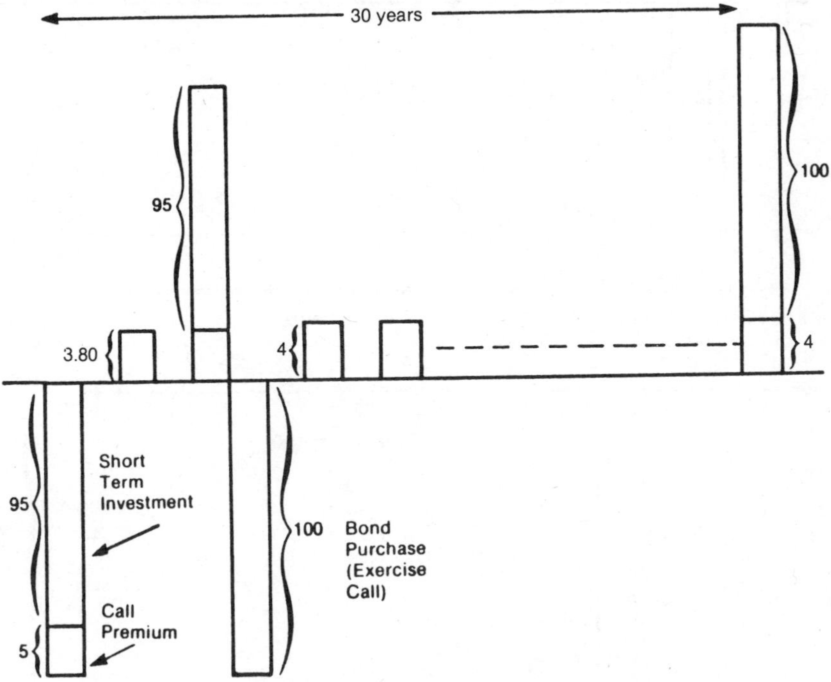

---

would be higher, resulting in a lower net cost for the call than is shown in Exhibit 14. Another way of looking at this is to say that the investor could pay more than five for the call but still have the same net cost.

If short-term rates were lower than long-term rates, the investor would pay not only the premium for the call, but would lose some yield on the remaining funds that were invested short term, thereby increasing the effective cost of the call. This effect is likely to lower the nominal dollar price that the investor would otherwise be willing to pay for the call. More discussion on this topic will be included in the Option Valuation section.

Using Puts to Protect Long Positions

The dramatic rise in rates and in rate volatility has made investors in long-term securities particularly vulnerable to large price swings. Hedging with futures can reduce downside risk, but at the expense of losing upside potential. Fixed-income puts also provide protection, but at a known cost, leaving any remaining upside profit intact.

EXHIBIT 14 The Cost of a Call: Premium and Forgone Interest

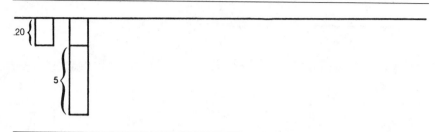

EXHIBIT 15 Cash Flows If Call Is Not Exercised

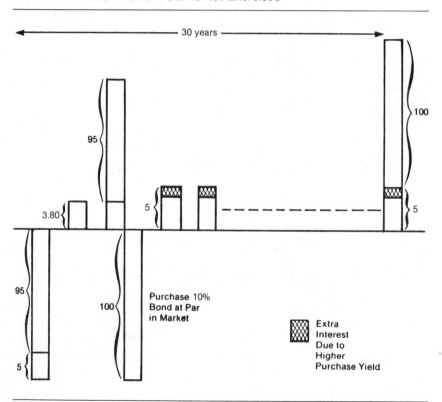

Let us utilize the securities introduced in the previous section, namely, a 30-year, 8 percent bond (at par) and the associated one-year put, struck at par. If the investor buys a put at the same time as he purchases the bond, he has the right to sell the bond at par anytime over the next year. If yields decline over the year, and the bond increases in price, the put will be allowed to expire worthless. But if yields increase

EXHIBIT 16 Call's Cost Can Be Offset by Higher Future Interest

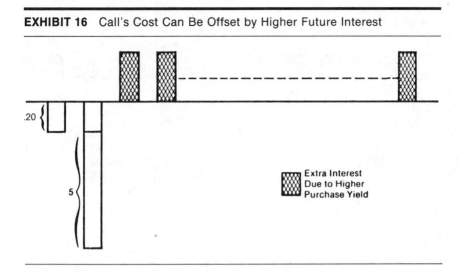

Extra Interest
Due to Higher
Purchase Yield

and drive down the price of the bond, the investor will be able to sell his bond at par and reinvest the proceeds in new, higher-coupon instruments at par.

To construct the cash-flow pattern, let us assume the following: The put costs 4 points, the yield curve is flat at 8 percent, the investor borrows the funds for the premium, pays interest semiannually and will repay the premium loan at expiration. If the option expires unexercised, the cash-flow pattern of the long bond (Exhibit 12) will be altered by the flows shown in Exhibit 17. If the option is exercised, and the investor reinvests his funds in a higher paying bond, the long bond flows will be altered by the flows shown in Exhibit 18. This clearly indicates the advantage of the put when yields increase.

Of course, it is not necessary to borrow the put premium, and that construct was used only to demonstrate the resemblance of Exhibits 17 and 18 to Exhibits 14 and 16.

EXHIBIT 17 The Cost of a Put: Premium and Interest

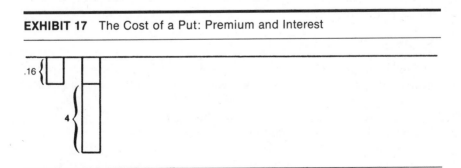

EXHIBIT 18 Put's Cost Can Be Offset by Higher Future Interest

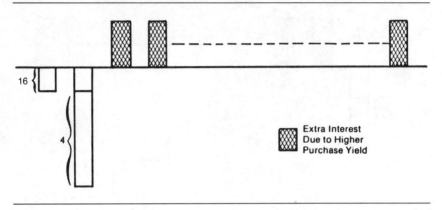

The similarity in these option-induced cash flows (Exhibit 16 and Exhibit 18) is another example of how nearly identical risk-return patterns can be constructed from various combinations of long and short positions in cash securities and options. In this case, protecting a long position with a put is nearly identical to protecting the absence of a long position with a call, shown in the last section.

Options in the Portfolio Context

The sections above have described several applications of options to particular security positions. In addition to these specific security transactions, options can have broader use in the adjustment of the risk position (i.e., the rate sensitivity) of the entire portfolio. Active managers can effectively "lengthen" the portfolio (i.e., increase the bullish rate sensitivity or performance) by purchasing calls. The portfolio can be "shortened" by buying puts.

Recent pension fund activity has heightened the interest in contingent immunization,[10] and fixed-income options can be used in the "active" and "near-immunized" modes of operation. Any investor desiring to adjust the rate sensitivity of a portfolio should evaluate the potentially useful role of options.

Equivalent Positions

Several examples have indicated that investors can achieve nearly identical profit patterns in alternative ways. For example, the put writer's

---

[10] See Martin L. Leibowitz and Alfred Weinberger, "Contingent Immunization," Salomon Brothers Inc, January 28, 1981.

profit pattern was shown to be similar to the covered call writer's profit pattern. In fact, there are a number of security positions that can be duplicated with options. Several are presented below.

Long position in underlying security = Long call + Short put
Equation I

This can be demonstrated by remembering that higher prices result in profits on the long position and on the long call, and lower prices result in losses on the long position and on the short put. By rearranging the components, other relationships can be found.

For example, if we add a short call to both sides of the equation (the long call and short call on the right cancel out), we have

Long position in underlying security + Short call = Short put
Equation II

The left side is the covered call writer, and the right side is the put writer. (See again Exhibits 8 and 11.)

By adding a long put to each side, the original Equation I becomes

Long position + Long put = Long call
Equation III

By reversing the position of each component in the original Equation I, we get

Short position in underlying security = Short call + Long put
Equation IV

Adding a long call to each side of Equation IV yields

Short position + Long call = Long put
Equation V

Note that the positions on either side of the equations may involve different cash outlays, and thus the higher outlay position must be financed, or the lower outlay position implicitly includes a short-term cash equivalent investment.

The equivalence of the positions shown above can be demonstrated by combining the individual profit patterns of the components. The availability of these equivalent positions may prompt investors to move from one to the equivalent if it can be achieved at cheaper cost, or may invite arbitrage between equivalent positions.

For example, Equation III suggests that

Long position + Long put + Short call = 0,

that is, a riskless position. In fact, the position is riskless and will be described later in the section on Conversions.

OPTION VALUATION

Determinants of Value

The determination of "fair" price or value for an option is important to both purchasers and sellers of options, regardless of the strategy they may be employing. For most equity options, variations of the Black-Scholes model are normally used in the valuation process. Although such models may be adapted to certain fixed income options with some degree of success, there are significant differences between the assumptions of the Black-Scholes framework and the reality of the fixed income market. First, a bond option valuation model must take account of the fact that the underlying instrument is changing over time. To cite an extreme example, a five-year option on a ten-year bond begins its life as an option on a ten-year bond but expires as an option on a five-year bond. It is clear that the price volatility of this security will change over time. Another requirement for a fixed income option valuation model is that it address the correlation of short-term interest rates and the yields which determine the price of the underlying security.

While it is not our purpose to explain these pricing models in detail, it is useful to present the basic inputs to these models and the logic behind their impact on value. These determinants of option value are: strike price, expected volatility of the underlying security, time to expiration, the cash flows of the underlying security (if any), short-term rates, and the current price of the underlying security.

The strike price. The strike price determines how far in- or out-of-the-money the option is when being valued. Other things being equal, an in-the-money option is worth more than one at-the-money, and the at-the-money option is worth more than one out-of-the-money. For a call option, this means the lower the strike price the higher the premium; for a put option, the higher the strike price the higher the option value.

Volatility of the underlying security. The expected volatility of the underlying security in the options valuation context refers to the expected variance of potential price moves of the underlying security.[11] Exhibit 19 is a probabilistic representation of two levels of expected volatility. From this illustration we will show why higher expected volatility translates to higher premiums on both puts and calls.

With Exhibit 19 as a point of reference, consider a call option with a strike price of 110, where the price of the underlying is 100. All else constant, it is evident that there is a higher probability that the call option expires in-the-money if expected volatility is 20 percent than if

---

[11] In debt option valuation, yield volatility is often the primary variable, and price volatility is derived from that.

EXHIBIT 19   Expected Price of Underlying Security under Different
Volatilities

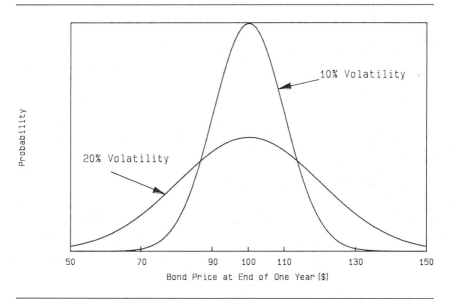

expected volatility is 10 percent. The fact that there is also a higher
probability of large negative price moves is of no concern to the call
option holder, since any adverse price moves below the strike price
represents zero intrinsic value at expiration, and no worse. The same
argument can be made for an out-of-the-money put option; for instance,
a put option struck at 90 is worth more if expected volatility is 20 percent
rather than 10 percent.

Higher expected volatility also increases the option premium for in-
the-money puts and calls. Perhaps the easiest way to make this argument is by referring to the earlier section discussing equivalent positions. Using the relationship which equates a long call position with a
long put position plus a long position in the underlying (Equation III), it
can be seen that if increased expected volatility raises the value of an
out-of-the-money call option, then the in-the-money put option on the
right-hand side of the equation must also increase in value. The same
argument shows that expected volatility and the price of an in-the-
money call option are positively related.

Estimating the volatility of the underlying security is perhaps the
most difficult task in the pricing of an option. It is the only variable
affecting the option premium which is not directly observable in the
market when the option is priced and is as elusive a quantity to predict

as the future price of the underlying security itself. Exhibit 20 shows an estimation method which involves both a measure of historic volatility as well as the current level of expected volatility as implied by the price of options traded in the market.

EXHIBIT 20   Historic versus Implied Volatility of Treasury Bond Futures

Time to expiration.   The time to expiration specifies the time constraint that the volatility of the security operates under and sets implicit limits to the range of potential prices likely to be realized. The time to expiration also determines the absolute dollar impact of the short-term rate and the cash flows of the underlying security on the price of the option. A longer time to expiration tends to increase the value of the option by extending the range of potential price movement, as does a higher volatility.[12]

Cash flows of the underlying security.   Depending on the structure of the option contract, cash flows on the underlying security may have a major impact on the option value. For example, while a zero-coupon bond can be expected to grow in price, even at a constant yield, a full-coupon bond yielding its coupon rate will not. If the strike price is fixed, the lack of price growth of the full-coupon bond (due to its return

---

[12] For European options, it is possible to increase time to expiration and decrease the value of the option.

in the form of periodic cash flows) will lower the value of a call option versus a call on the growing security. The nature of the strike price is also important in this regard. Even the "nongrowing" (constant yield) par bond will grow in total price (including accrued interest) between coupon payments. If the option contract specifies purchase or sale at the quoted price plus accrued interest, the inter-coupon growth will have little impact on value, because the strike price will rise along with accrued interest.

The short-term rate.[13] The role of the short-term rate has been mentioned earlier, when considering the financing of the premium. Another look is provided in this section.

Let us consider the purchase, for 4 points, of a one-year call on a 30-year, 8 percent bond when the yield curve is flat at 8 percent. To compare this case with the purchase of the bond at par, assume that the call buyer will also put 96 in one-year CDs at 8 percent. Thus, both investments (call plus CD and long bond) have equal outlays. The dollar returns for the two strategies, including income (but ignoring reinvestment), are shown in Exhibit 21.

EXHIBIT 21 Bond Purchase versus Call + CD Strategy

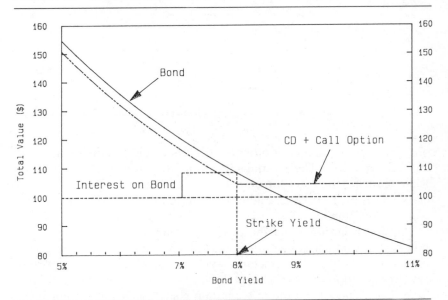

---

[13] The arguments presented here are based on market forces. Theoretical option valuation models incorporate the short-term rate in its effects on the present value of the strike price. This concept is considered in more detail in the valuation paper referenced earlier.

It is not difficult to see the impact that higher short-term rates would have if the premium remained constant at 4. If the short-term rate were 16 percent, for example, the total value of the CD (96 + interest) would exceed the bond's market value and earned interest, and the call + CD strategy would dominate the bond purchase; that is, the call + CD would be better for at least some possible yield levels at expiration and never worse. This is shown in Exhibit 22. All investors who were not

EXHIBIT 22   Dominance of Bond by Call + CD

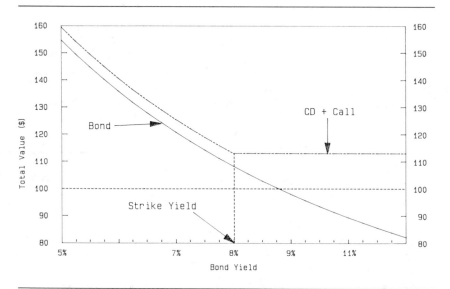

prohibited by regulatory or other constraints would sell their bonds and buy CDs and calls. These actions would tend to drive call prices higher while reducing the yield spread between bonds and CDs until the dominance disappeared. Thus, higher short-term rates would raise the level of call premiums.

Option premiums and the price of the underlying security.   The previous sections discussed the impact of a number of factors on option premiums. Most of these factors—such as volatility, short-term rates, time to expiration and expected cash flows—do not change significantly from day to day. The time to expiration changes, of course, but when the time to expiration is long, the slight daily decline has almost no impact on premium. When the time to expiration is short, the time premium is usually small, and declines in the time premium itself are small on an absolute basis. This leaves price changes in the underlying security as the most important determinant of changes in option premiums. In the discussion that follows, we will assume that all of the parameters other than price—namely volatility, short-term rates, expected cash flows and time to expiration—remain constant, and we will examine the option premium for various prices of the underlying security.

If the option is very far out-of-the-money, relative to the volatility of the underlying security, the option will have little value, because the possibility of going in-the-money is remote. If the option is very deep in-the-money, it will sell for close to its intrinsic value, with little time premium. The reasons for this lie in the basic appeal of the option itself—leveraged gains and limited losses. A deep in-the-money option must sell at a high price because of its high intrinsic value, thus exposing potential buyers to large losses if prices decline. In addition, the leverage is drastically reduced because of the high price paid for the option. Thus, while arbitrage will prevent the premium from falling below the intrinsic value by any appreciable amount, the lack of appeal to buyers and selling pressure from arbitrageurs (see the section on Early Exercises of Options) will prevent the premium from going much above the intrinsic value.

Somewhere between the extremes (deep in-the-money and deep out-of-the-money) described above, the time value reaches its greatest level. This level usually is realized when the option is close to being at-the-money. With these general statements as background, let us examine Exhibit 23, which relates the premium of a call to the various yields and corresponding prices of the underlying security. The horizontal axis of the figure is the yield to maturity of the underlying security. The left

EXHIBIT 23 Theoretical Value of a Call

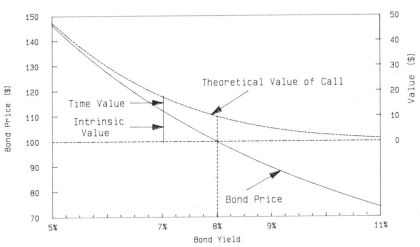

vertical axis shows the price of the underlying security. The right vertical axis shows the value of the option.

When the option is deep out-of-the-money (toward the right), the value is small because a large move in the security is necessary just to reach the strike price. The premium increases as the price gets higher (moving to the left in the figure). As the option becomes deep in-the-money, the premium approaches the intrinsic value.

A theoretical value of a put is developed in a like manner, except that the put increases in value as the underlying security declines in price. The pattern is similar otherwise, starting with a low value when out-of-the-money, and approaching the intrinsic value as the option becomes deeper in-the-money. This pattern is shown in Exhibit 24; note

EXHIBIT 24   Theoretical Value of a Put Relative to Bond Price

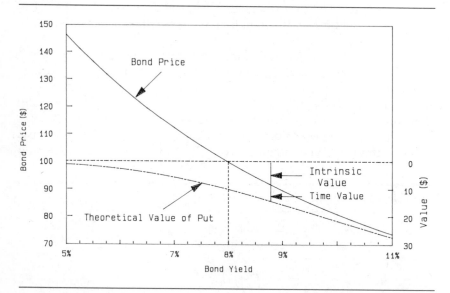

that the premium scale is inverted. The put's theoretical value can also be viewed against the intrinsic value that was first shown in Exhibit 10, and this comparison is shown in Exhibit 25. (The values shown are for puts that can be exercised at any time prior to expiration.)

While the pattern shown in Exhibit 25 is upright, with larger values appearing higher on the chart, the presentation in Exhibit 24 is more useful when discussing hedging. Thus, both Exhibit 23 (for calls) and Exhibit 24 (for puts) will be the basis for the discussions on hedging that follow.

EXHIBIT 25   Theoretical Value of a Put Relative to Intrinsic Value

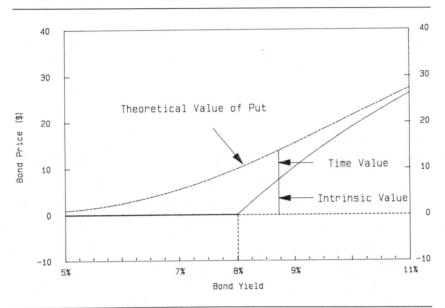

Conversions and Reversals

A somewhat different approach considers the relationship of put and call prices to each other through processes known as conversion and reverse conversion. In a conversion, an investor (usually a member firm) buys a put, buys the underlying security, and sells a call with the same strike price as the put. As described in the next paragraph, the investor takes on no risk, and removes puts from the market and provides calls to the market, as shown in Exhibit 26. The investor creates conversions to earn the difference, if large enough, between the price of the call sold and the put purchased. This difference must cover the net cost of carry on the long security. based on the current yield of the long security and the rate to finance it, and any excess is profit. Thus the short-term rate affects the spread in put and call premiums.

For example, assume that in June a December 100 put costs 5½, the December 100 call sells for 6, and that the underlying 8 percent bond is selling for 100. If the investor buys the bond, buys a put, and sells a call, he will be in a risk-free position. If the bond's price increases, it will be called away from him at 100, the price he paid for it. If the price declines, the investor will exercise his put and sell the bond for the strike price of 100. Thus, whether prices rally, decline, or remain constant, the investor will sell the bond for 100, the price he paid. (Note that the number

---

EXHIBIT 26 The Conversion Process

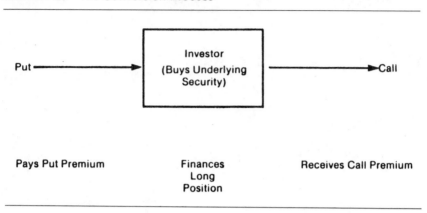

Put ⟶ Investor (Buys Underlying Security) ⟶ Call

Pays Put Premium   Finances   Receives Call Premium
                          Long
                          Position

---

following the expiration month is the strike price, and not the year of expiration. This might cause confusion if there is trading in December 86s, for example.)

Now let's examine the motivation for entering into conversion transactions. Assume that short-term financing rates are 8 percent. The calculations are shown in Exhibit 27.

EXHIBIT 27 Calculation of Profit From Conversion

Net Investment		
Buy security	−100.00	
Buy put	− 5.50	
Sell call	+ 6.00	
		−99.50
Net Cost of Carry		
Finance charge		
Amount × Rate × Time		
99½ × 8 percent × ½ year =	− 3.98	
Current Return on Security		
One coupon earned	+ 4.00	
		+ 0.02
Total Cost of Investment		−99.48
Sale Price of Investment		
Whether put or called		+100.00
Profit per Bond		+ 0.52

The net dollar return is thus $0.52 per bond purchased on a risk-free basis. If the financing (short-term) rate were higher, the spread between put and call premiums would have to be wider to maintain this profit. If the financing rate were much higher, the profit would become a loss. In that case, the positions would be reversed to earn the difference.

Normally, conversions (and reverse conversions) are done by dealers who can arbitrage differences in premiums that would be too small to be profitable to public investors. This section was intended to describe the relationship between put and call prices as well as to provide further explanation on the role of short-term rates on put and call premiums, not to suggest an option trading strategy for investors. It should also be noted that the conversion and reversal process described above involves the use of options which will not be exercised before the expiration date of the option. Where early exercise of an option is likely, the conversion and reversal processes will not be risk free.

Early Exercises of Options

In general, most options are worth more alive than dead, because an option that is sold will generate the intrinsic value (if any) plus the time premium (if any). If an option is exercised, however, only the intrinsic value is recovered from the position. Because most fixed income option exercise transactions incorporate accrued interest added to the strike price, coupon dates cause few exercises. This is in contrast to the equity market, where dividend payments (ex-dates) can trigger exercises, because the price of the stock changes but the strike is not adjusted.

Nevertheless, several factors can cause early exercise of puts and calls. Those that are specific to particular option contracts are discussed in papers covering those options. This section will present only one scenario to demonstrate that early exercise can be a rational action.

Consider a one-year call, with a strike of 70, on an 8 percent bond currently trading at 100. The option is obviously deep (30 points) in the money. Suppose that the relevant short-term (one-year) rate for an investor is 8 percent. We will examine the covered write under these conditions, that is, buy the bond and sell the call.

Assume that the call sells for only its intrinsic value of 30. If the investor feels that there is little possibility that the bond will sell for less than 70 at the end of a year, this transaction is similar to a futures "cash and carry." The investor would buy the security for 100 and sell the call for 30, resulting in a net cost of 70 (which will also be the sale price one year hence). Over the next year, the investor will earn 8 (two coupons) on an investment of 70 for a return of over 11 percent. This is clearly an attractive proposition.

If the attractiveness of selling calls causes many investors to sell calls and put downward pressure on the call price, the price might dip below the intrinsic value. If this happens, and the options can be exercised immediately, arbitrageurs will buy the options, exercise them, and sell the underlying security to earn the difference between the market price and the intrinsic value. Thus, the options may be exercised early.

On the other hand, holders of the calls will find that they have an asset worth $30 that is not going to produce interest over the year, but which will be subject to price changes that are approximately equal to the changes on the underlying bond. Thus, since they have the market risk of a bond position already, they might as well invest $70 and exercise the call, and earn 8 percent interest on the $100 face value of the bond. If they do not wish to take on the market risk of the bond, they can sell the call and earn interest on the resulting $30 inflow. This selling pressure will add to that described above, and may introduce more arbitrage.

Most of the actions discussed above involve selling the option, which induces a downward move in price. The only likely buyers at the high level of premium are arbitrageurs who buy the options in order to exercise them. Thus, the situation is basically unstable, and the only stabilizing force results in exercising the options. If this happens, the cash and carry investor would not earn the two coupons, because the security would be called away from him long before the one-year holding period originally expected. In any case, it can be seen that a variety of forces can result in early exercise of options. Holders of options should be aware of this and evaluate the attractiveness of exercising. ·Writers of options should be aware of the possibility of receiving an exercise notice long before expiration.

OPTIONS ON FUTURES

The highest volume of trading in debt options on the exchanges has been in options on futures contracts. These contracts include options on Treasury bond futures, options on Treasury note futures and options on Eurodollar time deposit rate futures.

Although an option on a futures contract may seem like a complicated security, in fact it is in many ways a simpler instrument to analyze and trade than an option on an actual cash instrument. This is because the impact of the cash flows of the cash security is already taken into account in the price of the futures contract, and hence need not be addressed in the pricing of the option.

When the holder of a call option on a futures contract exercises the option, he is delivered the futures contract at the current market price. Whereas exercise of a call option on an actual cash instrument requires the buyer to pay the full price of the underlying security, exercise of an in-the-money call option on the futures contract requires the option writer to pay the option holder the difference between the current price of the futures contract and the strike price. Essentially, a futures trade takes place at the strike price and then both parties are immediately marked to market. In the case of exercise of a put option on a futures contract, the holder of the option is assigned a short futures position at the current market price and the grantor of the option pays the holder the difference between the strike and the current futures price.

One way to think of the options on bond futures that captures the essence of the contract (though not the technicalities) is to view the futures contract as simply an index of government bond prices. Then the option can be thought of as a cash settlement option, where the seller of the option pays the holder the difference between strike and index value (market price) upon the exercise of an in-the-money option.[14]

The following example comparing an option on a cash bond and an option on the futures contract on that same cash bond will be used to illustrate the similarities between the two types of option contracts:

Option on Actual

Underlying Security:	8 Percent 30-Year Bond
Strike Price:	100
Expiration Date of Option:	Dec 19XX

Option on Futures

Underlying Security:	Futures Contract on 8 Percent 30-Year Bond Delivery Dec 19XX
Strike Price:	100
Expiration Date of Option:	Dec 19XX

Exhibit 28 shows the value of the call option on the futures contract at expiration, that is, the intrinsic value of the option, together with the profit pattern. Since the expiration of the option contract coincides with the delivery date of the futures contract[15] the cash price of the 8 percent, 30-year bond will equal the price of the futures contract on the 8 percent, 30-year bond. Hence, the intrinsic value patterns of the option on the futures and the option on the cash bond are identical. This is an important observation, because, if the buyer of the option is only concerned with the final payoff pattern of the option, he will be indifferent between the option on the futures and the option on the actual security so long as the premiums for the two options are the same. As shown in Exhibit 29, if the price of the option on the actual is greater than the price of the option on the futures, the profit pattern of the options on the futures

---

[14] In the unlikely event of an exercise of an out-of-the-money option, the holder of the option would pay the option writer.

[15] In practice there may be a short time period between the expiration of the options contract and the delivery date of the futures contract.

EXHIBIT 28   Intrinsic Value and Profit Pattern of a Call versus
Futures Price

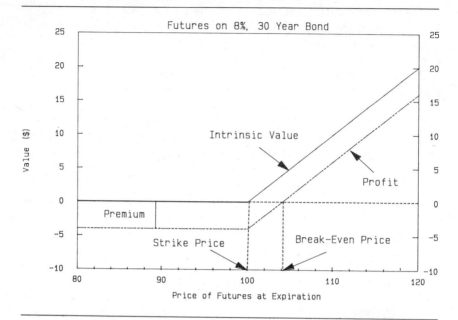

EXHIBIT 29   Dominance of Profit Pattern of Option on Futures over
Option on a Cash Bond

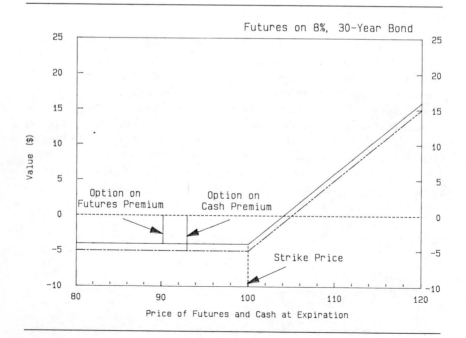

contract will always lie above the profit pattern for the option on the actual bond. This is an unstable situation in which selling of the option on the actual and buying of the option on the futures will realign the prices of the two options contracts.

In practice, there are certain forces which may cause the price of the option on the futures contract to be different from the price of an option on the corresponding cash security. First, the early exercise values for the two kinds of options will be different since the price of the futures is usually different from the price of the cash security to reflect the positive or negative cost of carry. Second, the multiple security delivery mechanism of the Treasury bond and Treasury note futures contracts on the CBOT often drives a wedge between the forward price of the relevant cash security and the price of the futures contract.[16,17]

The Hedge Ratio (Delta)

In most option valuation models developed for equities, the "hedge ratio" that is provided is simply the ratio of the change of the theoretical value of the option to the change in the current price of the stock. Because we have chosen to present theoretical value as a function of yield instead of price, the hedge ratio will be calculated somewhat differently, but it will have the same meaning, namely, the change in the value of the option for a given change in the price of the underlying security.

The price sensitivity of the underlying bond is the slope of the price yield curve at the current yield level, sometimes referred to as the "price value of one basis point." In effect, it is the price change that would occur in response to a one-basis-point change in the yield. The same calculation can be applied to the option to determine its price sensitivity, and the reader can see from Exhibits 23 and 24 that the option's price move per basis point yield change is always lower than or at most, equal to, that of the bond. The hedge ratio (defined consistently with its meaning in the equity market) is the ratio of the price sensitivity of the option to the price sensitivity of the bond.

$$\text{Hedge Ratio} = \frac{\text{Price Value per Basis Point of Option}}{\text{Price Value per Basis Point of Bond}}$$

The hedge ratio can be visualized in Exhibit 30, which enlarges a smaller section of Exhibit 23. The slopes of the two price curves are

---

[16] See Robert W. Kopprasch, Cal Johnson, Armand Tatevossian, *Strategies for the Asset Manager: Hedging and the Creation of Synthetic Assets*, Salomon Brothers Inc, October 1985.

[17] Although the above analysis was cast in terms of the options on bond and note futures contracts, the analysis of the option on the Eurodollar time deposit futures contract is basically the same.

EXHIBIT 30   The Price Responses of Call and Bond to a Change in Yield

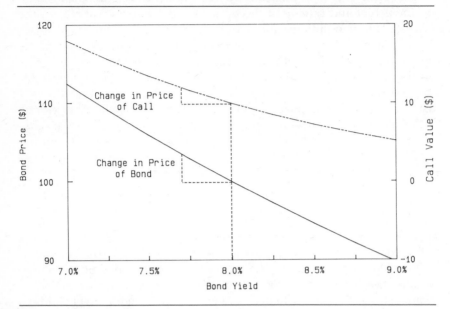

shown and the price response of the bond is greater. This is true for virtually all yield levels. However, when the option is deep in the money, the price responses are nearly identical and the hedge ratio is approximately one, its largest possible value.

While the above definition is consistent with the equity market definition, it is somewhat unfortunate that the term *hedge ratio* has that meaning, because the same term is used in futures hedging to mean something entirely different. As a result, we will introduce some new terminology later in the hedging sections to avoid the ambiguity that might otherwise develop in a discussion of hedging. The term hedge ratio will continue to be used as above.

USING OPTIONS IN HEDGING PROGRAMS

Some General Notes on Hedging

The general interpretation of hedging involves some element of protection against financial loss, and options can be used in several ways to accomplish this. The most obvious approach is the "one-for-one" hedge, where one option is used to hedge a position in the corresponding amount of underlying securities. Thus, a long position in $100,000 par amount in bonds might be hedged by purchasing one put, if each put covered $100,000 in bonds. If held to expiration, catastrophic losses would be avoided by use of the put, but the put buyer would lose the premium. This type of hedging protects against catastrophic loss at a known cost, much as fire insurance protects one's house for a specified time after payment of the premium.

These insurance-type hedges are basically concerned with large price movements in one direction. A long position can be hedged against declines by the purchase of a put, while a short position can be hedged against upside moves by purchase of a call. These hedges are straightforward and we will mention only a few relevant considerations.

When hedging a long-bond position with a put, the relationship of the strike price to the purchase price or current price of the bond is important. If the put is out-of-the-money (e.g., the bond is at par and the put's strike is 95), the initial downward move (5 points) will not be protected by the put. Of course, the out-of-the-money put costs less, so its lower degree of protection is understandable. (Continuing the insurance analogy, the 5 points would represent the "deductible.")

The same considerations apply to a one-for-one hedge of a short position with a long call. If the call is out-of-the-money, any initial upward price move up to the strike price (causing losses to the short position) would not be covered by the call. In-the-money options provide greater protection, but at the expense of higher premiums. (Of course, in-the-money options also provide immediate intrinsic value, which is the reason for the high premiums. Nevertheless, the cash outflow required is higher.)

If a hedged position is defined as one that does not change in value in response to yield changes, then a different approach to hedging is necessary. As shown in Exhibit 30, a given yield change produces different price changes in the option and the underlying security. If we attempt to insulate the portfolio from even small price changes, either up or down, more options are needed than in the one-for-one hedge. This calls for a ratio hedge.[18]

Hedging the Underlying Security

To hedge the underlying security, the investor will need to use more than one option for each underlying bond. For example, referring back to Exhibit 30, suppose that the price value per basis point was .05 for the bond at some yield, and .025 for the option at the same yield. The hedge

---

[18] For a description of the use of futures for this type of hedge, see Robert W. Kopprasch, *An Introduction to Financial Futures on Treasury Securities.*

position that would equate the dollar volatility of the two positions would be calculated as follows:

$$\frac{\text{Theoretical}}{\text{Hedge Position}} = \frac{\text{Volatility}}{\text{Ratio}} = \frac{\begin{array}{c}\text{Price Value per Basis Point of Security} \\ \text{to be Hedged (Bond)}\end{array}}{\begin{array}{c}\text{Price Value per Basis Point of Hedge} \\ \text{Vehicle (Option)}\end{array}}$$

$$.05 \div .025 = 2.0$$

Thus, if $1 million in bonds were to be hedged, options on $2 million would be required. The "Volatility Ratio" is simply the inverse of the hedge ratio.

The next aspect of the problem is to determine which option to use and whether it should be purchased or sold short. First, let us combine Exhibits 23 and 24 into one composite diagram, seen below as Exhibit 31. Put and call values are both read from the right-hand scale and are always positive.

EXHIBIT 31 Put and Call Theoretical Values Relative to Bond Price

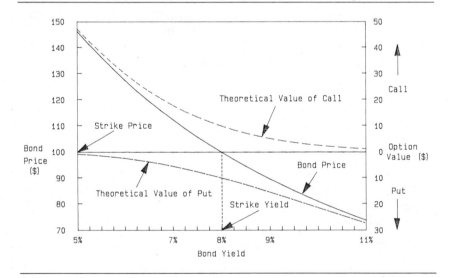

At some point along the horizontal yield axis, the slopes of the option value curves are identical. Assume that the condition takes place at the dotted line, and that the volatility ratio calculation above is for this point. Both the put and the call have an equal (but opposite) price response at this point. If the yield declines 10 basis points, we expect the call to increase in value by about 0.25, and we expect the put to decline by about 0.25. If yields increase, we expect both to change by the same value, but the call will decline by that value and the put will increase by that value. The theoretical hedge position for both puts and calls would be 2.0, though whether to buy or sell 2.0 depends on the nature of the position being hedged (long or short), and on which option is being employed. For example, assume that we wish to hedge a long position in the bond. We have to add to our portfolio a position that will have an approximately equal move that is opposite in direction to that of the bond, and there are two choices in the options arena. First, because calls move in the same direction as the bond, we can sell calls short. Second, because puts move in the opposite direction (increasing in value as the bonds decline), we can buy puts. Each of these tactics has advantages and disadvantages which we will describe.

Selling calls short has the obvious advantage of providing an inflow of funds, while buying puts results in an outflow. If the yield did not change, and we maintained the position to expiration, we would earn the income from selling the calls or lose the premium paid for the puts.

If yields move quickly in either direction, however, the advantage swings to the puts due to "second order" effects. Let us examine what happens if the bond price falls quickly, before our hedge position is changed. The calls that were shorted will also fall, but their rate of decline will become smaller the further the bond price falls, so that the profits on the short sale fail to fully compensate for losses on the long position. On the other hand, if the hedger were long puts, the puts would increase in price, but they increase at an accelerating rate. For example, if the price decline were swift and large, so that the resulting yield was on the right side of Exhibit 31, each put would be advancing in value as much as the bond retreated, and because the hedge position was greater than one, the hedger would probably show an absolute profit. The same type of analysis can be applied to hedging a short position in the underlying security, and similar asymmetries will be exposed. In addition, different margin rules apply, and this affects cash flows as the option prices change.

Uncertainties of the Hedge

In the theoretical discussion above, we have assumed that we could predict *accurately* the price response of the option to changes in the underlying security. It is unlikely that the real world will be so precise. Even if all market participants used the same valuation model (and they won't!), they would all have to input the identical short-term rate and volatility estimate to agree on the theoretical value of the option and its price sensitivity. It is likely that some investors would revise their volatility estimates as prices moved. In any case, the precision assumed above is not likely to be realized in the marketplace, so attempting to calculate volatility ratios (hedge positions) to a very high degree of accuracy is not likely to result in improved hedge effectiveness.

Cross Hedging

The uncertainties mentioned above are even more apparent when "cross hedging," that is, using an option to hedge something other than the underlying security. Nevertheless, because many securities do not have corresponding options, cross hedging is a common practice. When establishing a cross hedge, the position is determined as follows:

$$
\begin{array}{l}
\text{Theoretical} \\
\text{Cross Hedge} \\
\text{Position}
\end{array}
=
\begin{array}{l}
\text{Adjusted} \\
\text{Volatility} \\
\text{Ratio}
\end{array}
=
\dfrac{
\begin{array}{l}
\text{Price Value per Basis Point} \\
\text{of Security to be Hedged}
\end{array}
}{
\begin{array}{l}
\text{Price Value per Basis Point} \\
\text{of Option}
\end{array}
}
\times
\begin{array}{l}
\text{Relative} \\
\text{Yield} \\
\text{Volatility}
\end{array}
$$

The equation above is similar to the direct hedge of the underlying security but has the additional factor of Relative Yield Volatility. For example, if the options were on government bonds, and the bonds to be hedged were corporates, an estimate of relative yield volatility would be needed to determine the cross hedge position. A regression analysis of the yields is one way to approach this problem. Exhibit 32 shows the relation of the yield on a corporate issue versus the yield on the Treasury

---

EXHIBIT 32 Relative Yield Volatility Analysis (weekly data from 11/02/84 to 10/25/85)

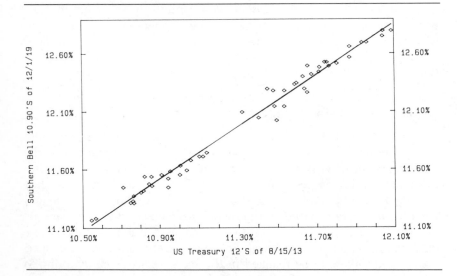

issue underlying the options contract which will be used to hedge the corporate issue. The regression shows that if the yield on the government bond increased 1 basis point, the yield on the corporate issue would be expected to move 1.1 basis point; hence the relative yield volatility would be 1.1, and the number of options used in the hedge would be increased by 10 percent over the unadjusted volatility ratio.

Hedging over Long Horizons

Typically it is not possible to buy or sell exchange-traded options on fixed income securities with more than one year to expiration. However, investors may wish to use options over a considerably longer horizon than one year, and will thus be forced to use a strip of shorter-term options over time to try to match the performance of a longer-term option that is not available.[19] The total cost of rolling options over time is impossible to quantify exactly at the start of such a program. However, it is possible to describe the cost as a function of several variables, including the expected volatility of the underlying security over time and the price path that the underlying security follows. Although the following analysis will be couched in terms of an option buying strategy, the framework is equally applicable to option writing programs.

Perhaps the most obvious source of uncertainty is the level of market expectations of volatility on each option roll date. All else constant, if the market's expectations of volatility of the underlying security increases over time, the cost of the program will rise relative to its cost at a constant volatility, and vice versa if expected volatility falls over the course of the program. It should be remembered that the greater (lesser) cost of the program reflects the increased (decreased) potential benefit from option purchasing.

An equally important determinant of the cost of such a program is the price path of the underlying security, where the points on the path are the prices of the security on the option roll dates. The following example of a rolling strategy will be used: Buy a one-year call option struck at par and, at the expiration of that option, buy another call option struck at par.

After one year has elapsed, the initial option position expires, paying the intrinsic value. The investor must now buy another one-year option struck at par. The out of pocket expense is the difference between the current price of the new one-year option and the intrinsic value of the expiring one-year option. This is illustrated graphically in Exhibit 33, which shows that the investor incurs increasingly lower cost the farther

---

[19] Dynamic hedging would be another way to try to achieve the protection afforded by a long-term option.

EXHIBIT 33   Cost of Rolling One-Year Options over Two-Year Horizon

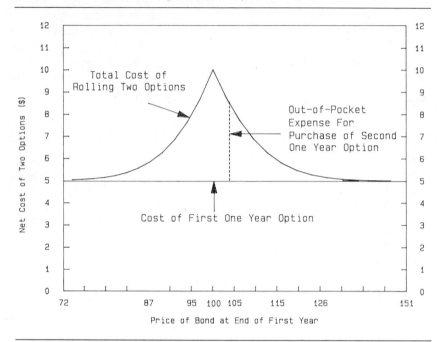

the price of the underlying security is from the strike price at the end of one year. The implication of the above analysis is that the cost of a rolling strategy which is aimed at protecting a terminal asset value depends on the price path of the underlying security. The cost of the program increases when the price path of the underlying security does not stray far from the path which starts at the current price and finishes at the final exercise price.

Intuitively this makes sense. As shown in Exhibit 23, the time premium of an option is greatest when the price of the underlying security is near the strike price of the option. If the time premium is viewed as an insurance premium, then the total cost of insurance over time will be greatest when the price of the underlying security stays close to being at-the-money at each option roll. For a given rolling strategy, a "worst case" cost and "best case" cost can be determined, assuming constant volatility. By making estimates of the variability of the price of the underlying security at option roll dates (which may be different than variance in the statistical sense), it is possible to determine the expected cost and the variability of the cost of more complicated multiperiod option rolling programs.

SUMMARY

The market in fixed income options offers a variety of approaches and alternatives to fixed income investing. We have attempted to provide a background for the analysis of these financial instruments. After carefully studying the details of specific contracts that may be relevant to them, potential investors will find that options offer new opportunities and applications in investing, arbitrage, and hedging. Options can be combined in a variety of ways with cash instruments and financial futures to create synthetic securities which may be attractive in their own right.

GLOSSARY

This glossary is intended to provide brief descriptions of option related terms. Please refer to the Option Clearing Corporation prospectus for precise legal meaning.

American Option: An option that can be exercised any time until it expires. (See European Option)

At-the-Money: When the market price of the underlying security is very close to an option's strike price, the option is "at-the-money."

Black-Scholes: Refers to an option valuation model developed by Fischer Black and Myron Scholes; the model utilizes the neutral hedge concept, and is widely used in the equity options market.

Call Option: The right (but not the obligation) to buy a particular security at a specified price (known as the strike price or exercise price). (See American Option and European Option)

Clearing Corporation: An organization that essentially stands between the long side and short side of the option transaction; the clearing corporation requires performance from the "short" if the option is exercised, and guarantees performance to the long.

Closing Purchase: An option purchase that closes out a short position. (See Opening Sale)

Closing Sale: An option sale that closes out a long position. (See Opening Purchase)

Conversion: A transaction in which an investor (usually a member firm in equities or a bond dealer) buys a put, buys the underlying security, and sells a call; from the viewpoint of the market, a put disappears and is replaced by a call.

Covered: A call writer is considered covered when he owns the security deliverable for a call. A put writer is considered covered when he owns another put with an equal or higher strike price and the same or later expiration.

Deliverable Security: A security that may be delivered when a put or call is exercised; also known as the Underlying Security.

European Option: An option that can be exercised only immediately prior to its expiration. (See American Option)

Exercise Price: See Strike Price.

Hedge Ratio: The ratio of the price change of an option to a change in price of the underlying security (all other factors held constant).

In-the-Money: When the price of the underlying security exceeds the strike price, a call is in the money; a put is in the money when the market price is below the strike price.

Intrinsic Value: The immediate exercise value of an option (but never less than zero).

"Long": Denotes ownership of a security, including options; also refers to the owner of an option.

Naked: An option writer is considered naked when the option's short position is not covered. (See Covered)

Neutral Hedge: A position involving two securities in which small changes in the price of one security are offset by changes in the price of the other security; in the context of option evaluation, the required option position is usually greater than (sometimes equal to) the stock position. (See Hedge Ratio) The neutral or riskless hedge is the basis for many option valuation models (e.g., Black Scholes).

Opening Purchase: An option purchase that initiates a long position. (See Closing Sale)

Opening Sale: An option transaction (short sale) that initiates a short position.

Out-of-the-Money: When the price of the underlying security is below the strike price, a call is out-of-the-money; a put is out-of-the-money when the market price is above the strike price.

Premium: The market price of an option.

Put Option: The right (but not the obligation) to sell a particular security at a specified price (known as the strike price or exercise price). (See American Option and European Option)

Reverse Conversion: A transaction that results in a call being removed from the market with a put taking its place. (See Conversion)

"Short": As a verb, means to engage in an Opening Sale; as a noun, refers to one who has written an option.

Spread: Any of a number of positions that involve more than one option with more than one strike price or more than one expiration month.

Straddle: A combination involving positions in one put and one call; one can be *long* a straddle (long both put and call) or *short* a straddle.

Strike Price: The price at which an exercise transaction takes place; the strike may be adjusted for options that allow delivery of one of a group of securities, and is sometimes quoted in terms of a strike yield. Also known as the Exercise Price.

Underlying Security: A security that can be delivered when a put or call is exercised.

Volatility Ratio: The number of options (per unit of underlying security) needed to hedge small price changes in the underlying security; the reciprocal of the Hedge Ratio.

Writer: An investor who is short an option contract; also known as the option Seller.

APPENDIX
Terms of Exchange Traded Options Contracts on Fixed Income Securities

	Option on Treasury Bond Future	Option on Treasury Note Future	Option on Eurodollar Future	Option on Treasury Bond	Option on 10-Year Treasury Note	Option on Five-Year Treasury Note	Option on 13-Week Treasury Bills
Contract size	$100,000 face value U.S. T-Bonds	$100,000 face U.S. T-Notes	$1,000,000 face value three-month time deposit	$100,000 face on specific Treasury bond	$100,000 face on specific 10-year Treasury note	$100,000 face on specific five-year Treasury note	$1,000,000 face on current 13-week Treasury bill
Expiration date	Saturday following the first Friday preceding by at least five business days, the first notice day of the bond, which is two business days prior to first day of the month.	Saturday following the first Friday preceding by at least five business days, the first notice day of the bond, which is two business days prior to the first day of the month.	6 P.M. EST on second London business day before third Wednesday. Same as underlying contract.	Saturday following third Friday of month.	Saturday following third Friday of month.	Saturday following third Friday of month.	Saturday following third Friday of month.
Settlement date on exercise	Position in underlying future effective the following business day.	Position in underlying future effective the following business day.	Position in underlying future effective the following business day.	Two business days after exercise.	Two business days after exercise.	Two business days after exercise.	Two business days after exercise.

Trading unit	1/64 pt.	1/64 pt.	1 b.p.	1/32 pt.	1/32 pt.	1/32 pt.	1 b.p.
Value of trading unit	$15.625	$15.625	$25	$31.25	$31.25	$31.25	$25
Exchange	CBOT	CBOT	IMM (CME)	CBOE	AMEX	CBOE	AMEX
Trading hours	9:00 A.M.–3:00 P.M. (EST)	9:00 A.M.–3:00 P.M. (EST)	8:30 A.M.–3:00 P.M. (EST)	9:00 A.M.–3:00 P.M. (EST)	9:00 A.M.–3:00 P.M. (EST)	9:00 A.M.–3:00 P.M. (EST)	9:00 A.M.–3:00 P.M. (EST)
Trading cycle	Mar, Jun, Sep, Dec, three most current months.	Mar, Jun, Sep, Dec, three most current months.	Mar, Jun, Sep, Dec, three most current months.	Mar, Jun, Sep, Dec, three most current months.	May, Aug, Nov, Feb, three most current months.	One and two month expirations plus two further out on Mar, Jun, Sep, Dec cycle.	Mar, Jun, Sep, Dec, three most current months.
Margin on naked short positions	Premium marked to market plus current futures margin less 1/2 amount out-of-the-money.	Premium marked to market plus current futures margin less 1/2 amount out-of-the-money.	Premium marked to market plus current futures margin less 1/2 amount out-of-the-money.	$3,500 plus premium less out-of-the-money amount.	$3,500 plus premium less out-of-the-money amount.	$3,500 plus premium less out-of-the-money amount.	$3,500 plus premium less out-of-the-money amount.
Minimum	$600	$600	$400	$500 plus premium	$500 plus premium	$500 plus premium	$500 plus premium

CBOT = Chicago Board of Trade
IMM (CME) = International Monetary Market, Chicago Mercantile Exchange
CBOE = Chicago Board Options Exchange
AMEX = American Stock Exchange

41

The Valuation and Exposure Management of Bonds with Imbedded Options*

Richard Bookstaber, Ph.D.
Vice President
Morgan Stanley & Company

INTRODUCTION

Many bonds have option-like features. Put bonds, bonds with bond warrants, and convertible bonds all include attached options to enhance their value. The call feature of corporate and Treasury bonds, and the prepayment option in mortgage-backed securities, represent a short call option position to the investor. Corporate debentures and other bonds with default risk are implicitly option-like instruments, having a payoff that is equal to a promised stream of payments or, if such payments are not made, a payoff that is equal to some claim on the underlying assets of the firm.[1]

Many other financial instruments share the characteristics of bonds with implicit options. In the insurance industry, Guaranteed Investment

---

* For complete citations, see **References** Section at the end of the chapter.

[1] The treatment of corporate debentures as bonds with option positions is found in Merton (1974), Galai and Masulis (1976), in Chapter 5 of Bookstaber (1981a), and in Chapter 7 of Cox and Rubinstein (1985). Such a bond can be viewed as a pure interest-rate vehicle combined with a short put option on the assets of the firm. The put option gives the issuer of the bond the right to put the assets of the firm to the bondholder in lieu of the promised payment. For a high-quality credit, this option is not likely to be exercised, since the value of the firm is far above the payments due the bondholders. However, understanding this option feature leads to a number of important insights for pricing and controlling the risk of high-yield bonds. See, for example, Bookstaber and Jacob (1986a, 1986b).

Contracts (GICs) and Single Premium Deferred Annuities (SPDAs) often have early redemption features which, like a put option, allow the holder to cash in the policy prematurely at par. In the thrift industry, certificates of deposit often have a similar put option attached through an early redemption feature. An analysis of the option features of fixed income securities can be applied to these financial liabilities as well.

Bonds with imbedded options can be viewed as a portfolio consisting of a pure bullet bond and an option. The techniques of fixed income analysis must be augmented by the use of option theory to effectively price and measure the exposure of these bonds.

For example, the conventional application of duration, the most popular measure of interest-rate sensitivity, is of limited value for bonds with implicit option positions. Since the price of an option does not move linearly with changes in the underlying bond's value, the convexity of any duration measure can become a severe problem. Also, a number of factors that are not important in determining bond pricing and interest-rate sensitivity, such as interest-rate volatility and the shape of the yield curve, are important for the valuation of the option.

The inability of most investors to successfully grapple with the pricing and exposure implications of these options leads to profit opportunities for those investors who can. The increased complexity that options add to the exposure measurement of fixed income instruments adds to their profit potential as well. Many investors are hesitant to take positions in bonds that are close to call or in mortgage-backed securities trading at a premium, since the impact of the option exercise is difficult to assess. Thus there is relatively greater demand for discount callable bonds and for deep-discount mortgage-backed securities, where the call feature has less impact. The simple economics of supply and demand lead the bonds trading near or above par to trade at more attractive yields.

Other bonds with option features, such as put bonds, are often mispriced simply because investors in the fixed income market are not familiar with option pricing and trading methods. Most fixed income investors view the option implicit in put bonds as an attractive added feature, but do not understand the trading methods for extracting the full value of the option.[2]

The potential for mispricing can be illustrated by considering the conventions used in pricing callable bonds. Callable bonds conventionally are priced either to call or to maturity, depending on how imminent the call is thought to be. It is clear, however, that both prices are incorrect, and in fact contain the upper and lower bounds on possible imbed-

---

[2] The persistent mispricing of put bonds and bonds with detachable bond warrants is discussed in detail in Bookstaber, Haney, and Norris (1984).

ded option prices. A callable bond will never be worth as much as a similar noncallable bond, since there is always the possibility of interest rates dropping to the point that the call will be exercised.[3] Similarly, a callable bond will never have a value as low as it would appear when it is priced to call, since until it is actually called, there is still some chance that rates will increase to make the exercise uneconomic.[4] Given the conventions in callable bond pricing, then, it is not surprising that many callable bonds will be either underpriced in the market, because they are priced to call, or overpriced, because they are priced to maturity.

The knowledge gap in the market, both in exposure management and option pricing, has opened up profit opportunities for those who can deal with these imbedded options. The purpose of this chapter is to lay out the pricing and exposure management issues, and point out the methods for bridging this gap.

PRICING

A bond with an imbedded option can be considered as a portfolio of two securities: a bullet bond without any option feature, and an option. To price these bonds, we first price the value of the underlying bond using the usual discounted cash-flow methods of bond pricing, and price the value of the option using option pricing theory. The net value of the bond will be the sum of the value of these two assets for a long option position, such as a put bond, or the value of the bullet less the value of the option for short option positions, such as callable bonds. The principle of value additivity leads the value of the sum of a set of assets to equal the sum of their individual values.

Yield Measurement for Bonds with Options: Adjusted Yield

Without adjustments, the yield of a bond with an attached option is not directly comparable to that of a pure bullet bond. We would clearly expect the yield on a callable bond to be higher than on a noncallable bond, since the call is to the detriment of the bondholder. Similarly, a bond with an attached warrant or a put bond would be expected to have a lower yield than a pure bullet bond, since the long option position

---

[3] The inaccuracies in pricing that arise from pricing a callable bond to maturity, thereby totally ignoring the negative impact of the call feature, are illustrated by considering the telephone issues, which often have 20 or more years of callability. No matter what the current interest-rate environment, it is hard to dismiss the value of an option with such a long time remaining to expiration.

[4] Furthermore, there may be internal issues in the firm which obviate the desirability to call an issue. For example, other issues with a higher coupon rate may be outstanding and may have a more pressing need to be called.

gives additional payoff potential. To compare the yield of these various bonds, an adjustment must first be made to net out these option features. The value additivity principle provides a natural means of comparing bonds with disparate option features.

Taking the price of a bond with an option position, we appeal to the additivity principle to separate out the option component by subtracting from the bond price the value of the option (in the case of a long option position), or adding back in the option component (in the case of a short option position).[5] The result will be the price of the remaining bullet bond after the attached option has been netted out at the theoretically fair price. The yield of the resulting bullet is then computed in the usual method. The result is called the *adjusted yield*.

In Table 1, suppose we want to compute the adjusted yield on a callable bond with 20 years to maturity and a 10 percent coupon. The

---

TABLE 1   Adjusted Yield

Assumptions

> 20-year, 10 percent coupon bond, callable after five years at 110.
> Bond is priced at par to yield 10 percent.
> Option premium is priced at $1.75.

Calculation of Adjusted Yield

Price of callable bond	$100.00
+ Price of call option	1.75
Price of bullet bond	101.75

Adjusted Yield = 9.80%

---

bond is currently priced at par. First we determine the price of the short call position. The bond is callable at 110, and has five years of call protection. Suppose we price this call option, using an option pricing model, and find it to be worth $1.75. Since the bondholder is short this call option, that implies the value of the bullet is par value plus $1.75, or $101.75. The call-adjusted yield on this bond is then equal to the yield on a 10 percent coupon, 20-year noncallable bond priced at $101.75, which is 9.80 percent.

---

[5] Getting the option price requires the use of an option pricing model. Obviously, this procedure will only be as accurate as the option model that is used in the pricing. Furthermore, the value additivity principle will not be applicable in more complex bond structures, where there are a number of options that interact. For example, the analysis is less straightforward when a callable bond also contains sinking fund provisions, or when a convertible bond is also callable.

The same analysis would be done to compute the adjusted yield on a put bond or a bond with a bond warrant. The only difference would be that the value of the option would be subtracted out, rather than being added in.

The Put/Call Parity Relationship for Bonds with Options

The pricing of the option component will obviously depend on the essential characteristics of the option position: whether the option is a put or a call, and whether the option position is long or short. In classifying option positions, the distinction between long and short positions is more important than the distinction between put and call options. Using the put/call parity relationship, it is easy to transform a position in a put into a call position with identical payoff characteristics. Thus we can look at a put bond, a bond with an attached put option, in the same way we look at a bond with an attached call warrant.

To see this, consider two bonds, one with a put option attached, the other with a call option attached. The first bond is a 10-year bullet, and the put option attached to it gives the holder the right to put the bond back to the issuer at par five years before the maturity date. The second bond is a bond with five years to maturity. It has the same par value and the same coupon payment schedule as the first bond. The call option attached to this bond has five years to expiration as well. It gives the holder the right, at its time of expiration in five years, to call a bond with five years of maturity and with coupon payments equal to the other two bonds. Both of these options are assumed to be European options, which means they can only be exercised at the time of expiration in five years.

Both bond-option packages will give the same coupon flow until year five, since they are assumed to have the same coupon rates, and since the options offer no opportunities to alter the cash flows before that time. What happens at year five depends on the bond price that exists at that time.

Suppose in five years bond yields have dropped, leading the bond prices to rise above par. The 10-year bond—which now has five years remaining to maturity—will not be put back to the issuer at par, since it is worth more than par. The put option will accordingly be left to expire unexercised, and the bondholder will end up with the bullet bond maturing in year 10. The bondholder with the call option package will see his five-year maturity bond mature, and, since the bond underlying his call option is priced above par, will take the proceeds and exercise the call option to call a five-year maturity bond at par. The net result is that if yields drops, both bondholders will have identical bullet bonds which mature in year 10.

Suppose now that rather than yields dropping at year five, they increase, leading the bond prices to drop below par. The holder of the 10-year bond will now exercise the put option to put the bond back to the issuer, since the resulting payoff of par will be greater than the value from continuing to hold the bond. The holder of the five-year bond will let the call option expire unexercised, since it would be uneconomic to exercise the right to pay par for a bond that is priced below par in the marketplace. The net result in the case of rising yields will also be identical for both the put and the call holder. They will both end up with par at year five. The payoffs of these two bond packages is summarized in Table 2.

TABLE 2 Put/Call Parity

Current Position
A. Call on a 10-year bond with five years to expiration
   Five-year bond
B. Put on a 10-year bond with five years to expiration
   10-year bond

Position in Five Years

	Case 1 Five-Year Bond Priced below Par	Case 2 Five-Year Bond Priced above Par
A.	Let call expire Bond matures	A. Exercise call Pay for five-year bond with matured bond
B.	Exercise Put Deliver bond	B. Let Put Expire Retain five-year bond
Net Result	Receive par value	Receive five-year Bond at par

Since the 10-year, bond-put option package gives the same payoff in all cases as the five-year, bond-call option package, the two packages must be priced identically today. Otherwise there would be arbitrage opportunities available. The investor would only need to buy the cheaper and sell the more expensive of the two packages to lock in a riskless profit.[6]

---

[6] The general formulation of the put/call parity relationship is:

$$B + P = C + E/(1 + r),$$

where B is the current price of the underlying asset (in this case a bullet bond), P is the current value of a put option with exercise price E, and C is the price of a call option on B with the same exercise price and time to expiration. The discount factor $(1 + r)$ is for a time period equal to the time to expiration of the option. As this expression indicates, for a bond currently selling at par, a call and put option with an exercise price E equal to par must have the same value. Further discussion of put/call parity for coupon-paying bonds is presented in Goodman (1985).

The Payoff Profile of Bonds with Option Positions

We will illustrate the pricing of bonds with option positions using two examples, one with a short option position, callable bonds, and the second with a long option position, put bonds.

Example 1: Callable bonds. The buyer of a callable bond is implicitly receiving a premium for the call option he has written to the issuer. This premium is paid out in the form of higher coupon payments, and therefore higher yield for the bond. As with any option writer, the holder of the callable bond will be best off if the option expires worthless. However, since the bondholder is a covered call writer, he will lose from any decline in bond price as well. The ideal world, therefore, is for the bond price to stay exactly at the exercise price of the option. This will lead the option value to decay to zero, allowing the bondholder to keep all of the premium, while at the same time preserving the greatest possible value for the underlying bond consistent with the zero value for the option. If the bond price moves above the exercise price, the bondholder will have to deliver the bond to the issuer, and will need to reinvest the proceeds in a lower interest-rate environment. If the bond price moves down, the option will not be exercised, but the bond itself will generate a loss.

The payoff profile for a callable bond is shown in Exhibit 1. The underlying bond has 10 years to maturity, and a coupon rate of 10 percent. There are five years to call at the time of issue. The exhibit shows the payoff as a function of bond yields when the option has one year to call, (top line), three years to call (middle line), and five years to call (bottom line). The closer the option comes to expiration, the greater the payoff in the event of no interest-rate changes. The curvature of the payoff profile also increases. The curvature tends to counteract the increasing peak of the profile, so that the break-even point is nearly the same for all three curves. However, a sizable change in interest rates will lead to a far greater potential loss as the time to call approaches.

In option strategy analysis, this type of payoff is called a "negative gamma" payoff, it has a payoff that will be adversely affected by volatile swings in the price of the underlying bond.[7] The trade-off in a gamma strategy is between the time decay of the option premium and the volatility of prices. In the case of a negative gamma strategy, the time decay

---

[7] The gamma of an option position is the second derivative of the option position value with respect to the underlying security price. That is, it is the change in the position delta with a change in the underlying security price. The gamma is thus a measure of the curvature of the payoff profile. It is a useful measure for delta neutral strategies, where the option position is unaffected by small changes in the value of the underlying security, i.e. where the position delta is zero.

EXHIBIT 1 Callable Bond Payoff versus Bond without Option

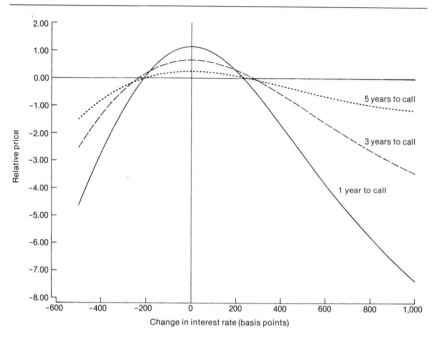

Change in interest rate (basis points)

is favorable. Since the option loses value over time, the option writer finds the payoff profile moves upward over time. On the other hand, volatility is undesirable. This payoff will be preferred by an investor who believes bond prices will be stable.

Example 2: Put bonds. The put bond sensitivity to interest-rate changes is opposite that of the callable bond. This would be expected, since, using put/call parity, a put bond can be restructured as a bond with a long call position, while a callable bond is obviously a bond with a short call position. If yields drop by the time the option expires, then the option will not be exercised. The bondholder will then have a longer maturity bond, which, in the lower yield environment, will be priced above par. If yields increase, the bond can be put at par, and the proceeds reinvested at the higher prevailing interest rate. If yields remain unchanged, then the option gives no benefit over holding a bullet, and the cost of the option premium will lead to a net lower yield for the put bond. The put bond holder has the option to trade off between short- and long-term rates, depending on which is more desirable.

EXHIBIT 2 Put Bond Payoff versus Bond without Option

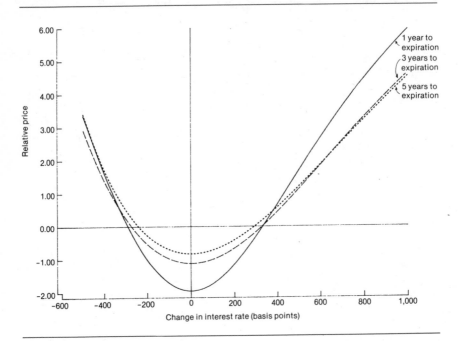

The payoff profile for a put bond is shown in Exhibit 2. This bond is a 15-year bond with a European put with 10 years to expiration. The bond has a 10 percent coupon rate.[8]

The payoff of this bond is as would be expected. The price is less than that of a comparable bullet if rates do not change. The price differential widens as the time to maturity of the bond and the time to maturity of the option approaches. The top line shows the option with five years remaining to expiration, the middle line three years, and the bottom line one year to expiration. The time decay increases at an increasing rate as expiration approaches, so the drop in value is more significant as we move from five to three and then to one year to expiration.

---

[8] The put bonds issued domestically generally have European-style puts, meaning these puts can only be exercised at the time of expiration. In contrast, the bonds with detachable bond warrants issued in Europe are American-style, in that they can be exercised any time before or at the time of expiration. This feature leads the maturity of the issue received upon exercise of the warrant to be a function of the time of exercise of the option. For example, if a seven-year warrant on a seven-year bond is exercised one year after issue, the holder will receive a bond with six years remaining to maturity. If it is exercised after three years, the holder will receive a bond with four years remaining to maturity.

The curvature of the payoff profile also increases as expiration approaches. As a result, the break-even point does not move appreciably as time to expiration approaches even though the gap in prices is increasing. A 250 basis point change in yield is necessary to break even.

This payoff profile is termed a *positive gamma* payoff in the option strategy literature. It benefits from increases in volatility, but is hurt by time decay in the option premium. Since the investor is long option premium, the drop in value of the option over time diminishes the value of his position. This is indicated by the downward movement in the payoff profile. If the underlying bond is more volatile than was assumed in determining the initial price of the option, profits from the volatility will more than compensate for this decay.

Taking Advantage of Mispricing

The objective in active bond management is to trade on yield differentials. Bonds with differentially higher yields are purchased, and those with differentially lower yields are sold. The returns from this strategy are immediately evident in the higher cash flow generated by the portfolio.

Bonds with options can be traded in the same way, using the adjusted yield to generate the trading signals. The difference from the usual active bond trading strategy is how the additional yield is realized in the portfolio. Higher adjusted yield does not immediately translate into higher cash flow. Adjusted yield may measure the mispricing of the option as well as of the bullet bond. If the option on a callable bond is overvalued, the adjusted yield will be higher. If the option on a put bond is overvalued, the adjusted yield will be lower. If the high adjusted yield is the result of the option being mispriced, profits from the mispricing rely on exploiting that option.

There are three ways to exploit the mispricing of a bond with an option.

First, as is done with equities and other misvalued securities, the bond can be purchased for sale once the market becomes aware of its value and corrects the price. Our empirical work has shown that, for many bonds, mispricing will correct over time. But for some bonds with active option features, the poor understanding of the market may lead to continued misvaluation of the option. The mispricing will not then be captured through a recovery in the price.[9]

Second, as with any option, it is possible to create an arbitrage hedge to extract the profit. The arbitrage profit opportunity arises because an option can be replicated synthetically through a dynamic hedg-

---

[9] The persistent undervaluation of put bonds is an example of this.

ing strategy in the underlying security.[10] If the price of the option in the market is not the same as the cost of creating the option synthetically, then an arbitrage can be executed by buying the cheaper and selling the higher priced of the market and the synthetic option. Since the payoff of the two options will be the same, the position, and hence the profit from the transaction, is riskless.

While this methodology is used extensively in trading listed options, there are several impediments to using it with options on bonds. First, most options on bonds are not detachable. Therefore, to execute the strategy, the investor must also carry around the bond as extra baggage. Buying a million dollars of mispriced options may require also holding one hundred million dollars of bonds. If the options are mispriced by 10 percent, capturing the mispricing amounts to only $1/10$ of 1 percent return on the total investment.

A second problem with the execution of a dynamic arbitrage strategy is the cost of trading in and out of the underlying bond. The dynamic trading strategy, as the name suggests, requires periodic adjustments in the position of the underlying security. Given the bid-asked spreads for many bonds, such adjustments could be costly. If the mispricing of the bond is expected to correct quickly, and the hedge only needs to be executed over a short time period, these problems are less important. Then the hedge can be used to lock in the mispricing against unforeseen changes in interest rates.

A third method is to play off the volatility of the interest-rate market, a method called a gamma strategy. As the callable bond and put bond examples show, the bond position includes an implicit bet on the range of movement of interest rates. For a callable bond, the bet is that rates will be stable, while for the long option position of the put bond the bet is that interest rates will be more volatile. Just as a bullet bond position can be used to profit from beliefs in the direction component of interest rates, so the option feature allows the investor to take positions and profit off of the nondirectional or volatility-related interest-rate movements.

The price of the option will dictate the attractiveness of the gamma strategy. For example, the callable bond strategy shown in Exhibit 1 will look more attractive the cheaper the option is, since the payoff will then move upward and be profitable for a wider range of interest rates. If a bond is mispriced, this implicitly means that the trade-off between time decay and volatility, and the expected return from the gamma strategy, is extraordinarily favorable.

---

[10] The dynamic strategy as the basis for option pricing and for extracting profits from mispriced options is discussed in Bookstaber (1981, 1985) and in Cox and Rubinstein (1985).

EXPOSURE MANAGEMENT

It is conventional to relate the interest-rate sensitivity of a fixed income security to the zero coupon bond with the same interest-rate sensitivity. This relationship is expressed as the security's *duration*. The duration of a bond measures interest-rate sensitivity in units of years. A duration of five years means the bond has the same interest-rate sensitivity as a zero coupon bond with five years to maturity. Since the price of a zero coupon bond is a convex function of time to maturity, its derivative with respect to interest rates will be an increasing function of time to maturity. A larger duration will therefore imply a greater price sensitivity to interest rates. The interest sensitivity of a bond can be related to its duration through the simple expression:[11]

$$D_B = -\frac{dP_B}{d(1 + r)} \frac{(1 + r)}{P_B},\tag{1}$$

where D_B is the duration of the bond. Since duration is defined as the maturity of the zero coupon bond with interest-rate sensitivity equivalent to that of the bond under analysis, this relationship is definitional.

A coupon-paying bond can be viewed as a portfolio of zero coupon bonds. Since the duration of each of these zero coupon bonds is immediately known, the duration of a coupon-paying bond can be easily determined as the sum of the durations of each of the zero coupon bonds in the replicating portfolio, each weighted by its share of the market price of the coupon-paying bond. That is,

$$D_B = \sum_t w_t \times t,\tag{2}$$

where w_t is the proportion of the market price of the coupon-paying bond attributed to the zero coupon bond maturing at date t.[12] This expression makes use of the additivity property of duration: the duration of a sum of cash flows is equal to the sum of the individual cash-flow's durations.

Changing Interest-Rate Sensitivity and the Convexity of Duration

The duration of a zero-coupon bond of given maturity is the maturity of that zero, and is therefore constant. The duration of other fixed income

---

[11] This expression shows duration to be the interest elasticity of the bond price.

[12] This equation assumes yield curves are flat and shift in a parallel fashion. Such an assumption is inconsistent with basic arbitrage condition for yield-curve generation, but is nonetheless a common assumption used in the professional finance literature. Other duration formulas have been developed based on more realistic yield curve assumptions. See, for example, Bierwag, Kaufman, and Toevs (1983).

securities will vary with changes in interest rates, and will also vary as the time to maturity of the security approaches. This can be seen from Equation (2) by recognizing that the weights are functions of both the interest-rate level and time, and that the replicating portfolio itself will change as coupon payments are made. The mathematical term for the change in interest-rate sensitivity manifest through the change in duration, the second derivative of P_B with respect to r, is the *convexity* of the bond.

While the convexity of zero coupon bonds is zero, the convexity of other bonds is not. This means that duration is only a linear approximation of their interest-rate sensitivity. In graphic terms, it only reflects the tangent line at a given interest rate and time to maturity of the price of the bond plotted as function of interest rates.

The convexity of duration places obvious limitations on its descriptive power. Despite the shortcomings that arise from duration being a linear approximation of interest-rate sensitivity, it still provides a highly intuitive and valuable tool for exposure measurement and asset liability management. With bonds with option positions, however, the problems with convexity loom larger, and the value and intuitive appeal of duration weaken.

Options are linked to interest rates through the underlying asset. The option price is a function of the price of the underlying instrument, which in turn is a function of interest rates. The relationship of an option to the underlying bond is expressed by the option's *delta*.[13] A delta of .5 means that a one point change in the price of the underlying bond will lead to a one-half-point change in the price of the option. The delta of a call option is positive, bounded by zero and one. The delta of a put option is negative, and is bounded by negative one and zero.[14] The further an option is out-of-the-money, the closer the delta is to zero. As an option moves far into-the-money, the option tends to move one-for-one with the underlying bond, and the delta approaches one for a call option, and minus one for a put option.[15]

---

[13] The delta is nothing more than the partial derivative of the option price with respect to the underlying bond price:

$$\Delta = \partial C / \partial P_B.$$

[14] Since a put option pays off more the further the underlying asset drops below the exercise price, its price moves in the direction opposite that of the underlying asset. While the delta of options are bounded by zero and one in absolute value terms, the absolute value of their percentage price changes will be bounded below by one. Since options are levered securities, their price will always change in percentage terms by more than the underlying asset. The percentage change in an option with a change in the underlying security can be measured by its price elasticity, $(dC/dP_B)(P_B/C)$. This measure of the option's leverage is also called the option's lambda.

[15] A call option is out-of-the-money when the price of the underlying asset is less than the exercise price, and is in-the-money when the price of the underlying asset is greater

Options are also related to interest rates through the cost-of-carry of the option position. Options provide a levered position in the underlying asset; the cost of the option is far below the value of the claim the option gives. The option holder gets the right to claim the asset from the option writer without needing to hold the asset physically. The option premium will compensate the option writer for the carrying cost of holding the asset for possible delivery through the option premium. Just as with futures contracts, the option price will include an implied cost-of-carry. The option premium will be greater the higher the carrying cost, and therefore the higher the interest rate. The interest-rate sensitivity of an option, then, expressed in terms of duration, includes two components—one for the effect of interest rates through the underlying asset, and one for the effect of interest rates on carrying costs:[16]

$$dC/dr = (\partial C/\partial P_B \times \partial P_B/\partial r) + \partial C/\partial r$$
$$= (\Delta \times -[D_B/(1 + r)]P_B) + \partial C/\partial r. \tag{3}$$

The additional link of the delta between the interest-rate sensitivity of the option and the duration of the underlying bond increases the potential range of movement in the option price for changes in the interest rate, and therefore increases the potential slippage in the application of duration as a measure of the interest-rate sensitivity. Since the option is a levered security, the change in the bond price with a change in interest rates will be magnified in percentage terms in its impact on the option price.[17]

Since the option price is itself a convex function of the underlying bond price, the problems that convexity brings to the applicability of duration will likewise be magnified. The increased convexity of duration for options is intuitively apparent when it is realized that options will generally be more dissimilar to a zero coupon bond than will the bonds underlying the options.

---

than the exercise price. A put option is out-of-the-money when the price of the underlying asset is greater than the exercise price, and is in-the-money when the price of the underlying asset is less than the exercise price. That is, an option is out-of-the-money when it has no intrinsic value, and is in-the-money when it has intrinsic value.

[16] The total derivative of the option price with respect to interest rates must include the impact of changing interest rates on the carrying cost of the option and on the present value of the terminal payment, as reflected in the discounting of the exercise price. The hedge ratio is conventionally expressed as the partial derivative of the option price with respect to the bond price. While the bond price will itself be determined by interest rates, this derivative does not take the impact of carrying cost changes into account.

[17] The leverage leads options to have unusually high values for duration. Durations on the order of 100 years are not uncommon. In the limit, options that are further out-of-the-money, and therefore that have greater leverage, resemble a forward contract, which has infinite duration. The possibility of very large, or even infinite, duration is merely an artifact of the way the duration measure is constructed. Since the duration divides the derivative of price with respect to interest rate by the price, a zero price will lead to an undefined duration. This, however, does not imply undefined interest-rate sensitivity.

The intuitive relationship between a coupon-paying bond and a zero coupon bond is strained when applied to options. An option cannot be so straightforwardly expressed as a portfolio of zeros; the option delta must be used as an intermediate input. While any instrument can be equated to the interest-rate sensitivity of a particular zero at any given point of time, if the relationship is unstable, it loses its explanatory value. For an option, the zero of equivalent interest-rate sensitivity is changing both due to the usual forces of convexity that relate to the underlying bond, and further due to the changes in the delta of the option.

The duration of the option can be seen by rewriting Equation (3):

$$D_C = (D_B \times \Delta \times P_B/C) - [\partial C/\partial r](1 + r)/C$$
$$= (D_B \times \lambda) - \rho, \tag{4}$$

where λ a measure of the leverage of the option, is the elasticity of the option price with respect to the underlying bond price, $\lambda = (dC/dP_B)(P_B/C)$, and ρ is the elasticity of the option price with respect to interest-rate changes, $\rho = [\partial C/\partial r](1 + r)/C$.

Exhibit 3 illustrates the sequence of effects that leads to the option's duration. The top panel shows the duration of the underlying bond. The second panel shows the delta of the option as a function of the various interest rates, and the third shows the ratio of the price of the underlying bond to the price of the option. As is shown by Equation (4), it is the product of these three that leads to the duration of the option, depicted in the last panel of the exhibit. The second term and the third term both contribute to the increased convexity of the options duration. It is the leverage of the option that leads to its high duration. Since lambda is always greater than one, the option will always have higher duration than the underlying bond. The leverage of an option, and therefore the duration of an option, increases as the option drops out-of-the-money.

Example 1: Callable bonds. The additivity of the duration measure allows us to express the duration of the callable bond as the sum of the duration of its parts. The callable bond will have a duration equal to the duration of the underlying bullet bond, D_B, less the duration of the short call position, D_C:

$$D = \alpha D_B - (1 - \alpha)D_C, \tag{5}$$

where α is the proportion of the callable bond value made up by the bullet, $\alpha = P_B/(P_B + C)$. Using Equation (4) for the duration of the call option, this can be rewritten as the simple expression

$$D = (\alpha - (1 - \alpha)\lambda)D_B + (1 - \alpha)\rho. \tag{6}$$

The duration of a callable bond will be bracketed by the duration of a bond with a time to maturity equal to the time to call, and a bond with a

EXHIBIT 3 The Components of Option Duration

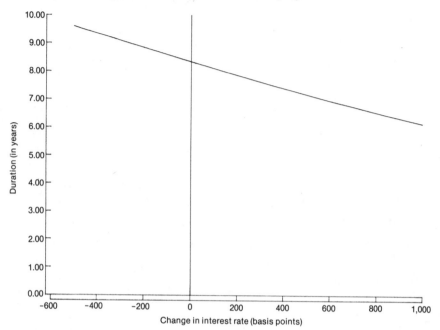

A. The Duration of the Underlying Bond

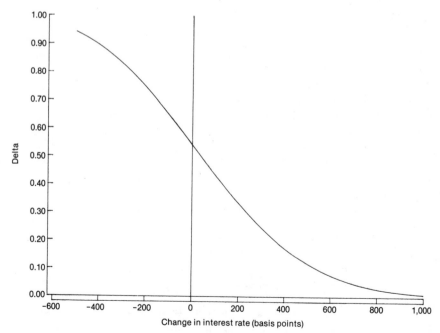

B. The Option Delta

EXHIBIT 3 *(concluded)*

C. Bond Price Divided by Option Price

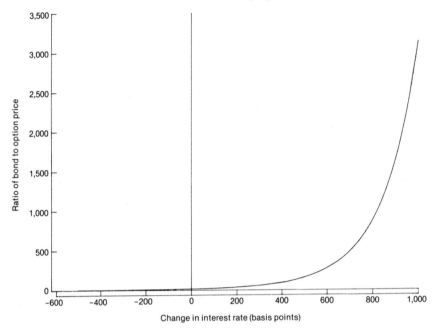

D. Duration of Option

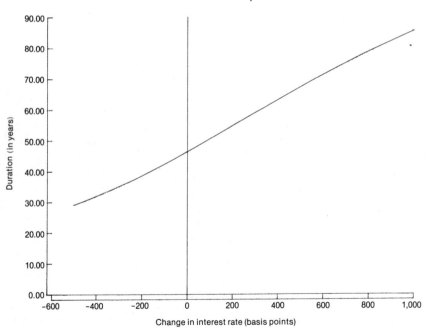

time to maturity equal to that of the bond itself. When the option is far out-of-the-money, the leverage of the option, λ, will be large, and the duration of the option will be as well. However, the larger duration of the option will be more than countered by its reduced weight in the duration calculation, as determined by $(1 - \alpha)$. When the bond is out-of-the-money, the duration of the bond will therefore move closer to that of the underlying bond. As the bond moves toward a premium, the duration will move closer to that of a bond with a time to maturity equal to the time to call. The time to call will have an impact on the sensitivity of the duration to the call feature. Obviously, the more time there is remaining to the call date, the smaller the effect the call provision will have.

Exhibit 4 illustrates the duration features of a callable bond. The underlying bond is a bond with 10 years to maturity, and a coupon rate

EXHIBIT 4 Duration of a Callable Bond

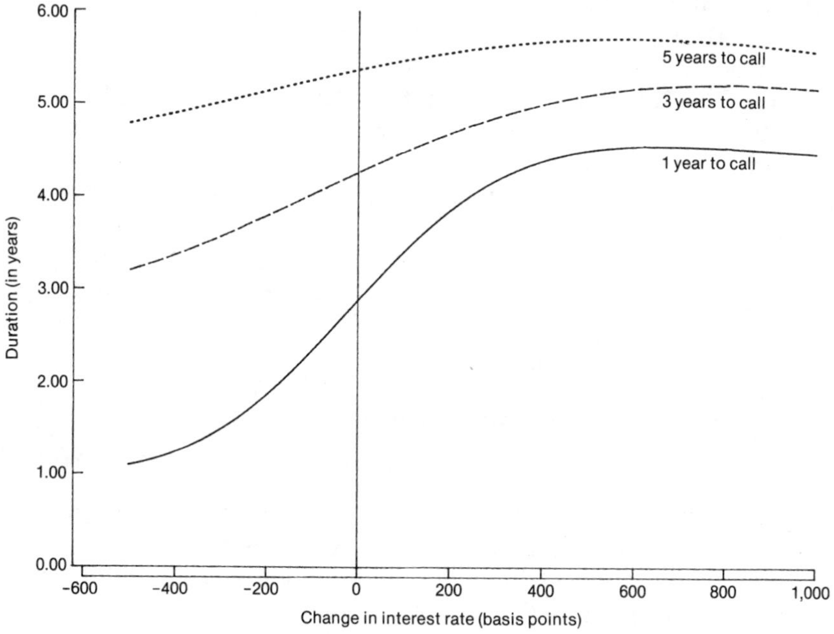

of 10 percent. The bond initially has five years of call protection. For simplicity, we assume the bond can then be called at par, and that the call option is European. Exhibit 4 shows the duration of this bond with 10 years remaining to maturity, and five years to call; with eight years remaining to maturity, and three years to call; and with six years remaining to maturity and one year to call. The base interest rate is 10 percent. An increase in interest rates of 400 basis points brings the option far enough out-of-the-money that the duration of the bond comes very close to that of the underlying bullet. A drop in interest rates pulls the duration down, with the effect being most dramatic for the case of only one year remaining to call. An interest-rate drop of over 400 basis points leads to a duration close to that of a one-year instrument.

Each of the curves is contained in an envelope of the duration of the bullet on the top and the duration of a similar coupon bond with a time to maturity equal to the time remaining to call on the bottom. The speed with which the curve shifts from one edge of the envelope to the other is a function of the time remaining to call, as well as the volatility of interest rates. The shorter the time remaining to expiration of the option, the quicker the shift will be.

The nonlinearity or convexity of duration is increasingly manifest as the time to call approaches. For an American option, the curve will dip to zero duration for interest rates that lead to values above par once the period of call protection is passed.[18]

Example 2: Put bonds. The key difference between callable bonds and put bonds is not that one has a call attached and the other has a put attached. The key difference is that the callable bond is *short* an option, while the puttable bond is *long* an option. Put/call parity tells us that the put and the call are different ways of looking at the same instrument. We can just as easily look at the puttable bond as a bond with an attached call option.

The long versus short option is evident when we decompose the puttable bond into its bullet and option parts, expressing the duration of the bond as

$$D = \alpha D_B + (1 - \alpha)D_P. \tag{7}$$

Applying Equation (4), this then becomes

$$D = (\alpha + (1 - \alpha)\lambda)D_B + (1 - \alpha)\rho. \tag{8}$$

This equation differs from Equation (6) only by λ here being additive.

Exhibit 5 traces the duration of a 15-year bond with a 10-year put as a function of interest rates. The bond and option have longer time to maturity in this example than in the callable bond example in order to give a comparison of lengthening time to maturity on the effect of the

---

[18] In practice, bonds are not optimally called. The bond may continue in force for a period of time after call should, theoretically, be made, and the actual duration effect will not be this dramatic.

EXHIBIT 5 Duration of a Put Bond with Option Position

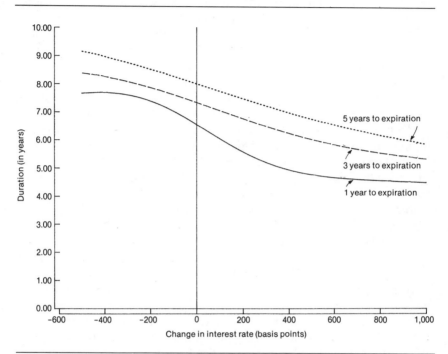

option.[19] Like the callable bond example, the exercise price of the put is at par. The duration for a time to maturity of 15, 13, and 11 years is plotted by the respective curves in Exhibit 5.

The long option position of the puttable bond leads, not unexpectedly, to duration effects that are the opposite of those of the callable bond's short option position. The envelope is the duration of a 15-year and a 10-year bond, with the top of the envelope being approached as interest rates drop, and the bottom of the envelope being approached as interest rates increase. The duration of the short side of this bond is identical to the duration of the long side of the callable bond depicted in Exhibit 4: a 10-year bond with a 10 percent coupon.[20]

---

[19] Using put/call parity, a 15-year bond with a put with 10 years to expiration is identical to a 10-year bond with a call option on a five-year bond, where the call has 10 years to expiration.

[20] This example is based on a European-style option, an option that can only be exercised at the time of expiration. Most put bonds issued domestically are European-style. The bonds with detachable bond warrants issued overseas are American-style op-

Example 3: Options on bonds and options on liabilities. The liabilities of many financial institutions can be viewed as interest sensitive cash-flow streams. The Guaranteed Interest Contracts (GICs) and Single Premium Deferred Annuities (SPDAs) issued by insurance companies, Certificates of Deposit (CDs) issued by banks and thrifts, as well as defined benefits pension plans can be viewed in a liability context in the same way coupon-paying bonds are in an asset context. A bullet GIC, for example, accrues all of its interest to a single maturity date, making its cash-flow analogous to a zero coupon bond. The pension benefits for the retired-lives portion of a defined benefits pension plan can be thought of as a type of coupon-paying bond.[21]

The goal of asset-liability matching is to match the interest-rate sensitivity of these liabilities to that of the assets backing them. When duration is used as the basis for measuring this sensitivity, the first objective is to construct a portfolio of assets with the same net duration as the liability cash flows. A secondary objective is to address the convexity of the asset and liability cash flows by using a set of assets whose duration will change with interest rates and with the passage of time in the same way as the liabilities. This second-order matching will lead to low net convexity, reducing the need to make adjustments in the asset/liability mix, and reducing the exposure from abrupt interest-rate changes.[22]

Just as there are bonds with options, so are there liabilities with options. SPDAs and GICs have a put option written to the issuer that allows the policyholder to put the policy back to the issuer at par value before maturity.[23] Bank CDs with early redemption privileges can similarly be viewed as a combination of a pure interest-rate instrument plus a put option written by the bank to the holder of the CD.

The effect of the option on the interest sensitivity and duration characteristics of these liabilities is clear. If interest rates rise, it will be in the interest of the option holder to exercise the option, put the instru-

---

tions, that can be exercised at any time on or before the expiration date. The American-style option can be exercised at any time, it is more sensitive to current changes in interest rates than is a European option with time remaining to expiration. The duration of an American-style option may drop to zero for a high enough interest rate, since a sufficiently high interest rate will trigger immediate exercise. The profile of an American-style option will differ from that of Exhibit 5 by dropping down more quickly with a positive change in interest rates, and by asymptoting the x-axis rather than the duration of the shorter-maturity bond.

[21] Typically, the pension benefits will be declining over time rather than being constant, and therefore are not analogous to a coupon-paying bond with level coupon payments. Also, many plans include cost-of-living adjustments that further complicate the analogy to bonds with payments set in nominal terms.

[22] Examples of asset/liability matching strategies are presented for banks and thrifts by Toevs and Haney (1986), and for insurance companies by Tilley and Latainer (1986).

[23] Some policies include a penalty for early exercise, which may be a function of time remaining to maturity. Such a penalty can be viewed as a transaction cost, and does not alter the essential nature of the option feature.

ment back to the issuer, and reinvest the proceeds at the higher market rate. If interest rates drop, it will be in the interest of the option holder to maintain the instrument until maturity. These instruments will therefore drop in duration as interest rates rise, and will extend in duration as interest rates decline.[24]

The interest-rate sensitivity of an SPDA contract is depicted in Exhibit 6-A. The GIC and CD will have a similar profile, approaching the duration of their option-free counterpart for low interest rates, and moving gradually to zero duration as interest rates increase.

Since these liabilities reflect a short put option position for the is-

EXHIBIT 6-A Interest Sensitivity of an SPDA

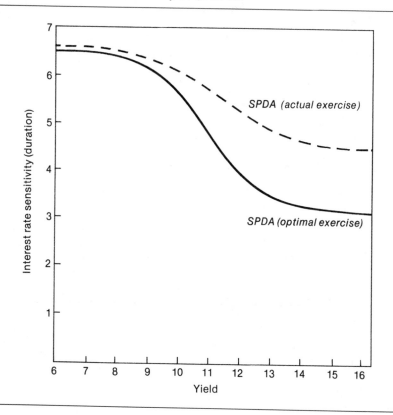

---

[24] The impact of the option is complicated by the fact that not all option holders will exercise at the theoretically optimal time. The change in the duration characteristics will therefore be somewhat less than predicted by a model that assumes optimal exercise by all option holders. We will treat the issue of nonoptimal exercise in more detail in the next section.

suer, a put bond will provide the best duration and convexity match. The long put option position of the put bond will net out with the short put position of the liability. The net result of matching a SPDA with a put bond is illustrated in Exhibit 6-B.

EXHIBIT 6-B   Covering an SPDA Liability with a Put Bond

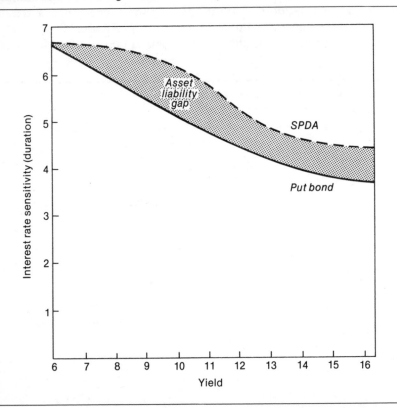

Many financial institutions are in the habit of funding their puttable liabilities with callable assets, assets such as callable bonds and mortgage-backed securities with prepayment options. The net result is a short straddle, a position consisting of both a short call option and a short put option. A short straddle will lose money if interest rates move in either direction. If interest rates rise, the put option on the liability side will be exercised, forcing the liquidation of assets that have declined in price. If interest rates drop, the call options on the asset side will be exercised, requiring the reinvestment of the proceeds at lower interest

EXHIBIT 6-C Covering an SPDA Liability with a Mortgage-Backed Security

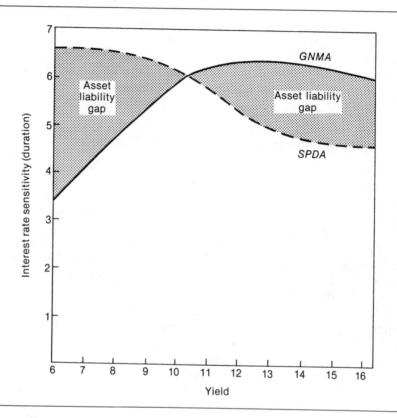

rates. This straddle is illustrated in Exhibit 6-C. Assuming the options are fairly priced in the market, this risk will be compensated for by an improved yield should interest rates remain stable, but the two-sided risk to the institution remains difficult to manage.[25]

---

[25] The risk of the short straddle position can be managed by careful dynamic adjustment of the asset and liability position to maintain a net neutral hedge ratio. There is always a point at which the positive change in the put option will be exactly counteracted by the negative change in the call option. If the asset position is adjusted to keep the put and call effect balanced, the result will be a "delta neutral" position, with the option effect washed out. Such dynamic adjustment strategies are common among option strategists working in the listed option markets, but are more difficult for fixed income securities where spreads and transactions costs are relatively high. The issues of dynamic hedging are presented in Bookstaber (1985).

POTENTIAL PITFALLS IN THE ANALYSIS OF BONDS WITH IMPLICIT OPTIONS

The principle of value additivity simplifies the pricing and exposure measurement of bonds with options. The bond and option features can each be analyzed separately, using the well-established tools for pricing cash flows and options. However, for those who are not well versed in option theory, a number of difficulties remain in the practical application of option tools to the interest-rate-sensitive options of the bond market. In this section we will address a few of these difficulties.

Assessing the Performance of Bonds with Options

The increased complexity that options add to the pricing and the exposure management of fixed income securities carries over to the evaluation of the performance of fixed income securities as well. Performance evaluation is based on the relative performance of comparable bond portfolios. Portfolios with similar characteristics are ranked against one another, or are compared to some other benchmark, such as the Becker Universe or the Shearson-Lehman Index. This evaluation process obviously only makes sense if the portfolios being compared truly are comparable. In the absence of option-like features, it is relatively simple to test for comparability. The quality, maturity, duration, and types of bonds in the portfolios are easily observed. With options imbedded in many bonds, the comparability begins to cloud.

We have already seen that options can have a dramatic effect on the interest-rate sensitivity of the bonds.[26] The duration of the bond will be far different when an option is out-of-the-money than when it moves into-the-money. Looking at the duration characteristics of the underlying bonds alone will inevitably misstate the true interest-rate sensitivity of the bonds.

The payoff distribution will also differ for bonds with different options. A bond with a short call option, such as a callable bond or a mortgage-backed security, will have truncated return potential. It will have limited opportunity for appreciation. The bondholder, as compensation for giving up the up-side potential, will receive a higher yield than he would for a comparable noncallable bond. A bond with a long put option will be truncated on down-side returns. The holder of a put bond has insurance against long-term declines in the bond price. As payment for this insurance protection, the holder of a put bond will receive a lower yield than a comparable nonputtable bond would give.

---

[26] The effect of option positions on portfolio returns is discussed in Bookstaber and Clarke (1981, 1983a, 1983b, 1984, and 1985).

It is difficult to rank two portfolios strictly on the basis of yield, since the higher yield of the one may have been achieved by selling off the upside potential, while the lower yield of the second may be moderated by protection against loss. These option features will not be apparent when the bonds are compared in a static environment. Even a comparison of returns over time will not give a complete indication of these features, since any such comparison is constrained to one particular interest-rate path. A portfolio heavily weighted toward put bonds will come out the winner if interest rates move substantially up or down, but will appear to be inferior if interest rates remain unchanged.[27] A portfolio weighted toward callable bonds will perform best if interest rates remain unchanged, since the bondholder receives the premium for the call option in the form of a higher coupon. However, if interest rates move up, the call feature will prove a detriment. The callable bondholders and puttable bondholders inherently are facing different risks, and are holding bonds with substantially different sensitivities to the interest-rate environment. It is difficult to lump the bonds together in terms of duration, convexity, and the distribution of payoff.

The payoff distribution of bonds with default risk, specifically corporate debentures, will be affected by option features in a way that may result in apparently superior performance for bonds with a higher risk of default. Bonds with default risk are hybrid instruments, part fixed income instrument, part equity of the firm. If the firm is successful in meeting its obligations to the bondholders, the bond remains a fixed income instrument, collecting the promised cash-flow payments. However, if the firm defaults on these payments, then the bondholder has recourse to the assets of the firm. The ownership of the firm reverts to the bondholders, who in effect become the equity holders of the firm.

Corporate debentures can be thought of as a pure interest-rate vehicle such as a Treasury bond combined with a short put option position on the equity of the firm. The put option gives the issuer of the bond, the current equityholders, the right to put the equity of the firm to the bondholder at an exercise price equal to the payments promised the bondholders. If the value of the firm drops below this exercise price, it will be in the interest of the equity holders to exercise the put option, and give the equity of the firm to the bondholders rather than give them the promised payment. If the value of the firm is above the exercise price, the equity holders will leave the option unexercised, since greater

---

[27] As we have seen in the previous section, the holder of a put bond has a straddle on interest rates. If rates rise, the put can be exercised, putting the investor into a bond with higher yield. If interest rates drop, the holder can let the option expire unexercised, and enjoy the appreciation in the longer-term bond.

value will be found in making the promised payment and retaining the ownership of the firm.[28]

The short put option position is undesirable from the standpoint of the bondholder, since in the event of default the bondholder faces a possible loss equal to the difference between the promised payment and the value of the assets of the firm. The bondholder is compensated for this through an option premium for the put option he has written. This premium is expressed in the spread between the yield of the corporate bond and the yield of a Treasury bond of comparable terms. The closer the option is to being in-the-money, the greater the option premium will be, and the higher the yield differential will be.

High-yield bonds, lower quality bonds with a higher risk of default, enjoy their yield advantage as a result of this option. The put option of high-yield bonds is closer to the money than is the option of higher quality corporate issues, and therefore has a higher premium. The implicit short put option of the high-yield bonds will lead to a return distribution that is more heavily weighted on the down-side, and is truncated on the up-side relative to other bonds without as strong a default component.[29]

The high-yield bondholder receives the value of the firm only when it is undesirable to receive it. This is obviously less desirable that a distribution that is symmetrically weighted toward receiving either higher or lower return as a result of changes in equity value. The short put option on the high-yield bond leads to variance being all "bad" variance: all the variability is on the down-side. As a result, the expected return is greater than for a bond with equal variance of return but with that variance being symmetric about the mean. Symmetric variance allows an equal chance for a favorable shock and for an unfavorable shock.

Virtually all studies of the performance of high-yield bonds have failed to note the need to consider not only the mean and variance of return, but where the variance is coming from. The result of most studies on high-yield bonds—that these bonds outperform higher quality bonds on a mean-variance basis—is not surprising when the source of that variance is considered. In a fair market, bonds with short put options should dominate unoptioned bonds in a mean variance context.[30] The inefficiency may not be with the bond market. Rather, it may be with the application of the mean-variance criterion to bonds with op-

---

[28] A description of high-yield bonds as bullet bonds with short put option positions is presented in Bookstaber and Jacob (1986).

[29] This distribution is similar to that of callable bonds, except that here the distribution is truncated in terms of equity rather than interest rates.

[30] The effect of option positions on the performance of securities measured in mean-variance space is discussed in Bookstaber and Clarke (1985).

tions. Options can truncate and skew the distribution in ways that require a consideration of more than just variance to assess risk. The higher moments of the distribution must also be considered.

Pitfalls in Option Model Design

Pricing and exposure measurement requires an option model. There are a number of option pricing models in the literature for options on interest-rate-sensitive instruments. It is beyond the scope of this chapter to consider these in depth, or to sketch out any particular model for applying the pricing and exposure concepts presented in the previous sections. However, here we will present some of the important considerations in using option models for interest-rate-sensitive instruments.

Developing a bond option pricing model requires overcoming a number of difficulties that are not present in models for a nonstochastic interest-rate environment. The most obvious difficulty is in depicting the relationship between the yield curve and the price of the interest-rate-sensitive instrument. A model requires both the interest rates for financing the arbitrage and the interest rate for pricing the underlying asset to be stochastic, and these rates must bear a relationship that preserves reasonable yield-curve structure. A second difficulty is the distributional assumptions for the interest rates and the underlying asset. The lognormal distribution conventionally used in option pricing models is inappropriate for modeling an interest-rate process, since interest rates tend to vary within a fairly narrow band.[31] Since bonds bear a complex relationship to interest rates, and furthermore are restricted to be priced at par at maturity, the usual assumption that bond prices are distributed lognormally is clearly inappropriate, even if interest rates are hypothesized to be lognormally distributed. These difficulties have been addressed in a number of models for interest-rate-sensitive assets.[32]

---

[31] Cox, Ingersoll, and Ross (1978) have used a mean-reverting process to model interest rates. There is reason to think interest rates are mean-reverting, since abnormally high rates will lead to a shift in monetary policy to reduce rates, while unusually low rates will lead to a less restrained policy which will lead rates to increase. By contrast, since in a lognormal process the variance grows linearly with time, a 20 percent standard deviation for rates over one year will imply a standard deviation of rates of over 60 percent in 10 years.

[32] The effect of stochastic interest rates and term structure has been the central topic of the models of Brennan and Schwartz (1982a, 1982b) and Courtadon (1982). Courtadon, relying on earlier work on the valuation of default-free bonds by Vasicek (1977), Cox, Ingersoll, and Ross (1978), and Dothan (1978), has developed models for the valuation of American calls and puts on bonds. Brennan and Schwartz follow a methodology similar to Courtadon, but use two bonds, a short-term bond and a long-term bond, to give a better picture of the term structure. As the authors of these papers note, their models are not preference free, greatly limiting their practical and theoretical appeal. Other models have

The most widely used approaches to modeling interest-rate-sensitive options are based on adaptations of the binomial option pricing model.[33] These approaches have been used to price bond options by those in academics, in the insurance industry, and in the investment banking community.[34] The binomial model is also similar in its computational procedure to other bond option pricing models which use numerical integration methods.

Because of the popularity of the binomial model, we will use it as an illustration of the difficulties inherent in developing consistent option pricing models for interest-rate-sensitive instruments. We will do this by illustrating one particularly perverse failure of such models: the failure to preserve put/call parity.

In the binomial approach, interest rates are assumed to follow a binomial process each period, and the value of the underlying bond is then computed as a function of the interest rate at each point on the binomial lattice. The option values at period T, the time of option expiration, are determined by the option contract specifications as a function of the underlying bond's prices at period t. The option prices for the periods before expiration are then found recursively. The option price in any period is found by solving the three equation system describing the no-net-investment and no-net-return conditions that are required to eliminate one-period arbitrage opportunities:

No net investment: $\quad \Delta_1 B_1^o + \Delta_s B_s^o - C^o = 0$

No net return: $\quad \Delta_1 B_1^u + \Delta_s B_s^u - C^u = 0$

$$\Delta_1 B_1^d + \Delta_s B_s^d = C^d = 0,$$

B_1, B_s, and C are the one-period bond prices, underlying bond prices, and option values for the current period (superscript 0), the next period

---

adapted the binomial framework of Cox, Ross, and Rubinstein (1979) to bond pricing. These include Rendleman and Bartter (1980), Clancy (forthcoming), and Pitts (1985).

The distributional implications for pricing debt options has been treated by Ball and Torous (1983), who attempt to overcome the restriction of bond prices approaching par at maturity by positing a Brownian bridge process as underlying bond price movements, and by Bookstaber and McDonald (1985), who develop a model based on a generalized return distribution for estimating the distributional characteristics of bond returns.

Although these models each meet some of the requirements of an option model for interest-rate-sensitive assets, inadequacies remain. The models of Courtadon and of Brennan and Schwartz, for example, are preference-dependent. Furthermore, these models do not adequately model the distributional properties of bonds. The models of Ball and Torous and Bookstaber and McDonald, while addressing these problems, are European models of limited value in assessing the options imbedded in bonds—options that are often American.

[33] The binomial model, first suggested by Sharpe (1978), is developed by Cox, Ross, and Rubinstein (1979), and by Rendleman and Bartter (1979).

[34] See Rendleman and Bartter (1980) for an academic paper, Clancy (forthcoming) for a paper from the insurance industry, and Pitts (1985) for an example of the work in investment banking.

the one-period arbitrage and the T-period arbitrage represented by the put/call parity relationship, there are possible arbitrage opportunities using the bonds with maturities of 2, 3, . . . , T-1 periods that must be addressed as well.

The failure of put/call parity is more than a curiosity. Put/call parity is a fundamental relationship that must exist between a put and call option, since this relationship can be exploited to reap arbitrage profits if it is violated. Furthermore, important strategies, such as conversions and reverse conversions, are related to the put/call parity relationship. A model that generates prices that violate put/call parity has generated prices that could not reasonably be expected to exist in the market place.[37]

The Problem of Nonoptimal Exercise

The theory of option pricing assumes all American options are exercised optimally, i.e. are exercised in such a way as to maximize the value of the option for the option buyer. Optimal exercise will occur when the option is worth more dead than alive; when the intrinsic value of the option is greater than the value unexercised.[38] The assumption of optimal exercise is not always a good one, however. When compared with the timing of theoretically determined optimal exercise, convertible bonds, callable bonds, and mortgage-backed securities all have their own characteristics of non-optimal exercise. Convertible bonds are often issued as a backdoor approach to the issue of equity. A firm, feeling the equity is undervalued by the market, or that it is not strong enough to attract investors for their equity, may issue convertible bonds in the hope that the bonds will later be converted, and in the end give the desired result of an equity issue.[39]

---

[37] This issue is discussed further in Bookstaber, Jacob, and Langsam (1986).

[38] Put options may be exercised early in order to capture the time value of the intrinsic value. For example, if a put option is far in-the-money, a greater return may be obtained by placing the proceeds of the exercise in the risk-free asset than can be obtained from further deterioration in the underlying security. For call options on bonds, early exercise may be desirable either because of favorable reinvestment rates on the proceeds of exercise relative to the return from continuing to hold the underlying security, or because of the effect of pull to maturity. As the bond approaches maturity, the potential for further large price increases diminishes. The volatility of the bond drops, and therefore the time value of the option drops as well.

[39] A casebook example of this is Novo Industry. Recognizing its domestic market, the Danish market, was too small to support its financing needs, Novo went out into the international market for capital. However, rather than issuing equity, which was not traded abroad, and therefore would not be received strongly by the market, Novo issued a number of convertible bond issues. After these issues converted, a large international holding of the equity was established, making it easier to get the equity listed. Novo is now listed on the New York Stock Exchange, and has options listed on the Chicago Board Option Exchange as well.

The objective of enhancing the equity position outweighs the objective of minimizing the cost of the firm's short option position. As a result, calling convertible bonds to force exercise of the equity option may not be done at what appears to be the optimal time. Other callable corporate bonds may remain unexercised after the optimal call date because the refinancing of other issues is more pressing.

Mortgage-backed securities suffer more from the problems of non-optimal exercise than any other type of security. Early exercise, which can occur either because of early prepayment or because of default, is the rule with mortgage-backed securities. The mortgage holder may prepay because of demographic concerns—a change in family size, a divorce, or a change in income level—or because the interest-rate environment makes the early exercise and refinancing attractive financially. The demographic component is relatively easy to predict, since it is largely independent of the interest-rate level, and is closely related to the age of the mortgage. The economic exercise component is also, in theory, predictable, since, as with any American option, the time of optimal exercise can be determined as a function of the time remaining to the option expiration and the current price of the underlying security. However, in practice mortgage holders do not appear to exercise optimally. The prepayment increases with a drop in interest rates, but the rate of prepayment remains distributionally related to the interest-rate level, leading to uncertainty of cash flows to the investors of mortgage-backed securities.

The uncertainty of prepayment leads to a second level of complexity in exposure management. Not only is the convexity of the bond affected by the prepayment option, the prepayment option itself behaves in an unpredictable way.[40]

CONCLUSION

The key feature options bring to the universe of fixed income instruments is flexibility of payoffs. Options provide the means to mold return distributions to meet investment objectives.

With long options, the investor can sell off undesirable return characteristics. Investors in put bonds truncate potential down-side loss in the event of interest-rate rises. Convertible bonds allow the investor to profit from equity while maintaining a known floor return (assuming the bond does not default).

Short option positions allow the investor to generate higher yield by selling off the desirable return characteristics. Callable bond holders sell the potential for appreciation in a lower interest-rate environment.

---

[40] The prepayment issues for mortgage-backed securities, and the methods of measuring prepayment, are discussed in Pinkus (1986).

Holders of debentures agree to absorb the difference between the promised payment and the value of the firm if the assets of the issuer drop to the point that the scheduled payments of principal and interest are not made.

Just as options allow the investor to alter returns to better meet investment objective, options can also be used to tailor interest-rate sensitivity to meet liability needs. We have illustrated how long option positions can help a bond position to better match the liability exposure from redeemable CDs, GICs, and other products with redemption features.

The increased flexibility that options bring comes at the price of greater complexity. The pricing of bonds now depends on option theory as well as the traditional methods of discounted cash flow analysis. Options exacerbate the measurement of interest-rate exposure, and magnify the convexity problems that arise in using duration for exposure management. For the investor who does not understand the role options play in bond pricing, the added complexity only leads to greater uncertainty and risk. For the investor who can use the option features intelligently, they open up an added dimension for the control of interest-rate risk, and for extracting profits from the market.

REFERENCES

Ball, C. and W. Torous. "Bond Price Dynamics and Options." *Journal of Financial and Quantitative Analysis*, 18, December 1983, pp. 517–31.

Bierwag, G.O., G.G. Kaufman, and A.L. Toevs. "Duration: Its Development and Use in Bond Portfolio Management." *Financial Analysts Journal*, July/August 1983.

Bookstaber, R. "The Use of Options in Performance Structuring." *Journal of Portfolio Management*, 11, Summer 1985, pp. 36–50.

_____. *Option Pricing and Strategies in Investing.* Reading, Mass.: Addison-Wesley, 1981.

Bookstaber, R., and R. Clarke. "Problems in Evaluating the Performance of Portfolios with Options." *Financial Analysts Journal*, January/February 1985, pp. 48–62.

_____. "Option Portfolio Strategies: Measurement and Evaluation." *Journal of Business*, 57, October 1984, pp. 469–92.

_____. "An Algorithm to Calculate with Return Distribution of Portfolios with Option Positions," *Management Science*, April 1983, pp. 419–29.

_____. *Option Strategies for Institutional Investment Management.* Reading, Mass.: Addison-Wesley, 1983.

_____. "Using Option Strategies to Alter Option Portfolio Distributions." *Journal of Portfolio Management*, Summer 1981, pp. 63–70.

Bookstaber, R., W. Haney, and P. Noris. "Are Options on Debt Issues Undervalued?" New York: Morgan Stanley, December 1984.

Bookstaber, R., and D. Jacob. "Controlling the Credit Risk of High-Yield Bonds." *Financial Analysts Journal*, March/April 1986, pp. 25–36.

Bookstaber, R., D. Jacob, and J. Langsam. "The Arbitrage-Free Pricing of Options on Interest Sensitive Instruments." *Advances in Futures and Options Research*. JAI Press, 1986.

Bookstaber, R., and J. McDonald. "A Generalized Option Valuation Model for the Pricing of Bond Options." *Review of Research in Future Markets*, 4, 1985, pp. 60–73.

Brennan, M. and E. Schwartz. "Alternative Methods for Valuing Debt Options." Working Paper 888. University of British Columbia. Vancouver, B.C., 1982a.

_____. "An Equilibrium Model of Bond Pricing and a Test of Market and Efficiency." *Journal of Financial and Quantitative Analysis*, 17 September 1982b, pp. 301–29.

Clancy, R. "Options on Bonds and Applications to Product Pricing." *Transactions of the Society of Actuaries*, forthcoming.

Courtadon, G. "The Pricing of Options on Default-Free Bonds." *Journal of Financial and Quantitative Analysis*, 17, March 1982a, pp. 75–100.

_____. "A More Accurate Finite Difference Approximation for the Valuation of Options." *Journal of Financial and Quantitative Analysis*, 17(5), December 1982b.

Cox, J., and J. Rubinstein. *Option Markets*. Englewood Cliffs, NJ: Prentice-Hall, 1985.

Cox, J., J. Ingersoll, and S. Ross. "A Theory of the Term Structure of Interest Rates." Research paper no. 468, Stanford University, Graduate School of Business, August 1978.

Cox, J., S. Ross, and M. Rubinstein. "Options Pricing: A Simplified Approach." *Journal of Financial Economics*, 7 1979, pp. 229–63.

Dothan, U. "On the Term Structure of Interest Rates." *Journal of Financial Economics*, January 1978.

Galai, D., and R. Masulis. "The Option Pricing Model and the Risk Factor of Stock." *Journal of Financial Economics*, 3, 1976, pp. 53–81.

Goodman, L. "Put-Call Parity with Coupon Instruments," *Journal of Portfolio Management*, 11, Winter, 1985, pp. 59–60.

Merton, R. C. "On the Pricing of Corporate Debt: The Risk Structures of Interest Rates." *Journal of Finance*, 29, May 1974, pp. 449–70.

Pinkus, S. "Mortgage Backed Securities: An Analytical Framework." In *Controlling Interest Rate Risk*, ed. R. Platt. New York: Wiley, 1986.

Pitts, M. "The Pricing of Options on Debt Securities," *Journal of Portfolio Management*, 11, Winter, 1985, pp. 41–50.

Platt, R., ed. *Controlling Interest Rate Risk*. New York: Wiley, 1986.

Rendelman, R., Jr., and B. Bartter, "Two State Option Pricing," *Journal of Finance*, 34, December 1979, pp. 1093–1110.

_____. "The Pricing of Options on Debt Securities." *Journal of Financial and Quantitative Analysis*, 9(4), December 1980.

Sharpe, W. *Investments*. Englewood Cliffs: Prentice Hall, 1979.

Tilley, J., and G. Latainer. "Risk Control Technique for Life Insurance Companies." in *Controlling Interest Rate Risk*. ed. R. Platt. New York: Wiley, 1986.

Toevs, A., and W. Haney, "Measuring and Managing Interest Rate Risk: A Guide to Asset/Liability Models Used in Banks and Thrifts." in *Controlling Interest Rate Risk*, ed. R. Platt. New York: Wiley, 1986.

Vasicek, O. "An Equilibrium Characterization of the Term Structure." *Journal of Financial Economics*, November 1977, pp. 177–88.

42

Managing Risk with Interest-Rate Futures

Mark Pitts, Ph.D.
Senior Vice President
Shearson Lehman Brothers

Futures on fixed income securities are now widely used throughout the debt markets. Banks, savings institutions, pension funds, money managers, security dealers, and corporations of every description are active users of fixed income futures contracts. While an impediment for many potential users has been regulatory and policy constraints, these constraints are now vanishing in many sectors. Other potential users have been deterred by a lack of knowledge and understanding of the futures markets. However, as more and more institutions learn about the futures markets and put them to effective use, those who remain outsiders find themselves at a competitive disadvantage.

This chapter addresses the primary concern of many institutional users: how the futures market can be used to hedge fixed income assets and liabilities. Other concerns such as pricing theory, trading strategies, and tax and accounting treatment of futures are addressed in other chapters of this section of the book. A discussion of the contracts is presented in Chapter 39.

The hedging process can be broken down into three phases: the preliminaries, defining and executing the strategy, and monitoring the hedge. The preliminaries are the steps that a manager should take before a hedge is ever initiated. In fact, to a large extent, these are the steps that a manager should take to decide if hedging is even the right decision. If hedging does appear to be the right decision, then a hedging strategy must be decided upon. Unfortunately, managers are bombarded with many different strategies that often appear contradictory. These include regression strategies, volatility weighting strategies, and strategies based on a presumed relationship between cash and futures prices. The hedging strategy that we present combines these strategies into one simple technique. We are able to do this because the various hedging strategies are not really contradictory techniques, although they are frequently presented as such. Finally, we conclude with a suggestion on how to manage and monitor a hedge once it is in place.

THE PRELIMINARIES

Before a hedge is ever initiated, there are several steps that the prudent manager should take in order to be completely comfortable with the hedging process. By taking these steps *before* the hedge is set, the potential hedger gains an understanding of what a hedge can and cannot accomplish, and ensures that if the hedge is set, it is set in the proper manner. Briefly, the preliminary steps are as follows:

1. Determine which futures contract is the most appropriate hedging vehicle.
2. Determine the target for the hedge—i.e., the rate or price which the manager should expect to lock in with the hedge.
3. Estimate the effectiveness of the hedge—i.e., the risk of a hedged position relative to an unhedged position.
4. Estimate the absolute (as opposed to relative) risk of the hedged position.
5. Determine the proper hedge ratio—i.e., the number of futures contracts needed to hedge the underlying risk.

A primary factor determining which futures contract will provide the best hedge is the degree of correlation between the rate on the futures contract and the interest rate which creates the underlying risk that the manager wants to eliminate. For example, a long-term corporate bond portfolio can be better hedged with Treasury bond (T-bond) futures than with Treasury bill (T-bill) futures because long-term corporate bond rates are more highly correlated with T-bond rates than with T-bill rates. Similarly, an anticipated sale of short-term liabilities tied to the T-bill rate could generally be more effectively hedged using T-bill futures than Eurodollar time deposit futures. Using the right delivery month is also important. Naturally, a manager trying to lock in a rate or price for June will use June futures contracts since June contracts will give the highest degree of correlation. Correlation is not, however, the only consideration if the hedging program is of significant size. If, for example, a manager wants to hedge $500 million of short-term liabilities in a single delivery month, liquidity in the futures market becomes an important consideration. In such a case, it might be necessary to spread the hedge across two or more different contracts. Consequently, a seller of liabilities tied to the T-bill rate might hedge by selling some T-bill futures and some Eurodollar time deposit futures, eventually rolling entirely into T-bill futures.

Having determined the right contract and the right delivery months, the manager should then determine what is expected from the hedge—that is, what rate will, on average, be locked in by the hedge. Obviously, if this rate is too high (if hedging a sale) or too low (if hedging a purchase), hedging is perhaps not the right strategy for dealing with unwanted risk. Determining what to expect (i.e., calculating the *target rate* for a hedge) is not always simple. However, this chapter explains how the manager should approach this problem for both simple and complex hedges.

Hedge effectiveness tells the manager what percentage of risk is eliminated by hedging. Thus, if the hedge is determined to be 90 percent effective, over the long run a hedged position will have only 10 percent of the risk (i.e., standard deviation) of an unhedged position. However, for any single hedge, it is possible that the hedged position will show more variation than the unhedged position.

The residual hedging risk, i.e., the absolute level of risk in the hedged position, tells the manager how much risk remains after hedging. While it may be comforting to know, for example, that 90 percent of the risk is eliminated by hedging, without additional statistics the hedger still does not know how much risk he faces. The residual risk in a hedged position is expressed most conveniently as a standard deviation. For example, it might be determined that the hedged position has a standard deviation of 10 basis points. Assuming a normal distribution of hedging errors, the hedger will then obtain the target rate plus or minus 10 basis points two times out of three. The probability of obtaining the target rate plus or minus 20 basis points is 95 percent, and the probability of obtaining the target rate plus or minus 30 basis points is greater than 99 percent.

The target rate, the hedge effectiveness, and the residual hedging risk determine the basic trade-off between risk and expected return. Consequently, these statistics give the manager the essential facts needed in order to decide whether or not to hedge. Using these figures he can construct confidence intervals for hedged and unhedged positions. Comparing these confidence intervals he can then determine whether hedging is the best alternative. Furthermore, if hedging is the right decision, his level of confidence in the hedge is well defined in advance.

The manager should also be aware that the effectiveness of a hedge and the residual hedging risk are not necessarily constant from one hedge to the next. Hedges that will be lifted near a futures delivery date will tend to be more effective and have less residual risk than those lifted on more distant dates. The life of the hedge, i.e., the amount of time between when the hedge is set and when it is lifted, also generally has a significant impact on hedge effectiveness and residual hedging risk. For example, a hedge held for six months might be 90 percent effective, while a hedge held for one month might be only 25 percent effective. The intuition behind this is that the security to be hedged and the hedging instrument might be highly correlated over the long run, but only weakly correlated over the short run.

Similarly, residual hedging risk usually increases as the life of the hedge increases. The residual risk on a six-month hedge may be 85 basis points even if the residual risk for a one-month hedge is only 35 basis points. It may seem surprising that the longer hedges have more risk if they are also more effective. However, hedge effectiveness is a measure of *relative* risk, and since longer time periods exhibit greater swings in interest rates, the greater percentage reduction in risk for longer hedges does not necessarily mean that there is less risk left over.

This concept is demonstrated in Exhibit 1 which shows the typical patterns of risk associated with hedged and unhedged positions. Because interest rates and spreads are generally less predictable further into the future, the risk (i.e., standard deviation) increases for longer holding periods for either position. Thus, residual hedging risk will tend to increase for longer holding periods. However, the effectiveness of the hedge is measured by the relative risk of the two positions. As shown, for shorter hedges the risk of the hedged position may be half as much as the risk of the unhedged position, leading to 50 percent hedge effectiveness (AB = ½ × AC). For longer periods, the risk of the hedged position is only about one third as much as the risk of the unhedged position, giving 66.7 percent effectiveness (DE = ⅔ × DF). Conse-

---

EXHIBIT 1   Risk as a Function of the Length of a Hedge

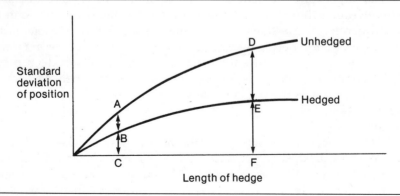

Note: AB = ½ × AC and DE = ⅔ × DF

quently, effectiveness increases as the length of the hedge increases even though the total risk of the hedged position also increases with the length of the hedge.

The target rate, residual risk, and the effectiveness of a hedge are relatively simple concepts. However, since these statistics are usually estimated using historical data, the potential hedger should be sure that these figures are estimated correctly. Statistics can be tricky business. Well-intentioned amateurs and not-so-well-intentioned professionals have been known to produce statistics that lead to overly optimistic estimates of what a hedge can do. Consequently, the potential hedger should not necessarily judge the skill of his broker by how much he promises to accomplish with a hedge.

The final factor that must be determined before the hedge is set is the *hedge ratio,* or the number of futures contracts needed for the hedge. Usually the hedge ratio is expressed in terms of relative face amounts. Accordingly, a hedge ratio of 1.20 means that for every $1 million face value of securities to be hedged, the manager needs $1.2 million face value of futures contracts to offset his risk. As the following pages demonstrate, hedge ratio calculations run the gamut from trivial to esoteric and may change from one hedge to the next. As will become apparent, it is very important for managers to be aware of all the factors that must be considered in calculating the hedge ratio.

HEDGING PRINCIPLES

Hedging is one of the primary ways that institutional accounts use interest-rate futures contracts. While it is difficult to concisely state the general principle that underlies futures hedging, a one-line attempt might be as follows: do in the futures market today what you anticipate needing (or wanting) to do on a future date. For instance, if a portfolio manager owns a long bond that he anticipates selling in six months, he hedges by selling today bond futures for delivery six months hence. If the same manager does not anticipate an actual sale, but wants to hedge the value of the bond six months forward, then the manager, in a sense, would like to sell the bond (as evidenced by the fact that he no longer wants the volatility of a long bond position), but may be constrained from doing so. His course of action should be the same: he should sell bond futures to hedge his position.

An asset manager can also use futures to hedge the rate at which anticipated cash flows will be invested. A manager expecting a cash inflow in one year might plan to buy long bonds when the cash is available, but he would like to hedge the rate at which that investment will be made. Anticipating a future purchase of bonds, the manager hedges by buying bonds in the futures market today. If, on the other hand, the manager plans to invest the cash in short-term securities, he would hedge by buying short-term debt futures, instead of bond futures.

Liability managers can apply the same hedging principle. The liability manager who funds his operations by continually rolling over short-term debt faces substantial interest-rate risk arising from the uncertainty of future rate levels. Since the manager anticipates having to sell new short-term debt in the future, he hedges by selling futures contracts on short-term debt.[1]

The liability manager who plans to sell long-term debt to fund his operations faces the risk that long-term rates will rise before the anticipated bond issuance. To hedge, he will enter into a trade in the futures market to mirror the trade he anticipates having to do on a future date; namely, he sells futures on long-term debt to hedge the subsequent sale of his own long-term debt.

Some managers are responsible for both the asset and liability side of the balance sheet. Frequently, one side of the balance sheet is more interest-rate sensitive than the other and the manager finds himself trying to manage an interest-rate gap. Usually, this occurs because the assets are of much longer maturity than the liabilities. Consequently, as interest rates rise, interest expense increases while interest income stays constant. To make matters worse, as rates rise long-term assets fall below their purchase price. Since a sale of assets would then result in losses, the manager often has few choices for correcting the imbalance.

The asset/liability manager can, however, control this exposure by combining the techniques used by asset managers and liability managers. Instead of reducing the interest-rate sensitivity of his assets by swapping into shorter maturity securities (and booking a loss), he can sell intermediate- or long-term debt futures and accomplish the same end. Alternatively, (or concurrently), he can increase the interest-rate sensitivity of his liabilities by lengthening their effective maturity. This is accomplished by selling short-term debt futures.

In each of the foregoing examples, the managers follow essentially the same rule. Whatever action they expect or want to take in the cash market, but are constrained from taking, they take instead in the futures market. At the risk of oversimplification, this rule can be followed by most, if not all, asset and liability managers.

RISK AND EXPECTED RETURN IN A HEDGE

When one enters into a hedge, the objective is to lock in a rate for the sale or purchase of a security. However, there is much disagreement as

---

[1] A manager who funds with floating-rate debt does not actually roll over short-term debt, but his interest-rate expense is determined by future short-term rates. Consequently, his best hedge will also be to sell short-term debt futures.

to what rate or price one should expect to lock in when futures are used in a hedge. One view is that the hedger can, on average, lock in the current spot rate for the security. The opposing view is that the hedger will, on average, lock in the rate at which the futures contracts are bought or sold. As it turns out, the truth usually lies somewhere in between these two positions. However, as the following examples illustrate, each view is correct in certain special situations.

The Target for Hedges Held to Delivery

Minimum variance hedges that are held until the futures delivery date provide an example of the hedge that locks in the futures rate of interest. A hedge with T-bill futures contracts is a straightforward illustration of this. Suppose an investor buys a $1 million six-month T bill at 8.50 percent and expects to sell it three months hence, at which time the bill will have three months of remaining life. To hedge his sale, the investor sells one $1 million three-month T-bill contract for delivery in three months. Suppose further that when the hedge is set, spot three-month bills are at 8.18 percent and three-month T-bill futures are at 9 percent. What rate does the hedger lock in for the sale of his T bill three months hence (on the futures delivery date)?

The process of *convergence* guarantees that the hedger locks in 9 percent (the futures rate) for his sale, while the spot rates of 8.18 percent and 8.50 percent are all but irrelevant. Convergence refers to the fact that at delivery there can be no discrepancy between the spot and futures price for a given security (or commodity).[2] If the futures price were higher than the spot price, one could buy in the cash market, immediately sell in the futures market, and take out money at no risk. If the futures price were lower than the spot price, one could buy in the futures market and immediately sell in the cash market, again taking out cash at no risk. Thus, arbitrage between the cash and futures market forces the cash and futures price to converge on the delivery date.

To see how convergence guarantees the hedger a price equal to the futures price on the day the hedge is set, consider the cash flows associated with a T-bill contract sold at 9 percent (quoted as 91.00). For each basis point increase in the futures rate above 9 percent (or .01 decrease in the quoted futures price below 91.00), the investor receives a margin inflow of $25. Now, if the investor targets 9 percent as the expected sale rate for his T bill (which will then have three months to maturity), every basis point above 9 percent at which he sells his T bill will cost him exactly $25 (from $1,000,000 × .0001 × 90/360). Thus, ignoring transaction costs, any short-fall relative to the targeted rate is just offset by gains on the futures contract. Conversely, if the hedger is able to sell his

---

[2] In the case of more than one deliverable, this is true only for the cheapest to deliver.

T bill at a price higher (or yield lower) than the target, losses on the futures contract just offset any windfall he experiences in the cash market. This guarantees that he does no worse than, and no better than, the target.[3] Table 1 illustrates this fact in more detail.[4]

TABLE 1 T-Bill Hedge, Held to Delivery

Rate on futures contracts when sold = 9 percent
Target rate = 9 percent
Target price = $977,500

Actual Sale Rate	Actual Sale Price	Gain (Loss) From Futures*	Effective Sale Price	Effective Sale Rate†
5.00%	$987,500	($10,000)	$977,500	9.00%
6.00	985,000	(7,500)	977,500	9.00
7.00	982,500	(5,000)	977,500	9.00
8.00	980,000	(2,500)	977,500	9.00
9.00	977,500	0	977,500	9.00
10.00	975,000	2,500	977,500	9.00
11.00	972,500	5,000	977,500	9.00
12.00	970,000	7,500	977,500	9.00
13.00	967,500	10,000	977,500	9.00
14.00	965,000	12,500	977,500	9.00
15.00	962,500	15,000	977,500	9.00

* By the process of convergence, the actual sale rate equals the final futures rate.
† Transaction costs and the financing of margin flows are ignored.

The domestic CD and Eurodollar time deposit futures work in very much the same fashion. In these cases as well, the hedger can lock in a rate or price for an anticipated purchase or sale. If the hedge is held until delivery, the only rate that he can lock in with certainty is the rate prevailing in the futures market. As the example above shows, the rate on the securities in the cash market does not affect the rate that can be locked in. However, it must be noted that while the hedge guarantees a sale rate equal to the futures rate, futures rates are often higher than cash rates. This is frequently referred to as the "cost of convergence."

The same principle holds true in the market for intermediate- and long-term debt, except that the situation is a little more complicated

---

[3] For this to be exactly true, one must ignore the fact that net margin inflows from the futures contract can be invested over the life of the hedge, and net margin outflows must be borrowed (or paid out at an opportunity loss) over the life of the hedge. To adjust for this fact, the total futures position should be reduced by the factor $(1 + r)^t$, where r is the rate for borrowing or lending margin flows, and t is the time until delivery.

[4] It must be emphasized, of course, that while a hedge may be perfect, futures losses—if any—must be met immediately, and in cash. Consequently, the institution should be very aware of the cash-flow considerations implicit in a futures position.

because the hedger does not know for sure when delivery will take place or which bond will be delivered. For the sake of simplicity, consider the T-bond contract and assume that it is obvious which bond will be delivered, and that delivery will take place on the last day of the delivery month (frequently the most advantageous day to make delivery). Consider the 7⅝ percent T bonds maturing on February 15, 2007. For delivery on the June 1985 contract the conversion factor for these bonds was .9660, implying that the investor who delivers the 7⅝ percent bonds would receive from the buyer .9660 times the futures settlement price, plus accrued interest. Consequently, at delivery, the (flat) spot price and the futures price times the conversion factor must converge. Otherwise, arbitrageurs would buy at the lower price and sell at the higher price and earn risk-free profits. Accordingly, a hedger could lock in a June sale price for the 7⅝ percent bonds by selling T-bond futures contracts equal to .9660 times the face value of the bonds. For example, $100 million face value of 7⅝ percent bonds would be hedged by selling $96.6 million face value of bond futures (966 contracts). Furthermore, the sale price that the hedger locks in would be .9660 times the futures price. Thus, if the futures price is 70-0 when the hedge is set, the hedger locks in a sale price of 67.62 (or approximately 67-20) for June delivery, regardless of where rates are in June. Table 2 shows the cash flows for a number of final prices for the 7⅝ percent bonds and illustrates how cash flows on the futures contract offset losses or gains relative to the target price of 67.62. In each case the effective sale price is very close to the target price (and, in fact, would be exact if enough decimal places were carried through the calculations). However, since the target price is determined by the futures price, the target price may be lower than the cash market price.

When we admit the possibility that bonds other than the 7⅝ of 2007 can be delivered, and that it might be advantageous to deliver other bonds, the situation becomes somewhat more involved. In this more realistic case the hedger may decide not to deliver the 7⅝, but if he does decide to deliver them, he is still assured of receiving an effective sale price of approximately 67.62. If he does not deliver the 7⅝, it would be because another bond can be delivered more cheaply.

In summary, if an investor sets a *risk minimizing* futures hedge *that is held until delivery*, he can be assured of receiving an effective sale price dictated by the *futures* rate (and *not* the spot rate) on the day the hedge is set.

The Target for Hedges with Short Holding Periods

Let us return to a variant of our original example of purchasing a $1 million six-month T bill at 8.50%. Now, however, we want to assume that the investor has no intention of holding the T bill for an extended period of time but intends to sell it in the very near term, say within a

TABLE 2 T-Bond Hedge, Held to Delivery

Instrument to be hedged: 7⅝ percent T bonds of 2/15/07
Conversion factor for June 1985 delivery = .9660
Price of futures contracts when sold = 70-0
Target price for 7⅝ percent T bonds = .9660 × 70 = 67.62

Actual Sale Price for 7⅝ Percent T Bonds	Final Futures Price*	Gain (Loss) on 966 Contracts ($10/.01/contract)†	Effective Sale Price‡
62-0	64.182	$5,620,188	$67,620,118
63-0	65.217	4,620,378	67,620,378
64-0	66.253	3,619,602	67,619,602
65-0	67.288	2,619,792	67,619,792
66-0	68.323	1,619.982	67,619,982
67-0	69.358	620,172	67,620,172
68-0	70.393	(379,638)	67,620,362
69-0	71.429	(1,380,414)	67,619,586
70-0	72.464	(2,380,224)	67,619,776
71-0	73.499	(3,380,034)	67,619,966
72-0	74.534	(4,379,844)	67,620,156
73-0	75.569	(5,379,654)	67,620,346
74-0	76.605	(6,380,430)	67,619,570
75-0	77.640	(7,380,240)	67,619,760

* By convergence, must equal bond price divided by the conversion factor.
† Bond futures trade in even increments of 1/32. Accordingly, the futures prices and margin flows are only approximate.
‡ Transaction costs and the financing of margin flows are ignored.

day. The investor still faces the risk that rates will rise and the sale price of the T bill will fall, and therefore he decides to hedge this risk by selling two of the nearby T-bill futures contracts, currently trading at 9 percent and calling for delivery in three months. (Two three-month T-bill contracts are required since at the time of sale the T bill will be approximately twice as volatile as a three-month T bill.) What rate should the hedger expect to lock in: the futures rate of 9.00 percent or the spot rate of 8.50 percent?

Since the hedge is lifted before delivery, the hedger can no longer be assured of locking in a rate—spot or future. However, the effective rate that he receives in this example is much more likely to approximate the current spot rate of 8.50 percent than the futures rate of 9.00 percent.

The critical difference between this hedge and the earlier example is that the hedge is not held until delivery and, therefore, convergence will generally not take place over the life of the hedge. In fact, since the futures delivery date is three months from the day the hedge is set and the hedge will be lifted in one day, it is much more realistic to assume that rates on the spot six-month T bill and the three-month T-bill future will move in a parallel fashion over the life of the hedge, rather than converge.

This example is not unique to T bills. Whether the hedger is hedging with one of the other short-term contracts or with the intermediate- and long-term contracts, he should expect the hedge to lock in the spot rate (or more exactly, the one-day forward rate), rather than the futures rate for very short-lived hedges (unless, of course, the short-lived hedge ends on a futures delivery date). To illustrate, returning to the simplified example in which the 7⅝ percent T bonds of February 15, 2007 were the only deliverable bonds on the T-bond futures contract, suppose that the hedge is set three months before delivery date and the hedger plans to lift the hedge after one day. It is much more likely that the spot price of the bond will move parallel to the converted futures price (i.e., the futures price times the conversion factor), than that the spot price and the converted futures price will converge by the time the hedge is lifted.

A one-day hedge is, admittedly, an extreme example. Other than underwriters and traders who reallocate assets very frequently, few investors are interested in such a short horizon. The very short-term hedge does, however, illustrate a very important point: the hedger should *not* expect to lock in a futures rate (or price) just because he is hedging with futures contracts. This would be true *only if the hedge is held until delivery,* at which point convergence must take place. If the hedge is held for only one day, the hedger should expect to lock in the one-day forward rate, which will very nearly equal the spot rate. Generally, of course, hedges are held for more than one day, but not necessarily to delivery. The proper target for these cases is examined in the next two sections.

How the Basis Affects the Target Rate for a Hedge

The *basis* is a concept used throughout the futures markets. The basis is defined as simply the difference between the spot price of a security (or commodity) and its futures price, that is:

$$\text{Basis} = \text{Spot Price} - \text{Futures Price}$$

In the fixed income markets two problems can arise when one tries to make practical use of the concept of the basis. First, the quoted futures price does not equal the price that one receives at delivery. In the case of intermediate- and long-term contracts, the actual futures price equals the quoted futures price times the appropriate conversion factor. In the case of the short-term contracts, the quoted futures price is actually 100 minus the annualized interest rate. The actual invoice price must be derived using the applicable yield to price conventions for the instrument in question. Consequently, to be useful, the basis in the fixed income markets should be defined using actual futures delivery prices rather than quoted futures prices.

A second problem arises due to the fact that fixed income securities (unlike most other commodities and securities) age over time. Thus, it is not exactly clear what is meant by the "spot price." Does the spot price mean the current price of the actual instrument that can be held and delivered in satisfaction of a short position, or does it mean the current price of an instrument that currently has the characteristics called for in the futures contract? For example, when the basis is defined for a three-month T-bill contract maturing in three months, should the spot price refer to the current price of a six-month T bill, which is the instrument that will actually be deliverable on the contract (since in three months it will be a three-month T bill), or should the spot price refer to the price of the current three-month T bill? Obviously, how this problem is resolved depends on the purpose one has in mind. The purpose here is to see how the basis affects the results of a hedge, and for hedging purposes, the only basis that really matters is the basis defined by the difference between the futures price and the current price of the security that can be held and actually delivered into the contract (the six-month T bill in this example).

For hedging purposes it is also frequently useful to define the basis in terms of interest rates rather than prices. Using the spot interest rate of the instrument that can be held and delivered, and the interest rate for that same instrument implied by the futures delivery price (as opposed to the quoted futures price), the *rate basis* is defined as:

$$\text{Rate Basis} = \text{Spot Rate} - \text{Futures Rate}$$

The rate basis is particularly useful for analyzing hedges of short-term instruments because it nets out all effects due solely to the aging process. For instance, if spot one-year T bills and three-month T-bill futures for delivery in nine months are both trading at 12 percent, the rate basis is zero since cash and futures are at the same interest rate. However, a one-year T bill at 12 percent has a price of 88, while a three-month T bill at 12 percent has a price of 97, giving a price basis of −9. Furthermore, because the cash security ages, a change in the price basis does not necessarily imply that there has been a change in the rate basis, or vice versa. Accordingly, the relationship between the price basis and the rate basis is not always an obvious one.

Both rate and price bases are helpful in explaining the two kinds of hedges examined in the preceding sections. The first hedge was a hedge of six-month T bills for a sale date three months in the future. By selling three-month T-bill futures for delivery in three-months, the hedger was able to lock in a rate equal to the rate at which the contract was sold (9 percent in the example). The second hedge was a hedge of the same T bill for a sale date only one day in the future. In this case, the hedger sells the same T-bill futures contract and expects to lock in a rate approximately equal to the current rate on his six-month T bill (8.50 percent in the example). To illustrate why the two hedges are expected to lock in such different rates, we define the *target basis* as the expected rate basis on the day the hedge is lifted. In the first case, a hedge lifted on the delivery date is expected to have, and by arbitrage activity will have, a zero rate basis when the hedge is lifted. Thus, the target rate for the hedge should be the rate on the futures contract. In the latter case, one would not expect the basis to change very much in one day and so the target rate basis approximates the current rate basis. Accordingly, the target rate for the hedge should be the futures rate plus the current rate basis, i.e., the current spot rate.

To generalize this concept, the hedger can set the target rate for any hedge equal to the futures rate plus the target rate basis:

$$\text{Target Rate} \atop \text{for Hedge} = {\text{Futures} \atop \text{Rate}} + {\text{Target Rate} \atop \text{Basis}}$$

This definition of the target rate is applicable to the intermediate- and long-term contracts as well as to the short-term contracts. (A numerical example is given in the next section.)

The target basis concept also explains why a hedge held until the delivery date locks in a rate with certainty and other hedges do not. It is often said that hedging substitutes basis risk for price risk, and the examples show that this is true. For the hedge held to delivery, there is no uncertainty surrounding the target basis; by convergence, the basis on the day the hedge is lifted is certain to be zero. For the short-lived hedge, the basis will probably approximate the current basis when the hedge is lifted, but its actual value cannot be known in advance. Thus, the uncertainty surrounding the outcome of a hedge is directly related to the uncertainty surrounding the basis on the day the hedge is lifted, i.e., the uncertainty surrounding the target basis.

A More General Approach to the Target

The discussion so far has centered on two special cases, the very short-term hedge and the hedge held to delivery. Many hedges fall somewhere between these two extremes. The problem then is to choose a target rate for hedges that are held for more than a few days, but are closed out prior to delivery. This is essentially a question of deriving the target basis since, as before, the target rate for the hedge should equal the futures rate plus the target basis.

To show how the target basis can be implemented in a general context, let us examine a simplified case in which we believe that the rate basis will decline linearly over time. The basis is thus expected to change by the same amount each day until, at delivery, the basis is zero.

To show how this assumption affects the target rate for the hedge, assume that the hedger who invests in six-month T bills at 8.50 percent plans to resell the T bills in 30 days, i.e., one third of the way between the purchase date and the futures delivery date. To account for the relative volatility of five-month T bills and three-month T bill futures, the investor should sell 1.67 contracts per $1 million invested. In these circumstances, what rate should the hedger target if the nearby T-bill contract is selling at 9.00 percent?

The rate basis at the outset of the hedge is $-.50$ percent. Assuming a linear decline in the basis, after 30 days the rate basis will equal $-.33$ percent. The target basis for the hedge is therefore $-.33$ percent. Using the formula for the target rate given in the last section, we have:

$$\frac{\text{Target Rate}}{\text{for Hedge}} = \frac{\text{Futures}}{\text{Rate}} + \frac{\text{Target Rate}}{\text{Basis}}$$

$$= 9.00 \text{ percent} - .33 \text{ percent}$$

$$= 8.67 \text{ percent}$$

As expected, since the hedge is lifted closer to the day the hedge is set than to the delivery date, the target rate is closer to the spot rate of 8.50 percent than to the futures rate of 9.00 percent.

The actual outcome of the hedge will be determined by how realistic it is to assume that the basis will decline linearly over time. However, as Table 3 shows, if this assumption is accurate, the target rate and price will be locked in by the hedge.

TABLE 3 T-Bill Hedge, Held for 30 Days

Rate on futures contracts when sold = 9 percent
Target rate = 8.67 percent
Target price = $963,875

Actual Sale Rate for T Bill	Actual Sale Price for T Bill	Futures Rate When Hedge Is Closed Out*	Gain (Loss) from 1⅔ Futures	Effective Sale Price for T Bill	Effective Sale Rate for T Bill†
5.00%	$979,167	5.33%	$(15,292)	$963,875	8.67%
6.00	975,000	6.33	(11,125)	963,875	8.67
7.00	970,833	7.33	(6,958)	963,875	8.67
8.00	966,667	8.33	(2,792)	963,875	8.67
9.00	962,500	9.33	1,375	963,875	8.67
10.00	958,333	10.33	5,542	963,875	8.67
11.00	954,167	11.33	9,708	963,875	8.67
12.00	950,000	12.33	13,875	963,875	8.67
13.00	945,833	13.33	18,042	963,875	8.67
14.00	941,667	14.33	22,208	963,875	8.67
15.00	937,500	15.33	26,375	963,875	8.67

* By assumption, equals the T-bill rate + .33 percent.
† Transaction costs and the financing of margin flows are ignored.

In the intermediate- and long-term markets it is somewhat easier (but not necessarily more accurate) to define the target for the hedge in terms of a price rather than an interest rate. Accordingly, in a hedge one might assume that the price basis, rather than the rate basis, will decline linearly over time. For example, suppose that 80 days before the assumed delivery date for the June 1985 T-bond futures contract a hedger wants to lock in a sale price for $100 million face value of 7⅝ percent T bonds of February 15, 2007, for a sale date 20 days in the future. (To simplify, assume the 7⅝ is the only deliverable bond.) The bonds, for example, may be selling at 67 in the cash market while the bond futures contract is at 68. Since the conversion factor for these bonds for the June 1985 contract was .9660, the price basis is calculated as 67 − (.9660 × 68) = 67 − 65.688 = 1.312. If the price basis declines linearly through time, on the day the hedge is lifted the basis will equal .9840. Thus, the target basis, in terms of price rather than yield, is .9840. Using a formula similar to the earlier one, the target price for the hedge is given by:

$$\frac{\text{Target Price}}{\text{for Hedge}} = \frac{\text{Futures Price}}{\times \text{ Conversion}} + \frac{\text{Target Price}}{\text{Basis}}$$
$$\text{Factor}$$

Or, in this example,

$$\text{Target Price} = 65.688 + .984$$
$$= 66.672$$

As in the earlier example, if the actual price basis on the day the hedge is closed out equals the target price basis, and the hedger shorts the appropriate number of futures contracts (966 in this case), the effective sale price for the hedged security will closely approximate the targeted price. Table 4 demonstrates this fact. (The effective sale price *exactly* equals the target price, except for rounding.)

Basis Risk

For a given investment horizon, hedging substitutes basis risk for price risk. Thus, one trades the uncertainty of the price of the hedged security for the uncertainty of the basis. Consequently, when hedges don't produce the desired results, it is customary to place all the blame on basis risk. However, basis risk is the correct explanation only if the target for the hedge is properly defined. Basis risk should refer only to the *unexpected* or *unpredictable* part of the relationship between cash and futures. The fact that this relationship changes over time does not in itself imply that there is basis risk. If, for example, the rate basis between a T-bill futures contract and the deliverable T bill is 1 percent, we know for certain that the basis will decline to virtually 0 percent on the delivery date. Thus, with respect to delivery date, there is no basis risk. The basis

---

TABLE 4 T-Bond Hedge, Held for 20 Days

Instrument to be hedged: 7⅝ percent T Bonds of 2/15/07
Conversion factor = .9660
Price of futures contracts when sold = 68-0
Target price for 7⅝ = (.9660 × 68) + .984 = 66.672

Actual Sale Price of Bonds	Future Price When Hedge Is Closed Out*	Gain (Loss) on 966 Contracts† ($10/.01/Contract)	Effective Sale Price‡
60-0	61.093	$6,672,162	$66,672,162
61-0	62.128	5,672,352	66,672,352
62-0	63.164	4,671,576	66,671,576
63-0	64.199	3,671,766	66,671,766
64-0	65.234	2,671,956	66,671,956
65-0	66.269	1,672,146	66,672,146
66-0	67.304	672,336	66,672,336
67-0	68.340	(328,440)	66,671,560
68-0	69.375	(1,328,250)	66,671,750
69-0	70.410	(2,328,060)	66,671,940
70-0	71.445	(3,327,870)	66,672,130
71-0	72.480	(4,327,680)	66,672,320
72-0	73.516	(5,328,456)	66,671,544

---

  * By assumption, when closed out, the futures price equals (Cash Price − Target Basis) ÷ Conversion Factor.
  † Bond futures trade in even 32nds. Thus the futures prices and the gains and losses are approximate.
  ‡ Transaction costs and the financing of margin flows are ignored.

will change by 1 percent, but since this change is completely predictable, there is no basis risk associated with the delivery date.

Basis risk, properly defined, refers only to the uncertainty associated with the target rate basis or target price basis. Accordingly, it is imperative that the target basis be properly defined if one is to correctly assess the risk and expected return in a hedge.

A Digression: Hedges that Do Not Minimize Risk

We have, until now, taken the minimum variance hedge as our point of departure and assumed that this is the desired hedge. In so doing, we have ignored expected return in our desire to minimize risk. A different approach can be taken to achieve different targets (i.e., different expected returns), but only at the cost of increasing risk.

A simple example is when the hedge ratio is set equal to zero, that is, when there is no hedge. The risk is then the risk of holding an unhedged cash security, and the target is the expected price of the security on the anticipated sale date. Futures prices in this case are irrelevant.

Alternatively, one can define the target, and then work backwards to find the hedge ratio that gives the desired target. For example, a hedger may want to hedge a deliverable security for a sale date corresponding to a futures delivery date (implying that he could lock in the sale price with no risk), but he wants the target to be the current price of the security. This may be possible: there is frequently some hedge ratio that on average (at least, historically) offsets changes in cash prices with changes in futures prices, thus making the current price the appropriate target. However, if the hedger uses a hedge ratio that makes the current price the target price, he must take on more risk than he would if he chose a hedge ratio that equates the target price to the futures price.

The important point is that it is imperative that the target and the risk be correctly defined, and both the target and the risk level depend on the hedge ratio. If the manager uses the minimum variance hedge ratio, then the target and risk level are determined as described in earlier sections. If, on the other hand, the target is set equal to the current price, a hedge ratio can usually be found to give this expected return, but the hedge will not generally be the minimum variance hedge. (The exception being very short-lived hedges and those cases in which the futures price equals the current price.) Thus the hedger may obtain a more desirable target rate for the hedge, but does so only by assuming incremental risk.

In subsequent sections, we will continue to assume that risk minimization is the primary concern of the hedger and set up hedges accordingly.

CROSS HEDGING

A cross hedge in the futures market is a hedge in which the security to be hedged is not deliverable on the futures contract used in the hedge.[5] For example, an investor or issuer who wants to hedge the sale price of long-term corporate bonds might hedge with the T-bond futures contract, but since corporate bonds cannot be delivered in satisfaction of the contract, this would be considered a cross hedge. Similarly, on the short end of the curve, a hedger might want to hedge a three-month rate that does not perfectly track the T-bill rate, domestic CD rate, or Eurodollar rate specified in the futures contracts. A hedger might also want to hedge a rate that is of the same quality as the rate specified in one of the contracts, but has a different maturity. For example, a hedger must cross hedge if he wants to hedge a Treasury bond, note, or bill with a maturity that does not qualify for delivery on any futures contract. Thus, when

---

[5] Since there is never actual delivery on the Eurodollar time deposit contract, a cross hedge is defined as one in which the rate to be hedged does not perfectly correspond to the three-month Libor rate underlying the futures contract.

the security to be hedged differs from the futures contract specification in terms of either quality or maturity, one is led to the cross hedge.

Conceptually, cross hedging is somewhat more complicated than hedging deliverable securities because it involves two relationships. First, there is the relationship between the most deliverable security and the futures contract. (This relationship was addressed in the foregoing sections.) Secondly, there is the relationship between the security to be hedged and the most deliverable security. Practical considerations may, at times, lead us to short cut this two-step relationship and focus directly on the relationship between the security to be hedged and the futures contract, thus ignoring the deliverable security altogether. However, in so doing, one runs the risk of miscalculating the target rate and the risk in the hedge. Furthermore, if the hedge does not perform as expected, the short cut makes it very difficult to tell why the hedge went awry.

The Hedge Ratio

The key to minimizing risk in a cross hedge is to choose the right hedge ratio. The key to the right hedge ratio is volatility weighting, or weighting by relative changes in value. The purpose of an asset hedge is to use gains or losses from the futures position to offset any difference between the target sale price and the actual sale price. Accordingly, the hedge ratio is chosen with the intention of matching the volatility (or dollar change) of the futures contract to the volatility (or dollar deviation from the target price) of the asset. The purpose of a liability hedge is to use futures gains or losses to offset any discrepancy between the target issue rate and the actual issue rate. Thus, the hedge ratio for a liability hedge is chosen with the intention of matching futures gains or losses to deviations of interest expense from the target level. In summary, then, the hedge ratio is determined by the expected relative volatility of the instrument to be hedged and the hedging instrument. Consequently, the hedge ratio is given by:

$$\text{Hedge Ratio} = \frac{\text{Volatility of Hedged Security}}{\text{Volatility of Hedging Instrument}}$$

As the formula shows, if the instrument to be hedged is more volatile than the futures contract (the hedging instrument), more than one futures contract will be needed.

While it might be fairly clear why volatility is the key variable in determining the hedge ratio, "volatility" has many definitions. For hedging purposes, however, we are concerned with volatility in absolute dollar terms.[6] To calculate the dollar volatility of a fixed income

---

[6] Duration and volatility in terms of percentage change in value may be helpful in deriving the hedge ratio, but offsetting actual dollars is always the bottom line.

security one must know the precise point in time that volatility is to be calculated (because volatility generally declines as a security ages) and the price or yield at which to calculate volatility (because higher yields generally lower dollar volatility for a given yield change). The relevant point in the life of the security for calculating volatility is the point at which the hedge will be lifted. Volatility at other points is essentially irrelevant since the goal is to lock in a price or rate only on that particular day. Similarly, the relevant yield at which to calculate volatility is the target yield. It is only the deviations from the target yield that are of concern to the hedger. Consequently, the "volatility of the hedged security" referred to in the formula is the price value of a basis point for the security on the hedge lift date, calculated at the target rate.

An example shows why volatility weighting leads to the proper hedge ratio. Suppose that on April 19, 1985 an investor buys the Southern Bell 11¾ percent bonds of 2023 and sells June 1985 T-bond futures as a hedge for the sale of the bonds. Since the telephone bonds are not deliverable, the investor must cross hedge. Suppose that the Treasury 7⅝ of 2007 is the most deliverable bond on the contract and that it is currently trading at 11.50 percent, the Southern Bell bonds at 12.40 percent, and the T-bond futures at a price of 70-0. To simplify, assume also that the yield spread between the two bonds will remain at 90 basis points and that the anticipated sale date is the end of June.

Since the sale date corresponds to the final futures delivery date, the target basis for the deliverable 7⅝ is zero, by convergence. Since the conversion factor for the 7⅝ for the June 1985 contract was .9660, the target price for hedging the 7⅝ would be 67.62 (from 70 × .9660) and the target yield would be 11.789 percent (the yield at a price of 67.62). Since the yield on the telephone bonds is assumed to stay at 90 basis points above the yield on the 7⅝, the target yield for the Southern Bell bonds would be 12.689 percent with a corresponding price of 92.628. At these target levels, the price values of a basis point (PVBP) for the 7⅝ and telephone bonds are, respectively, .056332 and .072564. As indicated earlier, all of these calculations are made using a settlement date equal to the anticipated sale date, in this case June 28, 1985. Thus, the relative price volatilities of the hedged security and the deliverable security are easily obtained from the assumed sale date and target prices.

However, in the formula for the hedge ratio we need the volatility, not of the deliverable security, but of the hedging instrument, i.e., of the futures contract. Fortunately, knowing the volatility of the hedged security relative to the most deliverable security, and the volatility of the most deliverable security relative to the futures contract, the relative volatilities that define the hedge ratio can be easily obtained as follows:

$$\frac{\text{Hedge}}{\text{Ratio}} = \frac{\text{Volatility of Hedged Security}}{\text{Volatility of Futures Contract}}$$

$$= \frac{\text{Volatility of Hedged Security}}{\text{Volatility of Most Deliverable}} \times \frac{\text{Volatility of Most Deliverable}}{\text{Volatility of Futures Contract}}$$

Or, more concisely, assuming a fixed yield spread between the security to be hedged and the most deliverable bond,

$$\text{Hedge Ratio} = \frac{\text{PVBP of Hedged Security}}{\text{PVBP of Most Deliverable}} \times \frac{\text{Conversion Factor}}{\text{for Most Deliverable}}$$

where PVBP stands for the price value of a basis point.

The hedge ratio in the example at hand is therefore approximately 1.24 (from .072564/.056332 × .9660). Table 5 shows that if the simplifying assumptions hold, a futures hedge using the recommended hedge ratio very nearly locks in the target price for $10 million face value of the telephone bonds. (Furthermore, most of the remaining error could be eliminated by frequent adjustments to the hedge ratio to account for the

---

TABLE 5 Hedging a Nondeliverable Bond to a Delivery Date

Instrument to be hedged: Southern Bell 11¾ of 4/19/23
Hedge ratio = 1.24
Price of futures contract when sold = 70-0
Target price for Southern Bell bonds = 92.628

Actual Sale Price of Telephone Bonds	Yield at Sale	Yield on U.S. 7⅝*	Price of U.S. 7⅝	Futures Price†	Gain (Loss) on 124 Contracts ($10/.01/ Contract)	Effective Sale Price‡
$8,200,000	14.338%	13.438%	59.313	61.401	$1,066,276	$9,266,276
8,400,000	13.996	13.096	60.887	63.030	864,280	9,264,280
8,600,000	13.671	12.771	62.451	64.649	663,524	9,263,524
8,800,000	13.359	12.459	64.018	66.271	462,396	9,262,396
9,000,000	13.061	12.161	65.580	67.888	261,888	9,261,888
9,200,000	12.776	11.876	67.134	69.497	62,372	9,262,372
9,400,000	12.503	11.603	68.683	71.100	(136,400)	9,263,600
9,600,000	12.240	11.340	70.233	72.705	(335,420)	9,264,580
9,800,000	11.988	11.088	71.773	74.299	(533,076)	9,266,924
10,000,000	11.745	10.845	73.312	75.892	(730,608)	9,269,392
10,200,000	11.512	10.612	74.839	77.473	(926,652)	9,273,348

* By assumption, the yield on the U.S. 7⅝ is 90 basis points lower than the yield on the Southern Bell bond.
† By convergence, the futures price equals the price of the U.S. 7⅝ divided by .9660 (the conversion factor).
‡ Transaction costs and the financing of margin flows are ignored.

fact that the price values of a basis point change as the bonds age and as rates move up or down.)

Although the example in Table 5 is constructed for a hedge held to the futures delivery date, the technique is equally valid for hedges lifted prior to delivery. The primary difference is that if the hedge is lifted before delivery, the target basis for the deliverable issue will not generally be zero and, thus, the target will be different. Such a hedge is illustrated in one of the examples that follow.

Changing Yield Spreads: The Regression

One final refinement in the hedging strategy is usually necessary for hedging nondeliverable securities. This refinement concerns the assumption about the relative yield spread between the most deliverable security and the security to be hedged. In the last section it was assumed that the yield spread was constant over time. However, yield spreads are not constant over time, but vary with the maturity of the instruments in question, the level of rates, and with many unpredictable and nonsystematic factors.

Regression analysis is a simple technique that allows the hedger to capture the relationship between yield levels and yield spreads and use it to his advantage. The regression is a statistical technique that can use historical data to model the imperfect relationship between two variables. For hedging purposes, the variables are the yield on the security to be hedged and the yield on the most deliverable security. Accordingly, the regression equation takes the form:

$$\text{Yield on Security to be Hedged} = a + b \times \text{Yield on Most Deliverable Security} + \text{error}$$

The regression procedure provides an estimate of b (beta), the expected relative yield change in the two securities. The "error" term accounts for the fact that the relationship between the yields is not perfect and contains a certain amount of noise. The regression will, however, give an estimate of a and b so that over the sample period the error is on average zero. The example in the previous section which uses constant spreads implicitly assumes that the beta in the regression equals 1.0 and a equals .90 (since .90 was the assumed spread).

For the two issues in question, i.e., the Southern Bell 11¾ and the Treasury 7⅝, the estimated beta over a recent period was 1.05. Thus, yields on the corporate issue are expected to move 5 percent more than yields on the Treasury issue. To correctly calculate the relative volatility of the two issues this fact must be taken into account; thus, the hedge ratio derived in the last section must be multiplied by the factor 1.05.

Consequently, instead of shorting 124 T-bond futures contracts to hedge $10 million of telephone bonds, the investor would short 130 contracts.

To generalize this concept, the formula for the hedge ratio is revised as follows to incorporate the impact of beta:

$$\frac{\text{Hedge}}{\text{Ratio}} = \text{beta} \times \frac{\text{PVBP of the Hedged Security}}{\text{PVBP of the Most Deliverable}} \times \frac{\text{Conversion}}{\text{Factor}}$$

where beta is derived from the yield of the hedged security regressed on the yield of the most deliverable security. As before, PVBP stands for the change in price for a single basis point change in yield, calculated at the target prices for settlement on the day the hedge is to be lifted.

This hedging strategy can also be applied to hedges of short-term assets or liabilities. However, since there are no conversion factors for short-term futures, the hedge ratio formula for the short-term contracts simplifies to:

$$\text{Hedge Ratio} = \text{beta} \times \frac{\text{PVBP of the Hedged Security}}{\text{PVBP of the Futures Contract}}$$

An example shows how this hedging strategy works in the short end of the curve and how to set up a cross hedge if the hedge is to be lifted before the futures delivery date. In the example illustrated in Table 3, a hedger used the T-bill contract to hedge the rate at which he would sell six-month T bills in 30 days (at which time the T bills would have five months to maturity). A similar example constructed to hedge a commercial paper rate can be used to illustrate the cross hedge technique. In the earlier example, it was assumed that spot six-month T bills were trading at 8.50 percent and that the T-bill futures contract settling in three months was trading at 9.00 percent. To illustrate the cross hedge, we assume that a hedger wants to hedge the six-month commercial paper rate 30 days out.[7] Suppose that the current rate on commercial paper is 9.40 percent and that the beta and intercept terms from the regression of commercial paper rates on T-bill rates are, respectively 1.05 and .50. Thus, the expected commercial paper rate, given the T-bill rate, is:

$$\text{Commercial Paper Rate} = .50 + 1.05 \times \text{T-Bill Rate}$$

It is important to note that, if possible, the rates that are used in the regression should be the rates on the securities as they will be when the hedge is lifted.[8]

---

[7] The hedger could be either an issuer who plans to issue six-month paper in 30 days, or an investor who owns seven-month paper which he intends to sell in 30 days.

[8] Obtaining the relevant data in this situation would be difficult, but ideally one would want to regress six-month commercial paper rates on five-month T-bill rates, since the security to be hedged and the deliverable security will be, respectively, six-month and five-month securities on the day the hedge is lifted. However, a reasonable alternative would be to use six-month T-bill rates as a proxy for five-month T-bill rates.

Using the formula, the hedge ratio is calculated as

$$\text{Hedge Ratio} = \text{beta} \times \frac{\text{PVBP of the Hedged Security}}{\text{PVBP of the Futures Contract}}$$

$$= 1.05 \times \frac{50.00}{25.00} = 2.10$$

The price value of a basis point is derived from the formula: PVBP = $1,000,000 × .0001 × (months to maturity/12). As always, the volatility (PVBP) figures are calculated for the securities as they will be on the day the hedge is lifted, not as they are on the day the hedge is set.

To show how well the hedge works, Table 6 shows the effective sale rate and price for the commercial paper given a range of market rates on

TABLE 6   Hedging Commercial Paper for 30 Days

Rate on futures contracts when sold = 9 percent
Face amount of commercial paper = $1 million

Actual Sale Rate for C. Paper	Actual Sale Price for C. Paper	Five Month T-Bill Rate*	Futures Rate When Hedge Is Closed Out†	Gain (Loss) on 2.1 Contracts	Effective Sale Price for C. Paper	Effective Sale Rate for C. Paper‡
5.00%	$975,000	4.29%	4.62%	$(22,995)	$952,005	9.60%
6.00	970,000	5.24	5.57	(18,008)	951,992	9.60
7.00	965,000	6.19	6.52	(13,020)	951,980	9.60
8.00	960,000	7.14	7.47	(8,033)	951,967	9.61
9.00	955,000	8.10	8.43	(2,993)	952,007	9.60
10.00	950,000	9.05	9.38	1,995	951,995	9.60
11.00	945,000	10.00	10.33	6,983	951,983	9.60
12.00	940,000	10.95	11.28	11,970	951,970	9.61
13.00	935,000	11.90	12.23	16,958	951,958	9.61
14.00	930,000	12.86	13.19	21,998	951,998	9.60
15.00	925,000	13.81	14.14	26,985	951,985	9.60

* From the regression, commercial paper rate = .50 + 1.05 × T-bill rate. Thus, T-bill rate = (commercial paper rate − .50)/1.05.
† When the hedge is set the rate basis is −.50 percent (from 8.50 percent − 9.00 percent). Given a linear decline in the basis, the basis will be −.33 when the hedge is lifted.
‡ Transaction costs and the financing of margin flows are ignored.

the day the hedge is lifted. In the table it is assumed that the six-month commercial paper rate exactly equals the rate that would be predicted by the regression (i.e., commercial paper rate = .50 + 1.05 × T-bill rate). Also it is assumed that the basis between the deliverable T bill and the futures contract declines linearly over time from its current level of −.50 percent. Thus, when the hedge is lifted in 30 days the futures rate will equal the cash rate plus .33 percent. (Recall, rate basis = cash rate − futures rate.) As the table shows, the hedge effectively locks in a rate of approximately 9.60 percent for the sale of the commercial paper, (and exactly 9.60 percent if all decimal places are carried through the calculations). Obviously, 9.60 percent should be the target rate for the hedge, not the spot commercial paper rate of 9.40 percent. The following section shows how a hedger could have easily derived this target when the hedge was set, without working through a large number of scenarios.

Deriving the Target for a Cross Hedge

It was shown earlier that the target rate for a hedge of a deliverable security should be defined as the sum of the futures rate and the target basis. That is,

$$\frac{\text{Target Rate}}{\text{for Hedge}} = \frac{\text{Futures}}{\text{Rate}} + \frac{\text{Target Rate}}{\text{Basis}}$$

The target rate basis is determined by the projected path of the basis through time. For simplicity, a linear decline in the basis was used in the examples. This formula is equally applicable to hedges of long-, short-, and intermediate-term debt securities.

When the discussion turned to cross hedging the relationship between the security to be hedged and the deliverable security was modeled using the regression equation. That equation was as follows:

$$\frac{\text{Yield on Security}}{\text{to be Hedged}} = a + b \times \frac{\text{Yield on}}{\text{Deliverable Security}} + \text{error}$$

On average, the error term is equal to zero. Combining these two equations, the target for a cross hedge is easily derived.[9]

$$\text{Target Rate} = a + b \times \left(\frac{\text{Futures}}{\text{Rate}} + \frac{\text{Target}}{\text{Basis}}\right)$$

To apply the formula to the commercial paper example, all the relevant information is on hand. The a and b coefficients from the regression were, respectively, .50 and 1.05; the target basis was −.33 percent, and the futures rate on the day the hedge was set was 9.00 percent. (See footnote † in Table 6.) Accordingly,

$$\text{Target Rate} = .50 + 1.05 \times (9.00 - .33)$$
$$= 9.60$$

---

[9] Since a regression of the deliverable security on itself would result in an intercept term equal to 0.0 and a beta equal to 1.0, this formulation includes the target rate for a deliverable security as a special case. Consequently, the original formula is derived when the cross hedge formula is applied to the deliverable security. The formula is also applicable if the hedger chooses to assume the yield spread will stay constant: setting the intercept (a) equal to the assumed yield spread and b equal to 1.0, the formula will give the correct target rate for constant yield spreads.

Thus, without working through any scenarios the hedger can see that the appropriate target for the hedge is 9.60 percent. As Table 6 shows, 9.60 percent is exactly what the hedge locks in if the assumptions are valid.

Cross Hedging Summarized

A cross hedge is more complicated than a hedge of a deliverable security because the security to be hedged is not directly tied to the futures contract, even on the delivery date. However, since the deliverable security and the futures contract are directly linked (at least at delivery), the cross hedger bridges the gap by estimating the relationship between the security to be hedged and the deliverable security (via the regression procedure), and estimating the relationship between the deliverable security and the futures contract (by projecting the future course of the basis). Combining these two estimates results in a forecast of the relationship between the security to be hedged and the futures contract. The combined estimates also give a forecast of what the hedger can expect from the hedge, i.e., the target rate. Exhibit 2 shows these relationships schematically.

It is sometimes necessary to take a short cut by focusing just on the relationship between the security to be hedged and the futures contract, leaving out the deliverable security. This relationship is just the convolu-

---

EXHIBIT 2 The Cross Hedge

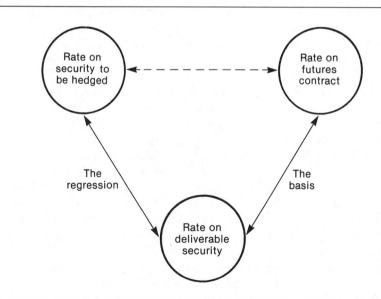

tion of the two relationships mentioned above—i.e., the relationship between the security to be hedged and the deliverable security, and the relationship between the deliverable security and the futures contract. The shorter route is sometimes the only practical approach, either because data is not available for the relevant regressions, or because there is a need to simplify. However, even when it is impossible to implement the hedge as a two-step process, the two-step process is probably the most accurate way to analyze a cross hedge.

MONITORING AND EVALUATING THE HEDGE

After a target is determined and a hedge is set, all that is left is to monitor the hedge during its life, and to evaluate it after it has been lifted. Most hedges require very little active monitoring during their life. In fact, overactive management poses more of a threat to most hedges than does inactive management. The reason for this is that the hedger usually will not receive enough new information during the life of the hedge to justify a change in the hedging strategy. For example, it is not advisable to readjust the hedge ratio every day in response to a new data point and a possible corresponding change in the estimated value of beta.

There are, however, exceptions to this general rule. As rates change, volatilities (i.e., PVBPs) change. Consequently, the hedge ratio may change slightly. In other cases, there may be sound economic reasons to believe that the beta has changed. In the commercial paper example, a financial crisis or rating change for the issuer could bring about a real change in the relationship between the commercial paper rate and the rate on the deliverable security. Consequently, it might be advisable to adjust the hedge ratio to conform to a new estimate of beta. However, these are exceptions, and the best approach is usually to let a hedge run its course while sticking to the original strategy.

Normally, a hedge can be evaluated only after it has been lifted. Evaluation involves, first, an assessment of how closely the hedge locked in the target rate, i.e., how much error there was in the hedge. To provide some meaningful interpretation of the error, the hedger should calculate how far from the target rate the sale (or purchase) would have been had there been no hedge at all. To illustrate, a hedger might set a target of 10 percent for a subsequent sale of bonds. Even with the hedge, he might find his effective sale rate to be 10.50 percent—a significantly higher rate than expected. However, it may be that without hedging, the bonds would have sold at 13 percent. Consequently, the hedge, although far from perfect, saved the seller 250 basis points.

The primary reason for evaluating a hedge after it has been lifted is to ascertain the sources of error in the hedge, hopefully to gain insights that can be used to the hedger's advantage in subsequent hedges. There are three major sources of hedging errors: the projected value of the basis at the lift date can be in error, the parameters estimated from the regression (i.e., a and b) can be inaccurate, and the error term in the regression may not equal zero. Frequently, at least in the short run, the last two sources of error are indistinguishable. The hedger will generally only know that the regression equation did not give an accurate estimate of the rate to be hedged. However, such inaccuracy could have occurred either from poor parameter estimates, or from very accurate parameter estimates in conjunction with a large error term. Only additional data will resolve the question.

The other major source of errors in a hedge—an inaccurate projected value of the basis—is the more difficult problem. Unfortunately, there are no simple models like the regression that can be applied to the basis. Simple models, it turns out, violate some equilibrium relationships for fixed income securities that we would expect to hold. On the other hand, theoretically rigorous models are very unintuitive and usually soluble only by complex numerical methods. Modeling the basis is undoubtedly one of the most important problems that hedgers face.

SUMMARY

There are many different ways to go about hedging and in the interest of prudence it is best to do some preliminary work before a hedge is ever initiated. Besides determining the appropriate number and types of contracts to use, we suggest that managers also obtain an estimate of the effectiveness of the hedge (i.e., risk reduction relative to an unhedged position), and the residual hedging risk (the absolute level of risk in a hedged position). While these are simple concepts, the subtleties of certain statistical procedures may make it difficult to derive reliable estimates of hedge effectiveness and residual hedging risk. The manager should be able to rely on his broker to help assess these parameters of the hedge.

The target of the hedge, i.e., the expected rate or price which the manager hopes to lock in, is another important variable that should be considered before the hedge is set. The target of the hedge depends on how long the hedge is held, the projected value of the basis, and the projected relationship between the security to be hedged and the deliverable security.

If the decision is made to hedge, the problem is then one of choosing a hedging strategy. Unfortunately, managers are exposed to many different strategies, including regression techniques, volatility weighting techniques, and techniques predicated on models of the basis. Each technique has certain advantages, but each also has its own target rate and hedge ratio. In this presentation we have suggested a strategy that combines these three techniques so that the hedger profits from the strong points of each.

43

A Comparison of Alternative Hedge Ratio Methodologies with Interest-Rate Futures

Alden L. Toevs, Ph.D.
Vice President, Director of Mortgage Research
Morgan Stanley & Co.

David P. Jacob
Research Manager
Morgan Stanley & Co.

This chapter compares the major estimation techniques for calculating hedge ratios when the hedging vehicle is a fixed income futures contact and the hedging objective is to minimize the variance of a target account for a fixed income portfolio. We find that the sophisticated hedging techniques come from a common theoretical base. They differ from one another in their estimates of the covariance between the hedging and target instruments and the variance of the hedging instruments. In practical applications these sophisticated techniques normally do not produce widely different returns. Their effectiveness does, however, often exceed more naive approaches. There are differences in computational costs among the sophisticated techniques. Based on an overall lower computational cost, an ability to handle extreme or unique pricing relationships, and the possibility of more carefully modeling the basis, we conclude that a hedge ratio computed using an instantaneous price sensitivity (duration) measure is better than regression-based hedging techniques.

We begin by classifying hedge types by the target account of concern. In the remainder of this chapter we devote most of our efforts to hedging one specific target: the market price of a portfolio of fixed income securities. This target was selected as an example because more alternative hedging techniques have been offered for this target than any other. We next list the various hedge ratio estimation methodologies that have been proposed to hedge market value. These vary from rules of thumb to regression-based hedge ratio techniques. Following a listing and theoretical critique of these estimation techniques, we study the successes of the hedging techniques in practice. Hedges are constructed and tested on several representative bonds for the period from mid-1982 to 1984.

CLASSIFICATION OF HEDGE TYPES

Many analysts have wrestled with the problem of producing an all encompassing definition of hedging. We forego this problem by defining a hedge to be any activity that minimizes the variance of return. Risk-minimizing hedges can be constructed for currently held positions or anticipated ones. And, the hedge may be in place for a known or uncertain period of time. Furthermore, hedges may be applied to asset or liability positions. Given all these possibilities, it helps to categorize hedge types. Exhibit 1 provides such taxonomy for asset hedges; liability hedges are similarly classified.

EXHIBIT 1 Hedge Classifications

	Time Uncertain	*Time Certain*
Currently Held Cash Position	*Weak Form Cash Hedge (Inventory Hedge)* Hedge Goal: Preserve capital on a daily basis. Hedge Strategy: Short the nearby futures contract.	*Strong Form Cash Hedge (Immunization)* Hedge Goal: Track daily the zero coupon bond due at the end of investment horizon. Hedge Strategy: Go long or short nearby futures contract.
Anticipated Cash Position	*Weak Form (Anticipatory Hedge)* Hedge Goal: Lock in currently available return or price at the uncertain cash inflow date. Hedge Strategy: Buy futures contract that expires nearest to the expected cash inflow date.	*Strong Form (Anticipatory Hedge)* Hedge Goal: Lock in currently available return or price at known cash inflow date. Hedge Strategy: Buy futures contract that expires nearest to the known cash inflow date.

The inventory hedge (weak form cash hedge) minimizes the price (market value) variance of an existing asset portfolio that is to be held for an indefinite period of time. An example is the hedge placed on a bond dealer's inventory. As indicated in Exhibit 1, an inventory hedge uses a short position in a futures contract. When interest rates rise, the cash position falls in value. A short position has offsetting price variation. The futures contract or contracts selected should have the highest possible covariance in prices with the inventory. Usually nearby futures contracts on securities similar to those in inventory maximizes this price covariance.

With a strong form cash hedge the investor knows the time the portfolio will be held. The hedging goal is to minimize the variance in the expected total return on the portfolio for a given investment period. To immunize portfolio returns, a cash and futures portfolio must be created and then maintained that has the same interest-rate sensitivity as a zero-coupon (pure discount) bond with an initial maturity equal to the investment period. Mirroring the zero coupon bond's initial value and its interest rate sensitivity at each point in time means that whenever the interest rate sensitivity of the cash portfolio is less than that of the zero-coupon bond, futures must be purchased to augment the price sensitivity of the cash portfolio. Conversely, whenever the cash portfolio is more interest rate sensitive than the zero-coupon bond, futures must be sold to reduce this level of sensitivity.

Strong form anticipatory hedges apply whenever a known amount of cash will be received at a certain future date and the portfolio manager wishes to minimize the variance of the acquisition prices of the cash securities. For example, suppose that the cash will be received on December 3, 1986 and the desire is to use this cash to purchase 90-day Treasury bills. The forward price of such a bill is, say, $97.05. Based on this price, these bills have a bond equivalent yield of 12.19 percent from their delivery to maturity.[1] The hedging position chosen is the one that most closely realizes this market-forecasted price and yield. This hedge appears to require the acquisition of future delivery rights to as many dollars of bills as the anticipated cash inflow. But, because margin calls on the long futures position must be financed, the appropriate hedge ratio is not an exact dollar match. An added complication arises if the futures contract offers a deliverable bond other than that desired by the future investor.

In the weak form anticipatory hedge, the goal is to minimize the variance in an acquisition price (a rate of return for a specified holding

---

[1] The quoted price of Treasury bills is based on the discount yield for a 360-day year. A "price" of 88.21 implies a discount from 100 of 11.79. This discount yield can be used to compute the corresponding price as follows: Price $= 100 - (90/360) \times 11.79$. Given the price, a bond equivalent yield can be calculated.

period) on asset flows to be received at an unknown date. Like the strong form anticipatory hedge, this hedge requires the purchase of futures contracts with an interest rate sensitivity equal to that of the security to be purchased. The uncertain timing of the cash receipt reduces the effectiveness of this type of anticipatory hedge. Nevertheless, futures can be used to narrow the range of possible outcomes.

The four-way classification in Exhibit 1 is incomplete. For example, an anticipatory hedge may be attempted when the cash to be received and the inflow date are both known with certainty, but the holding period for the investment is not. Alternatively, the cash inflow date and the holding period may be known with certainty, but the amount of cash to be received may be uncertain. We will not dwell here on these complications—to do so obscures the goal of developing an analytical foundation for the construction of variance minimizing hedge ratios for the more frequently encountered hedges.

THE THEORY OF MINIMUM VARIANCE HEDGE RATIOS

With a general classification of hedges behind us, we now turn to the determination of "optimal" hedge ratios. As noted above, we view the hedging goal to be the minimization of the variance of either the price or total return of existing or anticipated cash positions. Since the discussion of minimum variance hedge ratios for any one hedge classification substantially overlaps those of the other hedges, we will not discuss each hedge type in detail. We have chosen to critique the methods proposed for constructing minimum variance weak form cash hedges.[2] This type of hedge is instructive because the others are special cases of it and because this one has had more proposed hedge ratio methodologies than the others.

Hedge ratio estimation techniques will be illustrated using a simple historical situation. On June 24, 1982, a trader had a $10 million face value position (10,000 bonds) in the U.S. Treasury bond maturing on November 15, 2010. This bond pays a 12.75 percent coupon rate and was priced on June 24, 1982 at 90.125, which gives a market value of $9.0125 million. The trader selected the T-bond futures contract for delivery in September 1982 as the hedging instrument. This contract traded at 59.3125 on June 24, 1982. The problem is to determine the number of futures contracts to sell in order to minimize the price variation of the cash position. Five methods with two additional variations have been offered for estimating the hedge ratio in this instance. The major tech-

---

[2] Detailed analyses of the other three hedges can be found in A.L. Toevs and D.P. Jacob, *Interest Rate Futures: A Comparison of Alternative Hedge Ratio Methodologies* (New York: Morgan Stanley, June 1984).

niques are: dollar value matches, conversion factors, regression analyses using price changes, regression analyses using price levels, and an approach based on an instantaneous price sensitivity calculation. The following discusses the application of each technique to the situation existing on June 24, 1982.

Dollar Value Matches

A simple hedging strategy computes the hedge ratio using a dollar-valued exposure in futures contracts equal to the cash inventory market value. Since the trader was long $9.0125 million in cash securities on June 24, 1982, the short position selected with this method also was priced at $9.0125 million. Given a futures price of 59.3125, this requirement translates into a hedge ratio of 1.52.[3] In general, this hedge ratio methodology works well only when the interest rate characteristics of the cash bond closely match that of the futures market deliverable bond.

Conversion Factor Method

The conversion factor method is an extension of the dollar value match method when the futures exchange permits the short position holder to deliver several security grades to fulfill the futures contract. The conversion factor corrects the invoice amount for the required par delivery of bonds for the difference between the coupon of the security being delivered and that of the standard coupon specified by the contract. For example, Treasury bond and GNMA futures contracts allow many coupon/maturity combinations to be delivered.

The 12.75 percent T-bond maturing on November 15, 2010 has a conversion factor of 1.50 on June 24, 1982. This value indicates that the hedger should sell 1.50 times the number of futures contract "bonds" as held in inventory. Essentially, the conversion factor method presumes that if the cash bond could be delivered tomorrow, the hedge position would have as many dollars in short contracts as the cash position has in long contracts to "deliver." The accuracy of the conversion factor method increases when the delivery date nears and when the interest rate sensitivity of the cash bond approaches the interest rate sensitivity of the cheapest-to-deliver bond.

The above hedging techniques have convenience as their strong point. Neither method properly accounts for probable differences in the interest-rate sensitivities of cash securities and futures contracts. While

---

[3] This chapter will report the hedge ratio as the market value of the futures contract selected per market value dollar of the security to be hedged. This measure avoids having to deal with the minor complications introduced by various futures contracts representing different principal value commitments.

there are circumstances when these naive approaches produce effective hedges, sophisticated hedging techniques more often provide better results. We will now examine these alternative techniques.

The following expression represents the change in value of a portfolio consisting of a cash bond and a short position of N futures contracts:

$$\Delta V = \Delta P_c - (N \times \Delta P_f) \qquad \text{Equation I}$$

where ΔV, ΔP_c, and ΔP_f are the changes in the value of the portfolio, the cash bond, and the futures contract, respectively. If we define the optimal hedge ratio as the one that minimizes the variance of changes in portfolio value, it can be shown that

$$N^* = \text{covariance } (\Delta P_f \text{ with } \Delta P_c)/\text{variance } (\Delta P_f), \quad \text{Equation II}$$

where N^* is the optimal number of futures contracts to short. The mathematical proof is given in the Appendix.

The three remaining hedging methodologies considered in this paper are derived from Equation II. Each in its own way accounts for differential interest rate sensitivities in cash and futures contracts. The methods differ only in how they use available information to determine the covariance and variance terms in Equation II.

Regressions of Price Changes

This estimation methodology has its roots in early academic work on commodity hedging. A representative series of daily changes in price for a cash bond and a closely associated futures contract are graphed in Exhibit 2. Regression analysis is applied to this scatter of points to find the best fitting straight line. The equation used in the regression is

$$\Delta P_c = a + b\Delta P_f + error \qquad \text{Equation III}$$

The presumption in Equation III is that the changes in the cash and futures prices are linearly related to one another, subject also to random errors (basis risk). The estimated slope of the regression line (b in Equation III) gives the change in the value of the cash price per dollar move in the futures price. That is, it represents the market dollar amount of the futures contract to short per market dollar amount of inventory.

Ederington showed that the value of b equals the minimum variance hedge ratio provided that: (1) the futures contract selected for the regression has the highest possible correlation with the cash security; (2) ΔP_c and ΔP_f are related in a linear fashion; and (3) the historical data used in the regression are consistent with the current variance and covariance characteristics needed for use in Equation III.[4] This proof is discussed in

---

[4] Louis Ederington, "The Hedging Performances of the New Futures Markets," *Journal of Finance*, March 1979.

EXHIBIT 2 Daily Price Series, U.S. Treasury 12.75s of 2010 versus Nearby
T-Bond Futures Contract

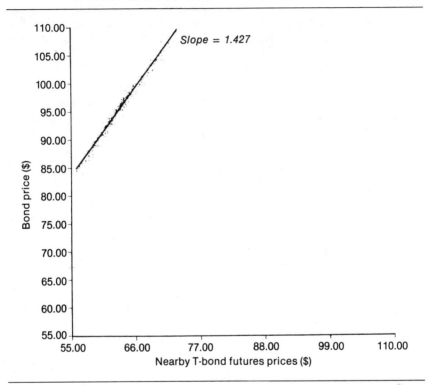

---

the Appendix. Any violation of these assumptions results in random or
systematic basis risk. Representative data series have to be long enough
to reflect true variance and covariance relationships, but they can also
be too long if the relationship between the cash and futures prices
evolves through time.

The data scatter in Exhibit 2 comes from daily price changes for the
240 trading days prior to 6/24/82 on the cash bond and the successively
nearby T-bond futures contracts. The slope of the best-fitting regression
line is 1.16 and means that the hedger of the 12.75s of 11/15/2010 should
short $1.16 in futures value per dollar of inventory.

Regressions of Price Levels

A different regression approach has recently been proposed. Here, the
regression fits a straight line to historical data series on cash and futures
price levels. Exhibit 3 depicts the historical relationship between the

EXHIBIT 3 Daily Change in Prices U.S. Treasury 12.75s of 2010 versus Nearby T-Bond Futures Contract

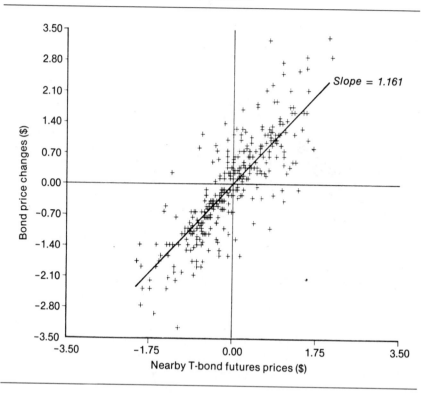

price levels on our cash bond and the successive nearby T-bond futures contracts. The estimated regression line for these data points is also graphed in Exhibit 3. (The scale differs significantly from Exhibit 2.) The regression equation that gives rise to this fitted line is

$$P_c = s + tP_f + \text{error} \qquad \text{Equation IV}$$

The slope of the line in Exhibit 3 is 1.43, which means that when P_f rises by one dollar, P_c rises by t dollars. Hence, the estimate of t can be thought of as a hedge ratio. (Note the substantial difference in this hedge ratio for that found using the same price data to run a regression of price changes.) The Appendix shows how t can be mathematically derived as a minimum variance hedge ratio.

Instantaneous Price Sensitivity Hedge Ratio

The price relationships depicted in Exhibit 3 can be exploited in a somewhat different manner. As shown by the broad, fuzzy line in Exhibit 4, a

EXHIBIT 4 Instantaneous Price Sensitivities

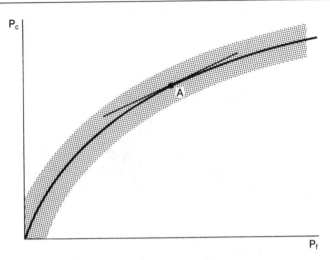

Slope of straight line estimates the hedge ratio
Slope is measured as in Equation (7) as $P_c D_{\tilde{c}}/P_f D_f$

close, but not precise, price relationship exists between cash and futures prices. The fuzziness of the relationship occurs because of basis risk. Rather than fitting a straight line through observed data points lying in this fuzzy band, one might ask the question: Given the current price position, does financial theory indicate how this position would change if interest rates slightly rise or fall?

Consider Point A in Exhibit 4. This position was chosen to lie on the center line of the band which indicates that current prices are such that futures are neither cheap nor rich to cash. The cash and futures prices are then reassessed after a small hypothetical movement in interest rates. This process is straightforward for cash bond prices, less so for futures prices. A futures price, however, implies a yield-to-maturity from the delivery date to the maturity date of the delivered bond. This yield is varied by one basis point, and the new futures (deliverable) price is computed. Dividing the instantaneous price change for the cash bond by that of the futures contract gives a hedge ratio.[5] This methodology produces the slope of the tangent to Point A in Exhibit 4. The Appendix

---

[5] Most contracts have a delivery month rather than a delivery date. In this case an expected delivery date must be used. A good rule of thumb is that delivery is expected to occur near the beginning (end) of the month when the yield curve is downward (upward) sloping.

shows this hedge ratio to be mathematically consistent with the minimum variance hedge ratio defined in Equation II.[6]

It is more difficult to compute the price sensitivity of futures contracts that permit several securities to be delivered. First the security that is expected to be cheapest to deliver must be identified. This bond's converted futures price (the quoted futures price times the conversion factor) coupled with its coupon rate, delivery date and maturity date provide sufficient information to compute a yield to maturity from the delivery date to the maturity date of the cheapest to deliver bond. Vary this yield by one basis point and find the new price of the deliverable. Convert this new price back into a future price by dividing it by the conversion factor. The new futures price relative to the original one gives the price sensitivity of the futures price for a one basis point change in yields.

The instantaneous price sensitivity hedge ratio can be expressed in terms of the "durations" of the cash and deliverable security. A useful property of duration is that it can express the price sensitivity of a bond in a convenient and simple expression: Change in P per unit change in r equals $-D^* \times P$, where D^* represents the duration of the bond divided by the quantity $(1 + (r/2))$, where r is the yield to maturity of the bond. (Some refer to D^* as the "modified" duration.)[7]

The instantaneous price hedge ratio is the price sensitivity of the cash security divided by the price sensitivity of the futures contract. Thus, an estimate of the minimum variance hedge ratio, expressed in terms of durations is

$$N^* = P_c \times D_c^*/P_f \times D_f^* \qquad \text{Equation V}$$

The subscripts refer to the cash or futures securities.

The literature on interpreting Equation V has been unclear in two respects. First, care has not been taken to specify what hedging objective is being sought through the application of this equation.[8] Second, there has been less than careful attention to the definitions of the prices and durations to be used in Equation V.[9] For weak form cash hedges, P_c is

---

[6] Under some circumstances the futures price may not be fully arbitraged. The interest-rate sensitivity of a mispriced contract can still be estimated using an assumption on what amount of the initial arbitrage premium remains after the interest rate shock.

[7] For a full explanation of duration, see G.O. Bierwag, G.G. Kaufman, and A.L. Toevs, "Duration: Its Development and Use in Bond Portfolio Management," *Financial Analysts Journal*, July/August 1983.

[8] See the critical comments of M. Pitts, "The Management of Interest Rate Risk: Comment," *Journal of Portfolio Management*, Fall 1985. These comments have been addressed in the Appendix where it is shown that duration and regression hedges have a common theoretical base.

[9] A number of papers by Chiang, Gay, and Kolb have contributed to the confusion on what prices and durations to use for the cash and futures contracts. (See, for example, G.D. Gay, and R.W. Kolb, "The Management of Interest Rate Risk," *Journal of Portfolio*

the current market value of the cash securities in the portfolio. D_c^* is the current modified duration of the cash portfolio. The price used for P_f when only one security is deliverable is the currently quoted futures price; otherwise, P_f is the current forward price of the cheapest-to-deliver security divided by the conversion factor of this security. D_f^* is the modified duration of the cheapest-to-deliver bond associated with P_f. It is calculated assuming the delivery date is today's date and using the cash flows associated with the deliverable bond from the delivery date to its maturity date.[10] Toevs and Jacob discuss the interpretations of prices and durations for other hedge classifications.[11]

On June 24, 1982, the September T-bond futures price was 59.3125 and the Treasury 8⅜ of 2008 was expected to be cheapest to deliver. This bond had a conversion factor of 1.0375, giving an estimated delivery price $61.537. At this price, the 8⅜ of 2008 has a yield to maturity, calculated from its delivery date, of 13.88 percent. Using this yield and price, the duration of the cash flows from the delivery date to 2008 is 7.75 years, which gives a modified duration of 7.25 for use in Equation V. The cash bond on June 24 had a price of 90.125 and a yield-to-maturity of 14.17 percent. This gives a duration of 7.34 years, 6.85 years in modified form. Substituting prices and durations into Equation V results in a hedge ratio of 1.38.

Some researchers have suggested adjusting durations for "relative yield volatilities". Rather than assuming a one basis point change in the yield on a benchmark security implies a one basis point change in the yield on any other security, these researchers assume that the yield changes are related proportionally. For example, if the benchmark is a

---

Management, Winter 1983, and R.W. Kolb, and R. Chiang, "Improving Hedging Performance Using Interest-Rate Futures," *Financial Management*, Autumn 1981.) This is surprising because a clearer statement of the problem is found in an earlier piece by McEnally and Rice, (See R.W. McEnally and M.L. Rice, "Hedging Possibilities in the Flotation of Debt Securities," *Financial Management*, Winter 1979.)

[10] The duration of a security that only promises future cash flows is interpreted somewhat differently than the duration of a cash security. A futures position does not constitute an investment; rather, it represents an instantaneous exposure of wealth, through changes in the variation margin, to changes in market perceptions of the expected course of interest rates. The futures contract's duration indexes the volatility of the variation margin to changes in the interest rates expected to prevail on the delivery date of the associated security. The simplest duration of a futures contract to compute is that of the T-bill futures contract. The duration of a 90-day Treasury bill at the delivery date of the contract equals .25 years. Thus, a T bill deliverable in one month and a T-bill futures contract deliverable in 21 months have equal durations. This does not necessarily imply that the hedge ratio computed with Equation V would be the same if the hedging security were either of these bill contracts. First, the prices of these two futures contracts may differ. Second, their modified durations would reflect any unequal interest rates implied by differing prices of these contracts. Third, as will be discussed in a moment, hedge ratios may also be adjusted for relative yield volatility estimates.

[11] See Toevs and Jacob, *Interest Rate Futures: A Comparison of Alternative Hedge Ratio Methodologies*.

one-year Treasury bill, then a proportionality factor of 0.9 for a two-year Treasury note indicates that when a basis point change in the bond equivalent yield occurs on the bill, the best guess is a 0.9 basis point change on the note.

The minimum variance hedge ratio obtained for situations when proportional yield changes occur in different securities can be constructed by making a simple adjustment to the hedge ratio reported in Equation V. It is

$$N^* = P_c \times D_c^* \times R_c/P_f \times D_f^* \times R_f, \qquad \text{Equation VI}$$

where R_c and R_f are the relative yield volatility factors for the cash and futures positions, respectively. On June 24, R_c/R_f was estimated to be 1.01.[12] This gives an adjusted hedged ratio of 1.39.

More comprehensive modeling of both duration and relative interest rate volatilities is possible. In the above, we have used a security's yield-to-maturity as the discounting rate for all cash flows associated with the security. Duration formulas exist that use individual discount factors (term structure rates). These formulas avoid having to make the assumption that yield curves are flat and change in a parallel fashion. Moreover, this approach allows the interest rate for each cash flow to have its own relative interest-rate volatility. The needed substitution in the above formulas is the more correctly computed duration and relative yield volatility values.

AN EVALUATION OF HEDGE RATIO METHODOLOGIES

Dollar matching and conversion factor hedge ratio estimation techniques, while convenient, apply in limited circumstances. All three of the remaining methods are theoretically consistent with the mathematics of minimizing the variance of a portfolio of futures and cash securities. The merits of these three estimation techniques must, then, depend on the empirical validity of their differing assumptions and the compromises that often arise in any associated empirical analyses.

Let us begin by analyzing hedge ratios constructed from regressions of price *levels*. Consider Exhibit 5. Here the deliverable has a different interest rate sensitivity than the cash bond. This is just the type of situation where nonsimple-minded hedge ratio estimation methodologies are expected to add value. If interest rates have, recently exceeded the interest rates giving rise to the current cash and futures prices (Point A), then the regression data are restricted to price combinations below those

---

[12] This was found by regressing the yield-to-maturity of the cash security against the yield from delivery to maturity of the cheapest to deliver security in prior periods.

EXHIBIT 5   Regression of Prices (historically low price experience)

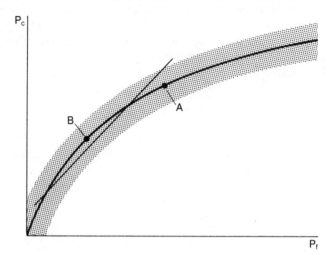

Slope of straight line estimates the hedge ratio
Hedge ratio too high

---

associated with Point A. The estimated hedge ratio overstates the current interest rate sensitivity of the cash security relative to the deliverable security—too many futures contracts will be shorted given our current price environment. Just the opposite conclusion holds when the available data systematically lies above Point A.

Only when a reasonable set of prices exists on both sides of the current prices of the cash and hedging instrument can the regression-based hedge ratio faithfully reflect the theoretically optimal hedge ratio. This is unfortunate because volatile and new price levels are normally situations when the correct execution of hedges adds the most value.[13]

The hedge ratio estimation technique derived from regressions of price *changes* also suffers from the same potential problem noted in Exhibit 5. In addition this regression technique assumes that the histori-

---

[13] Remember that this criticism holds when the interest-rate sensitivities of the cash and futures instruments differ from one another. If they did not do so, hedging is so simple that no sophisticated technique is required. In situations when the price relationship between cash securities and futures contracts is curved, as in Figure 5, a nonlinear regression equation might fit best. Toevs and Jacob examine this possibility, using a regression of the form $P_c = s + tP_f + vP_f^2 + \text{error}$. The empirical results for our example call for a hedge ratio of 1.53 as of June 24, 1982. In practice, we find the added complexity of this approach has little value.

cal pattern of the average size of price changes will hold in the future. The importance of this assumption can be illustrated rather simply. Recall that the hedge ratio estimated for June 24, 1982 using a regression of price *levels* was 1.43, but using a regression of price *changes* we obtained a ratio of 1.16. If the cash and futures price *pairs* are randomly scrambled and new regressions are run, the regression of price levels still produces a hedge ratio of 1.43, as the same pairs of prices are being fitted by the regression line, but the regression of price changes now produces a hedge ratio of 1.42! For regression of price changes to provide theoretically defensible hedge ratios, one must assume both that the prior price levels and the prior daily average price changes reflect today's potential price change magnitude. Only the former assumption need be made when using the regression of price levels.

A final deficiency of regression hedge ratios relative to the instantaneous price sensitivity methodology must be mentioned here. This issue helps make the transition from theory to practice. Advocates of regression techniques often ignore potential data problems of some importance. How would a bond portfolio manager deal with the data requirements needed to hedge a portfolio of 50–100 separate bonds? How can a regression be used to establish the hedge for a bond that has just been issued with a historically unusual coupon rate or maturity? How can regressions be conveniently performed for multiple bond portfolios? How can they be relied on should an unusual new issue become the cheapest-to-deliver security for existing futures contracts?

SOME EMPIRICAL RESULTS ON WEAK FORM CASH HEDGES

This section applies the hedge ratio estimation methodologies discussed above to recent market data. The time period analyzed starts in mid-1982 and continues to 1984. Data for 1981 through mid-1982 (240 days) are used to run the initial regressions. Regressions are updated every 20 trading days by dropping the oldest 20 days in the data set and adding the newest 20 days. Such frequently run regressions help place regression-based hedge ratios in a favorable light.

Four representative examples of weak form cash hedges are reported here. The first example hedges the 12.75 percent Treasury due in 2010. This security has an interest rate sensitivity during our sample period similar to that of the cheapest-to-deliver security associated with the T-bond futures contract. The second example hedges a Treasury note using the T-bond futures contract. The third and fourth examples examine the effectiveness of hedge ratio methodologies for single and double-A rated long-term corporate bonds.

Example 1: Hedging a Bond Similar to the T-Bond Futures Contract Deliverable Bond

From June 24, 1982 to January 1, 1984, daily hedges are constructed for the 12.75 Treasury of 2010, which ranged in price from 90 to 120. Table 1

TABLE 1 Percent Variance Reduced Cash Security: U.S. Treasury 12.75 of 2010

	10-Day Moving Average	30-Day Moving Average
Dollar matching	92%	96%
Conversion factor	92	96
Change in price regression	90	91
Price level regression	92	96
Price-sensitivity/duration	92	96
Price-sensitivity/duration (corrected for yield volatilities)	93	96
Curvilinear price regression*	92	96

* The hedge technique labeled "Curvilinear Price Regression" is that derived using a regression discussed in Footnote 13.

---

reports the percentage of the cash security's variance reduced by the alternative hedge ratios. Take, for example, the dollar match hedge ratio results for a 10-day moving average.[14] The reported variance reduction of 92 percent comes from the following four steps:

1. Compute for each trading day from 6/24/82 through 12/31/83 the hedged and unhedged portfolio returns.
2. Average these two series using a 10-day moving average.
3. Compute the variances of these 10-day average returns over the entire period.
4. Find the percentage variance of the unhedged position reduced in the hedged position.

Similar calculations are made based on a 30-day moving average of daily hedging outcomes. Because the interest-rate characteristics of the cash bond and the futures contract are so similar, all hedge ratio techniques produce similar and excellent results.

Example 2: Maturity/Duration Mismatched Hedge

Inventory positions may have duration characteristics dissimilar to those associated with the deliverable security underlying the best available

---

[14] Short time-span moving averages are used to remove the basis risk that is purely random in nature.

futures contract. After all, only three maturities are available in the Treasury futures contracts—the 90-day T-bill, the T-note, and the T-bond contracts. A relatively severe mismatch in maturities (durations) is studied in this example. The Treasury note paying 13 percent due in 1990 is hedged with the nearest to deliver T-bond futures contract. The results are reported in Table 2. This example reveals the weakness of the

TABLE 2 Percent Variance Reduced Cash Security: U.S. Treasury 13% of 1990

	10-Day Moving Average	30-Day Moving Average
Dollar matching	44%	68%
Conversion factor	50	72
Change in price regression	78	84
Price level regression	76	86
Price-sensitivity/duration	80	87
Price-sensitivity/duration (corrected for yield volatilities)	77	88
Curvilinear price regression	79	89

naive hedging strategies, i.e., ignoring the different interest rate sensitivities of the hedging and hedge instruments. As expected, the hedge performance for all hedge ratio methods falls below that experienced in Example 1, as no method perfectly estimates the influences of differential interest rate sensitivities.

As in Example 1, the more days in the moving average, the more random basis risk is offset. All techniques, other than dollar matching and conversion factor methods, remain tightly grouped. Note that the relative yield volatility correction in the price sensitivity hedge adds little value. This finding is explained by observing that variations in long-term cash market security yields are relatively close to the variations in intermediate-term yields. The curved line regression of prices technique modestly improves the hedging efficacy of the standard regression of price levels methodology. This is expected as the price relationships between the note and the T-bond futures contract has more distinct curvature—like that in Exhibit 5—than is present in Example 1.

Examples 3 and 4: Similar Maturity, Dissimilar Credit Quality Hedges

One can attempt to hedge inventories of long-term corporate bonds with T-bond futures contracts. In general, the greater the credit differential, the worse the hedge performance of T-bond futures contracts.[15] Suppose the cash security to be hedged is the double-A rated GMAC 8s of 2007. While this bond is callable, the high price discount of this low-coupon bond considerably reduces the chances of a call. Effectively, the duration of the bond is nearly that of a noncallable bond. Table 3 reports

---

TABLE 3   Percent Variance Reduced Cash Security: GMAC 8s of 2007

	10-Day Moving Average	30-Day Moving Average
Dollar matching	78%	89%
Conversion factor	75	86
Change in price regression	75	80
Price level regression	75	86
Price-sensitivity/duration	78	88
Price-sensitivity/duration (corrected for yield volatilities)	78	89
Curvilinear price regression	75	86

---

the relative performances of the various hedge ratios for the GMAC bond. Substantial portions of the variation in the naked position can be reduced by any means chosen to hedge. The convenience of dollar matching or price sensitivity hedge ratios argues for their use in practice. Given the poor performance of the naive dollar-matching strategy in other examples, however, price sensitivity hedge ratios provide a consistently superior methodology.

Table 4 examines the hedge effectiveness of alternative techniques when the corporate bond has a single A credit rating. The cash security in this example is the Tenneco 8⅜ of 2002. This bond trades at a substantial price discount which makes this callable bond effectively a long-term instrument. The lower credit quality of this bond reduces the hedge effectiveness for any hedge technique chosen, relative to the GMAC bond. Proportionally, more systematic interest-rate risk remains unhedged in this lower credit security than in the double-A rated bond examined above.[16]

---

[15] It should also be noted that it is more difficult to conduct regression analysis for corporate bonds than for Treasuries. Publicly available corporate bond price series have notable inaccuracies, making regression estimates for corporates much less accurate than those for Treasuries. We have minimized this problem here by using Morgan Stanley quotes on actively traded issues.

[16] A hedge methodology that takes into account the equity-like component of higher yielding bonds is discussed in R. Bookstaber and D.P. Jacob, *The Composite Hedge: Controlling the Credit Risk of High Yield Bonds* (New York: Morgan Stanley, 1985).

TABLE 4 Percent Variance Reduced Cash Security: Tenneco 8⅜ of 2002

	10-Day Moving Average	30-Day Moving Average
Dollar matching	64%	65%
Conversion factor	64	65
Change in price regression	64	69
Price level regression	64	69
Price-sensitivity/duration	64	69
Price-sensitivity/duration (corrected for yield volatilities)	64	70
Curvilinear price regression	64	70

The last two examples used deeply discounted callable securities. Hedge ratio construction for callable bonds priced at a premium, or bonds fluctuating between premium and discount prices is fraught with difficulties. Consider regression-based hedge ratios. If interest rates have been falling during the recent period, the bond to be hedged may have recently been trading at a discount or near par but is now trading at a premium. At these prior prices, the threat of a call is much less than current expectations. Since these expectations fundamentally influence the interest rate sensitivity of the callable bond, the regression-based hedge ratios may be severely misestimated. Price sensitivity hedge ratios can suffer equally if they continue to be calculated to the maturity date. But, as is shown by Toevs, the duration of a bond can be continuously and efficiently adjusted for the interest rate influences of its call provision.[17]

A final question can be raised about the above hedging examples. Given the problems with regression-based hedges discussed earlier, why do these hedge ratios have reasonable track records? First, great care was used to collect the data necessary to make the regression-based hedge ratios perform well. Second, call risk was minimized in our examples. Third, the data used in the regressions was from a period in time when there was sufficient ranges in price and the size of price changes to minimize some of the weaknesses noted for regression-based methodologies. Fourth, the assumptions made in the price sensitivity/duration based hedge ratio approach are often violated in practice. Yield curves are not flat, nor do they always shift in a parallel fashion. Thus, the simple Macaulay duration formula we used in the construction of these ratios is not strictly appropriate. More sophisticated duration formulas can add value. Fifth, the regression-based hedges captured any histori-

---

[17] A.L. Toevs, "Interest Rate Risk and Uncertain Lives." *Journal of Portfolio Management*, Spring 1985.

cal systematic basis risk, while our price sensitivity/duration approach was not so modified.

CONCLUSIONS

Sophisticated hedge ratio estimation methodologies have a common root—the mathematical minimization of the variance in a portfolio's value. In practice, all estimation techniques face empirical realities that are inconsistent with their theoretical assumptions. Naive hedge strategies can work well in some but not all instances. Their deficiencies lie in their assumption that the interest rate sensitivities of the hedging and cash instruments are equal.

We find that duration hedge is more conveniently constructed than any regression-based hedge. Neither historical data series nor regression analyses need be used. And, price-sensitivity/duration-based hedge ratios can be altered in numerous ways to increase hedging effectiveness (e.g., estimating relative *yield* volatilities, modeling the basis, accounting for the influences of call provisions on interest-rate sensitivities, and so on). By segmenting the sources of interest-rate risk in the price-sensitivity/duration framework, we have increased our ability to model the residual risks of futures hedges. In practice we find that simple price-sensitivity/duration hedges perform as well as any currently available techniques. Thus, simply constructed duration-based hedges appear to dominate the more elaborately constructed regression-based hedges. Finally, although not formally discussed in this paper, the application of hedges to the other hedge types—strong form cash hedges and anticipatory hedges—often make the use of naive and regression-based hedge ratios cumbersome if not impossible.

APPENDIX _____
Determination of the Minimum Variance Hedge Ratio

Minimum Variance Hedge Ratios

Let the unhedged position represent one unit of a cash security with a price of P_c. This price is a function of the maturity date and coupon rate of the cash security and of market determined interest rates. Let r_{c_0} represent the current market determined yield-to-maturity of the cash security. Let this yield change unexpectedly to $r_{c_0} + \lambda$, where $\lambda \gtrless 0$. This unexpected change in interest rates causes the cash security price to change. Since the size of this price change depends upon the value of λ, the price change can be functionally stated as $\Delta P_c(\lambda)$. The variance of the change in price is represented by var (ΔP_c).

Now, consider the influence any hedging instrument has on this cash position. Let the price of the hedging security be P_h and let this price reflect a yield of r_{h_0}. An unexpected change in this yield to $r_{h_0} + \gamma$, where $\gamma \geq 0$ produces a price change of $\Delta P_h(\gamma \cdot)$. The variance of the change in price is var (ΔP_h).

Given these variances, what is the variance of a portfolio of one unit of the cash security and N units of the hedging security? (The hedging security can be a cash, forward, or futures contract.) Using standard statistical relationships, the variance of $\Delta P_c + Nx_\Delta P_h$ is:

var($\Delta P_c + N\Delta P_h$)
$$= \text{var}(\Delta P_c + 2\,N\,\text{cov}(\Delta P_c, \Delta P_h) + N^2\text{var}(\Delta P_h) \quad \text{Equation A}$$

The number of units of the hedging securities that reduces this variance to a minimum is found by differentiating Equation A with respect to N and setting the result equal to zero. Thus,

$$N^* = -\text{cov}(\Delta P_c, \Delta P_h)/\text{var}(\Delta P_h) \qquad \text{Equation B}$$

This conclusion is similar to Equation II in the main text. In fact, Equations B and II are identical. If λ and γ are positively correlated, then ΔP_c and ΔP_h are positively correlated. The minus sign in Equation B indicates we should short sell N^* of the hedging security. Note that N^* represents the optimal number of hedging contracts to short per cash contract once the specific hedging contract has been selected. The optimal hedge requires that we first find the hedge security with highest net productive covariance and then establish N^* as the hedge ratio for this instrument.

The text notes that the regression of price levels and instantaneous price sensitivity/duration based hedge ratio estimation techniques are all consistent with the concept of a minimum variance hedge ratio. This assertion is demonstrated here.

Regression of Price Changes

The value of a hedged portfolio can be represented as

$$V_H = P_c + N \times P_h \qquad \text{Equation C}$$

The initial value for P_c, related through the regression equation to the price of the hedge, is

$$P_c = \hat{a} + \hat{b}P_h + \text{error} \qquad \text{Equation D}$$

where the ˆs indicate regression estimates of an intercept and slope. If interest rates change then the new P_c relates to the new P_h through the above equation. Thus,

$$P_c = P_c^* - P_c = a + bPh^* + \text{error}^* - a - bP_h - \text{error}$$
$$P_c = bP_h + (\text{error}^* - \text{error}) \qquad \text{Equation E}$$

The change in V_H derived from Equation C is, upon substitution of Equation E,

$$V_H = (b + N)P_h + (error^* - error) \qquad \text{Equation F}$$

The expected value of V_H due to a change in interest rates is zero and its variance, becomes

$$\text{var}(V_H) = (b + N)^2\text{var } P_h + \text{var error}^* - error \quad \text{Equation G}$$

To minimize this variance select the value for N that drives the derivative of Equation G to zero. The required derivative is

$$\partial \text{ var } V_H/\partial N = 2(b + N)\text{var } P_h = 0 \qquad \text{Equation H}$$

The only way this value equals zero is if $N = -b$. Thus, the minimum variance hedge ratio, N^*, equals the slope of the regression relating the price of the cash security to the price of the hedging instrument. If the hedging instrument is a futures contract, then the above analysis is not strictly correct. Portfolio value as expressed in Equation C becomes

$$V_H = P_c + N(P_f - P_f') \qquad \text{Equation I}$$

Where P_f' is the futures price established when the hedge was first put into place. $N(P_f - P_f')$ represents total allocation to the margin account. The substitutions and derivatives as found in Equations D through H ultimately eliminate the fixed term $-NP_f'$ and the result that $N^* = -b$ is maintained.

Duration Based Hedges

The duration based methodology asserts that $\Delta V_H = \Delta P_c + N\Delta P_h$; $\Delta r_c = k\Delta r_h = \varepsilon$; $\Delta P_c \cong -D_c P_c \Delta r_c/(1 + r_c/2)$; and $\Delta P_h \cong -D_h P_h \Delta r_h/(1 + r_h/2)$. Here k is the relative yield volatility factor and ε is a random error term that permits imperfect price arbitrage.

The duration approach, therefore, begins with the equation

$$\Delta V_h \cong -D_c^* P_c(k\Delta r_h + \varepsilon) - ND_h^* P_h \Delta r_h \qquad \text{Equation J}$$

where D_c^* and D_h^* are modified durations. For small changes in r_h, Equation J becomes exact.

Because Δr_h and ε are by definition uncorrelated and because the expectation of these two variables is zero, the variance of Equation J can be written as:

$$\text{var}[\Delta V_H] = [(D_c^* P_c k)^2 + 2kND_c^* P_c D_h^* P_h \\ + (ND_h^* P_h)^2]\text{var}[\Delta r_h] + (D_c^* P_c^*)^2 \text{var}[\varepsilon]$$

Minimizing this variance with respect to N produces

$$N^* = -D_c^* P_c k/D_h^* P_h$$

where k is the relative yield volatility factor, which may be equal to one.

44

Portfolio Insurance

Eric M. P. Tang
Vice President
Gifford Fong Associates

H. Gifford Fong
President
Gifford Fong Associates

An investor may want to ensure that his portfolio will produce at least a specified minimum return. To achieve this, the investor may consider purchasing insurance for his investment. An insured portfolio would allow him to participate in a rising market while limiting the down-side risk to a prespecified level.

There are several methods to insure a portfolio. First, the manager can purchase insurance directly. If the insured assets performed well, the investor would receive the return on those securities less the cost of insurance. If the insured assets performed poorly, the underwriter of the insurance would compensate the investor the difference between the actual return and the guaranteed minimum rate of return. An example of a directly insured portfolio would be the purchase of a put option contract against the existing portfolio. Under a declining market scenario the investor can exercise the put option. The gain in the put option would offset part or all of the losses on the underlying securities. In this case, the strike price of the put option effectively sets a floor to the portfolio's return.

In contrast, if the underlying assets performed well, the investor would let the put option expire without exercise and benefit from the appreciation of the underlying securities. The total return on the insured portfolio would be the profits on the actual portfolio minus the premium paid for the put option. Thus, the options premium is equivalent to an insurance premium.

Another method to insure a portfolio is to pursue a dynamic asset allocation strategy. This technique uses only the cash markets and does not rely on any option contract. The dynamic strategy would structure and rebalance various asset classes in the portfolio over the investment horizon in a fashion that the risk and return characteristics of the entire investment would replicate those of a portfolio protected by a put option. For instance, if an investor wants to insure a portfolio consisting of a risky or a volatile asset via the dynamic strategy, only part of the portfolio would be allocated to that asset. The rest of the portfolio would be invested in cash or a relatively risk-free security. When the risky asset performs poorly, the dynamic strategy would distribute more funds to the risk-free instrument. If the risky asset performs well, however, a larger portion of the portfolio would be invested in it. By properly rebalancing between the risky and the risk-free asset over the investment horizon, the return pattern on the overall investment would duplicate that of a portfolio protected by a put option.[1]

This alternative insurance method is valuable because direct portfolio insurance is not always feasible. Direct insurance is uncommon since publicly traded options are available only for a limited number of securities and asset types. Moreover, the expiration date and the strike price of traded option contracts are determined by the exchange. An investor may not always find a publicly traded option contract that is suitable for his portfolio. The dynamic strategy, on the contrary, allows the investor to insure any one or combination of assets at any strike price or expiration date that he desires. Thus, the dynamic asset allocation approach has a much wider appeal and more practical flexibility than direct portfolio insurance.

APPLICATIONS OF PORTFOLIO INSURANCE

There are several major uses for portfolio insurance. First, an investor (such as a pension fund sponsor) often wants to guarantee that the investment will generate a certain minimum rate of return that is required by the actuary. One way to satisfy the minimum rate is to immunize the portfolio.[2] An immunized portfolio would lock in the current spot rate of return on a fixed income portfolio over the investment horizon regardless of movements in interest rates. Immunization, however, is typically a passive strategy. Once a portfolio is immunized, the rate of return is fixed. The investor would not be able to earn a return significantly higher than the rate that the portfolio was originally immunized at.

---

[1] M. Rubinstein and H. E. Leland, "Replicating Options with Positions in Stock and Cash," *Financial Analyst Journal*, July/August 1981.

[2] See Chapter 31 for a discussion of immunization.

Portfolio insurance, on the contrary, allows an investor to participate in the movements of risky assets while setting a minimum return on the portfolio. If the risky assets perform well, the portfolio would achieve the return on these securities less the insurance cost. And the investor is not limited to just a fixed rate of return. Moreover, by setting the floor return on the portfolio at the appropriate level, the investor can be assured that the actuarially-set required rate of return will be satisfied. There is one drawback on portfolio insurance—the minimum floor return on the insured portfolio must be set at a level lower than the rate of the risk-free asset.

An alternative but similar strategy to portfolio insurance is contingent immunization.[3] Under contingent immunization an investor would invest the portfolio entirely in risky assets initially. If the risky securities produce a high return, the investor would benefit from it. But in order to avoid catastrophic losses, the investor would monitor the portfolio closely. If at any time the market value of the portfolio drops to the same amount as the portfolio's desired minimum terminal wealth, the investor would restructure the risky securities and immunize the entire portfolio. Therefore, even under a bear market, the manager can still be confident that the desired minimum rate of return will be met.

There is one major difference between contingent immunization and portfolio insurance, however. Contingent immunization is similar to a stop-loss order. For instance, suppose a portfolio is initially invested in risky assets. If the value of the risky securities drops to a point where the investor is forced to immunize, the portfolio can never be reactivated even if the risky assets recover. In contrast, a portfolio that is insured can participate in any rally of the risky assets—even after a major bear market. The insurance strategy is similar to a protective put option where the investor can be continuously exposed to the up-side potential of the risky securities. Thus, the advantage of insuring a portfolio is that the investment is never totally detached from the potential of the risky asset.

Besides ensuring a required rate of return, portfolio insurance is also a powerful analytical tool for dynamic asset allocation decisions. It is possible to extend the insurance program to the asset allocation process because the strategy of insuring a portfolio involves periodic redistribution of the assets in the portfolio. The assets are reallocated systematically over the investment horizon to pursue the initial investment objectives. For example, an investor may be very uncertain about future economic events. If the investor wants to protect the portfolio against major losses, an arbitrary amount of risky assets may be sold and the proceeds may be invested in cash or other risk-free instruments. This

---

[3] Martin L. Leibowitz and Alfred Weinberger, "The Uses of Contingent Immunization," *The Journal of Portfolio Management*, Fall 1981.

way, losses will be limited by the reduced proportion of the portfolio in the risky asset. Alternatively, the investor can employ a more systematic approach such as portfolio insurance. By using the dynamic asset allocation strategy, he can be assured of a minimum return on his portfolio regardless of the outcome in the risky asset.

Thus, portfolio insurance is a disciplined way to achieve the investment objectives of an actively managed portfolio. In the above example, the investor can measure the risk-return trade-off of his portfolio by how high the floor return is. A portfolio that has a high floor return is considered defensive because it guarantees a high minimum rate of return by sacrificing some up-side potential. Similarly, an offensive portfolio would have a low minimum floor rate. Such a portfolio would carry a lower insurance cost and hence, opportunity for greater appreciation. The down-side risk on an offensive portfolio, of course, is greater.

COMPARISON WITH TRADITIONAL ASSET ALLOCATION

There are several differences between portfolio insurance and other asset allocation methods. First, portfolio insurance is a dynamic strategy. The investor sets the investment objectives and the investment horizon in the beginning. The portfolio insurance program will determine the optimal allocation of assets over time. If one security is performing better than another, more funds will automatically be allocated to it. The investor simply follows the recommendations of the program in rebalancing his portfolio.

Most traditional methods of asset allocation utilize the static approach. The amount of investment in each security is decided initially. Reallocation among asset classes occurs only at the end of the investment horizon. If the investor changes his economic outlook, the assets may be redistributed prior to the horizon date. But any change in asset allocation would require new inputs in terms of the expected return and risk characteristics of the assets in the portfolio.

Another difference between portfolio insurance and other asset allocation approaches is that the dynamic strategy does not require an investor to generate the expected return of the risky securities in the portfolio. Anticipated returns are not needed because portfolio insurance relies on modern options pricing theory. The only inputs required to calculate the optimal asset allocation are the risk-free rate of return, the volatility, and the correlation of the return on the risky assets. This is a major advantage over the traditional static asset allocation procedure that requires the investor to estimate the expected return on every asset in the portfolio in addition to their risk characteristics. Thus, substantially less user inputs are needed to implement the dynamic asset allocation strategy.

THE MECHANICS OF INSURING A PORTFOLIO WITH THE DYNAMIC ASSET ALLOCATION STRATEGY

The main objective of the dynamic asset allocation strategy is to replicate the return pattern of a portfolio insured by a protective put option. To do so, the strategy relies on a property of an option contract which suggests that the return pattern of an asset protected by a put option is identical to a position that holds only cash plus a call option on the same security. This property is called the put/call parity of options.

To illustrate how this property works, consider the simple case where a portfolio consists of only one stock with a current market price of $100. Suppose the investor purchases a six-month put option on that stock with a strike price of $100 and an options premium of $5. The return pattern on this portfolio can be represented by Exhibit 1. If on the expiration date the market price of the stock drops below $100, the put option would be exercised and the terminal value of the portfolio would be the strike price of the options contract less the premium or $95. This return pattern is shown as line AB in Exhibit 1.

EXHIBIT 1

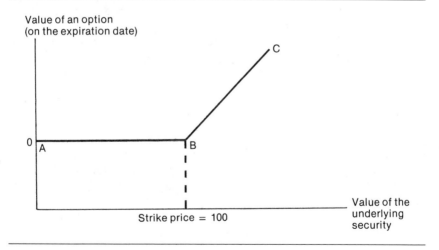

If the price of the stock rises above $100, the put option would expire without being exercised. The ending value of the portfolio would be the value of the stock less the option premium. This is shown as line BC in Exhibit 1. Thus, the line ABC represents the final payoff pattern of a stock protected by a put option.

Suppose instead of purchasing a protective put option, the investor decides to hold all cash plus a call option on the same stock. If the call option has the same strike price ($100) and the same premium ($5) as the put option, the return pattern of the cash plus call position would be exactly the same as in Exhibit 1.[4] To see why this is true, suppose the stock price rises above $100, the call option would be exercised. The terminal value of the portfolio would again be the value of the stock less the options premium as shown in line BC of Exhibit 1. If the price of the stock drops below $100, the call option would expire without being exercised. The ending value of the portfolio would be the amount of cash less the premium paid on the call option or $95. This can be represented by line AB. Therefore, the payoff distribution of a combined position in cash and call option is identical to holding the underlying security protected by a put option.

Because of the "put/call parity", an investor can insure a portfolio by either buying a protective put option against the existing assets or by holding only cash plus a call option. Similarly, a dynamic asset allocation strategy can insure a portfolio if the strategy reproduces the payoff pattern of a call option plus cash. It is possible to duplicate the payoff pattern of an option contract with only cash securities because there is a predictable relationship between the theoretical value of an option contract and the price of the underlying asset even prior to the expiration date. By varying the amount of the underlying cash securities that is held in the portfolio, one can reproduce the return distribution of an option.

The value of an option contract at any time is closely tied to the price of the underlying security. Consider the previous example where the strike price of the call option is $100. If the price of the underlying stock rises far above the strike price, the option would be considered "deep in-the-money". The value of a deep in-the-money option contract or the option premium is likely to move one-to-one with the price of the underlying stock.

If the price of the underlying stock drops substantially below the strike price, the option contract is considered "out-of-the-money". The value or the premium of an out-of-the-money option is likely to change very little in response to movements in the price of the underlying stock. In the extreme case where the price of the underlying stock falls close to zero, the value of the option approaches zero also.

This relationship between the price of the underlying stock and the value of the option is shown in Exhibit 2. Line ABC represents the value on the expiration date of a call option contract with a strike price of $100.

---

[4] This example assumes that the option can be exercised only on the expiration date and that the underlying stock does not pay dividends. Moreover, the interest rate on cash is assumed to be zero. The "put/call parity", however, still holds even if these restrictive assumptions were dropped. See John Cox and Mark Rubinstein, *Options Markets*, (Englewood Cliffs, N.J.: Prentice Hall, 1985).

EXHIBIT 2

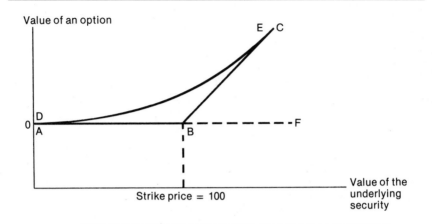

The value of the option prior to expiration is represented by the curve DE. At one extreme when the price of the underlying stock drops far below $100, the option premium falls toward zero. The curve DE becomes flat and its slope becomes zero. When the stock price rises significantly above $100, however, the option premium moves one-to-one with the underlying stock. In this case, curve DE approaches the 45 degree line BC. The slope of curve DE becomes 1.

The slope of curve DE is also known as the hedge ratio. (See the appendix for a formula of the curve DE and the hedge ratio.) The hedge ratio is an important concept in portfolio insurance or dynamic asset allocation because it suggests the proportion of the portfolio to be invested in the risky asset. Using the previous example, suppose the current price of the underlying stock is $100 and the slope of curve DE at that point is 0.5. If the price of the underlying stock changes, the value of the option would move by only half as much. Thus, a portfolio that is composed of 50 percent cash and 50 percent stocks would experience the same profit and loss as a position in cash plus a call option contract whose underlying value is equal to the value of the portfolio. To replicate the return pattern of the call option, half the portfolio should be allocated to stocks and the rest in cash. So, the correct hedge ratio is 0.5. Similarly, when the price of the underlying stock rises to $110, the hedge ratio will be increased. If the slope of curve DE is 0.8 at that point, 80 percent of the portfolio should be invested in stocks. The ratio is 0.8 because any change in the options premium will be 80 percent of the fluctuation of the stock price.

In summary, the value of an option contract will move with the price of the underlying stock. The sensitivity of the option's price relative to the stock price will depend on the slope of curve DE or the hedge ratio. By setting the strike price at the appropriate level to reflect the desired minimum floor return and by adjusting the hedge ratio continuously throughout the investment horizon, it is possible to duplicate the return pattern of the option contract.

Other Determinants of the Hedge Ratio

In addition to the difference between the price on the underlying stock and the strike price, the hedge ratio is also determined by the shape and position of the curve DE. The curve DE is the option value curve because it represents the value of an option contract or the size of the option premium. Under modern options pricing theory, the value of an option contract also depends on the following two factors: the volatility of the underlying stock and the time to expiration.[5]

The volatility of the underlying security is important because the greater the price fluctuates, the more likely the value of the stock will exceed the strike price prior to the expiration date. Since the potential of profits is higher, the contract is more valuable to the buyer of the option. Similarly, the value of an option contract is dependent on its remaining time to expiration. If a contract has a longer life, it is worth more to the buyer because there is more time for the price of the underlying asset to rise above the strike price. For the same reason, as a contract ages toward its expiration date, the "time premium", and hence the value of the option, declines. Thus, curve DE in Exhibit 2 will move downward over time. On the expiration date curve DE becomes the same as line ABC.

Rebalancing the Portfolio

The dynamic asset allocation strategy requires frequent rebalancing of the portfolio because the hedge ratio does not remain constant. Ideally, the portfolio should be rebalanced every time the hedge ratio changes. In practice, however, it is impossible to make instantaneous adjustments, and the actual frequency of rebalancing may range from daily to monthly.

The drawback of rebalancing infrequently, of course, is that the actual performance of the insured portfolio would be different from the theoretical prediction. For instance, if the risky securities performed well, the return on the portfolio may be lower than the risky asset less the insurance cost. This can happen because as the value of the risky

---

[5] Several other factors such as interest rates, cash dividends on the underlying stock, tax rate, margin requirement, transaction cost, and market structure also affect the value of an option contract.

security appreciates, the hedge ratio should be raised. (See Exhibit 2.) If the portfolio is not rebalanced fast enough, the actual hedge ratio of the portfolio would be lower than the required level. And the return to the portfolio would fall behind the risky securities by more than the cost of insurance.

If the portfolio is rebalanced very often, however, the transaction fee and the required management time would be substantially greater. The transaction cost can become an even bigger factor if the securities in the insured portfolio are not liquid. Thus, frequent rebalancing can narrow the difference between the theoretical and the actual return—but these gains must be evaluated against the higher transaction cost and the occupation of the manager's time.

One way to reduce transaction cost and improve portfolio liquidity is to use futures contracts. Futures contracts are valuable because they provide leverage in the portfolio. A small deposit (or margin requirement) on a futures contract would allow the investor to have a large exposure to the underlying asset. Thus, the hedge ratio of an insured portfolio can be adjusted easily and economically with the purchase or sale of a relatively small number of futures contracts. This tends to reduce the burden of rebalancing a portfolio frequently.

THE COST OF PORTFOLIO INSURANCE

One major consideration in dynamic asset allocation is the cost of this strategy. There is a cost to insure a portfolio because the program allows an investor to shun the down-side risk of a risky asset while capturing its up-side potential. The cost of insurance can be expressed as a percentage of the portfolio's value. For instance, if the cost of insurance is 2 percent per annum, the insured portfolio's return would be the return on the risky asset less 2 percent or the prespecified floor rate, whichever is higher.

Intuitively, the cost of insuring a portfolio is the price that the investor pays for not investing 100 percent in the risky asset. Under a dynamic asset allocation strategy the hedge ratio or the portion of the portfolio invested in the risky security will vary between zero and one depending on the performance of the risky asset. If the risky security earns a high return, the portfolio's return will be smaller because a certain portion of the portfolio is always invested in the lower-earning risk-free securities. Therefore, the implied cost of insuring a portfolio is the price the investor pays for not being fully invested in the risky security if the risky asset out performs the risk-free security.

The net cost of portfolio insurance, however, is lower than the implied cost. The implied cost is relevant only if the risky security is performing well. But if the return on the risky asset less the implied cost of insurance is lower than the minimum rate of return, the portfolio return will be the prespecified floor rate. In this case the investor recovers part or all of the insurance premium that he paid. At the inception of an insurance program, an investor would not know with certainty the future performance of the risky security. The expected price that he has to pay for this dynamic strategy versus holding 100 percent of the risky asset is the implied cost of insurance less the probability weighted amount of claims that he could collect if the risky securities performed poorly.

EXTENSIONS OF THE STRATEGY

The dynamic asset allocation strategy can be extended to insure a portfolio that contains more than one risky asset. For a multiple risky asset portfolio the insurance program would allow the portfolio to earn the highest return among all the risky assets less the cost of insurance. For example, if the risky assets are stocks and bonds, the return on the total portfolio would be the return on either stocks or bonds less the insurance premium, whichever is higher. If both risky securities performed poorly, the portfolio's return would be the prespecified minimum floor rate.[6]

The multiple risky asset approach offers investors several advantages. First, a diversified portfolio typically consists of numerous classes of assets. This strategy would help the portfolio manager to allocate the assets within that portfolio over the investment horizon. The allocation would be made in a systematic fashion that is consistent with the investment objectives. Furthermore, the potential for a very large return may be higher under the multiple risky asset than the single risky security strategy. This is true because the more classes of assets one includes into the portfolio, the more likely that at least one of them, and hence the portfolio, would earn a high return. An investor, however, would have to mitigate this extra opportunity against the additional cost—the insurance premium on a multiple risky security portfolio would be higher.

Another extension of the dynamic asset allocation strategy is to use an immunized portfolio rather than cash as the risk-free asset. The choice of the risk-free security is important because the minimum floor rate that an investor desires in an insured portfolio must be lower than the return on the risk-free asset on the inception date. The investor can be guaranteed a higher minimum rate of return if the yield on the risk-free security is higher. Thus, the minimum floor rate can be raised by using an immunized portfolio as the risk-free asset if the yield curve is upward sloping.

---

[6] Rene M. Stulz, "Options on the Minimum or the Maximum of Two Risky Assets," *Journal of Financial Economics*, July 1982.

Choosing an immunized portfolio as the risk-free security means that as the hedge ratio changes, funds will be withdrawn or added to the immunized portfolio. Since the withdrawals and contributions cannot be predicted in advance, the size of the immunized portfolio on each rebalancing date will be uncertain. And the actual return on the risk-free asset over the entire investment horizon may not be the same as the initial immunized interest rate. Therefore, a portfolio insured with an immunized asset must take this into consideration and allocate the assets differently than a portfolio using cash as the risk-free security.

AN EXAMPLE OF PORTFOLIO INSURANCE

Tables 1 and 2 show a simple example of insuring a portfolio using the dynamic asset allocation method. The initial value of the portfolio is $5 million and the investment horizon is two years. The portfolio consists of only one risky security and the risk-free asset is cash. The standard deviation of the return on the risky security is assumed to be 15 percent.

TABLE 1 Cost of Portfolio Insurance

Investment horizon: two years
Yield on cash: 8.0 percent

Minimum Return	Insurance Cost
6%	7.1%
5	5.4
4	4.2
3	3.3
2	2.7
1	2.1
0	1.7

To insure the portfolio, the investor would first decide on the minimum rate of return. One factor that may affect the investor's choice is the cost of insurance. If the floor rate is set high, the corresponding insurance premium would also be greater. Table 1 shows the insurance cost of several possible minimum rates.

Once the floor return is decided, the investor would follow the recommendation of the dynamic strategy in allocating the portfolio between cash and the risky security. An example of how the strategy would work and the performance of the insured portfolio under an assumed scenario is illustrated in Table 2. In this example, the investor is assumed to have chosen a minimum return of 3 percent and the implied

TABLE 2 An Example of Dynamic Asset Allocation

Investment horizon	: two years
Initial investment	: $5 million
Rebalancing frequency	: one month

| Minimum return | : 3 percent |
| Insurance cost | : 3.3 percent |

Yield on cash	: 8 percent
Standard deviation of risky asset	: 15 percent
Transaction cost	: 0.25 percent

Month	Monthly Return on Risky Asset	Cumulative Return on Risky Asset	Cumulative Return on Cash	Cumulative Return on Total	Hedge Ratio	Portfolio Value ($mil)
0					0.60	5.0
1	−0.4%	−0.4%	0.7%	0.1%	0.58	5.0
2	−3.1	−3.4	1.3	−1.4	0.49	4.9
3	0.3	−3.1	2.0	−1.0	0.49	4.9
4	1.6	−1.5	2.7	0.2	0.51	5.0
5	0.9	−0.6	3.3	0.9	0.52	5.0
6	3.7	3.0	4.0	3.2	0.59	5.2
7	−1.2	1.8	4.7	2.8	0.55	5.1
8	0.2	2.0	5.4	3.2	0.53	5.2
9	−0.5	1.5	6.1	3.2	0.50	5.2
10	2.2	3.7	6.8	4.7	0.55	5.2
11	0.1	3.8	7.5	5.0	0.53	5.2
12	−1.3	2.5	8.2	4.7	0.47	5.2
13	9.3	12.1	8.9	9.6	0.72	5.5
14	3.5	16.0	9.6	12.6	0.80	5.6
15	−1.3	14.5	10.3	11.6	0.77	5.6
16	5.6	20.9	11.0	16.5	0.89	5.8
17	7.8	30.2	11.8	24.6	0.98	6.2
18	2.0	32.9	12.5	27.1	0.99	6.3
19	−2.7	29.2	13.2	23.7	0.98	6.2
20	1.3	30.9	14.0	25.3	0.99	6.2
21	9.1	42.9	14.7	36.6	1.00	6.8
22	6.2	51.7	15.5	45.1	1.00	7.2
23	4.0	57.8	16.2	50.9	1.00	7.5
24	−2.9	53.3	17.0	46.6	1.00	7.3

insurance cost is 3.3 percent. The return on the risky security, however, was 23.8 percent per annum. Since the return on the risky security less the cost of insurance was higher than the floor rate, the portfolio's return was determined by the profitability of the risky asset.[7]

APPENDIX
Determining the Insurance Premium and the Hedge Ratio

The premium of an option and the hedge ratio can be determined by option pricing theory. For the simple case where the portfolio consists of only one risky security and the riskless asset is cash, the Black-Scholes formula can be used.[8] The exact formula is

$$C = S^*N(X) - Kr^{-t} N(X - \sigma \sqrt{t})$$

$$\text{where } X = \frac{\log(s/Kr^{-t})}{\sigma \sqrt{t}} + \frac{1}{2} \sigma \sqrt{t}$$

C = premium on a call option,

S = market price on the underlying security,

K = strike price,

t = time to expiration,

r = one plus the default-free interest rate,

σ = standard deviation of S, and

N = normal distribution function.

The hedge ratio is the slope of the option value curve or the derivative of C with respect to S. So,

$$\text{Hedge ratio} = \frac{\partial C}{\partial S} = N(X).$$

For extensions of the portfolio insurance strategy such as multiple risky assets or the use of an immunized portfolio as the risk-free security, other more advanced option pricing models would be used.

---

[7] The actual return on the portfolio may not be exactly the same as the difference between the return on risky asset and the insurance cost. Several factors such as non-instantaneous rebalancing of the portfolio and transaction cost may cause this difference.

[8] F. Black and M. Scholes, "The Pricing of Options and Corporate Liabilities," *Journal of Political Economy*, May-June 1973.

45

Strategies for Managing Bond Portfolios Using Futures and Options

Jess B. Yawitz, Ph.D.
Director, Financial Strategies Group
Goldman Sachs & Co.

William J. Marshall, Ph.D.
Associate Director, Financial Strategies Group
Goldman Sachs & Co.

Concern for interest-rate risk in the management of bond portfolios is no longer confined to the financial sector; it is widespread throughout the economy. Financial institutions, market makers, and money managers have long appreciated the importance of quantifying and actively managing this risk. More recently, pension plan sponsors and both corporate and household borrowers and lenders have realized the importance of understanding interest-rate risk.

Because of unprecedented interest-rate volatility that we have experienced during the last decade or so there is heightened awareness of interest-rate risk. Rate volatility is highly correlated with portfolio performance volatility, and many market participants have been adversely affected. Also, the increased concentration of funds among institutional investors, especially pension funds and insurance companies, stimulates awareness since the nature of the liabilities that must be funded makes these institutional investors especially sensitive to interest-rate risk. Accordingly, many of the new fixed income instruments and the development of new techniques for managing bond portfolios can be viewed as a direct response to an increased desire to cope with interest-rate risk.

Our purpose in this chapter is to discuss several methods of measuring and managing interest-rate risk. In the first section of this chapter we discuss the measurement of interest-rate risk for portfolios composed of default-free bonds. In the second section we review the concept of a hedged portfolio, followed by a discussion of the concept of duration as well as the use of futures in the immunization strategy. In the last section of this chapter, several hybrid investment strategies which combine elements of active and passive asset management are discussed.

SOURCES OF INTEREST-RATE RISK AND THE HOLDING PERIOD ASSUMPTION

We will consider only securities which offer known cash flows (i.e., are default free), and futures or options on such securities. By limiting ourselves in this way, we can reasonably view interest-rate risk to be the only relevant uncertainty about the portfolio's performance. We define interest-rate risk as the effect of unanticipated changes in interest rates on portfolio performance. The distinction between anticipated and unanticipated interest-rate changes is an important one. Most market participants agree that the shape of the yield curve embodies specific forecasts of future interest rates. For example, if the 90- and 180-day spot rates are 10 percent and 11 percent, respectively, the forward 90-day rate (beginning 90 days hence) is 12 percent. This is the so-called break-even rate which would result in identical 11 percent rates of return from buying the 180-day security and holding it to maturity or rolling over the 90-day security into a new 90-day instrument (at 12 percent). Since cash markets allow one to lock in this 12 percent rate (by buying the 180-day instrument and short-selling the 90-day instrument) a 200 basis point rise in the 90-day bill rate from 10 percent to 12 percent should not be viewed as the manifestation of interest-rate risk. Rather, deviations from the 12 percent figure constitute risk.

Our definition of interest-rate risk purposely leaves the concept of performance unspecified. If an investor measures performance by current market value, the length of his *holding period* or *investment horizon* is zero. For our purposes, the holding period is the length of time until a portfolio must be converted into cash to fund a specific liability. A zero holding period implies that the investor (perhaps a bond trader) implicitly or explicitly faces a daily settling up requirement. For such an investor, price changes are sufficient for measuring interest-rate risk.

In contrast, an investor who must fund a dollar outflow five years hence has a five-year holding period. For such an investor, portfolio performance is not measured by current market value, but rather by expected value five years hence. Accordingly, interest-rate risk refers to the effect of rate changes on this future value.

It should be evident from the above discussion that a particular security will not possess the same risk characteristics for investors with different length holding periods. The single payment security is a convenient vehicle for demonstrating how the interest-rate risk of a particular asset depends on the investor's holding period. Consider a claim to a single cash flow to be received n years hence that is owned by an investor with an m year holding period. If n is less than m, then this security subjects the investor to a particular type of interest-rate risk called *reinvestment risk*. The cash flow must be reinvested at the unknown rate at time n. The higher (lower) this rate, the greater (less) will be the contribution from this cash flow to the end-of-period value. Similarly, the claim to a cash flow to be received after the end of the holding period subjects the investor to *market risk* since it must be sold prior to maturity. Its contribution to end-of-period value (time m) will vary inversely with the interest rate at that time.

Thus, the claim to a single cash flow will subject the investor to reinvestment risk or market risk depending on whether its value at the end of the holding period is determined by "compounding forward" or "discounting back" from its maturity. While in the former case (m < n) the holding period value increases if rates rise, the value of an instrument that must be sold prior to its maturity increases with a decline in rates.

While we will have more to say about this later, the above discussion provides the basis for understanding the offsetting nature of the two types of interest-rate risk. For example, an increase in interest rates increases the end-of-period value of those cash flows received prior to the end of the holding period while reducing the value of cash flows received after the holding period. An understanding of this offset in the two types of interest-rate risk is important to understand the theoretical basis for procedures to be discussed later.

Time Profiles of Valuation

With a little imagination, the single payment instrument (zero) can be used to demonstrate the possible offset between the two types of interest-rate risk. The imagination is necessary since the strategy of purchasing a zero and holding it to maturity never requires one to reinvest cash or to liquidate securities. Yet, the time profile of the value of the zero under different interest-rate scenarios does demonstrate quite effectively how any price change that accompanies a change in the interest rate is precisely offset by more or less appreciation over the remaining life of the zero.

Exhibit 1 portrays the time profile of the value of a 10-year zero under three different interest-rate scenarios: (1) the interest rate remains at the initial level of 10 percent; (2) the rate rises to 11 percent, or (3) the rate falls to 9 percent. At a 10 percent rate, the investment of $100 will purchase a 10-year zero with a face value of $259. If the rate rises to 11 percent, the value of the instrument falls to $91. The loss of $9 is the effect of market risk. If the rate remains at 11 percent the valuation line remains below the value line for the 10 percent rate until maturity when,

EXHIBIT 1   Immunization with a 10-Year Holding Period

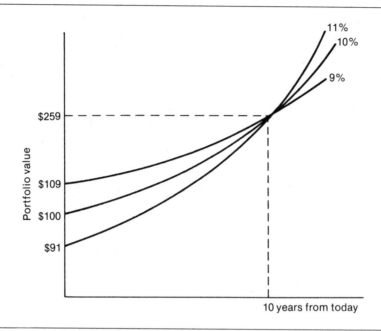

of course, the instrument matures for $259. The $9 loss is offset exactly by an additional $9 from the higher (implicit) reinvestment rate. For holding periods greater than 10 years, the 11 percent value line exceeds the 10 percent line, confirming the fact that the higher return from implicit reinvestment for the first 10 years and actual reinvestment thereafter exceeds the initial loss in present value.

If the rate falls to 9 percent, the zero's value increases to $109 and the value line remains above both the 10 percent and 11 percent lines for 10 years. For holding periods longer than 10 years, the 9 percent line is below the other two.

The purchase of a 10-year zero offers a guaranteed rate of return for an investor with a 10-year holding period. The zero represents a special case since the single cash payment is received on the last day of the holding period. However, the value profiles indicate the offsetting nature of reinvestment and market risk, and suggest the hedge that is in force with an immunized portfolio.

THE HEDGED PORTFOLIO

A hedged portfolio is one that does not subject the investor to interest-rate risk. In the case where an explicit liability stream is to be funded, the hedged portfolio has a zero probability of underfunding. When the liability is implicit, as with a specified holding period, the holding period rate of return is certain.

The hedged portfolio approach provides a useful benchmark for analyzing the new techniques for managing fixed income securities. The simplest of these techniques is the dedicated (cash-match) strategy. This approach funds a known stream of outflows with an identical stream of inflows. The simplest dedicated portfolio is a hedge: a single zero is purchased to fund a single liability, and the face value of the zero equals the dollar value of the future liability. Multiperiod liability streams are funded by purchasing an equal stream of zeros. This approach has proven quite useful as a means of funding "retired lives" with known pension benefits.

Before proceeding to consider more complex hedged portfolio strategies, we introduce futures and forward transactions in the dedicated strategy. This discussion will set the stage for the more detailed analysis of futures that follows.

Markets exist where one can contract today to receive (deliver) a particular zero coupon bond at a predetermined date in the future. An example is a three-month Treasury bill. For simplicity, assume there is no exchange of cash (or margin) until the date that the contract expires.

Consider an investor who has a five-year holding period for which there does not exist an appropriate maturity zero coupon security. As a result, an exact match is not possible using only the available cash market instruments. A match can be obtained, however, if there exist the appropriate forward contracts. For example, the purchase of a four-year, nine-month zero and the purchase of a three-month bill for delivery in four years and nine months would replicate a five-year zero. Similarly, the purchase of a five-year, three-month zero and the sale of a three-month bill for delivery in five years would also provide a match at five years. For these transactions the forward sale or purchase has the effect of transforming the risk of the cash position to obtain a hedged portfolio. An analogous risk transformation is the key to understanding the role of futures in the more complex applications that we consider later in the paper.

IMMUNIZATION

Immunization has been described as "a specialized technique for constructing . . . a bond portfolio to achieve a specified return target."[1] This technique *immunizes* the rate of return earned over a specified holding period against the effects of interest-rate risk.

---

[1] M. L. Leibowitz, "Specialized Fixed Income Security Strategies," *Financial Handbook, 5th Ed.*, ed. Edward Altman (New York: John Wiley, 1981), p. 3.

Immunization results from the offsetting nature of reinvestment risk and market risk. Immunization requires that one continuously maintain a hedged portfolio. This hedge is achieved by combining claims to cash flows so that the effects of reinvestment risk and market risk on the portfolio's holding period return will be offsetting. If interest rates increase, the additional end-of-period (holding period) return from the reinvested cash receipts from an immunized portfolio will at least offset the reduced end-of-period value of securities that must be sold. Similarly, if interest rates fall, the price appreciation on nonmatured securities will at least offset the reduced value of reinvested funds.

To provide a more thorough discussion of immunization, we consider the important concept of *duration*. We then examine the relation of this concept to immunization as well as the impact of futures. Throughout the analysis we maintain two assumptions, the effects from relaxing either[2] are "technical" issues that are beyond the scope of this paper:

1. The yield curve is initially flat.
2. Any interest-rate shock results in a parallel (equal) shift in the yield curve.

Additionally, we consider only default-free securities; and we ignore taxes.

Duration

Many of the more popular passive bond strategies use the concept of duration. We do not provide a rigorous analytical derivation of duration since most of the necessary understanding can be developed from simple examples. *The duration measure converts any series of cash flows into its single payment equivalent for the purposes of measuring price sensitivity to interest-rate changes.* For a zero the price change can be expressed as

$$\% \Delta P = -n\% \Delta R \qquad \text{Equation I}$$

where:

$\% \Delta P$ = percentage price change

n = maturity

$\% \Delta R$ = the change in the n period rate divided by one plus the rate times 100. For example, a 10 basis point increase from an initial value of 11% would imply a value of

---

[2] For a discussion of the effect of relaxing one or more of these assumptions on the implementation of immunization, see G. O. Bierwag and G. Kaufman, "Coping with the Risk of Interest-Rate Fluctuations," *Journal of Business*, July 1977, pp. 364–70; G. O. Bierwag and C. Khang, "An Immunization Strategy Is a Maximum Strategy," *Journal of Finance*, May 1979, pp. 389–414, and W. Marshall and J. Yawitz, "Lower Bounds on Portfolio Performance: An Extension of the Immunization Strategy," *Journal of Financial and Quantitative Analysis* March 1982, pp. 101–114.

$$\% \Delta R = \frac{.001}{1.11} .100 = .09\%.$$

Equation I indicates that for a given percentage change in the rate ($\% \Delta R$), the percentage price change on a zero is proportional to maturity—a 10-year zero experiences twice the percentage price change of a five-year zero.

One can express the price change on a security which offers two or more distinct cash payments easily by slightly modifying Equation I.

$$\% \Delta P = -D \% \Delta R \qquad \text{Equation II}$$

where:

$$D = \text{the security's duration.}$$

Notice that a proportional relationship exists between price change and duration, for a given value of $\% \Delta R$.

How is duration computed? As price change and maturity are linearly related for zeros, so also is the price change on a portfolio composed of several zeros linearly related to the "average" maturity of the zeros. In fact, duration is simply a weighted average of the maturity of each zero, where the weights represent each zero's contribution to the present value of the portfolio.

$$D = \sum_{t=1}^{n} (t) w_t \qquad \text{Equation III}$$

where:

t = the future period:

w_t = the ratio of the present value of the t year cash flow to the portfolio's present value;

n = the time to receipt of the most distant cash flow.

Notice that the sum of the weights equals one.

Examples Using Duration

1. Suppose one invested $100 in a three-year maturity and $200 in a six-year maturity zero. Since the present value weights are simply

$$w_3 = \frac{100}{300} = \frac{1}{3}$$

$$w_6 = \frac{200}{300} = \frac{2}{3}$$

the portfolio's duration is

$$D = \frac{1}{3}(3) + \frac{2}{3}(6) = 5 \text{ years}$$

This portfolio would experience the same percentage price change as a $300 investment in a five-year zero.

2. The computation of duration for coupon-bearing bonds is also straightforward. One approach is to weight the maturity of each coupon and par payment by its present value contribution. Alternatively, by viewing the bond as a combination of an annuity (coupon) and a zero (par), one can compute duration as a weighted average of the duration of these two instruments.

$$D_{B_n} = w_{A_n}D_{A_n} + w_{P_n}D_{P_n} \qquad\qquad \text{Equation IV}$$

where:

D_{B_n} = the duration of an n year bond

w_{A_n}, w_{P_n} = the present value weights of an n year annuity and an n year par payment, respectively

D_{A_n} = The duration of an n year annuity

D_{P_n} = n = the duration of an n year par payment

Table 1 provides several examples using this approach to compute a bond's duration. Notice that by varying the size of the coupon, holding constant the bond's maturity and yield, one simply changes the size of the weights in Equation IV. Since the annuity's duration (4.74) is less than the duration of the par payment (10), a higher coupon *reduces* duration by increasing the relative importance of the annuity in the present value of the bond.

The information in Table 1 can also be used to compute the duration of a portfolio composed of different coupon 10-year bonds. For example, suppose one purchased a $5 and a $15 coupon bond. The total cost of the portfolio is $200, $69.28 for the $5 and $130.73 for the $15. The portfolio's duration is simply

$$D = \left(\frac{69.28}{200}\right)7.66 + \left(\frac{130.73}{200}\right)6.28 = 6.76 \text{ years}$$

As expected, this is simply the duration of the $10 coupon par bond.

As the discussion of Exhibit 1 in the previous section indicated, immunization occurs when an investor purchases a zero with maturity equal to the investor's holding period. Duration equals maturity for a zero. Since the duration measure converts any series of cash flows into its single payment equivalent, when duration equals holding period for *any* portfolio, immunization is achieved. Returning to Exhibit 1, one can demonstrate that every portfolio with a 10-year duration and an initial value of $100 will fall in value to $91 if rates rise from 10 percent to 11

TABLE 1 Calculating Duration for Various Coupon Bonds (maturity = 10 Years, yield = 10 percent)

| (1) Coupon | Annual Coupon Payment | | (4) (2) + (3) Present Value of Bond | (5) Present Value Weights | | (6) Duration of | | (7) (5) × (6) Duration of Bond |
	(2) Present Value of Coupons	(3) Present Value of $100 Par Payment		(2) ÷ (4) Coupons	(3) ÷ (4) Par	Coupons	Par	
0	0	$38.55	$ 38.55	0%	100%	4.73	10	10
$ 5	$30.73	$38.55	$ 69.28	44.4	55.6	4.73	10	7.66
$10	$61.45	$38.55	$100.00	61.4	38.6	4.73	10	6.76
$15	$92.18	$38.55	$130.73	70.5	29.5	4.73	10	6.28

percent. This simply confirms the role of duration as a measure of price sensitivity. Furthermore, every portfolio worth $91 will be worth $91(1.11)^{10} = 259 ten years hence if rates remain at 11 percent. The valuation profiles of Exhibit 1 cross at the same point (10 years hence) for all 10-year duration portfolios, regardless of the change in the interest rate.

Financial Futures

Financial futures (and options) can aid in managing interest-rate risk. The buyer of a financial futures contract agrees to purchase a cash market instrument at a specific date and price. Each day, any change in the futures contract is settled in cash, and the contract is rewritten at the new price. The daily settling up is called "marking to the market." Thus, even though the contract specifies a cash-flow commitment (receipt or payment) at the delivery date, there can be immediate changes in it, which affect the cash position of the investor.

Marking to the market is particularly important in determining the effect of a futures position on portfolio performance. Specifically, the immediate cash-flow effect from a given change in a futures price is *independent* of the delivery date on the contract. For example, a 10 basis point fall in the discount yield on a 90-day Treasury bill futures contract will generate an immediate $250 cash inflow to the long position, regardless of whether the contract specifies delivery in 1 month or 13 months. Therefore, the futures contract has greater price risk (i.e., its value is more sensitive to changes in yields) than the corresponding forward contract where no settlement is required until expiration. That is, if one were to buy a six-month T bill and sell short an equal present value three-month bill, the resulting net position in the forward market would be less price volatile than the corresponding futures contract. Any change in the forward price affects the value of the cash market position only in proportion to the present value of the change, while the change in the value of the futures position is the change in the forward price.

Risk and Futures

Since no investment is required for a futures position (ignore margin), it is technically impossible to compute conventional risk surrogates for futures, such as duration, that measure risk as percentage changes in value. A useful conceptualization is to view a futures contract as simply changing the interest-rate risk of the portfolio in which it is contained. In the cash market a specific cash flow contributes reinvestment or market risk depending on whether its maturity is longer or shorter than the holding period. In contrast, regardless of the delivery date, the holding period, or the maturity of the underlying instrument, the purchase (sale) of a futures reduces (increases) the reinvestment risk of a portfolio since its effect on end-of-period value varies inversely (directly) with the level of interest rates. Equivalently, the purchase (sale) of a futures contract adds (reduces) market risk to the portfolio.

The purchase of a futures contract commits a specific future cash inflow (coupon or maturing security) to reinvestment at a specified rate and therefore reduces reinvestment risk. When viewed in a more general context, a futures purchase will reduce (increase) the total amount of funds to be reinvested over the entire life of the portfolio, should interest rates rise (decline). This is due to the immediate cash settlement required on the futures. That settlement offsets the effect of rate changes on the income from reinvested coupons and maturing securities.

Futures and Immunization

Exhibit 2 illustrates the effects of interest rate changes on a long position in futures.[3] If the rate remains at 10 percent, the "value" of the futures

EXHIBIT 2   The Valuation Effects from Purchasing Futures

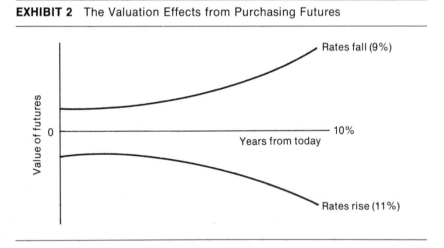

contract remains at zero. If the rate falls to 9 percent, the price of the security underlying the futures contract increases, and a cash inflow equal to the change in value of the underlying instrument is received. Over time, the incremental value of the futures position increases as the initial cash receipt grows at 9 percent. If the rate rises to 11 percent, a

---

[3] For a thorough discussion of the use of futures in immunization portfolios, see J. Yawitz and W. Marshall, "The Use of Financial Futures in Immunized Portfolios," *Journal of Portfolio Management* Winter 1985, pp. 51–8.

cash settlement outflow results, causing the futures position to have a negative value. Over time, this loss grows at the 11 percent rate.

Regardless of the holding period, the purchase (sale) of a futures contract reduces (increases) reinvestment risk, since the contract's value varies inversely with interest rates. However, the longer the holding period, the greater the effect on end-of-period value from the futures contract.

Futures can be combined with cash market securities to alter portfolio interest-rate risk. The purchase (sale) of futures will lengthen (shorten) the duration of a cash market portfolio. Recall that a cash market portfolio with a duration of 10 years has risk for an investor with a holding period longer than 10 years, say 12 years. Specifically, the performance of the portfolio will vary directly with the level of interest rates since the 10 year duration portfolio is "too short". Since the purchase of futures reduces reinvestment risk, there exists a futures position which would lengthen the duration of a 10-year cash portfolio to 12 years.

Exhibit 3 portrays the valuation profiles of a 10-year duration cash market portfolio and of another portfolio comprised of the cash market position plus a long futures position, for three interest-rate scenarios.

EXHIBIT 3 Immunization with Futures Purchases for a 12-Year Holding Period

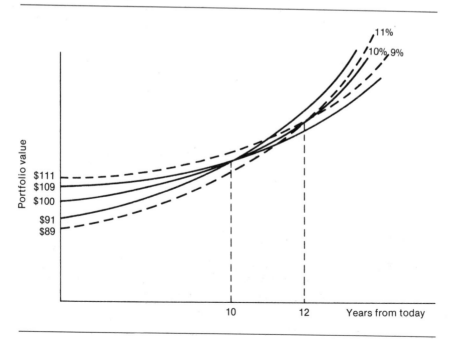

The three valuation lines for the cash-futures portfolio intersect at 12 years, indicating that the new portfolio has a duration of 12 years. The dotted lines in Exhibit 3 refer to the cash-futures portfolio. They are obtained by adding vertically the valuation lines in Exhibit 1 and the appropriate futures valuation lines, such as Exhibit 2.

Without futures, the present value of the portfolio is $109 at 9 percent, and $91 at 11 percent; the difference is $18. After 10 years, $91 invested to earn 11 percent will equal $109 invested at 9 percent. In other words, the initial $18 difference is exactly offset in 10 years by the 2 percent higher reinvestment rate. For holding periods shorter than 10 years, the $18 difference is less than offset; for holding periods exceeding 10 years, the $18 difference is more than offset.

Adding a long futures position increases the sensitivity of the portfolio's present value to a change in the interest rate. If sufficient futures contracts are purchased to increase duration to 12 years, rates of 9 percent and 11 percent result in present values of $111 and $89, respectively. The difference in value of $22 would be offset in 12 years by the different reinvestment rates. Thus, the portfolio is immunized for a 12-year holding period.

As a long futures position increases the duration of the portfolio, a short futures position must reduce duration. A 10-year duration portfolio subjects an investor with a shorter holding period to an excess of market risk. The sale of futures reduces the sensitivity of the portfolio's present value to a change in rates since the cash settlement on the contract is opposite to the price change on the cash market asset. The smaller present value effect of a change in the interest rate requires fewer periods to be offset by the change in the reinvestment rate. Exhibit 4 graphs the value lines for portfolios without and with the futures position necessary to reduce duration to eight years.

An additional insight can be gained by considering the effect on portfolio duration of additional short positions. By selling contracts, one could reduce the portfolio's duration to zero. This zero duration portfolio has an interesting characteristic in that its present value is *independent* of interest-rate changes. The independence is achieved by selling the number of futures necessary for the cash settlement effect from a rate change to exactly balance the interest-rate effect on the present value of the cash market position.

A "negative duration" portfolio is achieved by selling more contracts than required to achieve a zero duration portfolio. The present value of a negative duration portfolio varies *directly* with the level of interest rates. Obviously, such a position could not be achieved if one were limited only to purchases of cash market instruments (although short positions in cash market instruments could be used).

EXHIBIT 4 Immunization with Futures Sales for an 8-Year Holding Period

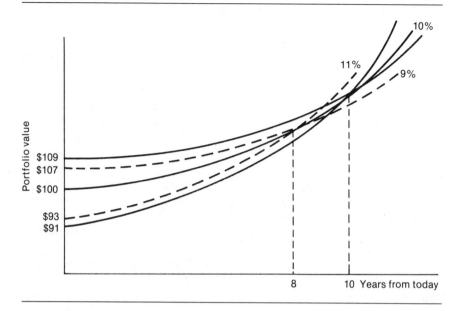

Managing an Immunized Portfolio

Thus far we have ignored issues involving the ongoing management, or rebalancing, of an immunized portfolio. To continuously maintain the desired hedge between the two sources of interest-rate risk one must restructure a portfolio as necessary to maintain the equality between duration and the remaining length of the holding period.[4] There are two reasons why a portfolio that is initially immunized may require rebalancing—maturation and rate changes. As a bond portfolio matures, its duration decreases. The duration of a zero decreases at the same rate as the holding period. Therefore, duration will always be equal to the remaining holding period for a portfolio immunized with a zero; no rebalancing is required. However, any portfolio consisting of two or more cash flows will require rebalancing as a result of maturation. For example, a portfolio composed of equal present values in a one-year and a nine-year maturity zero has a duration of five years. If the proceeds

---

[4] For an analysis of the rebalancing question, see J. Yawitz and W. Marshall, "The Investor's Holding Period and the Need to Rebalance an Immunized Portfolio," Working Paper #81–3, Washington University.

from the one-year zero are invested in overnight funds (zero maturity and duration), the portfolio will have a duration of two years at the end of the five-year holding period. This is the average of the zero duration of the overnight funds and the four-year duration of the longer zero. During the five-year period, rebalancing transactions will be required to maintain the equality between duration and holding period.

Interest-rate changes could also necessitate rebalancing. Consider again a portfolio with duration of five years, composed of equal present values in a one-year and a nine-year zero. An increase in the interest will cause both zeros to decrease in value, with the nine-year zero experiencing the greater price decline. The present value weights have changed: the shorter maturity security now has the greater weight. Thus the portfolio's duration is now less than five years. Rebalancing requires one to "lengthen" the portfolio by selling some of the shorter instrument and purchasing more of the longer instrument. Reestablishing the present value weights of 0.50 each will return the duration to five years.

Futures can be useful in rebalancing. Consider an immunized portfolio composed entirely of coupon-bearing securities. If an increase in the rate causes duration to fall (rise), one can rebalance by purchasing (selling) futures contracts. The increase in the rate increases reinvestment risk and reduces market risk. Purchasing futures reduces reinvestment risk to reestablish the balance. Similarly, as time passes, maturation causes the portfolio's market risk to exceed its reinvestment risk. Selling futures increases reinvestment risk and reestablishes the balance.

The use of futures in an immunization program also enhances the liquidity of the portfolio. Since futures transactions replace cash market transactions in the rebalancing process, one can maintain relatively large positions in fewer specific bond issues. If some unforeseen development necessitates liquidation of some of the portfolio, transactions costs will be lower.

COMBINING ACTIVE MANAGEMENT AND IMMUNIZATION

A number of portfolio strategies incorporate elements of active and passive management. While these strategies allow considerable choice in the types of assets purchased for the portfolio, they share the common characteristic that immunization could be required at some future date. We will refer to those strategies which utilize active management at the outset of the holding period while also guaranteeing a minimum holding period return as contingent immunization. More generally, contingent immunization[5] has denoted a strategy of active bond management that under certain circumstances would result in immunization before the end of the holding period. It is similar to immunization in that a specific holding period must be stated. In order to consider contingent immunization, the investor's minimum rate of return constraint must be below the rate available from conventional immunization. In principle, the management of a contingent immunization is straightforward. The portfolio is managed actively over the entire holding period or until the portfolio reaches a value in the future that is just sufficient to guarantee the minimum holding period return if it is immediately switched into a conventional immunization.

Further insight into contingent immunization can be gained from the valuation profiles in Exhibit 5. We assume the interest rate is initially

EXHIBIT 5 Contingent Immunization with a 10-Year Holding Period

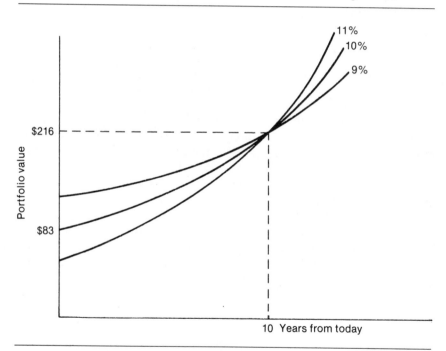

[5] The concept of "lower bound performance" that is the foundation of contingent immunization is developed in J. Yawitz and W. Marshall, "Lower Bounds on Portfolio Performance: An Extension of the Immunization Strategy." A thorough discussion of contingent immunization is found in M. L. Leibowitz and A. Weinberger, "Contingent Immunization—Part I: Risk Control Procedures," (New York: Salomon Brothers, 1981.)

10 percent, the investor has $100, the holding period is 10 years, and the minimum acceptable rate of return for the 10-year period is 8 percent. $100 invested for 10 years at 8 percent would result in $216; $83 invested at 10 percent in an immunized portfolio would guarantee the $216. The valuation profile beginning at $83 passes through $216 ten years hence if the interest rate remains at 10 percent. If the $83 was invested in a 10-year duration portfolio, the value lines corresponding to a new rate of either 9 percent or 11 percent would also pass through $216 after 10 years. Now, suppose the portfolio is actively managed. If rates remain constant and at some future date the portfolio's value touched the 10 percent value line (perhaps it was invested in equity or real estate), immunization would be undertaken. Similarly, if rates rise (fall) and the 11 percent (9 percent) value profile is touched, immunization is undertaken. The value line passing through $216 ten years hence and constructed using the current market rate serves as a lower bound or trigger point on portfolio performance. If the value of the actively managed portfolio ever touches this lower bound, immunization is undertaken.

Specific Applications of Contingent Immunization

One can view the extent of active management as the difference between the duration of the bond portfolio and the remaining length of the investor's holding period. When duration exceeds the holding period, performance will vary inversely with unanticipated changes in the interest rate. As a result, immunization will be invoked only if a rise in the interest rate causes portfolio value to fall to the point where the minimum return constraint can only be satisfied by switching to immunization. A parallel result holds for a fall in rates if the portfolio's duration is *less* than the holding period.

When portfolio duration differs from the length of the holding period, there need not exist an adverse rate change that will necessitate a switch to immunization. For any bond portfolio, one can determine a value for the interest rate which would result in the worst possible performance over a specific holding period. This worst case interest rate establishes a lower bound on the value of the portfolio at the end of the holding period.[6] If the lower bound on end-of-period value is at least as great as the value necessary to achieve the minimum performance constraint, a contingent immunization program will never require immunization. This condition will hold only if a portfolio's duration is "fairly close" to the length of the holding period.

Suppose that actively managed funds are invested in a bond portfolio with duration significantly different from the length of the holding

---

[6] For a rigorous analysis of this point, see: Marshall and Yawitz, "Lower Bounds on Portfolio Performance: An Extension of the Immunization Strategy."

period. If a sufficiently large adverse price change occurs soon after initiation of the investment program, a switch into immunization may not achieve the minimum return. This situation would occur if the value of the actively managed portfolio fell below the value necessary to achieve the minimum return with an immunized portfolio. The possibility of being "caught on the carry" represents a potentially serious shortcoming of contingent immunization.

Contingent immunization can also be achieved by combining cash market assets with futures and options. This approach affords several desirable features not found in portfolios limited only to cash market instruments.

Again, suppose the interest rate is 10 percent, the minimum acceptable rate of return over 10 years is 8 percent, and initial funds are $100. Active management within the framework of contingent immunization might immunize the $100 for 10 years, and buy or sell futures contracts depending on the rate forecast. If the forecast is correct, the profit from the futures position is used to add to the cash asset portfolio that is held. If the forecast is incorrect, the cash settlement is financed by liquidating enough cash assets, leaving the immunization in force.[7] As rate forecasts change, portfolio duration can be modified appropriately; the transactions costs will be considerably lower when futures rather than cash assets are used. Active management will automatically be terminated if the value of the cash assets ever equals the minimum value necessary to guarantee the 8 percent rate of return.

The use of futures in contingent immunization need not be limited to active bond management. Futures positions in commodities and stock indexes might be taken. However, one should realize that with futures there exists the possibility of violating the minimum return constraint if a rapid change in asset prices is experienced.

As with futures, options can be used to achieve contingent immunization. In the above example, one must invest $83 in an immunized portfolio to achieve the 8 percent minimum return on an initial investment of $100. The $17 difference is available for options purchases that are consistent with the specific rate forecast.[8] If the forecasts are correct, the realized return will exceed 8 percent. On the other hand, if forecasts are incorrect the value of the options portfolio will fall. If the option portfolio ever has a zero value, active management automatically ends. Since no restructuring of the cash position is required to immunize, one need not continually monitor the portfolio's value vis a vis the value necessary to achieve the minimum 8 percent return; the minimum value occurs when the option portfolio is valueless. In this situation the possibility of being caught on the carry has been eliminated.

---

[7] Any rate change would most likely require rebalancing of the portfolio.

[8] Purchase call (put) options on bonds if rates are expected to fall (rise).

As with futures, options on other than fixed income securities might be used. Also, the use of options could save management costs. Since the initial portfolio is partitioned into a passively managed ($83) and an actively managed ($17) component, one need only pay an active fee for the assets under management.

SUMMARY

In this paper we have provided a nontechnical analysis of several new techniques for managing bond portfolios. Immunization and several extensions of immunization dominated the discussion as these techniques have dominated modern practice. We also demonstrated how futures and options can be incorporated into portfolio strategies to produce important benefits. Specifically, futures (options) enable one to modify the risk parameters of a bond portfolio at a relatively low cost either to achieve immunization or to obtain a desired "at risk" position.

46

Spread Trading with Interest-Rate Futures

Mark Landau
Vice President
Wood Gundy Inc.

Benjamin Wolkowitz, Ph.D.
Vice President
Morgan Stanley & Co.

INTRODUCTION

Spread trading with futures contracts entails establishing two or more offsetting (i.e., short and long) futures positions simultaneously. Such spread positions typically have unique characteristics that distinguish them from an outright trade in one contract. Generally a spread position allows for a trade on an economic or financial factor that cannot be replicated with a position in only one contract. Moreover, spread trades frequently entail a lower level of risk than outright positions. For this reason, spread trades executed on one exchange require lower margin than an outright position. Spread trades have also been motivated by tax considerations although recent changes in the tax code have reduced the attractiveness of such trades.

Spread trades can be classified into several categories. A major distinction is between *intra* and *intermarket spreads*. Intramarket spreads refer to those spreads made up of two different delivery months in the same contract type. For example, short December Treasury bond futures and long March Treasury bond futures is an example of an intramarket spread. The difference between two different contract months can be conceived of as a short-term interest rate. (This will be explained in detail later). Opportunities for profitable trades may exist when these constructed short-term financing rates differ from actual market rates of comparable maturity. Intramarket spreads can also be constructed so as to replicate forward rates, and these forward rates when compared to cash market forward rates may suggest trades. Moreover, intermarket spreads can be constructed so as to take advantage of anticipated changes in the slope of the yield curve.

Spread trades constructed across contract types are known as *intermarket spreads*. Such trades are generally implemented because of quality differences, supply considerations, or maturity differences between the two instruments. Quality spreads refer to the difference between public and private credits. When the market's assessment of the quality of privately issued debt (generally Eurodollar or CD futures) is changing relative to the assessment of publicly issued debt (generally Treasury bills) the opportunity for a profitable trade may arise. Maturity differences refer to yield curve trades where the yield curve slope is expected to change, which would in turn affect the relative value of instruments at different points on the curve. A popular futures trade relating to maturity spreads depends on combining Treasury notes and Treasury bonds to take advantage of either changes in the yield curve or differences in price volatility.

A third catchall category of spreads is combination trades. These include *inter-intramarket spreads*, which as the name suggests are a combination of an intermarket and intramarket spread, to take advantage of characteristics inherent to each. Another type of combination spread, a *tandem spread*, positions an intramarket spread in one contract (e.g., a Treasury bill spread) against an intramarket spread in another contract (e.g., a Eurodollar spread). A final type of combination spread depends on a combination of two intramarket spreads in the same contract type. Such a spread is known as a *butterfly*. This type of spread has been motivated primarily by tax considerations; however, even though tax code changes have removed an incentive for such trades, they can still be employed profitably.

This chapter contains a consideration of all the major categories of futures spread trades except intermarket spreads due to maturity differences. This chapter is divided into the following sections: (1) a description and empirical evidence of the several types of intramarket spreads, (2) a review of a particular type of intramarket spread, the implied repo cost of carry spread trade, (3) a description and empirical evidence of several intermarket spreads, and (4) a review of combination spreads.

INTRAMARKET SPREADS—SHORT END OF THE MATURITY SPECTRUM

Implied Forward Rate—Futures Spread versus Cash Rates

A yield curve not only indicates the current cash market rates for various maturities of a given type of security(ies), but it also embodies forward rates for that security type. For example, a Treasury yield curve will reflect the current cash quotes for the entire maturity spectrum of Treasury securities, and it will also contain sufficient information to calculate a rate for a Treasury security of a given maturity for a certain period in the future. In effect, knowing two current rates enables you to solve for a third future rate. The yield curve provides the required information on the two current rates.

As an example, suppose you wanted to know the interest rate on a 90-day security 270 days from now. You could, from the yield curve, obtain a quote for a one-year security and for a 270-day security. The difference would be the yield on the 90-day security 270 days from now. Figure 1 illustrates that more generally, if R1 is the short-term rate and R3 is the long-term rate, the intermediate forward rate, R2, could be calculated from R1 and R3.

FIGURE 1

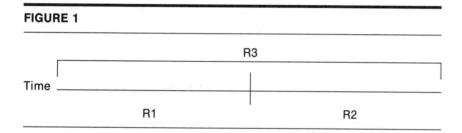

In general, if these rates apply to time periods, N1, N2, and N3, R2 (stated on a 360-day basis) can be calculated directly from the formula.

$$R2 = \left[\frac{1 + \dfrac{R3 * N3}{360}}{1 + \dfrac{R1 * N1}{360}} - 1 \right] * \frac{360}{N2}$$

Suppose for example that

R1 = 11.00% and N1 = 77 days
R3 = 11.50% and N3 = 168 days
R2 = the rate on a 91-day security,
  77 days from now

Using the formula above

$$R2 = \left[\frac{1 + \dfrac{.115 * 168}{360}}{1 + \dfrac{.11 * 77}{360}} - 1 \right] * \frac{360}{92} = 11.64\%$$

This procedure is applicable to any security type as long as it has a number of sufficiently different maturity and rate combinations quoted in the spot cash market to make the calculation of an implied forward rate feasible. The possibility for cash-futures trades exists when there are sufficient spot quotes available so that it is feasible to calculate implied forward rates corresponding to futures rates. If, for example, today were 87 days from the delivery date of a 90-day Eurodollar futures contract, a comparison between futures and cash would be possible if sufficient cash quotes were available to calculate a 90-day rate 87 days away. Using the terminology and symbols introduced earlier, we need an R2 and R3 for cash based on 87 days and 177 days so as to calculate an R1 based on 90 days.

Discrepancies between implied forward rates calculated from cash market quotes and futures quotes for the same time period suggest the existence of profitable trading opportunities. Certain differences in quotes may have a systematic pattern, however, suggesting that these are not trading opportunities but rather accurate reflections of different transaction costs and/or risks associated with the two markets. It is the unsystematic and presumably short-lived price discrepancies that afford real opportunities. Accurately disaggregating price differences into systematic and unsystematic components is difficult, but it is the key part of this type of trading activity. For example, there have been a number of studies of the cash-futures price relationships in the Treasury bill market directed at uncovering systematic and unsystematic price differences, but the results have been inconclusive.[1] The explanations for price differences seem at best to be accurate for short periods of time. In practice this type of spread trade depends less on scientific and more on subjective guidelines. Nevertheless, trading the difference between implied forward rates and actual future rates can be a profitable activity and it is worth pursuing.

At this juncture the reader may be somewhat confused—what first appeared to be a discourse on spreading futures contracts has begun with a description of a type of trade that requires taking two positions in cash, i.e., a cash market spread, against an outright single futures position. Thus, if anything, this is a cash market spread trade. In fact it can and often is put on in just that fashion. It can, under certain circumstances, be put on by using two futures positions and a single cash position. Referring to Figure 1 above, in general it is possible to use a combination of futures and cash to calculate R2 and then trade this position against another futures position. The feasibility of such a trade

---

[1] See Richard W. Lang and Robert H. Rasche, "A Comparison of Yields on Futures Contracts and Implied Forward Rates," *Federal Reserve Bank of St. Louis Monthly,* December 1978, pp. 21–30 and William Poole, "Using T-Bill Futures to Gauge Interest-Rate Expectations," *Federal Reserve Bank of San Francisco, Economic Review,* Spring 1978, pp. 7, 14, and 15.

depends on the periods N1 and N3 used to calculate an R2 for period N2. Two conditions must be met for the trade to be effective as a futures spread: (1) futures contracts must be available corresponding to either of the time periods N1 and N3, and (2) the prices for the futures contracts used as substitutes for a cash position must be sufficiently comparable to the cash price so as not to reduce the trade's effectiveness.

Obviously even if this trade were put on with two futures contracts it would not be a futures spread trade. The purpose of including this trade in our discussion is to highlight how futures and cash can be used interchangeably, and also to underscore what can be produced with a combination of instruments as opposed to a single instrument.

Yield Curve Spreads

Treasury bill and Eurodollar futures contracts offer significant intra-market spreading opportunities. The relationship of one contract month to another can be greatly affected by the shape of the front part of the yield curve (under two years) since, in concept, the contracts represent 90-day money out as long as contracts are listed, which is out to approximately two years.

A hypothetical example based on Eurodollar futures will illustrate how the slope of the yield curve affects the pricing of Eurodollar futures. At expiration, a Eurodollar futures contract will settle at a price equal to the offered side of the three-month Eurodollar deposit rate. For example, if the rate on a March contract is 10 percent, the contract will be priced at 90.00. At the same time, if six-month Eurodollar rates are offered at 11 percent, the June contract should be trading close to 88.00 because it would take an arithmetic average of 10 percent (the spot three-month rate) and 12 percent (the forward or future three-month rate) to produce the current 11 percent yield on six-month money.[2]

If the cash and futures markets were perfectly integrated and equally influenced by the same factors, futures spreads would reflect precisely the rates implied in the cash market. Indeed arbitrage activities would work to drive the futures and cash rates in line. These two markets will frequently be out of line, however, because of the influence of expectations on interest rates. Expectations will generally influence one of the markets ahead of the other setting up a lead-lag relationship. The effect of arbitrage activities will be to establish ranges within which cash

---

[2] This statement is not precisely correct because of the effect of compounding and arbitrage activity that will tend to keep the June contract priced around 88.00, but not force it to exactly that level. Nevertheless the concept is correct even if slight liberties were taken with the numerical example. Treasury bill futures will behave in a similar fashion except adjustments have to be made for the fact that it is not a cash settlement futures contract and it is quoted on a discount basis.

and futures prices will fall but equality of prices is unlikely because of the differential impact of expectations on these two markets.

During periods of very volatile interest rates, the slope of the yield curve will typically have the greatest influence on the behavior of spreads. A good illustration is provided by 1980, a year in which many short-term interest rates swung within a 10-point range. It was a period of dramatic changes in Federal Reserve policy which affected the slope of the short end of the yield curve. These curve changes influenced Treasury bill futures spread values (the Eurodollar contract had not yet been introduced).

In particular, in the spring of 1980, the Federal Reserve eased the availability of credit. This had the effect of changing the slope of the Treasury yield curve from inversion to very positive. At the same time Treasury bill futures spreads went from negative (lower prices nearby versus distant contracts) to extremely positive (higher prices nearby versus distant contracts). The Federal Reserve reversed its policy in the fall of 1980 by restricting the availability of credit. As a consequence the yield curve inverted. Treasury bill futures spreads narrowed, becoming negative again.

The first part of the impact of Fed actions is dramatically illustrated in Figure 2 which shows the behavior of the June 1980 Treasury bill futures contract. In a short period of time, this contract rallied more than 800 basis points. The impact on the June 1980–September 1980 Treasury bill spread is illustrated in Figure 3. This spread, widened by 150 basis points on the Treasury yield curve, changed from inverted to normal. As the data in Table 1 confirm, Fed tightening in the fall of 1980 resulted in the spread narrowing as the yield curve again inverted.

The period summarized in Table 1 is illustrative of classical capital markets theory. Federal Reserve influence on interest rates is most directly felt on short-term interest rates. After affecting short rates the influence of Federal Reserve policies will then work its way throughout the maturity spectrum. The appropriate way to profit from the policy moves summarized in Table 1 is to buy the spread (i.e., buy the nearby or front month and sell the distant month) in a bull market, and sell the spread (i.e., sell the nearby and buy the back month) in a bear market. These spread trading rules may be effective only during those periods when Federal Reserve policy dominates interest-rate movements.

During periods when expectations dominate interest-rate behavior, and in turn the slope of the yield curve, it is not uncommon for the shorter interest rates to be relatively stable in comparison to six-month and one-year rates. The markets are in effect adjusting to an anticipated change in Federal Reserve policy "down the road." Under such conditions the spread should be set up opposite to the way indicated above. For example, in a bull market case the expectation is that future rates will fall but immediate short-term rates are expected to be for the most part

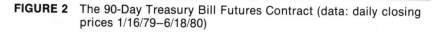

FIGURE 2 The 90-Day Treasury Bill Futures Contract (data: daily closing prices 1/16/79–6/18/80)

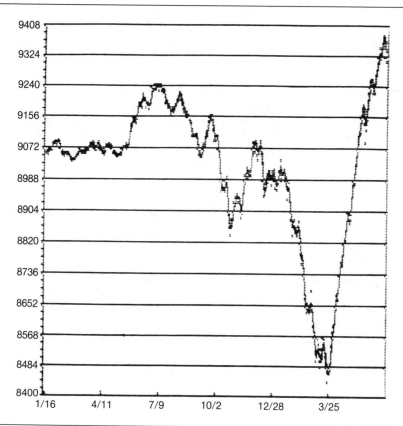

unchanged. Consequently one should sell the nearby contract and buy the distant contract. For similar reasons, in a bear market one should buy the nearby contract and sell the distant contract.

For example, in the bull credit markets that began in mid-1984, we saw the interest-rate movements indicated in Table 2. Since this particular bull market was in part the result of expectations it was characterized by a flattening cash curve as well as a contraction in futures spreads.

The profitability of futures spreads in expectationally driven markets will obviously be affected by the appropriate choice of contracts. The closer a Treasury bill or Eurodollar futures contract is to expiration, the more closely it behaves in the same manner as a three-month cash market rate. As discussed above such a short-term rate is less likely to be influenced by expectations than a more distant futures contract. There-

FIGURE 3 The June 1980–September 1980 Spread in Treasury Bill Futures Contracts (data: daily closing prices 1/16/79–6/18/80)

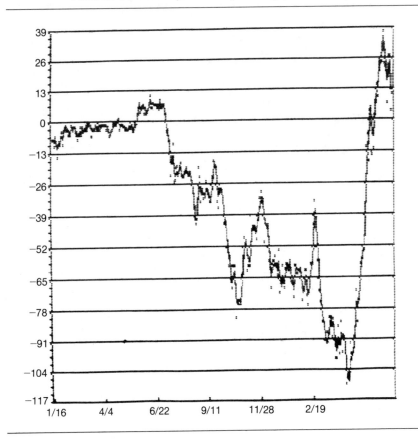

fore a contract close to expiration would be appropriate to sell under these economic circumstances. The next contract to the one expiring should more nearly replicate a six-month rate, and subsequent contracts will behave in the manner of progressively longer-term rates. These longer-term rate futures contracts are candidates to be bought. The behavior of spreads when the front month contract approaches expiration is demonstrated in Table 3.

Spread trading in an unchanged market is also feasible. If a nearby spread (March–June, for example) is at a different value than a more distant spread (Sept.–Dec. spread), and the trader anticipates the curve not changing, then the distant spread should have the same value as the nearby spread, when it is the nearby spread. A trade based on such

TABLE 1 The Changing Yield Curve and Bill Futures Spreads in a Volatile Period

	Bond Equivalent Yields for T bills			Price Spreads for Bill Futures			
	3 Mos.	6 Mos.	1 Yr.	Jun. 80–Sep. 80	Sep. 80–Dec. 80	Dec. 80–Mar. 81	Mar. 81–Jun. 81
01-02-80	12.34	12.92	12.55	−.68	−.32	−.06	0.03
02-01-80	12.34	12.98	13.00	−.74	−.45	−.25	−0.09
03-03-80	15.21	16.04	16.25	−.75	−.51	−.36	−0.21
04-01-80	15.25	16.31	16.52	−.96	−.58	−.27	−0.07
05-01-80	10.51	11.08	11.45	−.57	−.38	−.14	0.10
06-02-80	8.01	8.62	9.14	.24	.16	.18	0.18
07-01-80	8.15	8.43	8.78		.27	.26	0.18
08-01-80	8.82	9.29	9.65		.06	.14	0.11
09-02-80	10.01	10.70	11.21		.33	.17	0.14
10-01-80	11.61	12.35	12.69			.10	−0.12
11-03-80	13.36	14.36	14.54			−.21	−0.27
12-01-80	14.92	16.03	15.95			−.73	−0.58
01-02-81	14.86	15.19	14.58				−0.89
02-02-81	15.11	15.13	14.82				−1.60
03-02-81	14.73	15.56	15.49				−1.18

TABLE 2

	Eurodollar Deposit Rates		Sept. 1984–Dec. 1984 Eurodollar Futures Price Spread
	3 Mos.	6 Mos.	
June 15	11.63	12.25	.59
June 29	12.25	12.75	.82
July 16	12.00	12.63	.70
July 30	11.88	12.38	.51
Aug 15	11.88	12.13	.40
Aug 30	12.00	12.25	.48
Sept 14	11.75	11.94	.02

observations is known as "riding the yield curve." For example, suppose the following conditions prevailed on January 1,

3 Month Euros	6%	March Euro Futures	93.50
6 Month Euros	6.5%	June Euro Futures	92.60
12 Month Euros	6.75%	Sept Euro Futures	91.90
		Dec Euro Futures	91.30

TABLE 3

	Eurodollar Deposit Rates		Sept. 1984–Dec. 1984 Eurodollar Futures Price Spread
	3 Mos.	6 Mos.	
Aug 28	12.00	12.25	.47
Aug 29	12.00	12.25	.49
Aug 30	12.00	12.25	.48
Aug 31	12.00	12.44	.46
Sept 04	12.06	12.31	.50
Sept 05	12.13	12.44	.50
Sept 06	12.13	12.38	.41
Sept 07	12.00	12.25	.33
Sept 10	11.94	12.25	.22
Sept 11	11.88	12.06	.16
Sept 12	11.88	12.13	.18
Sept 13	11.81	12.13	.06
Sept 14	11.75	11.94	.02

The March–June spread had a value of 90 basis points, while the Sept.–Dec. spread had a value of 60 basis points. If in six months conditions had remained basically unchanged, then the Sept.–Dec. spread should have widened by 30 basis points. Thus on January 1, the Sept.–Dec. spread was a buy. Of course the various spreads had differing values because the market did not expect economic conditions to remain unchanged. To put on such a trade would require a contrary view of the market. In most any futures trade, however, the trader is establishing a position because of a belief that some event not reflected in the market will occur.

Deliverable Supply Spreads

Intramarket spreads in short maturity futures can be affected by the cash market "technicals" underlying the futures contracts. In particular, temporary high demand or shortages of supply of the underlying security will move the futures spread.

Knowing how the futures spread will react to a change in the supply or demand of the cash instrument requires knowing precisely what is deliverable in fulfillment of the obligation under the futures contract. For example, present rules of the Chicago Mercantile Exchange call for the delivery of a Treasury bill with either 90, 91, or 92 days to maturity from the time of delivery. Under the current Treasury issuance cycle, this means good delivery may be made with an old one-year bill, an old six-month bill, or a newly issued three-month bill. Under former contract specifications, a less generous supply of bills was eligible since an old one-year bill was not always acceptable for good delivery.

In spite of an increase in the categories of bills eligible for delivery, shortages can still occur. Such shortages are usually at most temporary, but they can cause the nearby contract to gain in price on more distant contract months, resulting in a widening of the spread. There are several possible events which may result in a bill shortage. The extent of the shortage will depend on whether these events occur in isolation or together. Several examples of such events include:

1. During extended periods of dollar weakness, foreign central banks may intervene in foreign exchange markets with dollar purchases. These dollars may then be invested temporarily in Treasury bills, either bought directly from the Federal Reserve, or from government security dealers;

2. The Federal Reserve's open market operations, affected by seasonal and/or policy considerations, can through outright purchases reduce the supply of Treasury bills;

3. The Treasury, in financing new government debt or refinancing (or paying down) outstanding debt, can greatly affect the supply of Treasury bills. The Treasury decides what maturities of debt to issue and in what size, all within the context of federal government needs. These needs are affected by fiscal policy and seasonal spending patterns.

These three events encompass both supply and demand considerations. Generally supply considerations will by themselves have only a slight impact on spreads. If, however, changes in the supply of Treasury bills accompany other factors influencing spreads in the same fashion, they will magnify the total effect. For example, a steepening of the yield curve could be made even more acute if accompanied by a temporary decrease in the supply of bills.

Supply conditions can also affect Eurodollar futures contracts even though the contract is a cash settlement instrument since the correct price is a function of economic factors influencing the underlying cash market. Unlike Treasury bills, however, the supply of Eurodollar deposits is affected by activities of numerous banking institutions, all able to create deposits at will. Thus the factors that will have to be tracked to determine the likely behavior of Eurodollar spreads include all the economic and financial factors influencing banks in their decisions regarding the issuance of Eurodollar deposits.

An example of how the Treasury bill spread can be influenced by various economic factors is provided by the experience of Spring 1978. That was a period when the Federal Reserve was easing at the same time there was weakness in the dollar in the international currency markets. Dollar support operations by foreign central banks meant they were buying dollars which they were often using to purchase Treasury bills.

Moreover, this was a seasonal paydown period for the U.S. Treasury which resulted in a reduction in the issuance of new Treasury bills. These events all contributed to Treasury bills appreciating in the cash market, which meant the nearby month in Treasury bill futures contracts gained on the back months. Figure 4 illustrates the widening in the June 1978–September 1978 Treasury bill futures spread.

FIGURE 4 The June 1978–September 1978 Treasury Bill Spread (data: daily closing prices 1/18/77 to 6/21/78)

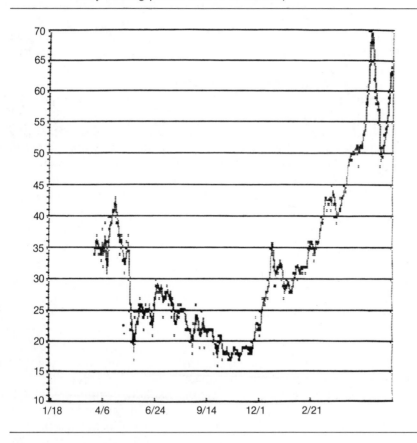

INTRAMARKET SPREADS—LONG END OF THE MATURITY SPECTRUM

Implied Repo—Cost of Carry Spreads

To understand the motivation behind intramarket spreads on the long end of the maturity spectrum, it is necessary to appreciate the distinction between carry commodities and those that are perishable. A carry commodity is one that can be delivered on several subsequent futures contracts. Gold is a key example of a futures contract that functions in this fashion. For agricultural contracts, a carry type commodity is one that can be stored such as grains, and is eligible for delivery on several contracts. The key issue for financial futures is that the deliverable has characteristics that permit it to be delivered on several contracts. For example, Treasury bond futures contracts allow for delivery of U.S. Treasury bonds with at least 15 years to call date and maturity. In concept, any newly issued 30-year Treasury bond would be deliverable for approximately 15 years (if noncallable).

Perishable agricultural commodities are not redeliverable for the obvious reason that they will not last. Live cattle is an example of a perishable agricultural commodity. Although live cattle do not literally perish, deliverable grade in futures specifies a limitation on weight which would be difficult to maintain from one contract delivery period to the next. The parallel in financials is exemplified by the certificate of deposit futures contract which has a maturity band about the deliverable which makes it impossible for a given certificate of deposit to satisfy deliverable grade on more than one contract.

Spread trades relying on commodities that can be carried are implemented in order to trade on the basis of the cost of carry. For nonfinancial commodities, the cost of carry is comprised of storage costs which generally contain two components; actual physical storage and insurance. In addition, there is an interest expense which comes from financing the storable inventory. This financing cost is nothing more than a short-term interest rate as graphically illustrated in Figure 5.

In the case of financial futures (and gold) practically the entire cost-of-carry will be the cost of financing the position. The cost of insurance and storage will be inconsequential relative to the value of the financial instruments. As a rule, the smaller is the ratio of physical bulk to value,

---

FIGURE 5

	Futures Contract Goes to Delivery	Futures Contract Goes to Delivery
T_0	T_1	T_2
SP_0	FP_1	FP_2

Notes: T_0 is the time period when a long position is established for a futures contract maturing in time period one (T_1) selling for a price of FP_1. Also a short position could be established in a futures contract maturing in time period two (T_2) selling for a price of FP_2.

Period of financing is $T_2 - T_1$. (Since futures contracts mature a minimum of four times a year, $T_2 - T_1$ is a three-month period assuming the trade is done over two subsequent contracts.)

the more important is the financing cost relative to the cost of insurance and storage in explaining the cost of carry.

Another way of characterizing the financing cost associated with the intramarket spread trade is as an implied repo rate. In the securities market, a common way of financing inventory is via repurchase or repo agreements. A dealer in long securities can lend them out with the understanding that the dealer will repurchase the securities at an agreed price at a specified time in the future. The difference between the price for the original lending of the securities and the repurchase price is the cost to the dealer of financing these securities.

In the intramarket spread trade, receiving securities on a long position and then delivering them in fulfillment of a short position is equivalent to the financing arrangement where the person who bought the first contract is the counterparty who loaned the dealer money using securities as collateral. The intramarket spread trader can then, in concept, pay a repo rate to finance the long position and earn a rate that is determined by the implied financing rate on the spread. The comparison between the actual repo rate in the market and the repo rate determined by the intramarket spread rate will indicate if the spread is a desirable trade.

Also during the period of carry there is likely to be a return depending on the characteristics of the instrument being carried. In particular, all coupon instruments will generate income during the carry period. On balance, it is possible that the carry income will exceed the financing costs generating positive carry. Such a situation is associated with a normal or positive yield curve when the longer the maturity of an instrument, the greater is the interest paid. Thus, for example, the financing cost of carrying a 30-year Treasury bond should be less than the coupon on such a bond. Alternatively, if the yield curve is inverted, carry is negative since short-term financing costs will be greater than the long-term yield.

These various points can be summarized symbolically with reference to Figure 5. In particular, the futures price at time period 1 (FP_1) should equal the spot price in period 0 (SP_0) plus the cost of carry from time period 0 to period 1 (CC01) minus the return to carry from time period 0 to time period 1 (RC01). That is,

$$FP_1 = SP_0 + CC01 - RC01$$

If the futures price exceeds the spot price adjusted for carry costs then it would be profitable to sell the relatively expensive futures and buy the relatively inexpensive spot commodity. A comparison of two successive futures contracts is a comparable exercise. In such a case, the futures price for period 2 (FP_2) should equal the futures price in period 1 (FP_1) adjusted for the cost of carry. That is,

$$FP2 = FP1 + CC12 - RC12$$

or solving for the implied repo rate CC12

$$CC12 = FP2 - FP1 - RC12$$

A comparison of CC12 with the cash market repo rate would indicate whether one should buy the spread (i.e., buy the period 1 contract and sell the period 2 contract) or sell the spread (i.e., sell the period 1 contract and buy the period 2 contract).

In a general sense the cost-of-carry trade relies on the spreading of futures contracts to construct a short-term rate. A comparison of the constructed rate with the actual short-term financing rate available in the market determines whether and in what fashion the trade should be done. Implicit in this discussion is the assumption that implied short-term rates and actual short-term rates should for the most part be equal. This would indeed be correct if the costs and risk associated with accomplishing something in the cash market were identical to those in the futures market. In fact this is not the case.

A commonly used financial futures contract for the purpose of the cash and carry trade is the Treasury bond futures contract. Establishing a short or long position in this contract is not equivalent to doing the same thing in futures and consequently there is a built-in systematic price discrepancy. In particular the futures contract gives a disproportionate advantage to the seller or short in the contract. The seller has complete discretion over which of several bonds satisfying deliverable grade will in fact be delivered. Moreover, during the delivery month, the short has until 8:00 P.M. Chicago time to notify of intention to make delivery. This is six hours after the futures market has closed which means that if the cash market price declined after the close of futures, the short could acquire the cash bond and make delivery based on a futures settlement price reflective of a higher cash market price. Finally the short has seven business days after the last trading day to make delivery, and the futures price is fixed over this period at the price the contract was finally settled. This is a variant on the daily 8:00 P.M. advantage. For these reasons there is a built-in downward bias in the price of the contract relative to cash. This bias will result in a lower than market implied repo rate which has to be considered when determining how best to put on the trade.

Deliverable Supply Spreads

Both the Treasury note and Treasury bond futures contracts listed on the Chicago Board of Trade are market basket deliverable contracts. That is, various cash instruments have the characteristics that make them deliverable on these contracts. However, events can occur that affect supply, either making a given cash instrument deliverable for a particular contract month, but not all others, or affecting the supply of a particularly popular deliverable issue. Such events will impact the value of spreads. This section contains a consideration of such events.

The Treasury note futures contract allows delivery of any noncallable Treasury issue with a maturity at delivery of 6½ to 10 years. Typically yield curve and coupon conditions favor the recently issued 10-year note as the cheapest to deliver, and the contract is priced accordingly.[3] Thus the March futures contract reflects where the new 10-year note issued in February will trade, the May contract is matched against the June issue, etc. Consequently, the spreads between the various note contracts reflect the Treasury issuance cycle. If the Treasury were to change the cycle with which it issues 10-year notes or if such notes were discontinued, then the value of the note contract spreads would change. For example, if the Treasury discontinued such notes entirely, the nearby contract would reflect the last issuance of such notes. Subsequent further out contracts would be priced on the basis of redelivery of the same issue or perhaps an older outstanding issue. This would impact the value of the spread.

Furthermore the spread values on the note contract might also change because of the impact the Treasury announcements would have on the cost and return from carrying the last 10-year note that was issued. Because the last 10-year note in the cycle would quickly become in short supply (i.e., tight) in the repo market, it would be at a premium, that is at a low cost of financing. This would in turn result in a higher return to carry because the coupon would be unaffected even though the cost of financing declined. This higher return to carry would affect the relative prices of distant contracts which would in turn affect the value of the spread.

The Treasury note futures spread can also be influenced by the type of note the Treasury elects to issue. There is no requirement that the Treasury issue a new note each quarter, rather an outstanding issue can be reopened. Because this decision affects the pricing and maturity of the note that is issued, it will also affect the price of the nearby futures contract. Contracts other than the nearby should be less affected than the nearby contract month. Thus the spreads will move. For example, if the announcement of a reopening comes as a surprise, it usually causes the nearby contract to gain on the back months thereby widening the spread. If, however, the market anticipated a possible reopening prior to the announcement, the spread would contract after the announcement of a new issue, or widen if the old issue were reopened.

---

[3] Recently The Treasury cycle has contained a 10-year note every three months—in February, May, August, and November.

The Treasury bond futures contract permits delivery on any issue with at least 15 years to call and maturity. The pricing of the issue depends on which issue is cheapest to deliver and expectations regarding which issue(s) will actually be delivered. Therefore, changes in cheapest to deliver against the contract and expectations about those changes can affect spreads.

On several occasions the bond spreads have been affected by the expectation that the Treasury was planning on issuing 40-year noncallable bonds.[4] A new 40-year bond could be the cheapest to deliver for the futures contract. For example, if the Treasury made an announcement in August that such an issue were contemplated for the November refunding, then the December Treasury bond futures would be repriced to where a 40-year bond would trade, assuming such a bond was the cheapest to deliver. The September futures contract would be unaffected, however, since this new proposed bond would not be deliverable on the September contract. Consequently, the September–December bond spread would be affected by this hypothetical issue and the timing of the announcement of this new longer maturity Treasury bond.

Treasury bond futures spreads are also affected when an outstanding cheapest-to-deliver issue, because of maturity requirements, is no longer deliverable on all outstanding contracts. In particular, at some point in time an outstanding issue will no longer have 15 years to maturity. Bond futures beyond that point will be priced to other issues. Thus the spreads will be affected because price movements in the different futures contracts will be dependent on different cash issues as well as differing expectations regarding the cost of carry.

INTERMARKET SPREADS

In the previous sections we examined intramarket spreads which depend on establishing opposite positions in two different contract months for the same type of contract, e.g., short March Treasury bills and long June Treasury bills. In this section we examine intermarket spreads, which depend on establishing opposite positions in two different contracts, but generally in the same month. Intermarket spreads are motivated by a perception that different markets will respond differently to a particular economic or financial event. Credit concerns, which have differential effects on different markets and may influence intermarket spreads, are considered in detail below.

Flight to Quality

The expression *flight to quality* is used generically in the securities markets to describe those situations in which credit considerations dominate

---

[4] Currently, the Treasury issues 30-year noncallable bonds each quarter.

market behavior. In particular, government securities become relatively more attractive than privately-issued securities for reasons of credit exposure. In futures, a flight to quality is evidenced by an appreciation in the value of Treasury bill contracts relative to the value of Eurodollar contracts resulting in a widening of the Treasury bill-Eurodollar futures spread or "TED" spread as it is commonly called.[5]

The value of the TED spread is also very much affected by the level of interest rates.[6] It could be conceived of as a trade to be used to profit from a move to a bull or bear market. This behavior is a direct consequence of the perceived impact of interest rates on bank profitability and financial stability. In particular, banks are generally viewed as benefiting from lower interest rates because the cost of funds and the risk of default are both directly related to the level of interest rates. Thus, as interest rates fall and banks are perceived as less risky, the risk premium built into bank rates declines. In such a situation the difference between the cost of Treasury debt and bank debt declines and the TED spread narrows.

As discussed above, the way to profit from a narrowing of the spreads generally is to sell the spreads; i.e., in this case sell Treasury bill futures and buy Eurodollar futures. If the implied interest rate on Eurodollar futures falls as a consequence of any improvement in the creditworthiness of banks, then the Eurodollar contracts will appreciate relative to the Treasury bill futures. Thus, the Eurodollar position could be liquidated at a greater gain than any loss resulting from the liquidating of the Treasury bill contracts.

The justification behind the changes in the TED spread when interest rates are changing is identical if rates are rising. A rising rate environment is indicative of possible bank funding and credit problems, which in turn, results in larger risk premiums for bank credits. Consequently the TED spread will widen. The appropriate trade to profit from a widening of the spread is to buy the spread.

Aside from changes in the level of interest rates, there are, of course, instances in which events directly affecting the creditworthiness of banks occur that in turn have a dramatic and direct impact on the cost of

---

[5] The flight-to-quality concept also affects the value of certificate of deposit futures contracts relative to Treasury bill futures; however, the CD contract is not nearly as liquid as the Eurodollar contract. Therefore, this section focuses on the TED spread.

[6] Interest on Treasury bills is quoted on a discount basis whereas interest on Eurodollar time deposits is quoted as a simple short-term or add-on rate. Thus the quote on Treasury bills is based on something less than a $1 million dollar instrument while interest on a Eurodollar time deposit is based on precisely a $1 million instrument. Futures market convention specifies the value of a basis point, an 01, as equal to $25 for both contracts. When trading on the basis of an 01, weighting both parts of the spread equally is appropriate. If, however, the trade is based on a bond equivalent yield basis, the trade has to be weighted differently to account for the different conventions used in quoting interest. In practice, however, the trade is rarely weighted.

bank liabilities and on quality spreads such as the TED spread. Such events include perceptions of credit problems among large banks. These events could be international in character, as when Third World nations have difficulty meeting their debt obligations; or they may be more regional in character, as when a group of banks lend money to an industry that falters. Alternatively the problems could be unique to a single large institution. Typically when a larger bank has problems, the resolution of the problem takes a long time and frequently has a spillover effect on the rest of the industry. The problems of Continental Illinois Bank and Trust Company in 1984 are a case in point. Events of this type influence the cost of all bank credits and in turn impact the TED spread.

Occasionally, both types of events—a change in the level of interest rates and a change in the general perception of bank creditworthiness as influenced by a particular event—may occur at approximately the same time. For example, an increase in the level of interest rates may occur at the same time the banking sector is affected by adverse publicity. In combination these events should have a greater impact than either one alone. The same logic holds for a situation where interest rates are eased because of news favorable to the banking sector.

It is of particular interest to examine periods when the effects on the TED spread are at least in concept offsetting. That is, when events influencing the perception of the creditworthiness of banks occur in a manner opposite to changes in the level of interest rates. Such a period occurred in the spring and summer of 1982. At that time the Federal Reserve had taken steps to ease the availability of credit which had the desired effect of resulting in a reduction in interest rates. At approximately the same time the capacity of Third World nations to meet their debt obligations to U.S. banks became an issue. Because of the size of their debt, there was concern over the impact such a default would have on the viability of U.S. banks.

The net effect of these two conceivably offsetting events is graphically presented in Figure 6. This graph presents the December Treasury bill–Eurodollar futures spread. At the beginning of 1982 this spread varied within a narrow range of approximately 20 basis points at a 180–200 basis point level. By the second quarter, the spread began to widen dramatically, gaining in excess of 100 basis points from low point values in the first quarter. During the summer of that year the spread continued to widen achieving a peak of approximately 350 basis points. Almost immediately after attaining this peak value, the spread began to narrow, even more dramatically than it had widened, rapidly falling back to the 160–180 basis point range, levels that had characterized the behavior of the TED spread during the first quarter.

An examination of what was happening to the December Treasury bill contract (one part of the spread) provides an explanation of why the TED behaved the way it did. At the outset of the period, the Treasury

FIGURE 6 (a)   December 1982 Treasury Bill Futures (data: daily closing prices July 23, 1981 to December 22, 1982)

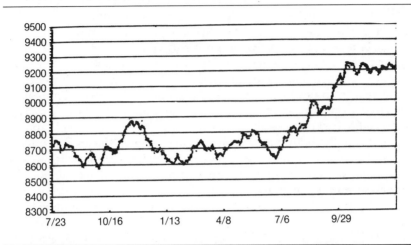

FIGURE 6 (b)   The December 1982 TED Spread (data: daily closing prices July 23, 1981 to December 22, 1982)

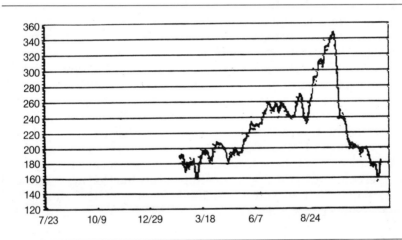

bill contract was also moving in a fairly tight range, although in absolute terms somewhat more than the spread itself. This suggests that the Eurodollar contract was moving along with the Treasury bill contract. This behavior changed by mid-second quarter when the TED spread widened while the Treasury bill contract actually fell in value thus implying that the Eurodollar contract fell even more than the Treasury bill contract. This changed by the end of the second quarter, and at the beginning of the third quarter the Treasury bill contract enjoyed a five point rally at the same time the TED spread widened to 350 basis points. Obviously the Eurodollar contract gained less during this period in response to the Fed easing, the reason being that bank credits were affected by adverse news.

The vagaries of money markets are such that it would be inappropriate to extrapolate from this discussion to predict how the TED spread might behave. This example does demonstrate that this spread can be very volatile over relatively short periods of time reflecting the principles of the flight to quality in the futures markets.

COMBINATION STRATEGIES

The "Whammy"

Combination spreads on the short end of the maturity spectrum typically involve a combination of the TED spread and the intramarket spread. The TED and intramarket combination is sufficiently popular that traders have a special name for it, the "whammy". Buying this spread (or buying the whammy) entails buying the nearby bill contract and selling the second Eurodollar contract out. Obviously the trader putting on this spread wants to take advantage of a movement in the intramarket spread as well as the TED spread; however the TED component usually incurs the bigger move. Thus in evaluating whether to put on the whammy, one should evaluate putting on the TED and then decide if the addition of the intramarket aspect can improve the trade's potential. Factors that have to be evaluated in determining whether to put on the whammy include the shape of the yield curve, deliverable supply considerations, the technicals of the underlying cash security, implied repo rates of deliverable securities, and expectations, all of which have been discussed in previous sections. Following are the optimal conditions that could make buying the whammy a successful trade, although it is unlikely that they would all occur simultaneously.

1. The time is within four weeks of the nearby contract going off the board.
2. The Fed is expected to be an outright purchaser of bills for open market operations as well as an agent for foreign central bank purchases.
3. The Treasury will be paying down Treasury bills because it is flush with funds.
4. There are growing private credit demands that the banks will be financing with externally raised funds.
5. The yield curve is steepening because of an expected bear market.
6. There is instability in the banking industry.

To make selling the whammy, i.e. selling a nearby T-bill future and buying a distant Eurodollar future, a successful trade would require that the opposite of some (if not all) of the above conditions hold (except for the first).

The "reverse whammy" which involves the nearby Eurodollar futures contract and the more distant Treasury bill futures contract is less popular because recently it has not been an effective trade. Many of the factors affecting the TED spread have had the same direction of impact on the intramarket, and these factors have induced the whammy to work more effectively than the reverse whammy. For example, reported difficulties in the banking sector not only cause the TED spread to widen but also the intramarket.

An example of how the whammy has actually behaved underscores the relationship between the cash and futures markets. Figure 7 illus-

FIGURE 7 The December 1984 Treasury Bill–March 1985 Eurodollar Futures Spread (data: daily closing prices for November 21, 1984 to December 19, 1984)

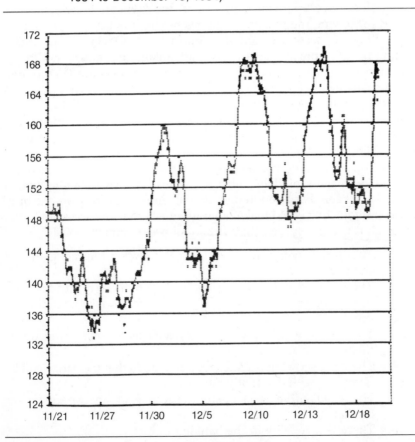

trates the spread between December 1984 Treasury bill futures and March 1985 Eurodollar futures for approximately one month—November 21, 1984 to December 19, 1984. Clearly the whammy was trending upward but in a very erratic fashion. At this time futures were dominated by bearish expectations resulting in a steepening of the yield curve and a widening of the intramarket spread. Moreover, since these expectations were in part based on anticipated increased credit demands, the TED spread was also widening. For these reasons the trend in the whammy was toward widening. The cash market, however, did not follow futures thus holding back the whammy. This dragging effect of the cash market explains the observed behavior in the whammy.

The Butterfly

A more involved category of spread trades includes those trades that are actually combinations of spreads. When such combinations involve intramarket spreads they are known as butterflies and when they involve intermarket spreads they are known as tandems. In either case evaluating these trades has to allow for relatively high commission and execution costs since so many positions are involved. Even so, under the proper circumstances these can be very effective trades. Moreover, even if these trades are not executed, evaluating these trades frequently will suggest effective, less complex, spread trades.

The butterfly is a combination of two intramarket spreads in which the nearby spread is put on in the opposite fashion to the more distant spread. In addition, both spreads must have the same difference in maturity and have one month in common. For example a butterfly spread could be comprised of being long one March T-bill futures contract, short two June T-bill futures contracts, and long one September T-bill futures contract. In effect the trader is long the March–June spread and short the June–September spread, that is, long the butterfly.

There are at least two reasons for becoming involved in the butterfly. One, is that it may be a reduced risk method of becoming involved in the front month spread. A reason for trading in any spread rather than in an outright position is because a spread involves a lower level of risk. For example, if a trader goes long a spread because rates are expected to fall and instead they rise, the loss incurred with a spread is likely to be less than the loss associated with an outright long position. In a similar fashion being long the front spread implies that the trader expects the spread to widen. Selling the back spread constrains the down-side potential on the trade, if the trader's expectations prove incorrect. Thus the butterfly is a reduced risk method of engaging in the front spread. Moreover, if the trader is correct the income reducing tendency associated with having the back spread on will not overwhelm the profitability of the front spread. Any factor influencing the front spread will of course also influence the back spread but it will generally do so to a diminished extent. Thus the impact on the back spread will be less than the effect on the front spread.

The second reason for becoming involved in the spread is arbitrage. That is, the butterfly is an appropriate strategy if a trader believes the nearby spread is out of line and wants to put on a trade to take advantage of the dislocation without the risk of movement in the intramarket spread from any new factors.

Both justifications for the butterfly have some appeal; however neither case is as riskless as it may at first appear. In the first case it is conceivable that some economic factor may have a greater impact the further out in the future you go rather than having the dampening effect on which the success of the trade depends. This is particularly true of the impact of expectations on interest-rate behavior. Thus a trader involved in a butterfly may find the second spread affected more than the nearby spread, and as a consequence the "losing" portion of the spread overwhelms the profitable portion. This justification for initiating a butterfly is more appealing, however, than arbitrage. At most one would expect the impact of arbitrage to result in a movement in the price range of a spread. It is unlikely that the arbitrage explanation can ever be used to predict a precise spread value. Profiting from changes in price ranges is so difficult as to be beyond recommending as a trading strategy especially when one considers the difficulty in executing a butterfly spread.

Figure 8 contains an illustration of an actual extreme movement in a butterfly. This particular butterfly is comprised of one position each in March 1985 and September 1985 Eurodollar futures contracts with the "body" of the butterfly comprised of two positions in June 1985 Eurodollar futures contracts. The period during which this butterfly is tracked, December 17, 1984 to March 7, 1985, was characterized by a bearish situation in the cash markets which resulted in a widening of the cash three-month to six-month Eurodollar rates. The front part of the spread was approaching maturity thus converging to cash, which meant that being long the butterfly implied a profitable return to at least the March–June part of the butterfly. Typically in such a situation the second leg of the butterfly, the June–September position, would lose but not by as much as the front part gained. This would happen because presumably bearish expectations would influence back months as well, but not by as much as front months. Interestingly, in this particular case June seemed to behave as a pivotal contract month in terms of market behavior. Thus the second part of the butterfly rather than detracting from the gains realized in the first part, actually was no worse than neutral and at times was slightly supportive. This combination of effects resulted in more than a typical movement in the butterfly.

FIGURE 8 A Butterfly Spread: One March 1985 Eurodollar Futures, Two
June 1985 Eurodollar Futures, and One September 1985
Eurodollar Futures (data: daily closing prices December 11,
1984 to March 1985)

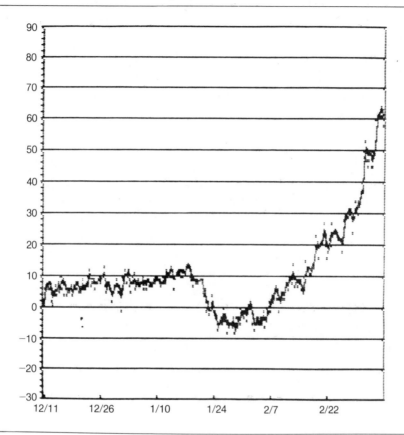

Tandems

Tandems are combinations of intermarket spreads, particularly the TED.
For example, buying the March–June TED tandem means buying the
March TED and selling the June TED. The actual positions are long one
March bill, short one March Euro, long one June Euro, and short one
June bill. One could also look at such a combination as two intramarket
spreads; long the March–June bill spread and short the March–June
Eurodollar spread. This combination trade is more clearly disaggregated
in Table 4.

The analyses previously described in this chapter can be used to
analyze this trade. Key factors influencing tandems are expectations and

TABLE 4 March–June TED Tandem

Long Bill Spread	{	long March bill short June bill	long March bill short March Euro	}	Long TED
Short Euro Spread	{	short March Euro long June Euro	short June bill long June Euro	}	Short TED

the technicals influencing the underlying market. If the tandem is analyzed as two intramarket spreads, then it can be seen that in order for the trade to be profitable some factor(s) must disproportionately influence one spread. This is conceivably the case when cash market technicals in the bill market influence bill futures and not Eurodollar futures. Although this is possible, the composition of the trade suggests that any

FIGURE 9 The March–June TED Tandem (data: daily closing prices December 11, 1984 to March 7, 1985)

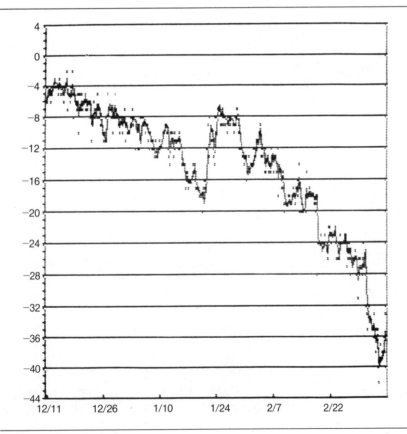

factors influencing short-term spreads generally will leave the value of the tandem unaffected.

Analyzing the tandem as a combination of two TED spreads is usually more meaningful. When the TED is close to maturity it trades in step with the cash market TED. Alternatively, second and further out TED spreads will be influenced more by expectations than by the cash market. For example, if conditions seem ripe for the TED to narrow, but the nearby contracts go off the board soon, and they are trading narrow to cash, then the second TED is likely to narrow more than the nearby TED. Consequently buying the tandem has the potential to be a profitable trade.

Figure 9 illustrates a period when selling the TED would have made for a profitable trade. During this particular period the June TED gained on the March TED. This behavior appears to be the result of the March and June TED spreads being influenced by different factors. The March TED appears to have been dominated by the effect of the cash market and by the convergence pattern. By comparison the June TED was affected by bearish expectations, widening more rapidly than the March portion of the spread.

Another way of analyzing the tandem, as discussed above, is as two intramarket spreads. Figure 10 illustrates the Eurodollar futures contract intramarket spread portion of the same tandem described above and illustrated in Figure 9. Obviously the Eurodollar portion of this tandem was widening because of the bearish expectations mentioned above. Although these same expectations affected the Treasury bill futures in-

FIGURE 10   The March 1985–June 1985 Eurodollar Futures Spread (data: daily closing prices December 11, 1984 to March 7, 1985)

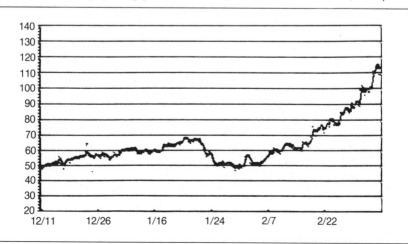

tramarket spread, this spread was widening less rapidly and as a consequence the tandem narrowed.

SUMMARY

This chapter has provided an extensive review of spread trades involving interest-rate futures contracts. Beginning with intramarket spreads on the short end of the maturity spectrum, Eurodollar, and Treasury bill futures contracts, attention was focused on implied forward rates, yield-curve movements and changes in deliverable supply factors influencing spreads. Separate attention was given to intramarket spreads on the long end of the maturity spectrum, that is, Treasury notes and Treasury bonds. In this section the cost-of-carry trade was described as was the impact of deliverable supply on longer maturity instruments. Inter-market spreads on the short end of the maturity spectrum were also reviewed. The flight-to-quality trade was the focus of this section. Finally, combination spread trades were discussed. Beginning with the relatively simple whammy (which is a combination inter/intramarket spread), we went on to the more complex butterfly and tandem spreads.

Throughout this chapter we have explained how to design these various spread trades. Our emphasis has always been on what factors to consider and how these factors should influence the behavior of a spread. Experience has indicated that there are no sure fire formulas that will always ensure success in spread trading. If it were that easy, spread trading would offer little or no challenge. Rather by observing spreads and trading them, one comes to appreciate the variety of ways one can trade futures. Perhaps more importantly, a spread trader inevitably develops a genuine appreciation of the interrelationships between the cash and futures markets.

47

Income Tax Treatment
of Interest-Rate Futures
and Debt Options

Lawrence A. Garber, LL.B., LL.M., C.P.A.
President
Woodcliff Consultants, Inc.
Woodcliff Lake, New Jersey

The tax laws have been radically revised since 1981 and now unique tax principles govern futures and nonequity option transactions. These rules are different from those pertaining to the taxation of other types of investments. The purpose of this chapter is to discuss the tax treatment of transactions involving interest-rate futures and debt options.

CAPITAL GAINS AND LOSSES—SOME BASICS[1]

Generally, for all but "Section 1256 contracts,"[2] realized gain or loss will be recognized for federal income tax purposes if there is a sale or exchange of a capital asset. There is a long-term capital gain/loss if the asset is held for more than six months. An asset held for six months or less is treated as a short-term capital gain/loss. The gain or loss is measured by the difference between the amount realized from the sale or exchange of a capital asset and the taxpayer's cost basis in the asset that was sold or exchanged. This complex sentence conveniently sets forth many of the terms used in the taxation of capital gains and losses.

---

[1] See Chapter 3 for a detailed explanation of capital gains and losses.

[2] Section 1256 contracts include nonequity options, equity options of dealers, certain foreign currency forward contracts, and "regulated futures contracts" (RFCs). A nonequity option is basically any listed option other than an option on a specific stock or an option on a narrow-based index of stocks. Thus, nonequity options include options on physical commodities, such as sugar; options on debt instruments, such as Treasury bonds; and options on broad-based stock indexes, such as the S&P 100. The term would

TAX TREATMENT OF INTEREST-RATE FUTURES AND DEBT OPTIONS

Interest-rate futures and debt options are *not* subject to the basic rules of capital gain/loss taxation because they qualify as "Section 1256 contracts." The tax laws treat Section 1256 contracts differently from other types of investments.

Section 1256 contracts are subject to a special year-end "mark-to-market" rule. Each contract held (long or short) by an individual at the close of the year is deemed to have been sold at its fair market value on the last trading day of the year. Therefore, all unrealized gains and losses from such contracts are taken into consideration and recognized for tax purposes at year-end. An adjustment is made to the cost basis of those contracts in the next year in order to prevent the recognition of the same gain or loss a second time.

Gains and losses from debt options that were either terminated (by exercise or being exercised, by lapse, by sale (which also is referred to as a closing or offsetting transaction), or otherwise) or owned at year-end are generally treated as short-term capital gain or loss to the extent of 40 percent of such gain or loss and long-term capital gain or loss to the extent of 60 percent of such gain or loss. The treatment is the same for gains and losses from interest-rate futures contracts that were either terminated (by offset, by transfer, or by taking or making delivery) or owned at year end. Thus, the maximum U.S. tax that an investor would pay on a debt option or interest-rate futures contract gain is 32 percent. This is computed as follows: 40 percent is a short-term capital gain on which the maximum tax rate is 50 percent (thus, 40 percent times 50 percent is 20 percent), and 60 percent is a long-term capital gain on which the maximum tax rate is effectively 20 percent (thus, 60 percent times 20 percent is 12 percent).[3]

The holding period of Section 1256 contracts is immaterial. Sixty percent of an individual's gain will be taxed as a long-term capital gain from a day trade and from a trade which has been held open for over six

---

not include an option on IBM stock or an option on the Computer Technology Index, which is a narrow-based index.

All listed options traded by dealers, professional market-makers, and specialists, in their normal course of activity of dealing in options, are treated as Section 1256 contracts. An RFC is generally any futures contract traded on a U.S. board of trade which has been designated as a contract market by the Commodity Futures Trading Commission. Thus, the term RFC includes agricultural futures, metal futures, interest-rate futures, currency futures, and stockmarket index futures. The Internal Revenue Service has ruled that contracts traded on the International Futures Exchange (Bermuda) and the Mercantile Division of the Montreal Exchange will qualify as Section 1256 contracts.

[3] If an individual is actively engaged in trading Section 1256 contracts and is registered with a U.S. futures exchange then his net income from trading Section 1256 contracts will be subject to self-employment taxes even though it is taxed at capital gains rates.

months. Gains and losses are taxed as such regardless of whether the individual was long or short the contract. A day trade gain from a short position is taxed 60 percent as long-term and 40 percent as short-term capital gains, and hence subject to a 32 percent maximum rate.[4]

There are no tax consequences associated with the opening of a position. There are no tax consequences resulting from an initial margin deposit or maintenance (variation) margin deposits, nor from receiving cash for selling an option, nor from the receipt of variation margin.

If an individual purchased a debt option, the premium paid is the cost basis. Upon a sale, the premium received is the sale proceeds. The difference represents gain or loss. If an individual writes a debt option (the grantor), the premium received is the sales price, and the premium paid upon a closing transaction is the cost. The difference is the gain or loss. If an option lapses, the purchaser has a loss equal to the premium paid, and the grantor has a gain equal to the premium received. The taxable event takes place on the date of expiration, unless the debt option was held at year-end in which case there is a taxable event in each of the two years and only the adjusted basis is taken into account in the second year.

If a debt option is exercised, there is a taxable event as of the day of exercise. The amount of gain/loss is determined as if the option was sold on the exercise date. This assumes that if the option was marked to market at the end of a prior year, an adjustment would be made to avoid double taxation.

If an individual has a net capital loss in a particular year, and if part or all of that loss consists of Section 1256 contract losses, then these Section 1256 contract losses (up to the amount of the net capital loss) can be carried back for up to three years to be offset against Section 1256 contract net gains (up to the amount of the net capital gain) of the earlier years. If the individual has no such carryback, then the capital losses are carried forward.

SPECIAL STRADDLE RULES

If an individual enters into what is known as a tax straddle, there are many special tax rules that come into play. The tax law defines a straddle as offsetting positions with respect to actively traded personal property. An individual would be considered to be in a straddle for tax purposes if there is a substantial diminution of risk of loss from holding any position by reason of holding one or more other positions. An example of a

---

[4] The tax treatment is different for equity options. A gain from an equity option that was held (long) for over six months is taxed as long-term capital gain with a maximum tax rate of only 20 percent. A gain or loss from a short (grantor) equity option results in short-term capital gain/loss regardless of the period of time the option was granted.

straddle would be an individual owning certain U.S. Treasury bonds and being short a Treasury bond futures contract. Tax rules similar to the short sale tax laws would be applicable to offsetting positions.

If an individual enters into a straddle consisting of at least one, but not all, Section 1256 contracts, he is entitled to make a "mixed straddle" election. This election removes the Section 1256 contracts forming part of the straddle from the mark-to-market and 60 percent long-term/40 percent short-term capital gain/loss rules. Therefore, if a debt option or interest-rate futures contract is part of a mixed straddle, by making the election, the contract is subject to the basic capital gain/loss rules. A person would want to make a mixed straddle election in order to avoid a situation that would require him to mark to market a gain on a Section 1256 contract, and have to recognize the gain for tax purposes, when there was an offsetting loss from a nonSection 1256 position that could not be recognized for tax purposes.

An individual is not allowed to recognize a loss for tax purposes to the extent of his unrecognized gains from one or more offsetting positions acquired before the recognition of the loss. The loss would be deferred and carried over to subsequent years until such time as the offsetting gain positions were closed out and the gains were recognized for tax purposes. For example, if one position is closed out during the year at a $17 loss and at year-end there is $8 of unrecognized gain in an offsetting position, then $9 can be currently deducted and $8 of the loss is deferred.

An individual can also make an "identified straddle" election. An identified straddle must be one of which all positions are acquired on the same day and disposed of on the same day and of which none of its positions are part of a larger straddle. If the election is made, an individual may not recognize a loss from part of the identified straddle before the day on which all of the positions making up that straddle are disposed of.

A person should consider making the identified straddle election in order to keep his straddle trades separate from his nonstraddle trades. This would prevent a position in the identified straddle from tainting, for tax purposes, a nonstraddle position. In addition, by making the election a person can avoid having to report, for tax purposes, the unrecognized gain in the identified straddle.

An individual must capitalize interest expense and carrying charges from straddle transactions. The expenses are offset against income before capitalization. For example, if an individual owns U.S. Treasury bonds, and sells short other similar bonds, a portion of the resulting short sale expenses must be capitalized. The individual can only deduct short sale expenses up to the amount of his interest income. This capitalization rule is a part of the anticonversion rules which attempt to prevent individuals from converting ordinary income and/or short-term capital gain into long-term capital gains.

TAX ASPECTS OF HEDGING WITH INTEREST-RATE FUTURES

There are very favorable tax rules applicable to those who use financial futures for hedging purposes. To qualify for these favorable tax rules, the transaction must fall within the strict technical tax definition of a hedge and must be properly identified, on a timely basis, as such on the books of the hedger.

If a futures transaction meets the strict tax law definition of a hedge and the proper elections and identifications are made, then the "mark to market" rule and the 40 percent short-term/60 percent long-term capital gain or loss rule do not apply. The gain or loss from the futures transaction is treated as ordinary income or loss and the timing of the recognition of that gain or loss is dependent on the taxpayer's method of tax accounting for the hedge.

The tax law definition of a hedge is found in Section 1256(e)(2) of the Internal Revenue Code. A transaction may qualify as a hedge for accounting purposes or may be generally referred to as a hedge in the business world, but unless it falls within the definition of a hedge in Section 1256(e)(2), it will not be considered a tax hedge.

If the futures transaction was entered into as a hedge against property that would normally be treated as a noncapital asset and if the futures transaction does not come within the strict tax law definition of a hedge, or was not properly identified as such by the taxpayer, then the mark to market rules apply but the 40 percent short-term/60 percent long-term capital gain or loss rules do not. Therefore, these hedges are marked to the market at year end and are taxed at ordinary income or loss rates.

If the transaction is to hedge a capital asset, then the futures contracts are marked to the market at capital gains rates. For example, if a bond investor hedges a bond investment with a bond futures contract, that futures contract could not be treated as a hedge for tax purposes and would therefore be subject to the year-end mark to market rules and the 60 percent–40 percent capital gain/loss tax rates.

In summary, gains and losses from transactions where noncapital assets or liabilities are being hedged are taxed as ordinary income or loss and not as capital gains or loss. The same is true for hedges that fall within the strict tax law definition of a hedge. A hedger would want to come within the strict tax law definition of a hedge (these hedges will be referred to as "technical tax hedges") for the following reasons.

The mark to market rules do not apply. If the hedge does not come within the definition of a "technical tax hedge," the open futures contracts would have to be valued at fair market value at the end of a taxpayer's fiscal year and recognized for tax purposes. If the hedge does qualify as a "technical tax hedge," other accounting rules might apply, which could result in the deferral of income or an adjustment to the tax basis of the hedged items. A taxpayer might be able to recognize income or loss when closing out the futures contract. The point is that a taxpayer could have a choice of accounting methods with a "technical tax hedge."

A hedger would file tax returns and use the method of accounting followed for book purposes. The book method would be acceptable for tax purposes as long as it did not result in a material distortion of income. If the hedger did not come within the rules of a "technical tax hedge," then the year-end mark to market rules would have to be followed regardless of the method used for book purposes.[5]

The loss deferral rules do not apply. The hedge can possibly qualify as a straddle for tax purposes if the hedged item is considered to be actively traded personal property. As explained in the previous section, a straddle is defined as offsetting positions with respect to actively traded personal property. A straddle would exist if there was a substantial diminution of risk of loss from holding any position by reason of holding one or more other positions. If the hedge qualifies as a straddle (and most hedges would qualify as straddles) then a loss on a postion could not be recognized for tax purposes to the extent of any unrealized gain from an offsetting position. Thus, even though the futures position may result in a loss, the loss may be deferred for tax purposes.

The expense capitalization rules do not apply. If a hedge qualifies as a straddle, then interest and certain other expenses would have to be capitalized rather than currently deducted. If the transaction qualifies as a "technical tax hedge," then the capitalization rules do not apply.

"Technical Tax Hedge" Defined

To qualify as a "technical tax hedge" the transaction must meet all of the following rules.

1. It must be entered into by a taxpayer in the *normal course* of the taxpayer's *trade or business*. The term normal course means a common occurrence rather than a very infrequent occurrence. The term *trade or business* means an active business rather than an investment activity and usually refers to an existing and continuing business rather than to a start-up operation. A problem can arise if a new entity is established. If a real estate developer sets up a new entity, would he be considered to be in a trade or business?

2. The transaction must have been entered into primarily to either
   a. reduce the risk of price changes or currency fluctuations with respect to property which is held or to be held by the taxpayer, *or*

---

[5] The Financial Accounting Standards Board has issued a release, *Statement of Financial Accounting Standards No. 80—Accounting for Futures Contracts*, which discusses hedge accounting for book purposes. This is discussed in the next chapter.

    b. reduce the risk of *interest rate* or price changes or currency fluctuations with respect to *borrowings made* or *to be made,* or *obligations incurred* or *to be incurred,* by the taxpayer. Thus, an anticipatory hedge is covered by these rules.[6]

3. The taxpayer must clearly identify the transaction as a hedge on its books before the close of the day on which such transaction was entered into. The Internal Revenue Service may issue regulations requiring the identification to be made at an earlier time. To date, no regulations have been issued. The intent of Congress was to "minimize bookkeeping identification requirements in as many cases as practicable."

4. The gain or loss from the transaction must be treated as ordinary income or loss rather than capital gain or loss. The underlying transaction and the hedge must both be treated as ordinary income or loss.

5. The transaction must not be entered into by or for a "syndicate."

The tax laws relating to commodities, including hedging transactions, were written with the intent to prevent taxpayers from claiming tax deductions from the use of certain types of straddles. Congress found that there were syndications, claiming to be involved in the commodities business, engaged in straddle trades. Many of the tax laws directed to straddles contain exceptions for hedgers. In order to prevent those syndications from using the umbrella of the hedging exception to continue straddles, Congress limited the hedging exception for certain syndicates. Thus, certain syndicates cannot qualify their hedges as "technical tax hedges."

A syndicate is any partnership or other entity (with the exception of a corporation which is not an S corporation) if more than 35 percent of the losses are allocable to limited partners or limited entrepreneurs. Included in the list of exceptions are those who actively participate in the management of the entity and certain of their relatives. Therefore, if you had a real estate limited partnership with more than 35 percent of the losses allocable to limited partners, who are not active in its management, that entity may not be able to use the "technical tax hedging" rules.

There is yet another exception to the syndication rules. The Internal Revenue Service (IRS) can issue tax regulations or public and private rulings to the effect that an interest should be *treated as* being held by an individual who actively participates in the management of such entity. The IRS would have to find that the entity was not being used for tax avoidance purposes.

---

[6] Item 2 does not apply to banks, so that even foreign currency trading of a bank could be considered a "technical tax hedge."

The IRS has not yet issued any regulations, and hopefully, when they do they will allow a "technical tax hedge" for real estate limited partnerships and similar entities that are using the futures markets for nontax avoidance hedging purposes.

Limitation on Losses from Hedging

There are limitations on the amount of hedging tax losses that a limited partner or limited entrepreneur can currently deduct. A tax loss from hedging can only be currently deductible by such a taxpayer to the extent of taxable income attributable to the trade or business in which the hedging transactions were entered into or to the extent that the hedging loss is an economic loss. To be an economic loss, the hedging loss must exceed the aggregate unrecognized gains from the hedging transactions. Any hedging losses that are not currently deductible are carried over to future years where the same tests will be applied.

These rules are very difficult to apply in the case of interest-rate hedging. If we assume that a limited partnership is engaged in an active trade or business, has variable-rate loans, and uses interest-rate futures contracts as a hedge, then what is the taxable income attributable to the trade or business in which the hedging transactions were entered into? If we merely look at the loan that is being hedged, there will only be interest expense and thus no taxable income. In this situation would a hedging loss be considered an economic loss? In this situation what would be the unrecognized gains from the hedging transactions? The answer is that the hedging loss should be an economic loss, and therefore, currently deductible unless the taxpayer has other unrecognized gains in his futures hedge account. Hopefully, this area will be clarified when tax regulations are issued.

Real Estate Development

Most interest expense incurred by real estate developers during the construction of their projects must be capitalized rather than currently deducted for tax purposes. The capitalized interest is subsequently amortized (deducted) over a period of years.

If a real estate developer is hedging its interest-rate exposure, it may be faced with the following results:

1. If interest rates rise during construction, there will be more interest expense to capitalize and hedging gains that may be currently taxable.
2. If interest rates decline during construction, there will be less interest expense to be capitalized and hedging losses which may be currently deductible.

A possible solution to the above timing problem would be to net the hedging gains or losses against the interest expense *prior* to its capitalization. If this method is followed for book purposes, it should also be allowed for tax purposes because it would not result in a distortion of income. Real estate developers may wish to request a ruling from the Internal Revenue Service to use this method of tax accounting.

VARIOUS TAX REFORM PROPOSALS

In November of 1984, the Treasury Department released a report it prepared for President Reagan on tax simplification and reform. One of the proposals was to eliminate the preferential tax treatment of realized capital gains. If this was enacted into law, the 60 percent long-term/40 percent short-term capital gain/loss rules for Section 1256 contracts would be eliminated. Therefore, gains or losses from Section 1256 contracts would be taxed at the same tax rates as all other income.

"The President's Tax Proposals to the Congress for Fairness, Growth, and Simplicity" released in May of 1985 did not call for the elimination of the preferential tax treatment of capital gains. This plan calls for a reduction in the top rate from 50 percent to 35 percent and a reduction in the long-term capital gain exclusion from 60 percent to 50 percent. This results in an effective maximum rate of 24.5 percent compared with the current 32 percent rate for Section 1256 contracts.

In May of 1986, the Senate Finance Committee adopted a proposal that would retain the mark to market rules and eliminate the preferential tax treatment of capital gains. This would result in a maximum rate of 27 percent for Section 1256 contracts.

SUMMARY

Interest-rate futures and debt options are treated as Section 1256 contracts. As such, they are subject to the year end mark-to-market rules and the 60 percent/40 percent long-term/short-term capital gain/loss rules.

The tax laws relating to hedging transactions are quite complex. Many hedges may fall within the tax law's definition of a "straddle" because a hedge is an offsetting position. The tax laws were written in a very restrictive fashion for straddles. Therefore, unless care is taken in making elections and identifications, a hedging transaction can result in unintended adverse tax consequences.

There have been no income tax regulations issued yet on the topic of hedging. It is hoped that when the regulations are issued they will be liberal with respect to true business hedges and restrictive only in those cases where a business may invest in the same types of futures contracts that they use for hedging purposes.

48

Accounting for
Interest-Rate Futures*

Arthur Andersen & Co.

Since the inception of the interest-rate futures market in 1975, all types
of enterprises have paid phenomenally increased attention to interest-
rate futures, especially to their use as a hedging tool. This growth in
interest and the tremendous growth in trading volume have led to the
development of new types of financial futures contracts as well as to
new marketplaces within and outside the United States. However, the
use of, and the accounting for, interest-rate futures contracts continue to
be topics of concern. Today, this controversial area finally seems to be
reaching a resolution. The FASB has released Statement of Financial
Accounting Standards No. 80, "Accounting for Futures Contracts,"
dated August 1984.

Statement No. 80 applies to all exchange-traded futures contracts,
except foreign currency futures contracts. This chapter deals exclusively
with interest-rate futures contracts and describes the accounting treatment prescribed by Statement No. 80 for interest-rate futures transactions, including several examples of this accounting applied to hedging
situations. The Appendix gives a summary of desirable internal controls
over trading in futures contracts.

OVERALL BASIS OF ACCOUNTING

Transactions in futures contracts involve a deposit of funds or the pledging of an acceptable security, representing a margin deposit. Funds
deposited as margin should be recorded simply as a "deposit." Consis-

tent with the accounting treatment for forward-type activities (e.g., foreign-exchange forward contracts), the gross amount of securities deliverable under futures contracts should not be reported in the balance sheet.

Generally, unrealized gains and losses resulting from a change in quoted market values of futures contracts, as well as realized gains and losses, should be recognized currently in the income statement. This basis of accounting (commonly referred to as "mark to market") should be followed when (1) futures contracts are entered into for speculation; (2) futures contracts represent hedges of asset positions, contemplated asset purchases or short positions, all of which are, or will be, carried at market value; or (3) the criteria for "hedge accounting" for specific hedging transactions, discussed below, are not met.

HEDGE ACCOUNTING

Statement No. 80 provides for different accounting treatment of certain futures contracts that are hedges. Futures contracts may be (1) hedges of existing assets, liabilities, or firm, fixed-price commitments to buy or sell financial instruments or (2) hedges of probable future financial transactions that an enterprise expects but may not be legally obligated to enter into (commonly referred to as "anticipatory hedges"). Hedge accounting treatment applies only if the criteria discussed in this section are met and if the related assets or liabilities are or will be accounted for on an historical cost or a lower-of-cost-or-market basis.

Hedge accounting is based on a concept of symmetry between the accounting for the futures contracts and the assets or liabilities being hedged. As explained in more detail later in this section, gains or losses on futures contracts entered into as hedges generally are deferred, rather than being recognized currently in income. Hedge accounting requires the designation of specific assets or liabilities to determine the appropriate time to recognize deferred gains and losses and/or the amortization period of such gains and losses. In addition, hedge accounting is appropriate if the enterprise can designate groups of like items (e.g., loans that have similar terms) to be hedged.

Criteria for Hedges of Existing Assets, Liabilities, or Firm Commitments

Futures contracts qualify as hedges of existing assets, liabilities, or firm, fixed-price commitments for accounting purposes if both the following conditions are met:

- The assets, liabilities, or firm, fixed-price commitments expose the company to interest-rate risk. The nature of the company's business and its other assets, liabilities, and commitments need to be considered to decide whether there is risk exposure. For example, a company that owns fixed-interest-rate financial instruments would not be exposed to interest-rate risk if the instruments are funded by fixed-interest-rate debt of similar maturity.

Some companies conduct their risk management on a decentralized basis and cannot assess their interest-rate risk on a company-wide basis. They can satisfy this criterion if the item to be hedged exposes the business unit that enters into the futures contract to interest-rate risk.

- The futures contracts reduce the interest-rate exposure and are designated as hedges. There must be a probable high correlation between changes in (1) the fair value of the hedged assets, liabilities, or firm commitments, and (2) the market value of the futures contracts.

The hedger needs to consider the correlation during relevant past periods and also the correlation that could be expected at higher or lower interest rates. The futures contract may be for a financial instrument different from the item to be hedged, if there is a clear economic relationship between their prices and high correlation is probable.

Criteria for Anticipatory Hedges

Futures contracts qualify as a hedge of anticipated transactions if both the criteria for hedges of existing assets, liabilities, or firm commitments and both of the following conditions are met:

- The significant terms of the anticipated transaction are identified, including the expected date, the type of financial instrument, the expected maturity and the quantity.
- The expected transaction is likely to occur. To determine that an anticipated transaction is likely, a company should consider the frequency of similar transactions in the past, the company's ability to carry out the transaction, the length of time until the anticipated transaction date, the loss or disruption of operations that could occur if the transaction is not consummated, and the likelihood that the same business purpose could be satisfied by a substantially different transaction (for example, a company planning to issue long-term bonds also could raise funds by selling common or preferred stock). Sometimes a company may have a choice among similar transactions to satisfy a business purpose (for example, issuing commercial paper, borrowing under a revolving credit agreement or selling short-term receivables with recourse). In such cases, futures contracts may qualify as hedges if all the other hedge criteria are satisfied for each of the possible transactions and the company is likely to enter into one of the possible transactions.

DISCUSSION OF HEDGE ACCOUNTING

Gains and losses on futures contracts that meet *all* the conditions described above are deferred as an adjustment to the carrying amount of the hedged item. If futures contracts hedge existing assets or liabilities, at each reporting date the deferred gains or losses are classified as an adjustment of the carrying amount of the hedged assets or liabilities. If the futures contracts hedge firm, fixed-price commitments, the deferred gains or losses are included in the measurement of the transactions that satisfy the commitments. Similarly, if futures contracts hedge expected transactions, the deferred gains or losses are included in the measurement of the transactions when they occur.

The deferred gains or losses on futures contracts are applied to adjust the carrying amount of an existing asset or liability, or will be applied to adjust the carrying amount of a future asset or liability. Those adjustments become an integral part of the carrying amount of the asset or liability and are accounted for as such. Thus, deferred gains or losses that adjust the carrying amounts of interest-bearing assets and liabilities are like discounts or premiums and are amortized to interest income or expense over the expected remaining lives of the instruments.

For hedges of firm commitments and anticipated transactions, the amortization starts when the anticipated transaction is entered into. For hedges of existing assets and liabilities, amortization must start no later than the date that a particular contract is closed out, regardless of whether the contract is replaced by a similar contract for later delivery ("rolled over").

If deferred gains or losses become part of the carrying amount of an asset carried at the lower of cost or market, they become part of cost in the cost versus market comparison.

A company must regularly assess the results of futures contracts designated as hedges to determine whether they continue to be highly correlated with changes in the values of the hedged items. If the expected high correlation has not occurred, the company stops accounting for the futures contract as a hedge and begins marking to market. The deferred gain or loss on the futures contract through that date continues to be treated as an adjustment to the carrying amount of the hedged item only to the extent the futures results have been offset by changes in the price of the hedged item. Any accumulated gain or loss on the futures contract in excess of the accumulated unrecognized loss or gain on the hedged item since the time the hedge transaction was entered is recognized in income.

If the financial instrument being hedged is deliverable under the futures contract and if it is likely that the company will hold both the hedged instrument and the futures contract until the contract's delivery date, Statement No. 80 allows, but does not require, separate accounting for the "premium" or "discount" on the futures contract (the difference between the spot price and the futures price of the instrument). The "premium" or "discount" on the futures contract may be amortized to income over the life of the contract rather than being included in the result of the cash transaction. This is illustrated in Example 5 beginning on page 1019. The FASB concluded that this "premium" or "discount" on the futures contract could be viewed as an adjustment to the yield of the hedged instrument during the life of the contract rather than during the period after the contract is closed.

If a company hedges an anticipated transaction and learns that the amount of the transaction is likely to be less than originally expected, a pro-rata portion of the futures gain or loss is recognized currently in income. If the hedge contract is closed before the anticipated transaction occurs, the futures gain or loss should continue to be deferred until the anticipated transaction takes place.

Disclosure

Statement No. 80 requires disclosure of (1) the nature of the items that are hedged with futures contracts, and (2) the method of accounting for the futures contracts (including a description of the events that result in recognizing the changes in value of futures contracts in income). Beginning on page 1013, we present five examples of hedging using futures contracts. Example 1 deals with a financial institution hedging an investment in bonds. Example 3 deals with a corporation hedging an anticipated investment in U.S. Treasury bills. These examples show how the financial institution and the corporation might disclose their hedging activities:

Example 1. During 19X1 and 19X0, the institution used financial futures to hedge the value of investments in fixed-interest-rate bonds. Gains and losses on futures contracts are accounted for as discount or premium on the investments in bonds. Amortization of the discount or premium begins when the futures contracts are closed.

Example 3. During 19X0, the Company entered futures contracts to "lock in" high interest rates on anticipated temporary cash investments. Gains and losses on those futures contracts were deferred and accounted for as discount or premium on the investments. The discount or premium was amortized to income over the period the investments were held.

HEDGING EXAMPLES

These examples have been somewhat simplified to illustrate the accounting requirements of Statement No. 80 while avoiding the complexities of transaction costs, accrued interest, etc.

Example 1: Short Hedge of an Asset Carried at Cost

This hedge strategy involves the sale of futures contracts to hedge against a market value decline of an existing fixed-rate asset. Examples of such a hedge include the selling of interest-rate futures contracts against an existing investment security or against existing fixed-rate loans in a financial institution environment. Gains and losses on futures contracts sold to hedge against market value declines for existing assets carried at cost should be deferred as an adjustment to the carrying amount of the asset.

Any premium or discount resulting from the adjustment to the carrying amount of the asset should be amortized to income over the expected remaining life of the asset as an adjustment to interest income. Following is an example of a hedge of an asset carried at cost, with the appropriate journal entries.

Situation. On August 15, 19X0, a financial institution pays par for a $1,000,000, 25-year, 14.00 percent bond with interest payable semiannually. On August 15, 19X1, interest rates have decreased, and the bonds are now selling at $107-10 (yield of 13.00 percent), or $1,073,125. The institution does not have any long-term, fixed-interest-rate liabilities and is, therefore, exposed to interest-rate risk.

Hedge. The treasurer of the institution, not wanting to sell the bond and fearing an increase in interest rates, decides to protect the value of the bond by selling December 19X2 Treasury bond contracts ($100,000 per contract) at a price of $65-00 (yield of 12.93 percent). The treasurer, having studied the price correlation between the bond position and the futures Treasury bond market, believes that their yield correlation is very high, i.e., over time, for every basis point move in the bond position yield, there is a basis point move in the yield of the futures bond contract. Therefore, in constructing the appropriate hedge ratio, the treasurer evaluates the effect of interest-rate changes on his bond position versus the futures market. For example, if by August 15, 19X2 the market value of the bond position rises to $115-17 (yield of 12.00 percent), the institution would experience an additional $82,187 in market value appreciation on the bond; however, the futures bond price would have increased similarly to $70-10 (yield of 11.93 percent), and the institution would experience a loss per bond contract of $5,312. Therefore, approximately 15.47 Treasury bond futures contracts would be the appropriate hedge ($82,187/$5,312). Conversely, if by August 15, 19X2, the market value of the bond position falls to $99-31 (yield of 14.00 percent), the institution would experience market value depreciation of $73,438 on the bond position; however, the futures bond price would have decreased similarly to $60-10 (yield of 13.93 percent), and the institution would experience a gain per bond contract of $4,688. Therefore, approximately 15.67 Treasury bond futures contracts would be the appropriate hedge ($73,438/$4,688). In summary, the treasurer determines that between 15 and 16 contracts should be used to hedge the $1,000,000 bond position. The treasurer decides to use 15 contracts.

Assumption. On August 15, 19X2, interest rates have increased, and the bonds are now selling at $82-23 (yield of 17.01 percent). The December bond contract price has decreased to $49-17 (yield of 16.85 percent).

The results of this hedge and the accounting journal entries are summarized in Table 1.

Example 2: Long Hedge of a Liability Carried at Cost

This hedge strategy involves the purchase of futures contracts to protect against the risk of falling interest rates. Examples of such a hedge include buying interest-rate futures contracts against existing fixed-interest-rate deposits that are used to fund floating-interest-rate loans, i.e., interest-rate "spread hedge." Gains and losses on futures contracts sold to hedge against falling interest rates for existing fixed-interest-rate liabilities should be deferred as an adjustment to the carrying amount of the liability. Any premium or discount resulting from the adjustment to the carrying amount of the liability should be amortized to income over the expected remaining life of the liability as an adjustment to interest expense. Following is an example of a hedge of a liability carried at cost, with the appropriate journal entries.

Situation. A bank issues $100 million of six-month "money market" certificates (MMCs) on September 1. The interest rate of 11.00 percent on the MMCs equals the discount rate on 180-day U.S. Treasury bills the last week of August. The MMCs are used to fund floating interest rate loans, currently yielding 13.00 percent.

Hedge. The bank is satisfied with the 2.00 percent spread between the current interest income on the loans and the interest cost of the MMCs and wants to protect against any reduction in the spread if interest rates fall before the MMCs mature. The asset/liability manager buys 100 December 90-day Treasury bill contracts ($1,000,000 per contract) at a price of $89.20 (discount rate of 10.80 percent).

Assumption. By December 1, the 90-day Treasury bill discount rate has fallen to 10.15 percent, and the December Treasury bill futures contract price has increased to $89.82 (discount rate of 10.18 percent).

The results of this hedge and the accounting journal entries are summarized in Table 2.

Example 3: Anticipatory Long Hedge of an Asset to Be Carried at Cost

This hedge strategy involves the purchase of futures contracts to protect against the risk of falling interest rates on expected purchases of fixed-

TABLE 1 Example 1: Summary of Results and Accounting Journal Entries

Summary of Results

Cash Market
August 15, 19X1
Decides to protect against deterioration of $73,125 unrealized gain on $1,000,000 bond position.

Futures Market
August 15, 19X1
Sells 15 December 19X2 bond contracts at a price of $65-00.

August 15, 19X2
Sells $1,000,000 bond at a price of $82-23.

August 15, 19X2
Buys 15 December 19X2 bond contracts at a price of $49-17.

Realized Loss
$172,812

Gain
$232,031

Unrecognized Loss Since Date Hedge Was Entered
$245,937

Had the treasurer not hedged on August 15, 19X1, and had he sold the bonds on August 15, 19X2, the institution would have realized a $172,812 loss. However, because he hedged, the institution has a net realized gain of $59,219 ($232,031 gain on the futures position less the $172,812 realized loss on the sale of the bond position). The unrealized gain of $73,125 at August 15, 19X1, was not fully protected because of an unfavorable basis movement of 9 basis points (the difference between the cash and futures yields increased from a difference of 7 basis points at August 15, 19X1 to a difference of 16 basis points at August 15, 19X2) and because the treasurer opted to use 15 bond contracts—the correct ratio was between 15 and 16 contracts.

The correlation between the futures result and the price change on the hedged bond position is 94 percent ($232,031 ÷ $245,937), which is high enough to support hedge accounting.

Accounting Journal Entries

August 15, 19X0

Investment in bonds	$1,000,000	
Cash		$1,000,000
(To record purchase of bonds)		

August 15, 19X1

Margin deposit with broker	$ 30,000	
Cash		$ 30,000
(To record cash margin deposit with broker of $2,000 per contract)		

August 16, 19X1–August 15, 19X2 (cumulative)

Cash	$ 232,031	
Unamortized discount on investment in bonds		$ 232,031
(Deferred gain on futures hedge)		
(To record gain on open futures position)		

August 15, 19X2

Cash	$ 30,000	
Margin deposit with broker		$ 30,000
(To record return of margin from broker when futures position is closed out)		
Cash	$ 827,188	
Unamortized discount on investment in bonds	$ 232,031	
Gain on sale of investment		$ 59,219
Investment in bonds		$1,000,000
(To record sale of bonds and recognize gain on futures position)		

TABLE 2   Example 2: Summary of Results and Accounting Journal Entries

---

Summary of Results

Cash Market	**Futures Market**
September 1	**September 1**
Decides to protect against deteriorating spread on repricing of loans funded with 180-day deposits. Objective is to lock in a 2.00 percent spread for the second half of the deposits' term, by effectively converting the 180-day deposits into two consecutive 90-day deposits.	Buys 100 December 90-day Treasury bill contracts at $89.20 (discount rate of 10.80 percent).
December 1	**December 1**
The bank does not make any cash market transaction. The carrying amount of the MMCs is $102,750,000 (including 90 days of accrued interest). The fair value of the MMCs is $102,889,187.	Sells 100 December 90-day Treasury bill contracts at $89.82 (discount rate of 10.18 percent).
Unrecognized Loss Since Date Hedge Was Entered	**Gain**
$139,187	**$155,000**

Had the asset/liability manager not hedged, he would have sustained a $139,187 unrecognized loss in the cash market. That loss would have been recognized in the form of a narrower spread between interest income on loans and interest expense on the MMCs over the 90 days from December 1 to March 1. However, because he hedged, the bank has a net gain of $15,813. The unrealized loss was more than offset because of a favorable basis movement.

The correlation between the futures result and the price change on the hedged MMCs is 90 percent ($139,887 ÷ $155,000), which is high enough to support hedge accounting.

Accounting Journal Entries

September 1

Cash	$100,000,000	
Deposits (180-day MMCs)		$100,000,000
(To record issuance of MMCs)		
Margin deposit with broker	$ 200,000	
Cash		$ 200,000
(To record cash margin deposit with broker of $2,000 per contract)		

September 2–December 1 (cumulative)

Cash	$ 155,000	
Unamortized premium on MMCs		$ 155,000
(To record gain on futures position)		

December 1

Cash	$ 200,000	
Margin deposit with broker		$ 200,000
(To record return of margin from broker when futures position is closed out)		

Note: The gain on the futures position ($155,000) was greater than the unrecognized loss on the MMCs ($139,187). If the correlation between the two had been insufficient to support continuation of hedge accounting, the $15,813 excess gain would have been recorded in income immediately rather than being amortized to income over the remaining 90-day term of the MMCs.

interest-rate assets. Examples of long anticipatory hedges include the purchase of futures contracts to protect against the risk of falling interest rates on the anticipated purchase of a fixed-rate investment security or the anticipated repricing of an existing asset, such as a loan held by a financial institution that, for instance, reprices (i.e., interest rates are adjusted) every three months. In the case of a long anticipatory hedge, gains and losses on futures contracts should be deferred and should be included in the measurement of the dollar basis of the asset acquired for which the hedge was intended. The gains and losses then would be amortized to income over the expected life of the asset as an adjustment to interest income. Following is an example of a long anticipatory hedge, with the appropriate accounting journal entries.

Situation.   On May 1, a corporate treasurer expects to have $5 million to invest on August 15. He plans to invest in 90-day Treasury bills and is satisfied with the current market yields of 12.08 percent (discount rate of 11.73 percent). The company has no short-term debt and is, therefore, exposed to interest-rate risk. The $5 million is needed for a sinking-fund payment on November 15, which limits the treasurer to a 90-day investment.

Hedge.   Fearing that by August 15 interest rates will decline, the corporate treasurer seeks protection from the risk of falling interest rates by buying five September Treasury bill futures contracts ($1,000,000 per contract) at a price of $88.17 (discount rate of 11.83 percent).

Assumption.   By August 15, when the $5 million becomes available for investment, the 90-day Treasury bill discount rate has fallen to 10.13 percent and the September Treasury bill futures contract price has increased to $89.54 (discount rate of 10.46 percent).

The result of this hedge and the accounting journal entries are summarized in Table 3.

Example 4: Anticipatory Short Hedge of a Liability to Be Carried at Cost

This hedge strategy involves the sale of futures contracts to protect against the risk of rising interest rates on the anticipated incurrence of a fixed-interest-rate liability. Examples of short anticipatory hedges include the selling of interest-rate futures contracts to protect against the risk of rising interest rates for the anticipated issuance of fixed-rate debt, for the anticipated rollover of fixed-rate debt, for the anticipated rollover of fixed-rate deposits by financial institutions or for the repricing of existing liabilities that are repriced, say, every three months. Gains and losses on futures contracts sold as an anticipatory hedge of a liability to be carried at cost should be deferred and should be included in the measurement of the dollar basis of the liability incurred for which the hedge was intended. Those gains and losses would then be amortized to

---

TABLE 3 Example 3: Summary of Results and Accounting Journal Entries

---

Summary of Results

Cash Market	**Futures Market**
May 1	**May 1**
Decides to protect current yield of 12.08 percent (discount rate of 11.73 percent) on $5 million anticipated purchase of 90-day Treasury bills.	Buys 5 September Treasury bill contracts at $88.17 (discount rate of 11.83 percent).
August 15	**August 15**
Buys $5 million of 90-day Treasury bills at 10.13 percent discount rate or at a price of $4,873,375.	Sells 5 September Treasury bill contracts at $89.54 (discount rate of 10.46 percent).
Opportunity Loss	**Gain**
$20,000	$17,125

Had the corporate treasurer not hedged, he would have sustained a $20,000 opportunity loss in the cash market. However, because he hedged, the opportunity loss is partially mitigated by a gain on the futures position. The loss was not fully offset because of an unfavorable basis movement of 23 basis points.

The correlation between the futures result and the price change on the Treasury bills is 86 percent ($17,125 ÷ $20,000), which is high enough to support hedge accounting.

Accounting Journal Entries

May 1

Margin deposit with broker	$ 10,000	
Cash		$ 10,000
(To record cash margin deposit with broker of $2,000 per contract)		

May 2–August 15 (cumulative)

Cash	$ 17,125	
Deferred gain on futures hedge		$ 17,125
(To record gain on open futures position)		

August 15

Cash	$ 10,000	
Margin deposit with broker		$ 10,000
(To record return of margin from broker when futures position is closed out)		
Investment	$4,856,250	
Deferred gain on futures hedge	$ 17,125	
Cash		$4,873,375
(To record purchase of 90-day Treasury bills and to include the gain on the futures hedge position in the measurement of the Treasury bills purchased)		

income over the expected life of the debt instrument as an adjustment to interest expense. Following is an example of a short anticipatory hedge, with the appropriate accounting journal entries.

Situation.   A financial institution is currently funding some long-term, fixed-rate loans yielding 16.00 percent with 180-day deposits bearing interest at a rate of 13.25 percent. On June 1, the financial institution's asset/liability manager identifies that $10 million of the 180-day deposit will mature on November 15 and anticipates that they will be "rolled over" into new 180-day deposits.

Hedge.   Interest rates have been creeping up, and 180-day deposits are now selling at an interest rate of 14.00 percent. Satisfied with a 2.00 percent spread between the interest income on the long-term, fixed-rate assets and a funding cost of 14.00 percent and fearing interest rates may increase, the asset/liability manager seeks protection against the risk of rising interest rates on the rollover of the deposits by selling 20 December 90-day CD contracts ($1,000,000 per contract) at a price of $85.75 (add-on yield of 14.25 percent). A two-to-one hedge ratio was selected because a 180-day exposure is being hedged with a 90-day futures instrument.

Assumption.   By November 15, when the 180-day deposits roll over, interest rates have fallen and the new deposits are issued at an interest rate of 12.00 percent. The December 90-day CD contract price has increased to $87.50 (add-on yield of 12.50 percent).

Table 4 summarizes the results of this hedge and the accounting journal entries.

Example 5: Short Hedge of an Asset Carried at Cost That Is Deliverable under the Terms of the Futures Contract

This hedge strategy involves the sale of futures contracts to "lock in" a higher return through arbitrage between the cash and futures markets. Examples of such a hedge include the selling of futures contracts on financial instruments that a company owns to take advantage of unusual basis differences between the cash and futures markets.

In this situation, Statement No. 80 allows the company to amortize the "premium" or "discount" on the futures contracts (the difference between the fair value of the asset and the contracted futures price) over their lives. Gains and losses on the contracts should be deferred as an adjustment to the carrying amount of the asset.

Any premium or discount resulting from the adjustment to the carrying amount of the asset should be amortized to income over the expected remaining life of the asset as an adjustment to interest income. Following is an example of a hedge of an asset carried at cost, with the appropriate journal entries. Note that the accounting illustrated here is

---

TABLE 4 Example 4: Summary of Results and Accounting Journal Entries

---

Summary of Results

Cash Market	Futures Market
June 1	**June 1**
Decides to protect against deteriorating spread on rollover of $10 million of 180-day deposits. Objective is to lock in a 14 percent interest cost, i.e., a 2.00 percent spread or spread income of $100,000 for six months.	Sells 20 December 90-day CD contracts at $85.75.
November 15	**November 15**
Issues $10 million of 180-day deposits at 12.00 percent interest rate.	Buys 20 December 90-day CD contracts at $87.50.
Opportunity Gain	**Loss**
$100,000	$87,500

Had the asset/liability manager not hedged, he would have had spread income of $200,000 over the six-month period starting November 15 (16.00 percent return on assets less 12.00 percent funding cost on $10,000,000 for 6 months). However, because he hedged, his opportunity gain of $100,000 was partially mitigated by a $87,500 loss on the futures position (the gain was not fully offset because of a favorable basis movement of 25 basis points). As a result, spread income over the six-month period starting November 15 would be $112,500.

The correlation between the futures result and the gain from the lower interest cost of the deposits is 88 percent ($87,500 ÷ $100,000), which is high enough to support hedge accounting.

Accounting Journal Entries

June 1

Margin deposit with broker	$ 40,000	
Cash		$ 40,000
(To record cash margin deposit with broker of $2,000 per contract)		

June 2–November 15 (cumulative)

Deferred loss on futures hedge	$ 87,500	
Cash		$ 87,500
(To record loss on open futures position)		

November 15

Cash	$ 40,000	
Margin deposit with broker		$ 40,000
(To record return of margin deposit when futures position is closed out)		
Deposits—old	$10,000,000	
Discount on deposits issued	$ 87,500	
Deferred loss on futures hedges		$ 87,500
Deposits—new		$10,000,000
(To record issuance (rollover) of new deposits and to include the loss on futures hedge position in the measurement of the dollar basis of the new deposits)		

---

optional. The company also could use the general hedge accounting method illustrated in Example 1.

Situation. A corporate treasurer has $10,000,000 of funds that will be needed for a specific capital project in 90 days. He wants to invest in U.S. Treasury bills for safety. 90-day Treasury bills are available at a discount rate of 8.60 percent (yield of 8.91 percent). However, he finds that if he simultaneously buys 180-day Treasury bills and sells 90-day U.S. Treasury bill futures for delivery in 90 days he can obtain a higher yield. Therefore, on December 15, 19X0, the treasurer buys $10,000,000 face amount of 180-day U.S. Treasury bills for $9,555,000 (discount rate of 8.90 percent).

Hedge. The Treasurer sells 10 March 19X1 Treasury bill contracts ($1,000,000 per contract) at a price of $90.80 (discount rate of 9.20 percent).

The treasurer expects to receive a yield of 9.13 percent from this hedged Treasury bill investment, considering the following factors:

- Original investment $9,555,000
- Futures price (sales price if Treasury bills are delivered to close the contracts) $9,770,000
- "Premium" on futures contracts $215,000

Assumption. On March 15, 19X1, 90-day Treasury bill discount rates have climbed to 10.60 percent, and the March Treasury bill contract price has decreased to $89.40 (discount rate of 10.60 percent). The treasurer delivers his Treasury bills (which are now 90 days from maturity) to close the futures contracts.

Table 5 summarizes the results of this hedge and the accounting journal entries.

The difference between the cash price and the futures price of a financial instrument is basically due to the interest cost of carrying the instrument. If the futures price is expensive or cheap relative to cash positions, arbitrageurs will buy cash instruments and sell futures, or vice versa, until the two markets are brought back into equilibrium. Statement No. 80 recognizes that some futures trades are arbitrage transactions and provides special accounting treatment to reflect their economics.

The arbitrage accounting method will not work well with U.S. Treasury bonds and Treasury bond futures because the Treasury bond futures contract is based on a theoretical benchmark 8 percent U.S. Treasury bond that does not exist. A conversion factor is used to create equivalence with this benchmark among bonds that differ in coupon rate or time to maturity. As a result, the hedge ratio for Treasury bond contracts is never 1:1 and, because the number of contracts used as hedges would not equal the Treasury bond position, the Treasury bonds futures could not all be closed out by delivery of the bonds.

TABLE 5   Example 5: Summary of Results and Accounting Journal Entries

---

Summary of Results

Cash Market
December 15, 19X0
Buys $10,000,000 face amount of 180-day U.S. Treasury bills for $9,555,000 (discount rate of 8.90 percent). Decides to lock in return by selling Treasury bill futures.

Futures Market
December 15, 19X0
Sells 10 March 19X1 Treasury bill futures at a price of $90.80 (discount rate of 9.20 percent).

March 15,19X1
Delivers Treasury bills to close contracts.

March 15, 19X1
Delivers Treasury bills to close contracts, which now have a price of $89.40 (discount rate of 10.60 percent).

Realized Gain
$180,000 ($9,735,000 implicit sales price less $9,555,000).

Gain
$35,000 ($90.80 − $89.40 × 10 contracts)

Accounting Journal Entries
December 15, 19X0

Investment in Treasury bills	$9,555,000	
Cash		$9,555,000
(To record purchase of the Treasury bills)		
Margin deposit with broker	$ 20,000	
Cash		$ 20,000
(To record cash margin deposit with broker of $2,000 per contract)		

December 16, 19X0–March 15, 19X1 (cumulative)

Investment in Treasury bills	$ 215,000	
Income		$ 215,000
(To record amortization of "premium" on futures contracts with contra entry to investment in Treasury bills)		
Cash	$ 35,000	
Investment in Treasury bills		$ 35,000
(To record gain on open futures position)		

March 15, 19X1

Cash	$ 20,000	
Margin deposit with broker		$ 20,000
(To record return of margin from broker when futures position is closed out)		
Cash	$9,735,000	
Investment in Treasury bills		$9,735,000
(To record delivery of the Treasury bills to close out the futures position)		

APPENDIX
Internal Control Considerations

In the past, several foreign-exchange scandals have resulted in multimillion dollar losses. Also, there have been reports of substantial losses in the securities "forward" market. Typically, these losses have resulted from attempts by individuals to recoup unrealized and unrecognized losses on previous trading activities.

Unauthorized trading is perhaps the largest exposure in the area of interest-rate futures, as well as "forward" trading (whether it be foreign exchange or the securities forward market). However, unlike the forward market, the characteristics of the interest-rate futures market provide for certain monitoring techniques that can be used to limit the exposure to unauthorized trading. The mechanics of futures contracts, transacted through a broker, require periodic cash settlements and related statements supporting trading activity, cash settlements, open positions, and deposits. Through a proper segregation of duties over cash settlements and the monitoring of related statements, the exposure to unauthorized trading can be limited. Equally important, senior management should have a clear understanding of how the company uses the interest-rate futures market and what controls have been established over such activities.

The objectives of internal controls over futures trading activities are to provide reasonable assurance that:

- Only authorized trades are executed.
- All trades are recorded properly in both the general ledger and supporting subsidiary ledgers.
- Management receives the proper information to evaluate the entire trading performance and hedging operation.

Before discussing specific control procedures, it is important to note that a company must give due consideration to the risks involved and the costs of maintaining the controls. Therefore, a system of internal controls for interest-rate futures contracts would differ from one company to another depending on such things as the reason for entering the interest-rate futures market, the volume of transactions involved and the sophistication of the system in effect covering other investment-related activity. The following is a brief description of certain basic internal control procedures and measures that a company engaging in the interest-rate futures market should consider.

POLICY AND PROCEDURES MANUAL

As with any system of internal control, the policy and procedures relating to interest-rate futures activity and accounting should be documented in a formalized procedures manual approved by senior management in the department or area using the futures contracts and also by top management in the accounting control and internal audit areas.

The objectives of the company's activity in futures contract trading, an approved list of brokers for transacting business, authorization and approval policies, and the matters discussed in the following sections all should be included in the procedures manual.

TRADER DUTIES

Only traders knowledgeable in the futures market and related company policies and procedures should be authorized to trade, and the company's brokers should be informed to trade only with these individuals. To ensure that the traders' knowledge and abilities are commensurate with the authority given to them, a comprehensive training program may be necessary.

TRADING LIMITS

Senior management should establish limits as to maximum open positions in futures contracts. These authorized limits should be set for the company in total and for each trader individually (if necessary). Overall limits on net open positions should be established and further consideration should be given to establishing "gap limits"—limits established for each contract maturity date rather than for all contract dates combined. The limits might not be set in terms of numbers of contracts because of hedge ratio considerations. Instead, limits could be set in relation to existing or anticipated interest rate risk.

TRADE TICKETS

As each trade is made, the trader should prepare a trade ticket, which becomes the starting point for the accounting information flow. Trade tickets should contain all the information needed to record the transaction properly in the company's records, such as trade date, buy or sell, contract description, quantity, price, trader, and reason for trade (i.e., the interest-rate risk being reduced, if applicable) and desirably should be prenumbered. As each ticket is prepared, a copy should be sent to the accounting personnel responsible for recording the activity.

ACCOUNTING RECORDS

The records necessary to account for and control interest-rate futures activity should be maintained by someone who is independent of the actual trading function. The records should contain all the information necessary to verify statements received from the enterprise's broker, to support entries to the general ledger for trading activity, and to generate the necessary internal reports needed to monitor interest rate futures activity.

The form of the records ordinarily will vary from entity to entity but typically a company might use "activity" ledgers segregated by maturity, type of activity, and broker. For each maturity, all trading activity would be recorded from the trade ticket, including trade date, trader, reason, buy or sell, quantity, price, and commission expense. The accounting clerk should verify each trade ticket by reference to the trade confirmation received directly from the broker. (The trader should not receive the trade confirmation directly.)

By recasting the information contained in the activity ledgers, subsidiary ledgers could be developed to support the deferred gains or losses on futures contracts and margin deposit amounts recorded in the general ledger. Also, reports to management on activity and positions taken by each trader can be generated.

If a company's intent is to use the futures transactions as a hedge, it is important to identify in the accounting records the existing or planned transaction with which the futures contract is associated. These records are necessary to document that this criterion of Statement No. 80 is satisfied and to choose the correct period to amortize any deferred gains or losses.

BROKER STATEMENTS

At least monthly, a company will receive a statement from its broker (futures commission merchant, or FCM) reflecting trading activity for the month, open positions at the end of the month, market value of open positions, unrealized gains and losses on open positions and cash balances in the account. Someone independent of both the trading and recordkeeping function should receive a copy of this statement. This individual should compare the monthly activity from the statement with the accounting records. Also, the open positions and contract prices should be compared with the trial balances. In addition, the market prices as reflected on the statement should be traced to the listed prices in a published source, and the unrealized gains and losses should be recomputed. Cash balances reflected in this statement should be reconciled to the deposit balance on the company's books and records.

REPORTING

The type and frequency of management reporting will vary by entity and by level of management; however, reports should be prepared, at least weekly, that show:

- All open positions on an issue-by-issue basis and on an operation-by-operation basis, along with the trading activity and related income effects, both current and historical. A review of the income trend can highlight the financial effect on current operations and the economic profitability of the hedging operation.
- Realized gains/losses and market appreciation/depreciation on open positions for the week and for a longer period to show trends and performance.
- A comparison of the actual performance to the targeted objective, including the actual correlation between the results of the futures contracts and the effects of interest-rate changes on the hedged items, as opposed to reporting only the gains or losses from the futures position.
- A comparison of open positions with authorized trading limits to determine that the limits are being complied with.
- If more than one trader is involved, a report of open positions, trading activity and gains/losses by individual trader, to permit evaluation of trader performance.

INTERNAL AUDIT DEPARTMENT

An extremely important internal control over any activity is the periodic operational review performed by an independent internal auditor. The responsibility of the internal auditor in reviewing interest-rate futures activity is to evaluate the internal control procedures and measures to determine whether they are adequate to properly record and report futures activity and to determine whether those procedures and measures are operating effectively.

Periodically during the year, an internal auditor should perform tests of trading activity. The work should be performed on a surprise basis; that is, the auditor should begin the work on an unannounced basis, immediately gaining control over appropriate records to preclude any unauthorized adjustments or alterations to the records. Procedures the internal auditor should consider in performing the audit are:

- A test of all aspects of the trade transactions through a physical examination and comparison of original trade tickets, entries recorded in the subsidiary ledger with supporting trade confirmations, entries recorded in general ledger memorandum accounts with corresponding commission expense entries and proper reflection in management reports.
- A test of the clerical accuracy of the subsidiary records.
- A test of the completeness and accuracy of management reports.
- A review of total positions to determine compliance with established trading and gap limits.

- A comparison of statements, obtained directly from the company's FCM, with the subsidiary records noting agreement on a trade-by-trade basis. Entries to record gains and losses also should be tested by tracing recorded gains and losses to the FCM's statement and examining evidence of payment.
- A review of manual adjustments affecting either trading positions or income recognition to determine the propriety of such adjustments along with the appropriate approval.
- A discussion with trading area management and control department personnel, along with a review of supporting records, to determine if management reports are being reviewed on a timely basis and if accounting entries and subsidiary ledgers are being reviewed.

All audit problems and exceptions noted by the internal auditor should be discussed with the appropriate level of management. A written report should be prepared describing the results of the audit and any recommendations. The internal auditor should obtain a written response from management describing the resolution of audit exceptions and the procedures implemented to prevent similar exceptions in the future. All significant problems noted by the internal auditor should be followed up by senior management on a timely basis to ensure prompt corrective action.

PART 6

International Bond Investing

49

Perspectives on International Bond Investing

Margaret Darasz Hadzima, C.F.A.
Vice President, Bonds
Scudder, Stevens & Clark

Cornelia M. Small
Managing Director
Scudder, Stevens & Clark

INTRODUCTION

In 1984, Eurobond volume exceeded, for the first time, U.S. domestic corporate bond volume, with Eurodollar bonds representing 80 percent of total new issue Eurobond volume. In the five years from 1980 to 1984, the total amount of funds raised by all issuers in the Eurobond market equalled approximately three quarters of the new-issue volume in the U.S. public corporate bond market. In this same period, the volume of nondollar foreign bonds sold by issuers outside their own domestic market, totaled about 30 percent of the U.S. new-issue public corporate bond volume. Although complete statistics on the entire size of the various worldwide domestic bond markets are not readily available, the total outstanding size of the U.S. bond market is now around half of the sum of the major bond markets.[1] Whether or not international bonds in

---

[1] This conclusion is supported by a study prepared by Richard Segal published July 24, 1985 by Salomon Brothers Inc entitled "How Big is the World Bond Market?" According to this study, which is based on 1984 figures, the United States represents 46 percent of the total government bond markets in 13 major countries including Japan, Germany, the United Kingdom, France, Canada, Switzerland, the Netherlands, Australia, Italy, Be-

any of their various forms have a place in U.S. portfolios, their sheer volume suggests that a general understanding of their characteristics is in order.

The term *international bonds* is often used to describe a number of different types of bonds with a variety of characteristics relating to issuer domicile, the nature of the underwriting syndicate, the location of the primary trading market, the domicile of the primary buyers, and/or currency denomination. Insofar as price movements are concerned, the most important characteristic is currency denomination. Regardless of the domicile of the issuer, the buyer, or the trading market, prices of issues denominated in U.S. dollars ("U.S. pay") are affected principally by the direction of U.S. interest rates, whereas prices of issues denominated in other currencies ("foreign pay") are determined primarily by movements of interest rates in the country of the currency denomination. Thus, analysis of international bond investing must be separated into two parts—U.S. pay and foreign pay.

U.S.-PAY INTERNATIONAL BOND INVESTING

The U.S.-pay international bond market can in turn be divided into issues for which the primary trading market is in the United States ("Yankees") and issues for which the primary trading market is abroad ("Eurodollar").

Eurodollar Bonds

The latter has come to be known as the *Eurodollar market*, and Eurodollar bonds are described as securities that are:

1. Denominated in U.S. dollars.
2. Underwritten by an international syndicate.
3. Sold at issue to non-U.S. investors.

Since offerings of Eurodollar bonds are not registered with the SEC, the expenses of bringing an issue to market are less than in the domestic U.S. bond market. However, because the securities are not registered, underwriters are legally prohibited from selling new issues to the U.S. public until the issue has "come to rest" and a cooling-off or seasoning period has expired. Most underwriters' counsels judge this period to range from three to nine months, depending on their legal interpretations. As a result, although U.S.-based investors may buy Eurodollar

---

lgium, Sweden, Denmark, and the United States. When agencies, municipals, corporates, and other domestic public issues are included, the United States represents 55 percent of the total; and when foreign and Eurobonds are added, the United States represents 57 percent of the total.

bonds after the seasoning period, the market remains dominated by foreign-based investors, and the primary trading center remains in London.

The size of the Eurodollar bond market has grown dramatically from a nominal new-issue volume in the early 1960s to more than $16 billion of new issues in 1980 and $63 billion in 1984. Marketability of Eurodollar bonds has improved over the years but is still limited. Although the size of recent straight fixed coupon Eurodollar issues has been about $200 million, most of the older issues are less than $50 million. In recent issues, trades of $10 million sometimes occur, but $2 to $5 million is normally a large trade. In older issues, trading volume of $200,000 per trade is considered good size. Eurodollar bonds pay interest only annually, so adjustment in the yield calculation must be made for comparison to domestic issues that pay interest semiannually.

Like the U.S. domestic market, which has seen a number of creative financing techniques over the last few years, the Eurodollar market has spawned a number of innovations, including floating-rate notes, original issue discounts, zero percent coupon issues, index-linked securities, and convertibles. When convertible into the stock of a foreign-based company, Eurodollar convertibles provide opportunities for currency gain related to prospects for increased conversion value while maintaining their bond-related denomination in U.S. dollars.

Yankee Bonds

The other portion of the U.S.-pay international bond market encompasses those foreign-domiciled issuers who register with the SEC and borrow U.S. dollars via issues underwritten by a U.S. syndicate for delivery in the United States. The principal trading market is in the United States, although foreign buyers can and do participate. Unlike the Eurodollar market, interest is paid semiannually. Marketability of these "foreign bonds" in the United States is usually quite good but can at times be limited depending largely on the quality of the issuer. This market has loosely been termed the *Yankee bond market*, although technically Yankee bonds are issues that would have been subject to the interest equalization tax (IET) prior to its elimination in 1974.[2] Canadian bonds, some South American issues, and issues of some supranational agencies (such as the World Bank, Inter American Development Bank, and Asian Development Bank) were not subject to the IET and therefore are not formally considered Yankee bonds.

---

[2] The interest equalization tax was imposed on purchases of foreign securities by U.S. residents during the years 1963 to 1974. The intent and effect of the tax was to discourage foreign borrowing in the United States by increasing the cost of capital. In order to make returns after the I.E.T. competitive with rates on domestic issues, gross rates on foreign borrowings had to be higher than would otherwise have been the case.

Since removal of the IET in 1974, sale of "foreign bonds" in the United States has been significant, although recent years have seen a decline in volume, coming in part as a response to the high borrowing rates in the United States compared with alternative markets. Annual new-issue volumes are shown in Exhibit 1.

Until July 1984 when the U.S. withholding tax on interest paid to foreigners was eliminated, U.S.-pay international bonds were generally more attractive to foreign buyers than were U.S. Treasury or corporate issues. The primary reason was that interest on these bonds—Eurodollar, Yankee, Canadian, and supranational agency bonds—was exempt from U.S. withholding tax. In contrast, interest on domestic bonds, including U.S. Treasury obligations, was subject to a 30 percent withholding tax unless that rate was reduced by a U.S. tax treaty with the holder's domicile country. In practice, the United States has tax treaties with most major countries, and thereby the effective withholding tax on interest received on domestic bonds by residents of these countries was significantly less than 30 percent. These treaties also apply to the withholding tax rate on dividends of U.S. corporations and generally provide that any withholding tax paid can be used as a partial offset to the investor's domestic income tax bill (see Exhibit 2). Certain foreign institutions with tax-exempt status in their own country are subject to reduced or eliminated withholding tax rates, and foreign central banks are exempt from all taxes. However, even when a purchaser could offset or reclaim the 30 percent withholding tax on domestic bond interest, it was often a tedious and time-consuming task, since a filing had to be made to the U.S. government in order to reclaim the withholding tax paid. Perhaps even more important, the filing process eliminated anonymity, which was an important concern for some foreign buyers. Thus securities that were themselves exempt from the withholding tax had an advantage to foreigners, an advantage that had no value to domestic buyers.

Even with the elimination of the withholding tax, there are a number of other less important factors that explain a preference of foreign buyers for U.S.-pay international bonds over Treasury or domestic corporate issues. The anonymity problem has not been eliminated with the elimination of the withholding tax, since purchase of most domestic issues now involves registration unless these issues have been specifically targeted for sale to foreigners. With the elimination of withholding tax, the Eurodollar market did cheapen relative to the domestic market, and one year later yields are higher than U.S. governments and some U.S. corporates, a definite advantage when coupled with the familiarity of Eurobond buyers with Yankee and Eurobond credits. Yankee and Eurodollar bond maturities are usually shorter than many U.S. domestic issues, and call protection is sometimes longer—both characteristics traditionally appeal to foreign bond buyers.

EXHIBIT 1 New-Issue Foreign Bonds Sold in the United States ($ millions)

	1973	1974	1975	1976	1977	1978	1979	1980	1981	1982	1983	1984
Canadian entities	$865	$1,962	$3,074	$ 6,138	$3,022	$3,142	$2,193	$2,136	$4,630	$3,330	NA	NA
International organizations	—	610	1,900	2,275	1,917	459	1,100	550	1,375	1,700	NA	NA
Other	95	719	1,488	2,191	2,489	2,194	1,222	743	1,547	1,066	NA	NA
Total	$960	$3,291	$6,462	$10,604	$7,428	$5,795	$4,515	$3,429	$7,552	$6,096	$4,545	$5,487

SOURCE: *World Financial Markets*, (New York: Morgan Guaranty).

EXHIBIT 2 Withholding Taxes on Dividends and Interest

Dividend Paying Company or Interest Paying Debtor in

Investor Resident in‖	South Africa*		Australia		Belgium*		Denmark*		France*		Germany*		Hong Kong		Italy*	
Australia	15	10			15	10	15	–	15	10	15	–	–	15	30	10–20
Belgium	15	10	15	10			15	–	§15	10	15	–	–	15	15	10–15
Denmark	15	10	15	10	15	15			–	–	15	–	–	15	15	10–20
France	15	10	15	10	15	15	–	–			15	–	–	15	15	10–15
Germany	15	10	15	10	15	–	15	–	§15	–			–	15	30	–
Hong Kong	15	10	30	10	25	25	30	–	25	25	25	–			30	10–20
Italy	15	10	30	10	15	15	15	–	15	25	25	–	–	15		
Japan	15	10	15	10	15	15	15	–	§15	10	15	–	–	15	15	10
Malaysia	15	10	15	10	15	10	–	–	§15	15	15	–	–	15	30	10–20
Netherlands	15	10	15	10	15	–	15	–	§15	10	15	–	–	15	30	10–20
Norway	15	10	15	10	15	15	15	–	§15	–	15	–	–	15	30	10–20
Singapore	15	10	15	10	15	15	30	–	15	10	15	–	–	15	10	10–12.5
Spain	15	10	30	10	15	15	15	–	§15	10	15	–	–	15	15	12
Sweden	15	10	15	10	15	15	15	–	§15	–	15	–	–	15	15	10–20
Switzerland	7.5	10	15	10	15	10	–	–	§15	10	15	–	–	15	15	10–12.5
U. K.	15	10	15	10	15	15	15	–	§15	10	15	–	–	15	15	10–20
U.S.A.	15	10	15	10	15	15	15	–	§15	10	15	–	–	15	15	10–20

A	B

A = Withholding tax on dividends
B = Withholding tax on interest
* Certain reductions or increases may apply in some cases and individual tax treaty should be consulted.
† Plus tax credit less 15 percent withholding tax
‡ Some gilts free of withholding tax
§ Plus avoir fiscal
‖ S. Africa has been excluded since residents are prohibited from purchasing foreign securities.
Compiled by Vickers da Costa Securities Inc. Reprinted by permission.

For these reasons, despite elimination of the tax advantage, there is a group of foreign buyers who prefer U.S.-pay international bond issues—Eurodollar, Yankee, Canadian, or supranational agencies—to domestic issues. As a result of this preference, the degree of interest of foreign buyers in U.S.-pay securities, or lack thereof, is often reflected in a narrowing or widening in the spread between U.S.-pay international

				Dividend Paying Company or Interest Paying Debtor in					
Japan*	Malay-sia	Nether-lands*	Nor-way*	Singa-pore	Spain*	Swe-den*	Switzer-land*	United King-dom‡	United States*
15 10	– 15	15 –	15 –	– 10	18 18	15 –	15 10	† – 10	15 –
15 15	– 10	15 –	15 –	– 15	15 15	15 –	15 10 ·	– 15	15 –
15 10	– 15	15 –	15 –	– 40	15 10	15 –	– –	† –	15 –
15 10	– 15	15 –	15 –	– 10	15 10	– –	5 10	† 10	15 –
15 10	– 15	15 –	15 –	– 10	15 10	15 –	15 –	– –	15 –
20 20	– 15	25 –	25 –	– 40	18 18	30 –	35 35	– 30	30 –
15 10	– 15	– –	25 –	– 12.5	15 12	15 –	15 12.5	– 30	15 –
	– 10	15 –	15 –	– 15	15 10	15 –	15 10	† 10	15 –
15 10		25 –	– –	– 40	18 18	– –	15 10	† 15	30 –
15 10	– 15		15 –	– 10	15 10	15 –	15 5	† –	15 –
15 10	– 15	15 –		– 40	10 10	15 –	5 5	† –	15 –
15 15	– 15	15 –	– –		18 18	15 –	15 10	† 15	30 –
15 10	– 15	15 –	15 –	– 40		15 –	15 10	† 12	30 –
15 10	– 15	15 –	15 –	– 15	15 15		5 5	† –	15 –
15 10	– 15	15 –	5 –	– 10	15 10	5 –		† –	15 –
15 10	– 15	15 –	15 –	– 15	15 12	5 –	15 –		15 –
15 10	– 15	15 –	15 –	– 40	18 18	15 –	15 15	† –	

bond yields and U.S. domestic yields. This is particularly true of Eurodollar bonds, since foreign interest governs this market to a greater extent than in the other types of international issues that are more broadly distributed in the United States. The attraction of Eurodollar bonds to foreigners is most often related to judgments on the prospects for the U.S. dollar, the level of interest rates in the United States relative to other foreign markets, and expectations for capital changes. Since the structure of bond markets in most other countries is geared to short or intermediate maturities (out to 10 years), foreign participants in the U.S. market usually prefer this range. Thus fluctuations in yield spreads of U.S.-pay international bonds versus Treasury obligations can be more pronounced in intermediate maturities than in longer-term bonds.

Whether foreign investors will continue to support a market with no tax advantage and that trades in an orbit to itself remains to be seen. Much institutional structure has been built around developing and maintaining a separate market by dealers. However, the growing internationalization of the investment world suggests the increased melding between the Euro and domestic markets should occur. Some evidence of this melding process has started to arise. In the year following the elimination of the withholding tax the volatility of the U.S. bond market had occasioned some foreign buyers to look to the U.S. market for short-term capital plays. Here, unsurpassed liquidity of U.S. Treasuries makes participation in the domestic market particularly attractive.

FOREIGN-PAY INTERNATIONAL BOND INVESTING

From the standpoint of the U.S. investor, foreign-pay international bonds encompass all issues denominated in currencies other than the dollar. There is a variety of types of issues available to the U.S. investor, but in all cases the primary trading market is outside the United States.

The Markets

Securities sold by a particular issuer within its own country and in that country's currency are typically termed *domestic issues*. These may include direct government issues, government agencies sometimes called semigovernments, or corporates. Corporate bonds clearly carry an additional risk beyond the currency, interest rate, and sovereign risks—that of company credit risk. Although a yield advantage to governments may be available from corporates, this margin relative to the total return expected must always be measured against their lesser marketability and additional credit concern. If a withholding tax is imposed by a particular country, all securities in the domestic bond market of that country are subject to withholding tax on interest when sold to nonresidents unless the rate is reduced or eliminated by a tax treaty with the country of the buyer. The withholding tax rates imposed by countries with the most developed bond markets are shown in Exhibit 2.

Another market is termed the *foreign bond market*, which includes issues sold primarily in one country and currency by a borrower of a different nationality. The Yankee market is the U.S.-dollar version of this market. Other examples are the Samurai market, which consists of yen-denominated bonds issued by non-Japanese issuers, and the Bulldog market, which is comprised of United Kingdom sterling-denominated bonds issued by non-British entities. Relative to the size of the domestic bond markets, these foreign bond markets are quite small, and liquidity can be limited. However, to the nonresident investor, these issues have the advantage of freedom from withholding taxes.

This tax advantage is shared by securities called *Eurobonds,* of which Eurodollar bonds are the U.S.-pay version. These securities are typically underwritten by international syndicates and are sold in a number of national markets simultaneously. They may or may not be obligations of or guaranteed by an issuer domiciled in the country of currency denomination, and the issuer may be a sovereign government, a corporation, or a supranational agency. Eurodollar bonds have consistently been the largest sector of this market, representing about 65 percent of the total over the last 15 years, and Euro deutsche mark issues have regularly been second, averaging above 15 percent of the total. Like the foreign bond market, liquidity of Eurobond issues is typically less than in domestic government issues.

Components of Return

To the dollar-based investor, there are only two components of return in U.S.-pay bond investing: income, and capital change resulting from interest-rate movements. In foreign-pay investing, a third component of return must be considered: foreign currency movements. Thus the U.S. investor must couple the domestic or internal price movement with income and then translate the total domestic return into dollars to assess the total return in U.S. dollars.

For the U.S. investor in foreign currency bonds, the prospects for return should not only be viewed in an absolute sense, but also be analyzed relative to returns expected in the U.S. market. The analysis can be separated into three different questions.

1. What is the starting yield level relative to yield levels on U.S. bonds? Where this spread is positive, the income advantage will, over time, provide a cushion against adverse movements of the foreign bond price relative to U.S. bonds or against deterioration in the value of the foreign currency. The longer the time horizon, the greater the cushion provided by this accumulating income advantage. If, on the other hand, the starting income level of the foreign currency issue is below that provided by U.S. bonds, this income deficiency must be offset continually by an appreciating currency or positive internal price movement relative to U.S. bonds in order to provide comparable returns. This may appear to be a difficult challenge, but the decade of the 1970s as a whole saw the best converted U.S. dollar total returns accruing to bond investments with the lowest income levels. The underlying rationale for this result was that bonds with low yields were denominated in currencies of countries with low inflation rates, which were ultimately translated to currency appreciation relative to the U.S. dollar.

2. What are the prospects for internal price movements relative to expectations for U.S. bond prices? This factor can be broadly discussed in terms of changing yield spreads of foreign pay bonds versus U.S. issues in the same way that changing yield spreads within the domestic U.S. market are discussed when describing changes in relative prices. However, several points should be considered in regard to this analogy. In the U.S. market, all bond prices generally move in the same direction, although not always to the same extent; whereas domestic price movements of foreign-pay bonds may move in a direction opposite to that of the U.S. market. Second, although yield spread relationships within the U.S. market may fluctuate broadly, in many cases there is a normal spread that has some repetitive meaning. However, changing economic, social, and political trends between the United States and other countries suggests that there are few normal relationships to serve as useful guidelines.

Finally, although both U.S. and international investors must be aware of differing price movements emanating from equal yield movements in securities of differing maturities, international bond investors must also be aware of the impact a given basis point change in yield has on the price movements of bonds with significantly different starting yield levels. For example, a 100-basis-point movement in a 10-year United Kingdom government issue starting at a 15 percent yield is about 5 percent, whereas the same 100-basis-point move equates to about a 7 percent price change for a 10-year Swiss Franc issue with a starting yield of 7 percent. When the more commonly analyzed effects of varying maturities and differing yield changes are added to the impact of different starting yield levels, the resulting changes in relative price movements are not intuitively obvious. For example, the various combinations of starting yield, maturity, and yield change shown in Exhibit 3 all result in the same 10 percent capital price increases.

EXHIBIT 3 Impact of Maturity and Starting Yield on Yield and Price Change Relationships

Starting Yield	Maturity (Years)	Yield Change	Price Change
15 percent	10	−1.83%	+10%
15	5	−2.73	+10
7	10	−1.32	+10
7	5	−2.27	+10

3. What are the prospects for currency gain or loss versus the dollar? The debate on whether or not foreign currency changes can be predicted and, if so, what factors determine such changes has been a continuing one. In many ways this debate is little different from that regarding the predictability of stock market movements or interest rates. Like the stock and bond markets, a number of factors can be identified as exerting a direct influence on foreign exchange rates. The common problems faced by forecasters are whether these factors have already been fully discounted in prices—be they stock, bond, or foreign exchange—and which factor will predominate at any given time. Those factors generally regarded to affect foreign currency movements include the following:

1. The balance of payments and prospective changes in that balance.
2. Inflation and interest differentials between countries.
3. The social and political atmosphere, particularly with regard to the impact on foreign investment.
4. Central bank intervention in the currency markets.

Some people have questioned whether returns for international bond investing are almost entirely a function of currency movements.

EXHIBIT 4 Average Annual Returns of International Bond Index* by Components

| | | Contribution to Return | | |
	Income	Domestic Capital Gain	Foreign Currency	Total Dollar-Converted Average Annual Return
1966–69	+6.3%	−2.3%	−.6%	+3.4%
1970–74	+7.9	−3.8	+5.4	+9.5
1975–79	+9.3	+.5	+3.1	+12.9
1980–84	+11.2	+.5	−9.6	+2.1
1966–84	+8.8	−1.2	−.5	+7.1

* Equally weighted in government bonds of Australia, Canada, France, Germany, Japan, Netherlands, Switzerland, United Kingdom. Rebalanced monthly.

Exhibit 4 shows that for the 19-year period 1966–1984 and for the four interim periods the income component of return has proven to be the largest of the three portions, as measured by an index of international bonds equally weighted in eight foreign countries.

However, for specific years, domestic capital change and/or foreign exchange at times played significantly larger roles, as shown in Exhibit 5. Domestic capital changes ranged from −9.0 percent in 1979 to +13.2 percent in 1982, and currency returns varied from −14 percent in 1984 to

---

EXHIBIT 5   Annual Returns of International Bond Index* by Components

		Contribution to Return		
	Income	Domestic Capital Gain	Foreign Currency	Total Dollar-Converted Average Annual Return
1966	+6.1%	−1.7%	−.3%	+4.1%
1967	+6.1	−.6	−1.5	+4.0
1968	+6.3	−1.3	−.1	+4.9
1969	+6.6	−5.6	−.3	+.7
1970	+7.6	−1.9	+1.1	+6.8
1971	+7.7	+3.3	+9.1	+20.1
1972	+7.1	−2.4	+1.7	+6.4
1973	+7.6	−8.5	+10.2	+9.3
1974	+9.5	−8.9	+5.1	+5.7
1975	+10.4	+4.5	−5.9	+9.0
1976	+9.9	+2.6	−1.0	+11.5
1977	+9.5	+7.8	+11.3	+28.6
1978	+8.3	−2.5	+11.9	+17.7
1979	+8.5	−9.0	+.3	−.2
1980	+10.4	−5.6	−2.1	+2.7
1981	+11.7	−6.5	−10.3	−5.1
1982	+13.5	+13.2	−12.1	+14.6
1983	+10.4	+0	−10.0	+.4
1984	+10.5	+2.6	−14.0	−.9

* Equally weighted in government bonds of Australia, Canada, France, Germany, Japan, Netherlands, Switzerland, United Kingdom. Rebalanced monthly.

+11.9 percent in 1978. For individual countries, the variation in components of return was even greater. The greatest capital price changes occurred in the United Kingdom, where losses and gains were −23.4 percent and +29.1 percent in 1974 and 1982, respectively. Currency changes for specific countries ranged from nearly +28 percent for the Swiss franc in 1974 to −20.7 percent for the French franc in 1981. These data show clearly that all three factors of return—income, capital change, and currency movement—are important and must be considered both absolutely and relative to U.S. alternatives.

THE RATIONALE FOR INTERNATIONAL BOND INVESTING

The rationale for foreign-pay international bond investing is two-fold. First, international bonds can from time to time enhance an investor's total rate of return relative to what is available from alternative U.S. domestic bond investments. The composition of return will, however, be variable as between income, domestic price change, and foreign currency change. Second, international bonds can reduce the risk or the volatility of return relative to a portfolio invested solely in U.S. fixed income securities.

In analyzing the case for international bonds, there is no a priori reason why one rationale for international bond investing should receive more emphasis than the other. The relative emphasis on these rationales is properly a function of the investment objectives of the investor, and these objectives should be reflected in the composition of an international bond portfolio. To some investors with long-term time horizons, the impact of international bonds on interim volatility of returns is unimportant. For these investors, embarking on a program of international bond investing is not appropriate unless international bonds can be expected to improve the rate of return. To others, particularly those with shorter time horizons who have been seared by the recent roller coaster in the U.S. fixed income markets, the attraction of international bonds may be their potential for a reduction in the volatility of overall portfolio returns.

Superior Rates of Return

One of the cornerstones of the rationale for international equity investing is that a portfolio of foreign equities should, over time, provide a higher return than a portfolio of U.S. equities, since many areas of the world are growing more rapidly than the United States and are experiencing higher rates of investment spending and productivity growth. Ultimately these superior growth characteristics should translate into more rapid increases in corporate profits and, in turn, stock prices assuming a degree of comparability in starting valuations.

No such strong fundamental arguments exist for international bonds. History has shown that there have been long periods (1966–78 excepting 1970 and 1976) where international bonds provided superior returns to U.S. instruments and long periods (1981–84) where the reverse was true. In the former period, foreign bonds benefited both by higher income levels than in the United States and strengthening currencies. Toward the end of this period, the United States was experiencing higher unanticipated inflation rates than other industrialized countries which explained part of the dollar weakening, but also led to poor domestic U.S. bond price movements relative to those abroad. In the 1981–84 period, U.S. bonds benefited from income streams much higher than in other markets coupled with the improvement in the inflation outlook which, with other forces, resulted in a rise in bond prices and a rise in the dollar.

These results strongly suggest that prospective returns from international bonds relative to the United States must be carefully analyzed by the three components—income advantage, relative domestic price movements, and prospective currency changes.

The best case for ongoing observance of international bonds lies in the continual array of opportunities and risks provided by the constant shifting of international exchange rate and interest-rate relationships. The range of starting yields is continuously changing; some foreign rates provide a yield cushion against a U.S. interest-rate bogey, and others provide a disadvantage. At any time, different countries will be at different points in their economic and interest-rate cycles. Similarly, foreign currency relationships are continuously shifting, sometimes moving with interest rates and sometimes against them.

Over time it should be possible to capitalize on these shifting relationships, which will, in the aggregate, supply a greater number of opportunities than can any one individual and relatively homogeneous market. This rationale is an opportunistic and selective one, which has at its heart the cyclicality of economic behavior worldwide.

In the analysis that follows, eight foreign bond markets are analyzed in relationship with the U.S. market. Included are the government bond markets of Australia, Canada, France, Germany, Japan, the Netherlands, Switzerland, and the United Kingdom. In the absence of published price data extending back historically, price movements have been imputed from monthly yield series.[3]

A comparison of eight foreign bond markets with the U.S. market shows that over the period 1966–84, foreign bonds provided a somewhat better 7.1 percent rate of return to that produced by a U.S. 10-year-bond average of 5.67 percent.[4] Exhibit 6 shows the total rates of return from nine bond markets in U.S.-dollar terms over the 19-year period. In that period the return on U.S. bonds was exceeded by five out of eight foreign markets. In the subperiods of 1966–69 and 1975–79, the return on U.S. bonds ranked seventh out of nine, outperforming only the

---

[3] Domestic government bond yields from 1966 to 1977 were compiled by Morgan Guaranty and published in their *World Financial Markets*. Yields for 1978–1984 were compiled by Scudder, Stevens and Clark.

[4] U.S. bond returns were calculated in a manner consistent with all other foreign markets. Returns were extrapolated from the government yield series described in Footnote 3, and 10-year maturities were assumed throughout.

EXHIBIT 6 International Bond Markets Compound Annual Rates of Return—1966–1984

	Total Return in U.S. Dollars	Components of Return			
		Domestic Capital Change	Income	Total Domestic Return	Foreign Exchange Change
Australia	4.65%	−2.99%	9.32%	6.33%	−1.58%
Canada	5.98	−2.42	9.56	7.14	−1.09
France	3.97	−2.42	10.14	7.72	−3.48
Germany	9.63	−.01	8.26	8.25	+1.27
Japan	9.89	−.17	7.99	7.82	+1.92
Netherlands	7.89	−.60	8.40	7.80	+.08
Switzerland	7.40	−.40	4.97	4.57	+2.71
United Kingdom	4.44	−2.11	11.51	9.40	−4.54
United States	5.67	−2.74	8.41	5.67	

United Kingdom and France in the first instance and Australia and Canada in the latter period. In the interim 1970–74, it ranked eighth out of nine just ahead of the United Kingdom. However in the most recent 1980–84 period, the United States has provided a return second only to Canada.

Over the 1966–80 15-year period, the superior performance of most foreign bond markets relative to the U.S. market was attributable to all three components of return: an income advantage, more favorable relative price trends, and positive currency changes. The period was one of rising interest rates worldwide and declining bond prices in domestic price terms in all nine markets analyzed. The percentage drop, however, was the least in the relatively low inflation countries of Germany, Switzerland, and Japan. The price performance was the worst in Australia, Canada, and the United Kingdom, but even these drops were exceeded by that of the U.S. bond market. With the exception of Switzerland, the return attributable to income was greater in each of the eight foreign markets than in the United States. Although long U.S. interest rates were among the highest by 1980, they were exceeded by many foreign rates during the first 10 years of the period when annual income from U.S. bonds averaged from 70 to 370 basis points less than that provided by foreign bonds. Combining these two variables, the return in local currency terms in each foreign market exceeded that of the U.S. bond market. When foreign exchange movements are factored in, the relative advantage of foreign bonds widened. Of eight foreign currencies considered, six appreciated against the dollar by amounts ranging from .4 percent to 6.16 percent per annum. Only the Canadian dollar and British pound declined relative to the U.S. dollar, but not by enough to offset the relative advantages of price and income.

The higher rate of return from foreign bond markets over the 1966–80 period relative to the U.S. market had no necessary repetitive significance. This period was obviously unique in many respects: the Vietnam War, the impact of the oil price rise in both 1973–74 and 1979–80, and a variance in political trends here and abroad that contributed to important differences in economic priorities and policy in the United States and in other industrial nations. In fact, events changed markedly in the next five years. The strong relative returns of U.S. bonds over foreign bonds in 1980–84 was due to the strong dollar as shown previously in Exhibit 5. On average, depreciating foreign currencies subtracted 9.6 percent annually from the total return of the international bond index. This, in addition to the 1.45 percent higher income of U.S. bonds over international bonds more than compensated for the 2.7 percent superior price performance in domestic terms of foreign bonds versus U.S. issues. All in all, 1980–84 provided a 10.5 percent return for U.S. bonds versus +2.1 percent for international issues.

The prospects for international bond returns relative to the United States will be a function of when the pattern of a strengthening dollar is broken and whether resulting foreign currency appreciation and relative domestic bond price movements can offset the year-end 1984 225 basis point disadvantage of foreign bonds relative to the U.S.

Analysis of the individual country returns from 1966–84 highlights the importance of the variability of the source of the return. For example, in the case of Switzerland, the rise in the value of the Swiss franc partially offset the relative income disadvantage of Swiss franc bonds. In contrast, although the value of pound sterling declined by 4.5 percent per annum, the 310 basis-point income advantage resulted in a United Kingdom bond return only about 1 percent less than a U.S. bond return.

The variability of the sources of return is even more evident in a comparison of annual data. The components of return for the two years 1976 and 1980 are shown in Exhibit 7. In each case, the U.S. bond market ranked fifth or sixth out of nine markets as measured by total return in U.S.-dollar terms. In 1976 the three top performers were the major hard currency countries of Europe: Germany, Switzerland, and the Netherlands. In 1980 these three countries trailed the list, and the United Kingdom, Japan, and Australia provided the best returns. In the case of the United Kingdom, the positive return in 1980 was accounted for by all three components of return; whereas the 18 percent rise in the value of the yen contributed 70 percent of the return on Japanese bonds, and in Australia the currency appreciation more than offset a poor domestic bond market. In 1976 the superior performance of German bonds was due to all three components of return; while in Switzerland currency and price movements offset the 300-basis-point income disadvantage; and in the Netherlands higher income and foreign exchange appreciation offset a lower capital change than in the United States.

EXHIBIT 7 The Variability of the Components of Returns

1976

		Components of Return		
	Total Return (Dollars)	Capital Change	Income	Foreign Exchange Change
Germany	32.24%	10.07%	9.07%	11.00%
Switzerland	24.96	11.12	5.75	6.92
Netherlands	20.53	.74	9.41	9.41
Canada	17.70	6.62	10.24	0.71
Japan	16.90	2.84	9.33	4.22
United States	14.48	5.85	8.63	
France	−5.11	−5.29	10.43	−9.75
United Kingdom	−5.68	−2.01	14.12	−15.87
Australia	−7.40	−3.23	10.38	−13.58

1980

		Components of Return		
	Total Return (Dollars)	Capital Change	Income	Foreign Exchange Change
United Kingdom	27.02%	2.94%	15.50%	7.24%
Japan	25.16	−3.20	9.20	18.07
Australia	3.36	−14.00	10.78	6.80
Canada	1.88	−8.11	12.31	−2.23
United States	−.10	−10.84	10.74	
Netherlands	−6.90	−5.63	9.67	−10.52
France	−7.24	−8.62	12.82	−10.98
Switzerland	−8.54	−2.62	4.56	−10.28
Germany	−10.30	−6.55	8.04	−11.62

Despite some evidence of variability in the components of return, a frequent challenge to international bond investing is that the favorable foreign bond returns in the 1970s were due primarily to the weak dollar and that the reverse has been true in the first half of the 1980s. Although there is considerable merit to this argument over short and intermediate time periods, the historical contribution of return from currency appreciation over long periods of time should not be over-emphasized. Exhibit 8 shows the contribution in basis points of currency movements to returns. For each of the last five-year periods, the impact of currency on return has been much higher than for the nineteen-year period as a whole. Whether this trend continues will have an important impact on the place of international bonds in U.S. portfolios. Exhibit 9 compares local currency returns and converted dollar returns for 1966–84. In half the cases, currency conversion added to the results and in half it subtracted.

EXHIBIT 8 Average Annual Contribution of Foreign Currency Changes to International Bond Returns (basis points)

	1966–84	1966–69	1970–74	1975–79	1980–84
Australia	−168	−1	+357	−390	−624
Canada	−116	+5	+171	−342	−274
France	−375	−318	+469	+222	−1848
Germany	+138	+223	+939	+752	−1237
Japan	+207	+23	+365	+511	−106
Netherlands	+ 9	−10	+815	+614	−1300
Switzerland	+283	0	+1154	+1089	−985
United Kingdom	−496	−393	−44	−124	−1437

EXHIBIT 9 Comparison of International Bond Returns

	Average Annual Return of Long Bonds Converted to U.S. Dollars 1966–1984	Average Annual Return of Long Bonds in Domestic Currency 1966–1984
Australia	4.6%	6.3%
Canada	6.0	7.1
France	4.0	7.7
Germany	9.6	8.3
Japan	9.9	7.8
Netherlands	7.9	7.8
Switzerland	7.4	4.6
United Kingdom	4.4	9.4
United States	5.7	5.7

A second challenge relating to foreign currency exposure relates to the fact that the foreign currency factor adds to the volatility of foreign bond returns. On a market-by-market basis, this has been true. Exhibits 10 and 11 show the standard deviation of monthly total returns in nine bond markets in both local currency and dollar-denominated terms. The data are presented for the 1966–84 period and are also broken down into five-year segments. In the period 1966–84, the volatility of returns in the United States was equal to or greater than in any other market in local currency terms except for the United Kingdom. In all cases, the volatility increased during the period; but the volatility of U.S. returns continued to be among the highest. When foreign exchange movements are factored in, the volatility of foreign bond returns increased substantially, and in fact for the 1966–84 period and for each sub-period the standard deviation of the U.S. return is about the lowest.

EXHIBIT 10   Standard Deviation of Monthly Domestic Total Returns

	1966–84	1970–74	1975–79	1980–84
Australia	2.002	2.160	.919	3.031
Canada	2.377	1.577	1.502	3.943
France	1.824	1.427	1.278	2.765
Germany	1.792	1.926	1.682	2.231
Japan	1.736	1.267	1.702	2.619
Netherlands	1.396	1.231	1.091	2.077
Switzerland	1.462	1.054	1.350	2.147
United Kingdom	3.064	2.786	4.133	2.939
United States	2.342	1.964	1.541	3.648

EXHIBIT 11   Standard Deviation of Monthly Total Return Converted to U.S. Dollars

	1966–84	1970–74	1975–79	1980–84
Australia	2.955	3.041	3.149	3.733
Canada	2.896	1.845	2.220	4.735
France	3.372	3.228	3.160	4.520
Germany	3.598	3.171	3.841	4.731
Japan	3.727	2.788	4.078	5.360
Netherlands	3.348	3.049	3.618	4.371
Switzerland	3.687	3.241	4.220	4.569
United Kingdom	4.313	3.486	5.548	4.792
United States	2.342	1.964	1.541	3.648

The fact that foreign currency movements add to the volatility of individual market returns suggests (and other evidence lends some credence to this theory) that foreign exchange movements reinforce returns in domestic price terms over long periods of time. This is not surprising considering the common long-term fundamental factors affecting both domestic prices and foreign exchange rates.

As discussed in the next section, however, the increase in volatility of individual market returns due to foreign exchange movements is significantly reduced in a diversified international bond portfolio.

Diversification

A second rationale for international bond investing is diversification. The inclusion of foreign bonds in a portfolio should reduce the risk or volatility of returns of a portfolio otherwise invested solely in U.S. fixed income securities. The fundamental reason for this is that foreign bond markets do not move with, or are not perfectly correlated with, the U.S.

EXHIBIT 12 Correlation Coefficients of Domestic Capital Change in Major Foreign Bond Markets—1966–1984 (based on monthly data)

	United States	Australia	Canada	France	Germany	Japan	Netherlands	Switzerland	United Kingdom
United States	1.00								
Australia	.14	1.00							
Canada	.75	.17	1.00						
France	.09	.09	.21	1.00					
Germany	.38	.14	.35	.19	1.00				
Japan	.36	.09	.40	.24	.43	1.00			
Netherlands	.43	.05	.38	.27	.53	.38	1.00		
Switzerland	.25	.12	.26	.15	.36	.40	.39	1.00	
United Kingdom	.23	.03	.27	.11	.21	.19	.13	.21	1.00

bond market. Intuitively this is obvious. The dynamics of the business cycle differ by country. The role of monetary policy in the arsenal of a government's economic weapons varies among countries. Institutional or structural forces, government financing practices, and tradition mean that the role of buyers and sellers differs between fixed income markets. The trend of inflation, a nation's tolerance of inflation, and the sources of inflationary pressure differ among countries, as does the impact of inflation on the trend and structure of interest rates.

Finally, there is a host of geopolitical, foreign policy, and societal forces that ensure that the movements of foreign bond prices are not perfectly correlated. Consequently, when foreign currency bonds are added to a portfolio of U.S. fixed income securities, the price movements often offset each other, and the overall volatility of returns can be reduced.

Exhibit 12 shows the correlation coefficients of monthly changes in bond prices in local currency terms between nine major bond markets, including the United States, over the 1966–84 period. The highest correlation with the U.S. market is Canada—not a surprising occurrence in view of the multilateral relationships between the two economies. The correlation is practically zero with Australia, which once again is reasonable in view of the lack of interdependence between the two economies. Between these two extremes lie the European markets and Japan. It should be noted that in most cases the correlation among the continental European markets is higher than that between those markets and the United States, reflecting the high degree of interdependence between the European economies and the existence of informal currency blocs.

Exhibit 13 shows the correlation coefficients of monthly domestic capital changes between the United States and foreign markets broken down by five-year time periods. In all cases except France, the degree of correlation or interdependence rose over the period. This is one more statistical manifestation of the degree to which the world is getting

---

EXHIBIT 13 Correlation Coefficient between U.S. and Foreign Bond Markets Domestic Capital Change (based on monthly data)

	1966–84	1966–69	1970–74	1975–79	1980–84
Australia	.14	−.21	.04	−.07	.24
Canada	.75	.71	.45	.66	.84
France	.09	.30	.05	−.28	.16
Germany	.38	.29	.09	.30	.58
Japan	.36	−.09	.17	.03	.53
Netherlands	.43	−.01	.03	.34	.62
Switzerland	.25	−.18	.13	.05	.38
United Kingdom	.23	.37	.16	.00	.45

smaller and the increased synchronization of economic behavior resulting from growing trade and capital flows. More specifically, it reflects the heavy and uniform impact of the sharp rise in oil prices in all industrialized countries in 1973–75 and 1979–80, particularly on the trend of inflation and interest rates and in later years, the very high level of U.S. rates, which through the currency link, held foreign rates up as well. To the extent the industrialized world succeeds in better coordinating national financial and economic policies, it is possible that the trend toward a somewhat higher interdependence between markets will continue. For reasons discussed above, however, international bond price trends should remain less than perfectly correlated.

Exhibits 14 and 15 show the correlation coefficients of the change in bond prices converted to U.S. dollars between the U.S. and foreign markets and the total return, including income, converted to U.S. dollars for the 1966–84 period overall, and again broken down into five-year segments. The inclusion of income had only a modest impact on the

EXHIBIT 14 Correlation Coefficients between United States and Foreign Bond Markets Capital Change Converted to U.S. Dollars (based on monthly data)

	1966–84	1966–69	1970–74	1975–79	1980–84
Australia	.12	−.20	.01	−.06	.26
Canada	.69	.71	.45	.50	.78
France	.16	.24	−.01	.00	.28
Germany	.30	.22	−.03	.29	.46
Japan	.27	−.10	.09	.03	.43
Netherlands	.30	−.06	.00	.27	.48
Switzerland	.23	−.26	−.10	.17	.45
United Kingdom	.26	.32	.12	.10	.43

EXHIBIT 15 Correlation Coefficient between United States and Foreign Bond Markets Total Return Converted to U.S. Dollars (based on monthly data)

	1966–84	1966–69	1970–74	1975–79	1980–84
Australia	.12	−.22	.00	−.06	.26
Canada	.69	.71	.45	.49	.78
France	.16	.23	−.01	.00	.28
Germany	.29	.22	−.03	.29	.46
Japan	.27	−.10	.08	.03	.42
Netherlands	.30	−.08	.00	.27	.48
Switzerland	.22	−.28	−.10	.17	.44
United Kingdom	.26	.32	−.11	.10	.43

degree of correlation between markets. Comparison of Exhibits 13 and 14 shows that the impact of currency movements on the correlation of returns was, however, more substantial but not tremendous by any means and varied significantly by country. In the 1966–84 period, in two cases (the United Kingdom and France) the degree of correlation was increased, and in six cases (Australia, Canada, Germany, Japan, Switzerland, and the Netherlands) it was reduced. The impact of currency movements was much more substantial in the post-1971 period once exchange rates started to float. The divergent effects of currency movements on the degree of correlation is understandable given the volatility of foreign exchange rates in the post-1971 period and the complexity of factors underlying foreign exchange-rate movements.

THE IMPACT OF FOREIGN BONDS ON A U.S. BOND PORTFOLIO

Given the risk/return characteristic of foreign bond investing outlined above, it is natural to question the impact of foreign bonds on a U.S. fixed income portfolio. Although the magnitude of future effects is uncertain, some guidance may be provided by analyzing, albeit somewhat hypothetically, what the impact of foreign bond investing would have been on a U.S. bond portfolio in the past.

Exhibit 16 shows the comparison of the compound rates of return of an international index equally weighted in the eight foreign markets

EXHIBIT 16 Compound Annual Rates of Return

	1966–84	1966–69	1970–74	1975–79	1980–84
International Index	7.10	3.44	9.52	12.94	2.12
United States	5.67	.66	5.03	5.69	10.49
Portfolio I	6.02	1.05	5.99	7.18	8.87
(80 percent United States, 20 percent International Index)					

studied and the U.S. bond market together with a portfolio assumed to be invested 80 percent in the U.S. market average and 20 percent in the international index. While for the period as a whole, international bonds provided about a 1.5 percent better return than U.S. bonds and added 35 basis points of return when a 20 percent commitment was added to an 80 percent commitment in U.S. bonds, the results were markedly different before and after 1980. In the first 14 years, international bonds added a clear increment to return. In the most recent five years, U.S. bonds provided an 8.4 percent annual increment of return over foreign bonds due, as shown in Exhibit 4, to a 9.6 percent appreciation of the dollar and a higher income stream in the United States.

Exhibit 17 shows the comparison of standard deviation of returns. Although Exhibit 11 demonstrated that dollar denominated returns from

---

EXHIBIT 17   Standard Deviations of Monthly Returns (in U.S. dollars)

	1966–84	1970–74	1975–79	1980–84
International Index	2.485	2.005	2.590	3.517
United States	2.342	1.964	1.541	3.648
Portfolio I	2.119	1.645	1.434	3.380
(80 percent United States, 20 percent International Index)				

---

individual foreign bond markets were significantly more volatile than U.S. bond returns, Exhibit 17 indicates that the standard deviation of an international bond portfolio was relatively low by comparison, reflecting the relatively low degree of correlations between foreign markets. In 1970–74 and 1975–79 coinciding with superior international bond returns, volatility of the international bond index was above the United States, with the reverse true in 1980–84. When international bonds are included in a portfolio, the volatility of returns is reduced relative to a portfolio invested 100 percent in the U.S. market average. Over the 1966–84 period as a whole and in each of the five-year periods, the variability of monthly returns of the internationally diversified portfolio was somewhat below that of the U.S. market average.

SUMMARY

International bonds, both U.S. pay and foreign pay, represent a significant portion of the world's fixed income markets, and an understanding of their characteristics is important for all bond investors.

Since U.S.-pay foreign bonds have particular appeal to non-U.S. buyers, knowledge of the reasons for this preference and an ongoing familiarity with the investment posture of non-U.S. buyers toward U.S.-pay bonds is necessary in order to effectively participate in that market.

Not only must investors in foreign-pay bonds consider income levels and prospective price movements both absolute and relative to U.S. alternatives, but the outlook for foreign currency changes must also be evaluated. The evidence indicates that over the 1966–79 period, foreign-pay bonds converted to U.S. dollars combined with U.S. bonds would have both reduced the overall volatility of a portfolio invested solely in U.S. issues and increased the returns. In the 1980–84 period volatility was again reduced, but at the expense of a substantially lower return. Although these facts have by themselves little repetitive significance, many of the factors leading to the low correlation in returns between the U.S.- and foreign-pay markets continue. It is more difficult to conclude whether or not international bonds in general will provide superior returns to U.S. bonds, but the variance of social, political, monetary, and fiscal trends and policies between countries suggest that there will from time to time be particular markets that offer better values than the U.S. market.

50

International Portfolio Management

Cornelia M. Small
Managing Director
Scudder, Stevens & Clark

Margaret Darasz Hadzima, C.F.A.
Vice President, Bonds
Scudder, Stevens & Clark

Chapter 49 presents the rationale for investment in foreign-pay bonds: opportunities for superior investment returns and a reduction in the volatility of returns when added to a U.S. portfolio. Once the investor accepts the basic justification for at least periodic investment in foreign-pay bonds and determines whether or not foreign-pay bonds are suitable for the portfolio objectives and requirements, the next question relates to the appropriate investment strategy. As in the U.S. stock and bond markets and in international equities, the investor must resolve the debate between active and passive investing.

PASSIVE VERSUS ACTIVE MANAGEMENT

There is little question that, with the benefit of hindsight, a strategy of active international bond portfolio management over the 19-year period beginning in 1966 could have provided a better return than a passive strategy. Exhibit 1 shows the range in international bond returns converted to U.S. dollars for each year between 1966 and 1984 in comparison with U.S. bond returns and an index equally weighted in eight major foreign markets. Of interest is the wide range of returns for each year and the variety of countries that headed the best and worst return scales. The average percentage spread from the best to worst return in each year was 27.9 percent and ranged from 56.6 percent to 8.8 percent. In the 19-year period, six of the eight foreign markets reviewed provided

EXHIBIT 1 Total Annual Return Converted to U.S. Dollars

	Best		Worst			
	Percentage	*Country*	*Percentage*	*Country*	*U.S.*	*Index I*
1984	14.7%	United States	−13.4%	United Kingdom	14.7	−.9
1983	11.4	Japan	−8.7	Germany	2.3	.4
1982	36.2	Canada	2.4	Switzerland	35.9	14.6
1981	5.9	Japan	−17.6	France	3.4	−5.1
1980	27.0	United Kingdom	−10.3	Germany	−.1	2.7
1979	14.8	United Kingdom	−24.2	Japan	1.8	−.1
1978	35.5	Switzerland	−6.0	Canada	1.6	17.7
1977	55.0	Japan	−1.6	Canada	2.2	28.6
1976	32.2	Germany	−7.4	Australia	14.5	11.5
1975	16.6	France	1.0	Australia	8.9	9.0
1974	28.7	Switzerland	−11.6	Japan	2.5	5.7
1973	21.6	Germany	−3.2	United States	−3.2	9.3
1972	18.0	Japan	−7.8	United Kingdom	5.7	6.4
1971	27.0	United Kingdom	10.0	United States	10.0	20.1
1970	25.7	Canada	−.9	Australia	10.8	6.8
1969	9.4	Germany	−10.4	France	−.7	.7
1968	9.3	Germany	.3	United Kingdom	1.6	4.9
1967	12.8	Germany	−10.0	United Kingdom	−2.0	4.0
1966	8.3	Germany	−.5	Switzerland	3.9	4.1

Note: Index I is equally weighted in government bonds of Australia, Canada, France, Germany, Japan, the Netherlands, Switzerland, and the United Kingdom.

the best total returns converted to U.S. dollars at least once, and seven of the eight were the worst at least once.

The crucial question, of course, is whether without such hindsight an actively managed portfolio can provide an incremental return over a passive portfolio without incurring a commensurate degree of risk. Although this can only be answered empirically, it is difficult to justify a passive approach to international bond investing on either a theoretical or practical basis. This conclusion is based on several different considerations.

Assumption of efficient markets. Underlying the theoretical basis of a passive approach to investing is the assumption of efficient markets. This assumption may be argued to be valid in the case of the U.S. capital markets, but the assumption does not hold when the definition is extended to the international fixed income markets. For a market to be efficient, information must be freely available, all participants must use the information similarly, and capital flows between investments must be free. It is obvious that these conditions do not apply to the various constituent markets making up the international bond market. The availability of information is probably freer in the case of international bonds than of international stocks, but it is scarcely complete. There are very different degrees of disclosure among countries regarding the various factors that influence the trend and level of interest rates: monetary policy, government financing requirements, foreign exchange policy, broad economic statistics. Furthermore, that information that is available is, for all practical purposes, not uniformly shared by all participants in the marketplace.

Use of market information. A variety of impediments prevent market information from being used in a similar fashion: differences in national character and tradition, legal differences, differences in tax treatment by countries and the tax situation of investors, and institutional differences between countries. Also, a number of obstacles (of which foreign exchange and capital controls are the most obvious) often impede the free flow of capital between markets.

Exchange-rate changes. As has been demonstrated in Chapter 49, foreign exchange-rate changes make up an important component of return. A passive approach would prevent the investor from implementing any independent judgment regarding currency movements. This consideration would be a minor one if the foreign exchange markets were, as is frequently argued, efficient. If they were, the bond returns of various countries when converted to a common currency would be roughly equivalent over time. In such a case, the interest differentials and currency changes would reflect differential inflation rates so that currency changes would equal the difference in income factors. In the 19-year period from 1966 to 1984, this did not prove to be the case. The average annual converted return ranged from about 4 percent for France to 9.9 percent for Japanese bonds. In fact, the variation was less in domestic prices than after conversion to a common currency, the U.S. dollar. These results are shown on Exhibit 2. In addition, it is intuitively obvious that the foreign exchange markets are not perfectly efficient. There is a myriad of special factors that determine exchange-rate movements; inflation differentials is only one of these factors. Official foreign exchange intervention and different perceptions of political forces are

---

EXHIBIT 2 Comparison of International Bond Returns

	Average Annual Return of 10 Year Bonds Converted to U.S. Dollars 1966–1984	Average Annual Return of 10 Year Bonds in Domestic Currency 1966–1984
Australia	4.7%	6.3%
Canada	6.0	7.1
France	4.0	7.7
Germany	9.6	8.3
Japan	9.9	7.8
Netherlands	7.9	7.8
Switzerland	7.4	4.6
United Kingdom	4.4	9.4
United States	5.7	5.7

among the many factors that distort fundamental exchange-rate relationships. In view of these inefficiencies, it is to be expected that active
decisions regarding foreign commitments can add incremental value to a
foreign bond portfolio.

Choice of market portfolio. An additional factor challenging the
case for a passive approach relates to the choice of a market portfolio. It
can be argued that an efficient market portfolio in its purest form should
include all investment assets, not just one class, such as bonds. Even if
the universe is confined to bonds, what is the appropriate market index?
Exhibit 3 shows the differences between two indexes over the 1966–84

EXHIBIT 3 A Comparison of Two International Indexes—Dollar
Denominated Total Return

	Index I	Index II	Difference
1966	4.14%	4.55%	−.41
1967	4.03	−2.02	6.05
1968	4.92	2.59	2.33
1969	.71	2.03	−1.32
1970	6.81	6.59	.22
1971	20.09	21.72	−1.63
1972	6.38	1.72	4.66
1973	9.25	5.59	3.66
1974	5.68	−1.18	6.86
1975	9.03	9.99	−.96
1976	11.52	10.37	1.15
1977	28.63	38.52	−9.89
1978	17.68	16.04	1.64
1979	−.15	−3.42	3.27
1980	2.68	11.98	−9.30
1981	−5.12	−4.92	−.20
1982	14.61	15.86	−1.25
1983	.39	2.94	−2.55
1984	−.90	−1.22	+.32
Average annual mean	7.10	6.80	
Monthly standard deviation of return	2.485	2.792	

period where Index I is based on equal weightings assigned to eight
foreign markets and Index II is based on the relative amounts of government debt outstanding. Because of the dominance of the Japanese and
British markets in the market capitalization index (accounting for more
than 50 percent combined), there are significant and frequent differences in returns between the two approaches, particularly on an annual
basis. In view of the special circumstances that pertain in each of these
countries, it is questionable whether the investor should be submitted to

such a weighting on an ongoing basis. In the case of both indexes, but particularly the equally weighted index, there is the additional complication of liquidity constraints in some markets that may prevent the investor from practically achieving a full investment position.

Specific investment objectives. A final drawback to a passive investment approach is that it removes any incorporation of specific investment objectives. The optimum portfolio will depend on the investment requirements of the investor. In some cases there may be a desire to tailor a portfolio so as to capitalize on the risk reduction capabilities of international investing, and in other cases incremental return should be emphasized. A passive approach treats all investors uniformly.

ACTIVE MANAGEMENT

A thorough understanding of the components of total return and their interrelationships is important to any international investor, but it is particularly important if active management is selected as the international investment technique. As discussed in Chapter 49, there are three factors in the return provided by international bonds—income, capital change, and currency. Of these, only income in local currency terms and the margin over the income bogey provided by U.S. alternatives are known initially, and even they are subject to change as exchange rates fluctuate. A positive yield advantage over alternative U.S. bonds will, over time, provide a cushion for deterioration in the domestic capital price or the currency relative to U.S. issues. By the same token, with time, a negative yield spread will have to be offset by relative appreciation of the domestic bond price or currency. This requirement may suggest that investment in lower-yielding foreign securities may necessitate a limited time horizon, since a longer time horizon demands continually increasing relative price or currency appreciation to offset the income disadvantage.

It is noteworthy that over the first 15 years of the period studied (1966–80), during which international bonds provided a higher return than U.S. bonds, the average income of international bonds was about 1 percent higher than in the United States. At the beginning of the period, the average yield of the eight foreign bond markets was 5.85 percent, whereas long United States rates were 4.5 percent. Over time that margin fluctuated, and narrowed as shown in Exhibit 4. By the end of 1980, U.S. rates were more than 1 percent higher than international rates. In the 1981–84 period, the yield spread averaged 138 basis points in favor of U.S. bonds. This income advantage, together with the appreciation of the dollar, were important in accounting for the more favorable investment performance of U.S. bonds—13.3 percent versus 2 percent for the international index. By year end 1984, the yield margin exceeded 200 basis points. For international bonds to achieve a return competitive

EXHIBIT 4 Domestic Government Yield Levels

	Average of International Bond Markets at Beginning of Year	U.S. Government Yields at Beginning of Year	Yield Spread (Basis Points)
1966	5.85%	4.49%	136
1967	6.08	4.59	149
1968	6.14	5.48	66
1969	6.33	5.97	36
1970	7.16	6.92	24
1971	7.42	6.42	100
1972	6.93	5.92	101
1973	7.32	5.95	137
1974	8.68	7.35	133
1975	10.21	8.13	208
1976	9.44	8.05	139
1977	9.08	7.20	188
1978	7.92	8.23	−31
1979	8.34	8.98	−64
1980	9.82	10.12	−30
1981	10.78	11.94	−116
1982	12.04	13.65	−161
1983	9.78	10.40	−62
1984	9.73	11.85	−212
1985	9.28	11.54	−226

with U.S. bonds in the future, this income disadvantage must be offset by higher currency appreciation or favorable movements in foreign domestic bond prices relative to U.S. bond prices.

The factors that have a bearing on currency fluctuation, the second component of return, are well known. By and large, most factors can be characterized as relating to one or more of the following:

1. The balance of payments and its circular relationship with exchange rates.
2. Inflation and interest-rate differentials, both current and expected.
3. Social and political developments.
4. Central bank intervention.

From a practical viewpoint, there are two main problems in using these factors to project currency trends. One relates to the analyst's ability accurately to perceive trends not already efficiently reflected in the present currency price. The second relates to the interaction of these factors and the ability to project which factors will predominate. As more fully pointed out in Chapter 49, the component of return provided by currency changes for an international bond index over long time periods has not been large, averaging −.5 percent for 1966–84, but becomes increasingly important as the time period is shortened. Breaking the 1966–84 period into four segments, the range of currency contribution increases to −9.6 percent to +5.4 percent. (See Exhibit 4 of Chapter 49.) For the one-year periods 1966–84, the range of currency contribution rises still further to −14.0 percent to +11.9 percent. (See Exhibit 5 of Chapter 49.) Currency changes can be even more significant for individual markets. Thus the international bond investor who opts for the active management approach must be willing to make judgments on foreign exchange.

The third component of return, domestic price movements, must be analyzed both absolutely and relative to expected U.S. movements. There are substantial differences between various markets regarding the extent of government influence on the level of interest rates. However, the common key variables affecting interest-rate movements are generally viewed to be the following:

1. Monetary policy, particularly with regard to exchange rates.
2. The level and direction of domestic inflation rates.
3. Demand for funds, which is often related to real GNP growth.
4. Supply of funds.
5. Fiscal policy and budget deficits.
6. Social and political developments.

The international bond investor must then assess these factors to make judgments on the likely direction of rates in each country. As in the United States, this assessment must distinguish between movements in short rates and long rates, which most often move in the same direction but not usually to the same extent. Interest-rate movements are typically magnified in the short-term area relative to long yield movements, with the degree of interest-rate movements for intermediate issues often somewhere in the middle. Projections of the extent of these movements can then be translated into possible price movements, and when coupled with income differentials, some judgments on appropriate maturity structure within each country can be made.

However, it is also important to view the maturity allocation of the portfolio as a whole. The 1980–84 experience reminds us of both the interrelationship between the interest-rate and currency levels and of the circular and interrelated nature of interest rates between countries with floating exchange rates. While domestic economic trends and apparent government desires would have suggested lower interest levels in a number of foreign economies, record high U.S. interest rates precluded lower rates abroad without precipitating even further foreign exchange deterioration. Increasingly, few projections of foreign interest-rate levels were made without reference to expectations for the United States. Only time will tell whether the increased interrelationship of all markets is a permanent change or a transitory one. A strong case can be made that it is transitory and precipitated by a rare and unusual event—extraordinarily high and volatile rates and prices in the largest bond market in the world as the U.S. economy attempted to break the inflationary spiral of the 1970s. In more normal times the pattern of differing social and political trends, monetary policy, inflation trends, and phases of the economic cycle may once again predominate.

Clearly then, an active approach to international bond management requires ongoing economic analysis and judgment to assess the prospective exchange rate and domestic price components of return. Even the most dedicated active manager is aware of the room for error in interest-rate and currency projections. Although a single economic forecast may suffice for an international economist, the portfolio manager must consider the alternatives should the preferred forecast prove to be wrong. Chapter 49 pointed out that the international bond expert had to deal not only with price changes resulting from interest-rate movements on differing maturities, but also with the impact of interest-rate movements on price for substantially different starting interest-rate levels. When currency changes and income levels are added, the problem is complicated further. For example, not even the most mathematically inclined bond specialist is likely to know intuitively whether the best one-year return is provided by a 7 percent, 10-year bond beginning at par with a 275-basis-point decline in yield and no currency change or a 14 percent, 20-year issue starting at par with a 25-basis-point decline in yield and a 10 percent currency gain. In both cases, the one-year returns are about equal at 27 percent. When the necessity for a variety of alternative currency and interest-rate forecasts is imposed, the problem is further magnified. Thus the active international bond manager quickly finds that the facility for simple computer modeling and sensitivity analysis may be required.

INTERNATIONAL BONDS—THEIR ROLE IN PORTFOLIO MANAGEMENT

The foregoing discussion focused on the case for and the techniques of active international bond management. A related issue is the role of international bonds in portfolio construction or management.

Traditionally, U.S. investors have viewed international bonds as an alternative to long U.S. bonds, if at all. There are two reasons for this. First, the U.S. investment community is bifurcated into two areas of specialization and expertise: stocks and bonds. This separation is reflected in the common division of portfolios into bonds and stocks, with the responsibility for investment management frequently divided. It is, therefore, natural that bond managers consider international bonds as part of their ken. Second, both international and domestic bonds share certain characteristics—most notably a fixed income stream. As shown in Exhibit 4 of Chapter 49, this income component proved to be the largest component of return over both intermediate and long-term periods.

Despite this frequent association, it is interesting to note the dissimilarities between international and domestic bonds. Both instruments have fixed income flows in local currency terms, but the income produced by foreign currency bonds when translated into dollars can be highly volatile. In addition, in the case of domestic bonds, their investment attraction in portfolio construction relative to stocks has traditionally been price stability and the income component of return. As was discussed in the prior section, income is only one of three components of foreign bond returns, and at any given time it may not represent the justification for purchasing foreign bonds.

It can be argued that foreign bonds at times are much more similar to international equities. Over short time periods, as seen in Exhibit 5 of Chapter 49, capital change and currency movements can dominate returns. It is these two components of return that are affected by the same economic factors the international equity manager must consider in the analysis of expected international equity returns. The exchange-rate movement is a direct common component, but those determinants of interest-rate movements—GNP growth, inflation prospects, fiscal and monetary policy, social and political developments, and supply of funds—are also considered in projecting price movements of the stock market or particular companies. In fact, the level of interest rates itself is of critical importance to the equity manager in assessing the appropriate discount rate. With all of these common denominators then, international bonds perhaps should be considered a direct alternative to international equities. This suggests that the use of international bonds should be considered within the context of an international balanced portfolio. Carrying this logic further, since both international equities and U.S. bonds are an alternative to U.S. equities, the transitive property suggests that international bonds, too, must be viewed as an alternative to U.S. equities.

The result of this argument is satisfying. In this day of investment specialization, all too often the investment process leads to acceptance of good returns relative to a particular bogey, without regard either to a broader spectrum of alternative returns or the absolute level of returns. It is not satisfactory for a long-term return on an actively managed international bond portfolio to be superior to a passively managed one if the absolute or real return over the inflation rate is not satisfactory or if alternative investment vehicles offer substantially better returns on a risk-adjusted basis. Between 1966 and 1984 international bonds provided an average annual converted dollar return of 7 percent: the return on 10-year U.S. bonds was 5.7 percent, and the CPI was around 6.6

percent. At the same time, U.S. equity returns (including dividends) were about 1 percent higher than the inflation rate and international equity returns converted to U.S. dollars were nearer to 10 percent. Relative to the alternatives, then, international bonds have provided a satisfactory return on a historical basis.

The long-term historical record is not sufficient to bestow on international bonds a permanent role in a portfolio of U.S. and foreign securities. A number of factors have changed over this period that had an important bearing on results in the last four years studied (13.3 percent U.S. return versus 2 percent international index return). Some of the factors may continue while some may reverse themselves completely. An assessment of prospective relative returns from international bonds and appropriate equity and U.S. bond alternatives must include consideration of the following:

1. In comparison with stocks, the relatively high level of starting interest rates.
2. In comparison with U.S. bonds, a starting yield about 2 percent lower than U.S. bonds, as opposed to an average 1 percent higher in the prior 1966–80 period.
3. In comparison with inflation, the starting level of interest rates relative to the long-term expected rate of inflation.
4. In comparison with U.S. investments of all types, the long-range judgment on the outlook of the dollar.

Investors considering international bonds must have a truly worldwide scope in assessing alternative prospective returns. The conclusions are not clear, and perhaps no final opinions can be drawn. In that event, perhaps a case for some international bond investments can be made simply on the basis of a diversification argument into a variety of asset classes. This is an acceptable rationale, as is an approach based on the reasoned belief that some of the factors leading to poor international bond results in the recent past will reverse, notably, a change in the currency trend against the dollar. The investor must avoid, however, blindly extrapolating these historical results into a world and investment environment that has changed dramatically in the 19-year period since 1966.

INTERNATIONAL BONDS—THEIR ROLE BY PORTFOLIO TYPE

The appropriate role of international bonds in a portfolio is in part a function of their investment characteristics relative to alternative assets (bonds or stocks) and in part a function of the investment objectives of the investor. Put simply, international bonds will play a different role in different kinds of portfolios.

Private employee benefit plans. The suitability of international bonds is probably the greatest in the case of private employee benefit plans. International investments in both stocks and bonds are generally viewed to be permitted under ERISA. In cases in which individual plan agreements prohibit international investing, amendment is frequently possible. A more common obstacle to international investing is emotion—an uneasiness attached to investing in a foreign security whose credit is not as well known as a comparable U.S. security and concern with vulnerability to sharp exchange-rate changes. These obstacles can be overcome with education regarding the investment risk-return characteristics of international bonds. Although the diversification characteristic of international bonds is of value to private pension plans, the typical plan characteristics of a long-term time horizon and improved total return are probably of paramount importance. International bond investing meshes well with these objectives. The reduced reliability of income flows from foreign pay bonds, both as to level and variability, is less of a deterrent to their use in private plans than in many other kinds of portfolios. Except in cases of mature plans where there is a net cash outflow, stipulated income requirements can usually be interpreted flexibly enough to accommodate foreign-pay bond investing.

Finally, foreign bond investments can be easily adapted to the investment structure of private plans. For example, in those cases in which the total portfolio has been divided into a core portfolio and special investment situations, the bulk of the portfolio may be effectively indexed and then above market return can be provided by small satellite portfolios. In situations of in-house management, although the complexity of foreign bond analysis may be too demanding for an in-house staff, a portion of a portfolio can easily be spun off for external international bond management without duplicating investment research and management effort.

Other pension plans. In many cases legal or political obstacles will prevent the use of international bonds in public funds and labor management or multiemployer funds.

Endowments and foundations. The suitability of international bonds in the investment of endowment and foundation portfolios will vary. When investment objectives focus on current income requirements, the use of international bonds will be limited, except as an equity substitute. In cases in which income requirements do not prevail, their use will depend on the same factors as in the preceding discussion under private employee benefit plans.

Individuals. In most cases direct investment in international bonds will play a limited role in individual portfolios. Income requirements, tax considerations, problems of custody, execution, and liquidity are likely to preclude effective active management of international bonds. These factors, which to some extent are matters of concern to all types of potential international investors, are discussed below.

THE OBSTACLES—PERCEIVED AND REAL

One of the common arguments used against international bond investing relates to perceived and real obstacles in dealing in foreign markets. Indeed international bond investing is more difficult than limiting oneself to the domestic U.S. market, but most concerns are surmountable, particularly given the opportunities available within this broader horizon.

Once a decision is made to invest internationally and to buy a certain bond market and currency, an appropriate vehicle must be identified. Thus international bond investors must have sufficient knowledge of the alternatives to select the appropriate type of issue.

Like investment in U.S.-dollar-denominated bonds, investments in foreign-pay bonds are divided into two classes as discussed in Chapter 49. One group includes domestic or internal issues that are obligations of domestic issuers, underwritten by domestic syndicates, and sold primarily within the particular country. The second group encompasses international bonds that are the equivalent of the Eurodollar and Yankee markets in the United States. Eurocurrency issues are underwritten by international syndicates and normally sold outside of the country of currency denomination. Foreign bonds, of which Yankee bonds are the U.S.-dollar version, are foreign issuers raising funds in a country and currency other than their own. These types of issues come under a variety of names ranging from the "bulldog" market for sterling-denominated foreign bonds to the "samurai" market for yen-denominated foreign bonds.

Like the U.S. market, a prime difference between domestic foreign-pay issues and international Eurocurrency and foreign credit bonds is that many domestic issues, when bought by foreigners, are subject to withholding tax by the host country. As pointed out in Chapter 49, the United States has tax treaties with a number of countries that reduce or eliminate these taxes, but they are still a factor to consider in selection of the investment vehicle. Methods of handling the withholding tax payments differ from country to country. For example, in Japan the 20 percent withholding tax rate on interest is reduced to 10 percent for U.S. investors by declaration of the selling dealer at the time of purchase. The Netherlands and Germany have no withholding tax on interest, and Canada has none on government issues and most other recently issued securities with original maturities of five or more years. Although the general rate of withholding on interest is 30 percent in the United Kingdom, a number of previously issued government securities are exempt from withholding tax when paid to non-United Kingdom residents who have made the appropriate filing. The withholding tax rates for most major bond markets and the reduction for U.S. residents under tax treaties are shown in Exhibit 2 of Chapter 49.

Although international equity investors are spared the vagaries of various interest calculation traditions, international bond investors must understand the variety of techniques and make adjustments to attain comparability. In most countries, bonds are traded at price plus accrued interest as in the United States. In the United Kingdom, however, security prices of bonds with maturities longer than five years include the accrued interest. Thus to calculate yield, the interest earned from the last payment date must be "stripped" from the price as in the case of preferred stocks. Adjustments in yield calculations are also required to equate the yields on bonds with annual coupons to the U.S. standard of semiannual payments. United Kingdom, Japanese, and Canadian interest on domestic issues is paid semiannually, but interest in most other domestic markets and in the Euromarkets is paid annually. Furthermore, yield calculations include a provision for compounding, be it annual or semiannual, but the standard Japanese method does not.

One factor that is regularly discussed as an obstacle in international equity investing is whether or not information on particular companies is adequate. This is not a real problem in the bond area, since there is a large supply of government paper available that allows one to invest internationally without having to evaluate the credit of particular companies. Relative to the income, currency, and capital change returns emanating from interest-rate movements, the gain to be added from selection of relatively undervalued corporate issues appears small.

Another key factor in the assessment of particular securities is marketability. Without exception, government securities in the domestic markets are more liquid than either corporate issues or the foreign type of securities. The United Kingdom gilt-edged market is renowned for its liquidity, and large holdings of government securities in Japan, Canada, and Germany are easily tradable. Euro DM bonds enjoy a reasonably liquid market, but Swiss franc foreign bonds at times trade in blocks no larger than 500,000 SF.

When an understanding of the tax situation in each market coupled with knowledge of the relative marketability of the various types of issues is joined with a comparison of yields and expectations, a decision can be made as to the appropriate investment vehicle.

Three additional factors that may cause some initial concern are custody of international securities, foreign exchange controls, and trading.

1. Custody. Some U.S. banks have improved substantially their ability to handle foreign-pay securities. Many have branches in a number of foreign cities, and others can arrange subcustodial relationships or utilize one of two book-entry clearing facilities for most Eurocurrency and foreign securities—Euroclear, managed by Morgan Guaranty Trust, and Cedel, owned by a consortium of banks around the world.

2. Foreign exchange controls. Foreign exchange controls remain a philosophical concern. In practice, they have rarely been imposed on foreign investors except to limit investment in securities of strong currencies to prevent further upward pressure on the currency. Still they are a risk that the international investor must consider and be willing to accept.

3. Execution. As in the U.S. market, there is no substitute for years of experience in dealing in particular markets to facilitate trades efficiently. However, in the past few years a number of foreign banks and brokerage firms have opened offices in the United States to accommodate U.S. investors. Additionally, several U.S. brokerage firms have expanded their abilities in this area so that execution of foreign trades has become easier for the U.S.-based investor. The normal period of time from trade to settlement varies between countries, but alternative arrangements can often be made if discussed before the transaction.

CONCLUSION

There is no question that international investing requires special expertise and acceptance of some uncertainties and structural impediments not required in investment in U.S. securities. However, it is these same factors that allow inefficiencies to exist, thereby providing the periodic potential for adding incremental return while reducing the overall volatility of a portfolio.

51

The Deutschemark Bond Market

Tran Q. Hung
Vice President
Merrill Lynch Capital Markets

There are two important reasons for international investors to take a new look at the Deutschemark (DM) fixed-income market at the time of this writing. First, after years of relentless appreciation, the dollar has begun to weaken. We expect the dollar to trend lower in the period ahead, mainly as a result of the decline in U.S. interest rates produced by a relaxation of the Federal Reserve's monetary policy and some effort to reduce the U.S. budget deficit. In the environment of a weaker dollar, we expect bonds denominated in the DM (or other DM-bloc currencies) to be among the best performing sectors of the international fixed-income markets.

Second, the German authorities have taken several steps since 1984 to liberalize the DM bond market, making it more attractive to international investors. One reason behind Germany's move, undoubtedly, is to remain competitive with other major financial centers in the United States, Japan and the United Kingdom which have gone through an extensive deregulation process in recent years. In addition, the situation which in the late 1970s caused the Bundesbank to strongly oppose any move to enhance the international investment and reserve currency role of the DM (namely, fear of a huge capital inflow that might have interfered with the central bank's tight monetary policy objectives) has been reversed recently. Due to high U.S. interest rates and the rising dollar, West Germany has suffered substantial net capital outflows in the past few years. Any move that could induce international investors to purchase more DM assets would help reduce this net capital outflow, allowing the Bundesbank more freedom to reduce domestic interest rates in the face of a post-war high unemployment rate in Germany.

Specifically, the German liberalization measures consist of the following:

1. A decision by the government to abolish the coupon tax (withholding tax) on interest income of nonresidents on domestic bonds, to be effective from August 1, 1984. Previously, the basic coupon tax rate was 25 percent for nonresidents from a nontax treaty country. This tax rate could have been reduced to as much as zero percent in many instances by application for refunds or tax credits by residents from countries with a tax treaty with West Germany.

2. On April 12, 1985, the Bundesbank released a statement on the issuance of Euro-Deutschemark bonds to become effective May 1, 1985. The statement permits all German banks, including legally independent foreign-owned domestic banks, to be lead managers of new Euro-DM bond issues. The only qualifying condition is that German-owned banks operating in the country of the foreign-owned bank in question be accorded reciprocal treatment. This agreement replaces the gentlemen's agreement of January 1980 according to which only German-owned banks were allowed to lead-manage Euro-DM bond issues. Also, in the place of a monthly new issue calendar approved by the Capital Market Subcommittee consisting of five leading German banks, lead managers are asked to inform the Bundesbank via telex by month-end of any intended Euro-DM issue (including private placements of more than DM 20 million) with a specific launch date during the subsequent calendar month. The notification should also contain the issue's terms and conditions, including the issuer's name, amount, final maturity, and the form and type of placement.

3. The Bundesbank's April 1985 statement also authorized a wide range of instruments which heretofore have not been available in the Euro-DM bond market. These included floating-rate notes, zero-coupon bonds (and original discount issues in general), convertible bonds, bonds with equity warrants, currency option bonds, dual currency bonds (or any currency swap-related bonds). In the case of foreign currency bonds with a Deutschemark option, or dual currency bonds where interest or principal payments are made in DM, it will be sufficient if a German bank is a co-lead manager of the underwriting syndicate. However, the Bundesbank reiterated its long-standing objection to the introduction of DM money market instruments such as certificates of deposit or units of DM money market funds. It also required that new publicly offered Euro-DM bonds must have a maturity of not less than five years and DM private placements a maturity of not less than three years.

These liberalization measures are likely to enhance the attractiveness of the DM bond market by opening up the primary market to more participants, making it easier to deal in the secondary market, and diversifying the range of instruments available to borrowers and investors.

This chapter will present an overview and anatomy of the DM bond market. It will then proceed to discuss the investment opportunities in the newly introduced instruments of the Euro-DM market and to reexamine the traditional trading relationships within the fixed-rate DM bond market in the aftermath of the coupon tax's removal. The chapter will then analyze other relevant factors having a bearing on the performance of the DM bond market, such as the orientation and operations of fiscal and monetary policies. The conclusion will touch on areas where further liberalization actions may take place in the future.

ANATOMY OF THE DEUTSCHEMARK BOND MARKET

The German bond market is the third largest in the world after the U.S. and Japanese bond markets. In terms of par value outstanding at the end of 1984, the DM bond market amounted to about $300 billion, accounting for slightly more than 6 percent of the world bond market. In comparison, the U.S. dollar bond market was close to $2.7 trillion (almost 57 percent of the world market) while the Japanese yen bond market was about $780 billion (17 percent of the total).

At the end of March 1985, the total outstanding value of the DM bond market was DM 982 billion. Bank bonds, including mortgage bonds, communal bonds and other bank bonds, comprised the largest segment of the DM bond market with an outstanding value of DM 639 billion, making up 65 percent of the total market. Mortgage bonds are issued by private mortgage banks to finance mortgage loans. Under the Mortgage Bond Act, mortgage bonds are subject to a "matching cover" requirement: they must be covered by mortgage loans of at least the same face value and yielding at least the same interest. Communal bonds are issued by public-law banks to finance loans to various public authorities at the Federal, state and local levels. Communal bonds must also be covered in a similar fashion by the public loans they finance. These two types of bonds are very popular in Germany, judging by their outstanding volumes. Public sector bonds, comprised mainly of bonds issued by the Federal government (Bundesobligationen), Federal Railways (Bundesbahn), Federal Post Office (Bundespost), State governments (Lander) and local authorities (Gemeinden), had a 24.5 percent market share with an outstanding value of DM 241 billion. Euro-DM bonds accounted for another 10.2 percent of the market with DM 100 billion outstanding (see Chart 1). Compared with the structure of the DM bond market at the end of 1980, public sector bonds have increased their market share while the relative size of the Euro-DM sector has shrunk moderately, reflecting the slower pace of new Euro-DM bond issuance in recent years.

Chart 2 shows the maturity structure of the domestic DM bond market. Short-term bonds (with remaining maturity of four years or less)

CHART 1 Structure of the Deutschemark Bond Market (as of March 1985, percentage share)

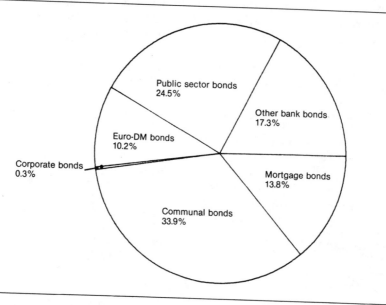

CHART 2 Maturity Structure of the Domestic DM Bond Market (as of March 1985, percentage share)

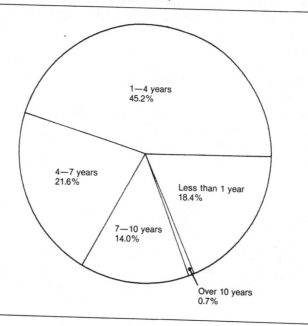

dominate the market with a 63.5 percent share. Long-term bonds (in the German context, with remaining maturity between 7 and 10 years) make up only 14 percent of the whole market. The small amount of bonds longer than 10 years is the remnant of 30-year mortgage bonds which were issued in earlier periods and which are in the process of being redeemed.

Federal government securities (Bundesobligationen) account for more than 75 percent of the public sector bond market (see Table 1).

TABLE 1 Outstanding Volume of Public Sector Bonds
(billions of Deutschemark)

	Total	Federal Gov't	Federal Railways	Federal Post	State Gov't	Local Authorities	Others
1973	48.7	18.5	8.9	10.2	9.2	0.9	1.0
1975	68.2	34.2	9.9	10.8	11.8	0.8	0.8
1980	130.7	94.3	15.2	8.7	12.2	0.3	0
1984	228.1	174.5	17.1	14.6	21.6	0.2	0
1985 : 3	240.7	186.7	17.5	14.6	21.7	0.2	0

Bonds issued by the Federal Railways Authority (Bundesbahn) and the Federal Post Office (Bundespost) account for another 7.3 percent and 6.1 percent, respectively. These three kinds of bonds trade interchangeably at the same yield level and therefore are equivalent to an investor. They are commonly referred to as Bund/Bahn/Post bonds. Bonds issued by the state governments (Lander) make up 9 percent of the total and their volume has risen rapidly in recent years.

The public authorities in Germany also raise a substantial amount of funds through bank loans, virtually all of them in the form of Schuldscheindarlehen. At the end of last year, public sector Schuldscheindarlehen totaled DM 520 billion, with the state and Federal governments being the major borrowers (see Chart 3). Schuldscheindarlehen issued by private sector borrowers are estimated to amount to more than DM 500 billion, making the total Schuldschein market larger than DM 1 trillion in size. Schuldscheindarlehen are not securities but debt certificates providing evidence of a loan agreement between a "first lender" bank and a borrower. As such, they are not subject to the various regulations governing German securities (no withholding and securities transfer taxes, no authorization needed for new issues, etc.). Investors in Schuldschein, essentially, take participations in the loan and thereby acquire contractual claims on the borrower. An investor can reassign his Schuldschein to other investors but the number of reassignments is limited to three or four times and it usually requires the consent of the borrower.

CHART 3   Schuldscheindarlehen Issued by Public Authorities (as of December 1984, percentage share)

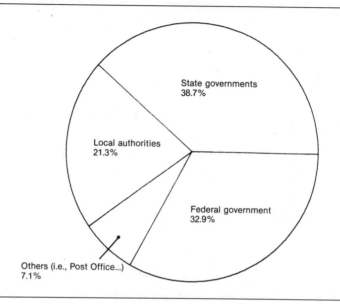

State governments
38.7%

Local authorities
21.3%

Federal government
32.9%

Others (i.e., Post Office...)
7.1%

Chart 4 portrays the borrower's profile in the Euro-DM bond market. Sovereign and supranational borrowers dominate this market with 64 percent of total outstanding volume. The remainder is made up by corporate nonbank and bank borrowers.

Table 2 shows the annual gross new issue volume and redemption in different sectors of the DM bond market. The redemption of maturing bonds in those sectors has been quite substantial, especially in the Euro-DM market, helping to facilitate the absorption of new paper.

TABLE 2   Gross Issuance and Redemption (in parentheses) of Deutschemark Bonds (billions of Deutschemark)

		Bank Bonds				Public	Euro
	Total	Mortgage Bonds	Communal Bonds	Other Bk. Bonds	Corporate Bonds	Sector Bonds	DM Bonds
1973	50.0	5.8	8.5	21.8	0.01	9.9	4.0
	(20.5)	(1.8)	(3.9)	(7.3)	(0.6)	(5.5)	(1.4)
1975	83.6	8.0	30.9	18.2	0.4	18.6	7.5
	(28.7)	(2.6)	(6.9)	(11.9)	(0.5)	(5.2)	(1.5)
1980	152.5	13.9	51.6	44.2	0.02	27.9	14.9
	(98.4)	(7.9)	(26.9)	(33.5)	(1.3)	(22.9)	(5.9)
1984	246.5	21.9	68.9	84.6	0.6	51.4	19.1
	(165.7)	(16.7)	(49.1)	(74.2)	(0.8)	(14.4)	(10.4)

CHART 4 Structure of the Euro-Deutschemark Bond Market (as of March 1985, percentage share)

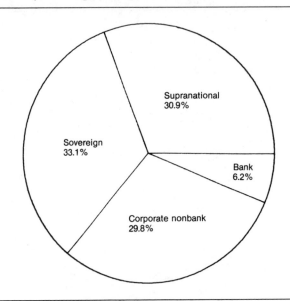

Supranational
30.9%

Sovereign
33.1%

Bank
6.2%

Corporate nonbank
29.8%

CHART 5 Ownership Structure of the Domestic DM Bond Market (as of December 1984, percentage share)

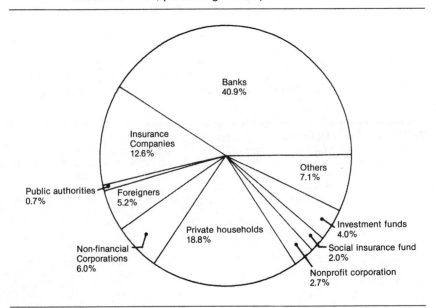

Banks
40.9%

Insurance
Companies
12.6%

Others
7.1%

Public authorities
0.7%

Foreigners
5.2%

Investment funds
4.0%

Non-financial
Corporations
6.0%

Private households
18.8%

Social insurance fund
2.0%

Nonprofit corporation
2.7%

In terms of the ownership structure of the domestic DM bond market, banks have been the major investor holding DM 348 billion or 40.9 percent of the market at the end of 1984 (see Chart 5). Private households (18.8 percent) and insurance companies (12.6 percent) are the next two important groups of investors. At the end of last year, foreign investors held DM 44 billion or 5.2 percent of the domestic DM bond market. This represents a slight increase from a 4.5 percent share at the end of 1983. (At the end of 1984, foreign investors held a total of DM 430 billion of DM-denominated securities in the domestic and Euro-DM markets.)

THE NEWLY INTRODUCED INSTRUMENTS IN THE EURO-DM MARKET

The newly authorized instruments have significantly enhanced the diversity of the Euro-DM bond market which hitherto had only offered fixed-rate bonds. As a consequence, investors can now look at different segments of the Euro-DM market to satisfy their various needs.

Floating-Rate Notes (FRNs)

Patterned after the hugely successful Eurodollar FRN market, DM floating-rate notes offer investors, for the first time, something close to a marketable money market instrument. (Even though an FRN is a long-dated security, the fact that its coupon is refixed every three or six months at a spread over the London interbank rate keeps its price quite stable. Consequently, in the Eurodollar market investors have come to treat FRNs as money market instruments.) For a variety of institutional reasons, West Germany does not have a well-developed money market. Commercial banks fund themselves with time deposits on which they have to maintain required reserves with the Bundesbank. Banks satisfy their monthly reserve requirements by borrowing from the Bundesbank through its various facilities such as the Lombard window or securities repurchase facilities. The interbank market is very active at the very short end (call money) to help banks bridge over their reserve deficiencies. The Bundesbank has traditionally opposed the development of any open money market instruments such as marketable certificates of deposit (CDs) on the grounds that first, Germany never has any interest-rate ceilings regulation similar to Regulation Q in the United States; and second, since CDs are classified as securities under German law, they are not subject to reserve requirements—hence their introduction might complicate the Bundesbank's control of money supply growth. Concerns about monetary control also led the Bundesbank to prohibit the sale of short-term German securities to foreigners (for many years, "short-term" was defined as having less than four years remaining to maturity. In early 1980, this period was reduced to one year. This restriction was then dropped in 1981.)

For foreign investors, who have been confined at the short end to the DM deposit market, Deutschemark FRNs have added greatly to their flexibility to play the DM yield curve. For example, investors can position themselves defensively when the outlook for the DM bond market is bearish by staying in FRNs; yet they have much more flexibility to extend maturities when it is opportune to do so. Similarly, foreign investors who like the prospects for the DM yet don't like the German bond market can keep their funds in FRNs. Owing to these attributes, the initial crop of Euro-DM FRNs was quite successful. Forming a natural investor base for these floaters are the international banks which have been major purchasers of Eurodollar FRNs. As prime quality Eurodollar floaters are now trading below LIBOR, these banks can earn a good spread buying Euro-DM FRNs with a basic margin of ⅟₁₆ to ⅛ over DM LIBOR and fund the positions in the Euro-DM interbank market.

Eventually, when the Euro-DM FRN market is sufficiently developed, it can give rise to interesting trading opportunities. One possibility is to swap FRNs by the same issuers between the Euro-DM and Eurodollar markets. As has been demonstrated in the fixed-rate bond

CHART 6 Yield Spread: Three-Month Euro-DM Less Three-Month Frankfurt Interbank Rate (basis points)

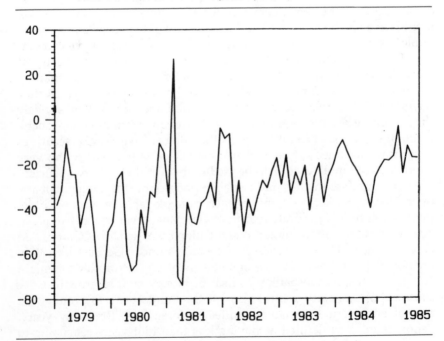

market, issues by the same borrower can trade differently in different markets due to different supply and demand conditions as well as different credit perceptions. This differentiation is also true in the FRN market. For example, the new Euro-DM floaters for Dresdner Bank and Sweden currently trade around 4.9 and 12.7 basis point discounted margins over DM LIBOR whereas their counterparts in the Eurodollar FRN market trade around 0 and 5.3 basis points, respectively, over dollar LIBOR. Thus investors can pick up incremental returns swapping from Eurodollar to Euro-DM FRNs for these names. The currency or interest-rate risk is limited in this kind of swap because most investors fund their FRN investments in the interbank market.

Another potentially active trading strategy emanates from the volatility of the yield differential between Euro-DM and domestic interbank rates (see Chart 6). Euro-DM deposit rates are normally lower than domestic (i.e., Frankfurt) interbank rates because Euro-DM deposits taken up by German banks are subject to the Bundesbank minimum reserve requirements (currently 7.15 percent) while domestic interbank liabilities are free of such reserve requirements. Consequently, the fluctuation of the Euro-DM deposit bid rate is bounded by the inward and outward arbitrage limits defined as follows[1]:

$$FIB_B (1 - RR_{EDM}) - EDM_S \leq EDM_B \leq FIB_O$$

FIB_B or $_O$: Frankfurt Interbank rate, bid or offer side
RR_{EDM} : Reserve requirement on Euro-DM deposits taken on by German banks
EDM_B or $_O$: Euro-DM deposit rate, bid or offer side
EDM_S : Bid/offer spread on Euro-DM deposits

The left-hand side represents the inward arbitrage limit, the right-hand side the outward arbitrate limit. Within these limits, the Euro-DM/domestic interbank rate differential has fluctuated a lot as a result of arbitrage activities by banks and changing demand/supply conditions in each market. Since Euro-DM FRNs are based on the Euro-DM deposit rate, their prices should be sensitive to the spread between Euro-DM and domestic interbank rates: prices are likely to fall when the spread widens and vice versa. When the domestic FRN market develops based on the Frankfurt interbank rate, the relative price movement between Euro-DM and domestic floaters will likely give rise to trading opportunities somewhat similar to those between LIBOR and T-bill based dollar FRNs.

German investors, particularly individual investors, have also been enthusiastic about Euro-DM FRNs. To them, these are attractive money

---

[1] See Ian H. Giddy, "EuroCurrency Arbitrage," in *Eurodollars and International Banking,* eds. Paolo Savona and George Sutija; (New York: St. Martin's Press, 1985).

market instruments, easily marketable and yielding a positive spread above the offered side of the Euro-DM interbank rate. At times, the Euro-DM interbank rate can be higher than the domestic time deposit rate, as has been the case for most of the past one and one-half years (see Chart 7). The domestic interest in FRNs has prompted several German

CHART 7 Yield Spread : Six-Month Euro-Deutschemark Less Six-Month Bank Time Deposit Rate (basis points)

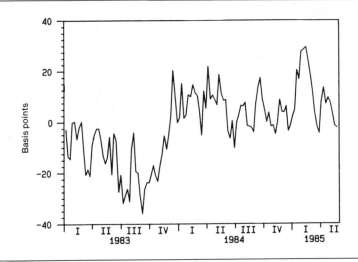

banks to actively consider issuing floaters, with coupon rates referenced to the Frankfurt interbank rate. This will open up a very advantageous source of long-term finances to German banks which have been major borrowers in the domestic bond market. As the German yield curve is normally positively sloped (long-term bond yield and short-term inter-bank rate differential has averaged about 150 basis points in the past year—see Chart 8), it is obviously cheaper to fund by FRNs than by long-term bank bonds. A major obstacle, however, currently stands in the way of any swift development of the German FRN market, espe-cially as far as individual investors are concerned. That is the stock exchange turnover tax (or securities transfer tax) which currently im-poses a 0.25 percent tax on nonbroker transactions in domestic securities and 0.10 percent on foreign securities listed on German stock exchanges. This tax has sharply reduced the incremental yield FRNs have to offer German investors. It also discourages active trading which may at times be an important feature in the management of a FRN portfolio.

CHART 8 Yield Spread : Ten-Year German Government Bonds Less
Three-Month Interbank (basis points)

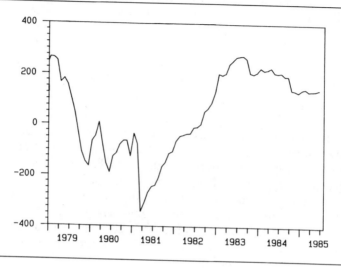

Zero Coupon Bonds

While zero coupon securities have gained widespread popularity in the
dollar bond market (both domestic and Euro), they were not available in
the DM market before. Consequently their introduction has been welcomed by DM investors who have wanted to take advantage of the
special attributes of zero coupon securities. Basically, these include:

1. The ability for long-term investors such as pension funds and
    insurance companies to lock in returns and avoid reinvestment
    rate risks.
2. The single payment feature of zero coupon instruments makes
    them very versatile to a whole range of portfolio applications
    such as dedication, immunization, etc. These passive portfolio
    management techniques having gained popularity in the United
    States, have begun to spread to other countries.
3. Finally, zero coupon instruments have the longest duration in
    any market, making their prices the most volatile. This charac-
    teristic is particularly desirable in a generally bullish bond mar-
    ket, but quite unattractive when interest rates are rising.

To German taxable investors, however, the appeal of zero coupon
bonds is limited somewhat by their current tax treatment. According to a
Ministry of Finance announcement on January 24, 1985, the price accretion on zero coupon bonds is no longer regarded as capital gains, free of

tax. Instead, the accrued interest income over the holding period is calculated, and is treated as taxable income. In contrast to the practice in the dollar market according to which zero coupon bonds are offered at a deep discount, DM zeros are usually offered at a par price and with a redemption value above par.

Euro-DM Convertible Bonds/Equity Linked Bonds

Even though Euro-DM convertible bonds have been available before, the Bundesbank's April 24 announcement formally recognized equity-linked issues (bonds with warrants exercisable into common shares of the borrowing company). Because equity-linked bonds offer investors the opportunity to benefit from any rally in the borrower's stock market, they usually carry a coupon rate three or four percentage points below the current level of coupons on full-coupon bonds. These low coupon instruments are attractive to German investors as the coupon income subject to taxation is low compared with both full-coupon issues and zero coupon bonds. This helped account for the substantial purchases of Euro-DM equity-linked bonds by German residents in late 1984 and early 1985.

Dual Currency Bonds/Bonds with Currency Swaps

The Bundesbank's easing move has lifted a ban on dual currency bonds which prevented the practice from spreading to the DM market in 1983. Early that year, dual currency bonds were introduced in the Swiss franc market whereby foreign bond issues could be denominated, and coupon payments made in the franc but payment of principal would be made in U.S. dollars, at a predetermined exchange rate. These instruments offered investors an opportunity to benefit if the Swiss franc depreciates against the dollar by more than the fixed exchange rate during the life of the bond. Since the dollar was generally strong during this period, dual currency bonds were welcomed by investors who wanted to speculate against the Swiss franc. Bonds linked to a foreign currency or offered with currency options have also been used in other markets. Prior to the recent liberalization move permitting them to issue Euroyen bonds, Japanese companies used to float yen-linked Eurodollar bonds as a means to raise long-term Euroyen funds. Eurosterling bonds have been issued with investors' options to take payments in dollars, essentially offering a currency option with a longer life than exchange-traded contracts.

A dual currency bond denominated in DM, which pays interest in DM and repays principal in dollars (at a fixed exchange rate relative to the nominal DM amount) will normally have a lower yield than a straight Eurodollar bond but a higher yield than a straight Euro-DM bond. The reason is that investors have to be compensated for the risk of taking payment of principal in dollars instead of DM while borrowers welcome the opportunity to borrow at a rate lower than dollar debt but with principal repayment already fixed in dollars and with the coupon payment stream in DM easily hedged in the forward market. In addition, the implicit DM/U.S. dollar conversion rate is usually higher (DM appreciation) than the current spot rate, but lower than the break-even exchange rate implied by the yield differential between the Eurodollar and Euro-DM bonds. For a DM-based investor, a dual currency bond is superior to a Euro-DM issue if the DM remains weaker at the bond's maturity than the implicit DM/dollar conversion rate adjusted further upward by the yield premium that the dual currency bond enjoys over the Euro-DM issue. If the DM appreciates strongly past the break-even exchange rate, the dual currency bond will start to outperform the Eurodollar issue as the DM coupon stream will be translated at an advantageous DM/dollar exchange rate. Thus from the point of view of a single currency investor, depending on his expectation for the DM/dollar exchange rate, a dual currency bond can offer some good value. But for multi-currency investors, it has been pointed out that it is always feasible to construct a portfolio of straight Eurodollar and Euro-DM bonds that will always perform at least as well as the dual currency bond and usually better than the dual currency issue.[2] Consequently, unless the coupon rate and implicit conversion rate offered on a dual currency issue are set correctly, a multi-currency investor can always do better by constructing his own portfolio of Eurodollar and Euro-DM bonds.

Of more interest to prospective borrowers is the permission to issue DM bonds with currency swap arrangements. This decision greatly enhances the already popular currency swap market, in which borrowers issue bonds in the market where they command a comparative advantage and swap the proceeds into another currency which they need, at competitive costs. As a consequence, the range of financing sources has been enlarged for both German and foreign borrowers.

STRAIGHT DM BONDS AFTER WITHHOLDING TAX REPEAL

Since August 1, 1984, the removal of the German withholding tax has enhanced the attractiveness of the domestic bond market to foreign investors. As a consequence, the trading relationship among various sectors of the DM bond market has been changed in the process. This should be kept in mind when investors assess relative values in the DM bond market.

---

[2] See *Currency and Bond Market Trends*, Vol. I, No. 28 and 29; Merrill Lynch Co., 1985.

Euro-DM versus Government Bonds

Euro-DM bonds used to be of particular interest to foreign investors since they were free of withholding tax and maturity restrictions which were imposed on foreign purchases of domestic securities. Euro-DM issues are also in bearer form, which may be of interest to some investors seeking anonymity. As a consequence of the predominant foreign interest in Euro-DM bonds, the yield spread between Euro-DM and German government bonds usually moved inversely with the strength of the Deutschemark (see Chart 9). The appreciation of the DM normally

CHART 9 Ten-Year Euro-Deutschemark and Government Bond Yield Spread and DM/U.S. Dollar Exchange Rate

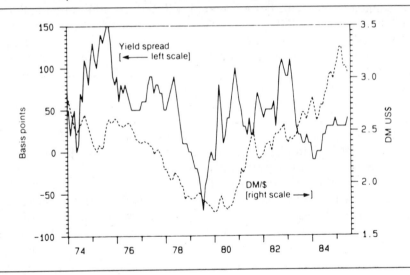

attracted foreign investors into DM bonds in general, but particularly into the Euro-DM bond market, narrowing the Euro-DM/government yield spread. Conversely, when the DM weakened, net selling or lack of buying by foreigners caused Euro-DM bonds to underperform the government sector. However, the yield spread was prevented from widening too far by buying interest from German residents who did not have any risk of currency losses and who could pick up yields swapping from domestic to Euro-DM bonds. This is confirmed by Chart 10 which shows that German residents increased their net purchases of Euro-DM bonds whenever this spread widened, and vice versa. In the past 10 years, the inverse relationship between the Euro-DM/government spread and the DM was observed both during periods when German bond yields fell and when they increased, confirming the importance of foreign investors with currency concerns in the Euro-DM market (see Chart 11).

CHART 10   Net Purchases of Euro-Deutschemark Bonds By German Residents and the 10-Year Euro-DM and Government Bonds Yield Spread

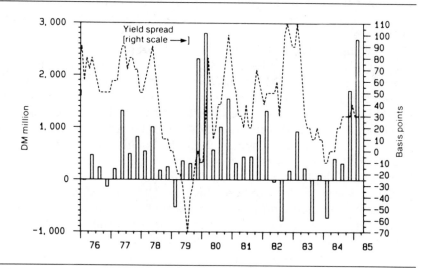

CHART 11   Ten-Year Euro-Deutschemark and Government Bond Yield Spread and the West German Government Bond Yield

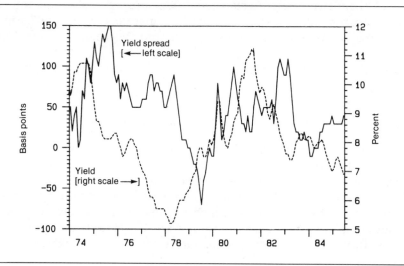

The trading relationship described above has changed since late 1984, now that the German withholding tax has been abolished. For example, in the first two months of 1985 when the DM was battered by the dollar in the foreign exchange markets, the Euro-DM/government spread narrowed unexpectedly by more than 50 basis points, a big move in this yield spread. Then since early March to the present when the dollar fell by 20 percent from its record level of DM 3.47 reached in late February, the spread widened. The breakdown in the traditional relationship between the DM exchange value and the Euro-DM/government spread suggests that while foreigners continue to base their investment in DM bonds on exchange-rate expectations, they don't have to rely as much on the Euro-DM sector like they had to before. Now that they are free of withholding tax, German domestic bonds, particularly government bonds, offer foreign investors a much bigger market with more liquidity and depth than the Euro-DM market was ever able to offer.

The relative performance of the Euro-DM and government bond markets has become a function of movement in German interest rates. As the price reaction in the smaller and relatively illiquid Euro-DM market lags behind the price movements in the much deeper government market, the Euro-DM/government yield spread can be expected to widen when German interest rates decline, and to narrow when rates rise. This is what has happened since mid-1984. During the second half of 1984, when German government bond yields fell from a high of 8.08 percent to 6.97 percent, the Euro-DM/government yield spread widened from 20 basis points to 50 basis points. In the first two months of 1985 when German bond yields backed up to 7.55 percent, the spread narrowed by about 40 basis points. Since then, as the German bond market has continued to rally, the spread has opened up again. An investment implication of this new trading relationship is that Euro-DM bonds should be viewed as more stable and therefore a defensive instrument than government issues. Consequently, if investors expect the German bond market to rally, they should switch into government bonds. Conversely, when interest rates are expected to increase modestly or when the outlook becomes uncertain, they should move into the Euro-DM sector.

German Bank Bonds versus Government Bonds

Even though bank bonds comprise the largest segment of the domestic DM bond market, many international investors have not paid much attention to this sector, partly because of the withholding tax problem before it was removed, but mainly because of the illiquidity of the secondary market. The market for the bank bonds is dominated by German institutional investors who buy these securities at issue and hold them till maturity. Consequently, secondary trading in these bonds is very thin. In their favor, bank bonds usually yield more than government securities. The bank bond/government yield spread usually fluctuates between 10 and 20 basis points, but at times it can widen to 40 basis points or more (see Chart 12). At these wide spread levels, bank bonds

CHART 12   Yield Spread: Ten-Year German Bank Bond Less German Government (basis points)

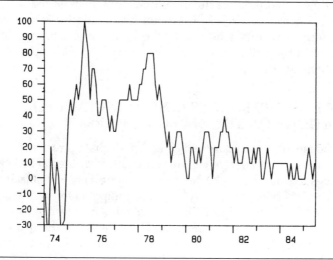

offer an attractive alternative to government issues on a yield basis as well as on a total return basis. In addition, the size of the bank bond market and that of individual issues is big enough to accommodate deals in a size which could prove difficult to accomplish in the Euro-DM bond market. Finally, the liquidity problem of the secondary market may eventually be improved, if the German bank bond market is able to attract more foreign participation whose investment attitude is likely to be different from the buy-and-hold attitude of the German institutional investors.

Schuldscheindarlehen versus Government Bonds

The abolishment of the German withholding tax is also likely to reduce the unique advantage of Schuldschein to foreigners. Foreign borrowers, mostly the European supranational institutions and governments, used to raise DM funds using this vehicle because of the relative ease in issuing Schuldschein and because they were able to do so in size. International investors were attracted to Schuldschein because of their relatively high yield (usually 50 basis points over bonds of comparable maturity and credit quality) which was free of withholding tax. The loss of the tax benefit enjoyed by Schuldschein is consequently focusing investors' attention to the limited marketability of Schuldschein. Investors invest in Schuldschein by obtaining a letter of agreement from the first lender bank. Subsequently, participations in a Schuldschein can be transferred to other investors, but the transfer usually requires the consent of the borrower and the number of assignments is limited to three or four times (two times in the case of Schuldschein issued by the Federal government). As a result, the Schuldschein market is more suitable to long-term investors who want to commit large amounts of funds without disturbing the market and who wish to pick up yields over government bonds.

IMPACT OF THE BUNDESBANK MONETARY POLICY OPERATIONS ON THE DM BOND MARKET

The Bundesbank's monetary policy stance exerts a direct and powerful impact on German short and long-term interest rates. The operating techniques the Bundesbank uses to implement its policy objectives also impact the DM bond market by providing impetus to trading activities on a short-term basis. Since February 1985, the Bundesbank has moved away from its reliance on official lending rates (i.e., the discount and Lombard rates) to guide movements in German interest rates. One drawback to the old approach was that the discount and Lombard rates had received so much visibility as signals of major policy moves that the Bundesbank only changed them infrequently and with a great deal of caution and deliberation. This institutional problem had reduced the flexibility of the Bundesbank in responding to developments in the money and foreign exchange markets. It had also resulted in heavy usage of the Lombard facility by commercial banks (borrowing from the Bundesbank using eligible securities as collateral), especially when the call money rate exceeded the Lombard rate. Under the new approach, the Lombard facility has been restored to its original function as a short-term (overnight) lending-of-last-resort facility by the fact that the Lombard rate has been kept substantially higher than the current call money rate. As such, the Lombard rate has become the ceiling on the movements of the call money rate. At the other extreme, any excess liquidity that develops in the banking system will be soaked up by the Bundesbank which stands ready to offer three-day Federal Treasury bills to banks at a predetermined rate which is much lower than the Lombard rate. The T-bill selling rate thus constitutes the floor of the tunnel within which the call money rate fluctuates (see Chart 13). The call money rate is most sensitive to the liquidity condition of the banking system as banks use the overnight segment of the interbank market to meet their minimum monthly reserve requirements with the Bundesbank.

CHART 13   Bundesbank Monetary Policy Operations

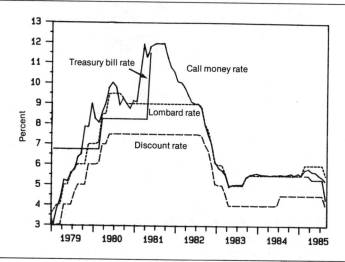

Under its new approach, the Bundesbank will focus on fine-tuning the availability of liquidity to the banking system, directly influencing the movement of the call money rate and sending a signal to the market as to the near-term policy intention of the central bank. Since February 1985, the Bundesbank has utilized a variety of liquidity measures in implementing this operating procedure. The most frequently used method to add temporary liquidity to the money market is via the securities repurchase facility. Using a tender system, the Bundesbank invites banks to submit bids for funds, normally for 30 days but occasionally for 62 days. The Bundesbank also usually announces a minimum rate for the tender, reserving the opportunity to look at the amount of the bids and their rates before deciding on the size and rate of the repo facility. If the new repo facility supplies more funds to the market and/or at a lower rate than the expiring facility, the Bundesbank can be inferred as wishing to ease monetary conditions and foster lower interest rates. The reverse holds true if the Bundesbank wants to firm up the money market. The Bundesbank can also make a more forceful statement of its near-term policy intention by announcing, instead of the minimum rate of the tender, a fixed rate which is higher or lower than the previous repo rate or the current level of call money rate. Recently, there have been several instances when concurrent repo facilities with their expiring dates staggered were used so that the Bundesbank had a frequent opportunity to provide liquidity and therefore direction to the market. To meet a sudden and very temporary shortage of liquidity, the Bundesbank can also shift deposits of the Federal authorities on its books to the commercial banks under the authority of section 17 of the Bundesbank

TABLE 3 Liquidity Policy Measures of the Bundesbank (average level during period, billions of Deutschemark)

	Unused Rediscount Facility	Lombard Borrowing	Balance of Short-Term Liquidity Measures
1974	4.1	2.8	0
1978	12.7	1.6	0
1980	4.4	6.5	8.2
1981	3.1	4.0	12.2
1982	6.6	4.1	12.4
1983	3.3	5.1	15.7
1984	4.3	5.4	23.4
1985 : 1Q	3.1	3.7	34.1
1985 : 2Q	3.4	0.6	35.5

Act. As illustrated in Table 3, the role of these short-term liquidity measures has increased noticeably while the borrowing by banks at the Lombard window has shrunk to a negligible level.

The liquidity measures discussed above are temporary in nature, allowing the Bundesbank to continuously adjust the desirable level of liquidity in the banking system. When the Bundesbank judges that economic circumstances require a permanent addition of liquidity, it can raise the rediscount quotas of the banks. This quota sets the limit on the amount of 90-day bills that eligible banks can discount at the Bundesbank. This amount is usually taken up in full by the banks as the discount rate is substantially lower than the call money rate or the Lombard rate. However, due to the revolving nature of the rediscount facility, a small amount (DM 2–3 billion) always remains unused. However, after the one-time impact of the rediscount quota increase is absorbed, this facility and the discount rate itself do not influence day-to-day trading conditions very much.

In short, the Bundesbank's liquidity approach to monetary policy is likely to produce a flexible German money market, and through arbitrages along the yield curve, a flexible bond market. In addition, investors will have more opportunity to gauge the Bundesbank's policy intentions by monitoring its money market operations.

The Bundesbank has also acted to smooth out fluctuations in the German bond market by its buying or selling of government bonds in the open market. However, owing to statutory limitations and the modest volume of bond holdings and daily bond market operations (see Table 4) the Bundesbank does not have the authority or the capability to influence DM bond yields in this manner. According to Chart 14, there has been no discernible relationship between the movement of German government bond yields and the net purchase or net sales of bonds by the Bundesbank.

TABLE 4   Securities Holdings of the Bundesbank (billions of Deutschemark)

End of Period	Federal and State Government Bonds	Bundesbank/Post Bonds
1980	2.3	1.6
1981	2.3	1.4
1982	3.8	1.6
1983	5.8	2.0
1984	2.9	1.4
1985 : 6	2.4	1.3

CHART 14   Public Sector Bond Sales/Purchases by the Bundesbank and the 10-Year Government Bond Yield

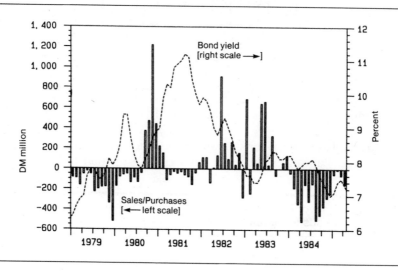

IMPACT OF FISCAL POLICY ON THE DM BOND MARKET

The stance of fiscal policy as measured by the public sector deficit as percentage of GNP has a direct impact on long-term interest rates. An increase in the public sector deficit (assuming there is no monetary accommodation) would tend to drive up interest rates by stimulating economic activities and by the government competing with the private sector for funds in the capital markets. The reverse takes place when the size of the deficit shrinks, and this is what has happened in West Germany in the past few years (see Chart 15). As the German government

CHART 15 Ten-Year German Government Bond Yield and Public Sector Deficits as a Percentage of Nominal GNP

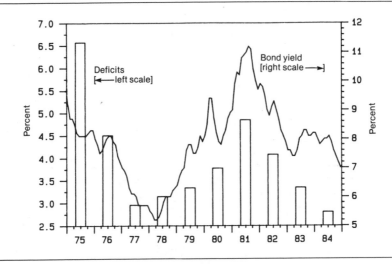

remains committed to consolidate its public finances, the fiscal policy factor continues to be positive for the DM bond market in the period ahead.

On a more technical consideration, the redemption and interest payment on outstanding public sector bonds is estimated to outpace the

CHART 16 Flow of Funds in Public Sector Bond Market: Gross Issuance versus Redemption plus Interest Payment

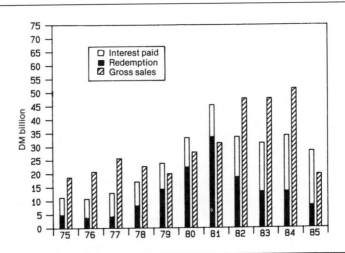

gross issuance of new public sector bonds (see Chart 16). This trend is likely to continue in the next few years as gross issuance of public bonds is expected to decline over time while redemption and interest payments remain substantial. The positive fund reflows expected for this year and beyond thus constitute another positive factor of the DM bond market.

CONCLUSION: FUTURE LIBERALIZATION MOVES

The recent liberalization measures authorized by the Bundesbank have greatly enhanced the flexibility and diversity of the DM bond market. However, these measures have created a momentum for further liberalization. Currently, market attention is focusing on a possible abolition of two outstanding obstacles, namely, the security transfer tax and the prohibition on issuance of DM Certificates of Deposits (CDs).

- Currently investors are levied a 0.25 percent securities transfer (or stock exchange turnover) tax on purchases of German securities and a 0.10 percent tax on purchases of foreign securities (i.e., Euro-DM bonds) listed on German stock exchanges. This tax, which is particularly onerous for the trading of the new Euro-DM floaters since their spread over the banks funding cost (LIBOR) is thin, has caused transactions in Euro-DM bonds to be shifted away from the German exchanges to offshore centers such as London or Luxembourg. Recently, this process has extended to the trading of German government bonds with international investors. Given the expressed wish of the Bundesbank to see the liberalized Euro-DM bond market to be anchored in Germany, it is natural to expect this tax to be abolished eventually.
- German banks are required to maintain minimum reserves with the Bundesbank on their liabilities of up to three years maturity. However, under current German law, marketable CDs are classified as securities and as such, they are not subject to the Bundesbank's minimum reserve requirement. As a result, the Bundesbank has been opposed to the introduction of CDs for fear of losing its monetary control. With a view to further develop the German money market, the German authorities are reportedly discussing changes to the minimum reserve requirement system so as to allow banks to issue CDs. One of the proposals being floated would make CDs subject to minimum reserve requirement as any other bank deposit but would reduce the maturity of reservable liabilities down to two years. The reason for this trade-off is that the amount of reserves needed by the German banking system would not change too greatly by the inclusion of CDs to the range of reservable liabilities.

Subsequent to the writing of this chapter, the Bundesbank authorized the issuance of Deutschemark CDs beginning May 1st, 1986.

52

The ECU Bond Market

Tran Q. Hung
Vice President
Merrill Lynch Capital Markets

The exceptional appreciation of the dollar in recent years has taken the U.S. currency to record levels against many major currencies. The current lofty level of the dollar's exchange value, however, has generated widespread investor concerns about the scope for its further strengthening. Yet experiences in recent years have rendered quite uncertain any prediction of a fall in the dollar's exchange rate.

In this environment, ECU bonds have become attractive to international investors. If the dollar does indeed depreciate, ECU bonds will provide investors with currency gains comparable to gains derived from investing in other major currencies such as the Deutschemark. However, if the dollar continues to be strong, investors can get some yield protection since ECU bonds currently yield about 250–500 basis points more than the DM, Swiss franc, and yen bond markets.

The recent interest in ECU bonds as an alternative to dollar assets has augmented more traditional demand for ECU bonds in Europe. The resulting strong investor demand has prompted many borrowers to issue ECU bonds. In addition to the supranational and sovereign borrowers within the EEC who have used the ECU bond market since 1981, new borrowers include commercial banks, corporations, and non-EEC institutions such as the World Bank. This has diversified the range of credits available in the ECU bond market and made it more attractive to investors.

DESCRIPTION OF THE ECU

The European Currency Unit (ECU) is the official composite currency unit of the European Monetary System (EMS). The EMS was established in March 1979 with the objective of fostering a European zone of exchange-rate stability and encouraging a convergence of economic policies among member countries. The ECU is essential to the attainment of those objectives, both as a cornerstone of a fixed, but adjustable, exchange-rate system and as a means of settlement among EMS member central banks in the course of their exchange market interventions to defend existing parities.

The ECU is currently defined as a basket containing fixed amounts of national currencies of the 10 member countries of the European Economic Community (EEC). The weight of each currency in the ECU is the percentage share of the U.S. dollar equivalent of the prescribed amount of that currency in the ECU basket (see Table 1). As is evident in the calculation, the weights change continuously as a function of both the prescribed amount of each currency in the ECU basket and the movement of those currencies' exchange value against the U.S. dollar.

Consequently, the currency that appreciates relative to the rest of the basket will have its weight in the ECU increasing over time, and vice versa. For example, between March 1979 and September 16, 1984 (when the composition of the ECU was revised), the weights of the Deutschemark, sterling, and Dutch guilder had risen noticeably as these currencies depreciated less severely against the dollar than other currencies. The remaining currencies, by contrast, experienced a shrinkage in their weights (quite sharply by 24.8 percent in the case of the lira).

The composition of the ECU can change periodically. In principle, the fixed amount of each currency making up the ECU basket is reviewed every five years when changes can be made with a view of restoring the original proportion of each currency in the ECU. Midterm reviews can also be carried out when either a new member joins the EEC or when the weight of any component currency changes by 25 percent due to cumulative exchange-rate movements. In all cases, any change in the composition of the ECU has to be unanimously approved by the EEC and has to result in no change of the ECU exchange rate immediately following the change in composition. The first such change in the composition of the ECU took place on September 16, 1984 at the first regular five-year review which took into account the new EEC membership of Greece (which joined in 1981) and the fact that the lira's weight had fallen by almost 25 percent.

The ECU serves as an anchor for the EMS fixed exchange-rate system. Exchange-rate parities for member currencies are set against the ECU, and are referred to as the central rates (see Table 2). Bilateral parity rates or cross rates among the EMS currencies can be calculated by

TABLE 1 Definition of the ECU

	Amount of Currency in Original Basket (From 3/79 to 9/84)	Weightings (Percent)		Amount of Currency in Revised Basket (Since 9/17/84)	As of October 16, 1985		
		Mar 79	9/16/84		Exchange Rate Against U.S. Dollar	Dollar Equivalent	Weightings (Percent)
Deutschemark	0.828	33.0	36.9	0.719	2.6855	0.26773	32.48
French Franc	1.15	19.9	16.7	1.31	8.1850	0.16005	19.42
Pound Sterling	0.0885	13.4	15.1	0.0878	1.4085	0.12367	15.00
Italian Lira	109.0	10.5	7.9	140.0	1808.5	0.07741	9.39
Dutch Guilder	0.286	9.5	11.3	0.256	3.0250	0.08463	10.27
Belgian Franc	3.66	9.1	8.1	3.71	54.25	0.06839	8.30
Luxembourg Franc	0.14	0.4	0.3	0.14	54.25	0.00258	0.31
Danish Krone	0.217	3.1	2.7	0.219	9.7275	0.02251	2.73
Greek Drachma	—	—	—	1.15	158.24	0.007267	0.88
Irish Pound	0.00759	1.0	1.0	0.00871	1.1542	0.01005	1.22
	100.0	100.0	100.0			0.82429	100.00

TABLE 2   ECU Central Rates and Divergence Indicators

	ECU Central Rates (Since July 1985)	Spot Exchange Rate against ECU (October 16, 1985)	Adjusted Change from Central Rates (Percent)*	Divergence Indicators (Percent)
Deutschemark	2.23840	2.21334	−0.48	+/−1.1455
French franc	6.86402	6.74646	−1.07	+/−1.3654
Italian lira	1520.60	1491.79	−1.81	+/−4.0856
Dutch guilder	2.52208	2.49445	−0.46	+/−1.5162
Belgian franc	44.8320	44.7619	+0.48	+/−1.5425
Danish krone	8.12857	8.02207	−0.67	+/−1.6421
Irish pound	0.724578	0.714995	−0.68	+/−1.6673

* Changes are adjusted for the fact that sterling and drachma are not members of the EMS and lira can move by +/−6 percent. Positive changes denote a weak currency.

dividing the ECU central rates into one another, forming a bilateral parity grid. The EMS member currencies are then subject to two exchange-rate constraints:

1. *Bilateral Parity Constraint* requires that no EMS currency may appreciate or depreciate by more than 2.25 percent against any other member currency. The lira, being the exception, may move by +/− 6 percent. The pound sterling and Greek drachma are subject to no constraints as the U.K. and Greece are not members of the EMS.

2. *Divergence limit from ECU central rates.* The ECU exchange rate for each EMS currency is not allowed to move beyond a maximum divergence from its ECU central rate. In fact, when a member currency moves by 75 percent of its maximum divergence and touches its divergence indicator, remedial action by the central bank involved will have to be taken.

In short, the bilateral parity constraint and the divergence limit require the monetary authorities of both the weakening and strengthening

TABLE 3   EMS Realignments Since Inception (March 13, 1979) (percent revaluation [R] or devaluation [D] from ECU central rates)

	Deutsche-mark	French Franc	Italian Lira	Dutch Guilder	Belgian Franc	Irish Pound	Danish Krone
9/24/79	—	—	—	—	—	—	4.00% D
11/30/79	—	—	—	—	—	—	5.00% D
3/22/81	—	—	6.00% D	—	—	—	—
10/05/81	5.50% R	3.00% D	3.00% D	5.50% R	—	—	—
2/22/82	—	—	—	—	8.50% D	—	3.00% D
3/21/83	5.50% R	2.50% D	2.50% D	3.50% R	1.50% D	3.50% D	2.50% R
7/21/85	6.00% R	6.00% R	2.00% D	6.00% R	6.00% R	6.00% R	6.00% R
4/06/86	3.00% R	3.00% D	—	3.00% R	1.00% R	—	1.00% R

currencies to take steps to prevent their currencies from exceeding the bilateral and divergence limits. Possible remedial actions include foreign exchange market interventions, changes in national monetary and fiscal policies and ultimately, realignments of the ECU central rates. Such realignments are expected to be carried out periodically to offset different price movements among the EMS countries. Since its inception, the EMS has experienced eight central rate realignments (see Table 3).

THE ECU BOND MARKET: THE BORROWERS

From the outset, the EEC and other community institutions such as the European Investment Bank (EIB) and the European Coal and Steel Community (ECSC) have been committed to supporting the ECU. The measures of support included asking commercial banks to accept time and demand deposits denominated in ECUs to facilitate EEC-wide transactions. Moreover, most EEC member countries and many non-EEC countries such as the United States, Japan, and Switzerland regard the ECU as a foreign currency subject to the same regulatory treatment as any other foreign currency. The only major exception is West Germany where ECU transactions among residents have to be authorized on a case by case basis. However, West German residents are allowed to have assets, but not liabilities, denominated in ECUs vis-à-vis nonresidents. The commercial banks, confronted with the task of having to decompose the ECU into its component currencies whenever an ECU transaction takes place, began to establish a clearing mechanism to settle ECU transactions as an integral unit. The clearing system which evolved is called "Mutual ECU Settlement Accounts" (MESA) where participating banks, by maintaining a MESA account with one another, net out total ECU credits or debits against one another on a daily basis. Only the net differences, reaching at least ECU 10 million, need to be settled by national currencies only if the payee so desires. This system has greatly facilitated the settlement of ECU-denominated transactions and helped foster the growing private use of the ECU as a currency, not just an accounting unit. Currently, commercial banks in Europe maintain an active foreign exchange market in the ECU, quoting spot and forward rates for up to one year against major currencies. The market is quite liquid with the typical bid/ask spread of five to seven pips for the dollar/ ECU exchange rate which is comparable to the spread for the DM/dollar exchange rate.

With market participants being able to borrow, invest, and hedge themselves in ECUs, an ECU money market for interbank deposits and CDs has developed and flourished, reaching an estimated size of ECU 10 billion with more than 300 banks participating. A syndicated loan market in ECUs is also quite active. In this environment, the first ECU bond was launched in March 1981. Since then, new issue activities in

ECU bonds have increased significantly, with the outstanding volume almost doubling in 1984 alone (see Chart 1). As a currency of denomination in the primary market for Eurobonds in 1984, the ECU ranked third after the dollar and DM. If foreign bonds were included, the ECU

CHART 1   New Issue Volume of ECU Bonds

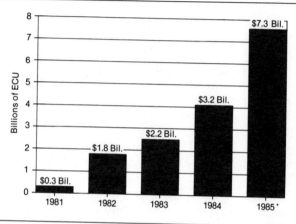

* January–September 1985 at an annualized rate.

ranked sixth, after the dollar, Swiss franc, DM, sterling, and yen; substantially ahead of other major currencies such as Canadian dollars and Dutch guilders.

Most of the ECU bonds offered so far carry a fixed coupon rate, ranging from 9¼ percent to 14¾ percent, with maturity mostly between 7 and 10 years even though there are a few 15-year issues. In addition, there are fifteen floating rate notes, totaling $1.2 billion, with coupons being set every three or six months at a spread of ¹⁄₁₆ to ¼ over ECU deposit rates.

The ECU bond market has appealed to a wide variety of borrowers.

- EEC official institutions, which can on-lend ECU funds directly, have been major issuers of ECU bonds because they want to expand the use of the ECU. This motive was particularly behind the EEC bond issue (ECU 200 million at 9⅞ percent coupon for 12 years) targeted to the U.S. investors and the EIB issue (ECU 200 million at 9¼ percent coupon for 10 years) targeted to French investors. These issues have helped to widen the investors' base for ECU bonds.
- Sovereign borrowers in EMS member countries with high inflation and high interest rates such as Italy, Ireland, and France have also

made repeated flotations in the ECU bond markets. To these borrowers, ECU bonds offer a cheaper source of finance compared with their respective domestic capital markets since ECU interest rates are roughly the weighted average of interest rates in all member countries. However, by issuing ECU bonds, they take on the risk that their respective currencies may depreciate against the ECU. In the absence of an EMS realignment, this currency exposure is limited to a narrow margin of fluctuation permissible within the EMS.

• European, Japanese, and to a lesser extent, U.S. banks have issued ECU bonds to fund their growing ECU assets. As the ECU syndicated loan market continues to expand, commercial banks will have a natural need to borrow in the ECU bond market.

• Nonbank corporations with their European operations increasingly denominated in ECUs may also want to have long-term ECU liabilities to match their ECU assets or income stream. Chrysler has recently joined GTE and became the second U.S. industrial corporation to issue an ECU bond (ECU 60 million at 10 percent for six years).

• Finally, other non-EEC borrowers such as the World Bank have used the ECU bond market as a competitive financing alternative to the dollar in their effort to diversify their borrowings.

Chart 2 presents a profile of major groups of borrowers in terms of percentage share of total outstanding.

CHART 2 Borrower Profile in the ECU Bond Market (at the end of 1984)

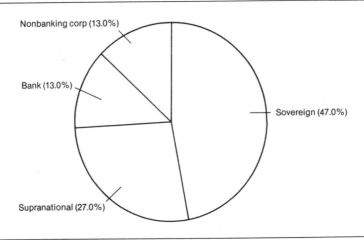

Nonbanking corp (13.0%)

Bank (13.0%)

Sovereign (47.0%)

Supranational (27.0%)

THE ECU BOND MARKET: THE INVESTORS

The dramatic growth of the ECU primary bond market since last year reflects strong investor interest in ECU bonds. From an investor's point of view, ECU bonds offer many attractions.

- For investors from countries like Belgium, Luxembourg, West Germany, Netherlands, and Switzerland who have traditionally favored the Deutschemark, Dutch guilder, and Swiss franc bond markets because of the low inflation in those countries, ECU bonds offer a hefty yield pick-up of 250 to 500 basis points over their respective markets at the moment. (See Chart 3 for a comparison of ECU and Euro DM bond yields.) The currency risk to these investors is limited to the permissible range of fluctuation within

CHART 3 Ten-Year ECU and Euro DM Bond Yields (percent)

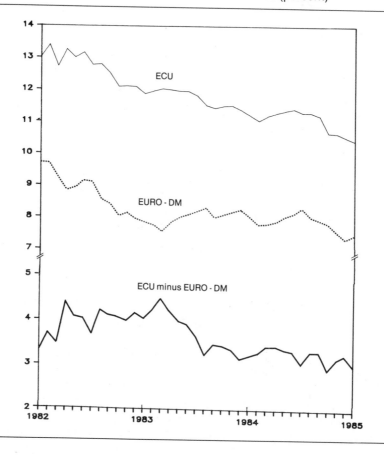

the EMS and to the infrequent realignments of the EMS central rates. In the past two years, this risk has been small as the DM/ECU exchange rate has been quite stable (see Chart 4). Until 1985, the yield inducement of ECU bonds was more attractive than the

---

CHART 4 Deutschemark/ECU Exchange Rate

weighted average of yields in the EMS member countries. According to Chart 5, throughout 1984 ECU bonds yielded about 20 to 25 basis points more than the weighted average yield, a result of the fact that there was a greater supply of ECU-denominated securities than there was natural demand for them. Since early 1985, ECU bond yields have been substantially lower than the weighted average yield as the investor base for ECU bonds is being established. The yield sacrifice on ECU bonds relative to the weighted average yield can be thought of as a convenience premium because it is quite difficult for investors to construct a portfolio of bonds to exactly duplicate the composition of ECU bonds.

To dollar investors (from the United States, Japan and other countries) who are concerned about the present lofty level of the dollar's exchange value, ECU bonds are an attractive alternative. If the dollar weakens, holders of ECU bonds will have full potential for currency gains since the dollar/ECU exchange rate moves similarly to the DM/dollar exchange rate and their volatilities are also comparable (see Chart 6). In fact, for the entire 1979–85 period, the volatility of the dollar/ECU exchange rate as measured by the coef-

CHART 5   Medium-Term ECU Bond Yields

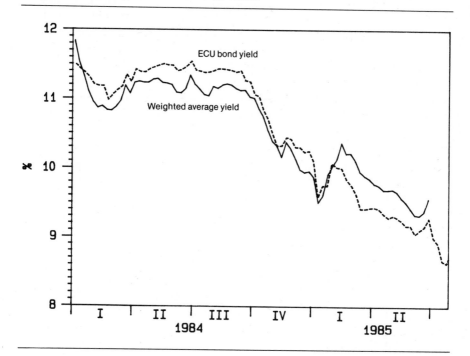

CHART 6   Selected Exchange Rates: U.S. Dollar Per ECU and U.S. Dollar per Deutschemark

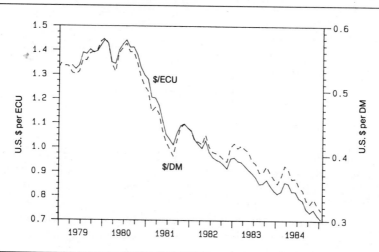

ficient of variation of 23.5 percent exceeded that of the DM/dollar rate of 18.5 percent. For this opportunity, investors currently have to give up only 125 basis points moving from dollar to ECU bonds, compared with a yield sacrifice of 350 to 650 basis points required to invest in the yen, DM, Dutch guilder, and Swiss franc bond markets (see Chart 7 for a comparison of ECU and Eurodollar bond

CHART 7 Ten-Year ECU and Eurodollar Bond Yields (percent)

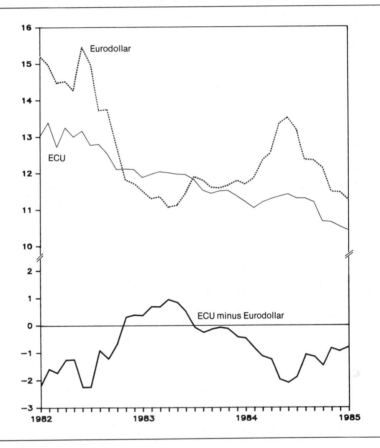

yields). Furthermore, ECU bond yields are less volatile than dollar bond yields, a result of the fact that ECU interest rates are a composite of rates in the EMS member countries. On a real yield basis, ECU bonds are slightly less attractive than many other major markets owing to the fact that the ECU weighted average inflation rate is 5 percent which reflects the high inflation rate in Italy, Greece and France (see Table 4).

TABLE 4 Real Bond Yield in Major Markets (ten-year bond yield minus 1984 inflation rate)

Yen	4.8%
ECU	5.2
DM	5.4
Dollar	6.4
Sterling	6.6

- For diversification purposes, ECU bonds offer investors the opportunity to be exposed to less-well-traded currencies such as the Danish krone, Irish pound, and lira, whose bonds are not normally available.
- Finally, owning an ECU asset can give investors an opportunity to swap or hedge into assets denominated in other currencies for yield pick-ups. Because of the stability of exchange rates within the EMS, investors can use cross currency hedging techniques to hedge an ECU asset and lock in attractive yield in their base currency. For example, at the present time, dollar investors can purchase one-year ECU deposit at 10.25 percent and sell DM forward at a 3 percent premium, creating a yield of 13.25 percent compared with 10.06 percent for one year Eurodollar deposit. This investment strategy is open to the risk that DM may appreciate by more than 3.2 percent against the ECU.

At the present time, with the ECU yield curve being slightly inverted which makes short-term ECU rates very attractive compared to dollar or DM rates relative to the ECU yield advantage of longer maturities (see Charts 8 and 9). Consequently, investors may be interested in ECU floating-rate notes. In addition to price stability, ECU FRNs give investors the same currency gain if the dollar tops out. However, if the dollar continues to be strong and forces European central banks to keep their short-term rates high to defend their currencies, the ECU yield curve may continue to be flat or inverted. In addition, investors may use the cross currency hedging technique mentioned above to sell DM forward against the stream of ECU coupon income every three or six months, further improving the yield pick-up. The cross currency hedge can be discontinued when the dollar starts to decline.

Table 5 summarized the performance of ECU bonds compared with other sectors of the Eurobond markets in 1983, 1984, and the first nine months of 1985. In local currency terms, ECU bonds provided the second highest return in each of these periods, helped by an excellent local currency performance by the French franc bond market. In dollar terms,

CHART 8   ECU and Eurodollar Yield Curves

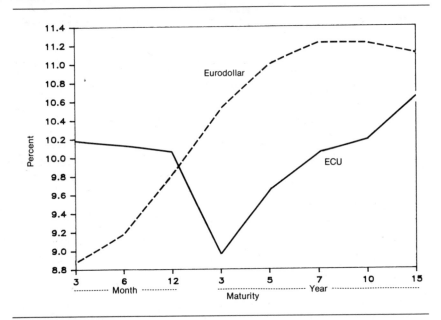

CHART 9   ECU and Euro—DM Yield Curves

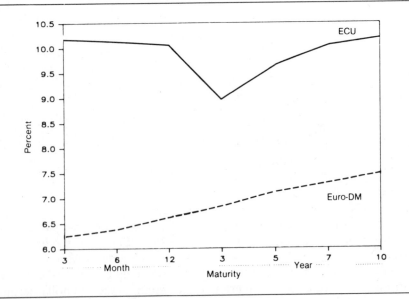

TABLE 5 Performance Comparison

	1983			1984			Jan.–Sept. 1985		
	Total Return in Local Currencies	Change versus the Dollar	Total Return in Dollar Terms	Total Return in Local Currencies	Change versus the Dollar	Total Return in Dollar Terms	Total Return in Local Currencies	Change versus the Dollar	Total Return in Dollar Terms
Eurodollar	9.8%	—	9.8%	9.5%	—	9.5%	12.5%	—	12.5%
ECU	14.7	−14.5%	−1.9	12.7	−14.1%	−3.2	12.0	16.8%	30.8
Eurosterling	16.6	−10.2	4.7	13.0	−20.0	−9.6	11.1	21.2	34.7
EuroDM	9.0	−12.8	−5.0	11.9	−13.6	−3.3	6.5	15.4	22.9
Euroguilder	5.6	−14.4	−9.6	10.5	−13.8	−4.7	8.4	15.1	24.8
Euroyen	7.4	1.2	8.7	6.8	−7.5	−1.2	8.0	13.0	22.0

SOURCE: AIBD, Merrill Lynch.

ECU bonds outperformed both EuroDM and Euroguilder confirming the attraction of ECU bonds to the Deutschemark-block investors.

ADDITIONAL ADVANTAGES AND RISKS OF HOLDING ECU BONDS

Two recent developments seem to indicate that the ECU market is likely to develop further in the future, thus adding to the potential advantages of holding ECU investments.

1. There has been renewed political support among major European countries for the ECU, both for official and private uses. The expectation is that if the ECU can be promoted to be viewed as an alternative to the dollar, it can help foster more stability in intra-European exchange rates by relieving the DM from the burden of adjusting to the dollar exchange rate movement. Normally, due to its status as a key investment currency beside the dollar, the DM strengthens or weakens more sharply against the dollar than other EMS currencies as speculative funds flow back and forth between DM and dollar assets. If the ECU is to take up some of these investment flows, the differentiated exchange rate movements of the ECU component currencies against the dollar will tend to diminish.

2. Related to the above aim, the EEC and the Bank for International Settlements (BIS) have discussed the possibility of the BIS becoming a central clearing house for ECU transactions. If realized, this arrangement would definitely enhance the status of the ECU as well as the efficiency of settling ECU transactions, contributing to wider use of the ECU.

The peculiar risk of holding ECU bonds is of course the risk that the ECU may cease to be used because it is officially abandoned by the EMS (or following the dissolution the EMS itself). A related risk would be the change in the composition of the ECU during the life of an ECU bond issue. In the foreseeable future, the composition of the ECU may be changed when Spain and Portugal become members of the EEC.

As regard to the risk that the ECU may cease to be used, ECU bond indentures usually provide for the Fiscal Agent to make payments in U.S. dollars or any other convertible currency equal to the dollar equivalent of the ECU based on its composition on the last day on which the ECU is in use. If this eventuality happens, the ECU bond market may be more cumbersome to trade and hence become less liquid, but otherwise ECU bonds still retain the same characteristics of a basket currency instrument.

PART 7

Interest-Rate Determinants and Interest-Rate Forecasting

53

The Term Structure of Interest Rates

Richard W. McEnally, Ph.D., C.F.A.
Professor of Finance
University of North Carolina

INTRODUCTION

Exhibit 1 contains a three-dimensional representation of yields on U.S. Treasury securities with different terms-to-maturity for each calendar month since 1950. Even the most casual observer of this plot cannot help but be struck by the facts that in each month these yields vary with maturity, and this yield-maturity relationship itself varies from month to month. Such relationships are generally referred to as the *term structure of interest rates*, or more properly, the term structure of *yields*. When plots of the yield-maturity relationship are examined for a single point in time, as in Exhibit 2, such a representation is frequently called the *yield curve*. Regardless of how it is examined or what it is called, awareness and appreciation of this relationship is absolutely essential in fixed income investment analysis and management.

Some of the uses of the term structure include the following:

1. *Analyzing the returns for asset commitments of different terms.* Fixed income investment managers vary their portfolios along many dimensions, including quality, coupon level, and type of issuer. But no dimension is more important than the maturity dimension; it has the greatest influence on whether the portfolio will gain or lose in today's volatile interest-rate environment. The yield curve shows what the rewards will be for commitments of different lengths if they are held to maturity. Properly interpreted, it can also be used to make judgments about the short-term rewards of different maturity strategies as interest rates change.

EXHIBIT 1a   Term Structure of Interest Rates, January 1950–December
1964

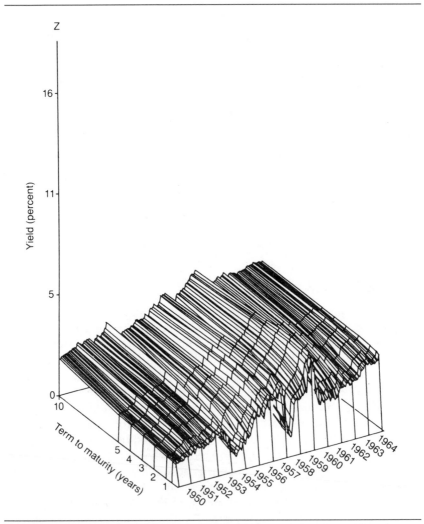

2. *Assessing consensus expectations of future interest rates.* In fixed income investment the manager who can make better predictions of future
interest rates than the consensus forecast—or even the manager who
can correctly identify the *direction of error* in the consensus forecast—can
profit immensely. But a strategy based on this principle requires a
knowledge of what the consensus expectation of future interest rates is.
Analysis of the term structure can provide this information.

EXHIBIT 1*b* Term Structure of Interest Rates, January 1965–March 1981

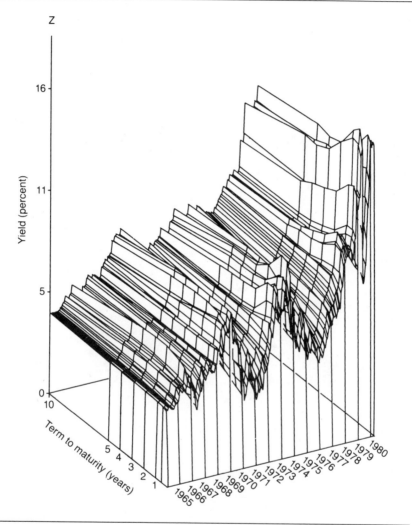

SOURCE: Data courtesy of Salomon Brothers Inc.

3. *Pricing bonds and other fixed-payment contracts.* The yield curve shows the pure price of time, a price that changes from hour to hour and day to day. In pricing financial obligations, it is essential that consideration be given to the yields available on alternative investments with a similar length of commitment. The yield curve shows what these alternative yields are. Today it is commonplace to price bonds and other contracts "off the yield curve."

EXHIBIT 2 Yields of Treasury Securities, December 31, 1980 (based on closing bid quotations)

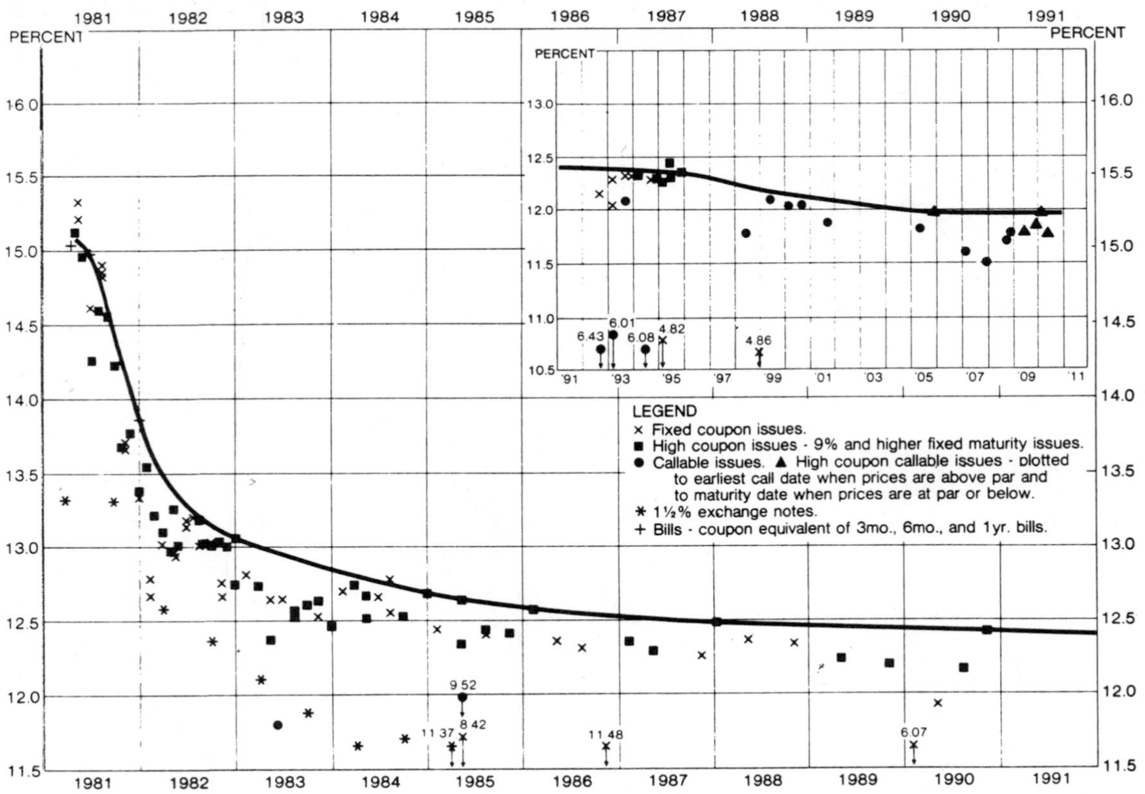

PERCENT
1981
1982
1983
1984
1985
1986
1987
1988
1989
1990
1991
16.0
15.5
15.0
14.5
14.0
13.5
13.0
12.5
12.0
11.5
13.0
11.0
10.5
'91
'93
'95
'97
'99
'01
'03
'05
'07
'09
'11
6.43
6.01
6.08
4.82
4.86
9.52
8.42
11.37
11.48
6.07
LEGEND
× Fixed coupon issues.
■ High coupon issues - 9% and higher fixed maturity issues.
● Callable issues. ▲ High coupon callable issues - plotted to earliest call date when prices are above par and to maturity date when prices are at par or below.
✱ 1½% exchange notes.
+ Bills - coupon equivalent of 3mo., 6mo., and 1yr. bills.

Note: The curve is fitted by eye and based only on the most actively traded issues. Market yields on coupon issues due in less than three months are excluded.

SOURCE: *U.S. Treasury Bulletin*, January 1981.

4. *Arbitraging between bonds of different maturities.* As explained in Chapter 29, swaps between similar bonds whose prices appear to be out of line is a traditional fixed income portfolio management technique. Appraising the effects of term is no problem if the maturities are virtually identical. When they are not, yield curve analysis can be used to make the yields more directly comparable and thereby facilitate yield spread analysis.

In this chapter we deal principally with two questions about the term structure: What causes it to be the way it is? And how can we measure, analyze, and interpret it? However, we should acknowledge at the outset that, despite the attention that has been given to the term structure (the term structure is a prime candidate for the title of "most studied topic in financial economics"), there are no firm answers to these questions. Nowhere is the well-known disagreement among economists more pronounced than in the term structure area. Thus about the best we can hope for is more insight and understanding.

DETERMINANTS OF THE SHAPE OF THE TERM STRUCTURE

Theories

If buyers of fixed income securities were indifferent among securities of differing maturity, there would be no meaningful term structure; all yields would be equal. Therefore, the fact that yield curves are not perfectly horizontal suggests that some maturity preferences must exist. Reasons that have been advanced for the shape of the term structure are in effect theories or hypotheses about maturity preferences among investors. Three such theories are prominent: the market segmentation hypothesis, the expectations hypothesis, and the liquidity premium hypothesis. Let us examine each of these in turn.

The market segmentation hypothesis. Suppose buyers of fixed income securities fall roughly into two groups, one with a strong preference for short-term securities and the other with a strong preference for long-term securities. If there is little overlap in the range of maturities each group considers acceptable for portfolio investment, then *the* market for fixed income securities will actually be separated or segmented into two separate submarkets. And if one group of investors gains on the other in terms of funds available for investment, then, in the absence of an offsetting response by borrowers, this group will bid up prices and thus force down security yields in its preferred submarket. The same result might occur from a relative increase in the quantity of bonds issued by borrowers in one of the maturity ranges.[1]

This, in a nutshell, is the *market segmentation, preferred habitat,* or *hedging pressure* theory of the term structure. It appears to be particularly popular among practicing investments professionals. The commercial bank is usually identified as the primary source of demand for short-term securities, and the demand for long-term securities is associated with life insurance companies. Advocates of this hypothesis acknowledge that these two types of institutions do not confine their investment exclusively to one end of the maturity spectrum. Moreover, they recognize the presence of other investors, including investors who will operate in either maturity range. But they also believe that banks and life insurers are so dominant and their maturity preferences are so pronounced that short- and long-term yields behave as if the markets were segmented along these lines.

It is usually asserted that life insurance company demand for long-term bonds is reasonably stable over time. On the other hand, bank demand for short-term securities is said to be more volatile. Banks prefer to lend directly to businesses and individuals when possible, only putting funds that are left over into securities. But demand for short-term loans by businesses and individuals is also quite volatile. In periods of strong economic activity, these borrowers demand funds for business expansion and consumption, banks sell securities to accommodate their demands, and short-term yields rise compared with long-term yields. In slack periods these borrowers pay down their loans, and banks have excess funds for which they seek an outlet in short-term securities, driving their yields downward in comparison with long-term yields.

Opposition to the market segmentation hypothesis is based primarily on a belief that some other hypothesis provides a better explanation for the behavior of the term structure. Advocates of other hypotheses also believe that the segmentation hypothesis understates the willingness of banks, insurance companies, and many other investors to gravitate to the segment of the maturity structure that appears to offer the highest return, thereby arbitraging away temporary yield differentials.

The "unbiased" or "pure" expectations hypothesis. This hypothesis stands in sharp contrast to the market segmentation hypothesis, for it is based on the assumption that fixed income investors in the aggregate act to eliminate any comparative attraction of securities of a particu-

---

[1] Alternatively, issuers might offset changes in the relative position of investors in the two submarkets by shifting their borrowing to the favored, lower interest-rate market, thereby restoring equality of interest rates. In the absence of strong maturity preferences, this is what we would expect rational borrowers to do, and there is evidence that some large borrowers—such as the U.S. Treasury—tend to behave in just this way. However, typical formulations of the market segmentation hypothesis assume that borrower behavior is unaffected by interest rates, or, as it is said, is "exogenously determined."

lar maturity. In effect, it acknowledges that maturity preferences may initially exist because of expectations about the future level of interest rates, but asserts that investors will respond in reasonable and rational ways to profit from these expectations. In the process they neutralize maturity preferences, but they also create yield differences among securities of different maturities.

A simple example will help us understand the expectations hypothesis. Suppose the yield curve is flat, "the" yield is 6 percent per annum, and investors are generally in agreement that yields will increase to 8 percent in one year. Under these conditions the yield curve would not remain flat but would become upward sloped. Plausible equilibrium or indifference yields to maturity are 6 percent on one-year (or short-term) securities and 7 percent on two-year (or long-term) securities.

To see why this is so, let us first consider an investor with a long-term, or two-year horizon. His objective is to earn the highest possible rate of return on his money over these two years, and yield aside he is indifferent between initially buying a two-year security and holding it for two years, or purchasing a one-year security, holding it one year, and then rolling over into another one-year security for the second year. Before yields adjust, the first alternative gives him 6 percent on his money in each year. Under the second alternative, he knows he can earn 6 percent on his money for the first year and expects that he can earn 8 percent on his money in the second year, for an average yield of approximately 7 percent per annum over the two years. Thus he will prefer the second alternative and will buy one-year securities at 6 percent rather than two-year securities at 6 percent. As he and other like-minded investors behave in this manner, prices on two-year securities will be driven down, and yields will be driven up. Only when they reach 7 percent will the investor consider their purchase as attractive as the series of two one-year securities.[2]

We can get to the same result by considering an investor who is seeking the largest total return (coupon yield plus price change) over the next year. She has a short-term horizon. Under our yield scenario she knows that her total return on the one-year security will be 6 percent, for it will pay off at par in one year. On the other hand, her expected total return on the two-year security over the next year is only 4 percent.

To see this, assume the two-year security has a 6 percent coupon. At the end of one year it will be a one-year security—that is, it will have one year of life remaining. If it is then to offer the expected yield-to-maturity of 8 percent, it must sell for approximately 98. At this price a purchaser

---

[2] In this example we are requiring that equilibrium be restored by movement in the yield of the long-term security. This is purely for expository convenience. Restoration of equilibrium might well involve both a decline in one-year yields and an increase in two-year yields.

will in the second year get a coupon of 6 and a capital gain of 2, for a total return of $(6 + 2)/98 \cong 8$ percent. But if the two-year security sells at 98 at the end of a year, its total return over the first year is only 4 percent because of the loss of value of 2; that is, $(6 - 2)/100 \cong 4$ percent.

The bottom line is that the investor oriented to one-year total return and having a one-year horizon will also prefer the one-year 6 percent security and avoid the two-year 6 percent security until the yield-to-maturity on the latter rises to 7 percent. At this yield she is indifferent, as the following tabulation shows.

	Maturity	
	1 Year	2 Years
Coupon	6%	6%
Initial yield-to-maturity	6%	7%
Initial price	100	98
Return over life	6/100 = 6%	$6 + 6 + 2/98 \cong 14\%$
		$\cong 7\%$ per annum
Price at end of year at		
8 percent	—	98
Return, year 1	6/100 = 6%	$6/98 \cong 6\%$
Return, year 2	—	$(6 + 2)/98 \cong 8\%$

At an initial price of 98, the two-year security offers an average yield-to-maturity of 7 percent per annum, based on its 6 percent coupon each year plus a capital gain of 2 spread out over the two years on an initial investment of 98. However, if the price at the end of the first year remains at 98, consistent with a yield-to-maturity of 8 percent in the second year, then its total return in the first year is only 6 percent ($\cong 6/98$); there is no capital gain or loss. Thus, its total rate of return in the first year is exactly equal to the total rate of return on the one-year security, even though the yields-to-maturity are different.

This example illustrates several significant implications of the pure expectations hypothesis. First, in each period total rates of return—coupon plus capital gain or loss—are expected to be identical on all securities regardless of their term-to-maturity. Second, the consensus expectation of future yields can be inferred from the presently observable term structure; e.g., in our example, observing a 6 percent yield-to-maturity on one-year securities and a 7 percent yield-to-maturity on two-year securities, we know that the consensus forecast of one-year yields in one year must be 8 percent. Third, yields on long-term securities are equal to an average of the present yield on a short-term security plus an expected future yield (or yields) on short-term securities.

This last implication is believed to account for the observable tendency of short-term yields to fluctuate more than long-term yields. This tendency is readily evident in Exhibit 1; it is also shown directly in Exhibit 3, which plots the mean absolute deviation (average deviation

EXHIBIT 3 Mean Absolute Deviation of Monthly Changes in U.S. Government Security Yields and Prices, January 1950–March 1981*

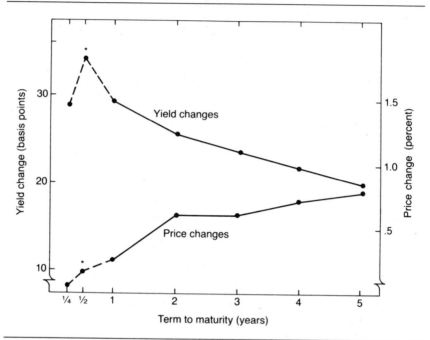

* Except for maturities of one-half year, which date from January 1959.
SOURCE OF DATA: Courtesy of Salomon Brothers Inc.

with sign ignored) of the same yields from month to month. At any given time short-term money may be cheap or dear. But the market believes it will not always be this way; tight credit periods tend to be followed by loose money periods, and conversely. And such fluctuations tend to be averaged out more and more in yields on progressively longer securities. This phenomenon leads to a common analogy of the yield curve with a person's waving arm: The arm is anchored to the shoulder (the long-maturity end), and the hand (short-term securities) moves up and down most as the arm is waved.

It is useful to formulate the pure expectations hypothesis algebraically, and over the years a somewhat standard notation has evolved for doing this. Let $_tR_n$ be the actual, observable yield on a security, with the prescript denoting the time at which it is observed and the postscript indicating term-to-maturity. In terms of our simple example, we have for the one-year security $_0R_1 = 6$ percent, and for the two-year security after adjustment, $_0R_2 = 7$ percent, where 0 means "now." These are frequently called *spot* rates. We also need something to represent unobservable but anticipated future yields; $_tr_{n,t}$ is used for this purpose, with the prescript representing the time at which the rate goes into effect, the first postscript indicating the term-to-maturity of the securities to which it applies, and the second postscript denoting the time at which the forecast is made. For example, instead of saying that "the presently expected yield on one-year securities in one year is 8 percent," we say $_1r_{1,0} = 8$ percent. Such rates are commonly referred to as *forward* rates.

Given this notation, and acknowledging the fact of interest compounding ignored in our simple example, the proposition that long rates are an average of observable and unobservable short rates can be stated as

$$(1 + {_t}R_n) = [(1 + {_t}R_1)(1 + {_{t+1}}r_{1,0})(1 + {_{t+2}}r_{1,0})$$
$$\ldots (1 + {_{t+n-1}}r_{1,0})]^{1/n} \quad \text{Equation I}$$

In terms of our example

$$(1 + {_0}R_2) = [(1 + {_0}R_1)(1 + {_1}r_{1,0})]^{1/2} \quad \text{Equation I(a)}$$

or

$$(1.07) \cong [(1.06)(1.08)]^{1/2} \quad \text{Equation I(b)}$$

Notice that the average on the right side of this equation is a *geometric average*, in which we take the nth root of the product of n values, as opposed to an arithmetic average, in which we divide the sum of n values by n. A geometric average is necessary because, with compounding, returns combine multiplicatively rather than additively. The product of 1.06 and 1.08 is 1.1448, implying that $1 invested for one year at 6 percent and the next at 8 percent would grow in value by 14.48 percent. Because of compounding, a yield slightly less than 7 percent earned in each of the two years would give the same appreciation. The geometric mean of 1.06 and 1.08 (that is, the square root of 1.1448) is actually 1.06995, and this is the value that belongs on the left side of Equation I(b).

We can use the same notation to derive the forward rate implicit in two observed spot rates. In terms of our example

$$(1 + {_1}r_{1,0}) = (1 + {_0}R_2)^2/(1 + {_0}R_1) \quad \text{Equation II(a)}$$

or

$$(1.08) \cong (1.07)^2/1.06 \quad \text{Equation II(b)}$$

or more generally

$$(1 + {_{t+m}}r_{n-m,t})^{n-m} = (1 + {_t}R_n)^n/(1 + {_t}R_m)^m \quad \text{Equation II}$$

Thus, if we know any two points on the yield curve, we can infer the yield that connects them. We can deduce the yield that is expected to prevail at the end of the shorter term to maturity (m) for the time interval that will be remaining (n − m) until the end of the longer term to maturity (n). For instance, if we know the yield on four-year obligations and five-year obligations, we can readily determine the implied yield on one-year obligations that is expected to prevail in four years; if we know the yield on one-year obligations and five-year obligations, we can obtain the yield expected on four-year securities in one year.

The liquidity or interest-rate risk hypothesis. For the moment, let us set aside our knowledge of the market segmentation and pure expectations hypotheses, and let us return to our simple situation in which there is a one-year bond and a two-year bond, each of which carries a 6 percent coupon in an environment in which the rate of interest is 6 percent. (Alternatively, think of this as a market in which institutional and expectations considerations are neutral.) Now, let us suppose the interest rate instantaneously goes to 7 percent: What happens to the prices of these two securities?

As we have already seen, the two-year security will drop to 98 in price. At this price it offers a capital gain of two spread over two years, or one per year, and a coupon of six each year. If the rate of interest remains at 7 percent, then the price at the end of the first year is 99; the return in the first year is $(6 + 1)/98 \cong 7$ percent and in the second year $(6 + 1)/99 \cong 7$ percent.

What about the one-year security? We would expect its price to drop immediately to 99. At this price it is like the two-year security after one year has elapsed; it offers a capital gain of 1, which when added to the coupon of 6 represents a total return $\cong 7$ percent on the initial investment of 99.

These price declines in response to a one percentage point increase in yields are 1 percent and 2 percent of the initial prices of the one- and two-year securities, respectively. For securities of even longer term, the price decline would be ever larger. Now in reality the price decline would not increase *quite* proportionately with the term-to-maturity. The intuition for this nonproportionality is that the more the price drops below par the smaller is the initial investment.[3]

Exhibit 4 plots the actual prices at which a 12 percent coupon security must sell to yield 14 percent to maturity when it has a term-to-maturity of one to twenty-five years. The necessary price decline does increase with maturity, but at a decreasing rate. Exhibit 4 also shows the prices needed for such securities to yield only 10 percent; compared with

---

[3] For example, $(6 + 1)/99$ is actually equal to 7.07 percent, and $(6 + 6 + 2)/98$ is actually equal to 14.28 percent; a price decline to 99.07 and to 98.25 are all that are necessary to give total returns of 7 percent and 14 percent respectively:

$$(6 + 100 - 99.07)/99.07 = (6 + .93)/99.07 = 7 \text{ percent}$$
$$(6 + 6 + 100 - 98.25)/98.25 = (12 + 1.75)/98.25 = 14 \text{ percent}$$

EXHIBIT 4   Price of a 12 Percent Coupon Bond of Various Maturities at Yields of 10 Percent and 14 Percent

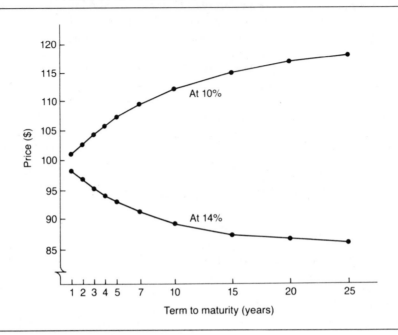

par, these represent increases in prices that rise with maturity but at a decreasing rate.

This price change/yield change relationship is purely mechanical in nature; it follows from the mathematics of bond price calculations. Therefore, if all yields fluctuated by the same amount, then long bonds should fluctuate more in price than short bonds. But we have already established that short-term yields fluctuate more than long-term yields; this was the message of Exhibit 3. Which of these influences is more important in terms of price fluctuation? That is, do short-term bonds actually vary more or less in price than long-term bonds? The answer, which can only be obtained by observation, turns out to be that longer-term bonds have greater price volatility. Exhibit 3 also shows mean absolute deviations of monthly bond price changes derived from yield changes for 1950 to the present. Here it is evident that bond price volatility increases with maturity, at first at a very rapid rate but then at a much lower rate as bond maturity lengthens.

This observation suggests a third reason investors might not be indifferent among bonds of different maturities. If most investors are adverse to fluctuations in the value of their portfolios, they will have some preference for short-term securities simply because their values are more stable. Therefore, in order to induce them to hold progressively longer-term bonds, they must expect to receive higher returns. Such a return increment is usually referred to as a *liquidity premium* on the basis that shorter-term securities are more money-like, and this is a premium for bearing illiquidity. For obvious reasons it might better be described as an interest-risk premium. But regardless of what it is called, its implication is the same: other considerations aside, longer-term bonds should offer higher yields.[4]

Because actual bond price fluctuations increase with maturity but at a decreasing rate, interest-rate risk premia should also increase with maturity but at a decreasing rate. Therefore, yields that would otherwise be equal regardless of maturity should increase but at a decreasing rate as maturity lengthens. In fact, individuals who are familiar with yield curves and yield curve analysis will recognize that the general shape of the classical textbook yield curve resembles the price volatility curve in Exhibit 3, always rising with increasing maturity but more and more gradually, so that the slope of the curve is very steep at short maturities but very gentle—almost unobservable—at long maturities.

A formal statement of the liquidity premium or interest-rate risk premium hypothesis is that the market adds increments L_t to yields that would otherwise exist, with

$$0 < L_t < L_{t+1} < L_{t+2} < \ldots < L_{t+n}$$

implying these liquidity premia are positive and rise with longer maturities. Moreover,

$$(L_{t+1} - L_t) > (L_{t+2} - L_{t+1}) > \ldots (L_{t+n} - L_{t+n-1})$$

That is, the liquidity premia increase at a decreasing rate with lengthening maturities.

An eclectic yield curve hypothesis. The market segmentation, unbiased expectations, and interest-rate risk premium hypotheses are not mutually exclusive ways of thinking about interest rates. It is probably fair to say the majority of those who watch the money and credit markets believe that at least two and possibly all three of these influences are present in the term structure from time to time. For example, one might be of the opinion that relative yields are usually determined by supply/

---

[4] This is the conventional wisdom. A large class of fixed income investors carry their securities at cost rather than market value and are possibly more concerned about reinvestment-rate risk than price risk—life insurers being a prime example. Such investors might well *prefer* long-term securities. These issues expose them to less risk of being forced to reinvest a large portion of their portfolio when yields are low. If such long-term investors dominated the markets, then there might actually be negative liquidity premia.

demand conditions in the short- and long-term securities markets with some tendency toward lower rates in the short end, yet still feel that at some particular time the expectation of sharply lower rates was also influencing the term structure.

One composite hypothesis, the *biased expectation hypothesis,* is particularly prominent. According to this theory, the yield curve reflects future interest-rate expectations of the moment and also persistent (but not necessarily stable) liquidity premia. Formally,[5]

$$(1 + {}_tR_n) = [(1 + {}_tR_1)(1 + {}_{t+1}r_{1,0} + L_2)(1 + {}_{t+2}r_{1,0} + L_3) \ldots$$
$$(1 + {}_{t+n}{}^-{}_1r_{1,0} + L_n)]^{1/n} \quad \text{Equation III}$$

This hypothesis is liked by many because, in addition to incorporating two elements they find intuitively appealing, it is readily able to account for "humped" yield curves, which can be observed in Exhibit 1—situations in which rates initially rise with lengthening maturity but then reach a peak and decline at the longer maturities. This pattern can be rationalized in the following way. Interest rates are expected to decline moderately, and this alone should produce a yield curve that declines over its entire length. However, liquidity premia, which have their largest marginal effects at short maturities, overpower this tendency toward a downward-sweeping yield curve at the short end. Toward the middle of the yield curve and at its long end, the expectations component is dominant. Exhibit 5 summarizes these effects.

Classical Yield Curves and Their Rationale

The yield curve in Exhibit 5 can be explained in other ways, and in fact almost any yield curve can be accounted for in a variety of ways. Exhibit 6 portrays four different yield curves that might be described as "classics" in the sense that they are prototypes of the forms into which all yield curves are supposed to fall. It is important to observe the level at which these yield curves are plotted as well as their shape, for the level

---

[5] This presentation follows the conventional practice of showing the liquidity premium as a series of constants that are added to the basic rates. However, many believe that such liquidity premia are more likely to be multiplicative in form, so that, for example, one term might be

$$(1 + {}_{t+1}r_{1,0})(1 + L_2)$$

The additive model implies that the incremental return for increased interest-rate risk is the same absolute amount regardless of the level of rates, whereas the multiplicative model is a constant relative to the level of rates. If L_2 is .005, we might have

additive: 1.04 + .005 = 1.045; 1.08 = .005 = 1.085
multiplicative: (1.04)(1.005) = 1.0452; (1.08)(1.005) = 1.0854

EXHIBIT 5   Expectations and Liquidity Effects in the Yield Curve

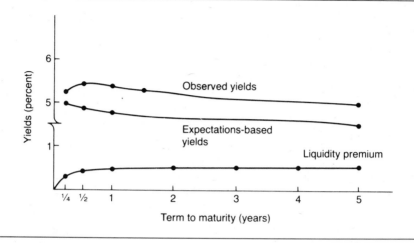

of rates plays an important role in the usual stories that are told to explain the shapes.

The four forms are these:

1. *Normal.* Interest rates are at moderate levels. Yields rise continuously with increasing maturity but with a gentle and continuously decreasing slope.
2. *Rising.* Interest rates are "low" by historical or other standards. Yields rise substantially with increasing term-to-maturity, but possibly with some reduction in the rate of increase at longer maturities.
3. *Falling.* Yields are extremely high by historical standards and decline over the entire maturity range of the yield curve.
4. *Humped.* This is the curve in Exhibit 5. Interest rates are high by historical standards. The yield curve at first rises with increasing maturity but then peaks and declines at the longer maturities.

Exhibit 6 also summarizes the stories that can be told under a variety of theories of the term structure to account for these shapes. Notice that in several cases there is no adequate stand-alone explanation for the yield curve shape under the liquidity premium hypothesis. This is consistent with the earlier discussion to the effect that the liquidity premium hypothesis is most often regarded as an "add on" rather than a "free standing" hypothesis.

EXHIBIT 6 Alternative Classical Yield Curves and Their Explanations

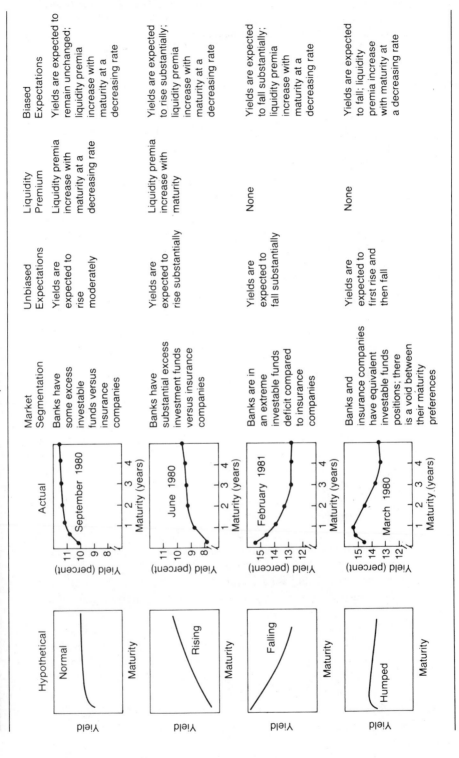

Hypothetical	Actual	Market Segmentation	Unbiased Expectations	Liquidity Premium	Biased Expectations
Normal	September 1980	Banks have some excess investable funds versus insurance companies	Yields are expected to rise moderately	Liquidity premia increase with maturity at a decreasing rate	Yields are expected to remain unchanged; liquidity premia increase with maturity at a decreasing rate
Rising	June 1980	Banks have substantial excess investment funds versus insurance companies	Yields are expected to rise substantially	Liquidity premia increase with maturity	Yields are expected to rise substantially; liquidity premia increase with maturity at a decreasing rate
Falling	February 1981	Banks are in an extreme investable funds deficit compared to insurance companies	Yields are expected to fall substantially	None	Yields are expected to fall substantially; liquidity premia increase with maturity at a decreasing rate
Humped	March 1980	Banks and insurance companies have equivalent investable funds positions; there is a void between their maturity preferences	Yields are expected to first rise and then fall	None	Yields are expected to fall; liquidity premia increase with maturity at a decreasing rate

Empirical Evidence on the Term Structure Hypotheses

In principle, it should be possible to look at the numerical record and establish which of these hypotheses is most nearly valid. But in practice such validation is extremely difficult for a variety of reasons.

First, market consensus expectations, which are needed to verify the expectations hypothesis, are not directly observable. We can actually observe future interest rates that are supposed to be predicted by forward rates embedded in the term structure, but there is nothing in the expectations hypothesis that guarantees that these forward rate predictions will come to pass.

Second, the two theories most at odds conceptually—the segmented markets and expectation hypothesis—often are both consistent with observed yield curves. For example, when the yield curve is low by historical standards but steeply upward sloping, the implication according to the expectations hypothesis is that yields are expected to rise. But periods when interest rates are low also tend to be periods of slack economic activity and low short-term loan demand, so banks are in a surplus funds position compared with life insurance companies. These conditions should produce upward-sloping yield curves according to the segmentation hypothesis. In the same manner, high but downward-sloped yield curves imply decreasing interest rates in the future. But periods when interest rates are high also tend to be characterized by strong economic activity and high demand for the type of loans that banks tend to make, so the price of short-term money should exceed the price of long-term money supplied by insurance companies. Unfortunately, if two theories can account for observed yield patterns equally well, then it is impossible to differentiate between them.

Third, and as we shall see, measurement of liquidity premia is extremely difficult in an uncertain world.

Nevertheless, it is useful to look at some of the evidence that has been brought forth on the various hypotheses.[6] This evidence does permit some general, tentative conclusions. And in a number of instances the form of the evidence should be of interest to fixed income investors in its own right.

Interest-rate risk or liquidity premia. This is the hypothesis on which the evidence is the most unequivocal, and it tends to add up to a strong case for the presence of interest-rate risk or liquidity premia.

Possibly the most obvious evidence is the behavior of yields over long periods of time. For example, analysis of the term structure num-

---

[6] A standard reference source on the term structure that reviews evidence bearing on the alternative theories in much more detail is James C. Van Horne's *Financial Market Rates and Flows* (Englewood Cliffs, N.J.: Prentice-Hall, 1978), especially Chapters 4 and 5.

bers underlying Exhibit 1 reveals that yields on securities of the shortest term have tended to be below those on longer-term securities the majority of the time over the past three decades as shown by the following tabulation:

	Number (Proportion) of Times –	
	Short Rate ≤ Long Rate	Short Rate > Long Rate
3-month Treasury bills versus 6-month Treasury bills*	256 (.959)	11 (.041)
3-month Treasury bills versus 1-year bonds	349 (.931)	26 (.069)
6-month Treasury bills versus 1-year bonds*	223 (.835)	44 (.165)

* Six-month Treasury bill series commenced January 1959.

It is also useful to look at long-run total returns, which consider changes in value as well as coupon income on longer-term securities. The well-known Ibbotson-Sinquefield total return series, which looked at monthly rates of return from the beginning of 1926 through the end of 1978, reveals an average annual rate of return on short-term bills (maturities of just over one month) of 2.5 percent per annum versus 3.4 percent per annum on long-term government bonds (maturities of 20 years).[7] This result obtains despite the general upward trend of interest rates over these years, which tended to produce capital losses on average from month to month in the long-term bond series.

The expectations hypotheses. It is evident that if the liquidity premium hypothesis is valid, then the pure or unbiased expectations hypothesis cannot be. What about the biased expectations hypothesis, in which the term structure reflects expected future interest rates as well as liquidity premia?

A popular form of test of the biased expectations hypothesis examines the pattern of revisions in yield curves with the passage of time. Such tests accept the validity of the so-called error-learning model of the formation of economic expectations. The essence of this model is that expectations of the more distant future will be revised when expecta-

---

[7] Roger G. Ibbotson and Rex A. Sinquefield, "Stocks, Bonds, Bills, and Inflation: Updates," *Financial Analysts Journal*, (July–August 1979,) pp. 40–44. It should be noted, however, that such higher returns for longer-term securities do not always show up in the short run, even when the short run is quite long. For example, over the January 1950–March 1981 period, three-month bills had higher actual holding period returns than long-term Treasury bonds.

tions of the more immediate future are found to be in error, and they will be revised in the same direction. As an example of this in the present context, suppose the market routinely forecasts some rate both three months into the future and six months into the future. If after three months have elapsed the actual rate is below the forecast made three months previously, then the market might be expected to revise downward its forecast that was formerly six months into the future but is now only three months out. If this indeed seems to happen, one is justified in concluding that (1) the error-learning model captures the way in which forecasts are made, and (2) expectations of future rates are embedded in present rates.

This test was devised by David Meiselman, and his work on the subject is a standard reference.[8] However, for our purposes it may be more useful to look at a recent study utilizing a variant of this technique by Richard Worley and Stanley Diller.[9]

Their results are summarized in Exhibit 7. The upper panel of this figure shows the errors in forecasts of three-month rates made three months earlier—that is, the actual three-month rate is subtracted from the three-month rate that was implied by the term structure three months earlier (or $_tr_{3,t-3} - {_tR_3}$). Notice that an inverted scale is used, so large underestimates of actual rates are near the top of the plot, and large overestimates are near the bottom. The lower panel shows the coincident changes in forecasted future rates—the difference in three-month rates expected in three months and the same three-month rate that was implied by the term structure three months previously (or $_{t+3}r_{3,t} - {_{t+3}r_{3,t-3}}$). These values are plotted in the usual way, so for example, a positive number means that the forecast for rates three months out has been raised. The plotted values are based on monthly observations for 1966 through most of 1976.

It is evident from the figure that there is close correlation between forecast errors and revisions in the forecasts. Underestimates in prior forecasts are associated with increases in forecasts of the future, and conversely for overestimates. Although such association does not prove that the term structure is based on expectations of future interest rates, it is consistent with the expectations hypothesis.

The market segmentation hypothesis.   Empirical evidence hearing on this hypothesis is limited. One of the more relevant studies, by Echols and Elliott,[10] was part of a larger study of term structure influ-

---

[8] David Meiselman, *The Term Structure of Interest Rates* (Englewood Cliffs, N.J.: Prentice-Hall, 1962).

[9] Richard B. Worley and Stanley Diller, "Interpreting the Yield Curve," *Financial Analysts Journal* (November–December 1976), pp. 37–45.

[10] Michael E. Echols and Jon Walter Elliott, "Rational Expectations in a Disequilibrium Model of the Term Structure," *American Economic Review* (March 1976), pp. 28–74.

EXHIBIT 7 Worley-Diller Analysis of the Influence of Forecast Errors on Forecast Changes

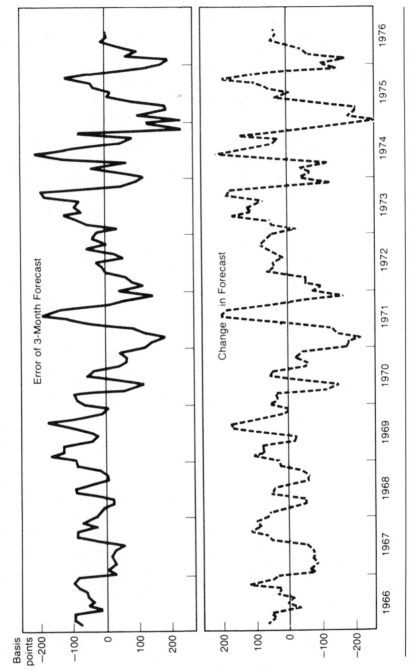

SOURCE: R. B. Worley and S. Diller, "Interpreting the Yield Curve," *Financial Analysts Journal*, Nov.–Dec. 1976, p. 43.

ences. These authors worked with monthly data from the beginning of 1964 through the end of 1971. They first made estimates of forward rates from a model that considers macroeconomic variables—changes in the money supply, the net budgetary position, net export deficit or surplus, and the like. These estimates were refined to include the measured effects of a liquidity premium. An effort was then made to explain differences in these estimated forward rates and forward rates that were actually observed by use of a supply and a demand variable. The supply measure was the ratio of the quantity of government bonds outstanding with 5 or fewer years to maturity to the quantity of bonds with 10+ years to maturity. The demand measure was the ratio of the stock of bank funds invested in U.S. government securities to the stock of insurance company funds invested in this way. Echols and Elliott found that an increase in bank holdings relative to insurance company holdings did tend to push down forward rates, especially at shorter maturities. This result is as predicted by the segmentation hypothesis. Increases in the relative supply of short-term bonds also tended to raise forward rates, particularly in shorter maturities, but this effect was not statistically significant. The authors considered these results to be consistent with the operations of preferred maturity habitats for the institutions.

The same variables were also used in an effort to explain actual yield spreads, the excess of 12-year bond yields over the three-month Treasury bill rate. In this investigation the spread was negatively related to relative institutional participation—more bank funds in government securities compared with insurance company funds meant *smaller* spreads. Moreover, here they found that an increase in the relative quantity of short-term bonds outstanding actually tended to *raise* the spread. Both these results are not consistent with the segmented market hypothesis as it is usually conceived.

A Related Issue—Forecasting Efficiency

Recall that one of the implications of the expectations hypothesis is that forecasts of future interest rates are imbedded in the present term structure of interest rates, or to state the same proposition another way, the term structure prices bonds in such a way that expected holding period returns across maturities are equal (interest-rate risk premium and market segmentation considerations aside). If the expectations considered tend to dominate the slope of the yield curve *and* if the market in the aggregate possesses adequate forecasting ability, then we should find that the term structure actually does forecast future interest rates with some degree of accuracy and that actual holding period returns across maturities do tend toward equality.

If the term structure doesn't forecast future rates well or holding period returns show little similarity across maturities, we cannot conclude unequivocally that the expectations hypothesis as a theory of the term structure is not valid. Interest-rate forecasting is an activity at which it is extremely easy to be very wrong! And it may simply be that the market forecast is consistently wrong. Nevertheless, evidence bearing on the forecasting ability of the term structures is extremely important to professional investors. For if the term structure displays little forecasting ability—either because it doesn't incorporate forecasts or because those forecasts aren't very good—then the investor can come out ahead on average by simply investing in maturities from the highest yielding portion of the yield curve.[11]

Many of the early investigations of the expectations hypothesis were actually joint tests of this hypothesis and the forecasting capabilities of the market. In one of the classic papers on the term structure, J. M. Culbertson examined holding weekly period returns on Treasury bills (the longest outstanding) and Treasury bonds (Culbertson used a bond of approximately 19 years' maturity) for 1953. Culbertson detected little evidence of parallel movements in holding period returns, and as a result indicated, "The conclusion to which we seem forced to turn is that speculative activity [i.e., activity that should equate holding period returns], dominant though it can be in very short-run movements, does not determine the broad course of interest rates or of interest-rate relationships."[12]

In contrast, Jacob Michaelson looked at weekly holding period returns on U.S. government securities with maturities ranging from one week to 10+-years over the 1951–1962 period.[13] He first observed a tendency for average realized total returns to increase with terms to maturity of from 1 to 13 weeks over this overall period and in a number of subperiods typified by cyclical upturns or downturns in interest rates. Since these results conformed closely to what one would expect in a market dominated by the biased expectation theory, he concluded that the realized returns on short-term securities conformed closely to anticipations. He then looked at the correlation between total returns on the

---

[11] If this is so, then the fixed income securities markets are not efficient in the "no easy money" or "no free lunch" sense, as excess profits can be obtained by the use of readily available strategies without the investor bearing extra risk. Note also that a frequent test of efficiency in the stock market—independence of price changes over time—is not appropriate in the fixed income markets. If fixed income security prices or yields do not display some dependence over time, then excess returns are possible provided the yield curve is not horizontal. Apparently there is confusion regarding this point, for authors occasionally describe the bond market as "efficient" when they are unable to disclose yield dependencies.

[12] J. M. Culbertson, "The Term Structure of Interest Rates," *Quarterly Journal of Economics*, (November 1957) pp. 485–517. This particular statement appears on pages 508 and 509.

[13] Jacob B. Michaelson, "The Term Structure of Interest Rates and Holding Period Yields in Government Securities," *Journal of Finance*, (September 1965) pp. 444–63.

13-week and the longer maturity series. The correlations obtained in this way were uniformly positive. On this basis he concluded that the expectations hypothesis was supported; his results also suggest that on average the market did possess some interest-rate forecasting ability.

Another implication of the expectations hypothesis is that long-term yields should lead short-term yields in time. This relationship follows from the assumption that long-term rates have expected future short-term rates embedded in them along with a belief that the market should have some meaningful interest-rate forecasting ability. This relationship was utilized by Frederick R. Macaulay in a test reported in his landmark volume *Some Theoretical Problems Suggested by the Movement of Interest Rates, Bond Yields, and Stock Prices in the United States Since 1856.*[14] Macaulay examined the relationship for the 1890–1913 period between yields on call money and on 90-day loans and found some evidence of the latter yield series leading the former. More recently, Thomas Sargent utilized the techniques of cross-spectral analysis (in essence, a technique for extracting all possible lead and lag relationships from two time series) to examine interrelationships between monthly yield series for the 1951–1960 period.[15] He also found a tendency for longer rates to lead the shorter ones.

The proposition that the market cannot forecast yield changes has recently been propounded with considerable vigor by Herbert Ayres and John Barry. As they express it, "For every real bond, the expected rate of change of yield-to-maturity is zero, hence the expected total rate of return for any real bond is its present yield-to-maturity."[16]

To test this proposition, they use the mathematical expression

$$\Delta y(m) = \Delta y(\infty) + \Delta S(m - \infty) \qquad \text{Equation IV}$$

which says that the changes in the yield of a security with a maturity of m, $\Delta y(m)$, is equal to the change in the yield on a perpetual bond, $\Delta y(\infty)$, plus the change in the spread between yields on the security with a maturity of m and the perpetuity, $\Delta S(m - \infty)$. They then show the following:

1. On monthly observations over the 1966–1974 period, the mean change in long-term bond yields (a proxy for the perpetuity) was not statistically different from zero. In other words, and despite the considerable drift upward in yield that occurred over those years, the monthly

---

[14] National Bureau of Economic Research, New York, 1938.

[15] Thomas J. Sargent, "Interest Rates in the Nineteen Fifties," *Review of Economics and Statistics* (May 1968) pp. 164–72.

[16] Herbert F. Ayres and John Y. Barry, "The Equilibrium Yield Curve for Government Securities," *Financial Analysts Journal* (May–June 1979) pp. 31–39. The quotation appears on page 34.

change in long-term yields could not have been reliably predicted to be positive.

2. Over the same period, the average change in spread between yields on long bonds and bonds of shorter maturities was not significantly different from zero, meaning it could not be reliably predicted to be other than zero.

3. Changes in the perpetuity rate and changes in the spread were uncorrelated. That is, there was no association between $\Delta y(\infty)$ and $\Delta S(m - \infty)$. This is the finding that is most at odds with the expectation hypothesis, for the hypothesis implies that there should be positive correlation between the two—that is, they should change in the same direction. For example, if short yields are initially above long yields, the yield spread $S(m - \infty)$ is positive, and the yield curve is downward sweeping; then the long yield should decline, and as it does the yield spread should become negative $[y(m) < y(\infty)]$ as the yield curve returns to its normal shape. As evidence on this point, Ayres and Barry examine changes in the five-year rate and changes in the spread on one- and five-year yields, in Exhibit 8. The data, which are standarized, display no statistically meaningful correlation.

Actually, the situation may not be quite so bleak as Ayres and Barry suggest. The relationship between $\Delta y(\infty)$ and $\Delta S(m - \infty)$ is only one of many that might be examined. Consider these additional comparisons:

$$\Delta S(m - \infty) \quad \text{and} \quad \Delta y(m)$$

This is similar to the Ayres-Barry comparison, but looks at changes in spreads and changes in short rates. The expectations hypothesis again predicts a positive correlation.

$$S(m - \infty)_t \quad \text{and} \quad \Delta y(\infty)_{t+1}$$

This comparison is actually more in the spirit of the expectations hypothesis. The expectation is for a negative correlation between an observed spread and the change in the long rate in the succeeding period. For example, if the spread is large and positive, with short rates above long rates, the implication is that long rates will decline. If the spread is large but negative, short rates are well below long rates, and long rates are expected to increase.

$$S(m - \infty)_t \quad \text{and} \quad \Delta y(m)_{t+1}$$

This is a restatement of the preceding comparison but in this statement an effort is made to predict short rates. For similar reasons the correlations should be negative.

$$S(m - \infty)_t \quad \text{and} \quad \Delta S(m - \infty)_{t+1}$$

This comparison is between observed spreads and changes in spreads in the succeeding period. The expectations hypothesis predicts a negative

EXHIBIT 8   Ayres and Barry's Correlations between Changes in Yield Spreads and Long Yields, January 1956–August 1978

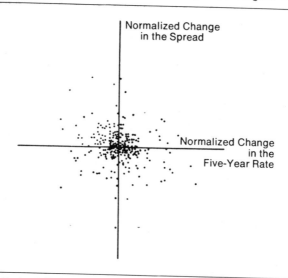

SOURCE: Herbert F. Ayres and John Y. Barry, "The Equilibrium Yield curve for Government Securities," *Financial Analysts Journal* (May–June 1979) p. 35.

relationship—a downward-sloped yield curve [S(m − ∞) > 0] should become less downward sloped, whereas a strongly upward-sloped yield curve [S(m − ∞) < 0] should become less upward sloped.

Exhibit 9 shows the simple correlation coefficients for each of these comparisons for intervals of 1, 3, 6, and 12 months over the same January 1956–August 1978 period examined by Ayres and Barry. The correlation for the comparison suggested by Ayres and Barry is the first value shown in Exhibit 9, and the result is quite consistent with what they report. However, as the interval is lengthened, this correlation becomes significant in the proper positive direction. The other correlations are also generally significant and in the direction the expectations hypothesis predicts, except for some of the one-month interval comparisons and the comparisons that attempt to predict changes in the long rate from the preceeding month's yield spread.[17]

These results, therefore, are consistent with a market that has some forecasting ability and that incorporates these forecasts into the term

---

[17] For holding period intervals in excess of one month, the successive observations are not independent; for example, 11 months in a given 12-month period overlaps with the preceeding period. Such nonindependence can make overlap correlation coefficients of the sort contained in Exhibit 9 and tests of other significance misleading. However, this analysis has been repeated with only nonoverlapping holding periods (e.g., January through December periods only) with similar results.

EXHIBIT 9 Selected Correlations between Yield Changes, Yield Spreads, and Changes in Yield Spreads, January 1956–August 1978

$\Delta y(\infty)$ versus $\Delta S(m - \infty)$:

Monthly	0.097
Quarterly	0.460*
Semiannually	0.547*
Annually	0.512*

$\Delta S(m - \infty)$ versus $\Delta y(m)$:

Monthly	0.698*
Quarterly	0.805*
Semiannually	0.839*
Annually	0.834*

$S(m - \infty)_t$ versus $\Delta y(\infty)_{t+1}$:

Monthly	.019
Quarterly	−0.044
Semiannually	−0.023
Annually	−0.028

$S(m - \infty)_t$ versus $\Delta y(m)_{t+1}$:

Monthly	0.125*
Quarterly	−0.191*
Semiannually	−0.238*
Annually	−0.281*

$S(m - \infty)_t$ versus $\Delta S(m - \infty)_{t+1}$:

Monthly	−0.222*
Quarterly	−0.324*
Semiannually	−0.460*
Annually	−0.594*

---

* Relationship is statistically significant at 5 percent level.

structure. Thus they support many of the more traditional tests of the expectations hypothesis. But there is a substantial difference between statistical tests and economic tests. It may well be, as Ayres and Barry suggest, that *for practical purposes* one can proceed as though the best guess regarding the holding period return from a bond of any maturity is its yield-to-maturity. Obviously much more testing is needed in this area, particularly testing that is more directly oriented toward the economic rewards of different investment strategies based on the predictive properties of the term structure.

MEASURING THE TERM STRUCTURE

For many investors an occasional rundown on yields on U.S. Treasury securities as published by *The Wall Street Journal* and other periodicals will be sufficient to keep an eye on the term structure. Others will want to be more formal in their analysis. In this section we review some of the ways for monitoring the term structures.

Published Yield Curves

Possibly the most frequently utilized representatives of the term structure are the yield curves published each month in the *U.S. Treasury Bulletin*; the yield curve in Exhibit 2 comes from this source. These curves are visually fitted to month-end yields to maturity on U.S. government securities by Treasury analysts; that is, they are drawn freehand or by eye without resort to statistical curve-fitting techniques. In fitting these curves only the yields on approximately current coupon bonds with no special features (e.g., flower bonds) are considered. Yields on low-coupon bonds are believed to be downward-biased representations of market yields because of the favorable taxation awarded to the capital gains component of their returns, and flower bond yields are also downward biased due to their favored treatment in payment of federal estate taxes.

The *Treasury Bulletin* yield curves provide an excellent means for keeping abreast of the general behavior of the term structure. However, for more detailed analytical purposes, they are not entirely satisfactory for two reasons. First, in the final analysis they are judgmentally derived, and there is always uncertainty about judgmental members—it is unlikely, for example, that any two analysts would usually fit exactly the same yield curve. Second, another problem arises when explicit numerical yield numbers are needed. Such numbers must be read off the yield curve, and this is an activity of uncertain precision. It is unlikely that these are serious problems, and in fact they are present to a greater or lesser degree in almost all yield curve analysis. But it has become more common to work with constructed or synthetic yield-maturity data series and to statistically fit yield curves in analyzing the term structure.

Sources of Yield-Maturity Series

A standard source of yields on U.S. government securities by maturity is a series published by Salomon Brothers Inc. The Salomon Brothers yields have been employed to construct many of the exhibits in this chapter. This series currently shows yields at 11 maturity points ranging from three months to 30 years in numerical form. It is published weekly in Salomon Brothers' *Bond Market Roundup,* and historical first-of-month (midmonth prior to 1959) yields are reported in Salomon Brothers' *An Analytical Record of Yields and Yield Spreads.* The Salomon Brothers data is prepared in much the same way as the *Treasury Bulletin* yield curves; that is, yield curves are fitted to actual bond yield data, following the yields of higher coupon bonds when a choice exists, and then the yields are read off at each maturity point. Thus the primary advantages of the Salomon Brothers series are its timeliness and that fact that the curve reading has already been done for the analyst.

In recent years the *Federal Reserve Bulletin* has contained a constant maturity yield series for U.S. government bonds and notes ranging from 1 to 30 years to maturity. This series is described as "yields on the more actively traded issues adjusted to constant maturities by the U.S. Treasury, based on daily closing bid prices." The yields are reported by calendar weeks ending on Wednesdays, by months, and by years; the weekly data represent averages of the undisclosed daily values, monthly data are averages of the weeks, and so on. Therefore, the *FRB Bulletin* numbers are not directly comparable with the Salomon Brothers data. Exhibit 10 contains the Salomon Brothers data for January 2, 1981 (the

EXHIBIT 10 A Comparison of Salomon Brothers and Federal Reserve Bulletin Yield Data

Term to Maturity	Yields, Salomon Brothers, January 2, 1981	Yields, Federal Reserve Bulletin, Week Ending January 2, 1981
3 months	15.02%	15.05%*
6 months	14.96	14.96*
1 year	13.97	13.86
2 years	13.01	13.00
3 years	12.65	12.81
4 years	12.68	—
5 years	12.57	12.54
7 years	12.47	12.43
10 years	12.43	12.36
20 years	11.96	12.05
30 years	11.94	11.95

* Treasury bill discounts converted to coupon-equivalent yields.
SOURCE: Data courtesy of Salomon Brothers Inc and from the *Federal Reserve Bulletin*, February 1981.

first was a holiday) and the *FRB* data for the week ending January 2, 1981. Although the two series are not identical, they are quite similar, especially in the yield-curve patterns they display.

Fitting Yield Curves

These yield series are probably more useful for investment decision making than the *Treasury Bulletin* yield curves because they have been reduced to numerical terms by someone who is experienced in doing this. The numbers themselves can be examined for yield patterns, or they can be plotted to obtain yield curves such as those in Exhibit 1, which are of the "connect the dots" variety.

Such curves are described as discontinuous. This means that they change shape at each measurement point and can do so abruptly. However, one would expect yield transitions from one maturity to another to be fairly smooth—that is, to be characterized by a continuous curve. In addition, one is often interested in maturities that lie away from measurement points. Such intermediate yields could be estimated by linear interpolation, but this is clumsy and at odds with the notion of yield curves that change shape continuously. For those reasons it is frequently desirable to fit mathematical curves to the yield points.

A number of models have been proposed for fitting such curves. All use the method of least squares to actually fit the curve. Where they differ is in the form of the equation that is fitted and its number of terms. With too few terms the estimated yield curve is excessively smooth—for example, with one term it would simply be a straight line. Too many terms will "overfit" the line—with as many terms as maturity points, the line will go precisely through each point.

One model that has been proved particularly effective for such applications is due to Stephen Bradley and Dwight Crane.[18] The Bradley-Crane model has the form

$$\ln(1 + R_M) = a + b_1(M) + b_2\ln(M) + e \quad \text{Equation V}$$

That is, values equal to the natural logarithm of one plus the observed yields for term-to-maturity of length M are regressed on two variables, the term-to-maturity and the natural log of the term-to-maturity. The last term represents the unexplained yield variation. Fitting this model is well within the capability of the typical scientific calculator. Once the estimated values of a, b_1, and b_2 are obtained, specific maturities of interest can be substituted to obtain estimated yields at these maturity points. Exhibit 11 shows the Salomon Brothers yield series as of January 2, 1981, along with a yield curve fitted by this method. It can be observed that the fit is not particularly good in the shorter maturities. Fortunately, Treasury bill yields are available in weekly maturity intervals out to approximately one year, so they can readily be used instead for many purposes.

Occasionally one wishes to fit yield curves directly to yield data for individual bonds rather than to homogenized yield series. This might be desirable as a means of avoiding possible distortions created in the process of arriving at the synthetic yield series. It might also be motivated by a particular interest in individual bonds—for example, when looking for arbitrage opportunities between underpriced or overpriced bonds by

---

[18] Stephen P. Bradley and Dwight B. Crane, "Management of Commercial Bank Government Security Portfolios: An Optimization Approach under Uncertainty," *Journal of Bank Research*, Spring 1973, pp. 18–30.

EXHIBIT 11 Bradley-Crane Yield Curve Fitted to Salomon Brothers Yield Data for January 2, 1981

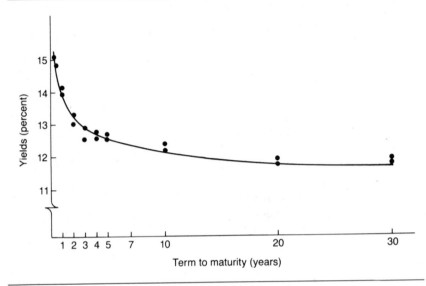

SOURCE: Salomon Brothers Inc; line estimated by author.

examining their yields in comparison with a fitted yield curve. A model for fitting such yield curves has been proposed by Elliot and Echols.[19]

The Elliot-Echols model has the form:

$$1n(1 + R_i) = a + b_1((1/M_i) + b_2(M_i) + b_3(C_i) + e_i \quad \text{Equation VI}$$

where R_i, M_i, and C_i are the yield-to-maturity, term-to-maturity, and coupon rate of the ith bond.

Notice that yield and maturity are related in somewhat different ways than in the Bradley-Crane model. This representation also differs by the inclusion of the individual bond's coupons. As was noted previously, low-coupon bonds tend to have yields that are subnormal for their term-to-maturity, presumably because of the favored tax treatment of their built-in capital gain. The coupon term adjusts for this effect.

Elliott and Echols suggested that in obtaining yield curves from this model the coupon term should be set equal to zero so as to avoid confounding coupon effects and maturity effects. The author believes that a more appropriate (if more cumbersome) procedure is to search for that

---

[19] Michael E. Echols and Jan Walter Elliott, "A Quantitative Yield Curve Model for Estimating the Term Structure of Interest Rates," *Journal of Financial and Quantitative Analysis*, March 1976, pp. 87–114.

coupon rate at which the coupon rate and the yield-to-maturity of a hypothetical bond of a given term-to-maturity would be the same. The resulting point on the yield curve is the estimated yield at which a current coupon bond would sell if one existed. (The Elliott-Echols method gives the estimated yield at which a zero-coupon bond would sell if one existed.) Exhibit 12 shows such a yield curve fitted to individ-

---

EXHIBIT 12 Elliot-Echols Yield Curve Fitted to Individual U.S. Government Bond and Note Yields, March 31, 1977

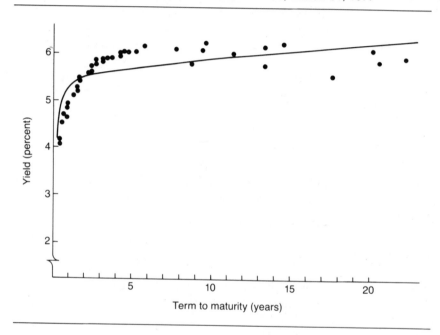

---

ual bond and note data for this method as of the end of March 1977. Note that because of this coupon effect there is no reason for the individual bonds to be scattered evenly around the line. Of course, a bond's actual coupon should be used in estimating its appropriate yield if the objective is to determine whether it is underpriced or overpriced.

Estimating Forward Rates

Many uses of term structure or yield curve do not require the estimation of forward rates. However, there will be occasions in which it is desirable to actually extract forward rates from the yield curve or other data in order to get some idea of interest rates the market consensus is forecasting.

If suitably spaced yields on either synthetic or actual securities are available, then forward rates can be estimated directly by the use of Equation II without the necessity for fitting yield curves. Recall that Equation II stated

$$(1 + {}_{t+m}r^b_{n-m,t})^{n-m} = (1 + {}_tR_n)^n / (1 + {}_tR_m)^m \quad \text{Equation II}$$

Use of this formula is extremely straightforward once the data are in proper form. The equation is written on the assumption that all yields are expressed in the same units of time, per annum yields being most common. For many purposes it will be useful to measure m and n in units that have the effect of making $m - n = 1$.

A simple example may help illustrate the process and clarify this last point. On January 2, 1981, three-month and six-month coupon-equivalent Treasury bill yields as reported in *The Wall Street Journal* were 15.31 percent and 15.00 percent per annum respectively. If we use Equation II with m and n expressed in years to estimate the three-month rate anticipated in three months, we have

$$(1 + {}_{1/4}r^b_{1/4,0})^{1/4} = \frac{(1.1500)^{1/2}}{(1.1531)^{1/4}} = \frac{1.0724}{1.0363} = 1.0349$$

This last value is one plus an annual rate, but is raised to the one-fourth power in accordance with it being for a quarter of a year. In order to make it apply to a whole year, we must raise it to the fourth power, or

$$[(1 + {}_{1/4}r^b_{1/4,0})^{1/4}]^4 = (1 + {}_{1/4}r^b_{1/4,0}]$$

When we do we get

$$(1.0349)^4 = 1.1469, \text{ or } 14.69 \text{ percent}$$

Alternatively, we might simply express m and n in three-month periods, since we are interested in a three-month forward rate:

$$(1 + {}_1r^b_{1,0})^1 = \frac{(1.1500)^2}{(1.1531)^1} = \frac{1.3225}{1.1531} = 1.1469$$

or 14.69 percent again.

Exhibit 13 continues the estimation of three-month forward rates as of January 2, 1981. The first rate in each series is unadjusted; the second has been adjusted for liquidity premia, as will be discussed subsequently. The exhibit also shows forward rates estimated using a simplified method proposed by Worley and Diller.[20,21]

$$_{t+m}r^b_{n-m,t} = \frac{({}_tR_n \cdot n) - ({}_tR_m \cdot m)}{n - m} \qquad \text{Equation VII}$$

---

[20] Worley and Diller, "Interpreting the Yield Curve," p. 45.

[21] The values in the first four columns of Exhibit 13 are computed by reference to the actual number of days in each period because the periods are not of equal length—principally because no Treasury bill traded on January 2 matured on October 2, making it necessary to use the bill maturing October 8.

EXHIBIT 13 Alternative Estimates of Three-Month Forward Rates, January 2, 1981

Forward Rates for Three Months Beginning	Actual Yields, Equation II		Actual Yields, Equation VII		Fitted Yields, Equation II	
	Unadjusted	Adjusted	Unadjusted	Adjusted	Unadjusted	Adjusted
April 2, 1981	14.69%	14.11%	14.69%	14.11%	13.88%	13.71%
July 2, 1981	13.02	12.76	13.01	12.77	13.40	13.19
October 8, 1981*	12.88	12.66	12.87	12.65	13.10	12.88
January 2, 1982					12.88	12.66
April 2, 1982					12.71	12.49
July 2, 1982					12.58	12.36
October 2, 1982					12.46	12.24
January 2, 1983					12.37	12.15
April 2, 1983					12.29	12.07
July 2, 1983					12.21	11.99
October 2, 1983					12.15	11.93

* October 2, 1981 for estimates based on fitted yields.

This equation, which does not require the use of exponents or assume compounding, is quite satisfactory provided the interval $n - m$ is not large.

Suppose suitably spaced yields are not available. Suppose, for example, we want to estimate forward rates for three-month intervals on out beyond a year in the future. This is where fitted yield curves become useful. After having estimated the appropriate coefficients, we can simply substitute in the appropriate values of m and n and use Equation V or VI to obtain the forward rate. For example, the Bradley-Crane model equation for January 2, 1981 (Exhibit 11), is

$$\ln(1 + R_M) = 0.129700 + 0.000425(M) - 0.008497 \ln(M)$$

If we are interested in the three-month rate one year into the future, at the beginning of January 1982, we substitute 1.0 and 1.25 (m and n, equal to 1 year and 1¼ years) in the equation, obtaining 13.8970 for R_1 and 13.6933 for $R_{1.25}$. Equation II gives

$$\left({}_1r^b{}_{.25,0}\right)^{.25} = \frac{(1.136933)^{1.25}}{(1.138970)^1}$$

$$= 1.030756$$

or 12.88 percent per annum.

Exhibit 13 contains forward rates for each three-month interval beginning three months through three years into the future in addition to the forward rates for the first three of those intervals obtained earlier. The differences in the two series, which are caused by differences in data as well as method, are initially large but converge rapidly. Both sets of numbers illustrate in striking fashion the decline that was expected in interest rates during 1981 as the year began.

Liquidity Premia Adjustment

The formulas for forward rates presented in the preceding section all had a superscript b attached to the r's representing forward rates. This superscript is intended as a reminder that these are "biased" forward rates; that is, to the extent that there are liquidity premia imbedded in the term structure, then forward rates are upward-biased estimates of yields the market consensus expects in the future. For many purposes these biased forward rates are acceptable or even desirable. For example, if our interest is in monitoring the pattern of changes in expected forward rates from month to month, we need not be concerned about the liquidity premia, since they are imbedded in both the beginning and ending series and probably don't change much over such short intervals. If we are attempting to price out a bond using forward rates, we would actually *prefer* rates with imbedded liquidity premia.

This is fortunate, because entirely satisfactory liquidity premia estimates are impossible to obtain. Ideally, we could estimate liquidity premia in any of the following ways:

1. Compute differences in yields along a long-run average yield curve.
2. Compute long-run differences in average total returns on bonds of different maturities.
3. Compute long-run differences in implied forward rates and actual outcomes.

In practice none of these approaches is entirely satisfactory. The problem is that there is no reason to believe liquidity premia remain stable over long periods of time, yet for shorter periods of time it is unlikely that on average interest rates are expected to remain unchanged [which makes approach (1) unsatisfactory] or that forecasted yields actually turn out as expected [which militates against the value of approaches (2) and (3)].

Using the third approach, Worley and Diller estimated liquidity premia for the 1966–1976 period as follows:

m	$n - m$	L
3 months	3 months	58 basis points
6	3	26
9	3	22
6	6	24

where

m = time in future when rate is effective
$n - m$ = maturity of security to which rate applies
L = liquidity premium in basis points

J. Houston McCulloch has employed a variant of this approach to make liquidity premium estimates for the largely nonoverlapping period March 1951–March 1966 contained in Exhibit 14.[22] Direct comparisons with the Worley-Diller estimates are possible. For the three-month rate in three months, the estimates are dramatically different—58 basis points for Worley-Diller versus 17 basis points for McCulloch. However, premia for three-month maturities further into the future are similar— for example, 21 and 26 basis points for rates to be effective in six months, and 22 basis points for both for rates effective in nine months.

---

[22] J. Houston McCulloch, "An Estimate of the Liquidity Premium," *Journal of Political Economy,* February 1975, pp. 95–119.

EXHIBIT 14 McCulloch Liquidity Premium Estimates, March 1951–March 1966

n − m / m	0	One Month	Two Months	Three Months	Six Months	Nine Months	1 Year	2 Years	3 Years	5 Years	10 Years	20 Years	30 Years
One month	0.17	0.13	0.11	0.09	0.05	0.04	0.03	0.01	0.01	0.01	0.00	0.00	0.00
Two months	0.28	0.22	0.17	0.14	0.09	0.06	0.05	0.02	0.02	0.01	0.00	0.00	0.00
Three months	0.34	0.27	0.21	0.17	0.11	0.07	0.06	0.03	0.02	0.01	0.01	0.00	0.00
Six months	0.41	0.32	0.26	0.21	0.13	0.09	0.07	0.03	0.02	0.01	0.01	0.00	0.00
Nine months	0.32	0.34	0.27	0.22	0.13	0.09	0.07	0.04	0.02	0.01	0.01	0.00	0.00
1 year	0.43	0.34	0.27	0.22	0.14	0.09	0.07	0.04	0.02	0.01	0.01	0.00	0.00
2 years	0.43	0.34	0.27	0.22	0.14	0.09	0.07	0.04	0.02	0.01	0.01	0.00	0.00
3 years	0.43	0.34	0.27	0.22	0.14	0.09	0.07	0.04	0.02	0.01	0.01	0.00	0.00
5 years	0.43	0.34	0.27	0.22	0.14	0.09	0.07	0.04	0.02	0.01	0.01	0.00	0.00
10 years	0.43	0.34	0.27	0.22	0.14	0.09	0.07	0.04	0.02	0.01	0.01	0.00	0.00
20 years	0.43	0.34	0.27	0.22	0.14	0.09	0.07	0.04	0.02	0.01	0.01	0.00	0.00
30 years	0.43	0.34	0.27	0.22	0.14	0.09	0.07	0.04	0.02	0.01	0.01	0.00	0.00

SOURCE: Adapted from J. Houston McCulloch, "An Estimate of the Liquidity Premium," *Journal of Political Economy*, February 1975, p. 113.

It is interesting that the incremental liquidity premia is for practical purposes zero for yields beyond about six months into the future in both series. If this property persists over time (and there is reason to believe that it should), it is good news. Even though forward rates derived from the term structures may be biased, the bias is internally consistent beyond six months or so into the future. Thus, for example, if the forward rates show 3-months money rising in price between 9 and 12 months into the future, it is likely that this reflects the market's expectation of higher future interest rates rather than effects of liquidity premia.

Exhibit 13 uses the Worley-Diller and McCulloch liquidity premia to adjust the forward rates for January 2, 1981, obtained previously.

Another Approach to Estimating the Term Structure

A problem with conventional yields-to-maturity and hence yield-curve analysis based on such yields is that they suffer from a "coupon effect" that is independent of any tax consequences of coupons and price discounts. Because of this coupon effect, the yield-to-maturity on any specific bond is probably *not* equal to the market's required rate of return over the bond's term-to-maturity. The essence of the problem is that bonds with different coupons have different cash flow patterns that yield-to-maturity calculations do not adequately reflect. It is analogous to the difficulties that can arise in using internal rate of return in ranking projects for capital budgeting purposes.

The problem is probably best understood via an example.[23] Suppose we have two two-period bonds, Bond A with a 9 percent coupon and Bond B with a 5 percent coupon. Assume that the spot rates the market is using to price the bonds are $_0R_1 = 0.04$ and $_0R_2 = 0.09$. That is, the market presently requires 4 percent per annum on money committed for one year and 9 percent on two-year money. Then the proper prices of these bonds are

$$P_A = \frac{9}{(1.04)} + \frac{109}{(1.09)^2} = 100.397$$

$$P_B = \frac{5}{(1.04)} + \frac{105}{(1.09)^2} = 93.184$$

At these prices the bonds will each provide the one- and two-period returns the market requires. But the conventionally computed yields to maturity are 8.78 percent for Bond A and 8.87 percent for Bond B!

Now this may be an extreme example—for instance, the implied rate on one-year money in one year is 14.24 percent. Moreover, this problem does not arise with zero-coupon securities, such as Treasury

---

[23] This example was provided to the author by James V. Jordan.

bills, so it creates no difficulties for analysis of near-term forward rates. Nevertheless, the principle is valid, and there is some evidence that it can be serious in forward-rate estimation.

A way around it that has been known to academics for some years and is beginning to be applied in fixed income decision-making applications works with discount factors rather than yields.[24] Discount factors are values equal to $1/(1 + R_t)^t$; they are the factors found in the familiar present value tables.

The essence of the approach is to estimate the d coefficients in the multiple regression

$$P_{i,0} = d_1 X_{i,1} + d_2 X_{i,2} + \cdots + d_t X_{i,T} + e_i$$

where

$$P_{i,0} = \text{the price of the } i^{th} \text{ bond at time zero}$$
$$X_{i,t}(t = 1, \ldots, T) = \text{the cash flows from the bond in period t}$$

In other words, prices of a number of bonds at a specific instant in time are regressed on their future coupons and maturity payments in a cross-sectional regression. The estimated values of d are discount factors, and from them yields that are free of coupon bias can be computed. For example, d_1 is an estimate of $1/(1 + R_1)$, d_2 is an estimate of $1/(1 + R_2)^2$, and so on.

Practical implementation of this approach involves dealing with some issues that are beyond the scope of this chapter, including data selection and constraints on the behavior of the d_t. However, those issues have been dealt with and largely resolved in the academic literature, and thus this method is worthy of consideration by persons contemplating serious term structure analysis.[25]

Financial Futures as a Guide to the Term Structure

The recent emergence of a viable market in interest-rate futures provides a means of observing forward interest rates that should be highly satis-

---

[24] Development and use of this methodology is reported in J. Houston McCulloch, "Measuring the Term Structure of Interest Rates," *Journal of Business*, January 1971, pp. 19–31; Stephen M. Schaefer, "On Measuring the Term Structure of Interest Rates," paper presented to the International Workshop on Recent Research in Capital Markets, Berlin, September 1973; and Willard T. Carleton and Ian A. Cooper, "Estimation and Uses of the Term Structure of Interest Rates," *Journal of Finance*, September 1976, pp. 1067–1083. The liquidity premia estimates appearing in Exhibit 14 were estimated by McCulloch utilizing this method.

[25] A good introduction to the implementation of this model appears in James V. Jordan, "Studies in Direct Estimation of the Term Structure," a dissertation completed at the University of North Carolina in 1980. It is unpublished, but copies are available from the author of this chapter.

factory for many purposes. There is currently an active market on the Chicago Board of Trade for Treasury bonds of 15+ years to maturity and Government National Mortgage Association mortgage pass-throughs (GNMAs) to be delivered up to 3 years in the future; futures contracts on three-month Treasury bills to be delivered as far as two years into the future trade on the International Monetary Mart. Those futures contracts trade on a price basis, but equivalent yield figures are usually provided along with price quotations. The delivery dates correspond to m, the date at which the forward rate becomes effective, and the maturities of the securities in question are the same as n − m. Thus forward rates for three-month money, money of approximately 6 to 8 years duration, and 15+ years can be read directly out of *The Wall Street Journal* or equivalent sources.[26]

Such numbers as of January 2, 1981, appear in Exhibit 15. These are biased forward rates.[27] This means that the caveats that are in order for

---

EXHIBIT 15   Yields on Financial Futures Instruments, January 2, 1981

Delivery Month	Treasury Bills*	GNMAs	Treasury Bonds
March 1981	12.97%	12.79%	11.66
June 1981	11.85	12.66	11.52
September 1981	11.42	12.63	11.45
December 1981	11.29	12.64	11.44
March 1982	11.28	12.65	11.43
June 1982	11.09	12.66	11.42
September 1982	11.00	12.67	11.41
December 1982	11.52	12.69	11.40

* Treasury bill yields have been converted from a discount to a coupon-equivalent basis.

---

[26] The life of GNMAs is not an obvious number. Conventional GNMA computations assume that all mortgages in the pool are paid down according to schedule until the 12th year of their life, at which time they are paid off entirely. Prepayment in recent years has been considerably more rapid than this. Moreover, since a mortgage is a constant paydown investment, the date of the last payment (maturity date) is much less relevant than for conventional bonds. The range of six to eight years encompasses a number of alternative measures of life estimated by Martin L. Leibowitz. These measures as well as a more general discussion of the problem appears in a memorandum entitled "Cash Flow Characteristics of Mortgage Securities," presented to the Financial Analysts Federation/Institute of Chartered Financial Analysts Symposium, Boston, 1979. It is reprinted in *CFA Readings in Financial Analysis*, 5th ed. (Charlottesville, Va.: The Institute of Chartered Finance Analysts, 1981), pp. 152–82.

[27] To see this, consider the fact that the cash flows of a six-month Treasury bill can be duplicated by buying a three-month bill and a contract for delivery of another three-month

biased forward rates also apply to financial futures yields. Nevertheless, financial futures quotations provide a readily accessible means of monitoring the market's consensus of future yields and tracing changes in these consensus forecasts.

---

bill in three months; under the latter scenario the proceeds on the maturing three month bills are used to pay for the bills delivered on the contract. Thus

$$(1 + \text{6-month bill yield})^{1/2} = (1 + \text{3-month bill yield})^{1/4}$$
$$(1 + \text{yield on three-month bill contract for delivery in three months})^{1/4}$$

If this relationship did not hold, then arbitragers would enter the market, buying the higher yielding side and shorting the lower yielding side. This relationship is the same as

$$(1 + {_0}R_{1/2})^{1/2} = (1 + {_0}R_{1/4})^{1/4}(1 + {_{1/4}}r^b{_{1/4}})^{1/4}$$

which can be written as

$$(1 + {_{1/4}}r^b{_{1/4}})^{1/4} = (1 + {_0}R_{1/2})^{1/2}(1 + {_0}R_{1/4})^{1/4}$$

a version of Equation II.

For this reason yields on the financial futures instruments are not independent of the present level of interest rates. They should tend to fall as interest rates between the observation point and the delivery date rise, all other things equal. And the liquidity premia that are imbedded in the spot three- and six-month rates will also affect these yields.

54

Corporate-to-Treasury Yield Spreads: A Cyclical Analysis

James L. Kochan
Vice President and Manager
Fixed Income Research
Merrill Lynch, Pierce, Fenner & Smith, Inc.

All managers of fixed income portfolios are accustomed to dealing with market risk—the probability that bond prices will rise and fall in an unpredictable manner. Managers of portfolios that include corporate bonds must also contend with credit risk and sector risk—the prospect of changes in the credit quality of the bonds they own, and changes in yield relationships between the corporate and Treasury markets. This chapter investigates the latter source of portfolio risk. Unanticipated shifts in corporate-to-Treasury yield spreads can be one of the most rewarding or painful factors to influence the total returns of a fixed income portfolio.

Because corporate debt entails credit risk while Treasury issues do not, and because corporates lack the high degree of market liquidity that Treasuries enjoy, yields on corporate bonds are always above those on Treasury issues of the same maturity. Investors demand and receive additional compensation for incurring the incremental risk and loss of liquidity that stems from owning corporates rather than governments. However, the market's evaluation of these factors changes dramatically over time. Even a casual analysis shows a high degree of variability in corporate/Treasury yield spreads. Spreads between long double-A rated utility bonds and the 20-year Treasury bond were as narrow as 25 basis points on several occasions during the 1950s and as wide as 275 basis points in 1981. Moreover, these spreads can change very rapidly. Perhaps the most vivid example of a rapid adjustment occurred in 1980, when spreads dropped over 100 basis points in the space of one month. (See Exhibits 1 and 2.)

EXHIBIT 1   Yields on a 20-Year Treasury Security

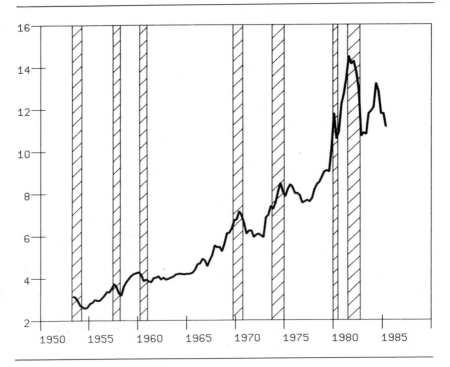

At first glance, it may appear that explaining and, therefore, predicting movements in corporate/Treasury yield spreads should be relatively straightforward. There is a pronounced cyclical pattern to the spreads—increasing when bond yields are in a cyclical uptrend and falling when yields are trending downward. Within this pattern, however, is a significant amount of variation that is difficult to explain.

THE VALUE OF YIELD RATIOS

The amplitude of the swings and indeed the *level* of the yield spreads are clearly a function of the *level* of yields. During the 1953–1964 period, the utility-to-Treasury yield spreads were generally in the 30–60 basis point range and rarely exceeded 100 basis points. During the past 10 years,

EXHIBIT 2   Yield Spreads between an AA Utility Bond and a 20-Year
Treasury Security

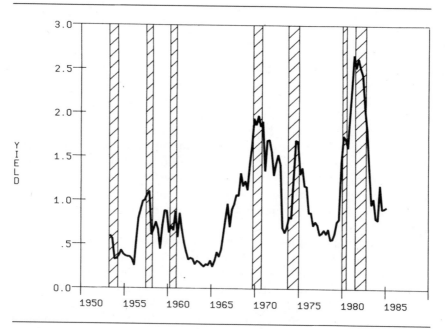

this spread has rarely been below 60 basis points, and has been above 200 basis points for quite a long time. Even in 1985, when bond yields were quite low by the standards of this decade, this yield spread typically moved within the 80–100 basis point range, well above the lowest spreads of the 1950s and 1960s.

Whenever the absolute levels of yields change as dramatically as during the past 20 years, absolute spread relationships lose a great deal of continuity and comparability. In the analysis of yield relationships, the yield ratios are the more useful statistics when interest rates move over a wide range. For example, in mid-1985, the ratio of utility-to-Treasury yields of 1.08 was not significantly greater than the low ratios of 1955–65. This suggests that at the current higher levels of bond yields, spreads of around 80 basis points are as narrow, on a relative basis, as the 25–35 basis point spreads of 1963–65. At times, the 1985 spreads were narrower (relatively) than the 30–50 basis point spreads that prevailed from 1953 to 1955.

Using yield ratios helps eliminate the effects of wide swings in yield levels from the analysis of sector spreads, but does not address the question of cyclical movements in these spreads. The ratios also show significant cyclical variation. The utility-to-Treasury ratio has been as low as 1.05 and as high as 1.35 during the past 30 years, a peak-to-trough differential of almost 30 percent. One key to successful portfolio management is to anticipate these cyclical movements.

THE CYCLE IN YIELD SPREADS

The fundamental pattern of the corporate/Treasury yield differentials is well-defined—the spreads typically widen as yields trend upward and fall when bond yields are in a cyclical downtrend. One possible explanation focuses on changes in credit risk. When interest rates are in a cyclical uptrend, investors begin to anticipate a business-cycle recession. A business recession, in turn, implies lower corporate profits, strains on corporate balance sheets, and perhaps cash-flow problems if the recession becomes severe. Periods of rising interest rates are also characterized by rising debt ratios, since one of the factors contributing to the higher rates is stronger demand for borrowed funds on the part of corporate business.

In combination, these factors spell potential reductions in credit ratings by the ratings agencies. Investors, anticipating these events, may decide to avoid these potential problems by shifting out of corporate debt into the Treasury sector. Then, as yields begin to trend lower, investors anticipate improvements in corporate earnings and cash flow and the cyclical restructuring of balance sheets in which short-term debt is retired with retained earnings or the proceeds of bond sales. These developments, in turn, spark investor expectations of prospective upgrades in credit ratings and encourage shifts in asset allocation toward corporates and out of governments.

Credit-quality considerations cannot be the only explanation for the observed movements of corporate/Treasury spreads. Investor perceptions of creditworthiness would be expected to change slowly and to create a *gradual* widening or narrowing in yield spreads. Instead, we often observe that when these spreads change, they do so very quickly and dramatically. This suggests that at some point in the bear-market interest-rate cycle, short-term factors trigger decisions to shift away from corporate bonds in favor of alternative, "safer" assets. The opposite response when yields are falling often produces an equally rapid collapse in corporate/Treasury spreads.

This market behavior has its roots in the portfolio management strategies employed by large institutional investors that are the principal buyers of corporate bonds—the insurance companies and the pension and retirement funds. In the past 20 years, as interest rates and bond prices have become more volatile, portfolio managers at these institutions have shifted from passive to active management strategies. The traditional "buy and hold" approach to corporate bonds has largely been replaced by a more aggressive approach that seeks to achieve acceptable total returns from the portfolio during each quarterly evaluation period.

The active manager will attempt to structure a portfolio that will earn the target rate of return with a minimum of risk. That means he is not wedded to the corporate sector if he can achieve his target return with a portfolio that entails less risk than one comprising only corporate notes and bonds. Such opportunities typically arise when yields are approaching cyclical peaks. For example, in mid-1979, an investor could capture yields of around 10 percent by purchasing long utility bonds but less than 9 percent by purchasing five-year governments. However, only two months later, the 10 percent yield was available on five-year governments, an issue offering far less credit and market risk than utility bonds.

There is a tendency, therefore, for investors to switch into the more liquid, less risky Treasury issues as yields reach levels that are unusually generous by past standards. This process typically gains additional momentum as yields move progressively higher, producing wider corporate/Treasury spreads as yields approach cyclical peaks.

This process apparently receives additional impetus when the Treasury yield curve becomes flat or inverted. When that happens, yields on the shortest, least volatile market instruments such as bills, CDs, or commercial paper may equal or even exceed those on the riskier long bonds. Moreover, at that configuration of the yield curve, owning the long maturities entails a very high degree of market risk.

A steep, positively sloped yield curve helps to cushion bond yields against the full impact of rising short-term rates. That is, bond yields may rise only slightly as short-term rates move upward when the curve is unusually steep. However, as the curve flattens, this cushion effect wanes until, when the curve becomes horizontal, any further rise in short rates may force bond yields upward by almost the same amount. And since bond prices are far more volatile for an identical move in rates than prices of short- to intermediate-term issues, the bond sector becomes exceedingly risky when the yield curve flattens. (See Exhibits 3 and 4.)

This is another reason portfolio managers seek the relative safety of short-term governments when yields are relatively high. Moreover, these considerations would help explain the tendency for the corporate/Treasury spreads to increase sharply and rapidly once the Treasury yield curve has become flat or inverted. A rapid widening of these spreads when the curve becomes inverted is evident in the past two interest-rate cycles.

The same factors that cause sector spreads to increase as yields rise work in the opposite direction during the bull market phase of the interest-rate cycle. As rates decline, portfolio managers seeking to capture relatively high long-term yields must shift from the Treasury to the

EXHIBIT 3   Ratio of Yields on an AA Utility Bond to a 20-Year
Treasury Security

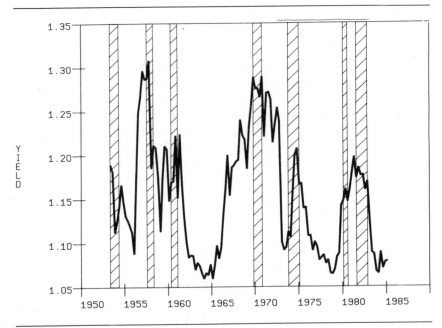

corporate market. For example, in mid-1982, investors captured yields
as high as 13 percent on five-year governments. By year-end 1982, yields
that generous were available only on long corporate bonds. Portfolio
managers seeking to lock in high yields for their clients were forced to
purchase corporates instead of governments and the corporate/Treasury
spreads moved lower.

However, the sharpest reductions in the corporate/Treasury spreads
did not occur until early 1983, a full six months after bond yields began a
dramatic cyclical decline. And between January and April, these spreads
narrowed by roughly 100 basis points. This lag illustrates that, while one
can predict with confidence that yield spreads will decline as bond
yields fall, the exact timing of that phenomenon is highly uncertain.

In this latest instance, the lag between the onset of the decline in
yields and the sharp reduction in spreads may have stemmed from the
bitter experiences of the recent past. In 1980, investors had seen a major
second-quarter decline in yields reversed almost immediately. Any portfolio managers who had regarded the 1980 rally as a signal to shift into
corporates were badly hurt in subsequent quarters. In 1982 they may
have waited for more convincing evidence that yields would not soon
reverse course.

EXHIBIT 4 The Slope of the Treasury Yield Curve: 20-Year Treasury Security Minus 6-Month Bill

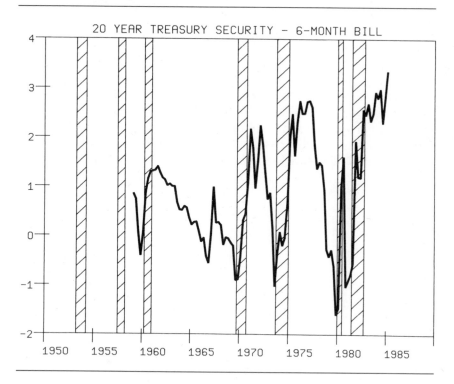

In addition, while yields are declining steadily, total returns are dominated by price gains and are typically as generous on Treasuries as on corporates, so there is little incentive to shift to the corporate sector. Once yields stop falling and investors must look to coupon income as the principal source of total return, the corporates become more attractive. This quest for incremental yield in a relatively stable market, in which the slope of the yield curve is again positive, is a major factor contributing to lower corporate/Treasury spreads during the final stages of a cyclical bull market.

CONCLUSION

As no two business or interest-rate cycles are identical, no two cycles of corporate/Treasury spreads are likely to be the same. Each cycle has special elements that result in considerable variation in the movement of sector spreads. One such element is the recent explosive growth in the market for mortgage-backed securities. In the past two years, a substantial number of portfolio managers have begun to use mortgage-backed securities as substitutes for corporate notes and bonds. Yield spreads to Treasuries on mortgage-backed securities are typically somewhat greater than for corporates of comparable duration.

The rapid growth in this new market has very likely kept corporate/ Treasury yield spreads somewhat wider than would normally prevail in a period of relatively low bond yields. Yield ratios that in the first half of 1985 were slightly above the lowest of earlier cycles provide some support to this hypothesis. Furthermore, the introduction of this competing market for investor assets will very likely alter subsequent cyclical patterns in yield spreads and yield ratios. This virtually guarantees that in future cycles, as in the past, anticipating the behavior of corporate/ Treasury yield differentials will be as much art as science.

55

Fedwatching and the Federal Funds Market

William C. Melton, Ph.D.*
Vice President and Senior Economist
IDS Financial Services, Inc.

Myriad factors affect the determination of interest rates, including the pace of economic activity, the mix of fiscal and monetary policies, the financing strategies of borrowers, and the preferences of investors. This chapter discusses a small subset of these factors—those directly affecting the rate on federal funds. The object is to present the basic concepts necessary to analyze the behavior of the major participants in the market as well as to describe some analytical techniques of interest to the practitioner.[1]

A proper understanding of the funds market is crucial to market participants, since it is the immediate locus of Federal Reserve operations to affect the availability of reserves to the banking system—and no other single factor so influences other money market interest rates as the funds rate. Moreover, in view of the significant rate volatility inherent in the Federal Reserve's operating procedures—the potential of which was amply demonstrated during 1979–82—it is also worthwhile to consider whether—and how—the market could be made to function more efficiently.

* Like many people, the author gets by with a little help from his friends. Critical comments and other assistance were generously provided by Irving Auerbach, Jeffrey Brummette, Louis V. B. Crandall, Kenneth D. Garbade, David S. Jones, William Jordan, Gerald Levy, Charles Lieberman, Jean M. Mahr, Christopher McCurdy, Paul Meek, Anne-Marie Meulendyke, Larry Ricciardelli, Madeleine D. Robinson, Marcia L. Stigum, Robert W. Stone, Thom B. Thurston, and Betsy B. White. Michele Farano labored mightily typing the manuscript, and Olga Vidal prepared the charts. The author alone bears responsibility for any remaining errors.

[1] For an expanded discussion, see: William C. Melton, *Inside the Fed: Making Monetary Policy* (Homewood, Ill.: Dow Jones-Irwin, 1985).

The chapter first discusses forces affecting the funds market "in the large"—during a reserves statement maintenance period taken as a whole. Once the special character of the reserves market has been roughed out, the focus of the analysis shifts to the market "in the small"—the day-to-day behavior of market participants and the relation of that behavior to the potentially highly volatile daily movements of the funds rate. Throughout, the emphasis is on the (in)ability of market participants to understand and quantify factors affecting the market and, thus, to estimate the equilibrium funds rate. In that activity (among others), "Fedwatchers"—an apt vernacular description of the (some-times) highly expert analysts of Fed policy—have a key role. In order to understand clearly the forecasting activities of Fedwatchers as they re-late to the funds market, the next two sections discuss the major factors affecting bank reserves positions as well as the strategy of Federal Re-serve open market operations. The chapter concludes with some thoughts on the inefficiencies created by the paucity of information available to market participants (relative to that in the hands of the Fed) together with suggestions as to how they might best be ameliorated.

Before proceeding to the analysis, a few definitional comments are in order. In referring to the federal funds market, most of the discussion actually has in mind the market for loans of immediately available funds typically settled via the Fed Wire. That market comprises not only fed-eral funds proper (i.e., typically unsecured loans of immediately avail-able funds through which member banks may secure reserve-free bal-ances from certain categories of financial institutions) but also the market for repurchase agreements (RPs).[2] Since the security involved in loans of immediately available funds is largely unimportant in the analy-sis, this distinction is ignored.

THE RESERVES MARKET: IN THE LARGE

One of the most powerful techniques in the economist's analytical tool-box is the concept of a market equilibrium defined by demand and supply functions. The simple model typically ignores all dynamic as-pects of price formation as well as risk aversion and the imperfect quality of available information—the very factors that account for some of the most interesting (and bizarre) behavior in the funds market. Neverthe-less, precisely because the model is so austere, it can, if properly ap-plied, focus the analysis on a set of fundamental determinants of the equilibrium interest rate that might otherwise be difficult to identify. In that spirit, this section uses a simple graphic model of the reserves market to illustrate some of the peculiarities of the supply and demand

---

[2] For a discussion of the regulatory and other distinctions between federal funds and repurchase agreements, see Marcia L. Stigum, *The Money Market* (Homewood, Ill.: Dow Jones-Irwin, 1983).

for reserves and to trace their consequences for the nature of equilibrium in the funds market as well as the Federal Reserve's implementation of monetary policy.

Supply of Reserves

The Federal Reserve controls the supply of reserves available to the banking system, though its control is imprecise in the very short run, principally due to the unpredictability of certain so-called operating factors (about which more later). For analytical purposes, the supply of reserves may be decomposed into two components: nonborrowed reserves and borrowed reserves. Nonborrowed reserves are those supplied by the Fed through acquisition of assets for its own account, other than through extension of accommodation credit through the discount window. Borrowed reserves are those supplied through accommodation lending.

Prior to October 6, 1979, the Fed attempted to alter the supply of nonborrowed reserves in whatever amount was required to maintain the federal funds rate at a target level. Afterward, the Fed adopted a reserves-oriented operating procedure—often described simply as "nonborrowed reserves targeting"—which, to a first approximation, required that the supply of nonborrowed reserves be kept on a target growth path.[3] In late 1982, that procedure was supplanted by an approach best described as "borrowed reserves targeting"; the supply of nonborrowed reserves is adjusted as necessary to make the volume of borrowed reserves equal a desired level. As a result, the supply of nonborrowed reserves is currently only indirectly unresponsive to the funds rate.

In contrast, the supply of borrowed reserves continues to respond to the funds rate, though in a complex fashion that is the result of the peculiar historical evolution of the Fed discount window.[4] In essence,

---

[3] The Fed continues to specify upper and lower bounds for the funds rate, but these differ from the pre-October 1979 bounds in that they are much wider and serve only to prompt consultations when they are breached. They do not constitute an operational constraint on the system account manager.

[4] A key purpose of the Federal Reserve Act of 1913 was to establish a "lender of last resort," a central bank function first clearly defined by Walter Bagehot, the prominent 19th-century English economist, historian, and literary critic, who is also credited with the invention of the Treasury bill and the founding of the *Economist* magazine. Bagehot viewed the central bank as the ultimate source of liquidity in a financial crisis and framed the principle that credit extended under such circumstances should be charged an above-market interest rate to ensure that the central bank would be the last resort of banks in trouble and the first of their borrowing sources to be paid off as the crisis waned. In contrast, the Federal Reserve generally has sought to maintain its discount rate below the funds rate and to empty the (implied) threat of nonaccommodation in order to maintain discipline over banks seeking assistance. The logic to this approach is that banks experiencing temporary difficulties ought not to be penalized by the Fed for their misfortune. Were Bagehot alive today, he surely would point out that such an approach also reduces the incentive of banks to take measures to forestall the occurrence of such events.

the Fed views borrowing as a privilege and not a right. Operationally, that principle generally means that one individual bank should not borrow too frequently; and when it does borrow, it should demonstrate an inability to secure funds in the market. The obvious way to do that is to bid aggressively for funds without successfully covering the reserves deficiency before applying to the discount window. Otherwise expressed, the willingness of a discount officer to accept a bank's request for accommodation is likely to be an increasing function of the spread of the funds rate over the discount rate.[5] However, the precise nature of that relationship depends on banks' *attitudes* toward borrowing from the Fed. For that reason, discount window borrowing has sometimes been viewed as demand determined, although it clearly is a channel for the supply of reserves.

It is now possible to assemble these two components of the Fed's supply of reserves in a diagram. As Exhibit 1 indicates, the supply schedule is vertical at lower levels of the funds rate and becomes positively sloped at higher rates.

Since borrowing is, for all practical purposes, the only channel for additions to the aggregate reserves of the banking system, the funds rate should not be above the discount rate when borrowing is at essentially "frictional" levels. Otherwise expressed, the reserves supply function begins to take on a positive slope at that approximate funds-rate level.

However, though this point is conceptually clear, a practical problem of interpretation arose from time to time when a surcharge on frequent borrowings by large institutions (those with deposits of $500 million or more) was applied.[6] Since the rules have provided that an institution must borrow in more than a specified number of statement weeks in the recent past in order to be subjected to the surcharge, the "effective" discount rate (i.e., the rate that banks perceive as the opportunity cost of reserves) was made a complex function of the volume of borrowing in past weeks as well as banks' inherently subjective appraisal of the likelihood that they might have to borrow in the future.[7]

---

[5] Discount window borrowings fall into two categories—short-term adjustment credit and extended credit. Extended credit includes long-term assistance provided by the Federal Reserve to certain troubled financial institutions. Since its volume is essentially unresponsive to the funds rate, it is best regarded as functionally a component of nonborrowed reserves, or the so-called operating factors. Short-term adjustment credit corresponds directly to the concept of borrowing employed in the text.

[6] Effective March 17, 1980, through May 7, 1980, the surcharge was set at 3 percent. Thereafter, it was eliminated, only to be reinstituted at a 2 percent level effective November 17, 1980, subsequently raised to 3 percent on December 5, 1980, and to 4 percent on May 5, 1981. Effective October 1, 1981, the surcharge was reduced to 3 percent, reduced again to 2 percent on October 13, 1981, and then eliminated entirely effective November 17, 1981.

[7] Specifically, until October 1, 1981, the rules stipulated that the surcharge would apply to an institution borrowing during (1) two successive statement weeks, or (2) more

EXHIBIT 1   Federal Reserve Supply of Reserves

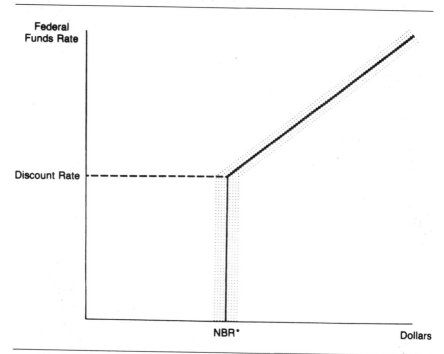

* Nonborrowed reserves target.

About all that could be said in practice was that the effective discount rate lay somewhere between the basic discount rate and that rate plus the surcharge.[8]

than four weeks during a *calendar* quarter. Such an arrangement had the effect that, in a quarter in which borrowing had been modest, banks found themselves possessed of excess "tickets" as the quarter end approached, with the result that their attitude toward borrowing became more aggressive, making the effective discount rate plunge toward the basic rate. That process was especially evident during the first and third quarters of 1981. The Fed responded by altering the rules effective October 1, 1981, to replace the calendar quarter with a "moving quarter" consisting of the current statement week plus the 12 prior weeks. That change meant that there could never be a glut of "tickets" unless borrowing were at essentially frictional levels for a protracted period of time.

[8] Two considerations apparently caused the Fed to view the surcharge as a useful supplement to the basic discount rate. First, since the stringency of discount window administration varies considerably from one Federal Reserve district to another, subjecting frequent users of accommodation credit to the surcharge guarantees at least a minimum of uniformity of treatment of similar banks in different districts. In addition, with the surcharge structure in place, the "effective" discount rate tends to rise toward the full (i.e., basic plus surcharge) rate as borrowing pressure increases. Other things equal, that feature made the funds rate more responsive to borrowing pressure and was at least superficially consistent with the spirit of the nonborrowed reserves targeting procedures in use at the time.

Finally, it is important to note that—for reasons that will be explored in more detail later on—the supply of nonborrowed reserves is not perfectly controlled by the Fed, at least over a period as short as a few weeks. As a result, the supply of nonborrowed reserves may actually fluctuate in a *range* around its estimated amount. In addition, though the relation of discount window borrowing to the funds rate is theoretically precise, in practice it is at times highly variable. The uncertainty thus introduced into the supply of nonborrowed and borrowed reserves is represented in Exhibit 1 by the shaded area around the supply schedule.

Demand for Reserves

Banks' demand for reserves is usefully decomposed into two components: required reserves and excess reserves. (Excess reserves are defined residually as the difference between total reserves and required reserves.)[9]

The computation of required reserves is fairly complex. Effective February 2, 1984, the reserves maintenance period was changed from seven days starting on Thursday and ending on Wednesday to fourteen days starting on Thursday and ending on the second Wednesday following. Simultaneously, reserve requirements on *transactions* deposits—demand deposits and so-called "other checkable deposits" (mainly NOW accounts)—were made almost contemporaneous with the new two-week reserves maintenance period. Specifically, a bank's average level of transactions deposits in the two-week period starting on Tuesday two days prior to the beginning of the maintenance period and ending on Monday two days prior to the end of the maintenance period is multiplied by the applicable reserve requirement percentage to calculate reserves required to support the bank's transactions deposits. Since the *deposit computation period* for transactions deposits thus overlaps with the *reserves maintenance period* on 12 out of 14 days, this system of reserve requirements is loosely described as "contemporaneous," in contrast to the previous "lagged" system in which weekly average deposits were used to compute required reserves in the one-week maintenance period two weeks later.

Under the current system, reserve requirements on nontransactions deposits are calculated on the basis of their two-week average four weeks prior to the maintenance period.

---

[9] Reserves can be maintained in two forms: collected deposits at a Federal Reserve Bank and holdings of vault cash. Deposits are measured during the current reserves maintenance period, but vault cash held approximately four weeks earlier counts as reserves during the current period.

In the current maintenance period, reserves required to support nontransactions deposits are completely predetermined by events of four weeks earlier. In principle, the almost-contemporaneous reserve requirement applied to transactions deposits allows banks in the aggregate to alter their transactions deposits—and thus their required reserves—by varying their extension of credit. The system is too new to permit a verdict as to the practical importance of this effect. However, most would probably agree that the responsiveness of deposits to changes in interest rates during a maintenance period is quite small. Consequently, banks' demand for reserves with which to cover their reserve requirements is probably quite unresponsive to interest rates during the reserves maintenance period.

The second component of reserves demand, excess reserves, is generally kept at the most minimal levels consistent with the state of the art of funds transfers and management of banks' reserves positions.[10] In general, the large money-center banks, which devote substantial resources to managing their reserves positions, maintain their average excess reserves in the neighborhood of zero. The bulk of excess reserves—which do not earn interest—is held by smaller banks, for whom the cost savings from more precise management of reserves positions is less than the expense of staffing themselves adequately to monitor their positions.

Although the cost incentive induces banks generally to maintain their excess reserves at "frictional" levels, a modest degree of interest sensitivity remains in their demand for excess reserves. The reason is that Federal Reserve regulations permit banks to carry into the next reserves maintenance period a deficiency or excess in the bank's reserves position—provided that it is within a specified percentage of the bank's required reserves and provided further that the bank does not post deficiencies for two weeks in succession.[11] Although banks may have excesses in successive periods, the carry-over from the prior period to the current one may not be counted toward the current period's reserve position in such a case. Thus, if the funds rate is abnormally high at the end of a period, a bank with a small deficiency can reduce its funding cost by covering it in the following period, when (it is hoped) the rate is lower. Similarly, a soft funds rate at the end of the period may prompt potential sellers of funds to carry over small excesses rather than

---

[10] For a review of the recent behavior of excess reserves, see "Monetary Policy and Open Market Operations in 1984," Federal Reserve Bank of New York *Quarterly Review*, Spring 1985, pp. 36–56.

[11] The regulations introduced in February 1984 provided that the "carry-over" percentage be 3 percent for six months, 2.5 percent for six months after that, and 2 percent from February 1985 onward.

to sell the funds at an abnormally low rate.[12] The result is that federal funds are not a completely perishable commodity; to a limited extent they can be "stored" in the current reserves maintenance period and "consumed" in the following period (alternatively, "consumed" this period and "replenished" in the next). That imparts a modest degree of interest sensitivity to banks' demand for excess reserves.

The amount of reserves required to support nontransactions deposits is known with great precision due to its computation from deposit levels in prior weeks. But that is not true of reserves required to support transactions deposits. Accordingly, the demand for total required reserves is uncertain during the maintenance period, and that fact is indicated in Exhibit 2 by the shaded area around the demand schedule for required reserves.

EXHIBIT 2 Demand for Total Reserves

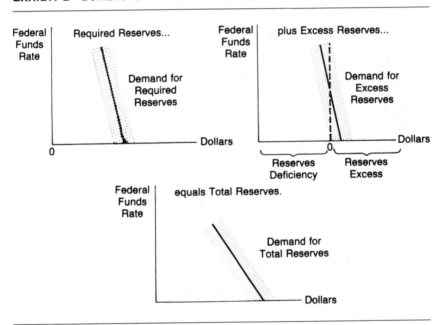

---

[12] Assuming a bank's reserves position in the current period is even and that it was even or deficient in the prior week, the expected profit from buying funds to carry into the next week is simply the spread of the rate expected to prevail next week over the current rate. However, if the bank carried in an excess from last week, that amount will be lost, thus reducing the expected profit. Consequently, for a bank contemplating "doubling up" in this way, the break-even funds rate (i.e., the current funds that makes the expected profit zero) can be found by using the following formula:

$$\text{Break-even funds rate} = \frac{\text{Carry-over from this period}}{\text{Carry-over from last period} + \text{Carry-over from this period}} \times \text{Funds rate expected next period}$$

In addition, the demand for excess reserves can be highly erratic at times, reflecting (among other things) banks' imperfect knowledge of their true reserves position as well as interest rate expectations. This uncertainty is indicated in Exhibit 2 by the shaded area around the demand schedule for excess reserves.

Summing banks' demand for required reserves and excess reserves, the demand for total reserves has the shape shown in Exhibit 3. Reflect-

---

EXHIBIT 3   Equilibrium in the Federal Funds Market

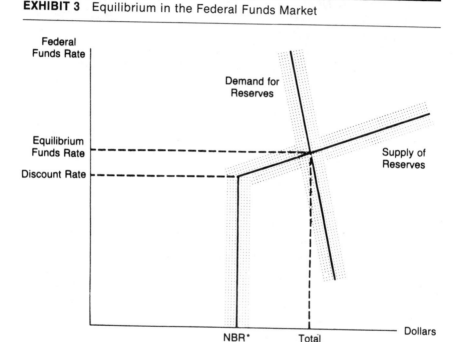

* Target for nonborrowed reserves including a small, frictional amount of borrowed reserves.

---

ing the limited ability of banks to store excess reserves, the function has a steeply negative slope, indicating a modest responsiveness of reserves demand to interest rates.

Market Equilibrium

Having defined the properties of the supply and demand for reserves during a statement week, it remains to put them together to analyze the nature of the market equilibrium and, in particular, the source of the potential volatility of the funds rate.

Exhibit 3 shows the equilibrium funds rate determined by the intersection of the supply and demand functions discussed earlier. The equilibrium is reasonably stable so long as the amount of borrowing from the discount window remains above frictional levels. In that case, the spread of the funds rate over the discount rate is determined by banks' reluctance to borrow (alternatively, the firmness of discount window administration).[13] Unanticipated shocks to the demand for excess reserves are offset by equal movements of borrowed reserves, with relatively modest impacts on the funds rate. Of course, if something should cause the slope of the borrowing function to increase (e.g., an increase of "discipline" exerted on banks by the Fed's discount officers) then the impact on the funds rate will be greater.

Moreover, if borrowing becomes depressed—perhaps as a result of slow growth of the money supply and, thus, of required reserves relative to the target for nonborrowed reserves—then the equilibrium funds rate is determined by the intersection of the vertical supply schedule for nonborrowed reserves with the *almost* vertical reserves demand schedule. In that situation, small errors in the Fed's supply of nonborrowed reserves and small shocks to banks' demand for excess reserves can produce large movements of the funds rate. Moreover, an attempt by the Fed to keep nonborrowed reserves greater than required reserves will enlarge excess reserves while forcing borrowing to frictional levels, so that a pell-mell drop of the funds rate may well ensue, reflecting the "perishability" of the excess funds.

In other words, though the funds market is always volatile due to shocks of various sorts, it is especially so when borrowing is so low that the discount rate may cease to serve as a prop under the funds rate. The Fed, of course, is well aware of that fact and is not likely to allow a "free-fall" to develop. It has several options available to forestall such a situation. Perhaps the most obvious is to revert to some kind of funds-rate targeting. That is essentially what was done in the May–June 1980 period, when borrowing was at frictional levels and the funds rate repeatedly challenged or breached the lower limit of the funds-rate band then in force. As noted earlier, targeting the funds rate causes the Fed to lose

---

[13] This underscores the radically different role of the discount rate in the post-October 6, 1979, period compared with its earlier function. Prior to that time, the funds-rate target set the trading range for the funds rate, and the discount rate was merely adjusted from time to time to keep it in line with the funds rate (i.e., to keep the spread from becoming enlarged). That helped enforce discipline at the discount window. In contrast, the discount rate now serves as the base for the funds-rate structure, with the spread determined by the degree of borrowing pressure. Consequently, although a discount-rate increase in the earlier period need have no impact on the funds rate, an increase now would be expected to lift the funds rate by an almost identical amount.

control of nonborrowed reserves through supplying or draining whatever amount is necessary to keep the funds rate at the desired level.
Another way to brake the decline of the funds rate without explicitly
targeting its level is to depress the supply of nonborrowed reserves
sufficiently to maintain borrowings—at least for a time—at an above-
frictional level. This approach was employed during March–April 1981
and again in autumn of that year. In terms of Exhibit 4, the policy shifts

EXHIBIT 4   Market-Equilibrium under Contemporaneous
Reserves Accounting

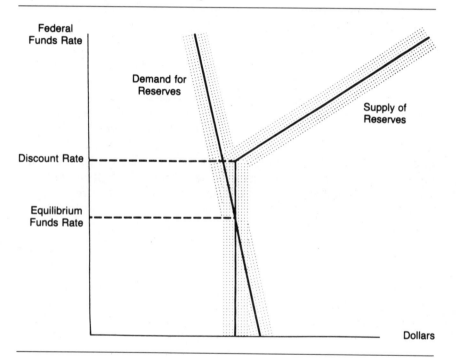

the whole supply function to the left, thereby keeping some distance
between the demand function and nonborrowed reserves. Such an approach is obviously akin to funds-rate targeting, but the key difference is
that the Fed does not "endogenize" its provision of nonborrowed reserves. Moreover, since the objective presumably is to allow the funds
rate to decline in a reasonably restrained fashion, a simultaneous reduction of the discount rate would be appropriate. That way, the funds rate
(in principle) will decline without entering the free-fall zone.
    Even more akin to funds-rate targeting was the approach followed
from late 1982 through the present (Summer 1985). The Fed for all practi-

cal purposes adopted discount-window borrowings as its operating target. Adjustments to the borrowings target were comparatively minor during the period, and the funds rate accordingly was significantly less volatile than it was under the nonborrowed reserves targeting procedure. While the Fed's supply of nonborrowed reserves was endogenized by the process of trying to hit a borrowed reserves target, the instability of the relationship between discount-window borrowing and the funds rate made the funds rate more volatile on a day-to-day basis than it had been prior to October 1979.[14]

Excursus: Total Reserves Targeting

In general, monetarist economists advocate tight control of the supply of reserves. That implies a role for the discount rate radically different from its role in targeting nonborrowed reserves or borrowed reserves. Instead of serving as a prop *under* the funds rate as in Exhibit 3, a "penalty" discount rate is advocated that would be kept well above the normal trading range of the funds rate. That way, as depicted in Exhibit 4, the relevant range of the reserves supply function is vertical, while the demand for reserves is sharply negatively sloped. As a result, the funds rate under total reserves targeting would be more volatile than currently, not because of the contemporaneous calculation of required reserves on transactions deposits—in fact, *despite* that feature—but because of the lack of interest sensitivity in the relevant portion of the reserves supply function. Control over the supply of reserves obviously would become more precise. However, there could well be substantial slippage between reserves and the money supply. In particular, if the enlarged reserves carry-over provisions introduced in February 1984 were retained, the increased interest sensitivity of demand for excess reserves will allow banks to temporarily defer adjustments in deposits, thus impairing somewhat the precision of monetary control.

Most econometric evidence suggests that total reserves targeting would at best improve monetary control marginally over the span of a month or so without affecting its precision over longer time horizons. Thus one's attitude toward the choice between total reserves targeting and nonborrowed reserves targeting is importantly conditioned on the importance one attaches to short-run monetary control as well as the greater interest rate volatility likely to be associated with total reserves targeting.

---

[14] For a discussion of the recent behavior of the relationship between discount window borrowing and the funds rate, see "Monetary Policy and Open Market Operation in 1984."

THE RESERVES MARKET: IN THE SMALL

This section changes the focus of the analysis from the supply and demand for reserves in the reserves maintenance period as a whole to the adjustment of banks' reserves positions and the Fed's provision of reserves *during* the period.

Supplying Reserves: The Fed's Problem

In supplying nonborrowed reserves during the reserves maintenance period, the Fed typically tries to hit its target.[15] That target may be derived from short-run growth objectives for primarily M1 as was the case during 1979–82, or it may be inferred from a desired level of "reserves pressure"—i.e., discount-window borrowings. In either case, the task is complicated by the at times highly erratic movements of the so-called operating factors. One of the most variable such factors is Federal Reserve float, the weekly average of which can swing by $1 billion or more in response to acute operational problems in the payments system. (Float and other operating factors are discussed in more detail below.) In contrast, the average weekly reserves provision called for by the growth path for nonborrowed reserves is only on the order of about $50 million. The upshot is that, for the most part, the Fed's open market operations are "defensive" in nature; that is, they are intended to offset a swing in reserves availability produced by float or some other operating factor rather than to provide the small increment of reserves called for by the target.

Moreover, given the overall need to add to or drain from the weekly average level of reserves, the Fed still must decide the *timing* of open market operations during the reserves maintenance period. Several factors influence the timing decision. First, the information available to the Fed's Open Market Desk (hereafter, Desk) concerning reserves supplies as well as the level of banks' required reserves generally becomes more complete and reliable as the period progresses. All other things equal, then, the Desk would probably prefer to delay arranging any open market operations.

Also, the Desk on occasion may attempt to smooth out swings in the availability of reserves during the period so as to avoid unnecessary volatility in the funds market. Since banks must meet reserve requirements on an average basis for the period as a whole, *intra*period swings in reserves availability in principle need have no impact on the funds rate. Indeed, if banks were able to anticipate the movement in availabil-

---

[15] For an excellent description of the daily routine of the Desk, see Paul Meek, *U.S. Monetary Policy and Financial Markets* (New York: Federal Reserve Bank of New York, 1982).

ity with confidence, they could passively allow their reserves positions to mirror the swing, and there would be no impact on the funds rate. In practice, banks are highly uncertain about their reserves positions—as is discussed further below—and the funds rate is likely to respond to major daily imbalances between banks' "normal" reserves positions and actual availability. Though such funds-rate movements may mislead some market participants, the Fed in recent years has been much less inclined than in the past to smooth out swings in availability. Nevertheless, if projections suggest a very large excess of reserves emerging prior to a weekend, the Desk probably would want to offset the glut on Thursday or Friday rather than see the funds rate temporarily depressed. Similarly, if the reserves market appears generally in balance prior to the weekend, with a major excess supply expected to emerge later, then the Desk's natural inclination would be to delay the reserves-draining operation until after the weekend. On the other hand, moderate intraperiod swings in reserves availability probably would be ignored.

Smoothing adjustments may also be necessitated by variations in the distribution of discount window borrowing during the period. The problem is rooted in the institutional phenomenon that virtually all discount window borrowing by large banks (abstracting from long-term credit extensions) is done on only two days: Friday and Wednesday.[16] If, as is usually the case, the discount rate is below the Fed funds rate, Friday is the preferred day to borrow. This is because borrowing on that day counts for three days, thus magnifying the favorable impact of the below-market discount rate on a bank's average funds cost for the week. (Primarily regional banks can succeed with such a tactic; discount window administration at the New York Federal Reserve Bank is generally acknowledged to be more stringent than in other Federal Reserve districts.) Indeed, as Exhibit 5 illustrates, the Wednesday percentage of total borrowing is negatively related to the overall level of borrowing. In 1976, when banks actually averaged net free reserves and the funds rate was low relative to the discount rate, Wednesday borrowing averaged about 40 percent of the total. During 1978–79, when borrowing traffic was much greater and the funds rate was correspondingly higher than the discount rate, the Wednesday percentage was about half as large, reflecting the greater attractiveness of Friday borrowing. However, during 1980–83 the Wednesday percentage on average was substantially higher than in 1978–79 and more erratic, despite the fact that average

---

[16] When small banks borrow from the discount window, they frequently do so for every day of the statement maintenance period. The reason is that such banks almost always are sellers of federal funds, so that if they have sustained a reserve drain so large that it cannot be covered by reducing funds sales, there may be no practical alternative to seeking accommodation for a number of days.

EXHIBIT 5   Behavior of Federal Reserve Adjustment Borrowing

| | Average Federal Funds Rate Less Discount Rate | Average Borrowed Reserves | Avg. Net Borrowed Reserves | Wednesday Borrowing as a Percentage of Week Total | | | |
				Mean	Std. Dev.	Min.	Max.
1976	−0.44%	$ 85	$−134	40.6%	24.4%	7.8%	82.1%
1977	0.06	464	250	29.4	22.4	7.6	92.8
1978	0.40	868	671	20.5	9.9	7.5	56.3
1979	0.88	1338	1116	19.6	9.0	7.0	47.7
1980	0.79	1232	934	28.1	24.0	4.1	97.2
1981	0.11	1266	964	27.2	15.6	7.5	89.2
1981	1.21	876	516	32.0	20.0	6.2	88.3
1983	0.59	664	167	33.5	21.7	3.7	86.3

Note: Borrowing data have been adjusted to remove extended credit advanced to certain institutions. The discount rate includes the discount-rate surcharges applied at various times during 1980–81. Since the surcharge was not binding for several months in 1981, the difference between the funds rate and the fully surcharged discount rate is deceptively small for that year.

borrowing was about the same in both periods. Though the reasons for that phenomenon are not clear, it is probably related to the advent of the reserves-oriented operating procedures in late 1979 and perhaps to the effect of the discount rate surcharge on banks' borrowing behavior.

The substantial variability of the distribution of borrowing traffic during the reserves maintenance period can create problems for the Desk. For example, if for some reason borrowing is unexpectedly high early in the period, the period's borrowing target may have been fulfilled—or even overfulfilled—leaving nothing to be done on the final Wednesday. The result would be downward pressure on the funds rate unless the Desk entered the market to drain out some of the excess.[17] Such an operation would involve a deliberate, though probably temporary, departure from the intended relative supplies of nonborrowed and borrowed reserves rather than merely a decision with regard to the timing of reserves availability during the maintenance period.

Once the Desk has formed a view with regard to the desirable timing of any operations affecting reserves availability, it must choose an instrument to accomplish the objective. Basically, the decision involves a choice between (1) permanent reserves operations versus temporary ones, and (2) various alternative kinds of temporary operations. In order

---

[17] In a sense, Friday borrowing is "demand-determined," largely reflecting banks' efforts to take advantage of a (possibly) below-market discount rate. By the final Wednesday afternoon, however, the total amount of borrowing remaining to be done is almost completely determined by reserves availability earlier in the period. That means that on the final Wednesday (and perhaps somewhat earlier) the funds rate responds to the scale of borrowing and not the other way around as on a Friday.

to avoid interfering with the market's determination of interest rates, the Desk tries to minimize its presence in the market. Thus, if there is a need to add reserves over a substantial period of time (e.g., during the late-year holiday season), the natural course is to make one or more outright purchases of securities. One way this can be done is to buy them from the foreign central banks for whom the New York Fed acts as agent and securities custodian. Such a transaction would be arranged internally and would involve no operations in the market; it thus serves as a convenient device to reduce the Fed's presence in the market. The major limitation of that kind of transaction is that the decision to buy or sell securities is made by the foreign customers, so that the Fed can take advantage of a timely opportunity to carry out its reserves-adding task this way, but it cannot create that opportunity itself. In the event that no such opportunity appears, the Fed must instead purchase the securities in the market by asking dealers for their offers.[18] Regardless of how the outright purchase (sale) of securities is arranged, its purpose is to relieve the Fed of the necessity of repeatedly carrying out temporary additions (drains) of reserves for a protracted period of time.

In the event of a need to drain reserves over a substantial time period, a sale of securities to foreign accounts, if possible, would be convenient. But in this case, there is another nonmarket option as well: The Fed can bid to redeem some of its maturing bills at the regular weekly auction of Treasury bills. To do so, the Fed submits a noncompetitive tender for an amount smaller than its holding of the maturing issues. The major limitation of this approach is that the Fed obviously can redeem only as much as it holds of the maturing issues and in practice would not want to disrupt the auction process by concentrating a large redemption in a single auction. Consequently, only reserves drains in amounts of $500 million or so are likely to be implemented in this fashion. Larger operations will involve outright sales of securities in the market.[19]

When a reserves need is perceived to be temporary, affecting only one or a few maintenance periods, The Fed's preferred action is to ar-

---

[18] By law, the Federal Reserve may not bid to increase its holdings of maturing Treasury bills or coupons in an auction. The original purpose of this restriction apparently was to prevent the Treasury from selling unlimited amounts of securities directly to the Fed; instead, the Treasury was to be subject to the discipline of the market. At present, the main practical justification for the restriction is that any attempt by the Fed to enlarge its holdings in an auction would, in effect, reduce the size of the offering to the public below the size announced, thus tending to produce an unexpectedly high price (low yield) on the issue. That could be disadvantageous to securities dealers and others submitting competitive bids for the issue.

[19] In practice, outright sales of securities are rather rare. They sometimes occur early in the year to implement a seasonal drain of reserves. In addition, outright sales tend to be associated with reductions of reserve requirements, which otherwise might produce a substantial reserve excess.

range repurchase agreements (RPs) with the dealers. That injects reserves for the duration of the RPs and is operationally simpler and less obtrusive than would be an outright purchase of securities followed by an outright sale.

RPs can be arranged by the Fed for its own account—so-called System RPs. Those arranged by the Fed as agent for foreign central bank customers are termed customer RPs.

The Federal Reserve Bank of New York performs a number of banking services for foreign central banks and several international organizations. Typically the Fed handles their very short-term investments by in effect doing RPs with them, using securities in the Fed's portfolio as collateral.[20] The total of such short-term investment balances is sometimes informally referred to as the "internal RP pool," reflecting the fact that the investments are processed internally at the Fed for the most part, with no private market participants involved. When the Desk wishes to inject reserves by reducing the portion of the pool invested with the Fed, it does so by executing some of the investment orders with the dealers as so-called "customer RPs." What remains of the pool is invested with the Fed and is described on the Fed's balance sheet as "matched sale-purchase transactions executed internally with customer accounts" (more on these below).

Since the Fed treats the pool as one of several operating factors affecting reserves availability, there is no difference between the reserves impact of System and customer RPs—though that fact is not always recognized by market participants. If they are functionally identical, then what explains the Fed's choice between them? As a rule, the Fed employs customer RPs when it estimates a reserves need to be small.[21] The largest customer RP ever arranged totaled only $3 billion, and the average size is $1–2 billion. In contrast, System RPs have been executed fairly often for amounts as great as $6–7 billion. The feasible size of customer RPs is fundamentally limited by the available volume of foreign investment orders, which generally average $2–3 billion. Furthermore, since the foreign orders primarily constitute working cash balances of central banks, it is rather unusual for the Desk to arrange multiday customer RPs, though some have occurred. Thus, if a multiday RP is needed, a System transaction is the most likely alternative. More-

---

[20] In effect, an RP is a collateralized loan. When a dealer arranges an RP, (s)he transfers title to a security to the lender in exchange for cash. At maturity, the transaction reverses. The security is returned to the dealer, and the lender receives the original principal plus interest due. A so-called "reverse RP" operates in exactly the same way, except the dealer temporarily lends out cash in exchange for a security.

For more details, see Stigum, *op. cit.*

[21] When the Fed was targeting the funds rate prior to October 1979, customer RPs frequently were employed to signal that the Fed had no objection to the current funds rate but wanted to add reserves to meet a modest estimated reserve need.

over, in the past, more restrictive conditions on the securities eligible to serve as collateral for customer RPs meant that when the "floating supply" of collateral was scarce, customer RPs could be more difficult for the Fed to arrange than System RPs.[22] Under such circumstances, the Fed naturally preferred to rely on System RPs. However, collateral standards are now uniform for both types of RPs.[23]

In the event of a severe collateral shortage, the Desk may experience difficulty in executing the desired amount of System RPs. When faced with such a situation in the past, the Desk frequently has preannounced its RPs (e.g., notified dealers on Wednesday afternoon of its intention to do RPs on the following Thursday) in order to encourage dealers and their customers to keep collateral available for use with the System RPs.

A temporary reserves-draining operation is simpler because matched sale-purchase transactions (MSPs), which are functionally equivalent to reverse repurchase agreements, can be used to remove the temporary reserves glut.[24] Here again, however, there may be a delicate problem of choice of technique. Frequently, market participants show relatively poor proposals to the Fed for multiday MSPs for an abundantly clear reason: They are being asked to extend the Fed a fixed-rate loan when they have at least some grounds for suspecting that the rationale for the MSPs might be to reduce the availability of reserves. All other things equal, such an operation would raise short-term interest rates and thus would increase their costs of funding that loan.[25] Pro-

---

[22] A collateral shortage may exist when the floating supply of eligible securities in the hands of dealers and their customers is relatively small, as when widespread expectations of rising interest rates cause dealers and banks to trim their holdings of securities.

[23] Until a few years ago, collateral for customer RPs was priced at market value, while collateral for System RPs was priced at par value. That meant that dealers required more collateral per dollar of customer RPs than of System RPs. Currently, collateral for both forms of RPs is priced at market value, including any accrued interest.

Until recently, there was also an important difference in the types of securities that were eligible collateral for customer and System RPs. Only Treasury and agency securities are eligible collateral for customer RPs, while those securities as well as certain bankers' acceptances were eligible for System RPs. As of July 1984, however, acceptances ceased to be eligible collateral for System RPs, so that there now are no remaining differences in collateral eligibility.

[24] Since the Federal Reserve Act prohibits the Federal Reserve banks from borrowing from the public, reverse RPs were and are viewed as an illegal transaction for the Fed. However, in 1966, a sudden temporary increase in float resulting from a disruption of airline service prompted the innovation of the matched (cash) sale- (forward) purchase agreement. The agreement is structured as two separate transactions and is therefore legal under the act's authorization to buy and sell securities. Moral: There's more than one way to skin a cat! Operationally, MSPs are less time-consuming for the Desk than are RPs, since the Fed controls the collateral. That is, the Fed can specify the one or two bill issues in its portfolio that are to be used in the MSPs and set the prices easily. For RPs, however, the Fed must accept whatever eligible collateral the dealers wish to offer, and the pricing task is commensurately greater.

[25] On the other hand, if the MSPs are widely perceived to be required to offset a reserve excess due to movements of the operating factors, then proposals likely will be more competitive.

posals are more competitive for overnight MSPs or for multiday MSPs when market participants generally recognize the need to drain reserves. As a result, the Fed may well encounter a situation in which it is simply unable to drain a sufficient amount of reserves via multiday MSPs arranged, for example, on Thursday (without, that is, accepting rates well above the going market rate) and thus must return for more on Friday. This problem can be alleviated somewhat by offering simultaneously overnight and multiday MSPs.

Finally, if inadequate proposals prevent the Desk from achieving the desired reserves add (drain), the Treasury may be asked to alter the balances in its account at the Fed. Such an operation would take care of the problem if an additional drain is called for, but there can be difficulties when Treasury balances are used to inject reserves. The reason is that Treasury deposits must be collateralized; and if banks have insufficient collateral available, they will remit the balances back to the Treasury's Fed account, thus frustrating the reserves injection. In any event, manipulation of Treasury balances to adjust reserves positions is done relatively infrequently; in general, balances in the Treasury's Fed account are maintained close to a weekly average of $3 billion.[26]

Bank's Problem: Managing Reserves Positions

The key objective of a bank in managing its reserves position during a reserves maintenance period is to maintain its weekly average level of excess reserves as close as possible to zero. The reason is that excess reserves earn no interest and may be applied to a bank's reserve requirement in the subsequent period only to a limited extent. The two principal areas of uncertainty affecting a bank as it begins the period are the scale of its needs for funds and the level of the federal funds rate during the course of the period. The latter was especially volatile during 1979–82. The former is the result of the net flow of collected funds to the bank during the period. For the most part, it reflects transfers in and out of deposit accounts; but it is also affected by maturing securities and other sources of funds. For a small bank serving primarily retail customers, uncertainty concerning its funds need may be minor. In contrast, large money-center banks sometimes sustain net increases or decreases of 20 percent or more in their demand deposits in a single day. If such movements are so erratic as to be essentially unpredictable, then the bank faces a difficult task in controlling its reserve position.

In addition, a bank's funds trader works under several major constraints as he or she attempts to home in on the zero excess reserves

---

[26] This procedure was reintroduced in November 1978, when new regulations were adopted governing Treasury tax and loan accounts. For details, see Joan E. Lovett, "Treasury Tax and Loan Accounts and Federal Reserve Open Market Operations." Federal Reserve Bank of New York *Quarterly Review*, Summer 1978, pp. 41–46.

target. First, as noted earlier, a modest deficiency of required reserves may be carried in from one maintenance period to the next, but significant penalties will be incurred if the bank is deficient in the second period. Thus, following a deficiency, a funds trader must exercise special care to end up even or in an excess position subsequently. If an excess is carried over in two consecutive periods, the first carry-over is lost, so that also involves a cost. Second, the Federal Reserve does not allow banks to have an overnight overdraft in their reserves accounts (that would constitute a loan by the Fed). Recently the Fed has gone even further and has discouraged banks from allowing overdrafts to occur in their accounts *during* the business day. That limits the ability of a funds trader to maintain a "short" position in a reserve account. Third, it is generally rather late in the day before the funds trader can know what the closing position in his or her Fed account will be; that operational constraints limits somewhat the trader's willingness to take a view in the funds market earlier in the day.

Most funds traders cope with these constraints by covering their reserves need incrementally during the two-week maintenance period, as available information concerning their average reserves need becomes more refined with each passing day.[27] Moreover, even if the trader feels confident about his or her reserves need and the direction of the funds rate, the inability to run a deficit in the reserves account limits the trader's ability to "take a view." For example, a trader who expects the funds rate to decline will want to have a "short" position in the reserves account (i.e., to have less reserves in the account than necessary to cover that day's normal portion of the total weekly reserve need), which the trader will cover later (it is hoped) at a lower rate. But the constraint on daylight and overnight overdrafts limits the trader's ability to do so. Similarly, a trader who expects the funds rate to increase will want to have a "long" position now, followed by a sufficiently short position later as to make the excess reserves average about zero over the period as a whole. Here again, the overdraft constraint limits the amount of funds that can be sold later and thus the size of the long position that can be taken now. In fact, even if they have a well-defined rate outlook, large money-center banks typically run deficit positions during most of the maintenance period, which they cover starting on the final Monday. That minimizes the risk that they may be caught with surpluses early in the period that would prevent making excess reserves average zero (or close to it) without running an overdraft later in the period. (The mirror image of this process is that small banks and other

---

[27] The major exception is that a funds trader consciously preparing to borrow from the Fed discount window will purposely try to stay in a deficit position before going to the window. In doing so, the trader will generally not sell funds—the Fed would frown on that—but rather will avoid buying funds by refusing to bid at the market rate.

sellers of funds that have much less uncertainty concerning their positions run surpluses during most of the period.)

To a very minor extent, the overdraft constraint may be offset by arranging transactions in the forward market for Federal funds. In the forward market, traders buy or sell funds today for settlement on future days when the transaction can be covered in the cash market. This device thus allows traders the possibility of realizing a potentially substantial spread between the rate at which they sell funds and the rate at which they buy them (if they guess right) without having to arrange all the transactions on the same day and without running an overdraft on any day.

However, volume in the forward funds market is very small relative to total transactions and is even smaller now than in the recent past. The primary reason for the decline in activity is the demise of so-called Eurodollar arbitrage, a technique by which large banks were able to reduce their effective required reserves.[28] Arbitrage created an incentive for forward funds transactions to be arranged for Friday and Monday in order to lock in the profit from the transaction. Before September 1980, such forward trades frequently accounted for 10 percent or more of total funds trades on those days.[29] However, by late 1981 forward trades—though more dispersed throughout the week—generally accounted for only about 1 percent of total volume; and on a fair number of days, there was no forward trading at all. Moreover, such trading as there was tended to be limited to a handful of banks.

Intraperiod Pattern of the Funds Rate

The preceding discussion has outlined the essential relationships a funds trader should consider when forming a view as to the likely course of the funds rate during the two-week reserves maintenance period. First, one needs to know the Fed's target for borrowing during the period. Assume also that actual borrowing closely approximates the target. Then, by solving the relationship between borrowing and the spread of the funds rate over the discount rate—a relationship that appears to have changed substantially since the introduction of contemporaneous reserve requirements in February 1984–a notion of the funds rate can be formed consistent with the borrowing target (given the discount rate). And *that* is the level at which a funds trader should expect to trade. Forming a view, in essence, is the process of gauging the extent to which the current funds rate differs from that equilibrium rate.

---

[28] The best description of Eurodollar arbitrage is Warren L. Coats, Jr., "The Weekend Eurodollar Game," *Journal of Finance*, June 1981, pp. 649–60.

[29] The basis for these statements is the author's inspection of the records of trades kept by one of the largest federal funds brokers.

Alas, it's not so simple in practice. To start with, as the period begins on Thursday, the funds trader knows neither the Fed's target for borrowed reserves nor the actual level of borrowing during the preceding period. Add to that the fact that the relation between borrowing and the funds rate is uncertain, particularly when the "effective" discount rate is unknown (as in the case of a surcharge applied to the basic rate), and it is apparent that several layers of uncertainty obscure the funds trader's perception of the equilibrium rate.

In this setting, many funds traders rely on a second-best approach. In effect, they filter recent movements of the funds rate in order to define the current equilibrium (or notionally "fair") rate.[30] This procedure makes a great deal of sense during the period, as an emerging reserve imbalance tends to persist for a while, causing serially correlated movements in the funds rate. From the informational point of view, the technique has much less merit in analyzing trading in two separate maintenance periods, since (as noted earlier) reserves provision is largely separated between them. Nevertheless, the initial Thursday opening rate is very strongly correlated with the rates at which funds traded on previous days. (Trading during the final Wednesday afternoon, when the market is generally thin and often erratic, seems to be ignored in setting the opening rate.)

As a result of traders' notional equilibrium—as well as the enlarged "carry-over" provisions in effect since February 1984—the funds rate is sometimes slow to adjust to a change in the degree of borrowing pressure in the banking system. One reason is that such a change may only begin to be evident in the reserves market in late Wednesday trading, and events at that time are erratic anyway and consequently are given little weight by funds traders. Moreover, in some cases, a reserves stringency (if widespread) may be manifested initially not as an increase of borrowing but as a negative excess reserves position. As banks seek to avoid reserves deficiencies in the subsequent period, the funds rate should belatedly increase. Finally, if borrowing has been at very low levels for some time, banks may feel little initial concern about seeking accommodation at the Fed window; and as long as that attitude persists, the full effect of increased borrowing pressure will be delayed.

The notional equilibrium funds rate is obviously compatible with the incremental approach to covering reserves positions discussed earlier, in that both depend on an assumption that it is impossible to determine precisely where the funds rate ought to trade. In the absence of such

---

[30] Conceptually, this process is similar to the way dealers in a thin market try to use transactions data to determine the equilibrium price of a security. For an excellent description and analysis of such behavior, see Kenneth D. Garbade, *Securities Markets* (New York: McGraw-Hill, 1982), Chapter 26.

well-defined knowledge, both techniques represent second-best methods with which funds traders can cope.

Nevertheless, it would be a mistake to assume that any sluggishness of the funds rate is solely attributable to funds traders. The Fed's Open Market Desk also from time to time uses movements in the funds rate as a check on its reserves projections. The logic of the approach is to use the information contained in funds-rate movements to verify the existence of an imbalance in the reserves market. Thus, if the borrowing target has not changed appreciably, but the funds rate is moving sharply higher (lower), that suggests that some disturbance to nonborrowed reserves has created a reserves shortage (excess). The Desk probably would use this kind of information only in relation to large movements of the funds rate, ignoring smaller changes. However, such a tactic should in principle induce a tendency toward serial correlation in the funds rate, since movements of the rate away from its previous level will be more likely to prompt offsetting open market operations. Ironically then, the existence of such second guessing on the part of the Fed lends some credence to funds traders' notional equilibrium funds rate. The Desk, for its part, has pointed to market expectations of open market operations as reducing the usefulness of the funds rate as an indication of reserve need.

During the reserves maintenance period, the funds rate responds to a *perceived imbalance* in the reserves market. Such an imbalance will be only temporary because as the funds rate adjusts to a level consistent with inducing the implied amount of borrowing from the discount window, the imbalance is relieved. As noted earlier, borrowed reserves to a large extent are provided at three points in the two-week period—two Fridays and the final Wednesday. Hence, in order to increase borrowing, the Fed generally will need to create a palpable reserve shortage early in the period in order to put upward pressure on the funds rate in time to induce the called-for traffic at the discount window on Friday night. If the funds rate does not respond immediately, for whatever reason, then pressure should intensify later in the period, as enlarged borrowing needs finally begin to become apparent to funds traders. If the funds rate is rising during the period's final days, the increased tightness will generally produce a higher rate at the following Thursday opening, which in principle could induce the desired average weekly volume of borrowing. The same basic procedure operates in reverse when the Fed is in process of easing pressure on bank reserves positions.

The principal problem this convoluted procedure presents to a funds trader is that of distinguishing the daily rate gyrations due only to unevenness of borrowing (given the period's total) from adjustments designed to create a change in the total. It is not an easy task, but it is greatly facilitated if one has a clear conception of the pattern of open market operations that would be most likely to produce an even distribution of borrowing at the pace of the previous period. A deviation from such a pattern may signal to a funds trader a possible shift in the funds rate before the end of the period.

ANALYTICS OF RESERVES: A CHILD'S GUIDE TO FLOAT AND OTHER MYSTERIES

The starting point for anticipating and interpreting open market operations is the ability to estimate the extent to which forces outside the direct control of the Fed are increasing or decreasing banks' needs for reserves. Exhibit 6 summarizes the most important such influences. The

---

EXHIBIT 6   Factors Affecting Reserves (statement week ended January 20, 1982; $ millions)

Factors Creating Reserves Need:		
1. Required reserves*	+2,268	
2. Excess reserves	+140	
3. Currency in circulation	−1,385	
4. Treasury deposits at Federal Reserve banks	+643	
5. Miscellaneous liabilities	−191	
6. Total		+1,475
Factors Reducing Reserves Need:		
7. Vault cash†	+111	
8. Float	+2,651	
9. Advances	−50	
10. Miscellaneous assets	+165	
11. Total		+2,877
12. Total reserve need (6 less 11)		−1,402

Note: Data are changes in weekly average levels. Beginning February 2, 1984, the reserves maintenance period was lengthened from one week to two weeks.

* Adjusted for required reserves covered through holdings of vault cash.

† Held by institutions maintaining reserves balances at a Federal Reserve bank; data reflect holdings two weeks prior to the statement week.

---

first category is those factors that create a reserves need for banks (i.e., those for which an increase implies an added need for the banking system to hold reserves in the form of deposits at the Federal Reserve banks). They include required reserves as well as excess reserves. In addition, certain factors drain funds from these reserve accounts, such as Treasury deposits at the Federal Reserve banks, currency in circulation, and a variety of other minor items. The mechanism involved is simple: An increase of Treasury deposits, for example, involves a transfer of funds from bank reserves accounts to the Treasury's account at the Fed, thus reducing reserve availability. Similarly, when the nonbank public increases its holdings of currency, banks must replenish their stocks by obtaining currency from the Fed (either directly or via a correspondent bank) in exchange for debits to their reserve accounts.

The second basic category of reserves factors includes those for which an increase reduces banks' reserves needs. Because vault cash (held four weeks ago) counts as reserves, an increase (other things equal) reduces the need for reserves from other sources. Easily one of the most variable factors in this category is Federal Reserve float (essentially the discrepancy between the *scheduled* availability of checks and other cash items presented to the Fed for collection versus the *actual* volume of collections posted). Since float for the most part reflects the degree to which the check-processing system is functioning smoothly, it swings erratically in response to acute disruptions of normal procedures (e.g., airport closures due to bad weather or computer malfunctions).[31] Last but not least, borrowings from the Fed obviously reduce the reserves needed by banks from other sources.

In order to compute the amount of reserves to be supplied (drained) during the maintenance period, the total change of the factor reducing reserves needs is subtracted from the total change of factors increasing reserves needs. If the result is positive (negative), the Fed needs to add (drain) reserves.

Of course, as a practical matter, both the Fed and Fedwatchers rely on estimates of factors that may diverge considerably from their actual values. For example, in 1984, projections of the total 14-day average of market factors made by the System Open Market Desk staff on the first Thursday morning of the period diverged from the actual by an average absolute amount of $810 million. By the second Thursday, the error was down to $320 million, and on the final day of the maintenance period, it was $75 million. Uncertainty is not confined to reserves supplied through market factors. Estimates of the reserve need are also prone to error primarily due to the system of contemporaneous reserve requirements introduced in February 1984. From late February through the end of the year, the average absolute revision to estimates of required reserves from the first to the last day of the period was $220 million; the average revision after the end of the period was $65 million.[32]

The information available to Fedwatchers compares very poorly with that available to the Fed itself. Fedwatchers, for example, receive

---

[31] The classic description of techniques used by the Fed and Fedwatchers to predict float is Irving Auerbach, "Forecasting Float," in *Essays in Money and Credit* (New York: Federal Reserve Bank of New York, 1964), pp. 7–13. Recently the Fed has begun to charge banks for float and its average level and variability have dropped substantially compared to previous years.

[32] "Monetary Policy and Open Market Operations in 1984."

data on discount-window borrowing and most operating factors on Thursday evening each week. Data for required reserves, excess reserves, and vault cash are computed as two-week averages and are released every other Thursday. The only daily data received by Fedwatchers is for Treasury balances, and that is available from the Treasury only with a two-day lag. Despite these handicaps, some of the more astute Fedwatchers achieve an impressive degree of forecast accuracy. But even they are often in error concerning open market operations, since they may lack vital information on the course of developments in the current maintenance period.

Once one knows the value of the reserves need as given on line 12 of Exhibit 6, there remain two additional steps to be taken before computing the amount of open market operations. First, if RPs (MSPs) were executed in the prior week, the runoff from their average level in that week to zero in the current week will create a reserves drain (add), in addition to that indicated on line 12. Second, as noted earlier, the Fed may execute internally the temporary investment orders of its foreign central bank customers, or it may pass them through to the market as customer RPs. If the volume of orders executed increases, the result is an increased reserves need. In that respect, the foreign orders resemble other factors creating a need. As a matter of simplicity, the Desk personnel add the change in foreign orders (i.e., the average level of orders available for execution in the current week minus the average level of orders *actually* executed in the previous week) to the reserves need given on line 12. If the Deity is disposed to ease the Desk's job, the result will be zero, and no operations in the market will be necessary. That does not happen often, however.

STRATEGY OF OPEN MARKET OPERATIONS

During the year, both the reserves need (line 12) and the reserves need adjusted for runoffs of RPs and MSPs and for changes in foreign investment orders, have a pronounced seasonal pattern. Currency and demand deposits follow distinct multiweek swings and also fluctuate around certain dates—for example, holidays and tax payment dates. In principle, even the large swings of reserves need could be met through arranging large amounts of RPs, but a number of considerations argue against such a tactic. First, the amount of collateral required easily approaches $10 billion or so and could well exceed the floating supply of "free" collateral in the hands of dealers and other financial institutions (mainly commercial banks). The result would be that the Desk would be unable to adhere to its nonborrowed reserves target. Moreover, even if the amount of collateral were adequate, the fact that banks would repeatedly begin the reserves maintenance period with a severe reserves deficiency (until the need was met through RPs) would probably create considerable upward pressure on the funds rate. For these reasons, provision of at least some portion of the reserves need through outright purchases of securities is desirable, and outright transactions are closely related to swings in seasonal reserve needs as well as changes in reserve requirements.

There are, of course, various ways to do outright transactions. First, as noted earlier, a suitable foreign customer order may present an opportunity for the Fed to effect the permanent addition (drain) of reserves without recourse to transactions with dealers. Such an approach is consistent with the Fed's desire to minimize its presence in the market; but it presents problems to Fedwatchers, who do not learn of the existence of the transaction until the Fed's release of reserves data following the maintenance period in which it was executed. Another means by which the Fed can achieve a permanent reserve drain is to bid to reduce its holdings of maturing bills in a Treasury auction—for example, the regular Monday auction of three- and six-month bills. In such a case, Fedwatchers will learn of the redemption when the results are announced in the evening of the day of the auction. Since settlement for the auctioned bills is the following Thursday, Fedwatchers in this case will know the size of the reserves impact a couple of days before it actually occurs. In many cases, the Fed will have no choice but to execute an outright transaction in the market. Such transactions usually are arranged on Wednesday for settlement the following day, though they do occur on other days as well, sometimes for skip-day settlement. (That might happen if Wednesday were a holiday, or if the Treasury were conducting an auction that day.) Fedwatchers can only guess at the size of the transaction, since the Fed does not announce it; typically, more than a week elapses before the size of the outright transaction becomes known to the market through the Fed's release of reserves data.

Given the decision to effect a permanent addition (drain) of reserves, the Fed must decide how many securities of what type to purchase (sell). The alternatives are Treasury bills, Treasury coupon securities, and federal agency securities. In general, bills are the preferred instrument. The bill market is more liquid than the market for any other money market instrument, so that the large transactions arranged by the Fed (frequently on the order of $1–2 billion) will not have much impact on rates in the market. Since the Fed prefers not to exercise undue influence on market rates, that is an important consideration. On the other hand, there is some incentive for the Fed to allocate at least some of its holdings to coupon securities so as to provide a core of permanent reserves without the need repeatedly to roll over large amounts of maturing issues. Operationally, the problem with coupon purchases is that the amounts in dealer hands are frequently rather modest relative to the size the Fed requires, so that the Fed generally must solicit offers for a wide variety of issues in order to have flexibility to obtain competitive rates and to maintain the desired maturity balance.[33] That means a sizable task of computing yields for a large number of issues and extends the time required for the transaction to be processed. Otherwise expressed, a coupon "pass" is an ordeal for the Desk. Even worse is an agency pass. Since supplies of agency issues in dealer hands are typically light, even for short-term issues, offers must be solicited for many maturities of each agency's issues, necessitating an arduous computation of yields, followed by comparison of spreads between the rates on issues of different agencies. Thus, it comes as no surprise that agency passes are infrequent.

In the final analysis, the desired mix of permanent and temporary reserve injections must inevitably depend on subjective judgments by the System account manager. Nevertheless, there are certain situations for which temporary reserves injections or drains are particularly appropriate. A good example would be a four-week period in which the first maintenance period requires, say, a $1 billion weekly average addition to reserves, followed by a $1 billion drain in the following period. This could be accomplished easily by executing $2.3 billion three-day RPs on each Friday ($2.3 billion × 3 days ÷ 7 days = $1 billion) and doing no RPs in the subsequent period, producing a $1 billion average reserves drain. That approach obviously has merit in that it minimizes the need for the Fed to enter the market.

In practice, of course, matters are rarely that straightforward. In the first place, estimates of reserves need are only that—estimates. Second, repeated execution of temporary reserves injection (drain) operations may at times serve an ancillary purpose by affecting the psychological attitude of funds traders. For example, in an environment in which the funds rate has declined substantially in past weeks, funds traders may be apt to anticipate still further declines in the current maintenance period. One way in which the Fed may temper such expectations without departing from the nonborrowed reserves path (i.e., without temporarily forcing higher borrowing) would be to arrange open market operations so that, for several weeks, RPs are necessary. Then banks would start each period short of reserves and would therefore probably bid more aggressively for funds.[34]

Needless to say, to monetary policy purists, such behavior smacks of the old procedure of funds-rate targeting, and some critics have suggested that the Fed should reduce the frequency with which it arranged

---

[33] This problem is obviously less severe in the period immediately following the settlement of an auction of Treasury coupon securities when dealer holdings typically are rather ample. Not coincidentally, most of the Fed's purchases of coupon securities are made at such times.

[34] A simpler way to achieve the same objective would be to undersupply nonborrowed reserves, but that approach obviously would involve a departure from the nonborrowed reserves path.

RPs.[35] Of course, the vast majority of temporary reserves injections (drains) are not related to the kind of expectations alteration described above but are required by very short-term movements in the operating factors. Even so, since late 1982 the Desk more often than not has executed some form of RP in the last three days of the reserves maintenance period, contributing to a level of RP activity substantially greater than that which drew the critics' ire. The object apparently is to guard against the possibility of the funds rate plunging due to an unintended, temporary excess of reserves. Whether one thinks the tactic justified or not has a great deal to do with whether or not one believes the Fed should do anything at all to damp interest-rate volatility.[36] Professional economists have sharply divided opinions on that issue.

Nevertheless, there is one respect in which the frequency of execution of RPs could be reduced with only a trivial change in techniques. It is not widely appreciated among market participants that multiday system RPs typically are "withdrawable"—that is, the dealer participating in the transaction may give notice to the Fed by 1:30 P.M. on the day the dealer wishes to terminate the agreement. As a result, if the Fed arranges, say, a seven-day RP on Thursday with a "stop" rate (the lowest accepted rate) of 10 percent, but the market RP rate declines to 9½ percent by Friday, then a substantial and essentially unpredictable portion of the dealers who entered into the RPs with the Fed on Thursday now have a palpable economic incentive to withdraw, leaving the Fed with the job of coming back into the market to arrange more RPs so as to prevent a reserves scarcity from emerging. Not only that, but if rates rise after Thursday and dealers respond by lightening their positions, then their reduced financing needs may also cause them to withdraw from the RPs, putting still further pressure on the funds market.

At this point, the reader may well be wondering why the Fed would allow its RPs to be withdrawable in the first place, especially since non-withdrawable RPs are standard among other market participants. The best explanation appears to be that the withdrawable RP is an institution that has survived the circumstances that originally made it useful. Before 1966, when the first MSPs were executed, any reserves draining was accomplished through outright sales of securities. Thus, if the Fed

---

[35] For example, Milton Friedman has criticized the Fed for an excessive amount of RP activity. See Milton Friedman, "Monetary Policy: Theory and Practice," *Journal of Money, Credit and Banking*, February 1982, pp. 98–118. For a critique and correction of Friedman's charges by two officers of the Open Market Desk, see Fred J. Levin and Anne-Marie Meulendyke, "A Comment," *Journal of Money, Credit and Banking*, August 1982, pp. 399–403, as well as Friedman's reply in the same issue, pp. 404–6.

[36] In terms of Exhibit 3, the object is to maintain banks' reserves demand schedule on the sloped portion of the reserves supply schedule *at all times* during the reserves maintenance period so that an unintended increase in nonborrowed reserves does not prompt a plunge in the funds rate. The likelihood of such an event is increased when the borrowing target is relatively low, as it has been from late 1982 to the present (Summer, 1985).

had done RPs early in the week in response to a perceived reserve need but later found itself faced with a need to drain reserves, then to the extent that the soft funds rate caused RPs to be withdrawn, the reserve drain would be accomplished automatically and, in particular, without requiring an outright sale of securities.[37] Obviously, however, MSPs make this particular feature of RPs redundant.

Presumably because of the interest-rate risk involved, dealers generally have participated in a smaller portion of the Fed's multiday MSPs and (very rare) multiday nonwithdrawable RPs than have their so-called customers (primarily banks). Consequently, if multiday RPs were made uniformly nonwithdrawable, a smaller volume of less attractively priced proposals generally would be submitted, and that might impair the Fed's ability to execute as many transactions as desired.[38] One way to cope with that problem would be to offer one-day and multiday RPs simultaneously, as is frequently done with MSPs. Another would be to execute outright transactions more often.

With the exception of customer RPs, the Fed does not disclose the size of a temporary addition (drain) of reserves, and that presents problems for Fedwatchers and other market participants. Some participants attempt to cope by monitoring the stop rate on the transaction. The conventional wisdom is that a low (high) stop on an RP (MSP) relative to the market rate indicates an "aggressive" operation. But in fact, monitoring the stop is a very poor substitute for knowing the size of the transaction relative to the size of the reserve need. The reason is that the stop rate in general depends on the size of the transaction *and* the distribution of proposals submitted to the Fed. As Exhibit 7 illustrates, the flatter the "tail" of the proposals (i.e., the narrower the range from the highest to the lowest rates shown to the Fed), the less responsive is the stop rate to variations in the size of the transaction. Consequently, there

---

[37] Sometimes, however, the withdrawal of RPs in those days was not altogether automatic. The story is told of a System open market account manager who was confronted with a need to drain reserves after multiday RPs had been executed earlier in the week. Though the funds rate was softening, no withdrawals were forthcoming. Upon investigation, it turned out that a large block of the RPs was held at a major dealer firm. Accordingly, the account manager telephoned the firm's head trader and asked whether he would like to withdraw his RPs. The head trader replied that he was not interested. Then the account manager said that he would appreciate it if the RPs were withdrawn. Again the offer was declined. Before hanging up, the account manager observed that he was certain to remember this event the next time the head trader was in a jam and needed a favor. About 10 minutes later, a phone call to the Desk announced the withdrawal of the RPs.

[38] Recall that dealers desire to do RPs primarily to finance their inventory of securities, though many do run a so-called matched book quite independently of their securities position. Consequently, if the inventory being financed by a multiday nonwithdrawable RP were liquidated, the dealer would suddenly be in a long funds position that could not be eliminated by the simple device of withdrawing from the RP. For the same reason, customers account for a larger than normal portion of multiday MSPs as well as RPs when dealers have very light or net short positions.

EXHIBIT 7 Hypothetical Distributions of Proposals for Repurchase
Agreements and Matched Sale-Purchase Agreements

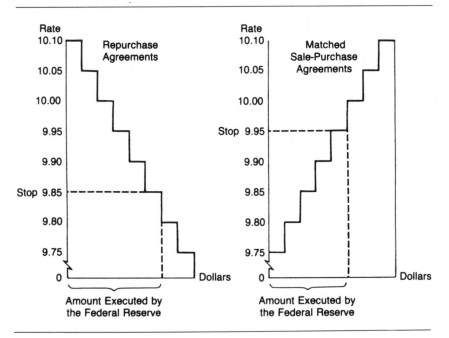

is no unique relation between the stop relative to the market and the aggressiveness of the operation. Moreover (as noted earlier), in some circumstances, dealers and perhaps also their customers are likely to be loath to submit very competitive proposals to the Fed—for example, multiday MSPs in general and RPs when dealers are holding negligible or short positions.

DOES FEDWATCHING MATTER?

Essentially, Fedwatching comprises three analytical techniques. First, like many other economists, a Fedwatcher makes projections, whether formally or subjectively, of the level of economic activity, especially as it bears on variables in which the Fed is thought to be particularly interested (e.g., the GNP, inflation, or one or more measures of the money stock). In this same general area, the federal budget may be analyzed both for its overall macroeconomic impact as well as for the more direct impact on financial markets of the scale and timing of Treasury financing needs. The second focus is the forecasting and interpretation of bank reserves positions and the Fed's open market operations. Most of this chapter has been devoted to explaining the objectives and techniques of such analysis. Flowing naturally from the first two is the third area of interest: the projection of interest rates in money and capital markets. As far as the operation of a financial institution in general and a securities dealer firm in particular is concerned, this is the most important of all.

The first and the last of these activities will always be necessary, but there is no intrinsic reason for projection of reserves positions and open market operations to be part of the job. In performing such an analysis, Fedwatchers merely duplicate and improve on, if possible, the projections routinely generated by the Fed staff to guide the Desk. Moreover, as the preceding discussion has illustrated, the best efforts of Fedwatchers often fall far short of the quality of the Fed staff's projections, primarily because of major delays in the receipt of information by market participants.

As noted earlier, the consequence of this lack of information is greater uncertainty among funds traders as to the degree of borrowing pressure being placed on banks and thus the equilibrium funds rate, so that funds traders are impelled to be more or less aggressive in bidding for funds than they otherwise would be. Indeed, in a sense, the quantity of information provided to the market has been sharply *reduced* since the advent of the nonborrowed reserves targeting procedures in 1979. Prior to that time, by targeting the funds rate, the Fed effectively communicated all information necessary to determine the equilibrium funds rate with precision. Market participants concentrated their analytical energies on divining the next change in the funds-rate target and had to do little more than watch the Fed's "intervention points" (the funds rate at which reserves were added or drained) to determine the equilibrium rate. Since late 1979, however, Fedwatchers and funds traders have had to process information on reserves to estimate the equilibrium rate. In principle, there is nothing wrong with that, and of course the procedures have advantages for monetary policy. The main disadvantage—potential volatility of the funds rate—is due in substantial part to the unavailability of current information concerning factors affecting reserves.

Suppose that market participants were perfectly informed concerning reserves factors and the Fed's intended supplies of nonborrowed reserves. Then they would have a fairly precise idea of the equilibrium funds rate, and any change of the Fed's policy with respect to reserves supplies would be followed immediately by a change in the perceived equilibrium funds rate—and thus of the actual funds rate. During 1979–82, when a nonborrowed reserves targeting procedure was used, the Fed seemed to be of two minds: On the one hand, its operating procedures were designed to speed the adjustment of the funds rate to deviations from monetary targets; but on the other hand, the information supplied to the market was—and is—far from adequate to allow participants to estimate confidently an equilibrium rate to which they can respond. As a result, when the equilibrium is changing, the actual funds rate probably will lag behind, but may even rush ahead. That kind of response is inconsistent with a fully efficient market. Moreover, even if the equilibrium rate is not changing, uncertainty caused by swings in intraperiod borrowing traffic contributes to a dispersion of trades around the equilibrium rate.

Needless to say, the flow of information to the market can never be perfect. But the Fed could supply to the market at almost negligible cost all daily information on factors affecting reserves, thus enhancing the ability of market participants to interpret their environment. Even better, the Fed could announce to the market its own projections of operating factors as well as the size of all open market operations carried out. Doing so would scarcely interfere with the Fed's ability to conduct its operations. On the contrary, it could facilitate them in certain cases (such as multiday MSPs).

Several considerations in addition to the usual bureaucratic inertia may account for the Fed's reluctance to provide such data. First, the Fed may suspect (no doubt correctly in some cases) that the wealth of data to be released would prove confusing to some market participants. Moreover, since the float data, for example, are subject to a variety of "as of" adjustments, the Fed could argue that on some occasions data released might be misleading if not supplemented with background information on the continuing flow of such adjustments. Another consideration that probably influences the Fed's attitude is that the occasional large size of revisions to factor estimates could be embarrassing. Finally, the Fed may believe that release of the full set of reserves data and projections might "tie the hands" of the Desk, conveying to the market an impression of a need for open market operations when the Desk had grounds to suspect that some other factor (such as a prospective swing in the volume of foreign investment orders) might invalidate a superficial interpretation of the data and projections. In such a case, the market might be misled by the Fed's abstaining from open market operations.

These are not trivial considerations, but their significance is unduly magnified when they are advanced with an implicit assumption that the market functions efficiently now. For example, coping with the complexity of reserves data and the revisions constantly being made would indeed tax the patience of almost anyone, but it could hardly be argued to be more trying than the patently inadequate techniques *currently* employed for the same purpose. Similarly, revisions to projections are a source of embarrassment to all forecasters, and all Fedwatchers regularly eat their humble pie in large portions; but that is merely evidence of the job's difficulty. In any event, the Fed regularly releases data on its major bi-weekly forecast errors anyway. Finally, the "tie our hands" argument only applies when the market is deprived of the knowledge that the Fed questions the accuracy or interpretation of the projections;

otherwise, it has no force. In sum, the objections typically advanced against timely release of reserves data have little merit. Ironically, they had more substance when the Fed was targeting the funds rate.

In view of the pivotal role of the funds market in implementing monetary policy, the market's striking inefficiencies are of major concern. Though the reserves-projecting activities of Fedwatchers constitute a logical and—under the circumstances—crucial response to the problems, this response is not the most effective way to improve the operation of the funds market.

56

Forecasting Interest Rates

W. David Woolford, C.F.A.
Vice President
Prudential Insurance Company of America

INTRODUCTION

There is no shortage of interest-rate forecasts, although only a small segment of the population dares to make this the sole basis for a career. Each day individuals buy and sell money for various time periods, both for their own account and as agent or investment advisor. Whether the analyses leading to their decisions were shallow or deep, rigorous or emotional, the outcome of these myriad decisions—in the cash markets, financial futures markets, with and without the assistance of financial intermediaries—is a series of interest rates for various maturities and types of securities. This series, in turn, can be decomposed—though imperfectly—into a consensus forecast for interest rates. That consensus provides a benchmark for successful forecasting. Improve on this consensus consistently (net of transaction and opportunity costs), and the forecast has been profitable. However, not everyone can succeed, for the consensus, by definition, has been established by an equal weighting of dollars on both sides.

For many market professionals, the difficulty in consistently correctly predicting shifts in the consensus has led to a refocus of their analysis toward topics outlined elsewhere in this volume. That new focus entails a goal not so much to outguess the consensus as to exploit even momentary adjustment lags, to arbitrage cash and futures markets, and to construct portfolios that offer significant upside potential but have already built-in limits to downside risk. These adjustments in focus are not free, however, and returns from such activity will not exceed the market average unless the professional can somehow combine this activity with better information, transaction or scale economies, or a cheaper access to financing.

This chapter, however, is intended to lay the groundwork for those daring (or foolish) enough to attempt to improve on the consensus. For those so determined, a large body of literature stands ready to prepare (and perhaps dissuade) the uninitiated. With few exceptions, methods can be catalogued in two groups.

At one extreme are multisector models, simplifications of the economy that seek to explain interest-rate behavior from the interactions of a wide range of hypothetical economic actors in a hypothetical economy containing various degrees of realism. Among the large multisector models providing users with excellent equation/sector descriptions and analyses are Wharton, Data Resources, and Chase Econometrics. Such models need not be composed of several hundred interacting equations. They may also be grossly oversimplified—a restatement of the demand for money to forecast interest rates, for example—but they share a common element that the forecast for interest rates is based on a pattern of causality from one or more economic variables that is expected to be reproduced, on average, in the future.

At the other extreme are projections that lack any causal specification but rather are based on an analysis of technical factors. Again, such technical activity may be limited to charting relationships or may be very sophisticated time series analyses. These models lack the structural specification that, say, conditions A, B, and C will be associated with result X in strength Y within time T. However, they share one commonality with structural models. Both seek to explain the future on the basis of the past. Furthermore, only a biased sample of past data can be used. When combined with the range of innovation in financial markets over the past century, and particularly in the past 25 years, this selection bias helps to explain why identical models in the hands of different forecasters can produce sharply varying results.

Just how different can be seen from a survey of interest rate forecasts. At the end of 1980, for example, a small group of forecasters, presumably with access to identical information and to each other, saw fit to disagree on the outlook for interest rates one year later to such an extent that the range of forecasts for the interest rate on federal funds spanned 900 basis points. For most cyclical experiences over the past two centuries, that range exceeds the actual trough-to-peak and peak-to-trough movements in interest rates. Of course, the final months of 1980 were exceptionally difficult times in which to forecast the level of interest rates, and forecasters generally agreed on their future direction (down). Recent forecasts, such as those made at the end of 1984 for year-end, 1985, are much more in agreement as to the level of interest rates one year later, and much less in agreement as to direction.

Consensus forecasts display considerably less variation, as might be expected from an average. An estimate of the consensus forecast, prepared roughly at the same time as the forecasts above, is shown in Exhibit 1. In retrospect, it proved to be a tough standard for 1981.

EXHIBIT 1 Forecasts for the Federal Funds Rate Prepared One Year
Earlier (actual data rounded)

Forecast for:	Year-End, 1981	Year-End, 1985
Estimate of market consensus	12.8%	10.0%
Forecast 1	8.0%	12.0%
Forecast 2	11.0	6.0
Forecast 3	14.0	8.0
Forecast 4	16.0	11.3
Forecast 5	17.0	9.3
Actual rate at year-end (weekly average)	12.9%	9.6%
Actual funds rate at time of forecast (monthly average)	18.9	8.4

Note: Identities of forecasters are not constant over time. The consensus has been
extrapolated from forward rates implicit in the Treasury yield curve and assumes that
funds carried a 100 basis point premium to Treasury instruments in 1981 and 50 basis
points in 1985.

Estimates of the market consensus cannot be prepared directly from
interest rates quoted in cash or futures markets, except in the case of
pure discount instruments. The usual specification of interest rates in
bond markets, however, is the conventional yield-to-maturity, an internal rate-of-return calculation that assumes that all coupon payments can
be reinvested at this internal rate of return until maturity. Furthermore,
the bond markets contain a vast heterogeneity of instruments bearing
differing call, default risk, liquidity premia, and other features.

The first difficulty with the conventional yield-to-maturity specification presents largely computational difficulties. A complete description
of the term structure can be created by estimating a well-defined concept, the *spot rate*. The spot rate is the rate that, compounded over the
period, gives the return that the market would demand for a pure discount instrument for that period, say T. (With pure discount instruments, reinvestment risk is eliminated.) As T is varied, the sequence of
spot rates traces out the term structure. Equivalently, this also describes
a series of forward rates—the incremental return in varying T. Hence
the spot rate, R_T, is equivalent to the geometric average of all forward
rates, r_i.

$$(1 + R_T) = (1 + r_1)(1 + r_2) \ldots (1 + r_R) \ldots (1 + r_T)$$

Any member of this series of forward rates, in turn, can be decomposed into an anticipated interest rate, F, and a liquidity premium, L.

$$(1 + r_k) = (1 + F_k)(1 + L_k) \qquad k = 1, 2, \ldots T$$

Until recently, spot rates had to be estimated from a sample of
securities. (In practice, the yield curve was estimated using Treasury
securities to minimize default risk and bias introduced by call features.)

However, major Wall Street investment bankers have introduced a series of spot rate products—bearing various trademarks—and the U.S. Treasury has recently seen fit to recognize the success of these products by agreeing that future Treasury issues will be capable of being disaggregated (stripped) into their spot rate components. The Treasury's decision makes the product more generic and easily transferable and should spawn a number of new academic studies.

This market will remove some of the errors in estimating spot rates but will not end the debate over the shape and magnitude of term premiums until more complete markets are available in forwards than the current futures markets contain. The advent of organized futures markets had been expected to provide an important laboratory for the study of financial markets and the market consensus. Results of initial experiments, however, were greeted with consternation when it became apparent that forward cash market and futures rates were not equal, despite their apparent theoretical equivalence. However, that apparent inconsistency has been resolved by noting, first, differences in tax treatments in cash and futures transactions and (a more fundamental difference) the cost of guaranteeing futures contracts in an organized market (Kane [43]).[1] Despite the reserves carried by the organized exchanges, residual risk does exist—a future contract on a default-free security does not make the contract default free. The price to be paid for bearing the residual risk is sufficient to generate differences in prices for cash market and futures claims.

Interest will continue to focus on the stability of liquidity, or term, premiums. There is some empirical support for the following argument: Although the postwar average liquidity (term) premium has ranged from perhaps 15 to 20 basis points in very short bill maturities, to 50 to 75 basis points for three-month rates six months forward, to perhaps 200 basis points or more at longer forwards, these liquidity premia will vary procyclically over the business cycle.[2]

For the interest-rate forecaster, however, each of these considerations might be judged to pale by contrast to the more difficult task of preparing an alternative to the consensus. Empirical research, particularly work by Roll [62] and Pesando [58], has shown that the consensus sets a high standard by which to be judged. Fame and fortune have accrued to those fortunate enough to top the consensus, but forecasts by

---

[1] For clarity, numbers in brackets are used to footnote references. Corresponding numbered references are contained in the bibliography at the end of this chapter.

[2] The origin of the liquidity premium is itself a source of debate. It may reflect moneyness, perceived default risk (including credit or interest-rate controls), or changes in the volatility of interest rates. For example, Throop [70] found that the standard deviation of rates is significantly related to a measure of the liquidity premium for Treasury bill rates in some specifications. In general, however, there is no hard agreement as yet on either the underlying cause(s) or the empirical size of liquidity premiums.

FORECASTING INTEREST RATES / **1197**

those less fortunate lie in unmarked graves. Thus an understanding of the consensus is important as a benchmark. The consensus is also useful as a neutral position when other methods offer no clear strategy, which occurs more frequently than most fixed income managers care to admit.

STRUCTURAL MODELS

The heart of all structural models used in interest-rate forecasting is a description of the supply of funds to the credit markets and the demand for these funds. This equilibrium has been summarized (and embellished in numerous ways) in the so-called Hicksian Cross, or IS–LM framework.[3] Exhibit 2 shows the determinations of interest rates and economic activity under this framework. This IS curve traces the locus of points along which savings (often assumed simply proportional to economic activity, although clearly responsive to interest rates as they reflect the reward for postponing expenditures, and not just anticipated inflation) is equal to investment (whose level is a function of some kind of hurdle rate derived from the marginal efficiency of capital). Clearly, both can be made conditional on various monetary and fiscal policies. This curve is downward sloping because lower interest rates would be found as higher levels of economic activity increased the flow of savings, and because increased investment reduces the marginal return on investment. (However, the slope is reversed in comparing interest rates and inflation. The anticipation of accelerated inflation rates reduces savings, forcing higher interest rates.) Similarly, LM measures the locus of points along which money supply and money demand are equal and is an upward-sloping function, reflecting a higher demand for money as economic activity increases.[4]

The intersection of the proximate determinants of increments to the flow of funds as expressed by the IS curve, and monetary factors determines the equilibrium interest rate. Forecasting interest rates would appear to be merely a matter of forecasting determinants of IS and LM. In fact, this is the route taken by early structural models and continued up to this day (though with a significant upgrading in sophistication) by many econometric model builders.

Structural models of which IS-LM is the major form offer the only means currently available to evaluate structural changes in the econ-

---

[3] This is also sometimes mistakenly called the Keynesian cross. Keynes himself may have felt that a somewhat different interpretation of the interest rate was in order. See Meltzer [48].

[4] This sidesteps both the precise definition of *moneyness* to be used in forecasting interest rates and the interest elasticity of the demand for money function. Despite the wealth of empirical tests of this elasticity, its value remains a matter of dispute. Recent discussions of the "stability" of the demand for money implicitly argue that with interest-rate volatility, estimation errors have increased.

EXHIBIT 2 IS-LM Relationships

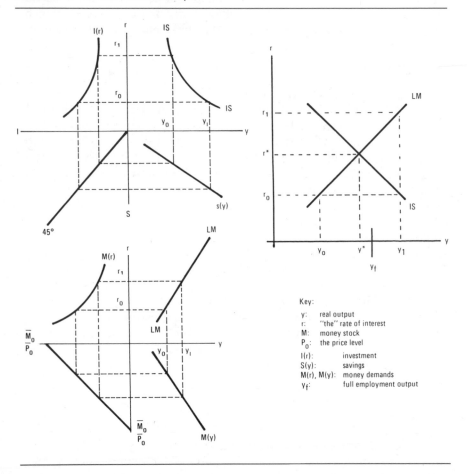

Key:

y:	real output
r:	"the" rate of interest
M:	money stock
P_0:	the price level
I(r):	investment
S(y):	savings
M(r), M(y):	money demands
y_f:	full employment output

---

omy, including changes in operating procedures for monetary and fiscal policies. Their failure to produce above-average forecasts, however (see Pesando [58] and McNees [50]), has produced a healthy skepticism directed at econometric models. Users of these models should be aware of a number of shortcomings. The following is only a partial catalogue.

Stability

Large econometric models include a substantial number and variety of feedback relations. Changes in farm prices, for example, alter trade balances and affect farm machinery sales, industrial orders and employment, personal income, food consumption, and farm prices. Lower interest rates (for example, from an unexpectedly expansionary monetary policy) initially increase investment and economic activity, increase prices of assets (including common stocks), and spur additional borrowing, thereby forcing interest rates to reverse their initial decline. Not infrequently, specification of individual feedback relationships produces simultaneity in which model specification must be altered (*add-factored* is the professional euphemism) to produce convergence. Usual practice is for model-building entrepreneurs to permit users to interact with the ultimate system, but such a "simulation" leaves the model's response *framework* unchanged; reestimation to explore alternative specifications is not particularly user-friendly. Some modelers do report dynamic Monte Carlo simulations that provide more accurate error bounds on forecasts, but again, these projections of forecast errors are conditional on the future appropriateness of the underlying model structure.

Several chapters in this book deal with the portfolio and specific problems introduced by optionable securities, especially mortgage instruments. Researchers in these securities are particularly sensitive to the dangers of assuming that an underlying model structure will persist into the future. As one analyst aptly put it, "The fact that a pool has recently experienced faster-than-expected prepayment may merely indicate that that pool's fast payers are now in someone else's pools."

Identification

The proverbial introductory economics examination question: "We observe a decline in interest rates. Investment demand must have fallen." In terms of Exhibit 2, a fall in investment demand (a shift to the right of I(r)) is consistent with a decline in interest rates, but this decline is also consistent with a host of other phenomena including a shifting savings behavior. Identification of the large model equivalents of IS and LM relationships usually involve simplifying assumptions on the determinants and specification of interest-sensitive relationships, in order to distinguish demand and supply.

Specification Error

Pressures for convergence and identification will lead to specification bias. Forecasts of an upturn in interest rates may be conditional on a prior upturn in inflation, for example, when there is considerable evidence that the reverse is true. Wage rates may *lead* rather than (correctly) *lag* inflation. Wealth effects may operate with unacceptably long or short lags to be consistent with other equilibrium conditions. Long-run, own-price elasticities may be estimated to be no larger than short-run responses. Of necessity, volatility will be damped. This is a necessary concomitant of regression procedures, but one that can have the unfortunate side effect of increasing the apparent explanatory power of one-factor models while failing to capture the unique characteristics that can distinguish a correct forecast from the consensus.

A full description of various models and their specific features cannot be attempted in this chapter. However, model builders and buyers should ask for some minimum requirements if the model is to be useful in answering hypotheses on the impact of structural changes on levels of interest rates:

1. Over long periods of time, inflation is essentially a monetary phenomenon. Over that same time frame, the primary determinant of the level of interest rates is inflation. Short-run relationships of money stock, inflation, and interest rates, however, are highly variable. Nevertheless, models that seek to forecast interest rates should have steady state characteristics consistent with the long-run rate of inflation having a consistent relationship with long-run growth in the money stock. One test is to double the growth rate of the quantity of money and maintain the new growth for a sustained period of time. Since no change has been made to the productivity function for money, long-run steady state should see the rate of inflation roughly double, because there is no reason in this context to expect a permanent increase in the underlying demand for money balances. Does the model show the predicted response?

2. Concerning the government budget constraint, how does the model close the identity that Treasury outlays must match receipts from taxes and debt issue, including debt sales through the intermediary of the central bank? What mechanism, if any, is there for the central bank's response to the deficit? Earlier mechanisms specified this response as one in which the central bank's willingness to absorb the deficit via open-market debt purchases was a positive function of the level of interest rates.[5] These mechanisms are perhaps appropriate so long as the central bank follows an interest-rate target, but their applicability was sharply reduced by recent changes in operating procedures. Specification of the central bank's reaction function is not an easy task. Moreover, heightened recognition of the central bank's importance in the inflationary process has increased the focus on this reaction function. For example, the fear that deficits will ultimately be monetized because of pressures from political or economic events can lead to substantial term premiums.

3. Under an interest-rate target, what mechanism exists to model the central bank's reaction function when the target is incompatible with

---

[5] Focus on this factor assumes that there is not a high interest elasticity of demand for money. If there is—Keynes' so-called liquidity trap—interest rates are insensitive to changes in money supply, and it is immaterial how the deficit is financed. Empirically, however, a liquidity trap has not characterized the postwar period.

price stability? Many models contain no such bridge, pretending that an infinitely elastic reserve supply procedure can nevertheless co-exist with a determinant price level. The fault generally lies in a failure to specify a clearing mechanism for *aggregate* demand, replacing this with n–1 clearing markets in a way that confuses relative prices with the aggregate price level. Such a model cannot capture interest-rate movements.

4. Is there a monetary explanation of the exchange rate (and, if applicable, central bank intervention)? External/internal balance is particularly important because of the potential to only partly specify credit demand if the Euromarket is ignored.[6] Hartman [37] found support for the hypothesis that a significant part of variation in short-term U.S. interest rates in the 1975–78 period was attributable to foreign influences. His work predates, but anticipates, the recent debate on the impact of the record U.S. trade deficit on domestic capital markets.

5. How is credit market equilibrium specified? Although money supply growth is the primary determinant of the long-term level of inflation, inflation is the rate of change of the purchasing power of money. Interest rates specify the price of credit—the rate for exchanging future claims on consumption for present claims. Clearly, their most important determinant will be the time path of anticipated price changes for these consumption claims over the period, and this explains the attention paid to projecting expectations of inflation rates and actual inflation rates in interest-rate-forecasting models. In the short run, however, other factors can combine to generate sharply different interest-rate conditions than would be projected on the basis of inflation expectations. Adjustment lags, institutional conditions (disintermediation, for example), central bank and Treasury financing activity, inventory adjustments, and other factors can all produce interest-rate environments that differ, short term, from what expectations of inflation might suggest.

Ultimately such temporary conditions will be arbitraged. Many models of credit market conditions provide such arbitrage. The user should be careful to analyze the following:

1. Analyze whether such arbitrage exists. Can interest rates permanently fail to reflect expected inflation? If so, the model is useful only for very short-term timing activities and is inconsistent with equilibrium.

2. Analyze whether or not the credit market specification closes the asset and liability sides of the relationship. For example, some flow-of-

---

[6] In principle, Walras' Law ensures that if n–1 markets can be shown to clear, the nth market must also be in equilibrium. Domestic asset markets, however, cannot be fully specified, so Walras' law cannot be used to justify omitting consideration of foreign influences on the domestic interest-rate environment. Indeed, for small countries with open capital markets, foreign influences are the most important determinant of interest rates.

funds models contain no constraint on loan growth from funding—
implicitly assuming an infinitely elastic supply of bank reserves by the
central bank. In such an environment, however, no meaningful specification of the level or movement in interest rates is possible, and the
entire model should be discarded. (In terms of the IS–LM framework,
such a model presumes a horizontal LM function.)

Rational Expectations

Even if these checks produce a satisfactory report, model users face a
potentially insurmountable obstacle to improving on the consensus forecast in the form of rational expectations.[7] Early models of expectations
merely specified some mechanically extrapolative formation of expectations—distributed lags, for example. No attempt was made to see if this
was consistent with competitive equilibrium in, say, the capital markets.
When such tests of equilibrium were performed, however, it became
clear that mechanical formulations of expectations (whether adaptive,
regressive, inertial, extrapolative, or some combination) would only be
accurate if markets offered unexploited profits.[8] Market participants
could consequently improve on mechanical extrapolations, and would if
markets were efficient. In an efficient market interest-rate forecasting
would be defined as the solution to the following exercise:

1. Assume the change in interest rates, dr, is linear in the information set, S, needed to forecast changes in interest rates. Then to a first
order approximation, the change in interest rates, dr, can be described
by:

$$dr = f(S,V) \tag{1}$$

where V is a serially uncorrelated error term independent of S.

2. By definition, S is not known to all or even a significant number
of capital market participants, or interest rates would already reflect this
information. This is equivalent to saying that data on interest-rate determinants, K, can be decomposed into two components, information already available (K_{-1}) and S:

$$K = f(K_{-1},S) \tag{2}$$

---

[7] There is a tendency to confuse rational expectations with market efficiency because
tests for these phenomena are joint tests. Market efficiency implies that prices already
efficiently use available information. Forecasters cannot expect to improve on the market
consensus unless they have access to new information at above-average efficiency or (what
amounts to the same thing) have additional information. Efficiency can be produced with
all market participants behaving irrationally—that is, in ways other than consistently in
their own best interests.

[8] Adaptive expectations adjust the new forecast by a proportion of the error between
forecast and actual values; regressive expectations projects the actual return will adjust to
its previous level (equilibrium) over a period of time. (See, for example, Dobson, Sutch,
and Vanderford [16].)

3. Statistically, an estimate for S can be derived from errors in (2). Efficient market theory would argue that estimates of S in (2) will be serially independent. Otherwise lagged values of S could be used to improve estimates in (2). These estimates of S can then be used in (1) to solve for dr. If the efficient markets hypothesis holds, lagged values of S will have no significance for dr in (1). Furthermore, at the margin, the cost of collecting S and estimating its impact should roughly equal its value in estimating dr.[9]

Note that this does not preclude improving on the market consensus in forecasting short-term rates, because there is no arbitrage opportunity in serial dependence to exploit—a one-period bond matures in the same period as information is available. References elsewhere in this chapter supporting apparent improvements on the market forecast, in fact, are uniformly limited to short-term rates. Furthermore, the longer the forecast horizon, the weaker is the evidence for market efficiency, in part because term premiums will display (cyclical) variability.[10]

The difficulty that rational expectations presents to model builders is that it hypothecates that market participants will *alter* their behavior to reduce unexploited profit opportunities—in terms of the above framework that participants consistently reduce the expected value of information needed to forecast changes in interest rates—$E(S/S_{-1})$—to zero. Profitable arbitrages cannot persist. This means that the response coefficients estimated from a structural model, which has been of necessity based on past reactions, will change depending on the actual outcome.

The reader interested in pursuing this problem with respect to the term structure should always be aware that since rationality is specified in the sense that expectations must be consistent with predictions deriving from economic and statistical theory, and since the term structure is also estimated from the same data set, the test will be a joint test of rational expectations formations and the hypothecated term structure.[11]

The question of rationality also has been addressed with regard to the Fisher equation. Irving Fisher postulated that the nominal rate of interest would equal the rate of return from holding real assets together with the expected rate of inflation on these assets. The Fisher equation is easily understood in theory. Its use in practical forecasting is largely limited to longer-term asset equilibrium. The equation is:

$$(1 + i_t) = (1 + r_t)(1 + p_t)(1 + g_t) \tag{3}$$

---

[9] For a further discussion, and some estimates, see Evans [19] and Pesando [58]. Evan's estimates, however, should be carefully reviewed because of statistical problems created by overlapping sample intervals reducing degrees of freedom.

[10] For a similar but more restrictive view on the potential for successful forecasting, see Pesando [58].

[11] See for example Modigliani and Shiller [53].

where

i_t = the nominal interest rate

r_t = the default-free real return

p_t = the anticipated rate of inflation

g_t = the "risk premium."

At this level of generality, g_t can be linked to many sources: default risk, term or other issuer options, the volatility of inflation, taxes, to name a few. Clearly, g_t can be positive or negative. Although there is no agreement on either the size or stability of r_t, Friedman and Schwartz [28], in an encyclopedic study of monetary developments in the United States and United Kingdom, argue that over the past century roughly a three percent figure would have been appropriate. Accepting this figure, a portfolio manager would choose a rate of inflation that he or she expected to persist at the end of a given period, set r_t equal to 300 basis points, and add any additional premiums to solve for i_t in (3). That solution could then be compared with forward rates available given the current term structure vector consistent with (1). The excess (deficient) available return, on a risk-adjusted basis, can then be used as an input in asset allocation. The real rate cannot be stimulated from averaging *ex post* data. For example, Ibbotson and Sinquefield [42] found that the average real return to an investment in long-term Treasury securities was 0.7 percent between 1926 and 1978. This is an estimate of the real rate if, over the period, average errors in estimating p were zero and the average value of g was zero. Realized real returns are heavily impacted by unanticipated inflation. (From 1926 to 1950, realized real returns were 2.7 percent—much closer to the 3 percent figure of Friedman and Schwartz.)

The tenuous short-term connection between inflation and interest rates limits the practical use of this relation to longer term asset equilibrium. The Fisher equation holds so long as real assets and bonds are arbitraged by investors—in other words, an efficient market. Tests by Fama [20] supported the joint test of rationality and a constant real rate, but this result has been the subject of significant criticisms, particularly Fama's use of the Consumer Price Index as an index of real asset prices. However, for those determined to forecast interest rates through forecasts of inflation, Fama's tests are disturbing because they appear to support the argument that current interest rates already contain *all* relevant information about inflation (in other words, interest rates may operate as the best predictor of inflation), but the reverse does not hold.

Such a finding would deal a harsh blow to forecasts based on projections of inflation, although it would still leave open the question of whether it was possible to develop projections of the real rate (whether the real rate should properly be treated as a constant, either in analytical or forecasting applications, remains an open question). Recent evidence questioning the cyclical constancy of the natural rate of unemployment, for example, indirectly supports the hypothesis that the real rate of interest also varies. Evidence along this same vein is now available from Great Britain, where the first large scale use of index-linked bonds in a moderate inflation environment (so that a long-term capital market exists) appears to show [76] that most of the movement in nominal interest rates reflects changes in expected inflation, but real interest rates are sensitive to expectations of the strength of economic activity.

A different question is addressed by the preferred habitat thesis, which argues that interest rates on different instruments will reflect demand and supply by major participants in these sectors. For example, this thesis would forecast that a major determinant of changes in negotiable certificate of deposit rates will be the future path of bank loan demand, or that prices for corporate bonds will reflect demand for these securities by such typical institutional purchasers as insurance and pension fund portfolios. Such a hypothesis is often implicitly used by flow-of-funds forecasts in projecting various kinds of new issue indigestion because traditional purchasers will be unable to absorb forthcoming supply. The Fisher equation, as noted, relies for its validity on arbitrage between real goods and bonds. As an aid to short-term run forecasts, preferred habitat rests on an even more fragile reed—the lack of arbitrage, except at substantial premiums, between various sectors of the debt markets. As initially proposed by Modigliani and Sutch [54], preferred habitat reflected differences in investor time period preferences for consumption. Cox, Ross, and Ingersoll's extension [14] to differing risk preferences does not alter the fundamental difficulty that forecasting interest rates on the basis of preferred habitat requires an institutional or other rationale for the absence of arbitrageurs. It is thus a disequilibrium situation, observable at times, but extremely difficult to forecast on a systematic basis. In fact, Singleton [67, p. 612] found no evidence that maturity-specific disturbances could explain a significant part of yield movements for Treasury securities. Except for the one-year bill, he said, "the specific processes appeared to be generated by serially uncorrelated processes and, thus, [were] of no value for forecasting future interest rates." Singleton was led to conclude that "if institutional variables have an effect, then it will be through their influence on liquidity premiums and expectations."

Projecting interest-rate movements by ascribing future twists in the yield curve to "preferred habitat" remains a popular, if questionable, practice. Some examples:

1. Bank portfolios tend to purchase Treasury securities in 2- to 7- (occasionally 10-) year maturities to speculate on interest-rate movements (by mismatching asset and liability durations). This speculation has historically been associated with weakening loan demand and

downward pressure on bank earnings; this correlation has weakened as banks have come to view their portfolio as less a source of liquidity for loan demand and more as a separate profit center. If the hypothesis is valid, one would expect to find, other things equal, upward pressure on these maturities when loan demand is very strong.

2. Insurance companies and pension fund managers are traditional buyers of longer term fixed income securities. Their asset allocation and available funding, then, should twist the yield curve up or down for these instruments relative to other maturities. (The author knows of no valid evidence for this statement.)

3. Many analysts view short-term interest rates as purely demand determined, arguing that the aggregate supply of short-term credit will be insensitive to interest rates because of a lack of liquid investment alternatives. The statement has been used to justify forecasts of short-term rates well below inflation rates. Though perhaps valid for some investors, it neglects the ability of other investors to alter their asset/liability structure. For example, inordinately high short-term interest rates will encourage borrowing long to lend short; the reverse will be true at levels of short-term rates viewed as excessively low.

4. The Euromarkets are typically viewed as financial markets for overnight to 15-year maturities, although the market's growth has brought a full spectrum of maturities. The view that strong foreign demand for dollars will reduce domestic interest rates is true, other things equal, but there is no reason to expect that particular maturities will not be arbitraged—by sales to other investors, for example. This arbitrage accounts for tightened links between domestic and Eurodollar markets. For example, recent investor demand for seven-year securities, and the consequent reshaping of the yield curve, has partly and perhaps largely reflected growth of the swap market. Frequently, the swap involves exchange of floating rate cash flows for fixed rate cash flows over a five-to-seven year period. The Euromarket's ability to offer strong domestic credits access to the seven-year maturity spectrum at a yield competitive with or even at a premium to Treasuries has facilitated this end of the swap and, in the process, led to much closer links by underwriters to the domestic market. Similarly, the evidence that new Eurodollar instruments will offer above-average returns has become more fleeting coincident with increased interest by nonbank institutions in this country and elsewhere in international dollar and nondollar fixed income vehicles.

Recap

This brief review of structural models may appear to have been a uniformly negative one. In fact, the scale of criticism that can be brought to bear is testimony to the wealth of knowledge that has been accumulated in this area. Future work directed at liquidity premia and rational expectations can pay further dividends in expanding knowledge, although it is clear that profitable forecasts are dependent on use of unprocessed or normally unavailable information, or as a side benefit to necessary participation in risk-bearing. There are several directions that this may take:

1. Improved processing of information. Time-series analysis has produced, in some instances, forecasts that improve on implicit forward rates. One recent states/space improvement on ARIMA is the contribution by Fildes and Fitzgerald [24]. Improved time-series models have become increasingly available to serious portfolio managers. Their appeal should be particularly strong to forecasters interested in constructing benchmark forecasts independent of their personal interpretation of history. There remains the hurdle of quantifying changing response patterns to new information. This is a fertile and productive field for Bayesian analysis.

2. There has now been sufficient empirical evidence to question the applicability of the simple one-factor capital asset pricing model in equity markets. Bond price variability has increased to reflect the increased variability of inflation. (This was predictable. With the acceleration of inflation, either yields could remain low and price variability low, giving bonds the character of a nominal option with a suboptimal return, or returns and risks could both rise.) Despite the more univariate character of bonds, this has spurred interest in an application of the arbitrage pricing theory [63] in which compensation for bearing risk is composed of several premia. Elsewhere in this volume, work reported on the respective values for call options, sinking funds, warrants, and other extendable/retractable features permit the price of a bond to be expressed as the sum of various risk premia. In turn, the term structure can be viewed as a piecewise continuous set of risk premia for capital and reinvestment risks.

3. Improvement in quantitative research into business cycles. A review of current methodology in the following pages makes the gaps in this area readily apparent. However, the need to estimate rational expectations models incorporating predictable response coefficients stands as a major stumbling block to useful forecasting improvements to this area.[12]

BUSINESS-CYCLE MODELS

A charitable view of less-than-perfect performance of large-scale forecasting models would be that their useful features are already incorpo-

---

[12] This point has been made in another context by Al Wojnilower [78, p. 278]: "Because of the major structural changes in finance between most successive cycles, the behavior of financial data, including monetary aggregates, also is likely to have different implications from cycle to cycle."

rated in the term structure, as market efficiency would suggest. Of course, this has also had the impact of maintaining interest in other forecasting procedures having various levels of naivete.

Any examination of the term structure over the business cycle should begin with Phillip Cagan's three intensive studies of cyclical movements in interest rates (in [34] and [35]) augmented by his exhaustive examination of trends and cycles in the quantity of money [11]. There has been a clear tendency for interest-rate cycles to better anticipate business cycles in more recent times. This undoubtedly reflects the improved frequency and quality of economic information. Just as noticeable is a tendency for the lag in cyclical swings in long- to short-term rates to tighten. Long-term rates now exhibit peaks and troughs coincident with or even in advance of swings in short-term rates. Growth in sophistication and activity of financial markets may be one explanation for this observation; another is the increased attention to monetary policy and attempts by portfolio managers to anticipate shifts in policy intent. To the extent these consensus expectations prove to be correct and shifts in policy intent are consistent with the economy's cyclical character, long-term rates can lead short-term rates. To the extent they are incorrect, rate movements will display a jagged trend, and each successive error in the direction of long-term rates will lead the market to extract greater risk premiums varying with the duration (interest sensitivity) of the security and produce a steeper (or for initially inverted cases, a flatter) yield curve. Forecasting interest-rate cycles in this formulation is thus a joint forecast of (1) the economy's underlying strength and (2) the reaction function of policymakers.

This is the lesson of the 1983–85 experience. The sharp drop in interest rates that accompanied the 1982 recession produced a yield curve that, in an environment of weak short-term credit demand, carried a term premium of roughly 225 basis points between three month and 25 year maturities. Over the next two years, short-term credit demands surged at record rates, but the impact of this pressure on the yield curve was more than offset by a fluctuation in the level of interest rates of some 350 basis points, while inflation rates remained low—and the term premium reached nearly 350 basis points.

Studies of the term structure over the business cycle have noted some general similarities, of which the following is a sampling.

1. Since business cycles incorporate an adjustment of actual inventory to desired inventory positions that typically involves some inventory liquidation (or at least a sharp reduction in accumulation), the cessation of the liquidation stage at or near the cycle trough typically produces a relatively sharp rebound in production activity and temporary sharp upward pressure on interest rates as working capital needs expand. This pressure relaxes for two reasons: The translation of raw

materials into finished products reduces the pressure on cash flow, and initial inflation expectations generated by the contemporaneous rebound in raw material and intermediate product prices (as these inventories contract to and below target levels) are softened by the evidence of more moderate price increases at the finished goods level. With the gain in productivity as capacity utilization begins to climb, expanded profit margins are possible, further contributing to moderating pressures to raise prices while improving cash flow.

2. This upward pressure on interest rates around and following the trough typically lasts at most 6 to 12 months. It is then followed by a sharp rally that will carry bond prices back to near (or through) previous highs and yields to near (or below) their previous cyclical lows. At this point, the postwar history has been one of rising demand for funds producing a fundamental inconsistency between the interest-rate targets sought by the central bank and economic reality. Since this result is perceived only with a lag, the result is a succession of policy adjustments until policy ultimately succeeds in either pricing sufficient participants out of the market or engages in direct allocation (via disintermediation, for example) to achieve this goal.

So long as the Federal Reserve persisted on pursuing an interest-rate target that permitted credit demands to continue to be met at prices that were generally below inflationary expectations, projections of interest-rate turning points at peaks were equivalent to finding evidence of the onset of disintermediation. In this respect, it is important to remember that financial institutions make forward commitments and, until recently, had no organized markets in which to offset this risk.[13]

The composite index of leading indicators is frequently followed as an indicator of the future pattern of credit demands. However, the index, despite its relatively good track record in tracing cyclical patterns, cannot be said to provide more than a rough gauge to interest-rate movements. Interest-rate turning points are more closely linked with the reference cycle, as reflected by the composite index of coincident indicators, particularly when adjusted for a lagging recognition that the economy had entered recession. Credit demands themselves, other expert opinion notwithstanding, do not give useful signals as to the peak in interest rates, save possibly over very short-run intervals. In part, this reflects the elasticity of balance sheets of financial intermediaries together with the fact that data to estimate supply and demand for funds are available on only a piecemeal basis for the financial system.

3. Interest rates themselves typically attempt to anticipate the peak in economic activity, resulting in a flattening and, in recent cycles, inver-

---

[13] Commitments are an option to the borrower that he may choose not to exercise. At this writing, markets for state-contingent claims of this sort, including the interest rate options markets, are still in their infancy.

sion in the yield curve. Inversion in prewar periods was generally linked to a liquidity crunch in the midst of monetary panic. More recently, the credit markets have exhibited sustained periods of substantial inversion. An inverted yield curve is a disequilibrium phenomenon that cannot persist in the absence of new information to alter expectations, since it projects future declines in rates. Persistent inversion requires that short-term rates continue to rise and, furthermore, is generally accompanied by more-than-proportional increases in long-term rates that will ultimately destroy the inversion. This process reflects the adjustments to:

> Disappointed expectations that rates will fall and produce capital appreciation (roughly) proportional to the duration of fixed income instruments.
>
> Larger risk premiums, since levels of interest rates have deviated more than expected and (generally) created a stretched financial fabric.
>
> Potential or actual political pressure for more (read: inflationary) expansionary monetary policies to relieve upward pressures on interest rates.

4. Postwar peak-to-trough declines in short-term interest rates have, on a percentage basis, been so similar as to enter the rule-of-thumb mythology. A similar stability in terms of percentage peak-to-trough declines in long-term interest rates during the postwar period can be seen in Exhibit 3. At the same time, however, the differential in call money and long-term Treasury yields at the trough has tended to shrink as shown in Exhibit 4. This may have reflected an implicit judgment on the part of the credit market at the trough that inflation would continue to decline—a judgment largely in error thus far in the postwar period.

EXHIBIT 3 Percent Decline in Interest Rates from Peak to Trough

	(1) Federal Funds	(2) Aaa Corporate Bonds	(3) Increases in Inflation Rate (CPI) in Prior Upturn	(4) (3) Divided by Trough Rate
1957–58	−82	−25	+5.7	1.57
1959–61	−71	−19	+2.6	0.59
1966–67	−34	−13	+4.1	0.77
1970–71	−59	−22	+5.4	0.71
1974–75	−64	−24	+9.9	1.25
1980	−49*	−21	+11.9	1.07
1981–83	−58	−29	—	—

* Decline approximated 60 percent using weekly data. No significant upturn in inflation.

SOURCE: *Business Conditions Digest*, U.S. Department of Commerce.

EXHIBIT 4   Relative Behavior of Call Money and Long-Term Treasury
Yields at Troughs

(1) Reference Cycle	(2) Federal Funds	(3) Long Treasury Bonds	(4) (3) − (2)
April 1958	0.63% (May 1958)	3.12% (April 1958)	2.49%
February 1961	1.16 (July 1961)	3.73 (May 1961)	2.57
November 1970	3.71 (March 1971)	5.71 (March 1971)	2.00
March 1975	5.22 (May 1975)	6.66 (February 1975)	1.44
July 1980	9.03 (July 1980)	9.40 (June 1980)	0.37
November 1982	8.51 (February 1983)	10.19 (April 1983)	1.68

Note: Dates in parentheses are trough months on a month-average basis.
SOURCE: *Business Conditions Digest*, U.S. Department of Commerce.

Another of the rules-of-thumb of the postwar period is that the cyclical decline in corporate bonds will typically retrace over half the preceding trough-to-peak basis-point rise (see Exhibit 5).

5. Until recently, the Federal Reserve has tended to follow a policy of targeting interest rates. Use of an interest-rate target, however, demands an accurate projection of the economic climate that will be produced by that target in conjunction with other factors. Exhibit 6 (from Poole, [59]) illustrates how an interest-rate target produces excessive shifts in monetary policy (as described by the LM function) in response to real shocks in economic activity (a shift from IS_0 to IS_1 is produced by a cyclical upswing). The interest-rate target, however, cushions shocks produced by instability in money demand (shifts in LM). Since the Federal Reserve has no special claim to prescience, its interest-rate targets were frequently inappropriate for economic conditions. One test of the appropriateness of the Federal Reserve's various targets was the target's relationship to inflation expectations. (See Exhibit 7.) Recall the Fisher equation (above). An attempt to maintain an interest-rate target below inflation expectations (here proxied by the average survey response to the Michigan Survey Research Center) implies an opportunity to arbitrage goods against borrowing and pressures for accelerating monetary growth, *ultimately* forcing higher interest rates. The question of just when is "ultimately" is not an easy one for which to find empirical regularities. The Federal Reserve has chosen to alter its interest-rate targets more frequently in recent years, and target adjustments now tend to be tied to actual money supply growth relative to interim targets

EXHIBIT 5 High-Grade Corporate Bond Yields

	(1) Trough	(2) Succeeding Peak	(3) Basis Points Rise	(4) Basis Points Decline	(5) (4)/(3)
1953–54	2.74 (54:3)	4.81 (57:6)	207	120	58%
1957–58	3.61 (58:6)	5.37 (59:10)	176	100	57
1960–61	4.37 (61:3)	6.14 (66:9)	177	79	45
1966–67	5.35 (62:2)	9.70 (70:6)	435	216	50
1970–71	7.54* (71:2)	10.44 (74:9)	290	254	88
1974–75	7.90 (76:12)	14.08 (80:3)	618	296	48
1980–81	11.12 (80:6)	16.97 (81:9)	585	568	97
7 Cycle Average					63%

Note: Dates in parentheses are dates of cyclical peaks and troughs in monthly average interest rates.
  * Trough in 1972 was disregarded due to price controls.
  SOURCE: *Business Conditions Digest*, U.S. Department of Commerce.

EXHIBIT 6 Impact on Output of Real and Monetary Shocks under Alternative Monetary Policies

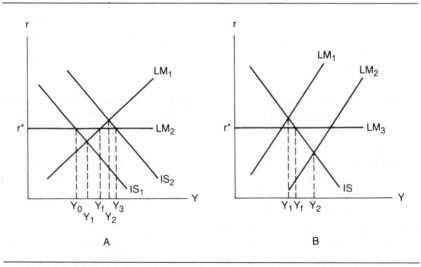

Notes: Definitions of variables are the same as for Exhibit 1. In Figure 7a, a real shock (IS_1 to IS_2) results in an income change of ($Y_3 - Y_0$ if monetary policy pegs interest rates (LM_2), but $Y_2 - Y_1$ if policy constrains reserves. However, (Figure 7b), a monetary shock will change income by $Y_2 - Y_1$. To justify a money stock (reserve) policy, one sufficient condition would be that real shocks are larger than monetary shocks (i.e., that money demand is more stable than net investment. See also [35]).
  SOURCE: Adapted from Poole [60].

EXHIBIT 7 Federal Funds Rate and Inflationary Expectations*
(quarterly averages)

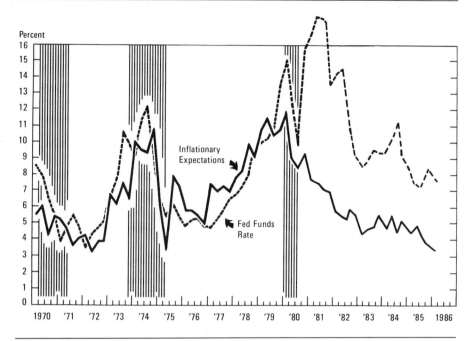

* University of Michigan Survey Research Center; mean expected price increase over next 12 months. Shaded areas indicate periods of contraction in business cycle activity.
SOURCE: Federal Reserve Board; Survey Research Center, the University of Michigan.

chosen by the Federal Reserve. Since these interim operating targets for money supply growth are not released until after the end of the interim period, however, they must be deduced by careful analysis of the operating factors within which monetary policy is conducted. These factors are particularly important for clues to the near-term (short-run) pressures on interest rates. They do not have good predictive power for longer-term trends in interest rates.

6. Cagan [35] found a "weak but significant association" between the lag in the upswing in interest rates and the duration of the following business expansion. A similar correlation was apparent for the depth of recession. The short recessions of 1960, 1970, and 1980 may reflect the nearly contemporaneous timing of reference-cycle and interest-rate peaks. For this to continue to be true, however, given the increased attention to anticipating business cycles by credit market participants, is to make an improbable statement about the future duration of business cycles.

Major interest-rate turning points have tended to complement business-cycle turning points and, increasingly, to anticipate these reference-cycle turning points. What analytical tools are available for this purpose?

The most visible and easily available is the composite index of leading economic indicators. The index is composed of indicators that tend to lead business activity and, moreover, were selected partly based on their ability to provide consistent leads with a minimum of false signals. Three consecutive one-month declines in the index do not necessarily signal impending recession; four are, however, rarely a false signal. The actual decline in the indicators prior to the peak in economic activity is not an indicator of the ultimate severity of the recession, but the author has found a good relationship between the peak-to-trough decline in the index and the depth of recession that has the intuitive appeal of rough correspondence to the cyclical component of overall economic activity.

Leading indicators have had a highly variable lead time (see Exhibit 8) and, during the ensuing period till recession, a substantial part of the cyclical upswing in interest rates is usually found, as credit demands become increasingly less easily postponed while credit supply is under pressure.

Interestingly, however, once the economy passes its peak, interest rates are generally already moving lower in an irregular fashion or have little upward momentum remaining. Exceptions to this statement in the 1970s tended to coincide with the clash of secularly rising inflation and still highly regulated credit markets; with deregulation, that phase may well have passed.

An important reason for this variation lies not in the variation in cyclical experience so much as in the discrepancy between cycle and chronological time. The stages identified by Arthur Burns and Wesley Mitchell [10] in pioneering work at the National Bureau are always found in each business cycle, but as circumstances vary, the *time* necessary to complete each stage can show wide variations. Consequently, the student of business cycles seeks evidence to support an argument that the economy has passed from one stage to the next, using these points as roadposts to the potential for major sustainable turning points in interest rates, including the flattening of the yield curve and sharp run-up in interest rates that typically accompanies the final stages of the economic expansion. That evidence has become easier to gather with the widening range of easily available information. However, inflation, by increasing the dispersion and volatility of relative prices, has offset this advantage by making it more difficult to measure reference-cycle phases.

As laid out by Burns and Mitchell, the analytical study of business cycles encompasses nine stages: trough, peak, and subsequent trough, three intermediate periods of expansion and three of contraction. For

EXHIBIT 8 Leading Indicators and Cyclical Increases in Interest Rates

(1) Cyclical Peak	(2) Lead in Months by Composite Index of Leading Economic Indicators	Proportion of Total Cyclical Upswing Following Peak in Composite Index of Leading Economic Indicators		Proportion of Total Cyclical Upswing Following Peak in Business Cycle	
		(3) Yield on New Issues on Long-Term High-Grade Corporate Bonds	(4) Three-Month Treasury Bills	(5) Yield on New Issues on Long-Term High-Grade Corporate Bonds	(6) Three-Month Treasury Bills
August, 1957	23	74	67	—	7
April, 1960	11	26	32	—	—
September, 1966*	6	42	25	—	1
December, 1969	8	50	24	11	5
November, 1973	8	87	47	81	11
January, 1980	10	72	56	39	33
July, 1981	3	34	24	11	11
Average, seven cycles	10	55	39	20	10

* Not an official business cycle peak.
SOURCE: U.S. Department of Commerce, *Handbook of Business Cycle Indicators*.

statistical purposes, their approach was to measure peaks and troughs on a centered three-month average, then divide expansions and contractions into three stages of (arbitrarily) equal length.

Much of these studies predated large-scale computers. Computers permit easy computation of inflection points, producing nine stages as before but with the initial, intermediate (inflexion), and terminal stages of unequal length. The final, more judgmental process is then to correlate various indicators as an aid to deciding the economy's current position in the cycle.

At times, cyclical indicators frequently used as indicators of interest-rate movements may have only a casual correlation to rates. Even business-cycle phases lack a perfect correlation: From 1910 to 1948 there were six cycle phases (expansions and contractions) in which there were no identifiable corresponding swings in interest rates.[14] An additional dramatic example has been provided by the behavior of spot commodity prices and long-term Treasury bond yields in 1979–81. (See Exhibit 9.) Casual empiricism would suggest that the weakening in commodity prices suggests an impending decline in interest rates, since either demand is weakening (lowering inflationary expectations) or supply is unexpectedly high (again with presumably beneficial effects on inflation). In 1979 and 1980 major shifts in commodity prices were nearly contemporaneous with interest-rate movements, but no such pattern was evident in 1981. The negative correlation observed in 1981 can be rationalized; high interest rates, by increasing the cost of carry, must either reduce cash prices, or be matched by a rise in prices for forward (future) delivery, or both.[15] The example illustrates the undesirability of using either forward or spot prices independently in analyzing interest rates. The relationship between spot and forward prices reflects the following:

- Carrying costs including storage.
- Normal backwardation (a risk premium offered cash holders).
- The risk premium for noncompliance with the forward contract specifications.
- The expected price change for the specific commodity.

Therefore the spot-futures arbitrage relationship will contain no new information about the *future* direction of interest rates. This also implies that analyses of the statistical relationships of spot and futures prices to forecast interest rates through inflation premia in commodity markets contain no new information. The residual information being offered by these markets as forecasts of interest rates is essentially "white noise"—

---

[14] Phillip Cagan, "The Influence of Interest Rates on the Duration of Business Cycles," Tables 1–2, p. 15 in [35].

[15] Foreign exchange interest parity relationships spring from the same root.

EXHIBIT 9 Long-Term Treasury Bonds and Spot Commodity Prices

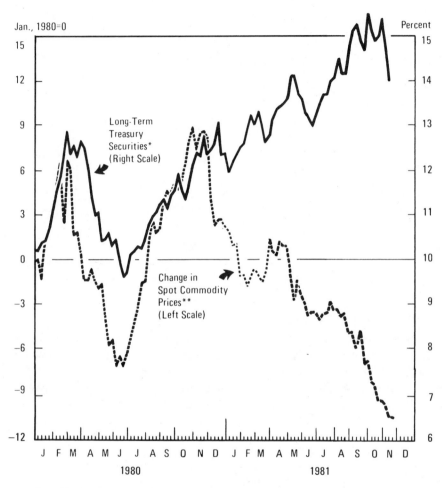

*   20 year constant maturity.
**   Journal of Commerce, 1947-49=100, change since 1/1/80. Index includes grains, food-
       stuffs, textiles and metals, but does not directly measure petroleum or precious metals.

a random walk that offers only the potential for arbitrage profits between markets.

Gauging a cyclical peak in economic activity has produced a relatively wide error bound on the basis of cyclical indices. Troughs can
usually be gauged much more closely—largely because postwar recessions have tended to be of relatively short duration. The following com-
pendium, by Roy Moor and Evelina Tainer of The First National Bank of

Chicago, notes 12 signals of economic recovery found in the six postwar recessions to 1979.

Signal of Recovery	Average Lead Time (months)
1. Upturn in composite index of leading indicators	3+ months
2. Downturn in composite index of lagging indicators	8 months
3. Slowdown in repayments of consumer installment credit	8+ months
4. Consumer savings rate reverses the initial recession decline	5 months
5. Employment declines	4 months
6. Treasury bill rates decline	8 months
7. Long-term corporate bond yields decline	7 months
8. Net borrowed (free) reserves rise	7+ months
9. Deceleration in production decline (three-month average)	3 months
10. Housing starts rise (year-to-year)	7+ months
11. Crude material prices ease (year-to-year)	11 months
12. Adjusted-for-inflation M2 declines	2 months

Spread Relationships

On the basis of published indices, business-cycle turning points are rarely identical for all types of fixed income instruments. Some frequently heard shibboleths:

Municipal markets lag taxable securities. This is a special case of the preferred habitat thesis. Banks, casualty companies, and individuals are the primary buyers of tax-exempt issues. For this statement to be correct, spreads between taxable and tax-exempt securities can tighten at and after interest rate peaks to the extent that buyers have a reduced need for tax-exempt income. Similarly, spreads could widen prior to the peak as demands for tax-exempt income mount, reflecting the heated pace of business activity and bracket creep. The key to arbitraging these relationships is estimating the extent to which bracket creep and tax losses will exist in upturns and downturns, respectively, and estimating the extent to which alternative vehicles, such as leasing credits, will be used to defer and manage taxes.

Current-coupon corporate bonds will lag Treasury securities with comparable maturities in declining interest-rate environments. Potential price appreciation in a declining rate environment will be smaller for current-coupon corporate issues than for Treasury issues because of differences in call features. Whenever interest rates are viewed to be high relative to their sustainable long-run level, the lesser call protection offered by corporate issues will cause spreads to current-coupon Treasuries to widen. To be true in a declining-rate environment for noncallable securities, however, credit quality concerns must force risk premiums to rise. This frequently happens in the initial stages of recession then reverses as rates drop, leverage ratios improve, and balance sheets are restructured. Call option values also play a role here. At lower rate (more normal) levels, projections of volatility decline, coupon call options have less value, and spreads can tighten, even though quality premiums remain high.

Seasonal factors tend to lead to interest-rate peaks near midyear and interest-rate troughs at the first of the new year. In relatively efficient markets, predictable seasonal fluctuations will be anticipated. What remains will be either so variable or so damped that there is little or no profitable information from estimating the seasonal. Diller's analysis of seasonals (in [34], Chapter 2) for the early postwar period (1948–1965) found repetitive seasonality in the 1955–60 period, but seasonal movements were either damped or irregular in earlier and later periods. In the 1955–60 period seasonals tended to peak near year-end, trough in June, and peak again in September. The evidence was consistent with seasonal characteristics in the money demand function. Lawler's [46] recent study found that the spread between negotiable certificate of deposit and bill yields displayed a seasonal peak in February, with a June trough. Though Lawler did not draw this conclusion, the seasonality again appears related as much to Federal Reserve activity as to private sector activity, reflected in management of commercial bank balance sheets.

Longer Run Influences: Kondratieff and Kuznets Waves

War, natural calamities, sweeping technological advances, and other shocks can result in cycles overlaid on the more seasonal and cyclical swings in interest rates. The theme of very long cycles in prices and economic activity is identified with Nicolai Kondratieff, who postulated that economies followed regular cycles of roughly 50 years' duration (Phelps Brown and Hopkins [9] presented evidence of 50-year cycles for prices in the United Kingdom over the past eight centuries). According to Kondratieff (see Exhibit 10) the first part of the 50-year cycle is typically composed of an upcycle lasting 20 years. In this up phase, inflation gradually accelerates as entrepreneurial confidence increases, economic policies are expansive, and capacity utilization—initially very low—increases, first to levels that encourage productivity improvements and new investment, but then to unsustainable levels. Economic volatility increases sharply, and the up phase usually terminates in heightened social tensions and even war. The termination of the up phase is gener-

EXHIBIT 10 U.S. Wholesale Prices and the Idealized Kondratieff Wave

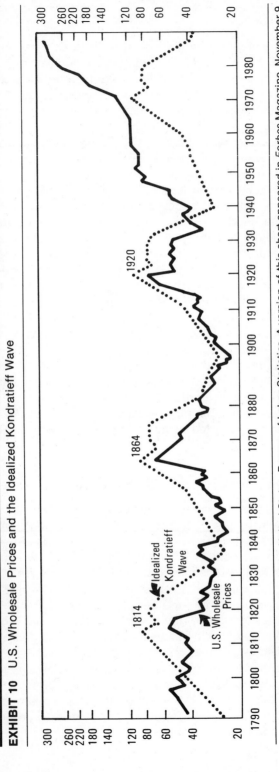

SOURCE: Historical Statistics of the United States, Bureau of Labor Statistics. A version of this chart appeared in *Forbes* Magazine, November 9, 1981.

ally followed by a 7- to 10-year interval of relative price stability, although bond prices remain close to their lows reached in the high inflation ending the up phase. The transition from recent excesses is typically accompanied by a swing to libertarian, laissez-faire, philosophies, and sustained attempts to cut government spending and deficits. The deflationary impact of these policies, on a financial system already strained by the prior inflation, sets off a self-feeding deflationary cycle that encompasses several business cycles with steep, lengthy counteractions, short recoveries, and sharply higher levels of bankruptcy.

To be sustainable, Kondratieff cycles must somehow involve systematic underprediction of inflation in the early up phase, and equally systematic errors in the deflation period. The improvement in the measurement and frequency of economic data and the safeguards built into the financial system in recent years have reduced the likelihood that we are entering the plateau phase of a Kondratieff-like cycle.

Kuznets' swings or "waves" occupy an intermediate position. In examining data over longer periods of time, Kuznets (for example [45]) found "long swings" in growth rates of real output and population spanning roughly 20 years. More recently, the same 20-year regularity has been observed in property casualty underwriter pricing. In the case of population, these swings have been linked to migration (which, given the selective character of international migration, has its own implications for growth rates) and technological change. Like Kondratieff cycles, moreover, Kuznets waves are associated with changes in capacity utilization. Immigration will lead to an accelerated demand for capital stock, rising real interest rates, and pressures for expansionary fiscal and monetary policies; outmigration can have the reverse effect. So long as international capital markets clear relatively efficiently, this need not have any long-term significance for interest rates, since international capital flows will shift capital from surplus to deficit countries (or asset prices will adjust). Neither labor nor capital market efficiency is perfect, however, and over/under building will produce cycles—long swings— that tend to produce unexpected pressures on credit markets over sustained periods of time.

Although an emphasis on long swing may seem at odds with the goal of predicting interest-rate movements over relatively short intervals, recall the discussion of market efficiency above. Success in forecasting the set of really *valuable* information (S) usually implies using information not generally variable or not generally used, or making use of new techniques to better understand existing information. To the extent that long waves have validity and are currently not being incorporated in existing models, they offer a relatively "cheap" source of new information, particularly since we might expect to find with efficient markets that *ex ante* changes in long-term rates increase with the forecast horizon.

FLOW–OF–FUNDS ANALYSIS

In contrast to those who forecast future interest rates on the basis of inflation and/or monetary policies, the flow-of-funds school projects supply and demand for credit by various participants.

Flow-of-funds methods do not forecast interest rates in a reduced-form relation. The goal instead is a more modest one, to anticipate directions in movements in interest rates as a result of an examination of the *sectoral* consistency of national income projections with the implication for financing. Underlying this approach is the implicit assumption that economic plans are being based on these national income projections and will be reflected in credit demands and supplies. Also implicit, however, is the assumption that sectoral financial flows change predictably and are only moderately sensitive to interest rates in other markets (preferred habitat). Otherwise, flow-of-funds models reverse the causality above, determining sector flows from wealth, NIA components, and interest rates, subject to aggregate constraints. Dependent and independent variables are reversed.

Emphasis on the various sources of and demands for loanable funds is in no way inconsistent with the emphasis on monetary variables by monetarists. Nobel laureate Sir John Hicks [40, p. 135], writing in 1938, made perhaps the most direct statement on this point:

> Is the rate of interest determined by the supply and demand for loanable funds (that is to say, by borrowing and lending); or is it determined by the supply and demand for money itself? This last view is put forward by Mr. Keynes in his *General Theory*. I shall hope to show that it makes no difference whether we follow his way of putting it, or whether we follow those writers who adopt what appears at present to be a rival view. Properly followed up, the two approaches lead to exactly the same results.

Hick's reconciliation noted that equilibrium was inconsistent with more than one set of spot rates.[16] Walras' Law could then be invoked to show that in an economy with n commodities (n − 1 relative prices), a loan or credit market, and money and, with equilibrium in the n − 1 relative prices, if the loan/credit market were in equilibrium, then the supply of money must equal the demand for money. Put another way, the n commodity markets and the supply and demand for money will determine the n − 1 relative prices and the price level that are consistent with only one interest rate; and that is the interest rate that clears the loan market, since only one spot rate can exist for a given maturity.

The differences between those who would forecast interest rates on

---

[16] If, in our n-commodity system, demands for n − 1 products equal the supplies of n − 1 products, then the nth demand must equal its supply. The proof uses the fact that only n − 1 relative prices need to be determined and that income to be spent on the products, at any point in time, is given.

the basis of the supply of and demand for money and those who would use the supply of and demand for credit are only superficial at this level of analysis. The *real* argument relates to how best to determine the interest rate that is also consistent with simultaneously clearing the n goods markets. Monetarists implicitly view expectations of inflation as the primary determinant of the level and direction of interest rates and focus on this component of the Fisher equation. This view carries over to policy recommendations, which emphasize that commodity (real or goods) markets will clear quickly and efficiently in the absence of government intervention. By implication, the real rate of interest, or marginal efficiency of capital, is relatively stable. Analysts preferring flow of funds do so because they view money demand as unstable (or money supply as undefineable, or both) and see the real rate of interest as both unstable and capable of being heavily influenced by activities in certain key markets.

Viewed objectively, these differences are often a matter of the time frame of analysis. Short term, there is a limited correlation of interest rates with inflation, and at least the appearance of instability in money demand relationships. Flow of funds, as a forecasting tool, has the apparent advantage of focusing on markets closely connected with credit demands and supply, and on particular regulatory barriers. Longer run, money demand appears stable, and inflation expectations become the proximate determinant of interest rates. One is tempted to say that which forecasting procedure to use depends primarily on the time reference.

However, it is important not to overemphasize this distinction. Monetarists refer to the impact of money on interest rates as having three stages: liquidity, income, and price expectations effects that partition the time path into short-term and long-run influences.[17]

---

[17] Studies of money demand generally support the contention that the demand for money is a stable function of a small number of variables—specifically, wealth or permanent income and an opportunity cost given by the real rate of return on alternative assets. A shift to a more expansionary monetary policy generates an initial drop in interest rates as economic actors attempt to shed excess balances through purchase of other assets. These purchases bid up the price of other assets (bid down the opportunity cost of money) to enable the initial increase to be held. However, it also encourages increased production of these assets (the income effect), which bids up the demand for money and lowers prices of the competing assets whose production has been increased (raising the real interest rate). Finally, by increasing capacity utilization and raising asset prices, this process produces an upward adjustment in price expectations and money interest rates. Empirical studies find the liquidity effect of an unanticipated monetary expansion to be at most six months and the income effect to be somewhat longer and more variable. For an anticipated expansion, however, liquidity and income effects have already been largely if not totally discounted. For an elaboration, see, for example, Friedman [27], Gibson and Kaufman [30], Barro [2], and Miskin [52]. However, the variability of liquidity and income effects (depending on the validity of expectations, initial economic conditions, etc.) and the evidence of market efficiency referred to earlier in this chapter are used to justify the monetarist focus on price expectations for interest-rate forecasts and a longer run perspective.

Beyond the forecasting horizon, it is often difficult to categorize flow-of-funds approaches to interest rates because different forecasters identify different pressure points at different points in the business cycle as the predominant determinant of the direction and level of interest rates.

Comments, below, are generally offered as a guide:

1. Flow-of-funds data are prepared by staff of the Board of Governors of the Federal Reserve from data produced by a large number of different sources. Data frequently must be massaged in one way or another to produce comparability.[18] The Board's personnel do an excellent job with this difficult task. Nevertheless, estimates are subject to wider error bounds than many financial data. For this reason, flow-of-funds forecasts tends to focus on Treasury financing, bank, bond, and mortgage borrowing, and consumer credit. One way to assess the potential for error is to study the statistical discrepancy between asset and liability statistics in the various sectors (see Exhibit 11). Even after sev-

---

EXHIBIT 11 Statistical Discrepancy for Selected Sectors
(three year averages)

| | Average Discrepancy | | | |
| | $ Billions | | As a Percent of Sector Net Increase in Liabilities | |
Sector	1979–81	1982–84	1979–81	1982–84
Households, personal trusts, and nonprofit organizations	−59	−31	39%	19%
Nonfinancial corporate business (excluding farms)	35	14	23	10
United States government	4	2	6	5
Commercial banking	−10	−9	8	7

SOURCE: Board of Governors of the Federal Reserve System, Flow of Funds Accounts, 1981 and 1985.

---

eral revisions, unresolved statistical discrepancies remain a large part of the estimated net increase in liabilities.

2. The concept of "crowding out" plays an important role in many flow-of-funds analyses. In Exhibit 12 higher Treasury borrowing raises interest rates from i_0 to i_1, reducing business external borrowing for

---

[18] For example, bond issuance volume in the public and private new-issue markets must be gathered; retired and maturing issues must then be netted from this gross total.

EXHIBIT 12 Crowding Out

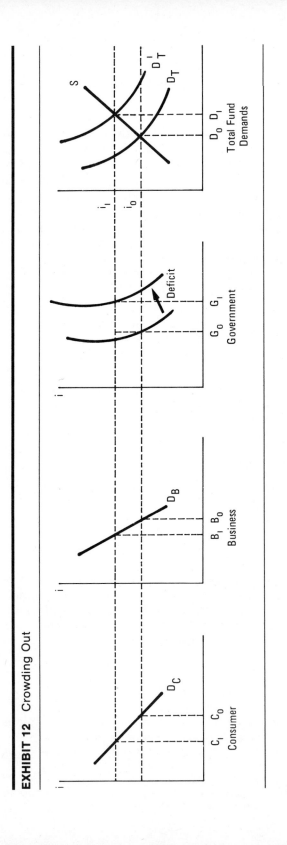

(e.g.) fixed investment by $B_0 - B_1$ and lowering consumer borrowing by $C_0 - C_1$. This neglects the cause of the initial deficit, which might have been lower tax receipts because reduced activity cut underlying consumer and business activity to levels consistent with C_1 and B_1, respectively. Furthermore, the analysis neglects the impact of a deficit created by expansionary fiscal policy on private output through operating on perceived wealth and asset values for underlying (more utilized) capital stock. The impact, for example, *might* be to produce additional internal funds, short term to fund the deficit. Longer run, of course, expansionary policies will increase external cash needs to increment capacity. It also helps to assume only a limited elasticity of supply of savings—an assumption that has considerable support empirically. Otherwise, "crowding out" must be relatively minor, and interest-rate forecasts based on flow of funds would show little variation.[19] On balance, Exhibit 12 contains a dangerous simplicity; the actual support for crowding out, short term, must be empirical.

3. Structural or regulatory constraints that prevent markets from arbitraging play a key role in many flow-of-funds forecasts. Regulation Q, which limited the monetary interest rates that banks and savings associations could pay on certain types of deposits, has been an effective throttle on home mortgage lending whenever market interest rates rose above these ceilings. This effectively increased credit supplies to other participants and subsidized their cost of credit in high interest-rate environments. In recent years several deposit forms not subject to Regulation Q have developed, and the regulation itself is scheduled to be totally phased out in stages to 1986. Another less documented "structural" constraint sometimes seen in flow-of-funds analyses conforms with preferred habitat by arguing that significant new Treasury debt can only be sold at a sharp concession to current debt holdings—in other words, a very inelastic demand function exists for additions to current holdings.

4. Within the flow-of-funds school are at least two disparate groups. One group emphasizes aggregate financial ratios. Current or prospective financial conditions, in this view, will result in financial ratios that are so extreme as to lead to extremely inelastic credit supplies thereby widening quality differentials and increasing the probability of a credit crunch as these stretched ratios strain the normal intermediary function. We might call this the intermediary school. The second group also uses ratios but emphasizes ratios dealing with wealth, maturity mismatch, and debt service capacity—the "real balance" school. This second group emphasizes (explicitly or implicitly) that interest rates are the "terms of trade" between consuming in the present and postponing current consumption. The major difference between the groups, then, is

---

[19] As a general rule, this is the typical result for model-based forecasts because of the need to damp the large statistical noise in the data.

that the intermediary school focuses on the potential for a given supply of savings to be channeled to various borrowers and the potential for key borrowers or intermediaries to be shut out of the credit market as a result of an actual or perceived deterioration in their risk-bearing ability. By contrast, the "real balance" group's focus is on how elastic this initial supply of savings will be to changes in economic conditions (both income and price effects), implicitly assuming the efficiency of the intermediation process.

5. In some ways the term *flow of funds* is a misnomer that tends to concentrate attention on sources of new funds and incremental demands at the expense of changes in asset allocation among existing assets. Such shifts have the potential to dwarf incremental flows. For example, money market funds total more than $200 billion; there are $450 billion in money market deposit accounts (MMDA's) and over $500 billion in six-month to 2½-year bank and thrift certificates. A 10 percent shift out of these funds is on the scale of 75 percent of personal savings flows. Furthermore, recent work on asset models has stressed that markets often clear by changes in price with modest flows. Arbitrage of international and domestic short-term money markets is a frequent example; so are the equity markets, in which net flows of funds are a miniscule part of outstanding market values.

PRODUCING A FORECAST

What might seem like the most difficult is actually the easiest part of this exercise, which is why it has been delayed until the end. Following are five ways of producing a forecast.

1. Forecasts can be read directly from the forward rate structure. In the absence of additional information or confidence in one's expertise, this is the rational choice. Exhibit 13 is an example of forward rates calculated by one analytical service near mid year, 1985. To these forward rates must be added any liquidity or term premiums. Furthermore, the geometric mean of a series of forward rates is the spot rate, and coupon premium, default, and call options must be added to produce a forecast of a particular interest rate. The latter are generally estimated from historical data of actual rates regressed on spot rates and proxy variables—sector and rating dummies for default risk and coupon scales, the theoretical value of the call option, and so on. (One approach to measuring the call option is found in Yawitz and Marshall [79].) For short-term rates, however, evidence to date supports using one or more of the techniques below or a survey of forecasters.

2. Use a large-scale econometric model. The evidence to date is ambiguous on this point. If experts have provided their judgemental review, there may be some gain in using this as a tool for forecasting short-term rates (e.g., Throop, [70] and Pesando [58]).

EXHIBIT 13 Estimated U.S. Treasury Term Structure, June 6, 1985

Maturity	Spot Rates	Current Yield on Par Bond	Discount Function	Forward Rates
1 mo.	7.27%	7.43%	.994%	7.27%
2 mo.	7.24	7.41	.988	7.21
3 mo.	7.23	7.39	.982	7.21
6 mo.	7.27	7.43	.965	7.31
12 mo.	7.58	7.74	.928	7.89
2 yr.	8.37	8.51	.849	9.16
3 yr.	8.74	8.87	.774	9.48
5 yr.	9.50	9.56	.629	10.65
7 yr.	9.72	9.76	.515	10.27
10 yr.	9.89	9.86	.381	10.28
15 yr.	10.41	10.24	.218	10.45
20 yr.	10.66	10.37	.125	11.41
30 yr.	10.59	10.40	.045	11.45

SOURCE: Gifford Fong & Associates.

---

3. Produce a "monetarist" forecast. These come in several variants. Perhaps the simplest solves for the interest-rate path consistent with a projected growth of the money stock, given the assumption of a stable money demand function. This involves projection of the price and income components for the money demand function and finding interest rates consistent with these projections. A variant on this method would assume some portion of the differential between money supply and money demand is made up each period that money supply growth is different than "expectations" (based either on publicly announced targets or distributed lags, for example, Barro [2]). Naturally, the success of this procedure is dependent on the ability to correctly predict income, price, and adjustment components—a further reason monetarists tend to focus their horizon for interest-rate forecasts on the two- to five-year period where price expectations become the most important determinant. For these longer-run forecasts, longer-run growth of the money stock, and its first and second derivatives, become the prime components of a forecast.[20]

A simple example of a short-term, monetarist forecast is given below. There is general agreement that a good specification of the demand for money in terms of a small number of variables, is:

$$\frac{M}{NP} = a + b\left(\frac{Y}{PN}\right) + c(R_0) + d(R_B) + e\left(\frac{M_{-1}}{P_{-1}N_{-1}}\right) \qquad (4)$$

---

[20] The fact that the second derivative of monetary growth is damped about zero has not, apparently, prevented its being an important part of the judgment on the direction of interest rates two to three years out!

where all variables are expressed in logarithmic form, and are defined as follows:

M = any variant of M_1 or M_2, depending on one's preference

Y = real (preferably permanent) income (often proxied by real GNP)

N = population

P = a broad-based price index, usually proxied by the GNP deflator because of the absence of a broad-based price index for assets.

R_0 = an interest-rate proxying for the opportunity cost of money. Both short-term and long-term rates have been used without real discrimination, though a "transactions" view of money demand would favor the short-term rate.

R_B = the "own" rate—passbook savings or (more recently), NOW accounts, preferably adjusted upward for nonpecuniary returns.

The subscript "-1" indicates a one period lag, to allow for partial adjustment in observed data.

Assuming one determined a desired specification (4), could be estimated over some prior period using R_0 as an independent variable, and incorporating any desired shift variables (for price controls, changing commitment pricing terms on bank lines, etc.) The use of a lagged term to capture serial correlation is a serious statistical weakness from a forecasting standpoint. Forecasts would use these estimated coefficients to solve for R_0:

$$R_0 = \frac{1}{c}\frac{M}{NP} - \frac{b}{c}\left(\frac{Y}{PN}\right) - \frac{d}{c}(R_B) + \frac{e}{c}\left(\frac{M_{-1}}{P_{-1}N_{-1}}\right) - \frac{a}{c} \qquad (5)$$

using forecasts of M/NP and Y/PN; R_B is (generally) slowly changing or predictable on the basis of legislation, and $M_{-1}/(P_{-1}N_{-1})$ is known. M can be forecast using Federal Reserve targets, if desired. N is predictable; forecasts of Y and P can be naive (last period's growth rate), sourced from consensus forecasts, or even based on recent and projected money stock growth. (A close correlation exists between nominal income growth over six-month spans and money supply growth over prior six-month spans.)

There is less agreement on stability of this relationship.[21] More important, unless consistent forecasts of M, Y, and P have been created, the solution for R_0 lacks validity, since the coefficients were calculated based on a certain consistency. (This is a variant of the previous descriptions of rational expectations.)

---

[21] Two solutions for the above equation are given in Hafer and Hein [35, pp. 13–14] and [25].

4. Forecasts using business cycle turning points, of course, rely on an ability to outperform the composite index of leading economic indicators or one of its variants (such as the ratio of composite coincident to composite lagging indicators). There have been a number of books on business cycles, but the Mitchell/Burns anthology and its offspring remains required reading for serious students. Also recommended is the critique of recent research by Lucas [47].

5. Different emphases, as noted, make it more difficult to precisely describe the creation of a forecast using flow of funds. Instead, major areas are detailed below.[22]

    a. The basic flow-of-funds forecast typically contains key trigger points:

        (1) The differential, *ex ante,* between investment demand and the flow of savings. To close this differential, prices and quantities must adjust (markets clear) and ensure *ex post* equality.

        (2) The size and timing of the federal government's financing needs, as a key component of *ex ante* savings flows.

        (3) The outlook for inventories and corporate cash flows as a guide to external cash needs.

        (4) In recent years, sources of funds from abroad.

        (5) Asset allocation by banks and insurance companies ("preferred habitat").

    b. Start with national income (NIA) projections as a guide to flow of funds and as a check on the internal consistency of the national income projections. (Refer to Exhibit 14 for NIA components to gross savings and investment.)

    Sources of savings include:

        (1) Household and personal savings. To personal savings from income from current production (NIA), add:

          • The surplus of railroad retirement and state and local retirement funds because these funds are also available for investment.

          • Capital gains distributions of investment companies.

          • Consumer durables (NIA, and thus gross of depreciation).

          • Depreciation on other household assets.

        (2) Nonfinancial business savings. To undistributed corporate profits, add capital consumption allowances, but subtract a minor item, capital gains dividends of investment companies, and the undistributed profits of the financial sector (including retained earnings of government entities).

---

[22] This discussion relies heavily on von Furstenberg [29].

EXHIBIT 14

	1980 ($billions)
Gross Savings:	
Personal savings	$101.3
Undistributed corporate profits	107.2
Corporate inventory valuation adjustment	−45.7
Capital consumption adjustment	−17.2
Corporate capital consumption allowance	175.4
Noncorporate corporate capital consumption allowance	111.9
Total gross private savings NIA	432.9
Plus	
Federal government surplus	−61.2
State and local surplus	29.1
Consumer durables	211.9
Equals: gross savings, flow of funds	612.7
Gross Investment:	
Consumer durables	211.9
Residential	105.3
Plant and equipment	296.0
Inventory change	−5.9
Oil leases/mineral rights (U.S. government sales)	6.5
Total gross investment	613.8
Statistical Discrepancy	1.1

SOURCE: Federal Reserve, November 1981, Flow of Funds Accounts.

(3) Foreign sector saving. This is the negative of net foreign investment.

(1), (2), and (3) constitute private sources; to this, to determine gross savings, (4) must be added.

(4) Government savings—both the federal government's overall cash surplus or deficit and the surplus or deficit of state and local governments.

Since gross savings must equal gross investment, the forecast of the sum of (1)–(4) is compared with uses for these funds:

- Residential construction.
- Nonresidential outlays for structures and equipment.
- Inventories.
- Consumer durables.

To this point, the forecast is basically equivalent to describing the IS relationship. This means that it is consistent with *any* level of interest rates, although a particular interest rate would be specified were a level of economic activity known. In fact, the IS relationship specifies jointly attainable combinations of output, y and interest

EXHIBIT 15 Derivation of Net Financial Investment, 1980 ($billions)

Line Number	Transactions Category	Households u	Households s	Business u	Business s	Net Foreign Sector u	Net Foreign Sector s	State and Local Governments u	State and Local Governments s	U.S. Government u	U.S. Government s	Federally Sponsored Credit Agencies u	Federally Sponsored Credit Agencies s	Monetary Authority u	Monetary Authority s	Commercial Banking u	Commercial Banking s	Private Nonbank Finance u	Private Nonbank Finance s	Total, All Sectors u	Total, All Sectors s
1	Gross saving	402.9		257.6			0.0		2.7		−70.0		0.9		0.4	8.2				612.7	
2	Capital consumption	302.8		225.0					—		—					5.0				465.4	
3	Net savings (1 − 2)	172.0		32.6					2.7		−70.0		0.9		0.4	3.2				147.3	
4	Gross investment (5 + 10)	402.9		257.7		0.0		2.7		−70.0		0.9		0.4		8.2				612.7	
5	Private capital expenditures (6 to 9)	313.1		285.4				0.0		—		0.0		0.0		11.3				612.7	
6	Consumer durables	211.9		—																211.9	
7	Residential construction	93.8		11.4																105.3	
8	Plant and Equipment	7.4		273.6												11.3		2.9		295.0	
9	Inventory change/ mineral rights	—		0.6																0.6	
10	Net financial investment (1 − 5) = (18 − 19)	89.8		−27.8		0.0		2.7		−70.0		0.9		0.4		−3.2		7.1		—	

11	Demand deposits and currency	10.9	2.4	0.7	-1.1	-3.6	0.1	2.3	9.0	0.7	4.9	3.7	2.1	16.0	16.0
12	Time/savings deposits	131.2	1.7	1.2	-1.7	-0.2					91.7	128	53.4	145.1	145.1
13	Money funds	29.2	—									29.2	29.2	29.2	29.2
14	Gold/foreign exchange/SDRs	—	—	5.5				3.9	2.6					8.1	8.1
15	Life insurance reserves	11.5				4.3							11.5	11.5	11.5
16	Pension fund reserves	77.5										42.3		77.5	77.5
17	Interbank items	—	—	-24.5	*	26.5	*	8.8	-1.9	-1.0	-4.5	-29.8	—	-30.8	-30.8
18	Net investment in liquidor insurance claims (11 to 17)	260.3	4.1	-28.1	-29.3	-8.3	0.1	-6.3	-70.6	-122.0				0	
19	Net investment in credit markets and related investments (10 – 18)	-170.5	-31.9	28.1	32.1	-61.7	0.8	+6.3	67.4	129.1				0	
20	Statistical discrepancy Incl. in (10)	-79.6	44.5	28.5	9.8	-0.8	0.6	—	-10.6	-0.9				-8.6	
21	= 19 – 20	90.0	-76.4	-0.4	22.3	-60.5	-1.5	-6.3	56.8	128.2				8.6	

Note: u = use; s = source. Details may not add to totals due to rounding.
* Included in household sector.

SOURCE: November, 1981 Flow of Funds Accounts, Board of Governors of the Federal Reserve System.

rates, r. Since y and r are jointly determined, however, it is not sufficient to form an interest-rate forecast. Even at this level of generality, however, two features might be noted:

- Personal savings are only a part of the economy's gross savings pool. International comparisons of savings that focus only on this subcomponent may seriously distort the overall relationship. Japan's substantially higher personal savings rate, for example, is partly offset by a much higher government deficit and more leveraged business sector.

- At this level of aggregation, savings and investment "appear" to be independent of financial markets. The role of financial markets is to channel or gather an excess of deficiency of funds from various sectors to ration across various sectors requiring net financial investment. Their success determines the ultimate combination of output and interest rates (y_0, r_0).

Exhibit 15 shows the derivation for 1980 of net financial investment. (Statistical discrepancies have been subsumed in net financial investment for each sector.)

c. From this point, the flow-of-funds forecast, whether econometric or intuitive, is successively disaggregative. That is partly because there is only a *weak* relationship between actual credit/GNP in aggregate and the trend in interest rates. (See Exhibit 16.)

Forecasts for NIA components, by sector, determine net financial investment for each sector (Exhibit 17).

Net financial investment, in turn, equals net acquisition of financial assets less debt issuance for each sector. In terms of Exhibit 17, this obviously places the onus on the household and financial sectors to finance business and government activities under most economic environments.

Also shown in Exhibit 15 are gross flows underlying net activity. These should also be carefully examined. Too small a proportion of gross to net flows *suggests* an unexpectedly greater degree of monetary stringency with consequent upward pressure on interest rates.

Once a sector-by-sector description of net financial investment has been created using NIA data, it is necessary to determine what funds will be available to or demanded from the credit markets. This involves projecting reasonable values for items in lines 11 through 17 of Exhibit 15, and comparing these items with net financial investment to arrive at net investment in credit markets and related instruments (line 19). Several of the line items in line 11 to 17 are linked to other forecasts. De-

EXHIBIT 16   Credit Demand and Long-Term Interest Rates

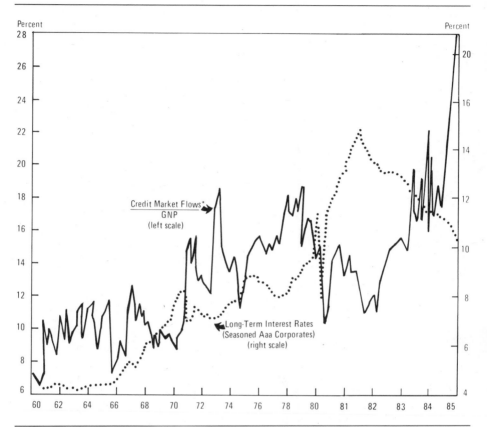

* Includes all debt obligations of business, household, and government sectors.
SOURCE: Federal Reserve Flow of Funds. Nonseasonally adjusted and nonannualized data.

mand deposit and currency growth, for example, must be consistent with one's view of the policy measures followed by the Federal Reserve. Insurance and pension reserves tend to follow a relatively predictable trend. The relatively unpredictable items are the distribution of household assets between money market funds and time deposits, and business demands for time deposits, particularly since distinguishing these demands from security R/P and other liquid assets is a very artificial one.

Line 19 of Exhibit 15 is the penultimate goal in creating a forecast. This is the forecast, by sector, of funds that will be provided to the credit markets and related instruments. Note the implication, for example, of

EXHIBIT 17 Net Financial Sector Investments, 1980 ($ billions)

Line Number	Transactions Category	Households u	Households s	Business u	Business s	Net Foreign Sector u	Net Foreign Sector s	State and Local Government u	State and Local Government s	U.S. Government u	U.S. Government s	Federally Sponsored Credit Agencies u	Federally Sponsored Credit Agencies s	Monetary Authority u	Monetary Authority s	Commercial Banking u	Commercial Banking s	Private Nonbank Finance u	Private Nonbank Finance s	Total, All Sectors u	Total, All Sectors s
17	Net investment in credit market and related investments (from table 8)	-17.5			-31.9		28.1		32.1		-61.7		0.8	6.3			67.4		129.1		0.0
22	Credit market investments (lines 22 to 31)	27.6	101.7	3.7	123.7	15.6	27.1	44.5	25.3	23.7	79.2	42.1	43.0	4.5	0.0	99.7	7.1	155.6	10.4	412.4	412.4
23	U.S. government securities	20.5		-2.1		10.5		23.6			79.3		43.0^{c,d}		4.5	25.6		39.7		122.3	122.3
24	State and local obligation	3.0		-0.2	25			0.3	24.4							13.6		10.1		26.9	26.9
25	Corporate/foreign bonds	3.6			30.4	5.1	0.8		9.7							0.6	1.5	20.1	5.6	38.4	38.4
26	Home mortgages	6.3	83.4		-1.6				8.0	2.7			25.6^c			11.3		27.1	-0.8	81.0	81.0
27	Other mortgages	1.8	1.5		38.9				2.8	4.8	-0.1		7.1^d			8.1		15.5	-0.1	40.1	40.1
28	Consumer credit	—	2.3	2.3	2.1											-9.7		9.9		2.3	2.3

29	Bank loans, not else-where classified	5.6	31.7	11.5		0.9							48.4	10.0	-0.5		48.4	48.4
30	Other loans[b]	8.9	15.2	4.7		16.2	10.4								7.1		36.6	36.6
31	Commercial paper/banker's acceptances	—	3.9	6.6	10.1			0.1		1.8	5.6	23.2	-0.9		21.4	21.4		
32	Related instruments (lines 33 to 37)	-89.2	7.1	98.9	10.4	42.6	3.0	2.8	-2.5	3.7	0.8	0.0	0.5	-1.3	-4.3	20.8	7.6	23.7	67.0	67.0
33	Corporate equity issuance (net)	-1.9		12.9	5.4	2.1	5.3				0.4	12.3	5.7	21.1	21.1
34	Security credit	4.1	5.0							0.8	5.1	4.9	10.0	10.0
35	Taxes payable	—	-6.7	-1.1		-2.8			0.5	3.1	-3.9	-3.9
36	Trade credit (net)	2.2	2.1	32.8	1.8	1.0	1.8	1.4	3.7	40.0	40.0
37	Equity in clinicorp enterprises	-18.3	-18.3			-18.3	-18.3
38	Other	-75.3	66.1	-10.3	35.4	6.8	-1.1	0.8	0.5	-1.3	-5.2	20.0	-9.9	10.0	-18.3	18.1
20	Statistical discrepancy incl. in lines 22, 32	-79.6	44.5	28.5	9.8	-0.8	0.6	-10.6	-0.9	-8.6

[a] Line 19 also equals the negative of net sources in Lines 21 and 32.
[b] Includes: Finance company loans to business, U.S. government loans, sponsored credit agency loans, and policy loans.
[c] Includes: $18.0 billion of mortgage pools.
[d] Includes: $16.0 billion of mortgage pools.
[e] Includes: 7.1 billion of advances from FHLB.

SOURCE: November, 1981 Flow of Funds Accounts, Board of Governors of the Federal Reserve System.

relatively large figure for the household sector in line 10 coupled with a decline in line 18. The implication is that much more of the household's credit acquisition will be direct or through nontraditional intermediaries.

Data in Exhibit 17 show that in 1980, household borrowing for consumer credit and home mortgage debt accounted for 46 percent of household net investment in credit markets and related instruments, a comparatively small proportion because of the negligible rise in consumer credit. Similarly, a growing projection of funds by commercial banks relative to nonbank finance (comparing 1980 to prior years, not shown here) would tend to suggest business would be "forced" to use more bank financing, or go directly to investors, bypassing intermediaries. To go from this statement to the implication that long-term interest rates would be under upward pressure, however, requires an additional assumption. This is that businesses will pay a premium to have the somewhat longer maturity offered by public debt markets, or that banks will refuse to offer longer term fixed-rate claims, or some combination of these factors. (One reason often given in recent years to expect such a premium has been the deterioration in business balance sheet flexibility.)

Comparing entries in Exhibit 17 over time also helps to pinpoint how Treasury and off-budget financing might be met. Again, some forecasters choose to draw implications, based strongly or weakly on preferred habitat, of the pressure on interest rates necessary to permit the Treasury to fund a greater-than-normal (let alone greater-than-expected) deficit, particularly if the distribution of funds for the credit markets deviates from normal and/or large inelastic entries can already be identified. (An example of the latter would be heavy business trade credit needs.)

Typical practice is to complete as many items of the array in Exhibit 17 from trend extrapolation or compatible figures to NIA extrapolations. Upward pressures on interest rates—and revisions to NIA estimates—are indicated by a failure of expected financial demands, whether from Treasury or private users, to meet sources. Usually, a first pass is made using only private sector uses cued to NIA projections. (For example, projections for housing sales and starts cue mortgage activity, consumer durables and employment gains can be related to consumer credit, and inventory activity will be reflected in business short-term credit needs.) These demands then leave remaining sources to meet the Treasury's deficit (or can be incremented by a surplus). This gap indicates whether pressures on interest rates, given the NIA projections, would be significant (and in some circumstances, the potential for declines in rates). A judgment on what sectors will prove most interest-elastic to meet Treasury funding requirements is then made, and NIA activity recalculated to arrive at new sources and uses. Computer simulation permits a simultaneous solution.

The problems that face all large models, described earlier, face modeling flow of funds. As noted previously, too, the size of the statistical discrepancy means that the standard errors attaching to projections of microelements of individual accounts must be considered to be very large. Successful flow-of-funds forecasters generally weld experience, subjective beliefs, and a substantial element of luck to detailed economic analysis.

Although this may appear to be more art than science and, as described, is a process of successive iteration, with each new entry requiring a cross-check of other projections, it must be emphasized again that flow-of-funds methods do not forecast interest rates in a reduced-form-equation fashion. The goal is a more modest one—to anticipate directions in the movement of interest rates as a result of the examination of the *sectoral* consistency of NIA projections with the implications, given institutional limitations, for financing sectoral demands. Underlying this approach is the implicit assumption that economic plans are being based on these NIA projections and will be reflected in credit demands and supplies. This need not be true. For example. Wojnilower's summation of his techniques (in [78, p. 232]) explicitly recognized that professional projections may dovetail poorly with results:

> The most interesting case of schizoid expectations comes from the financial community, although here my evidence is unfortunately entirely anecdotal. That financial managers in their professional capacities have had a more optimistic outlook than the public on security prices is surely attested by the fact that institutions have continued to acquire massive amounts of bonds in the face of virtually continual declines in real and all too often also nominal values. Meanwhile the public has clearly shifted its investment mix toward increasing its borrowings and its real estate assets, producing palpably superior investment performance.

Flow-of-funds models have a further advantage that also helps to account for their popularity. Like the "stories" that color perceptions of individual equity issues (despite the weight of evidence that on average these stories are fully discounted by current stock prices), flow of funds can be used to emphasize a particular component that the analyst views as the *current* crucial factor in interest-rate movements. The fallacy of composition, that what is true of the individual need not be true of the whole, is equally applicable for flow-of-funds analysis (personal versus gross savings for example), but flow of funds can add the emperor's new clothes to what is otherwise the naked and relatively efficient operation of Adam Smith's "invisible hand." By giving color to a view of the operation of the economy, flow-of-funds analysis can provide a service that is as much a marketing technique as an analytical underpinning. It is a technique that many special-interest groups have honed to near perfection in interaction with government to justify federal guarantees or other subsidies that ballooned total funding in recent years.

CONCLUSIONS

Serious studies generally indicate that short-term forecasts of long-term interest rates contain little or no value added. Forecasts of short-term interest rates, however, have been made successfully, by comparison with naive extrapolations, both because there is no theoretical necessity for short-term rates, short term, to follow a random walk and because the Federal Reserve has frequently chosen to act in a predictable fashion.

The evidence that short-term, long-term interest rates follow a random walk has been used to:

1. Support option strategies directed toward fixed income investments, such as immunization, that shift the forecast horizon to a longer term perspective (but may offset this advantage by concentrating reinvestment risk).
2. Relate interest rates and inflation over longer periods of time. Deregulation, in this writer's opinion, has only temporarily disturbed this relationship, and presumably shifted it to a different plateau.
3. Justify an approach that views flow of funds as primarily a consistency check and marketing guide, rather than an efficient tool for forecasting rates.

As in all other markets, however, the maxim in forecasts is *caveat emptor*.

REFERENCES

1. Barro, Robert J. "Rational Expectations and the Role of Monetary Policy." *The Journal of Monetary Economics*, January, 1976, pp. 1–32.
2. _____. "Unanticipated Money, Output, and the Price Level in the United States." *The Journal of Political Economy*, August 1978, pp. 549–80.
3. Black, Fischer. "The ABC's of Business Cycles." *Financial Analysts Journal*, November/December 1981, pp. 75–80.
4. Blanchard, Oliver J. and Lawrence H. Sumers. "Perspectives on High World Real Interest Rates." *Brookings Papers on Economic Activity*, No. 2, 1984, pp. 273–334.
5. Bodie, Zvi, Alex Kane, and Robert L. MacDonald. "Why Haven't Nominal Rates Declined?" NBER Reprint Series, #498, 1984.
6. Bodie, Zvi and John B. Shoven. *Financial Aspects of the U.S. Pension System.* Chicago: National Bureau of Economic Research, University of Chicago Press, 1982.
7. Blinder, Alan, and Stanley Fischer. "Inventories, Rational Expectations and the Business Cycle." National Bureau of Economic Research Working Paper, No. 381, August 1979.
8. Bomberger, William A., and W. J. Frazer. "Interest Rates, Uncertainty, and the Livingston Data." *The Journal of Finance*, June 1981, pp. 661–75.
9. Brown, Earnest Phelps, and Shiela Hopkins. "Seven Centuries of the Price of Consumables, Compared with Builders' Wage Rates." *Economica*, November 1956, pp. 296–314.
10. Burns, Arthur C., and Wesley C. Mitchell. *Measuring Business Cycles.* New York: National Bureau of Economic Research, 1947.

11. Cagan, Phillip. *Determinants and Effects of Changes in the Stock of Money 1875–1960*. New York: National Bureau of Economic Research, Columbia University Press, 1965.

12. Chow, G. C. "Multiplier, Accelerator, and Liquidity Preference." *Review of Economics and Statistics*, January 1967, pp. 1–15.

13. Cox, John C.; Jonathan E. Ingersoll, Jr.; and Steven A. Ross. "Duration and the Measurement of Basis Risk." *The Journal of Business*, January 1979, pp. 51–61.

14. _____. "A Reexamination of Traditional Hypotheses about the Term Structure of Interest Rates." *Journal of Finance*, September 1981, pp. 769–93.

15. Culbertson, John M. *Macroeconomic Theory and Stabilization Policy*. New York: McGraw-Hill, 1968.

16. Dobson, Steven W.; Robert C. Sutch; and David E. Vanderford. "An Evaluation of Altenative Empirical Models of the Term Structure of Interest Rates." *Journal of Finance*, September 1976, pp. 1035–65.

17. Dwyer, Gerald P. "Are Expectations of Inflation Rational?" *Journal of Monetary Economics*, February 1981, pp. 59–84.

18. Echols, Michael E., and Jan W. Elliot. "Rational Expectations in a Disequilibrium Model of the Term Structure." *American Economic Review*, March 1976, pp. 28–44.

19. Evans, Paul. "Why Have Interest Rates Been So Volatile?" Federal Reserve Bank of San Francisco, *Economic Review*, Summer 1981, pp. 7–20.

20. Fama, Eugene. "Short-Term Interest Rates as Predictors of Inflation." *American Economic Review*, June 1975, pp. 427–48.

21. Fama, Eugene, and G. William Schwert. "Inflation, Interest and Relative Prices." *Journal of Business*, April 1979, pp. 183–210.

22. Feldstein, Martin. "Inflation, Income Taxes and the Rate of Interest: A Theoretical Analysis." *American Economic Review*, December 1976, pp. 809–20.

23. Feldstein, Martin, and Otto Eckstein. "The Fundamental Determinants of the Interest Rate." *Review of Economics and Statistics*, August 1970, pp. 363–75.

24. Fildes, Robert A., and M. D. Fitzgerald. "Efficiency and Premiums in the Short-Term Money Market." *Journal of Money, Credit and Banking*, November 1980, Part I, pp. 615–29.

25. Fisher, Irving. *The Theory of Interest*. New York: MacMillan, 1930.

26. Friedman, Benjamin, and William G. Dewald. *Financial Market Behavior Capital Formation and Economic Performance*. Conference papers published by the *Journal of Money, Credit and Banking*, vol. 12, part 2 (May 1980).

27. Friedman, Milton. *The Optimum Quantity of Money and Other Essays*. New York: Aldine Publishers, 1969. (See especially essays 5, 6, 10.)

28. Friedman, Milton, and Anna J. Schwartz. *Monetary Trends in the United States and the United Kingdom*. Chicago: National Bureau of Economic Research, University of Chicago Press, forthcoming, 1982.

29. von Fustenberg, George M. "Flow of Funds Analysis and the Economic Outlook." *Annals of Economic and Social Measurement*, February 1977, pp. 1–25.

30. Gibson, William E., and George Kaufman. "The Sensitivity of Interest Rates to Changes in Money and Income." *The Journal of Political Economy*, May/June 1968, pp. 472–78.

31. Gordon, R. A., and L. Klein, eds. *Readings in Business Cycles*. Homewood, Ill.: Richard D. Irwin, 1965.

32. Gordon, Robert J. "Large-Scale Econometric Models." Mimeographed. Washington, D.C.: U.S. Department of the Treasury, 1970.

33. Grossman, Jacob. "The Rationality of Money Supply Expectations and the Short-Run Response of Interest Rates to Monetary Surprises." *Journal of Money, Credit and Banking*, November 1981, pp. 409–24.

34. Guttentag, Jack M., ed. *Essays on Interest Rates*. Vol. 2. New York: National Bureau of Economic Research, Columbia University Press, 1971. (Especially essays 1, 2.)

35. Guttentag, Jack M., and Phillip Cagan, eds. *Essays on Interest Rates*. Vol. 1. New York: National Bureau of Economic Research, Columbia University Press, 1969.

36. Hafer, R. W., and Scott Hein. "The Dynamics and Estimation of Short-Run Money Demand." Federal Reserve Bank of St. Louis *Review*, March 1980, pp. 26–35.

37. Hartman, David G. "The International Financial Market and U.S. Interest Rates." Working Paper No. 598, National Bureau of Economic Research, New York, 1981.

38. Hein, Scott. "Dynamic Forecasting and the Demand for Money." Federal Reserve Bank of St. Louis *Review*, June-July 1980, pp. 13–23.

39. Hicks, Sir John R. "Mr. Keynes and the Classics." *Econometrica*, April 1937, pp. 147–59.

40. _____ . *Value and Capital*. 2d ed. London: Oxford at the Clarendon Press, 1946.

41. Houglet, Michel X. *Estimating the Term Structure of Interest Rates for Nonhomogeneous Bonds*. Ph.D. dissertation, University of California, Berkeley, 1980.

42. Ibbotson, Roger G., and Rex, A. Sinquefield. *Stocks, Bonds, Bills, and Inflation: Historical Returns (1926–1978)*. 2d ed. Charlottesville, Va.: The Financial Analysts Research Foundation, 1979.

43. Kane, E. J. "Arbitrage Pressure and Divergences between Forward and Futures Interest Rates." Working Paper No. CSFM–21 Center for the Study of Futures Markets, Columbia Business School, New York, May 1980.

44. Kessel, Reuben A. *The Cyclical Behavior of the Term Structure of Interest Rates*. New York: National Bureau of Economic Research, Columbia University Press, 1965.

45. Kuznets, Simon. *Economic Growth of Nations*. Cambridge, Mass.: Harvard University Press, 1971.

46. Lawler, T. A. "Seasonal Movements in Short-Term Yield Spreads." Federal Reserve Bank of Richmond *Economic Review*, July/August 1978.

47. Lucas, Robert. "Methods and Problems of Business Cycle Theory." *The Journal of Money, Credit and Banking*, November 1980, Part II, pp. 696–715.

48. Lutz, F. A. *The Theory of Interest*. 2d ed. New York: Aldine Publishers, 1967.

49. McCulloch, J. Huston. "The Tax-Adjusted Yield Curve." *Journal of Finance*, June 1975, pp. 811–30.

50. McNees, Stephen K. "The Recent Record of Thirteen Forecasters." *New England Economic Review*, Federal Reserve Bank of Boston, September/October 1981.

51. Meltzer, Allan H. "Keynes' General Theory: A Different Perspective." *Journal of Economic Literature*, March 1981, pp. 34–64.

52. Miskin, Frederic. "Monetary Policy and Long-Term Interest Rates." *Journal of Monetary Economics*, February 1981, pp. 29–55.

53. Modigliani, Franco, and R. J. Shiller. "Inflation, Rational Expectations and the Term Structure of Interest Rates." *Economica*, February 1973, pp. 12–43.

54. Modigliani, Franco, and Richard Sutch, "Innovations in Interest Rate Policy." *American Economic Review, Papers and Proceedings*, May 1966, pp. 178–97.

55. Mundell, R. A. *Monetary Theory*. Pacific Palisades, Calif.: Goodyear Publishing, 1971.

56. Nelson, Charles R. *The Term Structure of Interest Rates*. New York: Basic Books, 1972.

57. Nelson, Charles R., and G. William Schwert. "Short-Term Interest Rates as Predictors of Inflation: On Testing the Hypothesis that the Real Rate Is Constant." *American Economic Review*, June 1977, pp. 478–86.

58. Pesando, James E. "On Forecasting Long-Term Interest Rates: Is the Success of the No-Change Prediction Surprising?" *Journal of Finance*, September 1980, pp. 1045–47.

59. Poole, William R. "Optimal Choice of Monetary Policy Instruments in a Simple Stochastic Macro Model." *Quarterly Journal in Economics*, May 1970, pp. 197–216.

60. _____ . The Relationship of Monetary Decelerations to Business Cycle Peaks: Another Look at the Evidence." *Journal of Finance*, June 1975, pp. 697–712.

61. Reinganum, Marc. "The Arbitrage Pricing Theory: Some Empirical Results." *Journal of Finance*, May 1981, pp. 313–21.

62. Roll, Richard. *The Behavior of Interest Rates*. Amsterdam: North Holland, 1970.

63. Ross, Stephen A. "The Arbitrage Theory of Capital Asset Pricing." *Journal of Economic Theory*, December 1976, pp. 341–60.

64. Salomon Brothers, *Prospects for Financial Markets*. Annual. New York: Salomon Brothers Bond Market Research.

65. Santoni, G. J., and Courtenay C. Stone. "What Really Happened to Interest Rates: A Longer-Run Analysis." Federal Reserve Bank of St. Louis *Review*, November 1981, pp. 3–14.

66. Shiller, Robert J.; John Y. Campbell; and Kermit Schoenholtz. "Forward Rates and Future Policy: Interpreting the Term Structure of Interest Rates." *Brookings Papers on Economic Activity*, No. 1, 1983. pp. 173–224.

67. Singleton, Kenneth J. "Maturity-Specific Disturbances and the Term Structure of Interest Rates." *Journal of Money, Credit and Banking*, November 1980, part 1, pp. 603–14.

68. Stokes, Houston H., and H. Neuberger. "The Effect of Monetary Changes on Interest Rates: A Box-Jenkins Approach." *Review of Economics and Statistics*, November 1979, pp. 534–48.

69. Telser, Lester G. "A Critique of Some Recent Empirical Research on the Explanation of the Term Structure of Interest Rates." *Journal of Political Economy*, August 1967, pp. 546–61.

70. Throop, Adrian W. "Interest-Rate Forecasts and Market Efficiency." Federal Reserve Bank of San Francisco, *Economic Review*, Spring 1981, pp. 29–43.

71. Tobin, James, and William Brainard. "Pitfalls in Financial Model Building." *American Economic Review, Papers and Proceedings*, May 1968, pp. 99–122.

72. Turnbull, Stuart M. "Measurement of the Real Rate of Interest and Related Problems in a World of Uncertainty." *Journal of Money, Credit and Banking*, May 1981, pp. 177–91.

73. Wecker, William. "Predicting the Turning Points of a Time Series." *The Journal of Business*, January 1979, pp. 35–50.

74. Wendel, Helmut F. "Interest-Rate Expectations." Washington, D.C.: Board of Governors of the Federal Reserve System, 1968.

75. Wenninger, John; Lawrence Radecki; and Elizabeth Hammond. "Recent Instability in the Demand for Money." Federal Reserve Bank of New York, *Quarterly Review*, Summer 1981, pp. 1–9.

76. Wilcox, James A. "Short-Term Movements of Long-Term Interest Rates: Evidence from the U.K. Indexed Bond Market." *National Bureau of Economic Research*, unpublished working paper, 1985.

77. _____. "Private Credit Demand, Supply and Crunches: How Different Are the 1980s?" *American Economic Review, Papers and Proceedings*, May 1985, pp. 351–6.

78. Wojnilower, Albert R. "The Central Role of Credit Crunches in Recent Financial History." *Brookings Papers on Economic Activity*, vol. 2 (1980), 30th Conference, pp. 277–326.

79. Yawitz, Jess B., and W. J. Marshall. "Measuring the Effect of Callability on Bond Yields." *Journal of Money, Credit and Banking*, February 1981, pp. 60–71.

PART 8

Interest-Rate Swaps

57

Interest-Rate Swaps: New Tools to Increase the Flexibility and Adaptability of Fixed Income Securities*

Carl R. Beidleman, Ph.D.
Allen C. DuBois Professor of Finance
Lehigh University
Bethlehem, Pennsylvania

The huge volumes of fixed income securities that have been issued in recent years reflect the preferences of issuers and investors in paying or receiving the level of interest rates at the time of issuance across varying periods marked by their respective maturities. In recent years, variable or floating-rate securities have become popular[1] where the coupon or interest rates are periodically redetermined based on some short-term market rate as opposed to paying or receiving a predetermined fixed rate over the life of a term instrument. While preferences to be either fixed or floating-rate payers or receivers may have been desirable at the time the securities were placed, conditions may change through time causing alternative coupon configurations to be more suitable. For instance, the fixed or floating-rate basis incorporated in an instrument may have lost its appeal, the floating-rate reset frequency may have become undesirable, or the overall level or term structure of interest rates may have changed making the contractual interest payments less desirable than alternative configurations currently available.

In addition, certain anomalies in markets have made it possible to utilize a particular type of financing or investment to obtain a lower cost or higher yield than otherwise available. These situations occur when

---

* Adapted from "The Role of Coupon Swaps in Floating Rate Markets," published in *Floating Rate Instruments: Characteristics, Valuation and Portfolio Strategies*, ed. Frank J. Fabozzi, Chicago: Probus Publishing Co., 1986.

[1] These instruments are discussed in Chapter 14.

certain markets are not equally accessible by all players or when regulatory, cultural, or market convention differences influence market availability.[2] For example, a player might find it propitious to use the fixed-rate markets together with swaps or swap-like instruments to assemble a financial package that reduces its all-in cost or enhances its all-in yield. Such simulated financing or investment strategies have become quite popular in recent years. In general, the key to their implementation has been the application of asset/liability management techniques using a recently developed set of instruments called interest-rate or coupon swaps.

ASSET/LIABILITY MANAGEMENT

Informed portfolio managers have always been ready to shift assets and asset categories to best fit the current objectives of their portfolio based on the set of market opportunities available at a given time. In implementing this process, they have developed complex managerial techniques to identify changes in actual or proposed portfolio content.

These concepts of modern portfolio management were primarily confined to asset portfolios until the early 1960s. Since then professionally astute banks and other financial intermediaries became aware that their liquidity needs and their risk-return preferences could be more effectively dealt with by actively managing their liabilities. As a result, sourcing and trading of liabilities became an active practice among funds managers of progressive financial institutions. If an institution was well-managed and had a good name, fluctuations in funding needs could be attended to by simply purchasing or selling liabilities. In terms of its impact on the risk-return calculus of the institutions, liability management was conceptually quite similar to asset portfolio management. Despite this similarity, liability management did not catch on as quickly as portfolio management. This may have been due to the lack of understanding or the lack of acceptance of these techniques as suitable to the liability side of the balance sheet.

Modern liability management as now practiced by banks and financial institutions can be employed by other types of players to reduce their cost of funds. Certain debt markets may be more accessible to some borrowers than others but despite their relative accessibility they may have undesirable debt service or coupon characteristics. Hence, natural fixed-rate payers may be advised to attach floating-rate funds in order to obtain finance, or natural floating-rate payers may find it propitious to tap fixed-rate markets in which they have an advantage. What remains

---

[2] See C. R. Beidleman, *Financial Swaps: New Strategies in Currency and Coupon Risk Management*, Chapter 4 (Homewood, Ill: Dow Jones-Irwin, Inc., 1985), for a more complete discussion of market inefficiencies and their impact on financial costs and returns.

is for each type of payer to swap its interest obligation with the other to obtain the market access and interest configuration that it prefers. The instruments needed to accomplish this exchange are called interest-rate or coupon swaps.

The use of interest-rate swaps to obtain a lower all-in cost of funds by accessing financial markets in which one has a relative advantage enables financial managers to tailor the interest configuration on their liabilities so as to be different from that of their initial financing. Similarly, portfolio managers can employ coupon swaps to alter the coupon characteristics of their portfolio and, in the process, simulate investments that have higher all-in yields than equivalent risk assets that are directly accessible. As before, the key link is the use of an interest-rate swap. In the next section, we examine the essential characteristics of interest-rate swaps. A brief description of the standardization of instruments and the growth in the swap market follows. A comprehensive section covering recent applications of coupon swaps to fixed income securities completes the chapter.

INTEREST-RATE SWAPS

A coupon or interest-rate swap provides a convenient means of altering the coupon cash flows on a debt instrument. Its primary objective is to exchange fixed-rate interest payments for floating-rate payments or vice versa. Prior to the advent of term floating-rate instruments, contractual coupon payments were fixed over the life of a debt security. More recently, however, debt issues that call for coupon payments that float or are reset periodically, say, each three or six months have abounded in world capital markets. The basis for these revisions is some well-documented market rate such as the London Interbank Offer Rate (Libor), some short-term Treasury bill rate, commercial paper, certificate of deposit composite rate, or other index of rates.

The quality or certainty of the level of coupon cash payments or receipts on floating-rate instruments is lower or more uncertain than it is on fixed-rate instruments. This difference in certainty of the coupon flows provides an attraction or an aversion for various types of market participants. That is, some players prefer to receive floating-rate payments over fixed-rate payments or vice versa. And on the financing side certain borrowers prefer to pay a fixed-rate of interest while others, because of their asset structures, are more inclined to pay floating-rates.[3] Despite these preferences, it frequently works out that players find it less onerous and costly to access debt markets that require coupon flows

---

[3] For an extended discussion of the preferences of coupon payers and receivers, see Beidleman, op. cit. pp. 203–9.

that conflict with their preferences. A natural solution to this financial dilemma rests in the use of an interest-rate swap.

An interest-rate or coupon swap may be defined as an exchange of a coupon or interest payment stream of one configuration for another coupon stream with a different configuration on the same notional principal amount. Interest-rate swaps in which payments are based on one floating-rate index or basis in exchange for a different floating-rate index or basis are also available, i.e., a floating-rate versus floating-rate swap in which Libor flows are exchanged for prime flows less some negotiated percentage. These swaps could be done in order to alter the quality or configuration of the coupon cash flows and to make them more compatible with the preferences of investors or issuers of debt instruments.

It is important to note that, in an interest-rate swap, the principal is only notional to the transaction. While the principal determines the size of the coupon flows, it is not swapped, and, hence, not at risk. This point significantly reduces the risk to the parties and to the market intermediaries. All that is at risk is the interest differential between the fixed and floating-rate coupon determinants. Because of the financial characteristics of the parties, this difference generally conforms to satisfying their underlying preferences.

MARKET DEVELOPMENT OF INTEREST-RATE SWAPS

As we have seen, the risk involved in interest-rate swaps excludes the risk of principal and is limited to the interest differential between the fixed and floating-rate basis of the coupon payments. This basis risk can be readily managed within reasonable limits, providing market makers with a means of limiting their exposure. As a result, the market in interest-rate swaps has developed rapidly, and has now become nearly standardized and fully productized.

The interest-rate swap product was originally introduced in the Euromarket in early 1982 as a modification of the currency or foreign exchange swap. These latter instruments had been in rather common use since 1976. However, their annual volume had reached only $4 to $5 billion by 1982. Because of a large volume of ready applications and reduced risk to the parties, interest-rate swaps took off quickly after their introduction. It has been estimated that approximately $5 billion of interest-rate swap transactions were done in 1982, followed by $25 billion in 1983 and $80 billion in 1984. 1985 is expected to show another near doubling in volume.

A major impetus to the initial rapid growth of the coupon swap market can be ascribed to the existence of a rather deep-seated anomaly between the fixed and floating-rate markets. This market anomaly or imperfection exists because of the differential premium for risk demanded by each market. For example, in 1982, a BBB-rated industrial company faced a 1.5 percent risk premium over a AAA bank in the fixed-rate market and only a 0.5 percent premium in the floating-rate Eurodollar market. The difference of 1 percent represented a credit arbitrage opportunity. That is, given these differential spreads, the bank should borrow fixed-rate funds at, say, 11 percent and pass this rate on to the BBB firm. The latter should borrow at, say, Libor plus 50 basis points and swap this floating-rate obligation with the bank. In this example, the swap would provide for the bank to receive 11 percent from the BBB with which to service its fixed-rate debt, and the BBB would receive Libor less 0.25 percent with which to service its floating-rate debt. Here, the bank saves 0.25 percent under its cost to access floating-rate funds directly (Libor) and the BBB firm sees a fixed-rate cost difference of 1.5 percent under its directly accessible cost of fixed-rate funds of 12.5 percent. This saving is reduced by the 0.75 percent difference between what the BBB pays and receives for floating-rate funds. It is further reduced by the fact that the BBB is required to pay the transactions costs of the swap and related credit intermediation fees. The net result is that the bank obtains a net saving of 0.25 percent and the BBB realizes an all-in saving of 0.43 percent. In addition to the saving, it is important to note that each party obtained the configuration of financing that it preferred.

CHARACTERISTICS OF THE INTEREST-RATE SWAP MARKET

The development of the interest-rate swap market was able to occur rapidly because the product could be standardized with relative ease and risk could be managed within relatively narrow limits by market makers. Standardized documentation was available, from an early date, drawing on the concepts used in currency swaps. Pricing was based on a dual threshold, with the fixed-rate quotation at some spread over term Treasuries of the same maturity as that of the interest-rate swap, versus the floating-rate index flat. An example of this pricing is presented in Figure 1.

FIGURE 1   Interest Rate Swap Spreads (October 24, 1985)*

	2 Yrs.	5 Yrs.	7 Yrs.	10 Yrs.
3 Month LIBOR	58	58	46	45
3 Month bill	−32	−40	−54	−66

* Quoted for generic swaps as a basis-point spread to the Treasury yield curve versus the floating index flat.
SOURCE: Salomon Brothers Inc, Bond Market Roundup, October 25, 1985.

FIGURE 2 The Interest-Rate Swap Market: Six Month LIBOR (Floating)
versus U.S. Treasuries (Fixed)

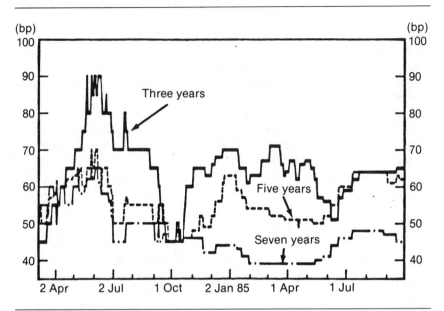

Note: Chart displays the fixed spread over U.S. Treasuries (for the indicated maturities) one would receive (or pay) in an interest-rate swap arrangement in return for paying (or receiving) six-month LIBOR.
SOURCE: Salomon Brothers Inc, *Floating-Rate Financing Quarterly*, September, 1985, October 22, 1985.

Figure 2 presents a record of interest-rate swap pricing for various maturities against the six-month Libor floating-rate index over a period of a year. These data reflect the degree of sophistication that the coupon swap market has achieved in a remarkably short period of time.

A principal reason for this rapid development of the interest-rate swap market was that the exposure to the market makers could be readily managed. There is very little risk on the floating-rate side. Here, price risk is limited to the short period until repricing occurs. Any basis risk present due to funding cost would not be excessive and could be controlled by careful management. The exposure on the fixed-rate side is similar to being long (short) in term bonds. This can be managed by selling (buying) sufficient Treasury bill or bond futures to obtain the needed offset protection.

Complete productization of interest-rate swaps also depends on the way in which credit risk can be managed. From the outset, credit risk to each of the parties could be handled by bringing a bank intermediary into the transaction to provide a letter of credit-like assurance that each of the parties would perform on its obligation. Of course, when a bank is one of the parties to the interest-rate swap it fills the credit risk function also. Other means of providing for the credit risk inherent in interest-rate swaps include the use of collateral or margin and a daily mark to market to determine the level of margin requirements.

Improved ability to manage credit risk has also contributed to the ability to trade or transfer interest-rate swaps in the secondary market. If the credit risk of an assignee or its guarantor is acceptable to a principal market maker, it is now possible to assign an interest-rate swap as may be required in a trading process. Thus, market sophistication has proceeded to the point where interest-rate swaps have become trading vehicles and gains or losses may be taken as the players seek to redress their balance sheets and/or income statements.

APPLICATIONS TO FIXED INCOME SECURITIES

The growth in annual volume of interest-rate swaps affirms the validity of the concept and its demand by both floating-rate and fixed-rate payers and receivers. A few actual case studies will be helpful in providing a clearer understanding of how interest-rate swaps can be used to reduce costs, increase yields, or revise the basis of coupon flows to better suit the preferences of the parties.

Liability Management

The first case study occurred in November, 1984. A rather small, regional commercial bank that faced a large increase in its money market deposit accounts sought to improve its interest sensitivity by buying a $5 million floating-rate note indexed to six-month Treasury bills and reset each six months. This floating-rate note (FRN) was acquired in 1983. Although it improved the gap management and interest sensitivity of the bank over investment in longer-term assets, some time after the FRN was acquired it became clear that two significant shortcomings still remained. First, each major credit crisis in the United States resulted in a flight to quality instruments, which, in turn, caused a decline in short-term Treasury interest rates. Thus the income from the FRN was depressed from time to time with a resultant adverse affect on the net interest margin of the bank. Second, the bank had some asset sensitivity at six months which it wanted to shorten up.

The solution was a floating versus floating-rate interest-rate swap where the bank received six-month Libor with a six-month reset and paid the bond equivalent rate on six-month Treasury bills plus 90 basis points (0.90 percent) with a weekly reset based on the weekly Treasury auction. The notional size of the swap was $5 million. In this way the bank eliminated its six-month asset sensitivity by effectively funding its six-month asset with weekly reset payments. In addition it converted its Treasury bill based FRN to a six-month Libor based FRN and no longer needed to fear the effects on net interest income from a domestic flight to quality.

Although its objective was to better balance its interest sensitivity and exposure to the effects of a domestic financial crisis, the bank earned an average of $4,000 a month on the swap during the first reset period. This occurred because of movements in the rates such that its Treasury bill funding costs plus the 90 basis point spread fell below the six-month Libor that the bank was receiving. The counterparty to this swap was a financial intermediary who, as a result of its market-making activities in interest-rate swaps, found itself with a long position in six-month Libor and a short position in six-month Treasury bills. After completion of this swap it neutralized both of these exposures and picked up a swap spread in the process.

Asset Swap

A second case study involves an asset or portfolio swap. This example can be used to highlight the limited risk features of an interest-rate swap. In this case a U.S. life insurance company purchased a five-year floating-rate CD in mid-1983 at six-month Libor plus 0.25 percent. The life insurance firm preferred term fixed-rate assets whose cash flows more nearly coincided with its expected disbursements and whose fixed-rate returns could be relied on to produce required returns for policyholders. Thus the life firm sought to swap its floating-rate CD interest income with a weak (BBB) corporate credit. Other logical counterparties would be thrift institutions or small banks. The BBB-rated firm in this case utilized existing floating-rate or short-term debt. It could also have sourced its funds from a bank, relying on the floating-rate interest payments from the life firm to service its floating-rate debt.

The BBB firm was interested in fixed-rate debt and was willing to pay a spread of 300 basis points over five-year Treasuries. Five-year Treasuries were yielding 10.5 percent, making the fixed-rate payment to the life firm 13.5 percent. In exchange, the life firm paid over to the BBB firm its floating-rate interest receipts of 0.25 percent over six-month Libor (10 percent at the time) or 10.25 percent in the first interest period. Of course, the six-month Libor rate would be reset each six months.

The advantages to the life firm were that it received fixed-rate income at a yield reflecting a BBB-rated credit as if it had lent the funds to a BBB-rated firm rather than investing them in a bank issued floating-rate CD. The BBB firm also enjoyed the benefits of obtaining fixed-rate finance at a time when fixed-rate funds were not otherwise available and at a cost which reflected no increase in its cost of debt capital.

The risk profile faced by the life firm in this example is of interest. First, the risk of principal was limited to that of the issuer of the CD, a bank in this case, since principal is not swapped in an interest-rate swap. Thus, the only risk that the insurance company was exposed to was the uncertainty that the BBB firm may not remit the required fixed-rate interest flows. Even then the level of exposure was only the difference between the 13.5 percent fixed-rate and the 10.25 percent and subsequent floating-rate payments. Moreover, this risk is really an opportunity type of risk, i.e., the risk that the insurance firm may have to reinvest its principal at a lower fixed-rate.

Capital Market Swap

A third example in which the interest-rate swap market provided an attractive financing alternative in the fourth quarter of 1985 is shown in Figure 3. Here we see that substantial spreads below Libor could have been obtained over a nine-month period by using the swap market to transform a fixed-rate obligation to a floating-rate obligation. The strategy would entail an AAA borrower tapping the five-year Eurodollar bond market at a fixed interest rate that is lower than it would receive on the fixed-rate side of a fixed for floating-rate coupon swap against six-month Libor. The positive spread that the borrower received could be used to reduce the effective floating-rate cost that must be borne for the financing. It can be seen from Figure 3 that at times, this cost savings has exceeded 100 basis points and has averaged about 50 basis points over the period. Figure 4 provides approximate cash flows that would have occurred if the swap were done in October, 1985. From this it can be seen that the use of an interest-rate swap enabled the borrower to obtain floating-rate finance at 50 basis points under the rate that first name Eurobanks charged one another for six-month funds.

Simulated Investment

A final example illustrates how an interest-rate swap can be utilized to construct a synthetic investment opportunity that can produce a more attractive yield than alternative investments with similar risk. On December 19, 1984 a commercial bank was offered a $5 million FRN issued by Republic Bank of New York at 98.55. The FRN matures on December 19, 2009 and resets quarterly at 0.125 percent over three-month Libor. The current rate had just been set at 9.1875 percent. On the same day the bank was offered a two-year coupon swap to pay three-month Libor and receive the two-year Treasury note yield plus 62 basis points. On that day, the two-year Treasury rate was 10.01 percent and three-month Libor was 9.0625 percent.

FIGURE 3 The Interest-Rate Swap Market: Effective Costs versus Six-Month
LIBOR

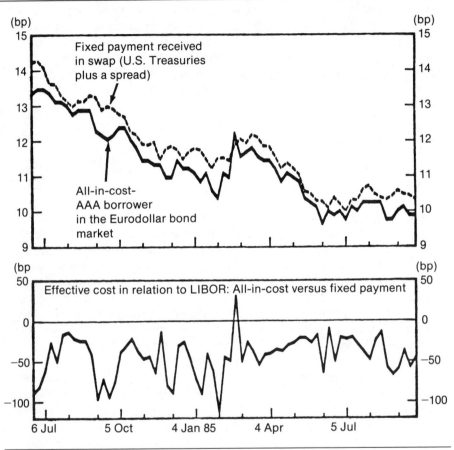

Note: The borrower in this example enters into a swap agreement where he agrees as a
"floating-rate payer" to pay six-month LIBOR and receive a fixed-rate which is five-year U.S.
Treasuries plus a spread. At the same time, he issues a fixed-rate Eurodollar bond. To the
extent that what he receives (U.S. Treasuries plus a spread) exceeds the all-in cost of this
bond, the borrower has achieved an effective cost below LIBOR.
    SOURCE: Salomon Brothers Inc., *Floating-Rate Financing Quarterly*, September, 1985,
October 22, 1985.

   The combined opportunity of the swap and the Republic of New
York FRN enabled the bank investor to effectively earn 10.76 percent on
its investment for the next two years. This was obtained from the sum of
the 10.63 percent fixed rate received on the swap plus the difference
between the Libor paid on the swap and the Libor plus 0.125 percent
received from Republic of New York. In addition, because the FRN

FIGURE 4 Capital Market Swap Illustrative Cash Flows

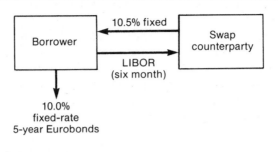

Summary

Fixed-rate paid by borrower (Eurobond liability)	10.0 percent
Fixed-rate received by borrower (swap inflow)	10.5 percent
Net fixed-rate payment received by borrower	0.5 percent
Floating-rate paid by borrower (swap outflow)	Six-month Libor
Effective floating-rate cost paid by borrower	Six-month Libor—0.5 percent

could be purchased at a discount from par, the current yield would be higher by 0.1352 percent, i.e., 9.3227 percent instead of 9.1875. Moreover, the bank could acrete the 1.45 point discount and further increase its yield for book purposes. In sum, the yield obtainable on this simulated investment exceeded 10.90 percent, more than 0.40 percent above the 10.50 percent available on an alternate Republic of N.Y. shelf registration bond at the time and a full 89 basis points above the yield curve on two-year treasuries. A negative factor lies in the fact that there is more credit exposure on the 25-year FRN because it doesn't mature until 2009, but the bank may already have had the credit risk or may be willing to assume it in a name like Republic of New York.

CONCLUSION

From these examples it becomes clear that fixed-income securities and interest-rate swaps can be combined to impose the flexibility and adaptability of fixed income markets from the points of view of both issuers and investors. Because they provide the opportunity to separate the coupon of an asset portfolio from the coupon originally contracted for, they improve their total rate of return to investors under appropriate conditions. Moreover, when applied in appropriate combinations, swaps enable issuers to obtain a lower all-in cost-of-capital and in the configuration which they wish ultimately to service it. Financial swaps enable portfolio managers to restructure their assets without incurring actual sales or purchases with their concomitant tax and cash flow implications. Swaps allow liability managers to adjust their liability and asset structures in order to improve interest sensitivity and strengthen gap management processes. And swaps facilitate the breaching of market anomalies in order to extract arbitrage opportunities where market inefficiencies exist. With the ongoing growth of fixed-income security markets in both the fixed and floating-rate categories, it is evident that the need for these types of transactions should continue to increase. Hence, interest-rate swaps can be expected to play a dominant role in fixed income securities markets for the foreseeable future.

58

The Interest Rate Swap Market: Yield Mathematics, Terminology, and Conventions*

Robert Kopprasch, Ph.D., C.F.A.
Bond Portfolio Analysis Group
Salomon Brothers Inc

John Macfarlane
Interest-Rate Swap Group
Salomon Brothers Inc

Daniel R. Ross
Interest-Rate Swap Group
Salomon Brothers Inc

Janet Showers, Ph.D.
Corporate Finance Department
Salomon Brothers Inc

* The authors would like to thank Daniel L. Schwartz for his contribution to the Appendix and to the development of the theories herein.

Since its inception in the late 1970s, the interest-rate swap[1] has developed from a negotiated device used primarily by international banks and their corporate counterparties, into a broadly based market instrument used by virtually every type of institution. The rapid growth of the over-the-counter swap market largely reflects the flexibility that it affords its participants in closing maturity, funding, and index mismatches on their balance sheets. In addition, market makers' willingness to structure swaps that meet individual counterparty needs has further stimulated the market's growth.

The expansion of the market, however, has not come without costs. Throughout this period, the market has failed to develop a consistently used yield mathematics for swaps. This lack of consistency, along with the wide variety of swap structures, has caused specific transactions to be misunderstood and mispriced.

This chapter will remove the uncertainty and imprecision that has surrounded this market and explain the mathematics fundamental to its understanding. The approach that we will use follows:

- First, we will present the terminology that is most frequently used when discussing swaps.
- Second, we will describe the *generic swap*, which can serve as the basis for structuring swaps and as the cornerstone of a valuation procedure for swaps.
- Third, we will discuss complexities of swap cash flows that initially appear to make the application of traditional bond analysis difficult.
- Fourth, we will suggest a valuation methodology for analyzing a generic interest-rate swap within the general bond math framework that is familiar to most market participants.
- Fifth, we will adapt our methodology for use in valuing nongeneric swaps.
- Finally, we will explore the typical nongeneric features actually found in the market and, using our methodology, describe their effect on a swap's "cost" or "value."

Because the mathematical techniques used in this chapter employ only traditional bond mathematics, we hope that institutions that are presented with a swap will use this approach as a framework to analyze the swap's particular features and to assess its value.

---

[1] An interest rate swap is an agreement between two institutions in which each commits to make periodic interest payments to the other based on an agreed-upon notional principal amount, maturity, and either a predetermined fixed rate of interest or an agreed-upon floating money market index. No principal amounts change hands. This chapter will discuss only fixed-for-floating U.S. dollar interest rate swaps, although many of the principles outlined apply to other swaps as well.

A PRIMER ON MARKET TERMINOLOGY

Mathematics has not been the sole source of confusion for swap market participants. The lack of consistently used terminology and the fact that some terminology initially appears to be counterintuitive have left institutions unsure of how to approach the market. Thus, before we discuss mathematics, we will briefly review the following market terminology:

- The terms used when discussing the anatomy of a particular swap;
- The terms associated with positioning or making markets in swaps; and
- The interpretation of market quotations for swaps.

An interest-rate swap is a contract between two participants or *counterparties*, in which interest payments are made based on the *notional principal amount*, which itself is never paid or received. The fixed-rate payment in the swap (often called the fixed-rate coupon) is made by the *fixed-rate payer* to the *floating-rate payer*. Similarly, the floating-rate payment in the swap is made by the floating-rate payer (or variable-rate payer) to the fixed-rate payer. Both fixed and floating interest start accruing on the swap's *effective date* and cease accruing on the swap's *maturity date*. The *trade date* is the date on which the counterparties commit to the swap. On this date, the transaction is priced for value as of the *settlement date*.[2]

The various money market index on which the floating-rate payment could be based are presented in Figure 6. The floating-rate payment stream will sometimes be calculated based on the index plus or minus an agreed-upon number of basis points, known as the floating *spread*. The overall value or cost of a swap is expressed as the *all-in-cost* (AIC), which will be discussed later. Although particular counterparties may supply credit enhancement devices (e.g., letter of credit, bank intermediaries, collateral or insurance), the cost of such devices is not included in the AIC.

While the language relating to the structure of an individual swap is straightforward, the terminology associated with positioning or market making initially can appear to be somewhat confusing. Historically, a market maker's bias has been to "buy" or "go long" swaps by being a fixed-rate payer.[3] A market maker who is long the swap market makes

---

[2] The settlement date is also the date on which any net cash payment—including any net accrued interest—changes hands. Such a cash payment could occur, for example, in secondary market or seasoned transactions as discussed in the section on nonpar swaps. In the case of entering into a swap, the settlement date is normally the same as the effective date whether or not any cash payment occurs.

[3] Given time, the market maker would "sell" his position to appropriate counterparties to offset these long positions. This trading strategy evolved because initially, floating-rate payers were limited in number and relatively inflexible in accommodating various swap structures.

fixed-rate payments and, therefore, can be considered short the bond market (as if he had issued fixed-rate debt). This market anomaly has resulted in the widely accepted terminology shown in Figure 1.

FIGURE 1   Terminology of the Swap Market

A Fixed-Rate Payer

Pays fixed in the swap.
Receives floating in the swap.
Has bought a swap.
Is long a swap.
Is short the bond market.
Has established the price sensitivities of a longer-term liability and a floating-rate asset.

A Floating-Rate Payer

Pays floating in the swap.
Receives fixed in the swap.
Has sold a swap.
Is short a swap.
Is long the bond market.
Has established the price sensitivities of a longer-term asset and a floating-rate liability.

The market convention for quoting swap levels is to quote the all-in-cost (or the internal rate of return) of the fixed side of the swap versus the opposite flow of the floating index flat.[4] The swap's all-in-cost can be expressed either as an absolute level on a semiannual basis or as a basis-point spread to the semiannual bond equivalent of the U.S. Treasury yield curve. For an example of the latter type of quote, a seven-year LIBOR swap might be quoted to a fixed-rate payer as "the Treasury yield curve plus 60 basis points versus three-month LIBOR flat." This means that the fixed-rate payer could enter into a swap in which he receives three-month LIBOR flat and makes fixed payments, the internal rate of return of which equates to 60 basis points over the semiannual bond equivalent yield of the Treasury yield curve on the trade date.[5]

Market participants use several methods to define the Treasury yield curve. The most predominant methods determine at the time of execution the yield of a principal amount of Treasury securities based

---

[4] The floating index *flat* means that the floating payments equal the index itself with no spread over or under the index.

[5] The cash flows for this internal rate of return calculation include, for analytical purposes, the price of the hypothetical fixed-rate bond and redemption of principal at maturity (see the section on valuation methodology).

upon the swap's notional principal amount.[6] One method defines the curve as the semiannual yield-to-maturity of the specific note or bond with maturity closest to that of the swap. This method unfortunately often results in anomalous levels because of thin trading in the particular security or because of the presence of a discount or premium in the particular security.

We believe that a better method involves using only current coupon "on-the-run" securities. If the swap's maturity is reasonably close to the maturity of such a security, then that security's yield defines the curve. If the swap's maturity lies between that of two on-the-run securities, then the curve would be defined by interpolation of the yields.[7]

THE GENERIC SWAP

Throughout the evolution of the market, we have observed one fundamental structure emerging as the point of reference against which all interest-rate swaps are compared. This generic (or "plain vanilla") swap may not be the final structure of most swaps completed, but it remains the single theme on which all of the countless swap variations are based. The generic swap, therefore, is a starting point for analysis.

The generic interest-rate swap combines the characteristics of a traditional fixed-income security on the fixed-rate side with the characteristics of a traditional floating-rate note on the floating side. These characteristics are outlined in Figure 2.

COMPLEXITIES OF SWAP ANALYSIS

Several factors complicate the analysis of cost or return of an interest-rate swap within the confines of traditional bond math. Two such complications affect even the generic swap, which is the most straightforward in terms of valuation: (1) An interest-rate swap involves neither an investment at settlement date nor a repayment of principal at maturity; and (2) a swap's future floating-rate payment stream is unknown. These two factors must be addressed first in setting forth a valuation technique for swaps.

---

[6] The price of the Treasury securities is negotiated at the time that the parties enter the swap. Market makers have historically wanted to use the bid side to determine the curve for fixed-rate payers and the offered side to determine the curve for floating-rate payers. This convention developed because a market maker selling a swap to a fixed-rate payer traditionally sold its hedge and, hence, used the bid side. Similarly, the market maker traditionally bought a hedge when buying a swap from a floating-rate payer and, thus, used the offered side.

[7] Interpolation is straight-line based on the actual number of days between the maturity of the swap and the two securities.

FIGURE 2 Terms of the Generic Swap

Terms	*Definition*
Maturity	One to fifteen years

Effective date	Five business days from trade date (corporate settlement). The effective date is such that the first fixed- and first floating-payment periods are full coupon periods (i.e., no long or short first coupons).

Settlement date	Effective date
Fixed payment	
Fixed coupon	Current market rate
Payment frequency	Either semiannually or annually
Day count	30/360
Pricing date	Trade date
Floating payment*	
Floating Index	Certain money market indexes
Spread	None
Determination source	Some publicly quoted source; for example, the *Reuter Monitor Money Rates Service* or the *Federal Reserve Statistical Release H.15 (519)*.
Payment frequency	The term of the floating index itself.
Day count	Actual/360 for private sector floating rate indexes and Actual/Actual for Treasury bills.
Reset frequency	The term of the floating index itself, except for Treasury bills, for which the index is reset weekly regardless of term.
First coupon	Current market rate for the index

Premium or discount	None†

All-in-cost	Semiannual equivalent of the internal rate of return of the fixed flows versus the floating index flat.‡

---

* For details on floating-rate generic standards, see Figure 6.
† This means that no cash payment is made by either party on the effective date (see the section on nonpar swaps).
‡ See Footnote 5.

Swapping Interest Payments or Swapping Securities?

The first obstacle to analyzing an interest-rate swap using bond math is overcome by viewing the swap as a simultaneous exchange of two separate hypothetical securities of equal maturity. This notion holds that the fixed-rate payer has sold a hypothetical fixed-rate security to the floating-rate payer and that the floating-rate payer has sold a hypothetical floating-rate note to the fixed-rate payer. Because the par amount of both "securities" is the notional principal amount of the swap, a netting of the two purchase prices upon settlement and of the two principal repayments at a maturity results in no net cash flow based upon principal dollars.[8]

This artificial construct allows us to look at the two "securities" separately for valuation purposes. Whether one thinks of a swap as an exchange of interest payments or an exchange of securities, the net cash flows of the swap are the same.

The Uncertainty of the Floating-Rate Payments

The uncertainty of the floating-rate payment stream presents a slightly more difficult problem to overcome. The fundamental question is how can one determine the market value of a swap without knowing the precise floating-rate payments. Specifically, would a technique like Simple Margin, Total Margin, Adjusted Total Margin, or Discount Margin be required?[9]

The structure of an interest-rate swap, however, suggests a simple answer to this fundamental question. Unlike a true floating-rate note, a swap has two-way cash flows: fixed versus floating. This feature allows the swap market to value the relative attractiveness of a swap's floating index by bidding the accompanying fixed rate up or down. Consequently, the floating-rate note valuation techniques mentioned are not required. The value of the floating-rate security is incorporated into the fixed cost quoted versus the floating payments. Therefore, valuation questions for swaps focus on the hypothetical fixed security.

THE VALUATION METHODOLOGY FOR GENERIC SWAPS

The basic valuation method for *generic* swaps is to find the internal rate of return of the hypothetical fixed-security flows. For analytical purposes these flows, from the perspective of the fixed-rate payer, are the "proceeds" received from the "sale" of the hypothetical fixed-rate security versus an outflow of the fixed-rate payments plus the notional principal amount at maturity.[10] The internal rate of return (expressed as a

---

[8] In a generic swap the prices of the exchanged "securities" are equal and, thus, no net cash payment is exchanged upon settlement. In nongeneric swaps, the prices may not be equal. In such a case, the net of the two purchase prices would determine the cash payment upon settlement (see the section on nonpar swaps).

[9] These tools attempt to measure a floater's return by quantifying an implicit change in the floating rate whenever the note deviates from par.

[10] The proceeds are not cash but instead are the value of the hypothetical floating-rate note received in exchange. In a generic swap the value of the floating-rate note is par. For nongeneric swaps the proceeds are the net of the value of the floater and any cash payment on the settlement date (see the section on nonpar swaps).

semiannual bond equivalent) of the hypothetical fixed security is quoted as the all-in-cost versus the floating flows that constitute the index flat.

THE VALUATION METHODOLOGY FOR NONGENERIC SWAPS: THE GENERIC EQUIVALENT CASH FLOW APPROACH (GECA)

The structuring of swaps to meet individual counterparty needs often results in nongeneric swaps. When a swap's floating side is not generic,[11] merely determining the internal rate of return of the fixed side would not produce a meaningful number. If the floating side could be adjusted to be generic, however, both generic and nongeneric swaps could be compared on an equivalent basis. To this end, we use the *Generic Equivalent Cash Flow Approach* (GECA) to value nongeneric swaps.

Under GECA we use the following procedure in analyzing a swap:

- First, we construct the cash flows of the two "securities" as specified in the swap contract.
- Second, we determine whether the floating payments are generic. If they are not, we artificially adjust the floating cash flows to correspond to a stream of payments satisfying the generic standard.[12] If the floating payments must be altered, we must alter the fixed cash flows by these same dollar amounts (the *adjustment flows*) so that the swap's net cash flows remain unchanged. We will refer to these adjusted cash flows as the *analytical flows* to distinguish them from the *contractual flows*.
- The final step in the GECA process is to determine the internal rate of return (on a semiannual-equivalent basis) of the analytical fixed flows. Because the floating cash flows were adjusted to be the generic standard, this internal rate of return is the swap's all-in-cost.

VARIATIONS ON THE GENERIC THEME

This section will discuss nongeneric swap features that often occur in the market. Where possible for each such feature, we will use our GECA methodology to describe the feature's effect on the swap's all-in-cost.

---

[11] The floating payments are generic if they fulfill the conditions set forth in the generic swap, namely: The payments equal the index flat; the payment frequency equals the index maturity; the reset frequency equals the index maturity (with the exception of Treasury bills, which are reset weekly); and the day-count convention is consistent with the basis on which the index is quoted (see Figure 6).

[12] For some nongeneric swaps, it is not possible to adjust the floating cash flows to the generic standard in a precise manner without knowing the level of the floating index. (For example, see the section on mismatches.)

Because GECA requires that the floating payments be adjusted to the generic standard, our discussion will begin with nongeneric floating-payment structures. We will then consider nongeneric fixed-payment structures.

For ease of discussion, we will use a particular generic swap as an example. Then, by varying the swap's terms, we will create nongeneric swaps and discuss how these nongeneric terms affect the all-in-cost.

The swap described in Figure 3 is clean analytically:

- The floating payment is the index flat;
- The floating rate is based on *Reuters*;
- The payment and reset frequencies of the floating payment are equal to the term of the index;
- There are no day-count discrepancies between payments and their standards;
- The initial floating coupon is a current rate;
- There is no premium or discount;

FIGURE 3   The Generic Swap—A Base Case Example

Notional principal amount	$10,000,000
Maturity	May 15, 1992
Trade date	May 8, 1985
Effective date	May 15, 1985
Settlement date	Effective date

Fixed Payment

Fixed coupon	12.50 percent
Payment frequency	Semiannual
Day count	30/360
Pricing date	Trade date

Floating Payment

Floating index	Six-month LIBOR
Spread	None
Determination source	*Reuter Monitor Money Rates Service*
Payment frequency	Semiannual
Day count	Actual/360
Reset frequency	Semiannual
First coupon	Six-month LIBOR quoted for value as of the settlement date.

Premium or discount	None

All-in-cost	12.50 percent (semiannual) versus six-month LIBOR flat.

- The swap settles "corporate";
- There are no short or long first coupon payments; and
- The swap is priced on the trade date.

Floating-Rate Variations

Spreads above or below the floating-rate index. Many swaps are structured with floating-rate payments based on the floating-rate index plus or minus an agreed-upon spread. For example, a swap might be structured with a fixed-rate payment of 12.50 percent semiannual and floating-rate payment of six-month LIBOR less 25 basis points. To express this swap's AIC according to market convention against the index flat, one is tempted simply to add 25 basis points to both sides and call it 12.75 percent semiannual versus six-month LIBOR flat. Unless the fixed rate and the floating rate are calculated on the same day-count basis and paid on the same frequency, however, this procedure would be inaccurate. Analyses of two different cases of this type of swap follow.

In swaps of the first case, fixed and floating payments have the same frequency. Consider our base case example described in Figure 3, with a spread under the floating index set at 25 basis points. To find the all-in-cost, we use GECA. First, the floating payments are artificially altered to become LIBOR flat, and then the fixed flows are altered by the same dollar amounts.

The first floating payment covers the period from May 15, 1985, until November 15, 1985—or 184 days. An increase in the LIBOR rate by 25 basis points changes the payment by:

$$0.0025 \times 10,000,000 \times 184/360 = 12,777.78$$

In terms of the fixed-note, this corresponds to 25.56 basis points higher on the first coupon. On the second coupon, the increase is 25.14 basis points because the next period covers only 181 days. Each fixed-rate payment must be adjusted in this way to determine the precise analytical cash flows and yield of the fixed-rate note. This procedure, when completed, shows the all-in-cost of this swap to be 12.7537 percent versus six-month LIBOR flat. Figure 4 depicts the contractual and analytical cash flows.

In swaps of the second case, fixed and floating payments have different frequencies. For this example, consider the generic base case swap with the floating rate changed to three-month LIBOR less 25 basis points reset and paid quarterly. As in the last example, the fixed-rate payer receives 25 basis points less on the floating payment. However, here this "loss" occurs quarterly instead of semiannually, which adds a compounding effect to the day-count effect of the last example. To analyze this swap structure, we must analytically add the dollar value of the 25 basis points onto the quarterly floating-rate payments to create three-

FIGURE 4 The Effect of a Floating Spread with the Same Payment Frequencies

Contractual flows

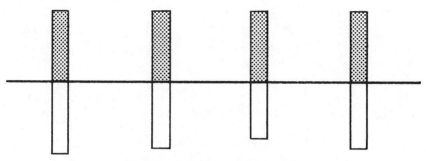

Floating index — 25 basis points

Analytical flows

$$\text{Fixed} + \left(\frac{25}{100} = \frac{\text{Actual}}{360} \right)$$

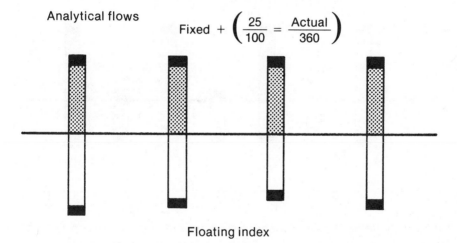

Floating index

month LIBOR flat and then adjust the fixed cash-flow stream by the same amounts. This procedure results in the analytical fixed-payment stream shown in Figure 5.

Figure 5 illustrates the Generic Equivalent Cash Flow Approach: The fixed-rate payer essentially makes small quarterly payments to the floating-rate payer, while the floating-rate payer analytically pays three-month LIBOR flat. This extra quarterly analytical payment increases the all-in-cost of the fixed-rate payer to 12.7577 percent versus three-month LIBOR flat. The compounding effect is 0.4 basis point in addition to the

FIGURE 5 The Effect of a Floating Spread with Different Payment Frequencies

Contractual flows

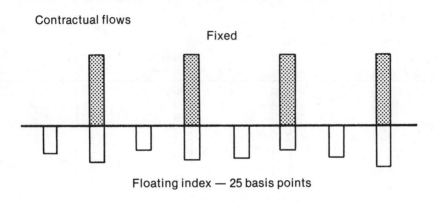

Fixed

Floating index — 25 basis points

Analytical flows

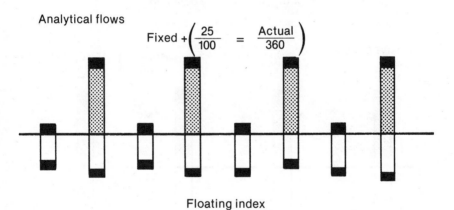

$$\text{Fixed} + \left(\frac{25}{100} = \frac{\text{Actual}}{360} \right)$$

Floating index

0.37-basis-point day-count effect seen in the previous example. Although both effects are small, it would be an error to ignore either one.

Mismatches. The characteristics of the floating-rate side of a generic swap are based on the cash market in the short-term instrument on which the index is based. Specifically, the swap's reset frequency and payment frequency equal the maturity of the underlying cash instrument, and the swap's floating rate accrues on a day count consistent with its form of quotation. For example, the floating rate in a generic three-month LIBOR swap resets quarterly, pays quarterly and accrues on an Actual/360 day count. The exception to this rule is a generic Treasury bill swap, which resets weekly.[13]

---

[13] While inconsistent with the cash market in bills themselves, this convention appears consistent with the structure of most bill-based floating-rate notes.

The flexibility of the interest-rate swap market, however, often creates transactions that have floating sides that deviate structurally from the underlying cash market. Any such deviation is called a *mismatch*. We will now discuss mismatches in payment frequency, day count and reset frequency.[14]

Payment-frequency mismatch. A payment-frequency mismatch occurs when the floating-rate payment frequency does not agree with the maturity of the floating-rate index. For example, a swap in which the fixed-rate payer receives interest based upon the three-month commercial paper index reset quarterly but paid semiannually is a payment-frequency mismatch swap.[15]

In this example, the fixed-rate payer loses the compounding of interest on interest that he would have received had he invested in the underlying cash instrument. Unfortunately, the precise cost of losing this "opportunity to compound" is difficult to calculate. An institution presented with a payment-frequency mismatch swap must make a largely qualitative assessment of both the amount of interest available to reinvest and the rate at which it should be compounded. Because both are impossible to determine completely in advance, no methodology can quantify precisely the effect of a payment-frequency mismatch on AIC.

Although this problem is difficult to assess, it does appear to have a reasonable solution. If the accrued floating-rate interest is compounded at the next floating rate until payment of the floating interest occurs, the fixed-rate payer should be satisfied.[16] If, however, the counterparties cannot agree on this or on some other compounding arrangement, they will be forced to make a qualitative judgment about the value of the payment-frequency mismatch.

Day-count mismatch. The generic interest-rate swap offers a day count consistent with the basis on which the floating-rate index is quoted. For example, if the certificate of deposit (CD) equivalent rate of one-month commercial paper is the basis for quoting the floating rate, then the floating-rate payment should accrue according to an Actual/360 day-count basis. Figure 6 outlines the most frequently used conventions.

Any inconsistencies between the swap conversion basis and the swap day count would alter the economics of the swap. Because the economic effect of a day-count mismatch varies with the absolute level

---

[14] One swap can possess more than one mismatch. For example, consider a swap in which three-month LIBOR is reset semiannually and paid semiannually.

[15] The receipt of a three-month index semiannually probably recurs because, for both credit and operational reasons, swap counterparties often prefer net transactions, i.e., where payment of both fixed and floating interest occurs on the same day.

[16] If there are more than two reset periods in each payment period (for example one-month commercial paper, which is reset monthly and paid semiannually), then the total accrued before a given reset period should be compounded forward through that period at that period's rate. This compounding should occur for all resets (after the first set).

FIGURE 6 Floating-Rate Generic Standards

Floating Index	Cash Market Quotation Basis	Swap Conversion Basis*	Swap Day Count	Payment Frequency	Reset Frequency
Treasury bills	Discount	BE	Actual/Actual	Term of index	Weekly
Commercial paper	Discount	CDE	Actual/360	Term of index	Term of index
Bankers' acceptances	Discount	CDE	Actual/360	Term of index	Term of index
LIBOR	CDE	CDE	Actual/360	Term of index	Term of index
Prime	CDE	CDE	Actual/360	Quarterly	Daily
Certificates of deposit	CDE	CDE	Actual/360	Term of index	Term of index
Federal funds	CDE	CDE	Actual/360	Compounded daily to mutually agreeable frequency	Daily

* In the case of indexes quoted on a discount basis, the actual number of days in a floating-rate period—and not a predetermined notion as to the maturity of the discount instrument—should be used when converting to a bond equivalent (BE) or CD equivalent (CDE) basis. (See the *Code of Standard Wording, Assumptions and Provisions for Swaps, 1985 Edition.*) For indexes with maturities of 182 days or less, the following formulas can be used to convert between a rate quoted on a discount basis (d), a bond equivalent basis (b) and a CD equivalent basis (c):

$$b = \frac{365 \times d}{360 - d \times t} \qquad c = b \times \frac{360}{365}$$

where t is the actual number of days in the floating-rate period.

---

of interest rates, no methodology can precisely quantify this nongeneric day-count effect. However, a counterparty can use GECA to estimate the magnitude of the day-count mismatch effect by making assumptions about the levels of the floating rate over the life of the swap.

Reset-frequency mismatch. A reset-frequency mismatch occurs when the reset frequency does not agree with the maturity of the floating-rate index.[17] An illustration of this nongeneric variation would be our base case example changed to require monthly resets of the six-month LIBOR index. In this revised swap, the interval between resets is shorter than the maturity of the index.

This nongeneric feature clearly changes the value of the swap. Resetting an index more frequently than its stated term ignores the fact that, by choosing a particular maturity, cash investors choose to forfeit more frequent repricing opportunities. Because the cash investor's repricing expectations are theoretically incorporated in the index, it is inappropriate to alter the reset frequency of the index without considering its impact on value.

The value of such a structure, however, depends on the investor's expectations and portfolio considerations. For example, a fixed-rate payer who wishes to match existing short-term liabilities that are reset weekly with a three- or six-month private-sector swap index might be willing to pay more for a swap with more frequent nongeneric resets

---

[17] Therefore, the generic Treasury bill swap, in which the floating rate resets weekly, is a reset-frequency mismatch. The structure nevertheless is considered to be generic because it is consistent with the underlying market in bill-based floating-rate notes.

than for a swap with a generic structure. Little can be done, however, to quantify the effect of this market anomaly on the pricing of interest-rate swaps. Such nongeneric reset features, however, certainly deserve qualitative consideration when they appear.

Short or long first floating-rate period. A swap may trade with a first floating-rate payment period that is either shorter or longer than those in the remainder of the swap.[18] In our base case generic example, this would occur if the effective date were July 15, 1985.[19] In this case, the appropriate floating-rate index for the first floating-rate period is at issue.

We believe that the correct index in this example would be four-month LIBOR flat. In general, if a private-sector swap has a short or long first floating-rate period and the structure of the floating side is otherwise generic, then the index for the first period should have a maturity equal to the time from the effective date until the first reset date.[20] This structure is consistent with the cash market. Furthermore, if there is a spread over or under the regular index, then the same spread should apply to the first-period index.

The presence of a payment-frequency or reset-frequency mismatch creates problems for determining the correct index for a long or short first coupon. For example, what would be the proper short first coupon for a five-week first floating-payment period on a swap with a regular floating-rate index of three-month LIBOR reset weekly and paid quarterly? Definitive market convention has not yet been established in this area. However, the rule proposed above for use with otherwise generic swaps could be a starting point for negotiating the appropriate short or long first coupon.

Fixed-Rate Variations

Payment frequencies. By definition generic swaps have semiannual or annual fixed-rate coupons. Although rare, other fixed-rate payment frequencies do exist. The rule for computing the all-in-cost is the same whether the fixed coupons are semiannual or nonsemiannual: The AIC equals the internal rate of return (expressed on a semiannual bond-equivalent basis) of the analytical fixed flows.

For a generic (par) swap with a semiannual fixed coupon, therefore, the AIC equals the fixed-coupon rate. For an otherwise generic swap

---

[18] This would most likely occur in the case of a secondary market trade or the sale of a seasoned swap. A *seasoned swap* is a swap held in a position by a market maker awaiting primary distribution.

[19] The trade date would be changed to July 8, 1985, to maintain corporate settlement. All other terms would remain the same.

[20] Because of the anomalies of the short Treasury bill market, Treasury bill swaps generally pay the stated index regardless of the term of the initial variable-rate period.

1274 / CHAPTER 58

with a nonsemiannual fixed coupon, the AIC equals the semiannual equivalent of the fixed-coupon rate.

For example, if the base case example is changed to pay a 12.50 percent coupon annually, the annual yield of the hypothetical fixed-rate note becomes 12.50 percent, but the swap would be quoted at the semi-annual all-in-cost of 12.132 percent. If one were to structure a generic swap with a 12.50 percent semiannual all-in-cost but with an annual fixed-rate coupon, the annual coupon would be 12.891 percent. (See the Appendix for conversion formulas.)

Short and long first fixed-rate period. Except when closing out an existing swap, swaps settle flat (i.e., with no accrued interest).[21] Conse-quently, when valuing a swap that settles on any date other than a fixed-coupon payment date, the present value calculation must incorporate a "long" or "short" first coupon period. The mathematics of this discount-ing is such that, on an otherwise generic swap, the all-in-cost will not equal the coupon rate if the first coupon is short or long. The Appendix contains formulas for the discounting process.

Day counts. Although the market convention is to structure swaps with fixed-rate payments accruing on a 30/360 day-count basis, other day-count methods are used. The Actual/360 day count, the Actual/365 and the Actual/Actual all appear. To determine the price or equivalent generic all-in-cost for such a nongeneric swap, the GECA method is applied to the actual fixed-coupon cash flows to construct the analytical fixed flows, which then are discounted on a 30/360 basis.

Effective Date

The generic swap provides for five business days to elapse between the trade date and the effective date. (For simplicity in this discussion, as-sume that the effective date is the settlement date.) Any variation of this "settlement period" alters the economics of the swap and, therefore, requires analysis.

The impact of an accelerated or delayed effective date is the oppor-tunity costs afforded each counterparty by entering into the swap with an irregular settlement period. One measure of this impact is the differ-ence between the fixed and floating interest that otherwise might have accrued. Typically, the two counterparties agree either to pay this ad-justment on the settlement date or to amortize it over the life of the swap.

---

[21] Closeouts are the termination of an existing swap between counterparties through a mutually agreeable cash payment. See "Secondary Trading: The Key to Further Develop-ment of the Interest Rate Swap Market," Patrick J. Dunlavy and Thomas W. Jasper, *Quarterly Statement*, November 1984.

Nonpar Swaps

Thus far we have examined swaps with no net cash payment at settlement and with both hypothetical securities valued at par. At this point we will generalize the GECA methodology to incorporate cash payments and situations in which the hypothetical securities are not at par. This methodology can then be applied to analyze any swap (except those with the features mentioned above that render precise analysis impossible). Figure 7 summarizes the sequence of steps in the analysis.

FIGURE 7   Summary of Generic Equivalent Cash Flow Approach (GECA)

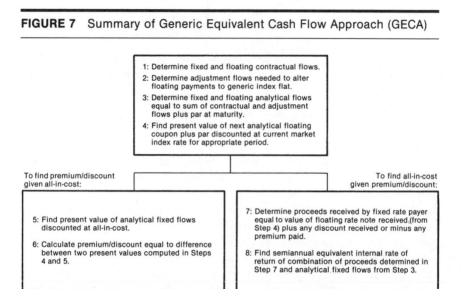

It may be useful to place the previously described GECA analysis into the framework of Figure 7. Steps 1, 2, and 3 are performed in the analysis of all swaps. Thus far, in our all-in-cost determination the floating-rate note has been assumed to be at par (Step 4), and there were no cash payments. Therefore, the proceeds in Step 7 have been par, and Step 8 could be completed with 100 as the proceeds.

Even swaps.   A swap with no cash payment at the settlement date occurs when, at pricing, the value of the hypothetical fixed-rate note equals the value of the hypothetical floating-rate note received in exchange. The two securities can be equal in two situations—when they both are at par or when they both are at the same nonpar price. We call the swap situation in which both hypothetical securities are at par a *par swap*. The second situation, in which the securities have equal but non-

FIGURE 8 Classification of Swaps by Pricing

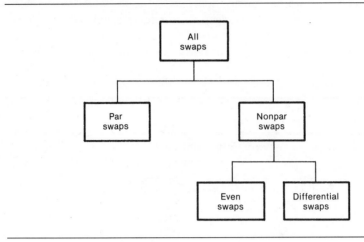

par prices, is called an *even swap* (see Figure 8). Note that because the hypothetical securities in a generic swap have current, regular coupons, they are at par. Therefore, generic swaps are par swaps.

Differential swaps: Premiums and discounts. A swap involving a cash payment at settlement occurs when the values of the two hypothetical securities are not equal at pricing. Because the payment compensates for the difference in value of the two securities, we call this swap a *differential* swap. By swap market convention, if a counterparty makes a payment at the settlement date of a swap, then that payment is referred to as a *premium*. If a counterparty receives a payment at the settlement date, then that payment is known as a *discount*.

Although this terminology has been borrowed from the bond market, its meaning in the swap market is distinct. In the bond market, these terms refer to the difference between the price of a security and its own par value. In the swap market, these terms refer to the difference in price between the two hypothetical securities involved in a swap. In a differential swap, the cash payment is both a premium (to the party that makes the payment) and a discount (to the party that receives the payment).

The valuation of even and differential swaps with GECA. The major procedural change that must be made when analyzing nonpar swaps is that we must determine the "proceeds" of the fixed-rate note sale. This step is not necessary in analyzing a par swap for which the proceeds are always par. In a nonpar swap, the proceeds of the sale of the hypothetical fixed-rate security are the value of the hypothetical floating-rate note received in exchange less any premium paid or plus any discount received. When solving for all-in-cost, the premium or discount is known, and the hypothetical floater must be valued to determine the fixed-rate payer's proceeds. Conversely, when determining the appropriate premium or discount, one must determine the value of both hypothetical securities.

Valuing the hypothetical floating-rate note. In interest-rate swap analysis, the hypothetical floating-rate note paying the index flat is considered to be at par on any of its payment dates. If at some point the index flat is not deemed to be an appropriate return in the market, the swap market will revalue the fixed security to reflect new conditions. Thus, the benchmark index-flat floater will remain at par on coupon dates.

Once a coupon rate is set, however, market variations of the appropriate maturity index can cause the hypothetical security to trade above or below par.[22] For example, in a generic swap, if three-month LIBOR is 9 percent at the reset but, one month later, two-month LIBOR is at 10 percent, the flat price of the floater will be worth less than par. To determine the full price of the floating-rate note between coupon payments, determine the present value of the next coupon, which has been previously set, plus par, which is the value of the floater on the next payment date. The discount rate used is the current market rate for the appropriate maturity of the index. In the example, the appropriate discount rate is 10 percent.

Determining all-in-cost of a nonpar swap. To determine the all-in-cost of a swap with a cash payment at settlement or with a nonpar floating-rate note, first the analytical fixed-bond flows paid versus the receipt of the generic index-flat note must be constructed using GECA (Steps 1, 2 and 3 of Figure 7). The proceeds of this hypothetical fixed-rate note are the value of the hypothetical floating-rate note plus any discount received or minus any premium paid by the fixed-rate payer. This is Step 7 of Figure 7. Then in Step 8, the all-in-cost is calculated by computing the internal rate of return of the fixed-bond flows.

For example, let us alter the base case example to include a payment of 0.6 percent of the notional principal amount to the floating-rate payer on the settlement date, and let us assume that the floating-rate note has a price of 99.6; all other terms of the base case remain the same. The analytical fixed-rate security (versus six-month LIBOR flat) is a seven-year bond paying 12.50 percent semiannually with a price of 99. The semiannual all-in-cost of this swap (equal to the yield on this hypothetical bond) is 12.72 percent.

Pricing secondary market or seasoned swaps with GECA. In secondary market or in seasoned-swap transactions, the terms of the fixed

---

[22] The appropriate maturity is the period from the settlement date to the next floating-rate reset date.

and floating payments have previously been negotiated. Current market levels determine the all-in-cost. The premium or discount is the unknown. The process of determining this payment is known as *pricing* a swap.

The procedure for pricing a swap is similar to that described for determining a swap's all-in-cost. Referring to Figure 7, Steps 1, 2, and 3 are performed as before to construct the analytical flows for the two hypothetical securities. At this point each of the two component securities is priced (Steps 4 and 5). The method for pricing the floating-rate note has been described. The fixed-rate note is priced using a conventional bond math approach discounting the analytical cash flows at the all-in-cost.

The difference between the prices of the hypothetical fixed-rate and floating-rate notes is the market price of the swap. If the floating security is worth more than the fixed security, then the fixed-rate payer would make a cash payment to the floating-rate payer when entering into the swap. In the same market situation, the fixed-rate payer would receive a cash payment if closing out the swap. Conversely, if the fixed security is worth more than the floating security, the floating-rate payer would make a cash payment to the fixed-rate payer when entering into the swap, or he would receive cash payment if closing out the swap. In addition to the cash payment, net accrued is also paid.

For example, suppose that the floating-rate note is worth 99 and the fixed-rate security is worth 95. The fixed-rate payer would receive a payment of four points (plus or minus the net accrued) if closing out the swap. In essence, the fixed-rate payer is repurchasing his fixed-rate security worth 95 with the floating-rate note that he holds that is worth 99. The excess of four points is returned.

CONCLUSION

As long as the interest-rate swap market operates as a negotiated over-the-counter market, swap structures will vary as widely as the counterparties themselves. In our approach to interest-rate swap mathematics and pricing, we do not intend to suggest that one structure is superior to another. Instead, we simply wish to establish a standard—the generic swap—against which the myriad varieties of swaps can be measured. We hope that the introduction of this standard, coupled with a fair and consistent framework for analysis of nongeneric swaps, will eliminate the uncertainty about interest rate swap mathematics. Ultimately, our goal is to increase understanding and encourage wider use of this valuable asset and liability management tool.

APPENDIX _____

This Appendix provides a technical description of how to price generic and nongeneric interest-rate swaps using standard bond pricing methodology.[1] These procedures are based upon the notion that an interest rate swap can be considered an exchange of a hypothetical fixed-income security for a hypothetical floating-rate note (see Figure 7 in the text). The Appendix will first discuss the pricing of the fixed side of the swap (including any adjustment flows required) and then describe the pricing of the floating side (which has been adjusted to the index flat). Each formula will be demonstrated through an example based upon the base case generic swap set forth in Figure 3. For simplicity, the Appendix assumes that the floating rate is based on a generic LIBOR index, with a spread introduced in the appropriate examples.

Discounting Methods

The pricing of the fixed and floating sides of a swap involves present value calculations. The discounting methods used are consistent with the pricing methods used in the corporate fixed-rate bond and floating-rate note markets, respectively. This means that the flows of a fixed-rate side of the swap, including any adjustment flows due to a spread under or over the floating index, are discounted scientifically on a 30/360 day-count basis. In contrast, the flows of the floating side, adjusted to have no spread, are discounted in a straight-line manner using the Actual/360 day-count basis in the case of private-sector indexes. Because the benchmark for quoting all-in-cost is the index flat, spreads under the index can be thought of as payments from the fixed-rate payer to the floating-rate payer. As such, these payments (the adjustment flows) should be discounted at the fixed-rate payer's all-in-cost. Only by using this convention can two swaps with the same all-in-cost (one with no spread and one with a spread under the index and a correspondingly lower fixed-rate coupon) truly be called equivalent in terms of yield.

Pricing the Hypothetical Fixed-Rate Security

The price of the fixed-rate side of a swap can be viewed as the sum of two components: (1) the present value or full price of a fixed-rate bond (the Fixed Bond) based on the fixed-rate payer's contractual payments and (2) the present value of those flows necessary to adjust the floating side to the generic standard if possible (the Adjustment Flows). The

---

[1] The Appendix discusses only the pricing methodology for swaps and not the computation of a swap's all-in-cost. All-in-cost is determined through an internal rate of return calculation. This calculation is usually an iterative procedure that prices the swap using trial values of all-in-cost until one results in the actual price.

discount rate for both present values is the swap's all-in-cost, and discounting is done using methods consistent with corporate fixed-rate bond pricing.

We begin by discussing the pricing of the Fixed Bond in a swap with semiannual fixed payments. For such a swap, the formula for the present value of the contractual fixed-rate swap payments plus the hypothetical principal repayment at maturity is:

$$\sum_{i=1}^{n} \frac{\dfrac{C}{2}}{\left(1 + \dfrac{AIC}{200}\right)^{P_i}} + \frac{100}{\left(1 + \dfrac{AIC}{200}\right)^{P_n}} \qquad \text{Equation I}$$

where

n = the number of fixed coupon payments from the settlement date to maturity,

C = the fixed coupon rate (expressed as a percentage),

AIC = the all-in-cost (expressed as a percentage), and

P_i = the number of whole and fractional fixed coupon periods from the settlement date to the ith fixed coupon payment date.

Using this formula to price the Fixed bond in the example for May 15, 1985 settlement, at an all-in-cost of 12.50%, we make the following calculations:

Present Value of the Fixed Bond =

$$\frac{\dfrac{12.50}{2}}{\left(1 + \dfrac{12.50}{200}\right)^{1}} + \frac{\dfrac{12.50}{2}}{\left(1 + \dfrac{12.50}{200}\right)^{2}} + \frac{\dfrac{12.50}{2}}{\left(1 + \dfrac{12.50}{200}\right)^{3}}$$

$$+ \cdots + \frac{\dfrac{12.50}{2}}{\left(1 + \dfrac{12.50}{200}\right)^{14}} + \frac{100}{\left(1 + \dfrac{12.50}{200}\right)^{14}} = 100$$

Equation I applies only to swaps that have no short or long first coupons. If the first fixed coupon is short or long and the remaining fixed payments are semiannual, the following formula is appropriate:

Present Value of the Fixed Bond =

$$\frac{\dfrac{C}{2} \times P_1}{\left(1 + \dfrac{AIC}{200}\right)^{P_1}} + \sum_{i=2}^{n} \frac{\dfrac{C}{2}}{\left(1 + \dfrac{AIC}{200}\right)^{P_i}} \qquad \text{Equation II}$$

$$+ \frac{100}{\left(1 + \dfrac{AIC}{200}\right)^{P_n}}$$

If the base case swap had an effective date of April 1, 1985, with a short first coupon payment on May 15, 1985, the price of the Fixed Bond for settlement on April 1, 1985, at an all-in-cost of 12.50 percent would be found as follows:

Present Value of the Fixed Bond =

$$\frac{\frac{12.50}{2} \times \frac{44}{180}}{\left(1 + \frac{12.50}{200}\right)^{\frac{44}{180}}} + \frac{\frac{12.50}{2}}{\left(1 + \frac{12.50}{200}\right)^{1 + \frac{44}{180}}}$$

$$+ \frac{\frac{12.50}{2}}{\left(1 + \frac{12.50}{200}\right)^{2 + \frac{44}{180}}} + \cdots + \frac{\frac{12.50}{2}}{\left(1 + \frac{12.50}{200}\right)^{14 + \frac{44}{180}}}$$

$$+ \frac{100}{\left(1 + \frac{12.50}{200}\right)^{14 + \frac{44}{180}}} = 100.034$$

For swaps in which the payment frequency is not semiannual, the following generalization of Equation II is used to price the Fixed Bond:

Present Value of the Fixed Bond =

$$\frac{\frac{C}{freq} \times P_1}{\left(1 + \frac{AIC_c}{(100 \times freq)}\right)^{P_1}} + \sum_{i=2}^{n} \frac{\frac{C}{freq}}{\left(1 + \frac{AIC_c}{(100 \times freq)}\right)^{P_i}} \quad \text{Equation III}$$

$$+ \frac{100}{\left(1 + \frac{AIC_c}{(100 \times freq)}\right)^{P_n}}$$

where freq =the number of fixed-rate payments per year, and
  AIC_c =the all-in-cost converted to the same compounding frequency as the number of fixed-rate payments per year (expressed as a percentage)

Under market convention, the all-in-cost is always quoted as a semiannual rate. To convert the all-in-cost to a rate with a compounding frequency consistent with the number of fixed coupon payments per year (as required in Equation III), use the following formula:

$$AIC_c = \left[\left(1 + \frac{AIC}{200}\right)^{\frac{2}{freq}} - 1\right] \times 100 \times freq \quad \text{Equation IV}$$

For the base case swap changed to have a coupon of 12.75 percent paid annually, the two steps in computing the price of the Fixed Bond for settlement on May 15, 1985, at an all-in-cost of 12.50 percent semiannual are the following:

First, the semiannual all-in-cost is converted to its annual equivalent using Equation 4:

$$\text{AIC}_c = \left[\left(1 + \frac{12.50}{200}\right)^{\frac{2}{1}} - 1\right] \times 100 \times 1 = 12.890625$$

Then the price of the Fixed Bond is computed using Equation III as follows:

Present Value of the Fixed Bond =

$$\frac{\dfrac{12.75}{1}}{\left(1 + \dfrac{12.890625}{(100 \times 1)}\right)^1} + \frac{\dfrac{12.75}{1}}{\left(1 + \dfrac{12.890625}{(100 \times 1)}\right)^2}$$

$$+ \ldots + \frac{\dfrac{12.75}{1}}{\left(1 + \dfrac{12.890625}{(100 \times 1)}\right)^7}$$

$$+ \quad \frac{100}{\left(1 + \dfrac{12.890625}{(100 \times 1)}\right)^7} = 99.376$$

If the swap has a spread under or over the index, we must determine the present value of the Adjustment Flows needed to alter the floating side to the index flat. These flows correspond to the spread that accrues during each floating payment period. Since the spred accrues on the same basis as the LIBOR index (Axtual/360), the actual number of days in the payment period determines the size of each Adjustment Flow. Since the adjustment for the spread is considered part of the hypothetical fixed security, the discount rate for the Adjustment Flows is the swap's all-in-cost. These ideas are reflected in the following formula for computing the present value of the Adjustment Flows:

Present Value of the Adjustment Flows =

$$\sum_{i=1}^{n} \frac{S \times \dfrac{D_i}{360}}{\left(1 + \dfrac{\text{AIC}_c}{(100 \times \text{freq})}\right)^{P_i}} \qquad \text{Equation V}$$

where n = the number of floating coupon payments from the settlement date to maturity,

S = the spread under the index (expressed as a percentage),

D_i = the actual number of days of interest accrual for the ith floating payment,

freq = the number of floating-rate payments per year,

AIC_c = the all-in-cost converted to the same compounding frequency as the number of floating-rate payments per year
(expressed as a percentage), and

P_i = the number of whole and fractional floating coupon periods
from the settlement date to the ith floating coupon payment
date.

If the base case swap had a spread of 25 basis points under the six-
month LIBOR index and was priced for settlement on May 15, 1985, at
an all-in-cost of 12.50 percent, the formulas for calculating the present
value of the Adjustment Flows (to convert the floating side to six-month
LIBOR flat) would be applied as follows:

Present Value of the Adjustment Flows =

$$
\frac{0.25 \times \dfrac{184}{360}}{\left(1 + \dfrac{12.50}{(100 \times 2)}\right)^1} + \frac{0.25 \times \dfrac{181}{360}}{\left(1 + \dfrac{12.50}{(100 \times 2)}\right)^2}
$$

$$
+ \frac{0.25 \times \dfrac{184}{360}}{\left(1 + \dfrac{12.50}{(100 \times 2)}\right)^3} + \ldots + \frac{0.25 \times \dfrac{182}{360}}{\left(1 + \dfrac{12.50}{(100 \times 2)}\right)^{14}} = 1.161
$$

Because the cash flows of the hypothetical fixed-income security are
the combination of the cash flows of the Fixed Bond and the Adjustment
Flows, the full price of the fixed side is simply calculated as follows:

Full Price of the Fixed Side =

Present Value of the Fixed Bond +

Present Value of the Adjustment Flows

When computing the price of a swap being closed out in the secondary market, the settlement date of the transaction will often not be the
beginning of a fixed or floating coupon period. The transaction, therefore, will involve accrued interest. A calculation of the accrued interest
on the fixed side must include accrued interest on the Adjustment Flows

to be consistent with our methodology. To compute the portion of the full price that is accrued interest, the following formulas are used:

$$\text{Accrued Interest on the Fixed Bond} = \frac{D_F}{360} \times C \quad \text{Equation VI}$$

$$\text{Accrued Interest on the Adjustment Flows} = \frac{D_A}{360} \times S \quad \text{Equation VII}$$

where D_F = the number of days (computed on a 30/360 basis) from the previous fixed payment[2] to the settlement date of the secondary market transaction,

D_A = the number of days (computed on an Actual/360 basis) from the previous floating payment date to the settlement date of the secondary market transaction,

C = the fixed coupon rate (expressed as a percentage),

S = the spread under the index (expressed as a percentage).

If the base case swap with a spread of 25 basis points under the index were priced for a closeout in the secondary market with a settlement date of June 1, 1985, at an all-in-cost of 12.75 percent, the full price and accrued interest for the fixed side would be found by applying Equations III, V, VI and VII as follows:

Present Value of the Fixed Bond =

$$\frac{\dfrac{12.50}{2}}{\left(1 + \dfrac{12.75}{200}\right)^{\frac{164}{180}}} + \frac{\dfrac{12.50}{2}}{\left(1 + \dfrac{12.75}{200}\right)^{1 + \frac{164}{180}}}$$

$$+ \frac{\dfrac{12.50}{2}}{\left(1 + \dfrac{12.75}{200}\right)^{2 + \frac{164}{180}}} + \ldots +$$

$$\frac{\dfrac{12.50}{2}}{\left(1 + \dfrac{12.75}{200}\right)^{13 + \frac{164}{180}}} + \frac{100}{\left(1 + \dfrac{12.75}{200}\right)^{13 + \frac{164}{180}}} = 99.409$$

---

[2] In this case (as well as in all cases that follow), if no payment has yet occurred, the number of days is counted from the swap's original effective date to the settlement date of this secondary market transaction.

Present Value of the Adjustment Flows =

$$\frac{0.25 \times \dfrac{184}{360}}{\left(1 + \dfrac{12.75}{(100 \times 2)}\right)^{\frac{164}{180}}} + \frac{0.25 \times \dfrac{181}{360}}{\left(1 + \dfrac{12.75}{(100 \times 2)}\right)^{1 + \frac{164}{180}}}$$

$$+ \frac{0.25 \times \dfrac{184}{360}}{\left(1 + \dfrac{12.75}{(100 \times 2)}\right)^{2 + \frac{164}{180}}} + \ldots +$$

$$\frac{0.25 \times \dfrac{182}{360}}{\left(1 + \dfrac{12.75}{(100 \times 2)}\right)^{13 + \frac{164}{180}}} = 1.159$$

Full Price of the Fixed Side = 99.409 + 1.159 = 100.568

Accrued Interest of the Fixed Bond = $\dfrac{16}{360} \times 12.50 = 0.566$

Accrued Interest of the Adjustment Flows = $\dfrac{17}{360} \times 0.25 = 0.012$

Total Accrued Interest of the Fixed Side = 0.556 + 0.012 = 0.568

Pricing the Hypothetical Floating-Rate Note

To price the floating-rate side of a swap, we use the discounting conventions for floating-rate notes. Since the floating-rate note is assumed to have a value of par at the next payment date, the price of the floating-rate side is the present value of the next payment plus par. The discount rate used to calculate the present value should be the current market rate of the appropriate maturity index for the period from the settlement date to the next floating payment date. For example, consider a swap with a floating side that resets and pays quarterly and floats off three-month LIBOR. When priced with two months to the next floating payment, the discount rate should be the current two-month LIBOR rate. The formula for the full price of the floating-rate side, adjusted to be the index flat, is:

$$\text{Present Value of the Floating Side} = \frac{100 + ER \times \dfrac{D_{PN}}{360}}{1 + \dfrac{CR}{100} \times \dfrac{D_{SN}}{360}} \qquad \text{Equation VIII}$$

where ER = the current rate in effect for the next floating coupon payment (expressed as a percentage),

D_{PN} = the actual number of days from the previous floating payment date to the next floating payment date,

CR = the current market rate of the index for the period from the settlement date to the next floating payment date (expressed as a percentage),

D_{SN} = the actual number of days from the settlement date to the next floating payment date.

The accrued interest portion of the full price of the floating side can be calculated using the following formula:

$$\text{Accrued Interest on the Floating Side} = \frac{ER \times (D_{PN} - D_{SN})}{360}$$

Equation IX

To price the floating-rate side of the base case swap with a settlement date of June 1, 1985, assuming the current floating rate in effect was set at 8.9375 percent on May 15, 1985, and that the current market rate for five and one-half month LIBOR is 9.00 percent, the aforementioned formulas would be applied as follows:

Full Price of the Floating Side =

$$\frac{100 + \left(8.9375 \times \frac{184}{360}\right)}{1 + \left(\frac{9.00}{100} \times \frac{167}{360}\right)} = 100.377$$

Accrued Interest on Floating Side =

$$8.9375 \times \frac{(184 - 167)}{360} = 0.422$$

Pricing the Swap

After calculating the present values of the fixed and floating sides, we can calculate the current market price of the entire swap. Recall that we have described a swap as an exchange of two securities: a hypothetical fixed-rate note (including analytical adjustment flows) and a hypothetical floating-rate note (adjusted to the index flat). Under this notion, on closing out a swap, each party will buy back the security originally sold and sell back the other party's security originally purchased. The price of the swap will be the difference in the prices of these two securities.

Expressed as a formula, the swap's full price paid by the fixed-rate payer on closing out the swap is:

Full Price Paid by the Fixed-Rate Payer =

Full Price of the Fixed Side − Full Price of the Floating Side

If this full price is negative, the cash payment is made by the floating-rate payer. The portion of the full price that is accounted for as accrued interest is given by the formula:

Net Accrued Interest Paid by the Fixed-Rate Payer =

Accrued Interest on the Fixed Side −

Accrued Interest on the Floating Side

If this net accrued interest is negative, the floating-rate payer has accrued a larger interest liability than the fixed-rate payer.

Consider again the base case swap with a spread of 25 basis points under six-month LIBOR and an original floating rate set at 8.9375 percent. To close out this swap on June 1, 1985, at an all-in-cost of 12.50 percent and a current market five and one-half month LIBOR rate of 9.00 percent, these equations show that the fixed-rate payer would pay the floating-rate payer 0.191 percent of the notional principal amount, of which 0.146 is net accrued interest. The calculations would be as follows:

Full Price Paid by the Fixed-Rate Payer = 100.568 − 100.377

$$= 0.191$$

Net Accrued Interest Paid by the Fixed-Rate Payer = 0.568 − 0.422

$$= 0.146$$

—————————— Appendix ——————————

Fixed Income Indexes

Arthur Williams III, C.F.A.
Managing Director
Simms Capital Management, Ltd.

Noreen M. Conwell
Assistant Vice President—Pension Fund Investments
Merrill Lynch, Pierce, Fenner & Smith, Inc.

INTRODUCTION

As investors become increasingly interested in analyzing their fixed income investments, the need for appropriate benchmarks against which to measure portfolios also grows. This trend has created the need for more accurate and more specific fixed income indexes to measure fixed income investments. Fortunately, the marketplace has recognized this need and has developed a large number of indexes for use by fixed income investors and analysts. Most of these indexes are listed in Exhibits 1 through 9 together with their most important characteristics.[1]

The development of an index to measure a phenomenon requires deciding what is to be measured, how each component is to be weighted

---

[1] Further information regarding some of the indexes may be obtained from the following representatives:

Carol M. Havdala, Fixed Income Analyst, Merrill Lynch, Pierce, Fenner & Smith, Inc., (212) 637-8369.

Henry Shilling, Director of Marketing, Lipper Analytical Securities Corp., (212) 269-4080.

George P. Parthemos, Senior Vice President and Director, Fixed Income Research, Shearson Lehman Brothers Inc., (212) 558-1500.

Ronald Ryan, Ryan Financial Strategy Group, (617) 491-3465.

Elliot Shurgin, Assistant Manager, Statistical Research Department, Standard & Poor's Corporation, (212) 248-3460.

Earl Stephens, Moody's Investors Service, Inc., (212) 553-0495.

Statistical Section, Barron's National Business and Financial Weekly, (413) 592-7761.

(equally or by some other method), and the statistical technique to be applied to the weighted data. For fixed income investments, this simple-sounding process is extremely complex. The problems in establishing bond indexes are the following:

1. It is difficult to find accurate and consistent information as to the prices of bonds at a point in time. Whereas most of the stocks in which institutional investors invest are traded on stock exchanges, bonds are traded over-the-counter, and hence it is difficult to establish the timing and price of transactions.
2. Bonds change characteristics as time passes. For instance, a 20-year bond today is a 19-year bond a year from today, and 19-year bonds behave somewhat differently from 20-year bonds.
3. The transition of bonds from one category to another creates the need to add and subtract bonds from categories.
4. Newly issued bonds being added to an index have different yield levels from existing bonds and thus perform slightly differently.

TYPES OF INDEXES

There are at least three types of indexes that might be of interest to investors: those relating to price, yield, and total return. Price indexes measure only the prices of bonds; yield indexes measure yield-to-maturity (although they could also measure current return); and total-return indexes show the return an investor would have achieved in a certain type bond over a given period through a combination of price change, coupon interest, and interest on interest. The total-return index, which is more comprehensive than the others, breaks out the return attributable to the three major factors impacting bonds and totals them to provide a true rate of return based on the assumption as to reinvestment rate.

MEASURING RISK OF INDEXES

Increasingly, investors are concerned not only with return but also with the risk taken in achieving that return. This has created the need to measure the riskiness of portfolios and indexes. A number of methods have been established for this purpose. Chapter 37 discusses how the risk in fixed income portfolios can be measured. Since bond indexes are really just specific portfolios, these techniques can be applied to indexes as well.

EXHIBIT 1 Corporate Bond Indexes

Index Name	Number of Securities	Total MV,PV (billions of dollars)	Securities Included	Type (Yield, Total Return, etc.)	Weighting	Calculation	Period and Base Amount	YTM or Coupon and Period	Number of Years to Maturity	Beginning Date of Index	Source of Bond Prices	Historical Information and Frequency
Salomon Brothers High-Grade LT AAA–AA	845	PV = $82.58	AAA–AA	Total return	Par value	Arithmetic	1978 = 100	y = 15.45% 11/1/81	23 years	1/1/69	Salomon trading desks	1969 monthly
Salomon Brothers LT A		PV = $58.00	A	Total return	Par value	Arithmetic	1978 = 100	c = 8.92 11/1/81	22 years	1/1/78	Salomon trading desks	1969 monthly
Salomon Brothers High-Grade LT AAA–AA–A		PV = $140.00	AAA–AA–A	Total return	Par value	Arithmetic	1978 = 100	c = 8.648 11/1/81	23 years	1/1/78	Salomon trading desks	1969 monthly
Barron's Best grade bonds	10	N/A	Aaa	YTM	Equally	Bond value tables	N/A	y = 13% 11/12/81 c = 5¼% 11/12/81	15 years 11/12/81	1/32	The Wall Street Journal	No
Barron's Intermediate grade bonds	10	N/A	Baa	YTM	Equally	Bond value tables	N/A	y = 14½% 11/12/81 c = 7⅜% 11/12/81	20 years 11/12/81	7/76	The Wall Street Journal	No
Dow Jones 20 bonds average	20	N/A	Aaa	YTM	Equally	Bond value tables	N/A	y = 14⅛% 11/12/81 c = 7½% 11/12/81	20 years 11/12/81	7/76	The Wall Street Journal	No

Index		Rating		Weighting	Method		Current level	Maturity	Base date	Source	Reinvestment
Dow Jones 10 Industrial bonds average	10	N/A	Aaa	YTM	Equally	Bond value tables	N/A	$y = 13\frac{3}{4}\%$ 11/12/81 $c = 6\frac{3}{4}\%$ 11/12/81	12 years 11/21/81	4/15	*The Wall Street Journal*	No
Dow Jones 10 Public utility bonds average	10	N/A	Aaa	YTM	Equally	Bond value tables	N/A	$y = 14\frac{1}{2}\%$ 11/12/81 $c = 8\frac{3}{8}\%$ 11/12/81	20 years 11/12/81	4/15	*The Wall Street Journal*	No
Standard & Poor's Corp. composite bond yield Average–AA	8-AA Ind. 8-AA Util. 16	N/A	AA	YTM	Equally	Arithmetic	N/A	10.98 6/12/85	10–30 years 6/12/85	1/37	Salomon Brothers	1971– weekly; 1937– monthly
Standard & Poor's Corp. composite bond yield Average–A	8-A Ind. 8-AA Util. 16	N/A	A	YTM	Equally	Arithmetic	N/A	$y = 11.11\%$ 6/28/85	15–30 years 6/12/85	1/37	Salomon Brothers	1971– weekly; 1937– monthly
Standard & Poor's Corp. composite bond yield Average–BBB	8-BBB Ind. 8-BBB Util. 15	N/A	BBB	YTM	Equally	Arithmetic	N/A	$y = 11.68\%$ 6/12/85	10–30 years 6/12/85	1/37	Salomon Brothers	1971– weekly; 1937– monthly
Standard & Poor's Industrial bond yield Average–AAA	5-Inds AAA 8-Util AAA 16	N/A	AAA	YTM	Equally	Arithmetic	N/A	$y = 10.49\%$ 6/12/85	15–20 years 6/12/85	1/37	Salomon Brothers	1971– weekly; 1900– monthly

EXHIBIT 1 (continued)

Index Name	Number of Securities	Total MV,PV (billions of dollars)	Securities Included	Type (Yield, Total Return, etc.)	Weighting	Calculation	Period and Base Amount	YTM or Coupon and Period	Number of Years to Maturity	Beginning Date of Index	Source of Bond Prices	Historical Information and Frequency
Standard & Poor's Industrial bond yield Average-AA	8-Inds AA	N/A	AA	YTM	Equally	Arithmetic	N/A	y = 11.06% 6/12/85	15–30 years 6/12/85	1/37	Salomon Brothers	1971– weekly; 1900– monthly
Standard & Poor's Industrial bond yield Average-A	7-Ind A	N/A	A	YTM	Equally	Arithmetic	N/A	y = 11.06% 6/12/85	15–20 years 6/12/85	1/37	Salomon Brothers	1971– weekly; 1900– monthly
Standard & Poor's Industrial bond yield Average-BBB	7-Ind BBB	N/A	BBB	YTM	Equally	Arithmetic	N/A	y = 11.70% 6/12/85	10–20 years 6/12/85	1/37	Salomon Brothers	1971– weekly; 1900– monthly
Shearson Lehman Brothers Corp. bond index	4,575.5	283.545	BBB,A, AA, AAA	Total return	Market value	Arithmetic	N/A	y = 11.28% 5/85	1 year +	12/72	Shearson Lehman Brothers	12/72– monthly
Shearson Lehman Brothers Intermediate corp. bond index	1,884.0	112.161	BBB,A, AA, AAA	Total return	Market value	Arithmetic	N/A	y = 10.85% 5/85	1–9.99 years	12/72	Shearson Lehman Brothers	12/72– monthly

Index			Rating	Return	Value	Mean		Yield	Maturity		Source	Period
Shearson Lehman Brothers Long-term corp. bond index	2,691.5	171.383	BBB,A, AA, AAA	Total return	Market value	Arithmetic	N/A	y = 11.57% 5/85	10 years +	12/72	Shearson Lehman Brothers	12/72– monthly
Shearson Lehman Brothers Indus-trial bond index	982.5	82.546	BBB,A, AA, AAA	Total return	Market value	Arithmetic	N/A	y = 11.35% 5/85	1 year +	12/72	Shearson Lehman Brothers	12/72– monthly
Shearson Lehman Brothers Utility bond index	2,728.5	129.445	BBB,A, AA, AAA	Total return	Market value	Arithmetic	N/A	y = 11.53% 5/85	1 year +	12/72	Shearson Lehman Brothers	12/72 monthly
Shearson Lehman Brothers Finance bond index	864.5	71.553	BBB,A, AA, AAA	Total return	Market value	Arithmetic	N/A	y = 10.76% 5/85	1 year +	12/72	Shearson Lehman Brothers	12/72– monthly
Shearson Lehman Brothers Aaa bond index	822	881.257	AAA	Total return	Market value	Arithmetic	N/A	y = 9.64% 5/85	1 year +	12/72	Shearson Lehman Brothers	12/72– monthly
Shearson Lehman Brothers Aa bond index	1,409.5	106.474	AA	Total return	Market value	Arithmetic	N/A	y = 11.02% 5/85	1 year +	12/72	Shearson Lehman Brothers	12/72– monthly
Lehman Brothers Kuhn Loeb A bond index	1,950.0	111.335	A+	Total return	Market value	Arithmetic	N/A	y = 11.26% 5/85	1 year +	12/72	Shearson Lehman Brothers	12/72– monthly
Lehman Brothers Kuhn Loeb Baa bond index	991.0	51.939	BBB+	Total return	Market value	Arithmetic	N/A	y = 12.03% 5/85	1 year +	12/72	Shearson Lehman	12/72– monthly

EXHIBIT 1 (continued)

Index Name	Number of Securities	Total MV,PV (billions of dollars)	Securities Included	Type (Yield, Total Return, etc.)	Weighting	Calculation	Period and Base Amount	YTM or Coupon and Period	Number of Years to Maturity	Beginning Date of Index	Source of Bond Prices	Historical Information and Frequency
Moody's Aaa Industrial bond average	7	N/A	Aaa	YTM	N/A	Arithmetic	N/A	$c = 9\tfrac{3}{8}\%$	20 years 2 mos.	1918	Newspaper, security dealers and other sources	1918–monthly
Moody's Aa Industrial bond average	10	N/A	Aa	YTM	N/A	Arithmetic	N/A	$c = 9\tfrac{5}{8}\%$	22 years 5 mos.	1918	Newspaper security dealers and other sources	1918–monthly
Moody's A Industrial bond average	10	N/A	A	YTM	N/A	Arithmetic	N/A	$c = 11\tfrac{7}{8}\%$	23 years 8 mos.	1918	Newspaper security dealers and other sources	1918–monthly
Moody's Baa Industrial bond average	10	N/A	Baa	YTM	N/A	Arithmetic	N/A	$c = 10\tfrac{1}{4}\%$	20 years 7 mos.	1918	Newspaper security dealers and other sources	1918–monthly

Moody's Industrial average	37	N/A	Aaa, Aa, A, Baa	YTM	N/A	Arithmetic	N/A	c = 10¼%	21 years 7 mos.	1918	Newspaper security dealers and other sources	1918– monthly
Moody's Aaa Public utility average	10	N/A	Aaa	YTM	N/A	Arithmetic	N/A	c = 8⅝%	21 years 9 mos.	1918	Newspaper security dealers and other sources	1918– monthly
Moody's Aa Public utility average	10	N/A	Aa	YTM	N/A	Arithmetic	N/A	c = 9⅝%	23 years 9 mos.	1918	Newspaper security dealers and other sources	1918– monthly
Moody's A Public utility average	10	N/A	A	YTM	N/A	Arithmetic	N/A	c = 10⅝%	24 years 5 mos.	1918	Newspaper security dealers and other sources	1918– monthly
Moody's Baa Public utility average	10	N/A	Baa	YTM	N/A	Arithmetic	N/A	c = 10¾%	24 years 2 mos.	1918	Newspaper security dealers and other sources	1918– monthly
Moody's Public Utility average	40	N/A	Aaa, Aa, A, Baa	YTM	N/A	Arithmetic	N/A	c = 9⅞%	23 years 5 mos.	1918	Newspaper security dealers and other sources	1918– monthly

EXHIBIT 1 *(continued)*

Index Name	Number of Securities	Total MV,PV (billions of dollars)	Securities Included	Type (Yield, Total Return, etc.)	Weighting	Calculation	Period and Base Amount	YTM or Coupon and Period	Number of Years to Maturity	Beginning Date of Index	Source of Bond Prices	Historical Information and Frequency
Moody's Aa Railroad bond average	5	N/A	Aa	YTM	N/A	Arithmetic	N/A	$c = 8\frac{3}{8}\%$	16 years 3 mos.	1918	Newspaper security dealers and other sources	1918– monthly
Moody's A Railroad bond average	5	N/A	A	YTM	N/A	Arithmetic	N/A	$c = 6\%$	17 years 1 month	1918	Newspaper security dealers and other sources	1918– monthly
Moody's Baa Railroad bond average	4	N/A	Baa	YTM	N/A	Arithmetic	N/A	$c = 6\frac{5}{8}\%$	28 years 5 mos.	1918	Newspaper security dealers and other sources	1918– monthly
Moody's Railroad bond average	14	N/A	Aa, A, Baa	YTM	N/A	Arithmetic	N/A	$c = 7\%$	22 years	1918	Newspaper security dealers and other sources	1918– monthly

Moody's Aaa Corp. composite	17	N/A	Aaa utilities and industrials	YTM	N/A	Arithmetic	N/A	c = 9%	21 years 1 month	1918	Newspaper security dealers and other sources	1918– monthly
Moody's Aa Corp. composite	20	N/A	Aa utilities and industrials	YTM	N/A	Arithmetic	N/A	c = 9⅝%	23 years 1 month	1918	Newspaper security dealers and other sources	1918– monthly
Moody's A Corp. composite	20	N/A	A utilities and industrials	YTM	N/A	Arithmetic	N/A	c = 11¼%	24 years	1918	Newspaper security dealers and other sources	1918– monthly
Moody's Baa Corp. composite	20	N/A	Baa utilities and industrials	YTM	N/A	Arithmetic	N/A	c = 10½%	22 years 4 mos.	1918	Newspaper security dealers and other sources	1918– monthly
Moody's Corp. average composite	77	N/A	Aaa, A, Baa utilities and industrials	YTM	N/A	Arithmetic	N/A	c = 10⅛%	22 years 6 mos.	1918	Newspaper security dealers and other sources	1918– monthly

EXHIBIT 1 (continued)

Index Name	Number of Securities	Total MV,PV (billions of dollars)	Securities Included	Type (Yield, Total Return, etc.)	Weighting	Calculation	Period and Base Amount	YTM or Coupon and Period	Number of Years to Maturity	Beginning Date of Index	Source of Bond Prices	Historical Information and Frequency
Merrill Lynch (C8A0) Long term (15 years+)	1741	MV = 131.6 PV = 152.6	BBB/ AAA	Total return	Market value	Arithmetic	12/31/72 = 100	c = 9.86% y = 11.60% 5/85	23.25 5/85	12/31/72	Merrill Lynch Bond Pricing	1973
Merrill Lynch (C8B0) Long term (15 years+), high quality	687	MV = 59.3 PV = 69.3	AA/AAA	Total return	Market value	Arithmetic	12/31/72 = 100	c = 9.56% y = 11.34% 5/85	23.92 5/85	12/31/72	Merrill Lynch Bond Pricing	1973
Merrill Lynch (C8H0) Long term (15 years+), high quality utilities	487	MV = 35.8 PV = 42.5	AA/AAA	Total return	Market value	Arithmetic	12/31/72 = 100	c = 9.39% y = 11.34% 5/85	25.58 5/85	12/31/72	Merrill Lynch Bond Pricing	1973
Merrill Lynch (C8H3) Long term (15 years+), high quality utilities-coupons 4–5.99 percent	35	MV = 1.1 PV = 2.0	AAA/ AAA	Total return	Market value	Arithmetic	12/31/72 = 100	c = 4.86 y = 2.0% 5/85	18.08 5/85	12/31/72	Merrill Lynch Bond Pricing	1973

117	Merrill Lynch (C8H4) Long term (15 years+), high quality utilities-coupons 6–7.99 percent	MV = 6.6 PV = 9.4	AA/AAA	Total return	Market value	Arithmetic	12/31/72 = 100	c = 7.32% y = 11.07% 5/85	21.50 5/85	12/31/72	Merrill Lynch Bond Pricing	1973
231	Merrill Lynch (C8H5) Long term (15 years+), high quality utilities-coupons 8–9.99 percent	MV = 15.5 PV = 19.3	AA/AAA	Total return	Market value	Arithmetic	12/31/72 = 100	c = 8.72% y = 11.1% 5/85	23.83 5/85	12/31/72	Merrill Lynch Bond Pricing	1973
37	Merrill Lynch (C8H6) Long term (15 years+), high quality utilities-coupons 10–11.99 percent	MV = 3.8 PV = 3.9	AA/AAA	Total return	Market value	Arithmetic	9/30/74 100	c = 11.15% y = 11.41% 5/85	31.08 5/85	9/30/74	Merrill Lynch Bond Pricing	1974
98	Merrill Lynch (C8E0) Long term (15 years+), high quality indus-trials	MV = 15.3 PV = 17.1	AA/AAA	Total return	Market value	Arithmetic	12/31/72 = 100	c = 10.00% y = 11.32% 5/85	20.5 5/85	12/31/72	Merrill Lynch Bond Pricing	1973

EXHIBIT 1 *(continued)*

Index Name	Number of Securities	Total MV,PV (billions of dollars)	Securities Included	Type (Yield, Total Return, etc.)	Weighting	Calculation	Period and Base Amount	YTM or Coupon and Period	Number of Years to Maturity	Beginning Date of Index	Source of Bond Prices	Historical Information and Frequency
Merrill Lynch (C8E4) Long term (15 years+), high quality industrials-coupons 6–7.99 percent	22	MV = 1.9 PV = 2.8	AA/AAA	Total return	Market value	Arithmetic	12/31/72 = 100	c = 7.10% y = 10.99% 5/85	18.42 5/85	12/31/72	Merrill Lynch Bond Pricing	1973
Merrill Lynch (C8E5) Long term (15 years+), high quality industrials-coupons 8–9.99 percent	38	MV = 5.7 PV = 6.9	AA/AAA	Total return	Market value	Arithmetic	12/31/72 = 100	c = 8.71% y = 11.04% 5/85	19.08 5/85	12/31/72	Merrill Lynch Bond Pricing	1973
Merrill Lynch (C8E6) Long term (15 years+), high-quality industrials-coupons 10–11.99 percent	20	MV = 2.8 PV = 2.9	AA/AAA	Total return	Market value	Arithmetic	12/31/72 = 100	c = 11.15% y = 11.32%	26.5 5/85	12/31/72	Merrill Lynch Bond Pricing	1973

Merrill Lynch index												
Merrill Lynch (C8K9) Long term (15 years+), high-quality finance coupons 16.0+ percent	3	MV = 147.8 PV = 131.4	AA/AAA	Total return	Market value	Arithmetic	12/31/72 = 100	c = 18.07% y = 15.93%	18.0 5/85	12/31/72	Merrill Lynch Bond Pricing	1973
Merrill Lynch (C8K4) long term (15 years+) high-quality finance-coupons 6–7.99 percent	2	MV = 247.3 PV = 431.8	AA/AAA	Total return	Market value	Arithmetic	12/31/72 = 100	c = 6.10% y = 11.20%	26.4 5/85	12/31/72	Merrill Lynch Bond Pricing	1973
Merrill Lynch (C8K5) Long term (15 years+), high-quality finance-coupons 8–9.99 percent	19	MV = 2.2 PV = 2.7	AA/AAA	Total return	Market value	Arithmetic	12/31/72 = 100	c = 8.72% y = 11.10% 5/85	19.1 5/85	12/31/72	Merrill Lynch Bond Pricing	1973
Merrill Lynch (C8K6) Long term (15 years+), high-quality finance-coupons 10–11.99 percent	12	MV = 1.2 PV =	AA/AAA	Total return	Market value	Arithmetic	9/30/74 = 100	c = 11.48% y = 11.32% 5/85	21.1 5/85	9/30/74	Merrill Lynch Bond Pricing	1973

EXHIBIT 1 (continued)

Index Name	Number of Securities	Total MV,PV (billions of dollars)	Securities Included	Type (Yield, Total Return, etc.)	Weighting	Calculation	Period and Base Amount	YTM or Coupon and Period	Number of Years to Maturity	Beginning Date of Index	Source of Bond Prices	Historical Information and Frequency
Merrill Lynch (C8K7) Long term (15 years+) high-quality finance-coupons 12–13.99 percent	15	MV = 859.2 PV = 827.2	AA/AAA	Total return	Market value	Arithmetic	1/31/83 = 100	c = 12.3% y = 11.8% 5/85	22 5/85	1/31/83	Merrill Lynch Bond Pricing	1973
Merrill Lynch (C8K8) Long term (15 years+) high-quality finance-coupons 14–15.99 percent	3	MV = 224.3 PV = 195.3	AA/AAA	Total return	Market value	Arithmetic	7/29/83 = 100	c = 15.1% y = 13.1% 5/85	23 5/85	1/31/83	Merrill Lynch Bond Pricing	1973
Merrill Lynch (C8I0) Long term (15 years+), medium-quality utilities	773	MV = 47.5 PV = 53.8	A/BBB	Total return	Market value	Arithmetic	12/31/72 = 100	c = 10.39% y = 11.88%	23.5 5/85	12/31/72	Merrill Lynch Bond Pricing	1973

Index	N	MV/PV	Rating	Return	Base	Coupon/Yield	Value	Date	Source	Year
Merrill Lynch (C813) Long term (15 years+), medium-quality utilities-coupons 4–5.99 percent	5	MV = .2 PV = .4	BBB/A	Total return Market value Arithmetic	12/31/72 = 100	c = 5.56% y = 11.06% 5/85	20.00 5/85	12/31/72	Merrill Lynch Bond Pricing	1973
Merrill Lynch (C814) Long term (15 years+), medium-quality utilities-coupons 6–7.99 percent	154	MV = 5.8 PV = 8.3	A/BBB	Total return Market value Arithmetic	12/31/72 = 100	c = 7.49% y = 11.45% 5/85	18.75 5/85	12/31/72	Merrill Lynch Bond Pricing	1973
Merrill Lynch (C815) Long term (15 years+), medium-quality utilities-coupons 8–9.99 percent	341	MV = 18.0 PV = 22.7	A/BBB	Total return Market value Arithmetic	12/31/72 = 100	c = 8.88% y = 11.53% 5/85	23.58 5/85	12/31/72	Merrill Lynch Bond Pricing	1973
Merrill Lynch (C816) Long term (15 years+), medium-quality utilities-coupons 10–11.99 percent	86	MV = 5.3 PV = 5.7	A/BBB	Total return Market value Arithmetic	12/31/72 = 100	c = 10.79% y = 11.75% 5/85	22.75 5/85	12/31/72	Merrill Lynch Bond Pricing	1973

EXHIBIT 1 (continued)

Index Name	Number of Securities	Total MV,PV (billions of dollars)	Securities Included	Type (Yield, Total Return, etc.)	Weighting	Calculation	Period and Base Amount	YTM or Coupon and Period	Number of Years to Maturity	Beginning Date of Index	Source of Bond Prices	Historical Information and Frequency
Merrill Lynch (C8F0) Long term (15 years+), medium-quality industrials	222	MV = 21.2 PV = 24.9	BBB/A	Total return	Market value	Arithmetic	12/31/72 = 100	c = 9.759% y = 11.745% 5/85	23.58 5/85	12/31/72	Merrill Lynch Bond Pricing	1973
Merrill Lynch (C8F4) Long term (15 years+), medium-quality industrials- coupons 6–7.99 percent	40	MV = 3.4 PV = 5.3	BBB/A	Total return	Market value	Arithmetic	12/31/72 = 100	c = 6.93% y = 11.64% 5/85	23.58 5/85	12/31/72	Merrill Lynch Bond Pricing	1973
Merrill Lynch (C8F5) Long term (15 years+), medium-quality industrials- coupons 8– 9.999 percent	96	MV = 7.7 PV = 9.6	BBB/A	Total return	Market value	Arithmetic	12/31/72 = 100	c = 8.866% y = 11.601% 5/85	21.58 5/85	12/31/72	Merrill Lynch Bond pricing	1973

Description	No.		Rating	Total return	Market value	Arithmetic		Coupon/Yield		12/31/72	Source	Year
Merrill Lynch (C8F6) Long term (15 years+), medium-quality industrials-coupons 10–11.99 percent	34	MV = 2.5 PV = 3.0	BBB/A	Total return	Market value	Arithmetic	12/31/72 = 100	c = 11.068% y = 11.694% 5/85	23.25 5/85	12/31/72	Merrill Lynch Bond Pricing	1973
Merrill Lynch (C8L0) Long term (15 years+), medium-quality finance	33	MV = 2.5 PV = 3.0	BBB/A	Total return	Market value	Arithmetic	12/31/72 = 100	c = 9.03% y = 11.47% 5/85	19.92 5/85	12/31/72	Merrill Lynch Bond Pricing	1973
Merrill Lynch (C8L4) Long term (15 years+), medium-quality finance-coupons 6–7.99 percent	5	MV = .4 PV = .6	BBB/A	Total return	Market value	Arithmetic	12/31/72 = 100	c = 6.40% y = 11.45% 5/85	21.42 5/85	12/31/72	Merrill Lynch Bond Pricing	1973
Merrill Lynch (C8L5) Long term (15 years+), medium-quality finance-coupons 8–9.99 percent	20	MV = 1.6 PV = 1.9	BBB/A	Total return	Market value	Arithmetic	12/31/72 = 100	c = 9.01% y = 11.34% 5/85	17.2 5/85	12/31/72	Merrill Lynch Bond Pricing	1973

EXHIBIT 1 *(continued)*

Index Name	Number of Securities	Total MV, PV (billions of dollars)	Securities Included	Type (Yield, Total Return, etc.)	Weighting	Calculation	Period and Base Amount	YTM or Coupon and Period	Number of Years to Maturity	Beginning Date of Index	Source of Bond Prices	Historical Information and Frequency
Merrill Lynch (C8L6) Long term (15 years+), medium-quality finance-coupons 10–11.99 percent	1	MV = .05 PV = .06	BBB/A	Total return	Market value	Arithmetic	12/31/72 = 100	c = 11.38% y = 12.70% 5/85	22.0 5/85	12/31/72	Merrill Lynch Bond Pricing	1973
Merrill Lynch (C6H0) intermediate term, (5–9.99 years) high-quality utilities	142	MV = 6.5 PV = 7.4	AA/AAA	Total return	Market value	Arithmetic	12/31/72 = 100	c = 8.33% y = 10.5% 5/85	7.83 5/85	12/31/72	Merrill Lynch Bond Pricing	1973
Merrill Lynch (C6H3) Intermediate term, (5–9.99 years) high-quality utilities-coupons 4–5.99 percent	81	MV = 2.3 PV = 3.2	AA/AAA	Total return	Market value	Arithmetic	12/31/72 = 100	c = 4.63% y = 10.02% 5/85	7.42 5/85	12/31/72	Merrill Lynch Bond Pricing	1973

Description										Source	
Merrill Lynch (C6H4) Interme-diate term, (5–9.99 years) high-quality utilities-coupons 6–7.99 percent	19	MV = .5 PV = .6	AA/AAA	Total return	Market value	Arithmetic	12/31/72 = 100	c = 6.7% y = 10.5% 5/85	7.8 5/85	12/31/72 Merrill Lynch Bond Pricing	1973
Merrill Lynch (C6H5) Interme-diate term, (5–9.99 years) high-quality utilities-coupons 8–9.99 percent	5	MV = .2 PV = .2	AA/AAA	Total return	Market value	Arithmetic	12/31/74 = 100	c = 8.37% y = 10.87% 5/85	9.25 5/85	9/30/74 Merrill Lynch Bond Pricing	1973
Merrill Lynch (C6H6) Interme-diate term, (5–9.99 years) high-quality utilities-coupons 10–11.99 per-cent	8	MV = 1.0 PV = 1.0	AAA/AA	Total return	Market value	Arithmetic	12/31/72 100	c = 10.62% y = 10.27% 5/85	6.0 5/85	12/31/72 Merrill Lynch Bond Pricing	1973
Merrill Lynch (C6E0) Interme-diate-term (5–9.99 years) high-quality industrials	40	MV = 4.2 PV = 4.3	AA/AAA	Total return	Market value	Arithmetic	12/31/72 100	c = 10.60% y = 11.33% 5/85	7.2 5/85	12/31/72 Merrill Lynch Bond Pricing	1973

EXHIBIT 1 (continued)

Index Name	Number of Securities	Total MV,PV (billions of dollars)	Securities Included	Type (Yield, Total Return, etc.)	Weighting	Calculation	Period and Base Amount	YTM or Coupon and Period	Number of Years to Maturity	Beginning Date of Index	Source of Bond Prices	Historical Information and Frequency
Merrill Lynch (C6E4) Intermediate-term (5–9.99 years), high-quality industrials-coupons 6–7.99 percent	7	MV = .7 PV = .9	AA/AAA	Total return	Market value	Arithmetic	12/31/74 100	c = 6.97% y = 10.62% 5/85	7.50 5/85	12/31/72	Merrill Lynch Bond Pricing	1973
Merrill Lynch (C6E5) Intermediate-term (5–9.99 years), high quality industrials-coupons 8–9.99 percent	4	MV = .2 PV = .2	AA/AAA	Total return	Market value	Arithmetic	12/31/72 = 100	c = 9.375% y = 10.369% 5/85	7.25 5/85	12/31/74	Merrill Lynch Bond Pricing	1975
Merrill Lynch (C6E6) Intermediate-term (5–9.99 years), high-quality industrials-coupons 10–11.99 percent	6	MV = .8 PV = .7	AA/AAA	Total return	Market value	Arithmetic	12/31/72 = 100	c = 11.06% y = 10.6% 5/85	6.50 5/85	12/31/72	Merrill Lynch Bond Pricing	1973

Name	No.		AA/AAA	Total return	Market value	Arithmetic	12/31/72 = 100			Date	Source	Year
Merrill Lynch (C6K0) Intermediate-term (5–9.99 years) high-quality finance	58	MV = 5.7 PV = 5.7	AA/AAA	Total return	Market value	Arithmetic	12/31/72 = 100	c = 11.63% y = 11.32% 5/85	7.33 5/85	12/31/72	Merrill Lynch Bond Pricing	1973
Merrill Lynch (C6K4) Intermediate-term (5–9.99 years) high-quality finance coupons 6–7.99 percent	8	MV = .7 PV = .8	AA/AAA	Total return	Market value	Arithmetic	12/31/72 = 100	c = 7.34% y = 10.87% 5/85	9.17 5/85	12/31/72	Merrill Lynch Bond Pricing	1973
Merrill Lynch (C6K5) Intermediate-term (5–9.99 years) high-quality finance coupons 8–9.99 percent	2	MV = .2 PV = .2	AA/AAA	Total return	Market value	Arithmetic	12/31/74 = 100	c = 8.01% y = 10.83% 5/85	8.00 5/85	6/30/74	Merrill Lynch Bond Pricing	1975
Merrill Lynch (C6K6) Intermediate-term (5–9.99 years), high-quality finance coupons 10–11.99 percent	15	MV = 1.2 PV = 1.2	AA/AAA	Total return	Market value	Arithmetic	12/31/72 = 100	c = 11.30% y = 11.01% 5/85	7.42 5/85	12/31/72	Merrill Lynch Bond Pricing	1973

EXHIBIT 1 (continued)

Index Name	Number of Securities	Total MV, PV (billions of dollars)	Securities Included	Type (Yield, Total Return, etc.)	Weighting	Calculation	Period and Base Amount	YTM or Coupon and Period	Number of Years to Maturity	Beginning Date of Index	Source of Bond Prices	Historical Information and Frequency
Merrill Lynch (C6C0) Intermediate-term (5–9.99 years), medium quality	629	MV = 41.3 PV = 41.0	A/BBB	Total return	Market value	Arithmetic	12/31/72 = 100	c = 11.76% y = 11.52% 5/85	7.42 5/85	12/31/72	Merrill Lynch Bond Pricing	1973
Merrill Lynch (C6I0) Intermediate-term (5–9.99 years), medium-quality utilities	324	MV = 16.1 PV = 15.9	A/BBB	Total return	Market value	Arithmetic	12/31/72 = 100	c = 12.13% y = 11.64% 5/85	6.67 5/85	12/31/72	Merrill Lynch Bond Pricing	1973
Merrill Lynch (C6I3) Intermediate-term (5–9.99 years), medium-quality utilities-coupons 4–5.99 percent	110	MV = 1.8 PV = 2.6	A/BBB	Total return	Market value	Arithmetic	12/31/72 = 100	c = 4.67% y = 10.80% 5/85	7.34 5/85	12/31/72	Merrill Lynch Bond Pricing	1973

Merrill Lynch (C6I4) Intermediate-term (5–9.99 years), medium-quality utilities-coupons 6–7.99 percent	33	MV = .5 PV = .7	A/A	Total return	Market value	Arithmetic	7/31/76 = 100	c = 7.08% y = 10.87% 5/85	7.42 5/85	7/31/76	Merrill Lynch Bond Pricing	1976
Merrill Lynch (C6I5) Intermediate-term (5–9.99 years), medium-quality utilities-coupons 8–9.99 percent	38	MV = .8 PV = .8	A/BBB	Total return	Market value	Arithmetic	12/31/72 = 100	c = 8.85% y = 15.21% 5/85	7.75 5/85	12/31/72	Merrill Lynch Bond Pricing	1973
Merrill Lynch (C6I6) Intermediate-term (5–9.99 years), medium-quality utilities-coupons 10–11.99 percent	17	MV = 1.3 PV = 1.3	A/BBB	Total return	Market value	Arithmetic	6/30/74 = 100	c = 11.22% y = 10.78% 5/85	7.17 5/85	6/30/74	Merrill Lynch Bond Pricing	1974
Merrill Lynch (C6F4) Intermediate-term (5–9.99 years), medium-quality industrials	164	MV = 1.5 PV = 1.5	BBB/A	Total return	Market value	Arithmetic	12/31/72 = 100	c = 11.39% y = 11.48% 5/85	7.67 5/85	12/31/72	Merrill Lynch Bond Pricing	1973

EXHIBIT 1 *(continued)*

Merrill Lynch (C6F4) Intermediate-term (5–9.99 years), medium-quality industrials coupons 6–7.99 percent	29	MV = .2 PV = .3	BBB/A	Total return	Market value	Arithmetic	6/30/74 = 100	$c = 6.72\%$ $y = 15.34\%$ 5/85	7.83 5/85	6/30/74	Merrill Lynch Bond Pricing	1974
Merrill Lynch (C6F5) Intermediate-term (5–9.99 years), medium-quality industrials coupons 8–9.99 percent	17	MV = 1.6 PV = 1.9	BBB/A	Total return	Market value	Arithmetic	6/30/74 = 100	$c = 9.39\%$ $y = 11.96\%$ 5/85	9.08 5/85	6/30/74	Merrill Lynch Bond Pricing	1974
Merrill Lynch (C6F6) Intermediate-term (5–9.99 years), medium-quality industrials coupons 10–11.99 percent	38	MV = 2.8 PV = 2.8	BBB/A	Total return	Market value	Arithmetic	9/30/74 = 100	$c = 10.99\%$ $y = 10.99\%$ 5/85	6.67 5/85	9/30/74	Merrill Lynch Bond Pricing	1974

Description	No.	MV/PV	Rating			Base	c/y	Value	Date	Source	Year
Merrill Lynch (C6L0) Intermediate-term (5–9.99 years), medium-quality finance	104	MV = 7.6 PV = 7.5	BBB/A	Total return	Market value	Arithmetic 12/31/72 = 100	c = 11.66% y = 11.41% 5/85	7.42 5/85	12/31/72	Merrill Lynch Bond Pricing	1973
Merrill Lynch (C6L4) Intermediate-term (5–9.99 years), medium-quality finance-coupons 6–7.99 percent	18	MV = .7 PV = .8	A/BBB	Total return	Market value	Arithmetic 12/31/72 = 100	c = 7.69% y = 10.98% 5/85	7.25 5/85	12/31/72	Merrill Lynch Bond Pricing	1973
Merrill Lynch (C6L5) Intermediate-term (5–9.99 years), medium-quality finance-coupons 8–9.99 percent	25	MV = .8 PV = .9	A/BBB	Total return	Market value	Arithmetic 12/31/73 = 100	c = 8.86% y = 11.04% 5/85	6.92 5/85	12/31/73	Merrill Lynch Bond Pricing	1974
Merrill Lynch (C6L6) Intermediate-term (5–9.99 years), medium-quality finance-coupons 10–11.99 percent	18	MV = .4 PV = .5	BBB/A	Total return	Market value	Arithmetic 12/31/74 = 100	c = 11.23% y = 11.11% 5/85	7.98 5/85	12/31/74	Merrill Lynch Bond Pricing	1975

EXHIBIT 1 *(concluded)*

Merrill Lynch (C1A0) Short term (1–2.99 years)	337	MV = 23.3 PV = 23.4	BBB/ AAA	Total return	Market value	Arithmetic	12/31/75 = 100	c = 9.89% y = 9.92% 5/85	2.0 5/85	12/31/75	Merrill Lynch Bond Pricing	1976
Merrill Lynch (C1B0) Short term (1–2.99 years), high-quality	121	MV = 11.1 PV = 11.1	AA/AAA	Total return	Market value	Arithmetic	12/31/75 = 100	c = 7.85% y = 15.61% 5/85	2.0 5/85	12/31/75	Merrill Lynch Bond Pricing	1976
Merrill Lynch (C1C0) Short term (1–2.99 years), medium-quality	216	MV = 12.2 PV = 12.3	A/BBB	Total return	Market value	Arithmetic	12/31/75 = 100	c = 9.93% y = 10.12% 5/85	1.92 5/85	12/31/75	Merrill Lynch Bond Pricing	1976
Merrill Lynch (C2A0) intermediate-term (3–4.99 years)	287	MV = 18.7 PV = 18.7	BBB/ AAA	Total return	Market value	Arithmetic	12/31/75 = 100	c = 10.79% y = 10.76% 5/85	4.08 5/85	12/31/75	Merrill Lynch Bond Pricing	1976

Merrill Lynch (C2B0) Intermediate-term (3–4.99 years), high quality	109	MV = 8.1 PV = 9.0	AA/AAA	Total return	Market value	Arithmetic	12/31/75 = 100	c = 10.50% y = 10.52% 5/85	3.92 5/85	12/31/75	Merrill Lynch Bond Pricing	1976
Merrill Lynch (C2C0) Intermediate-term (3–4.99 years), medium quality	178	MV = 9.8 PV = 8.1	BBB/A	Total return	Market value	Arithmetic	12/31/75 = 100	c = 11.05% y = 10.97% 5/85	3.92 5/85	12/31/75	Merrill Lynch Bond Pricing	1976
Merrill Lynch (C7A0) Intermediate-term (10–14.99 years)	795	MV = 30.5 PV = 38.3	BBB/ AAA	Total return	Market value	Arithmetic	12/31/75 = 100	c = 8.13% y = 11.19% 5/85	13.42 5/85	12/31/75	Merrill Lynch Bond Pricing	1976
Merrill Lynch (C7B0) Intermediate-term (10–14.99 years) high quality	255	MV = 11.9 Pv = 15.4	AA/AAA	Total return	Market value	Arithmetic	12/31/75 = 100	c = 7.45% y = 10.84% 5/85	13.42 5/85	12/31/75	Merrill Lynch Bond Pricing	1973
Merrill Lynch (C7C0) Intermediate-term (10–14.99 years) medium quality	540	MV = 18.6 PV = 22.9	A/BBB	Total return	Market value	Arithmetic	12/31/75 = 100	c = 8.58% y = 11.43% 5/85	13.58 5/85	12/31/75	Merrill Lynch Bond Pricing	1973

EXHIBIT 2 U.S. Government Bond Indexes

Index Name	Number of Securities	Total MV,PV (billions of dollars)	Securities Included	Type (Yield, Total Return, etc.)	Weighting	Calculation	Period and Base Amount	YTM or Coupon and Period	Number of Years to Maturity	Beginning Date of Index	Source of Bond Prices	Historical Information and Frequency
Salomon Brothers long-term govts	N/A	N/A	All but flower bonds	Total return	Par value	Arithmetic	1978 = 100	c = 9.51% 11/1/81	12 years	1/1/78	Salomon Brothers	3 months monthly
Salomon Brothers medium-term 3–5	N/A	N/A	All but flower bonds	Total return	Par value	Arithmetic	1978 = 100	c = 10.09 11/1/81	3–5 years	1/1/78	Salomon Brothers	3 months monthly
Salomon Brothers medium-term 6–8	N/A	N/A	All but flower bonds	Total return	Par value	Arithmetic	1978 = 100	c = 9.44 11/1/81	6–8 years	1/1/78	Salomon Brothers	3 months monthly
Salomon Brothers medium-term 9–11	N/A	N/A	All but flower bonds	Total return	Par value	Arithmetic	1978 = 100	c = 10/46 11/1/81	9–11 years	1/1/78	Salomon Brothers	3 months monthly
Salomon Brothers U.S. Govt. index	36	N/A	U.S. Treasury bonds	Total return	N/A	Arithmetic	12/31/77 = 100	N/A	14 years	1/1/78	Salomon Brothers	12/77 monthly
Salomon Brothers U.S. Treasury Bill index	N/A	N/A	U.S. Treasury bills	Total return	N/A	Arithmetic	12/31/77 = 100	N/A	3 months	1/1/78	Salomon Brothers	12/77 monthly
Standard & Poor's Long-term govt. bond yield average	4	N/A	N/A	YTM	Equally	Arithmetic	N/A	y = 10.31% 6/12/85	10 years 6/12/85	1/42	The Wall Street Journal (YTM)	1942 monthly 1971 weekly

Standard & Poor's Long-term govt. bond price index	4	N/A	Price	N/A	Equally	YTM is converted into a price assuming 3 percent coupon + 15 years to maturity (Dollars per $100 par value)	N/A	p = 44.77 6/12/85	15 years 6/12/85	1/42	*The Wall Street Journal* (convert yields into price)	1942 monthly 1971 weekly
Standard & Poor's Intermediate-term govt. bond yield average	4	N/A	YTM	N/A	Equally	Arithmetic	N/A	y = 10.04% 6/12/85	6–9 years 6/12/85	1/42	*The Wall Street Journal* (YTM)	1942 monthly 1971 weekly
Standard & Poor's Intermediate-term govt. bond price index	4	N/A	Price	N/A	Equally	YTM is converted into a price assuming 3 percent coupon and 7 1/2 years to maturity (Dollars per $100 par value)	N/A	p = 63.48 6/12/85	7 1/2 years 6/12/85	1/42	*The Wall Street Journal* (convert yields into price)	1942 monthly 1971 weekly

EXHIBIT 2 (continued)

Index Name	Number of Securities	Total MV, PV (billions of dollars)	Securities Included	Type (Yield, Total Return, etc.)	Weighting	Calculation	Period and Base Amount	YTM or Coupon and Period	Number of Years to Maturity	Beginning Date of Index	Source of Bond Prices	Historical Information and Frequency
Standard & Poor's Short-term govt. bond yield average	4	N/A	N/A	YTM	Equally	Arithmetic	N/A	y = 8.80% 6/12/85	2–4 years 6/12/85	1/42	The Wall Street Journal (YTM)	1942 monthly 1971 weekly
Standard & Poor's Short-term govt. bond price index	4	N/A	N/A	Price	Equally	YTM is converted into a price assuming 3 percent + 3 1/2 years to maturity (Dollars per $100 par value)	N/A	p = 82.82 6/12/85	3 1/2 years 6/12/85	1/42	The Wall Street Journal (convert yields into price)	1942 monthly 1971 weekly
Shearson Lehman Brothers Treasury bond index	145.0	707.570	AAA	Total return	Market value	Arithmetic	N/A	y = 9.61% 7/85	1 year+	12/72	Shearson Lehman Brothers	N/A

Shearson Lehman Brothers Intermediate Treasury bond index	105	563.282	AAA	Total return	Market value	Arithmetic	N/A	y = 9.34% 7/85	1-9.99 years	12/72	Shearson Lehman Brothers	N/A
Shearson Lehman Brothers Long term Treasury bond index	40	144.288	AAA	Total return	Market value	Arithmetic	N/A	y = 10.70% 7/85	10 years +	12/72	Shearson Lehman Brothers	N/A
Merrill Lynch (GOAO) Govt. master	389	MV = 883.2 PV = 850.9	AAA/ AAA	Total return	Market value	Arithmetic	3/31/72 100	c = 11.3% y = 9.83% 7/85	8 years	12/31/72	Merrill Lynch Bond Pricing	1973
Merrill Lynch (G802) U.S. Treasury long-term (15+)	35	MV = 164.4 PV = 15.9	AAA/ AAA	Total return	Market value	Arithmetic	3/31/73 100	c = 11.5% y = 10.9% 7/85	24 years	3/31/73	Merrill Lynch Bond Pricing	1973
Merrill Lynch (G202) Govt-U.S. Treasury intermediate term (3-4.99 years)	24	MV = 132.2 PV = 125.6	AAA/ AAA	Total return	Market value	Arithmetic	12/31/72 100	c = 11.6% y = 9.8% 7/85	4 years	12/31/72	Merrill Lynch Bond Pricing	1973
Merrill Lynch (G302) Govt-U.S. Treasury intermediate term (5-6.99 years)	15	MV = 83.8 PV = 76.6	AAA/ AAA	Total return	Market value	Arithmetic	12/31/72 100	c = 12.6% y = 10.4% 7/85	6 years	12/31/72	Merrill Lynch Bond Pricing	1973

EXHIBIT 2 (concluded)

Index Name	Number of Securities	Total MV,PV (billions of dollars)	Securities Included	Type (Yield, Total Return, etc.)	Weighting	Calculation	Period and Base Amount	YTM or Coupon and Period	Number of Years to Maturity	Beginning Date of Index	Source of Bond Prices	Historical Information and Frequency
Merrill Lynch (G402) Govt-U.S. Treasury intermediate term (7–9.99 years)	21	MV = 80.1 PV = 78.0	AAA/ AAA	Total return	Market value	Arithmetic	12/31/72 100	c = 10.9% y = 10.5% 7/85	9 years	12/31/72	Merrill Lynch Bond Pricing	1973
Merrill Lynch (G102) Govt-U.S. Treasury short term (1–2.99 years)	42	MV = 284.9 PV = 276.1	AAA/ AAA	Total return	Market value	Arithmetic	12/31/72 100	c = 11.0% y = 8.9% 7/85	2 years	12/31/72	Merrill Lynch Bond Pricing	1973
Merrill Lynch (G7PO) Govt-U.S. Treasury intermediate term (10–14.99 years)	12	MV = 2.7 PV = 2.7	AAA/ AAA	Total return	Market value	Arithmetic	7/31/77 100	c = 8.4% y = 10.6% 7/85	12 years	7/31/77	Merrill Lynch Bond Pricing	1973

EXHIBIT 3 U.S. Government/Agencies Bond Indexes

Index Name	Number of Securities	Total MV,PV (billions of dollars)	Securities Included	Type (Yield, Total Return, etc.)	Weighting	Calculation	Period and Base Amount	YTM or Coupon and Period	Number of Years to Maturity	Beginning Date of Index	Source of Bond Prices	Historical Information and Frequency
Shearson Lehman Brothers Govt. bond index	597	867.461	AAA	Total return	Market value	Arithmetic	N/A	9.62% 5/85	1 year+	12/72	Shearson Lehman Brothers	12/72 monthly
Shearson Lehman Brothers Govt. intermediate bond index	458.0	713.296	AAA	Total return	Market value	Arithmetic	N/A	9.39% 5/85	1–9.99 years	12/72	Shearson Lehman Brothers	12/72 monthly
Shearson Lehman Brothers Govt. long-term bond index	139.0	154.165	AAA	Total return	Market value	Arithmetic	N/A	10.70% 5/85	10 years+	12/72	Shearson Lehman Brothers	12/72 monthly
Shearson Lehman Brothers GNMA Pass-through bond index	17.0	N/A	AAA	Total return	Market value	Arithmetic	N/A	N/A 11/81	N/A	12/72	Shearson Lehman Brothers	12/72 monthly
Merrill Lynch (G702) Govt-federal agencies intermediate term (10–14.99 years)	4	MV = 6.2 PV = 7.3	AAA/ AAA	Total return	Market value	Arithmetic	12/31/75 100	c = 8.9% y = 10.6% 5/85	13 years 5/85	12/31/75	Merrill Lynch Bond Pricing	1973

EXHIBIT 3 *(concluded)*

Index Name	Number of Securities	Total MV, PV (billions of dollars)	Securities Included	Type (Yield, Total Return, etc.)	Weighting	Calculation	Period and Base Amount	YTM or Coupon and Period	Number of Years to Maturity	Beginning Date of Index	Source of Bond Prices	Historical Information and Frequency
Merrill Lynch (G8P0) Govt-federal agencies long term (15 years+)	18	MV = 1.8 PV = 2.2	AAA/AAA	Total return	Market value	Arithmetic	12/31/75 100	c = 8.9% y = 10.9% 5/85	24 years 5/85	12/31/75	Merrill Lynch Bond Pricing	1973
Merrill Lynch (G1P0) Govt-federal agencies short term (1–2.99 years)	118	MV = 74.5 PV = 71.8	AAA/AAA	Total return	Market value	Arithmetic	12/31/75 100	c = 11.5% y = 9.0% 5/85	2 years 5/85	12/31/75	Merrill Lynch Bond Pricing	1973
Merrill Lynch (G2P0) Govt-federal agencies intermediate term (3–4.99 years)	65	MV = 34.4 PV = 32.5	AAA/AAA	Total return	Market value	Arithmetic	12/31/75 100	c = 11.8% y = 9.8% 5/85	4 years 5/85	12/31/75	Merrill Lynch Bond Pricing	1973

				Total return	Market value	Arithmetic					
Merrill Lynch (G3P0) Govt-federal agencies intermediate term (5–6.99 years)	30	MV = 15.3 PV = 14.4	AAA/ AAA				12/31/75 100	c = 11.8% y = 10.3% 5/85	6 years 5/85	12/31/75	Merrill Lynch Bond Pricing	1973
Merrill Lynch (G402) Govt-federal agencies intermediate term (7–9.99 years)	21	MV = 81.9 PV = 74.4	AAA/ AAA				12/31/75 100	c = 11.1% y = 10.3% 5/85	9 years 5/85	12/31/75	Merrill Lynch Bond Pricing	1973

EXHIBIT 4 U.S. Government/Agencies/Corporates and Corporates/Governments Bond Indexes

Index Name	Number of Securities	Total MV,PV (billions of dollars)	Securities Included	Type (Yield, Total Return, etc.)	Weighting	Calculation	Period and Base Amount	YTM or Coupon and Period	Number of Years to Maturity	Beginning Date of Index	Source of Bond Prices	Historical Information and Frequency
Shearson Lehman Brothers Long-term, high-quality govt. agency corp. bond index	1147.0	228.198	AAA	Total return	Market value	Arithmetic	N/A	y = 10.91% 5/85	10 years+	12/72	Shearson Lehman Brothers	12/72 monthly
Shearson Lehman Brothers Intermediate govt/corporate bond index	2342.0	825.458	AAA	Total return	Market value	Arithmetic	N/A	y = 9.59% 5/85	1–9.99 years	12/72	Shearson Lehman Brothers	12/72 monthly
Shearson Lehman Brothers Long-term govt/corporate bond index	2830.5	325.548	AAA	Total return	Market value	Arithmetic	N/A	y = 11.16% 5/85	10 years +	12/72	Shearson Lehman Brothers	12/72 monthly
Shearson Lehman Brothers Govt/corporate bond index	5172.5	1151.006	AAA	Total return	Market value	Arithmetic	N/A	y = 10.03% 5/85	1 year+	12/72	Shearson Lehman Brothers	12/72 monthly
Merrill Lynch Corp. (BOAO) and Govt. Master	4686	MV = 1175.0 PV = 1178.2	AA/AA	Total return	Market value	Arithmetic	12/31/72 100	y = 10.03% 7/85	9 years 7/85	12/72	Merrill Lynch Bond Pricing	1973

EXHIBIT 5 Municipal Bond Indexes

Index Name	Number of Securities	Total MV,PV (billions of dollars)	Securities Included	Type (Yield, Total Return, etc.)	Weighting	Calculation	Period and Base Amount	YTM or Coupon and Period	Number of Years to Maturity	Beginning Date of Index	Source of Bond Prices	Historical Information and Frequency
Lipper general municipal bond fund index	10	7.4	Representative general munibond funds	Principal only	Dollar weighted	Arithmetic	12/31/80 = 100	N/A	N/A	12/31/80	Bond fund prices-NASD	12/31/80 daily
Lipper short-term municipal bond fund	10	21.9	10 largest short-term munibond funds	7-day average yield; 30-day average yield; average days to maturity	Unweighted	Arithmetic	N/A	N/A	N/A	9/2/81	Call funds directly	9/2/81 weekly
Bond Buyer rev. bond index	Potential issuers 25	N/A		YTM	Equally	Arithmetic	Coupon-par in 30 years	N/A	N/A	Thursday to Thursday	Traders from 10-15 firms are asked their yield values each Thursday	Weekly 1979-Present

EXHIBIT 5 *(concluded)*

Index Name	Number of Securities	Total MV,PV (billions of dollars)	Securities Included	Type (Yield, Total Return, etc.)	Weighting	Calculation	Period and Base Amount	YTM or Coupon and Period	Number of Years to Maturity	Beginning Date of Index	Source of Bond Prices	Historical Information and Frequency
Bond Buyer 20-bond index	20	N/A		YTM	By rating	Arithmetic	Coupon-par in 20 years	N/A	N/A	Thursday to Thursday	Traders from 10–15 firms are asked their yield values each Thursday	Monthly 1917–45 Weekly 1946–Present
Bond Buyer 11-bond index	11	N/A		YTM	By rating	Arithmetic	Coupon-par in 20 years	N/A	N/A	Thursday to Thursday	Traders from 10–15 firms are asked their yield values each Thursday	Monthly 1917–45 Weekly 1946–Present

Standard & Poor's municipal bond yield index	15	N/A	General obligation Bonds AAA,AA,A	YTM	Equally	Arithmetic	N/A	y = 8.75% 6/12/85	20 years	N/A	Phone survey	1900 monthly 1971 weekly
Standard & Poor's municipal bond price index	15	N/A	AAA,AA,A	Price	Equally	Convert YTM into price assuming 4 percent coupon, 20 years to	N/A	p = 55.51 6/12/85	20 years	N/A	Phone survey	1900 monthly 1971 weekly

EXHIBIT 6 Yankee Bond Indexes

Index Name	Number of Securities	Total MV,PV (billions of dollars)	Securities Included	Type (Yield, Total Return, etc.)	Weighting	Calculation	Period and Base Amount	YTM or Coupon and Period	Number of Years to Maturity	Beginning Date of Index	Source of Bond Prices	Historical Information and Frequency
Shearson Lehman Brothers Yankee bond index	99	8954	AAA	Total return	Market value	Arithmetic		YTM = 10.53% 5/85	1 year+	12/72	Sherson Lehman Brothers	12/72 monthly
Shearson Lehman Brothers Yankee intermediate bond index	53	5118	AAA	Total return	Market value	Arithmetic		YTM = 10.27% 5/85	1–9.99 years	12/72	Shearson Lehman Brothers	12/72 monthly
Shearson Lehman Brothers Yankee long-term bond index	46	3836	AAA	Total return	Market value	Arithmetic		YTM = 10.88% 5/85	10 years+	12/72	Shearson Lehman Brothers	12/72 monthly
Merrill Lynch Corp–Yankee bonds (CONO) ALL	133	MV = 17.7 PV = 17.9	AAA/AAA	Total return	Market value	Arithmetic	12/31/75 = 100	c = 11.4% y = 10.7%	9 years 7/85	12/75	Merrill Lynch Bond Pricing	1973

EXHIBIT 7 Eurodollar and Foreign Bond Indexes

Index Name	Number of Securities	Total MV,PV (billions of dollars)	Securities Included	Type (Yield, Total Return, etc.)	Weight-ing	Calculation	Period and Base Amount	YTM or Coupon and Period	Number of Years to Maturity	Begin-ning Date of Index	Source of Bond Prices	Historical Information and Frequency
Shearson Lehman Brothers Int'l global index	987	87.372	Publicly traded	Total return	Market value	Arithmetic	N/A	11.12% 5/85	1 year+	12/76	AIBD quotations	12/72 monthly
Shearson Lehman Brothers Int'l short-term global index	813	68.687	Publicly traded	Total return	Market value	Arithmetic	N/A	11.04% 5/85	1–7 years	12/76	AIBD quotations	12/72 monthly
Shearson Lehman Brothers Int'l long-term global index	174	18.685	Publicly traded	Total return	Market value	Arithmetic	N/A	11.38% 5/85	7 years+	12/76	AIBD quotations	12/72 monthly
Shearson Lehman Brothers Int'l high grade public sector index	213	20.289	AAA	Total return	Market value	Arithmetic	N/A	10.77% 5/85	1 year+	12/76	AIBD quotations	12/72 monthly
Shearson Lehman Brothers Int'l short-term, high-grade public sector index	159	14.81	AAA	Total return	Market value	Arithmetic	N/A	10.55% 5/85	1–7 years	12/76	AIBD quotations	12/72 monthly
Shearson Lehman Brothers Int'l long-corp. index public sector index	54	5.479	AAA	Total return	Market value	Arithmetic	N/A	11.22% 5/85	7 years+	12/76	AIBD quotations	12/72 monthly

EXHIBIT 7 (continued)

Index Name	Number of Securities	Total MV,PV (billions of dollars)	Securities Included	Type (Yield, Total Return, etc.)	Weighting	Calculation	Period and Base Amount	YTM or Coupon and Period	Number of Years to Maturity	Beginning Date of Index	Source of Bond Prices	Historical Information and Frequency
Shearson Lehman Brothers Int'l U.S. corp. index	295	29.295	Obligations of U.S. corp.	Total return	Market value	Arithmetic	N/A	11.28% 5/85	1 year+	12/76	AIBD quotations	12/72 monthly
Shearson Lehman Brothers Int'l U.S. short-term corp. index	242	22.732	Obligations of U.S. corp.	Total return	Market value	Arithmetic	N/A	11.26% 5/85	1–7 years	12/76	AIBD quotations	12/72 monthly
Shearson Lehman Brothers Int'l U.S. long-term corp. index	53	6.562	Obligations of U.S. corp.	Total return	Market value	Arithmetic	N/A	11.34% 5/85	7 years+	12/76	AIBD quotations	12/72 monthly
Shearson Lehman Brothers Int'l European corporate index	213	13.949	European, Australia, and New Zealand commercial banks	Total return	Market value	Arithmetic	N/A	11.22% 5/85	1 year+	12/76	AIBD quotations	12/72 monthly

Shearson Lehman Brothers Int'l European corp. short-term index	190	11.969	European, Australia, and New Zealand commercial banks	Total return	Market value	Arithmetic	N/A	11.15% 5/85	1–7 years	12/76	AIBD quotations	12/72 monthly
Shearson Lehman Brothers Int'l European corp. long-term index	23	1.980	European, Australia, and New Zealand commercial banks	Total return	Market value	Arithmetic	N/A	11.66% 5/85	7 years+	12/76	AIBD quotations	12/72 monthly
Shearson Lehman Brothers Int'l Canadian public sector index	121	13.591	Obligations of Canadian provinces	Total return	Market value	Arithmetic	N/A	11.08% 5/85	1 year+	12/76	AIBD quotations	12/72 monthly
Shearson Lehman Brothers Int'l short-term Canadian public sector index	94	10.569	Obligations of Canadian provinces	Total return	Market value	Arithmetic	N/A	11.00% 5/85	1–7 years	12/76	AIBD quotations	12/72 monthly
Shearson Lehman Brothers Int'l long-term Canadian public sector index	27	3.022	Obligations of Canadian provinces	Total return	Market value	Arithmetic	N/A	11.35% 5/85	7 years+	12/76	AIBD quotations	12/72 monthly

EXHIBIT 7 *(continued)*

Index Name	Number of Securities	Total MV,PV (billions of dollars)	Securities Included	Type (Yield, Total Return, etc.)	Weighting	Calculation	Period and Base Amount	YTM or Coupon and Period	Number of Years to Maturity	Beginning Date of Index	Source of Bond Prices	Historical Information and Frequency
Shearson Lehman Brothers Int'l short-term Japanese index	75	6.952	Japanese private sector banks	Total return	Market value	Arithmetic	N/A	10.98% 5/85	1–7 years	12/76	AIBD quotations	12/72 monthly
Handelsblatt bond fund index	N/A	N/A	German F.I. mutual funds—bond and cash equivalents	Price	N/A	N/A	12/31/66 = 100	N/A	N/A	1966	Redemption prices	N/A
Financial Times actuaries fixed interest index	11	N/A	U.K. govt. securities	Price	Equally	Geometric	10/15/26 = 100	N/A	N/A	10/15/26	London Stock Exchange	N/A
Financial Times actuaries fixed interest index	87	70.453	Govt. bonds	Price	Market value	Geometric	12/31/75 = 100	N/A	N/A	12/31/75	London Stock Exchange	N/A
Nikkei Bond Index	N/A	N/A	Long-, medium- and short-term bonds	YTM	Equally	Arithmetic	N/A	N/A	N/A	N/A	N/A	N/A

Index	Number	Value	Quality	Return	Valuation	Averaging	Base	Yield/Coupon	Maturity	Start date	Source	Frequency
Merrill Lynch Corporate-Canadian (U.S.) (COMO) payable AAA	214	MV = 21.8 PV = 22.3	AA/AA	Total return	Market value	Arithmetic	12/31/75 = 100	c = 11.2% y = 11.3% 7/85	22.17 10/81	12/31/75	Merrill Lynch Bond Pricing	N/A
Salomon Brothers World bond index (weighted)	448	N/A	Prime quality, publicly traded	Total return	Market value	Arithmetic	12/31/77 = 100	N/A	9 years	12/77	Salomon Brothers Index	12/77 monthly
Salomon Brothers World bond index (unweighted)	448	N/A	Prime quality, publicly traded	Total return	Market value	Arithmetic	12/31/77 = 100	N/A	9 years	12/77	Salomon Brothers Index	12/77 monthly
Salomon Brothers World money mkt. index (un-weighted)	N/A	N/A	Money market instruments traded	Total return	Market value	Arithmetic	12/31/77 = 100	N/A	N/A	12/77	Salomon Brothers Index	12/77 monthly
Salomon Brothers Foreign dollar bond index	38	N/A	Prime Foreign Dollar Bonds (Yankees)	Total return	N/A	Arithmetic	12/31/77 = 100	N/A	18 years	12/77	Salomon Brothers Index	12/77 monthly
Salomon Brothers Eurodollar bond index	75	N/A	Prime quality Eurodollar bonds	Total return	N/A	Arithmetic	12/31/77 = 100	N/A	7 years	12/77	Salomon Brothers Index	12/77 monthly

EXHIBIT 7 *(continued)*

Index Name	Number of Securities	Total MV,PV (billions of dollars)	Securities Included	Type (Yield, Total Return, etc.)	Weighting	Calculation	Period and Base Amount	YTM or Coupon and Period	Number of Years to Maturity	Beginning Date of Index	Source of Bond Prices	Historical Information and Frequency
Salomon Brothers Eurodollar FRN index	32	N/A	Prime quality Eurodollar FRN's (3 and 6 months)	Total return	N/A	Arithmetic	12/31/77 = 100	N/A	7 years	12/77	Salomon Brothers Index	12/77 monthly
Salomon Brothers Canadian govt. index	11	N/A	Canadian Treasury bonds	Total return	N/A	Arithmetic	12/31/77 = 100	N/A	17 years	12/77	Salomon Brothers Index	12/77 monthly
Salomon Brothers Euro Canadian dollar bond index	8	N/A	Prime quality Euro Canadian dollar bonds	Total return	N/A	Arithmetic	12/31/77 = 100	N/A	8 years	12/77	Salomon Brothers Index	12/77 monthly
Salomon Brothers German government index	15	N/A	Bundes- and republics & Bundes-posts	Total return	N/A	Arithmetic	12/31/77 = 100	N/A	7 years	12/77	Salomon Brothers Index	12/77 monthly

Salomon Brothers Euro Deutsche Mark bond index	48	N/A	Prime quality Euro DM bonds	Total return	N/A	Arithmetic	12/31/77 = 100	N/A	7 years	12/77	Salomon Brothers Index	12/77 monthly
Salomon Brothers Japanese govt. index	10	N/A	Canadian govt. bonds	Total return	N/A	Arithmetic	12/31/77 = 100	N/A	7 years	12/77	Salomon Brothers Index	12/77 monthly
Salomon Brothers Samurai bond index	24	N/A	Prime quality Samurai bonds	Total return	N/A	Arithmetic	12/31/77 = 100	N/A	9 years	12/77	Salomon Brothers Index	12/77 monthly
Salomon Brothers Euroyen bond index	6	N/A	Prime quality Euroyen bonds	Total return	N/A	Arithmetic	12/31/77 = 100	N/A	8 years	12/77	Salomon Brothers Index	12/77 monthly
Salomon Brothers UK Gilt index	19	N/A	UK gilt-edged stocks	Total return	N/A	Arithmetic	12/31/77 = 100	N/A	16 years	12/77	Salomon Brothers Index	12/77 monthly
Salomon Brothers Eurosterling bond index	10	N/A	Prime quality Eurosterling bonds	Total return	N/A	Arithmetic	12/31/77 = 100	N/A	8 years	12/77	Salomon Brothers Index	12/77 monthly
Salomon Brothers Swiss govt. index	9	N/A	Swiss Confederation bonds	Total return	N/A	Arithmetic	12/31/77 = 100	N/A	8 years	12/77	Salomon Brothers Index	12/77 monthly

EXHIBIT 7 *(continued)*

Index Name	Number of Securities	Total MV,PV (billions of dollars)	Securities Included	Type (Yield, Total Return, etc.)	Weight-ing	Calculation	Period and Base Amount	YTM or Coupon and Period	Number of Years to Maturity	Begin-ning Date of Index	Source of Bond Prices	Historical Information and Frequency
Salomon Brothers Foreign Sfr. bond index	50	N/A	Prime quality foreign Sfr. bonds	Total return	N/A	Arithmetic	12/31/77 = 100	N/A	9 years	12/77	Salomon Brothers Index	12/77 monthly
Salomon Brothers Dutch govt. index	18	N/A	Netherlands govt. bonds	Total return	N/A	Arithmetic	12/31/77 = 100	N/A	6 years	12/77	Salomon Brothers Index	12/77 monthly
Salomon Brothers Foreign Dff. bond index	11	N/A	Prime quality foreign Dff. bonds	Total return	N/A	Arithmetic	12/31/77 = 100	N/A	6 years	12/77	Salomon Brothers Index	12/77 monthly
Salomon Brothers Euro Dff. bond index	13	N/A	Prime quality Euro Dff. bonds	Total return	N/A	Arithmetic	12/31/77 = 100	N/A	5 years	12/77	Salomon Brothers Index	12/77 monthly
Salomon Brothers French govt. index	7	N/A	Prime quality French govt. bonds	Total return	N/A	Arithmetic	12/31/77 = 100	N/A	6 years	12/77	Salomon Brothers Index	12/77 monthly

Salomon Brothers Euro Ffr. bond index	10	N/A	Prime Quality Euro Ffr. bonds	Total return	N/A	Arithmetic	12/31/77 = 100	N/A	5 years	12/77	Salomon Brothers Index	12/77 monthly
Salomon Brothers Domestic U.S. Dollar C.D. index	N/A	N/A	Domestic Dollar CD	Total return	N/A	Arithmetic	12/31/77 = 100	N/A	3 months	12/77	Salomon Brothers Index	12/77 monthly
Salomon Brothers Eurodollar CD index	N/A	N/A	Eurodollar DC	Total return	N/A	Arithmetic	12/31/77 = 100	N/A	3 months	12/77	Salomon Brothers Index	12/77 monthly
Salomon Brothers Eurodollar deposit index	N/A	N/A	Eurodollar Deposit	Total return	N/A	Arithmetic	12/31/77 = 100	N/A	3 months	12/77	Salomon Brothers Index	12/77 monthly
Salomon Brothers Canadian treasury bill index	N/A	N/A	Canadian treasury bill	Total return	N/A	Arithmetic	12/31/77 = 100	N/A	3 months	12/77	Salomon Brothers Index	12/77 monthly
Salomon Brothers Euro Canadian dollar deposit index	N/A	N/A	Euro Canadian dollar deposit	Total return	N/A	Arithmetic	12/31/77 = 100	N/A	3 months	12/77	Salomon Brothers Index	12/77 monthly
Salomon Brothers Domestic Yen C.D. Index	N/A	N/A	Domestic yen CD	Total return	N/A	Arithmetic	12/31/77 = 100	N/A	3 months	12/77	Salomon Brothers Index	12/77 monthly
Salomon Brothers Yen Gensaki index	N/A	N/A	Yen Gensaki	Total return	N/A	Arithmetic	12/31/77 = 100	N/A	3 months	12/77	Salomon Brothers Index	12/77 monthly

EXHIBIT 7 *(concluded)*

Index Name	Number of Securities	Total MV,PV (billions of dollars)	Securities Included	Type (Yield, Total Return, etc.)	Weighting	Calculation	Period and Base Amount	YTM or Coupon and Period	Number of Years to Maturity	Beginning Date of Index	Source of Bond Prices	Historical Information and Frequency
Salomon Brothers Euroyen deposit index	N/A	N/A	Euroyen deposit	Total return	N/A	Arithmetic	12/31/77 = 100	N/A	3 months	12/77	Salomon Brothers Index	12/77 monthly
Salomon Brothers U.K. Treasury bill index	N/A	N/A	U.K. Trea-sury bill	Total return	N/A	Arithmetic	12/31/77 = 100	N/A	3 months	12/77	Salomon Brothers Index	12/77 monthly
Salomon Brothers Domestic L CD index	N/A	N/A	Domestic L CD	Total return	N/A	Arithmetic	12/31/77 = 100	N/A	3 months	12/77	Salomon Brothers Index	12/77 monthly

Salomon Brothers Eurosterling deposit index	N/A	N/A	Domestic L CD	Total return	N/A	Arithmetic	12/31/77 = 100	N/A	3 months	12/77	Salomon Brothers Index	12/77 monthly
Salomon Brothers Domestic Sfr. deposit index	N/A	N/A	Domestic Sfr. deposit	Total return	N/A	Arithmetic	12/31/77 = 100	N/A	3 months	12/77	Salomon Brothers Index	12/77 monthly
Salomon Brothers Euro Sfr. deposit index	N/A	N/A	Euro Sfr. deposit	Total return	N/A	Arithmetic	12/31/77 = 100	N/A	3 months	12/77	Salomon Brothers Index	12/77 monthly
Salomon Brothers Domestic Ffr. deposit index	N/A	N/A	Domestic Ffr. deposit	Total return	N/A	Arithmetic	12/31/77 = 100	N/A	3 months	12/77	Salomon Brothers Index	12/77 monthly
Salomon Brothers Euro Ffr. deposit index	N/A	N/A	Euor Ffr. deposit	Total return	N/A	Arithmetic	12/31/77 = 100	N/A	3 months	12/77	Salomon Brothers Index	12/77 monthly

EXHIBIT 8 Zero-Coupon Bond Indexes

Index Name	Number of Securities	Total MV,PV (billions of dollars)	Securities Included	Type (Yield, Total Return, etc.)	Weighting	Calculation	Period and Base Amount	YTM or Coupon and Period	Number of Years to Maturity	Beginning Date of Index	Source of Bond Prices	Historical Information and Frequency
Merrill Lynch Zero-Coupon 2-Year Tigr (T101)	N/A	N/A	N/A	N/A	N/A	N/A	8/30/85	N/A	N/A	8/85	Merrill Lynch bond pricing	8/85 monthly
Merrill Lynch Zero-Coupon 5-Year Tigr (T301)	N/A	N/A	N/A	N/A	N/A	N/A	8/30/85	N/A	N/A	8/85	Merrill Lynch bond pricing	8/85 monthly
Merrill Lynch Zero-Coupon 7-Year Tigr (T401)	N/A	N/A	N/A	N/A	N/A	N/A	8/30/85	N/A	N/A	8/85	Merrill Lynch bond pricing	8/85 monthly
Merrill Lynch Zero-Coupon 10-Year Tigr (T701)	N/A	N/A	N/A	N/A	N/A	N/A	8/30/85	N/A	N/A	8/85	Merrill Lynch bond pricing	8/85 monthly
Merrill Lynch Zero-Coupon 20-Year Tigr (T801)	N/A	N/A	N/A	N/A	N/A	N/A	8/30/85	N/A	N/A	8/85	Merrill Lynch bond pricing	8/85 monthly

EXHIBIT 9 High-Yield Bond Indexes

Index Name	Number of Securities	Total MV, PV (billions of dollars)	Securities Included	Type (Yield, Total Return, etc.)	Weighting	Calculation	Period and Base Amount	YTM or Coupon and Period	Number of Years to Maturity	Beginning Date of Index	Source of Bond Prices	Historical Information and Frequency
Merrill Lynch High-yield utilities, long-term (J9H0)	159	MV = 65.8	C3/BB1	Total yield	Market value	Arithmetic	10/31/84 = 100	c = 11.6%	20.0	10/84	Merrill Lynch bond pricing	10/84 monthly
Merrill Lynch High-yield finance and banks, long-term (J9K0)	21	MV = .9	C3/BB1	Total yield	Market value	Arithmetic	10/31/84 = 100	c = 12.8%	15.0	10/84	Merrill Lynch bond pricing	10/84 monthly
Merrill Lynch All high-yield bonds (J0A0)	671	MV = 33.8	C3/BB1	Total yield	Market value	Arithmetic	10/31/84 = 100	c = 12.3%	13.0	10/84	Merrill Lynch bond pricing	10/84 monthly
Merrill Lynch All high-yield transportation bonds (J0W0)	18	MV = 11.5	C3/BB1	Total yield	Market value	Arithmetic	4/30/85 = 100	c = 13.0%	12.0	4/85	Merrill Lynch bond pricing	4/85 monthly

EXHIBIT 9 *(concluded)*

Index Name	Number of Securities	Total MV,PV (billions of dollars)	Securities Included	Type (Yield, Total Return, etc.)	Weighting	Calculation	Period and Base Amount	YTM or Coupon and Period	Number of Years to Maturity	Beginning Date of Index	Source of Bond Prices	Historical Information and Frequency
Merrill Lynch High-yield industrials, intermediate-term (J5E0)	138	MV = 75.9	C3/BB1	Total yield	Market value	Arithmetic	10/31/84 = 100	c = 12.2%	13.0	10/84	Merrill Lynch bond pricing	10/84 monthly
Merrill Lynch High-yield industrials, intermediate-term (J5H0)	79	MV = 44.9	C3/BB1	Total yield	Market value	Arithmetic	10/31/84 = 100	c = 12.2%	6.0	10/84	Merrill Lynch bond pricing	10/84 monthly
Merrill Lynch High-yield finance and banks, intermediate-term (J5K0)	27	MV = 14.5	C3/BB1	Total yield	Market value	Arithmetic	10/31/84 = 100	c = 13.1%	6.0	10/84	Merrill Lynch bond pricing	10/84 monthly
Merrill Lynch High-yield industrials, long-term (J9E0)	227	MV = 11.6	C3/BB1	Total yield	Market value	Arithmetic	10/31/84 = 100	c = 12.6%	15.0	10/84	Merrill Lynch bond pricing	10/84 monthly

Name Index

Subject Index